FUNDAMENTALS OF PSYCHOLOGY

FUNDAMENTALS OF PSYCHOLOGY

EDWARD E. SMITH
UNIVERSITY OF MICHIGAN

DARYL J. BEM
CORNELL UNIVERSITY

SUSAN NOLEN-HOEKSEMA
UNIVERSITY OF MICHIGAN

Harcourt College Publishers

Fort Worth   Philadelphia   San Diego   New York   Austin   Orlando   San Antonio
Toronto   Montreal   London   Sydney   Tokyo

Publisher	Earl McPeek
Acquisitions Editor	Brad Potthoff
Market Strategist	Katie Matthews
Developmental Editor	Michelle Vardeman
Project Editor	Jim Patterson
Art Director	David A. Day
Production Manager	Linda McMillan

Cover image: Christie's Images/SuperStock

ISBN: 0-15-501225-8

Library of Congress Catalog Card Number: 00-104764

Address for Domestic Orders
Harcourt College Publishers, 6277 Sea Harbor Drive, Orlando, FL 32887-6777
800-782-4479

Address for International Orders
International Customer Service

Harcourt, Inc., 6277 Sea Harbor Drive, Orlando, FL 32887-6777
407-345-3800
(fax) 407-345-4060
(e-mail) hbintl@harcourt.com

Address for Editorial Correspondence
Harcourt College Publishers, 301 Commerce Street, Suite 3700, Fort Worth, TX 76102

Web Site Address
http://www.harcourtcollege.com

Printed in the United States of America

0 1 2 3 4 5 6 7 8 9   032   9 8 7 6 5 4 3 2 1

Harcourt College Publishers

Preface

Fundamentals of Psychology is a new text with a rich heritage behind it. As the authors of *Hilgard's Introduction to Psychology*—often touted as the gold standard of introductory psychology textbooks around the world—we have crafted *Fundamentals* to carry on this grand tradition in its own unique way. At the request of many colleagues, we've created *Fundamentals of Psychology* to fulfill a specific vision for introductory psychology—to provide comprehensive, in-depth, balanced, accurate, and most of all, *applicable* coverage of both classical and modern psychology in one concise text. You'll find scholarly sophistication, thorough coverage, and clarity in our brief, fourteen-chapter presentation, handily designed to fit the college term.

The pedagogy in *Fundamentals* will incite interest, enhance learning, and is set forth in a style that we believe will be both engaging and challenging to students. Additionally, each year, more and more studies are revealing the physiological foundations of psychological phenomena. The integration of these new discoveries has been a primary focus in our writing of *Fundamentals,* and examples pertinent to our everyday lives may be found throughout the text.

We've also worked to include in *Fundamentals of Psychology* topics not typically found in many brief introductory texts. For example, we've included:

- full coverage of all sensory systems—not simply the visual—in Chapter 4, *Sensation and Perception* (p. 100)
- an analysis of drug tolerance, the Rescorla-Wagner model, the relationship of learning to biology and cognition, and the role of prior beliefs in Chapter 6, *Learning* (p. 189)
- an introduction to working and repressed memory in Chapter 7, *Memory* (p. 224)
- expansive coverage of the physiology of motivation, the facial feedback hypothesis, and the very latest on sexuality and sexual orientation in Chapter 9, *Motivation and Emotion* (p. 298)
- the role of stress in modern culture and the effect of attribution styles on physical and psychological health in Chapter 12, *Stress, Health, and Coping* (p. 406)
- antisocial and borderline personality theories, case studies, and narratives in Chapter 13, *Abnormal Psychology* (p. 452)
- a discussion of commitment to mental health facilities against one's will, an overview of the legal guidelines for the insanity defense, and many practical suggestions for staying mentally happy in Chapter 14, *Treatment* (p. 480)

Frontiers of Psychology examines research that is expanding the limits of our knowledge about the field of psychology. Examples include *The Effects of Day Care* (Chapter 3), *Neurotransmitters and Psychology* (Chapter 10), and *Herbal Remedies for Psychological Problems* (Chapter 13). This feature explores how basic research and theories in psychology address some of the most important practical problems that people face today.

A detailed guide to help you locate specific pages in the text covering these and many other topics may be found on the companion website under Instructor Resources at www.harcourtcollege.com/psych/Fundamentals.

Throughout *Fundamentals of Psychology,* we present highlights of the primary theories and research that have shaped psychology historically, plus cutting-edge coverage of trends and the latest research being done in the field. Two special features that call attention to trends of particular interest to students include **Frontiers of Psychology** (see previous page) and **Contemporary Voices in Psychology** (below).

Contemporary Voices are essays written by leading researchers in psychology addressing controversial issues, such as "Are We Naturally Selfish?" "Is ADHD Overdiagnosed?" and "Problems with the Evolutionary Model of Sex Differences in Mate Preferences." This feature is geared to help students understand how psychologists use theory and research to approach unresolved issues in the field.

Aligned with learning theories such as PQRST, which emphasize the importance of Previewing and Reviewing, **Chapter Outlines and Summaries** serve as structural "bookends" within each subject area. Chapter Outlines set the stage for upcoming content by providing students with a preview of the major issues covered and chapter organization as a whole. Chapter Summaries provide a review of key concepts in each chapter, helping students synthesize what they have learned and serving as a study tool in preparation for exams.

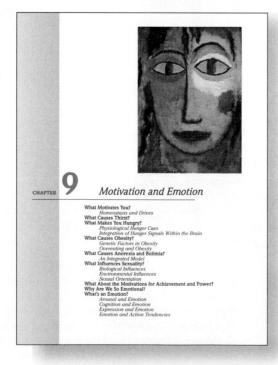

Another primary goal in writing *Fundamentals of Psychology* was to make the learning, comprehension, and retention of introductory psychology as easy, and as effective, as possible. A number of pedagogical tools reflect this focus:

---

tion procedure—might also influence their later competence as preschoolers. (For a discussion of the effects of day care on attachment, see the Frontiers of Psychology feature on page 89.)

Thinking Critically

1. Would your parents have characterized your infant personality as "easy," "difficult," or "slow to warm up"? Which aspects of your current personality seem to be primarily a reflection of your inborn temperament, which seem to reflect the way you were raised, and which seem to reflect a blend or interaction between "nature" and "nurture"?

2. Some psychologists have suggested that our earlier childhood attachment styles can influence the kinds of romantic relationships we form as adults. What form might the attachment styles discussed in this chapter assume in an adult romantic relationship? Can you relate your own adult "attachment styles" to your early childhood attachment style or to features of your childhood environment?

How Does Development Continue in Adolescence?

adolescence the period of transition from childhood to adulthood

Adolescence refers to *the period of transition from childhood to adulthood.* It extends roughly from age 12 to the late teens, when physical growth is nearly complete. During this period, the young person becomes sexually mature and establishes an identity as an individual apart from the family.

Conventional wisdom holds that adolescence is a period of "storm and stress"

Thinking Critically sections throughout the text encourage students to master one content area before proceeding to the next, thereby enhancing understanding and improving recall. These sections also challenge students to apply the material just covered to new questions in the field of psychology and to their own lives.

---

res and compares the actual perfor-
money produces better performance.
d is called the **independent variable**
hat the participant does. Performance
ecause it is *a variable that is hypothe-*
variable. Thus, the independent vari-
ipulates, and the dependent variable
The dependent variable is almost al-
vior. The phrase "is a function of" is
e on another. For this experiment, we
the tasks is a function of the amount
hat are paid money are usually called
e condition under study is present. The
trol group, or *the group in which the*
rol group serves as a baseline against

st described is random assignment of
hen the experimenter cannot rule out

independent variable
a variable independent of what the participant does

dependent variable
the variable hypothesized to depend on the value of the independent variable

experimental group
a group in which the condition under study is present

control group a group in which the condition under study is absent

---

Marginal glossaries throughout the text alert students to the most important terms and concepts within each section, provide unambiguous definitions so that students are confident about their meaning, and are placed near material discussing their applications.

Enhance and Explore

To enhance your understanding of the psychological concepts found in this chapter, please consult the following aids:

Study Guide

Learning Objectives, p. 66
Define the Terms, p. 70
Test Your Knowledge, p. 75
Essay Questions, p. 83
Thinking Independently, p. 85

PowerPsych CD-ROM

WHAT IS THE BASIS OF VISION?
Anatomy of the Eye
HOW DO WE KEEP THE PERCEPTUAL WORLD CONSTANT?
Size Constancy Illusions
The Ames Room
The Moon Illusion

PsychCentral

For more information concerning the topics found in this chapter, access psychology links on the Word Wide Web made through the Harcourt Web page at:
http://www.harcourtcollege.com/psych/Fundamentals

www.harcourtcollege.com
http://www.harcourtcollege.com/psych/index.html

Enhance and Explore sections at the end of each chapter encourage students to cement what they have covered in the text by using the Study Guide, *PowerPsych* CD-ROM, and companion Web site for further study. For each chapter, page references to key sections of the Study Guide and major concepts covered on *PowerPsych* are listed here for quick reference.

Suggested Readings

There are numerous good general texts on sensory processes and perception. A particularly clear one is Goldstein, *Sensation and Perception* (3rd ed., 1989). Other useful texts include Barlow and Mollon, *The Senses* (1982); Coren and Ward, *Sensation and Perception* (3rd ed., 1989); Schiffman, *Sensation and Perception* (3rd ed., formance: Vol. 1, Sensory Processes and Perception* (1986), edited by Boff, Kaufman, and Thomas; and Stevens's *Handbook of Experimental Psychology: Vol. 1* (1988), edited by Atkinson, Herrnstein, Lindzey, and Luce. For general texts that emphasize perception, see Kosslyn, *Invitation to Cognitive Science: Vol. 2, Visual Cog-

For students who want to find additional information on topics covered in the chapter, **Suggested Readings** are given at the end of each chapter.

Ancillaries

Fundamentals of Psychology is complemented by a full range of exciting teaching and learning supplements:

For Instructors

- **Instructor's Manual** by Mark Harvey, University of North Carolina, Asheville, is geared to assist both new and seasoned Instructors. Four major sections are aligned to each chapter of the text: Teaching Objectives (tied directly to the Learning Objectives found in the Study Guide); Lecture Ideas; Class Activities, Demonstrations, Exercises and Discussion Suggestions; and Suggested Media. All are focused on helping instructors to provide their students with the most comprehensive and cohesive learning experience possible.

- **Test Bank** prepared by Jutta Street, Barton College. Each chapter of the Testbank contains 170 multiple-choice, 20 fill-in-the-blank, and 10 essay questions. Multiple-choice items are rated by cognitive level (F = factual, C = conceptual, A = application), by difficulty level (1 = easy, 2 = moderate, 3 = difficult), and keyed to the page number in the main text where the concept is discussed. To allow instructors to challenge students beyond the memorization level, the majority of the multiple-choice questions are conceptual or application items. Specifically, cognitive levels are classified according to the first three levels of Benjamin Bloom's Taxonomy. Factual items (F) require students to recognize or recall certain facts, terms, rules, classifications, principles, and methods. Conceptual items (C) require students to translate, interpret, predict, generalize, or explain the theories and concepts that have been presented; these items may also require students to identify examples of psychological concepts that have been introduced. Applied items (A) require students to employ psychological concepts, methods, and principles in unique problem-solving situations. The fill-in-the-blank items are standard recall items that instructors might choose to include in an exam, but can also serve as quick, end-of-lecture quiz items to keep students alert. The essay items require students to apply, analyze, synthesize, or evaluate the theories and concepts that have been discussed. Answer guidelines for these items provide instructors with key concepts that should be included in a complete answer.

- **Computerized Test Banks** for Mac and Windows platforms are also available. The Testbank software, *EXAMaster+*™, offers three unique features to the instructor. EasyTest creates a test from a single screen in just a few easy steps. FullTest offers a range of options that includes selecting, editing, adding, or linking questions or graphics; random selection of questions from a wide range of criteria; creating criteria; blocking questions; and printing up to 99 different versions of the same test and answer sheet. EXAMRecord™ records, curves, graphs, and prints out grades according to criteria the instructor selects. Grade distribution displays as a bar graph or plotted graph.

- **PowerPoint Slide Presentation** prepared by Gordon K. Hodge, University of New Mexico, brings psychology to life through this easy-to-use, fully customizable, overhead lecture software consisting of approximately 300 slides conveniently organized according to the text outline. Illustrations and video clips appear frequently, vividly depicting essential concepts found in the book.

- **Films for the Humanities and Sciences.** Choose from films in the areas of biopsychology, developmental psychology, abnormal psychology, social psychology, and more. Qualifying criteria apply.

- **The Whole Psychology Catalog,** Fifth Edition, prepared by Michael B. Reiner of Kennesaw State College, easily supplements the course with work and assignments. This ancillary has perforated pages containing experiential exercises, questionnaires, and visual aids. Each activity is classified by one of eight learning goals central to the teaching of psychology. Also included in the fifth edition is an informative section on using the World Wide Web.

For Students

- **Study Guide** by Fred Whitford, University of Montana, provides students with a solid reinforcement of key terms and concepts found in the main text. The Study Guide features five major sections, each successive section building upon the last: Learning Objectives (tied directly to the Teaching Objectives found in the Instructor's Manual); Define the Terms; Test Your Knowledge; Essay Questions; and Thinking Independently. This structure not only helps students prepare for exams, but goes further to equip them with the tools needed to apply the tenets of psychology to their individual lives.

- **PowerPsych CD-ROM** prepared by Gordon K. Hodge, University of New Mexico, offers students an opportunity to learn the core concepts in Psychology in an interactive and fun environment. It contains exciting graphics, tutorials and even a "Check Mastery" self-test section which accompanies each major feature. Use of virtual reality technology and 3D-rendered animations and simulations allows students to view and manipulate structures. For example, they may view the brain to study functions such as ion movement prior to action potentials, and to review concepts such as classical conditioning and systematic desensitization.

- **WebCT General Psychology Course** includes all major topics covered in introductory psychology and can be used to provide Web-based learning environment for the students. Student features include:
  - Course content aligned specifically to *Fundamentals,* organized by chapter
  - Online self-quizzing and testing
  - Psychology Glossary
  - Communications Tools—mail, bulletin board, chat, and white board

  WebCT also includes Instructor Course Management tools. You can build course calendars, provide online testing and grading, and track your students' progress—all available at the click of a button. Try it for yourself with a live demonstration! Go to http://webct.harcourtcollege.com/public/genpsychdemo/

Both Instructors and students can benefit from visiting Harcourt's PsychCentral Web site and the text's companion Web site, www.harcourtcollege.com/psych/Fundamentals.

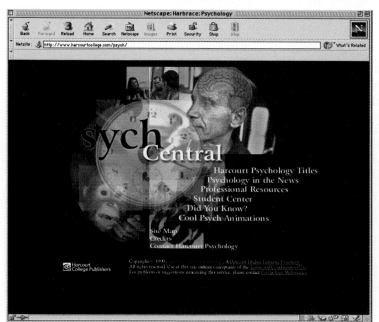

PsychCentral offers

- **Psychology in the News.** Read about how psychological research affects our everyday lives through a variety of article links.
- **Professional Resources.** Here are links to sites all over the Web to help students become familiar with professional journals and organizations in psychology, as well as the many paths one can pursue with a psychology degree.
- **Student Center.** Here are tips on studying, becoming a better student, how to master difficult material, improve memory, and become a better writer.

- **Did You Know?** A collection of fascinating facts from the world of psychology.
- **Cool Psych Animations.** Explore Mendel's experiments, The Gestalt Principle of Continuity, Perceptions of Causality, and more! These interactive figures can help improve understanding of psychological principles.

Check this site frequently for updates and new features!

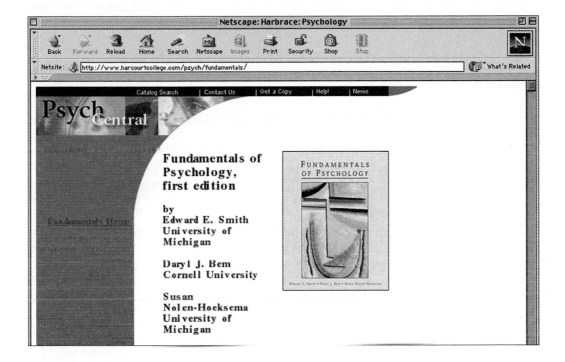

The *Fundamentals of Psychology* site offers

Student Resources

- Interactive Quizzing and Testing
- Contemporary Voices in Psychology Further Study contains links to further information about the experts featured in the textbook and the topics they discuss
- Web Activities aligned specifically to the text
- Internet Links featuring some of the most interesting psychology sites on the Web for students to explore, organized by chapter topic
- Research covering the latest in psychology field research along with some helpful tips on how to read a journal article
- Glossary for quick reference while on line

Instructor Resources

An abundance of teaching aids are available, including

- Electronic, downloadable version of the Instructor's Manual
- Teaching tips from Eric Landrum's *Guide to Teaching Introductory Psychology*
- Film Guide to help dramatically illustrate psychological concepts in the classroom
- Full-color Overhead Transparencies and accompanying guide provide more than 100 images for use in your introductory psychology course
- Course management tools

Acknowledgments

We would like to acknowledge our colleagues and peers who contributed substantially to this first edition of *Fundamentals of Psychology*. Kent Berridge of University of Michigan provided the groundwork for Chapter 2: The Biological Basis of Psychology, and was assisted by Sheila Reynolds, also from the University of Michigan. Carla Grayson of the University of Michigan solicited and organized the Contemporary Voices essays from leading researchers throughout the world. Carolyn D. Smith, a professional writer and editor, did a wonderful job helping us to develop this first edition.

We'd also like to thank James Calhoun, University of Georgia; Helena M. Carlson, Lewis & Clark College; Michelle M. Chandrasekhar, Florida State University; Mark Fineman, Southern Connecticut State University; Carol Hayes, Delta State University; Kevin Larkin, West Virginia University; Stephen Madigan, University of Southern California; Ron Mulson, Hudson Valley Community College; Rebecca Regeth, Stephen F. Austin State University; James Rotenberg, Mohawk Valley Community College; Ann Weber, University of North Carolina, Asheville. Their insightful comments helped make this first edition the best.

Special thanks to Michelle Vardeman, Harcourt developmental editor, for shepherding this project so competently and patiently. We also thank the many other people at Harcourt for their valuable contributions to this volume, including Earl McPeek, publisher; Brad Potthoff, senior aquisitions editor; Linda McMillan, production manager; Jim Patterson, project editor; David Day, art director; Caroline Robbins, permissions editor; and Katie Matthews, marketing strategist. This book could not have come into being without them.

About the Authors

The highly distinguished authors of *Fundamentals of Psychology* blend theory, research, and real-world application in a way that is eaily accessible to the student.

Edward E. Smith is the Arthur W. Melton Professor of Psychology at the University of Michigan. Having published well over a hundred articles and a dozen books, he is currently Distinguished University Professor and director of the program in cognitive science and cognitive neuroscience.

He received a B.A. in psychology from Brooklyn College and a Ph.D. in psychology from the University of Michigan. Dr. Smith's research has focused on concepts, categorization, and reasoning, as well as the structure of human memory. Present interests center on the neural bases of memory and higher-level cognition, particularly as revealed through brain-scanning.

Dr. Smith has been elected into the American Academy of Arts and Sciences and the National Academy of Sciences. He has received a Guggenheim Fellowship, the American Psychological Association Distinguished Scientific Contribution Award, and the American Psychological Society William James Fellow Award.

Daryl J. Bem, professor of psychology at Cornell University, began his academic career with a B.A. in physics from Reed College in Portland, Oregon and graduate work in physics at MIT. However, in witnessing the birth of the civil rights movement, Dr. Bem became so intrigued with changing attitudes toward desegregation in the American South, he decided to pursue a career as a social psychologist specializing in attitudes and public opinion.

Dr. Bem obtained his Ph.D. in social psychology from the University of Michigan and has since taught at Carnegie-Mellon University, Stanford, Harvard, and Cornell University, where he has been since 1978. Professor Bem has presented testimony to a subcommittee of the United States Senate on the psychological effects of police interrogation and has served as an expert witness in several court cases involving sex discrimination.

Dr. Bem has published on diverse topics in psychology, including group decision making, self-perception, personality theory, ESP, and sexual orientation. He is the author of *Beliefs, Attitudes, and Human Affairs* (1970) and *Exotic Becomes Erotic: Explaining the Enigma of Sexual Orientation* (forthcoming).

Susan Nolen-Hoeksema is professor of psychology at the University of Michigan, having earned a B.A. in psychology from Yale University and a Ph.D. in clinical psychology from the University of Pennsylvania.

Dr. Nolen-Hoeksema's research focuses on emotion regulation, stress and coping, and depression. She is the recipient of an early career award from the American Psychological Association, numerous research grants, and two major teaching awards.

Dr. Nolen-Hoeksema has published 5 books and over 40 research articles in the last 14 years. She currently directs the Gender and Mental Health Training Program at the University of Michigan, which trains pre- and post-doctoral students in research on the intersection of gender and mental health.

Brief Contents

Contents

A Word to the Student

A central topic in psychology is the analysis of learning and memory. Almost every chapter of this book refers to these phenomena; Chapter 6 ("Learning") and Chapter 7 ("Memory") are devoted exclusively to learning and memory. In this section we review a method for reading and studying information presented in textbook form. The theoretical ideas underlying this method are discussed in Chapter 7; the method is described here in greater detail for readers who wish to apply it in studying this textbook.

This approach for reading textbook chapters, called the PQRST method, has been shown to be very effective in improving a reader's understanding of and memory for key ideas and information. The method takes its name from the first letter of the five steps one follows in reading a chapter—Preview, Question, Read, Self-recitation, Test. The first and last stages (Preview and Test) apply to the chapter as a whole; the middle three stages (Question, Read, Self-recitation) apply to each major section of the chapter as it is encountered.*

Stage P (Preview) In the first step, you preview the entire chapter by skimming through it to get an idea of major topics. This is done by reading the chapter outline and then skimming the chapter, paying special attention to the headings of main sections and subsections and glancing at pictures and illustrations. The most important aspect of the preview stage is to read carefully the summary at the end of the chapter once you have skimmed through the chapter. Take time to consider each point in the summary; questions will come to mind that should be answered later as you read the full text. The preview stage will give you an overview of the topics covered in the chapter and how they are organized.

Stage Q (Question) As noted earlier, you should apply Stages Q, R, and S to each major section of the chapter as it is encountered. The typical chapter in this textbook has five to eight major sections, each section beginning with a heading set in large letters. Work through the chapter one section at a time, applying Stages Q, R, and S to each section before going on to the next section. Before reading a section, read the heading of the section and the headings of the subsections. Then turn the topic headings into one or more questions that you should expect to answer while reading the section. Ask yourself: "What are the main ideas the author is trying to convey in this section?" This is the Question Stage.

Stage R (Read) Next, read the section carefully for meaning. As you read, try to answer the questions you asked in Stage Q. Reflect on what you are reading, and try to make connections to other things you know. You may choose to mark or underline key words or phrases in the text. Try, however, not to mark more than 10 to 15% of the text. Too much underlining defeats the intended purpose, which is to make key words and ideas stand out for later review. It is probably best to delay taking notes until you have read the entire section and encountered all the key ideas, so you can judge their relative importance.

Stage S (Self-Recitation) After you have finished reading the section, try to recall the main ideas and recite the information. Self-recitation is a powerful means of fixing the material in your memory. Put the ideas into your own words and recite the information (preferably aloud or, if you are not alone, to yourself). Check against the text to be sure that you have recited the material correctly and completely.

---

* The PQRST method as described here is based on the work of Thomas and H. A. Robinson (1982) and Spache and Berg (1978); their work, in turn, is based on the earlier contributions of R. P. Robinson (1970). In some sources, the name SQ3R is used instead of PQRST. The S, the Q, and the three Rs stand for the same five steps, but are relabeled as Survey, Question, Read, Recite, and Review. We find PQRST to be easier to remember than SQ3R.

Self-recitation will reveal blanks in your knowledge and help you organize the information in your mind. After you have completed one section of the chapter in this way, turn to the next section and again apply Stages Q, R, and S. Continue in this manner until you have finished all sections of the chapter.

Stage T (Test)   When you have finished reading the chapter, you should test and review all of the material. Look over your notes and test your recall for the main ideas. Try to understand how the various facts relate to one another and how they were organized in the chapter. The test stage may require that you thumb back through the chapter to check key facts and ideas. You should also reread the chapter summary at this time; as you are doing so, you should be able to add details to each entry in the summary. Don't put off the test stage until the night before an examination. The best time for a first review of the chapter is immediately after you have read it.

Research indicates that the PQRST method is very helpful and definitely preferable to simply reading straight through a chapter (Thomas & Robinson, 1982). Self-recitation is particularly important; it is better to spend a significant percentage of study time in an active attempt to recite than it is to devote the entire time to reading and rereading the material (Gates, 1917). Studies also show that a careful reading of the summary of the chapter before reading the chapter itself is especially productive (Reder & Anderson, 1980). Reading the summary first provides an overview of the chapter that helps organize the material as you read through the chapter. Even if you choose not to follow every step of the PQRST method, special attention should be directed to the value of self-recitation and reading the chapter summary as an introduction to the material.

FUNDAMENTALS OF PSYCHOLOGY

The Nature and History of Psychology

What Are the Interdisciplinary Approaches to Psychology?
    Cognitive Neuroscience
    Evolutionary Psychology
    Cognitive Science
    Cultural Psychology
What Are the Major Subfields of Psychology?
Overview of the Book

Psychological questions touch virtually every aspect of our daily lives: Does the way our parents raised us affect the way we raise our own children? Can we recover a traumatic childhood experience in more detail under hypnosis? How should instruments in a nuclear power plant be designed to minimize human error? What effect does prolonged stress have on the immune system? Is psychotherapy more effective than drugs in treating depression? Psychologists are working to answer these and many other questions.

Psychology also affects our lives through its influence on laws and public policy. Psychological theories and research have influenced laws concerning discrimination, capital punishment, pornography, sexual behavior, and personal responsibility for actions, among many others.

Because psychology affects so many aspects of our lives, even people who do not intend to specialize in the field should know something about its basic facts and research methods. An introductory course in psychology will give you a better understanding of why people think and act as they do, and it will provide insights into your own attitudes and reactions. It should also help you evaluate the many claims made in the name of psychology. Everyone has seen newspaper headlines like these:

- New Form of Psychotherapy Facilitates Recovery of Repressed Memories
- Anxiety Controlled by Self-Regulation of Brain Waves
- Proof of Mental Telepathy Found
- Hypnosis Effective in the Control of Pain
- Emotional Stability Closely Related to Family Size
- Homosexuality Linked to Parental Attitudes
- Transcendental Meditation Facilitates Problem Solving
- Multiple Personality Linked to Childhood Abuse

There are two things you need to know to evaluate such claims. First, you need to know what psychological facts are already firmly established so that you can determine whether the new claim is compatible with those facts; if it is not, there is reason to be cautious. Second, you need to know the kind of evidence necessary to give credence to a new claim or discovery, so that you can determine whether the arguments in support of the new claim meet the usual standards of scientific evidence; if they do not, again there is reason for skepticism. This book tries to supply both kinds of knowledge. First, it reviews the current state of knowledge in psychology—that is, it tries to present the most important findings in the field so that you know the established facts. Second, it examines the nature of research—that is, how a psychologist designs a research program that is capable of providing strong evidence for or against a hypothesis—so that you know the kind of evidence needed to back up a new claim.

In this chapter we first consider the kinds of *topics* that are studied in psychology and briefly describe its *historical origins*. Next we discuss the *perspectives* that psychologists adopt in investigating these topics. Then we describe the *research methods* used in psychological investigations, and after that, we turn to various *interdisciplinary approaches* that involve psychology and look at the *professional specializations* within the field. Finally, we briefly describe the contents of the rest of the book.

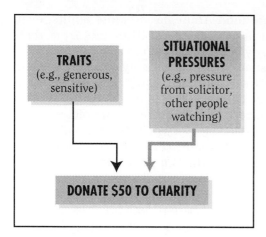

Figure 1-1

Trait Attribution In deciding whether a substantial donation to charity is caused by the giver's traits or by the situation, we are biased toward believing that a trait was the critical factor.

What Is Psychology About?

Psychology can be defined as *the scientific study of behavior and mental processes.* An astonishing variety of topics fits this definition. To give you some idea of this variety, we briefly describe five representative problems examined by psychologists.

psychology the scientific study of behavior and mental processes

Brain Damage and Face Recognition It is no surprise that when people suffer brain damage, they typically show impairment in their behavior. What is surprising is that sometimes, when the damage is in a specific part of the brain, the person's behavior may change in one way while appearing normal in all other ways. In some such cases, for example, people are unable to recognize familiar faces as a result of damage to a particular region on the right side of their brain—yet they can do just about everything else normally. A famous example of this condition, termed *prosopagnosia,* was described by the neurologist Oliver Sacks[1] (1985) in his book *The Man Who Mistook His Wife for a Hat.* In another case, a person with prosopagnosia complained to a restaurant waiter that someone was staring at him, only to be informed that he was looking in a mirror! Such cases tell us a lot about the way the normal brain works. They indicate that some psychological functions, such as face recognition, are *localized* in particular parts of the brain.

Attributing Traits to People Suppose that in a crowded department store, a person soliciting for a charity approaches a customer and implores her to make a contribution; the woman proceeds to write a $50 check to the charity. Would you think the woman was generous? Or would you think that she had been pressured into making the donation because so many people witnessed her action? Experiments designed to study situations like this one indicate that most people would consider the woman generous. We tend to see other people's actions as caused by their personal traits, not by the situations in which they find themselves—even though some situational pressures can be so great that they cause just about everybody to act in predictable ways (see Figure 1-1).

---

[1] Throughout this book you will find references, cited by author and date, that document or expand the statements made here. Detailed publishing information on these studies appears in the reference list at the end of the book.

Events that happen early in childhood usually are not remembered. This little girl probably will not remember the events surrounding the birth of her baby brother.

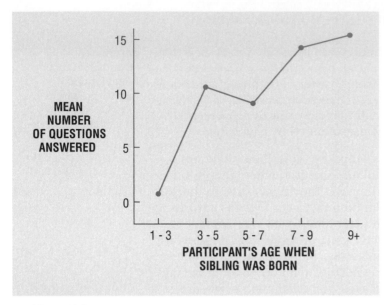

Figure 1-2

Recall of an Early Memory   In an experiment on childhood amnesia, college-age participants were asked 20 questions about the events surrounding the birth of a younger sibling. The average number of questions answered is plotted as a function of the participant's age when the sibling was born. If the birth occurred before the participant's fourth year of life, no participant could recall a thing about it; if the birth occurred after that, recall increased with the participant's age at the time of the event. (After Sheingold & Tenney, 1982)

Figure 1-3

The Relationship Between Childhood Viewing of Violent Television and Adult Aggression   A classic study shows that preference for viewing violent TV programs by boys at age 9 is related to aggressive behavior as rated by peers at age 19. (After Eron, Huesmann, Lefkowitz, & Walder, 1972)

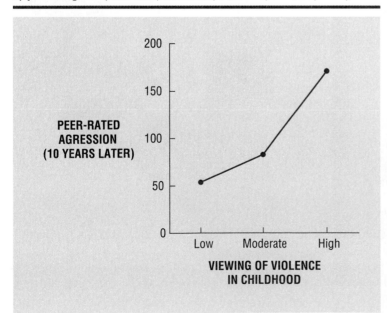

Childhood Amnesia   Most adults, even elderly ones, can recall events from their early years, but only up to a certain point. Almost no one can accurately recall events from the first 3 years of life. Consider a significant event like the birth of a sibling. If the birth occurred after you were 3 years old, you may have some memory of it, the amount you recall being greater the older you were at the time of the birth. But if the birth occurred before age 3, you probably would remember very little about it, if anything at all (see Figure 1-2). This phenomenon is called *childhood amnesia*. It is particularly striking because our first 3 years are so rich in experience: We develop from helpless newborns to crawling, babbling infants to walking, talking children. But these remarkable transitions leave little trace on our memory.

Obesity   Roughly 35 million Americans are obese—that is, their weight is 30% or more above the weight that would be appropriate for their body structure and height. Obesity is dangerous—it increases vulnerability to diabetes, high blood pressure, and heart disease. Psychologists are interested in what factors lead people to eat too much. One factor seems to be a history of deprivation. If rats are first deprived of food, then allowed to feed back to their normal weight, and finally allowed to eat as much as they want, they eat more than other rats that have no history of deprivation.

Effects of Media Violence on Children's Aggression   The question of whether watching violence on television causes children to be more aggressive has long been controversial. Although many observers believe that televised violence affects children's behavior, others have suggested that watching violence might have a *cathartic* effect—that is, it might actually reduce aggression by allowing children to express it vicariously, thereby "getting it out of their system." But research evidence does not support this view. In one experiment, one group of children was randomly assigned to watch violent cartoons while another group was randomly assigned to watch nonviolent cartoons for the same amount of time. The children who watched violent cartoons became more aggressive in their interactions with peers, whereas those who viewed nonviolent cartoons showed no change in aggressive behavior (Steuer, Applefield, & Smith, 1971). These effects can persist over time: The more violent programs a boy watches at age 9, the more aggressive he is likely to be at age 19 (see Figure 1-3).

Figure 1-3 displays the results of a classic study showing that a preference for viewing violent TV programs by boys at age 9 is related to aggressive behavior at age 19. Why does this study fail to demonstrate that watching violence on TV makes boys more aggressive? Does the other experiment on TV violence described in the text demonstrate the point? What is the crucial difference between the two studies?

Thinking Critically

What Are the Historical Origins of Psychology?

The roots of modern psychology can be traced to the great philosophers of ancient Greece. The most famous of them, Socrates, Plato, and Aristotle, posed fundamental questions about mental life. What is consciousness? Are people inherently rational or irrational? Is there really such a thing as free choice? These questions, and many similar ones, are as important now as they were 2,000 years ago. They deal with the nature of mind and mental processes, and, as we will see in the next section, they are key elements of the cognitive perspective.

Other psychological questions deal with the nature of the body and human behavior, and they have an equally long history. Hippocrates, often called the "father of medicine," lived at around the same time as Socrates. He was very interested in **physiology,** *the study of the functions of the living organism and its parts*. He made many important observations about how the brain controls various organs of the body. These observations set the stage for what became the biological perspective in psychology.

physiology the study of the functions of the living organism and its parts

Nativism vs. Empiricism

One of the earliest debates about human psychology is still raging today. It is the question of whether human capabilities are inborn or acquired through experience. The *nativist* view holds that human beings enter the world with an inborn store of knowledge and understanding of reality. Early philosophers believed that this knowledge and understanding could be accessed through careful reasoning and introspection. In the 17th century, the French philosopher René Descartes, supported the nativist view by arguing that some ideas (such as God, the self, geometric axioms, perfection, and infinity) are innate. Descartes is also notable for his conception of the body as a machine that can be studied in much the same way that other machines are studied. This is the root of modern-day *information-processing* perspectives on the mind, discussed later in the chapter.

The *empiricist* view holds that knowledge is acquired through experience and interactions with the world. Although some of the early Greek philosophers held this view it is most strongly associated with the 17th-century English philosopher John Locke. According to Locke, at birth the human mind is a *tabula rasa,* or blank slate, onto which experience "writes" knowledge and understanding as the individual matures. This perspective gave birth to *associationist psychology*. Associationists denied that there were inborn ideas or capabilities of the mind. Instead, they argued that the mind is filled with ideas that enter by way of the senses and then become associated with one another through such principles as similarity,

The ancient Greek philosopher Socrates posed fundamental questions about mental life. Many of these questions are as important today as they were in Socrates' time.

Archives of the History of American Psychology, The University of Akron

Wilhelm Wundt established the first psychological laboratory at the University of Leipzig. Here he is shown in the laboratory with his associates.

contrast, and contiguity. Current research on memory and learning is related to early association theory.

These days the debate between nativism and empiricism is referred to as the *nature-nurture* debate. Although some psychologists would still argue that human thought and behavior are either the result primarily of biology or primarily of experience, most psychologists take a more integrated approach, acknowledging that biological processes (such as heredity or processes in the brain) affect thoughts, feelings, and behavior, but that experience leaves its mark on these as well. We will encounter the nature-nurture issue at numerous points in later chapters.

The Beginnings of Scientific Psychology

Although philosophers and scholars continued to be interested in the functioning of both the mind and the body through the centuries, scientific psychology is usually considered to have begun in 1879, when Wilhelm Wundt established the first formal psychological laboratory at the University of Leipzig in Germany. The impetus for the establishment of Wundt's lab was the belief that mind and behavior, like planets or chemicals or human organs, could be the subject of scientific analysis. Wundt's own research was concerned primarily with the senses, especially vision, but he and his coworkers also studied attention, emotion, and memory.

introspection an individual's observation and recording of the nature of his or her own perceptions, thoughts, and feelings

Wundt relied on introspection as a method for studying mental processes. **Introspection** refers to *an individual's observation and recording of the nature of his or her own perceptions, thoughts, and feelings*—for example, reflections on one's immediate sensory impressions of a stimulus, such as the flash of a colored light. The introspective method was inherited from philosophy, but Wundt added a new dimension to it. Pure self-observation was not sufficient; it had to be supplemented by experiments. Wundt's experiments systematically varied some physical dimension of a stimulus, such as its intensity, and used the introspective method to determine how these physical changes modified the participant's conscious experience of the stimulus.

The reliance on introspection, particularly for very rapid mental events, proved unworkable. Even after extensive training in introspection, different people produced very different introspections about simple sensory experiences, and few conclusions could be drawn from these differences. As a result, introspection is not a central part of the current cognitive perspective. And as we will see, some psychologists' reactions to introspection played a role in the development of other modern perspectives.

Structuralism and Functionalism

During the 19th century, chemistry and physics made great advances by analyzing complex compounds (molecules) into their elements (atoms). These successes encouraged psychologists to look for the mental elements of more complex experiences. Just as chemists analyzed water into hydrogen and oxygen, perhaps psychologists could analyze the taste of lemonade (perception) into elements such as sweet, bitter, and cold (sensations). The leading proponent of this approach in the United States was E. B. Titchener, a Cornell University psychologist who had been trained by Wundt. Titchener introduced the term **structuralism**—meaning *the analysis of mental structures*—to describe this brand of psychology.

structuralism the analysis of mental structure

But some psychologists opposed the purely analytic nature of structuralism. William James, a distinguished psychologist at Harvard University, felt that less emphasis should be placed on analyzing the elements of consciousness and more on

William James, John B. Watson, and Sigmund Freud were key figures in the early history of psychology. James developed the approach known as functionalism, while Watson was the founder of behaviorism and Freud originated the theory and method of psychoanalysis.

understanding its fluid, personal nature. His approach was named **functionalism,** which refers to *the study of how the mind works so that an organism can adapt to and function in its environment.*

Nineteenth-century psychologists' interest in adaptation stemmed from the publication of Charles Darwin's theory of evolution. It was argued that consciousness had evolved only because it served some purpose in guiding the individual's activities. To find how the organism adapts to its environment, functionalists argued that it was necessary to observe actual behavior. Thus, functionalism broadened the scope of psychology to include behavior as an object of study. But both structuralists and functionalists still regarded psychology as the science of conscious experience.

functionalism the study of how the mind works so that an organism can adapt to and function in its environment

Behaviorism

Structuralism and functionalism played important roles in the early development of psychology. Because each viewpoint provided a systematic approach to the field, the two were considered competing *schools of psychology.* By 1920, however, structuralism and functionalism were being displaced by three newer schools: *behaviorism, Gestalt psychology,* and *psychoanalysis.*

Of the three new schools, behaviorism had the greatest influence on scientific psychology in North America. Its founder, John B. Watson, reacted against the view that conscious experience was the province of psychology. Watson made no assertions about consciousness when he studied the behavior of animals and infants. He decided not only that animal psychology and child psychology could stand on their own as sciences, but also that they set a pattern that adult psychology might follow.

For psychology to be a science, Watson believed, psychological data must be open to public inspection like the data of any other science. Behavior is public; consciousness is private. Science should deal only with public facts. Because psychologists at this time were growing impatient with introspection, behaviorism caught on rapidly.

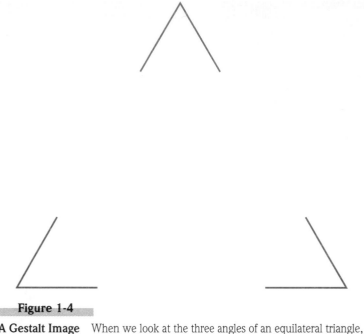

Figure 1-4

A Gestalt Image   When we look at the three angles of an equilateral triangle, we see a single large triangle rather than three small angles.

Many younger psychologists in the United States called themselves "behaviorists." (The Russian physiologist Ivan Pavlov's research on the conditioned response was regarded as an important area of behavioral research, but it was Watson who was responsible for behaviorism's widespread influence.)

Watson argued that nearly all behavior is the result of conditioning and that condiioned stimuli from the environment elicit specific responses or habits. For example, a toy previously associated with a loud noise will elicit fear and withdrawal from a child. The conditioned response was viewed as the smallest unit of behavior from which more complicated behaviors could be created. All types of complex behavior patterns arising from special training or education were regarded as nothing more than an interlinked fabric of conditioned responses.

Behaviorists tended to discuss psychological phenomena in terms of stimuli and responses, giving rise to the term *stimulus-response (S-R) psychology*. Note, however, that S-R psychology itself is not a theory or perspective but a set of terms that can be used to communicate psychological information. S-R terminology is often used in psychology today.

Gestalt Psychology

Around 1912, at about the same time that behaviorism was catching on in America, Gestalt psychology was appearing in Germany. *Gestalt* is a German word meaning "form" or "configuration," and it was used to refer to the approach favored by Max Wertheimer and his colleagues Kurt Koffka and Wolfgang Köhler, all of whom emigrated to the United States.

The Gestalt psychologists were interested primarily in perception, and they believed that perceptual experiences depend on the *patterns* formed by stimuli and on the *organization* of experience (see Chapter 4). What we actually see is relative to the background and other aspects of the whole pattern of stimulation. The whole is different from the sum of its parts since the whole depends on the relationships among the parts. For example, when we look at Figure 1-4, we see it as a single large triangle—as a single form or Gestalt—rather than as three small angles.

The Gestalt psychologists were interested in the perception of motion, in how people judge size, and in the appearance of colors under changes in illumination. These interests led them to a number of perception-centered interpretations of learning, memory, and problem solving that helped lay the groundwork for current research in cognitive psychology.

The importance of perception to all psychological events has led those psychologists influenced by Gestalt psychology to a number of perception-centered interpretations of learning, memory, and problem solving. These interpretations, referred to as forms of cognitive theory, helped lay the groundwork for current developments in cognitive psychology.

Psychoanalysis

Psychoanalysis is both a theory of personality and a method of psychotherapy. It originated with Sigmund Freud around the turn of the 20th century.

At the center of Freud's theory is the concept of the **unconscious**—that is, *the thoughts, attitudes, impulses, wishes, motivations, and emotions of which we are unaware.* Freud believed that the unacceptable (i.e., forbidden or punished) wishes of childhood are drives out of conscious awareness and become part of the unconscious, where they continue to influence our thoughts, feelings, and actions. Unconscious thoughts are expressed in various ways, including dreams, slips of the tongue, and physical mannerisms. During therapy with patients, Freud used the method of *free association,* in which the patient is instructed to say whatever comes to mind as a way of bringing unconscious wishes into awareness. The analysis of dreams serves the same purpose.

In classical Freudian theory, the motivations behind unconscious wishes almost always involve sex or aggression. It is for this reason that Freud's theory was not widely accepted when it was first proposed. But while most contemporary psychologists do not completely accept Freud's view of the unconscious, they tend to agree that individuals are not fully aware of some important aspects of their behavior.

unconscious the thoughts, attitudes, impulses, wishes, motivations, and emotions of which we are unaware

Modern Developments

Despite the important contribution of Gestalt psychology and psychoanalysis, until World War II psychology was dominated by behaviorism, particularly in the United States. After the war, interest in psychology increased. Sophisticated instruments and electronic equipment became available, and a wider range of problems could be examined. It became evident that earlier theoretical approaches were too restrictive.

This viewpoint was strengthened by the development of computers in the 1950s. Computers, properly programmed, were able to perform tasks—such as playing chess and proving mathematical theorems—that previously could be done only by human beings. It became apparent that the computer offered psychologists a powerful tool for theorizing about psychological processes. In a series of papers published in the late 1950s, Herbert Simon (who was later awarded a Nobel prize) and his colleagues indicated how psychological phenomena could be *simulated* using the computer. Many psychological issues were recast in terms of *information-processing systems.* The notion of the human being as a processor of information provided a more dynamic approach than S-R theory. Similarly, the information-processing approach made it possible to formulate some of the ideas of Gestalt psychology and psychoanalysis in a more precise fashion. In this way, earlier ideas about the nature of the mind could expressed in concrete terms and checked against actual data. For example, we can think of the operation of memory as analogous to the way a computer stores and retrieves information. Just as a computer can transfer information from temporary storage in its internal memory chips (RAM) to more permanent storage on the hard disk, so, too, our short-term memory can act as a way station to long-term memory (Atkinson & Shiffrin, 1971; Raaijmakers & Shiffrin, 1992).

Another important influence on psychology in the 1950s was the development of modern linguistics. Linguists began to theorize about the mental structures required to comprehend and to speak a language. Work in this area was pioneered by Noam Chomsky, whose book *Syntactic Structures,* published in 1957, stimulated the first significant psychological analyses of language and the emergence of the field of *psycholinguistics,* which is a collaboration between psychologists and linguists.

At the same time, important advances were occurring in *neuropsychology.* Various discoveries about the brain and the nervous system revealed clear relationships between neurobiological events and mental processes. In recent decades, with the aid of advances in biomedical technology, rapid progress has been made in research with

Herbert Simon

these relationships. In 1981 Roger Sperry was awarded a Nobel prize for demonstrating the links between specific regions of the brain and particular thought and behavioral processes, which we discuss in Chapter 2.

The development of information-processing models, psycholinguistics, and neuropsychology has produced a psychology that is highly cognitive in orientation. But while its principal concern is the scientific analysis of mental processes and structures, cognitive psychology is not exclusively concerned with thought and knowledge. As we will see throughout this book, this approach has been expanded to many other areas of psychology, including motivation, perception, personality, and social psychology.

In sum, during the past century the focus of psychology has come full circle. After rejecting conscious experience as ill-suited to scientific investigation and turning to the study of overt, observable behavior, psychologists are once again theorizing about covert aspects of the mind—but this time with new and more powerful tools.

What Are the Contemporary Perspectives in Psychology?

Now that we have explored the historical background of psychology, let us examine some of the discipline's major contemporary perspectives. What is a perspective? Basically it is an approach, a way of looking at a topic. Any topic in psychology can be approached from a variety of perspectives. Indeed, this is true of any action a person takes. Suppose that you walk across the street. From a *biological perspective,* this act can be described as involving the firing of the nerves that activate the muscles that move your legs. From a *behavioral perspective,* the act can be described without reference to anything within your body; rather, the green light is a stimulus to which you respond by crossing the street. One may also take a *cognitive perspective* of crossing the street, focusing on the mental processes involved in producing the behavior. From a cognitive perspective, your action might be explained in terms of your goals and plans: Your goal is to visit a friend, and crossing the street is part of your plan for achieving that goal.

Although there are many possible ways to describe any psychological act, the five perspectives described in this section represent the major approaches to the modern study of psychology (see Figure 1-5). Because these five perspectives are discussed throughout the book, here we provide only a brief description of some main points for each of them. Also keep in mind that these approaches need not be mutually exclusive; rather, they may focus on different aspects of the same complex phenomenon.

The Biological Perspective

The human brain contains well over 100 billion nerve cells and an almost infinite number of interconnections between those cells. It may well be the most complex structure in the universe. In principle, all psychological events can be related to the activity of the brain and nervous system. The biological approach to the study of human beings and

Figure 1-5

Perspectives in Psychology   The analysis of psychological phenomena can be approached from several perspectives. Each offers a somewhat different account of why individuals act as they do, and each can make a contribution to our conception of the total person. The Greek letter psy, "Ψ," is sometimes used as an abbreviation for "psychology."

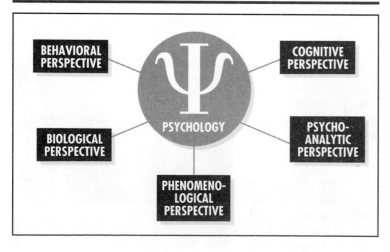

other species attempts to relate overt behavior to electrical and chemical events taking place inside the body. Thus, research from this perspective seeks to specify the neurobiological processes that underlie behavior and mental processes. The biological approach to depression, for example, seeks to understand this disorder in terms of abnormal changes in levels of neurotransmitters, which are chemicals produced in the brain that make communication between nerve cells possible.

We can use one of the problems described earlier to illustrate this perspective. The study of face recognition in patients with brain damage indicates that particular regions of the brain are specialized for face recognition. The human brain is divided into right and left hemispheres, and the regions devoted to face recognition seem to be located mainly in the right hemisphere. It turns out that there is considerable hemispheric specialization in humans; for example, in most right-handed people the left hemisphere is specialized for understanding language and the right hemisphere is specialized for interpreting spatial relations. The biological perspective has also assisted in the study of memory. It emphasizes the importance of certain brain structures, including the hippo-

By studying the brain activity of animals, researchers gain insight into the human brain. In this single-cell recording experiment, a microelectrode, which monitors the electrical activity of a single neuron, is implanted in the visual system of a monkey.

campus, which is involved in consolidating memories. Childhood amnesia may be partly due to an immature hippocampus, since this brain structure is not fully developed until a year or two after birth.

The Behavioral Perspective

As described in our brief review of the history of psychology, the behavioral perspective focuses on observable stimuli and responses. For example, an S-R analysis of your social life might focus on which people you interact with (these would be the social stimuli), the kinds of responses you make to them (rewarding, punishing, or neutral), the kinds of responses they in turn make to you (rewarding, punishing, or neutral), and how the rewards sustain or disrupt the interaction.

We can use our sample problems to further illustrate the approach. With regard to obesity, some people may overeat (a specific response) only in the presence of specific stimuli, and learning to avoid those stimuli is part of many weight control programs. With regard to aggression, children are more likely to make aggressive responses, such as hitting another child, when those responses are rewarded (the other child withdraws) than when their responses are punished (the other child counterattacks).

Historically, the strict behavioral approach did not consider the individual's mental processes at all, and even contemporary behaviorists usually do not conjecture about the mental processes that intervene between the stimulus and the response. Nevertheless, psychologists other than strict behaviorists will often record what a person says about his or her conscious experiences (a verbal report) and draw inferences about the person's mental activity from these objective data. Although few psychologists today would define themselves as strict behaviorists, many modern developments in psychology have evolved from the work of the earlier behaviorists (Skinner, 1981).

The Cognitive Perspective

The modern cognitive perspective is in part a return to the cognitive roots of psychology and in part a reaction to the narrowness of behaviorism and the S-R view (both of which tend to neglect complex human activities like reasoning, planning, decision making, and communication). Like the 19th-century version, the modern study of cognition is concerned with mental processes such as perceiving, remembering, reasoning, deciding, and problem solving. Unlike the 19th-century version, however, modern cognitivism is not based on introspection. Instead, it assumes that (1) only by studying mental processes can we fully understand what organisms do, and (2) we can study mental processes in an objective fashion by focusing on specific behaviors (just as the behaviorists do) but interpreting them in terms of underlying mental processes.

In making these interpretations, cognitive psychologists often rely on an analogy between the mind and a computer. Incoming information is processed in various ways: It is selected, compared and combined with other information already in mem-

Cognitive psychologists often use the computer as an analog of the brain. Information can be taken in, filtered, temporarily stored in short-term memory (RAM), moved to long-term memory (a hard disk), combined with information already stored in memory, rearranged, and so on. Humanistic psychologists believe that a major human motivation is self-actualization, striving to grow psychologically and to fulfull one's full potential. They emphasize the unique human qualities that distinguish healthy people from both disturbed patients and animals.

ory, transformed, rearranged, and so on. Consider the phenomenon of childhood amnesia described at the beginning of the chapter. Perhaps we cannot remember events from the first few years of life because of a major developmental change in the way we organize our experience in memory. Such changes may be particularly pronounced around age 3 because at that point there is a major increase in our language abilities, and language offers a new way of organizing our memories.

The Psychoanalytic Perspective

As mentioned earlier, the psychoanalytic conception of human behavior was developed by Sigmund Freud in Europe at about the same time that behaviorism was evolving in the United States. In some respects psychoanalysis was a blend of the 19th-century versions of cognition and physiology. In particular, Freud combined cognitive notions of consciousness, perception, and memory with ideas about biologically based instincts to forge a bold new theory of human behavior.

The basic assumption of Freud's theory is that much of our behavior stems from unconscious processes—the beliefs, fears, and desires that a person is unaware of but that nonetheless influence his or her behavior. Freud believed that many of the impulses that are forbidden or punished by parents and society during childhood are derived from innate instincts. Because each of us is born with these impulses, they exert a pervasive influence that must be dealt with in some manner. Forbidding them merely forces them out of awareness into the unconscious. They do not disappear, however; they may manifest themselves as emotional problems, symptoms of mental illness, or, on the other hand, socially approved behavior such as artistic and literary activity. For example, if you feel a lot of anger toward a person whom you cannot afford to alienate, your anger may become unconscious, perhaps being expressed in a dream about that person.

Freud believed that we are driven by the same basic instincts as animals (primarily sex and aggression) and that we are continually struggling against a society that stresses the control of these impulses. Thus the psychoanalytic perspective suggests new ways of looking at some of the problems described at the beginning of the chapter. For example, Freud claimed that aggressive behavior stems from an innate instinct. Although this proposal is not widely accepted in human psychology, it is in agreement with the views of some biologists and psychologists who study aggression in animals.

The Phenomenological Perspective

The phenomenological perspective focuses on a person's subjective experiences and has been associated with social psychologists, who are interested in how we perceive, understand, and interpret our social worlds. Within the domain of personality psychology, the phenomenological approach characterizes those who call themselves *humanistic* psychologists. Humanistic psychologists reject the assumptions about human nature made by the psychoanalytic and behavioral approaches. Instead, they emphasize the unique human qualities that distinguish healthy people from both disturbed patients and animals. For example, according to humanistic theories, an individual's principal motivational force is a tendency toward growth and self-actualization. All of us have a basic need to develop our potential to the fullest, to progress beyond where we are now. Although we may be blocked by environmental and social obstacles, our natural tendency is toward actualizing our potential. For example, a woman in a traditional marriage who had been raising her children for 10 years may come to feel a strong desire to pursue an outside career, perhaps to develop a long-dormant interest in science that she feels the need to actualize.

Phenomenological or humanistic psychology has been more aligned with literature and the humanities than with science. For this reason, it is difficult to give detailed descriptions of what the phenomenological perspective would say about our sample problems, such as face recognition and childhood amnesia, because these are not the kinds of problems that phenomenologists study. Phenomenological and humanistic psychologists have contributed most to the study of personality, and we will discuss their approach more fully in Chapter 10.

Relationships Between Psychological and Biological Perspectives

The behavioral, cognitive, psychoanalytic, and phenomenological perspectives all rely on concepts that are purely psychological (such as perception, the unconscious, and self-actualization). Although these perspectives sometimes offer different explanations for the same phenomenon, those explanations are always psychological in nature. The biological perspective is different. In addition to using psychological concepts, it employs concepts (such as neurons, neurotransmitters, and hormones) that are drawn from physiology and other branches of biology.

reductionism reducing psychological notions to biological ones.

There is a way, though, in which the biological perspective makes direct contact with the psychological perspectives. Biologically oriented researchers attempt to explain psychological concepts and principles in terms of their biological counterparts. For example, researchers might attempt to explain the normal ability to recognize faces solely in terms of neurons and their interconnections in a certain region of the brain. Such attempts are called **reductionism** because they involve *reducing psychological notions to biological ones.* Throughout this book we will present examples in which reductionism has been successful—that is, situations in which what was once understood at only the psychological level are now understood at least in part at the biological level.

If reductionism can be successful, why bother with psychological explanations at all? To put it another way, is psychology just something to do until the biologists figure everything out? The answer is no.

First, psychological findings, concepts, and principles direct biological researchers in their work. Given that the brain contains billions of cells and countless interconnections between these cells, biological researchers cannot hope to find something interesting by arbitrarily selecting some brain cells to study. Rather, they must have a way of directing their search to relevant groups of brain cells. Psychological findings can supply this direction. For example, if psychological research indicates that our ability to discriminate among spoken words (that is, to tell when they differ) obeys different principles from our ability to discriminate among various spatial positions, biological psychologists might look in different regions of the brain for the neural basis of these two kinds of discrimination (the left hemisphere for word discrimination and the right for spatial-position discrimination). As another example, if psychological research indicates that learning a motor skill is a slow process that is hard to undo, biological psychologists can direct their attention to brain processes that are relatively slow but permanently alter connections between neurons (Churchland & Sejnowski, 1988).

Second, our biology always acts in concert with our past circumstances and current environment. For example, obesity can be the result of both a genetic predisposition to gain weight (a biological factor) and the learning of bad eating habits (a psychological factor). The biologist can seek to understand the former, but it is still up to the psychologist to explore and explain the past experiences and current circumstances that influence a person's eating habits.

Nevertheless, the push for reductionism goes on at an ever-increasing rate. For many topics in psychology we now have both psychological explanations and biological knowledge about how the relevant psychological concepts are implemented or executed in the brain (for example, what parts of the brain are involved and how they are interconnected). This kind of biological knowledge typically falls short of total reductionism, but it is still very important. Memory researchers, for example, have long distinguished between short-term memory and long-term memory (which are psychological notions), but now they also know that these two kinds of memory

Nature and Nurture: Obesity can be the result of both a genetic predisposition to gain weight and the learning of bad eating habits.

are actually coded differently in the brain. Hence, for many of the topics discussed in this book, we will review what is known about a topic at the biological level as well as at the psychological level.

Indeed, a central theme of this book, and of contemporary psychology in general, is that psychological phenomena can be understood at both the psychological and biological levels, where the biological analysis shows how the psychological notions can be implemented in the brain. Both levels of analysis are clearly needed (although for some topics, including many having to do with social interactions, only psychological analyses have much to say).

How might the different perspectives outlined in this section approach the question, "What are the determinants of an individual's sexual orientation?"

Thinking Critically

How Is Psychological Research Done?

Now that we have some idea of the topics studied by psychologists and the perspectives from which they may approach the study of those topics, we can consider the research strategies they use to investigate them. In general, doing research involves two steps: (1) generating a scientific hypothesis, and (2) testing that hypothesis.

Generating Hypotheses

hypothesis   a statement that can be tested

The first step in any research project is to generate a **hypothesis**—*a statement that can be tested*— about the topic of interest. If our concern is childhood amnesia, for example, we might generate the hypothesis that people can retrieve more memories of early family life if they are back in the same place where the incidents originally occurred. How does a researcher arrive at such a hypothesis? There is no single answer. A person who is an astute observer of naturally occurring situations may have an advantage in coming up with hypotheses. For example, you might have noticed that you can remember more about your high school years when you are back home; this could generate the hypothesis just mentioned. It also helps to be familiar with the relevant scientific literature—that is, previously published books and articles about the topic of interest.

theory   an interrelated set of propositions about a particular phenomenon

The most important source of a scientific hypothesis, however, is often a scientific **theory,** *an interrelated set of propositions about a particular phenomenon.* For example, one theory of sexual orientation (discussed in Chapter 9) proposes that there is a genetic predisposition toward heterosexuality or homosexuality. This leads to the testable scientific hypothesis that pairs of identical twins—who have identical genes—should be more likely to share the same sexual orientation than pairs of fraternal twins, who share only about half their genes. A competing theory emphasizes childhood events as the source of an individual's sexual orientation and generates a competing set of hypotheses that can also be tested. As we will see throughout this book, the testing of hypotheses derived from competing theories is one of the most powerful ways of advancing scientific knowledge.

The term *scientific* means that the research methods used to collect the data are (1) *unbiased,* in that they do not favor one hypothesis over another; and (2) *reliable,* in that they allow other qualified people to repeat the observations and obtain the same results. The various methods to be considered in this section have these two characteristics. Although some of these methods are better suited to certain perspectives than others, each method can be used with each perspective. The major exception is that some phenomenological psychologists do not believe that such methods advance our understanding of the topics in which they are interested.

Experiments

variable   something that can occur with different values

The most powerful scientific method is the experiment. The investigator carefully controls certain conditions—often in a laboratory—and takes measurements in order to discover relationships among variables (a **variable** is *something that can occur with different values*). (See Table 1-1.) For example, an experiment might seek to discover the relationship between the variables of memory and sleep (more specifically, whether the ability to recall childhood events decreases with lack of sleep). To the extent that memory changes systematically with sleep, an orderly relationship between these two variables has been found to exist.

The ability to exercise precise control over a variable distinguishes the experimental method from other methods of scientific observation. For example, if the hypothesis being tested is that individuals will perform better on mathematics problems if they are offered more money for good performance, then the experimenter might randomly assign participants to one of three conditions: One group is told that they will be paid $10 if they perform well; the second group is told that they will be paid $5 if they perform well; the third group is not offered any money for their

Table 1-1

Terminology of Experimental Research

Hypothesis: a statement that can be tested.
Theory: an interrelated set of propositions about a particular phenomenon.
Variable: something that can occur with different values.
Independent variable: a variable that is independent of what the participant does.
Dependent variable: a variable whose values depend on the value of the independent variable.
Experimental group: a group in which the condition under study is present.
Control group: a group in which the condition under study is absent.
Measurement: a system for assigning numbers to variables.

performance. The experimenter then measures and compares the actual performance of all three groups to see if, in fact, more money produces better performance.

In this study, the amount of money offered is called the **independent variable** because it is *a variable that is independent of what the participant does.* Performance on the task is called the **dependent variable** because it is *a variable that is hypothesized to depend on the value of the independent variable.* Thus, the independent variable is the variable that the experimenter manipulates, and the dependent variable is the variable that the experimenter observes. The dependent variable is almost always some measure of the participant's behavior. The phrase "is a function of" is used to express the dependence of one variable on another. For this experiment, we could say that the participants' performance on the tasks is a function of the amount of money they had been offered. The groups that are paid money are usually called the **experimental groups,** or *groups in which the condition under study is present.* The group that is not paid would be called the **control group,** or *the group in which the condition under study is absent.* In general, a control group serves as a baseline against which experimental groups can be compared.

One important feature of the experiment just described is random assignment of participants to conditions. If this is not done, then the experimenter cannot rule out

independent variable
a variable independent
of what the participant
does

dependent variable
the variable hypothe-
sized to depend on the
value of the indepen-
dent variable

experimental group
a group in which the
condition under study
is present

control group a
group in which the
condition under study
is absent

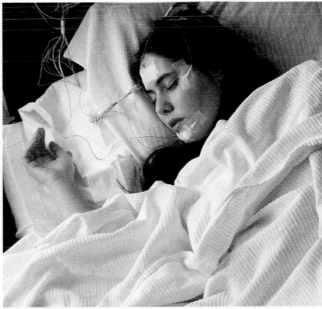

A researcher in a sleep laboratory monitors the brain activity of a sleeping woman.

the possiblity that other, unintended variables might have produced the results. For example, an experimenter should never let participants choose which group they would like to be in. Although most participants might choose to be in the highest-paid group, those who are made nervous by pressure might choose to be in a "casual" group that was not paid. In any case, the problem is that the groups would now contain different kinds of people and the differences in their personalities, rather than the amount of money offered, might be the reason that one group does better than another. Or suppose that an experimenter runs all the paid groups first and runs the no-payment groups afterward. This introduces a whole host of potential problems. Perhaps performance varies as a function of the time of day (morning, afternoon, or evening); maybe those who participate later in the experiment are closer in time to their midterm exams than earlier participants. In addition to these uncontrolled variables, there may be many others of which the experimenter is unaware. All such problems are resolved by randomly assigning participants to conditions.

The experimental method can be used outside the laboratory as well. For example, in research on obesity it is possible to investigate the effects of different methods of weight control by trying these methods on separate but similar groups of obese individuals. The experimental method is a matter of logic, not location. Still, most experiments take place in laboratories, chiefly because it is possible to measure behavior more precisely and to control the variables more completely. And, again, it is often random assignment that is at issue: If two obesity clinics use different methods and achieve different results, we cannot conclude with confidence that the different methods are responsible because the clinics might attract different kinds of people to their programs.

The experiments we have described so far examine the effect of one independent variable on one dependent variable. Limiting an investigation to only one independent variable, however, is too restrictive for some problems. **Multivariate experiments**—that is, *studies involving the manipulating of several variables*—are frequently used in psychological research. Thus, in the hypothetical study just described, in which the participants were offered different amounts of money for solving math problems, the experimenter might also vary the level of difficulty of the problems. Now there would be six groups of participants, each combining one of three different amounts of money with one of two levels of difficulty (easy versus difficult).

Measurement   Psychologists using the experimental method often find it necessary to make statements about amounts or quantities. Sometimes the variables can be measured by physical means—for example, number of hours of sleep deprivation or the dosage level of a drug. At other times variables have to be scaled in a manner that places them in some sort of order; in rating a patient's feelings of aggression, for example, a psychotherapist might use a five-point scale ranging from "never" through "rarely," "sometimes," "often," and "always." Thus, for purposes of precise communication, numbers are assigned to variables; this process is referred to as **measurement,** *a system for assigning numbers to variables.*

Experiments usually involve making measurements on many participants, not just one. The results, therefore, consist of data in the form of a set of numbers that can be summarized and interpreted. To accomplish this task, one needs to use **statistics,** *mathematical methods for sampling data from a population of individuals and then drawing inferences about the population from those data.* Statistics play an important role not only in experimental research but in other methods as well.[2] The most common statistic is the **mean,** which is simply *the technical term for an arithmetic average.* It is the sum of a set of scores divided by the number of scores in the set. In studies involving experimental and control groups, there are two means to be compared: a mean for the scores of the participants in the experimental group and a

multivariate experiment   a study involving the simultaneous manipulation of several variables

measurement   a system for assigning numbers to variables

statistics   mathematical methods for sampling data from a population of individuals and then drawing inferences about the population from those data

mean   technical term for an arithmetic average

---

[2] This discussion is designed to introduce the problems of measurement and statistics. A more thorough discussion is provided in the Appendix.

Not all questions of concern to psychologists can be studied using the experimental method. Many studies ask participants to describe their own thoughts, feelings, behaviors, and personalities on questionnaires, surveys, and tests. These responses are then correlated with other information obtained in the study or are used to categorize the participants into different groups for statistical analysis.

mean for the scores of the participants in the control group. The difference between these two means is, of course, what the experimenters are interested in. If the difference between the means is large, it can be accepted at face value. But what if the difference is small? What if the measures used are subject to error? What if a few extreme cases are producing the difference? Statisticians have solved these problems by developing tests for determining the significance of a difference. A psychologist who says that the difference between the experimental group and the control group is "statistically significant" means that a statistical test has been applied to the data and that the observed difference is unlikely to have arisen by chance or because there were a few extreme cases.

Correlation

Not all problems can be easily studied using the experimental method. There are many situations in which the investigator has no control over which participants go in which conditions. For example, if we want to test the hypothesis that anorexic people are more sensitive to changes in taste than normal-weight people, we cannot select a group of normal-weight participants and require half of them to become anorexic! Rather, we select people who are already anorexic or already of normal weight and see if they also differ in taste sensitivity. More generally, we can make use of correlation to determine whether some variable that is not under our control is associated, or *correlated,* with another variable of interest.

In the example just given there were only two values of the weight variable—anorexic and normal. It is more common to have many values of each variable, and to determine the degree to which values on one variable are correlated with values on another. This determination is made by using a statistic called the **correlation coefficient,** *an estimate of the degree to which two variables are related.* The correlation

correlation coefficient
an estimate of the degree to which two variables are related

coefficient, symbolized by r, is expressed as a number between -1 and $+1$. A perfect relationship is indicated by 1 ($+1$ if the relationship is positive and -1 if the relationship is negative); if there is no relationship at all, this is indicated by 0. As r goes from 0 to 1, the strength of the relationship increases.

A correlation can be either $+$ or $-$. The sign of the correlation indicates whether the two variables are positively correlated (the values of the two variables either increase together or decrease together) or negatively correlated (as the value of one variable increases, the value of the other decreases). For example, suppose that the number of times a student is absent from class correlates $-.40$ with his or her final course grade (the more absences, the lower the grade). On the other hand, the correlation between the number of classes attended and the course grade would be $+.40$. The strength of the relationship is the same, but the sign indicates whether we are looking at classes missed or classes attended.[3]

To get a clearer picture of a correlation coefficient, consider the hypothetical study presented in Figure 1-6. As shown in Figure 1-6a, the study involves patients with brain damage leading to problems in face recognition (prosopagnosia). What is of interest is whether the degree of deficit, or error, in face recognition increases with the amount of brain tissue that is damaged. Each point on the graph in Figure 1-6a represents the percentage of errors made by one patient on a test of face recognition. For example, a patient who had only 10% brain damage made 15% errors on the face recognition test, but a patient who had 55% brain damage made 76% errors. If errors in face recognition *always* increase with the percentage of brain damage, the points in the graph would consistently increase in moving from left to right; if the points had fallen on the diagonal line in the figure, the correlation would have been: $r = 1.0$—a perfect correlation. A couple of points fall on either side of the line, however, so the correlation is about .90. A correlation of .90 indicates that there is a very strong relationship between amount of the brain damage and errors in face recognition. In Figure 1-6a, the correlation is positive because more errors go with more brain damage.

If, instead of focusing on errors, we plot the percentage of correct responses on the face recognition test, we end up with the diagram in Figure 1-6b. Now the correlation is negative—about $-.90$—because *fewer* correct responses are associated with *more* brain damage. The diagonal line in Figure 1-6b is simply the inverse of the one in Figure 1-6a.

Finally, consider the diagram in Figure 1-6c. Here we have graphed errors on the face recognition test as a function of the patient's height. Of course, there is no reason to expect a relationship between height and face recognition, and the graph shows that there is none. The points neither consistently increase nor consistently decrease in moving from left to right, but rather bounce around a horizontal line. The correlation is 0.

In psychological research, a correlation coefficient of .60 or more is considered to be quite high. Correlations in the range from .20 to .60 are of practical and theoretical value and useful in making predictions. Correlations between 0 and .20 must be judged with caution and are only minimally useful in making predictions.

Tests   The familiar use of correlation involves tests that measure aptitudes, achievement, or other psychological traits. A test presents a uniform situation to a group of people who vary in a particular trait (such as mathematical ability, manual dexterity, or aggression). The variation in scores on the test can be correlated with variations on another variable. For example, people's scores on a mathematical ability test can be correlated with their subsequent grades in a college math course; if the correlation is high, the test score may be used to determine which students should be placed in advanced sections of the course.

---

[3] The numerical method for calculating a correlation coefficient is described in the Appendix.

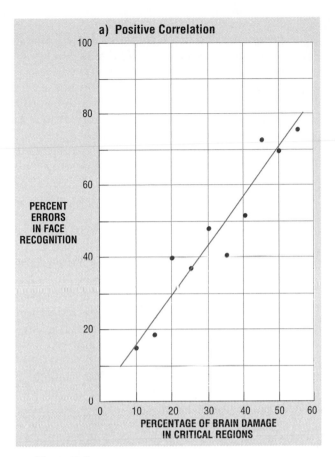

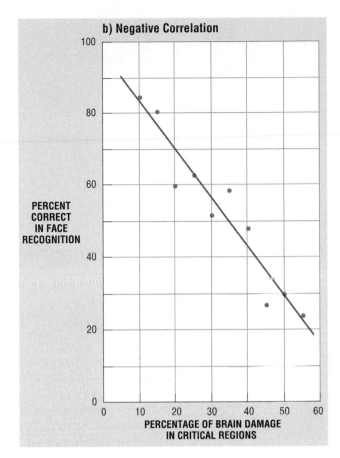

Figure 1-6

Scatter Diagrams Illustrating Correlations   These hypothesized data are based on 10 patients, all of whom have some damage in regions of the brain known to be involved in face recognition. In Figure 1-6a the patients are ordered along the horizontal axis with respect to the amount of brain damage, with the patient represented by the leftmost point having the least brain damage (10%) and the patient represented by the rightmost point having the most brain damage (55%). Each point on the graph represents a single patient's score on a test of face recognition. The correlation is a positive .90. In Figure 1-6b the same data are depicted, but we now focus on the percent of correct responses (rather than errors). Now the correlation is a negative .90. In Figure 1-6c the patient's performances on the face recognition test are graphed as a function of their height. Now the correlation is 0.

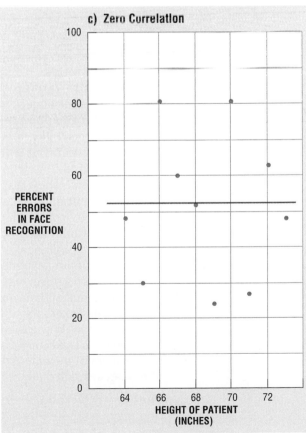

Correlation and Causation   There is an important distinction between experimental and correlational studies. In a typical experiment, one variable (the independent variable) is systematically manipulated in order to determine its *causal* effect on some other variable (the dependent variable). Such cause-and-effect relationships cannot be inferred from correlational studies. This point can be illustrated with a couple of examples. Studies have shown that the more TV violence a young boy watches, the more aggressive he is.

The early observation that smoking was correlated with lung cancer could not by itself demonstrate that smoking causes cancer. Additional evidence was required to establish the causal link.

But does watching violent TV cause the aggression or do more aggressive boys choose to watch more violent TV? If all we have is a correlation, we cannot say which variable is cause and which is effect. (Although recall that another study described earlier in this chapter demonstrated a causal relationship between watching violent TV and aggression. It was able to do so because the experimenters randomly assigned participants to different conditions in which the violence of the TV scenes was manipulated as an independent variable.)

It is also possible for two variables to be correlated when neither is the cause of the other. For example, many years before careful medical studies demonstrated that cigarette smoking actually causes cancer, it was known that there was a correlation between smoking and lung cancer. That is, it was already known that people who smoked were more likely to contract cancer. But—as the tobacco companies rushed to point out—this left open the possibility that some third cause was responsible. For example, if people who live in smoggy urban areas are more likely to smoke than people who live in clean rural air then it could be air pollution rather than smoking that causes the higher cancer rates in smokers.

In short, when two variables are correlated, variation in one may possibly be the cause of variation in the other, but without further experiments no such conclusion is justified.

Observation

Direct Observation   In the early stages of research, the most efficient way of making progress toward an explanation may be simply to observe the phenomenon under study as it occurs naturally. Careful observation of animal and human behavior is the starting point for a great deal of research in psychology. For example, observation of primates in their natural environment may tell us things about their social organization that will help in later laboratory investigations (see Figure 1-7). Motion pictures of newborn babies reveal details of their activity and the types of stimuli to which they respond. It is important to note that investigators observing naturally occurring behavior must be trained to observe and record events accurately so as to avoid letting their own biases influence what they report.

Observational methods may be used in a laboratory if the problem being studied is partly a biological one. For example, in their classic study of the physiological aspects of human sexuality, Masters and Johnson (1966) developed techniques that permitted direct observation of sexual responses in the laboratory. The data included (1) observations of behavior, (2) recordings of physiological changes, and (3) responses to questions asked about the participants' sensations before, during, and after sexual stimulation. While the researchers agreed that human sexuality has many dimensions besides the biological one, their observations of the anatomical and physiological aspects of sexual response have been very helpful in understanding the nature of human sexuality, as well as in solving sexual problems.

The Survey Method   Some problems that are difficult to study by direct observation may be studied by indirect observation through the use of questionnaires or interviews. That is, rather than observe people engaging in a particular behavior, such as exercising regularly, researchers simply ask them if they engage in that behavior. Because people may be trying to present themselves in a favorable light (for example, by saying that they exercise more than they actually do), this method is more open to bias than direct observation. Still, the survey method has produced many important results. For example, before Masters and Johnson conducted their research on sexual response, most of the available information on how people behave sexually (as opposed to how laws, religion, or society say they should behave) came from extensive surveys conducted by Alfred Kinsey and his associates 20 years earlier. Information from thousands of interviews was analyzed, resulting in the publication of two pioneering works: *Sexual Behavior in the Human Male* (Kinsey, Pomeroy, & Martin, 1948) and *Sexual Behavior in the Human Female* (Kinsey, Pomeroy, Martin, & Gebhard, 1953).

Surveys have also been used to discover people's political opinions, product preferences, health care needs, and so on. The Gallup poll and the U.S. census are probably the most familiar surveys. An adequate survey requires that a carefully pretested questionnaire be presented to a sample of people selected in such a way that they are representative of the larger population being studied.

Figure 1.7

Baboons Observed in Their Natural Habitat   Field studies can often tell us more about social behavior than experimental studies. Professor Shirley Strum has observed the same troop of baboons in Kenya for more than 20 years, identifying individual animals and making daily recordings of their behaviors and social interactions. Her data have provided remarkable information about the mental abilities of baboons and the role of friendships in their social system.

Case Histories   Still another means of indirect observation is to obtain a partial biography of a particular individual. This involves asking people to recall relevant experiences from their past. For example, if the research is concerned with the childhood antecedents of adult depression, the researcher might begin by asking questions about earlier life events. These **case histories** are *biographies obtained for scientific use,* and they are important sources of data for psychologists studying individuals.

case history   a biography obtained for scientific use

A major limitation of case histories is that they rely on the person's memories and reconstructions of earlier events, which are frequently distorted or incomplete. Sometimes other data can be used to corroborate information obtained in a case history. For example, written records, such as death certificates, can be used to check on specific dates, or relatives of the person being interviewed can be asked to report their own memories of the relevant events. Even so, their limitations make case histories less useful for testing a theory or proving a hypothesis than for suggesting hypotheses that can then be tested in more rigorous ways or checked with a larger sample of participants. In this way, scientists use the case history in much the same way that a therapist or physician might when trying to formulate a diagnosis and treatment of a particular individual.

Ethical Issues in Psychological Research

Because psychologists study living beings, they need to be sensitive to ethical issues that can arise in the conduct of research. Accordingly, the American Psychological Association (APA) and its counterparts in Canada and Great Britain have established guidelines for the care and treatment of both human participants and animal subjects (American Psychological Association, 1990). In the United States, federal regulations require any institution that conducts federally funded research to establish an internal review board, which reviews proposed studies to ensure that all participants will be treated properly.

minimal risk   the principle that the risks anticipated in the research should be no greater than those ordinarily encountered in daily life

The first principle governing the ethical treatment of human participants is **minimal risk.** The federal guideline specifies that, in most cases, *the risks anticipated in the research should be no greater than those ordinarily encountered in daily life.* Obviously, a person should not be exposed to physical harm or injury, but deciding how much psychological stress is ethically justified in a research project is not always so clearcut. In everyday life, of course, people may lie, be impolite, or make other people anxious. Under what circumstances is it ethically justifiable for a researcher to do these same things to a participant in order to meet the goals of a research project? These are the kinds of questions that the review boards consider on a case-by-case basis.

informed consent   the principle that participants must enter a study voluntarily and be permitted to withdraw from it at any time without penalty if they so desire

The second principle governing the ethical treatment of human participants is **informed consent,** meaning that *participants must enter a study voluntarily and be permitted to withdraw from it at any time without penalty if they so desire.* They must also be told ahead of time about any aspects of the study that could be expected to influence their willingness to cooperate. Like the principle of minimal risk, informed consent is not always easy to implement. In particular, informed consent is sometimes at odds with another common requirement of research: that participants be unaware of the hypotheses being tested in a study. If a researcher plans to compare participants who learn lists of familiar words with participants who learn lists of unfamiliar words, no ethical problem arises by simply telling participants that they will be learning lists of words: They do not need to know how the words vary from one participant to another. Nor are any serious ethical issues raised if participants are given a "surprise quiz" on words that they hadn't expected to be tested on. But what if the researcher seeks to compare participants who learn words while in a neutral mood with participants who learn words while they are angry or embarrassed? Clearly, the research would not yield valid conclusions if participants had to be told ahead of time that they would be intentionally angered (by being treated rudely) or intentionally embarrassed (by being led to believe that they had accidentally broken a piece of equipment). Accordingly, the guidelines specify that if such a study is permitted to proceed at all, participants must be *debriefed* about it as soon as possible afterwards. The reasons for keeping them in ignorance—or deceiving them—about the procedures must be explained, and any residual anger or embarrassment must be dealt with so that the participants leave the study with their dignity intact and their appreciation for the research enhanced. The review board must be convinced that the debriefing procedures are adequate to this task.

right to privacy   the principle that information about a participant that might be acquired during a study must be treated as confidential and not made available to others without his or her consent

A third principle of ethical research is the **right to privacy.** *Information about a participant that might be acquired during a study must be treated as confidential and not made available to others without his or her consent.* A common practice is to separate the names or other information used to identify participants from the data collected in the study. The data are then identified only by code or case numbers. In that way, no one other than the experimenter has access to how any particular participant responded.

Even if all these ethical conditions are met, it is still necessary for the researcher to weigh the costs of the study against the potential benefits—not the economic costs, but the costs in human terms. Is it really necessary to conduct a study in which participants will be deceived or embarrassed? In other words, will the potential findings be worth the human costs? Only if the researcher is fairly certain that the study will uncover worthwhile information—either practical or theoretical—can the research be fully justified.

Another area in which ethical standards must be observed is research using animals. About 7% to 8% of psychological studies employ animals (mostly rodents and birds), and very few of these involve painful or harmful procedures. Nevertheless, concern over the use, care, and treatment of animal subjects has increased in recent years, and both federal and APA guidelines require that any painful or harmful procedures imposed upon animals must be thoroughly justified in terms of the knowledge to be gained from the study. Specific rules also govern the living conditions and maintenance of laboratory animals.

Aside from the specific guidelines, a central principle of research ethics is that those who participate in psychology studies should be considered as full partners in the research enterprise. Some of the research discussed in this text was conducted before the ethical guidelines just described were formulated and would not be permitted by most review boards today.

What Are the Interdisciplinary Approaches to Psychology?

Other disciplines besides psychology are interested in mind and behavior—biology, linguistics, and philosophy, to name just a few. Increasingly, researchers from these disciplines are joining with psychologists to forge new approaches to the study of psychological phenomena. These approaches promise to be of great importance in the next few decades. Of particular interest are cognitive neuroscience, evolutionary psychology, cognitive science, and cultural psychology. Here we briefly describe each of these approaches, with examples of the kinds of research being done in each field.

Informed Consent *Before entering a psychological study, participants are often asked to sign a consent form indicating that they understand in general terms what they will be doing during the study and that they are free to withdraw from it at any time without penalty if they so desire.*

Cognitive Neuroscience

Cognitive neuroscience focuses on cognitive processes, relying heavily on the methods and findings of neuroscience (the branch of biology that deals with the brain and the central nervous system). In essence, it attempts to discover how mental activities are executed in the brain. The key idea is that cognitive psychology provides hypotheses about specific cognitive capacities—such as recognizing faces—and neuroscience supplies proposals about how these capacities might be executed in the brain.

What is particularly distinctive about cognitive neuroscience is its reliance on new techniques for studying the brains of normal individuals (as opposed to brain-damaged ones) while they are performing a cognitive task. These neuroimaging or brain scanning techniques create visual images of a brain in action, with an indication of which regions of the brain show the most neural activity during a particular task. An example is studies of how people remember information for either brief or long periods. When people are asked to remember information for a few seconds, neuroimaging results show increases in neural activity in regions in the front of the brain; when they are asked to remember information for a long period, there is an increase in activity in an entirely different region, one closer to the middle of the brain. Thus, different mechanisms seem to be used for the short-term and long-term storage of information (Smith & Jonides, 1994; Squire et al., 1993).

Evolutionary Psychology

Evolutionary psychology is concerned with the biological origins of cognitive and other psychological mechanisms. In addition to psychology and biology, the other disciplines involved in this approach include anthropology and psychiatry. The key idea behind evolutionary psychology is that, just like biological mechanisms, psychological mechanisms must have evolved over millions of years through a process of natural selection. This implies that those mechanisms have a genetic basis and have proved useful in the past in increasing the organism's chances of surviving and reproducing. To illustrate, consider a liking for sweets. Such a preference can be thought of as a psychological mechanism, and it has a genetic basis. Moreover, we have this preference because it increased our ancestors' chances of survival: The fruit that tasted the sweetest had the highest nutritional value, so by eating it they increased the chances of continued survival of the relevant genes (Symons, 1992).

There are a couple of ways in which an evolutionary perspective can affect the study of psychological issues. For one thing, from an evolutionary perspective certain topics are of particular importance because of their link to survival or successful reproduction. Such topics include how we select our mates and how we handle our aggressive feelings (Buss, 1991). An evolutionary perspective can also provide some new insights on familiar topics. We can illustrate this point with the example of obesity. We noted earlier that a history of deprivation can lead to overeating in the future. Evolutionary theory provides an interpretation of this puzzling phenomenon. Until comparatively recently in human history, people experienced deprivation only when food was scarce. An adaptive mechanism for dealing with scarcity is overeating when food is available. Hence evolution may have favored the tendency to overeat following deprivation.

Cognitive Science

Cognitive science describes areas of psychological research that (1) are concerned with cognitive processes like perceiving, remembering, reasoning, and problem solving, and (2) overlap with other disciplines interested in these processes, such as computer science. The field's major objectives are to discover how information is represented in the mind (mental representations) and what types of computations can be carried out on these representations to bring about perceiving, remembering, reasoning, and so on. In addition to psychology, the disciplines involved are anthropology, linguistics, philosophy, neuroscience, and artificial intelligence. (The latter is a branch of computer science concerned with developing computer programs that can simulate human thought processes.)

A central idea behind cognitive science is that the human cognitive system can be understood as though it were a giant computer engaged in a complex calculation. Just as a computer's complex calculation can be broken down into a set of simpler computations, such as storing, retrieving, and comparing symbols or representations, so a person's action can be broken down into a set of elementary mental components. Moreover, those components may involve storing, retrieving, and comparing symbols. There is a further parallel between a computer's calculations and a person's mental computations. A computer's activity may be analyzed at different levels—including the level of hardware with its emphasis on chips and the level of representation-and-algorithm with its emphasis on data structures and processes. Similarly, human cognitive activity may be analyzed at the level of "hardware," or neurons, and the level of mental representations and processes. The ideas of mental computation and levels of analysis, then, are among the cornerstones of cognitive science (Osherson, 1990).

Cultural Psychology

Scientific psychology in the West has often assumed that the same psychological processes occur in all cultures. Increasingly, this assumption is being challenged by proponents of cultural psychology, an interdisciplinary movement involving psychologists, anthropologists, sociologists, and other social scientists. Cultural psychology is concerned with how the culture in which an individual lives—its tradi-

Because of their emphasis on collectivism rather than individualism, Asian students are more likely than American students to study together.

tions, language, and worldview—influences that person's mental representation and psychological processes.

Here is an example. In the West—North America and much of western and northern Europe—we think of ourselves as separate and autonomous agents, with unique abilities and traits. In contrast, many cultures in the East—including those of India, China, and Japan—emphasize the interrelationships among people, rather than their individuality. Moreover, Easterners tend to pay more attention to social situations than Westerners do. These differences lead Easterners to explain the behavior of an other person differently from the way Westerners do. Rather than explaining a piece of behavior solely in terms of a person's traits, Easterners explain it in terms of the social situation in which it occurred. This has implications for trait attribution, one of the sample problems discussed at the beginning of the chapter. These differences between East and West in explaining behavior can also have educational implications. Because of their emphasis on collectivism rather than individualism, Asian students tend to study together more than American students. Such group study may be a useful technique, and it may be part of the reason why Asian students outperform their American counterparts in mathematics and some other subjects. In addition, when an American student is having difficulty in mathematics, both the student and the teacher tend to attribute the difficulty to the student's abilities; when a comparable case arises in a Japanese school, the student and the teacher are more likely to look to the situation—the student–teacher interaction in the instructional context—for an explanation of the poor performance (Stevenson, Lee, & Graham, 1993).

An earlier Thinking Critically question asked how the different perspectives might approach the question, "What are the determinants of an individual's sexual orientation?" How might evolutionary psychology and cultural psychology approach this same question?

Thinking Critically

What Are the Major Subfields of Psychology?

In this chapter we have gained a general understanding of psychology by looking at its topics, perspectives, and methods. We can further our understanding by looking at what different kinds of psychologists do.

About half the people who have advanced degrees in psychology work in colleges and universities. In addition to teaching, they may devote much of their time to research or counseling. Other psychologists work in schools, hospitals or clinics, research institutes, government agencies, or business and industry. Still others are in private practice and offer their services to the public for a fee. We now turn to a brief description of some of the subfields of psychology.

Biological Psychology   Biological psychologists (also referred to as *physiological psychologists*) seek to discover the relationships between biological processes and behavior.

Experimental Psychology   Experimental psychologists usually conduct research from a behaviorist or cognitive perspective and use experimental methods to study how people (and other animals) react to sensory stimuli, perceive the world, learn and remember, reason, and respond emotionally.

Developmental, Social, and Personality Psychology   These three subfields overlap. Developmental psychologists are concerned with human development and the factors that shape behavior from birth to old age. They might study a specific ability, such as how language develops in children, or a particular period of life, such as infancy.

Social psychologists are interested in how people perceive and interpret their social worlds and how their beliefs, attitudes, and behaviors are influenced by others. They are also concerned with social relationships between and among people and with the behavior of groups.

Personality psychologists study the thoughts, emotions, and behaviors that define an individual's personal style of interacting with the world. Accordingly, they are interested in differences between individuals, and they also attempt to synthesize all the psychological processes into an integrated account of the total person.

Clinical and Counseling Psychology   The largest number of psychologists are clinical psychologists; they apply psychological principles to the diagnosis and treatment of emotional and behavioral problems—including mental illness, drug addiction, and marital and family conflict.

Counseling psychologists serve many of the same functions as clinical psychologists, although they often deal with less serious problems. They often work with high school or university students.

School and Educational Psychology   Because the beginnings of serious emotional problems often make their first appearances in the early grades, many elementary schools employ psychologists whose training combines courses in child development, education, and clinical psychology. These school psychologists work with individual children to evaluate learning and emotional problems. In contrast, educational psychologists are specialists in learning and teaching. They may work in the schools, but more often they are employed by a university's school of education, where they do research on teaching methods and help train teachers.

Industrial and Engineering Psychology   Industrial psychologists (sometimes called *organizational psychologists*) typically work for a company. They are concerned with such problems as selecting people who are most suitable for particular jobs or developing job training programs.

Engineering psychologists (sometimes called *human factors engineers*) seek to improve the relationship between people and machines; they help design machines that will minimize human errors. One way they help improve human–machine interaction is by designing machines with the most efficient placement of gauges and controls, which leads to improved performance, safety, and comfort.

School psychologists work with individual children to evaluate learning and emotional problems. Their training combines courses in child development, education, and clinical psychology.

Overview of the Book

Today psychologists are investigating thousands of different phenomena. These phenomena range from how individual brain cells change during learning to the effects of population density and overcrowding on social behavior. We have tried to arrange the topics in this book so that an understanding of the issues in each chapter will provide a background for the study of topics presented in the next one.

To understand how people interact with their environment, we need to know something about their biological equipment. We also need to provide some background about biology so that you can understand research done from a biological perspective. Chapter 2 ("The Biological Basis of Psychology") describes how the nervous and endocrine systems function to integrate and control behavior. Because behavior also depends on the interaction between inherited characteristics and environmental conditions, this chapter includes a discussion of genetic influences on behavior.

Chapter 3 ("Psychological Development") provides an overview of the individual's psychological development from infancy through adolescence and adulthood. By noting how cognitive abilities, attitudes, and personality develop, including the problems that must be faced at different stages of life, we can appreciate more fully the kinds of questions to which psychology seeks answers.

With this as background, we move on to Chapter 4 ("Sensation and Perception"), in which we survey how humans and other species acquire information about the external world. Such information must first be registered by the sense organs, which mediate the sensations of light, sound, touch, smell, and taste. We first discuss the nature of sensory information and then consider how such information is organized into meaningful patterns and recognized as instances of familiar objects or events.

Organization and recognition are parts of the *process* of perception. The *products* of perception often emerge in consciousness, and we examine the characteristics of human consciousness under both normal and altered states in Chapter 5 ("Consciousness").

In Chapter 6 ("Learning"), we first consider how organisms learn about their environment, ranging from the learning of simple relationships like red light follows yellow light to the complex knowledge taught in college courses. In Chapter 7 ("Memory"), we consider how such information is remembered both in short-term and long-term memory. In Chapter 8 ("Thought and Language"), we discuss how remembered information is used for purposes of reasoning and problem solving. In addition, we take up the critical problem of language—how we communicate what we know.

Chapter 9 ("Motivation and Emotion") deals with the forces that energize and direct behavior. Such forces include basic motives such as hunger and sex, as well as emotions such as joy, fear, and anger.

The ways in which individuals differ is the substance of Chapter 10 ("Individual Differences, Intelligence, and Personality"). We consider differences in both mental abilities and personality, paying close attention to how these differences are measured. Chapter 10 also surveys formal theories of personality, focusing on the different perspectives outlined in this chapter.

Dealing with stress is the major topic of Chapter 11 ("Stress, Health, and Coping"). We consider the ways in which stressful events can affect both emotional and physical health. In Chapter 12, ("Abnormal Psychology"), we discuss the biological and psychological causes of severe mental disorders, and in Chapter 13 ("Treatment of Psychological Disorders"), we review the various therapies that have been developed to deal with such disorders.

The final chapter, Chapter 14 ("Social Behavior"), is concerned with social perception, interaction, and influence. We discuss how people think, feel, and act in social situations, including how they perceive and interpret the behaviors of other people. We also examine how other people influence our thoughts, feelings, and actions. And finally, we consider how people select their friends and lovers.

Summary

1. *Psychology* is the scientific study of behavior and mental processes.
2. The roots of psychology can be traced to the 4th and 5th centuries B.C. The Greek philosophers Socrates, Plato, and Aristotle posed fundamental questions about the mind, and Hippocrates, the "father of medicine," made many important observations about how the brain controls other organs. One of the earliest debates about human

psychology focused on the question of whether human capabilities are inborn (the nativist view) or acquired through experience (the empiricist view). Scientific psychology was born in the latter part of the 19th century with the idea that mind and behavior could be the subject of scientific analysis. The first experimental laboratory in psychology was established by Wilhelm Wundt at the University of Leipzig in 1897.

3. Among the early "schools" of psychology were *structuralism* (the analysis of mental structures), *functionalism* (the study of how the mind works so that an organism can adapt to and function in its environment), behaviorism (the study of behavior without reference to consciousness), Gestalt psychology (which focuses on the patterns formed by stimuli and on the organization of experience), and psychoanalysis (which emphasizes the role of unconscious processes in personality development and motivation).

4. Modern developments in psychology include information-processing theory, psycholinguistics, and neuropsychology.

5. The study of psychology can be approached from several perspectives. The biological perspective relates actions to events taking place inside the body, particularly the brain and nervous system. The behavioral perspective considers external activities of the organism that can be observed and measured. The cognitive perspective is concerned with mental processes such as perceiving, remembering, reasoning, deciding, and problem solving, and with relating these processes to behavior. The psychoanalytic perspective emphasizes unconscious motives stemming from sexual and aggressive impulses. The phenomenological perspective focuses on the person's subjective experiences and interpretations of the world. A particular area of psychological investigation often can be analyzed from more than one of these perspectives.

6. The biological perspective differs from the other viewpoints in that its principles are partly drawn from biology. Often biological researchers attempt to explain psychological principles in terms of biological ones; this is known as *reductionism.* Behavioral phenomena are increasingly being understood at both the biological and psychological levels.

7. Doing psychological research involves generating a hypothesis and then testing it using a scientific method. When applicable, the experiment is preferred for studying problems because it seeks to control all variables except the ones being studied. The *independent variable* is the one that is manipulated by the experimenter; the *dependent variable* (usually some measure of the participant's behavior) is the one that is being studied to determine whether it is affected by changes in the independent variable. In a simple experiment, the experimenter manipulates one independent variable and observes its effect on one dependent variable; in *multivariate experiments,* the experimenter manipulates several independent variables and observes their separate and joint effects on the dependent variable. An important element of most experiments is the random assignment of participants to experimental and control groups.

8. In many experiments the independent variable is something that is either present or absent. The simplest experiment includes an *experimental group* (with the condition present for one group of participants) and a *control group* (with the condition absent for another group of participants). If the difference in *means* between the experimental and control groups is statistically significant, we know that the experimental condition had a reliable effect—that is, the difference is due

to the independent variable, not to chance factors or a few extreme cases.

9. If an investigator has no control over which participants experience which conditions or in situations in which an experiment is not feasible, *correlation* may be used. This method determines whether a naturally occurring difference is correlated, or is associated with another difference. The degree of correlation between two variables is measured by the *correlation coefficient.* The correlation coefficient, represented by *r,* is a number between -1 and $+1$. A perfect relationship is indicated by 1; the absence of any relationship is indicated by 0. As *r* goes from 0 to 1, the strength of the relationship increases. The correlation coefficient can be positive or negative, depending on whether one variable increases with another $(+)$ or one variable decreases as the other increases $(-)$.

10. Another approach to research is observation, in which one observes the phenomenon of interest. Researchers must be trained to observe and record accurately in order to avoid projecting their own biases into what they report. Phenomena that are difficult to observe directly may be observed indirectly by means of surveys (questionnaires and interviews) or by reconstructing a *case history.*

11. The basic principles governing the ethical treatment of human participants are *minimal risk, informed consent,* and the *right to privacy.* Any painful or harmful procedures imposed upon animals must be thoroughly justified in terms of the knowledge to be gained from the study.

12. Two interdisciplinary approaches to psychology—cognitive neuroscience and evolutionary psychology—take a biological perspective.

Cognitive neuroscience involves attempts by cognitive psychologists and neuroscientists (biologists who specialize in the brain and nervous system) to discover how mental activities are executed in the brain. The key idea is to integrate information from cognitive psychology about specific psychological functions with information from neuroscience about how these functions might be implemented in the brain. Evolutionary psychology is concerned with the evolutionary origin of cognitive and other psychological mechanisms. Its key idea is that such mechanisms have evolved over millions of years through a process of natural selection. This approach has led psychologists to look at topics that are significant from an evolutionary perspective, such as the choosing of a mate.

13. Two other interdisciplinary approaches—cognitive science and cultural psychology—take a more psychological perspective. Cognitive science deals with the nature of intelligent processes; in addition to psychology, it involves disciplines like artificial intelligence, linguistics, and philosophy. Its key ideas are that mental processes may be understood as computations and that mental activity may be analyzed at various levels. Cultural psychology is a joint venture of psychologists, anthropologists, and other social scientists. It deals with how the culture in which an individual lives influences that person's mental representations and processes.

14. Among the major subfields of psychology are biological psychology; experimental psychology; developmental, social, and personality psychology; clinical and counseling psychology; school and educational psychology; and industrial and engineering psychology.

Suggested Readings

The topical interests and theories of any contemporary science can often be understood best according to its history. Several useful books are Hilgard, *Psychology in America: A Historical Survey* (1987); Wertheimer, *A Brief History of Psychology* (3rd ed., 1987); and Schultz, *A History of Modern Psychology* (4th ed., 1987). Also of interest is Kimble, Wertheimer, and White's *Portraits of Pioneers in Psychology* (1991).

The various conceptual approaches to psychology are discussed in Medcof and Roth (eds.), *Approaches to Psychology* (1988); Anderson, *Cognitive Psychology and Its Implications* (3rd ed., 1990); Peterson, *Personality* (1988); Royce and Mos (eds.), *Humanistic Psychology: Concepts and Criticism* (1981); and Lundin, *Theories and Systems of Psychology* (3rd ed., 1985).

The methods of psychological research are presented in Wood, *Fundamentals of Psychological Research* (3rd ed., 1986); Snodgrass, Levy-Berger, and Haydon, *Human Experimental Psychology* (1985); Ray and Ravizza, *Methods Toward a Science of Behavior and Experience* (3rd ed., 1988); and Elmes, Kantowitz, and Roediger, *Research Methods in Psychology* (3rd ed., 1989). For more of an emphasis on the thinking skills needed to do psychological research, see Stanovich's *Thinking Straight About Psychology* (1992).

A simple but elegant introduction to basic concepts in statistics is Phillips, *How to Think About Statistics* (rev. ed., 1992). A good introduction to cognitive neuroscience is provided by Kosslyn and Koenig, *Wet Mind: The New Cognitive Neuroscience* (1992). For an introduction to evolutionary psychology, see Barkow, Cosmides, and Tooby, *The Adapted Mind* (1990).

A general introduction to cognitive science is given in Gardner, *The Mind's New Science: A History of the Cognitive Revolution* (1985); and Osherson, *Invitation to Cognitive Science* (Vols. 1–3) (1990). For an introduction to cultural psychology see Shewder's *Cultural Psychology* (1990).

To find out more about career opportunities in psychology and the training required to become a psychologist, write to the American Psychological Association (1400 North Uhle Street, Arlington, VA 22201) for a copy of the booklet, "A Career in Psychology."

Enhance and Explore

To enhance your understanding of the psychological concepts found in this chapter, please consult the following aids:

Study Guide

Learning Objectives, p. 2
Define the Terms, p. 4
Test Your Knowledge, p. 11
Essay Questions, p. 15
Thinking Independently, p. 18

PowerPsych CD-ROM

HOW IS PSYCHOLOGICAL RESEARCH DONE?
Experimental Design: Effects of Marijuana on Memory
Measures of Central Tendency: How Does My Salary
Compare to Everyone Else's?

PsychCentral

For more information concerning the topics found in this chapter, access psychology links on the Word Wide Web made through the Harcourt Web page at:
http://www.harcourtcollege.com/psych/Fundamentals

www.harcourtcollege.com
http://www.harcourtcollege.com/psych/index.html

The Biological Basis of Psychology CHAPTER 2

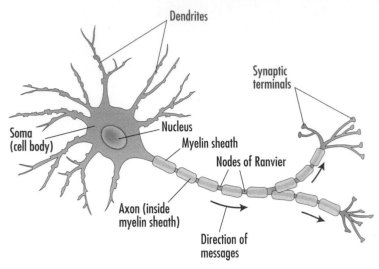

Dendrites

Synaptic terminals

Soma (cell body)

Nucleus

Myelin sheath

Nodes of Ranvier

Axon (inside myelin sheath)

Direction of messages

Figure 2-1

Schematic Diagram of a Neuron   Arrows indicate the direction of the nerve impulse. Some axons are branched; the branches are called collaterals. The axons of many neurons are covered with an insulating myelin sheath that helps increase the speed of the nerve impulse.

All behavior, from blinking an eye to playing basketball to writing a computer program, depends on millions of operations performed by the nervous system. Consider, for example, what must happen for you to stop your car at a red light. First you must see the light; this means that the light must register on a set of sense organs, your eyes. Neural impulses from your eyes are relayed to your brain, where the stimulus is analyzed and compared with information stored in your memory: You recognize that a red light in this context means "stop." The process of moving your foot to the brake pedal and pressing it is initiated by motor areas of your brain. In order to send the proper signals to these muscles, the brain must know where your foot is as well as where you want it to go. As you begin to make the movement, your brain receives continuous feedback from leg and foot muscles to control how much pressure is being exerted. At the same time, your eyes and some of your other senses tell you how quickly the car is stopping. If the light turned red as you were speeding toward the intersection, some of your endocrine glands would also be activated, leading to increased heart rate, more rapid respiration, and other metabolic changes associated with fear; these processes speed your reactions in an emergency. Your stopping at a red light happens quickly, yet it involves a variety of complex messages and adjustments. The information for these activities is transmitted by large networks of nerve cells.

Virtually all aspects of behavior and mental functioning can be better understood with some knowledge of the underlying biological processes. Elsewhere in this book, as we encounter such topics as perception, motivation, and language, we will go into more detail on the specific biological mechanisms involved. The purpose of this chapter is not to provide a comprehensive survey of the linkages between biology and psychology; instead, it is to serve as an introduction to some basic neurophysiological ideas that will be elaborated upon later as we discuss various psychological phenomena.

What Are the Properties of Neurons?

neuron   a specialized cell that transmits neural impulses or messages to other neurons, glands, and muscles

The basic unit of the nervous system is the **neuron,** *a specialized cell that transmits neuronal impulses or messages to other neurons, glands, and muscles.* It is important to understand neurons because they hold the secrets to how the brain works. We know their role in the transmission of nerve impulses, and we know how some neural circuits work; but we are just beginning to unravel the more complex functioning of neurons in memory, emotion, and thought.

Neurons and Nerves

Although neurons differ markedly in size and appearance, they have certain common characteristics (see Figure 2-1). Projecting from the cell body (the central part of the neuron) are a number of short branches called *dendrites* (from the Greek word *dendron,* meaning "tree"). Dendrites serve as "receiving antennae" for the neuron. The dendrites and cell body receive neural impulses from adjacent neurons. If the

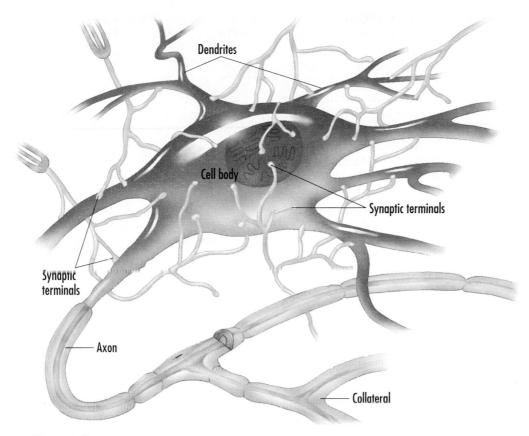

Dendrites

Cell body

Synaptic terminals

Synaptic terminals

Axon

Collateral

Figure 2-2

Synapses at the Cell Body of a Neuron   This diagram shows many different axons, each of which branches repeatedly, and synapses on the dendrites and cell body of a single neuron. Each branch of an axon ends in a swelling, called a synaptic terminal that contains chemicals called neurotransmitters. When released, neurotransmitters transmit the nerve impulse across the synapse to the dendrites or cell body of the receiving cell.

neuron "decides" to send a message of its own, the message is transmitted to other neurons (or to muscles and glands) by a tubelike extension of the cell called an *axon.* At its end the axon splits into a number of tiny branches that end in small swellings called *terminal buttons,* which send the signal to other neurons.

The terminal button does not actually touch the neuron that it will stimulate. Rather, there is a slight gap between the terminal button and the cell body or dendrites of the receiving neuron. The junction of two neurons is called a *synapse,* and the gap itself is called the *synaptic gap.* When a neural impulse travels down the axon and arrives at the terminal buttons, it triggers the secretion of a **neurotransmitter,** *a chemical that diffuses across the synaptic gap and stimulates the next neuron,* thereby carrying the impulse from one neuron to the next. The axons from a great many neurons synapse on the dendrites and cell body of a single neuron (see Figure 2-2).

Although all neurons have these general features, they vary greatly in size and shape (see Figure 2-3). A neuron in the spinal cord may have an axon 3 to 4 feet long, running from the end of the spine to the muscles of the big toe; a neuron in the brain may cover only a few thousandths of an inch.

Neurons are classified into three categories based on their general function. *Sensory neurons* transmit impulses received by sensory receptors to the brain. The receptors are specialized cells in the sense organs, muscles, skin, and joints that are activated by physical or chemical stimuli. *Motor neurons* carry outgoing signals from

neurotransmitter a chemical that diffuses across the synaptic gap and stimulates the next neuron

the brain or spinal cord to muscles and glands. *Interneurons* receive the signals from the sensory neurons, decide whether to respond, and send the resulting impulses to other interneurons or to motor neurons. Interneurons are found only in the brain, eyes, and spinal cord; most neurons in the brain are interneurons.

nerve a bundle of elongated axons belonging to hundreds or thousands of neurons

A **nerve** is *a bundle of elongated axons belonging to hundreds or thousands of neurons.* Similar bundles that run through the brain are called *neural tracts.* A single nerve or tract may contain axons from both sensory and motor neurons.

In addition to neurons, the nervous system consists of a large number of cells, called *glial cells,* that are not neurons but are interspersed among—and often surround—neurons. Glial cells outnumber neurons by 9 to 1 and take up more than half the volume of the brain. The name *glia,* derived from the Greek word for "glue," suggests one of their functions—namely, providing structural support to hold neurons in place. In addition, they provide nutrients that are crucial to the neurons' health, and they appear to "keep house" in the brain by gathering and packaging up waste products and gobbling up dead neurons and foreign substances, thereby maintaining the signaling capacity of neurons (Sontheimer, 1995). Uncontrolled proliferation of glial cells is the cause of almost all brain tumors.

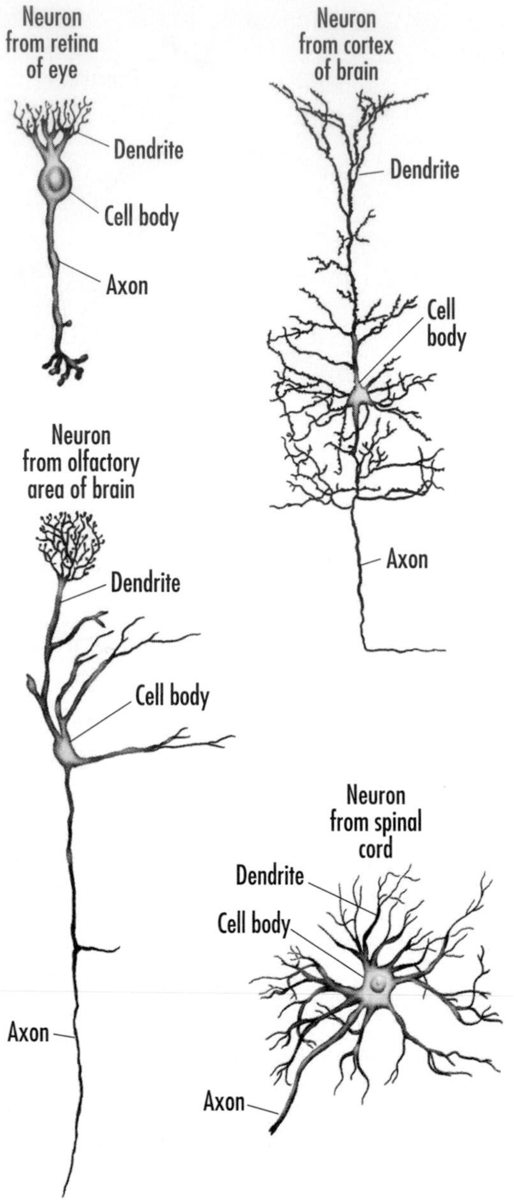

Estimates of the number of neurons and glial cells in the human nervous system vary widely, depending on the method used to make the estimate; scientists do not agree on the best estimate. In the human brain alone, the estimates range from 10 billion to 1 trillion neurons, and whatever the estimate for neurons, the number of glial cells is about 10 times that number (Groves & Rebec, 1992). These are astronomical figures, but this number of cells is undoubtedly necessary to support the complexities of human behavior.

Figure 2-3

Shapes and Relative Sizes of Neurons   The axon of a spinal cord neuron (not shown in its entirety in the figure) may be several feet long.

Action Potentials

action potential an electrochemical impulse that travels from the dendritic area down to the end of the axon

Information moves along a neuron in the form of a neural impulse called an **action potential**—*an electrochemical impulse that travels from the dendritic area down to the end of the axon.* Each action potential is the result of movements by electrically charged molecules, known as *ions,* in and out of the neuron. The following electrical and chemical processes lead to an action potential.

The cell membrane of the neuron is *semipermeable,* which means that some chemicals can pass through the cell membrane easily and others are not allowed to pass through except when special passageways in the membrane are open. These passageways, called *ion channels,* are doughnut-shaped protein molecules that form pores across the cell membrane. These protein structures regulate the flow of ions such as sodium (Na^+), potassium (K^+), calcium (Ca^{++}), and chloride (Cl^-) in and out of the neuron. Each ion channel is selective, permitting only one type of ion to flow through it when it is open.

When a neuron is not transmitting information, it is referred to as a *resting neuron.* In a resting neuron separate protein structures, called *ion pumps,* help maintain an uneven distribution of various ions across the cell membrane by pumping them into or out of the cell. For example, the ion pumps transport Na^+ out of the neuron whenever it passes into the neuron, and pumps K^+ back into the neuron whenever it gets out. In this way the resting neuron maintains high concentrations of Na^+ outside the cell and low concentrations inside it. The overall effect of these ion channels and pumps is to electrically polarize the cell membrane of the resting neuron, making the inside of the neuron more negative than the outside.

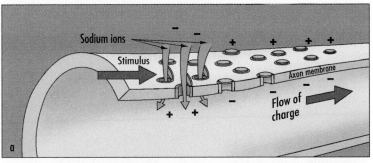

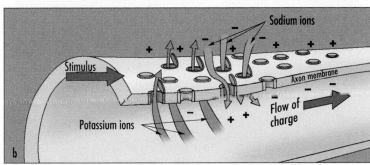

Figure 2-4

Action Potential (a) During an action potential, sodium gates in the neuron membrane open, and sodium ions enter the axon, bringing a positive charge with them. (b) After an action potential occurs at one point along the axon, the sodium gates close at that point and open at the next point along the axon. When the sodium gates close, potassium gates open, and potassium ions flow out of the axon, carrying positive charge with them, and causing the neuron to become negative again. (modified from Starr and Taggart, 1989).

When the neuron is stimulated, the voltage difference across the cell membrane is reduced. If the voltage drop is large enough, Na^+ channels open briefly at the point of stimulation and Na^+ ions flood into the cell. This process is called *depolarization.* Now the inside of that area of the cell membrane becomes positive relative to the outside. Neighboring Na^+ channels sense the voltage drop and open, causing the adjacent area to depolarize. This process of depolarization, repeating itself down the length of the axon, is a neural impulse. As the impulse travels down the axon, the Na^+ channels close behind it and the various ion pumps are activated to quickly restore the cell membrane to its resting state (see Figure 2-4). The importance of Na^+ channels is shown by the effect of local anesthetic agents such as Novocaine or Xylocaine: These prevent Na^+ channels from opening, thus stopping the action potential and preventing sensory signals from reaching the brain (Ragsdale et al., 1994).

The speed of the neural impulse as it travels down the axon can vary from about 2 to 200 miles per hour, depending on the diameter of the axon; larger ones generally are faster. The speed can also be affected by whether or not the axon is covered with a *myelin sheath.* This sheath consists of specialized glial cells that wrap themselves around the axon, one after another, with small gaps between them (refer back to Figure 2-1). These tiny gaps are called *nodes of Ranvier.* The insulation provided by the myelin sheath allows the nerve impulse to jump from one node of Ranvier to the next in a process known as *saltatory conduction,* which greatly increases the speed of transmission of the action potential down the axon. (*Saltatory* comes from the Latin word *saltare,* which means "to leap." In saltatory conduction, the action potential leaps from one node of Ranvier to another.) The myelin sheath is particularly prevalent in areas of the nervous system where rapid transmission of the action potential

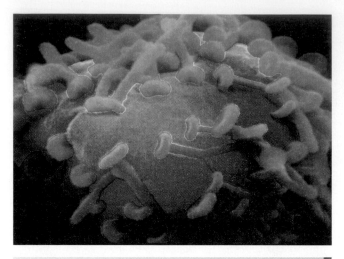

An electron micrograph of a neuron densely packed with synapses.

Figure 2-5

Release of Neurotransmitters into a Synaptic Gap   The neurotransmitter is carried to the presynaptic membrane in synaptic vesicles, which fuse with the membrane and release their contents into the synaptic gap. The neurotransmitters diffuse across the gap and combine with receptor molecules in the postsynaptic membrane.

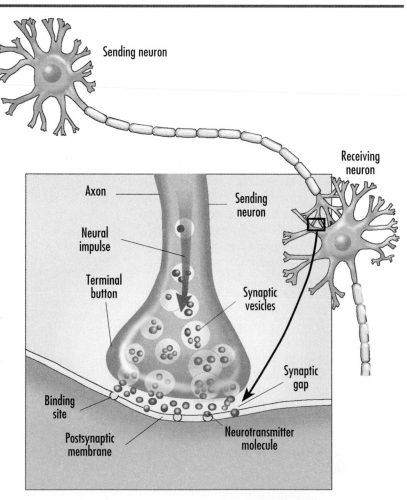

Sending neuron

Receiving neuron

Axon

Sending neuron

Neural impulse

Terminal button

Synaptic vesicles

Synaptic gap

Binding site

Postsynaptic membrane

Neurotransmitter molecule

is critical—for example, along axons that stimulate skeletal muscles. In *multiple sclerosis,* a disorder in which symptoms first become evident between the ages of 16 and 30, the immune system attacks and destroys the body's own myelin sheaths, producing severe motor nerve dysfunction.

Synaptic Transmission

The synaptic junction between neurons is of tremendous importance because it is there that nerve cells transfer signals. A single neuron discharges, or *fires,* when the stimulation reaching it via multiple synapses exceeds a certain threshold. The neuron fires in a single, brief pulse and then is inactive for a few thousandths of a second. The strength of the neural impulse is constant: It is always the same size, regardless of how strong the stimulus was; this is referred to as the *all-or-none principle of action.* The nerve impulse, once started, travels down the axon to its many terminal buttons.

As mentioned earlier, neurons do not connect directly at a synapse; there is a slight gap across which the signal must be transmitted (see Figure 2-5). When the action potential moves down the axon and arrives at the terminal buttons, it stimulates *synaptic vesicles* located in the terminal buttons. The synaptic vesicles are small spherical structures that contain neurotransmitters; when they are stimulated, they discharge the neurotransmitters into the synapse. The neurotransmitters diffuse across the synaptic gap and bind to *receptor sites* in the cell membrane of the receiving neuron. The neurotransmitter and the receptor site fit together like the pieces of a jigsaw puzzle or a key and a lock. This lock-and-key action causes a change in the permeability of ion channels in the receiving neuron. When bound to their receptors, some neurotransmitters have an *excitatory effect,* meaning that they allow positively charged ions, such as Na^+, to enter, thereby depolarizing the receiving neuron and making the inside of the cell more positive relative to the outside. Other neurotransmitters are *inhibitory,* meaning that they make the inside of the receiving neuron more negative relative to the outside, either by allowing positively charged ions, such as K^+, to leave the neuron or by letting negatively charged

Molecular Psychology

As discussed in the text, when the neural impulse reaches the end of an axon, neurotransmitters are released that cross the synaptic gap and combine with receptors in the membrane of the receiving neuron. The lock-and-key action of the neurotransmitter and its receptor changes the electrical properties of the target cell, making firing either a bit more likely (excitation) or a bit less likely (inhibition). To serve its function, every key requires a lock and every neurotransmitter requires a receptor. Many commonly used drugs interact with receptor molecules in very much the same way as neurotransmitters. Molecules of these drugs are shaped enough like those of the neurotransmitters to work as if they were keys to the locks of receptors.

A good example of look-alike molecules is the class of drugs called *opiates,* which includes heroin and morphine. In molecular shape, opiates resemble a group of neurotransmitters called *endorphins,* which have the effect of blocking pain. The discovery that opiates mimic naturally occurring substances in the brain has prompted considerable research on the chemical control system that copes with stress and pain. Individuals who appear to be indifferent to pain may have an unusual ability to increase the production of these natural painkillers when they are needed.

Research with one of the endorphins, called enkephalin, has helped explain why a painkiller like morphine can be addictive. Under normal conditions, enkephalin binds to a certain number of opiate receptors. Morphine relieves pain by binding to the receptors that are left unfilled. Too much morphine can cause a drop in enkephalin production, leaving opiate receptors unfilled. The body then requires more morphine to fill the unoccupied receptors and

to reduce pain. When morphine is discontinued, the opiate receptors are left unfilled, causing painful withdrawal symptoms.

The fact that the brain synthesizes substances that resemble opiates has been invoked to explain all sorts of effects. Joggers tout the theory that physical exertion increases enkephalin production to induce a "runner's high." Acupuncturists say that their needles actuate enkephalins, which then act as natural anesthetics. Some evidence to support this claim comes from observations that acupuncture-like stimulation appears to reduce pain responses and actuate enkephalin neural systems even when it is administered to animals (Chen, Geller, & Adler, 1996). Since animals are unlikely to show placebo effects, such studies are perhaps the strongest grounds for concluding that acupuncture directly activates neural enkephalin systems, although how it does this remains unclear.

Drugs that influence mental functioning and mood, such as opiates, are referred to as *psychoactive drugs.* By and large, they produce their effects by altering one of the various neurotransmitter-receptor systems. Different drugs can have different actions at the same synapse. One drug might mimic the effect of a specific neurotransmitter, another might occupy the receptor site so that the normal neurotransmitter is blocked out, and still others might affect the reuptake or degradation processes. The drug action will either increase or decrease the effectiveness of synaptic transmission.

Two drugs, chlorpromazine and reserpine, have proved useful in treating schizophrenia. Both drugs act on norepinephrine and dopamine systems, but their antipsychotic action is due primarily to their effect on the neurotransmitter dopamine. It appears that

chlorpromazine blocks dopamine receptors and that reserpine reduces dopamine levels by destroying storage vesicles in the synaptic terminals. The effectiveness of these drugs in treating schizophrenia has led to the formulation of the *dopamine hypothesis,* which states that schizophrenia is due to an excess of dopamine activity in critical cell groups within the brain. The key evidence for this hypothesis is that antipsychotic drugs seem to be clinically effective to the extent that they block the transmission of impulses by dopamine molecules.

Research on neurotransmitter-receptor systems has increased our understanding of how drugs work. In the past, psychoactive drugs were discovered almost entirely by accident and their development took years of research. Now, as we gain more knowledge about neurotransmitters and receptors, new drugs can be designed and developed in a systematic way. For example, during the last 10 years a great deal has been learned about the molecular basis of interneural communication. The emerging picture is that thousands of different types of molecules are involved—not just transmitter and receptor molecules, but also the enzymes that manufacture and degrade them and various other molecules that modulate their action. Of course, each time a new molecule is identified, we have discovered the potential for at least two diseases or forms of mental illness; some people will surely have too much of that molecule and others too little. Research on these problems has proved so productive that the field has been given the name *molecular psychology* (Franklin, 1987). The basic idea behind this new discipline is that mental processes and their aberrations can be analyzed in terms of the molecular interplay that takes place between neurons.

ions, such as Cl⁻, enter the cell. Thus, the excitatory effect increases the likelihood that the neuron will fire, whereas the inhibitory effect decreases the likelihood of firing.

A given neuron may receive neurotransmitters from many thousands of synapses with other neurons. Depending on their pattern of firing, different axons will release their neurotransmitters at different times. If—at a particular moment and at a particular place on the cell membrane—the excitatory effects on the receiving neuron become large enough relative to the inhibitory effects, depolarization occurs and the neuron fires.

Once a neurotransmitter is released and diffuses across the synaptic gap, its action must be very brief. Otherwise, it will exert its effects for too long, and precise control will be lost. The brevity of the action is achieved in one of two ways. For some neurotransmitters, the synapse is almost immediately cleared of the chemical by *reuptake,* a process in which the neurotransmitter is reabsorbed by the neuron from which it was released. Reuptake cuts off the action of the neurotransmitter and spares the axon terminals from having to manufacture more of the substance. Another way of removing neurotransmitters from the cleft is *degradation,* a process in which enzymes in the gap destroy the neurotransmitter molecule and make it inactive.

Neurotransmitters

More than 70 different neurotransmitters have been identified, and others surely will be discovered. Moreover, some neurotransmitters can bind to more than one type of receptor molecule, causing different effects. For example, glutamate can activate at least 16 different types of receptor molecules, allowing neurons to respond in distinct ways to the same neurotransmitter (Westbrook, 1994). Certain neurotransmitters are excitatory at some sites in the nervous system and inhibitory at other sites because two different types of receptor molecules are involved (Westbrook, 1994). In this chapter we obviously cannot discuss all the neurotransmitters that are found in the nervous system; instead, we will focus on a few that have important psychological roles.

Acetylcholine (ACh) is a neurotransmitter that is found at many synapses throughout the nervous system. Generally it is excitatory, but it can also be inhibitory, depending on the type of receptor in the membrane of the receiving neuron. ACh is particularly prevalent in an area of the forebrain called the hippocampus, which plays a key role in the formation of new memories (Squire, 1996).

Alzheimer's disease, a devastating disorder that affects many older people, involves impairment of memory and other cognitive functions. It has been demonstrated that neurons in the forebrain that produce ACh tend to degenerate in Alzheimer patients, and consequently the brain's production of ACh is reduced; the less ACh present in the forebrain, the greater the memory loss.

ACh is also released at every synapse at which a neuron terminates at a muscle fiber to trigger movement. The ACh stimulates muscles to contract, and drugs that interfere with ACh can produce muscle paralysis. For example, botulinum toxin, which is formed by bacteria in improperly canned foods, blocks the release of ACh at nerve–muscle synapses and can cause death when the muscles used for breathing become paralyzed. Some nerve gases developed for warfare, as well as many pesticides, cause paralysis by destroying the enzyme that degrades ACh once the neuron has been fired; when the degradation process fails, there is an uncontrolled buildup of ACh in the nervous system and normal synaptic transmission becomes impossible.

Norepinephrine (NE) and *dopamine (DA)* are two neurotransmitters that are important to motivation and reward. Drugs such as cocaine and amphetamines prolong the action of DA and NE in the synapse either by stimulating their release or by slowing down their reuptake process. Facilitation of DA and NE neurotransmission causes the stimulating psychological effects of these drugs.

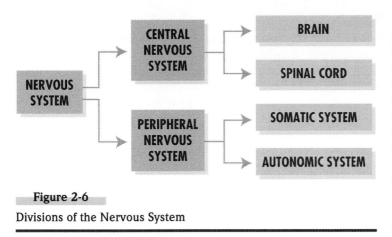

Figure 2-6

Divisions of the Nervous System

Another neurotransmitter, *serotonin,* is chemically related to DA and NE. Many mood-altering drugs act on this neurotransmitter as well as on DA and NE. Some psychotherapeutic drugs act specifically on serotonin synapses. For example, drugs like Prozac, which are prescribed for depression and other disorders, inhibit reuptake of serotonin from the synaptic cleft, leading to increased stimulation of serotonin receptors. Hallucinogenic drugs such as LSD also act primarily on serotonin synapses.

The excitatory neurotransmitter *glutamate* is present in more neurons of the central nervous system than any other transmitter. There are at least three subtypes of glutamate receptors, and one of these is believed to play a role in learning and memory. It is called the NMDA receptor after the chemical (N-methyl D-aspartate) that is used to detect it. Neurons in the hippocampus (an area near the center of the brain) are particularly rich in NMDA receptors, and there is considerable evidence that this area is critical in the formation of new memories.

Divisions of the Nervous System

All parts of the nervous system are interrelated. But for purposes of discussion, the nervous system can be separated into two major division, each having two subdivisions (see Figure 2-6).

The **central nervous system** includes *all the neurons in the brain and spinal cord.* The **peripheral nervous system** consists of *the nerves connecting the brain and spinal cord to the other parts of the body.* The peripheral nervous system is further divided into the **somatic system,** which *carries messages to and from the sense receptors, muscles, and the surface of the body,* and the **autonomic system**, which *connects with the internal organs and glands.*

---

1. Only about one tenth of the cells in your brain are neurons (the rest are glial cells). Does this mean that you use only one tenth of your brain when you think? Perhaps not. What other possibilities are there?

2. Local anesthetics, such as the one you might receive in a dentist's office, work by blocking Na$^+$ gates in the neurons near the point of injection. Of course, dentists and physicians typically inject the anesthetics into a part of the body near the source of pain. What do you think such a drug would do if it were injected into the brain? Would it still block pain and touch, and nothing else? Or would its effect be different?

What Is the Nature of the Central Core and Limbic System?

There are a number of ways to conceptualize the brain. One way to think about the brain is to divide it into three regions based on location: (1) the **hindbrain,** which includes *all the structures located in the hind, or posterior, part of the brain, closest to the spinal cord;* (2) the **midbrain,** which is located in *the middle of the brain;* and (3) the **forebrain,**

central nervous system   all the neurons in the brain and spinal cord

peripheral nervous system   the nerves connecting the brain and spinal cord to the other parts of the body

somatic system   the portion of the peripheral nervous system that carries messages to and from the sense receptors, muscles, and the surface of the body

autonomic system   the portion of the peripheral nervous system that connects with the internal organs and glands

Thinking Critically

hindbrain   all the structures located in the hind, or posterior, part of the brain, closest to the spinal cord

midbrain   the middle of the brain

forebrain   the structures located in the front, or anterior, part of the brain

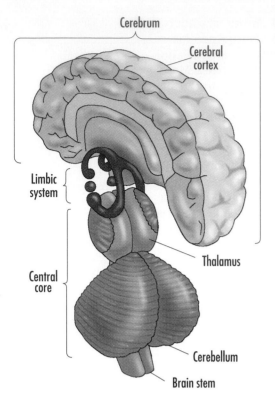

Cerebrum

Cerebral cortex

Limbic system

Central core

Thalamus

Cerebellum

Brain stem

Figure 2-7

Three Concentric Layers of the Human Brain   The central core and the limbic system are shown in their entirety, but the left cerebral hemisphere has been removed. The cerebellum of the central core controls balance and muscular coordination; the thalamus serves as a switchboard for messages coming from the sense organs; the hypothalamus (not shown but located below the thalamus) regulates endocrine activity and such life-maintaining processes as metabolism and temperature control. The limbic system is concerned with actions that satisfy basic needs and with emotion. The cerebral cortex (an outer layer of cells covering the cerebrum) is the center of higher mental processes, where sensations are registered, voluntary actions initiated, decisions made, and plans formulated.

which includes *the structures located in the front, or anterior, part of the brain.* The Canadian investigator Paul MacLean proposed another framework for organizing the brain that is based on the function of the brain structures rather than on their location. According to MacLean, we can think of the human brain as composed of three concentric layers: (1) the *central core,* which regulates our most primitive behaviors; (2) the *limbic system,* which controls our emotions, and (3) the *cerebrum,* which regulates our higher intellectual processes. Figure 2-7 shows how these layers fit together; compare it with the more detailed cross section in Figure 2-8. We will use MacLean's organizational framework as we discuss the various structures in the brain and their functions. (See also Table 2-1.)

The Central Core

The central core, also known as the *brain stem,* controls involuntary behaviors like coughing, sneezing, or gagging, as well as "primitive" behaviors that are under vol-

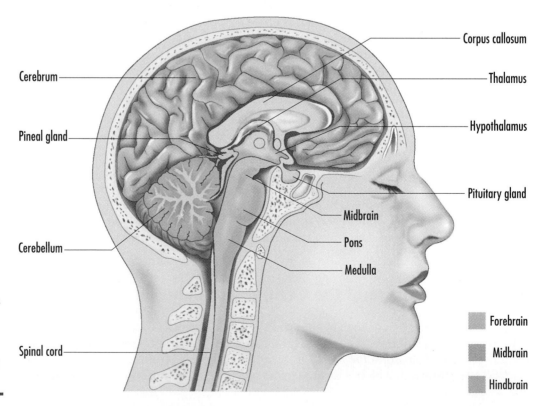

Corpus callosum

Cerebrum

Thalamus

Pineal gland

Hypothalamus

Pituitary gland

Cerebellum

Midbrain

Pons

Medulla

Spinal cord

Forebrain

Midbrain

Hindbrain

Figure 2-8

The Human Brain   This schematic drawing shows the main structures of the central nervous system. (Only the upper portion of the spinal cord is shown.)

Table 2-1

Parts of the Human Brain

Structure	Function
Cerebral cortex	Consists of several cortical areas: the primary motor area, the primary somatosensory area, the primary visual area, the primary auditory area, and association area.
Corpus callosum	Connects the two hemispheres of the cerebrum.
Thalamus	Directs incoming information from the sense receptors to the cerebrum; plays a role in the control of sleep and wakefulness.
Hypothalamus	Mediates eating, drinking, and sexual behavior; regulates endocrine activity and maintains homeostasis; plays a role in emotion and response to stress.
Reticular formation	Plays a role in controlling arousal and in the ability to focus attention on particular stimuli.
Hippocampus	Plays a special role in memory; also involved in emotional behavior.
Cerebellum	Concerned primarily with the coordination of movement.
Medulla	Controls breathing and some reflexes that help the organism maintain an upright posture.

untary control, such as breathing, vomiting, sleeping, eating, drinking, temperature regulation, and sexual behavior. The brain stem includes all the structures in the hindbrain and midbrain and two structures in the forebrain, namely, the hypothalamus and the thalamus. This means that the central core of the brain stretches from the hindbrain to the forebrain. In this chapter we will limit our discussion to four brain stem structures—the medulla, the cerebellum, the thalamus, and the hypothalamus—which are responsible for the regulation of the most important primitive behaviors necessary for survival.

The Medulla   The first slight enlargement of the spinal cord as it enters the skull is the *medulla,* a narrow structure that controls breathing and some reflexes that help maintain upright posture. Also at this point the major nerve tracts coming up from the spinal cord cross over so that the right side of the brain is connected to the left side of the body and the left side of the brain to the right side of the body.

The Cerebellum   Attached to the rear of the brain stem, slightly above the medulla, is a convoluted structure, the *cerebellum.* The cerebellum is concerned primarily with the coordination of movement. Specific movements may be initiated at higher levels, but their smooth coordination depends on the cerebellum. Damage to the cerebellum results in jerky, uncoordinated movements.

Until recently, most scientists thought that the cerebellum was concerned almost exclusively with movement and nothing else. However, recent research has identified direct neural connections between the cerebellum and frontal parts of the brain involved in memory, language, planning, and reasoning (Middleton & Strick, 1994). These connecting circuits are much larger in human beings than in monkeys and other animals. This, along with other evidence, suggests that the cerebellum may play a role in the control and coordination of more complex mental functions as much as it does in the coordination of movements.

The Thalamus and Hypothalamus   Located just above the midbrain inside the cerebral hemispheres are two egg-shaped structures (one on the left side of the brain and the other on the right), pressed together to make up the *thalamus.* Regions of the thalamus act as a relay station for different sensations (vision, hearing, touch, and taste) arriving in the brain; they direct incoming information from the sense receptors to the cerebrum.

The hypothalamus, located just below the thalamus, is a much smaller structure that is crucial to motivation and emotions. Centers in the hypothalamus control eating, drinking, and sexual behavior. The hypothalamus also regulates *endocrine* activity—the activity of glands that secrete substances directly into the bloodstream to affect distant targets—to control normal body temperature, heart rates, hormonal secretions, digestive reflexes, and blood pressure. Under stress, the hypothalamus's control over the secretion of hormones is disturbed, leading to physiological changes appropriate to emergency situations (the "fight-or-flight" response). The hypothalamus has therefore been called the body's "stress center."

The Limbic System

limbic system a set of structures that are closely interconnected with the hypothalamus and appear to impose additional controls over some of the instinctive behaviors regulated by the hypothalamus and brain stem

Around the central core of the brain are a number of structures that together are called the **limbic system,** *a set of structures closely interconnected with the hypothalamus, which appears to impose additional controls over some of the instinctive behaviors regulated by the hypothalamus and the brain stem* (refer back to Figure 2-7). One part of the limbic system, the *hippocampus,* plays a special role in memory. The effects of surgical removal of, or accidental damage to, the hippocampus demonstrate that it is critical for the storage of new events such as lasting memories but is not necessary for the retrieval of older memories. Upon recovery from such an operation, patients will have no difficulty recognizing old friends or recalling experiences from earlier in life. However, they will have little, if any, recall of events that occurred in the year or so just prior to the operation. They will not remember events and people they meet after the operation at all. For example, they will fail to recognize a new person with whom they may have spent many hours earlier in the day. They will do the same jigsaw puzzle week after week, never remembering having done it before, and will read the same newspaper over and over without remembering the contents (Squire, 1996).

The limbic system is also involved in emotional behavior. Monkeys with lesions (damage) in some regions of the limbic system react with rage at the slightest provocation, suggesting that the destroyed area was exerting an inhibiting influence. Monkeys with lesions in other areas of the limbic system no longer express aggressive behavior and show no hostility, even when attacked. They simply ignore the attacker and act as if nothing had happened.

Thinking Critically

According to MacLean, the brain is organized into three concentric layers with each higher layer imposing some control over lower layers. The limbic system modulates some of the brain stem's instinctive behaviors and in turn is itself modified by the higher information-processing cortical areas. Why does the brain have this type of organization and layering of control mechanisms? How could this type of organization be evolutionarily adaptive for animals with larger cortical areas?

What Is the Nature of the Cerebrum?

cerebrum the brain's two cerebral hemispheres

The **cerebrum**—*the brain's two cerebral hemispheres*—is larger and more complex in human beings than in any other organism. Its outer layer is called the *cerebral cortex* (in Latin, *cortex* means "bark"). The cerebral cortex (often simply called the cortex) of a preserved brain appears gray because it consists largely of nerve cell bodies and unmyelinated (lacking a myelin sheath) fibers—hence the term "gray matter." The inside of the cerebrum, beneath the cortex, is composed mostly of myelinated axons and appears white.

The Structure of the Cerebrum

Each of the sensory systems projects information to specific areas of the cortex. The movements of body parts (motor responses) are controlled by another area of the

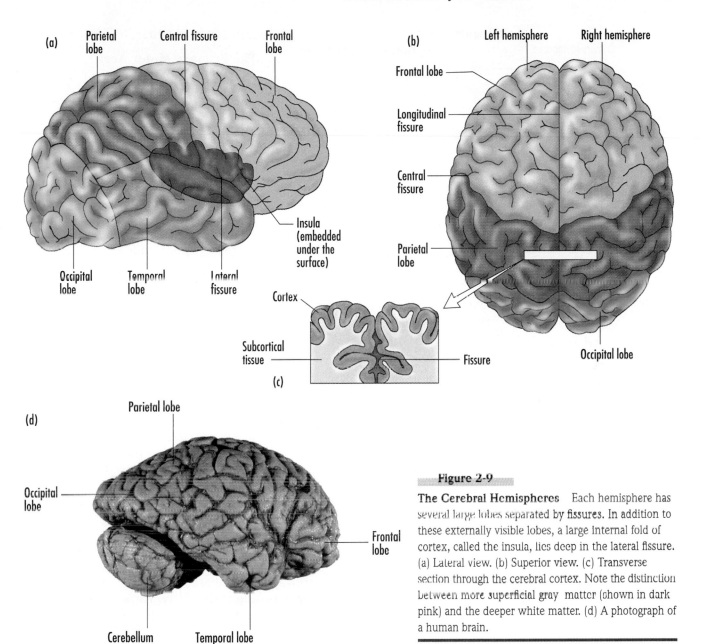

Figure 2-9

The Cerebral Hemispheres Each hemisphere has several large lobes separated by fissures. In addition to these externally visible lobes, a large internal fold of cortex, called the insula, lies deep in the lateral fissure. (a) Lateral view. (b) Superior view. (c) Transverse section through the cerebral cortex. Note the distinction between more superficial gray matter (shown in dark pink) and the deeper white matter. (d) A photograph of a human brain.

cortex. The rest of the cortex, which is neither sensory nor motor, consists of *association areas*. These areas are concerned with other aspects of behavior—memory, thought, and language—and occupy the largest portion of the human cortex.

Before discussing some of these locations, we need to describe the cerebral hemispheres themselves. The left and right sides of the brain are basically symmetrical, with a deep division between them running from front to rear. So we commonly refer to the right and left *hemispheres* of the brain. The cortex of each hemisphere is divided into four lobes: *frontal, parietal, occipital,* and *temporal.* The divisions between these lobes are shown in Figure 2-9. The frontal lobe is separated from the parietal lobe by the *central fissure,* which runs from near the top of the head sideways to the ears. The division between the parietal lobe and the occipital lobe is less clear-cut; for our purposes it suffices to say that the parietal lobe is at the top of the brain behind the central fissure and that the occipital lobe is at the rear of the brain. The temporal lobe is at the side of the brain, separated from the rest by the *lateral fissure.*

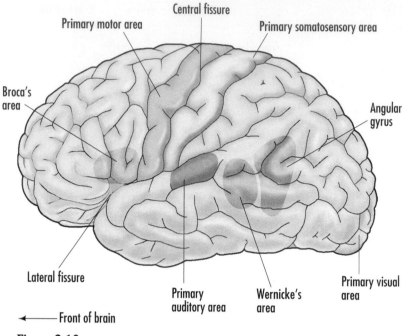

Central fissure

Primary motor area

Primary somatosensory area

Broca's area

Angular gyrus

Lateral fissure

Primary visual area

Front of brain

Primary auditory area

Wernicke's area

Figure 2-10

Specialization of Function in the Left Cortex   A major part of the cortex is involved in generating movements and in analyzing sensory inputs. These areas (which include motor, somatosensory, visual, auditory, and olfactory areas) are present on both sides of the brain. Other functions are found on only one side of the brain. For example, Broca's area and Wernicke's area are involved in the production and understanding of language, and the angular gyrus is involved in matching the visual form of a word with its auditory form. These language functions exist only on the left side of the human brain.

Cortical Areas

The Primary Motor Area   The *primary motor area* of the cortex is the back portion of the frontal lobe, just in front of the central fissure (see Figure 2-10). It controls the voluntary movements of the body. Electrical stimulation at certain spots on the motor cortex produces movement of specific body parts; when these spots on the motor cortex are injured, movement of those parts of the body is impaired. The body is represented on the motor cortex in approximately upside-down form. For example, movements of the toes are controlled near the top of the head, while tongue and mouth movements are controlled near the bottom of the motor area. Movements on the right side of the body are governed by the motor cortex of the left hemisphere; movements on the left side are governed by the right hemisphere.

The Primary Somatosensory Area The sense of touch is processed in the parietal lobe, behind the motor area and in back of the central fissure. If this area is stimulated electrically, it produces a sensory experience somewhere on the opposite side of the body. It is as though a part of the body were being touched. This is called the *primary somatosensory area* (body- sense area). Heat, cold, touch, pain, and the sense of body movement are all represented here.

Most of the nerve fibers in the pathways that radiate to and from the somatosensory and motor areas cross to the opposite side of the body. Thus, the sensory impulses from the right side of the body go to the left somatosensory cortex, and the muscles of the right foot and hand are controlled by the left motor cortex.

In general, the amount of somatosensory or motor area associated with a particular part of the body is directly related to its sensitivity and use. For example, among four-footed mammals the dog has only a small amount of cortical tissue representing the forepaws; the raccoon—which makes extensive use of its forepaws in exploring and manipulating its environment—has a much larger representative cortical area, including regions for the separate fingers of the forepaw. The rat, which learns a great deal about its environment by means of its sensitive whiskers, has a separate cortical area for each whisker.

The Primary Visual Area   At the back of each occipital lobe is an area of the cortex known as the *primary visual area*. Figure 2-11 shows the optic nerve fibers and neural pathways leading from each eye to the visual cortex. Notice that some of the optic fibers from the right eye go to the right cerebral hemisphere, whereas others cross over at the bottom of the brain at a junction called the *optic chiasm* and go to the opposite hemisphere; the same arrangement holds true for the left eye. Fibers from the right sides of both eyes go to the right hemisphere of the brain, and fibers from the left sides of both eyes go to the left hemisphere. Consequently, damage to the visual area of one hemisphere (say, the left) will result in blind fields in the left sides of both eyes, causing a loss of vision to the right side of the environment. This fact is sometimes helpful in pinpointing the location of a brain tumor or other abnormalities.

The Primary Auditory Area   The *primary auditory area* (located on the surface of the temporal lobe at the side of each hemisphere) is involved in the analysis of complex auditory signals. It is particularly concerned with the temporal patterning of sound, as in human speech. Both ears are represented in the auditory areas on both sides of the cortex; however, connections to the opposite side are stronger.

Association Areas   The many large areas of the cerebral cortex that are not directly concerned with sensory or motor processes are called *association areas.* The *frontal association areas* (the parts of the frontal lobes in front of the motor area) appear to play an important role in the thought processes required for problem solving. In monkeys, for example, lesions in the frontal lobes destroy the ability to solve a delayed-response problem. In this kind of problem, food is placed in one of two cups while the monkey watches, and the cups are then covered with identical objects. Next an opaque screen is placed between the monkey and the cups; after a specified period the screen is removed and the monkey is allowed to choose one of the cups. Normal monkeys can remember the correct cup after delays of several minutes, but monkeys with frontal lobe lesions cannot solve the problem if the delay is more than a few seconds. Normal monkeys have neurons in the frontal lobe that fire action potentials during the delay, thus possibly mediating their memory of an event (Goldman-Rakic, 1996).

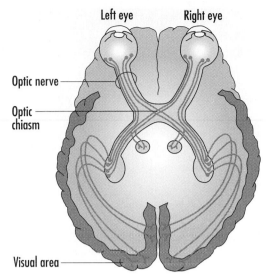

Figure 2-11

Visual Pathways   Nerve fibers from the inner, or nasal, half of the retina cross over at the optic chiasm and go to opposite sides of the brain. Thus, stimuli falling on the right side of each retina are transmitted to the right hemisphere, and stimuli falling on the left side of each retina are transmitted to the left hemisphere.

The posterior association areas are located near the various primary sensory areas and appear to consist of subareas, each of which serves a particular sense. For example, the lower portion of the temporal lobe is related to visual perception. Lesions (that is, brain damage) in this area produce deficits in the ability to recognize different forms. A lesion here does not cause loss of visual acuity, as would a lesion in the primary visual area of the occipital lobe; the individual "sees" the forms (and can trace the outline) but cannot identify the shape or distinguish it from a different form (Goodglass & Butter, 1988).

Pictures of the Living Brain

A number of brain scan techniques have been developed to obtain detailed pictures of the living human brain without causing distress or damage to the patient. Before these techniques were perfected, the precise location and identification of most types of brain injury could be determined only by exploratory neurosurgery, complicated neurological diagnosis, or an autopsy after the patient's death. For that reason, most knowledge about how brain systems control psychological functions and behavior has come from studies of animals. The new techniques for scanning human brain structure and activity depend on sophisticated computer methods that only recently have become feasible.

One such technique is *computerized axial tomography* (abbreviated CAT or simply CT), which reveals the neuroanatomy of a living brain. This procedure involves sending a narrow X-ray beam through the patient's head and measuring the amount of radiation that gets through. The revolutionary aspect of the technique is that measurements are made at hundreds of thousands of different orientations (or *axes*) through the head. These measurements are then fed into a computer. By making

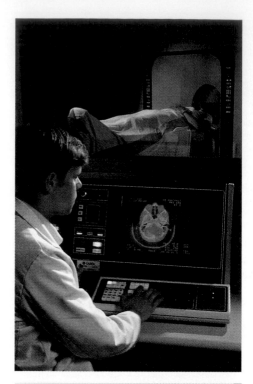

A technician administering a magnetic resonance imaging procedure. An image of the patient's brain appears on the computer screen.

appropriate calculations, a technician can construct a cross-sectional picture of the brain that can be photographed or displayed on a television monitor. The cross-sectional slice can be at any level and angle desired. The term *computerized axial tomography* refers to the critical role of the computer, the many axes at which measurements are made, and the resulting image that is a cross-sectional slice through the brain (*tomo* is an ancient Greek word meaning "slice" or "cut").

A newer and even more powerful technique is *magnetic resonance imaging* (abbreviated MRI). In this procedure, scanners use strong magnetic fields, radio-frequency pulses, and computers to compose the image. The patient lies in a doughnut-shaped tunnel surrounded by a large magnet that generates a powerful magnetic field. When the anatomic part to be studied is placed in the strong magnetic field and exposed to a certain radio-frequency pulse, the tissues emit a signal that can be measured. As with the CT scanner, hundreds of thousands of such measurements are made and then manipulated by a technician to produce a two-dimensional image of the anatomic part. Among scientists, the technique is usually called *nuclear magnetic resonance* because what is being measured are variations in the energy level of hydrogen atom nuclei in the body caused by the radio frequency pulses. However, many physicians prefer to drop the term *nuclear* and simply call it magnetic resonance imaging, since they fear that the public may confuse the reference to the nucleus of an atom with nuclear radiation.

MRI offers greater precision than the CT scanner in the diagnosis of diseases of the brain and spinal cord. For example, the MRI cross section of the brain shows features characteristic of multiple sclerosis that would not be detected by a CT scanner; previously, diagnosis of this disease required hospitalization and a test in which dye is injected into the canal around the spinal cord. MRI is also useful in the detection of abnormalities in the spinal cord and at the base of the brain, such as herniated disks, tumors, and birth malformations.

While CT and traditional MRI both provide a picture of the anatomical detail of the brain, it is often desirable to assess the level of neural activity at different locations in the brain. Two new techniques allow us to do this. One is a modification of the MRI technique, called *functional MRI (fMRI)* because it measures brain activity or function. This modification makes it possible to detect the rate at which oxygen is absorbed from the blood by various regions of brain tissue. The use of oxygen is proportional to the rate of neural activity, so it provides a measure of brain activity.

Another computer-based scanning procedure, *positron emission tomography (PET),* measures the brain's use of its principal fuel, glucose (obtained from

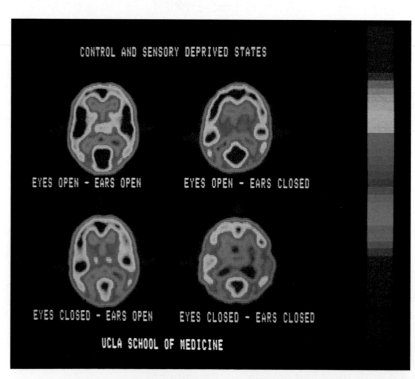

Red areas indicate maximum brain activity; blue areas show minimum activity.

the bloodstream). A small amount of a radioactive tracer compound can be mixed with glucose so that each molecule of glucose has a tiny speck of radioactivity (that is, a *label*) attached to it. If this harmless mixture is injected into the bloodstream, after a few minutes the brain cells begin to absorb the radiolabeled glucose in the same way that they use regular glucose. The most active neurons absorb more glucose, and the PET scan detects the level of radio-labeled glucose in different regions of the brain. The PET scan is essentially a highly sensitive detector of radioactivity (it is not like an X-ray machine, which emits X rays, but rather like a Geiger counter, which measures radioactivity). The PET scan measures the amount of radioactivity and sends the information to a computer, which draws a color cross-sectional picture of the brain with different colors representing different levels of neural activity. The measurement of radioactivity is based on the emission of positively charged particles called positrons—hence the term *positron emission tomography.*

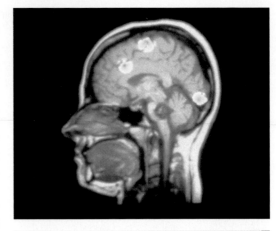

This PET image shows three areas in the left brain that are active during a language task.

Comparison of PET scans of normal individuals with those of individuals with neurological disorders indicates that a variety of brain problems (epilepsy, blood clots, brain tumors, and so on) can be identified using this technique. For psychological research, the PET scan has been used to compare the brains of schizophrenic individuals with those of normal individuals and has revealed differences in the metabolic levels of certain cortical areas (Andreasen, 1988). It has also been used to investigate the brain areas that are activated during higher mental functions such as listening to music, doing mathematical problems, or speaking, the goal being to identify the brain structures involved (Posner, 1993).

The CT, fMRI, and PET scanners are proving to be invaluable tools for studying the relationship between the brain and behavior. These instruments provide an example of how progress in one field of science forges ahead because of technical developments in another (Pechura & Martin, 1991; Raichle, 1994). For example, PET scans can be used to study differences in neural activity between the two cerebral hemispheres. These hemispheric differences in activity are known as brain asymmetries.

The cerebrum processes each sensory modality and motor movement in discreet, unique areas. Thus movements of the limbs, processing of visual information, and analysis of auditory signals are each processed in segregated regions of the cortex. How might this type of organization lead to optimal analysis and integration of incoming information and control over behavior? What problems might arise if all sensory, motor, and association functions were controlled by the exact same populations of neurons?

Thinking Critically

What Do We Know About Asymmetries in the Brain?

On casual examination, the two halves of the human brain look like mirror images of each other. But closer examination reveals asymmetries. When brains are measured during autopsies, parts of the left hemisphere are almost always larger than their counterparts in the right hemisphere. Also, the right hemisphere contains many long neural fibers that connect widely separate areas of the brain, whereas the left hemisphere contains many shorter fibers that provide rich interconnections within a limited area (Hillige, 1993).

As early as 1861, the French physician Paul Broca examined the brain of a patient who had suffered speech loss; he found damage in an area of the left hemisphere just above the lateral fissure in the frontal lobe. This region, known as *Broca's area* and shown in Figure 2-10, is involved in the production of speech. Destruction

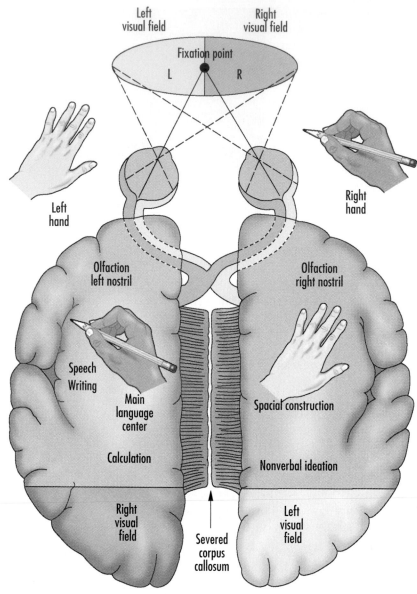

Figure 2-12

Sensory Inputs to the Two Hemispheres   With the eyes fixated straight ahead, stimuli to the left of the central fixation point go to the right cerebral hemisphere, and stimuli to the right go to the left hemisphere. The left hemisphere controls movements of the right hand, and the right hemisphere controls the left hand. Hearing is largely crossed in its input, but some sound representation goes to the hemisphere on the same side as the ear that registered it.

of the equivalent region in the right hemisphere usually does not result in speech impairment. A few left-handed people have speech centers located in the right hemisphere, but the great majority have language functions in the left hemisphere (as do right-handed individuals).

Although the left hemisphere's role in language has been known for some time, only in recent decades has it been possible to investigate what each hemisphere can do on its own. In a normal individual the brain functions as an integrated whole; information in one hemisphere is immediately transferred to the other by way of a broad band of connecting nerve fibers called the *corpus callosum*. This connecting bridge can cause a problem in some forms of epilepsy because a seizure starting in one hemisphere may cross over to the other. In an effort to prevent such generalized seizures in some severe epileptics, neurosurgeons have surgically severed the corpus callosum. The operation has proved successful for some individuals, resulting in a decrease in seizures. In addition, there appear to be no obvious undesirable aftereffects; the patients seem to function in everyday life as well as individuals whose hemispheres are still connected.

Split-Brain Research

It took some very special tests to demonstrate that mental functions were affected by separating the two hemispheres in so-called "split-brain" patients. A little more background information is needed to understand the experiments we are about to describe.

You already know that the sensory and motor nerves cross over from left to right, and vice versa, as they enter the brain. You also know that speech (Broca's area) is located in the left hemisphere. When the eyes are fixated directly ahead, images to the left of the fixation point go through both eyes to the right side of the brain and images to the right of the fixation point go to the left side of the brain (see Figure 2-12). Thus, each hemisphere has a view of the half of the visual field in which "its" hand normally functions. For example, the left hemisphere sees the right hand in the right visual field.

Roger Sperry pioneered work on split-brain patients and in 1981 was awarded the Nobel prize in neuroscience for this research. In one of Sperry's test situations, a patient who has undergone a split-brain operation is seated in front of a screen that

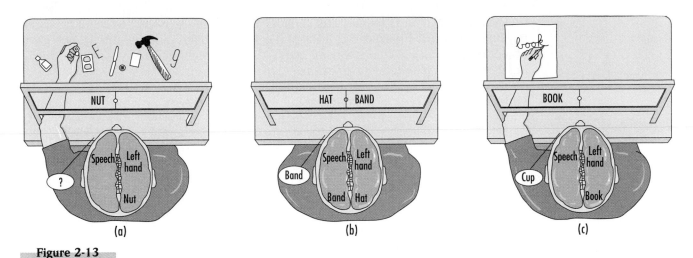

(a)   (b)   (c)

Figure 2-13

Testing the Abilities of the Two Hemispheres   (a) The split-brain subject correctly retrieves an object by touch with the left hand when its name is flashed to the right hemisphere, but he cannot name the object or describe what he has done. (b) The word "hatband" is flashed so that "hat" goes to the right cerebral hemisphere and "band" goes to the left hemisphere. The subject reports that he sees the word "band" but has no idea what kind of band. (c) A list of common objects (including "book" and "cup") is initially shown to both hemispheres. One word from the list ("book") is then projected to the right hemisphere. When given the command to do so, the left hand begins writing the word "book," but when questioned the subject does not know what his left hand has written and guesses "cup."

hides his hands from view (see Figure 2-13a). His gaze is fixed on a spot on the center of the screen and the word "nut" is flashed very briefly (one tenth of a second) on the left side of the screen. Remember that this visual signal goes to the right side of the brain, which controls the left side of the body. With his left hand, the subject can easily pick up the nut from a pile of other objects hidden from view. But he cannot tell the experimenter what word flashed on the screen because speech is controlled by the left hemisphere and the visual image of "nut" was not transmitted to that hemisphere. When questioned, the split-brain patient seems unaware of what his left hand is doing. He can only guess when asked to name the word he saw or what is in his hand. Since the sensory input from the left hand goes to the right hemisphere, the left hemisphere receives no information about what the left hand is feeling or doing.

It is important that the word be flashed on the screen for no more than one tenth of a second. If it remains longer, the patient's eyes move so that the word is also projected to the left hemisphere. If the patient can move his eyes freely, information goes to both cerebral hemispheres; this is one reason why the deficiencies caused by severing the corpus callosum are not readily apparent in a person's daily activities.

Further experiments demonstrate that a split-brain patient can use speech to communicate only what is going on in the left hemisphere. Figure 2-13b shows another test situation. The word "hatband" is flashed on the screen so that "hat" goes to the right hemisphere and "band" to the left. When asked what word he saw, the patient replies "band." When asked what kind of band, he makes all sorts of guesses— "rubber band," "rock band," "band of robbers," and so forth—and hits on "hatband" only by chance. Tests with other word combinations (such as "keycase" and "suitcase") show similar results. What is perceived by the right hemisphere is not transferred to the conscious awareness of the left hemisphere. With the corpus callosum severed, each hemisphere seems oblivious to the experiences of the other.

If the patient is blindfolded and a familiar object (such as a comb, toothbrush, or keycase) is placed in his left hand, he appears to know what it is; for example, he can demonstrate its use with appropriate gestures. But he cannot express his knowledge in speech. If asked what is going on while he is manipulating the object, he has no idea. This is true as long as any sensory input from the object to the left (speaking) hemisphere is blocked. But if the subject's right hand inadvertently touches the object or if it makes a characteristic sound (like the jingling of a keycase), the speaking hemisphere immediately gives the correct answer.

Although the right hemisphere cannot speak, it does have some linguistic capabilities. It recognized the meaning of the word "nut," as we saw in our first example, and it can write a little. In the experiment illustrated in Figure 2-13c, a split-brain patient is first shown a list of common words such as *cup, knife, book,* and *glass.* This list is displayed long enough for the words to be projected to both hemispheres. Next, the list is removed, and one of the words (for example, "book") is flashed briefly on the left side of the screen so that it goes to the right hemisphere. If the patient is asked to write what he saw, his left hand will begin writing "book." If asked what his left hand has written, he has no idea and will guess at any of the words on the original list. The patient knows that he has written something because he feels the writing movements through his body. But because there is no communication between the right hemisphere, which saw and wrote the words, and the left hemisphere, which controls speech, the subject cannot tell you what he wrote (Sperry, 1970, 1968; see also Gazzaniga, 1995; Hellige, 1994).

Hemispheric Specialization

The right hemisphere has a highly developed spatial and pattern sense. When tested in split-brain patients, it is superior to the left hemisphere in constructing geometric and perspective drawings. It can assemble colored blocks to match a complex design much more effectively than the left hemisphere. When split-brain patients are asked to use their right hand (controlled by the left brain) to assemble the blocks according to a picture design, they make numerous mistakes. Their left hand does much better. Sometimes they have trouble keeping their left hand from automatically correcting the mistakes being made by the right hand.

Studies with normal individuals tend to confirm the different specializations of the two hemispheres. For example, verbal information (such as words or nonsense syllables) can be identified faster and more accurately when flashed briefly to the left hemisphere (that is, in the right visual field) than when flashed to the right hemisphere. In contrast, the identification of faces, facial expressions of emotion, line slopes, or dot locations occurs more quickly when the information is flashed to the right hemisphere (Hellige, 1994). And electroencephalogram (EEG) studies indicate that electrical activity from the left hemisphere increases during a verbal task, whereas during a spatial task EEG activity increases in the right hemisphere (Kosslyn, 1988; Springer & Deutsch, 1989).

One should not infer from this discussion that the two hemispheres ordinarily work independently of each other. Just the opposite is true. The hemispheres differ in their specializations, but they integrate their activities at all times. As noted by Levy,

> These differences are seen in the contrasting contributions each hemisphere makes to all cognitive activities. When a person reads a story, the right hemisphere may play a special role in decoding visual information, maintaining an integrated story structure, appreciating humor and emotional content, deriving meaning from past associations and understanding metaphor. At the same time, the left hemisphere plays a special role in understanding syntax, translating written words into their phonetic representations and deriving meaning from complex relations among word concepts and syntax. But there is no activity in which only one hemisphere is involved or to which only one hemisphere makes a contribution. (1985, p. 44)

Language and the Brain

A great deal of our information about brain mechanisms for language comes from observations of patients who have suffered brain damage. The damage may be due

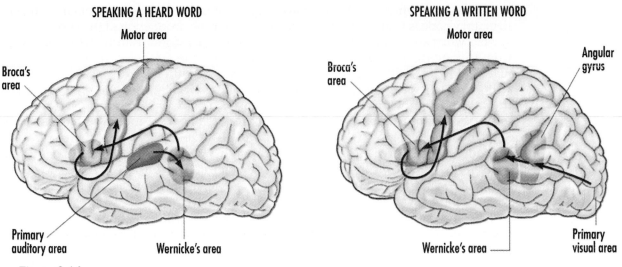

SPEAKING A HEARD WORD

Motor area

Broca's area

Primary auditory area

Wernicke's area

SPEAKING A WRITTEN WORD

Motor area

Angular gyrus

Broca's area

Wernicke's area

Primary visual area

Figure 2-14

The Wernicke-Geschwind Model The left panel illustrates the sequence of events when a spoken word is heard and the individual repeats the word in spoken form. Neural impulses from the ear are sent to the primary auditory area, but the word cannot be understood until the signal is next transmitted to Wernicke's area. In Wernicke's area, the word's acoustical code is retrieved and transmitted via a bundle of nerve fibers to Broca's area. In Broca's area, an articulatory code for the word is activated, which in turn directs the motor area. The motor area drives the lips, tongue, and larynx to produce the spoken word. In the right panel, a written word is presented and the individual is to speak the word. The visual input to the eye is first transmitted to the primary visual cortex and then relayed to the angular gyrus. The angular gyrus associates the visual form of the word with the related acoustical code in Wernicke's area. Once the acoustical code is retrieved and the meaning of the word is established, speaking the word is accomplished through the same sequence of events as before.

to tumors, penetrating head wounds, or the rupture of blood vessels. The term **aphasia** is used to describe *the language deficits of patients with brain damage.*

aphasia the language deficits of patients with brain damage

As already noted, Broca observed that damage to a specific area on the side of the left frontal lobe was linked to a speech disorder called *expressive aphasia.* Individuals with damage in Broca's area have difficulty enunciating words correctly, and they speak in a slow, labored way. Their speech often makes sense, but it includes only key nouns and verbs. Even nouns are generally expressed only in the singular, and adjectives, adverbs, articles, and conjunctions are likely to be omitted. However, these individuals have no difficulty understanding either spoken or written language.

In 1874 a German investigator, Carl Wernicke, reported that damage to another site in the cortex (also in the left hemisphere, but located behind Broca's area in the temporal lobe) was linked to a language disorder called *receptive aphasia.* People with damage in this location, known as *Wernicke's area,* are unable to comprehend words. Although they can hear the words, they do not recognize their meaning. When they speak, they can produce strings of words without difficulty and with proper articulation, but they make errors in word usage and their speech tends to be meaningless.

On the basis of an analysis of these defects, Wernicke developed a model for language production and understanding. Although the model is more than 100 years old, its general features still appear to be correct. An American neurologist, Norman Geschwind, built on these ideas to develop the theory known as the *Wernicke-Geschwind model* (Geschwind, 1979). According to this model, Broca's area is assumed to store articulatory codes that specify the sequence of muscle actions required to pronounce a word. When these codes are transferred to the motor area, they activate the muscles of the lips, tongue, and larynx in the proper sequence and produce a spoken word (see Figure 2-14). Wernicke's area, on the other hand, is where auditory codes and the meanings of words are stored. If a word is to be spoken, its auditory code must be activated in Wernicke's area and transmitted by a bundle of nerves to Broca's area, where it activates the corresponding articulatory code. In turn, the articulatory code is transmitted to the motor area for the production of the spoken word.

If a word spoken by someone else is to be understood, it must be transmitted from the auditory area to Wernicke's area, where the spoken form of the word is matched to its auditory code, which in turn activates the word's meaning. When a written word is presented, it is first registered in the visual area and then relayed to the *angular gyrus,* which associates the visual form of the word with its auditory code in Wernicke's area; once the word's auditory code has been found, so has its meaning. Thus, the meanings of words are stored in Wernicke's area along with their acoustical codes. Broca's area stores articulatory codes, and the angular gyrus matches the written form of a word to its auditory code; neither of these two areas, however, stores information about word meaning. The meaning of a word is retrieved only when its acoustical code is activated in Wernicke's area.

The model explains many of the language deficits shown by aphasics. Damage restricted to Broca's area disrupts speech production but has less effect on the comprehension of spoken or written language. Damage to Wernicke's area disrupts all aspects of language comprehension, but the individual can still articulate words properly (since Broca's area is intact), even though the output is meaningless. The model also predicts that individuals with damage in the angular gyrus will not be able to read but will have no problem in comprehending speech or in speaking. Finally, if damage is restricted to the auditory area, a person will be able to read and speak normally, but he or she will not be able to comprehend spoken speech.

There are some research findings that the Wernicke-Geschwind model does not adequately explain. For example, when the language areas of the brain are electrically stimulated in the course of a neurosurgical operation, both receptive and expressive functions may be disrupted at a single site. This suggests that some brain areas may share mechanisms for producing and understanding speech. We are still a long way from a comprehensive model of language function, but there can be no doubt that some aspects of language function are highly localized in the brain (Geschwind & Galaburda, 1985; Hellige, 1994).

Thinking Critically

1. Why is your brain symmetrical (meaning that the left and right sides look alike)? You have a left and a right motor cortex, a left and a right hippocampus, a left and a right cerebellum, and so on. In each case the left side is a mirror image of the right side (just as your left eye is a mirror image of your right eye, your left ear a mirror image of your right ear, etc.). Can you think of any reason why your brain is symmetrical in this way?

2. In "split-brain" patients, whose corpus callosum has been cut, the left and right sides of the brain seem to work independently after the operation. For example, a word shown to one side may be read and responded to without the other side knowing what the word was. Does such a person have two minds, each capable of knowing different things? Or does the patient still have only one mind?

What Is the Nature of the Autonomic Nervous System?

We noted earlier that the peripheral nervous system consists of two divisions. The somatic system controls movements and receives sensory information (touch, pain, etc.). The autonomic system controls the glands, heart, and other internal organs. The autonomic nervous system derives its name from the fact that many of the activities it controls—such as digestion and circulation—are autonomous, or self-regulating and continue even when a person is asleep or unconscious.

The autonomic nervous system has two divisions, the sympathetic and the parasympathetic, whose actions are often antagonistic. Figure 2-15 shows the contrasting effects of the two systems on various organs. For example, the parasympathetic

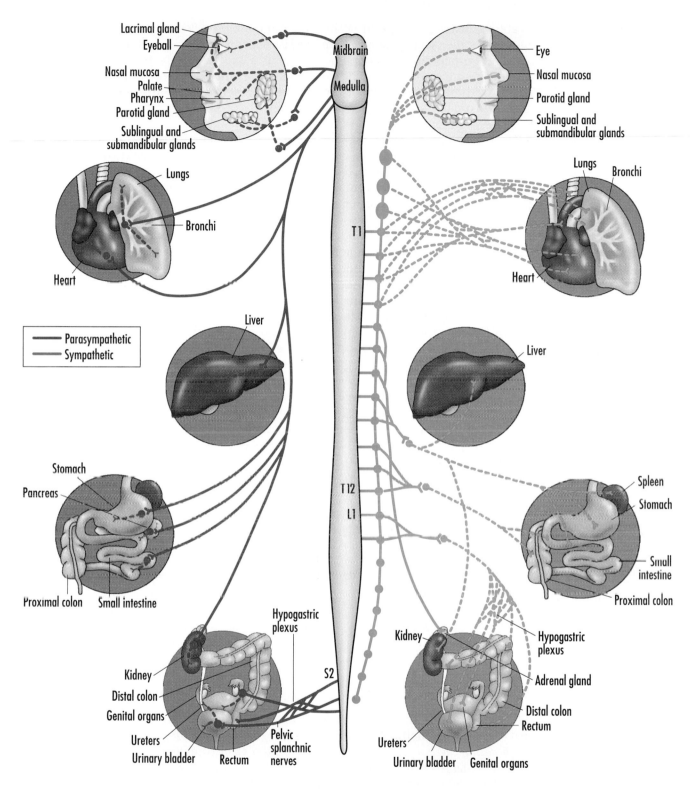

Figure 2-15

Motor Fibers of the Autonomic Nervous System   In this diagram the sympathetic division is indicated in blue and the parasympathetic is in red. Solid lines indicate preganglionic fibers and dashed lines indicate postganglionic fibers. Neurons of the sympathetic division originate in the spinal cord; they form synaptic junctions with ganglia lying just outside the cord. Neurons of the parasympathetic division exit from the medulla region of the brainstem and from the lower end of the spinal cord; they connect with ganglia near the organs stimulated. Most internal organs are innervated by both divisions.

system constricts the pupil of the eye, stimulates the flow of saliva, and slows the heart rate; the sympathetic system has the opposite effect in each case.

The sympathetic division tends to act as a unit, preparing the body for "fight or flight." During emotional excitement it simultaneously speeds up the heart, dilates the arteries of the skeletal muscles and heart, constricts the arteries of the skin and digestive organs, and causes perspiration. It also activates certain endocrine glands to secret hormones that further increase arousal.

Unlike the sympathetic system, the parasympathetic division tends to affect one organ at a time. Whereas the sympathetic system may be thought of as dominant during violent and excited activity, the parasympathetic system may be thought of as dominant during quiescence. It participates in digestion and, in general, maintains the functions that conserve and protect the body's resources. For example, a decreased heart rate and slowed breathing, which are maintained by the parasympathetic nervous system, require far less energy than a fast heartbeat and rapid breathing, which are by-products of activating the sympathetic system.

While the sympathetic and parasympathetic systems are usually antagonistic to each other, there are some exceptions to this principle. For example, the sympathetic system is dominant during fear and excitement; however, a not-uncommon parasympathetic symptom during extreme fear is involuntary discharge by the bladder or bowels. Another example is the complete sex act in the male, which requires erection (parasympathetic) followed by ejaculation (sympathetic). Thus, although the two systems are often antagonistic, they interact in complex ways.

─────────────

Thinking Critically

The autonomic nervous system controls our heart rate, breathing rate, blood pressure, perspiration, and other bodily activities without our conscious awareness. Indeed we often find that conscious control of these functions is either very difficult or impossible. Yet in many situations, the ability to control our heart rate or perspiration might be very helpful; we could conceal our fright of public speaking for example. Why have our autonomic systems developed to unconsciously control our internal functions?

What Do We Know About Genetic Influences on Behavior?

To understand the biological foundation of psychology, we need to know something about hereditary influences. The field of **behavior genetics** *combines the methods of genetics and psychology to study the inheritance of behavioral characteristics* (Plomin, 1994). We know that many physical characteristics—height, bone structure, hair and eye color, and so on—are inherited. Behavioral geneticists are interested in the degree to which psychological characteristics—mental ability, temperament, emotional stability, and so on—are transmitted from parent to offspring (Bouchard, 1994).

Chromosomes and Genes

The hereditary units that we receive from our parents and transmit to our offspring are carried by structures known as **chromosomes**—*structures found in the nucleus of each cell in the body.* Most body cells contain 46 chromosomes. At conception, the human being receives 23 chromosomes from the father's sperm and 23 chromosomes from the mother's ovum. These 46 chromosomes form 23 pairs, which are duplicated each time the cells divide (see Figure 2-16).

Each chromosome is composed of many individual hereditary units called genes. A **gene** is *a segment of a deoxyribonucleic acid (DNA) molecule,* which is the actual carrier of genetic information. The DNA molecule looks like a twisted ladder or a double-stranded helix (spiral), as shown in Figure 2-17.

Each gene gives coded instructions to the cell, directing it to perform a specific function (usually to manufacture a particular protein). Although all cells in the body carry the same genes, the specialized nature of each cell is due to the fact that only

behavior genetics a field of study that combines the methods of genetics and psychology to study the inheritance of behavior characteristics

chromosomes structures found in the nucleus of each cell in the body

gene a segment of a deoxyribonucleic acid (DNA) molecule

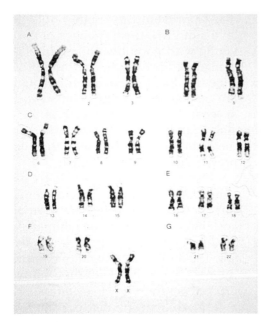

Figure 2-16

Chromosomes   This photo (greatly enlarged) shows the 46 chromosomes of a normal human female. A human male would have the same pairs 1 through 22, but pair 23 would be XY rather than XX.

5% to 10% of the genes are active in any given cell. In the process of developing from a fertilized egg, each cell switches on some genes and switches off all others. When "nerve genes" are active, for example, a cell develops as a neuron because the genes are directing the cell to make the products that allow it to perform neural functions (which would not be possible if genes that are irrelevant to a neuron, such as "muscle genes," were not switched off).

Genes, like chromosomes, exist in pairs. One gene of each pair comes from the sperm chromosomes, and one gene comes from the ovum chromosomes. Thus, a child receives only half of each parent's total genes. The total number of genes in each human chromosome is around 100,000. Because the number of genes is so high, it is extremely unlikely that two human beings would have the same heredity, even if they were siblings. The only exception is identical twins, who, because they developed from the same fertilized egg, have exactly the same genes.

Dominant and Recessive Genes   A gene pair can be composed of dominant or recessive genes. When one gene is dominant and the other recessive, the individual manifests the form of the trait specified by the dominant gene. When both genes are recessive, the recessive form of the trait is expressed. The genes that determine eye color, for example, act in this way; blue is recessive and brown is dominant. Thus a blue-eyed child may have two blue-eyed parents, or one blue-eyed parent and one brown-eyed parent (who carries a recessive gene for blue eyes), or two brown-eyed parents (each of whom carries a recessive gene for blue eyes). A brown-eyed child, in contrast, never has two blue-eyed parents.

Most human characteristics are not determined by the actions of a single gene pair, but there are some striking exceptions in which a single gene has enormous importance. Of special interest from a psychological viewpoint are diseases like phenylketonuria and Huntington's disease, both of which involve deterioration of the nervous system and related behavioral and cognitive problems. Geneticists have identified the genes responsible for both diseases.

Phenylketonuria (PKU) results from the action of a recessive gene that is inherited from each parent. The infant cannot digest an essential amino acid (phenylalanine), which then builds up in the body, poisoning the nervous system and causing irreversible brain damage. If left untreated, PKU children are severely retarded and usually die before the age of 30. However, if the disorder is discovered at birth and the infants are placed on a low-phenylalanine

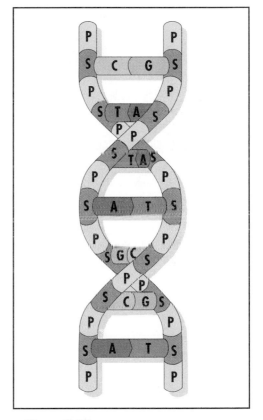

Figure 2-17

Structures of the DNA Molecule   Each strand of the molecule is made up of an alternating sequence of sugar (s) and phosphate (P); the rungs of the twisted ladder are made up of four bases (A, G, T, C). The double nature of the helix and the restriction on base pairings make possible the self-replication of the DNA. In the process of cell division, the two strands of the DNA molecule come apart with the base pairs. Each strand then forms a new complementary strand using excess bases available in the cell. By this process, two identical molecules of DNA come to exist where previously there was one.

The famous folk singer Woody Guthrie died of Huntington's disease at the age of 55.

diet to prevent the buildup of high levels of PKU, their chances of surviving with good health and intelligence are fairly high. Until the PKU gene was located, the disorder could not be diagnosed until an infant was at least 3 weeks old. Now it is possible to determine prenatally whether the fetus has the PKU gene so that the proper diet can begin at birth.

Huntington's disease (HD) is caused by a single dominant gene. The disease causes degeneration of certain areas in the brain, ultimately leading to death. Victims gradually lose the ability to talk and to control their movements, and they show marked deterioration in memory and mental ability. The disease usually strikes when a person is 30 to 40 years of age. Before then there are no symptoms or other evidence of the disease. Once HD strikes, victims will typically live for 10 to 15 years with progressive deterioration and the agonizing experience of knowing what is happening to them. Now that the Huntington gene has been isolated, geneticists can test individuals who are at risk for the disease and determine with virtual certainty whether or not they carry the gene. As yet there is no cure for HD, but the protein produced by the gene has been identified. This protein must be responsible for HD in some way and it may provide a key to treating the disease.

Sex-Linked Genes   A normal female has two similar-looking chromosomes in pair 23, called X chromosomes. A normal male has one X chromosome in pair 23 and one that looks slightly different, called a Y chromosome (refer back to Figure 2-16). Thus, the normal female chromosome pair 23 is represented by the symbol XX and the normal male pair by XY.

Women, who carry two X chromosomes, are protected from recessive traits carried on the X chromosome—because a recessive trait must be on both X chromosomes to be expressed—unless the recessive gene is on both their chromosomes. Men, who carry one X chromosome and one Y chromosome, express more recessive traits because a gene that occurs on one of these chromosomes will not be countered by a dominant gene on a similar chromosome. For example, color blindness is a recessive sex-linked characteristic. A man will be color-blind if he inherits a color-blind gene on the X chromosome that he receives from his mother. Females are less often color-blind, because a color-blind female has to have both a color-blind father and a mother who either is color-blind or carries a recessive gene for color blindness. A number of genetically determined disorders are linked to the 23rd chromosome pair; these are called *sex-linked disorders*.

Genetic Studies of Behavior

Some traits are determined by single genes, but most human characteristics are influenced by many genes; these are called *polygenic traits*. Polygenic traits such as intelligence, height, and emotionality do not fall into distinct categories but show continuous variation across the population. For example, most people are neither dull nor bright; intelligence is distributed over a broad range, with most individuals located near the middle. Sometimes a specific genetic defect can result in mental retardation, but in most instances a person's intellectual potential is determined by a large number of genes that interact with environmental conditions (Plomin, Owen, & McGruffin, 1994).

Selective Breeding   One method of studying the heritability of traits in animals is *selective breeding,* in which animals that are high or low in a certain trait are mated with each other. For example, in an early study of inheritance of learning ability in rats, females that did poorly in learning to run a maze were mated with males that did poorly; females that did well were mated with males that did well. The offspring of these matings were tested on the same maze. After a few rodent generations, "bright" and "dull" strains of rats were produced (see Figure 2-18).

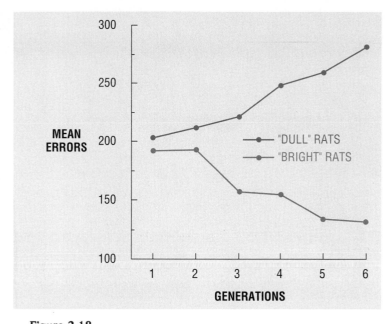

Figure 2-18

Inheritance of Maze Learning in Rats   Mean error scores of "bright" (green line) and "dull" (purple line) rats selectively bred for maze-running ability. (After Thompson, 1954)

Twin Studies   Since ethical considerations prevent psychologists from conducting breeding experiments with human beings, we must look instead at similarities in behavior among individuals who are related. Certain traits often run in families. But families are not only linked genetically, they also share the same environment. If musical talent runs in a family, we do not know whether inherited ability or parental emphasis on music is more important. Sons of alcoholic fathers are more likely than sons of nonalcoholic fathers to develop alcoholism. Do genetic tendencies or environmental conditions play the major role? In an effort to answer questions of this sort, psychologists have turned to studies of twins, especially twins who have been adopted and raised in different environments.

Identical twins develop from a single fertilized egg and therefore have exactly the same genes (they are called *monozygotic* twins because they come from a single *zygote,* or fertilized egg). Fraternal twins develop from different egg cells and are no more alike genetically that ordinary siblings; they are called *dizygotic* twins because they come from two zygotes. Fraternal twins are about twice as common as identical twins.

Studies comparing identical and fraternal twins help sort out the influence of environment and heredity. Identical twins are found to be more similar in intelligence than fraternal twins, even when they are separated at birth and reared in different homes (see Chapter 10). Identical twins are also more similar than fraternal twins in some personality characteristics and in susceptibility to the mental disorder of schizophrenia (see Chapter 12). Twin studies have proved to be a useful method of investigating genetic influences on human behavior.

A surprising finding from studies of adopted children suggests that genetic influences may actually become stronger as people age. Young children are not particularly similar either to their biological parents or to their adoptive parents in many psychological traits. As they grow older, one might expect them to become more like their adoptive parents in traits like general cognitive ability and verbal ability, and even less like their biological parents. But on the contrary, as adopted children approach

Identical twins are referred to as monozygotic because they develop from a single fertilized egg; fraternal or dizygotic twins develop from different egg cells and therefore are no more similar genetically than ordinary siblings.

age 16 they actually become more like their biological parents in these traits (Plomin, 1997), suggesting that genetic influences are operating.

It has been suggested that a number of human traits, such as personality factors, are influenced by specific genes, which are thought to influence particular neurotransmitter receptors (Zuckerman, 1995). In most studies of this sort, family members who have a particular trait are identified and compared to other members who lack the trait. Using techniques from molecular genetics, researchers attempt to find particular genes or chromosomes segments that are correlated with the psychological trait. For example, the tendency to score high on personality scales as "impulsive," "exploratory," and "quick-tempered" (forming a combination associated with "novelty seeking") has been reported to be linked to a gene that controls a type of receptor for dopamine (Benjamin, 1996).

Occasionally this type of gene/neurotransmitter analysis has been applied to very specific human behavioral traits. For example, as mentioned earlier, the sons of alcoholics are more likely to become alcoholics themselves than are people chosen at random. It has been reported that when they drink alcohol the sons of alcoholics also tend to release greater amounts of endorphin (the natural opiate neurotransmitter related to reward) than other people (Gianoulakis, 1996), suggesting the possibility of a biological factor that might predispose the individual toward alcoholism.

But these types of analyses can sometimes be misleading and must be treated with caution. For example, it was once claimed that a specific gene for a different dopamine receptor (the D2 receptor) occurred only in severe alcoholics and was a genetic basis for alcoholism. More recent studies of this gene, however, indicate that it also occurs in individuals who pursue many other types of pleasure and that it may be linked to drug abuse, obesity, compulsive gambling, and a wide range of "unrestrained behavior" (Blum, 1996). Our understanding of the role of this gene, and of its relationship to behavior, clearly has changed already in the few years since its discovery, and may change again as further evidence emerges. This highlights the need to treat reports of "the gene for behavior X" as intriguing, but to await further confirmation before concluding that the genetic basis for the behavior has been discovered. In several cases, what first seemed to be a clear genetic explanation has later been found to be spurious. In a rapidly developing area of research such as this, caution is needed to avoid leaping to a rash conclusion.

Environmental Influences on Genes Action   The inherited potential with which an individual enters the world is very much influenced by the environment that he or she encounters. Even individuals who have identical genes may still differ markedly in their psychological traits. For example, if one identical twin is schizophrenic, the chance that the other twin will exhibit some signs of mental disturbance is higher than usual. But in many cases the identical twin of a schizophrenic may show no signs of schizophrenia or other mental disorders and may lead a perfectly normal life. Whether or not the other twin develops the full-blown disorder will depend on a number of environmental factors. Thus, genes may predispose the individual to a particular condition, but environment also shapes the outcome.

————————————

It seems that every year the discovery of a new "gene for alcoholism"—or for addiction, schizophrenia, sexual orientation, impulsiveness, or some other complex psychological trait—is reported. But it often turns out after further studies that the gene is related to the trait in some people but not in everyone. And often the gene also turns out to be related to other behavioral traits besides the one to which it was originally linked. Can you think of any reasons why genes might affect psychological traits in this way? In other words, why isn't there a perfect one-to-one match between the presence of a gene and the strength of a particular psychological trait?

Thinking Critically

Summary

1. The basic unit of the nervous system is the *neuron,* a specialized type of cell. Projecting from the cell body of the neuron are a number of short branches called dendrites, which receive information, and a slender tube called the axon, which transmits information to other neurons. Stimulation of the dendrites and cell body creates a neural impulse, the *action potential,* which travels down the length of the axon. Sensory neurons transmit signals from sense organs to the brain; motor neurons transmit signals away from the brain.

2. The action potential travels along the neuron as an electrochemical impulse caused by a self-propagating mechanism called depolarization. Depolarization changes the permeability of the cell membrane to different types of ions (electrically charged atoms and molecules), allowing them to enter or leave the neuron.

3. An action potential causes the small swellings at the end of the axon, called terminal buttons, to release chemical substances called *neuro-*

transmitters. Neurotransmitters are responsible for transferring the signal from one neuron to an adjacent one. The neurotransmitters diffuse across a small gap between the juncture of the two neurons (called the synapse) and bind to receptors in the cell membrane of the receiving neuron. The occurrence of the action potential is an all-or-none event. There are many different kinds of neurotransmitters, and they help explain a range of psychological phenomena and many effects of psychoactive drugs.

4. The nervous system is divided into the *central nervous system* (the brain and spinal cord) and the *peripheral nervous system* (the *nerves* connecting the brain and spinal cord to other parts of the body). Subdivisions of the peripheral nervous system are the *somatic system* (which carries messages to and from the sense receptors, the muscles, and the surface of the body) and the *autonomic system* (which controls the internal organs and glands).

5. The human brain is composed of three concentric layers: the *central core,* the *limbic system,* and the *cerebrum.*
   a. The central core includes the medulla, cerebellum, hypothalamus, and thalamus. The medulla is responsible for respiration and postural reflexes; the cerebellum is concerned with motor coordination; the hypothalamus is important in emotion and in maintaining homeostasis; and the thalamus is a relay station for incoming sensory information.
   b. The limbic system controls instinctive activities such as feeding, attacking, fleeing from danger, and mating. Parts of the limbic system also play an important role in emotion and memory.
   c. The cerebrum is divided into two cerebral hemispheres. The convoluted surface of these hemispheres, the cerebral cortex, plays a critical role in higher mental processes such as thinking and decision making. Certain areas of the cerebral cortex serve as centers for specific sensory inputs or for the control of specific movements. The remainder of the cerebral cortex consists of association areas.
6. When the corpus callosum (the band of nerve fibers connecting the two cerebral hemispheres) is severed, significant differences in the functioning of the left and right hemispheres can be observed. The left hemisphere is most skilled in language and mathematical abilities. The right hemisphere can understand some language but cannot communicate through speech; it has a highly developed spatial and pattern sense.

7. The autonomic nervous system is made up of the sympathetic and the parasympathetic divisions. Because its fibers control the action of glands and internal organs, the autonomic system is particularly important in emotional reactions. The sympathetic division is active during excitement, and the parasympathetic division during quiescence.
8. An individual's hereditary potential, transmitted by *chromosomes* and *genes,* influences his or her psychological and physical traits. Genes are segments of DNA molecules, which store genetic information. Some genes are dominant, some recessive, and some sex-linked. Most human traits are polygenic— that is, determined by many genes acting together rather than by a single gene pair.
9. Selective breeding (mating animals that are high or low in a certain trait) is one method of studying the influence of heredity. Another method for sorting out the effects of environment and heredity in humans is twin studies, in which the characteristics of identical twins (who share the same heredity) are compared with those of fraternal twins (who are no more alike genetically than ordinary siblings) or others.
10. Genes may influence specific types of human behavior by controlling neurotransmitter receptors that have a special role in reward, emotionality, or other psychological traits. Behavior depends on the interaction between heredity and environment; the genes set the limits of the individual's potential, but what happens to that potential depends on the environment in which he or she grows up.

Suggested Readings

Introductions to physiological psychology are Kalat, *Biological Psychology* (6th ed., 1998); Rosenzweig, Leiman, & Breedlove, *Biological Psychology* (1996); and Pinel, *Biopsychology* (3rd ed., 1997).

For a discussion of the neural basis for memory and cognition, see Schacter, *Searching for Memory: the Brain, the Mind, and the Past* (1996); for a discussion of the neural basis of emotion, see LeDoux, *The Emotional Brain* (1996); for discussions of the neural bases of cognition, see Gazzaniga (Ed.), *The Cognitive Neurosciences* (1995); for a survey of research on the function of the two cerebral hemispheres, see Hellige, *Hemispheric Asymmetry: What's Right and What's Left* (1994); and for a discussion of human consciousness in terms of neural mechanisms, see Crick, *The Astonishing Hypothesis: The Scientific Search for the Soul* (1994).

A survey of genetic influences on behavior is provided by Steen, *DNA and Destiny: Nature and Nurture in Human Behavior* (1996); and Plomin, *Genetics and Experience: The Interplay Between Nature and Nurture* (1994).

For a review of psychoactive drugs and their effects on the body, brain, and behavior, see Feldman, Meyer, & Quenzer, *Principles of Neuropsychopharmacology* (1997); and Julien, *A Primer of Drug Action* (8th ed., 1998).

Enhance and Explore

To enhance your understanding of the psychological concepts found in this chapter, please consult the following aids:

Study Guide

Learning Objectives, p. 26
Define the Terms, p. 28
Test Your Knowledge, p. 33
Essay Questions, p. 38
Thinking Independently, p. 40

PowerPsych CD-ROM

WHAT ARE THE PROPERTIES OF NEURONS?

The Neuron
Action Potentials
Neurotransmission

WHAT IS THE NATURE OF THE CENTRAL CORE, LIMBIC SYSTEM, AND CEREBRUM?

Viewing the Brain: Planes of Section
Structure and Function
Cerebral Cortex

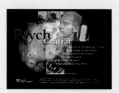

PsychCentral

For more information concerning the topics found in this chapter, access psychology links on the Word Wide Web made through the Harcourt Web page at:
http://www.harcourtcollege.com/psych/Fundamentals

www.harcourtcollege.com

http://www.harcourtcollege.com/psych/index.html

Psychological Development

Of all mammals, human beings require the longest period of maturation and learning before they are self-sufficient. In general, the more complex an organism's nervous system is, the longer the time required to reach maturity. A lemur (a primitive primate) can move about on its own shortly after birth and is soon able to fend for itself; an infant monkey is dependent on its mother for several months, a chimpanzee for several years. But even a chimpanzee—one of our closest relatives—becomes a functioning adult member of its species long before a human of the same age.

Developmental psychologists are concerned with how and why different aspects of human functioning develop and change across the life span. They focus on *physical development,* such as changes in height and weight and the acquisition of motor skills; *cognitive development,* such as changes in thought processes, memory, and language abilities; and *personality and social development,* such as changes in self-concept, gender identity, and interpersonal relationships. The development of particular psychological abilities and functions is treated in more detail in later chapters. In this chapter, we provide a general overview of psychological development across the life span and consider two central questions: (1) How do biological factors interact with events in the child's environment to determine the course of development (often called the *nature-nurture question*)? and (2) Is development best understood as a gradual, continuous process of change or as a series of abrupt, qualitatively distinct stages?

How Do Nature and Nurture Interact to Affect Development?

The question of whether heredity ("nature") or environment ("nurture") is more important in determining the course of human development has been debated for centuries. The 17th-century British philosopher John Locke rejected the prevailing notion that babies were miniature adults who arrived in the world fully equipped with abilities and knowledge and simply had to grow in order for these inherited characteristics to appear. On the contrary, Locke believed that the mind of a newborn infant is a *tabula rasa* (Latin for "blank slate"). What gets written on this slate is what

Both John Locke and Charles Darwin influenced the nature-nurture debate, but in different ways. Locke emphasized the role of the senses in the acquisition of knowledge, arguing that knowledge is provided only by experience. Darwin emphasized the biological basis of human development, leading to renewed interest in the role of heredity.

the baby experiences—what he or she sees, hears, tastes, smells, and feels. According to Locke, all knowledge comes to us through the senses. It is provided entirely by experience; there is no built-in knowledge.

Charles Darwin's theory of evolution (1859), which emphasizes the biological basis of human development, led many theorists to place renewed emphasis on heredity. With the rise of behaviorism in the 20th century, however, the environmentalist position once again gained dominance. Behaviorists such as John B. Watson and B. F. Skinner argued that human nature is completely malleable: Early training can turn a child into any kind of adult, regardless of his or her heredity. Watson stated the argument in its most extreme form:

> Give me a dozen healthy infants, well-formed, and my own specified world to bring them up in, and I'll guarantee to take any one at random and train him to be any type of specialist I might select—doctor, lawyer, artist, merchant-chief, and, yes, even beggar-man and thief, regardless of his talents, penchants, tendencies, abilities, vocations, and race of his ancestors (1930, p. 104).

Today most psychologists agree not only that both nature and nurture play important roles but that they interact continuously to guide development. For example, we will see in Chapter 10 that the development of many personality traits, such as sociability and emotional stability, appears to be influenced about equally by heredity and environment; similarly, we shall see in Chapter 12 that psychiatric illnesses can have both genetic and environmental determinants.

Even forms of development that seem to be determined by innate biological timetables can be affected by environmental events. At the moment of conception, a remarkable number of personal characteristics are already determined by the genetic structure of the fertilized ovum. Our genes program our growing cells so that we develop into a person rather than a fish or chimpanzee. They determine our sex, the color of our skin, eyes, and hair, and our overall body size, among other things. These genetically determined characteristics are expressed in development through the process of **maturation**—*innately determined sequences of growth and change that are relatively independent of environmental events.* Thus, the human fetus develops according to a fairly fixed time schedule, and fetal behavior, such as turning and kicking, also follows an orderly sequence that depends on the stage of growth. However, if the uterine environment is seriously abnormal in some way, maturational processes can be disrupted. For example, if the mother contracts rubella during the first 3 months of pregnancy (when the fetus's basic organ systems are developing according to the genetically programmed schedule), the infant may be born deaf, blind, or brain-damaged, depending on which organ system was in a critical stage of development at the time of infection. Maternal malnutrition, smoking, and consumption of alcohol and drugs are other environmental factors that can affect the maturation of the fetus.

Motor development after birth also illustrates the interaction between genetically programmed maturation and environmental influence. Virtually all children go through the same sequence of motor behaviors in the same order: rolling over, sitting without support, standing while holding onto furniture, crawling, and then walking. But they go through the sequence at the different rates, and developmental psychologists have long wondered whether learning and experience play important roles in such differences.

Although early studies suggested that the answer is no, more recent studies indicate that practice or extra stimulation can accelerate the appearance of motor behaviors to some extent. For example, newborn infants have a stepping reflex; if they are held in an upright position with their feet touching a solid surface, their legs will make stepping movements that are similar to walking. A group of infants who were given stepping practice for a few minutes several times a day during the first 2 months of life began walking 5 to 7 weeks earlier than babies who did not receive such practice (Zelazo, Zelazo, & Kolb, 1972).

maturation innately determined sequences of growth and change that are relatively independent of environmental events

Virtually all children go through the same sequence of motor behaviors in the same order, but they go through the sequence at different rates.

The development of speech provides another example of the interaction between genetically determined characteristics and experience. In the course of normal development, all human infants learn to speak, but not until they have attained a certain level of neurological development; with rare exception, infants less than a year old cannot speak in sentences. But children reared in an environment in which people talk to them and reward them for making speech-like sounds speak earlier than children who do not receive such attention. For example, children reared in middle-class American homes begin to speak at about 1 year of age. Children reared in San Marcos, a remote village in Guatemala, have little verbal interaction with adults and do not utter their first words until they are over 2 years old (Kagan, 1979). Note that it is the *rate* that is affected by the environment, not the ultimate skill level.

Are There Stages of Development?

In explaining the sequence of development, several psychologists have proposed that there are discrete, qualitatively distinct steps or stages of development. The concept of stages implies that (1) behaviors at a given stage are organized around a dominant theme or coherent set of characteristics; (2) behaviors at one stage are qualitatively different from behaviors that appear at earlier or later stages; and (3) all children go through the same stages in the same order. Environmental factors may speed up or slow down development, but the order of stages does not vary; a child cannot enter a later stage without going through an earlier one first. As we will see later, not all psychologists agree that development proceeds according to a fixed sequence of qualitatively distinct stages.

critical or sensitive periods stages in development during which the organism is optimally ready to acquire certain abilities

Closely related to the concept of stages is the idea that there may be **critical** or **sensitive periods** in human development—*stages in development during which the organism is optimally ready to acquire certain abilities*. Critical periods have been identified for some aspects of the physical development of the human fetus. For example, the period 6 to 7 weeks after conception is critical for normal development of the sex organs. Whether the primitive sex organ develops into a male or female sexual structure depends on the presence of male hormones, regardless of the XX or XY arrangement of chromosomes. The absence of male hormones means that female sexual organs will develop in either case. If male hormones are injected later in development, they cannot reverse the changes that have already taken place.

During postnatal development, there is a critical period for the development of vision. If children who are born with cataracts have them removed before the age of 7, their vision will develop fairly normally. But if a child goes through the first 7 years without adequate vision, extensive permanent disability will result (Kuman, Fedrov, & Novikova, 1983).

Are there critical or sensitive periods in the *psychological* development of the child? It is known that if certain behaviors are not well established at particular periods during the development, they may not develop to their full potential. For example, the first year of life appears to be such a period for the formation of close interpersonal attachments. (Tizard & Rees, 1975). The preschool years may be especially significant for intellectual development and language acquisition (Cardon et al., 1992; Curtiss, 1977, 1989). Children who have not had enough exposure to language before age 6 or 7 may fail to acquire it altogether (Goldin-Meadow, 1982). The experiences of the child during such critical or sensitive periods may shape his or her future course of development in a manner that will be difficult to change later.

What Are the Capacities of the Newborn?

At the end of the 19th century, psychologist William James suggested that the newborn child experiences the world as a "buzzing, blooming confusion," an idea that was still prevalent as late as the 1960s. We now know that newborn infants enter the world with all of their sensory systems functioning and are well prepared to learn about their new environment.

Because babies cannot explain what they are doing or tell us what they are thinking, developmental psychologists have had to design some ingenious procedures to study the capacities of young infants. The basic method is to change the baby's environment in some way and observe the responses. For example, an investigator might present a tone or a flashing light and see if there is a change in heart rate or if the baby turns its head or sucks more vigorously on a nipple. In some instances, the researcher will present two stimuli at the same time to determine whether infants look longer at one than the other. If they do, it indicates that they can tell the stimuli apart and may indicate that they prefer one over the other. In this section we describe some of the findings of research on infant capacities, beginning with studies of infants' vision.

Vision

As we will see in Chapter 4, newborns have poor visual acuity, their ability to change focus is limited, and they are very nearsighted. It is not until they are 2 years of age that they see as well as an adult (Courage & Adams, 1990). But, despite the immaturity of their visual system, newborns spend a lot of time actively looking about. They scan the world in an organized way and pause when their eyes encounter an object or some change in the visual field. They are particularly attracted to areas of high contrast, such as the edges of an object. Instead of scanning the entire object, as an adult would, they keep looking at areas that have the most edges. They also prefer complex patterns over plain ones and patterns with curved lines over patterns with straight lines.

The possibility that there is an inborn, unlearned preference for faces initially aroused great interest, but later research showed that infants are not attracted to faces per se but to stimulus characteristics such as curved lines, high contrast, interesting

Although infants love to explore the faces of those who care for them, research has shown that they are attracted not to faces per se but to such characteristics as curved lines, movement, and complexity.

edges, movement, and complexity—all of which faces possess (Aslin, 1987; Banks & Salapatek, 1983). Newborns look mostly at the outside contour of a face, but by 2 months they focus on the inside of the face—the eyes, nose, and mouth (Haith, Bergman, & Moore, 1977). At this point parents may notice with delight that the baby has begun to make eye contact.

Hearing

Newborn infants will startle at the sound of a loud noise. They will also turn their heads toward the source of a sound. Interestingly, the head-turning response disappears at about 6 weeks and does not reemerge until 3 or 4 months, at which time the infants will also search with their eyes for the source of the sound. The temporary disappearance of the head-turning response probably represents a maturational transition from a reflexive response controlled by subcortical areas of the brain to a voluntary attempt to locate the source of the sound. By 4 months, infants will reach toward the source of a sound in the dark; by 6 months they show a marked increase in their responsiveness to sounds that are accompanied by interesting sights and are able to pinpoint the location of sound more precisely, an ability that continues to improve into their second year (Ashmead et al., 1991; Field, 1987; Hillier, Hewitt, & Morrongiello, 1992).

Newborn infants can also detect the difference between very similar sounds, such as two tones that are only one note apart on the musical scale (Bridger, 1961), and they can distinguish between the human voice and other kinds of sounds. We will see in Chapter 8 that they can also distinguish a number of critical characteristics of human speech. For example, 1-month-old infants can tell the difference between similar sounds such as "pa" and "ba." Interestingly, infants can distinguish between some speech sounds better than adults can. These are sounds that adults "hear" as identical because there is no distinction between them in their native language (Aslin, Pisoni, & Jusczyk, 1983). For example, "ra" and "la" are separate sounds in English but not in Japanese. Japanese infants can distinguish between them, but Japanese adults cannot.

By 6 months of age the child will have picked up enough information about the language that it too will have begun to "screen out" sounds it does not use (Kuhl et al., 1992). Thus, human infants appear to be born with perceptual mechanisms already tuned to the properties of human speech that will help them in learning language (Eimas, 1975).

Taste and Smell

Infants can discriminate among different tastes shortly after birth. They prefer sweet-tasting liquids over those that are salty, bitter, sour, or bland. The characteristic response of the newborn to a sweet liquid is a relaxed expression resembling a slight smile, sometimes accompanied by lip-licking. A sour solution produces pursed lips and a wrinkled nose. In response to a bitter solution, the baby will open its mouth with the corners turned down and stick out its tongue in what appears to be an expression of disgust.

Newborns can also discriminate among odors. They will turn their heads toward a sweet smell, and their heart rate and respiration will slow down; these are indicators of attention. Noxious odors, such as those of ammonia or rotten eggs, cause them to turn their heads away; heart rate and respiration accelerate, indicating distress. Infants are even able to discriminate subtle differences in smells. After nursing for only a few days, an infant will consistently turn its head toward a pad saturated with its mother's milk in preference to one saturated with another mother's milk (Russell, 1976). Only breast-fed babies show this ability to recognize the mother's odor (Cernoch & Porter, 1985). When bottle-fed babies are given a choice between the smell of their familiar formula and the smell of a lactating breast, they will choose the latter (Porter et al., 1992). Thus, there seems to be an innate preference for the odor of breast milk. In general, the ability to distinguish among smells has a clear adaptive value: It helps infants avoid noxious substances, thereby increasing their likelihood of survival.

Learning and Memory

It was once thought that infants could neither learn nor remember. This is not the case; evidence for early learning and remembering comes from several studies. In one, infants only a few hours old learned to turn their heads right or left, depending on whether they heard a buzzer or a tone. In order to taste a sweet liquid, the baby had to turn to the right when a tone sounded and to turn to the left when a buzzer sounded. After only a few trials, the babies were performing without error—turning to the right when the tone sounded and to the left when the buzzer sounded. The experimenter then reversed the situation so that the infant had to turn the opposite way when either the buzzer or the tone sounded. The babies mastered this new task quickly (Siqueland & Lipsitt, 1966).

By the time they are 3 months old, infants have good memories. When a mobile over an infant's crib was attached to one of the baby's limbs by a ribbon, 3-month-old infants quickly discovered which arm or leg would move the mobile. When the infants were placed in the same situation 8 days later, they remembered which arm or leg to move (Hayne, Rovee-Collier, & Borza, 1991; Rovee-Collier & Hayne, 1987) (see Figure 3-1).

More startling is evidence that infants have already learned and remembered sensations they experienced before birth, while still in the uterus. We noted earlier that newborn infants can distinguish the sound of the human voice from other sounds. They also prefer the human voice over other sounds. A few days after birth infants will learn to suck on an artificial nipple in order to turn on recorded speech or vocal music, sucking more vigorously to hear speech sounds than to hear nonspeech sounds or instrumental music (Butterfield & Siperstein, 1972). They also prefer heartbeat sounds and female voices over male voices, and they prefer their mother's voice to those of other women. But they do not prefer their father's voice to those of other men (Brazelton, 1978; DeCasper & Fifer, 1980; DeCasper & Prescott, 1984) (see Figure 3-2).

These preferences appear to stem from the infant's prenatal experience with sounds. For example, the mother's voice can also be heard in the uterus, which would appear to explain why a newborn infant prefers her voice over others. Perhaps most surprising is evidence that the unborn infant may actually be learning to discriminate among some of the sounds of individual words. In an extraordinary experiment, pregnant women recited speech passages from children's stories each

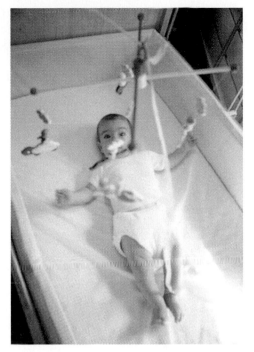

Figure 3-1

Early Learning   If a mobile is attached so that the infant's movements activate the mobile, the infant soon discovers this relationship and seems to delight in activating the mobile with the appropriate kick. Two-month-old babies can learn to do this, but soon forget. Three-month-old babies can remember the correct action for several days.

Figure 3-2

Preference for Sounds   A newborn can indicate a preference for certain sounds—such as the mother's voice—by sucking more vigorously on a nipple when it causes the preferred sounds to be played through the earphones.

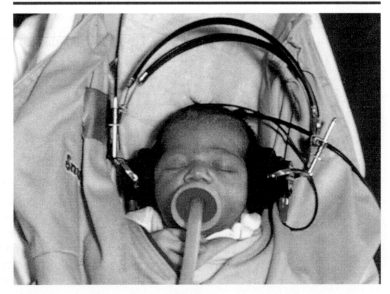

day during the last 6 weeks of pregnancy. For example, some women recited the first 28 paragraphs of Dr. Seuss's story *The Cat in the Hat*. Others recited the last 28 paragraphs of the same story, but with the main nouns changed so that it was now about "the dog in the fog" instead of the "cat in the hat." By the time the infants were born, they had heard one of the selected stories for a total of about 3½ hours.

Then, 2 or 3 days after the infants were born, they were permitted to suck on a special pacifier wired to record sucking rates (like the apparatus shown in Figure 3-2). Sucking on the pacifier turned on a tape recording of either their mother's voice or an unfamiliar woman's voice reciting either the story the infants had heard before birth or the story they had not heard previously. As in previous experiments, the infants showed by their sucking rates that they preferred their mother's voice to the stranger's. The startling finding, however, was that they also preferred the familiar story over the unfamiliar story (DeCasper & Spence, 1986).

In sum, the research we have described challenges the view of the newborn as experiencing the world as "buzzing, blooming confusion" as well as the view that the child enters the world as a "blank slate." Clearly, the infant enters the world well prepared to perceive and learn.

How Does Cognitive Development Proceed?

Although most parents are aware of the intellectual changes that accompany their children's physical growth, they would have difficulty describing the nature of these changes. The ways in which contemporary psychologists describe these changes have been most profoundly influenced by the Swiss psychologist Jean Piaget (1896–1980), who is widely acknowledged to be one of the 20th century's most influential thinkers. Prior to Piaget, psychological thinking about children's cognitive development was dominated by the biological-maturation perspective, which gave almost exclusive weight to the "nature" component of development, and by the environmental-learning perspective, which gave almost exclusive weight to the "nurture" component. In contrast, Piaget focused on the interaction between the child's naturally maturing abilities and his or her interactions with the environment. In this section we outline Piaget's stage theory of development and then turn to some more recent approaches. We also discuss the work of Lev Vygotsky, a Russian psychologist whose ideas about cognitive development, originally published in the 1930s, have attracted renewed interest in recent years.

Piaget's Stage Theory

Partly as a result of his observations of his own children, Piaget became interested in the relationship between the child's naturally maturing abilities and his or her interactions with the environment. He saw the child as an active participant in this process, rather than as a passive recipient of biological development or external stimuli. He viewed the children as "inquiring scientists" who experiment with objects and events in their environment to see what will happen ("What does it feel like to suck on the teddy-bear's ear?" "What happens if I push my dish off the edge of the table?"). The results of these "experiments" are used to construct **schemas**—*theories about how the physical and social worlds operate*. Upon encountering a novel object or event, the child attempts to *assimilate* it—that is, to understand it in terms of a preexisting schema. If the new experience does not fit the existing schema, the child—like any good scientist—modifies the schema and thereby extends his or her theory of the world. Piaget called this process of revising the schema *accommodation* (Piaget & Inhelder, 1969).

schemas theories about how the physical and social worlds operate

Piaget's first job as a postgraduate student in psychology was as an intelligence tester for Alfred Binet, inventor of the IQ test (see Chapter 10). In the course of this work, he began wondering why children made the kinds of errors they did. What distinguished their reasoning from that of adults? He observed his own children closely as they played, presenting them with simple scientific and moral problems and asking them to explain how they arrived at their answers. Piaget's observations convinced him that children's ability to think and reason progresses through a series of qualitatively distinct stages. He divided cognitive development into four major stages and a number of substages. The major stages are the *sensorimotor* stage, the *preoperational* stage, the stage of *concrete operations,* and the stage of *formal operations* (see Table 3-1).

The Sensorimotor Stage   Piaget designated the first 2 years of life as the **sensorimotor stage,** *a period in which infants are busy discovering the relationships between their actions and the consequences of those actions.* They discover, for example, how far they have to reach to grasp an object and what happens when they push their food dish over the edge of the table. In this way, they begin to develop a concept of themselves as separate from the external world.

Children often are as eager to play with empty boxes as with the toys they contained. Piaget believed that children act as "inquiring scientists," experimenting with objects in their environment to see what will happen.

An important discovery during this stage is the concept of **object permanence,** *the awareness that an object continues to exist even when it is not present to the senses.* If a cloth is placed over a toy that an 8-month-old is reaching for, the infant immediately stops reaching and appears to lose interest in the toy. The baby seems neither surprised nor upset, makes no attempt to search for the toy, and acts as if the toy has ceased to exist (see Figure 3-3). In contrast, a 10-month-old will actively search for an object that has been hidden under a

sensorimotor stage
a period in which infants are busy discovering the relationships between their actions and the consequences of those actions

object permanence
the awareness that an object continues to exist even when it is not present to the senses

Table 3-1

Piaget's Stages of Cognitive Development   The ages given are averages. They may vary considerably depending on intelligence, cultural background, and socioeconomic factors, but the order of the progression is assumed to be the same for all children. Piaget has described more detailed phases within each stage; only a general characterization of each stage is given here.

Stage	Characterization
1. Sensorimotor (birth–2 years)	Differentiates self from objects
	Recognizes self as agent of action and begins to act intentionally; for example, pulls a string to set a mobile in motion or shakes a rattle to make a noise
	Develops object permanence, the awareness that an object continues to exist even when it is not present
2. Preoperational (2–7 years)	Learns to use language and to represent objects by images and words
	Thinking is still egocentric: has difficulty taking the viewpoint of others
	Classifies objects by a single feature; for example, groups together all the red blocks regardless of shape or all the square blocks regardless of color
3. Concrete operational (7–11 years)	Can think logically about objects and events
	Achieves conservation of number (age 6), mass (age 7), and weight (age 9)
	Classifies objects according to several features and can order them in series along a single dimension, such as size
4. Formal operational (11 years and up)	Can think logically about abstract propositions and test hypotheses systematically
	Becomes concerned with the hypothetical, the future, and ideological problems

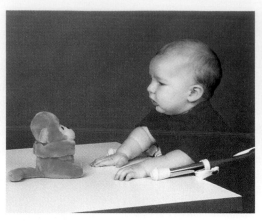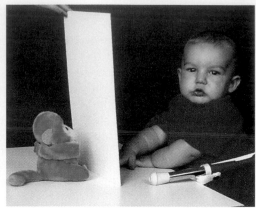

Figure 3-3

Object Permanence   When the toy is hidden by a screen, the infant acts as if the toy no longer exists. From this observation Piaget concluded that the infant had not yet acquired the concept of object permanence.

cloth or behind a screen. The older baby seems to realize that the object exists even though it is out of sight; thus, the infant has attained the concept of object permanence. This implies that the baby possesses a *mental representation* of the missing object. But even at this age, search is limited. If the infant has had repeated success in retrieving a toy hidden in one place, he or she will continue to look for it in that spot even after watching an adult conceal it in a new location. Not until about 1 year of age will a child consistently look for an object where it was last seen to disappear, regardless of what happened on previous trials.

The Preoperational Stage   By about 1½ to 2 years of age, children have begun to use symbols. Words can represent things or groups of things, and one object can represent another. Thus, a 3-year-old may treat a stick as if it were a horse and ride it around the room; a block of wood can become a car; one doll can become a father and another a baby. But although 3- and 4-year-olds can think in symbolic terms, their words and images are not yet organized in a logical manner. During this **preoperational stage** of cognitive development, *the child does not yet comprehend certain rules or operations*. An **operation** is *a mental routine for separating, combining, and otherwise transforming information mentally in a logical manner*. For example, if water is poured from a tall narrow glass into a short wide one, adults know that the amount of water has not changed because they can reverse the transformation in their minds; they can imagine pouring the water from the short glass back into the tall glass, thereby arriving back at the original state. In the preoperational stage of cognitive development, a child's understanding of reversibility and other mental operations is absent or weak. As a result, according to Piaget, preoperational children have not yet attained **conservation**—*the understanding that the amount of a substance remains the same even when its form is changed.* Thus, they fail to understand that the amount of water is conserved—that is, remains the same—when it is poured from the tall glass into the short one.

The lack of conservation in preoperational children is also illustrated by a procedure in which a child is given some clay to make into a ball that is equal to another ball of the same material. After doing this, the child declares them to be "the same." Then, leaving one ball for reference, the experimenter rolls the other into a long sausage shape while the child watches. The child can plainly see that no clay has been added or subtracted. In this situation, 4-year-olds will say that the two objects no longer contain the same amount of clay: "The longer one contains more" (see Figure 3-4). Not until age 7 do most children say that the amount of clay in the longer object is equal to the amount in the ball.

preoperational stage a period when the child does not yet comprehend certain rules or operations

operation a mental routine for separating, combining, and otherwise transforming information mentally in a logical manner

conservation the understanding that the amount of a substance remains the same even when its form is changed

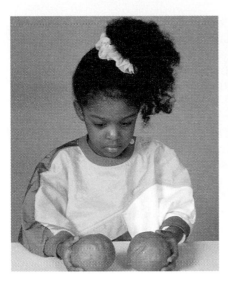

Figure 3-4

The Concept of Conservation   A 4-year-old acknowledges that the two balls of clay are the same size. But when one ball is rolled into a long, thin shape, she says that it contains more clay. Not until she is several years older will she state that the two different shapes contain the same amount of clay.

Piaget believed that preoperational thinking is dominated by visual impressions. A change in the visual appearance of the clay influences the preoperational child more than less obvious but more essential qualities, such as mass or weight. This reliance on visual impressions is illustrated by an experiment on the conservation of number. If two rows of checkers are matched one-for-one against each other, young children will say, correctly, that the rows have the same number of checkers (see Figure 3-5). If the checkers in one row are brought closer together to form a cluster,

Figure 3-5

Conservation of Number   When the two rows of seven checkers are evenly spaced, most children report that they contain the same amount. When one row is then clustered into a small space, children under age 6 or 7 will say that the original row contains more.

5-year-olds say there are now more checkers in the straight row—even though no checkers have been removed. The visual impression of a long row of checkers overrides the numerical equality that was obvious when the checkers appeared in matching rows. In contrast, 7-year-olds assume that if the number of objects was equal before, it must remain equal. At this age, numerical equality has become more significant than visual impression.

Another key characteristic of preoperational children, according to Piaget, is *egocentrism*. Preoperational children are unaware of perspectives other than their own—they believe that everyone else perceives the environment the same way they do (Piaget, 1950). To demonstrate this, Piaget created the "three-mountain problem." A child is allowed to walk around a table on which are arranged three mountains of different heights. Then the child stands on one side of the table while a doll is placed on the table at various locations (and therefore has a view of the three mountains different from that of the child). The child is asked to choose a photograph that shows what the doll is seeing. Before the age of 6 or 7, most children choose the photograph that illustrates their own perspective on the three mountains (Piaget & Inhelder, 1948/1956).

Piaget believed that egocentrism explains the rigidity of preoperational thought. Because young children cannot appreciate points of view other than their own, they cannot revise their schemas to take into account changes in the environment—hence their inability to reverse operations or conserve quantity.

Operational Stages   Between the ages of 7 and 12, children master the various conservation concepts and begin to perform other logical manipulations. They can place objects on the basis of a dimension, such as height or weight. They can also form a mental representation of a series of actions. Five-year-olds can find their way to a friend's house but cannot direct you there or trace the route with paper and pencil. They can find their own way because they know they have to turn at certain places, but they have no overall picture of the route. In contrast, 8-year-olds can readily draw a map of the route. Piaget calls this period the **concrete operational stage:** *Although children are using abstract terms, they are doing so only in relation to concrete objects*—that is, objects to which they have direct sensory access.

At about the age of 11 or 12, children arrive at adult modes of thinking. This is the **formal operational stage,** in which *the person is able to reason in purely symbolic terms.* In one test for formal operational thinking, the child tries to discover what determines the amount of time that a pendulum takes to swing back and forth once (its period of oscillation). The child is presented with a length of string suspended from a hook and several weights that can be attached to the lower end. He or she can vary the length of the string, change the attached weight, and alter the height from which the bob is released. In contrast to children who are still in the concrete operational stage—who will experiment by changing some of the variables, but not in a systematic way—adolescents of even average ability will set up a series of hypotheses and proceed to test them systematically. They reason that if a particular variable (weight) affects the period of oscillation, the effect will appear only if they change one variable and hold all others constant. If this variable seems to have no effect on the period of oscillation, they rule it out and try another. Considering all the possibilities—working out the consequences for each hypothesis and confirming or denying these consequences—is the essence of what Piaget called formal operational thought.

An Evaluation of Piaget's Theory

Piaget's theory is a major intellectual achievement; it has revolutionized the way we think about children's cognitive development. However, newer and more sophisticated methods of testing the intellectual functioning of infants and preschool children reveal that Piaget underestimated their abilities. Many of the tasks designed to test stage theories actually require several underlying information-processing skills

concrete operational stage   a period when, although children are using abstract terms, they are doing so only in relation to concrete objects

formal operational stage   a period in which a person has the ability to reason in purely symbolic terms

if the child is to succeed at them, such as attention, memory, and specific factual knowledge. A child may actually have the ability being tested, but be unable to perform the task because he or she lacks one of the other required skills.

These points are sharply illustrated by studies of object permanence. As we saw earlier, when infants younger than 8 months are shown a toy that is then hidden or covered while they watch, they act as if it no longer exists; they do not attempt to search for it. Note, however, that successful performance on this test requires the child not only to understand that the object still exists, but also to remember where the object was hidden and to show through some physical action that he or she is searching for it. Because Piaget believed that early cognitive development depends on sensorimotor activities, he did not consider the possibility that the infant might know the object still exists but be unable to show this knowledge through searching behavior.

In a study designed to test this possibility, children were not required to actively search for the hidden object. As shown in the top section of Figure 3-6, the apparatus consisted of a screen hinged at one edge to the top of a table. At first, the screen lay flat on the table. As the infant watched, the screen was slowly rotated away from the infant through a complete 180-degree arc until it was again lying flat on the table. The screen was then rotated in the opposite direction, toward the infant.

When the infants were first shown the rotating screen, they looked at it for almost a full minute; but after repeated trials, they lost interest and turned their attention elsewhere. At that point, a brightly painted box appeared on the table beyond the hinge, where it would be hidden as the screen moved into its upright position. (The infant was actually seeing a reflected image of a box, not the actual box.) As shown in Figure 3-6, the infants were then shown either a possible event or an impossible event. One group of infants saw the screen rotate from its starting position until it reached the point where it should bump against the box; at that point, the screen stopped and then moved back to its starting position. The other group saw the screen rotate to the upright position but then continue to rotate all the way to the other side of the 180-degree arc just as though there were no box in the way. The investigators reasoned that if the infants thought the box still existed even when it was hidden by the screen, they would be surprised when it seemed to pass through the box—an impossible event—and, hence, look at the screen longer than they would when the screen seemed to bump into the box before returning to its starting point. This is exactly what happened. Even

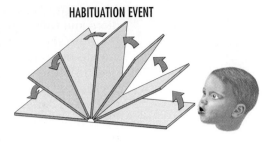

HABITUATION EVENT

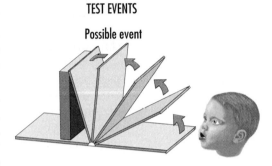

TEST EVENTS

Possible event

Impossible event

Figure 3-6

Testing Object Permanence   Infants are shown a rotating screen until they no longer attend to it. A box is placed where it can be hidden by the screen. The infants then see either a possible event (the screen rotates until it would hit the box and return to its starting position) or an impossible event (the screen appears to pass right through the box). Infants attend more to the impossible event, indicating that they realize that the hidden box still exists. (Adapted from Baillargeon)

though the impossible event was perceptually identical to an event they had seen repeatedly and lost interest in, they found it more interesting than a physically possible event they had never seen before—the screen stopping halfway through the arc and then reversing direction (Baillargeon, Spelke, & Wasserman, 1985).

It should be noted that the infants in this experiment were only 4½ months old; they thus displayed object permanence 4 to 5 months earlier than Piaget's theory predicts. Replications of this study have found that some infants as young as 3½ months display object permanence (Baillargeon, 1987; Baillargeon & DeVos, 1991).

More recent experiments using Piaget's conservation tasks have also yielded evidence that children's mental capacities develop earlier than he thought. In one study of number conservation, two sets of toys were lined up in one-to-one correspondence (as in Figure 3-5 described earlier). The experimenter then said, "These are your soldiers and these are my soldiers. What's more, my soldiers, your soldiers, or are they both the same?" After the child answered this question correctly, the experimenter spread out one of the rows of toys and repeated the question. As Piaget and others had previously reported, 5-year-old children failed to conserve, stating that the spread-out row contained more soldiers. But then the investigator introduced a second set of conditions. Instead of describing the toys as individual soldiers, she said, "This is my army and this is your army. What's more, my army, your army, or are they both the same?" With this simple change of wording, most of the children were able to conserve, judging the two "armies" to be the same size, even when one of them was spread out. Thus, when children are prompted to interpret the display as an aggregate or collection rather than as a set of individual items, their judgments of equality are less likely to be influenced by irrelevant perceptual transformations (Markman, 1979).

Other research has identified a variety of factors that can influence the development of concrete operational thought. For example, specific cultural practices influence children's mastery of Piagetian tasks (Rogoff, 1990). In addition, the experience of going to school seems to promote mastery of those tasks (Artman & Cahan, 1993). This and other evidence suggests that concrete operational reasoning may not be a universal stage of development that emerges during middle childhood but, instead, a product of the cultural setting, schooling, and the specific wording of questions and instructions (Gellatly, 1987; Light & Perrett-Clermont, 1989; Robert, 1989).

Alternatives to Piaget's Theory

Developmental psychologists generally agree that the kinds of findings we have just reviewed show that Piaget underestimated children's abilities, and his theory has been challenged on many grounds. However, there is no consensus on which is the best alternative to pursue. Some psychologists favor information-processing approaches, while others have pursued knowledge-acquisition and sociocultural approaches. We will now look briefly at these alternatives to Piaget's theory.

Information-Processing Approaches   We have already noted that many of the experiments challenging Piaget's views were inspired by investigators who view cognitive development as the acquisition of several separate information-processing skills. Accordingly, they believe that the standard Piagetian tasks fail to separate these several skills from the critical skill that the task is allegedly designed to assess. But they disagree among themselves about how exactly their views challenge Piaget's theory. For example, they disagree on the important question of whether development is best understood as a series of qualitatively distinct stages or as a continuous process of change. Some believe that the entire notion of stages should be abandoned (for example, Klahr, 1982). In their view, the separate skills develop smoothly and continuously rather than in a series of discrete stages. But other theorists believe that gradual changes in information-processing skills do, in fact, lead to discontinuous, stagelike changes in children's thinking (for example, Case, 1985). These theorists are sometimes referred to as *neo-Piagetians*. Some neo-Piagetians agree that there are genuine stages but believe that they occur only within more narrow domains of knowledge. For example, a child's language skills, mathematical understanding, social reasoning, and so forth may all develop in stagelike fashion, but each domain proceeds at its own pace, relatively independently of the others (for example, Mandler, 1983).

Knowledge-Acquisition Approaches   Some developmental psychologists believe that after infancy, children and adults have essentially the same cognitive processes and capacities and that the difference between them is primarily the adult's more extensive knowledge base. By *knowledge,* they do not just mean a larger collection of facts, but a deeper understanding of how facts in a particular domain are organized.

This distinction between facts and the organization of facts is illustrated by a study that compared a group of 10-year-olds who were competing in a chess tournament with a group of college students who were chess amateurs. When asked to memorize and recall lists of random numbers, the college students easily outperformed the 10-year-olds. But when tested on their ability to recall actual game positions of the chess pieces on the board, the 10-year-old chess experts did better than the 18-year-old chess amateurs (Chi, 1978). Thus the relevant difference between the two groups is not different stages of cognitive development or different information-processing abilities (for example, memory capacity), but domain-specific knowledge. Because the 10-year-olds had a deeper grasp of the underlying structure of chess, they were able to organize and reconstruct the arrangements from memory by "chunking" the separate pieces of information into larger meaningful units (for example, a king-side attack by white) and eliminating from consideration implausible placements of the pieces. (We discuss experts versus amateur problem solvers in Chapter 8.)

Increasing knowledge of the world rather than a qualitative shift in cognitive development may also account for children's increasing ability to solve Piaget's conservation tasks as they get older. For example, a child who does not know that mass or number is the critical feature that defines what is meant by "more clay" or "more checkers" is likely to judge that the quantity has changed when only its visual appearance has changed. An older child may simply have learned the essential defining feature of "more." This hypothesis is confirmed in studies showing that a child who fails to show conservation in one domain can show conservation in another domain in which he or she has more knowledge (Keil, 1989).

Sociocultural Approaches   Although Piaget emphasized the child's interaction with the environment, the environment he had in mind was the immediate physical environment. The social and cultural context plays virtually no role in Piaget's theory. Yet much of what children must learn consists of the particular ways in which their culture views reality, what roles different persons—and different sexes—are expected to play, and what rules and norms govern social relationships in their particular culture. In these areas, there are no universally valid facts or correct views of reality. Thus according to those who take a sociocultural approach to development, the child should be seen not as a physical scientist seeking "true" knowledge but as a newcomer to a culture who seeks to become a native by learning how to look at social reality through the lenses of that culture (Bem, 1987, 1993; Shweder, 1984).

The origins of this view of cognitive development can be seen in the work of the Russian scholar Lev Vygotsky (1934/1986). Vygotsky believed that we develop understanding and expertise primarily through what might be described as *apprenticeship*—we are guided by more knowledgeable individuals who help us understand more and more about our world and develop new skills. He also distinguished between two levels of cognitive development: the child's actual level of development, as expressed in problem-solving ability, and the child's level of potential development, as determined by the kind of problem solving the child can do when guided by an adult or a more knowledgeable peer. According to Vygotsky, we need to know both the actual and potential levels of development in a particular child if we are to fully understand his or her level of cognitive development and provide appropriate instruction.

According to Vygotsky, children develop understanding and expertise through a form of apprenticeship in which they are guided by more knowledgeable individuals. For example, an older child may help a younger one develop new skills.

Because language is the primary means by which humans exchange social meanings, Vygotsky viewed language development as central to cognitive development; in fact, he regarded the acquisition of language as the most important aspect of children's development (Blanck, 1990). Language plays an important role in developing new skills and knowledge. As adults and peers help children master new tasks, the communication between them becomes part of the children's thinking. The children then use their language ability to guide their own actions as they practice the new skill. Thus, what Piaget referred to as egocentric speech, Vygotsky considered an essential component of cognitive development: Children speak to themselves in order to give themselves guidance and direction. This kind of self-instruction is termed *private speech*. You can observe this process in a child who gives herself instructions about how to perform a task, such as tying her shoes, that she previously heard from an adult (Berk, 1997).

The Development of Moral Judgment

In addition to studying the development of children's thought, Piaget was interested in how children develop moral judgment. He believed that children's understanding of moral rules and social conventions would have to match their overall level of cognitive development. On the basis of observations he made of children of different ages playing games with rules, such as marbles, he proposed that children's understanding of rules develops in a series of four stages (Piaget, 1932/1965). The first stage emerges at the beginning of the preoperational period. Children at this stage engage in "parallel play," in which each child follows his or her own set of idiosyncratic rules. For example, the child might sort the marbles of different colors into groups or roll the big ones across the room, followed by all the small ones. These "rules" give the child's play some regularity, but they are frequently changed, and they serve no collective purpose such as cooperation or competition.

Beginning about age 5, the child develops a sense of obligation to follow rules, treating them as absolute moral imperatives handed down by some authority such as God or the child's parents. Rules are permanent, sacred, and not subject to modification. Obeying them to the letter is more important than any human reason for changing them. For example, children at this stage reject the suggestion that the position of the starting line in the marble game might be changed to accommodate younger children who might want to play. From this and other studies, Piaget came to the view that children at this stage subscribe to a **moral realism,** *a confusion between moral and physical laws.* Moral rules are predetermined and permanent aspects of the world—just like the law of gravity. When asked what would happen if they violated some moral rule (like lying or stealing), children at this stage often expressed the view that punishment would surely result—God would punish them or they would be hit by a car.

moral realism   a confusion between moral and physical laws

At this same stage, children judge an act more by its consequences than by the intentions behind it. For example, Piaget told children several pairs of stories. In one pair, a boy broke a teacup while trying to steal some jam when his mother was not home; another boy, who was doing nothing wrong, accidentally broke a whole trayful of teacups. "Which boy is naughtier?" Piaget asked. Preoperational children tended to judge as naughtier the person in the stories who did the most damage, regardless of the intentions or motivation behind the act.

In Piaget's third stage of moral development, the child begins to appreciate that some rules are social conventions—cooperative agreements that can be arbitrarily decided and changed if everyone agrees. Children's moral realism also declines: When making moral judgments, children now give weight to subjective considerations like a person's intentions, and they see punishment as a human choice, rather than as an inevitable, divine retribution.

The beginning of the formal operational stage coincides with the fourth and final stage in children's understanding of moral rules. Youngsters now show an interest in

Although young children participate in parallel play with one another, it is only when they become older that they begin to understand the rules that govern social interaction.

generating rules to deal even with situations that they have never encountered. This stage is marked by an ideological mode of moral reasoning, which addresses wider social issues rather than just personal and interpersonal situations.

The American psychologist Lawrence Kohlberg extended Piaget's work on moral reasoning to include adolescence and adulthood (Kohlberg, 1969, 1976). He sought to determine whether there are universal stages in the development of moral judgments by presenting participants with moral dilemmas in the form of stories. For example, in one story a man whose dying wife needs a drug he cannot afford pleads with a druggist to let him buy the drug at a cheaper price. When the druggist refuses, the man decides to steal the drug. Participants are asked to discuss the man's action.

By analyzing answers to several such dilemmas, Kohlberg arrived at six developmental stages of moral judgment which he grouped into three levels: *preconventional, conventional,* and *postconventional* (see Table 3-2). The answers are scored on the basis of the reasons given for the decision, not on the basis of whether the action is judged right or wrong. For example, agreeing that the man should have stolen

---

Table 3-2

Stages of Moral Reasoning   Kohlberg believed that moral judgment develops with age according to these stages. (After Kohlberg, 1969)

Level I:	Preconventional Morality
Stage 1	Punishment orientation (Obeys rules to avoid punishment)
Stage 2	Reward orientation (Conforms to obtain rewards, to have favors returned)
Level II:	**Conventional Morality**
Stage 3	Good-boy/good-girl orientation (Conforms to avoid disapproval of others)
Stage 4	Authority orientation (Upholds laws and social rules to avoid censure of authorities and feelings of guilt about not "doing one's duty")
Level III:	**Postconventional Morality**
Stage 5	Social-contract orientation (Actions guided by principles commonly agreed on as essential to the public welfare; principles upheld to retain respect of peers and, thus, self-respect)
Stage 6	Ethical principle orientation (Actions guided by self-chosen ethical principles, which usually value justice, dignity, and equality; principles upheld to avoid self-condemnation)

the drug because "If you let your wife die, you'll get in trouble" or disagreeing because "If you steal the drug, you'll be caught and sent to jail" are both scored at Stage 1. In both cases, the man's actions are evaluated as right or wrong on the basis of anticipated punishment.

Kohlberg believed that all children are at Level I until about age 10, when they begin to evaluate actions in terms of other people's opinions (Level II). Most youngsters can reason at this level by age 13. Following Piaget, Kohlberg argues that only those who have achieved formal operational thought are capable of the kind of abstract thinking necessary for Level III, postconventional morality. The highest stage, Stage 6, requires the ability to formulate abstract ethical principles and uphold them in order to avoid self-condemnation.

Kohlberg reports that fewer than 10% of his adult participants show the kind of "clear-principled" Stage 6 thinking that is exemplified by the following response of a 16-year-old to the story described earlier: "By the law of society [the man] was wrong but by the law of nature or of God the druggist was wrong and the husband was justified. Human life is above financial gain. Regardless of who was dying, if it was a total stranger, man has a duty to save him from dying" (Kohlberg, 1969, p. 244). Before he died, Kohlberg eliminated Stage 6 from his theory; Level III is now sometimes simply referred to as *high-stage principled reasoning.*

Kohlberg presented evidence for this sequence of stages in children from several cultures, including America, Mexico, Taiwan, and Turkey (Colby, Kohlberg, Gibbs, & Lieberman, 1983; Nisan & Kohlberg, 1982). On the other hand, there is evidence that people use different rules for different situations and that the stages are not sequential (Kurtines & Greif, 1974). The theory has also been criticized for being "male centered," because it places a "masculine" style of abstract reasoning based on justice and rights higher on the moral scale than a "feminine" style of reasoning based on caring and concern for the integrity and continuation of relationships (Gilligan, 1982).

Piaget's assertion that young children cannot distinguish between social conventions (rules) and moral prescriptions has also been challenged. In one study, 7-year-old children were given a list of actions and asked to indicate which ones would be wrong even if there were no rules against them. Most of the children agreed that lying, stealing, hitting, and selfishness would be wrong even if there were no rules against them. In contrast, they thought that there was nothing wrong with chewing gum in class, addressing a teacher by his or her first name, boys entering the girls' bathroom, or eating lunch with one's fingers—as long as there were no rules against these acts (Nucci, 1981).

Thinking Critically

What levels of moral reasoning seem to be embedded in campaigns designed to discourage young people from using drugs or from being sexually active? Can you think of campaign themes that would appeal to a "higher" stage of moral reasoning?

How Do Personality and Social Development Proceed?

First-time parents are often surprised that their newborn seems to possess a distinctive personality from the very beginning; when they have a second child, they are often surprised at how different the second child is from the first. As early as the first weeks of life, infants show individual differences in activity level, responsiveness to change in their environment, and irritability. One infant cries a lot; another cries very little. One endures diapering or bathing without much fuss; another kicks and thrashes. One is responsive to every sound; another is oblivious to all but the loudest noises. Infants even differ in "cuddliness": Some seem to enjoy being cuddled and mold their bodies to the person holding them; others stiffen and squirm (Korner, 1973). The term **temperament** is used to refer to such *mood-related personality characteristics.*

temperament mood-related personality characteristics

Temperament

The study of temperament is a very active research area, and there are disagreements over how temperaments should be defined, identified, and measured. It also is not clear to what extent temperament in early childhood is reflected in the individual's later personality (Kohnstamm, Bates, & Rothbart, 1989).

The observation that temperamental differences arise early in life challenges the traditional view that all of an infant's behaviors are shaped by the early environment. Parents of a fussy baby, for example, tend to blame themselves for their infant's difficulties. But research with newborns makes it increasingly clear that many temperamental differences are inborn, and that the relationship between parent and infant is reciprocal—in other words, the infant's behavior also shapes the parent's response. An infant who is eas-

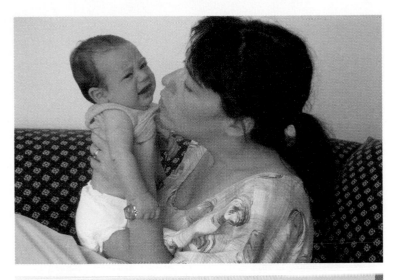

Some infants are more readily soothed than others. Such differences are due to differences in temperament.

ily soothed, who snuggles and stops crying when picked up, increases the parent's feelings of competence and attachment. An infant who stiffens and continues to cry, despite efforts to comfort it, makes the parent feel inadequate and rejected. The more responsive a baby is to the stimulation provided by the parent (snuggling and quieting when held, attending alertly when talked to or played with), the easier it is for the parent and child to establish a loving bond.

A pioneering study of temperament began in the 1950s with a group of 140 middle- and upper-class infants. The initial data were gathered through interviews with parents and were later supplemented by interviews with teachers and by scores on tests administered to the children. The infants were scored on nine traits, which were later combined to define three broad temperament types: Infants who were playful, regular in their sleeping and eating patterns, and adapted readily to new situations were classified as *easy* (about 40% of the sample); infants who were irritable, irregular in sleeping and eating patterns, and responded intensely and negatively to new situations were classified as *difficult* (about 10% of the sample); infants who were low in activity level, tended to withdraw from new situations in a mild way, and required more time than easy infants to adapt to new situations were classified as *slow to warm up* (about 15% of the sample). The remaining 35% of the infants were not rated high or low on any of the defining dimensions (Thomas et al., 1963).

Of the original sample, 133 participants have been followed into adult life and have again been assessed on temperament and psychological adjustment. The results provide mixed evidence for the continuity of temperament. On the one hand, temperament scores across the first 5 years of these children's lives were correlated with one another; moreover, children with "difficult" temperaments were more likely than "easy" children to have school problems later on. Adult measures of both temperament and adjustment were also also correlated with the measures of childhood temperament obtained at ages 3, 4, and 5. On the other hand, all the correlations were low (about .3), and when considered separately, most of the nine traits that were measured showed little or no continuity across time (Chess & Thomas, 1984; Thomas & Chess, 1977, 1986).

The researchers emphasize that continuity and discontinuity of temperament are functions of the interaction between the child's genotype (inherited characteristics) and the environment. In particular, they believe that the key to healthy development is the degree of fit between the child's temperament and the home environment.

Infants throughout the world begin to smile at about the same age—as do blind children—implying that maturation is more important than the conditions in which a child is reared in determining the onset of smiling.

When parents of a difficult child provide a happy, stable home life, the child's negative, difficult behaviors decrease with age (Belsky, Fish, & Isabella, 1991). Thomas and Chess cite the case of Carl, a boy who displayed a very difficult temperament from the first few months of life through age 5. Because Carl's father took delight in his son's "lusty" temperament and allowed for his initial negative reactions to new situations, Carl flourished and became increasingly "easy." At age 23 he was classified in the "easy" temperament group. Nevertheless, Carl's original temperament often emerged briefly when his life circumstances changed. For example, when he started piano lessons in late childhood, he again showed an intense negative response, followed by slow adjustment, and eventually positive involvement. A similar pattern emerged when he entered college (Thomas & Chess, 1986).

Another study provides further evidence of continuity of temperament. Seventy-nine children were categorized at 21 months as either extremely inhibited or uninhibited. At age 13, those who had been categorized as inhibited at 21 months of age scored significantly lower on a test of delinquent and aggressive behavior (Schwartz, Snidman, & Kagan, 1996). Other research has found that the tendency to approach or avoid unfamiliar events, which is an aspect of temperament, remains moderately stable over time (Kagan & Snidman, 1991).

Early Social Behavior

By 2 months of age, the average child will smile at the sight of its mother's or father's face. Delighted with this response, parents will go to great lengths to encourage repetition. Indeed, the infant's ability to smile at such an early age may have evolved historically precisely because it strengthened the parent–child bond. Parents interpret these smiles to mean that the infant recognizes and loves them, encouraging them to be even more affectionate and stimulating in response. A mutually reinforcing system of social interaction is thus established and maintained.

Infants all over the world begin to smile at about the same age, suggesting that maturation plays an important role in determining the onset of smiling. Blind babies also smile at about the same age as sighted infants, indicating that smiling is an innate response (Eibl-Eibesfeldt, 1970).

By their third or fourth month, infants show that they recognize and prefer familiar members of the household by smiling or cooing more when seeing these familiar faces or hearing their voices, but they are still fairly receptive to strangers. At about 7 or 8 months, however, many infants begin to show wariness or distress at the approach of a stranger and protest strongly when left in an unfamiliar setting or with an unfamiliar person. Parents are often disconcerted to find that their formerly gregarious infant, who had always happily welcomed the attentions of a baby-sitter, now cries inconsolably when they prepare to leave—and continues to cry for some time after they have left. Although not all infants show this *stranger anxiety,* the number of infants who do show it increases dramatically from about 8 months of age until the end of the first year. Similarly, distress over separation from the parent reaches a peak between 14 to 18 months and then gradually declines. By the time they are 3 years old, most children are secure enough in their parents' absence to be able to interact comfortably with other children and adults.

The waxing and waning of these two fears appears to be only slightly influenced by conditions of child rearing. The same general pattern has been observed among American children reared entirely at home and among those attending a day care center. Figure 3-7 shows that although the percentage of children who cry when their mother leaves the room varies across different cultures, the age-related pattern of onset and decline is very similar (Kagan, Kearsley, & Zelazo, 1978).

How do we explain the systematic timing of these fears? Two factors seem to be important in both their onset and their decline. One is the growth of memory capacity. During the second half of the first year infants become better able to remember past events and to compare past and present. This makes it possible for the baby to detect, and sometimes to fear, unusual or unpredictable events. The emergence of stranger anxiety coincides with the emergence of fears to a variety of

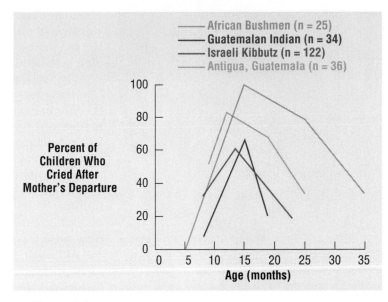

Figure 3-7

Children's Stress at Mother's Departure   Even though the percentages of children who cry when their mothers leave the room varies from one culture to another, the age-related pattern of onset and decline of such distress is similar across cultures. (From Kagan, Kearsley, & Zelazo, 1978)

stimuli that are unusual or unexpected; a weird-looking mask or a jack-in-the-box that brings smiles to a 4-month-old often causes an 8-month-old to look apprehensive and distressed. As children learn that strangers and unusual objects are not generally harmful, such fears gradually diminish.

It also seems reasonable to assume that memory development is involved in separation anxiety. The infant cannot "miss" the parent unless he or she can recall that parent's presence a minute earlier and compare this with the parent's absence now. When the parent leaves the room, the infant is aware that something is amiss—a kind of object permanence—which can lead to distress. As the child's memory for past instances of separation and return improves, the child becomes better able to anticipate the return of the absent parent, and anxiety declines.

The second factor is the growth of autonomy. One-year-olds are still highly dependent on care from adults, but children of 2 or 3 can head for the snack plate or toy shelf on their own. They can also use language to communicate their wants and feelings. Thus, dependence on caregivers in general and on familiar caregivers in particular decreases, and the issue of the parent's presence becomes less critical for the child.

Attachment

The term **attachment** is used to describe *an infant's tendency to seek closeness to particular people and to feel more secure in their presence.* Psychologists theorized at first that attachment to the mother developed because she was the source of food, one of the infant's most basic needs. But some facts did not fit. For example, ducklings and baby chicks feed themselves from birth, yet they still follow their mothers about and spend a great deal of time with them. The comfort they derive from the mother's presence cannot come from her role in feeding. A series of well-known experiments with monkeys showed that there is more to mother–infant attachment than nutritional needs (Harlow & Harlow, 1969).

Infant monkeys were separated from their mothers shortly after birth and placed with two artificial "mothers" constructed of wire mesh with wooden heads. The torso

attachment an infant's tendency to seek closeness to particular people and to feel more secure in their presence

Figure 3-8

A Monkey's Response to an Artificial Mother
Although it is fed via a wire mother, the infant spends
more time with the terry-cloth mother. The terry-cloth
mother provides a safe base from which to explore
strange objects.

of one mother was bare wire; the other was covered with foam
rubber and terry cloth, making it more cuddly and easy to cling
to (see Figure 3-8). Either mother could be equipped to provide milk by means of a bottle attached to its chest.

The experiment sought to determine whether the "mother"
that was always the source of food would be the one to which
the young monkey would cling. The results were clear-cut: No
matter which mother provided food, the infant monkey spent
its time clinging to the terry-cloth mother. This purely passive
but soft-contact mother was a source of security. For example,
the infant monkey's obvious fear when placed in a strange environment was allayed if it could make contact with the cloth
mother. While holding on to the cloth mother with one hand
or foot, the monkey was willing to explore objects that were
otherwise too terrifying to approach.

Although contact with a cuddly, artificial mother provides
an important aspect of "mothering," it is not enough for satisfactory development. Infant monkeys raised with artificial mothers and isolated from other monkeys during the first 6 months
of life showed various types of bizarre behavior in adulthood.
They rarely engaged in normal interaction with other monkeys
later on (either cowering in fear or showing abnormally aggressive behavior), and their sexual responses were inappropriate. When female monkeys that had been deprived of early
social contact were successfully mated (after considerable effort), they made poor mothers, tending to neglect or abuse
their first-born infants—although they became better mothers with their later-born children. Note, however, that these
monkeys were deprived of all social contact. Monkeys with artificial mothers do fine as adults if they are allowed to interact
with their peers during the first 6 months.

Although we should be careful in generalizing from research
on monkeys to human development, there is evidence that the
human infant's attachment to the primary caregiver serves the same functions. Most
of the work on attachment in human infants originated with the psychoanalyst John
Bowlby in the 1950s and 1960s. His research convinced him that a child's failure to
form a secure attachment to one or more persons in the early years is related to an
inability to develop close personal relationships in adulthood (Bowlby, 1973).

Mary Ainsworth, one of Bowlby's associates, made extensive observations of
children and their mothers in Uganda and the United States and then developed
a laboratory procedure for assessing the security of a child's attachments from about
12 to 18 months of age (Ainsworth, Blehar, Waters, & Wall, 1978). The procedure,
called the *Strange Situation,* consists of a series of episodes in which a child is observed as the primary caregiver leaves and returns to the room (see Table 3-3).
Throughout this sequence, the baby is observed through a one-way mirror during
the entire sequence, and several observations are recorded: the baby's activity level
and play involvement, crying and other distress signs, proximity to and attempts
to gain attention of the mother, proximity to and willingness to interact with the
stranger, and so on. On the basis of their behaviors, babies are categorized into three
main groups:

- *Securely attached:* Regardless of whether they are upset at the mother's departures (episodes 3 and 5), babies who are classified as securely attached seek
to interact with her when she returns. Some are content simply to acknowledge her return from a distance, while continuing to play with the toys. Others

Frontiers of Psychology

Effects of Day Care

Day care is a controversial subject in the United States because many people have doubts about its effects on very young children; also, many Americans believe that children should be cared for at home by their mothers. But in a society where the vast majority of mothers are in the labor force, day care is a reality; in fact, more 3- and 4-year-olds (43%) attend day care than are cared for in either their own home or another home (35%).

Many researchers have attempted to discover what effects, if any, day care has on children. One well-known study (Belsky & Rovine, 1988) found that infants who received more than 20 hours of nonmaternal care per week were slightly more likely to be insecurely attached to their mothers; however, this finding applied only to male infants with unresponsive mothers who felt that their infants had a difficult temperament. Similarly, Clarke-Stewart (1989) found that infants receiving nonmaternal care were somewhat less likely to be securely attached to their mothers than infants who were cared for by their mothers (47% versus 53%). Other researchers found that children's development is not affected adversely by good-quality nonmaternal care (Phillips et al., 1987).

In recent years research on day care has focused less on the effects of day care versus maternal care than on the effects of high-quality versus low-quality day care. For example, children who receive high-quality day care from an early age have been found to be more competent socially in elementary school (Andersson, 1992; Field, 1991; Howes, 1990) and more assertive (Scarr & Eisenberg, 1993) than children who enter day care later. On the other hand, poor-quality care may have negative effects on adjustment, particularly in boys, especially if the child comes from a highly stressed home environment (Garrett, 1997). Good-quality day care can reduce the effects of growing up in such an environment (Phillips et al., 1994).

What constitutes good-quality day care? Several factors have been identified. They include a relatively low number of children in a single space, a favorable ratio of caregivers to children, low turnover among caregivers, and the completion of higher-level education and training programs by the caregivers. Under these conditions caregivers tend to be more attentive to children and sensitive to their needs, as well as more verbally stimulating, and as a result the children perform better on measures of intelligence and social development (Galinsky et al., 1994; Helburn, 1995; Howes, Phillips, & Whitebook, 1992). Other research has found that centers that are well equipped and provide a wide variety of activities have positive effects (Scarr et al., 1993).

A recent large-scale study of more than 1,000 children in 10 day care centers found that in the better centers (as measured by the qualifications of the caregivers and the amount of individual attention given to the children) children actually made greater gains in language and thinking abilities than children from similar backgrounds who were not receiving high-quality day care. This was especially true of children from lower-income households (Garrett, 1997).

In sum, it appears that children are not significantly affected by nonmaternal care. Any negative effects tend to be emotional in nature, whereas positive effects are more likely to be social; cognitive development is usually affected either positively or not at all. However, these findings apply to day care of reasonable quality. Poor quality care usually has negative effects on children, regardless of their home environment.

Table 3-3

Episodes in the Strange Situation Procedure

1. A mother and her child enter the room. The mother places the baby on the floor, surrounded by toys, and goes to sit at the opposite end of the room.
2. A female stranger enters the room, sits quietly for a minute, converses with the mother for a minute, and then attempts to engage the baby in play with a toy.
3. The mother leaves the room unobtrusively. If the baby is not upset, the stranger returns to sitting quietly. If the baby is upset, the stranger tries to soothe him or her.
4. The mother returns and engages the baby in play while the stranger slips out of the room.
5. The mother leaves again, this time leaving the baby alone in the room.
6. The stranger returns. If the baby is upset, the stranger tries to comfort him or her.
7. The mother returns and the stranger slips out of the room.

seek physical contact with her. Still others are completely preoccupied with the mother throughout the entire session, showing intense distress when she leaves. In all, 60% to 65% of American babies fall into this category.

- *Insecurely attached, avoidant:* These babies avoid interacting with the mother in the reunion episodes. Some ignore her almost entirely; some display mixed attempts to interact and to avoid interacting. Avoidant babies may pay little attention to the mother when she is in the room and often do not seem distressed when she leaves. If distressed, they are as easily comforted by the stranger as by the mother. About 20% of American babies fall into this category.
- *Insecurely attached, ambivalent:* Babies are classified as ambivalent if they show resistance to the mother during the reunion episodes. They simultaneously seek and resist physical contact. For example, they may cry to be picked up and then squirm angrily to get down. Some act very passive, crying for the mother when she returns but not crawling toward her and then showing resistance when she approaches. About 10% of American babies are classified into this category.

Because some babies did not seem to fit any of these categories, more recent studies have included a fourth category, called *disorganized* (Main & Solomon, 1986). Babies in this category often show contradictory behaviors. For example, they may approach the mother while taking care not to look at her, approach her and then show dazed avoidance, or suddenly cry out after having first settled down. Some seem disoriented, appear emotionless, or look depressed. About 10% to 15% of American babies fall into this category, with the percentages being much higher among babies who are maltreated or whose parents are being treated for mental disorders.

In attempting to account for differences in attachment among babies, researchers have directed most of their attention to the behavior of the primary caregiver, usually the mother. The main finding has been that a caregiver's "sensitive responsiveness" to the baby's needs produces secure attachment. Mothers of securely attached babies usually respond promptly when the baby cries and behave affectionately when they pick him or her up. They also tailor their responses closely to the baby's needs (Clarke-Stewart, 1973). In feeding, for example, they use an infant's signals to determine when to begin and end feeding and attend to the baby's food preferences. In contrast, mothers of babies who show either type of insecure attachment respond according to their own needs or moods rather than according to signals from the baby. For example, they will respond to the baby's cries for attention when they feel like cuddling the baby but will ignore such cries at other times (Stayton, 1973).

Not all developmental psychologists agree that the caregiver's responsiveness is the major cause of an infant's attachment behaviors. They call attention to the baby's own inborn temperament (Campos et al., 1983; Kagan, 1984). For example, perhaps the temperaments that make some babies "easy" also make them more securely attached than do the temperaments of "difficult" babies. And, as noted earlier, a parent's response to a child is often itself a function of the child's own behavior. For example, mothers of difficult babies tend to spend less time playing with them

"Sensitive responsiveness" to a baby promotes secure attachment. Mothers of securely attached babies tend to respond promptly when the baby cries, behave affectionately when they pick him or her up, and tailor their responses closely to the needs and moods of the child.

(Green, Fox, & Lewis, 1983). Attachment patterns may reflect this interaction between a baby's temperament and the parent's responsiveness.

In reply, attachment theorists point to data that support the "sensitive responsiveness" hypothesis. For example, it has been found that in the first year of life an infant's crying changes much more than the mother's responsiveness to the crying does. Moreover, the mother's responsiveness over a 3-month period predicts the infant's crying over the next 3 months significantly better than the infant's crying predicts the mother's subsequent responsiveness to crying. In short, the mother appears to influence the infant's crying more than the infant influences the mother's responsiveness to crying (Bell & Ainsworth, 1972). In general, the mother's behavior appears to be the most important factor in establishing a secure or insecure attachment (Isabella & Belsky, 1991).

Other findings may resolve this debate. Recall that the attachment classification is based not on the baby's distress when the mother leaves but on how the baby reacts when she returns. It now appears that an infant's temperament predicts the former but not the latter (Frodi & Thompson, 1985; Vaughn, Lefever, Seifer, & Barglow, 1989). For example, babies with "easy" temperaments are not typically distressed when the mother leaves. When she returns, they either tend to greet her happily—thus showing secure attachment—or they show the avoidant type of insecure attachment. Babies with "difficult" temperaments are typically distressed when the mother leaves. When she returns, they either tend to seek her out and cling to her—thus showing secure attachment—or they show the ambivalent type of insecure attachment (Belsky & Rovine, 1987). Thus children's overall reaction to the departure and return of their primary caregiver is a function of both the caregiver's responsiveness to the child and the child's temperament.

Attachment and Later Development   A baby's attachment classification has been found to remain quite stable when retested in the Strange Situation several years later—unless the family experiences major changes in life circumstances (Main & Cassidy, 1988; Thompson, Lamb, & Estes, 1982). Stressful life changes are likely to affect parental responsiveness to the baby that, in turn, affects the baby's feelings of security.

Early attachment patterns also appear to be related to how children cope with new experiences. For example, in one study, 2-year-olds were given a series of problems requiring the use of tools. Some of the problems were within the child's capacity; others were quite difficult. The toddlers, who had been rated as securely attached when they were 12 months of age, approached the problems with enthusiasm and persistence. When they encountered difficulties, they seldom cried or became angry; rather, they sought help from adults. Children who had been rated earlier as insecurely attached behaved quite differently. They became easily frustrated and angry, seldom asked for help, tended to ignore or reject directions from adults, and quickly gave up trying to solve the problems (Matas, Arend, & Sroufe, 1978).

This and similar studies suggest that children who are securely attached by the time they enter their second year are better equipped to cope with new experiences. However, we cannot be certain that the quality of children's early attachments is directly responsible for their later competence in problem-solving. Parents who are responsive to their children's needs in infancy probably continue to provide effective parenting during early childhood—encouraging autonomy and efforts to cope with new experiences, yet ready with help when needed.

Children who were rated as insecure in their attachment relationships at 15 months of age tended to be socially withdrawn and hesitant about participating in activities in later years, when they were in nursery school.

Thus, the child's competence may reflect the current state of the parent–child relationship rather than the relationship that existed 2 years earlier. Moreover, children's temperaments—which, as we saw earlier, affect their behavior in the Strange Situation procedure—might also influence their later competence as preschoolers. (For a discussion of the effects of day care on attachment, see the Frontiers of Psychology feature on page 89.)

see the Frontiers of Psychology feature on page 89.)

Thinking Critically

1. Would your parents have characterized your infant personality as "easy," "difficult," or "slow to warm up"? Which aspects of your current personality seem to be primarily a reflection of your inborn temperament, which seem to reflect the way you were raised, and which seem to reflect a blend or interaction between "nature" and "nurture"?

2. Some psychologists have suggested that our earlier childhood attachment styles can influence the kinds of romantic relationships we form as adults. What form might the attachment styles discussed in this chapter assume in an adult romantic relationship? Can you relate your own adult "attachment styles" to your early childhood attachment style or to features of your childhood environment?

How Does Development Continue in Adolescence?

adolescence the period of transition from childhood to adulthood

Adolescence refers to *the period of transition from childhood to adulthood.* It extends roughly from age 12 to the late teens, when physical growth is nearly complete. During this period, the young person becomes sexually mature and establishes an identity as an individual apart from the family.

Conventional wisdom holds that adolescence is a period of "storm and stress" characterized by moodiness, inner turmoil, and rebellion. But research findings do not support this pessimistic view. One study followed more than 300 adolescents as they progressed from the sixth through the eighth grades, assessing them and their parents twice a year by means of interviews and psychological tests. They were assessed again during their last year of high school (Petersen, 1989). Most of the adolescents made it through this period without major turmoil. The data indicate, however, that puberty does have significant effects on body image, self-esteem, moods, and relationships with parents and members of the opposite sex.

Some of these effects may be linked directly to the hormonal changes of puberty (reviewed in detail by Buchanan, Eccles, & Becker, 1992), but most are related to the personal and social effects of the body's physical changes and, most important, the timing of those changes. Being an early or late maturer (one year earlier or later than average) affects an adolescent's satisfaction with his or her appearance and body image. In general seventh- and eighth-grade boys who have reached puberty report positive moods more often than their prepubertal male classmates, and they tend to be more satisfied with their weight and their overall appearance than later-maturing boys—a reflection of the importance of strength and physical prowess for males in our society. But early-maturing boys also tend to have less self-control and emotional stability than later-maturing boys; they are more likely to smoke, drink, use drugs, and be in trouble with the law (Duncan et al., 1985). In contrast, late-maturing boys feel the worst about themselves in seventh grade, but typically end up as the healthiest group by their senior year in high school (Petersen, 1989).

Early maturation has the opposite effect on the self-esteem of girls. Compared with later maturers, early maturers experience more depression and anxiety (Brooks-Gunn & Ruble, 1983), have lower self-esteem (Simmons & Blyth, 1988), and are generally less satisfied with their weight and appearance. They tend to be embarrassed by the fact that their bodies are more womanly in shape than those of their female classmates—particularly since the current standards for female attractiveness as promoted by the media emphasize the lean look. Although early maturers also achieve

There is wide variation in the age at which puberty begins and the rate at which it progresses. As a result, some adolescents may be much taller and more physically mature than others of the same age.

early popularity, this is partly because they are seen as sexually precocious. They are also more likely to have conflict with their parents, to drop out of school, and to have both emotional and behavioral problems (Caspi & Moffitt, 1991; Stattin & Magnusson, 1990).

Again, however, it is important to emphasize that in the study just mentioned, early adolescence was relatively trouble-free for more than 50% of both males and females. About 30% of the participants had only intermittent problems. Only 15% were caught in a "downward spiral of trouble and turmoil"; emotional and academic problems that were evident in the eighth grade continued or worsened during the high school years (Petersen, 1989).

Identity Development   The psychoanalyst Erik Erikson believed that the major task confronting the adolescent is to develop a sense of identity, to find answers to the questions "Who am I?" and "Where am I going?" Although Erikson coined the term **identity crisis** to refer to this *active process of self-definition,* he believed that it is an integral part of healthy psychosocial development. Similarly, most developmental psychologists believe that adolescence should be a period of "role experimentation" in which young persons can explore alternative behaviors, interests, and ideologies. Many beliefs, roles, and ways of behaving may be "tried on," modified, or discarded in an attempt to shape an integrated concept of the self.

Adolescents try to synthesize these values and appraisals into a consistent picture. If parents, teachers, and peers project consistent values, the search for identity is easier. In a simple society in which adult models are few and social roles are limited, the task of forming an identity is relatively easy. In a society as complex as ours, it is a difficult task for many adolescents. They are faced with an almost infinite array of possibilities of how to behave and what to do in life. As a result, there are large differences among adolescents in how the development of their identity proceeds.

identity crisis
active process of self-definition

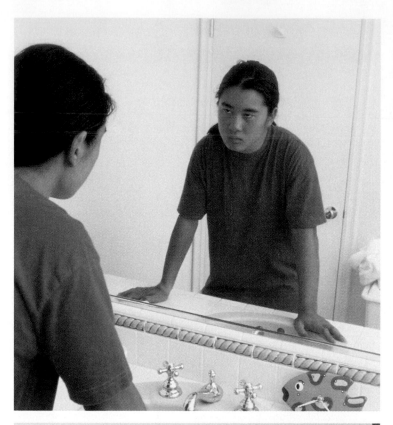

Developing a personal identity—an answer to the questions "Who am I?" and "Where am I going?"—is a major task of adolescence.

Moreover, any particular adolescent's identity may be at different stages of development in different areas of life (for example, sexual, occupational, ideological).

Ideally the identity crisis should be resolved by the early or mid-twenties so that the individual can move on to other life tasks. When the process is successful, the individual is said to have *achieved an identity;* this usually means having arrived at a coherent sense of one's sexual identity, vocational direction, and ideological worldview. Until the identity crisis is resolved, the individual has no consistent sense of self or set of internal standards for evaluating his or her self-worth in major areas of life.

Erikson's theory about adolescent identity development has been tested and extended by James Marcia (1966, 1980). On the basis of open-ended interviews, Marcia concluded that there are four identity statuses or positions based on whether the person perceives an identity issue and whether a resolution has been reached:

- *Identity achievement:* Individuals in this status have passed through an identity crisis, a period of active questioning and self-definition. They have committed to ideological positions that they have worked out for themselves and they have decided on an occupation. They have begun to think of themselves as a future doctor, not just a pre-med chemistry major. They have reexamined their family's religious and political beliefs and discarded those that don't seem to fit their identity.
- *Foreclosure:* Those in this status are also committed to occupational and ideological positions, but they show no signs of ever having gone through an identity crisis. They have accepted their family's religion without question. When asked about politics, they often say they have never given it much thought. Some of them seem committed and cooperative, others rigid, dogmatic, and conforming. They give the impression that they would be lost if a major event occurred to challenge their unexamined rules and values.
- *Moratorium:* These are the young people currently in the midst of an identity crisis. They are actively seeking answers but have not resolved the conflicts between their parents' plans for them and their own interests. They may express a set of political or religious beliefs with great intensity for a while, only to abandon them after a period of reconsideration. At best, they seem sensitive, ethical, and open-minded; at worst, they appear anxiety ridden, self-righteous, and vacillating (Scarr, Weinberg, & Levine, 1986).
- *Identity diffusion:* This is Marcia's term for what Erikson called *identity confusion.* Some individuals in this category may have had an identity crisis; some have not. But in either case, they still have no integrated sense of themselves. They say that it might be "interesting" to go to law school or start a business, but they are not taking steps in either direction. They say that they are not interested in religion or politics. Some seem cynical, others shallow and confused. Some, of course, are still too young to have reached the identity development of adolescence.

As expected, the percentage of adolescents who have attained identity achievement steadily increases from the years just prior to high school through the late college years, while the percentage of those remaining in identity diffusion steadily decreases. The state of identity crisis—moratorium—peaks during the first 2 years of college. In general, studies show that the level of identity achievement is considerably higher for vocational choice than for political ideology (Waterman, 1985).

Using Marcia's categories of identity achievement, foreclosure, moratorium, and identity diffusion, can you identify how and when your religious, sexual, occupational, and political identities have developed and changed over time?

Thinking Critically

Summary

1. Two central issues in developmental psychology are (1) how biological factors ("nature") interact with environmental experiences ("nurture") to determine the course of development, and (2) whether development is best understood as a continuous process of change or as a series of qualitatively distinct stages. A related issue is whether there are *critical* or *sensitive periods* during which specific experiences must occur for psychological development to proceed normally.

2. An individual's genetic heritage is expressed through the process of *maturation,* innately determined sequences of growth or bodily changes that are relatively independent of the environment. Motor development, for example, is largely a maturational process because all children master skills such as crawling, standing, and walking in the same sequence and at roughly the same age. But even these can be modified by an atypical or inadequate environment.

3. Infants are born with all their sensory systems functioning. They are well prepared to learn about their environment. There is even some evidence that newborns respond differentially to sounds that they had heard while still in the uterus.

4. Piaget's theory describes stages in cognitive development. These proceed from the *sensorimotor stage* (in which an important discovery is *object permanence*), through the *preoperational stage* (when symbols begin to be used) and the *concrete operational stage* (when conservation concepts develop), to the *formal operational stage* (when hypotheses are tested systematically in problem solving).

5. New methods of testing reveal that Piaget's theory underestimates children's abilities, and some alternative approaches have been proposed. Information-processing approaches view cognitive development as reflecting the gradual development of processes such as attention and memory. Other theorists emphasize the child's domain-specific knowledge. Still others focus on the influence of the social and cultural context.

6. Piaget believed that children's understanding of moral rules and judgments develops along with their cognitive abilities. Kohlberg extended Piaget's work to include adolescence and adulthood. He proposed three levels of moral judgment: preconventional, conventional, and postconventional.

7. As early as the first weeks of life, infants show individual differences in activity level, responsiveness to change in their environment, and irritability. Such mood-related personality characteristics are called *temperament* and appear to be inborn. It is not yet clear to what extent they constitute the building blocks for the individual's later personality. Continuity of temperament across the life span is a function of the interaction between the child's inherited characteristics and the environment.

8. Some early social behaviors, such as smiling, reflect innate responses that appear at about the same time in all infants, including blind infants. The emergence of many later social behaviors—including wariness of strangers and distress over separation from primary caregivers—appears to depend on the child's developing cognitive skills.

9. An infant's tendency to seek closeness to particular people and to feel more secure in their presence is called *attachment.* Attachment can be assessed through a procedure called the Strange Situation, a series of episodes in which a child is observed as the primary caregiver leaves and returns to the room. On the basis of the child's reactions, he or she is classified as (1) securely attached; (2) insecurely attached, avoidant; or (3) insecurely attached, ambivalent. Securely attached infants tend to have primary caregivers who respond sensitively to their needs. A child's temperament also influences his or her behavior in the Strange Situation. Later in childhood, securely attached children tend to cope with new experiences better than insecurely attached children.

10. Puberty has significant effects on an adolescent's body image, self-esteem, moods, and relationships; but most adolescents make it through this period without major turmoil. Compared with their prepubertal classmates, early-maturing boys report greater satisfaction with their appearance and more frequent positive moods; in contrast, early-maturing girls report more depression, anxiety, family conflict, and dissatisfaction with their appearance than do their prepubertal classmates. According to the psychoanalyst Erik Erikson, forming a personal sense of identity is the major task of *adolescence.*

Suggested Readings

Comprehensive textbooks on development include Berk, *Child Development* (4th ed., 1997), and Newcombe, *Child Development: Change Over Time* (8th ed., 1996). A general text on development through the life course is Rice, *Human Development* (3rd ed., 1998). For a discussion of the major approaches to the study of development, see Miller, *Theories of Developmental Psychology* (3rd ed., 1993).

Books focusing on infancy include Osofsky (ed.), *Handbook of Infant Development* (2nd ed., 1987); Lamb and Bornstein, *Development in Infancy: An Introduction* (2nd ed., 1987); and Rosenblith, *In the Beginning: Development from Conception to Age Two Years* (2nd ed., 1992). A four-volume overview of the major theories and research in child development may be found in Mussen (ed.), *Handbook of Child Psychology* (4th ed., 1983).

Cognitive Development (3rd ed., 1992) by Flavell presents a thorough introduction to this topic. *The Development of Memory in Children* (3rd ed., 1989) by Kail provides a readable summary of research on children's memory. *Children's Thinking* (2nd ed., 1991) by Siegler is written from the perspective of information-processing theories. For a brief introduction to Piaget, see Phillips, *Piaget's Theory: A Primer* (1981).

Two books on children's moral and social reasoning are Damon, *Social and Personality Development: From Infancy Through Adolescence* (1983), and Turiel, *The Development of Social Knowledge: Morality and Convention* (1983). Kohnstamm, Bates, and Rothbart (eds.), *Temperament in Childhood* (1989) provides a good summary of research in this active area.

Adolescent development is dealt with in Steinberg, *Adolescence* (4th ed., 1996), and Kimmel and Wiener, *Adolescence: A Developmental Transition* (1985).

Enhance and Explore

To enhance your understanding of the psychological concepts found in this chapter, please consult the following aids:

Study Guide

Learning Objectives, p. 48
Define the Terms, p. 50
Test Your Knowledge, p. 54
Essay Questions, p. 57
Thinking Independently, p. 59

PowerPsych CD-ROM

HOW DOES COGNITIVE DEVELOPMENT PROCEED?

PIAGET'S STAGE THEORY
Sensorimotor Stage
Preoperational Stage
Concrete Stage
Formal Operations Stage

PsychCentral

For more information concerning the topics found in this chapter, access psychology links on the Word Wide Web made through the Harcourt Web page at:
http://www.harcourtcollege.com/psych/Fundamentals

www.harcourtcollege.com
http://www.harcourtcollege.com/psych/index.html

How instrumental are parents in the development of their children?

Parents Have No Lasting Influence on the Personality or Intelligence of Their Children

Judith Rich Harris

Your parents took good care of you when you were little. They taught you many things. They are leading players in your memories of childhood. All these things could be true, and yet your parents may have left no lasting impression on your personality or intelligence or on the way you behave when they're not around.

Hard to believe? Try, for a moment, to put aside your preconceptions and consider the evidence. For example, the studies designed to separate the effects of genes from those of the home environment show that if you eliminate the similarities due to genes, two people who grew up in the same home are not noticeably more alike in personality or intelligence than two people picked at random from the same population. Almost all the similarities between brothers or sisters reared together are due to the genes they have in common. If they are adoptive siblings, they are not more alike than adopted people reared in different homes. On average, an adopted child reared by agreeable parents is no nicer than one reared by grouches, and one reared by parents who love books is no smarter than one reared by parents who love soap operas.

Because these results don't fit the popular theories of child development, many psychologists ignore them or try to explain them away. But results that don't fit the theories have been piling up (Harris, 1995, 1998). A recent study showed that children who spent most of their first three years in day-care centers do not differ in behavior or adjustment from children who spent that time at home (NICHD Early Child Care Research Network, 1998). Children who must vie with their siblings for their parents' attention do not differ in personality from only children (Falbo & Polit, 1986). Boys and girls behave as differently today as they did a generation ago, even though today's parents try hard to treat their sons and daughters alike (Serbin, Powlishta, & Gulko, 1993). Children who speak Korean or Polish at home but English with their peers end up as English speakers. The language learned outside the home takes precedence over the one their parents taught them, and they speak it without an accent (Harris, 1998).

But what about the evidence that dysfunctional parents tend to have dysfunctional offspring and that children who are treated with affection tend to turn out better than children who are treated harshly? The trouble with this evidence is that it comes from studies that provide no way to distinguish genetic from environmental influences or causes from effects. Are the offspring's problems due to the unfavorable environment provided by the dysfunctional parents or to personality characteristics inherited from them? Did the hugs cause the child to develop a pleasant personality, or did her pleasant personality make her parents want to hug her? Judging from studies that use more advanced techniques, it appears that the problems were at least partly inherited and that the child's pleasant personality evoked the hugs (Plomin, Owen, & McGuffin, 1994; Reiss, 1997).

There is no question that parents influence the way their children behave at home, and this is another source of confusion. Is the way children behave at home a good indication of how they'll behave in the classroom or the playground? When researchers discover that children behave differently in different social contexts, they usually assume that the way they behave with their parents is somehow more important or long-lasting than the way they behave elsewhere. But the children who speak Korean or Spanish at home and English outside the home use English as their primary language in adulthood. A boy whose cries evoke sympathy when he hurts himself at home learns not to cry when he hurts himself on the playground, and as an adult he seldom cries. A child who is dominated by her older sibling at home is no more likely than a firstborn to allow herself to be dominated by her peers. Children learn separately how to behave at home and outside the home, and it's their outside-the-home behavior they bring with them to adulthood—which makes sense, since they are not going to spend their adult lives in their parents' house.

Children have to learn how to get along in the world outside the home, and out there the rules are different. Children are not putty in their parents' hands.

Judith Rich Harris

The Unquestionable Influence of Parents

Jerome Kagan, *Harvard University*

The development of the skills, values, and social behaviors that maximize adaptation to the society in which a particular child grows requires the orchestration of many relatively independent forces. The most important of these include the temperamental biases that the child inherits; the class, ethnic, and religious affiliations of the child's family; relationships with siblings; the historical era in which childhood is spent; and always the behaviors and personality of the parents.

Parental influences on the child assume two different forms. Parental actions with the child are the most obvious. Parents who regularly talk and read to their children usually produce children with the largest vocabularies, the highest intelligence scores, and the best academic grades (Gottfried, Fleming, & Gottfried, 1998; Ninio, 1980). Parents who reason with their children while making requests for obedience usually end up with more civil children (Baumrind, 1967). The power of the family is seen in the results of a study of over 1,000 children from 10 different cities in the United States who were studied extensively by a team of scientists. Some of these children were raised at home, and some attended daycare centers for varied amounts of time. The main result was that the family had the most important influence on the three-year-old child's personality and character (NICHD Early Child Care Research Network, 1998). One of the most important illustrations of the power of parental behavior is the fact that some children who were orphaned and made homeless by war were able to regain intellectual and social skills they failed to develop during their early privation if they were adopted by nurturant families (Rathburn, DiVirglio, & Waldfogel, 1958).

Parents also influence their children through their own characteristics. Children come to the conclusions about themselves, often incorrect, because they assume that since they are the biological offspring of their mother and father, they possess some of the qualities that belong to their parents. This emotionally tinged belief is called identification, and it is the basis for national pride and loyalty to ethnic and religious groups. Thus, if a parent is perceived by her child as affectionate, just, and talented, the child assumes that she, too, probably possesses one or more of these desirable traits and, as a result, feels more confident than she has a right to, given the evidence. By contrast, the child who perceives a parent who is rejecting, unfair in doling out punishment, and without talent feels shame because he assumes that he probably is in possession of some of these undesirable characteristics (Kagan, 1998).

Support for this last claim is fact that all children become upset if someone criticizes their family. The anxiety or anger that follows such criticism is strong because children assume, unconsciously, that any criticism of their parents is also a criticism of them.

The provocative suggestion in Harris's "The Nurture Assumption" that parents have minimal influences on their children's personality and character, while peers have a major influence, is undermined by two sets of facts. First, peers are of little influence until the child is five or six years of age, but six year olds from varied cultures or children living in different historical eras are very different in their behavior and personality. Puritan children living in New England in the 17th century were more obedient than contemporary Boston children because of parental behaviors toward them.

Jerome Kagan

Second, children select friends who share their values and interests. A child who values school work will choose friends with similar interests. If such a child becomes an academically successful adult, it is not logical to assume that this outcome is due to the influence of friends because the child chose that type of friend in the first place.

It is rare to find a belief that all societies, ancient and modern, share. I know of no society that claimed that the family's influence on the child's mind was without much significance. This degree of consensus implies that it might be a universal truth. To declare that parents have little influence on children, in light of the scientific evidence and every parent's daily experiences, is a little like declaring on a foggy September morning that all the trees have disappeared because you cannot see them.

CHAPTER 4

Sensation and Perception

What Is the Role of Attention?
Selective Looking and Listening
The Neural Bases of Attention
How Does Perception Develop?
Discriminatory Capacities in Infants
Effects of Rearing With Controlled Stimulation
Learning Perceptual–Motor Coordination

Your face is the most distinctive part of you. The shape and size of your eyes, ears, nose, and mouth are what make you look so different from other people. But the primary purpose of your facial features is not to make you recognizable; it is to enable you to sense the world. Our eyes see it, our ears hear it, our noses smell it, our mouths taste it—and these, along with a few other senses, provide us with most of our knowledge about the world. The next time you look at your face in a mirror, think of it as an elaborate sensing system, mounted on the platform you call your body, that allows you to explore the world.

The world that we know through our senses is not the same as the world that other species know through their senses. Each of our sense organs is tuned to receive a particular range of stimuli that are relevant to our survival, but each organ is insensitive to stimuli outside this range. Different species have different ranges of sensitivity because they have different survival needs. Dogs, for example, are far more sensitive to smells than we are because they rely heavily on odors for activities that are critical to their survival, such as locating food, marking trails, and identifying kin.

In this chapter we discuss some of the major properties of human senses and how information obtained through our senses is converted into perceptual experience. These two topics are commonly referred to as *sensation* and *perception*. While there is no sharp dividing line between them, **sensations** are *experiences associated with simple stimuli,* such as a brief red light, and focus on people's reactions to single attributes, such as color. In contrast, **perception** is *the integration and meaningful interpretation of sensations.* Studies of perception typically involve real objects, such as a pictured fire engine, and focus on people's reactions to the whole object. At a biological level, sensory processes primarily involve the sense organs (e.g., the retina) and the neural pathways that run from the sense organs to the cerebral cortex; in contrast, perceptual processes involve various regions of the cortex itself.

sensations experiences associated with simple stimuli

perception the integration and meaningful interpretation of sensation

The senses that we consider include vision, hearing, smell, taste, and the skin senses (pressure, temperature, and pain). In everyday life, a number of senses may be involved in a single action—we see a peach, feel its texture, taste and smell it as we bite into it, and hear the sounds of our own chewing. For purposes of analysis, though, we often want to keep the senses separate. Before beginning our analysis of individual senses, we will discuss some properties that are common to all the senses. Then we consider the different senses, excluding vision, individually. This survey will give us an idea of how the various senses work. The rest of the chapter focuses on vision, our most finely developed sense and the one about which we know the most. We first discuss visual sensation and then

The world we know through our senses is different from that of other species. Each of our sense organs is tuned to receive a particular range of stimuli relevant to human survival (such as the ability to perceive the utility and beauty of the sun), and insensitive to stimuli outside this range.

move on to visual perception. We will analyze how human beings localize and recognize objects, then consider how the perceptual system keeps the appearance of objects constant, and then consider the role of attention in perception. We conclude the chapter with a brief discussion of sensory and perceptual development.

What Properties Are Common to All the Senses?

In this section we consider two properties that are common to all the senses. The first one describes senses at a psychological level, while the second focuses on the biological level.

Our Senses Are Finely Tuned

One of the most striking aspects of our senses is that they are extremely good at detecting the presence of an object or event or a change in an object or event. Some indication of this sensitivity is given in Table 4-1. For five of the senses, we have provided an estimate of the minimal stimulus that they can detect. What is most noticeable about these minimums is how low they are—that is, how sensitive.

absolute threshold
the minimum magnitude of a stimulus that can be reliably discriminated from no stimulus at all

Absolute Thresholds   Suppose that you came across an alien creature and wanted to determine how sensitive it is to light. What would you do? Perhaps the most straightforward thing to do would be to determine the minimum amount of light the creature could detect. This is the key idea behind measuring sensitivity. That is, the most common way to assess the sensitivity of a sensory system is to determine the **absolute threshold,** *the minimum magnitude of a stimulus that can be reliably discriminated from no stimulus at all*—for example, the weakest light that can be reliably discriminated from darkness.

Psychophysical methods are the procedures used to determine absolute thresholds. In one commonly used method, the experimenter first selects a set of stimuli with magnitudes varying around the threshold (for example, a set of dim lights that vary in intensity). The stimuli are presented to a participant one at a time in random order, and the participant is instructed to say "yes" if the stimulus is detected and "no" if it is not. Each stimulus is presented many times, and the percentage of "yes" responses is determined for each stimulus magnitude.

Figure 4-1 is a graph of the percentage of "yes" responses as a function of stimulus magnitude such as light intensity. The data are typical of those obtained in this kind of experiment; the percentage of "yes" responses rises gradually as intensity is increased. The participant detects some stimuli with intensities as low as 3 units, yet occasionally fails to detect some with intensities of 8 units. When performance is characterized by such a graph, psychologists have agreed to define the absolute threshold as the value of the stimulus at which it is detected 50% of the time.

The notion of an absolute threshold is misleading in one respect, though. Such a notion suggests a fixed sensory barrier: Above it, people can detect a stimulus; below it, they cannot. This conception is too simple in that people may experience some random activity in their sensory system even when no stimulus is present. Hence, rather than just reporting whether a stimulus crossed a fixed barrier, participants may have to make a decision about whether their sensory experience is due to a stimulus or to random activity in their sensory systems (Green & Swets, 1966). Still, for our purposes we can continue to talk about thresholds, keeping in mind that subtle decisions may also be involved.

◼︎ Table 4-1 ◼︎

Minimum Stimuli   Approximate minimum stimuli for various senses. (After Galanter, 1962)

Sense	Minimum Stimulus
Vision	A candle flame seen at 30 miles on a dark, clear night
Hearing	The tick of a clock at 20 feet under quiet conditions
Taste	One teaspoon of sugar in 2 gallons of water
Smell	One drop of perfume diffused into the entire volume of six rooms
Touch	The wing of a fly falling on your cheek from a distance of 1 centimeter

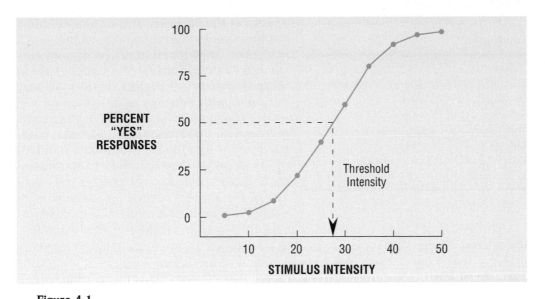

Figure 4-1

Psychophysical Function From a Detection Experiment   Plotted on the vertical axis is the percentage of times the participant responds, "Yes, I detect the stimulus"; on the horizontal axis is the measure of the magnitude of the physical stimulus. Such a graph may be obtained for any stimulus dimension to which an individual is sensitive.

Detecting Changes in Intensity   The world is constantly changing, and being able to spot these changes has obvious survival value. Not surprisingly, psychologists have devoted a good deal of effort to studying our ability to detect changes in intensity.

Just as there must be a certain minimum stimulus before we can perceive anything, so there must be a certain difference between two stimulus magnitudes before we can reliably distinguish one from the other. For instance, two tones must differ in intensity by a certain amount before one is heard as louder than the other; they must also differ in frequency by a certain amount before one is heard as different in pitch from the other. The **difference threshold,** or **just noticeable difference (jnd),** is *the minimum difference in stimulus magnitude or quality necessary to tell two stimuli apart.* Like the absolute threshold, the jnd is defined statistically. Using an experimental method like the one described earlier, the jnd is the amount of change necessary for a participant to detect a difference between two stimuli on 50% of the trials.

An experiment to determine a jnd might proceed as follows. A spot of light (standard) is flashed, and above it another spot of light (increment) is flashed for a shorter duration. The standard spot is the same on every trial, but the increment spot varies in intensity from one trial to the next. The participant responds "yes" or "no" to indicate whether the increment seems more intense than the standard. If the participant can discriminate an intensity of 51 watts in the increment from a standard of 50 watts on half the trials, the jnd is 1 watt under these conditions.

Experiments like this have a long history. In 1834 Ernst Weber, a German physiologist, performed such a study and found that the more intense the stimulus is to begin with, the larger the change must be for the participant to notice it. Finding that a jnd increased with the intensity of the standard, he proposed what is now known as *Weber's law,* which states that the jnd is a constant fraction of stimulus intensity. For example, if a jnd is 1 at an intensity of 50, it will be 2 at 100, 4 at 200, and so forth (the jnd is always 0.02 of the intensity of the standard in this example). This relationship between the intensity of a standard and a jnd may be written as follows:

$$\frac{\ddot{A}I}{I} = k$$

difference threshold or **just noticeable difference (jnd)**   the minimum difference in stimulus magnitude or quality necessary to tell two stimuli apart

Table 4-2

Weber's Constants for Different Senses

Stimulus Dimension	Weber's Constant
Sound frequency	.003
Sound intensity	.15
Light intensity	.01
Odor concentration	.07
Taste concentration	.20
Pressure intensity	.14

where I is the intensity of the standard, $\ddot{A}I$ is the increase in the intensity for a jnd, and k is a constant proportion called *Weber's constant* (0.02 in this case). An example should make this principle clear. Consider a 3-way lightbulb with settings of 50, 100, and 150 watts. The jump from 50 to 100 watts seems greater than that from 100 to 150 watts. Why? Because the first jump starts from a standard of 50 watts while the second starts from a standard of 100 watts, and the greater the intensity of the standard, the bigger the change needed to produce a noticeable difference.

The values of Weber's constants can be used to contrast the sensitivity of different senses. The smaller the constant, the more tuned we are to a change in intensity in that sense. Table 4-2 provides Weber's constants for different senses; it shows, for example, that we are more sensitive to smell than to taste. This means that as you add more spice to a dish you are cooking, you will be able to smell the difference before you can taste it.

Sensory Information Must Be Coded Into Neural Impulses

Now that we know something about the sensitivity of the different senses, we can inquire into the biological bases of sensation.

From Receptors to the Brain   The brain has a formidable problem in sensing the world. Each sense responds to a certain kind of stimulus—light energy for vision, mechanical energy for audition and touch, chemical energy for smell and taste. But the brain understands none of this. It speaks only the language of electrical signals associated with neural discharges. Somehow each sense must achieve **transduction**— that is, it must *translate physical energy into electrical signals* so that these signals can eventually make their way to the brain. Transduction is carried out by specialized cells in the sense organs called *receptors.* The receptors for vision, for instance, are located in a thin layer on the inside of the eye; each visual receptor contains a chemical that reacts to light, and this reaction triggers a series of steps that result in a neural impulse. The receptors for audition are fine hair cells located deep in the ear; the vibrations in the air that are the stimulus for sound succeed in bending these hair cells, which results in a neural impulse. Similar descriptions apply to the other senses.

transduction   the translation of physical energy into electrical signals in the brain

Once it has been activated, a receptor passes its electrical signal to connecting neurons. The signal travels until it reaches its receiving area in the cortex, with different receiving areas for different sensory modalities. Somewhere in the brain—perhaps in the cortical receiving area, perhaps elsewhere in the cortex—the electrical signal results in conscious sensory experience. Thus, when we experience a touch, the experience is "occurring" in our brain, not in our skin. However, the electrical impulses in our brain that directly mediate the experience of touch are themselves caused by electrical impulses in touch receptors located in the skin. Similarly, our experience of a bitter taste occurs in our brain, not in our tongue; but the brain impulses that mediate the taste experience are themselves caused by electrical impulses in taste receptors on the tongue. In this way our receptors play a major role in relating external events to conscious experience. Numerous aspects of our conscious perceptions are caused by specific neural events that occur in the receptors. For these reasons, we emphasize receptor events in our discussion of sensation.

Coding Intensity and Quality   The receptors and their neural pathways to the brain code both the intensity and quality of objects and events in the world. The question is: How do they do this? Researchers who study these coding processes need a way of determining which specific neurons are activated by which specific stimuli. The usual means is to record from single cells in the receptors and neural pathways to the brain while presenting various inputs or stimuli. By such means, one can determine exactly which attributes of a stimulus a particular neuron is responsive to.

A typical single-cell recording experiment is illustrated in Figure 4-2. This is a vision experiment, but the procedure is similar for studying other senses. Before the experiment, the animal (in this case a monkey) has undergone a surgical procedure in which thin wires are inserted into selected areas of its visual cortex. (The surgery, of course, is done under sterile conditions and by surgeons using appropriate anesthesia.) The thin wires are microelectrodes, insulated except at their tips, that can be used to record the electrical activity of the neurons they are in contact with. Once implanted, these microelectrodes cause no pain, and the monkey moves around and lives quite normally. During the experiment itself, the monkey is placed in a testing apparatus and the microelectrodes are connected to recording and amplifying devices. The monkey is then exposed to various visual stimuli. For each stimulus, one can determine which neurons respond to it by seeing which microelectrodes produce sustained signals. Because the electrical signals are tiny, they must be amplified and displayed on an oscilloscope, which converts the electrical signals into a graph of the changing electrical voltage. Most neurons emit a series of nerve impulses that appear on the oscilloscope as vertical spikes. Even in the absence of a stimulus, many cells will respond at a slow rate *(spontaneous activity)*. If a stimulus is presented to which the neuron is sensitive, a fast train of spikes will be seen.

With the aid of single-cell recordings, researchers have learned a good deal about how sensory systems code intensity and quality. The primary means for coding the intensity of a stimulus is in terms of the number of neural impulses in each unit of time—that is, the rate of neural impulses. We can illustrate with touch. If someone lightly touches your arm, a series of electrical impulses will be generated in a nerve fiber. If the pressure is increased, the impulses stay the same in size but increase in number per unit of time. The same story holds for other senses. In general, the greater the intensity of the stimulus, the higher the rate of neural firing and the greater the perceived magnitude of the stimulus.

Another means of coding intensity is by the sheer number of neurons activated; the more intense the stimulus, the more neurons are recruited.

Coding the quality of a stimulus is a more complex matter, and one that will continually crop up in our discussion. The key idea behind coding of quality is due to Johannes Müller, who in 1825 proposed that the brain can distinguish between information coming from different senses—for example, distinguishing lights from sounds—because they involve different sensory nerves (some nerves lead to visual experiences, others to auditory experiences, and so on). Müller's idea of specific nerve energies received support from subsequent research demonstrating that neural pathways originating in different receptors terminate in different areas of the cortex. There is now a good deal of consensus that the

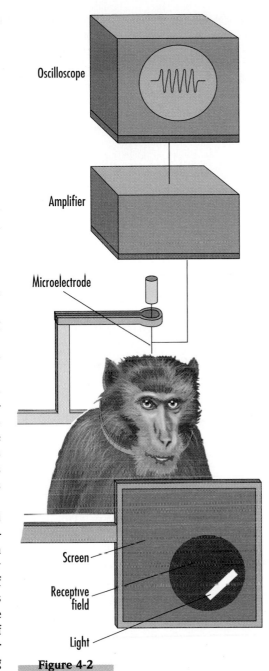

Figure 4-2

Single-Cell Recording An anesthetized monkey is placed in a device that holds its head in a fixed position. A stimulus, often a flashing or moving bar of light, is projected onto the screen. A microelectrode implanted in the visual system of the monkey monitors activity from a single neuron, and this activity is amplified and displayed on an oscilloscope.

brain codes the qualitative differences between senses by the specific neural pathways involved.

But what about the distinguishing qualities *within* a sense? How do we tell red from green or sweet from sour? It is likely that again the coding is based on the specific neurons involved. To illustrate, there is evidence that we distinguish sweet tastes from sour ones by virtue of the fact that each kind of taste has its own nerve fibers. Thus, sweet fibers respond primarily to sweet tastes, sour fibers primarily to sour tastes, and ditto for salty fibers and bitter fibers.

But specificity is not the only plausible coding principle. A sensory system may also use the pattern of neural firing to code the quality of a sensation. While a particular nerve fiber may respond maximally to a sweet taste, it may respond to other tastes as well, but to varying degrees. One fiber may respond best to sweet tastes, less to bitter tastes, and even less to salty tastes; a sweet-tasting stimulus would thus lead to activity in a large number of fibers, with some firing more than others, and this particular pattern of neural activity would be the system's code for sweet. A different pattern across neural fibers would be the code for bitter. As we will see when we discuss the senses in detail, both specificity and patterning are used in coding the quality of a stimulus.

What Do We Know About the Individual Senses?

In this section we present some basic facts about audition, smell, taste, and the skin senses (we leave vision for a more extensive treatment in the next section). For each of the senses that we survey, we first consider what kind of stimulus energy triggers the sense; next we describe the basic physical system involved, with emphasis on how the receptors carry out the transduction process; then we consider how the sense processes information about intensity and quality.

The Nature of Audition

Along with vision, audition—hearing—is our major means of obtaining information about the environment. For most of us it is the primary channel of communication and the vehicle for music. As we will see, it all comes about because small changes in sound pressure can move a membrane in our inner ear back and forth.

Sound Waves Are the Stimuli for Audition   Sound originates from the motion or vibration of an object, as when the wind rushes through the branches of a tree. When something moves, the molecules of air in front of it are pushed together. These molecules push other molecules and then return to their original position. In this way, a wave of pressure changes (a *sound wave*) is transmitted through the air, even though the individual air molecules do not travel far. This wave is analogous to the ripples set up by throwing a stone into a pond.

A sound wave may be described by a graph of air pressure as a function of time. A pressure-versus-time graph of one type of sound is shown in Figure 4-3. The graph depicts a *sine wave* (so called because it corresponds to a sine wave function in mathematics). Sounds that correspond to sine waves are called *pure tones*. Pure tones vary with respect to a couple of aspects that determine how we experience the tone. One aspect is the tone's frequency. The **frequency** of a tone is *the number of cycles per second* (called hertz), which reflects the rate at which the molecules move back and forth. Frequency is the basis of our perception of pitch—and as we will see in a moment, pitch is one of the most noticeable qualities of a sound.

Another aspect of a pure tone is its **intensity,** *the pressure difference between the peak and the trough* in a pressure-versus-time graph. Intensity underlies our sensation of loudness. Sound intensity is usually specified in decibels; an increase of 10 decibels corresponds to a change in sound power of 10 times; 20 decibels, a change

frequency in sound, the number of cycles per second in a pure tone

intensity in sound, the pressure difference between the peak and the trough in a pressure-versus-time graph

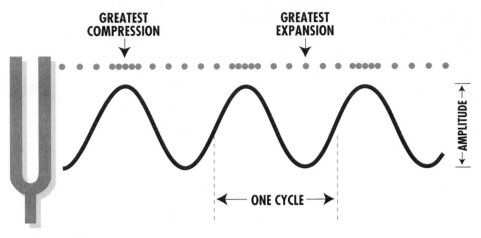

Figure 4-3

A Pure Tone   As the tuning fork vibrates, it produces successive waves of compression and expansion of the air, which correspond to a sine wave. Such a sound is called a pure tone. It can be described by giving its frequency and intensity. If the tuning fork makes 100 vibrations per second, it produces a sound wave with 100 compressions per second and a frequency of 100 hertz. The intensity (or amplitude) of a pure tone is the difference in pressure between the peaks and the troughs. The waveform of any sound can be decomposed into a series of sine waves of different frequencies with various amplitudes and phases. When these sine waves are added together, the result is the original waveform.

of 100 times; 30 decibels, a change of 1,000 times; and so forth. Table 4-3 shows the intensities of some familiar sounds and indicates that some of them are so intense as to endanger our hearing. Note in particular that the sound level at a rock concert is 10,000 times the level necessary to produce deafness, given enough time. (The difference between 80 decibels and 120 decibels is 4 log steps, or 10,000 times.)

Table 4-3

Decibel Ratings and Hazardous Time Exposures of Common Sounds   This table gives the intensities of common sounds in decibels. An increase of 3 decibels corresponds to a doubling of sound power. The sound levels given correspond approximately to the intensities that occur at typical working distances. The right-hand column gives the exposure times at which one risks permanent hearing loss.

Intensities of Some Familiar Sounds		
Decibel Level	Example	Dangerous Time Exposure
0	Lowest sound audible to human ear	—
30	Quiet library, soft whisper	—
40	Quiet office, living room, bedroom away from traffic	—
50	Light traffic at a distance, refrigerator, gentle breeze	—
60	Air conditioner at 20 feet, conversation, sewing machine	—
70	Busy traffic, office tabulator, noisy restaurant (constant exposure)	—
Critical Level Begins		
80	Subway, heavy city traffic, alarm clock at 2 feet, factory noise	More than 8 hours
90	Truck traffic, noisy home appliances, shop tools, lawn mower	Less than 8 hours
100	Chain saw, boiler shop, pneumatic drill	12 hours
120	Rock concert in front of speaker, sandblasting, thunderclap	Immediate danger
140	Gunshot blast, jet plane	Any exposure is dangerous
180	Rocket launching pad	Hearing loss inevitable

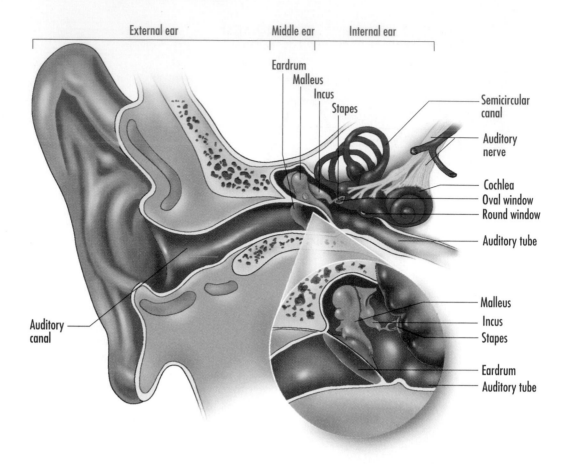

Figure 4-4

A Cross Section of the Ear   This drawing shows the overall structure of the ear. The inner ear includes the cochlea, which contains the auditory receptors, and the vestibular apparatus (semicircular canals and vestibular sacs), which is the sense organ for our sense of balance and body motion.

The Auditory System   The auditory system consists of the ears, parts of the brain, and the various connecting neural pathways. Our primary concern will be with the ears, including not just the appendages on the sides of the head but the entire hearing organ, most of which lies within the skull (see Figure 4-4).

The ear contains two systems. One system amplifies and transmits the sound to the receptors, whereupon the other system takes over and transduces sound into neural impulses. The *transmission system* involves the outer ear, which consists of the external ear along with the *auditory canal,* and the middle ear, which consists of the *eardrum* and a chain of three bones. The *transduction system* is housed in a part of the inner ear called the *cochlea,* which contains the receptors for sound.

Let us take a more detailed look at the transmission system (see Figure 4-4 again). The outer ear aids in the collection of sound and funnels it through the auditory canal to a taut membrane, the *eardrum.* The eardrum is the outermost part of the middle ear. It is caused to vibrate by sound waves funneled to it through the auditory canal. The middle ear's job is to transmit these vibrations of the eardrum across an air-filled cavity to another membrane, the *oval window,* which is the gateway to the inner ear and the receptors. The middle ear accomplishes this transmission by means of a mechanical bridge of three tiny bones. This mechanical arrangement not only transmits the sound wave but greatly amplifies it as well.

Now consider the transduction system. The cochlea is a coiled tube of bone. It is divided into sections of fluid by membranes, one of which, the *basilar membrane,* sup-

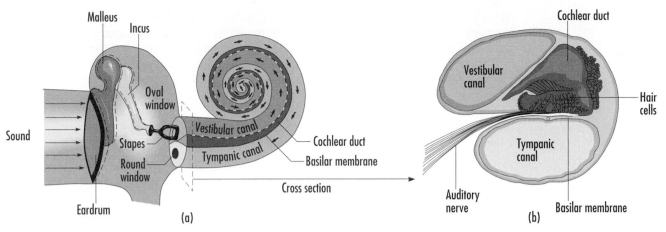

Figure 4-5

A Schematic Diagram of the Middle and Inner Ear   (a) Movement of the fluid within the cochlea deforms the basilar membrane and stimulates the hair cells that serve as the auditory receptors. (b) A cross section of the cochlea showing the basilar membrane and the hair cell receptors.

ports the auditory receptors (see Figure 4-5). The receptors are called *hair cells* because they have hairlike structures that extend into the fluid. Pressure at the oval window (which connects the middle ear and the inner ear) leads to pressure changes in the cochlear fluid, which in turn causes the basilar membrane to vibrate, resulting in a bending of the hair cells and an electrical impulse. Through this complex process a sound wave is transduced into an electrical impulse. The neurons that synapse with the hair cells have long axons that form part of the auditory nerve. The auditory pathway from each ear goes to both sides of the brain and has synapses in several nuclei before reaching the auditory cortex.

How We Hear Sound Intensity and Quality (Pitch)   We are more sensitive to sounds of intermediate frequency than we are to sounds near either end of our frequency range. This is illustrated in Figure 4-6, which shows the absolute threshold for sound intensity as a function of frequency. Many people have some deficit in hearing and consequently have a higher threshold than those shown in Figure 4-6. There are two basic kinds of hearing deficits. In one, thresholds are elevated roughly equally at all frequencies as a result of poor conduction in the middle ear *(conduction loss)*. In the other kind of hearing loss, the threshold elevation is unequal, with large elevations occurring at higher frequencies. This pattern is usually a consequence of inner-ear damage, often involving some destruction of the hair cells *(sensory-neural loss)*. Once they have been destroyed, hair cells do not regenerate.

Sensory-neural loss occurs in many older people. That is why the elderly often have trouble hearing high-pitched sounds. Sensory-neural loss is not reserved for the elderly, though. It occurs in young people who are exposed to excessively loud sound. Rock musicians, airport runway crews, and pneumatic drill operators commonly suffer major,

Figure 4-6

Absolute Threshold for Hearing   The lower curve shows the absolute intensity threshold at different frequencies. Sensitivity is greatest in the vicinity of 1,000 hertz. The upper curve describes the threshold for pain. (Data are approximate, from various determinations.)

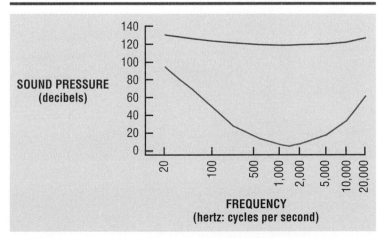

permanent hearing loss. For example, Pete Townsend, the well-known guitarist of the rock group The Who, suffered severe sensory-neural loss because of his continuous exposure to loud rock music; he has since alerted many people to this danger.

When hearing a pure tone, we experience not only its loudness but also its pitch. **Pitch** is *the prime quality of sound, ordered on a scale from low to high*. It is determined by the sound's frequency. As frequency increases, pitch increases. We are very good at discriminating among sounds of different frequencies. Young adults can hear frequencies between 20 and 20,000 hertz (cycles per second), with the jnd less than 1 hertz at 100 hertz and increasing to 100 hertz at 10,000 hertz.

pitch the prime quality of sound, ordered on a scale from low to high

Theories of Pitch Perception   How do our receptors turn frequency information into pitch? One major theory holds that frequency is coded into pitch by *resonance* (Green & Wier, 1984). To appreciate this idea, it is helpful to first consider a familiar example of resonance. When a tuning fork is struck near a piano, the piano string that is tuned to the frequency of the fork will begin to vibrate. To say that the ear works the same way is to say that the ear contains a structure like a stringed instrument, with different parts of this structure tuned to different frequencies, so that when a frequency is presented to the ear, the corresponding part of the structure vibrates. This idea is roughly correct. The structure involved is the basilar membrane, and the *place theory* of pitch perception holds that each specific place along the basilar membrane will, when it responds, lead to the sensation of a particular pitch. The place of maximum movement depends on the specific frequency sounded. High frequencies cause vibration at the near end of the basilar membrane; as frequency increases, the vibration pattern moves toward the oval window (Bekésy, 1960). Note that place theory does not imply that we hear with our basilar membrane; rather, the places on the membrane that vibrate most determine what neural fibers are activated, and that determines the pitch we hear. This is an example of a sensory system coding quality by the specific nerves involved.

The Nature of Smell

Smell is one of the most primitive, yet most important, of the senses. The sense organ for smell has a position of prominence in the head appropriate to a sense intended to guide the organism. Smell has a more direct route to the brain than any other sense: The receptors, which are in the nasal cavity, are connected to the brain without synapse. Moreover, unlike the receptors for audition, the receptors for smell are exposed directly to the environment—they are right there in the nasal cavity, with no protective shield in front of them. (In contrast, the receptors for audition are protected by the outer and middle ears.)

Smell (or *olfaction*) aids in the survival of our species; it is needed for the detection of spoiled food or escaping gas, and loss of smell can lead to a dulled appetite. Still, smell is even more essential for the survival of many other animals. Not surprisingly, therefore, a larger area of the cortex is devoted to smell in other species than in our own. In fish, the olfactory cortex takes up almost all of the cerebral hemispheres; in dogs, about one-third; in humans, only about one-twentieth. These differences are related to differences in sensitivity. Taking advantage of the superior smell capability of dogs, both the U.S. Postal

Dogs are far more sensitive to smells than humans, and for this reason they are often used in police work, search-and-rescue operations, and drug and bomb detection, as well as hunting.

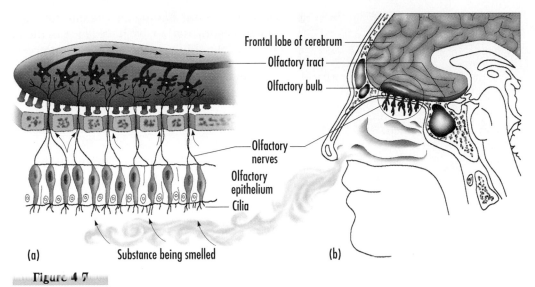

Frontal lobe of cerebrum
Olfactory tract
Olfactory bulb
Olfactory nerves
Olfactory epithelium
Cilia

(a)   Substance being smelled   (b)

Figure 4-7

Olfactory Receptors   (a) Detail of a receptor interspersed among numerous supporting cells. (b) The placement of the olfactory receptors in the nasal cavity.

Service and the Bureau of Customs have trained them to check unopened packages for heroin. Specially trained police dogs can sniff out hidden explosives.

Because smell is so well developed in other species, it is often used as a major means of communication. Insects and some higher animals secrete **pheromones,** *chemicals that float through the air to be sniffed by other members of the species.* For example, a female moth can release a pheromone so powerful that males are drawn to her from a distance of several miles. Do we humans have a remnant of this primitive communication system? There is evidence that we do, and that we may communicate subtle matters by means of odor. Women who live or work together seem to communicate where they are in their menstrual cycle by means of smell, and over time this results in a tendency for their menstrual cycles to synchronize and begin at the same time (McClintock,1971; Russel, Switz, & Thompson, 1980).

pheromones chemicals that float through the air to be sniffed by other members of the species

The Olfactory System   The volatile molecules given off by a substance (odorant) are the stimulus for smell. The molecules leave the substance, travel through the air, and enter the nasal passage (see Figure 4-7). The olfactory system consists of the receptors in the nasal passage, certain regions of the brain, and interconnecting neural pathways. The receptors for smell are located high in the nasal cavity. When the *cilia* (hairlike structures) of these receptors are contacted by molecules of odorant, an electrical impulse results; this is the transduction process. This impulse travels along nerve fibers to the *olfactory bulb,* a region of the brain that lies just below the frontal lobes. The olfactory bulb in turn is connected to the olfactory cortex on the inside of the temporal lobes. Interestingly, there are direct connections between the olfactory bulb and the part of the brain involved in the formation of long-term memories—the hippocampus—and a part of the brain involved in emotional experience—the amygdala. These connections may explain why a distinctive smell is a powerful cue for remembering both the content of a previous event and the emotional experience of that event (Herz & Cupchik, 1995).

How We Sense Intensity and Quality   Human sensitivity to the intensity of a smell depends greatly on the substance involved. Absolute thresholds can be as low as 1 part per 50 billion parts of air. Still, as noted earlier, we are far less sensitive to smell than other species. Dogs, for example, can detect substances at 0.01 the concentration necessary for human detection (Moulton, 1977). Our relative lack of sensitivity

Humans vary in their sensitivity to different tastes. Some people, like this coffee taster, are able to discriminate among very subtle differences in the tastes of particular substances.

is not due to our having less sensitive olfactory receptors. Rather, we have fewer of them: roughly 10 million receptors for people versus 1 billion for dogs.

Although we rely less on smell than other species do, we are capable of sensing many different qualities of odor. Estimates vary, but a healthy person appears to be able to distinguish among 10,000 to 40,000 different odors, with women generally doing better than men (Cain, 1988). Professional perfumers and whiskey blenders can probably do even better—perhaps discriminating among 100,000 odors (Dobb, 1991). Moreover, we know something about how the olfactory system codes the quality of odors at the biological level. Many kinds of receptors seem to be involved; an estimate of 1,000 kinds of olfactory receptors is not unreasonable in light of recent research (Buck & Axel, 1991). Rather than coding a specific odor, each kind of receptor may respond to many different odors (Matthews, 1972). So quality may be coded partly by the pattern of neural activity even in this receptor-rich sensory modality.

The Nature of Taste

Taste gets credit for a lot of experiences that it does not provide. We say that a meal "tastes" good; but when smell is eliminated by a bad cold, our food becomes far less tasty and we may have trouble telling red wine from vinegar. Still, taste (or *gustation*) is a sense in its own right. Even with a bad cold, we can tell salted from unsalted food.

The Gustatory System   The stimulus for taste is a substance that is soluble in saliva, which is a fluid much like salt water. The gustatory system includes receptors that are located on the tongue as well as on the throat and the roof of the mouth; the system also includes parts of the brain and interconnecting neural pathways. In what follows, we focus on the receptors on the tongue. These taste receptors occur in clusters, called *taste buds,* on the bumps of the tongue and around the mouth. At the ends of the taste buds are short, hairlike structures that extend outward and make contact with the solutions in the mouth. This contact results in an electrical impulse; this is the transduction process. The electrical impulse then travels to the brain.

How We Sense Intensity and Quality   Sensitivity to different taste stimuli varies from place to place on the tongue. While any substance can be detected at almost any place on the tongue (except the center), different tastes are best detected in different regions. Sensitivity to salty and sweet substances is best near the front of the tongue; sour is best along the sides; and bitter is best on the soft palate (see Figure 4-8). In the center of the tongue is a region that is insensitive to taste (this is the place to put an unpleasant pill). While absolute thresholds for taste are generally very low, jnds for intensity are relatively high. If you are increasing the amount of spice in a dish, you usually must add more than 20% or you will not taste the difference.

There is an agreed-upon vocabulary for describing tastes. Any taste can be described as one or a combination of the four basic taste qualities: sweet, sour, salty, and bitter (McBurney, 1978). These

Figure 4-8

Taste Areas   Although any substance can be detected anywhere on the tongue—except in the center—different areas are maximally sensitive to different tastes. Thus, the area labeled "sweet" is most sensitive to sweet tastes.

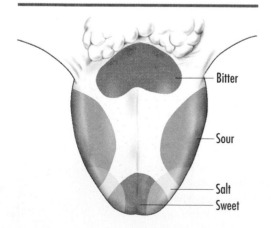

Bitter

Sour

Salt

Sweet

four tastes are best revealed in sucrose (sweet), hydrochloric acid (sour), sodium chloride (salty), and quinine (bitter). When people are asked to describe the tastes of various substances in terms of just the four basic tastes, they have no trouble doing this; even if they are given the option of using additional qualities of their own choosing, they tend to stay with the four basic tastes (Goldstein, 1989).

The gustatory system codes taste in terms of both the specific nerve fibers activated and the pattern of activation across nerve fibers. There appear to be four types of nerve fibers corresponding to the four basic tastes. While each fiber responds somewhat to all four basic tastes, it responds best to just one of them. Hence, it makes sense to talk of "salty fibers," whose activity signals saltiness to the brain. Thus, there is a remarkable correspondence between our subjective experience of taste and its neural coding.

The Nature of the Skin Senses

Traditionally, touch was thought to be a single sense. Today, it is considered to include three distinct skin senses, one responding to pressure, another to temperature, and the third to pain.

Pressure   The stimulus for the sensation of pressure is physical pressure on the skin. Although we are not aware of steady pressure on the entire body (such as air pressure), we can discriminate among variations in pressure over the body surface. Some parts of the body are more effective than others at sensing the intensity of pressure; the lips, nose, and cheek are most sensitive to pressure, while the big toe is least sensitive. These differences are closely related to the number of receptors that respond to the stimulus at each of these locations. However, like other sensory systems, the pressure system shows profound adaptation effects. If you hold a friend's hand for several minutes without moving, you will become insensitive to it and cease to feel it.

Temperature   The stimulus for the sensation of temperature is the temperature of the skin. The receptors are neurons with free nerve endings just under the skin. In the transduction stage, *cold receptors* generate a neural impulse when there is a decrease in skin temperature, while *warm receptors* generate an impulse when there is an increase in skin temperature (Duclauz & Kenshalo, 1980; Hensel, 1973). Hence, different qualities of temperature can be coded primarily by the specific receptors activated. However, this specificity of neural reaction has its limits. Cold receptors respond not only to low temperatures but also to very high temperatures (above 45 degrees centigrade). Consequently, a very hot stimulus will activate both warm and cold receptors, which in turn evoke a hot sensation.

Because maintaining body temperature is crucial to our survival, it is important that we can sense small changes in our skin temperature. When the skin is at its normal temperature, we can detect a warming of only 0.45 degrees centigrade and a cooling of just 0.15 degrees centigrade (Kenshalo,

After being in a swimming pool for a while, our temperature sense adapts to the change in temperature. However, when first dangling a foot into the water we can detect the cooler temperature.

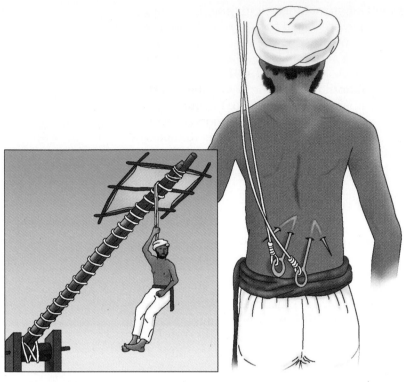

Figure 4-9

Culture and Pain   Right: Two steel hooks are inserted in the back of the celebrant in the Indian hook-swinging ceremony. Left: The celebrant hangs onto the ropes as a cart takes him from village to village. As he blesses the village children and crops, he swings freely suspended by the hooks in his back. (After Kosambi, 1967)

Nafe, & Brooks, 1961). Our temperature sense adapts completely to moderate changes in temperature, so that after a few minutes the stimulus feels neither cool nor warm. This adaptation explains the strong difference of opinion about the temperature of a swimming pool between those who have been in it for a while and those first dipping a toe in it.

Pain   Of all our senses, none captures our attention like pain. We may sometimes be blasé about the other sensations, but it is hard to ignore the sensation of pain. Yet for all the discomfort it causes, we would be at risk if we had no sense of pain. It would be difficult for children to learn not to touch a hot stove or to stop chewing their tongues. In fact, some people are born with a rare genetic disorder that makes them insensitive to pain; they typically die young, from tissue deterioration resulting from wounds that could have been avoided if they had a sense of pain.

Any stimulus that is intense enough to cause tissue damage is a stimulus for pain. It may be pressure, temperature, electric shock, or irritant chemicals. The effect of such a stimulus is to cause the release of chemical substances in the skin, which in turn stimulate receptors (the transduction stage); the receptors are neurons with specialized free nerve endings (Brown & Deffenbacher, 1979).

More than any other sensation, the intensity and quality of pain is influenced by factors other than the immediate stimulus. These factors include the person's culture, expectations, and previous experience. The striking influence of culture is illustrated by the fact that some non-Western societies engage in rituals that seem unbearably painful to Westerners. A case in point is the hook-swinging ceremony practiced in some parts of India:

> The ceremony derives from an ancient practice in which a member of a social group is chosen to represent the power of the gods. The role of the chosen man (or "celebrant") is to bless the children and crops in a series of neighboring villages during a particular period of the year. What is remarkable about the ritual is that steel hooks, which are attached by strong ropes to the top of a special cart, are shoved under his skin and muscles on both sides of his back [see Figure 4-9]. The cart is then moved from village to village. Usually the man hangs on to the ropes as the cart is moved about. But at the climax of the ceremony in each village, he swings free, hanging only from the hooks embedded in his back, to bless the children and crops. Astonishingly, there is no evidence that the man is in pain during the ritual; rather, he appears to be in a "state of exaltation." When the hooks are later removed, wounds heal rapidly without any medical treatment other than the application of wood ash. Two weeks later the marks on his back are scarcely visible (Melzak, 1973).

Clearly, pain is more than a matter of sensory receptors.

Phenomena like this have led to the *gate control theory* of pain (Melzak & Wall, 1965, 1982). According to the theory, the sensation of pain requires not only that

Ending Pain in an Arm That No Longer Exists

Derek Steen lost his left arm as a result of a motorcycle crash that tore all the nerves that attached the arm to his spine. The arm was hopelessly paralyzed, and a year later it was amputated. But Steen experienced a phenomenon that has been reported by many amputees, known as the "phantom limb." He had the sensation that the missing arm was pressing against his body, and it ached horribly.

Pain or discomfort in a phantom limb is exceedingly difficult to treat. After an amputation the brain modifies its sensory maps. The region mapping a missing arm no longer receives inputs from the arm, but it does receive stimuli from adjacent body parts, and these stimuli fool the brain into thinking that the arm is still there.

Vilayanus S. Ramachandran, a professor of neuroscience at the University of California at San Diego, began wondering why Steen was experiencing the phantom limb sensation even though the arm had been paralyzed prior to the amputation. He concluded that in the first few weeks after the accident, Steen had developed "learned paralysis"; his brain kept sending signals to the arm, commanding it to move, but although he could see that the arm was there, it did not move. "His brain constantly got information that his arm was not moving, even though it was there," Ramachandran comments.

If paralysis can be learned, is it possible that it can be unlearned? Ramachandran decided to test this idea. Like a magician, he "did it with mirrors." He built a box without a front or a lid and placed a vertical mirror in the middle of it. By placing his right arm in the box, Steen could see a mirror image of his missing left arm.

"I asked him to make symmetric movements with both hands, as if he were conducting an orchestra," Ramachandran said. "He started jumping up and down and said, 'Oh, my God, my wrist is moving, my elbow is moving!'" But when asked to close his eyes, Steen groaned and said. "Oh, no, it's frozen again."

Ramachandran told Steen to take the box home with him and play around with it. Three weeks later Steen called him and said, "Doctor, it's gone!"

According to Ramachandran, the reason the phantom limb pain disappeared probably has to do with tremendous sensory conflict. "His vision was telling him that his arm had come back and was obeying his commands. But he was not getting feedback from the muscles in his arm. Faced with this type of conflict over a protracted period, the brain says: 'This doesn't make sense. I won't have anything to do with it.'"

Ramachandran emphasizes that his technique needs to be tested further and that his conclusions are speculative. But he has succeeded in treating patients with other kinds of phantom limb pain. These results, along with similar findings in other areas of neuroscience, make it abundantly clear that an individual's perceptions can be quite different from the actual stimuli received from the sensory systems (Ramachandran & Blakeslee, 1998).

---

pain receptors on the skin be active but also that a "neural gate" in the spinal cord be open and allow the signals from the pain receptors to pass to the brain (the gate closes when critical fibers in the spinal cord are activated). Because the neural gate can be closed by signals sent down from the cortex, the perceived intensity of pain can be reduced by the individual's mental state, as in the hook-swinging ceremony. What exactly is the "neural gate"? It appears to involve a region of the midbrain called the *periaqueductal gray,* or PAG for short; neurons in the PAG are connected to other neurons, which inhibit cells that would normally carry the pain signals arising in the pain receptors (Jesell & Kelly, 1991). So when the PAG neurons are active, the gate is closed; when the PAG neurons are not active, the gate is open.

Interestingly, the PAG appears to be the main place where strong painkillers like morphine affect neural processing. Morphine is known to increase neural activity in the PAG, which should result in a closing of the neural gate. Moreover, the body produces certain chemicals, called *endorphins,* that act like morphine to reduce pain, and these chemicals too are believed to have their effect by acting on the PAG in such a way as to close the neural gate.

At the psychological level, then, we have evidence that drugs, cultural beliefs, and various nonstandard medicinal practices can dramatically reduce pain. All of these factors, though, may have a common locus at the biological level. This is another case in which research at the biological level may actually unify findings at the psychological level.

Thinking Critically

How would your life change if you did not have a sense of pain? How would it change if you did not have a sense of smell? Which do you think would be worse, and why?

What Is the Basis of Vision?

Only vision, audition, and smell are capable of obtaining information that is at a distance from us (and often vital to our survival); of this group, vision is the most finely tuned sense in the human species. In discussing vision, we proceed as we did with the other senses: First we consider the nature of the stimulus energy to which vision is sensitive; next we describe the visual system, with particular emphasis on how its receptors carry out the transduction process; and then we consider how the visual system processes information about intensity and quality.

Light Is the Stimulus for Vision

Each sense responds to a particular form of physical energy, and for vision the physical stimulus is light. Light is *electromagnetic radiation,* a kind of energy that emanates from the sun and the rest of the universe, and that constantly bathes our planet. Electromagnetic energy travels in waves and includes not only visible light but also cosmic rays, X rays, ultraviolet and infrared rays, and radio and television waves. Our eyes are sensitive to only a tiny bit of this continuum—wavelengths of approximately 350 to 750 nanometers—which we call *visible light.*

The Visual System

The human visual system consists of the eyes, several parts of the brain, and the pathways connecting them. (Go back to Chapter 2, Figure 2-11, for a simplified illustration of the visual system.) Our primary concern here will be with the inner workings of the eyes. The eye contains two systems, one for forming the image and the other for transducing the image into electrical impulses. The critical parts of these systems are illustrated in Figure 4-10.

The image-forming system works something like a camera. Its function is to focus light reflected from objects so as to form an image of the object on the *retina,* a thin layer at the back of the eyeball (see Figure 4-11). The image-forming system itself consists of the cornea, the pupil, and the lens. Without them, we could see light but not pattern. The *cornea* is the transparent front surface of the eye; light enters here, and rays are bent inward by it to begin image formation. The *lens* completes the process of focusing the light on the retina. To focus objects at different distances, the lens changes shape. It becomes more spherical for near objects and flatter for far ones. In some eyes, the lens does not become flat enough to bring far objects into focus, although it focuses near objects well; people with such eyes are said to be *myopic* (nearsighted). In other eyes, the lens does not become spherical enough to focus on near objects, although it focuses well on far objects; people with such eyes are said to be *hyperopic* (farsighted). Such optical defects are common and can easily be corrected with eyeglasses or contact lenses. The *pupil,* the third

Figure 4-10

Top View of the Right Eye   Light entering the eye on its way to the retina passes through the cornea, the aqueous humor, the lens, and the vitreous humor. The amount of light entering the eye is regulated by the size of the pupil, a small hole toward the front of the eye formed by the iris. The iris consists of a ring of muscles that can contract or relax, thereby controlling pupil size. The iris gives the eyes their characteristic color (blue, brown, and so forth).

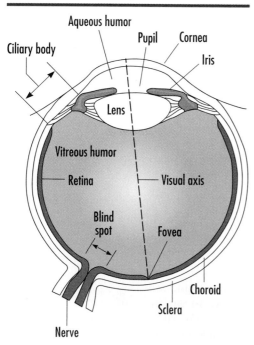

component of the image-forming system, is a circular opening that varies in diameter in response to the light level. It is largest in dim light and smallest in bright light, thereby ensuring enough light to maintain image quality at different light levels.

The image-forming system serves to focus the image on the back of the eyeball, on the retina. There the transduction system takes over. The heart of the system is the receptors. There are two types of receptor cells, *rods* and *cones*, so called because of their distinctive shapes (see Figure 4-12). The two kinds of receptors are specialized for different purposes. Rods are designed for seeing at night; they operate at low intensities and lead to colorless sensations. Cones are best for seeing during the day; they respond to high intensities and result in sensations of color.

When we want to see the details of an object, we routinely move our eyes so that the object projects onto a region in the center of the retina called the *fovea*. We do this because the receptors are plentiful and closely packed in the fovea; outside the fovea, in the *periphery*, there are fewer receptors.

When light reflected from an object has made contact with a receptor cell, how does the receptor transduce the light into electrical impulses? The rods and cones contain chemicals called *photopigments* that absorb light. The absorption of light by the photopigments starts a process that results in a neural impulse. Once this transduction step is completed, the electrical impulses must make their way to the brain via connecting neurons. The responses of the rods and cones are first transmitted to *bipolar cells* and then from bipolar cells to other neurons called *ganglion cells* (refer again to Figure 4-12). The long axons of the ganglion cells extend out of the eye to form the *optic nerve* to the brain. At the place where the optic nerve leaves the eye, there are no receptors; we are blind to a stimulus in this region. We do not notice this partial blindness—this hole or "blind spot" in our visual field—because the brain automatically fills it in (Ramachandran & Gregory, 1991).

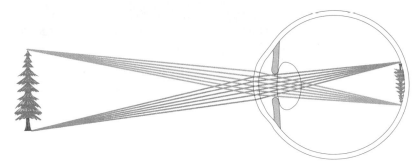

Figure 4-11

Image Formation in the Eye   Each point on an object sends out light rays in all directions, but only some of these rays actually enter the eye. Light rays from the same point on an object pass through different places on the lens. If a sharp image is to be formed, these different rays have to be brought back together (converge) at a single point on the retina. For each point on the object, there will be a matching point in the retinal image. Note that the retinal image is inverted and is generally much smaller than the actual object. Note also that most of the bending of light rays occurs in the cornea.

Figure 4-12

A Schematic Picture of the Retina   This is a schematic drawing of the retina based on an examination with an electron microscope. The bipolar cells receive signals from one or more receptors and transmit those signals to the ganglion cells, whose axons form the optic nerve. Note that there are several types of bipolar and ganglion cells. There are also sideways or lateral connections in the retina. Neurons called horizontal cells make lateral connections at a level near the receptors; neurons called amacrine cells make lateral connections at a level near the ganglion cells. (After Dowling & Boycott, 1966)

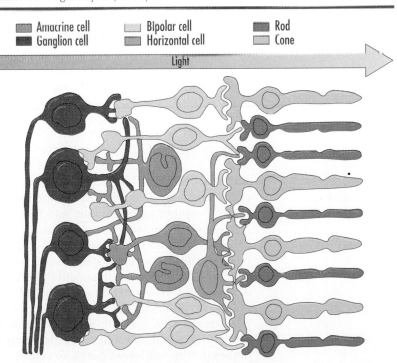

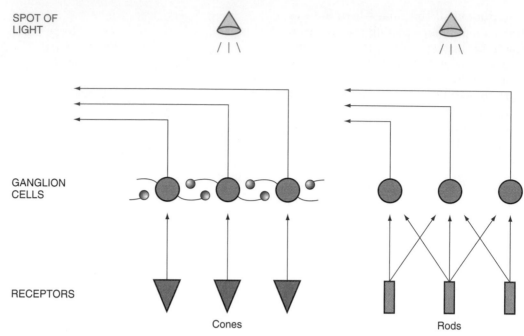

SPOT OF LIGHT

GANGLION CELLS

RECEPTORS

Cones   Rods

Figure 4-13

How Cones and Rods Connect to Ganglion Cells   This diagram shows a single spot of light shining onto a cone and a rod. To simplify matters, we have omitted several other types of cells located between receptors and ganglion cells. Arrows represent a signal to increase neuronal firing. Dots represent a signal to decrease neuronal firing. The long arrows emanating from the ganglion cells are axons that become part of the optic nerve.

How We See Light

Sensitivity and Acuity   Our sensitivity to a light's intensity is determined by the rods and cones. There is a critical difference between rods and cones that explains a number of phenomena involving perceived intensity, or *brightness*. On average, more rods than cones connect to a single ganglion cell; rod-based ganglion cells therefore receive more inputs than cone-based ones. As a result, vision is more sensitive when based on rods than on cones. Exactly how this comes about it illustrated in Figure 4-13. The left side of the figure shows three adjacent cones, each of which is connected (indirectly) to a single ganglion cell; the right side contains three adjacent rods, all of which are connected (indirectly) to the same ganglion cell. To see the implication of these differences in the "wiring" of cones and rods, suppose that three very dim adjacent spots of light are presented to either the rods or the cones. When presented to the cones, each spot of light may be too weak to lead to a neural impulse in its associated receptor, and consequently no neural response will occur in the ganglion cell. But when these dim spots are presented to the rods, the activation from the three receptors can combine, and the sum may be strong enough to lead to a neural response in the ganglion cell. Thus, connecting multiple rods to a single ganglion cell allows for a convergence of neural activation, and this convergence is why rod-based vision is more sensitive than cone-based vision.

But this advantage in sensitivity comes at a price—namely, that rod-based vision is less acute than cone-based vision (acuity is our ability to see details). Look again at the two diagrams in Figure 4-13, but now suppose that the three adjacent spots of light are relatively bright. When presented to the cones, each spot of a light may lead to a neural response in its associated receptor, which in turn will lead to neural impulses in three different ganglion cells; these three messages will be sent to the brain, and the system will therefore have a way of knowing that there are three different things out there. In contrast, when the three adjacent bright spots of light are presented to the rods, the neural activation in each receptor again converges with that in the others, leading to the activation of a single ganglion cell; hence, only one message is sent to the brain, and the system has no way of knowing that there is more than one thing out there. In short, the way receptors connect to ganglion cells explains the differences between rods and cones in sensitivity and acuity.

Light Adaptation   Thus far we have emphasized that we are sensitive to changes in stimuli. The other side of the coin is that if a stimulus does not change we adapt to it. A good example of light adaptation occurs when you enter a dark movie theater from a bright street. At first you can see hardly anything in the dim light reflected from the screen. However, in a few minutes you are able to see well enough to find a seat. Eventually you are able to recognize faces in the dim light. When you reenter the bright street, almost everything will seem painfully bright at first and it will be impossible to discriminate among these bright lights. Everything will look normal in less than a minute, though, because adaptation to this higher light level is rapid. The rod system takes much longer to adapt, but it is sensitive to much dimmer lights.

How We See Color

All light is alike except for wavelength. Our visual system does something wonderful with wavelength—it turns it into color, with different wavelengths resulting in different colors. For example, *short-wavelength* lights (450 to 500 nanometers) appear blue; *medium-wavelength* lights, (roughly 500 to 570 nanometers) appear green; and *long-wavelength* lights, (about 620 to 700 nanometers) appear red (see Figure 4-14). In what follows, our discussion of color perception considers only wavelength. This is adequate for cases in which the origin of a color sensation is an object that emits light, such as the sun or a lightbulb. Usually, however, the origin of a color sensation is an object that reflects light when a light source illuminates it. In these cases our perception of the object's color is determined partly by the wavelengths the object reflects and partly by other factors, particularly the characteristic color of the object. Thus, we tend to see a rose as red even when it is illuminated by yellow-green light.

The Appearance of Color   Seeing color is in some ways a subjective experience. But to study color scientifically we have to use the same terms to describe it. Consider a spot of light seen against a dark background. From a phenomenological standpoint it can be described by three dimensions: lightness, hue, and saturation. **Lightness** refers to *how white a light appears*. **Hue** refers to *the quality described by the color*

lightness how white a light appears

hue the quality of light described by a color name

Figure 4-14

The Solar Spectrum   The numbers given are the wavelengths of the various colors in nanometers (nm).

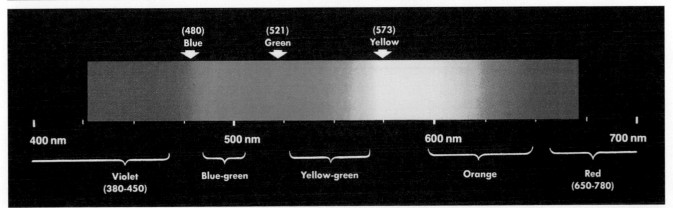

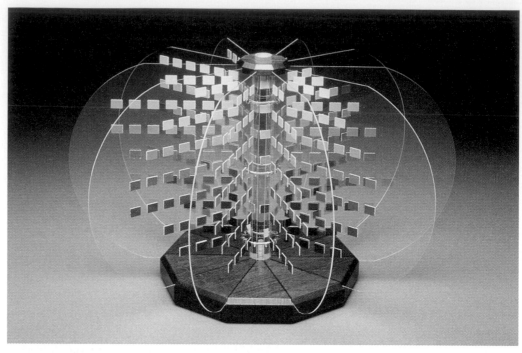

Figure 4-15

The Color Solid   The three dimensions of color can be represented on a double cone. Hue is represented by points around the circumference, saturation by points along the radius, and brightness by points on the vertical axis. A vertical slice taken from the color solid will show differences in the saturation and lightness of a single hue.

saturation   the color-fulness or purity of light

name, such as red or greenish-yellow. **Saturation** means *the colorfulness or purity of the light;* unsaturated colors, such as pink, appear pale, whereas saturated colors appear to contain no white. Albert Munsell, an artist, proposed a scheme for specifying colored surfaces by assigning them one of ten hue names and two numbers, one indicating saturation and the other brightness. The colors in the Munsell system are represented by the color solid (see Figure 4-15). (The key characteristics of color and sound are summarized in Table 4-4.)

How many colors are we capable of seeing? We can discriminate among 150 hues, suggesting we can distinguish among about 150 wavelengths. Given that each of the 150 discriminable colors can have many different values of lightness and many different values of saturation, the estimated number of colors that we can discriminate among is more than 7 million, and we have names for about 7,500 of them (Goldstein, 1989; Judd & Kelly, 1965).

Table 4-4

The Physics and Psychology of Light and Sound

Stimulus	Physical Attribute	Measurement Unit	Psychological Experience
Light	Wavelength	Nanometers	Hue
	Intensity	Photons	Brightness
	Purity	Level of Gray	Saturation
Sound	Frequency	Hertz	Pitch
	Amplitude	Decibels	Loudness
	Complexity	Harmonics	Timbre

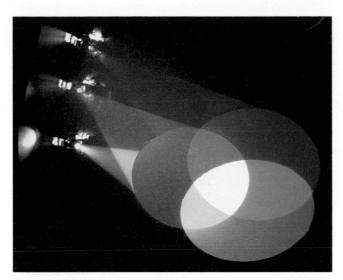

Figure 4-16

Additive and Subtractive Color Mixtures   Additive color mixture (illustrated by the figure on the left) combines lights. Red and green lights are mixed to appear yellow; green and purple appear blue; and so on. In the center where the three colors overlap, the mixture appears white.

Subtractive color mixture (illustrated in the figure at the right) takes place when pigments are mixed or when light is transmitted through colored filters placed one over another. Usually, blue-green and yellow will mix to give green, and complementary colors such as blue and yellow will combine to appear black.

Color Mixture   Remarkably, all the hues that we can discriminate among can be generated by mixing together just a few basic colors. Suppose that we project different-colored lights to the same region of the retina. The result of this light mixture will be a new color. For example, a mixture of red and green lights in the proper proportion will look yellow. Note that we are referring to mixing lights, called an *additive* mixture; we are not referring to mixing paints or pigments, a *subtractive* mixture (see Figure 4-16). In general, *three wavelengths of light can be combined to match almost any color* of light as long as one is drawn from the long-wave end of the spectrum (red), another is drawn from the middle (green or green-yellow), and the third is from the short end (blue or violet). This finding is sometimes referred to as the *three primaries law.*

To illustrate the three primaries law, a participant in an experiment on color matching might be asked to match the color of a test light by mixing together three other colored lights. As long as the three mixture lights are drawn from the three parts of the spectrum, the participant will always be able to match the test light. The participant will not, however, be able to match any test light if he or she is provided with only two mixture lights—for example, the 450- and 640-nanometer lights. The number three, therefore, is significant. Because some lights that are grossly different physically look identical to humans, we have to conclude that we are blind to the differences. Without this blindness, color reproduction would be impossible. Realistic color reproduction in television or photography relies on the fact that a wide range of colors can be produced by mixing just a few colors. For example, if you examine the picture on your television screen with a magnifying glass you will find that it is composed of tiny dots of only three colors (blue, green, and red). Additive color mixture occurs because the dots are so close together that their images on your retina overlap.

Color Deficiency   While most people match a wide range of colors with a mixture of three primaries, other people can match a wide range of colors by using mixtures

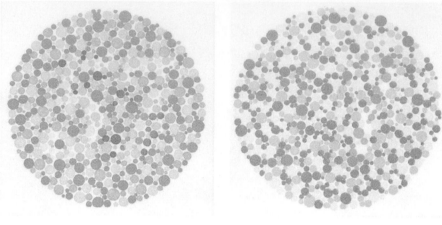

Figure 4-17

Testing for Color Blindness   Two plates used in color blindness tests. In the left plate, individuals with certain kinds of red-green blindness will see only the number 5; others see only the 7; still others, no number at all. Similarly, in the right plate, people with normal vision will see the number 15, whereas those with red-green blindness see no number at all.

of only two primaries. Such people, referred to as *dichromats,* have deficient color vision, as they confuse some colors that people with normal vision *(trichromats)* can distinguish. But dichromats can still see color. This is not so for *monochromats,* who are unable to discriminate wavelength at all. Monochromats are truly color-blind. (Screening for color blindness is done with tests like that shown in Figure 4-17.) Most color deficiencies are genetic in origin. Color blindness occurs much more frequently in males (2%) than in females (.03%) because the critical genes are recessive genes on the X chromosome (Nathans, Thomas, & Hogness, 1986).

Theories of Color Vision   How do our receptors turn wavelength into color? One of the major theories of color vision was developed in the 19th century. According to this *trichromatic theory,* even though there are many different colors that we can discriminate, there are only three types of receptors (cones) for color. Each receptor is sensitive to a wide range of wavelengths but is most responsive in a narrow region. As shown in Figure 4-18, the *short-wavelength receptor* is maximally sensitive to short wavelengths (blues), the *medium-wavelength receptor* is most sensitive to

Figure 4-18

The Trichromatic Theory   Response curves for the short-, medium-, and long-wave receptors proposed by trichromatic theory. These curves enable us to determine the relative response of each receptor to light of any wavelength. In the example shown here, the response of each receptor to a 500-nanometer light is determined by drawing a line up from 500 nanometers and noting where this line intersects each curve. (Smith, V. C. and J. Porkorny, 1975. "Spectral sensitivity of the foveal cone photopigments between 400 and 500 nm." *Vision Research,* 15:161–171.)

medium wavelengths (greens and yellows), and the *long-wavelength receptor* is maximally sensitive to long wavelengths (reds). The joint action of these three receptors determines the sensation of color. That is, a light of a particular wavelength stimulates the three receptors to different degrees, and the specific ratios of activity in the three receptors leads to the sensation of a specific color. Hence, with regard to our earlier discussion of coding of quality, the trichromatic theory holds that the quality of color is coded by the pattern of activity of three receptors rather than by specific receptors for each color.

The trichromatic theory explains the facts about color vision that we mentioned previously. First, we can discriminate among different wavelengths because they lead to different responses in the three receptors. Second, the law of three primaries follows directly from trichromatic theory. We can match a mixture of three widely spaced wavelengths to any color, because the three widely spaced wavelengths will activate the three different receptors, and activity in these receptors is what lies behind perception of the test color. (Now we see the significance of the number

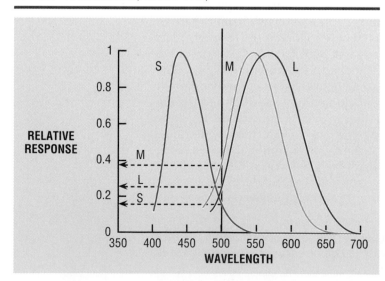

three.) Third, the trichromatic theory explains the various kinds of color deficiencies by positing that one or more of the three types of receptors is missing: Dichromats are born missing one type of receptor, whereas monochromats are born missing two of the three types of receptors. In addition to accounting for these long-known facts, trichromatic theory led biological researchers to a successful search for three kinds of receptors. We now know that there are three kinds of cones in the human retina.

How Is Visual Perception Accomplished?

Up to this point, we have been concerned with individual aspects of vision, notably intensity and color. While this piecemeal approach is critical for understanding vision, it cannot tell us the whole story. Information may enter our senses in bits and pieces, but that is not how we perceive the world. We perceive a world of three-dimensional objects and people, a world of integrated wholes, not piecemeal sensations. It is to the perception of objects that we now turn. This change in emphasis from sensation to perception will lead to a change in what we emphasize at the biological level. Rather than focusing on receptors and the pathways emanating from them, our attention now moves to the cortex because that is where perception is based.

Both auditory and visual perception involve determining (1) what objects or sounds are out there (apples, cats, ringing telephone, siren) and (2) where these objects or sounds are in relation to ourselves (object straight ahead, sound from the rear). Thus we perceive not simply piecemeal sensations, but a world of integrated wholes.

Researchers studying visual perception ask what problems the perceptual system is designed to solve. Two general problems are often mentioned. The perceptual system must determine (1) what objects are out there (apples, tables, cats, and so on) and (2) where these objects are (arm's length on my left, hundreds of yards straight ahead, and so on). The same two problems are involved in auditory perception (What was that sound, a phone or a siren? Where was it coming from, the front or the back?), and in other sensory modalities as well.

In vision, the process of **object recognition,** or *recognition,* refers to *determining what objects are.* It is crucial for survival because often we have to know what an object is before we can infer its properties. Once we know that an object is an apple, we know that it is edible; once we know that an object is a wolf, we know not to disturb it. **Spatial localization,** or *localization,* refers to *determining where visual objects are.* It is also necessary for survival. Localization is the means we use to navigate through our environment. Without such an ability, we would constantly bump into objects, fail to grasp things we are reaching for, and move into the path of dangerous objects and predators.

object recognition
determining what objects are

spatial localization
determining where objects are

In what follows, we first set the stage for our discussion by considering how the brain divides its perceptual tasks. Then we turn to what is known about localization and recognition. While we will focus primarily on visual perception because this is the area that has been investigated most, keep in mind that the goals of localization and recognition seem to apply to all the senses. With regard to recognition, for example, we can use hearing to recognize a Mozart sonata, smell to recognize McDonald's fries, touch to recognize the quarter in our pants pocket, and the body senses to recognize how well we are following our aerobics instructor's directions.

Division of Labor in the Brain

In the past decade a great deal has been learned about the neural processes that underlie perception. At a general level, the part of the brain concerned with vision—the *visual cortex*—operates according to a *division-of-labor* principle. Rather than all of the visual cortex participating in all or most aspects of perception, different regions

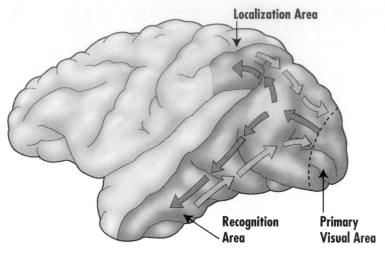

Localization Area

Recognition Area   **Primary Visual Area**

Figure 4-19

Two Cortical Visual Systems   The arrows going from the back of the brain toward the top depict the localization system; the arrows going from the back toward the bottom of the brain depict the recognition system. (After Mishkin, Ungerleider, & Macko, 1983)

of the visual cortex are specialized to carry out different perceptual functions (Kosslyn & Koenig, 1992).

Localization and Recognition Are Separate Systems   The idea that localization and recognition are qualitatively different tasks is supported by findings showing that they are carried out by different regions of the visual cortex. Recognition of objects depends on a branch of the visual system that includes the cortical receiving area for vision (the first area in the cortex to receive visual information) and a region near the bottom of the cerebral cortex. In contrast, localization of objects depends on a branch of the visual system that includes the cortical receiving area for vision and a region of the cortex near the top of the brain (see Figure 4-19). Studies with nonhuman primates show that if the recognition branch of an animal's visual system is impaired, the animal can still perform tasks that require it to perceive spatial relationships between objects (one in front of the other, for example), but it cannot perform tasks that require it to discriminate between objects—for example, tasks that require discriminating a cube from a cylinder. If the location branch is impaired, the animal can perform tasks that require it to distinguish a cube from a cylinder, but it cannot perform tasks that require it to know where the objects are in relation to each other (Mishkin & Appenzeller, 1987).

More recent research has used brain scanning techniques to document the existence of separate object and location systems in the human brain. One widely used technique is PET (discussed in Chapter 2). Recall its basic logic. A radioactive tracer is injected into a person's bloodstream and the individual is placed in a PET scanner while he or she performs various tasks. The PET scanner measures increases in radioactivity in various regions of the brain; those increases indicate increases in blood flow to those regions. Regions that show the greatest increase in blood flow presumably are the ones that control performance in the task.

In one PET study, participants performed two tasks, one a test of face recognition, which taps object recognition, and the other a test of mental rotation, which reflects localization. In the face recognition task, on each trial participants saw a *target* face and, beneath it, two *test* faces (see Figure 4-20a). One test face was of the same person as that depicted by the target, except for changes in orientation and lighting; the other test face was of a different person. The task was to decide which test face was the same as the target. While the participant was engaging in this task, there was an increase in blood flow in the recognition branch of the cortex (the branch terminating near the bottom of the cortex) but not in the localization branch (the branch terminating near the top of the cortex). Very different results were obtained with the mental rotation task. In this task, on each trial participants saw a target display of a dot at some distance from a double line; beneath that were two test displays (see Figure 4-20b). One test display was the same as the target, except that it had been rotated, and the other test display contained a different configuration of the dot and lines. While engaging in this task, participants showed an increase in blood flow in the localization branch of the cortex but not in the recognition branch. Localization and recognition therefore are carried out in entirely different regions of the visual cortex (Grady et al., 1992; Haxby et al., 1990).

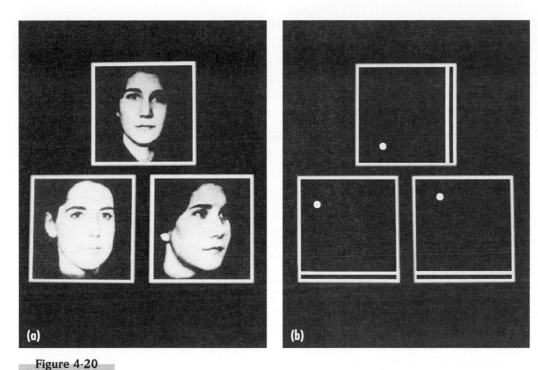

Figure 4-20

Recognition and Localization Tasks   Sample items from the face matching (a) and dot-location (b) matching tasks. (From Grady et al., 1992)

Components of Recognition   The division of labor in the visual cortex does not end with the split between localization and recognition. The different kinds of information that are used in recognition—color, shape, and texture, for example—appear to be processed by different subregions or cells of the recognition branch of the cortex.

Some evidence for this claim comes from studies with nonhuman primates. These studies record electrical activity from single cells while the animal is exposed to various stimuli (refer back to Figure 4-2 for a description of single-cell recording). Such studies indicate that different attributes of an object are processed by different regions of the brain or by different cells within a region. Thus, within the primary receiving area of the visual cortex some cells respond only to simple shapes like lines and edges, while other cells respond only to colors and still others only to movement (Keki, 1992).

By using brain-scanning techniques (PET and fMRI), researchers have been able to find comparable results with humans. Participants in these experiments have their brains scanned while being presented with either lines and edges, various colored objects, or objects in motion. Different areas of the cortex are activated by these different inputs, again with lines and edges being processed in one area, color in another, and motion in still another (Haxby et al., 1991). These specialized regions seem to be located in roughly the same place in the human brain as in the monkey brain. Thus, when it comes to the neural bases of object recognition, we have much in common with other primates.

Hierarchical Organization   Given that information about the different attributes of an object are processed in different, specialized regions of the brain, how are these regions organized? It appears that the organization is **hierarchical,** *progressing from lower-level to higher-level attributes.* That is, low-level attributes such as lines and edges are fed into a higher-level region that is sensitive to a global attribute like shape, which in turn is fed into an even higher-level region that is sensitive to a specific object. Remarkably, this progression from lower-level to higher-level attributes

hierarchical   an organizational system that progresses from lower-level to higher-level attributes

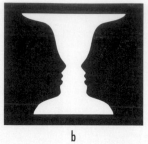

a   b   c

Figure 4-21

Reversible Figure and Ground   Three patterns in which either a white vase or a pair of black faces can be seen. Note that it is impossible to see both organizations at the same time, even though you know that both are possible percepts. When the white area is smaller (a), the vase is more likely to be seen; when the black area is smaller (c) the faces are more likely to be seen.

occurs as one moves from the back of the brain forward. We can illustrate this with the recognition of faces. At the back *(posterior)* end of the temporal cortex, which governs object recognition, there are regions that are sensitive to shapes in general; they are as likely to be activated by pictures of scrambled faces as by pictures of normal faces. As one moves farther forward *(anterior)* in the temporal lobe, one finds regions that respond to intact faces but not to scrambled ones; and as one moves still farther forward, one finds regions that respond only to specific faces. Thus, as one moves in a backward-to-forward (posterior to anterior) direction, one moves from regions that are specialized for elementary attributes to regions specialized for whole objects (e.g., Courtney et al., 1995).

The upshot is that the visual cortex consists of numerous *processing modules,* each of which is specialized for a particular task. The more we learn about the neural basis of other perceptual systems, the more this modular, or division-of-labor, approach seems to hold.

How We Localize Objects

To know where the objects in our environment are, the very first thing that we have to do is segregate the objects from one another and from the background. Then the perceptual system can determine the position of the objects in a three-dimensional world, including their distance from us and their movement patterns. The idea that these three perceptual abilities—segregation, determining distance, and determining movement—belong together is supported by physiological findings indicating that all three abilities are controlled by the same branch of the visual system (Livingstone & Hubel, 1988). We will discuss each of these perceptual abilities in turn.

Figure 4-22

Perceptual Grouping

The proximity of the lines that appear to be in pairs leads us to see three pairs and an extra line at the right.

The same lines as above, but with extensions, lead to the opposite pairing; three broken squares and an extra line at the left.

How We Segregate Objects   The image projected on our retina is a mosaic of varying brightness and colors. Somehow our perceptual system organizes the mosaic into a set of discrete objects projected against a background. This kind of organization was of great concern to *Gestalt psychology,* an approach to psychology that began in Germany early in the 20th century. The Gestalt psychologists emphasized the importance of perceiving whole objects or forms. They proposed a number of principles of how we organize objects, some of which we discuss in the following paragraphs.

Figure and Ground   In a stimulus that contains two or more distinct regions, we usually see part of it as a *figure* and the rest as *ground.* The regions seen as a figure contain the objects of interest—they seem more solid than the ground and appear in front of the ground. This is the most elementary form of perceptual organization. Figure 4-21 illustrates that figure–ground organization can be reversible. If you look at this picture for a few seconds, you will note that you can see as the figure either a vase or two profiles. Thus, you can see the same contour as part of one object or as part of another. (Note that we can perceive figure–ground relations in senses other than vision. For example, we may hear the song of a bird against a background of outdoor noises, or the melody played by the violin against the harmonies of the rest of the orchestra.)

Grouping of Objects   We see not only objects against a ground, but a particular grouping of the objects as well. Even simple patterns of lines or dots fall into groups when we look at them. In the top part of Figure 4-22, for example, we tend to see three pairs of lines, with an extra line at the right. But notice that the stimulus can be described equally well as three pairs beginning at the right, with an extra line at the left. The slight modification of the lines shown in the lower part of the figure causes us to perceive the second grouping.

The Gestalt psychologists identified a number of factors that determine grouping. One is *proximity:* Elements that are near one another tend to be grouped together. This principle explains the preferred grouping of the lines in the top part of Figure 4-22. *Closure,* the tendency to group elements so as to complete figures in which there are gaps, explains the grouping preferred in the bottom part of the figure. There, closure is a stronger factor than proximity.

Although perceptual grouping has been studied mainly in visual perception, the same determinants of grouping appear in audition. Proximity clearly operates in audition (although it is proximity in time rather than in space): Four drumbeats with a pause between the second and third will be heard as two pairs.

The research on perceptual grouping only scratches the surface of the Gestalt psychologists' contributions to our current understanding of perception. Other Gestalt insights will be noted throughout the remainder of this chapter.

Perceiving Distance   To know where an object is, we must know its distance or *depth.* Although perceiving an object's depth seems effortless, it is a remarkable achievement given the physical structure of our eyes. The retina, the starting point of vision, is a two-dimensional surface. This means that the retinal image is flat and has no depth at all. This fact has led many students of perception (artists as well as scientists) to the idea of **distance cues,** *two-dimensional aspects that a perceiver uses to infer distance in a three-dimensional world.* There are a number of distance cues that combine to determine perceived distance. The cues can be classified as *monocular* or *binocular,* depending on whether they involve one or both eyes.

People using only one eye can perceive depth remarkably well by picking up monocular depth cues. Figure 4-23 illustrates four of these cues. The first is *relative size.* If an image contains an array of similar objects that differ in size, people interpret the smaller objects as being farther away (see Figure 4-23a). A second monocular cue is *superposition.* If one object is positioned so that it obstructs the view of the other, people perceive the overlapping object as being nearer (see Figure 4-23b). A third cue is *relative height.* Among similar objects, those that appear higher are perceived as being farther away (see Figure 4-23c). A fourth cue is *linear perspective.* When parallel lines appear to converge, they are perceived as vanishing in the

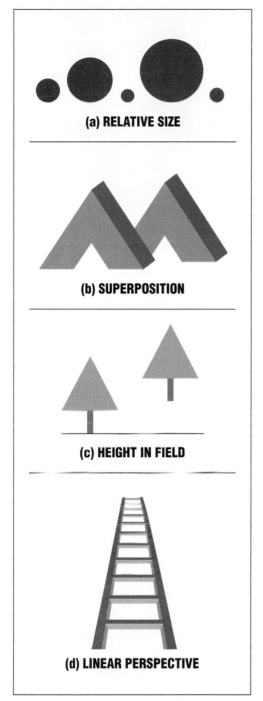

(a) **RELATIVE SIZE**

(b) **SUPERPOSITION**

(c) **HEIGHT IN FIELD**

(d) **LINEAR PERSPECTIVE**

Figure 4-23

Monocular Distance Cues   The figure illustrates four monocular distance cues. These are used by artists to portray depth on a two-dimensional surface and are also present in photographs.

distance cues   two-dimensional aspects that a perceiver uses to infer distance in a three-dimensional world

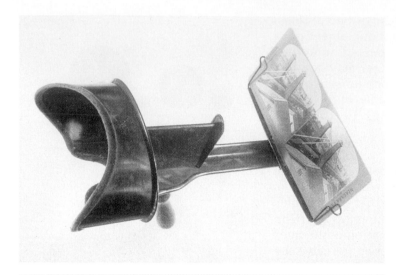

The Holmes-Bates stereoscope, invented by Oliver Wendell Holmes in 1861 and manufactured by Joseph Bates, creates a vivid perception of depth.

binocular parallax
the fact that any visible point will differ slightly in its direction to the two eyes

binocular disparity
the difference between the retinal images on the two eyes when we look at an object from a distance

distance (see Figure 4-23d). These four cues have been known to artists for centuries—they are called *pictorial cues* for this reason—and a single painting will often use more than one of them.

Seeing with both eyes rather than one has advantages for *depth perception.* Because the eyes are separated in the head, each eye perceives a three-dimensional object from a slightly different angle. Consequently, each eye has a slightly different view of the object. Fusing these two views gives rise to an impression of depth. This can be demonstrated by a device called a *stereoscope.* The stereoscope displays a different photograph or drawing to each eye. If the two pictures are taken from slightly separated camera positions or drawn from slightly different perspectives, the viewer will experience vivid depth.

Binocular parallax is one cue that is responsible for this perception of depth. It hinges on *the fact that any visible point will differ slightly in its direction to the two eyes.* A related cue is **binocular disparity;** it is based on *the difference between the retinal images on the two eyes when we look at an object from a distance.* You can easily demonstrate these cues to yourself. Hold a pencil about a foot in front of you. With only one eye open, line it up with a vertical edge of the wall opposite you. Then close that eye and open the other. The pencil will now appear in a different location; the difference between the two locations is binocular parallax. Also, the two edges that were lined up in the first eye will appear separated when you open the second eye, and indeed the images in the second eye are separated; the difference between the retinal images in the two eyes is binocular disparity.

The idea behind distance cues is that the observer notes a critical cue—for instance, that one object appears larger than another—and then unconsciously infers distance information from the cue. This notion of unconscious inference was introduced by Helmholtz in 1909. While it continues to be a key idea in the study of perception (Rock, 1983), some psychologists have argued that we do not infer depth, but rather perceive it directly (Gibson, 1950, 1966, 1979).

Figure 4-24

Stroboscopic Motion   The sequence of still frames in (a), shown at the appropriate intervals, will result in the percept shown in (b). The illusion of continuous motion resulting from successively viewed still pictures is the basis of motion in movies, videos, and television.

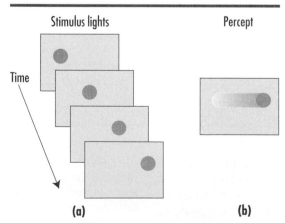

Stimulus lights

Percept

Time

(a)   (b)

Perceiving Motion   If we are to move around our environment effectively, we need to know not only the locations of static objects but also the trajectories of moving ones. We need to know, for example, not only that the object located a few feet in front of us is a softball but also that it is coming toward us at a fast clip. This brings us to the issue of how we perceive motion.

What causes us to perceive motion? The simplest idea is that we perceive an object as being in motion whenever its image moves across our retina. This answer turns out to be too simple, though, for we can see motion even when *nothing* moves on our retina. This phenomenon was demonstrated in 1912 by Wertheimer in his studies of stroboscopic motion (see Figure 4-24). Stroboscopic motion can be produced by flashing a light in darkness and then, a few milliseconds later, flashing another light near the location of the first light. The light will seem to move from one place to the other in a way that is indistinguishable from real motion.

The motion that we see in movies is stroboscopic. The film is actually a series of still photographs (frames), each slightly different from the preceding. The frames are projected on the screen in rapid sequence, with dark intervals in between. The rate at which the frames are presented is critical. In the early days of motion pictures, the frame rate was 16 per second. This was too slow, and as a consequence movement in these early films appears too rapid, as well as jerky and disjointed. Today the rate is usually 24 frames per second (with each frame typically shown a few times in succession to further reduce jumpiness).

Another case in which we perceive motion in the absence of movement across our retina is the phenomenon of *induced motion.* When a large object surrounding a smaller one moves, the smaller object may appear to be the one that is moving, even if it is static. This phenomenon may be at play on a windy night when the moon seems to be racing through the surrounding clouds.

Of course, our visual system is also sensitive to *real motion*—that is, motion induced by an object moving across the retina. Some aspects of real motion are coded by specific cells in the visual cortex. These cells respond to some motions and not to others, and each cell responds best to one direction and speed of motion. The best evidence for the existence of such cells comes from studies with animals, in which the experimenter records from single cells in the visual cortex while the animal is presented with stimuli containing different patterns of motion (refer to Figure 4-2 again). Such single-cell recording studies have found cortical cells tuned to particular directions of movement. There are even cells specifically tuned to detect an object moving toward the head, an ability that clearly is useful for survival (Regan, Beverly, & Cynader, 1979). Again, it is striking how the visual cortex distributes its various jobs over different areas and cells.

However, there is more to the neural basis of real motion than the activation of specific cells. We can see motion when we track a luminous object moving in darkness (such as an airplane at night). Because our eyes follow the object, the image makes only a small, irregular motion on the retina (due to imperfect tracking), yet we perceive a smooth, continuous motion. Why? The answer seems to be that information about how our eyes are moving is sent from motor regions in the front of the brain to the visual cortex and influences the motion that we see. In essence, the motor system is informing the visual system that it is responsible for the lack of regular motion on the retina, and the visual system then corrects for this lack. In more normal viewing situations, there are both eye movements and large retinal-image movements. The visual system must combine these two sources of information to determine the perceived motion.

Sometimes the motion of objects tells us not only about where the objects are but also about what they are doing. Thus our perception of motion is directly tied to our perception of events. A barking dog racing toward an intruder is perceived not just as a "moving dog" but as the event "a dog is attacking." Motion is particularly important in our perception of simple causal events. When two objects are in motion, we may perceive one as having caused the motion of the other. In a demonstration of this, Michotte (1963) used squares like those in Figure 4-25 as stimuli. When square A moves to square B and B immediately begins to move in the direction that A was moving, participants report that A caused B's movement; more specifically, A seems to launch B. (This perception of causality, however, occurs only when the interval between when A reaches B and when B starts to move is very brief—roughly, less than one-fifth of a second.)

Figure 4-25

Motion and the Perception of Causality
When square A moves to square B, and B then immediately begins to move, participants report that A "launches" B (a). The perception of causality is somewhat different when A stops before it reaches B (b).

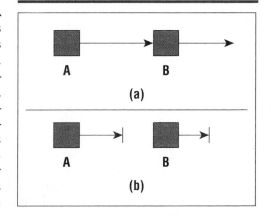

Such perception of causality appears to occur directly, without any conscious reasoning (Goldstein, 1989).

How We Recognize Objects

We turn now to the second major function of perception: recognizing what an object is. Recognizing an object amounts to assigning it to a category—that's a shirt, that's a cat, that's a daisy, and so on. Of course, we can also recognize people, which amounts to assigning the visual input to a particular individual—that's Ben Murphy, or this is Irene Paull. In either case, objects or people, recognition allows us to infer many hidden properties of the object—if it's a shirt then it's made of cloth and I can wear it; if it's Ben Murphy he'll want to tell me about his latest exploits. Recognition is what allows us to go beyond the information provided by our senses.

What attributes of an object do we use to recognize it—shape, size, color, texture, orientation? While all of these attributes may make some contribution, shape appears to play the critical role. We can recognize a cup, for example, regardless of whether it is large or small (a variation in size), brown or white (a variation in color), smooth or bumpy (a texture variation), presented upright or tilted slightly (an orientation variation). In contrast, our ability to recognize a cup is strikingly affected by variations in shape; if part of the cup's shape is hidden, we may not recognize it at all. One piece of evidence for the importance of shape in recognition is that we can recognize many objects about as well from simple line drawings, which preserve only the shapes of the objects, as from detailed color photographs, which preserve many attributes of the objects (Biederman & Ju, 1988).The critical question then becomes: How do we use the shape of an object to assign it to its appropriate category?

Early Stages of Recognition   We can distinguish between *early* and *late* stages in recognizing an object (Marr, 1982).These stages are characterized by what they accomplish. In early stages, the perceptual system uses information on the retina, particularly variations in intensity, to describe the object in terms of primitive components like lines, edges, and angles. The system uses these primitive components to construct a description of the object itself. In later stages, the system compares the object's description with shape descriptions of various categories of objects stored in visual memory, and selects the best match. To recognize a particular object as the letter B, for example, is to say that the object's shape matches that of B better than it matches that of other letters. Most of the processing in both the early and late stages of recognition are not available to consciousness. For now, our concern is with the early stages, which construct the shape description of the object.

Much of what is known about the primitive features of object perception comes from biological studies of other species (cats, monkeys) that use single-cell recordings in the visual cortex (refer back to Figure 4-2). These studies examine the sensitivity of specific cortical neurons when different stimuli are presented to the regions of the retina associated with these neurons; such a retinal region is called a *receptive field* of a cortical neuron. These single-cell studies were pioneered by Hubel and Wiesel (1968), who shared a Nobel prize in 1981 for their research.

Hubel and Wiesel identified cells in the visual cortex that can be distinguished by the features to which they respond. *Simple cells* respond when the eye is exposed to a line stimulus (such as a thin bar or straight edge between a dark and a light region) at a particular orientation and position within their receptive field. Figure 4-26 illustrates how a simple cell will respond to a vertical bar and to bars tilted away from the vertical. The response decreases as the orientation varies from the optimal one. Other simple cells are tuned to other orientations and positions. A *complex cell* also responds to a bar or edge in a particular orientation, but it does not require that the stimulus be at a particular place within its receptive field. A complex cell responds to the stimulus anywhere within its receptive field, and it responds continuously as the stimulus is moved across its receptive field. Since Hubel and Wiesel's

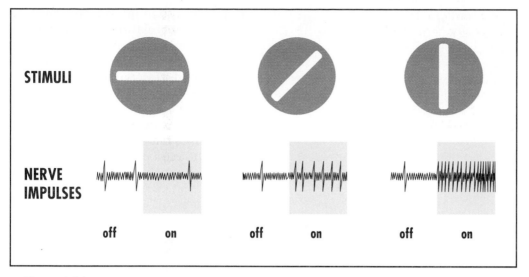

Figure 4-26

The Response of a Simple Cell   This figure illustrates the response of a simple cortical cell to a bar of light. The stimulus is on the top, the response on the bottom; each vertical spike on the bottom corresponds to one nerve impulse. When there is no stimulus, only an occasional impulse is recorded. When the stimulus is turned on, the cell may or may not respond, depending on the position and orientation of the light bar. For this cell, a horizontal bar produces no change in response, a bar at 45 degrees produces a small change, and a vertical bar produces a very large change.

initial reports, investigators have found cells that respond to shape features other than single bars and edges—for example, cells that respond to corners or angles of a specific length (DeValois & DeValois, 1980; Shapley & Lennie, 1985). All of these cells are referred to as *feature detectors*. Because the edges, bars, corners, and angles to which these detectors respond can be used to approximate many shapes, the feature detectors might be thought of as the building blocks of shape perception. As we are about to see, these primitive features may be used to derive more complex features of objects.

The shape features of natural objects are more complex than lines and curves; they are more like simple geometric forms. The features must be such that they can combine to form the shape of any recognizable object. The features of objects must also be such that they can be determined or constructed from more primitive features, such as lines and curves, because primitive features are the only information the system initially has available.

One proposal is that the features of objects include a number of geometric forms, such as cylinders, cones, blocks, and wedges, as illustrated in Figure 4-27a. These features, referred to as *geons* (for *geometric ions*), were developed by Irv Biederman (1987). Biederman argues that a set of 36 geons like those

Figure 4-27

A Possible Set of Features (Geons) for Natural Objects   (a) Wedges, cubes, cylinders, and cones may be features of complex objects. (b) When the features (geons) are combined, they form natural objects. Note that when the arc (geon 5) is connected to the side of the cylinder, it forms a pail. (After Biederman, 1990)

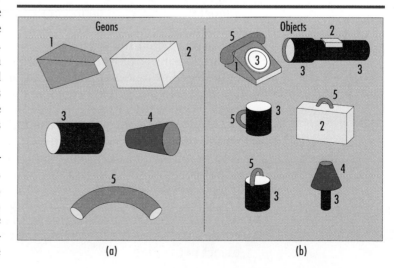

(a)   (b)

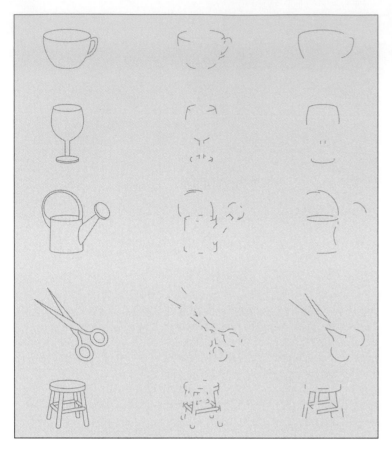

in Figure 4-27a, combined according to a small set of spatial relations, is sufficient to describe the shapes of all objects that people can possibly recognize. Moreover, geons like those in Figure 4-27a can be distinguished solely in terms of primitive features. For example, geon 2 in Figure 4-27a, the cube, differs from geon 3, the cylinder, in that the cube has straight edges but the cylinder has curved edges; straight and curved edges are primitive features.

Evidence that geons are features comes from experiments in which participants try to recognize pictured objects that are presented briefly. The general finding is that recognition of an object is good to the extent the geons of the object are perceptible (see Figure 4-28).

The description of an object includes not just its features but also the relationships between them. This is evident in Figure 4-27b. When the arc is connected to the side of the cylinder, it forms a cup; when connected to the top of the cylinder, it forms a pail. Once the description of an object's shape has been constructed, it is compared to an array of geon descriptions stored in memory to find the best match.

Figure 4-28

Object Recognition and Geon Recovery   Items used in experiments on object recognition. The left column shows the original intact versions of the objects. The middle column shows versions of the objects in which regions have been deleted, but the geons are still recoverable. The right column shows versions of the objects in which regions have been deleted and the geons are not recoverable. Recognition is better for the middle versions than for the rightmost versions. (After Biederman, 1987)

Matching and Top-Down Processing   The late stage of object recognition involves (unconsciously) comparing a description of the object we are looking at to stored shape descriptions (or representations) of various categories of objects, and selecting the best match. To recognize a particular object as a banana, for example, is to decide that the object's shape matches that of a banana better than it matches that of other objects. Because there are so many stored representations to consider, the matching process almost certainly goes on in parallel; that is, multiple stored representations are simultaneously matched with the object. Also, we may use context (again, unconsciously) to limit the number of stored representations we consider; for example, if we are looking at objects in the produce section of a grocery store, we may consider only stored representations of fruits and vegetables.

This use of context is referred to as *top-down processing*. Whereas *bottom-up processes* are driven solely by the input, *top-down processes* are driven by a person's knowledge and expectations. To illustrate, recognizing that an object is a lamp solely on the basis of its geon description involves only bottom-up processes; one starts with primitive features of the input, determines the geon configuration of the input, and then compares this input description with stored shape descriptions. In contrast, recognizing that the object is a lamp partly on the basis of its being on a night table next to a bed involves some top-down processes; one brings to bear information other than the information in the input. While most of the processes we have considered so far are bottom-up ones, top-down processes also play a major role in object perception.

Top-down processes are what lie behind the powerful effects that context has on our perception of objects and people. You expect to see your chemistry lab partner Sarah at the lab every Tuesday at 3 P.M., and when she enters the lab at that moment you hardly need to look to tell that it is she. Your prior knowledge has led to a powerful expectation, and little input is needed for recognition. But should Sarah suddenly appear in your hometown during winter break, you may have considerable trouble recognizing her. She is out of context—your expectations have been violated, and you must resort to extensive bottom-up processing to tell that it is in fact she. (We experience this as "doing a double take.") As this example makes clear, when the context is appropriate (that is, when it predicts the input object), it facilitates perception; when the context is inappropriate, it impairs perception.

The effects of context are particularly striking when the stimulus object is ambiguous—that is, when it can be perceived in more than one way. An ambiguous figure is presented in Figure 4-29; it can be perceived either as an old woman or as a young woman (although the old woman is more likely to be seen initially). If you have been looking at unambiguous pictures that resemble the young woman in Figure 4-29 (that is, if young women are the context), you will tend to see the young woman first in the ambiguous picture. This effect of temporal context is illustrated with another set of pictures in Figure 4-30. Look at the pictures as you would at a comic strip, from left to right and top to bottom. The pictures in the middle of the series are ambiguous. If you view the figures in the sequence just suggested, you will tend to see these ambiguous pictures as a man's face. If you view the figures in the opposite order, you will tend to see the ambiguous pictures as a young woman.

Because of top-down processing, our motives and desires can potentially affect our perceptions. If we are very hungry, a quick glance at a red ball on the kitchen table may register as a tomato. Our desire for food has led us to think about food, and these expectations have combined with the input (a red, round object) to yield the perception of a tomato.

Neural Organization   Are the visual object descriptions (or representations) that are stored in visual memory organized in any way? It appears that they are organized by content—with, say, representations of faces being separate from representations of words. The best evidence for this comes from studies of the neural bases of object recognition.

Different parts of the brain are devoted to the recognition of words and faces, as shown by studies of neurological patients who have a selective deficit in recognizing objects (referred to as *agnosics*). Some

Figure 4-29

An Ambiguous Stimulus   An ambiguous drawing that can be seen either as a young woman or as an old woman. Most people see the old woman first. The young woman is turning away, and we see the left side of her face. Her chin is the old woman's nose, and her necklace is the old woman's mouth. (After Boring, 1930)

Figure 4-30

Effects of Temporal Context   What you see here depends on the order in which you look at the pictures. The pictures in the middle of the series are ambiguous. If you have been looking at pictures of a man's face, they will appear to be distorted faces. If you have been looking at pictures of a woman, they will look like a woman.

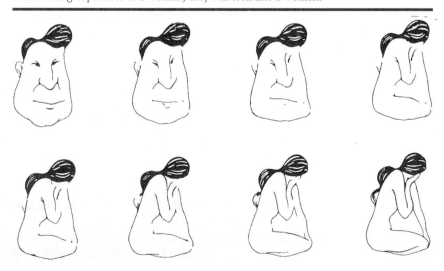

Brain scanning techniques suggest that representations of animals and tools are stored separately in the brain. Recognition of common animals sparks more activation in the occipital cortex while activation in parts of the temporal cortex occurs when naming tools.

agnosic patients have lost just the ability to recognize faces; they can do just about everything else normally (this deficit is called *prosopagnosia*). The deficit can be very severe, as when the patient is unable to recognize his wife or children, or even himself when looking in a mirror. Usually the brain damage accompanying this deficit is in a region connecting the occipital and temporal cortices, particularly in both hemispheres (Farah, 1990). There are other patients whose main symptom is inability to recognize words (called *pure alexia*). Patients with this deficit typically have no trouble recognizing faces and other common objects. They can even identify individual letters. What they cannot do is recognize whole words. When presented with a word, they attempt to read it letter by letter and can take as long as 10 seconds to recognize a familiar but long word (Bub, Blacks, & Howell, 1989). The brain damage accompanying pure alexia is typically in the left-hemisphere temporal-occipital region. These findings with patients strongly suggest that visual representations of faces and words are stored in different regions. Brain scanning experiments with normal individuals confirm this suggestion, as the regions of the brain that are activated when participants recognize faces are different from those activated when they recognize words (Haxby et al., 1991; Petersen et al., 1989).

What about objects other than words or faces? Again, there is evidence for organization by content. For one thing, there are neurological patients who are more impaired in the recognition of common objects like animals and artifacts than in the recognition of faces (Farah, 1990). Even more dramatically, there are neurological patients who are markedly impaired in their ability to recognize common animals but are relatively normal in the recognition of tools, whereas there are other patients who show the reverse deficit (Warrington & Shallice, 1984). This suggests not only that representations of common objects are kept distinct from those of faces and words, but further that representations of animals and tools are separate. Again, there are brain scanning results with normal individuals that provide converging evidence for these content differences. When normal individuals have to name pictures of common animals and tools while having their brains scanned, they show more activation in the occipital cortex when naming animals, and more activation in certain parts of the temporal cortex when naming tools (Martin et al., 1996). The division-of-labor principle that we discussed earlier with respect to simple features of objects appears to extend to representations of whole objects as well.

Thinking Critically

1. The Gestalt psychologists were fond of saying, "The whole is different from the sum of its parts." What exactly do you think they meant by this? Can you think of examples of this principle that came up in the discussion of perception?

2. Can you think of implications of top-down processing in perception for the validity of eyewitness testimony in legal trials?

3. Much of the processing that goes on in object recognition seems to be very rapid and not available to consciousness. Why do you think we have evolved so that this is so?

How Do We Keep the Perceptual World Constant?

In addition to localization and recognition, our perceptual system seems to have another goal: to keep the appearance of objects constant even though their impressions on our retinas are changing. By and large, we perceive an object as remaining relatively constant regardless of changes in lighting, the position from which we view it, or its distance from us. Your car does not appear to grow larger as you walk toward it, distort in shape as you walk around it, or change in color when you view it in artificial light, even though the image on your retina does undergo these changes. The term **perceptual constancy** is used to refer to this *tendency toward constancy in perceiving the appearance of objects.* Although constancy is not perfect, it is a salient aspect of visual experience.

Lightness and Brightness Constancy

When an object is illuminated, it reflects a certain amount of the light. The amount reflected is related to the apparent *lightness* of the object. The phenomenon of **lightness constancy** refers to *the fact that the perceived lightness of a particular object may barely change even when the amount of reflected light changes dramatically.* Thus, a black velvet shirt can look just as black in sunlight as in shadow, even though it reflects thousands of times more light when it is directly illuminated by the sun. Why?

When we perceive objects in natural settings, several other objects are usually visible, and lightness constancy depends on the relationships among the intensities of light reflected from the different objects. Thus, normally we continue to see black velvet as black even in sunlight because the velvet continues to reflect a lower percentage of its light than its surroundings do. It is the relative percentage of light reflected that determines its brightness (Gilchrist, 1978).

Similar principles apply to color. **Color constancy** refers to the *tendency for an object to remain roughly the same color with different light sources.* As with lightness constancy, color constancy depends on a heterogeneous background (Land, 1977; Maloney & Wandell, 1986).

Shape and Location Constancy

When a door swings toward us, the shape of its retinal image goes through a series of changes (see Figure 4-31). The door's rectangular shape produces a trapezoidal image, with the edge toward us wider than the hinged edge; then the trapezoid grows thinner, until finally all that is projected on the retina is a vertical bar the thickness of the door. Nevertheless, we perceive an unchanging door swinging open. The fact that *the perceived shape is constant while the retinal image changes* is an example of **shape constancy.**

Still another constancy involves the locations of objects. Despite the fact that a series of changing images strike the retina as we move, the positions of fixed objects

perceptual constancy
the tendency toward constancy in perceiving the appearance of objects

lightness constancy
the tendency for the perceived lightness of an object to remain roughly the same even when the amount of reflected light changes dramatically

color constancy
the tendency for the perceived color of an object to remain roughly the same with different light sources

shape constancy
the tendency for the perceived shape of an object to remain roughly the same when the retinal image changes

Figure 4-31

Shape Constancy   The various retinal images produced by an opening door are quite different, yet we perceive a door of constant rectangular shape.

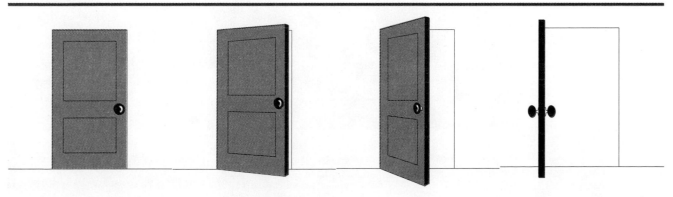

location constancy
the tendency for the perceived positions of fixed objects to remain roughly the same when the retinal image changes

appear to remain constant. We tend to take for granted this **location constancy**—*the tendency for the positions of fixed objects to be perceived as constant*—but it requires that the visual system take account of both our movements and the changing retinal images.

Shape constancy and location constancy also have implications for our earlier discussion of localization and recognition. In general, the constancies make the tasks of localization and recognition easier. If an object appeared to change its location every time we moved our eyes, determining its depth (an important part of localization) might be exceedingly difficult. If the shape of an object appeared to change every time it or we moved, the description of the object that we construct in the early stages of recognition would also change, and recognition might be impossible.

Size Constancy

size constancy the tendency for an object's perceived size to remain relatively constant no matter what its distance

The most studied of all the constancies is **size constancy,** *the fact that an object's perceived size remains relatively constant no matter what its distance.* As an object moves farther away from us, we generally do not see it as decreasing in size. Hold a quarter a foot in front of you and then move it out to arm's length. Does it appear to get smaller? Not noticeably. Yet the retinal image of the quarter when it is 24 inches away is half the size of the retinal image of the quarter when it is 12 inches away.

Dependence on Depth Cues   The example of the moving quarter indicates that when we perceive the size of an object, we consider something in addition to the size of the retinal image. That additional something is the perceived distance of the object.

It turns out that the perceived size of an object increases with both (1) the retinal size of the object and (2) the perceived distance of the object. More specifically, perceived size is equal to the product of retinal size multiplied by perceived distance. This is known as the *size–distance invariance principle,* and it explains size constancy. To illustrate: When a person walks away from you, the size of her image on your retina gets smaller but her perceived distance gets larger; these two changes cancel each other out, and your perception of the person's size remains relatively constant.

The moon looks much larger when it is near the horizon than when it is high in the sky, even though in both locations its retinal image is the same size.

Figure 4-32

The Ames Room   A view of how the Ames room looks to an observer viewing it through the peephole. The sizes of the boy and the dog depend on which one is in the left-hand corner of the room and which one is in the right-hand corner. The room is designed to wreak havoc with our perceptions. Because of the perceived shape of the room, the relative sizes of the boy and the dog seem impossibly different. Yet the same boy and dog appear in both photographs.

Illusions   The size–distance principle seems to be fundamental to understanding a number of size illusions. (An **illusion** is a *perception that is false or distorted.*) A good example of a size illusion is the *moon illusion.* When the moon is near the horizon, it looks as much as 50% larger than when it is at its zenith, even though in both locations the moon produces the same size retinal image. One explanation of this illusion is that the perceived distance to the horizon is judged to be greater than that to the zenith; hence, it is the greater perceived distance that leads to the greater perceived size (Rock & Kaufman, 1962).

illusion a perception that is false or distorted

Another size illusion is the Ames room (named after its inventor, Adelbert Ames). Figure 4-32 shows a view of how the Ames room looks to an observer seeing it through a peephole. When the boy is in the left-hand corner of the room (photograph on the left), he appears much smaller than when he is in the right-hand corner (photograph on the right). Yet it is the same boy in both pictures. Here we have a case in which size constancy has broken down. Why? The reason lies in the construction of the room. Although the room looks like a normal rectangular room to an observer seeing it through the peephole, it is in fact shaped so that its left corner is almost twice as far from us as its right corner (see Figure 4-33). Hence, the boy is in fact much farther away when he is on the left than when he is on the right, and consequently projects

Figure 4-33

The True Shape of the Ames Room   This figure shows the true shape of the Ames room. The boy on the left is actually almost twice as far away as the boy on the right; however, this difference in distance is not detected when the room is viewed through the peephole. (After Goldstein, 1984)

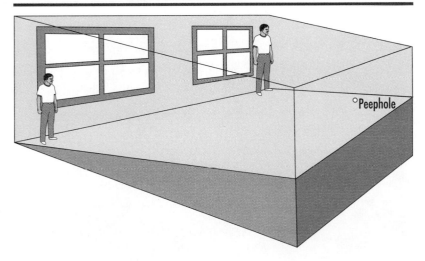

a smaller retinal image. We do not correct for this difference in distance, though, because we have been led to believe that we are looking at a normal room and thus assume that both boys are the same distance from us. Our assumption that the room is normal blocks our usual application of the size–distance invariance principle, and size constancy breaks down.

What Is the Role of Attention?

Our discussions of localization and recognition have often presupposed the notion of attention. To determine the motion of a plane, one must attend to its path; and to recognize a particular object, one must first attend to it. Attention thus involves selectivity. Most of the time we are bombarded with so many stimuli that we are unable to recognize all of them. As you sit reading, stop for a moment, close your eyes, and attend to the various stimuli that are reaching you. Notice, for example, the tightness of your left shoe. What sounds do you hear? Is there an odor in the air? You probably were not aware of these inputs before, because you had not selected them for recognition. **Selective attention** is *the process by which we select stimuli to attend to*. In what follows, we first discuss the psychological means by which we accomplish selectivity and then consider what is known about the neural basis of attention.

selective attention
the process by which we select stimuli for further processing

Selective Looking and Listening

Selective Looking   How exactly do we direct our attention to objects of interest? The simplest means is by reorienting our sensory receptors so as to favor those objects. For vision, this means moving our eyes until the object of interest falls on the most sensitive region of the retina.

Studies of visual attention often involve observing a participant looking at a picture or scene. If we watch the participant's eyes, it is evident that they are not stationary; rather, they are scanning. Scanning is not a smooth continuous motion; rather, it involves a series of eye movements or *fixations*. There are a number of techniques for recording these eye movements. The simplest method is to monitor the eyes with a television camera in such a way that what the eye is gazing at is reflected on the cornea so that it appears on television superimposed on the image of the eye. From this superimposed image, the experimenter can determine the point in the scene where the eye is fixated.

The eye movements used in scanning a picture ensure that different parts of the picture will fall on the fovea so that all of its details can be seen. (As noted earlier in the chapter, the fovea has the best resolution.) The points on which the eyes fixate are not random. They tend to be places that are most informative about the picture, places where important features are located. For example, in scanning a photograph of a face, many fixations are in the regions corresponding to the eyes, nose, and mouth (see Figure 4-34).

Figure 4-34

Eye Movements in Viewing a Picture   Next to the picture of the young girl is a record of the eye movements made by an individual inspecting the picture. (After Yarbus, 1967)

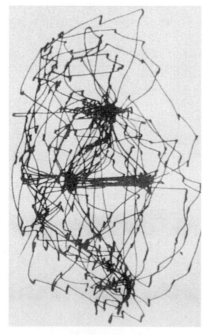

Although we may hear a number of conversations around us, as at a cocktail party, we remember very little of what we do not attend to. This is known as selective listening.

Selective Listening   In audition, the closest thing to eye movements is moving our head so that our ears are directed at the source of interest. This mechanism of attention is of limited use in many situations, though. Consider a crowded party. The sounds of many voices reach our ears, and their sources are not far enough apart that reorienting our ears would allow us to selectively follow one conversation. We are able, however, to use purely mental means to selectively attend to the desired message. Some of the cues that we use to do this are the direction of the sound, the lip movements of the speaker, and the particular voice characteristics of the speaker (pitch, speed, and intonation). Even in the absence of any of these cues we can, with difficulty, select one of two messages to follow on the basis of its meaning.

Research indicates that we remember very little of auditory messages that we do not attend to. A common procedure is to put earphones on a participant and play one message through one ear and another message through the other ear. The participant is asked to repeat (or *shadow*) one of the messages as it is heard. After a few minutes the messages are turned off and the listener is asked about the unshadowed message. Usually the listener can report only whether the voice was high or low, male or female, and so forth; he or she can say almost nothing about the content of the message (Moray, 1969).

The fact that we can report so little about unattended auditory messages initially led researchers to the idea that nonattended stimuli are filtered out completely (Broadbent, 1958). However, there is now considerable evidence that our perceptual system processes nonattended stimuli to some extent (in vision as well as audition), even though those stimuli rarely reach consciousness. One piece of evidence for partial processing of nonattended stimuli is that we are very likely to hear the sound of our own name even when it is spoken softly in a nonattended conversation. This could not happen if the entire nonattended message were lost at lower levels of the perceptual system. Hence, lack of attention does not block messages entirely, but rather attenuates them, much like a volume control that is turned down but not off (Treisman, 1969).

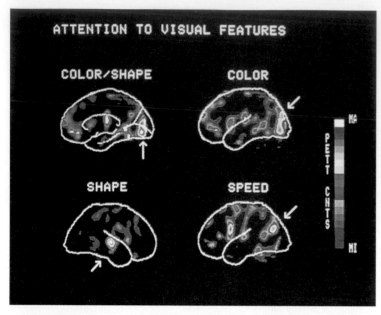

Figure 4-35

PET Images Reveal Differences in Cortical Activity   The image on the top right is from the condition in which participants attended to changes in color, whereas the images in the bottom row are from the conditions in which individuals attended to changes in shape or speed.

The Neural Bases of Attention

In the past several years there have been breakthroughs in our understanding of the neural basis of attention, particularly for visual attention. The research has concerned two major questions: (1) What brain structures control the psychological act of selecting an object to attend to? and (2) How does the subsequent neural processing differ for attended and nonattended stimuli? Let's consider these questions in turn.

It appears that the brain contains two separate systems that guide the selection of inputs. One system is geared to locations; it is responsible for selecting one location among many and for shifting from one location to the next. It is referred to as the *posterior system* because the brain structures involved are in the back of the brain. Thus, when people are instructed to shift their attention from one location to another while having their brain scanned, the cortical areas that show the greatest increase in blood flow—and hence neural activity—are the parietal lobes at the back of the brain (Corbetta et al., 1993). The other attentional system is geared to attributes of an object other than its location—for example, its shape or color. It is referred to as the *anterior system* because the structures involved are in the front of the brain. In short, we can select an object for attention by focusing either on its location or on some other attribute, and two entirely different regions of the brain are used to implement these two kinds of selectivity (Moran & Desimone, 1985; Posner, 1988).

Once an object has been selected for attention, what changes occur in its neural processing? To make things concrete, suppose that you are presented with a set of colored objects and instructed to attend only to the red ones. The anterior system will shift attention to color, but what else changes in your neural processing of each stimulus? The answer is that the regions of the visual cortex that process color become more active than they would be if you were not selectively attending to color. More generally, the activity of brain regions relevant to the attribute being attended to (be it color, shape, texture, motion, and so forth) will be *amplified* (Posner & Dehaene, 1994). Evidence for this amplification comes from brain scanning studies. In one experiment (Corbetta et al., 1993), participants viewed moving objects of varying color and form while having their brains scanned. In one condition, participants had to detect changes among the objects in motion; in another, they had to detect changes among objects in color; hence, motion is the attended attribute in the first condition, color in the second. Even though the physical stimuli were identical in the two conditions, cortical areas known to be involved in the processing of motion were found to be more active in the first condition, whereas areas involved in color processing were more active in the second condition (see Figure 4-35). Attention, then, amplifies what is relevant, not only psychologically but neurologically as well.

How Does Perception Develop?

An age-old question about perception is whether our perceptual abilities are learned or innate. Psychologists no longer believe that this is an either-or question. No one doubts that both genetics and learning influence perception; rather, the goal is to pinpoint the contribution of each and spell out their interaction. For the modern researcher, the question "Must we learn to perceive?" has given way to more specific questions: (1) What discriminatory capacity do infants have (which tells us something about inborn capacities), and how does this capacity change with age under normal child-rearing conditions? (2) If animals are reared under conditions that restrict what they can learn (referred to as *controlled stimulation*), what effects does this have on their later discriminatory capacity? (3) What effects does rearing under controlled conditions have on perceptual–motor coordination?

Discriminatory Capacities in Infants

Perhaps the most direct way to find out what perceptual capacities are inborn is to determine what capacities an infant has. At first, you might think that the research should consider only newborns, because if a capacity is inborn it should be present from the first day of life. This idea turns out to be too simple, though. Some inborn capacities, such as form perception, can appear only after other more basic capacities, such as seeing details, have developed. Other inborn capacities may require that there be some kind of environmental input for an appreciable time in order for the capacity to mature. Thus the study of inborn capacities traces perceptual development from the first minute of life through the early years of childhood.

Methods of Studying Infants   Because infants cannot talk or follow instructions, it is hard to know what they perceive. A researcher needs to find a form of behavior through which an infant indicates what it can discriminate. One behavior used for this purpose is an infant's tendency to look at some objects more than others. Psychologists make use of this behavior in the *preferential looking method:* Two stimuli, side by side, are presented to the infant. The experimenter, who is hidden from the infant's view, looks through a partition behind the stimuli and, by watching the infant's eyes, measures the amount of time the infant looks at each stimulus. Occasionally, the stimulus positions are switched randomly. If an infant consistently looks at one stimulus more than the other, the experimenter concludes that the infant can tell them apart—that is, discriminate between them.

A related technique is the *habituation method* (Frantz, 1966; Horowitz, 1974). It takes advantage of the fact that, although infants look directly at novel objects, they soon tire of doing so; in other words, they habituate. Suppose that a novel object is presented for a while and then replaced by another object. To the extent that the second object is perceived as identical or highly similar to the first one, the infant should spend little time looking at it; conversely, to the extent that the second object is perceived as substantially different from the first one, the infant should spend a lot of time staring at it. By these means, an experimenter can determine whether two physical displays look the same to an infant.

Using these techniques, psychologists have studied a variety of perceptual capacities in infants. Some of these capacities are needed to perceive forms, and hence are used in the task of recognition; other capacities studied in infants, particularly depth perception, are involved in the task of localization.

Perceiving Forms   To be able to perceive an object, one must first be able to discriminate one part of it from another—this is *visual acuity.* Related to acuity is the ability to discriminate between dark and light stripes under various conditions. (The dark and light stripes can correspond to different parts of a pattern.) The method typically used in studying acuity is preferential looking, with a pattern of stripes as one stimulus and a uniform gray field as the other stimulus. Initially, the stripes are relatively wide, and the infant prefers to look at the pattern rather than at the uniform field. Then the researcher decreases the width of the stripe until the infant no longer shows a preference. Presumably, at this point the infant can no longer discriminate a stripe from its surroundings so the pattern of stripes no longer has perceptible parts and looks like a uniform field. When first studied at about 1 month of

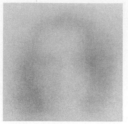

Figure 4-36

Visual Acuity and Contrast Sensitivity   Simulations of what 1-, 2-, and 3-month-old infants see
when they look at a woman's face from a distance of about six inches; the far right photograph is what
an adult sees. The simulations of infant perception were obtained by first determining an infant's contrast
sensitivity and then applying this contrast-sensitivity function to the photograph on the far right. (After
Ginsberg, 1983)

age, infants can see some patterns, but their acuity is very low. Acuity increases rapidly over the first 6 months of life; then it increases more slowly, reaching adult levels between 1 and 5 years of age (Pirchio et al., 1978; Teller et al., 1974).

What do studies like this tell us about the infant's perceptual world? At 1 month
infants can distinguish no fine details; their vision can discriminate only relatively
large objects. Such vision is sufficient, though, to perceive some gross characteristics of an object, including some of the features of a face (which create something
like a pattern of dark and light stripes). Figure 4-36 uses the results of acuity experiments to simulate what 1-, 2-, and 3-month-old infants see when viewing a woman's
face from a distance of 6 inches. At 1 month, acuity is so poor that it is difficult to
perceive facial expressions (and indeed newborns look mostly at the outside con-
tours of a face). By 3 months, acuity has improved to the point where an infant can
decipher facial expressions (Goldstein, 1989). No wonder infants seem so much more
socially responsive at 3 months than at 1 month.

Being able to discriminate dark edges from light ones is critical for seeing forms,
but what about other aspects of object recognition? Our sensitivity to some of the
shape features of objects is manifested early. When presented with a triangle, even a
3-day-old infant will direct its eye movements toward the edges and vertices, rather
than looking randomly over the form (Salapatek, 1975). Also, infants find some
shapes more interesting than others. They tend to look more at forms that resemble
human faces (Fantz, 1961, 1970). By 3 months, an infant can recognize something
about the mother's face, even in a photograph, as revealed by an infant's preference
for looking at a photograph of the mother rather than at one of an unfamiliar woman
(Barrera & Maurer, 1981).

Perceiving Depth   Depth perception begins to appear at about 3 months of age
but is not fully established until about 6 months. Thus, at 5½ months, but not before, infants will reach for the nearer of two objects, where nearness is signaled by
the monocular cue of relative size. Further evidence about the development of
monocular depth perception comes from studies of the *visual cliff.* The visual cliff (illustrated in Figure 4-37) consists of a board placed across a sheet of glass, with a
surface of patterned material located directly under the glass on the shallow side
and at a distance of a few feet below the glass on the deep side. (The appearance of
depth—the cliff—is created by an abrupt change in the texture gradient.) An infant
old enough to crawl (6 to 7 months) is placed on the board; a patch is placed over
one of her eyes to eliminate binocular depth cues. When the mother calls or beckons from the shallow side, the infant will consistently crawl toward her; but when
the mother beckons from the deep side, the infant will not cross the "cliff." Thus,
when an infant is old enough to crawl, depth perception is relatively well developed.

Figure 4-37

The Visual Cliff The "visual cliff" is an apparatus used to show that infants and young animals are able to see depth by the time they are able to move about. The apparatus consists of two surfaces, both displaying the same checkerboard pattern and covered by a sheet of thick glass. One surface is directly under the glass; the other is several feet below it. When placed on the center board between the deep side and the shallow side, the kitten refuses to cross to the deep side but will readily move off the board onto the shallow side. (After Gibson & Walk, 1960)

Effects of Rearing With Controlled Stimulation

We turn now to the question of how specific experiences affect perceptual capacities. To answer this question, researchers have systematically varied the kinds of perceptual experiences a young organism has, and then looked at the effects on subsequent perceptual performance. While the intent of these studies has usually been to study learning, the variations in experiences sometimes affect innate processes.

Absence of Stimulation The earliest experiments sought to determine the effects of rearing an animal in the total absence of visual stimulation. The experimenters kept animals in the dark for several months after birth until they were mature enough for testing. The idea behind these experiments was that if animals have to learn to perceive, they would be unable to perceive when first exposed to the light. The results turned out as expected: Chimpanzees reared in darkness for their first 16 months could detect light but could not discriminate among different patterns (Riesen, 1947). However, subsequent studies showed that prolonged rearing in the dark does more than prevent learning; it causes neurons in various parts of the visual system to deteriorate. It turns out that a certain amount of light stimulation is necessary to maintain the visual system. Without any light stimulation, nerve cells in the retina and visual cortex begin to atrophy.

Although these findings do not tell us much about the role of learning in perceptual development, they are important in themselves. In general, when an animal is deprived of visual stimulation from birth, the longer the time of deprivation, the greater the deficit. Adult cats, on the other hand, can have a patch over one eye for a long period without losing vision in that eye. These observations led to the idea of a critical period for the development of inborn visual capacities. Recall from Chapter

critical or sensitive periods stages in development during which the organism is optimally ready to acquire certain abilities

3 that a **critical period** is *a stage in development during which the organism is optimally ready to acquire certain abilities.* Lack of stimulation during a critical period for vision can permanently impair the visual system.

Limited Stimulation   Researchers no longer deprive animals of stimulation for long periods; instead, they study the effects of rearing animals with only certain kinds of stimulation. Researchers have raised kittens in an environment in which they see only vertical stripes or only horizontal stripes. The kittens become blind to stripes in the orientation—horizontal or vertical—that they do not experience (Blakemore & Cooper, 1970; Hirsch & Spinelli, 1970). This blindness seems to be caused by degeneration of cells in the visual cortex.

Of course, researchers do not deprive humans of normal visual stimulation, but sometimes this happens naturally or as a consequence of medical treatment. For example, after eye surgery the operated eye is usually patched. If this happens to a child in the first year of life, the acuity of the patched eye is reduced (Awaya et al., 1973). This suggests that there is a critical period early in the development of the human visual system similar to that in animals; if stimulation is restricted during this period, the system will not develop normally. The critical period is much longer in humans than in animals. It may last as long as 8 years, but the greatest vulnerability occurs during the first 2 years of life (Aslin & Banks, 1978).

None of these facts indicates that we have to learn to perceive. Rather, they show that certain kinds of stimulation are essential for the development of perceptual capacities that are present at birth. But this does not mean that learning has no effect on perception. For evidence of such effects we need only consider our ability to recognize common objects. The fact that we can more readily recognize a familiar object than an unfamiliar one—a dog versus an aardvark, for example—must certainly be due to learning. (If we had been reared in an environment that was rich in aardvarks and sparse in dogs, we could have recognized the aardvark more readily than the dog.)

Figure 4-38

The Importance of Self-Produced Movements   Both kittens receive roughly the same visual stimulation, but only the active kitten had this stimulation produced by its own movement. (After Held & Hein, 1963)

Learning Perceptual–Motor Coordination

When it comes to coordinating perceptions with motor responses, learning plays a major role. The evidence for this comes from studies in which participants receive normal stimulation but are prevented from making normal responses to that stimulation. Under such conditions, perceptual–motor coordination does not develop.

For example, in one classic study, two kittens that had been reared in darkness had their first visual experience in the "kitten carousel" illustrated in Figure 4-38. As the active kitten walked, it moved the passive kitten riding in the carousel. Although both kittens received roughly the same visual stimulation, only for the active kitten was this stimulation produced by its own movement. And only the active kitten successfully learned sensory–motor coordination;

for example, when picked up and moved toward an object, only the active kitten learned to put out its paws to ward off a collision.

Similar results have been obtained with humans. In some experiments people have worn prism goggles that distort the directions of objects. Immediately after putting on these goggles, a person temporarily has trouble reaching for objects and bumps into things. If a person moves about and attempts to perform motor tasks while wearing the goggles, he or she learns to behave adaptively. The person is learning to coordinate his or her movements with the actual locations of objects rather than with their apparent locations. On the other hand, if the person is pushed in a wheelchair, he or she does not adapt to the goggles. Apparently, self-produced movement is essential to prism adaptation (Held, 1965).

In sum, the evidence indicates that we are born with considerable perceptual capacities. The natural development of some of these capacities may require years of normal input from the environment; hence, environmental effects early in development are often more indicative of innate processes than of learned ones. But there clearly are learning effects on perception as well, and these are particularly striking when perception must be coordinated with motor behavior.

Some people are skeptical about the value of studying a psychological phenomenon at the biological level. Given what you have learned about the visual sense, how would you argue against such skeptics?

Thinking Critically

Summary

1. The major senses are vision; hearing (audition); smell (olfaction); taste (gustation); and the skin senses, which include pressure, temperature, and pain. Studies of *sensation* typically focus on single attributes of simple stimuli, whereas studies of *perception* typically focus on reactions to whole objects. A property that is common to all senses is sensitivity to change. Sensitivity to intensity is measured by the *absolute threshold,* the minimum amount of stimulus energy that can be reliably detected. Sensitivity to a change in intensity is measured by the *difference threshold* or *just noticeable difference,* the minimum difference between two stimuli that can be reliably detected.

2. Every sense modality must recode its physical energy into neural impulses; this *transduction* process is accomplished by the receptors. The receptors and connecting neural pathways code the *intensity* of a stimulus primarily by the rate of neural impulses and their patterns; they code the quality of a stimulus by the specific nerve fibers involved and their pattern of activity.

3. The stimulus for audition is a wave of pressure changes (a sound wave), and the sense organs are the ears. The ear includes the outer ear (the external ear and the auditory canal); the middle ear (the eardrum and a chain of bones); and the inner ear. The inner ear includes the cochlea, a coiled tube that contains the basilar membrane, which supports the hair cells that serve as the receptors for sound. Sound waves transmitted by the outer and middle ear cause the basilar membrane to vibrate. This results in bending of the hair cells and produces a neural impulse. *Pitch,* the most striking quality of sound, increases with the *frequency* of the sound wave.

4. The stimuli for smell are the molecules given off by a substance, which travel by air and activate the olfactory receptors in the nasal cavity. There are many kinds of receptors (on the order of 1,000). A normal person can discriminate among 10,000 to 40,000 different odors.

The stimulus for taste is a substance that is soluble in saliva; many of the receptors occur in clusters on the tongue (taste buds). Sensitivity varies from place to place on the tongue. Any taste can be described as one or a combination of four qualities: sweet, sour, salty, and bitter. Different qualities of taste are coded partly in terms of the specific nerve fibers activated and partly in terms of the pattern of fibers activated.

5. The skin senses include pressure, temperature, and pain. Sensitivity to pressure is greatest at the lips, nose, and cheeks. We are very sensitive to temperature, being able to detect a change of less than 1 degree centigrade. We code different kinds of temperatures primarily by whether hot or cold receptors are activated. Any stimulus that is intense enough to cause tissue damage is a stimulus for pain. Sensitivity to pain is influenced by factors other than the stimulus, including cultural beliefs. These factors seem to have their influence by opening or closing a neural gate in the spinal cord and midbrain; pain is felt only when pain receptors are activated and the gate is open.

6. The stimulus for vision is electromagnetic radiation with wavelengths from 350 to 750 nanometers, and the sense organs are the eyes. Each eye contains a system for forming the image (including the cornea, pupil, and lens) and a system for transducing the image into electrical impulses. The transduction system is in the retina, which contains the visual receptors, the rods and cones. Cones operate at high intensities, lead to sensations of color, and are found only in the center (or fovea) of the retina; rods operate at low intensities, lead to colorless sensations, and predominate in the periphery of the retina.

7. Different wavelengths of light lead to sensations of different colors. A mixture of three lights widely separated in wavelength can be made to match almost any color of light.

This fact and others led to the development of trichromatic theory, which holds that the perception of color is based on the activity of three types of receptors (cones), each of which is maximally sensitive to wavelengths in a different region of the spectrum.

8. The study of perception deals with two major functions of the perceptual system: localization, or determining where objects are, and recognition, or determining what objects are. To accomplish these functions, the visual cortex operates according to a division-of-labor principle. Localization and recognition are carried out by different regions of the brain, with localization controlled by a region near the top of the cortex and recognition controlled by a region near the bottom of the cortex. Recognition processes are further subdivided into separate modules—for example, color, shape, and texture.

9. To localize objects, we first segregate them from one another and then organize them into groups. Gestalt psychologists were the first to propose principles of organization. One such principle is that we organize a stimulus into regions corresponding to figure and ground. Other principles concern the bases that we use to group objects together, including proximity and closure. Localizing an object also requires that we know its depth. Depth perception is usually thought to be based on depth cues. Monocular depth cues include relative size, superposition, relative height, and linear perspective. Binocular depth cues include *parallax* and *disparity*.

10. Localizing an object sometimes requires understanding the motion of moving objects. Motion perception can be produced in the absence of an object moving across our retina; an example is stroboscopic motion, in which a rapid series of still images induces apparent movement; another case of motion perception without a moving object is

induced motion, in which movement of a large object induces apparent movement of a smaller stationary object. Real motion (induced by an object moving across the retina) is implemented in the brain by specific cells in the visual system.

11. Recognizing an object amounts to assigning it to a category and is based mainly on the shape of the object. In early stages of recognition, the visual system uses retinal information to describe the object in terms of features like lines and angles; neurons that detect such features (feature detectors) have been found in the visual cortex. These primitive features may be used to derive the shape features of natural objects, which are simple forms such as cylinders, cones, blocks, and wedges. In the late stages of recognition, the system matches the description of the object with shape representations stored in memory to find the best match. The stored representations appear to be organized by content, with, for example, face representations separate from representations of other objects.

12. Bottom-up recognition processes are driven solely by the input, whereas top-down recognition processes are driven by a person's knowledge and expectations. Top-down processes lie behind context effects in perception: The context sets up a perceptual expectation, and when this expectation is satisfied, less input information than usual is needed for recognition.

13. Another major function of the perceptual system is to keep the appearance of objects the same in spite of large changes in the stimuli received by the sense organs. *Lightness constancy* refers to the fact that an object appears equally light regardless of how much light it reflects; *color constancy* means that an object looks roughly the same color regardless of the light source illuminating it. In both cases, constancy depends on relationships between object and background elements; this is also true of two other well-known constancies, *shape constancy* and *location constancy. Size constancy* refers to the fact that any object's size remains relatively constant no matter how far away it is. The perceived size of an object increases with both the retinal size of the object and the perceived distance of the object, in accordance with the size–distance invariance principle. Thus, as an object moves away from the perceiver, its retinal size decreases but the perceived distance increases; the two changes cancel each other out, resulting in constancy.

14. *Selective attention* is the process by which we select some stimuli for further processing while ignoring others. In vision, the primary means for directing our attention are eye movements. Most eye fixations are on the more informative parts of a scene. In audition, we are usually able to selectively listen by using cues like the direction of the sound and the voice characteristics of the speaker. Two separate brain systems seem to guide the psychological act of selecting an object to attend to. The posterior system is responsible for selecting on the basis of localization, and the anterior system controls selection on the basis of other attributes, such as shape and color. PET studies show that once an object has been selected, the activity of brain regions relevant to the attribute being attended to is amplified.

15. Research on perceptual development is concerned with the extent to which perceptual capacity is inborn and/or learned by experience, and it relies on methods like preferential looking and habituation. Acuity, which is critical to recognition, increases rapidly over the first 6 months of life and then increases more slowly. Depth perception begins to appear at about 3 months of age but is not fully established until about 6 months. Animals raised in

darkness suffer permanent visual impairment, and animals raised with a patch over one eye become blind in that eye. Adult animals do not lose vision even when deprived of stimulation for long periods. These results suggest a *critical period* early in life during which lack of normal stimulation produces impairment in an innate perceptual capacity. Perceptual–motor coordination must be learned, however. Both animals and people require self-produced movement to develop normal coordination.

Suggested Readings

There are numerous good general texts on sensory processes and perception. A particularly clear one is Goldstein, *Sensation and Perception* (3rd ed., 1989). Other useful texts include Barlow and Mollon, *The Senses* (1982); Coren and Ward, *Sensation and Perception* (3rd ed., 1989); Schiffman, *Sensation and Perception* (3rd ed., 1990); and Sekuler and Blake, *Perception* (1985).

Introductory books on audition include Moore, *An Introduction to the Psychology of Hearing* (2nd ed., 1982); and Yost and Nielson, *Fundamentals of Hearing* (2nd ed., 1985). For smell, see Engen, *The Perception of Odors* (1982); for touch, *Tactual Perception* (1982), edited by Schiff and Foulke; and for pain, *The Psychology of Pain* (2nd ed., 1986), edited by Sternbach. For treatments of color vision, see Boynton, *Human Color Vision* (1979); and Hurvich, *Color Vision* (1981).

For reference works on sensory processes, there are a number of multivolume handbooks, each of which has several chapters on sensory systems. They are the *Handbook of Physiology: The Nervous System: Section 1, Vol. 3, Sensory Processes* (1984), edited by Darian-Smith; the *Handbook of Perception and Human Performance: Vol. 1, Sensory Processes and Perception* (1986), edited by Boff, Kaufman, and Thomas; and Stevens's *Handbook of Experimental Psychology: Vol. 1* (1988), edited by Atkinson, Herrnstein, Lindzey, and Luce.

For general texts that emphasize perception, see Kosslyn, *Invitation to Cognitive Science: Vol. 2, Visual Cognition* (2nd ed., 1995); Coren and Ward, *Sensation and Perception* (3rd ed., 1989); and Rock, *The Logic of Perception* (1983). Gibson's distinctive direct-perception approach is presented in *The Ecological Approach to Visual Perception* (1986). Marr's equally distinctive, cognitive-science approach to perception is given in his book *Vision* (1982).

Problems of recognition and attention are discussed in Spoehr and Lehmkuhle, *Visual Information Processing* (1982). Studies of brain mechanisms involved in recognition are discussed in Farah, *Visual Agnosia: Disorders of Object Recognition and What They Tell Us About Normal Vision* (1990); and Posner and Marin (eds.), *Mechanisms of Attention* (1985). Recent advances in brain scanning are described in Posner and Raichle, *Images of Mind* (1994).

Enhance and Explore

To enhance your understanding of the psychological concepts found in this chapter, please consult the following aids:

Study Guide

Learning Objectives, p. 66
Define the Terms, p. 70
Test Your Knowledge, p. 75
Essay Questions, p. 83
Thinking Independently, p. 85

PowerPsych CD-ROM

WHAT IS THE BASIS OF VISION?
Anatomy of the Eye

HOW DO WE KEEP THE PERCEPTUAL WORLD CONSTANT?
Size Constancy Illusions
The Ames Room
The Moon Illusion

PsychCentral

For more information concerning the topics found in this chapter, access psychology links on the Word Wide Web made through the Harcourt Web page at:
http://www.harcourtcollege.com/psych/Fundamentals

www.harcourtcollege.com
http://www.harcourtcollege.com/psych/index.html

CONTEMPORARY VOICES IN PSYCHOLOGY

Is perceptual development an innate or socially acquired process?

Perceptual Development Is an Intrinsic Process

Elizabeth S. Spelke, *Massachusetts Institute of Technology*

Human beings have a striking capacity to learn from one another. This capacity already is evident in the 1-year-old child, who can learn the meaning of a new word by observing just a few occasions of its use and who can learn the functions of a new object simply by watching another person act on it. The rapid and extensive learning that occurs in early childhood suggests that much of what humans come to know and believe is shaped by our encounters with other things and people. But is our very ability to perceive things and people itself the result of learning? Or, does perception originate in intrinsically generated growth processes and develop in relative independence of one's encounters with things perceived?

For two millennia, most of the thinkers who have pondered this question have favored the view that humans learn to perceive, and that the course of development proceeds from meaningless, unstructured sensations to meaningful, structured perceptions. Research on human infants nevertheless provides evidence against this view. For example, we now know that newborn infants perceive depth and use depth information as adults do, to apprehend the true sizes and shapes of objects. Newborn infants divide the speech stream into the same kinds of sound patterns as do adults, focusing in particular on the set of sound contrasts used by human languages. Newborn infants distinguish human faces from other patterns and orient to faces preferentially. Finally, newborn infants are sensitive to many of the features of objects that adults use to distinguish one thing from another, and they appear to combine featural information in the same kinds of ways as do adults.

How does perception change after the newborn period? With development, infants have been found to perceive depth, objects, and faces with increasing precision. Infants also come to focus on the speech contrasts that are relevant to their own language in preference to speech contrasts relevant to other languages. (Interestingly, this focus appears to result more from a decline in sensitivity to foreign language contrasts than from an increase in sensitivity to native language contrasts.) Finally, infants become sensitive to new sources of information about the environment, such as stereoscopic information for depth, configural information for object boundaries, and new reference frames for locating objects and events. These developments bring greater precision and richness to infants' perceptual experience, but they do not change the infant's world from a meaningless flow of sensation to a meaningful, structured environment.

The findings from studies of human infants gain further support from studies of perceptual development in other animals. Since the pioneering work of Gibson and Walk, we have known that depth perception develops without visual experience in every animal tested: Innate capacities for perceiving depth allow newborn goats to avoid falling off cliffs, and they allow dark-reared rats and cats to avoid bumping into approaching surfaces. More recent studies reveal that newborn chicks perceive the boundaries of objects much as human adults do, and they even represent the continued existence of objects that are hidden. Studies of animals' developing brains reveal that both genes and intrinsically structured neural activity are crucial to the development of normally functioning perceptual systems, but encounters with the objects of perception—external things and events—play a much lesser role. As with human infants, normal visual experience enriches and attunes young animals' perceptual systems, and abnormal visual experience may greatly perturb their functioning. Like human infants, however, other animals do not need visual experience to transform their perceptual world from a flow of unstructured sensations into a structured visual layout.

In sum, perception shows considerable structure at birth and continuity over development. This continuity may help to explain why young human infants are so adept at learning from other people. Consider an infant who watches an adult twist a lid off a jar while saying, "Let's open it." If the infant could not perceive the lid and jar as distinct movable and manipulable objects, she would not be able to make sense of the adult's action. If she could not perceive the sounds that distinguish "open" from other words, she could not begin to learn about this distinctive utterance. And if she could not perceive the person as an agent in some way like herself, then watching the person's action and listening to his speech would reveal nothing about what the infant herself could learn to do or say. Infants' prodigious abilities to learn, therefore, may depend critically on equally prodigious, unlearned abilities to perceive.

Elizabeth S. Spelke

Perceptual Development Is an Activity-Dependent Process

Mark Johnson, *University of London*

Most developmental scientists now agree that both nature and nurture are essential for the normal development of perception. However, there is still much dispute about the extent to which either nature or nurture is the more important factor. Points of view on this issue are more than just philosophical musings; they affect the kinds of experiments that are undertaken. In this essay I will argue that classifying particular aspects of perceptual development as being either innate or learned presents us with an overly passive view in which either genes or environment impose structure on the developing brain. In contrast, I suggest that perceptual development is better characterized as an activity-dependent process involving complex and subtle interactions at many levels.

To begin to illustrate my point, let's consider some recent neurobiological work on the prenatal development of the visual cortex in rodents. The neurons studied in these experiments are those involved in binocular vision. Experiments show that the prenatal tuning of these neurons arises through their response to internally generated waves of electrical activity from the main inputs to the visual cortex, the LGN and eye (Katz & Shatz, 1996). In other words, the response properties of these visual cortical neurons are shaped by a kind of "virtual environment" generated by cells elsewhere in the brain and eye. While it is possible to stretch this term *innate* to cover this example of development, we could equally well describe this process as the cortical cells "learning" from the input provided by their cousins in the LGN and eye. Further, after birth the same cortical neurons continue to be tuned in the same way, except that now their input also reflects the structure of the world outside the infant. Thus, when we examine development in detail it becomes harder to argue, as some theorists do (Spelke, 1998), that "innate knowledge" is fundamentally different from learning.

Another example of the role of activity-dependent processes in perceptual development comes from the ability to detect and recognize faces. Since it is known that there are regions of the human cortex specialized for processing faces, some have argued that this ability is innate. However, experiments with infants reveal a more complex story (Johnson, 1997). The tendency for newborns to look more toward faces turns out to be based on a very primitive reflex-like system that is triggered by a stimulus as simple as three high-contrast blobs in the approximate locations of the eyes and mouth. This simple bias is sufficient to ensure that newborns look much more at faces than at other objects and patterns over the first weeks of life. One consequence of this is that developing circuits on the visual recognition pathway of the cortex get more input related to faces and thus are shaped by experience with this special type of visual stimulus. We can now study this process by using new brain imaging methods. Such studies have shown that the brains of young infants show less localized and less specialized processing of faces in the cortex than do the brains of adults. It is not until 1 year old that infants show the same patterns of brain specialization for processing faces as adults, by which time they have had as much as 1,000 hours of exposure to human faces.

Another example comes from the study of infants' eye movements to visual targets. While newborns are capable of some primitive reflexive eye movements, it is not until much later in the first year that they can make most of the kinds of complex and accurate saccades seen in adults. One view is that the very limited ability present in newborns is just sufficient to allow them to practice and develop new brain circuits for the more complex integration of visual and motor information necessary for adult eye movements. And

Mark Johnson

practice they do! Even by 4 months, babies have already made over 3 million eye movements. Once again, it appears that infants actively contribute to their own subsequent development.

These considerations should make us skeptical about the many claims for innate perceptual abilities based on experiments with babies of 4 months and older. In fact, it has often turned out that when the same experiments were done with younger infants, quite different results were obtained, suggesting dramatic changes in perceptual abilities over the first few weeks and months after birth (Haith, 1998).

To conclude, infants are not passively shaped by either their genes or their environment. Rather, perceptual development is an activity-dependent process in which, during postnatal life, the infant plays an active role in generating the experience it needs for subsequent development.

When we concentrate, we are unaware of background stimuli such as other people's conversations. This ability to select stimuli to focus on enables us to avoid information overload.

must again be defined exclusively as the study of consciousness; it means only that a complete science of psychology cannot afford to neglect consciousness. If one can develop a theory about the nature of consciousness, and that theory leads to testable predictions about behavior, then such theorizing is a valuable contribution to understanding how the mind works.

Consciousness

Many textbooks define *consciousness* as the individual's current awareness of external and internal stimuli—that is, of events in the environment and of body sensations, memories, and thoughts. This definition identifies only one aspect of consciousness. It ignores the fact that we are also conscious when we try to solve a problem or deliberately select one course of action over others in response to environmental circumstances and personal goals. Thus, we are conscious not only when we monitor the environment (internal and external), but also when we seek to control ourselves and our environment. In short, **consciousness** involves (1) *monitoring ourselves and our environment so that perceptions, memories, and thoughts are represented in awareness;* and (2) *controlling ourselves and our environment so that we are able to initiate and terminate behavioral and cognitive activities* (Kihlstrom, 1984).

consciousness monitoring ourselves and our environment so that perceptions, memories, and thoughts are represented in awareness, and controlling ourselves and our environment so that we are able to initiate and terminate behavioral and cognitive activities

Monitoring   Processing information from the environment is the main function of the body's sensory systems. This processing leads to awareness of what is going on in our surroundings as well as within our own bodies. However, we could not possibly attend to all the stimuli that impinge on our senses; if we did, we would experience an information overload. Our consciousness therefore focuses on some stimuli and ignores others. Often the information selected has to do with changes in our external or internal worlds. While concentrating on this paragraph, for example, you are probably unaware of numerous background stimuli. But should there be a change—the lights dim, the air begins to smell smoky, or the noise of the air-conditioning system ceases—you would suddenly be aware of such stimuli.

Our attention is selective; some events take precedence over others in gaining access to consciousness and initiating action. Events that are important to survival usually have top priority. If we are hungry, it is difficult to concentrate on studying; if we experience a sudden pain, we push all other thoughts out of consciousness until we have done something to make the pain go away.

Controlling   Another function of consciousness is to plan, initiate, and guide our actions. Whether the plan is simple and readily completed (such as meeting a friend for lunch) or complex and long-range (such as preparing for a career), our actions must be guided and arranged to coordinate with events around us. In planning, events that have not yet occurred can be represented in consciousness as future possibilities; we may envision alternative scenarios, make choices, and initiate appropriate activities (Johnson-Laird, 1988).

Not all actions are guided by conscious decisions, nor are the solutions to all problems carried out at a conscious level. One of the tenets of modern psychology is that mental events involve both conscious and nonconscious processes and that many decisions and actions are conducted entirely outside the range of consciousness. The solution to a problem may occur "out of the blue" without our being aware that we have been thinking about it. And once we have the solution, we may be unable to say how the solution was obtained. One can cite many examples of decision making and problem solving that occur at a nonconscious level, but this does not mean that all such behaviors occur without conscious reflection. Consciousness is not only a monitor of ongoing behavior; it plays a role in directing and controlling that behavior as well.

Preconscious Memories

As just noted, we cannot focus on everything that is going on around us at any given time, nor can we examine our entire store of knowledge and memories of past events. At any given moment we can focus on only a few stimuli. We ignore, select, and reject all the time, so that the contents of consciousness are continually changing. Nevertheless, objects or events that are not the focus of attention can still have some influence on consciousness. For example, you may not be aware of hearing a clock strike the hour. After a few strokes, you become alert; then you can go back and count the strokes that you did not know you heard. Another example of peripheral attention (or nonconscious monitoring) is the lunch-line effect (Farthing, 1992)—also called the "cocktail party effect." You are talking with a friend in a cafeteria line, ignoring other voices and general noise, when the sound of your name in another conversation catches your attention. Clearly, you would not have detected your name in the other conversation if you had not, in some sense, been monitoring that conversation; you were not consciously aware of the other conversation until a special signal drew your attention to it. A considerable amount of research indicates that we register and evaluate stimuli that we do not consciously perceive (Greenwald, 1992; Kihlstrom, 1987). These stimuli are said to influence us *subconsciously,* or to operate at a nonconscious level of awareness.

Many memories and thoughts that are not part of your consciousness at this moment can be brought to consciousness when needed. At this moment you may not be conscious of the vacation you took last summer, but the memories are accessible if you wish to retrieve them; then they become a part of your consciousness. The term **preconscious memories** is used to refer to *memories that are accessible to consciousness.* They include specific memories of personal events as well as the information accumulated over a lifetime, such as one's knowledge of the meaning of words, the layout of the streets of a city, or the location of a particular country. They also include knowledge about learned skills such as the procedures involved in driving a car or the sequence of steps in tying one's shoelaces. These procedures, once mastered, generally operate outside conscious awareness, but when our attention is called to them we are capable of describing the steps involved.

preconscious memories memories that are accessible to consciousness

The Unconscious

One of the earliest theories of consciousness—and one that has been subject to considerable criticism over the years—is the psychoanalytic theory of Sigmund Freud. Freud and his followers believed that there is a portion of the mind, the **unconscious,** that contains *some memories, impulses, and desires that are not accessible to consciousness.* Freud believed that some emotionally painful memories and wishes are *repressed*—that is, diverted to the unconscious, where they may continue to influence our actions even though we are not aware of them. Repressed thoughts and impulses cannot enter our consciousness, but they can affect us in indirect or disguised ways—through dreams, irrational behaviors, mannerisms, and slips of the tongue. The term "Freudian slip" is commonly used to refer to unintentional remarks that are assumed to reveal hidden impulses. Saying "I'm sad you're better" when intending to say "I'm glad you're better" is an example of such a slip.

unconscious a portion of the mind that contains some memories, impulses, and desires that are not accessible to consciousness

"Good morning, beheaded—uh, I mean beloved."

Drawing by Dana Fradon; ©1979 The New York Times Magazine.

Freud believed that unconscious desires and impulses are the cause of most mental illnesses. He developed the method of *psychoanalysis,* whose goal is to draw the repressed material back into consciousness and, in so doing, cure the individual (see Chapter 13). Most psychologists accept the idea that there are memories and mental processes that are inaccessible to introspection and hence may be described as unconscious. However, many would argue that Freud placed undue emphasis on the emotional aspects of the unconscious and not enough on other aspects. They would include in the unconscious a large array of mental processes that we constantly depend on in our everyday lives but to which we have no conscious access (Kihlstrom, 1987). For example, during perception the viewer may be aware of two objects in the environment but have no awareness of the mental calculations that he or she performed almost instantaneously to determine that one of them is closer or larger than the other (see Chapter 4). Although we have conscious access to the outcome of these mental processes in that we are aware of the size and distance of the object, we have no conscious access to their operations (Velmans, 1991).

A study of the stereotypes people hold about the elderly (for example, that they are slow and weak) provided a striking demonstration of how cues from the environment can influence our behavior without our conscious knowledge. Participants were first given a "language test" in which they had to decipher a number of scrambled sentences. Some participants were given sentences that contained words such as *forgetful, Florida,* and *bingo*—words that the researchers believed would subconsciously evoke or "prime" the elderly stereotype in their minds; control participants saw sentences that did not contain these words. After the language test was completed, each participant was thanked and allowed to leave. A research assistant—who did not know which participants had been in the experimental group or the control group—surreptitiously measured how long it took each of them to walk down the 40-foot hallway to the exit. The researchers found that participants who had been primed with the elderly stereotype words walked more slowly than control participants. (The word *slow* had not appeared in the sentences.) Interviews with the participants showed that they had no awareness of this influence on their behavior (Bargh, Chen, & Burrows, 1996).

Automaticity and Dissociation

An important function of consciousness is the control of our actions. However, some activities are practiced so often that they become habitual or automatic. Learning to drive a car requires intense concentration at first. We have to concentrate on coordinating the different actions (shifting gears, releasing the

For experienced drivers, the actions involved in driving have become so automatic that they can carry on a phone conversation while driving.

clutch, accelerating, steering, and so forth) and can scarcely think about anything else. However, once the movements become automatic we can carry on a conversation or admire the scenery without being conscious of driving—unless a potential danger appears that quickly draws our attention to the operation of the car. The term **automaticity** refers to this *habituation of responses that initially required conscious attention.*

Skills, such as driving a car or riding a bike, once well learned no longer require our attention. They become automatic, thereby permitting a relatively uncluttered consciousness to focus on other matters. Such automatic processes may have negative consequences on occasion—for example, when a driver cannot remember landmarks passed along the way.

The more automatic an action becomes, the less it requires conscious control. Another example is the skilled pianist who carries on a conversation with a bystander while performing a familiar piece. The pianist is exercising control over two activities—playing and talking—but does not think about the music unless a wrong key is hit, drawing her attention to it and temporarily disrupting the conversation. You can undoubtedly think of other examples of well-learned, automatic activities that require little conscious control. One way of interpreting this is to say that the control is still there (we can focus on automatic processes if we want to) but it has been *dissociated* from consciousness.

The French psychiatrist Pierre Janet (1889) originated the concept of **dissociation,** in which *under certain conditions some thoughts and actions become split off, or dissociated, from the rest of consciousness and function outside of awareness.* Dissociation differs from Freud's concept of repression because the dissociated memories and thoughts are accessible to consciousness. Repressed memories, in contrast, cannot be brought to consciousness; they have to be inferred from signs or symptoms such as slips of the tongue.

When faced with a stressful situation, we may temporarily put it out of our minds in order to be able to function effectively; when bored, we may lapse into reverie or daydreams. These are mild examples of dissociation; they involve dissociating one part of consciousness from another. More extreme examples of dissociation can be seen in cases of dissociative identity disorder, or multiple-personality, which is discussed in Chapter 12.

automaticity habituation of responses that initially required conscious attention

dissociation a condition in which some thoughts and actions become split off, or dissociated, from the rest of consciousness and function outside of awareness

---

Many amateur pianists memorize a piece for a recital by playing it over and over until they can play it automatically, without paying attention to it. Unfortunately, they still often get stuck or forget parts of it during the actual recital. In contrast, some professional pianists deliberately memorize the music away from the piano so that their "mind and not just their fingers" know the piece. What does this imply about automatic processes and the controlling function of consciousness?

Thinking Critically

What Is Known About Sleeping and Dreaming?

We continue our discussion of consciousness with a state that seems to be its opposite: sleep. But while sleep might seem to have little in common with wakefulness, there are similarities between the two states. The phenomenon of dreaming indicates that we think while we sleep, although the type of thinking we do in dreams differs in various ways from the type we do while awake. We form memories while sleeping, as we know from the fact that we remember dreams. Sleep is not entirely quiescent: Some people walk in their sleep. People who are asleep are not entirely insensitive to their environment: Parents are awakened by their baby's cry. Nor is sleep entirely planless: Some people can decide to wake at a given time and do so. In this section we explore several facts of sleep and dreaming.

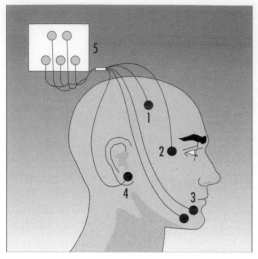

Figure 5-1

Arrangement of Electrodes for Recording the Electrophysiology of Sleep   This diagram shows the way in which electrodes are attached to the person's head and face in a typical sleep experiment. Electrodes on the scalp (1) record the patterns of brain waves. Electrodes near the person's eyes (2) record eye movements. Electrodes on the chin (3) record tension and electrical activity in the muscles. A neutral electrode on the ear (4) completes the circuit through amplifiers (5) that produce graphical records of the various patterns.

Stages of Sleep

Some people are readily aroused from sleep; others are hard to awaken. Research begun in the 1930s (Loomis, Harvey, & Hobart, 1937) has produced sensitive techniques for measuring the depth of sleep and determining when dreams are occurring (Dement & Kleitman, 1957). This research uses devices that measure electrical changes on the scalp associated with spontaneous brain activity during sleep, as well as eye movements that occur during dreaming. The graphic recording of the electrical changes, or brain waves, is called an *electroencephalogram,* or EEG (see Figures 5-1 and 5-2). The EEG measures the rapidly fluctuating average electrical potential of thousands of neurons that lie on the surface of the cortex under the electrode; it is a rather crude measure of cortical activity, but it has proved very useful in sleep research.

Analysis of the patterns of brain waves suggests that there are five stages of sleep: four differing depths of sleep and a fifth stage, known as rapid eye movement (or REM) sleep. When a person closes his or her eyes and relaxes, the brain waves characteristically show a regular pattern of 8 to 12 hertz (cycles per second); these are known as *alpha waves.* As the individual drifts into Stage 1 sleep, the brain waves become less regular and are reduced in amplitude. Stage 2 is characterized by the appearance of *spindles*—short runs of rhythmical responses of 12 to 16 hertz—and an occasional sharp rise and fall in the amplitude of the whole EEG (referred to as a *K-complex*). The still deeper Stages 3 and 4 are characterized by slow waves (1 to 2 hertz), which are known as *delta waves.* Generally it is hard to awaken the sleeper during Stages 3 and 4, although he or she can be aroused by something personal, such as a familiar name or a child crying. A more impersonal disturbance, such as a loud sound, may be ignored.

The Succession of Sleep Stages   After an adult has been asleep for an hour or so, another change occurs. The EEG becomes very active (even more so than when the person is awake), but the person does not wake. The electrodes placed near the eyes detect rapid eye movements; these eye movements are so pronounced that one can even watch the sleeper's eyes move around beneath the closed eyelids. This stage is known as **REM sleep** (for "rapid eye movement"); the other four stages are known collectively as **non-REM sleep** (or NREM).

REM sleep   a stage of sleep in which the sleeper's eyes move rapidly beneath the closed eyelids

non-REM sleep   stages of sleep other than REM sleep

These stages of sleep alternate throughout the night. Sleep begins with the NREM stages and consists of several sleep cycles, each containing some REM and some NREM sleep. Figure 5-3 illustrates a typical night's sleep for a young adult. As you can see, the person goes from wakefulness into a deep sleep (Stage 4) very rapidly. After about 70 minutes, Stage 3 recurs briefly, immediately followed by the first REM period of the night. Notice that the deeper stages (3 and 4) occurred during the first part of the night, whereas most REM sleep occurred in the last part. This is the typical pattern: The deeper stages tend to disappear in the second half of the night as REM becomes more prominent. There are usually four or five distinct REM periods over the course of an 8-hour night, with an occasional brief awakening as morning arrives.

The pattern of the sleep cycles varies with age. Newborn infants spend about half their sleeping time in REM sleep. This proportion drops to 20% to 25% of total sleep time by age 5 and remains fairly constant until old age, when it drops to 18% or less. Older people tend to experience less Stage 3 and 4 sleep (sometimes these stages disappear) and more frequent and longer nighttime awakenings. A natural kind of insomnia seems to set in as people grow older (Gillin, 1985).

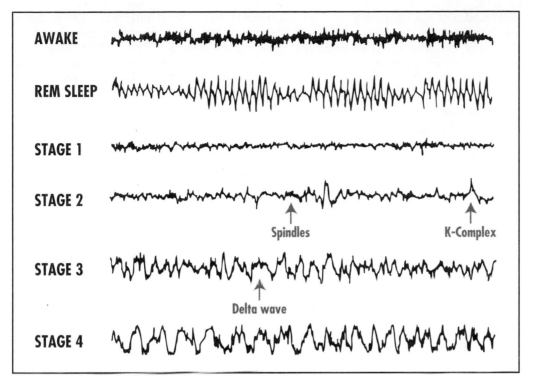

Spindles

K-Complex

Delta wave

Figure 5-2

Electrophysiological Activity During Sleep   This figure presents EEG recordings during wakefulness and during the various stages of sleep. The Awake Stage (relaxed with eyes closed) is characterized by alpha waves (8–12 hertz). Stage 1 is basically a transition from wakefulness to the deeper stages of sleep. Stage 2 is defined by the presence of sleep spindles (brief bursts of 12–16 hertz waves) and K-complexes (a sharp rise and fall in the brain-wave pattern). Stages 3 and 4 are marked by the presence of delta waves (1–2 hertz) and the only difference between these two stages is the amount of delta waves found. Stage 3 is scored when 20% to 50% of the record contains delta waves, and Stage 4 when the percentage of delta waves is 50% or more.

Figure 5-3

The Succession of Sleep Stages   This graph provides an example of the sequence and duration of sleep stages during a typical night. The individual went successively through Stages 1 to 4 during the first hour of sleep. He then moved back through Stage 3 to REM sleep. Thereafter he cycled between NREM and REM periods, with two brief awakenings at about 3½ and 6 hours of sleep.

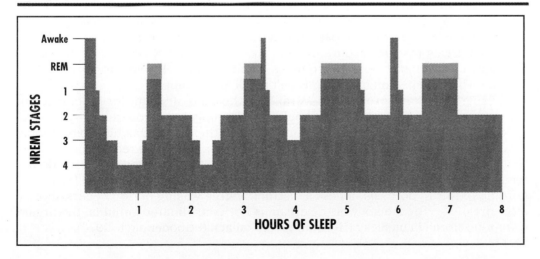

REM and NREM Compared   The two types of sleep, REM and NREM, are as different from each other as each is from wakefulness. Indeed, some investigators believe that REM is not sleep at all but a third state of existence. During NREM sleep, eye movements are virtually absent, heart and breathing rates decrease markedly, the muscles are relaxed, and the metabolic rate of the brain decreases by 25% to 30% compared to wakefulness. In contrast, during REM sleep very rapid eye movements occur in bursts lasting 10 to 20 seconds, the heart rate increases, and the brain's metabolic rate increases somewhat compared to wakefulness. Further, during REM sleep we are almost completely paralyzed—only the heart, diaphragm, eye muscles, and smooth muscles (such as the muscles of the intestines and blood vessels) are spared. To summarize, NREM sleep is characterized by an idle brain in a very relaxed body, while REM sleep is characterized by a brain that appears to be wide awake in a virtually paralyzed body.

Physiological evidence indicates that in REM sleep the brain is largely isolated from its sensory and motor channels; stimuli from other parts of the body are blocked from entering the brain, and there are no motor outputs. Nevertheless, the brain is still very active, being spontaneously driven by the discharges of giant neurons that originate in the brain stem. These neurons extend into parts of the brain that control eye movements and motor activities. Thus, during REM sleep the brain registers the fact that the neurons normally involved in walking and seeing are activated, even though the body itself is doing neither of these things (Hobson, 1994).

Sleepers who are awakened during REM sleep almost always report having a dream, but when awakened during NREM sleep they will report a dream only about 50% of the time (Antrobus, 1983; Cavallero et al., 1992; Foulkes & Schmidt, 1983). The dreams reported when a person is roused from REM sleep tend to be visually vivid and have emotional and illogical features—they represent the type of experience we typically associate with the word "dream." The longer the person has been in REM sleep before being aroused, the longer and more elaborate the reported dream. In contrast, NREM dreams are neither as visual nor as emotionally charged as REM dreams; they are more directly related to what is happening in the person's waking life. Thus, mental activity is different in REM and NREM periods, as indicated by the types of dreams we report and the frequency of reporting dreams.

Dreaming

dreaming an altered state of consciousness in which remembered images and fantasies are temporarily confused with external reality

Dreaming is *an altered state of consciousness in which remembered images and fantasies are temporarily confused with external reality.* Investigators do not yet understand why people dream at all, much less why they dream what they do. However, modern methods of study have answered a great many questions about dreaming. Some of them are explored here.

Does Everyone Dream?   Although many people do not recall their dreams in the morning, REM sleep evidence suggests that nonrecallers do as much dreaming as recallers. If you take people who have sworn that they never dreamed in their life, put them in a dream research laboratory and wake them from REM sleep, you will get dream recall at rates comparable to those of other people. If someone says "I never dream," what that person means is "I can't recall my dreams."

Researchers have proposed several hypotheses to account for differences in dream recall. One possibility is that nonrecallers simply have more difficulty than recallers in remembering their dreams. Another hypothesis suggests that some people awaken relatively easily in the midst of REM sleep and therefore recall more dreams than those who sleep more soundly. The most generally accepted model for dream recall supports the idea that what happens upon awakening is the crucial factor. According to this hypothesis, unless a distraction-free waking period occurs shortly after dreaming, the memory of the dream is not consolidated—that is, the dream cannot be stored in memory (Hobson, 1988; Koulack & Goodenough, 1976).

If upon awakening we make an effort to remember what we were dreaming at the time, some of the dream content will be recalled at a later time. Otherwise, the dream will fade quickly; we may know that we have had a dream but will be unable to remember its content. If you are interested in remembering your dreams, keep a notebook and pencil beside your bed. Tell yourself that you want to wake up when you have a dream. When you do, immediately try to recall the details and write them down. As your dream recall improves, look for patterns. Underline anything that strikes you as odd and tell yourself that the next time something similar happens, you are going to recognize it as a sign that you are dreaming. (Of course, you will lose some sleep if you follow this regimen!)

Research indicates that everyone dreams. Those who report that they never dream are actually reporting that they don't recall their dreams.

How Long Do Dreams Last?   Some dreams seem almost instantaneous. The alarm clock rings and we awaken to complex memories of a fire breaking out and fire engines arriving with their sirens blasting. Because the alarm is still ringing, we assume that the sound must have produced the dream. Research suggests, however, that a ringing alarm clock or other sound merely reinstates a complete scene from earlier memories or dreams. This experience has its parallel during wakefulness when a single cue may tap a rich memory that takes some time to tell. The length of a typical dream can be inferred from a REM study in which participants were awakened and asked to act out what they had been dreaming (Dement & Wolpert, 1958). The time it took them to pantomime the dream was almost the same as the length of the REM sleep period, suggesting that the incidents in dreams commonly last about as long as they would in real life.

Do People Know When They Are Dreaming?   The answer to this question is: Sometimes yes. People can be taught to recognize that they are dreaming, and their awareness does not interfere with the dream's spontaneous flow. For example, participants have been trained to press a switch when they notice that they are dreaming (Salamy, 1970).

Some people have *lucid dreams,* in which events seem so normal (lacking the bizarre and illogical character of most dreams) that the dreamers feel as if they are awake and conscious. Lucid dreamers report doing various "experiments" within their dreams to determine whether they are awake or dreaming. They also report an occasional "false awakening" within a dream. For example, one lucid dreamer discovered that he was dreaming and decided to call a taxicab as an indication of his control over events. When he reached into his pocket to see if he had some change to pay the driver, he thought that he woke up. He then found the coins scattered about the bed. At this point he really awoke and found himself lying in a different position and, of course, without any coins (Brown, 1936). Note, however, that relatively few people achieve lucidity with any regularity (Squier & Domhoff, 1997).

Can People Control the Content of Their Dreams?   Psychologists have demonstrated that some control of dream content can be achieved by making suggestions to participants in the presleep period and then analyzing the content of their dreams. In a carefully designed study of an implicit predream suggestion, researchers tested the effect of wearing red goggles for several hours before going to sleep. Although the researchers made no actual suggestion and the participants did not understand the purpose of the experiment, many participants reported that their visual dream worlds were tinted red (Roffwarg et al., 1978). In a study of the effect of an overt predream suggestion, participants were asked to try to dream about a personality characteristic that they wished they had. Most of the participants had at least one dream in which the intended trait could be recognized (Cartwright, 1974). Despite these findings, however, there is little evidence that dream content can actually be controlled (Domhoff, 1985).

Theories of Dream Sleep

One of the earliest theories of the function of dream sleep was suggested by Sigmund Freud. In *The Interpretation of Dreams* (1900), Freud proposed that dreams provide a "royal road to a knowledge of the unconscious activities of the mind." He believed that dreams are a disguised attempt at wish fulfillment. By this he meant that the dream touches on wishes, needs, or ideas that the individual finds unacceptable and has repressed to the unconscious (for example, the desire to hurt one's parent). These wishes and ideas are the *latent content* of the dream. Freud used the metaphor of a censor to explain the conversion of latent content into *manifest content* (the characters and events that make up the actual narrative of the dream). In effect, Freud said, the censor protects the sleeper, enabling him or her to express repressed impulses symbolically while avoiding the guilt or anxiety that would occur if they were to appear consciously in undisguised form.

According to Freud, the transformation of latent content into manifest content is done by "dream work," whose function is to code and disguise material in the unconscious in such a way that it can reach consciousness. However, sometimes dream work fails, and the resulting anxiety awakens the dreamer. The dream essentially expresses the fulfillment of wishes or needs that are too painful or guilt-inducing to be acknowledged consciously (Freud, 1933, 1965).

Subsequent research challenged several aspects of Freud's theory. After surveying dozens of studies of dreaming, Fisher and Greenberg (1977, 1996) concluded that while there is good evidence that the content of dreams has psychological meaning, there is none that supports Freud's distinction between manifest and latent content. Thus, while most psychologists would agree with Freud's general conclusion that dreams focus on emotional concerns, they question the concept of "dream work" and the idea that dreams represent wish fulfillment.

Since Freud's time a variety of theories have been advanced to explain the role of sleep and dreams. Evans (1984), for example, views sleep, particularly REM sleep, as a period when the brain disengages from the

"Can you describe this china shop?"

Freud believed that dreams express wishes or needs that the individual finds unacceptable and has repressed to the unconscious.

external world and uses this "offline" time to sift through the information that was input during the day and to incorporate it into memory. We are not consciously aware of the processing that occurs during REM sleep. During dreaming, however, the brain comes back online for a brief time and the conscious mind observes a small sample of the modification and reorganization of information that is taking place. The brain attempts to interpret this information the same way it would interpret stimuli coming from the outside world, giving rise to the kinds of pseudo-events that characterize dreams. Thus, according to Evans, dreams are nothing more than a small subset of the vast amount of information that is being scanned and sorted during REM sleep, a momentary glimpse by the conscious mind that we remember if we awaken. Evans believes that dreams can be useful in making inferences about the processing that occurs during REM sleep, but that they represent an extremely small sample on which to base such inferences.

Other researchers take different approaches. Hobson (1997), for example, notes that dreaming is characterized by formal visual imagery (akin to hallucination), inconstancy of time, place, and person (akin to disorientation), and inability to recall (akin to amnesia). Dreaming thus resembles delirium. It has also been suggested that dreams may have a problem-solving function (Cartwright, 1978, 1991, 1996), but this theory has been challenged on methodological grounds (Antrobus, 1993; Foulkes, 1993). Moreover, the content of dreams tends to differ according to the culture, gender, and personality of the dreamer, suggesting that dreams have some psychological meaning (Domhoff, 1996; Hobson, 1988). That is, dream content may reflect personal conflicts, but this does not mean that dreams function to resolve those conflicts (Squier & Domhoff, 1998).

In this regard, it is worth noting that only about half of all dreams include even one element related to events of the previous day (Botnam & Crovitz, 1992; Hartmann, 1968; Nielson & Powell, 1992). Moreover, systematic analyses of dream content have found that rates of aggression are higher than rates of friendly interactions; in fact, the murder rate in dreams is 2,226 per 100,000 characters, far above real world rates (Hall & Van de Castle, 1966)! In addition, there are more negative than positive emotions. Thus, dreams cannot be viewed as simple extensions of the activities of the previous day. On the other hand, researchers have repeatedly found great consistency in what people dream about over years or decades. For instance, G. William Domhoff and Adam Schneider (1998) report the following:

> Our analyses of lengthy dream journals reveal that there is an astonishing degree of consistency in what a person dreams about over several months or years, even 40 or 50 years in the two longest dream series analyzed to date. There are also striking continuities between dream findings and waking life, making possible accurate predictions about the concerns and interests of the dreamers. These findings suggest that dreams have "meaning."

Analyses of dreams have also found significant age, gender, and cross-cultural similarities and differences in their content, leading some theorists to propose that dreaming is a cognitive process (Antrobus, 1991; Domhoff, 1996; Foulkes, 1985). An early researcher in this field pointed out that dreams seem to express conceptions and concerns (Hall, 1947, 1953). However, dreaming differs from waking sleep in that it lacks intentionality and reflectiveness (Blagrove, 1992, 1996; Foulkes, 1985). Thus, in the view of these theorists it is unlikely that dreaming has a problem-solving function. Instead, it is a cognitive activity, as is evidenced by the continuity between dream content and waking thoughts and behavior. As Domhoff notes, "The concerns people express in their dreams are the concerns they have in waking life. What they dream about is also what they think about or do when they are awake" (1996, p. 8). Parents dream of their children; aggressive dream content is more common among people under age 30 than in older people; and women are more often victims of aggression. These patterns support what Domhoff and others refer to as the "continuity theory" of dreaming, in which dreaming is an imaginative process that reflects the individual's conceptions, concerns, and emotional preoccupations.

What Is the Nature of Meditation?

meditation achieving an altered state of consciousness by performing certain rituals and exercises

Meditation refers to *achieving an altered state of consciousness by performing certain rituals and exercises.* These include controlling and regulating breathing, sharply restricting one's field of attention, eliminating external stimuli, assuming yogic body positions, and forming mental images of an event or symbol. The result is a pleasant, mildly altered subjective state in which the individual feels mentally and physically relaxed. After extensive meditation, some individuals may have mystical experiences in which they lose self-awareness and gain a sense of being involved in a wider consciousness, however defined. The belief that such meditative techniques may cause a change in consciousness goes back to ancient times and is represented in every major world religion. Buddhists, Hindus, Sufis, Jews, and Christians all have literature describing rituals that induce meditative states.

Traditional forms of meditation follow the practices of *yoga,* a system of thought based on the Hindu religion, or those of *Zen,* which is derived from Chinese and Japanese Buddhism. Two common techniques of meditation are an *opening-up meditation,* in which the participant clears his or her mind for receiving new experiences, and a *concentrative meditation,* in which the benefits are obtained by actively attending to some object, word, or idea. The following is a representative statement of opening-up meditation:

> This approach begins with the resolve to do nothing, to think nothing, to make no effort of one's own, to relax completely and let go of one's mind and body . . . stepping out of the stream of ever-changing ideas and feelings which your mind is in, watch the onrush

The rituals of meditation include regulating breathing, restricting one's field of attention, eliminating external stimuli, and forming mental images of an event or symbol. Traditional forms of meditation follow the practices of yoga or Zen.

Frontiers of Psychology

Meditation for Relaxation

A somewhat commercialized and secularized form of meditation has been widely promoted in the United States and elsewhere under the name of *transcendental meditation* or TM (Forem, 1973). The technique is easily learned from a qualified teacher, who gives the novice meditator a *mantra* (a special sound) and instructions on how to repeat it over and over to produce the deep rest and awareness that are characteristic of TM.

A similar state of relaxation can be produced without the mystical associations of TM. Developed by Benson and his colleagues, the technique includes the following steps:

1. Sit quietly in a comfortable position and close your eyes.
2. Deeply relax all your muscles, beginning at your feet and progressing to your face. Keep them deeply relaxed.
3. Breathe through your nose. Become aware of your breathing. As you breathe out, say the word "one" silently to yourself. For example, breathe in . . . out, "one"; in . . . out, "one"; and so on. Continue for 20 minutes. You may open your eyes to check the time, but do not use an alarm. When you finish, sit quietly for several minutes, first with closed eyes and later with opened eyes.
4. Do not worry about whether you are successful in achieving a deep level of relaxation. Maintain a passive attitude and permit relaxation to occur at its own pace. Expect other thoughts. When these distracting thoughts occur, ignore them by thinking "oh well" and continue repeating "one." With practice, the response should come with little effort.
5. Practice the technique once or twice daily but not within 2 hours after a meal, since the digestive processes seem to interfere with the subjective changes. (Benson et al., 1977, p. 442)

During this kind of meditation, a person develops a reduced state of physiological arousal. Participants report feelings quite similar to those generated by other meditative practices: peace of mind, a feeling of being at peace with the world, and a sense of well-being.

Meditation is an effective technique for inducing relaxation and reducing physiological arousal. Almost all studies of the phenomenon report a significant lowering of the respiratory rate, a decrease in oxygen consumption, and less elimination of carbon dioxide. The heart rate is lowered, blood flow stabilizes, and the concentration of lactate in the blood is decreased (Dillbeck & Orme-Johnson, 1987). Also, there is a change in EEG activity suggesting that cortical arousal is decreased during meditation, reflecting a reduced level of mental activity (Fenwick, 1987). Meditation has also proved effective in helping people with chronic feelings of anxiety (Eppley, Abrams, & Shear, 1989) and improving self-esteem (Alexander, Rainforth, & Gelderloos, 1991).

A number of people involved in *sports psychology* believe that meditation can be useful in getting maximum performance from athletes (Cox, Qiu, & Liu, 1993). Engaging in meditation helps reduce stress before an event, and with experience the athlete can learn to relax different muscle groups and appreciate subtle differences in muscle tension. The meditation may also involve forming mental images of the details of an upcoming event, such as a downhill ski race, until the athlete is in total synchrony with the flow of actions. The skier visualizes the release from the starting platform, speeding down the hill, and moving between the gates, and goes through every action in his or her mind. By creating visual sensations of a successful performance, the athlete is attempting to program the muscles and body for peak efficiency.

The research literature on meditation is of mixed quality, and some claims, particularly by those with a commercial interest in the outcome, are suspect. Nevertheless, on balance the evidence suggests that meditation can reduce arousal (especially in easily stressed individuals) and may be valuable for people suffering from anxiety and tension.

Many sports psychologists believe that meditation can help athletes achieve maximum performance.

of the stream. Refuse to be submerged in the current. Changing the metaphor . . . watch your ideas, feelings, and wishes fly across the firmament like a flock of birds. Let them fly freely. Just keep a watch. Don't let the birds carry you off into the clouds. (Chauduri, 1965, pp. 30–31)

Here is a corresponding description of concentrative meditation:

> The purpose of these sessions is to learn about concentration. Your aim is to concentrate on the blue vase. By concentration I do not mean analyzing the different parts of the vase, but rather, trying to see the vase as it exists in itself, without any connections to other things. Exclude all other thoughts or feelings or sounds or body sensations. (Deikman, 1963, p. 330)

After a few sessions of concentrative meditation, participants typically report a number of effects: an altered, more intense perception of the vase; some time shortening, particularly in retrospect; conflicting perceptions, as if the vase fills the visual field and does not fill it; decreasing effectiveness of external stimuli (less distraction and eventually less conscious registration); and an impression of the meditative state as pleasant and rewarding.

Experimental studies of meditation provide only limited insight into the alterations of consciousness that a person can achieve after many years of meditative practice. In his study of the *Matramudra,* a centuries-old Tibetan Buddhist text, Brown (1977) has described the complex training required to master the technique. He has also shown that cognitive changes can be expected at different meditative levels. (In this type of meditation, people proceed through five levels until they reach a thoughtless, perceptionless, selfless state known as *concentrative samadhi.*)

What Is Hypnosis?

Of all altered states of consciousness, none has raised more questions than hypnosis. Once associated with the occult, hypnosis has become a subject of rigorous scientific investigation. As in all fields of psychological investigation, uncertainties remain, but by now many facts have been established. In this section we explore what is known about this controversial phenomenon.

Induction of Hypnosis

hypnosis   a condition in which a willing and cooperative participant relinquishes some control over his or her behavior to the hypnotist and accepts some reality distortion

In **hypnosis,** *a willing and cooperative participant* (the only kind that can be hypnotized under most circumstances) *relinquishes some control over his or her behavior to the hypnotist and accepts some reality distortion.* The hypnotist uses a variety of methods to induce this condition. For example, the participant may be asked to concentrate all his or her thoughts on a small target (such as a thumbtack on the wall) while gradually becoming relaxed. A suggestion of sleepiness may be made because, like sleep, hypnosis is a relaxed state in which a person is out of touch with ordinary environmental demands. But sleep is only a metaphor. The participant is told that he or she will not really go to sleep but will continue to listen to the hypnotist.

The same state can be induced by methods other than relaxation. A hyperalert hypnotic trance is characterized by increased tension and alertness, and the trance-induction procedure is an active one. For example, in one study, participants riding a stationary laboratory bicycle while receiving suggestions of strength and alertness were as responsive to hypnotic suggestions as conventionally relaxed participants (Banyai & Hilgard, 1976). This result denies the common equation of hypnosis with relaxation, but it is consistent with the trance-induction methods used by the whirling dervishes of some Muslim religious orders.

Modern hypnotists do not use authoritarian commands. Indeed, with a little training, participants can hypnotize themselves (Ruch, 1975). The participant enters the hypnotic state when the conditions are right; the hypnotist merely helps set the con-

ditions. The following changes are characteristic of the hypnotized state:

- *Planfulness ceases.* A deeply hypnotized
  participant does not like to initiate activity and would rather wait for the hypnotist to suggest something to do.
- *Attention becomes more selective than
  usual.* A participant who is told to listen only to the hypnotist's voice will
  ignore any other voices in the room.
- *Enriched fantasy is readily evoked.* Participants may find themselves enjoying
  experiences at a place distant in time
  and space.
- *Reality testing is reduced and reality distortion is accepted.* A participant may
  uncritically accept hallucinated experiences (for example, conversing with
  an imagined person believed to be sit-

*A therapist induces a hypnotic state. Not all individuals are equally
responsive to hypnosis.*

ting in a nearby chair) and will not check to determine whether that person
is real.
- *Suggestibility is increased.* A participant must accept suggestions in order to be
  hypnotized at all, but whether suggestibility is increased under hypnosis is a
  matter of some dispute. Careful studies have found some increase in suggestibility following hypnotic induction, though less than is commonly supposed
  (Ruch, Morgan, & Hilgard, 1973).
- *Posthypnotic amnesia is often present.* When instructed to do so, a highly responsive hypnotic participant will forget all or most of what took place during
  the hypnotic session. When a prearranged release signal is given, the memories are restored.

Not all individuals are equally responsive to hypnosis. Roughly 5% to 10% of the
population cannot be hypnotized even by a skilled hypnotist, and the remainder
show varying degrees of susceptibility. However, if a person is hypnotized on one
occasion, he or she probably will be equally susceptible on another (Hilgard, 1961;
Piccione, Hilgard, & Zimbardo, 1989).

Hypnotic Suggestions

Suggestions given to a hypnotized participant can result in a variety of behaviors
and experiences. The person's motor control may be affected, new memories may
be lost or old ones reexperienced, and current perceptions may be radically altered.

Control of Movement   Many hypnotic participants respond to direct suggestion
with involuntary movement. For example, if a person stands with arms outstretched
and hands facing each other and the hypnotist suggests that the participant's hands
are attracted to each other, the hands will soon begin to move together, and the participant will feel that they are propelled by some force that he or she is not generating. Direct suggestion can also inhibit movement. If a suggestible participant is told
that an arm is stiff (like a bar of iron or an arm in a splint) and then is asked to bend
the arm, it will not bend, or more effort than usual will be needed to make it bend.
This response is less common than suggested movement.

Participants who have been roused from hypnosis may respond with movement
to a prearranged signal from the hypnotist. This is called a *posthypnotic response.*
Even if the suggestion has been forgotten, participants will feel a compulsion to carry

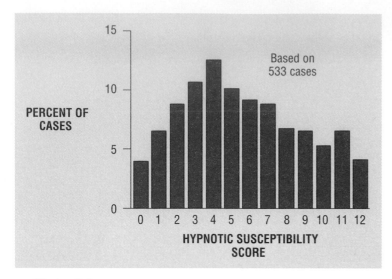

Figure 5-4

Individual Differences in Hypnotizability   After using a standard procedure designed to induce hypnosis, researchers administered 12 test suggestions from the Stanford Hypnotic Susceptibility Scale to 533 participants. The object of the experiment was to test the appearance of hypnotic responses such as those described in the test (for example, being unable to bend one's arm or separate interlocked fingers when the hypnotist suggests these possibilities). The response was scored as present or absent, and the present responses were totaled for each participant to yield a score ranging from 0 (totally unresponsive) to 12 (most responsive). Most individuals fell in the middle ranges, with a few very high and a few very low. (After Hilgard, 1965)

out the behavior. They may try to justify such behavior as rational, even though the urge to perform it is compulsive. For example, a young man searching for a rational explanation of why he opened a window when the hypnotist took off her glasses (the prearranged signal) remarked that the room felt a little stuffy.

Posthypnotic Amnesia   At the suggestion of the hypnotist, events that occur during hypnosis may be "forgotten" until a signal from the hypnotist enables the participant to recall them. This is called *posthypnotic amnesia*. Participants differ widely in their susceptibility to posthypnotic amnesia. In one study, participants were asked to recall 10 actions they had performed while hypnotized. A few participants forgot none or only one or two items; most participants forgot four or five. However, a sizable number of participants forgot all 10 items. Similar results have been found in many studies of posthypnotic amnesia. The group of participants with the higher recall is larger and presumably represents the average hypnotic responder; the smaller group, the participants who forgot all 10 items, has been described as hypnotic virtuosos.

Differences in recall between the two groups following posthypnotic suggestion do not appear to be related to differences in memory capacity: Once the amnesia is canceled at a prearranged signal from the hypnotist, highly amnesic participants remember as many items as those who are less amnesic. Some researchers have suggested that hypnosis temporarily interferes with the person's ability to retrieve a particular item from memory but does not affect actual memory storage (Kihlstrom, 1987).

Positive and Negative Hallucinations   Some hypnotic experiences require a higher level of hypnotic talent than others. The vivid and convincing perceptual distortions known as hallucinations, for instance, are relatively rare. Two types of suggested hallucinations have been documented: *positive hallucinations,* in which the participant sees an object or hears a voice that is not actually present; and *negative hallucinations,* in which the participant does not perceive something that normally would be perceived. Many hallucinations have both positive and negative components. In order not to see a person sitting in a chair (a negative hallucination), a participant must see the parts of the chair that would ordinarily be blocked from view (a positive hallucination).

Hallucinations can also occur as the result of posthypnotic suggestion. For example, participants may be told that upon being aroused from the hypnotic state they will find themselves holding a rabbit that wants to be petted, and that the rabbit will ask, "What time is it?" Seeing and petting the rabbit will seem natural to most of the participants. But when they find themselves giving the correct time of day, they are surprised and try to provide an explanation for the behavior: "Did I hear someone ask the time? It's funny, it seemed to be the rabbit asking, but rabbits can't talk!" is a typical response.

Negative hallucinations can be used to control pain. In many cases hypnosis eliminates pain, even though the source of the pain—a severe burn or a bone fracture, for example—continues. The failure to perceive something (pain) that would normally be perceived qualifies this response as a negative hallucination. The pain reduction need not be complete in order for hypnosis to be useful in giving relief. Reducing pain by 20% can make the patient's life more tolerable. Experimental studies have shown that the amount of pain reduction is closely related to the degree of measured hypnotizability (Crasilneck & Hall, 1985; Hilgard & Hilgard, 1975).

What Are the Effects of Psychoactive Drugs?

In addition to meditation and hypnosis, drugs can be used to alter a person's state of consciousness. Since ancient times people have used drugs to stimulate or relax, to bring on sleep or prevent it, to enhance ordinary perceptions, or to produce hallucinations. The word *drug* can be used to refer to any substance (other than food) that chemically alters the functioning of an organism. The term **psychoactive drugs** refers to *drugs that affect behavior, consciousness, and/or mood.* These drugs include not only illegal "street" drugs such as heroin and marijuana but also legal drugs such as tranquilizers and stimulants. Familiar, widely used drugs such as alcohol, nicotine, and caffeine are also included in this category.

It should be noted that whether or not use of a particular drug is legal does not accurately reflect the risks and dangers associated with the drug. For example, caffeine (coffee) is totally accepted, and its use is unregulated; nicotine (tobacco) is minimally regulated; alcohol is subject to numerous regulations but is legal; and

psychoactive drugs
drugs that affect behavior, consciousness, and/or mood

Although alcohol and tobacco are legal, they are included in the category of psychoactive drugs because they affect behavior, consciousness, and mood.

Table 5-1

Psychoactive Drugs That Are Commonly Used and Abused   Only a few examples of each class of drug are given. The generic name (for example, psilocybin) or the brand name (Xanax for alprazolam; Seconal for secobarbital) is used, depending on which is more familiar.

Depressants (Sedatives)	Stimulants
Alcohol (ethanol)	Amphetamines
Barbiturates	Benzedrine
Nembutal	Dexedrine
Seconal	Methedrine
Minor tranquilizers	Cocaine
Miltown	Nicotine
Xanax	Caffeine
Valium	**Hallucinogens**
Inhalants	
Paint thinner	LSD
Glue	Mescaline
Opiates (Narcotics)	Psilocybin
	PCP (Phencyclidine)
Opium and its derivatives	**Cannabis**
Codeine	
Heroin	Marijuana
Morphine	Hashish
Methadone	

marijuana is illegal. Yet it could be argued that of all these substances nicotine is the most harmful, since it is responsible for about 360,000 deaths per year. One could well ask whether nicotine would even be accepted as a legal drug if someone tried to introduce it today.

Table 5-1 lists and classifies the psychoactive drugs that are commonly used and abused. Drugs that are used to treat mental disorders (see Chapter 13) also affect mood and behavior and therefore might be considered psychoactive. They are not included here, however, because they are seldom abused. By and large, their effects are not immediate (for example, most of the drugs used to treat depression take days or weeks before they begin to lift the individual's mood); also, they usually are not experienced as particularly pleasant. An exception is the minor tranquilizers, which may be prescribed for the treatment of anxiety disorders and are sometimes abused. Caffeine and nicotine are also listed in the table. Although both substances are stimulants and can have negative effects on health, they do not significantly alter consciousness and hence are not discussed in this section.

The use of illegal drugs such as marijuana, particularly among young people, was not common before the 1950s, but since then there have been major changes in patterns of drug use. Beginning in the 1960s, drug use

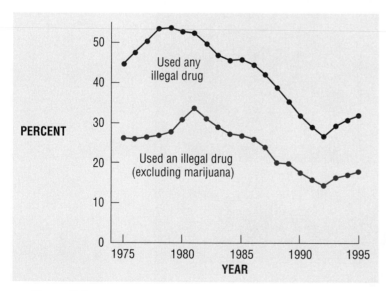

Figure 5-5

Illegal Drug Use   The percentage of American high-school seniors who reported using an illegal drug in the 12-month period prior to graduation. Drugs included in the upper curve are marijuana, hallucinogens, cocaine, heroin, and any nonprescribed use of opiates, stimulants, sedatives, and tranquilizers. The lower curve excludes marijuana. (After Johnston, O'Malley, & Bachman, 1995)

increased steadily, peaking in the late 1970s. In the 1980s, however, drug use gradually declined, a trend that continued until 1992 (see Figure 5-5). Efforts to educate young people about the hazards of drug use contributed to this decline. The turnaround that occurred in 1992 is a cause for concern because the percentage of teenagers who disapprove of drug use appears to have decreased (Johnston, O'Malley, & Bachman, 1995).

The drugs listed in Table 5-1 are assumed to affect behavior and consciousness because they act on the brain in specific biochemical ways. With repeated use, an individual can become dependent on any of them. **Drug dependence** has three key characteristics: (1) *tolerance*—with continued use, the individual must take more and more of the drug to achieve the same effect; (2) *withdrawal*—if use is discontinued, the person experiences unpleasant physical and psychological reactions; and (3) *compulsive use*—the individual takes more of the drug than intended, tries to control use but can't, and spends a great deal of time trying to obtain the drug.

The degree to which tolerance develops and the severity of withdrawal symptoms varies from one drug to another. Tolerance for opiates, for example, develops fairly quickly, and heavy users can tolerate a dosage that would be lethal to a nonuser; in contrast, marijuana smokers seldom build up much tolerance. Withdrawal symptoms are common and easily observed following heavy and sustained use of alcohol, opiates, and sedatives. They are common, but less apparent, for stimulants, and nonexistent after repeated use of hallucinogens. (American Psychiatric Association, 1994).

Although tolerance and withdrawal are the primary characteristics of drug dependence, they are not necessary for a diagnosis. A person who shows a pattern of compulsive use without any signs of tolerance or withdrawal, as some marijuana users do, would still be considered drug dependent.

Drug dependence is usually distinguished from **drug abuse,** which refers to *continued use of a drug by a person who is not dependent on it (that is, shows no symptoms of tolerance, withdrawal, or compulsive craving) yet continues to use it despite serious consequences.* For example, an individual whose overindulgence in alcohol results in repeated accidents, absenteeism from work, or marital problems (without signs of dependence) would be said to abuse alcohol.

In this section we now look at several types of psychoactive drugs and the effects they may have on those who use them.

Depressants

Depressants are *drugs that depress the central nervous system.* They include tranquilizers, barbiturates (sleeping pills), inhalants (volatile solvents and aerosols), and ethyl alcohol. Of these, the one that is most frequently used and abused is alcohol, and we will focus on it here.

Alcohol and Its Effects   People in most societies, whether primitive or industrialized, consume alcohol in some form. Alcohol can be produced by fermenting a wide variety of materials: grains, such as rye, wheat, and corn; fruits, such as grapes, apples, and plums; and vegetables, such as potatoes. Through the process of distillation, the alcoholic content of a fermented beverage can be increased to obtain "hard liquors" such as whiskey or rum.

The alcohol used in beverages is called ethanol and consists of relatively small molecules that are easily and quickly absorbed into the body. Once a drink is swallowed, it enters the stomach and small intestine, where there is a heavy concentration of small blood vessels. These give the ethanol molecules ready access to the blood. Once they enter the bloodstream, they are rapidly carried throughout the body and to all of its organs. Although the alcohol is fairly evenly distributed through the whole body, its effects are likely to be felt most immediately in the brain because a substantial portion of the blood that the heart pumps at any given time goes to the

drug dependence a condition in which an individual develops tolerance for a drug, suffers withdrawal upon discontinuing use of the drug, and engages in compulsive use of the drug

drug abuse continued use of a drug by a person who is not dependent on it, yet continues to use it despite serious consequences

depressants drugs that depress the central nervous system

Alcohol related automobile accidents are the leading cause of death among 15- to 24-year-olds. When some states lowered the legal drinking age from 21 to 18, traffic fatalities among 18- and 19-year-olds increased by 20% to 50%.

brain and the fatty tissue in the brain absorbs alcohol very well (Kyhn, Swartzwelder, & Wilson, 1998).

Measuring the amount of alcohol in the air we exhale (as in a breath analyzer) gives a reliable index of alcohol in the blood. Consequently, it is easy to determine the relationship between blood alcohol concentration (BAC) and behavior. At concentrations of .03% to .05% in the blood (30 to 50 milligrams of alcohol per 100 milliliters of blood), alcohol produces lightheadedness, relaxation, and release of inhibitions. People say things that they might not ordinarily say; they tend to become more sociable and expansive. Self-confidence may increase, but motor reactions will begin to slow (a pair of effects that makes it dangerous to drive after drinking).

At a BAC of .10%, sensory and motor functions become noticeably impaired. Speech becomes slurred, and people have difficulty coordinating their movements. Some people tend to become angry and aggressive; others grow silent and morose. The drinker is seriously incapacitated at a level of .20%, and a level above .40% may cause death. The legal definition of intoxication in most states is a BAC of .10% (one-tenth of 1%).

How much can a person drink without becoming legally intoxicated? The relationship between BAC and alcohol intake is not a simple one. It depends on a person's sex, weight, and speed of consumption. Age, metabolism, and experience with drinking are also factors. Although the effects of alcohol intake on BAC vary a great deal, the average effects are shown in Figure 5-6. Moreover, it is not true that beer or wine is less likely to make someone drunk than so-called hard liquor. A 4-ounce glass of wine, a 12-ounce can of beer, and 1.2 ounces of 80-proof whiskey have about the same alcohol content and will have about the same effect.

Alcohol Usage   Many college students view drinking as an integral part of social life. It promotes conviviality, eases tension, releases inhibitions, and generally adds to the fun. Nevertheless, social drinking can create problems in terms of lost study time, poor performance on exams on "the morning after," and arguments or accidents while intoxicated. Clearly the most serious problem is accidents: Alcohol-related automobile accidents are the leading cause of death among 15- to 24-year-

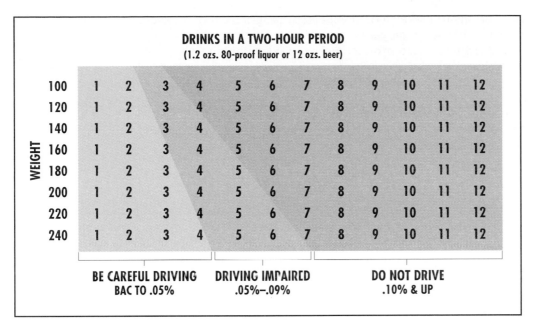

DRINKS IN A TWO-HOUR PERIOD
(1.2 ozs. 80-proof liquor or 12 ozs. beer)

WEIGHT												
100	1	2	3	4	5	6	7	8	9	10	11	12
120	1	2	3	4	5	6	7	8	9	10	11	12
140	1	2	3	4	5	6	7	8	9	10	11	12
160	1	2	3	4	5	6	7	8	9	10	11	12
180	1	2	3	4	5	6	7	8	9	10	11	12
200	1	2	3	4	5	6	7	8	9	10	11	12
220	1	2	3	4	5	6	7	8	9	10	11	12
240	1	2	3	4	5	6	7	8	9	10	11	12

BE CAREFUL DRIVING	DRIVING IMPAIRED	DO NOT DRIVE
BAC TO .05%	.05%–.09%	.10% & UP

Figure 5-6

BAC and Alcohol Intake Approximate values of blood-alcohol concentration as a function of alcohol consumption in a 2-hour period. For example, if you weigh 180 pounds and had 4 beers in 2 hours, your BAC would be between .05% and .09% and your driving ability would be seriously impaired. Six beers in the same 2-hour period would give you a BAC of over .10%—the level accepted as proof of intoxication. (After National Highway Traffic Safety Administration)

olds. When the legal drinking age was lowered from 21 to 18 in a number of states, traffic fatalities among 18- and 19-year-olds increased by 20% to 50%. All states have since raised their minimum drinking age, and the number of traffic accidents has decreased significantly.

About two-thirds of American adults report that they drink alcohol. At least 10% of them have social, psychological, or medical problems resulting from alcohol use. Probably half of that 10% are dependent on alcohol. Heavy or prolonged drinking can lead to serious health problems. High blood pressure, stroke, ulcers, cancers of the mouth, throat, and stomach, cirrhosis of the liver, and depression are some of the conditions associated with regular use of substantial amounts of alcohol.

Despite the fact that it is illegal for anyone under age 21 to purchase alcoholic beverages, experience with alcohol is almost universal among young people (67% of eighth graders, 81% of high school seniors, and 91% of college students have tried it). More disturbing is the widespread occurrence of "binge drinking" (having five or more drinks in a row). In national surveys, 28% of high school seniors and 44% of college students report binge drinking (Wechsler et al., 1994, 1998). Lost study time, missed classes, injuries, engaging in unprotected sex, and trouble with police are some of the problems reported by college students who engage in binge drinking. Because of these problems, an increasing number of universities no longer permit alcohol on campus. The Drug Free School and Campuses Act, passed by Congress in 1989, requires

*A mother's drinking during pregnancy can cause **fetal alcohol syndrome** in her child, a condition characterized by mental retardation and deformities of the face and mouth.*

institutions to make alcohol education programs and counseling services available to students and employees.

Alcohol can also produce risks for a developing fetus. Mothers who drink heavily are twice as likely to suffer repeated miscarriages and to produce low birth weight babies. **Fetal alcohol syndrome,** *a condition characterized by mental retardation and multiple deformities of the face and mouth,* is caused by drinking during pregnancy. The amount of alcohol needed to produce this syndrome is unclear, but it is thought that as little as a few ounces of alcohol a week can be detrimental (Streissguth, Clarren, & Jones, 1985).

fetal alcohol syndrome a condition characterized by mental retardation and multiple deformities of the face and mouth

Opiates

opiates drugs that diminish physical sensation and the capacity to respond to stimuli by depressing the central nervous system

Opium and its derivatives, collectively known as **opiates,** are *drugs that diminish physical sensation and the capacity to respond to stimuli by depressing the central nervous system.* (These drugs are commonly called narcotics, but *opiates* is the more accurate term; the term *narcotics* is not well defined and covers a variety of illegal drugs.) Opiates are medically useful for their painkilling properties, but their ability to alter mood and reduce anxiety has led to widespread illegal consumption. Opium, which is the air-dried juice of the opium poppy, contains a number of chemical substances, including morphine and codeine. The effects of codeine, a common ingredient in prescription painkillers and cough suppressants, are relatively mild (at least at low doses). Morphine and its derivative, heroin, are much more potent. Most illegal opiate use involves heroin because, being more concentrated, it can be concealed and smuggled more easily than morphine.

All opiate drugs bind to the same molecules in the brain, known as opiate receptors. The differences among them depend on how quickly they reach the receptors and how much it takes to activate them—that is, their potency. The rate at which opiates enter the body depends on how they are taken. When opiates are smoked or injected, they reach peak levels in the brain within minutes. The faster this occurs, the greater the danger of death by overdose. Drugs that are "snorted" are absorbed more slowly because they must pass through the mucous membranes of the nose to the blood vessels beneath (Kuhn, Swartzwelder, & Wilson, 1998).

Opiates can be smoked, injected, or inhaled. When smoked or injected, opiate levels in the brain reach peak levels quickly, increasing the danger of overdose.

Heroin Usage   Heroin can be injected, smoked, or inhaled. At first the drug produces a sense of well-being. Experienced users report a special thrill, or "rush," within a minute or two after an intravenous injection. Some describe this sensation as intensely pleasurable, similar to an orgasm. Young people who sniff heroin report that they forget everything that troubles them. After this, the user feels "fixed," or gratified, and has no awareness of hunger, pain, or sexual urges. The person may "go on the nod," alternately waking and drowsing while comfortably watching television or reading a book. Unlike a person intoxicated by alcohol, the heroin user can readily produce skilled responses to agility and intellectual tests and seldom becomes aggressive or assaultive.

The changes in consciousness produced by heroin are not very striking; there are no exciting visual experiences or feelings of being transported elsewhere. It is the change in mood—the feeling of euphoria and reduced anxiety—that prompts people to start using this drug. However, heroin is very addictive; even a brief period of usage can create physical dependence. After a person has been smoking or "sniffing" (inhaling) heroin for a while, tolerance builds up, and this method no longer produces the desired effect. In an attempt to regain the original high, the individual may progress to "skin popping" (injecting under the skin) and then to "mainlining" (injecting into a vein). Once the user starts mainlining, stronger and stronger doses are required to produce the high, and the physical discomforts of withdrawal from the drug become intense (chills, sweating, stomach cramps, vomiting, headaches). Thus, additional motivation to continue using the drug stems from the need to avoid physical pain and discomfort.

The hazards of heroin use are many; the average age at death for frequent users is 40 (Hser, Anglin, & Powers, 1993). Death is caused by suffocation resulting from depression of the brain's respiratory center. Death from an overdose is always a possibility because the concentration of street heroin fluctuates widely. Thus, the user can never be sure of the potency of the powder in a newly purchased supply. Heroin use is generally associated with serious deterioration in the user's personal and social life. Because maintaining the habit is costly, the user often becomes involved in illegal activities to acquire money to purchase the drug.

Additional dangers of heroin use include AIDS (acquired immunodeficiency syndrome), hepatitis, or other infections associated with unsterile injections. Sharing drug needles is an extremely easy way to become infected with the AIDS virus; blood from an infected person can be trapped in the needle or syringe and injected directly into the bloodstream of the next person who uses the needle. Sharing of needles and syringes by people who inject drugs is the primary means by which the AIDS virus is spreading today.

Opioid Receptors   In the 1970s researchers made a major breakthrough in understanding opiate addiction when they discovered that opiates act on very specific neuroreceptor sites in the brain. Neurotransmitters travel across the synaptic junction between two neurons and bind to neuroreceptors, triggering activity in the receiving neuron (see Chapter 2). In molecular shape, the opiates resemble a group of neurotransmitters called *endorphins*. These endorphins bind to opioid receptors, producing sensations of pleasure as well as reducing discomfort (Julien, 1992). Heroin and morphine relieve pain by binding to opioid receptors that are unfilled (see Figure 5-7). Repeated heroin use causes a drop in endorphin production; the body then needs more heroin to fill the unoccupied opioid receptors in order to reduce pain. When heroin is discontinued, the person experiences painful withdrawal symptoms because many opioid receptors are left unfilled. In essence, the heroin has replaced the body's own natural opiates (Koob & Bloom, 1988).

These findings have led to the development of new drugs that operate by modulating the opioid receptors. These drugs are of two basic types: agonists and antagonists. *Agonists* bind to the opioid receptors to produce a feeling of pleasure, thereby reducing the craving for opiates; but they cause less psychological and physiological impairment than the opiates. *Antagonists* also lock onto the opioid receptors, but in a way that does not activate them;

Figure 5-7

Drug-Abuse Medications   (a) Heroin binds to opioid receptors and produces a feeling of pleasure, mimicking the action of the body's naturally occurring endorphins. (b) Methadone, an agonist drug, will also bind to opioid receptors and produce a pleasant sensation. The drug reduces both the craving for heroin and the associated withdrawal symptoms. (c) Naltrexone, an antagonist drug, acts to block the opioid receptors so that heroin cannot gain access to them. The craving for heroin is not satisfied, and the drug has not proved generally effective as a treatment method.

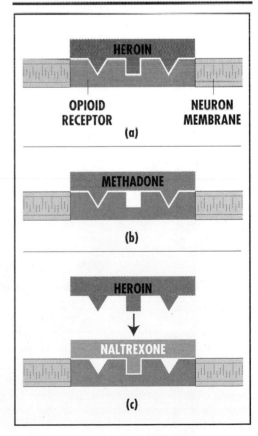

the drug serves to "block" the receptors so that the opiates cannot gain access to them. Thus, there is no feeling of pleasure and the craving is not satisfied (see Figure 5-7).

Methadone is the best-known agonist drug for treating heroin-dependent individuals. It is addictive in its own right, but it produces less psychological impairment than heroin and has few disruptive physical effects. When taken orally in low doses, it suppresses the craving for heroin and prevents withdrawal symptoms. Naltrexone, an antagonist drug, blocks the action of heroin because it has a greater affinity for the opioid receptors. Naltrexone is often used in hospital emergency rooms to reverse the effects of a heroin overdose, but it has not proved generally effective as a treatment for heroin dependence. Interestingly, naltrexone does reduce the craving for alcohol. Alcohol causes the release of endorphins, and naltrexone, by blocking opioid receptors, reduces the pleasurable effects of alcohol and consequently the desire for it (Winger, Hoffman, & Woods, 1992).

Stimulants

stimulants drugs that increase alertness and general arousal

In contrast to depressants and opiates, **stimulants** are *drugs that increase alertness and general arousal.* They increase the amount of monoamine neurotransmitters (norepinephrine, epinephrine, dopamine, and serotonin) in the synapse; the effects resemble what would happen if every one of the neurons that released a monoamine fired at once. The result is to arouse the body both physically, by increasing heart rate and blood pressure, and mentally, causing the person to become hyperalert (Kuhn, Swartzwelder, & Wilson, 1998).

Amphetamines   *Amphetamines* are powerful stimulants; they are sold under such trade names as Methedrine, Dexedrine, and Benzedrine and are known colloquially as "speed," "uppers," and "bennies." The immediate effects of consuming such drugs are an increase in alertness and a decrease in feelings of fatigue and boredom. Strenuous activities that require endurance seem easier after taking amphetamines. As with other drugs, the ability of amphetamines to alter mood and increase self-confidence is the principal reason for their use. People also use them to stay awake.

Low doses that are taken for limited periods to overcome fatigue (for example, when driving at night) seem to be relatively safe. However, as the stimulating effects of amphetamines wear off, there is a period during which the user feels depressed, irritable, and fatigued, and may be tempted to take more of the drug. Tolerance develops quickly, and the user needs increasingly larger doses to produce the desired effect. Because high doses can have dangerous side effects—agitation, confusion, heart palpitations, and elevated blood pressure—medications containing amphetamines should be used with caution.

When tolerance develops to the point at which oral doses are no longer effective, many users inject amphetamines into a vein. Large intravenous doses produce an immediate pleasant experience (a "flash" or "rush"); this sensation is followed by irritability and discomfort, which can be overcome only by an additional injection. If this sequence is repeated every few hours over a period of days, it will end in a "crash," a deep sleep followed by a period of lethargy and depression. The

Some herbal compounds and mild stimulants containing caffeine, legally available without a prescription, can temporarily reduce fatigue and increase alertness and energy levels.

amphetamine abuser may seek relief from this discomfort by turning to alcohol or heroin.

Long-term amphetamine use is accompanied by drastic deterioration in physical and mental health. The user, or "speed freak," may develop symptoms that are indistinguishable from those of acute schizophrenia (see Chapter 12), including persecutory delusions (the false belief that people are persecuting you or out to get you) and visual or auditory hallucinations. The delusions may lead to unprovoked violence. For example, in the midst of an amphetamine epidemic in Japan in the early 1950s (when amphetamines were sold without prescription and advertised for "elimination of drowsiness and repletion of the spirit"), 50% of the murders that occurred in a 2-month period were related to amphetamine abuse (Hemmi, 1969).

Cocaine   Like other stimulants, *cocaine,* or "coke," a substance obtained from the dried leaves of the coca plant, increases energy and self-confidence; it makes the user feel witty and hyperalert. Early in the 20th century, cocaine was widely used and easy to obtain; in fact, it was an ingredient in the original recipe for Coca-Cola. Its use then declined, but recently its popularity has increased, even though it is now illegal.

Cocaine can be inhaled or "snorted," or made into a solution and injected directly into a vein. It can also be converted into a flammable compound known as "crack," which is smoked.

One of the earliest studies of the effects of cocaine was conducted by Freud (1885).

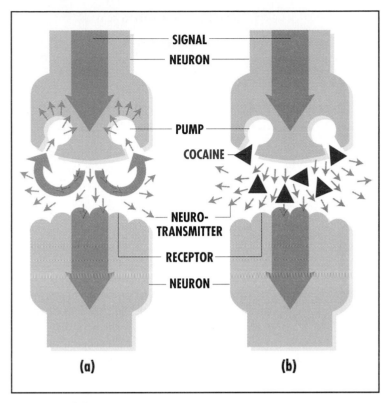

Figure 5-8

Molecular Effects of Cocaine   (a) A nerve impulse causes the release of neurotransmitters that carry the signal across the synapse to a receiving neuron. Some of the neurotransmitters are then reabsorbed into the originating neuron (reuptake process), while the rest are broken up chemically and made inactive (degradation process). These processes are discussed in Chapter 2. (b) Research findings indicate that cocaine blocks the reuptake process for three neurotransmitters (dopamine, serotonin, and norepinephrine) that are involved in the regulation of mood. With reuptake hampered by cocaine, the normal effects of these neurotransmitters are amplified; in particular, an excess of dopamine is associated with feelings of euphoria.

In an account of his own use of cocaine, he was at first highly favorable toward the drug and encouraged its use. However he changed his mind after using cocaine to treat a friend, with disastrous results. The friend developed a severe addiction, demanded ever larger dosages of the drug, and was debilitated until his eventual death.

Despite earlier reports to the contrary, and as Freud soon discovered, cocaine is highly addictive. In fact, it has become even more addictive and dangerous in recent years with the emergence of crack. Tolerance develops with repeated use, and withdrawal effects, while not as dramatic as with the opiates, do occur. The restless irritability that follows the euphoric high becomes, with repeated use, a feeling of depressed anguish. The down is as bad as the up was good and can be alleviated only by more cocaine (see Figure 5-8).

Heavy cocaine users can experience the same abnormal symptoms as people who use amphetamines heavily. A common visual hallucination is flashes of light ("snow lights") or moving lights. Less common—but more disturbing—is the feeling that bugs ("cocaine bugs") are crawling under one's skin. The hallucination may be so strong that the individual will use a knife to cut out the bugs. These experiences occur because cocaine is causing the sensory neurons to fire spontaneously (Weiss, Mirin, & Bartel, 1994).

Hallucinogens

hallucinogens drugs whose main effect is to change perceptual experience

Hallucinogens, or *psychedelics,* are *drugs whose main effect is to change perceptual experience.* They typically change the user's perception of both the internal and the external world. Usual environmental stimuli are experienced as novel events— for example, sounds and colors seem dramatically different. Time perception is so altered that minutes may seem like hours. The user may experience auditory, visual, and tactile hallucinations and reduced ability to differentiate between self and surroundings.

Some hallucinogenic drugs are derived from plants—such as mescaline from cactus and psilocybin from mushrooms. Others, such as LSD (lysergic acid diethylamide) and PCP (phencyclidine) are synthesized in the laboratory.

LSD   LSD, or "acid," is a colorless, odorless, tasteless substance that is often sold dissolved on sugar cubes or pieces of paper. It is a potent drug that produces hallucinations at very low doses. Some users have vivid hallucinations of colors and sounds; others have mystical or semireligious experiences. Anyone can have an unpleasant, frightening reaction, or "bad trip," even those who have had many pleasant LSD experiences. Another adverse LSD reaction, which may occur days, weeks, months, or even years after the last use of the drug, is the *flashback:* The person experiences illusions or hallucinations similar to those experienced when using the drug. Because LSD is almost completely eliminated from the body within 24 hours after it is taken, the flashback is probably a restoration of memories of the prior experience.

More threatening is the loss of reality orientation that can occur with LSD use. This alteration in consciousness can lead to irrational and disoriented behavior and, occasionally, to a panic state in which users feel that they cannot control what they are doing or thinking. People have jumped to their deaths from high places when in this state. LSD was popular during the 1960s, but its use subsequently declined, probably due to widespread reports of severe drug reactions. There are some indications, however, of renewed interest in LSD and other hallucinogens (Johnston, O'Malley, & Bachman, 1995).

PCP   Although it is sold as a hallucinogen (under street names like "angel dust," "Shermans," and "superacid"), PCP is technically classified as a *dissociative anesthetic.* It may cause hallucinations, but it also makes the user feel dissociated or apart from the environment. PCP was first synthesized in 1956 for use as a general anesthetic. It had the advantage of eliminating pain without producing a deep coma. However, its legal manufacture was discontinued when doctors found that the drug produced agitation, hallucinations, and a psychotic-like state resembling schizophrenia in many patients. Because the ingredients are cheap and the drug is relatively easy to manufacture in a kitchen laboratory, PCP is widely used as an adulterant of other, more expensive street drugs. Much of what is sold as THC (the active ingredient of marijuana) is really PCP.

PCP can be taken in liquid or pill form, but more often it is smoked or snorted. In low doses it produces an insensitivity to pain and an experience similar to a moderately drunken state—one characterized by confusion, loss of inhibition, and poor psychomotor coordination. Higher doses produce a disoriented, comalike condition. Unlike the person who experiences LSD, the PCP user is unable to observe his or her drug-induced state and frequently has no memory of it.

Cannabis

The cannabis plant has been harvested since ancient times for its psychoactive effects. The dried leaves and flowers are used to produce *marijuana,* the form in which it is most often used in this country, while the solidified resin of the plant, called *hashish* ("hash"), is commonly used in the Middle East. Marijuana and hashish are usually smoked but may also be taken orally mixed with tea or food. The active ingredient in both substances is THC (tetrahydrocannabinol). Taken orally in small doses (5 to 10 milligrams), THC produces a mild high; larger doses (30 to 70 milligrams) produce severe and longer-lasting reactions that resemble those of hallucinogenic drugs. As with alcohol, the reaction often has two stages: a period of stimulation and euphoria followed by a period of tranquility and sleep.

When marijuana is smoked, THC is rapidly absorbed by the rich blood supply of the lungs. Blood from the lungs goes directly to the heart and then to the brain, causing a high within minutes. However, THC also accumulates in other organs, such as the liver, kidneys, spleen, and testes. The amount of THC reaching the body varies according to how the user smokes: A cigarette allows for the transfer of 10% to 20% of the THC in the marijuana, whereas a pipe allows about 40% to 50% to transfer. A water pipe, or bong, traps the smoke until it is inhaled and therefore is

When marijuana is smoked, the psychoactive ingredient, THC, is rapidly absorbed, causing a high within minutes. Marijuana smoke contains larger amounts of known carcinogens than tobacco, but because marijuana users tend to smoke less than cigarette smokers, the total intake of these substances is lower.

a highly efficient means of transferring THC. Once in the brain, the THC binds to cannabinoid receptors, which are especially numerous in the hippocampus. Because the hippocampus is involved in the formation of new memories, it is not surprising that marijuana use inhibits memory formation (Kuhn, Swartzwelder, & Wilson, 1998).

Regular users of marijuana report a number of sensory and perceptual changes: a general euphoria and sense of well-being, some distortions of space and time, and changes in social perception. Not all marijuana experiences are pleasant. Sixteen percent of regular users report anxiety, fearfulness, and confusion as a "usual occurrence," and about one-third report that they occasionally experience such symptoms as acute panic, hallucinations, and unpleasant distortions in body image (Halikas, Goodwin, & Guze, 1971; Negrete & Kwan, 1972). Individuals who use marijuana regularly (daily or almost daily) often report both physical and mental lethargy; about a third show mild forms of depression, anxiety, or irritability (American Psychiatric Association, 1994). It should also be noted that marijuana smoke contains even larger amounts of known carcinogens than tobacco, but because marijuana users tend to smoke less than cigarette smokers, the total intake of these substances is lower.

Marijuana use interferes with performance on complex tasks. Motor coordination is significantly impaired by low to moderate doses; and reaction time for automobile braking and the ability to negotiate a twisty road course are adversely affected (Institute of Medicine, 1982). These findings make it clear that driving while under the drug's influence is dangerous. The number of automobile accidents related to marijuana use is difficult to determine because, unlike alcohol, blood levels of the drug decrease rapidly, as it is quickly absorbed by fatty tissues and organs. A blood analysis 2 hours after a heavy dose of marijuana may show no signs of THC, even though an observer would judge the person to be clearly impaired. It is estimated that one-fourth of all drivers involved in accidents are under the influence of marijuana alone or marijuana in combination with alcohol (Jones & Lovinger, 1985).

The effects of marijuana may persist long after the subjective feelings of euphoria or sleepiness have passed. A study of aircraft pilots using a simulated flight-landing task found that performance was significantly impaired as much as 24 hours after

Table 5-2

Effects of Major Psychoactive Drugs

Alcohol	Lightheadedness, relaxation, release of inhibitions
	Increased self-confidence
	Slowing of motor reactions
Heroin	Sense of well-being
	Feeling of euphoria
	Reduced anxiety
Amphetamines	Drowsiness
	Increased alertness
	Decreased fatigue and boredom
Cocaine	Increased energy and self-confidence
	Euphoric high
	Restless irritability
	High likelihood of dependence
LSD	Hallucinations
	Mystical experiences
	"Bad trips"
	Flashbacks
PCP	Feelings of dissociation from the environment
	Insensitivity to pain
	Confusion
	Loss of inhibition
	Poor coordination
Cannabis	Stimulation and euphoria followed by tranquility and sleep
	Sense of well-being
	Distortions of space and time
	Changes in social perception
	Impaired motor coordination
	Disruption of memory

the pilots had smoked one marijuana cigarette containing 19 milligrams of THC—despite the fact that the pilots reported no awareness of any aftereffects on their alertness or performance (Yesavage et al., 1985). These findings have led to concern about marijuana use by those whose jobs involve public safety.

It is well known that marijuana disrupts memory functions. Marijuana has two clear effects on memory: First, it makes short-term memory more susceptible to interference. For example, people under the influence of marijuana may lose the thread of a conversation or forget what they are saying in the middle of a sentence because of momentary distractions (Darley et al., 1973a). Second, marijuana disrupts learning; that is, it interferes with the transfer of new information from short-term to long-term memory (Darley et al., 1973b, 1977). These findings suggest that it is not a good idea to study while under the influence of marijuana; later recall of the material will be poor.

Table 5-2 summarizes the effects of the major psychoactive drugs described in this section. By and large, these are short-term effects. The long-term effects of most drugs other than nicotine and alcohol are largely unknown. However, the history of these two common drugs should lead us to be cautious in the use of any drug over a long period.

Thinking Critically

1. It has recently been demonstrated that the ancient Asian medical practice of acupuncture, in which needles are inserted into the skin at different "acupuncture points," stimulates the brain's production of endorphins. How might this explain why acupuncture seems to help people overcome addiction to heroin?

2. Laws that criminalize some psychoactive drugs (e.g., marijuana, cocaine) but not others (e.g., alcohol, tobacco) do not seem well matched to the actual dangers of using these drugs. If you were to redesign our society's drug policies from scratch, basing them only on current scientific knowledge, which drugs would you want to discourage most vigorously (or criminalize)? Which drugs would you worry least about? What widely held beliefs about the various drugs seem to be contradicted by the scientific evidence presented in this chapter? Were any of your own beliefs contradicted?

Does Psi (ESP) Exist?

No discussion of consciousness would be complete without considering some extraordinary claims about the mind that have long attracted widespread public attention. Of particular interest are questions about whether or not human beings (1) can acquire information in ways that do not involve stimulation of the known sense organs or (2) can influence physical events by purely mental means. These questions are the source of controversy over the existence of **psi,** *anomalous processes of information and/or energy transfer that cannot currently be explained in terms of known biological or physical mechanisms.* The phenomena of psi are the subject matter of *parapsychology* ("beside psychology") and include the following:

1. *Extrasensory perception (ESP):* Response to external stimuli without any known sensory contact.

    a. *Telepathy:* Transference of thought from one person to another without the mediation of any known channel of sensory communication (e.g., identifying a playing card that is merely being thought of by another person).

    b. *Clairvoyance:* Perception of objects or events that do not provide a stimulus to the known senses (e.g., identifying a concealed playing card whose identity is unknown to anyone).

    c. *Precognition:* Perception of a future event that could not be anticipated through any known inferential process (e.g., predicting that a particular number will come up on the next throw of a pair of dice).

2. *Psychokinesis (PK):* Mental influence over physical events without the intervention of any known physical force (e.g., willing that a particular number will come up on the throw of a pair of dice).

Experimental Evidence

Most parapsychologists consider themselves to be scientists who apply the usual rules of scientific inquiry to admittedly unusual phenomena. Yet the claims for psi are so extraordinary and so similar to what are widely regarded as superstitions that some scientists declare psi to be impossible and reject the legitimacy of parapsychological inquiry. Such a priori judgments are out of place in science; the real question is whether the empirical evidence is acceptable by scientific standards. Many psychologists who are not convinced that psi has been demonstrated are nonetheless open to the possibility that new evidence might emerge that would be more persuasive. For their part, many parapsychologists believe that several recent experimental procedures either provide that evidence or hold the potential for doing so. Here we will examine the most promising of these, the ganzfeld procedure.

The *ganzfeld procedure* tests for telepathic communication between a participant acting as the "receiver" and another participant who serves as the "sender." The receiver is sequestered in an acoustically isolated room and placed in a mild form of perceptual isolation: Translucent Ping-Pong ball halves are taped over the eyes, and headphones are placed over the ears; red light is directed toward the eyes and white noise is played through the headphones. (*White noise* is a random mixture of sound frequencies similar to the hiss made by a radio tuned between stations.) This homogeneous visual and auditory environment is called the *ganzfeld,* a German word meaning "total field."

The sender sits in a separate acoustically isolated room, and a visual stimulus (picture, slide, or brief videotape sequence) is randomly selected from a large pool of similar stimuli to serve as the "target" for the session. While the sender concentrates on the target, the receiver attempts to describe it by providing a verbal report of his or her ongoing imagery and free associations. Upon completion of the session, the receiver is presented with four stimuli, one of which is the target, and asked to rate the degree to which each matches the imagery and associations experienced during the ganzfeld session. A "direct hit" is scored if the receiver assigns the highest rating to the target stimulus.

More than 75 experiments have been conducted since this procedure was introduced in 1974; the typical experiment involves about 30 sessions in which a receiver attempts to identify the target transmitted by the sender. An overall analysis of 28

psi anomalous processes of information and/or energy transfer that cannot currently be explained in terms of known biological or physical mechanisms

The receiver (left) and the sender (right) in a ganzfeld experiment.

studies (comprising a total of 835 ganzfeld sessions conducted by investigators in 10 different laboratories) reveals that participants were able to select the correct target stimulus 38% of the time. Because a participant must select the target from 4 alternatives, we would expect a success rate of 25% if only chance were operating. Statistically, this result is highly significant; the probability that it could have arisen by chance is less than one in a billion (Bem & Honorton, 1994).

Debate Over the Evidence

In 1985 and 1986 the *Journal of Parapsychology* published an extended examination of the ganzfeld studies, focusing on a debate between Ray Hyman, a cognitive psychologist and a critic of parapsychology, and Charles Honorton, a parapsychologist and a major contributor to the ganzfeld database. Hyman and Honorton agreed on the basic quantitative results but disagreed on points of interpretation (Honorton, 1985; Hyman, 1985, 1994; Hyman & Honorton, 1986). In what follows, we use their debate as a vehicle for examining the issues involved in evaluating claims of psi.

The Problem of Replication   In scientific research, a phenomenon is not considered established until it has been observed repeatedly by several researchers. Accordingly, the most serious criticism of parapsychology is that it has failed to produce a single reliable demonstration of psi that can be replicated by other investigators. Even the same investigator testing the same individuals over time may obtain statistically significant results on one occasion but not on another. The ganzfeld procedure is no exception; fewer than half (43%) of the 28 studies analyzed in the debate just described yielded statistically significant results.

The parapsychologists' most effective response to this criticism actually comes from within psychology itself. Many statisticians and psychologists are dissatisfied with psychology's focus on the statistical significance level as the sole measure of a study's success. As an alternative, they are increasingly adopting the technique of **meta-analysis,** *a statistical technique that treats the accumulated studies of a particular phenomenon as a single grand experiment and each study as a single observation.* Thus, any study that obtains results in the positive direction—even though it may not be statistically significant itself—contributes to the overall strength and reliability of the phenomenon rather than being dismissed as a failure to replicate (Glass, McGaw, & Smith, 1981; Rosenthal, 1984).

meta-analysis a statistical technique that treats the accumulated studies of a particular phenomenon as a single grand experiment and each study as a single observation

From this perspective, the ganzfeld studies provide impressive replicability: 23 of the 28 studies obtained positive results, an outcome whose probability of occurring by chance is itself less than one in a thousand.

The ability of a particular experiment to replicate an effect also depends on how strong the effect is and how many observations are made. If an effect is weak, an experiment with too few participants or observations will fail to detect it at a statistically significant level—even though the effect actually exists. In the ganzfeld situation, if the effect actually exists and has a true direct-hit rate of 38%, then statistically we should expect studies with 30 ganzfeld sessions (the average for the 28 studies discussed earlier) to obtain a statistically significant psi effect only about one-third of the time (Utts, 1986).

In short, it is unrealistic to demand that any real effect be replicable at any time by any competent investigator. The replication issue is more complex than that, and meta-analysis is proving to be a valuable tool for dealing with some of those complexities.

Inadequate Controls   The second major criticism of parapsychology is that many, if not most, of the experiments have inadequate controls and safeguards. Flawed procedures that would permit a participant to obtain the communicated information in normal sensory fashion either inadvertently or through deliberate cheating are particularly fatal. This is called the problem of *sensory leakage.* Inadequate procedures for *randomizing* (randomly selecting) target stimuli are another common problem.

Methodological inadequacies plague all sciences, but the history of parapsychology is embarrassingly full of promising results that collapsed when the procedures were examined from a critical perspective (Akers, 1984). One common charge against parapsychology is that whereas preliminary, poorly controlled studies often obtain positive results, as soon as better controls and safeguards are introduced, the results disappear.

Once a flaw is discovered in a completed experiment, there is no persuasive way of arguing that the flaw did not contribute to the positive outcome; the only remedy is to redo the experiment correctly. In a database of several studies, however, meta-analysis can evaluate the criticism empirically by checking to see if, in fact, the more poorly controlled studies obtained more positive results than did the better controlled studies. If there is a correlation between a procedural flaw and positive results across the studies, there is a problem. In the case of the ganzfeld database, both critic Hyman and parapsychologist Honorton agreed that flaws of inadequate security and possible sensory leakage do not correlate with positive results. Hyman claimed to find a correlation between flaws of randomization and positive results, but both Honorton's analysis and two additional analyses by nonparapsychologists disputed his conclusion (Harris & Rosenthal, 1988; Saunders, 1985). Moreover, a series of 11 new studies designed to control for flaws identified in the original database yielded results consistent with the original set of 28 studies (Bem & Honorton, 1994).

The File-Drawer Problem   Suppose that each of 20 investigators independently decides to conduct a ganzfeld study. Even if there were no genuine ganzfeld effect, there is a reasonable probability that at least one of these investigators would obtain a statistically significant result by pure chance. That lucky investigator would then publish a report of the experiment, but the other 19 investigators—all of whom obtained "null" results—would become discouraged, put their data in a file drawer, and move on to something more promising. As a result, the scientific community would learn about the one successful study but have no knowledge of the 19 null studies buried in the file drawers. The database of known studies would thus be seriously biased toward positive studies, and any meta-analysis of that database would arrive at similarly biased conclusions. This is known as the *file-drawer problem*.

The file-drawer problem is a tricky one because by definition it is impossible to know how many unknown studies are languishing in file drawers. Nevertheless, meta-analysis provides an empirical approach to the problem. By knowing the overall statistical significance of the known database, it is possible to compute the number of studies with null results that would have to exist in file drawers to cancel out that significance. This is known as the *fail-safe number*. In the case of the ganzfeld database, the fail-safe number is now over 700; that is, there would have to be more than 700 unreported studies with null results to cancel out the statistical significance of the known studies (Bem & Honorton, 1994). A 1980 survey of all known parapsychologists uncovered only 19 unreported ganzfeld studies, and the proportion of those that were statistically significant was virtually identical to the proportion of studies in the known database that were statistically significant. It is generally agreed, therefore, that the overall significance of the ganzfeld studies cannot reasonably be explained by the file-drawer effect (Hyman & Honorton, 1986).

Rather than continue their debate, Hyman and Honorton issued a joint communiqué in which they set forth their areas of agreement and disagreement and made a series of suggestions for the conduct of future ganzfeld studies (Hyman & Honorton, 1986). Their debate and the subsequent discussion provide a valuable model for evaluating disputed domains of scientific inquiry.

Anecdotal Evidence

In the public's mind, the evidence for psi consists primarily of personal experiences and anecdotes. From a scientific standpoint such evidence is unpersuasive because it suffers from the same problems that jeopardize the experimental evidence—the replication problem, inadequate controls, and the file-drawer problem.

The replication problem is acute because most such evidence consists of single occurrences. A woman announces a premonition that she will win the lottery that day—and she does. You dream about an unlikely event, and it actually occurs a few days later. A "psychic" correctly predicts the assassination of a public figure. Such incidents may be subjectively compelling, but there is no way to evaluate them because they are not repeatable.

The problem of inadequate controls and safeguards is decisive because such incidents occur under unexpected and ambiguous conditions. There is therefore no way of ruling out alternative interpretations such as coincidence (chance), faulty memories, and deliberate deception.

Finally, the file-drawer problem also occurs with anecdotal evidence. The lottery winner who announced ahead of time that she would win is prominently featured in the news. But the thousands of others with similar premonitions who did not win are never heard from; their "evidence" remains in the file drawer. It is true that the probability of this woman's winning the lottery was very low. But the critical criterion in evaluating this case is not the probability that *she* would win but the probability that *any one* of the thousands who thought they would win would do so. That probability is much higher. Moreover, this woman has a personal file drawer that contains all the past instances in which she had similar premonitions but did not win.

The same reasoning applies to *precognitive dreams* (dreams that anticipate an unlikely event, which actually occurs a few days later). We tend to forget our dreams unless and until an event happens to remind us of them. We therefore have no way of evaluating how often we might have dreamed of similar unlikely events that did *not* occur. We fill our database with positive instances and unknowingly exclude the negative instances.

Perhaps the fullest file drawers belong to the so-called psychics who make annual predictions in the tabloid news-

©Bill Yates; reprinted with special permission of King Features Syndicate, Inc., 1971.

papers. Nobody remembers the predictions that fail, but everybody remembers the occasional direct hits. In fact, these psychics are almost always wrong (Frazier, 1987; Tyler, 1977).

Skepticism About Psi

If some of the experimental evidence for psi is as impressive as it seems, why isn't the existence of psi more widely accepted? Psychologists are a particularly skeptical group. A survey of more than 1,000 college professors found that about 66% believe that ESP is either an established fact or a likely possibility. Moreover, these favorable views were expressed by a majority of professors in the natural sciences (55%), the social sciences excluding psychology (66%), and the arts, humanities, and education (77%). The comparable figure for psychologists was only 34% (Wagner & Monnet, 1979).

There are several reasons for the skepticism of psychologists. First, most scientists believe that extraordinary claims require extraordinary evidence. A study reporting that students who study harder get higher grades will be believed even if the study was seriously flawed, because the data accord well with our understanding of how the world works. But the claim that two people in a ganzfeld study communicate telepathically is more extraordinary; it violates most people's a priori beliefs about reality. We thus rightly demand a stronger evidence from parapsychologists because their claims, if true, would require us to radically revise our model of the world—something we should not undertake lightly. In this way, science is justifiably conservative. Many open-minded nonparapsychologists are genuinely impressed by the ganzfeld studies, but reasonably they can and do ask to see more evidence before committing themselves to the reality of psi.

But even though most scientists would agree that extraordinary claims require extraordinary evidence, psychologists are probably more familiar with the methodological and statistical requirements for concluding that the evidence being presented is in fact "extraordinary." Psychologists are also more familiar than most scientists with past instances of extraordinary claims within psychology that turned out to be based on flawed experimental procedures, faulty inference, or even fraud and deception. Over the history of research on parapsychology, there have been a disturbing number of cases in which research claims have later proved to be based on flawed or fraudulent data. Those who follow developments in this field have so often encountered charlatans—some of whom were very clever—that they have good reason to be skeptical of new claims (Gardner, 1981; Randi, 1982).

Second, psychologists know that popular accounts of psychological findings are frequently exaggerated. For example, the remarkable findings from research on asymmetries in the human brain have spawned a host of pop-psychology books and media reports containing unsubstantiated claims about left-brained and right-brained persons. Irresponsible reports about states of consciousness—including hypnosis and psi—appear daily in the media. It is worth noting, therefore, that when the college professors in the survey cited earlier were asked to name the sources for their beliefs about ESP, they most frequently cited reports in newspapers and magazines.

Third, research in cognitive and social psychology has sensitized psychologists to the biases and shortcomings in our abilities to draw valid inferences from our everyday experiences (see Chapter 14). This makes psychologists particularly skeptical of anecdotal reports of psi, where, as we have seen, our judgments are subject to many kinds of errors.

Finally, like most professional scholars, academic psychologists tend to be most familiar with the research in their own areas of specialization. Because contemporary research on psi is not usually summarized in the professional journals, handbooks, or introductory textbooks, most psychologists are not aware of recent research in the area. In fact, you are now more familiar with the ganzfeld studies than most academic psychologists.

Summary

1. A person's perceptions, thoughts, and feelings at any moment in time constitute that person's *consciousness*. An altered state of consciousness is said to exist when mental functioning seems changed or out of the ordinary to the person experiencing the state. Some altered states of consciousness, such as sleep and dreams, are experienced by everyone; others result from special circumstances, such as meditation, hypnosis, or the use of drugs.

2. The functions of consciousness are (1) monitoring ourselves and our environment so that we are aware of what is happening within our bodies and in our surroundings, and (2) controlling our actions so that they are coordinated with events in the outside world. Not all events that influence consciousness are at the center of our awareness at a given moment. Memories of personal events and knowledge that are accessible but are not currently part of one's consciousness are called *preconscious memories*. Events that affect behavior even though we are not aware of perceiving them influence us subconsciously.

3. According to psychoanalytic theory, some emotionally painful memories and impulses are not available to consciousness because they have been repressed—that is, diverted to the *unconscious*. Unconscious thoughts and impulses influence our behavior even though they reach consciousness only in indirect ways—through dreams, irrational behavior, and slips of the tongue.

4. *Automaticity* refers to the habituation of responses that initially required conscious attention, such as driving a car. *Dissociation* refers to the observation that under certain conditions some thoughts and actions become split off, or dissociated, from the rest of consciousness and function outside of awareness.

5. Sleep, an altered state of consciousness, is of interest because of the rhythms that are evident in sleep schedules and depth of sleep. These rhythms are studied with the aid of the electroencephalogram (EEG). Patterns of brain waves show four stages (depths) of sleep, plus a fifth stage characterized by rapid eye movements (REMs). These stages alternate throughout the night. Dreams occur more often during *REM sleep* than during the other four stages *(NREM sleep)*.

6. Freud attributed psychological causes to dreams, distinguishing between their manifest and latent content and suggesting that dreams are wishes in disguise. Other theories see *dreaming* as a reflection of the information processing that the brain is doing while asleep. Recently some theorists have concluded that dreaming is a cognitive process that reflects the individual's conceptions, concerns, and emotional preoccupations.

7. *Meditation* consists of efforts to alter consciousness by following planned rituals or exercises such as those of yoga or Zen. The result is a somewhat mystical state in which the individual is extremely relaxed and feels divorced from the outside world.

8. *Hypnosis* is a responsive state in which participants focus their attention on the hypnotist and the hypnotist's suggestions. Some people are more readily hypnotized than others, although most people show some susceptibility. Characteristic hypnotic responses include enhanced or diminished control over movements, distortion of memory through posthypnotic amnesia, and positive and negative hallucinations. Reduction of pain, as a form of negative hallucination, is one of the beneficial uses of hypnosis.

9. *Psychoactive drugs* have long been used to alter consciousness and mood. They include *depressants*, such as alcohol, tranquilizers and inhalants; opiates, such as heroin

and morphine; *stimulants,* such as amphetamines and cocaine; *hallucinogens,* such as LSD and PCP; and cannabis (marijuana and hashish).

10. Repeated use of any of these drugs can result in *drug dependence,* which is characterized by tolerance, withdrawal, and compulsive use. *Drug abuse* refers to continued use of a drug, despite serious consequences, by a person who has not reached the stage of dependence.

11. There is controversy over the existence of *psi,* anomalous processes of information or energy transfer that cannot currently be explained in terms of known biological or physical mechanisms. The phenomena of psi include extrasensory perception (ESP) in its various forms (telepathy, clairvoyance, precognition) and psychokinesis (PK), mental influence over objects and events.

12. The results of a number of carefully controlled studies (called ganzfeld experiments) designed to test for the existence of telepathy suggest the possibility of a real ESP effect. For a number of reasons, however, the majority of academic psychologists remain skeptical about the existence of psi.

Suggested Readings

Farthing, *The Psychology of Consciousness* (1992), provides a very readable overview of the problems of consciousness and its alterations. See also Hobson, *The Chemistry of Conscious States* (1994). For philosophical/psychological discussions of consciousness, see Jackendoff, *Consciousness and the Computational Mind* (1990); and Churchland, *The Engine of Reason, the Seat of the Soul* (1995).

Useful books on sleep and dreams include Booztin, Kihlstrom, and Schacter (eds.), *Sleep and Cognition* (1990); Anch et al., *Sleep: A Scientific Perspective* (1988); and Hobson, *The Dreaming Brain* (1988). Maas, *Power Sleep* (1998), gives detailed advice on getting sufficient restful sleep.

There are a number of books on hypnosis. Presentations that include methods, theories, and experimental results are Hilgard, *The Experience of Hypnosis* (1968), and Gheorghiu et al. (eds.), *Suggestion and Suggestibility: Theory and Research* (1989).

General books on drugs include Julien, *A Primer of Drug Action* (6th ed., 1992); Goldstein, *Addiction: From Biology to Drug Policy* (1994); and Winger, Hofmann, and Woods, *A Handbook on Drug and Alcohol Abuse* (3rd ed., 1992). For a discussion of cocaine, see Weiss, Mirin, and Bartel, *Cocaine* (2nd ed., 1994). *Buzzed,* by Kuhn, Swartzwelder, and Wilson (1998), is an excellent, straightforward presentation of the known facts about psychoactive drugs.

For a review of parapsychology, see Wolman, Dale, Schmeidler, and Ullman (eds.), *Handbook of Parapsychology* (1986); Radin, *The Conscious Universe* (1997); and Broughton, *Parapsychology: The Controversial Science* (1991).

Enhance and Explore

To enhance your understanding of the psychological concepts found in this chapter, please consult the following aids:

**Study
Guide**

Learning Objectives, p. 94
Define the Terms, p. 96
Test Your Knowledge, p. 100
Essay Questions, p. 104
Thinking Independently, p. 106

**PowerPsych
CD-ROM**

WHAT IS KNOWN ABOUT SLEEPING AND DREAMING?

Stages of Sleep
Circadian Rhythms: Owls and Larks

WHAT ARE THE EFFECTS OF PSYCHOACTIVE DRUGS?

Actions of Psychoactive Drugs at the Synapse

PsychCentral

For more information concerning the topics found in this chapter, access psychology links on the Word Wide Web made through the Harcourt Web page at:
http://www.harcourtcollege.com/psych/Fundamentals

www.harcourtcollege.com

http://www.harcourtcollege.com/psych/index.html

Learning

Learning pervades our lives. Think of the years you spend in school; think of the time you've devoted to learning to play sports, learning to ride a bicycle, or learning to dance. Learning is involved not only in mastering a new skill or academic subject but also in emotional development, social interaction, and even personality development. We learn what to fear, what to love, how to be polite, how to be intimate, and on and on. Given the pervasiveness of learning in our lives, it is not surprising that we have already discussed many instances of it—how, for example, children learn to perceive the world around them, to identify with their own sex, and to control their behavior according to adult standards. Now, however, we turn to a more systematic analysis of learning.

learning   a relatively permanent change in behavior that results from practice

   Learning may be defined as *a relatively permanent change in behavior that results from practice*. Not included in this definition are behavior changes that are due to maturation, rather than practice, or to *temporary* conditions such as fatigue or drug-induced states. Not all cases of learning are the same, and four different kinds may be distinguished: (1) *habituation,* (2) *classical conditioning,* (3) *operant conditioning,* and (4) *complex learning*. Habituation, the simplest kind of learning, amounts to learning to ignore a stimulus that has become familiar and has no serious consequences—for example, learning to ignore the ticking of a new clock. Classical and operant conditioning both involve forming associations—that is, learning that certain events go together. In classical conditioning, an organism learns that one event follows another; for example, a baby learns that the sight of a breast will be followed by the taste of milk. In operant conditioning, an organism learns that a response it makes will be followed by a particular consequence; for example, a young child learns that striking a sibling will be followed by disapproval from his or her parents. Complex learning involves something in addition to forming associations—for example, applying a strategy when solving a problem, or constructing a mental map of one's environment. Our main focus will be on the last three kinds of learning. Before beginning our discussion of conditioning and learning, though, we need to consider how the various perspectives on psychology have been applied to the study of learning.

Learning an academic subject in a classroom is a common experience. Learning a motor skill seems to be a special kind of learning.

CHAPTER 6

Why Is Learning Studied From Multiple Perspectives?

Recall from Chapter 1 that three of the most important perspectives on psychology are the behaviorist, cognitive, and biological perspectives. As much as any area in psychology, the study of learning has involved all three of these perspectives.

Much of the early research on learning, particularly on conditioning, was done from a behaviorist perspective. Researchers studied how nonhuman organisms learn an association between stimuli or an association between a stimulus and a response. The focus was on external stimuli and responses, in keeping with the behaviorists' belief that behavior is better understood in terms of external causes than in terms of mental ones. The behaviorist approach to learning made other key assumptions as well. One was that simple associations of the classical or operant kind are the building blocks of all learning. Thus something as complex as acquiring a language was thought to be a matter of learning many associations (Staats, 1968). Another assumption was that the same basic laws of learning operate regardless of what is being learned or who is doing the learning—be it a rat learning to run a maze or a child mastering long division (Skinner, 1938, 1971).

Much of what we know about associative learning—particularly reward and punishment constructs—was revealed through behaviorist experiments on non-human organisms such as rats and pigeons.

These views led behaviorists to focus on how the behaviors of nonhuman organisms, particularly rats and pigeons, are influenced by rewards and punishments in simple laboratory situations. This research uncovered a wealth of findings and phenomena that form the basis of much of what we know about associative learning. But as we will see, the behaviorists' assumptions have had to be modified in light of subsequent findings. Understanding conditioning, not to mention complex learning, requires us to consider what the organism *knows* about the relationships between stimuli and responses (even when the organism is a rat or a pigeon), thereby ushering in the cognitive perspective. Also, in cases of complex learning, strategies, rules, and the like must be considered in addition to associations, and again this requires us to adopt a cognitive approach. Moreover, it now appears that there is no single set of laws that underlies learning in all situations and for all organisms. In particular, different mechanisms of learning seem to be involved in different species, thereby ushering in the biological perspective.

The upshot is that the contemporary study of learning integrates the three perspectives just mentioned. Our treatment of both classical and operant conditioning will consider behaviorist, cognitive, and biological factors (our treatment of complex learning will concern mainly cognitive factors). We begin our discussion with classical conditioning, which has been studied primarily from the behaviorist perspective.

What Are the Main Ideas Behind Classical Conditioning?

Classical conditioning is *a learning process in which a previously neutral stimulus becomes associated with another stimulus through repeated pairing of the two stimuli.*

classical conditioning a learning process in which a previously neutral stimulus becomes associated with another stimulus through repeated pairings

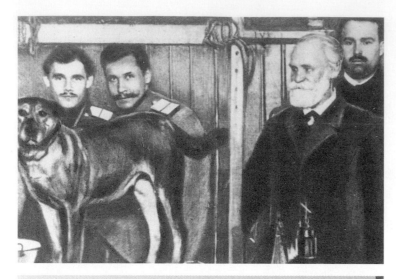

Ivan Pavlov with his assistants.

The study of classical conditioning began in the early 20th century when Ivan Pavlov, a Russian physiologist who had already won the Nobel prize for research on digestion, turned his attention to learning. While studying digestion, Pavlov noticed that a dog began to salivate at the mere sight of a food dish. While any dog will salivate when food is placed in its mouth, this dog had learned to associate the sight of the dish with the taste of food. Pavlov had happened upon a case of associative learning, and he decided to see whether a dog could be taught to associate food with other things, such as a light or a tone.

Pavlov's Experiments and Basic Findings

In Pavlov's basic experiment, a researcher first attaches a capsule to the dog's salivary gland to measure salivary flow. Then the dog is placed in front of a pan, in which meat powder can be delivered automatically. A researcher turns on a light in a window in front of the dog. After a few seconds, some meat powder is delivered to the pan and the light is turned off. The dog is hungry, and it salivates copiously (the recording device registers this). This salivation is an **unconditioned response (UCR),** for no learning is involved; by the same token, the meat powder is an **unconditioned stimulus (UCS).** The procedure is repeated a number of times—light then food, light then food, and so on. Then, to determine whether the dog has learned to associate the light with food, the experimenter turns on the light but does not deliver any meat powder. If the dog salivates, it has learned the association. This salivation is a **conditioned response (CR),** while the light is a **conditioned stimulus (CS).** (See Table 6-1.) The dog has been taught, or *conditioned,* to associate the light with food and to respond to it by salivating. Pavlov's experiment is diagrammed in Figure 6-1.

Experimental Variations   Over the years psychologists have devised many variations of Pavlov's experiments. To appreciate these variations, we need to note some critical aspects of the conditioning experiment. Each paired presentation of the conditioned stimulus (CS) and the unconditioned stimulus (UCS) is called a *trial.* The trials during which the organism is learning the association between the two stimuli make up the *acquisition stage* of conditioning. During this stage, repeated pairings of the CS (light) and the UCS (food) are said to strengthen, or *reinforce,* the association

unconditioned response (UCR) the response originally given to the unconditioned stimulus, used as the basis for establishing a conditioned response to a previously neutral stimulus

unconditioned stimulus (UCS) a stimulus that automatically elicits a response, typically via a reflex, without prior conditioning

conditioned response (CR) the learned or acquired response to a stimulus that did not evoke the response originally (i.e., a conditioned stimulus)

conditioned stimulus (CS) a previously neutral stimulus that comes to elicit a conditioned response through association with an unconditioned stimulus

Table 6-1

Elements of Classical Conditioning

Unconditioned stimulus (UCS)	A stimulus that automatically elicits a response, typically via a reflex, without prior conditioning.
Unconditioned response (UCR)	The response originally given to the unconditioned stimulus, used as the basis for establishing a conditioned response to a previously neutral stimulus.
Conditioned stimulus (CS)	A previously neutral stimulus that comes to elicit a conditioned response through association with an unconditioned stimulus.
Conditioned response (CR)	The learned or acquired response to a stimulus that did not evoke the response originally (i.e., a conditioned stimulus).

between the two, as illustrated in the left-hand curve of Figure 6-2. If the association is not reinforced (that is, if the UCS is omitted repeatedly), the response will gradually diminish; this is called *extinction* and is illustrated by the right-hand curve in Figure 6-2.

Acquisition and extinction make intuitive sense if we view classical conditioning as learning to predict what will happen next. (This is the heart of the cognitive approach to conditioning that we will consider later.) When the prediction is successful (reinforced), the animal learns to keep making that prediction (acquisition); when things change so that the prediction is outdated (not reinforced), the animal learns to inhibit that prediction (extinction).

Conditioning in Different Species   Classical conditioning is pervasive in the animal kingdom and can occur with organisms as primitive as the flatworm. Flatworms contract their bodies when subjected to mild electric shock, and if they experience sufficient pairings of shock (the UCS) and light (the CS), eventually they will contract in response to the light alone (Jacobson, Fried, & Horowitz, 1967).

Numerous human responses can also be classically conditioned. Many of these are involuntary responses. To illustrate, consider the plight of cancer patients who are undergoing chemotherapy treatments to stop the growth of their tumors. Chemotherapy involves injecting toxic substances into the patients, who as a result often become nauseated. After a number of chemotherapy sessions, patients sometimes become nauseated and sick upon entering the treatment room. The repeated pairing of the chemotherapy (the UCS) and the sight of the treatment room (the CS) has led them to associate the room with the chemotherapy, and as a result they experience intestinal upset before their treatment even begins. A related phenomenon arises with young cancer patients who are given ice cream before chemotherapy sessions. The ice cream may have been intended to lighten the child's distress about the impending treatment, but

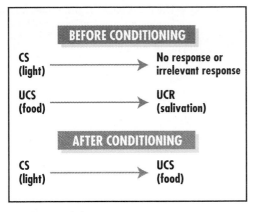

Figure 6-1

A Diagram of Classical Conditioning   The association between the unconditioned stimulus and the unconditioned response exists at the beginning of the experiment and does not have to be learned. The association between the conditioned stimulus and the unconditioned stimulus is learned. It arises through the pairing of the conditioned and unconditioned stimuli. (An association may also be learned between the conditioned stimulus and the conditioned response.)

Figure 6-2

Acquisiton and Extinction of a Conditioned Response   The curve in the panel on the left depicts the acquisiton phase of an experiment. Drops of salivation in response to the conditioned stimulus (prior to the onset of the UCS) are plotted on the vertical axis; the number of trials is plotted on the horizontal axis. After 16 acquisition trials the experimenter switched to extinction; the results are presented in the panel at the right. (After Pavlov, 1927)

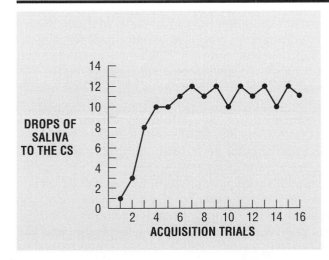
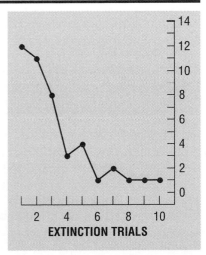

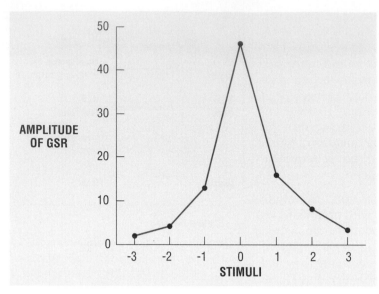

AMPLITUDE
OF GSR

STIMULI

Figure 6-3

The Gradient of Generalization   Stimulus 0 denotes the tone to which the galvanic skin response (GSR) was originally conditioned. Stimuli +1, +2, and +3 represent test tones of increasingly higher pitch; stimuli –1, –2, and –3 represent tones of lower pitch. Note that the amount of generalization decreases as the difference between the test tone and the training tone increases.

alas, it becomes conditioned to the chemotherapy experience (now ice cream is the CS and chemotherapy the UCS). The upshot is that the children will be less likely to eat ice cream, even outside the chemotherapy setting (Bernstein, 1978).

Phenomena and Applications

A number of phenomena greatly increase the generality of classical conditioning and make it an important kind of learning. In the following pages we examine some of those phenomena.

Second-Order Conditioning   Thus far in our discussion, the UCS has been biologically significant, such as food, cold, or shock. However, other stimuli can acquire the power of a UCS by being consistently paired with a biologically significant UCS. Recall the example of Pavlov's dog being exposed to a light (the CS) followed by food (the UCS), where the light comes to elicit a conditioned response. Once the dog is conditioned, the light acquires the power of a UCS. Thus, if the dog is now put in a situation in which it is exposed to a tone followed by the light (but no food) on each trial, the tone alone will eventually elicit a conditioned response even though it has never been paired with food.

The existence of such *second-order conditioning* greatly increases the scope of classical conditioning, especially for humans, for whom biologically significant UCSs occur relatively frequently. Now all that is needed for conditioning to occur is the pairing of one stimulus with another, which has previously been paired with a biologically significant event. Consider again our chemotherapy example. Suppose that for a particular patient the sight of the treatment room has become conditioned to the chemotherapy experience (a biologically significant event). If the patient is repeatedly presented with a neutral stimulus—say, a tone—followed by a picture of the treatment room, the patient may start to experience some unpleasant feeling in response to the tone alone.

Generalization and Discrimination   When a conditioned response has been associated with a particular stimulus, other similar stimuli will evoke the same response. Suppose that a person is conditioned to have a mild emotional reaction to the sound of a tuning fork producing a tone of middle C. (The emotional reaction arises because the tone is followed by a shock; the reaction is measured by the *galvanic skin response,* or GSR, a change in the electrical activity of the skin that occurs during emotional stress.) The person will also show a GSR to higher or lower tones without further conditioning (see Figure 6-3). *The more similar the new stimuli are to the original CS, the more likely they are to evoke the conditioned response.* This principle, called **generalization,** accounts in part for an individual's ability to react to novel stimuli that are similar to familiar ones.

A complementary process is called discrimination. Whereas generalization is a reaction to similarities, **discrimination** is *a reaction to differences between stimuli.* Conditioned discrimination is brought about through selective reinforcement, as shown in Figure 6-4. Instead of just one tone, for instance, now there are two. The low-pitched tone, CS_1, is always followed by a shock, and the high-pitched tone, CS_2,

generalization   the principle that the more similar new stimuli are to the original CS, the more likely they are to evoke the conditioned response

discrimination   a reaction to differences between stimuli

is not. Initially, participants will show a GSR to both tones. During the course of conditioning, however, the amplitude of the conditioned response to CS_1 gradually increases while that of the response to CS_2 decreases. Through this process of *differential reinforcement,* participants are conditioned to discriminate between the two tones. The high-pitched tone, CS_2, has become a signal to inhibit the learned response.

Generalization and discrimination occur in everyday life. A young child who has learned to associate the sight of her pet dog with playfulness may initially approach all dogs. Eventually, through differential reinforcement, the child may expect playfulness only from dogs that look like hers. The sight of a threatening dog has come to inhibit the child's response of approaching dogs.

Conditioned Fear   Classical conditioning plays a role in emotional reactions like fear. Suppose that a rat is placed in an enclosed compartment in which it is periodically subjected to electric shock (by electrifying the floor). Just before the shock occurs, a tone sounds. After repeated pairings of the tone (the CS) and the shock (the UCS), the tone alone will produce reactions in the rat that are indicators of fear, including stopping in its tracks and crouching; in addition, its blood pressure increases. The rat has been conditioned to be fearful when exposed to what was previously a neutral stimulus.

It has long been known that humans, too, can be conditioned to be fearful (Watson & Rayner, 1920). Many human fears may be acquired in this way, particularly in early childhood (Jacobs & Nadel, 1985). Perhaps the best evidence that they can be classically conditioned is that some of these fears, especially irrational ones, can be eliminated by means of therapeutic techniques based on classical conditioning principles. A person with an intense fear of cats, for example, may overcome the fear by gradually and repeatedly being exposed to cats. Presumably, a cat was a CS for some noxious UCS a long time ago, and when the person later repeatedly experiences the CS without the UCS, the conditioned fear is extinguished. Note that if the person were not treated, he or she would simply avoid cats; consequently, extinction would not occur and the phobia would persist. (See Chapters 12 and 13 for a discussion of conditioning of phobias and conditioning therapies.)

Conditioning and Drug Tolerance   In most of our examples thus far, the conditioned response resembles the unconditioned response. Pavlov's dogs salivate in response to the light (the CR) just as they do in response to the food (the UCR), cancer patients become nauseated at the sight of the treatment room (the CR) just as they do in response to the chemotherapy treatment (the UCR), and so on. But

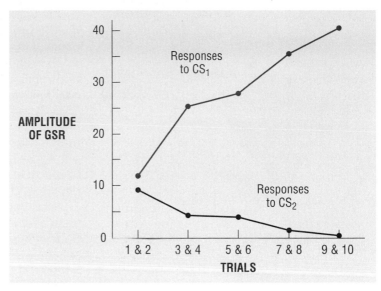

Figure 6-4

Conditioned Discrimination   The discriminative stimuli were two tones of clearly different pitch (CS_1 = 700 hertz and CS_2 = 3,500 hertz). The unconditioned stimulus, an electric shock applied to the left forefinger, occurred only on trials when CS_1 was presented. The strength of the conditioned response, in this case the GSR, gradually increased following CS_1 and extinguished following CS_2. (After Baer & Fuhrer, 1968)

Sometimes we learn to fear things that are not really dangerous.

Intravenous drug use involves classical conditioning.

this is not always the case. There are situations in which the CR is the opposite of the UCR, and some of the most dramatic of these situations involve the use of drugs.

Consider a case in which someone regularly takes injections of morphine. Since the sight of the injection is repeatedly followed by the morphine, the injection functions as a CS and morphine as a UCS, and classical conditioning occurs. That is, the sight of the injection will be associated with the intake of morphine. However, while the response to morphine (the UCR) is reduced sensitivity to pain, the response to the sight of the injection (the CR) is an increase in sensitivity to pain. Surprisingly, the CR is the opposite of the UCR.

This phenomenon is part of what goes on in the development of *drug tolerance.* It is well known that as a person continues to use a drug like morphine, a given dose of the drug becomes less effective; the person must increase the dosage level to get the desired effect. This is partly a matter of classical conditioning. With continued use of morphine, conditioning occurs between the sight of the injection and the intake of morphine. As noted, this results in an increase in pain sensitivity; hence, increasingly more morphine is needed to obtain the desired level of painkiller. It is not that the painkilling effect of morphine has decreased, but rather that the level of pain sensitivity has increased. The same process presumably operates in the use of heroin for nonmedical purposes. After repeated injections, the drug user's conditioned response to the injection is the opposite of the desired effect (a sense of well-being); consequently, he must take a higher and higher dosage to produce the desired effect (Siegel, 1979, 1983).

The Role of Predictability and Cognitive Factors

Up to this point we have analyzed classical conditioning solely in terms of external events—one stimulus is consistently followed by another, and the organism comes to associate them with each other. In contrast to this behaviorist view is the cognitive view: Classical conditioning provides an organism with new knowledge about the relationship between two stimuli; given the CS, it has learned to *expect* the UCS. In what follows, we consider the role of cognitive factors in classical conditioning.

Contiguity Versus Predictability   Since Pavlov's time, researchers have tried to determine the critical factor needed for classical conditioning to occur. Pavlov thought the critical factor was *temporal contiguity* of the CS and UCS—that is, the two stimuli must occur close together in time for an association to develop. There is, however, an alternative—namely, that the CS be a *reliable predictor* of the UCS. In other words, for conditioning to occur, there must be a higher probability that the UCS will occur when the CS has been presented than when it has not. This notion is a cognitive one.

In an important experiment, Robert Rescorla (1967), contrasted contiguity and predictability. On certain trials of the experiment he exposed dogs to shock (the UCS), and on some of these trials he preceded the shock by a tone (the CS). The procedures for two of the groups from the experiment are illustrated in Figure 6-5. The number of temporally contiguous pairings of tone and shock was the same in both groups. The independent variable was that all shocks were preceded by tones in Group A, whereas in Group B shocks were as likely to be preceded by no tones as by tones; hence, the tone had no predictive power. The predictive power of the tone proved critical: Group A rapidly became conditioned, whereas Group B did not (as determined by whether the dog responded to the tone in such a way as to avoid the

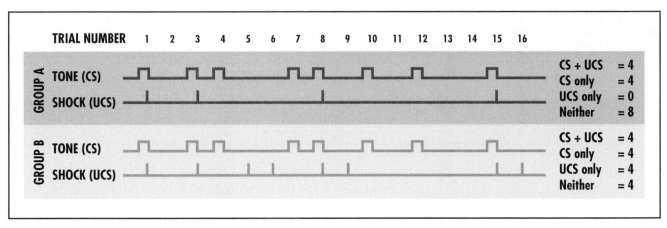

Figure 6-5

Rescorla's Experiment   This figure presents a schematic representation of two groups from Rescorla's study. For each group, the events for 16 trials are presented. Note that on some trials the CS occurs and is followed by the UCS (CS + UCS), on the other trials the CS or UCS occurs alone; and on still other trials, neither the CS nor the UCS occurs. The boxes to the far right give a count of these trial outcomes for the two groups. The number of CS + UCS trials is identical for both groups, as is the number of trials on which only the CS occurs. But the two groups differ in the number of trials on which the UCS occurred alone (never in Group A and as frequently as any other type of trial in Group B). Thus, for Group A the experimenter established a situation in which the tone was a useful (but not perfect) predictor that shock would follow shortly, whereas for Group B the tone was of no value in predicting subsequent shock. A conditioned response to CS developed readily for Group A but did not develop at all for Group B.

shock). The results of subsequent experiments support the conclusion that the predictive relationship between the CS and the UCS is more important than either temporal contiguity or the frequency with which the CS and the UCS are paired (Rescorla, 1972).

What a dog is doing in the preceding experiment is analogous to what a scientist usually does. Confronted with the possibility of an important negative occurrence like a thunderstorm, a meteorologist tries to find something that predicts the event. It cannot be something that merely occurs contiguously with thunderstorms, because many innocuous events will do so (such as clouds and even the presence of trees). Rather, the meteorologist must search for events that are predictive of thunderstorms in that they tend to occur prior to thunderstorms but not at other times. Likewise, when a dog in the preceding experiment has to deal with the important, negative occurrence of shock, it too tries to find some event that can predict it. And like the meteorologist, the dog does not focus on events that merely co-occur with shock (such as the sight of the experimental apparatus, or the tone in Group B of the experiment); rather, the dog looks for an event that tends to occur prior to any shock but not at other times (the tone in Group A of the experiment) and hence is truly predictive of the shock.

The importance of predictability is also shown by the phenomenon of *blocking,* discovered by Leo Kamin (1969). Kamin showed that if a CS is redundant, providing information that an organism already has, the organism will not be conditioned to the UCS.

Kamin's experiment is outlined in Table 6-2. It involved three stages. In the first stage, an experimental group of animals was repeatedly presented with a light (the CS) followed by a shock (the UCS). The experimental animals easily learned the light–shock association. The control group of animals received no training in this stage. In the second stage, both the experimental and control groups were repeatedly presented with a light plus a tone (a compound CS) followed by a shock (the UCS). For the experimental animals, which had already learned to associate the light with shock, the tone was redundant. For the control animals, which had no prior learning, the compound CS was informative. In the third and final stage of the experiment, the

Table 6-2

An Experiment on Blocking   This table presents the design of Kamin's experiment, which shows that a previously learned association can block the learning of a new association. (After Kamin, 1969)

	Stage 1	Stage 2	Stage 3
Experimental Group	Light → Shock	Light + Tone → Shock	Tone → No Conditioned Response
Control Group		Light + Tone → Shock	Tone → Conditioned Response

tone was presented alone to see whether it would produce a conditioned response. The control animals showed conditioned responses, but the experimental animals did not. For the experimental animals, the previously learned light–shock association blocked the learning of the new tone–shock association. Why? Presumably because the earlier learning made the shock predictable, and once a UCS is predictable there is little possibility of further conditioning.

Predictability and Emotion   Predictability is especially important for emotional reactions. If a particular CS reliably predicts that pain is coming, the absence of that CS predicts that pain is not coming and the organism can relax. The CS therefore is a "danger" signal and its absence a "safety" signal. When such signals are erratic, the emotional toll on the organism can be devastating. When rats have a reliable predictor that shock is coming, they respond with fear only when the danger signal is present; if they have no reliable predictor, they appear to be continually anxious and may even develop ulcers (Seligman, 1975).

There are clear parallels to human emotionality. If a dentist gives a child a danger signal by telling him that a procedure will hurt, the child will be fearful until the procedure is over. In contrast, if the dentist always tells a child "It won't hurt" when in fact it sometimes does, the child has no danger or safety signals and may become terribly anxious whenever he is in the dentist's office. As adults, many of us have experienced the anxiety of being in a situation in which something disagreeable is likely to happen but no warnings exist to enable us to predict it. Unpleasant events are by definition unpleasant, but unpredictable unpleasant events are downright intolerable. (Further discussion of this point is included in Chapter 11.)

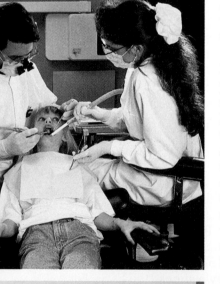

Knowing when pain may occur can help us deal with it.

Models of Classical Conditioning   The findings about predictability have led to a number of models of classical conditioning. The best known of these was developed by Rescorla and Wagner (1972), and it focuses on the cognitive notions of predictability and surprise. According to the *Rescorla-Wagner model,* the amount of conditioning on any trial depends on how surprising the UCS is, which in turn depends on how much the UCS is associated with possible CSs. The more surprising the UCS, the greater the amount of conditioning on that trial. Early in learning, the UCS is very surprising (no CSs yet predict it), and hence a good deal should be learned on each trial. Late in learning, there is at least one CS that predicts the UCS, and hence the UCS is not very surprising and rather little is learned on each trial. This pattern—bigger learning gains early, smaller gains later on—in fact characterizes the acquisition of a classically conditioned response (refer back to Figure 6-2).

Another assumption of the Rescorla-Wagner model is that the predictability of the UCS on any trial is determined by all the CSs present on that trial. For example, if there are two CSs present on a trial—say, a light and a tone—the amount of conditioning possible for one of the CSs—say, the tone—is less the more that conditioning has already occurred to the other (the light). This explains the blocking phenomenon described earlier. Essentially, CSs that occur together compete for association strength, where the amount to be won in the competition is the amount of unpredictability left in the UCS.

Another cognitive model views classical conditioning as the generation and testing of rules about what events are likely to follow other events (Holyoak, Koh, & Nisbett, 1989). According to this *rule model,* an animal is likely to generate a rule whenever two unexpected events occur in close proximity or whenever an old rule fails. For a rat in a classical conditioning experiment, an unexpected light followed closely by an unexpected shock would lead to the generation of the rule, "If light, then shock." Once a rule is formed, it is strengthened every time it leads to a correct prediction and weakened every time it leads to an incorrect one. The "If light, then shock" rule, for example, will be strengthened whenever the light is in fact followed by the shock, and weakened whenever it is not.

According to the rule model, predictability is necessary for conditioning to occur, since only correct predictions can strengthen a rule. The model also accounts for the blocking phenomenon: As long as a UCS is predicted by a known rule, no new rule involving that UCS will be generated.

Evolutionary Constraints on Conditioning

We mentioned earlier that different species sometimes learn the same thing through different mechanisms. These phenomena were discovered by **ethologists,** *biologists and psychologists who study animal behavior in the natural environment.* The phenomena reveal that what an organism can learn through conditioning is constrained by its biology.

ethologists biologists and psychologists who study animal behavior in the natural environment

The Ethological Approach Ethologists, like behaviorists, are concerned with the behavior of animals, but ethologists place more emphasis on evolution and genetics than on learning. This emphasis has led ethologists to take a distinctive approach to learning—namely, to assume that learning is rigidly constrained by an animal's genetic endowment and to show that different species will learn different things in different ways. As ethologists put it, when an animal learns, it must conform to a genetically determined "behavioral blueprint." That is, animals are preprogrammed to learn particular things in particular ways.

Constraints in Classical Conditioning Some of the best evidence for constraints in classical conditioning comes from studies of *taste aversion.* Consider first the basic phenomenon of taste aversion. In a typical study, a rat is permitted to drink a flavored solution—say, vanilla. After drinking it, the rat is mildly

"Oh, not bad. The light comes on, I press the bar, they write me a check. How about you?"

Table 6-3

An Experiment on Constraints and Taste Aversion   The design of an experiment showing that taste is a better signal for sickness than shock, where as light-plus-sound is a better signal for shock than sickness. (After Garcia & Koelling, 1966)

	Stage 1	Stage 2	Stage3
Experimental group	Taste and light + click	Sickness	Taste → Avoid ——————————— Light + click → Don't avoid
Control group	Taste and light + click	Shock	Taste → Don't avoid ——————————— Light + click → Avoid

poisoned and becomes ill. When the rat recovers, it is again presented with the vanilla solution. Now the rat scrupulously avoids the solution because it has learned to associate the vanilla taste with feeling ill. There is good evidence that such avoidance is an instance of classical conditioning: The initial taste of the solution is the CS; the feeling of being sick is the UCS; and after conditioning, the taste signals that sickness is on the way.

According to early behaviorist ideas, a light or a sound might be expected to play the same signaling role as taste. That is, if a light is as effective a stimulus as taste, an association between a light and feeling sick should be no more difficult to establish than an association between a taste and feeling sick. But the facts turn out to be otherwise. This is shown by the experiment diagrammed in Table 6-3.

In the first stage of the experiment, an experimental group of rats is allowed to lick a tube that contains a flavored solution; each time the rat licks the tube, a click and a light are presented. Thus, the rat experiences three stimuli simultaneously: the taste of the solution, the light, and the click. In the second stage of the experiment, rats in the experimental group are mildly poisoned. The question is: What stimulus—the taste or the light-plus-click—will become associated with feeling sick? To answer this, in the third and final stage of the study, rats in the experimental group are again presented with the tube; sometimes the solution in the tube has the same flavor as before but there is no light or click, while at other times the solution has no flavor but the light and click are presented. The animals avoid the solution when they experience the taste, but not when the light-plus-click is presented; hence, the rats have associated only taste with feeling sick. These results cannot be attributed to taste being a more potent CS than light-plus-click, as shown by the control condition of the experiment, diagrammed in the bottom of Table 6-3. In the second stage, instead of being mildly poisoned, the rat is shocked. Now, in the final stage of the study, the animal avoids the solution only when the light-plus-click is presented, not when it experiences the taste alone (Garcia & Koelling, 1966).

Thus, taste is a better signal for sickness than for shock, and light-plus-click is a better signal for shock than for sickness. Why does this selectivity of association exist? It does not fit with the early behaviorist idea that equally potent stimuli can substitute for one another. But it fits perfectly with the ethological perspective and its emphasis on an animal's evolutionary adaptation to its environment. In their natural habitat, rats (like other mammals) rely on taste to select their food. Consequently, there may be a genetically determined, built-in relationship between taste and intestinal reactions, which fosters an association between taste and sickness but not between light and sickness. Moreover, in a rat's natural environment pain resulting from external factors like cold or injury is invariably due to external stimuli. Consequently, there may be a built-in relationship between external stimuli and "external pain," which fosters an association between light and shock but not one between taste and shock.

If rats learn to associate taste with sickness because it fits with their natural means of selecting food, another species with a different means of selecting food might have trouble learning to associate taste with sickness. This is exactly what happens. Birds naturally select their food on the basis of appearance rather than taste, and they readily learn to associate a light with sickness but not to associate a taste with sickness (Wilcoxin, Dragoin, & Kral, 1971). Here, then, is a perfect example of different species learning the same thing—what causes sickness—by different means. In short, if we want to know what may be conditioned to what, we cannot consider the CS and UCS in isolation; rather, we must focus on the two in combination and consider how well that combination reflects built-in relationships.

Sometimes a person may feel fearful of a neutral object (e.g., loose buttons) but not know why. How could you explain this in terms of the principles and ideas presented in this chapter?

**Thinking
Critically**

What Are the Neural Bases of Learning?

Up to this point, our discussion of biological factors in learning has focused on evolutionary theory. But the biology of neurons and neural structures, which proved so important in our analyses of sensation and perception, is again relevant. In the last several years, there has been an upsurge in research on the neural bases of learning. Some of this research is done at the level of individual neurons and focuses on events occurring within a cell or at the juncture between cells. Other research is done at the level of neural structures (which are composed of many neurons) and focuses on the function of these structures and their interconnections. We first review research at the cellular level and then consider research on larger neural structures.

Structural Changes at the Cellular Level

It is useful to start by considering what kinds of approaches to the neural basis of learning will *not* work. One possibility is to look for a specific region in the cortex that is solely responsible for learning (much as there appear to be specific cortical regions that are responsible for processing color). However, researchers today do not believe in such a "learning center." Rather, the evidence indicates that the products of long-term learning are distributed all over the cortex, with the visual aspects of what is learned being stored in mainly visual regions of the brain, the motor aspects being stored in motor regions, and so on (Squire, 1982).

Another approach that will not work is to assume that whatever brain regions and neurons are involved in learning something will remain active *thereafter*. While this idea seems to hold for short-term learning or memory (as discussed in the next chapter), researchers agree that it cannot apply to long-term learning (Carlson, 1986). If everything we learned led to a permanent increase in neural activation, our brains would become increasingly active each day; this clearly is not the case.

So what kind of neurological approach *will* work? Researchers believe that the neural basis of learning consists of structural changes in the nervous system, and increasingly they are looking for these changes at the level of neural connections.

To appreciate their ideas, you need to recall from Chapter 2 the basic structure of a neural connection and how it transmits an impulse. An impulse is transmitted from one neuron to another by the axon of the sender. Because the axons are separated by the *synaptic gap,* the sender's axon secretes a *neurotransmitter,* which diffuses across the gap and stimulates the receiving neuron. More precisely, when the neural impulse travels down the sender's axon, it triggers terminals at the end of the axon to release the neurotransmitter, which is picked up by receptors on the receiving neuron. This entire structure is called a *synapse.*

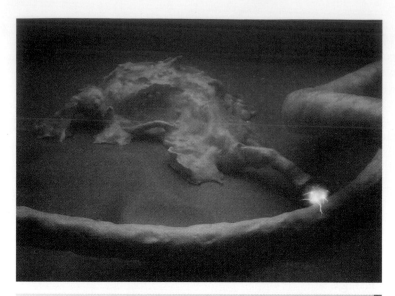

At the neural level, learning appears to cause a structural change in the synapse, which in turn makes the synapse more efficient, firing more quickly with each subsequent stimulation.

The key ideas regarding learning are that (1) some structural change in the synapse is the neural basis of learning and (2) the effect of this structural change is to make the synapse more efficient. What would constitute evidence for this proposal? One approach would be to demonstrate that after a learning episode a synapse becomes more efficient—that is, fires more readily when stimulated again. At present this is difficult to demonstrate with organisms of any complexity: If you recorded from some specific neurons, how could you find a learning task that affects exactly those neurons? Researchers have chosen the strategy of first electrically stimulating a particular set of neurons (presumably this simulates learning) and then checking for an increase in the rate of activity of these same neurons when they are subsequently stimulated. Such increases have been found in a number of regions of the rabbit brain, including regions known to be involved in learning. The increases can last for several months. This phenomenon is referred to as *long-term potentiation,* and it provides indirect support for the structural-change view of learning (Berger, 1984; Bliss & Lomo, 1973).

Cellular Changes in Simple Learning

We have not been very specific about what *kinds* of structural changes increase synaptic efficiency. There are several possibilities. One is that learning results in an increase in the amount of neurotransmitter secreted by the sending neuron. Alternatively, there may be an increase in the amount of neurotransmitter taken up by the receiving neuron. Other possibilities are that the synapse could change in size or that entirely new synapses could be established (Carlson, 1986). Several possibilities may be correct, with different kinds of structural changes underlying different kinds of learning.

To study learning processes at this level of neural detail, researchers have to work with elementary forms of learning and with organisms that have simple nervous systems. One kind of elementary learning, mentioned at the beginning of the chapter, is **habituation.** This is *the process through which an organism learns to weaken its reaction to a weak stimulus that has no serious consequences,* such as tuning out the sound of a loud clock. A related case of learning is **sensitization,** *the process whereby an organism learns to strengthen its reaction to a weak stimulus if a threatening or painful stimulus follows.* For instance, we learn to respond more intensely to the sound of a piece of equipment if it is frequently followed by a crash. Habituation and sensitization are found at virtually all levels of the animal kingdom, but our concern here is with the snail. Snails have a simple and accessible nervous system, which makes them well suited for studying structural changes in the synapse that accompany elementary learning.

When a snail is lightly touched repeatedly, it initially responds, but within about 10 trials it habituates to the touch. Researchers have shown that this habituation learning is accompanied by a decrease in the amount of neurotransmitter secreted by a sending neuron. The snail also manifests sensitization. Now a light touch to the body is accompanied by a strong stimulus to the tail, and after a few trials of this procedure, the snail's response to the touch becomes more pronounced. Sensitization learning has been shown to be accompanied by an increase in the amount of neuro-

habituation   the process through which an organism learns to weaken its reaction to a weak stimulus that has no serious consequences

sensitization   the process whereby an organism learns to strengthen its reaction to a weak stimulus if a threatening or painful stimulus follows

Genetic Improvement of Learning and Memory in Mice

In some very recent research, scientists have used genetic techniques to show that cellular changes can lead to changes in learning and memory. This research establishes direct links between genes and cellular changes, on one hand, and learning and memory, on the other (Tang et al., 1999).

To appreciate the work, which was done with mice, recall the basic mechanisms of a synapse: A neural impulse travels down a sender axon and triggers terminals at the end of that axon to release a neurotransmitter, which is then picked up by receptors in the receiver neuron. The research of interest focuses on the receptors on the receiving neuron and shows that improving their efficacy improves learning. More specifically, the researchers focused on NMDA receptors (N-methyl-D-asparate receptors), which are found in the hippocampus and cortex and are known to be involved in learning. The NMDA receptor is itself composed of a variety of subunits, one of which is the NR2B subunit. This subunit is more common in young mice than in older ones, and it produces a more sensitive receptor. Because scientists know the gene that directs the production of the NR2B subunit, it was possible for researchers to create strains of mice

that had extra copies of this gene, and to cause these extra copies to be expressed in the cortex and the hippocampus, thereby increasing the sensitivity of NMDA receptors in these regions. In short, it was possible to genetically alter mice so that they have more effective NMDA receptors. The question is: Do they learn faster than normal mice?

The answer is yes, as shown by the results of several different memory tasks. In one task, genetically altered and normal mice were first trained on a set of objects to make the objects somewhat familiar. Sometime after training, the mice were exposed to three objects, two of which were trained and one of which was novel. To the extent that the mice remember the trained objects, they should spend most of their time exploring the novel object (Mice, like the rest of us, are known to explore novel objects more than familiar ones.) When tested an hour after training, the genetically altered and normal mice spent the same amount of time with the novel object; but when tested more than an hour after training, the genetically altered mice spent more time exploring the novel objects. Hence, the genetically altered mice seem to have better long-term memories of the trained objects.

Similar results were obtained with a very different test of learning, one in which the mice were classically conditioned to fear a context in which they had experienced a foot shock. The measure of fear conditioning was the extent to which the mice "froze" when in that context. There was no difference between the genetically altered mice and the normal ones in freezing responses immediately after training, but when tested hours after training, the genetically altered mice showed more freezing. Again, a genetically engineered improvement in NMDA receptors led to an improvement in long-term memory.

In still another kind of learning task, the mice were placed in a vat of water and had to learn to find their way to a submerged platform on which they could rest. (Although mice can swim, they prefer the comfort of the platform.) This is a frequently used test of spatial learning and memory. Again, the genetically altered mice learned faster than normal mice.

These results dramatically show that components of neural receptors are directly linked to learning and memory. They also raise the possibility that genetic manipulations may someday be used to improve learning and memory.

transmitter secreted by the sending neuron (Kandel, Schwartz, & Jessel, 1991). These findings provide relatively direct evidence that elementary learning is based on structural changes at the neuronal level. Similar structural changes may underlie classical conditioning (Hawkins & Kandel, 1984).

Neural Systems in Fear Conditioning

In addition to research at the level of individual neurons, a great deal of research on the neural bases of learning focuses on neuroanatomical structures—each of which can be composed of hundreds or thousands of individual neurons—and the pathways that connect these structures. A good example of this kind of research concerns the neural bases of fear conditioning.

For more than 60 years it has been suspected that the critical brain structure involved in learning to be fearful is the *amygdala,* an almond-shaped group of nuclei buried deep within the temporal lobes (*amygdala* is Greek for "almond") (Kluver & Bucy, 1937). Recent research has turned up detailed evidence that the amygdala is critically involved in learning and expressing fear. In species ranging from rats to primates, damage to the amygdala leads to a reduction of fearful behavior in general and to difficulties in fear conditioning in particular. Rats whose amygdalas have been surgically removed show fewer signs of fear—that is, fewer fear-based responses such as freezing and crouching—when exposed to aversive stimuli and have great difficulty acquiring a classically conditioned fear response (Aggleton & Passingham, 1981). In normal rats with intact amygdalas, learning of a conditioned fear response is accompanied by increased neuronal firing in certain regions of the amygdala (Quirk, Repa, & LeDoux, 1995). And when normal organisms are administered a drug that blocks the functioning of the amygdala, fear conditioning is disrupted (Maren & Fanselow, 1995). Taken together, these findings build a strong case that in mammals the amygdala is the key brain structure involved in learning to be fearful.

Another study shows that what holds for other mammals applies to us as well (Bechera et al., 1995). This study involved a human patient, referred to as S.M., who had a rare disorder (Urbach-Wiethe disease) that results in degeneration of the amygdala. S.M. was exposed to a fear-conditioning situation in which a neutral visual stimulus (the CS) was predictably followed by the noxious sound of a loud horn (the UCS). Despite repeated trials, S.M. showed no evidence of fear conditioning. Yet S.M. had no trouble recalling the events associated with the fear conditioning, including the relationship between the conditioned and unconditioned stimuli. In sharp contrast, another patient, who had a normal amygdala but had suffered damage to a brain structure known to be involved in the learning of factual material, showed normal fear conditioning but was completely unable to recall the events associated with the conditioning. Thus, the two patients had the opposite problems, indicating that the amygdala is involved in the learning of fear but not in learning in general.

Learning Motor Sequences

For a different kind of example of the role of specific neural structure in learning, consider the case of learning a sequence of motor movements. Learning to make one particular movement after another is an instance of associative learning (though the kind of conditioning involved is operant, not classical, conditioning—see the next section). In an illustrative experiment, participants learned to make a sequence of finger movements and were given several weeks of training on the sequence. Since the participants were learning motor responses, we would expect that the part of the cortex involved in making motor movements—the "motor cortex"—would be activated. What was of interest, though, was the nature of the changes in the motor cortex that occurred with learning, particularly in the region known to control hand and finger movements. To determine the nature of these changes, at weekly intervals participants' brains were scanned (in an MRI scanner) while they performed either the trained motor sequence or a novel control sequence. Each control sequence required the same finger movements as the trained sequence, albeit in a different order.

At the very beginning of training, both the training and control sequences produced a patchy pattern of activation in the hand region of the motor cortex. As training progressed, the neural representation of the trained sequence changed: The patches of activation expanded, and the spaces between them were filled (Karni et al., 1995). Thus, as one learns a sequence better and better, more and more neural tissue is devoted to it. This neural expansion occurred only for the trained sequence, not for control sequences consisting of the same finger movements. So it was not the neural representation of the individual finger movements that expanded, but rather the neural representation of the sequence itself (Ungerleider, 1995).

1. Given that various drugs can affect neurotransmitters, mention some different ways in which a drug might facilitate learning—say, classical conditioning.

2. People sometimes say, "So-and-so is the way he is either because of his biological nature or because of what he's learned." They mean that it's one or the other, but not both. Is there really a dichotomy between biology and learning?

What Are the Main Ideas Behind Operant Conditioning?

In classical conditioning, the conditioned response often resembles the normal response to the unconditioned stimulus: Salivation, for example, is a dog's normal response to food. But when you want to teach an organism something novel—such as teaching a dog a new trick—you cannot use classical conditioning. What unconditioned stimulus would make a dog sit up or roll over? To train the dog, you must first persuade it to do the trick and *afterward* reward it with either approval or food. If you keep doing this, eventually the dog will learn the trick.

Much real-life behavior is like this: *Responses are learned because they operate on, or affect, the environment.* Referred to as **operant conditioning,** this kind of learning occurs in our own species as well as in others. Alone in a crib, a baby may kick and twist and coo spontaneously. When left by itself in a room, a dog may pad back and forth; sniff; or perhaps pick up a ball, drop it, and play with it. Neither organism is responding to a specific external stimulus. Rather, they are operating on their environment. Once the organism performs a certain behavior, however, the likelihood that the action will be repeated depends on its consequences. The baby will coo more often if each coo is followed by parental attention, and the dog will pick up the ball more often if this action is followed by petting or a food reward. If we think of the baby as having a goal of parental attention, and the dog as having a goal of food, operant conditioning amounts to learning that a particular behavior leads to attaining a particular goal (Rescorla, 1987).

operant conditioning a learning process in which responses are learned because they operate on, or affect, the environment

The Law of Effect

The study of operant conditioning began just over a century ago with a series of experiments by E. L. Thorndike (1898). Thorndike was trying to show that learning in animals is continuous with learning in humans. A typical experiment proceeded as follows. A hungry cat is placed in a cage whose door is held fast by a simple latch,

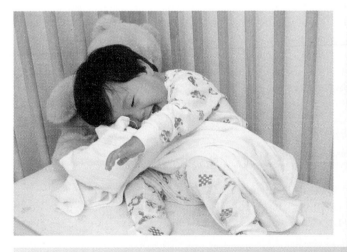

Operant conditioning occurs even in a crib. Dogs, too, learn by operant conditioning.

E. L. Thorndike's experiments in operant conditioning yielded the law of effect, *which demonstrates that reward, immediately following a specific behavior, results in increased learning of that behavior.*

and a piece of fish is placed just outside the cage. Initially the cat tries to reach the food by extending its paws through the bars. When this fails, the cat moves about the cage, engaging in a variety of behaviors. At some point it inadvertently hits the latch, frees itself, and eats the fish. The researchers then place the cat back in its cage and put a new piece of fish outside. The cat goes through roughly the same set of behaviors until once more it happens to hit the latch. The procedure is repeated again and again. Over a number of trials the cat eliminates many of its irrelevant behaviors, until eventually it opens the latch and frees itself as soon as it is placed in the cage. The cat has learned to open the latch in order to obtain food.

It may sound as if the cat is acting intelligently, but Thorndike argued that there is little "intelligence" operating here. There is no moment in time at which the cat seems to have an insight about the solution to its problem. Instead, the cat's performance improves gradually over a series of trials. Rather than insight, the cat appears to be engaging in *trial-and-error* behavior, and when a reward immediately follows one of these behaviors, the learning of that action is strengthened. Thorndike referred to this strengthening as the *law of effect.* He argued that in operant learning, the law of effect selects from a set of random responses just those that are followed by positive consequences. The process is similar to evolution, in which the law of *survival of the fittest* selects from a set of random species variations just those that promote survival of the species. The law of effect, then, promotes the survival of the fittest responses (Schwartz, 1989).

Skinner's Experiments and Basic Findings

B. F. Skinner was responsible for a number of changes in how researchers conceptualize and study operant conditioning. His method of studying operant conditioning is simpler than Thorndike's—there is only one response involved—and it has been widely accepted.

Experimental Variations   In a Skinnerian experiment, a hungry animal—usually a rat or a pigeon—is placed in a box like the one shown in Figure 6-6, which is popularly called a "Skinner box." The inside of the box is bare except for a protruding bar with a food dish beneath it. A small light above the bar can be turned on at the experimenter's discretion.

Left alone in the box, the rat moves about, exploring. Occasionally it inspects the bar and presses it. The rate at which the rat first presses the bar is the *baseline level*. After establishing the baseline level, the experimenter activates a food magazine located outside the box. Now every time the rat presses the bar a small food pellet is released into the dish. The rat eats the food pellet and soon presses the bar again; the food is said to *reinforce* bar pressing, and the rate of pressing increases dramatically. If the food magazine is disconnected so that pressing the bar no longer delivers food, the rate of bar pressing will diminish. Hence an operantly conditioned response (or, simply, an *operant*) undergoes *extinction* with nonreinforcement just as a classically conditioned response does. The experimenter can set up a *discrimination* test by presenting food only if the rat presses the bar while the light is on, hence conditioning the rat through selective reinforcement. In this example, the light serves as a *discriminative stimulus* that controls the response.

Thus operant conditioning increases the likelihood of a response by following the behavior with a reinforcer (often something like food or water). Because the bar is always present in the Skinner box, the rat can respond to it as frequently or infrequently as it chooses. The organism's *rate of response* therefore is a useful measure of the operant's strength; the more frequently the response occurs during a given time interval, the greater its strength.

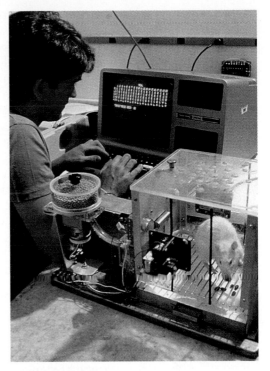

Figure 6-6

Apparatus for Operant Conditioning   This photograph shows a Skinner box with a magazine for delivering food pellets. The computer is used to control the experiment and record the rat's responses.

Implications for Child Rearing   Although rats and pigeons have been the favored experimental participants, operant conditioning applies to many species, including our own. Indeed operant conditioning has a good deal to tell us about child rearing. Consider the following case. A young boy had temper tantrums if he did not get enough attention from his parents, especially at bedtime. Since the parents eventually responded, their attention probably reinforced the tantrums. To eliminate the tantrums, the parents were advised to go through the normal bedtime rituals and then to ignore the child's protests, painful though that might be. If the reinforcer (the attention) was withheld, the tantrums should extinguish—which is just what happened. The time the child spent crying at bedtime decreased from 45 minutes to not at all over a period of only 7 days (Williams, 1959).

Another application of operant conditioning to child rearing focuses on the temporal relationship between a response and its reinforcer. Laboratory experiments have shown that immediate reinforcement is more effective than delayed reinforcement; the greater the interval between an operant response and a reinforcer, the weaker the response. Many developmental psychologists have noted that delay of reinforcement is an important factor in dealing with young children. If a child acts kindly to a pet, the act can best be strengthened by praising (rewarding) the child immediately rather than waiting until later. Similarly, if a child hits someone without provocation, this behavior will more likely be eliminated if the child is punished immediately rather than later.

Shaping   Suppose that you want to use operant conditioning to teach your dog a trick—for instance, to press a buzzer with its nose. You cannot wait until the dog does this naturally and then reinforce it, because you may wait forever. When the desired behavior is truly novel, you have to condition it by taking advantage of natural variations in the animal's actions. To train a dog to press a buzzer with its nose, you can give the animal a food reinforcer each time it approaches the area of the buzzer, requiring it to move closer and closer to the desired spot for each reinforcer until finally

shaping conditioning that is accomplished by reinforcing only variations in response that deviate in the direction desired by the experimenter

the dog's nose is touching the buzzer. This technique—*reinforcing only variations in response that deviate in the direction desired by the experimenter*—is called **shaping.**

Animals can be taught elaborate tricks and routines by means of shaping. Two psychologists and their staff trained thousands of animals of many species for television shows, commercials, and county fairs (Breland & Breland, 1966). One popular show featured "Priscilla, the Fastidious Pig." Priscilla turned on the TV set, ate breakfast at a table, picked up dirty clothes and put them in a hamper, vacuumed the floor, picked out her favorite food (from among foods competing with that of her sponsor!), and took part in a quiz program, answering questions from the audience by flashing lights that indicated yes or no. She was not an unusually bright pig; in fact, because pigs grow so fast, a new "Priscilla" was trained every 3 to 5 months. The ingenuity was not the pig's but the experimenters', who used operant conditioning and shaped the behavior to produce the desired result. Pigeons have been trained by means of shaping of operant responses to locate persons lost at sea (see Figure 6-7), and porpoises have been trained to retrieve underwater equipment.

Phenomena and Applications

There are a number of phenomena that greatly increase the generality of operant conditioning and show its applications to human behavior. We look at some of them briefly here.

Conditioned Reinforcers   Most of the reinforcers we have discussed are called *primary* because, like food, they satisfy basic drives. If operant conditioning occurred only with primary reinforcers, it would not be that common in our lives because primary reinforcers are not that common. However, virtually any stimulus can become a *secondary* or *conditioned reinforcer* by being consistently paired with a primary reinforcer; conditioned reinforcers greatly increase the range of operant conditioning (just as second-order conditioning greatly increases the range of classical conditioning).

Our lives abound with conditioned reinforcers. Two of the most prevalent are money and praise. Presumably, money is a powerful reinforcer because it has been paired so frequently with so many primary reinforcers—we can buy food, drink, and comfort, for examples. And mere praise, without even the promise of a primary reinforcer, can sustain many activities.

Figure 6-7

Search and Rescue by Pigeons   The Coast Guard has used pigeons to search for people lost at sea. Shaping methods are used to train the pigeons to spot the color orange—the international color for life jackets. Three pigeons are strapped into a plexiglas chamber attached to the underside of a helicopter. The chamber is divided into thirds so that each bird faces in a different direction. When a pigeon spots an orange object, or any other object, it pecks a key that buzzes the pilot. The pilot then heads in the direction indicated by the bird that responded. Pigeons are better suited than people for the task of spotting distant objects at sea. They can stare over the water for a long time without suffering eye fatigue; they have excellent color vision; and they can focus on a 60- to 80-degree area, whereas a person can focus only on a 2- to 3-degree area. (After Simmons, 1981)

Pigeon sitting

Pigeon pecking key

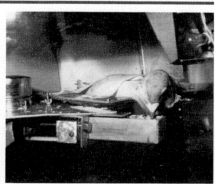
Pigeon rewarded

Generalization and Discrimination

Again, what was true for classical conditioning holds for operant conditioning as well: Organisms generalize what they have learned, and generalization can be curbed by means of discrimination training. If a young child is reinforced by her parents for petting the family dog, she will soon generalize this petting response to other dogs. Since this can be dangerous (the neighbors might have a vicious watchdog), the child's parents may provide some discrimination training: The child is reinforced when she pets the family dog but not when she pets the neighbor's dog.

Discrimination training will be effective to the extent that there is a discriminative stimulus (or set of them)

Operant conditioning and shaping are used in training animals to perform tricks of various kinds.

that clearly distinguishes between cases in which the response should be made and cases in which it should be suppressed. Our young child will have an easier time learning which dog to pet if her parents can point to an aspect of dogs that signals their friendliness (a wagging tail, for example). In general, a discriminative stimulus will be useful to the extent that its presence predicts that a response will be followed by reinforcement while its absence predicts that the response will not be followed by reinforcement (or vice versa). Just as in classical conditioning, the predictive power of a stimulus seems to be critical for conditioning to occur.

Partial Reinforcement

In real life, it is rare for every instance of a behavior to be reinforced; for example, sometimes hard work is followed by praise, but often it goes unacknowledged. If operant conditioning occurred only with continuous reinforcement, it might play a limited role in our lives. It turns out, however, that once a behavior has been established, it can be maintained when it is reinforced only a fraction of the time. This phenomenon is known as *partial reinforcement,* and it can be illustrated in the laboratory by a pigeon that learns to peck at a key for food. Once this operant has been established, the pigeon continues to peck at a high rate even if it receives only occasional reinforcement. In some cases, pigeons that were rewarded with food on the average of once every 5 minutes (12 times an hour) pecked at the key as often as 6,000 times per hour! Moreover, extinction following the maintenance of a response on partial reinforcement is much slower than extinction following the maintenance of a response on continuous reinforcement; this phenomenon is known as the *partial-reinforcement effect.* It makes intuitive sense because there is less difference between extinction and maintenance when reinforcement during maintenance is only partial.

When reinforcement occurs only some of the time, there is a question of how to schedule it—after every third response? after every 5 seconds? It turns out that different kinds of schedules are used. Some are **ratio schedules,** in which *reinforcement is available only after a certain number of responses have been made,* whereas others are **interval schedules,** in which *reinforcement is available only after a certain time interval has elapsed.*

To illustrate, on a ratio schedule, an organism might be reinforced after every five responses (this would be called a "fixed ratio five schedule" because the number of responses needed for reinforcement is fixed rather than variable), whereas on an interval schedule the organism might be reinforced only after 2 minutes have elapsed since its last reinforcement (this would be called a "fixed interval 2 minute schedule" because the critical time interval remains fixed rather than varying). Being

ratio schedules
schedules of reinforcement in which reinforcement is available only after a certain number of responses have been made

interval schedules
schedules of reinforcement in which reinforcement is available only after a certain time interval has elapsed

on a fixed ratio schedule is like being a factory worker who gets paid for piecework—you need to do a number of things to get the reinforcement; being on a fixed-interval schedule is like picking up your mail when there are only two delivery times a day—you have to wait a certain time before the reinforcement becomes available. Schedules of reinforcement are important because different schedules lead to different patterns of responding. Thus, on either a fixed ratio or a fixed interval scale the organism pauses in responding right after a reinforcement, but the pause is significantly longer on the interval schedule.

The Use of Aversive Events in Conditioning

We have talked about reinforcement as if it were almost always positive (food, for example). But negative or aversive events, such as shock or a painful noise, are often used in conditioning. There are different kinds of *aversive conditioning,* depending on the role of the unpleasant stimulus. In **punishment,** the *aversive event is used to weaken an existing response,* whereas in **escape** (or **avoidance**) the event is used *to cause the organism to learn a new response.*

punishment use of an aversive event to weaken an existing response

escape (avoidance) use of an aversive event to cause the organism to learn a new response

Punishment   In punishment training, a response is followed by an aversive stimulus, which results in the response being weakened or suppressed. Suppose that a young child who is learning to use crayons starts drawing on the wall (this is the undesirable response); if he is slapped on the hand when he does this (the punishment), he will learn not to do so. Similarly, if a rat learning to run a maze is shocked whenever it chooses a wrong path, it will soon learn to avoid past mistakes. In both cases, punishment is used to decrease the likelihood of an undesirable behavior.[1]

Although punishment can suppress an unwanted response, it has several disadvantages. First, its effects are not as predictable as the results of reward. Reward essentially says, "Repeat what you have done"; punishment says, "Stop it!" but fails to provide an alternative. As a result, the organism may substitute an even less desirable response for the punished one. Second, the by-products of punishment may be negative. Punishment often leads to dislike or fear of the punishing person (parent, teacher, or employer) and of the situation (home, school, or office) in which the punishment occurred. Finally, an extreme or painful punishment may elicit aggressive behavior that is more serious than the original undesirable behavior.

These cautions do not mean that punishment should never be employed. It can effectively eliminate an undesirable response if an alternative response is rewarded. Rats that have learned to take the shorter of two paths to reach food will quickly switch to the longer path if they are shocked in the shorter one. The temporary suppression produced by punishment provides the opportunity to learn to take the longer path. In this case, punishment is an effective means of redirecting behavior because it is informative, and this seems to be the key to the humane and effective use of punishment. A child who gets a shock from an electrical appliance may learn which connections are safe and which are hazardous.

In punishment training, an undesirable response (such as a child drawing on her bedroom wall) is followed by an aversive stimulus (such as spanking) which results in the response being weakened or suppressed.

---

[1] It is worth noting the relationship between the terms *reward* and *punisher* on the one hand, and *positive* and *negative* reinforcers on the other. *Reward* can be used synonymously with *positive reinforcer*—an event whose occurrence following a response increases the probability of that response. But a punisher is not the same as a negative reinforcer. *Negative reinforcement* means termination of an aversive event following a response; this increases the probability of that response. *Punishment* has the opposite effect: It decreases the probability of a response. (See Table 6-4.)

Table 6-4

Types of Reinforcement and Punishment

Type	Definition	Effect	Example
Positive reinforcement	A pleasant stimulus that follows a desired behavior	Increases the likelihood of the desired behavior	A high grade on an exam
Negative reinforcement	Removal of an unpleasant stimulus after a desired behavior occurs	Increases the likelihood of the desired behavior	Allowing a child to leave his or her room when no longer having a temper tantrum
Positive punishment	Presentation of an unpleasant stimulus after an undesired behavior occurs	Decreases the likelihood of the undesired behavior	A low grade on an exam
Negative punishment	Removal of a pleasant stimulus after an undesired behavior occurs	Decreases the likelihood of the undesired behavior	Canceling TV viewing privileges for a child who misbehaves

Escape and Avoidance   Aversive events can also be used in the learning of new responses. Organisms can learn to make a response in order to terminate an ongoing aversive event, as when a child learns to turn off a faucet to stop hot water from flowing into his bath. This is called *escape learning*. Organisms can also learn to make a response in order to prevent an aversive event from even starting, as when we learn to stop at red lights to prevent accidents (and traffic tickets). This is called *avoidance learning*.

Often escape learning precedes avoidance learning, as illustrated by the following experiment. A rat is placed in a box consisting of two compartments divided by a barrier. On each trial the animal is placed in one of the compartments. At some point a warning tone is sounded, and 5 seconds later the floor of that compartment is electrified; to get away from the shock, the animal must jump the barrier into the other compartment. Initially the animal jumps the barrier only when the shock starts—this is escape learning. But with practice the animal learns to jump upon hearing the warning tone, thereby avoiding the shock entirely—this is avoidance learning.

There is something very puzzling about avoidance learning. What exactly is reinforcing the avoidance response? In the study just described, what reinforces the animal for jumping the barrier? Intuitively, it seems to be the absence of shock, but this is a nonevent. How can a nonevent serve as a reinforcer? One solution to this puzzle holds that the learning occurs in two stages. The first stage involves classical conditioning: Through repeated pairings of the warning (the CS) and the punishing event or shock (the UCS), the animal learns a fear response to the warning. The second stage involves operant conditioning: The animal learns that a particular response (jumping the barrier) removes an aversive event, namely fear. In short, what first appears to be a nonevent is actually fear, and we can think of avoidance as escape from fear (Mowrer, 1947; Rescorla & Solomon, 1967).

The threat of punishment is an effective motivator.

The Role of Control and Cognitive Factors

Our analysis of operant conditioning has tended to emphasize external factors—a response is consistently followed by a reinforcing event, and the organism learns to associate the response and the reinforcement. However, cognitive factors also play an important role in operant conditioning, just as they do in classical conditioning. As we will see, it is often useful to view the organism in an operant conditioning situation as acquiring new knowledge about response–reinforcer relationships.

Contiguity Versus Control   As with classical conditioning, we want to know what factor is critical for operant conditioning to occur. Again, one of the options is temporal contiguity: An operant is conditioned whenever reinforcement immediately follows the behavior (Skinner, 1948). A more cognitive option, closely related to predictability, is *control:* An operant is conditioned only when the organism interprets the reinforcement as being controlled by its response. Some important experiments by Steve Maier and Martin Seligman (1976) provide more support for the control view than for the temporal contiguity view. (See also the discussion of control and stress in Chapter 11.)

Their basic experiment has two stages. In the first stage, some dogs learn that whether or not they receive a shock depends on—that is, is controlled by—their behavior, while other dogs learn that they have no control over the shock. Think of the dogs as being tested in pairs. Both members of a pair are in a harness that restricts their movements, and occasionally they receive an electric shock. One member of the pair, the "control" dog, can turn off the shock by pushing a nearby panel with its nose; the other member of the pair, the "yoked" dog, cannot exercise any control over the shock. Whenever the control dog is shocked, so is the yoked dog; and whenever the control dog turns off the shock, the yoked dog's shock is also terminated. The control and yoked dogs therefore receive the same number of shocks.

To find out what the dogs learned in the first stage, a second stage is needed. In this stage the experimenter places both dogs in a new apparatus—a box divided into two compartments by a barrier. This is the same avoidance-testing device that we considered a moment ago. As before, on each trial a tone is first sounded, indicating that the compartment that the animal currently occupies is about to get an electric shock; to avoid the shock, the animal must learn to jump the barrier into the other compartment when it hears the warning tone. Control dogs learn this response rapidly. But the yoked dogs are another story. Initially they make no movement across the barrier; as trials progress, their behavior becomes increasingly passive, finally lapsing into utter helplessness. Why? Because during the first stage of the experiment the yoked dogs learned that the shocks were not under their control, and this belief in noncontrol made conditioning in the second stage impossible. If a belief in noncontrol makes operant conditioning impossible, a belief in control may be what makes it possible. Many other experiments support the notion that operant conditioning occurs only when the organism perceives reinforcement as being under its control (Seligman, 1975). (See Chapter 11 for a detailed discussion of learned helplessness.)

Contingency Learning   We can also talk about these results in terms of *contingencies.* We can say that operant conditioning occurs only when the organism perceives a contingency between its responses and reinforcement. In the first stage of the preceding study, the relevant contingency is between pushing a panel and the ending of the shock; perceiving this contingency amounts to determining that the likelihood of shock ending is greater when the panel is pushed than when it is not. Dogs that do not perceive this contingency in the first stage of the study appear not to look for any contingency in the second stage. This contingency approach makes it clear that the results with operant conditioning fit with the findings about the importance of predictability in classical conditioning: Knowing that a CS predicts a UCS can be interpreted as showing that the organism has detected a contingency between the two stimuli. Thus, in both classical and operant conditioning, what the organism seems to learn is a contingency between two events.

Our ability to learn contingencies develops very early, as is shown by the following study of 3-month-old infants. All infants in the experiment were lying in their cribs, with their heads on pillows. Beneath each pillow was a switch that closed whenever the infant turned his or her head. For infants in the control group, whenever they turned their heads and closed the switch, a mobile on the opposite side of the crib was activated. For these infants, there was a contingency between head-turning and the mobile moving—the mobile being more likely to move with a head turn than without. These infants quickly learned to turn their heads, and they reacted to the moving mobile with signs of enjoyment (they smiled and cooed).

The situation was quite different for infants in the experimental group. For these infants, the mobile was made to move roughly as often as it did for the infants in the control group, but whether or not it moved was *not* under their control: There was no contingency between head-turning and the mobile moving. These infants did not learn to turn their heads more frequently. Moreover, after a while they showed no signs of enjoying the mobile moving. When infants had no control over the mobile, it appears to lose some of its reinforcing character.

Evolutionary Constraints on Conditioning

As with classical conditioning, evolution imposes constraints on what may be learned in operant conditioning. The constraints involve response–reinforcer relationships. To illustrate, consider pigeons in two experimental situations: *reward learning,* in which the animal learns a response that is reinforced by food; and *escape learning,* in which the animal learns a response that is reinforced by the termination of shock. In the case of reward, pigeons learn much faster if the response is pecking a key rather than flapping their wings. In the case of escape, the opposite is true: Pigeons learn faster if the response is wing flapping rather than pecking (Bolles, 1970).

As in the case of classical conditioning, the results seem to be inconsistent with the assumption that the same laws of learning apply to all situations, but they make sense from an ethological perspective. The reward case with the pigeons involved eating, and pecking (but not wing flapping) is part of the bird's natural eating activities. Hence, it is reasonable to assume that there is a genetically determined connection between pecking and eating. Similarly, the escape case involved a danger situation, and the pigeon's natural reactions to danger include flapping its wings (but not pecking). Birds are known to have a small repertoire of defensive reactions, and they will quickly learn to escape only if the relevant response is one of these natural defensive reactions. In sum, rather than being a means for learning arbitrary associations, operant conditioning also honors the behavioral blueprint.

Suppose that you are taking care of an 8-year-old who won't make his own bed; in fact, he does not even seem to know how to begin the task. How might you use operant conditioning techniques to teach him to do this?

**Thinking
Critically**

What Is Involved in Complex Learning?

According to the cognitive perspective, the crux of learning—and of intelligence in general—lies in an organism's ability to mentally represent aspects of the world, and then to operate on these mental representations rather than on the world itself. (This is analogous to a computer being able to represent data and to operate on these data representations.) In many cases, what we represent mentally are associations between stimuli or events; these cases correspond to classical and operant conditioning. In other cases, what we represent seems more complex. It might be a map of one's environment or an abstract concept like *cause.*

Also, there are cases in which the operations performed on mental representations are more complex than associative processes. The operations may take the form of a mental trial-and-error process, in which the organism tries out different

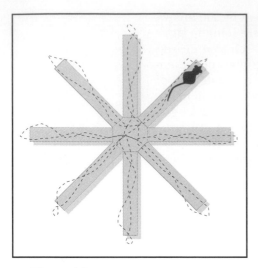

Figure 6-8

A Maze for Studying Cognitive Maps   With food placed at the end of every arm, the rat's problem is to find all the food without retracing its steps. The pattern shown here reflects perfect learning: this rat visited each arm of the maze only once, eating whatever it found there; it did not go back to an empty arm even one time.

possibilities in its mind. Or they may make up a *multistep strategy*, in which we take some mental steps only because they enable us to take subsequent ones. The idea of a strategy in particular seems at odds with the assumption that complex learning is built out of simple associations.

In what follows, we consider phenomena that point to the need to consider non-associative representations and operations. Some of these phenomena involve animals, whereas others involve humans performing tasks that are similar to conditioning.

Learning Cognitive Maps and Abstract Concepts

An early advocate of the cognitive approach to learning was Edward Tolman, whose research dealt with the problem of rats learning their way through complex mazes (Tolman, 1932). In his view, a rat running through a complex maze was not learning a sequence of right- and left-turning responses but rather was developing a *cognitive map*—a mental representation of the layout of the maze.

More recent research provides strong evidence for cognitive maps in rats. Consider the maze diagrammed in Figure 6-8. The maze consists of a center platform with eight identical arms radiating outward. On each trial, the researcher places food at the end of each arm; the rat needs to learn to visit each arm (and obtain the food there) without returning to those it has already visited. Rats learn this remarkably well; after 20 trials, they will virtually never return to an arm they have already visited. (Rats will do this even when the maze has been doused with after-shave lotion to eliminate the odor cues about which arms still have food.) Most important, a rat rarely employs the strategy that would occur to humans—such as always going through the arms in an obvious order, say clockwise. Instead, the rat visits the arms randomly, indicating that it has not learned a rigid sequence of responses. What, then, has it learned? Probably it has developed a maplike representation of the maze that specifies the spatial relations between arms, and on each trial it makes a mental note of each arm it has visited (Olton, 1978; 1979).

Other studies, which involve primates rather than rats, provide even stronger evidence for complex mental representations. Particularly striking are studies showing that chimpanzees can acquire abstract concepts that were once believed to be the sole province of humans. In a typical study, chimpanzees learn to use plastic tokens of different shapes, sizes, and colors as words. For example, they might learn that one token refers to "apples" and another to "paper," even though there is no physical resemblance between the token and the object. The fact that chimpanzees can learn these references suggests that they understand concrete concepts like "apple" and "paper." More impressively, they also understand abstract concepts like "same," "different," and "cause." Thus chimpanzees can learn to use their "same" token when presented with either two "apple" tokens or two "orange" ones, and their "different" token when presented with one "apple" token and one "orange" token. Likewise, chimpanzees seem to understand causal relationships. They will apply the token for "cause" when shown scissors and cut paper, but not when shown scissors and intact paper (Premack, 1985a; Premack & Premack, 1983).

Learning Through Insight

While many early researchers tried to study complex learning with species far removed from humans (such as rats and pigeons), others assumed that the best evidence for complex learning would come from studies with other primate species. Wolfgang Köhler's work with chimpanzees, carried out in the 1920s, remains particularly important. The problems that Köhler set for his chimpanzees left some room for insight, because no parts of the problem were hidden from view (in contrast, the workings of a food dispenser in a Skinner box are hidden from the animal's view). Köhler placed a chimpanzee in an enclosed area with a desirable piece of fruit, often a banana, out of reach. To obtain the fruit, the animal had to use a nearby object as a tool. Usually the chimpanzee solved the problem, and did it in a way that suggested it had some insight. The following description by Köhler is typical:

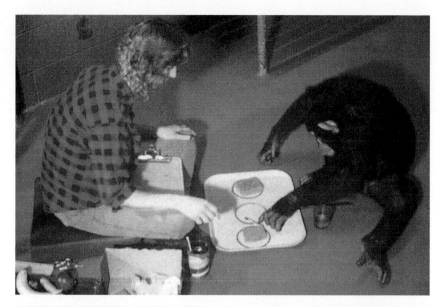

Using the technique developed by Premack, an experimenter tests a chimpanzee's ability to use language by manipulating plastic chips that represent specific words.

> Sultan [Köhler's most intelligent chimpanzee] is squatting at the bars but cannot reach the fruit which lies outside by means of his only available short stick. A longer stick is deposited outside the bars, about two meters on one side of the object and parallel with the grating. It cannot be grasped with the hand, but it can be pulled within reach by means of the small stick. [See Figure 6-9 for an illustration of a similar multiple-stick problem.] Sultan tries to reach the fruit with the smaller of the two sticks. Not succeeding, he tears at a piece of wire that projects from the netting of his cage, but that too is in vain. Then he gazes about him (there are always in the course of these tests some long pauses, during which the animals scrutinize the whole visible area). He suddenly picks up the little stick once more, goes up to the bars directly opposite to the long stick, scratches it towards him with the "auxiliary," seizes it, and goes with it to the point opposite the objective (the fruit), which he secures. From the moment that his eyes fall upon the long stick, his procedure forms one consecutive whole, without hiatus, and although the angling of the bigger stick by means of the smaller is an action that could be complete and distinct in itself, yet observation shows that it follows, quite suddenly, on an interval of hesitation and doubt—staring about—which undoubtedly has a relation to the final objective, and is immediately merged in the final action of the attainment of the end goal. (Köhler, 1925, pp. 174–175)

Several aspects of these chimpanzees' performance are unlike those of Thorndike's cats or Skinner's rats and pigeons. For one thing, the solution was sudden, rather than being the result of a gradual trial-and-error process. Another point is that once a chimpanzee solved a problem, thereafter it would solve the problem with few irrelevant moves. This is most unlike a rat in a Skinner box, which continues to make irrelevant responses on many trials. Also, Köhler's chimpanzees could readily transfer what they had learned to a novel situation. For example, in one problem Sultan was not caged, but some bananas were placed too high for him to reach, as shown in Figure 6-10. To solve the problem, Sultan stacked some boxes strewn around

Figure 6-9

The Multiple Stick Problem   Using the shorter sticks, the chimpanzee pulls in a stick long enough to reach the piece of fruit. It has learned to solve this problem by understanding the relationship between the sticks and the piece of fruit.

Figure 6-10

A Chimpanzee Constructing a Platform   To reach the bananas hanging from the ceiling, the chimpanzee stacks boxes to form a platform.

him, climbed the "platform," and grabbed the bananas. In subsequent problems, if the fruit was again too high to reach, Sultan found other objects to construct a platform; in some cases he used a table and a small ladder, and in one case he pulled Köhler himself over and used the experimenter as a platform.

The chimpanzee's solution, therefore, has three critical aspects: its suddenness, its availability once discovered, and its transferability. These aspects are at odds with trial-and-error behaviors of the type observed by Thorndike, Skinner, and their students. Instead, the chimpanzee's solutions may reflect a process of *mental trial and error*. That is, the animal forms a mental representation of the problem, manipulates components of the representation until it hits upon a solution, and then enacts the solution in the real world. The solution appears sudden because the researchers do not have access to the chimpanzee's mental process. The solution is available thereafter because a mental representation persists over time. And the solution is transferable because the representation is either abstract enough to cover more than the original situation or malleable enough to be extended to a novel situation.

Köhler's findings suggest that complex learning often involves two phases. In the initial phase, problem solving is used to derive a solution; in the second phase, the solution is stored in memory and retrieved whenever a similar problem presents itself. Hence complex learning is intimately related to memory and thinking (the topics of the next two chapters). Moreover, this two-phase structure characterizes not just chimpanzee learning but also many cases of complex learning in humans. Indeed it has been incorporated into artificial intelligence programs that try to simulate human learning (Rosenbloom, Laird, & Newell, 1991).

The distinction between a problem-solving phase and a memory phase also shows up at the neural level: Brain scanning studies reveal changes in the neural circuitry between the time one first does a task and the times one does it repeatedly. In one experiment, participants were presented with a sequence of nouns while their brains were scanned by PET. For each noun they had to supply a verb that went with it (given "apple," they might say "eat," for example). While this is an easy problem, it still requires some thought. When participants first did the task, one of the brain regions that was activated most was in the frontal cortex, a region known to be involved in problem solving. But as participants did the task again and again, with the same nouns being repeated, the frontal cortex became silent and other cortical areas became active (Petersen et al., 1996). These findings fit with the interpretation that when first confronted with a noun participants have to do a bit of thinking to generate an appropriate verb, but after they have seen that noun a couple of times they can just retrieve the appropriate verb from memory.

The Role of Prior Beliefs

While much of the research on associative learning has been done with other species, many experiments have been done with humans (Shanks, 1987; Wasserman, 1990). Such experiments typically use less salient associations than those employed with animals—rather than having to learn that one stimulus always goes with another, human participants might be given a situation in which one stimulus goes with another 60% of the time, and be asked to estimate the degree to which the two stimuli are associated. It turns out that how well people do at learning such subtle associations depends greatly on how compatible the association is with the person's *prior beliefs*. This indicates that learning involves other processes besides those that form associations between inputs.

In these experiments a different pair of stimuli is presented on each trial—say, a picture and a description of a person—and the participant's task is to learn the relationship between the members of the pairs—say, that pictures of tall men tend to be associated with brief descriptions. Some striking evidence for the role of prior beliefs comes from cases in which, objectively, there is *no* relationship between the stimuli, yet participants "learn" such a relationship.

In one experiment, participants were concerned with the possible relationship between the drawings that mental patients made and the symptoms that the patients manifested. On each trial participants were presented with a patient's drawing of a person and one of six symptoms, including the symptoms "suspiciousness of other people" and "concerned with being taken care of." The participant's task was to determine whether any of the signs in the drawing—some aspect of the eyes or mouth, for instance—were associated with any of the symptoms. In fact, the six symptoms had been randomly paired with the drawings so that there was no association between sign (drawing) and symptom. Yet participants consistently reported such relationships, and the relationships they reported were ones that they believed *before* participating in the experiment: for example, that large eyes are associated with suspiciousness, or that a large mouth is associated with a desire to be taken care of by others. These nonexistent but plausible relationships are referred to as *spurious associations* (Chapman & Chapman, 1967).

The preceding study shows us the power of prior beliefs when there is no objective association. What about the effects of prior beliefs when there is in fact an objective association to be learned? This question was analyzed in the following research.

On each of a set of trials, participants were presented with two measures of an individual's honesty, taken from two completely different situations. For example, one measure might have been how often a young boy copied another student's homework in school, and the second measure might have been an indication of how often that same boy was dishonest at home. It is well known that most people believe (erroneously) that two measures of the same trait (such as honesty) will always be highly correlated. This is the critical prior belief. In fact, the objective relationship between the two measures of honesty varied across conditions of the experiment, sometimes being quite low, and the participants' task was to estimate the strength of this relationship by choosing a number between 0 (which indicated no relationship) and 100 (a perfect relationship). The results showed that participants consistently overestimated the strength of the relationship. Their prior belief that an honest person is honest in all situations led them to see more than was there (Jennings, Amabile, & Ross, 1980).

In the preceding studies, the association to be learned and the participants' prior beliefs were in conflict. In such situations people typically go with their prior beliefs. If people believe that two different measures of an individual's honesty should be highly related, for example, they may "detect" such a relationship even when there is no objective association. However, other studies show that as the objective association is made increasingly salient, eventually our prior beliefs will capitulate, and we learn what is in fact out there (Alloy & Tabachnik, 1984). In the preceding study, for example, if 90% of the time that a boy was dishonest at school he was honest at home, participants would soon realize that there was a negative relationship between the two measures of honesty.

The results of the preceding studies are reminiscent of what we called *top-down processing in perception* (see Chapter 4). Recall that top-down processing refers to situations in which perceivers combine their expectation of what they are likely to see with the actual input to yield a final percept. In *top-down processing in learning,* learners combine their prior belief about an associative relationship with the objective input about that relationship to yield a final estimate of the strength of that relationship.

The effects of prior beliefs on learning have important implications for education. In particular, when teaching someone about a topic—say the biology of digestion—one cannot ignore his or her prior beliefs about the subject matter. The student will often try to assimilate the new information to the earlier beliefs. Educationally, it may be best to get these prior beliefs out in the open so that they can be confronted by the instructor if they are in fact erroneous (Genter & Collins, 1983).

In sum, this line of research demonstrates the importance of prior beliefs in human learning, thereby strengthening the case for a cognitive approach to learning. However, the research also has a connection to the ethological approach. Just as rats and pigeons may be constrained to learn only the kinds of associations for which evolution has prepared them, so we humans seem to be constrained to learn associations for which our prior beliefs have prepared us. Without prior constraints of some sort, perhaps there would simply be too many potential associations to consider, and associative learning would be chaotic, if not impossible.

Thinking Critically   Do you think that there are qualitative differences between how we learn facts and how we learn motor skills? What would some of the differences be?

Summary

1. *Learning* may be defined as a relatively permanent change in behavior that results from practice. There are four basic kinds of learning: (1) *habituation,* in which an organism learns to ignore a familiar and inconsequential stimulus; (2) *classical conditioning,* in which an organism learns that one stimulus follows another; (3) *operant conditioning,* in which an organism learns that a response leads to a particular consequence; and (4) complex learning, in which learning involves more than the formation of associations.

2. Research on learning was initially done from a behaviorist perspective but today is heavily influenced by the biological and cognitive perspectives as well. Thus, it is now assumed that (1) behavior needs to be understood in terms of internal (mental) causes as well as external ones; (2) while associations underlie a great deal of learning, more than associations is involved in com-

plex learning; and (3) the laws of learning may differ for different species and different situations.

3. In Pavlov's experiments, if a *conditioned stimulus (CS)* consistently precedes an *unconditioned stimulus (UCS)*, the CS comes to serve as a signal for the UCS and to elicit a *conditioned response (CR)* that often resembles the *unconditioned response (UCR)*. Stimuli that are similar to the CS also elicit the CR to some extent, although such *generalization* can be curbed by *discrimination* training. These phenomena occur in organisms as diverse as flatworms and humans. There are a number of important human applications of classical conditioning, including conditioned fear and conditioned drug tolerance.

4. For classical conditioning to occur, the CS must be a reliable predictor of the UCS; that is, there must be a higher probability that the UCS will occur when the CS has been presented than when it has not. The importance of predictability is also evident in the phenomenon of blocking: If one CS reliably predicts a UCS, and another CS is added, the relationship between the added CS and the UCS will not be learned. Models of classical conditioning center on the cognitive notions of predictability and surprise.

5. The research of ethologists shows that the laws of learning differ for different species and for different situations that a given species encounters. According to ethologists, what an animal learns is constrained by its genetically determined "behavioral blueprint." Evidence for such constraints on classical conditioning comes from studies of taste aversion. While rats readily learn to associate the feeling of being sick with the taste of a solution, they cannot learn to associate sickness with a light. Conversely, birds can learn to associate light and sickness but not taste and sickness. These differences are the result of innate differences between rats and birds in their food-gathering activities.

6. The neural bases of learning have been studied at the cellular level. Here the critical processes involve structural changes in the synapse that make it more efficient. In line with this general principle, once neurons have been stimulated for a substantial period they will show an increase in their rate of activity when subsequently stimulated (long-term potentiation). In simple organisms like snails, the structural changes that accompany *habituation* and *sensitization* learning consist of decreases and increases in the amount of neurotransmitter secreted by the sending neuron. The neural bases of learning have also been studied at the level of neural systems. In the classical conditioning of fear, the evidence indicates that the critical brain structure is the amygdala.

7. *Operant conditioning* deals with situations in which the response operates on the environment rather than being elicited by an unconditioned stimulus. The earliest systematic studies were performed by Thorndike, who showed that animals engage in trial-and-error behavior and that any behavior followed by reinforcement is strengthened (the law of effect).

8. In Skinner's experiments, typically a rat or pigeon learns to make a simple response, such as pressing a lever, to obtain reinforcement. The rate of response is a useful measure of response strength. *Shaping* is a training procedure used when the desired response is novel; it involves reinforcing only variations in response that deviate in the direction desired by the experimenter.

9. A number of phenomena increase the generality of operant conditioning, including conditioned reinforcement, generalization and discrimination, and the partial reinforcement effect. In conditioned reinforcement, a stimulus associated with a reinforcer acquires its own reinforcing properties. Generalization refers to the fact that organisms generalize responses to similar situations,

although this generalization can be brought under the control of a discriminative stimulus. Finally, in the partial reinforcement effect, once a behavior has been established it can be maintained when reinforced only part of the time. Exactly when the reinforcement comes is determined by its schedule of reinforcement.

10. The reinforcement in operant conditioning can be an aversive event like shock. There are three different kinds of aversive conditioning. In *punishment,* a response is followed by an aversive event, which results in the response being suppressed. In *escape,* an organism learns to make a response in order to terminate an ongoing aversive event. In *avoidance,* an organism learns to make a response in order to prevent the aversive event from even starting.

11. For operant conditioning to occur, the organism must believe that reinforcement is at least partly under its control; that is, the organism must perceive a contingency between its responses and reinforcement. This shows the importance of cognitive factors. Biological constraints also play a role in operant conditioning. There are constraints on what reinforcers can be associated with what responses. With pigeons, when the reinforcement is food, learning is faster if the response is pecking a key rather than wing flapping; but when the reinforcement is termination of shock, learning is faster when the response is wing flapping rather than pecking a key.

12. According to the cognitive perspective, the crux of learning is an organism's ability to represent aspects of the world mentally and then to operate on these mental representations rather than on the world itself. In complex learning, the mental representations depict more than associations, and the mental operations may constitute a strategy. Studies of complex learning in animals indicate that rats can develop a cognitive map of their environment, as well as acquire abstract concepts like cause. Other studies demonstrate that chimpanzees can solve problems through insight and then generalize these solutions to similar problems.

13. When humans learn associations between stimuli, they often invoke prior beliefs about the relationships, and these beliefs can have a dramatic effect on learning the new association. This can lead to the detection of relationships that are not objectively present (spurious associations). When the relationship is objectively present, having a prior belief about it can lead to overestimating its predictive strength; when an objective relationship conflicts with a prior belief, the learner may favor the prior belief.

Suggested Readings

Pavlov, *Conditioned Reflexes* (1927), is the definitive work on classical conditioning. Skinner, *The Behavior of Organisms* (1938), is the corresponding statement on operant conditioning. The major points of view about conditioning and learning, presented in their historical settings, are summarized in Bower and Hilgard, *Theories of Learning* (5th ed., 1981). For a general introduction to learning, a number of textbooks are recommended. Schwartz, *Psychology of Learning and Behavior* (3rd ed., 1989), is a particularly well-balanced review of conditioning, including discussions of ethology and cognition. Other useful textbooks are Gordon, *Learning and Memory* (1989); Schwartz and Reisberg, *Learning and Memory* (1991); and Domjan and Burkhard, *The Principles of Learning and Behavior* (1985). At the advanced level, the six-volume Estes (ed.), *Handbook of Learning and Cognitive Processes* (1975–1978), covers most aspects of learning and conditioning; and Honig and Staddon (eds.), *Handbook of Operant Behavior* (1977), provides a comprehensive treatment of operant conditioning.

The early cognitive approach is well described in two classics: Tolman, *Purposive Behavior in Animals and Men* (1932; reprint ed. 1967); and Köhler, *The Mentality of Apes* (1925; reprint ed. 1976). For a more recent statement of the cognitive approach to animal learning, see Roitblat, *Introduction to Comparative Cognition* (1986). For up-to-date treatments of the cognitive approach to human learning, see Anderson, *Cognitive Psychology and its Implications* (4th ed., 1997); and Medin and Ross, *Cognitive Psychology* (2nd ed., 1996).

Interest in the neural bases of learning is expanding rapidly, and some textbooks provide a good account of this work. One such text is McPhail, *The Neuroscience of Animal Intelligence* (1993). Another is Dudai, *The Neurobiology of Memory* (1989). These books discuss research on numerous species and learning mechanisms that are beyond the scope of this introductory chapter.

Enhance and Explore

To enhance your understanding of the psychological concepts found in this chapter, please consult the following aids:

Study Guide

Learning Objectives, p. 112
Define the Terms, p. 115
Test Your Knowledge, p. 118
Essay Questions, p. 122
Thinking Independently, p. 124

PowerPsych CD-ROM

WHAT ARE THE MAIN IDEAS BEHIND CLASSICAL CONDITIONING?
The Basics of Classical Conditioning
Phases and Features of Classical Conditioning
Classical Conditioning and Emotional Responses

WHAT ARE THE MAIN IDEAS BEHIND OPERANT CONDITIONING?
Successive Approximations: Shape a Rat to Lever Press

PsychCentral

For more information concerning the topics found in this chapter, access psychology links on the Word Wide Web made through the Harcourt Web page at:
http://www.harcourtcollege.com/psych/Fundamentals

www.harcourtcollege.com

http://www.harcourtcollege.com/psych/index.html

CONTEMPORARY VOICES IN PSYCHOLOGY

Is a predisposition to phobias innate, or are phobias a conditioned response?

Conditioning Sensitizes a Preexisting Fear

N. J. Mackintosh, *University of Cambridge*

John Watson, the founding father of behaviorism, believed that the human infant had only a handful of innate fears—two of the main ones being a fear of loud noises and of loss of support. All other fears, he argued, were learned as a result of conditioning. And to prove his point, Watson and his student, Rosalie Rayner, demonstrated the conditioning of fear in an 11-month infant, Albert B (Watson & Rayner, 1920). Albert was initially happy to reach out and touch any small animal brought close to him, but after seven conditioning trials on which a white rat (the CS) was presented and, if Albert reached toward it, a steel bar was sharply struck immediately behind him (the UCS), Albert began to cry and withdraw from the rat. The fear conditioned to the rat generalized to other stimuli—a rabbit, a dog, and a sealskin coat. Since then, hundreds of laboratory experiments have shown that the pairing of an arbitrary and initially neutral CS with an aversive event, such as a brief electric shock or a very loud noise, will establish a conditioned fear reaction to that CS.

Watson and Rayner's study has often been cited (see Harris, 1979) as evidence that adult phobias, whether of snakes or spiders, open spaces or confined places, are based on one or more past episodes of conditioning, in which, for example, a snake has been associated with some aversive consequence. There are several difficulties with this simple application of conditioning theory—one of which, it is worth noting (if only to defend Watson and Rayner against a charge of gross cruelty), is that little Albert never showed much more than mild fretting and withdrawal, even when the rat was allowed to crawl over him, and that even this modest level of fear

showed little generalization when he was tested in a different room.

Studies of "vicarious conditioning" have shown that the mere sight of a conspecific showing a fear reaction to a particular CS can act as a sufficient UCS to reinforce the conditioning of fear to that CS. Wildborn rhesus monkeys tend to be afraid of snakes. This is not an innate fear, since laboratory-born infant rhesus monkeys show no such fear. But a single experience of watching an adult displaying a fear reaction to a snake will condition a fear of snakes in the infant (Mineka, 1987). Here, then, may be one way in which parents can, unwittingly, influence the behavior of their children.

The traditional behaviorist view was that any detectable stimulus can become associated with any consequence. On the face of it, this implies another serious problem for a conditioning account of phobias, since by far the most common phobias are those directed toward animals or social situations, rather than to the myriad other objects or events (electrical outlets, the sight of one's own blood) that are more likely to have been associated with painful consequences. Does this mean that the predisposition to phobias is genetically determined? Not if that is taken to imply that we are all born with an innate fear of spiders—or else we would all have a spider phobia. Surely, it is at least in part the differences among our individual experiences that cause one person to develop a phobia of spiders, another, one of snakes, and another, none at all. But why just of spiders, snakes, and so on? Some conditioning experiments have suggested some answers to this question.

In a series of studies, Ohman and his colleagues have shown

that conditioned GSRs in people are more resistant to extinction when the CS is a picture of a snake or spider than when it is a picture of flowers or mushrooms (Ohman, 1986). Cook and Mineka (1990) have provided evidence of similar selective fear in monkeys. Infant monkeys developed a fear of snakes after watching a video clip of an adult monkey displaying fear reactions to a snake, but showed no fear of flowers after watching a cleverly edited video clip showing an adult monkey apparently having a panic attack at the sight of a flower.

Results such as these have been widely interpreted as evidence of a biological predisiposition to associate certain classes of stimuli with certain consequences: In the evolutionary history of early hominids or other African primates, snakes and spiders were potentially dangerous, while flowers and mushrooms were not. For the learning theories, there are other questions left unanswered. Ohman's experiments have established only that fear of snakes extinguishes more slowly than fear of flowers, not that it is acquired more rapidly in the first place. Other experiments have shown that pictures of snakes are just as easily established as safety signals as are pictures of flowers (McNally & Reiss, 1984). Cook and Mineka's infant monkeys, having watched a video of adults showing fear reactions to flowers but not to snakes *did* then show significant fear of a live snake (although no fear of flowers). Some of these findings suggest that what is happening is sensitization of a pre-existing fear to certain classes of stimuli under conditions of stress or threat, rather than more rapid conditioning of fear (Lovibond, Siddle, & Bond, 1993).

Phobias Are an Innate Defense Mechanism

Michael S. Fanselow, *University of California, Los Angeles*

The emotional experience of fear can be overwhelmingly powerful. Why does it exist? The reason must lie in the fact that fear serves some biologically important function. Fear in the face of a serious threat organizes our resources to protect against that threat. From such a vantage fear becomes a behavioral system that evolved for the purpose of defense against environmental threats. For many animal species one of the most serious threats is becoming the food of another species. If one fails to defend against a predator, the ability for future contributions to the gene pool is nil. Thus it is not surprising that very effective systems for defending against a predator have evolved. Certain brain regions are dedicated to this function, and those brain regions serve fear in species ranging from at least mice and rats to monkeys and humans. If natural selection is responsible for fear, it seems reasonable that genetic factors shape this experience.

So fear is in part defined by its biological function. But to be useful to a behavioral scientist, there need to be two other aspects to the definition. The conditions that give rise to fear must be specified—what turns on the defensive behavioral system. Also, the behaviors that result as a consequence of fear must be detailed. Natural selection has shaped the answer to these questions with genetic encoding of what we are born to fear, what we come to fear, and how we behave when afraid.

Defending against predation is urgent; you must react quickly with effective behavior. Slow, trial-and-error learning by reinforcement simply will not do. A species that relied on such learning would likely be the subject of a paleontologist rather than a psychologist.

First, you must recognize threats quickly. Animals have an uncanny ability to recognize their natural predators. In one study, deermice were trapped on two sides of the Cascade Mountains of Washington. Snakes are a natural predator of the eastern mice but not the western mice. On the other hand, western mice have to contend with weasels. The mice were bred for one generation in the laboratory, and their offspring were tested for fear of a range of predators and nonpredators. While these animals had no experience outside the lab and had never encountered a predator before, they displayed defensive responses specifically to the predators of their parent's habitat. This innate "phobia" is not lost when selection pressure is eased; even the highly domesticated laboratory rat shows fear on its first encounter with a cat. While it is not possible to perform such experiments with humans, the fact that phobias are far more common for some stimuli than others suggests that we have similar dispositions.

This is not to say that fear of environmental stimuli is never learned. But this learning is genetically constrained and specialized. Learning of fear is rapid and occurs with a single aversive experience, reflecting the evolutionary urgency of defense. Despite the rapidity of this learning, the sort of stimuli we learn to fear is heavily constrained. In the famous "little Albert study" described by Dr. Mackintosh, Watson and Rayner conditioned a baby boy to fear a white rat by pairing it with a loud noise. But while fear of a rat is easily acquired, the same methods do not result in conditioned fear to many other stimuli. Similar predispositions are found in other primates, for as Dr. Mackintosh also explained, monkeys readily learn to become afraid of snakes but not of flowers. Even when a researcher chooses a domesticated laboratory rat and uses a seemingly arbitrary stimulus such as electric shock, there is selectivity in association formation. Rats more readily learn to fear noises than lights, which fare better as safety signals.

If fear has to protect us against a very imminent threat, we are unlikely to have the opportunity to learn what behaviors are effective and what behaviors are not. The trial-and-error learner is doomed. Rather, specialized defensive behaviors are already programmed into the species; they are executed as soon as fear is activated. A rat freezes the first time it encounters a cat—cats are attracted to moving targets. These are responses to fear, as the rat will show the same freezing response to a noise that has been paired with shock. Although rats are known to be adept lever pressers when asked to work for food, they are horrendous if asked to make the same response to avoid shock. Of course, manipulation of small objects probably never did much for the rats' ancestors when they were faced with a predator. Similarly, I speculate that I would be more likely to solve a complex calculus problem if the inducement was a fine wine rather than avoidance of an armed attacker.

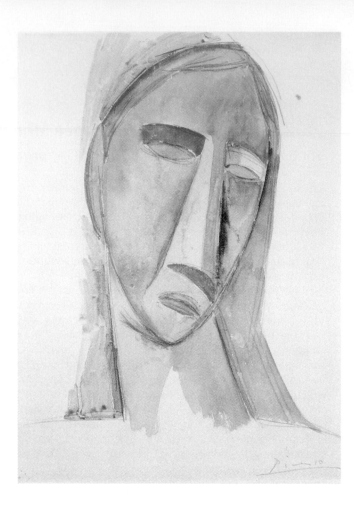

CHAPTER 7 *Memory*

It seems, then, that we owe to memory almost all that we either have or are; that our ideas and conceptions are its work, and that our everyday perception, thought, and movement is derived from this source. Memory collects the countless phenomena of our existence into a single whole; and, as our bodies would be scattered into the dust of their component atoms if they were not held together by the attraction of matter, so our consciousness would be broken up into as many fragments as we had lived seconds but for the binding and unifying force of memory. (Hering, 1920)

These words, spoken by Ewald Hering in a lecture to the Vienna Academy of Sciences many years ago, attest to the importance of memory in mental life. As Hering's comments about consciousness suggest, it is memory that gives us the sense of continuity on which our very notion of a *self* depends. When we think of what it means to be human, we must acknowledge the centrality of memory.

To appreciate the scientific study of memory, first we need to understand how researchers divide the field into manageable units, such as *working memory* and *long-term memory*. After describing the key distinctions, we will review the major findings about working memory, long-term memory, and what is called *implicit memory* (the kind of memory involved in learning a skill). Then we will take up a question of universal interest: How can memory be improved? We will conclude with a discussion of situations in which our memories are partly constructed.

How Do Psychologists Divide Up Memory?

While people often talk about memory as if there was only one kind, research findings indicate that there are in fact several kinds; moreover, within any memory system, there are different *stages* of memory. More specifically, in discussing memory, psychologists make three important distinctions. The first concerns the three stages of any memory system: *encoding, storage,* and *retrieval*. The second distinction deals with different memories to store information for short versus long periods. The third distinction deals with different memories to store different kinds of information (for example, one system for facts and another for skills). For each of these distinctions, there is evidence that the entities being distinguished—say, working memory versus long-term memory—are controlled by different structures in the brain.

encoding transforming a physical input into the kind of code or representation that memory accepts, and placing that representation in memory

Three Stages of Memory

Suppose that one morning you are introduced to a student and told that her name is Barbara Cohn. That afternoon you see her again and say something like, "You're Barbara Cohn. We met this morning." Clearly, you have remembered her name. But how exactly did you remember it?

Your minor memory feat can be broken down into three stages (see Figure 7-1). First, when you were introduced, you somehow entered Barbara Cohn's name into memory. This is the **encoding** stage; it consists of

Figure 7-1

Three Stages of Memory Theories of memory attribute forgetting to a failure at one or more of these stages. (After Melton, 1963)

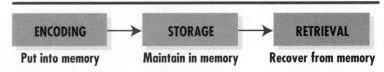

ENCODING	STORAGE	RETRIEVAL
Put into memory	**Maintain in memory**	**Recover from memory**

transforming a physical input (in this case, sound waves that correspond to a spoken name) into the kind of code or representation that memory accepts, and "placing" that representation in memory. Second, you stored the name during the time between the two meetings. This is the **storage** stage; it consists of *retaining an item in memory.* Third, you remembered the name at the time of your second meeting. This is the **retrieval** stage; which consists of *recovering an item from memory.*

storage retaining an item in memory

retrieval recovering an item from memory

Memory can fail at any of these three stages. Had you been unable to recall Barbara's name at the second meeting, this could have reflected a failure in either encoding, storage, or retrieval. Much current research on memory attempts to specify the mental operations that occur at each of these stages and to explain how these operations can go awry and result in memory failure.

A number of recent studies suggest that the different stages of memory are controlled by different structures in the brain. The most striking evidence comes from brain-scanning studies that look for neuroanatomical differences between the encoding and retrieval stages. These experiments have two parts. In part 1, which taps encoding, participants study a set of verbal items—for example, pairs consisting of categories and uncommon instances *(furniture–sideboard).* In part 2, which taps retrieval, participants have to recognize or recall the items when cued with the category name. In both parts, PET measures of brain activity are recorded while participants are engaged in their task. The most striking finding is that during encoding most of the activated brain regions are in the left hemisphere, whereas during retrieval most of the activated brain areas are in the right hemisphere (Shallice et al., 1994; Tulving et al., 1994). Thus the distinction between encoding and retrieval has a clear-cut biological bias.

Working Memory Versus Long-Term Memory

The three stages of memory do not operate the same way in all situations. Memory seems to differ between situations in which we keep material active for a matter of seconds and situations that require us to store material for longer intervals—from minutes to years. The former are said to tap *working memory*—previously referred to as "short-term memory"—whereas the latter reflect long-term memory.

What exactly do we mean by "working memory," and why the change in name? **Working memory** refers to *a system that keeps a limited amount of information in an active state for a brief period and performs mental operations on it;* usually it is a matter of maintaining and processing three to five items for a few seconds. For years it was thought that the main purpose of this system was merely to retain material until we could recall it, as when we keep active a phone number we have just looked up until we can dial it. More recently, it has become apparent that this memory system has other functions that are important for problem solving and thought. These other functions include: (1) keeping active information that is needed to solve a problem even though that information need not be explicitly recalled, and (2) performing operations on this temporarily stored information.

working memory a system that keeps a limited amount of information in an active state for a brief period and performs mental operations on it

An example should clarify these points. Suppose that you had to mentally multiply 35×8. You might start by determining that $8 \times 5 = 40$. You would then have to store that product for couple of seconds while doing the next step, multiplying 8×3; this temporary storage occurs in working memory. Moreover, combining these two numbers is a working-memory operation. Thus, working memory is a system that both stores and processes information, and this is why psychologists changed its name from "short-term memory" to "working memory" (Baddeley, 1992). In our discussion of this system, we initially focus on its immediate-memory function and then turn to its role in problem solving.

We can illustrate the distinction between working memory and long-term memory by amending our earlier story about meeting Barbara Cohn. Suppose that during the first meeting, as soon as you had heard her name a friend came up and you said, "Have you met Barbara Cohn?" In this case, remembering Barbara's name would be an example of working memory: You retrieved the name after only a second or two. Remembering her name at the time of your second meeting would be an example of long-term memory, because then retrieval would take place hours after the name was encoded. When you recall a name immediately after encountering it, retrieval often seems effortless as the name is still in your consciousness. But when you try to recall the same name hours later, retrieval is often difficult because the name is no longer in your consciousness and, in some sense, has to be brought back.

It is worth noting the existence of another short-term storage system, one that differs from working memory in that it holds a detailed sensory image of any stimulus that has just been presented, but only for a few milliseconds. For example, if a set of 12 letters is briefly flashed, a person will have a detailed visual image of *all* the letters for a few hundred milliseconds (Sperling, 1960). Such a *visual, sensory memory* or **iconic memory** is clearly useful in extending the life of briefly presented stimuli, but it plays far less of a role in thought and conscious recollection than the memory systems that we focus on in this chapter.

iconic memory
visual, sensory memory

It has been known for some time that working memory and long-term memory are implemented by different structures in the brain. In particular, the *hippocampus*, a structure located beneath the cortex and near the middle of the brain (see Chapter 2), is critical for long-term memory but not for working memory. In contrast, there are regions in the front of the brain that seem to be more critical for working memory than for long-term memory.

Much of the relevant evidence comes from experiments with rats and other non-human species. In some experiments, one group of rats is first subjected to damage in the hippocampus and the surrounding cortex while a second group is subjected to damage in a completely different region, the front of the cortex. Both groups of rats then perform a *delayed-response* task: On each trial, first one stimulus is presented (say, a square); then, after a delay, a second stimulus is presented (say, a triangle). The animal is supposed to respond only when the second stimulus *differs* from the first. How well the animal does on this task depends both on the kind of brain damage it has suffered and on the length of the delay between the two stimuli.

When the delay is long (15 seconds or more), animals with damage in the hippocampus perform poorly, but those with damage in the front of the cortex perform relatively normally. Because a long delay between stimuli requires long-term memory for storage of the first stimulus, these results fit with the idea that the hippocampus is critical for long-term memory. When the delay between the two stimuli is short (just a few seconds), the results are reversed: Now animals with damage in the front of the cortex perform poorly while those with hippocampal damage perform relatively normally. Because a short delay between stimuli requires working memory for storage of the first stimulus, these results indicate that regions in the frontal cortex are involved in working memory. Hence, different brain regions implement working memory and long-term memory (Goldman-Rakic, 1987; Zola-Morgan & Squire, 1985).

Is there evidence for this distinction in humans? Patients who have suffered damage in certain regions of the brain provide a "natural experiment." Some patients have suffered damage in the hippocampus and surrounding cortex, and consequently show severe memory loss. Because the hippocampus is located in the middle of the temporal lobe, these patients are said to have *medial-temporal-lobe amnesia.* Such patients have great difficulty remembering material for long intervals but rarely have any trouble remembering material for a few seconds. Thus, a patient with medial-temporal-lobe amnesia may be unable to recognize his doctor when she enters the room—even though the patient has seen this doctor every day for years—yet will have no trouble repeating the physician's full name when she is reintroduced (Milner, Corkin, & Teuber, 1968). Such a patient has a severe impairment in long-term memory but a normal working memory.

Other neurological patients, however, show the opposite problem: They cannot correctly repeat a string of even three words, yet they are relatively normal when tested on their long-term memory for words. Such patients have an impaired working memory but an intact long-term memory. And their brain damage is never in the medial temporal lobe (Shallice, 1988). Thus, for humans as well as for other mammals, working memory and long-term memory are controlled by different brain structures.

Different Memories for Different Kinds of Information

Until about 15 years ago, psychologists generally assumed that the same memory system was used for all materials. For example, the same long-term memory was presumably used to store both one's recollection of a grandmother's funeral and the skill one needs to ride a bike. Recent evidence indicates that this assumption was incorrect. In particular, we seem to use a different long-term memory for storing *facts* (such as information about a funeral) than we do for retaining *skills* (such as how to ride a bike). The evidence for this difference, as usual, includes both psychological and biological findings, but we will defer consideration of these findings until later in the chapter, when we discuss in detail the kind of memory that stores skills.

We have, then, three important distinctions. Given these differences, ideally we would like to proceed as follows: For both the kind of memory that stores facts (called explicit memory) and the kind that stores skills (implicit memory), we would like to describe the nature of the encoding, storage, and retrieval stages in both its working memory and long-term memory systems. At present however, we can do this only for explicit memory; we do not yet know enough about implicit memory. Explicit memory, therefore, is the focus of most sections of the chapter. The next two sections consider the nature of encoding, storage, and retrieval in working memory and in long-term explicit memory. Then we will examine what is known about implicit memory.

What Is the Nature of Working Memory?

Even in situations in which we must remember information for only a few seconds, memory involves the three stages of encoding, storage, and retrieval. Let us look more closely at how these processes operate in working memory.

Encoding Information

To encode information into working memory, we must attend to it. Since we are selective about what we attend to (see Chapter 4), our working memory will contain only what we have selected. This means that much of what we are exposed to never even enters working memory and, of course, will not be available for later retrieval. Indeed, many so-called memory problems are really lapses in attention. For example, if you bought some groceries and someone later asked you the color of the checkout clerk's eyes, you probably would be unable to answer, not because of a failure in your memory but because you had not paid attention to the clerk's eyes in the first place.

Phonological Coding   When information is encoded into memory, it is entered in a certain type of code or representation. For example, when you look up a phone number and retain it until you have dialed it, in what form do you represent the digits? Is the representation *visual*—a mental picture of the digits? Is it *phonological*—the sounds of the names of the digits? Or is it *semantic* (based on meaning)—some meaningful association that the digits have? Research indicates that we can use any of these types of representations to encode information into working memory, although we favor a phonological code when we are trying to keep information active by rehearsing it—that is, *by saying it over and over to ourselves*. **Rehearsal** is a particularly popular strategy when the information consists of verbal items such as digits, letters, or words. In trying to remember a phone number, we are most likely to encode the number as the sounds of the digit names and to rehearse these sounds to ourselves until we have dialed the number.

rehearsal   saying an item over and over to oneself

Figure 7-2

Testing for Eidetic Images   This test picture was shown to elementary-school children for 30 seconds. After the picture was removed, one boy saw his eidetic image "about 14" stripes in the cat's tail. The painting, by Marjorie Torrey, appears in Lewis Carroll's *Alice in Wonderland,* abridged by Josette Frank.

In a classic experiment that provided evidence of the existence of a phonological code, researchers briefly showed participants a list of six consonants (for example, RLBKSJ); when the letters were removed, the participants had to write all six letters in order. Although the entire procedure took only a second or two, participants occasionally made errors. When they did, the incorrect letter tended to be similar in sound to the correct one. For the list just mentioned, a participant might have written RLTKSJ, replacing the B with the similar-sounding T (Conrad, 1964). This finding supports the hypothesis that the participants encoded each letter phonologically (for example, "bee" for B), sometimes lost part of this code (only the "ee" part of the sound remained), and then responded with a letter ("tee") that was consistent with the remaining part of the code. This hypothesis also explains why it is more difficult to recall the items in the correct order when they are acoustically similar (for example, TBCGVE) than when they are acoustically distinct (RLTKSJ).

Visual Coding   If need be, we can also maintain verbal items in a visual representation. Experiments indicate that although we can use a visual code for verbal material, the visual details fade quickly. When a person must store nonverbal items (such as pictures that are difficult to describe and therefore difficult to rehearse acoustically), the visual code becomes more important. While most of us can maintain some kind of visual image in working memory, a few people are able to maintain images that are almost photographic in clarity. This ability occurs mainly in children. Such children can look briefly at a picture and still experience the image before their eyes after it has been removed. They can maintain the image for as long as several minutes and, when questioned, provide a wealth of detail, such as the number of stripes on a cat's tail (see Figure 7-2). Such children seem to be reading the details directly from an eidetic image (Haber, 1969, 1979). Such *eidetic imagery* is very rare, though. Some studies with children indicate that only about 5% report visual images that are long-lasting and have sharp detail. The visual code in working memory, then, is something short of a photograph.

The existence of both phonological and visual codes had led researchers to argue that working memory itself consists of two distinct stores or *buffers.* One is a *phonological buffer,* which briefly stores information in a phonological code; the second is a *visual-spatial buffer,* which briefly stores information in a visual or spatial code (Baddeley, 1986). Some recent brain-scanning studies indicate that the two buffers are controlled by different brain structures.

In one experiment, on every trial participants saw a sequence of letters in which both the identity and the position of the letter varied from one item to the next (see Figure 7-3). On some trials, participants

Figure 7-3

An Experiment on Acoustic and Visual Buffers   Participants had to decide whether each item was identical to the one three back in the sequence. The top half of the figure shows a typical sequence of events in which participants had to attend only to the identity of the letters, along with the responses required to each item. The bottom half of the figure shows the trial events when individuals had to attend only to the position of the letters, along with the responses required to each item. (After Smith et al., 1995)

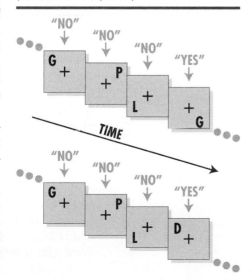

had to attend only to the name of the letters; their task was to determine whether each letter presented had the same name as the one presented three back in the sequence (see top portion of Figure 7-3). On other trials, participants had to attend only to the position of the letters; their task was to determine whether each letter's position was identical to that of the letter presented three back in the sequence (see bottom portion of Figure 7-3). Thus, the actual stimuli were identical in all cases. What varied was whether the participants were storing verbal information (the names of the letters) or spatial information (the positions of the letters). Presumably, the verbal information was being kept in the phonological buffer and the spatial information in the visual-spatial buffer.

On both name and spatial trials, PET measures of brain activity were recorded. The results indicated that the two buffers are in different hemispheres. On trials in which participants had to store verbal information (phonological buffer), much of the brain activity occurred in the left hemisphere; on trials in which participants had to store spatial information (visual-spatial buffer), much of the brain activity occurred in the right hemisphere. The two buffers seem to be distinct systems (Smith, Jonides, & Koeppe, 1996).

Storing Information

Perhaps the most striking fact about working memory is that it has a very limited capacity. On the average, the limit is seven items, give or take two (7 ± 2). Some people can keep only five items active in working memory; others can retain as many as nine. It may seem strange to give such an exact number to cover all people when it is clear that individuals differ greatly in their memory abilities. These differences, however, are due primarily to long-term memory. For working memory, most normal adults have a capacity of 7 ± 2. This constancy is often referred to as the "magic number seven" (Miller, 1956).

Psychologists determined this number by showing people various sequences of unrelated items (digits, letters, or words) and asking them to recall the items in order. The items are presented rapidly, so the participant does not have time to relate them to information stored in long-term memory; hence, the number of items recalled reflects only the storage capacity of working memory. On the initial trials, participants have to recall just a few items—say, three or four digits—which they can easily do. Then, over a series of trials, the number of digits increases until the experimenter determines the maximum number that a participant can recall in perfect order. The maximum (almost always between five and nine) is that individual's **memory span,** *the number of items the person can retain in working memory.* This task is so simple that you can easily try it yourself. The next time you come across a list of names (such as a directory in a university building), read through the list once and then look away and see how many names you can recall in order. The number will probably be between five and nine.

memory span   the number of items a person can retain in working memory

Chunking   As just noted, the memory-span procedure discourages participants from connecting the items to be remembered to information in long-term memory. When such connections are possible, performance on the memory-span task can change substantially.

To illustrate this change, suppose that you were presented the letter string SRUOYYLERECNIS. Because your memory span is 7 ± 2, you would probably be unable to repeat the entire letter sequence, which contains 14 letters. However, if you noticed that these letters spell the phrase SINCERELY YOURS in reverse order, your task would become easier. By using this knowledge, you have decreased the number of items that must be held in working memory from 14 to 2 (the two words). But where did this spelling knowledge come from? From long-term memory, where knowledge about words is stored. Thus, you can use long-term memory to recode new material into larger, more meaningful units and then store those units in working memory. Such units are called *chunks,* and the capacity of working memory is best expressed as 7 ± 2 chunks (Miller, 1956).

Forgetting   We may be able to hold on to seven items briefly, but in most cases they will soon be forgotten. Forgetting occurs either because the items *decay* with time or because they are *displaced* by new items.

Information may simply decay over time. We can think of the representation of an item as a trace that fades within a matter of seconds. One of the best pieces of evidence for this hypothesis is that our working memory span holds fewer words when the words take longer to say; for example, the span is less for long words such as "harpoon" and "cyclone" than for shorter words such as "bishop" and "pewter" (try saying the words to yourself to see the difference in their duration). Presumably this effect arises because as the words are presented we say them to ourselves, and the longer it takes to do this, the more likely it is that some of the words' traces will have faded before they can be recalled (Baddeley, Thompson, & Buchanan, 1975).

The other major cause of forgetting in working memory is the displacement of old items by new ones. The notion of *displacement* fits with the idea that working memory has a fixed capacity. Being in working memory may correspond to being in a state of activation. The more items we try to keep active, the less activation there is for any one of them. Perhaps only about seven items can be simultaneously maintained at a level of activation that permits all of them to be recalled. Once seven items are active, the activation given to a new item will be usurped from items presented earlier; consequently, the earlier items may fall below the critical level of activation needed for recall (Anderson, 1983).

Retrieving Information

Although the contents of working memory are active, retrieval of these contents is not immediate; in fact, it depends on the number of items in working memory. Evidence shows that the more items there are in working memory, the slower retrieval becomes. Most of the evidence for this comes from a type of experiment introduced by Saul Sternberg (1966).

On each trial of the experiment, a participant is shown a set of digits, called the *memory list,* that he or she must temporarily maintain in working memory. It is easy for the participant to maintain the information in working memory because each memory list contains between one and six digits. The memory list is then removed from view and a probe digit is presented. The participant must decide whether that digit was on the memory list. For example, if the memory list is 3 6 1 and the probe is 6, the participant should respond "yes"; given the same memory list and a probe of 2, the participant should respond "no." Participants rarely make errors on this task; what is of interest, however, is the *decision time,* the elapsed time between the onset of the probe and when the participant presses a "yes" or "no" button. Figure 7-4 presents data

Figure 7-4

Retrieval as a Search Process   Decision times increase in direct proportion to the number of items in short-term memory. Green circles represent "yes" responses; purple circles, "no" responses. The times for both types of decision fall along a straight line. Because the decision times are so fast, they must be measured with equipment that permits accuracy in milliseconds (thousandths of a second). (After Sternberg, 1966)

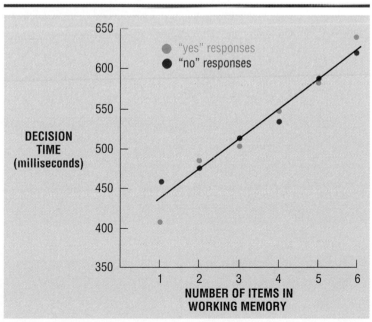

DECISION TIME (milliseconds)

● "yes" responses
● "no" responses

NUMBER OF ITEMS IN WORKING MEMORY

from such an experiment. The data indicate that decision time increases directly with the length of the memory list. What is remarkable about these decision times is that they fall along a straight line. This means that each additional item in working memory adds a fixed amount of time to the retrieval process—approximately 40 milliseconds, or one twenty-fifth of a second. The same results are found when the items are letters, words, auditory tones, or pictures of people's faces (Sternberg, 1975).

These results have led researchers to hypothesize that retrieval of an item in working memory may depend on the activation of that item reaching a critical level. That is, often a person decides that a probe is in working memory if its representation is above a critical level of activation. The more items in working memory, the less activation there is for any one of them (Monsell, 1978).

The Role of Working Memory in Thought

As noted earlier, working memory does more than hold information for later recall; it plays an important role in thought. When we consciously try to solve a problem, we often use working memory as a mental work space: We use it to store and process parts of the problem as well as information accessed from long-term memory that is relevant to the problem. To illustrate, consider again what it takes to multiply 35 by 8 in your head. You need working memory to store the numbers (35 and 8), the nature of the operation required (multiplication), and arithmetic facts such as $8 \times 5 = 40$ and $8 \times 3 = 24$. Not surprisingly, performance on mental arithmetic declines substantially if you simultaneously have to remember some words or digits in working memory; try doing the above mental multiplication while remembering the phone number 745-1739 (Baddeley & Hitch, 1974). Because of its role in mental computations, researchers think of working memory as a kind of blackboard on which the mind performs its computations and posts the partial results for later use (Baddeley, 1986).

Other research shows that working memory is used not only in doing numerical calculations but also in solving complex problems. One class of complex problems consists of geometric analogies, which are sometimes used in tests of intelligence (Ravens, 1955). An illustrative geometric analogy is presented in Figure 7-5. Try to solve it so that you can get an intuitive idea of the role of working memory in problem solving. You may note that you need working memory to store (1) the similarities and differences that you observe among the forms in a row and (2) the rules that you come up with to account for these similarities and differences and that you then use to select the correct answer. It turns out that the larger one's working memory, the better one does on problems like these. Moreover, when individuals solve these problems while having their brains scanned,

Figure 7-5

Illustration of a Geometric Analogy   The task is to inspect the forms in the 3 × 3 matrix, in which the bottom right entry is missing, and to determine which of the 8 alternatives given below is the missing entry. To do this, you have to look across each row and determine the rules that specify how the forms vary, and then do the same thing for each column. (After Carpenter, Just, & Shell, 1990)

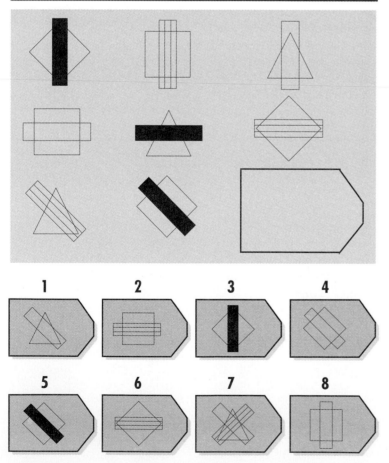

many of the brain areas found to be active are those that are activated when people have to store verbal or spatial material for brief periods (Prabhakaran et al., 1997). There seems to be little doubt that part of the difficulty in solving many complex problems is the load they place on working memory (Carpenter, Just, & Shell, 1990).

Working memory is also crucial for language processes like following a conversation or reading a text. When reading for understanding, we often must consciously relate new sentences to material that appeared earlier in the text. This relating of new to old seems to occur in working memory because people who have more working-memory capacity score higher than others on reading comprehension tests (Daneman & Carpenter, 1980; Just & Carpenter, 1992).

In summary, working memory is a system that can hold roughly 7 ± 2 chunks of information in either a phonological or a visual format. Information is lost from working memory through either decay or displacement, and information is retrieved from this system by a process that is sensitive to the total number of items being kept active. Last, and perhaps most important, working memory is used to store and process information needed during problem solving, and therefore is critical for thought.

How might an increase in the size of your working memory affect your performance on a standardized test of comprehension, such as the SAT? Don't just talk about "increases" and "decreases"; rather, try to explain how underlying comprehension processes might be affected.

What Is the Nature of Long-Term Memory?

Long-term memory is involved *when information has to be retained for intervals as brief as a few minutes* (such as a point made earlier in a conversation) *or as long as a lifetime* (such as an older adult's childhood memories). In experiments on long-term memory, psychologists generally have studied forgetting over intervals of minutes, hours, or weeks, but a few studies have looked at memory over periods of years or even decades. Experiments that use intervals of years often involve recall of personal experiences (what is called *autobiographical memory*) rather than of laboratory materials. In what follows, studies using both kinds of material are intermixed because they seem to reflect the same principles.

Our discussion of long-term memory will again distinguish among the three stages of memory—encoding, storage, and retrieval—but this time there is a wrinkle. It is often difficult to know whether forgetting from long-term memory is due to a loss from storage or to a failure in retrieval. To deal with this problem, we will delay our discussion of storage until after we have considered retrieval. That way we will have a clearer idea of what constitutes good evidence for a storage loss.

long-term memory a system that retains information for intervals ranging from a few minutes to a lifetime

Encoding Information

For verbal materials, the dominant long-term memory representation is neither acoustic nor visual; instead, it is based on the meanings of the items. Encoding items according to their meanings occurs even when the items are isolated words, but it is more striking when the items are sentences. Several minutes after hearing a sentence, most of what you can recall or recognize is the sentence's meaning. Suppose that you heard the sentence, "The author sent the committee a long letter." Two minutes later you would do no better than chance in telling whether you had heard that sentence or one that has the same meaning: "A long letter was sent to the committee by the author" (Sachs, 1967).

Encoding of meaning is pervasive in everyday memory situations. When people report on complex social situations, they may misremember many of the specifics (who said what to whom, when something was said, who else was there), yet they can accurately describe the basic situation (Neisser, 1981).

The early stages of learning to play the piano involve committing movement sequences to long-term explicit memory (the later stages involve implicit memory).

Although meaning may be the dominant way of representing verbal material in long-term memory, we sometimes code other aspects of the material as well. We can, for example, memorize poems and recite them word for word. In such cases we have coded not only the meaning of the poem but the words themselves. We can also use a phonological code in long-term memory. When you get a phone call and the other party says "hello," you often recognize the voice. In a case like this, you must have coded the sound of that person's voice in long-term memory. Visual impressions, tastes, and smells are also coded in long-term memory. Thus, long-term memory has a preferred code for verbal material (namely, meaning), but other codes can be used as well.

Adding Meaningful Connections

Often the items that we have to remember are meaningful but the connections between them are not. In such cases memory can be improved by creating real or artificial links between the items. For example, people learning to read music must remember that the five lines in printed music are referred to as EGBDF; although the symbols themselves are meaningful (they refer to notes on a keyboard), their order seems arbitrary. What many learners do is convert the symbols into the sentence "Every Good Boy Does Fine"; the first letter of each word names each symbol, and the relationships between the words in the sentence supply meaningful connections between the symbols. These connections aid memory because they provide retrieval paths between the words: Once the word "Good" has been retrieved, for example, there is a path or connection to "Boy," the next word that has to be recalled.

One of the best ways to add connections is to elaborate on the meaning of the material while encoding it. The more deeply or elaborately one encodes the meaning, the better memory will be (Craik & Tulving, 1975). If you have to remember a point made in a textbook, you will recall it better if you concentrate on its meaning rather than on the exact words. And the more deeply and thoroughly you expand on its meaning, the better you will recall it. Thus, there is an intimate connection between understanding and memory. The better we understand some material, the more connections we see between its parts. These connections can serve as retrieval links, so the better we understand, the more we remember.

Organization   The more we organize the material we encode, the easier it is to retrieve. Suppose that you were at a conference at which you met various professionals—doctors, lawyers, and journalists. When you try to recall their names at a later time, you will do better if you initially organize the information by profession. Then you can ask yourself, "Who were the doctors I met?" "Who were the lawyers?" And so forth. A list of names or words is far easier to recall when we encode the information into categories and then retrieve it on a category-by-category basis (e.g., see Bower et al., 1969).

Retrieving Information

Many cases of forgetting from long-term memory result from loss of access to the information rather than from loss of the information itself. That is, poor memory often reflects a retrieval failure rather than a storage failure. (Note that this is unlike working memory, where retrieval is thought to be relatively error-free.) Trying to retrieve an item from long-term memory is like trying to find a book in a large library. Failure to find the book does not necessarily mean that it is not there; you may be looking in the wrong place, or it may simply have been misfiled.

Evidence for Retrieval Failures   At some point everyone has been unable to recall a fact or an experience, only to have it come to mind later. How many times have you taken an exam and not been able to recall a specific name, only to remember it after the exam? Another example is the "tip-of-the-tongue" experience, in which a particular word or name lies tantalizingly outside our ability to recall it (Brown & McNeill, 1966). We may feel quite tormented until a search of memory (dredging up and then discarding words that are close but not quite right) finally retrieves the correct word.

A more striking example of retrieval failure is the occasional recovery in psychotherapy of a memory that had previously been forgotten. Although we lack firm evidence for these observations, they at least suggest that some seemingly forgotten memories are not lost. They are just difficult to get at and require the right kind of **retrieval cue,** which is *anything that can help retrieve a memory.*

For stronger evidence that retrieval failures can cause forgetting, consider the following experiment. Participants were asked to memorize a long list of words. Some of the words were names of animals, such as *dog, cat, horse;* some were names of fruits, such as *apple, orange, pear;* some were names of furniture, and so on (see Table 7-1). At the time of recall, the participants were divided into two groups. One group was supplied with retrieval cues such as "animal," "fruit," and so on; the other group, the control group, was not. The group that was given the retrieval cues recalled more words than the control group. In a subsequent test, both groups were given the retrieval cues. Now they both recalled the same number of words. Hence, the initial difference in recall between the two groups must have been due to retrieval failures.

Thus, the better the retrieval cues, the better our memory. This principle explains why we usually do better on a recognition test of memory than on a recall test. In a recognition test, we are asked whether we have seen a particular item before (for example, "Was Bessie Smith one of the people you met at the wedding?"). The test item itself is an excellent retrieval cue for our memory of that item. In contrast, in a recall test we have to produce the memorized items with minimal retrieval cues (for example, "Recall the name of the woman you met at the party"). Since the retrieval cues in a recognition test are generally more useful than those in a recall test, performance is usually better on recognition tests than on recall tests (Tulving 1974).

Interference   Among the factors that can impair retrieval, the most important is **interference,** *a condition in which the ability to retrieve an item is reduced because other items are associated with the same cue.* If we associate different items with the same cue, when we try to use that cue to retrieve one of the items (the target item), the

retrieval cue anything that can help retrieve a memory

interference a condition in which the ability to retrieve an item is reduced because other items are associated with the same cue

Table 7-1

Examples From a Study of Retrieval Failures
Participants who were not given the retrieval cues recalled fewer words from the memorized list than other participants who were given the cues. This finding shows that problems at the retrieval stage of long-term memory are responsible for some memory failures. (After Tulving & Pearlstone, 1966)

Lists to Be Memorized		
dog	cotton	oil
cat	wool	gas
horse	silk	coal
cow	rayon	wood
apple	blue	doctor
orange	red	lawyer
pear	green	teacher
banana	yellow	dentist
chair	knife	football
table	spoon	baseball
bed	fork	basketball
sofa	pan	tennis
knife	hammer	shirt
gun	saw	socks
rifle	nails	pants
bomb	screwdriver	shoes
Retrieval Cues		
animals	cloth	fuels
fruit	color	professions
furniture	utensils	sports
weapons	tools	clothing

When you look up a phone number and retain it until you have dialed it, do you retain it visually, phonologically, or semantically?

other items may become active and interfere with our recovery of the target. For example, if your friend Dan moves and you finally learn his new phone number, you will find it difficult to retrieve his old number. Why? You are using the cue "Dan's phone number" to retrieve the old number, but instead this cue activates the new number, which interferes with recovery of the old one. Or suppose that your reserved space in a parking garage, which you have used for a year, is changed. You may initially find it difficult to retrieve your new parking location from memory. Why? You are trying to learn to associate your new location with the cue "my parking place," but this cue retrieves the old location, which interferes with the learning of the new one. In both examples the power of retrieval cues ("Dan's phone number" or "my parking place") to activate particular target items decreases with the number of other items associated with those cues. The more items associated with a cue, the more overloaded it becomes and the less effective it is in retrieving a target item.

One way to think about interference is in terms of searching memory. Suppose that you are given a cue and have to retrieve some target information associated with it (as in our phone-number and parking-space examples). The more items associated with the cue, the more items you have to consider before finding your target and the greater the chances that you will fail to find it (see Figure 7-6). If the associations are stronger for recently experienced items and stronger associations are considered before weaker ones, this explains why we are more likely to find target information that has occurred more recently; this phenomenon is referred to as a *recency effect*. Alternatively, we can think about interference in terms of activation processes like those involved in retrieval from working memory. Now, retrieving a target item amounts to getting it sufficiently activated. The more items that are associated with a cue, the more the activation produced by the cue must be subdivided among its associations and the less likely it is that the target will be sufficiently activated for retrieval to occur (see Figure 7-6) (Anderson, 1983; Raaijmakers & Shiffrin, 1981).

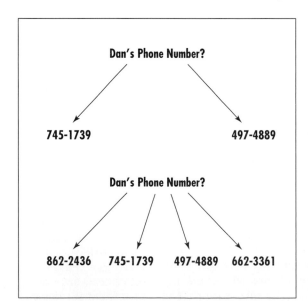

Figure 7-6

Retrieval as a Search Process Versus an Activation Process   In the situation depicted at the top, only two of Dan's phone numbers are stored in memory; in the situation depicted at the bottom, four of Dan's phone numbers are in memory. There is more interference in the bottom case than in the top case. If retrieval involves a search process, there are more paths to be searched in the bottom case than in the top case, and hence there are more chances for an error in the bottom case. If retrieval involves an activation process, the activation from the cue ("Dan's phone number") must be divided between only two paths in the top case but among four paths in the bottom case. Hence, less activation will reach each phone number in the bottom case.

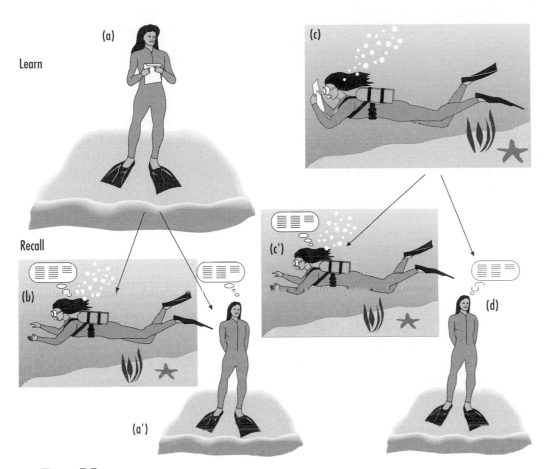

Figure 7-7

Effects of Environmental Context on Retrieval In an experiment to demonstrate how context affects retrieval, one group of deep-sea divers learned a list of words while they were on the beach (panel a), whereas another group of divers learned the list while they were beneath 15 feet of water (panel c). Later, each group was divided in half and tried to recall the words either in the same environment in which they had learned them (panels a' and c') or in a different environment (panels b and d). Whether the divers originally learned the words on land or under water had no overall effect. But divers who were tested in an environment different from the one in which they learned the words recalled 40% less than divers who learned and recalled in the same environment. (Godden & Baddeley, 1975)

Context It is easier to retrieve a particular fact or episode if you are in the same context in which you encoded it (Estes, 1972). For example, it is a good bet that your ability to retrieve the names of your classmates in the first and second grades would improve if you were to walk through the corridors of your elementary school. Similarly, your ability to retrieve an emotional moment with a close friend—say, an argument with her in a restaurant—would be greater if you were back in the place where the incident occurred. This may explain why we are sometimes overwhelmed by memories about our earlier life when we visit a place where we once lived. The context in which an event was encoded is itself one of the most powerful retrieval cues possible, and there is a great deal of experimental evidence for this (see Figure 7-7 for an extreme example).

Context is not always external to the memorizer; that is, it is not always a matter of environment. What is happening inside us when we encode information is also part of context. For example, if we experience an event while under the influence of a drug such as alcohol or marijuana, perhaps we can best retrieve it when we are again in that drug-induced state. In such cases, called **state-dependent learning,**

state-dependent learning a condition in which memory is partly dependent on the internal state prevailing during learning

memory is partly dependent on the internal state prevailing during learning. While the evidence for state-dependent learning is controversial, it suggests that memory does indeed improve when our internal state during retrieval matches that which prevailed during encoding (Eich, 1980).

Storing Information

Retrieval failures are unlikely to be the only cause of forgetting. The fact that some forgetting is due to retrieval failures does not imply that all forgetting is. It seems most unlikely that everything we ever learned is still present in memory, just waiting for the right retrieval cue. Some information is almost certainly lost from storage (Loftus & Loftus, 1980).

Some evidence for storage loss comes from people who receive electroconvulsive therapy to alleviate severe depression (a mild electric current applied to the brain produces a brief epileptic-like seizure and momentary unconsciousness; see Chapter 13). In such cases the patient loses some memory for events that occurred in the months just prior to the shock, but not for earlier events (Squire & Fox, 1980). These memory losses are unlikely to be due to retrieval failures; if the shock disrupted retrieval, all memories should be affected, not just recent ones. More likely, the shock disrupts storage processes that *consolidate* new memories over a period of months or longer, and information that has not been consolidated is lost from storage.

Most research on storage in long-term memory is done at the biological level. Researchers have made substantial progress in determining the neuroanatomical bases of consolidation. The critical brain structures involved seem to be the hippocampus (discussed at the beginning of the chapter) and the cortex surrounding the hippocampus. The hippocampus's role in consolidation seems to be that of a cross-referencing system, linking aspects of a particular memory that are stored in separate parts of the brain (Squire, 1992). While a global memory loss usually occurs only when the surrounding cortex as well as the hippocampus is impaired, damage to the hippocampus alone can result in severe memory disturbance.

A study with monkeys provides strong evidence that the function of the hippocampus is to consolidate relatively new memories. In the study, a group of experimental monkeys learned to discriminate between 100 pairs of objects. For each pair, there was food under one object, which the monkey got only if it chose that object. Since all the objects differed, the monkeys essentially learned 100 different problems. Twenty of these problems were learned 16 weeks before the researchers removed each monkey's hippocampus; additional sets of 20 problems were learned either 12, 8, 4, or 2 weeks before surgery. Two weeks *after* surgery, the researchers tested the monkeys' memory with a single trial of each of the 100 pairs.

The critical finding was that, whereas the experimental monkeys remembered discriminations learned 8, 12, or 16 weeks before surgery as well as normal control monkeys did, they remembered the discriminations learned 2 or 4 weeks before surgery less well than the control monkeys. Moreover, the experimental monkeys actually remembered less about the discriminations learned 2 to 4 weeks before surgery than they did about the discriminations learned earlier. These results suggest that memories need to be processed by the hippocampus for a period of a few weeks, for it is only during this period that memory is impaired by removal of the hippocampus. Permanent long-term memory storage is almost certainly localized in the cortex, particularly the regions in which sensory information is interpreted (Squire, 1992; Zola-Morgan & Squire, 1990).

There are also brain-scanning studies with humans that show that a normal hippocampus is active when learning new information. While having their brains scanned, participants had to learn word lists that varied in length. One of the brain areas activated was the hippocampus; the longer the list to be learned, the greater the activation in the hippocampus (Grasby et al., 1994). There is little doubt, then, that the hippocampus is critical for the storage of new information in species ranging from rats to monkeys to humans (Squire, 1992).

These findings have an interesting implication for the development of memory. Since the hippocampus is not mature until roughly a year or two after birth, events that take place during the first 2 years of life cannot be sufficiently consolidated by the hippocampus, and consequently they cannot be recalled well later. This may be part of the reason why virtually no one can remember events from the first 2 to 3 years of life, a phenomenon that was first discussed by Freud (1905) and is referred to as *childhood amnesia.*

How Emotion Affects Memory

So far we have treated memory as if it were divorced from emotion. But don't we sometimes remember (or forget) material because of its emotional content? There has been a great deal of research on these questions. The results suggest that emotion can influence long-term memory in at least five distinct ways. Thus, we now take a detailed look at the ways in which emotion affects memory.

Rehearsal   The simplest idea is that we tend to think about emotionally charged situations, negative as well as positive, more than we think about neutral ones. We rehearse and organize exciting memories more than bland ones. For example, you may forget where you saw a particular movie; but if a fire breaks out while you are in a theater, that incident will dominate your thoughts for a while and you will describe the setting over and over to friends, thereby rehearsing and organizing it. Since we know that rehearsal and organization can improve retrieval from long-term memory, it is not surprising that memory is often better for emotional situations than for unemotional ones (Neisser, 1982; Rapaport, 1942).

flashbulb memory
a vivid and relatively permanent record of the circumstances in which one learned of an emotionally charged, significant event

Flashbulb Memories   The second way emotion can affect memory is via flashbulb memories. A **flashbulb memory** is *a vivid and relatively permanent record of the circumstances in which one learned of an emotionally charged, significant event.* An example for people over age 20 would be the explosion of the space shuttle *Chal-*

lenger in 1986, which was witnessed by millions of people on television. Many people in their late twenties and older remember exactly where they were when they learned of the *Challenger* disaster and exactly who told them about it, even though these are the kinds of details that we usually forget quickly. Americans over 50 may have flashbulb memories of the assassinations of John F. Kennedy and Martin Luther King, Jr., in the 1960s. Remarkably, there is even a published report indicating that a century ago Americans had flashbulb memories of the assassination of Abraham Lincoln. When Colegrove (1899) interviewed 179 people, 127 of them were able to give full particulars as to where they were and what they were doing when they heard of Lincoln's assassination.

What is responsible for such memories? According to Roger Brown and James Kulik (1977), extremely important events trigger a special memory mechanism, one that makes a permanent record of everything the person

Many people in their mid-twenties and older have flashbulb memories of the Challenger *explosion that occurred in 1986.*

We are more likely to remember emotional events than non-emotional ones. The memory of a particularly poignant funeral can last a lifetime.

is experiencing at the moment. It is as if we took a picture of the moment, which is why the recollection is dubbed a "flashbulb memory."

Perhaps the most striking evidence for a special memory mechanism comes from a study that focused on the biological bases of memory. The key idea is that the storage of emotional memories involves the hormones adrenaline and noradrenaline (which can serve as neurotransmitters), whereas the storage of normal memories does not. Consequently, if the biochemical effects of these two hormones are blocked, people should have trouble remembering emotional material but no problem remembering nonemotional material. These ideas were tested in an experiment in which participants watched a slide presentation accompanied by either an emotional narration (about a boy being taken to a hospital for emergency surgery) or a neutral narration (about a boy going to a hospital to visit his father, who works there). Before hearing the stories, half the participants were given a drug (propranolol) that is known to block the effects of adrenaline and noradrenaline; the other half were given a placebo. One week later all participants were given a memory test for the stories. The participants who had taken the hormone-blocking drug recalled less information about the emotional story than did the participants who had taken the placebo, but the two groups of participants showed no difference on recall of the neutral story. These results imply that emotional material is indeed stored by a different mechanism from that used with neutral memories (Cahill et al., 1994).

We know what hormones are involved, but what neural structures are being affected by these hormones? In Chapter 6 we saw that the *amygdala* is involved in emotional learning. It turns out that this structure is also involved in emotional memory. The evidence for this comes from recent brain-scanning studies. While having their brains scanned, participants viewed slides accompanied by an emotional narration. The amygdala was activated, but participants differed with regard to how much activation they showed. The more amygdala activation a participant showed, the better he or she recalled the emotional information later. This is good evidence that the amygdala controls memory for emotional material (Cahill et al., 1996).

Retrieval Interference   There are also cases in which negative emotions hinder retrieval, which brings us to the third way emotion can affect memory. An experience that many students have at one time or another illustrates this concept:

> You are taking an exam about which you are not very confident. You can barely understand the initial question, let alone answer it. Signs of panic appear. Although the second question really isn't hard, the anxiety triggered by the previous question spreads to this one. By the time you look at the third question, it wouldn't matter if it just asked for your phone number. There's no way you can answer it. You're in a complete panic.

What is happening to memory here? Failure to deal with the first question produced anxiety. Anxiety is often accompanied by extraneous thoughts, such as "I'm going to flunk out" or "Everybody will think I'm stupid." These thoughts fill your consciousness and interfere with any attempt to retrieve the information relevant to the question; this may be why memory fails. According to this view, anxiety does not directly cause memory failure; rather, it causes, or is associated with, extraneous thoughts, and these thoughts cause memory failure by interfering with retrieval (Holmes, 1974).

Context   Emotion may also affect memory through a kind of *context effect.* As noted earlier, memory is best when the context at the time of retrieval matches that at the time of encoding. Since our emotional state during learning is part of the context, if the material we are learning makes us feel sad, perhaps we can best retrieve that material when we feel sad again. Experimenters have demonstrated such an emotional-context effect in the laboratory.

Sometimes when taking a difficult exam, you can get anxious, and that anxiety will interfere with your ability to retrieve the information you need.

In one study, participants agreed to keep diaries for a week, recording every emotional incident that occurred and noting whether it was pleasant or unpleasant. One week after they handed in their diaries, the participants returned to the laboratory and were hypnotized (they had been preselected to be highly hypnotizable). Half the participants were put in a pleasant mood and the other half in an unpleasant mood. All were asked to recall the incidents recorded in their diaries. For participants in a pleasant mood, most of the incidents they recalled had been rated as pleasant when they were experienced; for participants in an unpleasant mood at retrieval, most of the incidents recalled had been rated as unpleasant when they were experienced. As expected, recall was best when the dominant emotion during retrieval matched that during encoding (Bower, 1981).

Repression   A fifth view of emotion and memory is Freud's theory of the unconscious. Freud proposed that some emotional experiences in childhood are so traumatic that allowing them to enter consciousness many years later would cause the individual to be totally overwhelmed by anxiety. (This is different from the example of the exam, in which the anxiety is tolerable to consciousness.) Such traumatic experiences are said to be stored in the unconscious, or *repressed;* they can be retrieved only when some of the emotion associated with them is defused. Repression therefore represents the ultimate retrieval failure: Access to the target memories is *actively* blocked. This notion of active blocking makes the repression hypothesis qualitatively different from the ideas about forgetting discussed earlier. (For a discussion of Freud's theory, see Chapter 10.)

Repression is such a striking phenomenon that we would like to study it in the laboratory, but this has proved difficult to do. To induce true repression in the laboratory, the experimenter must have the participant experience something extremely traumatic; of course, ethical considerations prohibit this. The studies that have been done have exposed subjects to only mildly upsetting experiences, and the evidence from these studies lends mixed support to the repression hypothesis (Baddeley, 1990; Erdelyi, 1985).

In sum, long-term memory is a system that can hold information for days, years, or decades, typically in a code based on meaning, although other codes are possible. Retrieval of information from this system is sensitive to interference; many apparent "storage losses" are really retrieval failures. Storage in this system involves consolidation, a process that is controlled by the hippocampal system. Many aspects of long-term memory can be influenced by emotion; such influences may reflect selective rehearsal, retrieval interference, the effects of context, or two special-purpose mechanisms, flashbulb memories and repression.

1. We reviewed various proposals about how emotion affects explicit long-term memory. Some of these proposals implied that emotion helps memory, whereas others suggested that emotion hurts memory. How can you reconcile these apparent differences?

2. We noted that most people can remember very little about their first two to three years of life, and that this childhood amnesia is related to the development of the hippocampus. What psychological factors might also contribute to childhood amnesia? (Think of things that change dramatically around age 3.)

What Is the Nature of Implicit Memory?

explicit memory
memory that is manifested in conscious recollection of the past

Thus far we have been concerned mainly with situations in which people remember personal facts. These are cases of **explicit memory,** *manifested by consciously recollecting the past.* But there seems to be another kind of memory, which shows up as an improvement on some perceptual, motor, or cognitive task without conscious recollection of the experiences that led to the improvement. For example, with practice we can steadily improve our ability to recognize words in a foreign language, but at the moment that we are recognizing a word, and thereby demonstrating our skill, we need not have any conscious recollection of the lessons that led to our improvement. These are cases of **implicit memory,** *manifested in the performance of a skill* (Schacter, 1989).

implicit memory
memory that is manifested in the performance of a skill

Memory in Amnesia

amnesia   partial loss of memory

Much of what is known about implicit memory has been learned from people who suffer **amnesia,** or a *partial loss of memory.* Amnesia can result from very different causes, including accidental injuries to the brain, strokes, encephalitis, alcoholism, electroconvulsive shock, and surgery. Whatever its cause, its primary symptom is a profound inability to remember day-to-day events and, hence, to acquire new factual information; this is referred to as *anterograde amnesia,* and it can be extensive. There is an intensively studied patient, identified as NA, who is unable to participate in a normal conversation because he loses his train of thought with the least distraction. Another patient, identified as HM—the most intensively studied of all amnesiacs—reads the same magazines over and over and continually needs to be reintroduced to doctors who have been treating him for decades.

A secondary symptom of amnesia is inability to remember events that occurred *prior* to the injury or disease. The extent of such *retrograde amnesia* varies from one patient to another. Aside from retrograde and anterograde memory losses, the typical amnesiac appears relatively normal: He or she has a normal vocabulary, displays the usual knowledge about the world (at least prior to the onset of the amnesia), and in general shows no loss of intelligence.

Skills and Priming   A striking aspect of amnesia is that not all kinds of memory are disrupted. While amnesiacs are generally unable to either remember old facts about their lives or learn new ones, they have no difficulty remembering and learning perceptual and motor skills. This suggests that there is a different memory for facts than for skills. More generally, it suggests that explicit and implicit memory (which encode facts and skills, respectively) are different systems.

The skills that are preserved in amnesia include *motor skills,* such as tying one's shoelaces or riding a bike, and *perceptual skills,* such as normal reading or reading words that are projected into a mirror (and hence reversed). Consider the ability to read mirror-reversed words. Doing this well takes a bit of practice (try holding this book in front of a mirror and reading it). Amnesiacs improve with practice at the *very same rate* as normal individuals, although they may have no memory of having participated in prior practice sessions (Cohen & Squire, 1980). They show normal memory for the skill but virtually no memory for the learning episodes that developed it (the latter being *facts*).

A similar pattern emerges in situations referred to as **priming,** in which *prior exposure to a stimulus facilitates or primes later processing of that stimulus.* This pattern is illustrated in the experiment outlined in Table 7-2. In stage 1 of the experiment, amnesiac and normal participants were presented with a list of words to study. In stage 2, stems of words on the list and stems of words not on the list were presented, and participants tried to complete them. The normal participants performed as expected, completing more stems when they were drawn from words that were on the list. Thus, the words presented in stage 1 facilitated or primed performance on the stem-completion problems of stage 2.

An important point is that amnesiacs *also* completed more stems in stage 2 when they were drawn from words that were on the list than when they were drawn from words that were not on the list. In fact, the degree of priming for amnesiacs was exactly the same as that for normal individuals! This finding indicates that when memory is manifested implicitly, as in priming, amnesiacs perform normally. Lastly, in stage 3 of the experiment, the original words were presented again along with some novel words, and participants had to recognize which words had appeared on the list. Now amnesiacs remembered far fewer words than normal participants. Thus, when memory is tested explicitly, as in recognition, amnesiacs perform far below normal individuals.

There is an interesting variation of the preceding study that further strengthens its conclusion. Suppose that in stage 2 participants are instructed that it will help them in the stem-completion task to try to think of the words presented earlier. This instruction turns stem completion into an explicit memory task because conscious recollection is being emphasized. Now amnesiacs show substantially less priming than do normal individuals (Graf & Mandler, 1984).

A Variety of Memory Stores

On the basis of work with brain-damaged patients, researchers have proposed that both explicit and implicit memory have different forms. One such proposal is presented in Figure 7-8. The basic distinction is between explicit and implicit memory. With regard to implicit memory, a further distinction is made between perceptual–motor skills, such as reading

priming a condition in which prior exposure to a stimulus facilitates or primes later processing of that stimulus

Table 7-2

Procedure for an Experiment to Study Implicit Memory in Amnesia (After Warrington & Weiskrantz, 1978)

Stage 1	Example
Present list of words for study	MOTEL
Stage 2	
Present stems of list words and nonlist words for completion. Number of list words completed minus number of nonlist words completed = Priming	MOT BLA
Stage 3	
Present original list of words plus new words for recognition	MOTEL STAND

Figure 7-8

A Proposed Classification of Memory Stores Squire et al. (1995) propose that there are several different memory systems. The basic distinction is between explicit and implicit memory (which they refer to as declarative and nondeclarative, respectively).

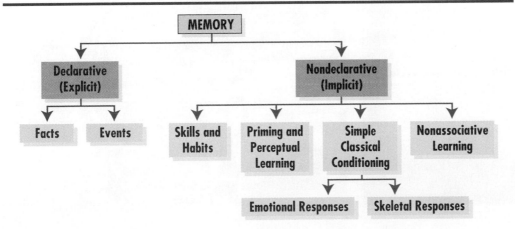

mirror-reversed words, and priming, as occurs in word-stem completions. The reason for assuming that skills and priming may involve different memory stores is that there are patients with brain damage (those in the early stages of Alzheimer's disease) who are normal at learning motor skills but show less priming than normal. In contrast, there are other brain-damaged patients (those with Huntington's disease) who show normal priming but are impaired in learning new motor skills (Schacter, 1989).

The theory depicted in Figure 7-8 also posits two kinds of explicit memory, which are referred to as *episodic* and *semantic*. Episodic facts refer to personal episodes, and semantic facts refer to general knowledge. To illustrate, your memory of your high school graduation is an episodic fact, and so is your memory of what you had for dinner last night. In each of these cases the episode is encoded with respect to you the individual (*your* graduation, *your* dinner), and often the episode is coded with respect to a specific time and place as well. All of this is in contrast to semantic facts, examples of which include your memory, or knowledge, that the word *bachelor* means an unmarried man and that September has 30 days. In these cases the knowledge is encoded in relation to other knowledge rather than in relation to yourself, and there is no coding of time and place (Tulving, 1985). This distinction between semantic and episodic memory fits with the fact that although amnesiacs have severe problems remembering personal episodes, they seem relatively normal in their general knowledge.

Implicit Memory in Normal Individuals

There are fundamental differences in how explicit and implicit memories are implemented in the normal brain. The critical evidence comes from brain-scanning experiments (PET). In one experiment (Squire et al., 1992), participants first studied a list of 15 words and then were exposed to three different conditions. The implicit-memory condition was the stem-completion task. Half the stems were drawn from the 15 words originally studied; the other half were new. Participants were instructed to complete the stems with the first words that came to mind. The second condition of interest involved explicit memory. Again word stems were presented, but now par-

Figure 7-9

Priming Reduces Neural Activation   The neural consequences of priming are illustrated in the pair of images below. The image on the left shows the areas activated when novel verbal items are presented, as in the control condition of the experiment described in the text. The image on the right shows the areas activated when the same verbal items are re-presented, as in the priming condition of the experiment in the text. Note that priming is accompanied by a marked decrease in activation.

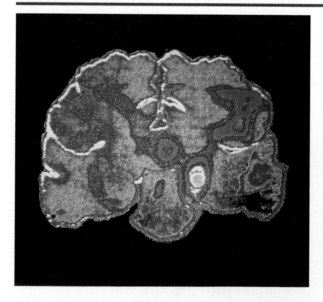
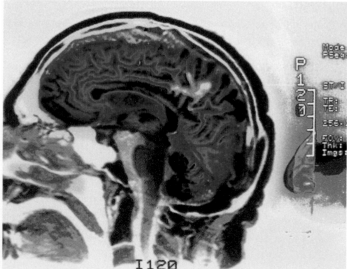

ticipants were instructed to use them to recall words from the initial list of 15. The third condition was a control. Word stems were presented and participants were instructed to complete them with the first words that came to mind, but now none of the stems were drawn from the words initially studied. The control condition, then, requires no memory. Participants performed all three of these conditions while their brains were being scanned.

Consider first what the brain is doing during the explicit-memory task. From the material presented in the first section of this chapter, we might expect that (1) the hippocampus is involved (remember, this structure is critical to the formation of long-term memories), and (2) most of the brain activity will be in the right hemisphere (because the task emphasized retrieval, and long-term retrieval involves mainly right-hemisphere processes). This is exactly what was found. More specifically, when the brain activity in the explicit-memory condition was compared to that in the control condition, there was increased activation in right-hemisphere hippocampal and frontal regions. Now consider the implicit-memory condition compared to the control condition; it showed *decreases* in activation rather than increases. That is, priming is reflected in less-than-usual neural activity, as if there has been a "greasing of the neural wheels" (see Figure 7-9). Implicit memory, then, has opposite neural consequences to those of explicit memory, which demonstrates a biological difference between the two kinds of memory. (This is the biological evidence for the explicit–implicit distinction that we alluded to in the first section of the chapter.)

How Can We Improve Memory?

Having considered the basics of working, long-term memory, and implicit memory, we are ready to tackle the question of improving memory. We will consider mainly explicit memory (partly because we are not sure what, other than sheer practice, can improve implicit memory). First we will consider how to increase the working memory span. Then we will turn to a variety of methods for improving long-term memory; these methods work by increasing the efficiency of encoding and retrieval.

Chunking and Memory Span

For most of us, the capacity of short-term memory cannot be increased beyond 7 ± 2 chunks. However, we can enlarge the size of a chunk and thereby increase the number of items in our memory span. To illustrate: Given the string 149-2177-620-01, we can recall all 12 digits if we recode the string into 1492-1776-2001 and store these three chunks in working memory. Although recoding digits into familiar dates works nicely in this example, it will not work with most digit strings because we have not memorized enough significant dates. But if a recoding system could be developed that worked with virtually *any* string, the memory span for numbers could be dramatically improved.

There is a study of a particular individual referred to as SF, who discovered such a general purpose recoding system and used it to increase his memory span from 7 to almost 80 random digits (see Figure 7-10). SF had

Figure 7-10

Number of Digits Recalled by SF SF greatly increased his memory span for digits by devising a recoding system using chunking and hierarchical organization. Total practice time was about 215 hours. (After Ericsson, Chase, & Faloon, 1980)

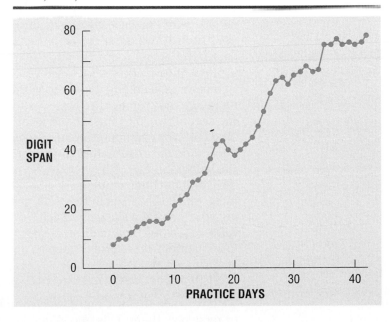

average memory abilities and intelligence for a college student. For a year and a half he engaged in a memory-span task for about 3 to 5 hours per week. During this extensive practice, SF, a good long-distance runner, devised the strategy of recoding sets of four digits into running times. For example, SF would recode 3492 as "3:49.2—world class time for the mile," which for him was a single chunk. Since SF was familiar with many running times (that is, he had them stored in long-term memory), he could readily chunk most sets of four digits. In cases in which he could not do so (for example, 1771 cannot be a running time because the third digit is too large), he tried to recode the four digits into either a familiar date or the age of some person or object.

Use of these recoding systems enabled SF to increase his memory span from 7 to 28 digits (because each of SF's seven chunks contains four digits). SF then increased his memory span to nearly 80 digits by hierarchically organizing the running times. Thus, one chunk in SF's short-term memory might have pointed to three running times; at the time of recall, SF would go from this chunk to the first running time and produce its four digits, then move to the second running time in the chunk and produce its digits, and so on. One chunk was therefore worth 12 digits. In this way SF achieved his remarkable span of nearly 80 digits. This feat was due to increasing the *size* of a chunk (by relating the items to information in long-term memory), not to increasing the *number* of chunks that working memory can hold. For when SF switched from digits to letters, his memory span went back to seven—that is, seven letters (Ericsson, Chase, & Faloon, 1980).

This research reflects psychologists' current interest in how to improve working memory. By contrast, there is a long history of research on how to improve long-term memory, the focus of the rest of this section. We will look first at how material can be encoded to make it easier to retrieve. Then we will consider how the act of retrieval itself can be improved.

Imagery and Encoding

We mentioned earlier that we can improve recall of unrelated items by adding meaningful connections between them at the time of encoding, for these connections will facilitate later retrieval. Mental images turn out to be particularly useful for connecting pairs of unrelated items, and for this reason imagery is the major ingredient in many **mnemonic systems,** or *systems for aiding memory.*

mnemonic systems
a system for aiding memory

One famous mnemonic system is the *method of loci* (*loci* is a Latin word meaning "places"). The method works especially well with an ordered sequence of arbitrary items, such as unrelated words. The first step is to commit to memory an ordered sequence of places—say, the locations you would come upon during a walk through your house. You enter through the front door into a hallway, then move to the bookcase in the living room, then to the television in the living room, then to the curtains at the window, and so on. Once you can easily take this mental walk, you are ready to memorize as many unrelated words as there are locations on your walk. You form an image that relates the first word to the first location, another image that relates the second word to the second location, and so on. If the words are items on a shopping list—for example, "bread," "eggs," "beer," "milk," and "bacon"—you might imagine a slice of bread nailed to your front door, an egg hanging from the light cord in the hallway, a can of beer in the bookcase, a milk commercial playing on your television, and curtains made from giant strips of bacon (see Figure 7-11). Once you have memorized the items in this way, you can easily recall them in order by simply taking your mental walk again. Each location will retrieve an image, and each image will retrieve a word. The method clearly works, and it is a favorite among those who perform memory feats professionally.

Elaboration and Encoding

We have seen that the more we elaborate items, the more we can subsequently recall or recognize them. This phenomenon occurs because the more connections we establish between items, the larger the number of retrieval possibilities. The practical implications of these findings are straightforward: If you want to remember a fact, expand on its meaning. To illustrate, suppose that you read a newspaper article about an epidemic in Brooklyn, New York, that health officials are trying to contain. To expand on this, you could ask yourself questions about the causes and consequences of the epidemic: Was the disease carried by a person or an animal? Was the disease transmitted through the water supply? To contain the epidemic, will officials go so far as to stop outsiders from visiting Brooklyn? How long is the epidemic likely to last? Questions about the causes and consequences of an event are particularly effective elaborations because each question sets up a meaningful connection, or retrieval path, to the event.

Context and Retrieval

Since context is a powerful retrieval cue, we can improve our memory by restoring the context in which the learning took place. If your psychology class always meets in a particular room, your recall of the lecture material may be better when you are in that room than when you are in a different building, because the context of the room serves as a retrieval cue for the lecture material. Most often, though, when we have to remember something we cannot physically return to the context in which we learned it. If you are having difficulty remembering the name of a particular high school classmate, you are not about to go back to your high school just to recall it. In such situations you can try to recreate the context mentally. To retrieve the long-forgotten name, you might think of different classes, clubs, and other activities in which you participated when you were in high school to see whether any of these bring to mind the name you are seeking. When participants in an experiment used these techniques, they were often able to recall the names of high school classmates whom they were sure they had forgotten (Williams & Hollan, 1981).

Figure 7-11

A Mnemonic System   The method of loci aids memory by associating items (here, entries on a shopping list) with an ordered sequence of places.

Organization

We know that organization during encoding improves subsequent retrieval. This principle can be put to great practical use: We are capable of storing and retrieving a massive amount of information if only we organize it.

Some experiments have investigated organizational devices that can be used to learn many unrelated items. In one study, participants memorized lists of unrelated words by organizing the words in each list into a story, as illustrated in Figure 7-12. Later, when tested on 12 such lists (a total of 120 words), participants recalled more than 90% of the words. Participants in a control group, who did not use an organizational strategy, recalled little more than 10% of the words! The performance of the participants in the experimental group appears to be a remarkable memory feat, but anyone armed with an organizational strategy can do it.

At this point you might concede that psychologists have devised some ingenious techniques for organizing lists of unrelated items.

Figure 7-12

Organizing Words Into a Story   Three examples in which a list of 10 unrelated words is turned into a story. The capitalized items are the words on the list. (After Bower & Clark, 1969)

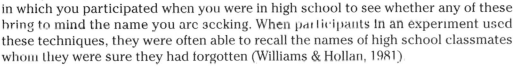

A LUMBERJACK DARTed out of a forest, SKATEd around a HEDGE past a COLONY of DUCKs. He tripped on some FURNITURE, tearing his STOCKING while hastening toward the PILLOW where his MISTRESS lay.

A VEGETABLE can be a useful INSTRUMENT for a COLLEGE student. A carrot can be a NAIL for your FENCE or BASIN. But a MERCHANT of the QUEEN would SCALE that fence and feed the carrot to a GOAT.

One night at DINNER I had the NERVE to bring my TEACHER. There had been a FLOOD that day, and the rain BARREL was sure to RATTLE. There was, however, a VESSEL in the HARBOR carrying this ARTIST to my CASTLE.

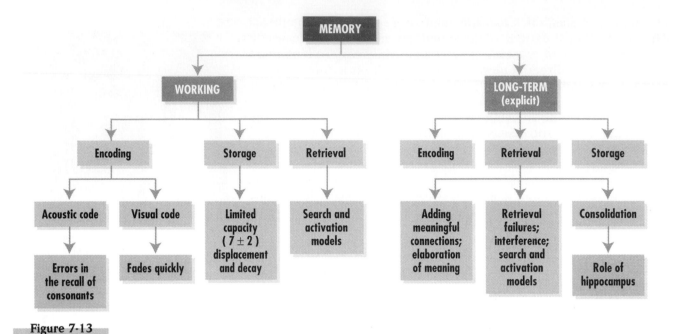

Figure 7-13

A Hierarchical Tree   Creating hierarchical trees of chapters in textbooks can help students retrieve information about those chapters. This tree represents the organization of part of this chapter.

But, you argue, what you have to remember are not lists of unrelated items but stories you have been told, lectures you have heard, and chapters you have read. Isn't this kind of material already organized, and doesn't this mean that the previously mentioned techniques are of limited value? Yes and no. Yes, this chapter is more than a list of unrelated sentences, but—and this is the critical point—there is always a problem of organization with any lengthy material intended to be read and remembered, including this chapter. Later you may be able to recall that elaborating meaning aids learning, but this may not bring to mind anything about, say, phonological coding in working memory. The two topics do not seem to be closely related, but there is a relationship between them: Both deal with encoding phenomena. The best way to see that relationship is to note the headings and subheadings in the chapter, because these show how the material in the chapter is organized.

A most effective way to study is to keep this organization in mind. You might, for example, try to capture part of the organization of this chapter by sketching a hierarchical tree like the one shown in Figure 7-13. Then you can use the hierarchy to guide your memory search whenever you have to retrieve information about this chapter. It may be even more helpful, though, to make your own hierarchical outline of the chapter.

Practicing Retrieval

Another way to improve retrieval is to practice it—that is, to ask yourself questions about what you are trying to learn. Suppose that you have 2 hours in which to study an assignment that can be read in approximately 30 minutes. Reading and rereading the assignment four times is generally less effective than reading it once and asking yourself questions about it. You can then reread selected parts to clear up points that were difficult to retrieve the first time around, perhaps elaborating these points so that they become particularly well connected to each other and to the rest of the assignment. Attempting retrieval is an efficient use of study time. This was demonstrated long ago by experiments using material like that actually learned in courses (see Figure 7-14).

A procedure akin to practicing retrieval may be useful in implicit memory situations. This procedure, referred to as **mental practice,** involves *the imagined rehearsal of a perceptual–motor skill in the absence of any gross body movements.* For example, you might imagine yourself swinging at a tennis ball, making mental corrections when the imagined swing seems faulty, without really moving your arm. Such mental practice can improve performance of the skill, particularly if the mental practice is alternated with physical practice (Swets & Bjork, 1990).

mental practice   the imagined rehearsal of a perceptual–motor skill in the absence of any gross body movements

The PQRST Method

Thus far we have considered particular principles of memory and their implications for improving memory. However, we can also proceed in the opposite direction: We can start with a well-known technique for improving memory and show how it is based on principles of memory.

One of the best-known techniques for improving memory is the PQRST method, which is intended to improve a student's ability to study and remember material presented in a textbook (Thomas & Robinson, 1982). The method takes its name from the first letters of its five stages. *Preview, Question, Read, Self-Recitation,* and *Test.* We can illustrate the method by showing how it would apply to studying a chapter in this textbook. In the first stage (Preview), students survey the material in a chapter to get an idea of its major topics and sections. Previewing involves reading the outline at the beginning of the chapter, skimming the chapter while paying special attention to the headings of main sections and subsections, and carefully reading the summary at the end of the chapter. This kind of preview induces students to organize the material in the chapter, perhaps even leading to the rudiments of a hierarchical organization like that shown a little earlier, in Figure 7-13. As we have repeatedly noted, organizing material increases the ability to retrieve it.

The second, third, and fourth stages (Question, Read, and Self-Recitation) apply to each major section of the chapter. In this book, for example, a chapter typically has five to eight major sections, and students would apply the Question, Read, and Self-Recitation stages to each section before going on to the next one. In the Question stage, students carefully read the section and subsection headings and turn these into questions. In the Read stage, students read the section with an eye toward answering these questions. And in the Self-Recitation stage, the reader tries to recall the main ideas in the section and recites the information. For example, if you were applying the method to this section, you might look at the headings and make up questions such as "How much can the memory span be increased?" or "What exactly is the PQRST method?" Next you would read the section and try to answer your questions (for example, "One person was able to increase his memory span to nearly 80 digits"). Then you would try to recall the main ideas (for example, "You can increase the size of a chunk but not the number of chunks"). The Question and Read stages induce students to elaborate the material while encoding it; the Self-Recitation stage induces students to practice retrieval.

The fifth, or Test, stage occurs after an entire chapter has been read. Students try to

Figure 7-14

Practicing Retrieval   Recall can be improved by spending a large proportion of study time attempting retrieval rather than silently studying. Results are shown for tests given immediately and four hours after completing study. (After Gates, 1917)

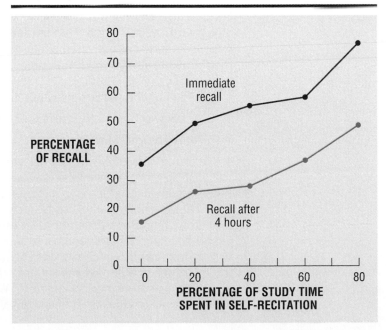

recall the main facts and to understand how they relate to one another. This stage induces elaboration and offers further practice at retrieval.

In summary, the PQRST method relies on three basic principles for improving memory: organizing the material, elaborating the material, and practicing retrieval. (For a more in-depth description of the method, see "A Word to the Student" at the beginning of this text.)

<hr>

Thinking Critically

On the basis of what you have learned about explicit long-term memory and ways to improve it, how would you study for an exam that emphasizes factual recall?

In What Ways Is Memory Constructed?

In previous chapters we distinguished between bottom-up and top-down processes; bottom-up processes are driven by input, whereas top-down processes are driven by prior knowledge and expectancies. This distinction can be applied to memory as well. Bottom-up processes work only on the input information—that is, the actual items that have to be remembered—while top-down processes bring other knowledge to bear on the task. Most of the material we have covered in this chapter deals with bottom-up processes. In this final section we consider **constructive memory,** in which *top-down processes add information to the input in creating a memory.*

constructive memory a condition in which top-down processes add information to the input in creating a memory

When we hear a sentence or story, we often take it as an incomplete description of a real event, and we use our general knowledge about how the world works to construct a more detailed description of the event. How do we do this? By adding to the input sentences statements that are likely to follow from them. For example, on hearing "Mike broke the bottle in a barroom brawl," we are likely to infer that it was a beer or whiskey bottle, not a milk or soda bottle. We add this inference to our memory of the sentence itself. Our total memory therefore goes beyond the original information given. We fill in gaps in the original information by using our general knowledge about what goes with what. We do this because we are trying to explain to ourselves the events we are hearing about. Constructive memory, then, is a by-product of our need to understand the world. Many, if not most, real-life memory situations are constructive ones.

Simple Inferences

Often when we read a sentence we draw inferences from it and store the inferences along with the sentence. This tendency is particularly strong when reading real text because inferences are often needed to connect different lines. To illustrate, consider the following story, which was presented to participants in an experiment:

1. Provo is a picturesque kingdom in France.
2. Corman was heir to the throne of Provo.
3. He was so tired of waiting.
4. He thought arsenic would work well.

When reading this story, participants draw inferences at certain points. At line 3, they infer that Corman wanted to be king, which permits them to connect line 3 to the preceding line. But this is not a necessary inference (Corman could have been waiting for the king to receive him). At line 4, participants infer that Corman had decided to poison the king, which permits them to connect this line to what preceded it. Again, the inference is not a necessary one (there are people other than the king to poison, and there are other uses of arsenic). When participants' memories were later tested for exactly which lines had been presented, they had trouble distinguishing the story lines from the inferences we just described. It is hard to keep what was actually presented separate from what we added to it (Seifert, Robertson, & Black, 1985).

Inferences can also affect memory of visual scenes. This point is strikingly illustrated in the following study. Participants were shown a film of a traffic accident and then were asked questions about their memory of the accident. One question was asked in two different ways. Some participants were asked, "How fast were the cars going when they smashed into each other?" whereas others were asked, "How fast were the cars going when they hit each other?" Participants who were asked the "smashed" question might infer that the accident was a very destructive one, perhaps more destructive than they had actually remembered. These participants were likely to use this inference to alter their memory of the accident to make it more destructive (see Figure 7-15). Participants who were asked the "hit" question, however, should be less likely to do this, since "hit" implies a less severe accident than does "smashed."

This line of reasoning was supported by the results of a memory test given a week later. In this test, participants were asked, "Did you see any broken glass?" There was no broken glass in the film of the accident, but participants who had been asked the "smashed" question were more likely to say that there had been glass than were participants who had been asked the "hit" question. The "smashed" question may have led to a reconstruction of the memory of the accident, and the reconstructed memory contained details, such as broken glass, that were never actually part of the accident (Loftus, Schooler, & Wagenaar, 1985). These results have important implications for eyewitness identification. A question phrased in a particular way ("smashed" rather than "hit") can alter the memory structures that an attorney is trying to probe.

Figure 7-15

Reconstructing a Memory of an Accident The picture at the top represents the subject's original memory of the accident. Then comes the "smashed" question, which leads the subject to draw inferences about the destructiveness of the accident. These inferences may be used to reconstruct the original memory so that it looks more like the picture on the bottom. (After Loftus & Loftus, 1975)

The Influence of Stereotypes

Another means by which we fill in, or construct memories is through the use of social stereotypes. A *stereotype* is a set of inferences about the personality traits or physical attributes of a whole class of people. We may, for example, have a stereotype of the typical German (intelligent, meticulous, serious) or of the typical Italian (artistic, carefree, fun-loving). These descriptions rarely apply to many people in the class and can often be misleading guides for social interaction. Our concern here, however, is not with the effects of stereotypes on social interaction (see Chapter 14 for a discussion of this) but with the effects of stereotypes on memory.

When presented with information about a person, we sometimes stereotype that person (for example, "He's your typical Italian") and then combine the input information with the information in our stereotype. Our memory of the person thus is partly constructed from the stereotype. To the extent that our stereotype does not fit the person, our recall can be seriously distorted. A British psychologist provides a firsthand account of such a distortion:

> In the week beginning 23 October, I encountered in the university, a male student of very conspicuously Scandinavian appearance. I recall being very forcibly impressed by the man's nordic, Viking-like appearance—his fair hair, his blue eyes, and long bones. On several occasions, I recalled his appearance in connection with a Scandinavian correspondence I was then conducting and thought of him as the "perfect Viking," visualizing him at the helm of a longship crossing the North Sea in quest of adventure. When I again saw the

man on 23 November, I did not recognize him, and he had to introduce himself. It was not that I had forgotten what he looked like but that his appearance, as I recalled it, had become grossly distorted. He was very different from my recollection of him. His hair was darker, his eyes less blue, his build less muscular, and he was wearing spectacles (as he always does). (Hunter, 1974, pp. 265–266)

Hunter's stereotype of Scandinavians seems to have so overwhelmed any information he actually encoded about the student's appearance that the result was a highly constructed memory. It bore so little resemblance to the student that it could not even serve as a basis for recognition.

The Influence of Schemas

schema a mental representation of a class of people, objects, events, or situations

Psychologists use the term **schema** to refer to *a mental representation of a class of people, objects, events, or situations*. Stereotypes are a kind of schema because they represent classes of people. Schemas can also be used to describe our knowledge about how to act in certain situations. For example, most adults have a schema for how to eat in a restaurant (enter the restaurant, find a table, get a menu from the waiter, order food, and so on). Perceiving and thinking in terms of schemas permits us to process large amounts of information swiftly and economically. Instead of having to perceive and remember all the details of each new person, object, or event we encounter, we can simply note that it is like a schema already in our memory and encode and remember only its most distinctive features. The price we pay for such "cognitive economy," however, is that an object or event can be distorted if the schema used to encode it does not fit well.

Bartlett (1932) was perhaps the first psychologist to study the effect of schemas on memory in a systematic fashion. He suggested that memory distortions can occur when we attempt to fit stories into schemas. Research has confirmed Bartlett's suggestion. For example, after reading a brief story about a character going to a restaurant, participants are likely to recall statements about the character eating and paying for a meal, even when those actions were never mentioned in the story (Bower, Black, & Turner, 1979).

Recovered Memories or Constructed Memories?

The findings about constructive memory, particularly studies like the "hit" versus "smashed" one, have important implications for a controversy involving reports of sexual abuse. In recent decades there have been numerous cases in which an adult claims to have recovered a previously forgotten—that is, repressed—memory of sexual abuse during childhood, the recovery often occurring in the context of therapy or a therapy-like situation. In some of these cases the person who has supposedly recovered the memory takes legal action against the alleged perpetrators (often the person's parents). These emotionally charged cases have attracted intense media coverage. The controversy arises because some professionals are convinced that the memories are authentic whereas others are convinced that they are false.

To make the controversy concrete, consider a variant of an actual case (described in Loftus, 1993). A woman in her late twenties began having recollections of being sexually abused by her father when she was between

SPECIAL REPORT

Tragic Delusions

How "recovered" memories tear families apart

Some have argued that the events described in "recovered memories" never really occurred, and that the accusations based on such "memories" can destroy families.

the ages of 5 and 8. She claimed that because of the trauma of that experience, her memories had been repressed for 20 years and were brought out only by counseling and therapy. She then sued her father for damages. Since the father vehemently denied the allegations, and since there were no witnesses to the abuse and no physical evidence of it, everything hinged on whether a jury would believe that the woman's memory was authentic.

Experts, as well as jurors, might have difficulty determining whether the woman's memory was authentic. There are reasons for taking her charges very seriously. For one thing, there is independent evidence that, regrettably, sexual abuse of children is relatively common in our society (Daro, 1988). In addition, there are many clinical reports of repression of traumatic events (Mack, 1980). But these considerations would not be decisive if the woman did not appear totally sincere in her allegations. Subjective impressions about a witness's honesty are critical because for many people, including professionals, if someone is not reporting a true memory, that person is lying.

This is where research on constructive memory comes in. These studies show there is an alternative to either reporting a true memory or intentionally lying—namely, that the person may be reporting a reconstructed memory. Earlier we described an experiment in which participants were led to believe that an accident they had witnessed was more serious than it initially appeared, and as a result the participants apparently embellished their memories of the accident to include some broken glass that was never there. When these participants later recalled the presence of broken glass, they were not reporting something that had actually happened, nor were they lying; they were reporting from a memory representation that was reconstructed rather than being an accurate record of the events. In the same way, the woman in our story may be sincerely and truthfully reporting the contents of her memory representations, but these representations may be based on a reconstruction of the past, one that is *not* an accurate record of the events that actually occurred.

What kinds of external influences would lead someone to reconstruct memories of childhood so as to include abuse? A major possibility stems from the fact that many of the cases involve people who are in therapy. Some therapists may unwittingly suggest that the client was abused in childhood, and then lead the client to elaborate this reconstructed abuse (Ganaway, 1989; Loftus, 1993). One therapist makes the following recommendation: "When the client does not remember what happened to her, the therapist's encouragement to 'guess' or 'tell a story' will help the survivor regain access to the lost material" (Olio, 1989, p. 6). And a well-known self-help book tells its readers: "To say 'I was abused,' you do not need the kind of recall that would stand up in a court of law. Often the knowledge that you were abused starts with a tiny feeling, an intuition. Assume your feelings are valid" (Bass & Davis, 1988, p. 22). These kinds of suggestions, though well intentioned, may be the stuff that reconstructed memories are made of. Moreover, some therapists may encourage the person who supposedly was abused to try to visualize the details of the episode. Even if we have not been abused, we may be able to visualize and feel what it would be like to have

Allegations of sexual abuse based on recovered memories can lead to court cases.

An Herbal Remedy for Memory Loss?

It has been called "the elixir of youth" and "memory mate." It has been found effective by both ancient healers and modern scientists. These days it is receiving a great deal of attention in the medical journals as well as the popular press.

This much-heralded substance is an extract from the ginkgo tree, an ornamental tree that has survived for more than 250 million years and is frequently planted as a shade tree along city streets. The Chinese have used ginkgo nuts for thousands of years to increase sexual energy and as a remedy for diseases ranging from venereal disease to cancer. Modern medical researchers have found evidence that ginkgo extract can be effective in treating a variety of ailments, including asthma, depression, impotence, and retinal damage. Perhaps most significant is the potential of gingko for the treatment of memory loss due to Alzheimer's disease, multi-infarct dementia (mini-strokes), and normal aging.

Much of the research on the health benefits of gingko extract has been conducted in Europe, where herbal medicine is more accepted than in the United States. Laboratory studies have found that gingko extract improves brain functioning and prevents or treats circulatory disorders such as stroke. These benefits stem largely from ginkgo's effects on the blood: It thins blood viscosity and lowers platelet adhesiveness, thereby increasing blood flow to the brain and extremities; it also regulates blood vessel elasticity. Because of these effects, it can counteract some of the most common conditions associated with aging, particularly decreased blood flow to the brain, which can adversely affect memory, concentration, and intellectual ability.

Laboratory studies of the effects of ginkgo extract on memory are usually set up as double-blind studies in which some participants receive ginkgo extract while others receive a placebo. The results have shown small but significant positive effects of ginkgo extract on short-term memory, degenerative dementia of the Alzheimer type, and multi-infarct dementia. One group of researchers concluded that ginkgo "was safe and appears capable of stabilizing and, in a substantial number of cases, improving the cognitive performance and the social functioning of demented patients for 6 months to 1 year" (Le Bars et al., 1997, p. 1327).

Some experts warn against excessive enthusiasm for ginkgo extract. They note that it is beneficial in the *early* treatment of Alzheimer's disease and that it can cure dementia only when the condition is caused by lack of blood flow to the brain. Claims that ginkgo extract is an "elixir of youth" are clearly overstated. Others note that ginkgo extract has not been subjected to extensive clinical trials nor has it received approval from the Food and Drug Administration. Nevertheless, the evidence from controlled research lends support to the ancient Chinese belief that ginkgo use can enhance health and longevity.

---

such an experience. Subsequently we may find it difficult to distinguish between what we imagined and what actually occurred, as has repeatedly been shown in experimental studies (Johnson, 1990).

It is quite a stretch, though, from laboratory studies of memories about relatively mundane events, such as broken glass in an automobile accident, to the kinds of traumatic memories that are at stake in allegations of sexual abuse. What we need are convincing studies that reconstruction goes on even when the events involved are significant. Such experiments are beginning to appear. In one study, a teenager is convinced by trusted family members that he was lost in a shopping mall when he was 5, an event that in fact never happened. Days after this brainwashing, the teenager starts recounting facts and feelings about the episode that were not even mentioned in the family members' account! He is embellishing a suggestion, thereby constructing a vivid memory of an event that never occurred (Loftus & Coan, 1994). Other studies suggest that younger children are particularly susceptible to the implantation of false memories (Ceci et al., 1981). The upshot, then, is that "recovered" memories of traumatic events may sometimes be reconstructions, induced in part by others' suggestions and embellished by one's own top-down processes.

We note in closing that progress in the study of memory has been made possible by dividing the field into manageable units—such as encoding in working memory or retrieval from explicit long-term memory—and that these divisions rest on the interplay of psychological and biological approaches. We have used three basic distinctions to structure this chapter—three stages of memory, working memory versus long-term memory, and explicit versus implicit memory—and in each case we have supplied biological as well as psychological (cognitive) evidence. Interestingly, in all three cases the psychological evidence was obtained first and used to direct the subsequent biological work. Thus the cognitive distinction between working memory and long-term memory was made clearly in papers published years ago, yet it is only relatively recently that biologically oriented researchers have been able to demonstrate some of the neural bases for this key distinction.

Showing us how to divide up the field of memory is by no means the only contribution of biological research. Increasingly, researchers are determining the neural bases of various kinds of memories. For example, we now know something about the biological basis of storage in explicit, long-term memory (specifically, the role of the hippocampal system) and about storage in visual and verbal buffers of short-term memory. Such knowledge is not only useful in its own right but may also prove helpful in combating the ravages of memory brought about by diseases of aging such as stroke, senility, and Alzheimer's disease.

We discussed several studies suggesting that false memories can be implanted in anyone. Do you think these studies offer critical evidence regarding the controversy over recovery of repressed memories? Try to defend your position in detail.

Thinking Critically

Summary

1. There are three stages of memory: encoding, storage, and retrieval. *Encoding* refers to the transformation of information into the kind of code or representation that memory can accept; *storage* is the retention of the encoded information; and *retrieval* refers to the process by which information is recovered from memory. The three stages may operate differently in situations that require us to store material for a matter of seconds *(working memory)* and in situations that require us to store material for longer intervals *(long-term memory)*. Moreover, different long-term memory systems seem to be involved in storing facts, which are part of *explicit memory,* versus skills, which are part of *implicit memory.*

2. There is biological evidence for these distinctions. Brain-scanning studies of long-term memory indicate that most of the brain regions activated during encoding are in the left hemisphere and that most of the regions activated during retrieval are in the right hemisphere. Evidence from both animal studies and studies of humans with brain damage indicates that different regions of the brain may control working memory and long-term memory. In particular, in both humans and other mammals, damage to the hippocampal system impairs performance on long-term memory tasks but not on working-memory tasks.

3. Information in working memory tends to be encoded phonologically, although we can also use a visual code. The most striking fact about working memory is that its storage capacity is limited to 7 ± 2 items, or chunks. While we are limited in the number of chunks we can store, we can increase the size of a chunk by using information in long-term memory to recode incoming material into larger meaningful units. Information can be lost from working memory because of either decay with time or displacement by new items. Retrieval slows down as the number of items in working memory increases.

4. Working memory seems to serve as a mental "work space" that is used in solving various kinds of problems, such as mental arithmetic, geometric analogies, and answering questions about text. The larger one's working memory, the better one does in solving problems.

5. Information in long-term memory is usually encoded according to its meaning. If the items to be remembered are meaningful but the connections between them are not, memory can be improved by adding meaningful connections that provide retrieval paths. Memory can also be improved by organizing the information during encoding. In addition, the context in which encoding occurs has an effect on subsequent memory: Subsequent recall will be better when the same context is established during retrieval.

6. Many cases of forgetting in long-term memory are due to retrieval failures (the information is there but cannot be found). Retrieval failures are more likely to occur when there is *interference* from items associated with the same *retrieval cue.* Such interference effects suggest that retrieval from long-term memory may be accomplished by a search process or by a spreading activation process.

7. Some forgetting from long-term memory is due to losses from storage, particularly when there is a disruption of the processes that consolidate new memories. The biological locus of consolidation includes the hippocampus, a brain structure located below the cerebral cortex, and the surrounding cortex. Recent research suggests that consolidation takes a few weeks.

8. Emotional factors affect long-term memory in at least five ways: (1) *Rehearsing* and thinking about emotionally charged events can facilitate their later recall; (2) some emotional events can lead to *flashbulb memories,* which result in very accurate recall of the event; (3) when the emotion experienced during an event is present again during retrieval, memory will be improved; (4) anxious thoughts at the time of retrieval can interfere with retrieval; and (5) particularly traumatic memories can be actively blocked (repression hypothesis).

9. *Explicit memory* refers to the kind of memory that is manifested in recall or recognition, in which we consciously recollect the past; *implicit memory* refers to the kind of memory that manifests itself as an improvement on some perceptual, motor, or cognitive task, with no conscious recollection of the experiences that led to the improvement. While explicit memory—particularly recall and recognition of facts—breaks down in *amnesia,* implicit memory is usually spared. This suggests that there may be separate storage systems for explicit and implicit memory. Brain-scanning studies with normal individuals support this suggestion. They show that explicit memory is accompanied by increased neural activity in certain regions, whereas implicit memory is accompanied by a decrease in neural activity in critical regions.

10. Although we cannot increase the capacity of working memory, we can use recoding schemes to enlarge the size of a chunk and thereby increase the *memory span.* Long-term memory for facts can be improved at the encoding and retrieval stages. One way to improve encoding and retrieval is to use imagery, which is the basic principle underlying *mnemonic systems* like the method of loci. Other ways to improve encoding (and subsequent retrieval) are to elaborate the meaning of the items and to organize the material during encoding. The best ways to improve retrieval are to attempt to reestablish the encoding context at the time of retrieval and to practice retrieving information while learning it. Most of these principles for improving encoding and retrieval are incorporated into the PQRST

method of studying a textbook; the five stages of this method are Preview, Question, Read, Self-Recitation, and Test.

11. Memory for complex materials, such as stories, is often *constructive* in that we use our general knowledge of the world to construct a more elaborate memory of a story or event. Construction can involve adding simple inferences to the material presented; it can also involve fitting the material into stereotypes and other kinds of *schemas* (mental representations of classes of people, objects, events, or situations). Some cases of supposedly "recovered" memories of traumatic events may actually involve constructions induced by suggestions made by therapists and others.

Suggested Readings

There are several introductory books on memory and cognition that are readable and informative: Baddeley, *Human Memory* (1990); Anderson, *Cognitive Psychology and Its Implications* (4th ed., 1995); Barsalou, *Cognitive Psychology for Cognitive Scientists* (1992); Medin and Ross, *Cognitive Psychology* (2nd ed., 1996); Haberlandt, *Cognitive Psychology* (1993); and Best, *Cognitive Psychology* (1992). In addition to these textbooks, Neisser (ed.), *Memory Observed* (1982), provides a survey of remembering in natural contexts.

For an advanced treatment of theoretical issues in memory, see Anderson, *Rules of the Mind* (1993); Tulving, *Elements of Episodic Memory* (1983); the second volume of Atkinson, Herrnstein, Lindzey, and Luce (eds.), *Stevens' Handbook of Experimental Psychology* (2nd ed., 1988); and Baddeley, *Working Memory* (1986).

For a review of research on the biological bases of memory and learning, see Squire and Butters (eds.), *The Neuropsychology of Memory* (1984); Squire, *Memory and Brain* (1987); Cohen and Eichenbaum, *Memory, Amnesia, and the Hippocampal System* (1993); and Fuster, *Memory in the Cerebral Cortex* (1995).

For a review that combines biological and cognitive work in a readable fashion, see Schacter, *Searching for Memory* (1996).

Enhance and Explore

To enhance your understanding of the psychological concepts found in this chapter, please consult the following aids:

Study Guide

Learning Objectives, p. 130
Define the Terms, p. 133
Test Your Knowledge, p. 136
Essay Questions, p. 139
Thinking Independently, p. 141

PowerPsych CD-ROM

WHAT IS THE NATURE OF WORKING MEMORY?
Testing Your Short-Term Memory

HOW CAN WE IMPROVE MEMORY?
Using Mnemonics

PsychCentral

For more information concerning the topics found in this chapter, access psychology links on the Word Wide Web made through the Harcourt Web page at:
http://www.harcourtcollege.com/psych/Fundamentals

www.harcourtcollege.com

http://www.harcourtcollege.com/psych/index.html

Thought and Language

CHAPTER 8

You're in a math class, and the professor has just asked you to determine the probability that two people in your class have exactly the same birthday.

You're walking to class and daydreaming about what you're going to say to someone you've been having a rough time with.

You're planning dinner for tonight, and trying to figure out exactly what you need to pick up at the grocery store on your way home.

In all of these cases you are engaged in some form of thought. Thinking includes a wide range of mental activities, running from the mundane to the creative. At its best, thinking has led to the greatest accomplishments of our species.

There is more than one way to think. One mode of thought corresponds to the stream of sentences that we "hear in our mind"; we refer to this as *symbolic thought* (it's not quite language, but it's close). Another mode corresponds to images, particularly visual ones, that we can "see" in our mind; this is *imaginal thought*. We will consider both modes of thought in this chapter, emphasizing the symbolic mode because we know more about it.

In the first section of the chapter, we will focus on *concepts*, which have both perceptual and symbolic components and are the building blocks of thought. We will emphasize the use of concepts in classifying objects; this is the study of *concepts and categorization*. Then we will consider some fundamental thinking processes, including some that seem to be symbolic, such as evaluating arguments or hypotheses, and some that involve imagery, such as rotating objects in our mind. Next we move to more complex cases of thinking, which may mix symbolic and imaginal modes in order to solve a problem; this is the study of *problem solving*. In the final two sections we will consider how thoughts are explicitly communicated, which is the study of *language*, and how such communication develops, which is the study of *language acquisition*.

How Do Concepts Help Us Divide Up the World?

Many symbolic thoughts express a factual claim. "Mothers are hard workers" is one such thought. "Cats are animals" is another. It is easy to see that such a thought con-

Students locked in thought, either while studying or walking to class.

sists of concepts—such as "mothers" and "hard workers" or "cat" and "animal"—that have been combined in a particular way. To understand thought, therefore, we need to understand the concepts that compose it.

Functions of Concepts

A **concept** represents an entire class—it is *the set of properties that we associate with the class.* The concept of "cat" for example, includes, among other things, the properties of having four legs and whiskers. Concepts serve some major functions in mental life. They divide the world into manageable units (this is referred to as *cognitive economy*). The world is full of so many different objects that if we treated each one as distinct we would soon be overwhelmed. If we had to refer to every single object we encountered by a different name, our vocabulary would have to be gigantic—so immense that communication might be impossible. (Think of what it would be like if we had a separate name for each of the 7 million colors among which we can discriminate!) Fortunately, we do not treat each object as unique; rather, we see it as an instance of a concept. Thus, many different objects are seen as instances of the concept "cat," many others as instances of the concept "chair," and so on. By treating different objects as members of the same concept, we reduce the complexity of the world that we have to represent mentally.

Assigning an object to a concept is called **categorization.** When we categorize an object, we treat it as if it has many of the properties associated with the concept, including properties that we have not directly perceived. Hence a second major function of concepts is that they allow us to predict information that we cannot readily perceive. For example, our concept of "apple" is associated with such hard-to-perceive properties as having seeds and being edible, as well as with visible properties like being round, having a distinctive color, and being found on trees. We may use the visible properties to categorize some object as an "apple" (the object is red, round, and hangs from a tree), and then infer that the object has the less visible properties as well (it has seeds and is edible). Concepts and categorization, then, enable us to go beyond the information given (Bruner, 1957).

If it's the right color and shape, and it grows on a tree, we categorize it as an apple.

concept the set of properties that we associate with a class

categorization assigning an object to a concept

Prototypes for Concepts

There seem to be two parts to a concept. One part is the **prototype,** which describes *the best examples of the concept.* In the concept "bachelor," for example, your prototype might include such properties as a man who is in his thirties, lives alone, and has an active social life. The prototype is what usually comes to mind when we think of the concept. But while the prototype properties may be true of the typical examples of a bachelor, they are clearly not true of all instances (think of an uncle in his sixties who boards with his sister and rarely goes out). This means that a concept must contain something in addition to a prototype; this additional something is a **core,** which includes *the properties that are most important for defining the concept.* Your core of the concept "bachelor" would probably include

prototype the best example of a concept

core the properties that are most important for defining a concept

Table 8-1

Different Kinds of Concepts

Well-Defined Concepts (e.g., "bachelor")	Fuzzy Concepts (e.g., "bird")
Determine core properties	Determine similarity to prototype

the properties of being adult, male, and unmarried; these properties are essential for being a member of the concept (Armstrong, Gleitman, & Gleitman, 1983).

As another example, consider the concept "bird." Your prototype likely includes the properties of flying and chirping—which works for the best examples of "bird," such as robins and blue jays, but not for other examples, such as ostriches and penguins. Your core would likely specify something about the biology of birds—that being a bird involves having certain genes, or at least having parents that are birds.

Note that in both our examples—"bachelor" and "bird"—the prototypes are salient but not reliable indicators of concept membership, whereas the cores are more defining of concept membership. However, there is an important difference between a concept like "bachelor" and a concept like "bird." The core of "bachelor" is a real definition and can be easily applied. Thus, anyone who is adult, male, and unmarried must be a "bachelor," and it is relatively easy to determine whether someone has these defining properties. Concepts like this are said to be *well defined* (see Table 8-1). Categorizing a person or object into a well-defined category involves determining whether it has the core or defining properties. In contrast, the core of "bird" is hardly a definition—we may know only that genes are involved, for example—and the core properties are hidden from view. Thus, if we happen upon a small animal, all we can do is check whether it does certain things, such as fly and chirp, and use this information to decide whether it is a bird. Concepts like "bird" are referred to as *fuzzy* (refer again to Table 8-1). Deciding whether an object is an instance of a fuzzy concept often involves determining its similarity to the concept's prototype (Smith, 1989). It is important to note that most natural concepts seem to be fuzzy—they lack true definitions, and their categorization relies heavily on prototypes.

Some instances of fuzzy concepts will have more prototype properties than other instances. Among birds, for example, a robin will have the property of flying whereas an ostrich will not. The more prototype properties an instance has, the more typical of the concept it is considered to be. Thus, in the case of "bird," most people rate a robin as more typical than an ostrich; in the case of "apple," they rate red apples as more typical than green ones (since red seems to be part of the prototype for "apple"); and so on.

Do flying and chirping make a bird? Your prototype for "bird" probably includes these features; however, they do not apply to certain kinds of birds, such as penguins and ostriches.

The *typicality* of an instance has a major effect on its categorization. When people are asked whether or not a pictured animal is a "bird," a robin produces an immediate "yes," whereas a chicken requires a longer decision time. When young children are asked the same question, a robin is almost invariably classified correctly, whereas often a chicken is declared a nonbird. Typicality also determines

Typical and atypical red color patches.

what we think of when we encounter the name of the concept. Hearing the sentence "There is a bird outside your window," we are far more likely to think of a robin than a vulture, and what comes to mind will obviously influence what we make of the sentence (Rosch, 1978).

Universality of Prototypes   Are our prototypes determined mainly by our culture, or are they universal? For some concepts, such as "bachelor," culture clearly has a big impact on the prototype. But for other more natural concepts, prototypes are surprisingly universal.

Consider color concepts, such as "red." This is a fuzzy concept (no layperson knows its defining properties) and one with a clear prototype: People in our culture agree in choosing which hues are typical reds and which are atypical. People in other cultures agree with our choices. Remarkably, this agreement is found even among people whose language does not include a word for "red." When speakers of these languages are asked to pick the best example from an array of red hues, they make the same choice we would. Even though the range of hues for what they would call "red" may differ from ours, their idea of a *typical* red is the same as ours (Berlin & Kay, 1969).

Further research suggests that the Dani (a New Guinea people), whose language has terms only for black and white, perceive color variations in exactly the same way as English-speaking people who have terms for many colors. Dani participants were given a set of red color patches to remember; the patches varied in how typical they were of "red." Later the participants were presented with a set of color patches and asked to decide which ones they had seen before. Even though they had no word for "red," they recognized more typical red colors better than less typical ones. This is exactly what American participants do (Rosch, 1974). Color prototypes, then, seem to be universal.

More recent experiments suggest that prototypes for animal concepts may also be universal. The experiments compared U.S. students and members of the Maya Itza, a culture in the Guatemala rain forest that is relatively insulated from Western influences. The U.S. participants were from southeastern Michigan, which happens to have a number of mammalian species that are comparable to those found in the Guatemala rain forest. Both groups of participants were presented with the names of these comparable species. They were asked first to group them into sets that go together, then to group these sets into higher-order groups that were related, and so on until all the species were in one group (corresponding to "mammals"). These groupings were determined by the similarity of the prototypes involved—in the first pass, participants would group together only species that seemed very similar. By making these groupings, each participant creates a kind of tree, with the initial groupings at the bottom and "mammal" at the top; this tree reflects the taxonomy of animals.

The trees or taxonomies created by the Maya Itza were quite similar to those created by the U.S. students. In fact, the correlation between the average Itza and average U.S. tree was about .6. Moreover, both the Itza and U.S. taxonomies were highly correlated with the true scientific taxonomy. Apparently, all people base their prototypes of animals on properties that they can easily observe (overall shape or distinctive features like a bushy tail, movement pattern, or coloring). These same properties are indicators of the evolutionary history of the species, which is what the scientific taxonomy is based on (Lopez et al., 1997).

Processes of Categorization

Categorization decisions are ubiquitous: We categorize every time we recognize an object (as discussed in Chapter 4), every time we diagnose a problem (e.g., "That's a power failure"), and so on. How do we use our concepts to categorize the world? As already noted, the answer depends on whether the concept is well defined or fuzzy.

For well-defined concepts like "bachelor" or "grandmother," we may sometimes determine how similar the person of interest is to our prototype ("She's sixtyish and has white hair, so she looks like a grandmother"); but if we are trying to be accurate, we can determine whether the person has the defining properties of the concept ("Is she the female parent of a parent?"). The latter amounts to applying a rule—"If she's the female parent of a parent, she's a grandmother." There have been many studies of rule-based categorization of well-defined concepts, and they show that the more properties there are in the rule, the more error-prone and slower the categorization process is (Bourne, 1966). This may be caused by the properties being processed one at a time.

For fuzzy concepts like "bird" and "chair," we do not know enough defining properties to use rule-based categorization, so we rely on *similarity* instead. As already mentioned, one thing we may do is determine the similarity of the object of interest to the prototype of the concept ("Is this object similar enough to my prototype to call it a chair?"). What is the evidence that people categorize objects in this fashion? The evidence involves three steps (Smith, 1995):

 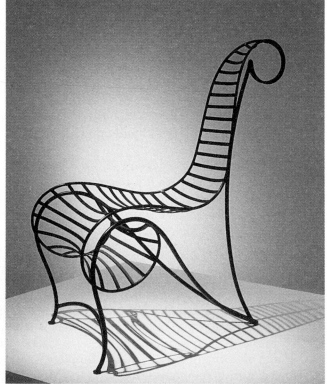

The chair on the left is a typical one, that on the right is atypical. Children learn to categorize the typical one first, and adults categorize the typical faster.

1. First the researcher determines the properties of a concept's prototype and of various instances of that concept (the researcher might ask one group of participants to describe the properties of their prototypical chair and of various pictures of chairs).

2. Then the researcher determines the similarity between each instance (each pictured chair) and the prototype by determining their shared properties; this provides a *similarity-to-prototype* score for each instance.

3. Finally the researcher shows that the similarity-to-prototype score is highly correlated with how accurately and quickly participants can correctly categorize that instance. This shows that similarity to prototype plays a role in categorization.

There is another kind of similarity calculation that we can use to categorize objects. We can illustrate it with our chair example. Since we have stored in long-term memory some specific instances or *exemplars* of chairs, we can determine whether the object of interest is sufficiently similar to our stored chair exemplars; if it is, we can declare it a chair. Thus, we have two means of categorization based on similarity—similarity to prototypes and similarity to stored exemplars. There is considerable evidence that children make extensive use of the exemplar strategy. Because young children know only typical exemplars, they often think that atypical exemplars are not members of the category (Mervis & Pani, 1981). Adults, too, will use the exemplar strategy when acquiring new concepts (Estes, 1994).

Sometimes the different means of categorization can lead to different conclusions, as when an object is similar to the prototype of a concept but lacks that concept's core, or rule-like, properties. In such cases we have to learn to go with the core properties. It takes children quite long to learn this, as is demonstrated by the following study.

Children between the ages of 5 and 10 were presented with descriptions of items and asked to decide whether or not they belonged to particular well-defined concepts. We can illustrate this process with the concept of "robber." One description of "robber" depicted a person who matched its prototype but not its defining properties:

> A smelly, mean old man with a gun in his pocket who came to your house and took your TV set because your parents didn't want it anymore and told him he could have it.

Another description depicted a person who matched the core of the concept but not its prototype:

> A very friendly and cheerful woman who gave you a hug, but then disconnected your toilet bowl and took it away without permission and no intention to return it.

The younger children often thought the prototypical description was more likely than the core description to be an instance of the concept. Not until age 10 did children show a clear shift from the prototype to the core as the final arbitrator of categorization decisions (Keil & Batterman, 1984).

Neural Bases of Concepts and Categorization

While we have emphasized the difference between well-defined and fuzzy concepts, research at the neurological level indicates that there are important differences among fuzzy concepts. In particular, the brain seems to store concepts of animals and concepts of artifacts in different neural regions. We mentioned some of the evidence for this in our discussion of perception

Parents can teach children to name and classify objects. Later, when the child sees another object, she may determine whether it is in the same category as the stored exemplar.

(Chapter 4). There we noted that some neurological patients are impaired in their ability to recognize pictures of animals but relatively normal in their recognition of pictured artifacts (like tools), whereas other patients show the reverse pattern (normal on animals but impaired on tools). We now add that what holds for pictures holds for words as well. Many patients who are selectively impaired on naming pictures also cannot tell you what the corresponding word means; for example, a patient who cannot name a pictured giraffe also cannot tell you anything about giraffes when presented with the word. The fact that the deficit appears with both words and pictures indicates that the deficit has to do with concepts—the patient has lost part of the concept "giraffe" (Farah & McClelland, 1991).

Other studies have focused on categorization processes. One line of research shows that determining the similarity between an object and a concept's prototype involves different regions of the brain from those involved in determining the similarity between an object and stored exemplars of the concept. The logic behind these studies goes as follows: The exemplar process involves retrieving items from long-term memory; as we saw in Chapter 7, such retrieval depends on structures in the medial temporal lobe; it follows that a patient with damage in these structures will not be able to effectively categorize objects by a process that involves exemplars, although that patient might be relatively normal in the use of prototypes. This is exactly what has been found.

One study tested patients with medial-temporal-lobe damage as well as normal individuals on two different tasks. One task required participants to learn to sort dot patterns into two categories (see Figure 8-1 for examples); the other task required participants to learn to sort paintings into two categories corresponding to two different artists. Independent evidence indicated that only the painting task relied on retrieval of exemplars. The patients learned the dot-pattern concepts as easily as

Figure 8-1

Examples of Dot Patterns Used to Study Categorization in Amnesiac Patients   Individuals learned that the study items all belonged to one category and then had to decide whether each of the test items belonged to that category. (Adapted from Squire & Knowlton, 1995)

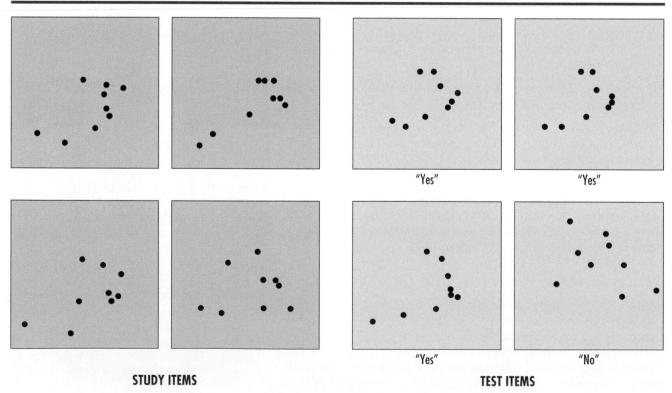

STUDY ITEMS   TEST ITEMS

Rule: An animal lives on VENUS if it has at least 3 out of the following 5 features:
hoofed feet, curly tail, long legs, red, and antennae ears. Otherwise, it lives on SATURN.

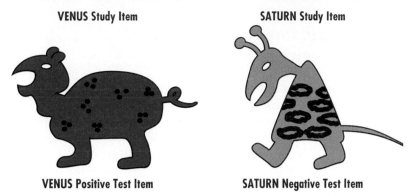

VENUS Study Item   **SATURN Study Item**

VENUS Positive Test Item   **SATURN Negative Test Item**

Figure 8-2

Examples of Imaginary Animals Used to Study Categorization   Individuals learned that some study items were from Venus, others from Saturn. They then had to decide to which category each test item belonged, while having their brains scanned.

the normal individuals, but performed far worse in acquiring the painting concepts (Kolodny, 1994). Thus, the use of exemplars depends on the brain structures that mediate long-term memory, but the use of prototypes in categorization must depend on other structures. Other research reports on a patient who is essentially incapable of committing *any* new information to long-term memory, yet this patient performs normally on the dot-pattern task. Clearly, prototype-based categorization does not depend on the structures that control long-term memory (Squire & Knowlton, 1995).

The findings just described show that there are neural differences between categorization based on prototypes and categorization based on stored exemplars. What about the difference between either of these processes (similarity processes) and categorization based on rules? A recent study shows that rule use involves different neural circuits from those involved in similarity processes. Two groups of participants were taught to categorize the imaginary animals shown in Figure 8-2 into two categories corresponding to whether the animals were from Venus or Saturn. One group learned to categorize the animals on the basis of a complex rule—for example, "An animal is from Venus if it has antennae ears, curly tail, and hoofed feet, otherwise it's from Saturn." The second group was instructed to learn to categorize the animals by relying solely on memory (the first time they saw an animal they would have to guess, but on subsequent trials they would be able to remember its category). After training, both groups were given novel animals to categorize while their brains were scanned. The rule group continued to categorize by rule; the memory group had to categorize a novel animal by retrieving the stored exemplar most similar to it and then selecting the category associated with that exemplar.

For the memory group, most of the brain areas activated were in the back of the brain, in the visual cortex. This fits with the idea that these participants were relying on retrieval of visual exemplars. Participants in the rule group also showed activation in the back of the brain, but they showed activation in some frontal regions as well. These regions are often damaged in patients who have trouble doing rule-based tasks. Hence, categorization based on rules relies on different neural circuitry from categorization based on similarity (Smith, Patalano, & Jonides, 1998).

In this section we have considered cases in which prototypes seem to be universal, largely unaffected by culture. Can you think of cases in which prototypes would be greatly influenced by culture? Give some examples. Do you have any ideas about

Thinking Critically

which kinds of concepts are associated with universal prototypes and which kinds with culturally varying prototypes?

What Are the Fundamental Processes of Symbolic and Imaginal Thinking?

Now that we know something about the building blocks of thought, we can consider how concepts are deployed in fundamental thinking processes. We first focus on symbolic thought and consider how people evaluate arguments and hypotheses; these are relatively simple reasoning tasks, and in real life we do them all the time. Such evaluation processes often involve a symbolic mode of thought. To find out about fundamental imagery processes, we must consider other kinds of tasks, and this is the second topic we cover in this section.

Symbolic Processes in Reasoning

Evaluating Deductive Arguments and Hypotheses   Logicians are much concerned with the evaluation of arguments. They have long noted that the strongest arguments are *deductively valid,* which means that the conclusion of the argument must be true if its premises are true (Skyrms, 1986). An example of such an argument is the following:

1. a. If it's raining, I'll take an umbrella. [premise]
   b. It's raining. [premise]
   c. Therefore, I'll take an umbrella. [conclusion]

How does the reasoning of ordinary people line up with that of the logician? When asked to decide whether an argument is deductively valid, people are quite accurate in their assessments of simple arguments. How do we make such judgments? Some theories of deductive reasoning assume that we operate like intuitive logicians, using logical rules in trying to prove that the conclusion of an argument follows from its premises. One piece of evidence that people are using such rules is that the number of rules an argument requires is a good predictor of the argument's difficulty. The more rules that are needed, the more likely it is that people will make an error, and the longer it will take them when they do make a correct decision (Rips, 1983, 1994).

But just as there was more to categorization than explicit rules, so logical rules cannot capture all aspects of normal deductive reasoning. Logical rules are triggered only by the logical *form* of statements, yet our ability to evaluate a deductive argument often depends on the *content* of the statements as well. We can illustrate this point with the following experimental problems. Participants are presented with four cards. In one version of the problem, each card has a letter on one side and a digit on the other (see top half of Figure 8-3). The participant must decide which cards to turn over to evaluate the following hypothesis: "If a card has a vowel on one side, then it has an even number on the other side." Most participants correctly choose the "E" card; it's clearly critical, since if it has a "7" on the other side the hypothesis is false. But fewer than 10% of the participants also choose the "7" card, which is the other correct choice. To see that the "7" card is critical, note that if it has an "E" on its other side, the hypothesis is again false. Instead of choosing the "7" card, many participants pick the "2" card. Although

Figure 8-3

Content Effects in Deductive Reasoning

The top row illustrates a version of the problem in which participants had to decide which two cards should be turned over to test the hypothesis, "If a card has a vowel on one side, it has an even number on the other side." The bottom row illustrates a version of the problem in which participants had to decide which cards to turn over to test the hypothesis, "If a person is drinking beer, he or she must be over 19." (After Griggs & Cox, 1982; Wason & Johnson-Laird, 1972)

the "2" card *seems* relevant, it can never disconfirm the hypothesis; if it has an "E" on the other side it's consistent with the hypothesis, while if it has a "K" on the other side it has no bearing on the hypothesis.

Performance improves drastically, however, in another version of the problem (see bottom half of Figure 8-3). Now the hypothesis that participants must evaluate is this: "If a person is drinking beer, he or she must be over 19." Each card has a person's age on one side and what he or she is drinking on the other. This version of the problem is logically equivalent to the preceding version (in particular, "Beer" corresponds to "E" and "16" corresponds to "7"); but now most participants make the correct choices (they turn over the "Beer" and "16" cards). Thus, the content of the hypotheses affects our reasoning.

Participants may solve the drinking problem by setting up a concrete representation of the situation, called a *mental model*. They may, for example, imagine two people, each with a number on his back and a drink in his hand. Making the problem concrete in this way helps the participants reason and increases their chances of getting the correct answer. In contrast, the abstract version (top of Figure 8-3) does not suggest a concrete model of the problem, and participants have difficulty reasoning about it (Johnson-Laird, 1989).

Evaluating Inductive Arguments and Estimating Probabilities   Logicians have noted that an argument can be good even if it is not deductively valid. Such arguments are *inductively strong,* which means that it is *probable* that the conclusion is true if the premises are true (Skyrms, 1986). An example of an inductively strong argument is as follows:

2. a. Mitch majored in accounting in college.
    b. Mitch now works for an accounting firm.
    c. Therefore, Mitch is an accountant.

This argument is not deductively valid (Mitch may have tired of accounting courses and taken a night-watchman's job in the only place he had contacts). Inductive strength, then, is a matter of *probabilities,* not certainties; and (according to logicians) inductive logic should be based on the theory of probability.

We make and evaluate inductive arguments all the time. In doing this, do we rely on the rules of probability theory as a logician or mathematician would? One probability rule that is relevant is the *base-rate rule.* It states that the probability of something being a member of a class (such as Mitch being a member of the class of accountants) is greater the more class members there are (that is, the higher the base rate of the class). Thus, it is more likely that Mitch is an accountant if 90% of the people working in his firm are accountants than if only 30% are. Another relevant probability rule is the *conjunction rule:* The probability of a statement cannot be less than the probability of that statement combined with another statement. For example, the probability that "Mitch is an accountant" cannot be less than the probability that "Mitch is an accountant and makes more than $50,000 a year." (Adding more constraints to an event can never increase its probability.) The base-rate and conjunction rules are rational guides to inductive reasoning—they are endorsed by logic— and most people will defer to them when they are made explicit. However, in the rough-and-tumble of everyday reasoning, people frequently violate these rules, as we are about to see.

Heuristics   In a series of ingenious experiments, Amos Tversky and Daniel Kahneman (1973, 1983) have shown that people violate some basic rules of probability theory when making inductive judgments. Violations of the base-rate rule are particularly common.

In one experiment, one group of participants was told that a panel of psychologists had interviewed 100 people—30 engineers and 70 lawyers—and had written descriptions of their personalities. These participants were then given a few descriptions and for each one were asked to indicate the probability that the person described was an engineer. Some of the descriptions were prototypical of an engineer (for example, "Jack shows no interest in political issues and spends his free time on home carpentry"); others were neutral (for example, "Dick is a man of high ability and promises to be quite successful"). Not surprisingly, these participants rated the prototypical description as more likely to be that of an engineer than the neutral description. Another group was given the identical instructions and descriptions, except that participants were told that the 100 people included 70 engineers and 30 lawyers (the reverse of the first group). The base rate of engineers therefore differed greatly between the two groups. This difference had virtually no effect: Participants in the second group gave essentially the same ratings as those in the first group. For example, participants in both groups rated the neutral description as having a 50-50 chance of being that of an engineer (whereas the rational move would have been to rate the neutral description as more likely to be in the profession with the higher base rate). Participants completely ignored the information about base rates (Tversky & Kahneman, 1973).

People pay no more heed to the conjunction rule. In one study, participants were presented with the following description:

> Linda is 31 years old, single, outspoken, and very bright. In college, she majored in philosophy . . . and was deeply concerned with issues of discrimination.

Participants then estimated the probabilities of the following two statements:

3. Linda is a bank teller.

4. Linda is a bank teller and is active in the feminist movement.

Statement 4 is the conjunction of statement 3 and the statement "Linda is active in the feminist movement." Yet, in flagrant violation of the conjunction rule, most participants rated statement 4 as *more* probable than statement 3. Note that this is a fallacy because every feminist bank teller is a bank teller, but some female bank tellers are not feminists, and Linda could be one of them (Tversky & Kahneman, 1983).

Participants in this study based their judgments on the fact that Linda seems more *similar* to a prototypical feminist bank teller than to a bank teller. Although they were asked to estimate *probability,* they instead estimated the *similarity* of Linda to the prototype of the concepts "bank teller" and "feminist bank teller." This is, of course, the same process that people use in categorizing with fuzzy concepts. Thus, estimating similarity is used as a heuristic for estimating probability; a **heuristic** is *a short-cut procedure that is relatively easy to apply and can often yield the correct answer but does not inevitably do so.* That is, people use the *similarity heuristic* because similarity is often related to probability but is easier to calculate.

Use of the similarity heuristic also explains why people ignore base rates. In the engineer-lawyer study described earlier, participants may have considered only the similarity of the description to their prototypes of "engineer" and "lawyer." Hence, given a description that matched the prototypes of "engineer" and "lawyer" equally well, participants judged that engineer and lawyer were equally probable. Reliance on the similarity heuristic can lead to errors even by experts.

Similarity is not our only strong heuristic; another is the *causality heuristic.* People estimate the probability of a situation by the strength of the causal connections between the events in the situation. For example, people judge statement 6 to be more probable than statement 5:

5. Sometime during the year 2004, there will be a massive flood in California, in which more than 1,000 people will drown.

6. Sometime during the year 2004, there will be an earthquake in California, causing a massive flood in which more than 1,000 people will drown.

heuristic   a short-cut procedure that is relatively easy to apply and can often yield the correct answer but does not inevitably do so

Judging statement 6 to be more probable than statement 5 is another violation of the conjunction rule (and hence another fallacy). This time, the violation arises because in statement 6 the flood has a strong causal connection to another event, the earthquake; whereas in statement 5 the flood alone is mentioned and hence has no causal connections.

In sum, our reliance on heuristics often leads us to ignore some basic rational rules, including the base-rate and conjunction rules. But we should not be too pessimistic about our level of rationality. For one thing, the similarity and causality heuristics probably lead to correct decisions in most cases. Another point is that under the right circumstances we can appreciate the relevance of certain logical rules to particular problems and use them appropriately (Nisbett et al., 1983). Thus, in reading and thinking about this discussion you were probably able to see the relevance of the base-rate and conjunction rules to the problems at hand.

Imaginal Processes in Reasoning

Evaluating arguments and hypotheses may occasionally involve the use of imagery, but most of the time the reasoning seems to be highly symbolic. When estimating the probability of earthquakes, for example, many of us will not experience images; and even if we do, our image may have little to do with how we derive our estimate. But there are other reasoning situations in which most people report using visual imagery to solve the problem or answer the question. Such situations are our next topic, for they tell us about fundamental operations in the imaginal mode of thought.

Answering Questions   To answer certain questions, sometimes we have to retrieve past perceptions, or parts of them, and then operate on them as we would on a real perception. To appreciate this point, try to answer the following three questions.

1. What shape are a German shepherd's ears?
2. What new letter is formed when an uppercase N is rotated 90 degrees?
3. How many windows are there in your parents' living room?

When answering the first question, most people report that they form a visual image of a German shepherd's head and "look" at the ears to determine their shape. When answering the second question, people report first forming an image of a capital N and then mentally "rotating" it 90 degrees and "looking" at it to determine its identity. And when answering the third question people report imagining the room and then "scanning" the image while counting the windows (Kosslyn, 1983; Shepard & Cooper, 1982).

These examples rest on subjective impressions, but combined with stronger evidence they suggest that imagery involves the same representations and processes that are used in perception (Finke, 1985). Our images of objects and places have visual detail: We see the German shepherd, the letter N, or our parents' living room in our "mind's eye." Moreover, the mental operations that we perform on these images seem to be analogous to the operations that we carry out on real visual objects: We scan the image of our parents' room in much the same way that we would scan a real room, and we rotate our image of the N the way we would rotate the real object.

Imaginal Operations   We have noted that the mental operations performed on images seem to be analogous to those we carry out on real visual objects. Numerous experiments provide objective evidence for these impressions.

One operation that has been studied intensively is *mental rotation*. In a classic experiment, participants saw the capital letter R on each trial. The letter was presented either normally (R) or backward and in its usual vertical orientation or rotated various degrees (see Figure 8-4). The participants had to decide whether the letter was normal or backward. The more the letter had been rotated from its vertical orientation, the longer it took the participants to make the decision (see Figure 8-5). This

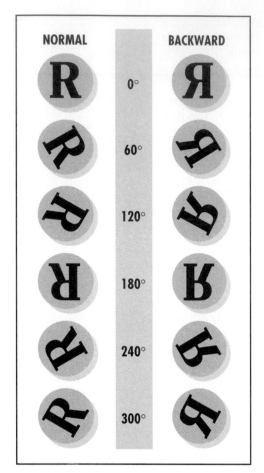

Figure 8-4

A Study of Mental Rotation   Shown are examples of the letters presented to participants in studies of mental rotation. On each presentation, participants had to decide whether the letter was normal or backward. Numbers indicate deviation from the vertical in degrees. (After Cooper & Shepard, 1973)

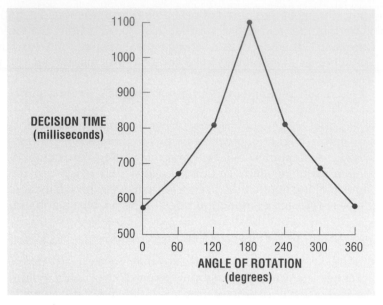

Figure 8-5

Decision Times in the Mental Rotation Study   The time taken to decide whether a letter had a normal or reversed orientation was greatest when the rotation was 180 degrees so that the letter was upside down. (After Cooper & Shepard, 1973)

finding suggests that participants made their decisions by mentally rotating the image of the letter until it was vertical and then checking to see whether it was normal or backward.

Another operation that is similar in imagery and perception is that of scanning an object or array. In an experiment on scanning an image, participants first studied a map of a fictional island that contained seven critical locations. The map was removed, and participants were asked to form an image of it and fixate on a particular location (for example, the tree in the southern part of the island; see Figure 8-6). Then the experimenter named another location (for example, the tree at the northern tip of the island). Starting at the fixated location, the participants were to scan their images until they found the named location, and to push a button upon "arrival" there. The greater the distance between the fixated location and the named one, the longer the participants took to respond. This suggests that they were scanning their images in much the same way that they scan real objects.

Another commonality between imaginal and perceptual processing is that both are limited by grain size. On a television screen, for instance, the grain of the picture tube determines how small the details of a picture can be and still remain perceptible. While there is no actual screen in the brain, we can think of our images as occurring in a "mental medium" whose grain limits the amount of detail we can detect in an image. If this grain size is fixed, smaller images should be more difficult to inspect than larger ones. A good deal of evidence supports this claim. In one experiment, participants first formed an image of a familiar animal—say, a cat. Then they were asked to decide whether or not the imaged object had a particular property. Participants made decisions faster for larger properties, such as the head, than for smaller ones, such as the claws. In another study, participants were asked to image an animal at different relative sizes—small, medium, or large. They were then asked to decide whether their images had a particular property. Their decisions were faster for larger images than for smaller ones. Thus, in imagery as in perception, the larger

Neural Bases of Decision Making

One of the most important functions of reasoning is to make decisions—particularly deciding which course of action to take when outcomes are uncertain. For a number of years now, neurologists have noted that certain kinds of neurological patients seem to be impaired when it comes to making decisions even though in all other ways the patients' cognition is normal. The patients of interest have lesions in the lower part of their frontal cortex, what is technically referred to as the "ventromedial prefrontal cortex" (we'll refer to the patients as "ventromedial patients"). Such patients retain normal intelligence, language memory, and perception, but they have severe problems when it comes to planning future activities, which severely limits them in holding jobs. They repeatedly select courses of action that are not in their best interest in the long run, and they generally act as if they have lost the ability to ponder different courses of action and select the one that promises the best outcome (Tranel, Bechera, & Damasio, 2000).

Recently, researchers have come up with a task for studying ventromedial patients' decision making in the laboratory, so that they can more precisely characterize their problem. The task involves a gambling situation (Bechera et al.,1994). Participants are presented four decks of cards—labeled A, B, C, and D—and on each trial they select a card from one of the four decks, and then find out how much they have won, or sometimes lost, from the selection. The game requires a hundred such selections, so participants have an opportunity to learn the payoffs and losses associated with each deck. In fact decks A and B have high payoffs—$100 on each trial—whereas decks B and C have lower payoffs—$50 on each trial. However, the penalties are also higher in decks A and B, and it turns out that in the long run one will make more money if one selects from decks C and D. When normal participants are tested in this task, initially (first 20 trials) they make most of their selections from the disadvantageous decks—apparently, they are being pulled by the higher payoffs. But eventually, normal participants learn that the C and D decks are the better ones, and by the last 40 trials most of their selections are from the good decks. When ventromedial patients are tested, however, the results are very different. Like the normals, their initial choices are from the high-payoff bad decks, but unlike the normals they never learn to favor the good C and D decks. And their problem seems to be due to the fact that their brain damage is in the ventromedial area, because patients with brain damage in other regions behave like normals when tested in the gambling task and eventually learn to make their selections from the C and D decks.

Why don't the ventromedial patients learn that the A and B decks will lead to substantial penalties? It appears that their problem is that they cannot anticipate the negative consequence of selecting from the A and B decks. This account was suggested by a follow-up study (Bechera, Tranel, Damasio, & Damasio, 1996), in which normals and patients performed the gambling task while the experimenters recorded activity in the autonomic nervous system—specifically skin conductance responses (SCRs). Three types of SCRs were of particular interest: (1) payoff SCRs, which are generated after a participant has turned a card for which there was a payoff and no penalty; (2) penalty SCRs, which are generated after a participant turns a card for which there was a penalty as well as a payoff; and (3) anticipatory SCRs, which are generated immediately prior to the point at which the participant turned a card from any deck, (i.e., during the time period when the participant is deciding which deck to choose). Both ventromedial and normal participants generate payoff and penalty SCRs—they react comparably to experienced rewards and punishments. But as they became experienced with the task, normal participants began to generate anticipatory SCRs, which were more pronounced prior to selection from the bad decks. Not so for the ventromedial patients; they never got to the point of generating SCRs in anticipation of payoffs and penalties. Presumably, this lack of anticipatory SCR is a physiological correlate of the patients' insensitivity to future outcomes.

But what does all this have to do with the ventromedial cortex? The ventromedial cortex receives and sends inputs from the autonomic nervous system. Damasio (1994) has suggested that the ventromedial cortex is needed to learn associations between higher-order stimuli, like the recognition that one has just lost money, and internal states that are experienced in conjunction with those stimuli, like the negative feeling that goes with selecting an option that frequently loses money. Patients who have damage in their ventromedial cortex cannot learn such associations, and without such associations they cannot anticipate the negative feeling when selecting the option of a bad deck. In contrast, normal participants can learn such association, will experience something of a negative feeling when thinking about making a selection from a bad deck, and this gut-level feeling will guide their choice. According to this analysis, part of what is good about normal decision making is its reliance on feeling.

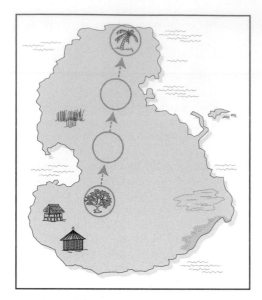

Figure 8-6

Scanning Mental Images   The person scans the image of the island from south to north, looking for the named location. It appears as though the individual's mental image is like a real map and that it takes longer to scan across the mental image if the distance to be scanned is greater. (After Kosslyn, Ball, & Reiser, 1978)

the image, the more readily we can see the details of an object (Kosslyn, 1980).

Visual Creativity   There are innumerable stories about scientists and artists producing their most creative work through visual thinking (Shepard & Cooper, 1982). Although they are not solid evidence, these stories are among the best indicators we have of the power of visual thinking. Visual thinking appears to be quite effective in highly abstract areas like mathematics and physics. Albert Einstein, for example, said that he rarely thought in words; rather, he worked out his ideas in terms of "more or less clear images which can be 'voluntarily' reproduced and combined." Thus, Einstein claimed that he had his initial insight into the theory of relativity when he thought about what he "saw" when he imagined chasing after and matching the speed of a beam of light.

Perhaps the most celebrated example of visual thinking occurred in the field of chemistry. Friedrich Kekule von Stradonitz was trying to determine the molecular structure of benzene (which turned out to have a ring structure). One night he dreamed that a writhing, snakelike figure suddenly twisted into a closed loop, biting its own tail. The structure of the snake proved to be the structure of benzene. A dream image had provided the solution to a major scientific problem. Visual images can also be a creative force for writers. Samuel Coleridge's famous poem "Kubla Khan" supposedly came to him in its entirety as a prolonged visual image.

The Neural Basis of Imagery   Perhaps the most persuasive evidence for imagery being like perception are demonstrations that both processes are governed by the same brain structures. Substantial evidence for this has accumulated in recent years. Some of the evidence comes from studies of brain-damaged patients and shows that any problem the patient has in visual perception is often accompanied by a parallel problem in visual imagery (Farah et al., 1988). A particularly striking example arises with patients who have suffered damage in the parietal lobe of the right hemisphere. As a result of this damage, they develop *visual neglect* of the left side of the visual field. Although they are not blind, these patients ignore everything on the left side of their visual fields. A male patient, for example, may neglect to shave the left side of his face. The Italian neurologist Bisiach showed that this visual neglect extends to imagery (Bisiach & Luzzatti, 1978). Bisiach asked patients with visual neglect to imagine a familiar square in their native Milan as it looks when one stands in the square facing the church. The patients reported most objects on their right but few on their left. When asked to imagine the scene from the opposite perspective—that is, when one stands in front of the church and looks out into the square—the patients neglected the objects that they had previously reported (those objects were now on the left side of the image). Thus, these patients manifested the same kind of neglect in imagery that they did in perception, suggesting that the damaged brain structures normally mediate imagery as well as perception.

Some studies have used brain-scanning methods to demonstrate that in normal people, the parts of the brain involved in perception are also involved in imagery. An experiment by Stephen Kosslyn and colleagues (1993) provides an example. While their brains were being scanned, participants performed two different tasks, a perception task and an imagery task. In the perception task, first a block capital letter was presented on a background grid and then an X was presented in one of the grid cells; the task was to decide as quickly as possible whether or not the X fell on part of the block letter (look at the left side of Figure 8-7). In the imagery task, the background grid was again presented, but without a block capital letter. Under the grid was a lowercase letter, and participants had to generate an image of the capital version of the lowercase letter and project their image onto the grid. Then an X was presented in one of the grid cells, and participants had to determine whether or not the X fell on part of the imagined block letter (look at the right side of Figure 8-7).

Not surprisingly, the perception task resulted in heightened neural activity in parts of the visual cortex. But so did the imagery task. Indeed, the imagery task resulted in increased activity in brain structures that are known to be among the first regions of the cortex to receive visual information. Thus, imagery is like perception from the early stages of cortical processing. Moreover, when the neural activations from the two tasks were compared directly, there was actually more activation in the imagery task than in the perception task, presumably because the imagery task required more "perceptual work" than the perception task. These results leave little doubt that imagery and perception are controlled by the same neural mechanisms.

In sum, fundamental thinking processes come in two flavors: symbolic and imaginal. Both types rely on concepts. This was particularly evident in our discussion of inductive reasoning (a form of symbolic thought), where we saw that people often use prototypes and a similarity heuristic when evaluating arguments. But concepts are also involved in other cases of symbolic reasoning, including evaluating deductive arguments. The fact that people are so affected by the content of a deductive problem means that they are dealing with the underlying concepts. And concepts are equally involved in visual thinking. For example, when we answer a question about the shape of a German shepherd's ears by visualizing the animal, we are drawing on our concept of German shepherd and using the perceptual information contained in it.

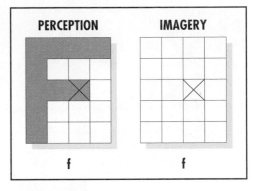

Figure 8-7

Imagery and Perception Tasks used to determine whether visual imagery involves the same brain structures as visual perception. In the perception task, participants must decide whether or not the X fell on part of the block letter. In the imagery task, participants generate an image of the block letter and then decide whether or not the X fell on part of the (image of the) block letter. The person knows which letter to image because the lowercase version of it is presented below the grid (the lowercase version is also presented in the perception task, just to keep things comparable). (After Kosslyn et al., 1993)

Thinking Critically

1. We considered studies showing that people use heuristics that violate rules of probability. How might you teach or train people to reason otherwise—that is, to reason in accordance with the rules of probability? Think of explicit things that you would do.

2. In this section, we focused on visual imagery. By analogy, how would you find evidence for auditory imagery? Try to come up with either a psychological or a biological study that would show that auditory imagery is like auditory perception.

How Do We Solve Complex Problems?

The thinking situations that we have considered thus far are relatively simple. For example, deciding whether a person is more likely to be a bank teller or a feminist bank teller involves only a few mental calculations (determining the similarity of the person to prototypes for bank teller and feminist bank teller) and takes only a few seconds; likewise, deciding whether a rotated letter is in its normal or backward form requires just one process (mental rotation) and takes only a second or two. Most thinking situations are far more complex than this, often involving novel circumstances, and requiring real problem solving. In this section we consider how people solve more complex problems.

In real problem solving, we are striving for a goal but have no ready means of obtaining it. (This is unlike most of the situations discussed previously, such as mental rotation, where we know what to do from the moment the task is presented to us.)

Solving a simple problem—trying to figure out the (forgotten) combination of a lock.

To reach a goal, we must break the goal into subgoals and perhaps divide these subgoals into smaller subgoals until we reach a level that we have the means to obtain (Anderson, 1990).

We can illustrate these points with a simple problem. Suppose that you need to figure out the combination for an unfamiliar lock. You know only that the combination has four numbers and that whenever you come across a correct number you will hear a click. Your overall goal is to find the combination. Rather than trying four numbers at random, most people decompose the overall goal into four subgoals, each corresponding to one of the numbers in the combination. Your first subgoal is to find the first number, and you have a procedure for accomplishing this—namely, turning the lock slowly while listening for a click. Your second subgoal is to find the second number, and you can use the same procedure; and so on for the remaining subgoals.

The strategy that people use to decompose goals into subgoals is a major issue in the study of problem solving. Another issue is how people represent the problem to themselves (a *mental representation*), because this also affects how readily we can solve the problem. The following discussion considers both of these issues.

Problem-Solving Strategies

Much of what we know about strategies for decomposing goals is derived from the research of Alan Newell and Herb Simon (1972). Typically, the researchers ask participants to think aloud while trying to solve a difficult problem. Then, they analyze the participants' verbal responses for clues to the underlying strategy. A number of general purpose strategies have been identified in this way.

One strategy is to reduce the difference between our current state in a problem situation and our goal state, in which a solution is obtained. Consider again the combination lock problem. Initially, our *current state* includes no knowledge of any of the numbers, while our *goal state* includes knowledge of all four numbers. We therefore set up the subgoal of reducing the difference between these two states; determining the first number accomplishes this subgoal. Our current state now includes knowledge of the first number. There is still a difference between our current state and our goal state, and we can reduce it by determining the second number, and so on. Thus, the critical idea behind *difference reduction* is that we set up subgoals that, when obtained, put us in a state closer to our goal.

A similar but more sophisticated strategy is *means–ends analysis.* Here we compare our current state to the goal state in order to find the *most important* difference between them; eliminating this difference becomes our main subgoal. We then search for a means or a procedure for achieving this subgoal. If we find such a procedure but discover that something in our current state prevents us from applying it, we introduce a new subgoal: eliminating the obstacle. Many commonsense problem-solving situations involve this strategy. Here is an example:

> I want to take my son to nursery school. What's the [most important] difference between what I have and what I want? One of distance. What [procedure] changes distance? My automobile. My automobile won't work. What is needed to make it work? A new battery. What has new batteries? An auto repair shop. (After Newell & Simon, 1972, as cited in Anderson, 1990, p. 232)

Means–ends analysis is more sophisticated than difference reduction because it allows us to take action even if it results in a temporary *decrease* in similarity between our current state and the goal state. In our example, the auto repair shop may be in the opposite direction from the nursery school. Going to the shop thus temporarily increases the distance from the goal, yet this step is essential for solving the problem.

Another strategy is *working backward* from the goal. This is particularly useful in solving mathematical problems such as that illustrated in Figure 8-8. The problem is this: Given that ABCD is a rectangle, prove that AD and BC are the same length. In working backward, one might proceed as follows:

> What could prove that AD and BC are the same length? I could prove this if I could prove that the triangles ACD and BDC are congruent. I can prove that ACD and BDC are congruent if I could prove that two sides and an included angle are equal. (After Anderson, 1990, p. 238)

We reason from the goal to a subgoal (proving that the triangles are congruent), from that subgoal to another subgoal (proving that the sides and angle are equal), and so on, until we reach a subgoal that we have a ready means of obtaining.

We have considered three strategies: difference reduction, means–ends analysis, and working backward. In each case, the only evidence we have supplied consists of the participants' verbal responses while solving a problem. Researchers have gone beyond this kind of evidence by using computer simulations. The researcher first programs a computer to use one of the three strategies, next inputs a problem into the computer, and then compares the output from the computer to aspects of people's performance on the problem—say, the sequence of moves. Researchers have found that people's performance generally matches the output from the computer, suggesting that the strategy that people are using is the same as the one that the computer has been programmed to follow (Newell & Simon, 1972).

The three strategies we have considered are extremely general and can be applied to virtually any problem. These strategies, which are often referred to as *weak methods,* do not rest on any specific knowledge and may even be innate. People may be especially likely to rely on these weak methods when they are first learning about an area and are working on problems whose content is unfamiliar. We will soon see that when people gain expertise in an area they develop more powerful domain-specific procedures (and representations), which come to dominate the weak methods (Anderson, 1987).

Representing the Problem

Being able to solve a problem depends not only on our strategy for decomposing it but also on how we represent it. Sometimes a symbolic representation works best; at other times a visual representation or image is more effective. To illustrate, consider the following problem:

> One morning, exactly at sunrise, a monk began to climb a mountain. A narrow path, a foot or two wide, spiraled around the mountain to a temple at the summit. The monk ascended at varying rates, stopping many times along the way to rest. He reached the temple shortly before sunset. After several days at the temple, he began his journey back along the same path, starting at sunrise and again walking at variable speeds with many pauses along the way. His average speed descending was, of course, greater than his average climbing speed. Prove that there exists a particular spot along the path that the monk will occupy on both trips at precisely the same time of day. (Adams, 1974, p. 4)

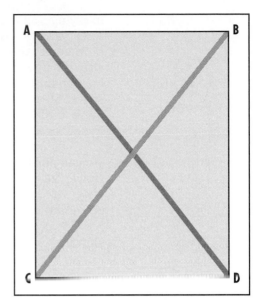

Figure 8-8

An Illustrative Geometry Problem   Given that ABCD is a rectangle, prove that the line segments AD and BC are the same length.

Learning aids help students visualize a math problem.

In trying to solve this problem, many people start with a symbolic representation. They may even try to write out a set of equations and soon confuse themselves. The problem is far easier to solve when it is represented visually. All you need do is visualize the upward journey of the monk superimposed on the downward journey. Imagine one monk starting at the bottom and the other at the top. No matter what their speed, at some time and at some point along the path the two monks will meet. Thus, there must be a spot along the path that the monk occupied on both trips at precisely the same time of day. (Note that the problem did not ask you where the spot was.)

Some problems can be readily solved by manipulating either symbols or images. We can illustrate with the following simple problem: "Ed runs faster than David but slower than Dan; who's the slowest of the three men?" To solve the problem symbolically, note that we can represent the first part of the problem as "David slower than Ed" and the second part as "Ed slower than Dan." In general, if x is slower than y and y is slower than z, then x must be slower than z; hence, we can deduce that David is slower than Dan, which makes David the slowest. To solve the problem by means of imagery, we might, for example, imagine the three men's speeds as points on a line, like this:

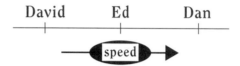

David   Ed   Dan

speed ▶

Then we can simply "read" the answer to the question directly from the image. Apparently, some people prefer to represent such problems as symbols while others tend to represent them visually (Johnson-Laird, 1985).

In addition to the issue of symbols versus images, there are questions about what is represented (which are questions about concepts). Often we have difficulty with a problem because we fail to include something critical in our representation or because we include something in our representation that is not an important part of the problem. We can illustrate this point with an experiment. One group of participants was given the problem of supporting a candle on a door, using only the materials depicted in Figure 8-9. The solution was to tack the box to the door and use the box as a platform for the candle. Most participants had difficulty with the problem, presumably because they represented the box as a container, not as a platform. This is because the property of being a container is a very salient part of the concept of boxes. Another group of participants was given the identical problem, except that the contents of the box were removed. These participants had more success in solving the problem because they were less likely to include the box's container property in their representation and more likely to include its supporter property. Studies like this give some inkling of why many experts believe that representing a problem in a useful manner—which amounts to activating the useful properties of the relevant concepts—is half the battle in solving the problem.

Figure 8-9

Materials for the Candle Problem   Given the materials depicted, how can you support a candle on a door? (After Glucksberg & Weisberg, 1966)

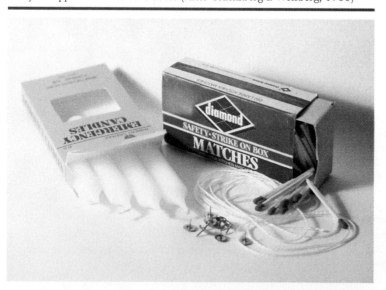

Experts Versus Novices

In a given content area (physics, geography, or chess, for instance), experts solve problems in a qualitatively different fashion from novices. These differences are due to differences in the representations and strategies that experts and novices use. Experts have many more specific representations stored in memory, which they can bring to bear on a problem. A master chess player, for example, can look for 5 seconds at a complex configuration of more than 20 pieces and reproduce it perfectly; a novice in this situation can reproduce only the usual 7 ± 2 items (see Chapter 7). Experts can accomplish this memory feat because through years of practice they have developed representations of many possible configurations; these representations permit them to encode a complex configuration in just a few chunks. Presumably these representations are what underlies their superior chess game. A master may have stored as many as 50,000 configurations and has learned what to do when each one arises. Thus, master chess players can essentially "see" possible moves; they do not have to think them through the way novices do (Chase & Simon, 1973).

Even when confronted with a novel problem, experts represent it differently from the way novices do. This point is illustrated in studies of problem solving in physics. An expert (say, a physics professor) represents a problem in terms of the physical principle needed to solve it—for example, "This is one of those every-action-has-an-equal-and-opposite-reaction problems." In contrast, a novice (say, a student taking a first course in physics) tends to represent the same problem in terms of its surface features—for example, "This is one of those inclined-plane problems" (Chi, Glaser, & Rees, 1982). Thus, the experts and novices are using different concepts in their representations (e.g., actions versus inclined planes).

Experts and novices also differ in the strategies they employ. In studies of physics problem solving, experts generally try to formulate a plan for attacking the problem before generating equations, whereas novices typically start writing equations with no general plan in mind (Larkin et al., 1980). Another difference is that experts tend to reason from the givens of a problem toward a solution, while novices tend to work in the reverse direction (the working-backward strategy). This difference in the direction of reasoning has also been obtained in studies of how physicians solve problems. More expert physicians tend to reason in a forward direction—from symptom to possible disease—while the less expert tend to reason in a backward direction—from possible disease to symptom (Patel & Groen, 1986).

The characteristics of expertise that we have just discussed—a multitude of representations, representations and concepts based on principles, planning before acting, and working forward—make up some of the domain-specific procedures that come to dominate the weak methods of problem solving discussed earlier.

Think of some activity (an academic subject, a game, a sport, or a hobby) in which you have gained or are gaining some expertise. How would you characterize the changes that you went through in becoming better at that activity? How do these changes line up with those described under the heading of "expertise"?

Thinking Critically

What Is the Nature of Language?

It is one thing to have a thought, but unless we can communicate it to others it will have a limited effect. Language is our primary means for communicating thought and hence there is an intimate connection between thought and language. Moreover, language is a universal means of communication: Every human society has a language, and every human being of normal intelligence acquires his or her native language and uses it effortlessly. The naturalness of language sometimes lulls us into thinking that language use requires no special explanation. Nothing could be further from the truth. Some people can read, while others cannot; some can do arithmetic, while others cannot; some can play chess, while others cannot. But virtually everyone can master and use an enormously complex linguistic system. Why this should be so is among the fundamental puzzles of human psychology.

Levels of Language

language production the process of translating a symbolic thought into a sentence and expressing the sentence with sounds

Language use has two aspects: production and comprehension. In **language production,** we *start with a symbolic thought, somehow translate it into a sentence, and end up with sounds that express the sentence.* In **language comprehension,** we *start by hearing sounds, attach meanings to the sounds in the form of words, combine the words to create a sentence, and then somehow extract a thought from it.* Thus, language use seems to involve moving through various levels, as shown in Figure 8-10. At the highest level are *sentence units,* including sentences and phrases. The next level is that of *words and parts of words* that carry meaning (the prefix "non" or the suffix "er," for example). The lowest level contains *speech sounds.* The adjacent levels are closely related to each other: The phrases of a sentence are built from words and prefixes and suffixes, which in turn are constructed from speech sounds. Language therefore is a multilevel system for relating thoughts to speech by means of word and sentence units (Chomsky, 1965).

language comprehension the process of hearing sounds, attaching meanings to them in the form of words, combining the words to create a sentence, and extracting a thought from the sentence

There are striking differences in the number of units at each level. All languages have only a limited number of speech sounds; English has about 40 of them. But rules for combining these speech sounds make it possible to produce and understand thousands of words (a vocabulary of 40,000 words is not unusual for an adult). Similarly, rules for combining words make it possible to produce and understand millions of sentences. Thus, two of the basic properties of language are that it is *organized at multiple levels* and that it is *productive:* Rules allow us to combine units at one level into a vastly greater number of units at the next level. Every human language has these properties.

Language Units and Processes

Let us now consider the units and processes involved at each level of language. In what follows, we usually take the perspective of a person comprehending language (a *listener*), although occasionally we switch to the perspective of a language producer (a *speaker*).

phoneme a discrete speech sound

Speech Sounds   If you could attend to just the sounds someone makes when talking to you, what would you hear? You would not perceive a continuous stream of sound; but rather, you would hear a sequence of *discrete speech sounds,* called **phonemes.** A phoneme is a category in the sense that sounds that differ physically can be perceived as the same phoneme. The sound corresponding to the first letter in "boy" is an instance of a phoneme symbolized as /b/. (Note that while phonemes may correspond to letters, they are speech sounds not letters; hence the slashes around the letter.) In English, we divide all speech sounds into about 40 phonemes.

We are good at discriminating between different sounds that correspond to different phonemes in our language, but poor at discriminating between different sounds that correspond to the same phoneme. Consider, for example, the sound of the first letter in "pin" and the sound of the second letter in "spin"; they are the same phoneme, /p/, and they sound the same to us even though they have different physical characteristics. The /p/ in "pin" is accompanied by a small puff of air, but the /p/ in "spin" is not (try holding your hand a short distance from your mouth as you say the two words). Thus, our phonemic categories act like filters, converting a continuous stream of speech into a sequence of familiar phonemes (Liberman et al., 1967).

Every language has a different set of phonemes, which is one reason why we often have difficulty learning to pronounce foreign words. Another language may use phonemes that never appear in ours. It may take us a while even to hear the new phonemes, let

Figure 8-10

Levels of Language   At the highest level are sentence units, including phrases and sentences. The next level is that of words and parts of words that carry meaning. The lowest level contains speech sounds.

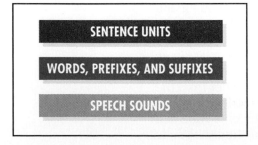

SENTENCE UNITS

WORDS, PREFIXES, AND SUFFIXES

SPEECH SOUNDS

alone produce them. For example, in Hindi the two different /p/ sounds just illustrated correspond to two different phonemes. Or another language may not make a distinction between two sounds that our language treats as two phonemes. For example, in Japanese, the English sounds corresponding to "r" and "l" (/r/ and /l/) are perceived as the same phoneme.

When phonemes are combined in the right way, we perceive them as words. Each language has its own rules about which phonemes can follow others. In English, for example, /b/ cannot follow /p/ at the beginning of a word (try pronouncing "pbet"). Such rules show their influence when we listen, and perhaps even more so when we speak. For example, we have no difficulty pronouncing the plurals of nonsense words that we have never heard before. Consider "zuk" and "zug." In accordance with a simple rule, the plural of "zuk" is formed by adding the phoneme /s/, as in "hiss." In English, however, /s/ cannot follow "/g/" at the end of a word, so to form the plural of "zug" we must use another rule—one that adds the phoneme /z/, as in "fuzz." We may not be aware of these differences in forming plurals, but we have no difficulty producing them. It is as if we "know" the rules for combining phonemes even though we are not consciously aware of the rules.

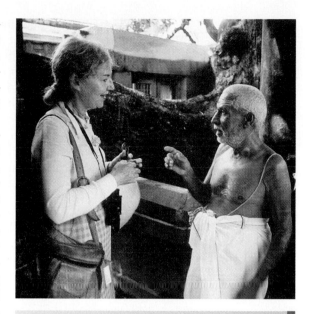

When learning a new language, we may experience difficulty discriminating between sounds that correspond to different phonemes in the new language, but not in ours.

Word Units   What we typically perceive when listening to speech are not phonemes but words. Unlike phonemes, words carry meaning. A **word** can be thought of as *the name of a concept;* hence, its meaning is the concept it names. However, words are not the only small linguistic units that convey meaning. Suffixes such as "ly" or prefixes such as "un" also carry meaning (e.g., "un" names the abstract concept "negation"); suffixes and prefixes can be added onto words to form more complex ones with different meanings, as when "un" and "ly" are added on to "time" to form "untimely." Any small linguistic unit that carries meaning is called a *morpheme.*

word the name of a concept

Most morphemes are words. While most words denote some specific content, such as "house" or "run," a few primarily serve to make sentences grammatical; such grammatical words, or *grammatical morphemes,* include articles and prepositions, such as "a," "the," "in," "of," "on," and "at." Some prefixes and suffixes, like the suffixes "ing" and "ed" also play primarily a grammatical role. They are also grammatical morphemes. Grammatical morphemes may be processed in a qualitatively different manner from content words. One piece of evidence for this is that there are forms of brain damage in which the use of grammatical morphemes is impaired more than the use of content words (Zurif, 1990).

Sentence Units   As listeners, we effortlessly combine words into sentence units, which include sentences as well as phrases. An important property of these units is that they can correspond to parts of a single symbolic thought. Such correspondences allow a listener to "extract" thoughts from sentences.

To understand these correspondences, one must first recognize that any symbolic thought can be divided into a *subject* and a *predicate* (a description). In the thought corresponding to "Audrey has curly hair," "Audrey" is the subject and "has curly hair" is the predicate. In the thought corresponding to "The tailor is asleep," "the tailor" is the subject and "is asleep" is the predicate. And in "Teachers work too hard," "teachers" is the subject and "work too hard" is the predicate. It turns out that any sentence can be broken into phrases in such a way that each phrase corresponds either to the subject or predicate of a thought (both of which are made up of concepts) or to an entire thought. For example, intuitively we can divide the simple sentence

"Irene sells insurance" into two phrases, "Irene" and "sells insurance." The first phrase specifies the subject of an underlying symbolic thought, while the second gives the predicate of the thought.

Thus, when listening to a sentence, people seem to first divide it into phrases and then extract thoughts from these phrases. There is a good deal of evidence that we divide sentences into phrases and treat the phrases as units. Some of this evidence comes from memory experiments. In one study, participants listened to sentences such as "The poor girl stole a warm coat." Immediately after each sentence was presented, participants were given a probe word from the sentence and asked to say the word that came after it. People responded faster when the probe and the response words came from the same phrase ("poor" and "girl") than when they came from different phrases ("girl" and "stole"). Thus, each phrase acts as a unit in memory. When the probe and response are from the same phrase, only one unit needs to be retrieved (Wilkes & Kennedy, 1969).

syntax   an analysis of the relations between words in phrases and sentences

Analyzing an incoming sentence into its constituent phrases (often called "noun phrases" and "verb phrases"), and then dividing these phrases into smaller units like nouns, adjectives, and verbs, is called *syntactic analysis* (**syntax** *deals with the relations between words in phrases and sentences*). Usually, in the course of understanding a sentence we perform such an analysis effortlessly and unconsciously. Sometimes, however, our syntactic analysis goes awry and we become aware of the process. Consider the sentence, "The horse raced past the barn fell." Many people have difficulty understanding this sentence. Why? Because on first reading, we assume that "The horse" is one phrase and "raced past the barn" is the other, and we have no place for the word "fell." To correctly understand the sentence, we have to repartition it so that the entire sequence "The horse raced past the barn" is one phrase, and "fell" is another—that is, the sentence is just a shortened version of "The horse *who* was raced past the barn fell" (Garrett, 1990).

Effects of Context on Comprehension and Production

By way of summary, Figure 8-11 presents an amended version of the levels of language. The figure suggests that producing a sentence is the inverse of understanding a sentence.

To understand a sentence, we hear phonemes, use them to construct the morphemes and phrases of a sentence, and finally extract the thought from the sentence unit. We work from the bottom level up. To produce a sentence, we move in the opposite direction. We start with a propositional thought, translate it into the phrases and morphemes of a sentence, and finally translate these morphemes into phonemes.

Although this analysis describes some of what occurs in understanding and producing sentences, it is oversimplified because it does not consider the *context* in which language processing occurs. Often the context makes what is about to be said predictable. After comprehending just a few words, we jump to conclusions about what we think the entire sentence means; we then use our guess to help us understand the rest of the sentence. In such cases, understanding proceeds from the highest level down as well as from the lowest level up (Adams & Collins, 1979).

Indeed, there are cases in which language understanding is nearly impossible without some context. To illustrate, try reading the following paragraph:

The procedure is actually quite simple. First you arrange things into different groups. Of course, one pile may be sufficient, depending on how much there is to do. If you have to go somewhere else due to lack of facilities, that is the next step; otherwise you are pretty well set. It is important

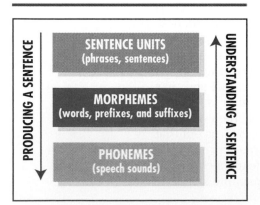

Figure 8-11

Levels of Understanding and Producing Sentences   In producing a sentence, we translate a propositional thought into the phrases and morphemes of a sentence and translate these morphemes into phonemes. In understanding a sentence, we go in the opposite direction—we use phonemes to construct the morphemes and phrases of a sentence and from these units extract the underlying propositions.

PRODUCING A SENTENCE

SENTENCE UNITS
(phrases, sentences)

MORPHEMES
(words, prefixes, and suffixes)

PHONEMES
(speech sounds)

UNDERSTANDING A SENTENCE

not to overdo things. That is, it is better to do too few things at once than too many. . . . At first the whole procedure will seem complicated. Soon, however, it will become just another facet of life. (After Bransford & Johnson, 1973)

In reading the paragraph, you no doubt had difficulty understanding exactly what it was about. But given the context of "washing clothes," you can use your knowledge about washing clothes to interpret all the cryptic parts of the passage. The "procedure" referred to in the first sentence is "washing clothes"; the "things" referred to in the first sentence are "clothes"; the "different groups" are "groups of clothing of different colors"; and so on. Thus, we can replace abstract concepts with more concrete ones. Reread the paragraph; your understanding of it should now be excellent.

Language production depends on context. You would probably use different language when giving directions to a group of tourists than when telling a neighbor where a particular restaurant or store is located.

Perhaps the most salient part of the context, though, is the person (or persons) we are communicating with. In understanding a sentence, it is not enough to understand its phonemes, morphemes, and phrases; we must also understand the speaker's *intention* in uttering that particular sentence (often referred to as the *pragmatic* aspect of language). For example, when someone at dinner asks you, "Can you pass the potatoes?" you usually assume that the intention was not to find out whether you are physically capable of lifting the potatoes but, rather, to get you to actually pass the potatoes. However, had your arm been in a sling, then given the identical question you might assume that the speaker's intention was to determine your physical capability. In both cases the sentence is the same; what changes is the speaker's goal in uttering the sentence (Grice, 1975). There is abundant evidence that people consider the speaker's intention as part of the process of comprehension (Clark, 1984).

There are similar effects in the production of language. If someone asks you, "Where is the Empire State Building?" you will say different things depending on the physical context and the assumptions you make about the questioner. If the question is asked of you in Detroit, for example, you might answer, "In New York"; if the question is asked in Brooklyn, you might say, "In midtown Manhattan"; and if the question is asked in Manhattan, you might say, "On 34th Street." In speaking, as in understanding, one must determine how the utterance fits the context.

The Neural Bases of Language

It has been known for well over 100 years that certain regions of the human brain are specialized for language. For almost all right-handers and for most left-handers, these regions are in the left hemisphere. In Chapter 2 we noted that damage to these regions results in *aphasia,* or language deficits. Also in that chapter, we emphasized the relationship between the site of the brain damage and whether the resulting deficit was primarily one of production or comprehension. Here we focus on the relationship between the site of the damage and whether the deficit involves syntactic or semantic knowledge.

Recall from Chapter 2 that two regions of the left hemisphere of the cortex are critical for language: *Broca's area,* which lies in the frontal lobes, and *Wernicke's area,* which lies in the temporal region (refer back to Figure 2-10). Damage to either of these areas leads to specific kinds of aphasia. The disrupted language of a patient with *Broca's aphasia* is illustrated by the following interview, in which "E" designates the interviewer and "P" the patient:

E: Were you in the Coast Guard?

P: No, er, yes, yes . . . ship . . . Massachu . . . chusetts . . . Coast Guard . . . years. [Raises hands twice with fingers indicating "19"]

E: Oh, you were in the Coast Guard for 19 years.

P: Oh . . . boy . . . right . . . right.

E: Why are you in the hospital?

P: [Points to paralyzed arm] Arm no good. [Points to mouth] Speech . . . can't say . . . talk, you see.

E: What happened to make you lose your speech?

P: Head, fall, Jesus Christ, me no good, str, str . . . oh Jesus . . . stroke.

E: Could you tell me what you've been doing in the hospital?

P: Yes sure. Me go, er, uh, P.T. nine o'cot, speech . . . two times . . . read . . . wr . . . ripe, er, rike, er, write . . . practice . . . get-ting better. (Gardner, 1975, p. 61)

The speech lacks fluency. Even in simple sentences, pauses and hesitations are plentiful. This is in contrast to the fluent speech of a patient with *Wernicke's aphasia:*

Boy, I'm sweating, I'm awful nervous, you know, once in a while I get caught up. I can't mention the tarripoi, a month ago, quite a little, I've done a lot well, I impose a lot, while, on the other hand, you know what I mean, I have to run around, look it over, trebin and all that sort of stuff. (Gardner, 1975, p. 68)

In addition to fluency, there are other marked differences between Broca's and Wernicke's aphasias. The speech of a Broca's aphasic consists mainly of content words. It contains few grammatical morphemes and complex sentences and, in general, has a telegraphic quality that is reminiscent of the language of very young children. In contrast, the language of a Wernicke's aphasic preserves syntax but is remarkably devoid of content. There are clear problems in finding the right noun, and occasionally words are invented for the occasion (as in the use of "tarripoi" and "trebin" in the example above). These observations suggest that Broca's aphasia involves a disruption at the syntactic stage whereas Wernicke's aphasia involves a disruption at the semantic level of words and concepts.

These characterizations of the two aphasias are supported by the results of experiments. In a study that tested for a syntactic deficit, participants had to listen to a sentence on each trial and show that they understood it by selecting a picture (from a set) that the sentence described. Some sentences could be understood without using much syntactic knowledge. For example, given "The bicycle the boy is holding is broken," one can figure out that it is the bicycle that is broken and not the boy, solely from one's knowledge of the concepts involved. Understanding other sentences requires extensive syntactic analysis. In "The lion that the tiger is chasing is fat," one must rely on syntax (word order) to determine that it is the lion who is fat, not the tiger. On sentences that did not require much syntactic analysis, Broca's aphasics did almost as well as normal individuals, scoring close to 90% correct. But with sentences that required extensive analysis, Broca's aphasics fell to the level of guessing (for example, given the sentence about the lion and tiger, they were as likely to select the picture with a fat tiger as the one with the fat lion). In contrast, the performance of Wernicke's aphasics did not depend on the syntactic demands of the sentence. Thus, Broca's aphasia, but not Wernicke's, seems to consist in part of disruption of syntax (Caramazza & Zurif, 1976).

Other experiments have tested for a semantic deficit in Wernicke's aphasia. In one study, participants were presented with three words at a time and asked to select the two that were most similar in meaning. The words included animal terms, such as "dog" and "crocodile," as well as human terms, such as "mother" and "knight." Normal participants used the distinction between humans and animal concepts as the major basis for their selections; given "dog," "crocodile," and "knight," for example, they selected the first two. Wernicke's patients, however, ignored this basic distinction. Although Broca's aphasics showed some differences from normals, their selections at least respected the human–animal distinction. A semantic deficit thus is more pronounced in Wernicke's aphasics than in Broca's aphasics (Zurif et al., 1974).

Although Broca's and Wernicke's aphasias have been studied the most, numerous other kinds of aphasias exist (Benson, Heilman, & Vallenstein, 1985). One of these is referred to as *conduction aphasia.* In this condition, the aphasic seems relatively normal in tests of both syntactic and conceptual abilities but manifests a severe problem when asked to repeat a spoken sentence. A neurological explanation of this curious disorder is that while the brain structures governing basic aspects of comprehension and production are intact, the neural connections between these structures are damaged. Hence, the patient can understand what is said because Wernicke's area is intact, and can produce fluent speech because Broca's area is intact, but cannot transmit what was understood to the speech center because the connecting links between the areas are damaged (Geschwind, 1972).

The preceding discussion presupposes that each kind of aphasia is caused by damage to a specific area of the brain. This idea may be too simple, though: The region that controls a particular linguistic function may vary from one person to another. The best evidence for such individual differences comes from the findings of neurosurgeons preparing to operate on patients with uncontrollable epilepsy. The neurosurgeon needs to remove some brain tissue but first has to be sure that this tissue is not controlling some critical function, such as language. Accordingly, before the surgery and while the patient is awake, the neurosurgeon delivers small electric charges to the area in question and observes their effects on the patient's ability to name things. If electrical stimulation disrupts the patient's naming, the neurosurgeon knows to avoid this location in the operation.

These locations are of great interest to students of language. Within a single patient, these language locations seem to be highly localized. A language location might be less than 1 centimeter in all directions from locations where electrical stimulations do not disrupt language. But—and this is the critical point—different brain locations have to be stimulated to disrupt naming in different patients. For example, one patient's naming may be disrupted by electrical stimulation to locations in the front of the brain but not by stimulation toward the back of the brain, whereas another patient

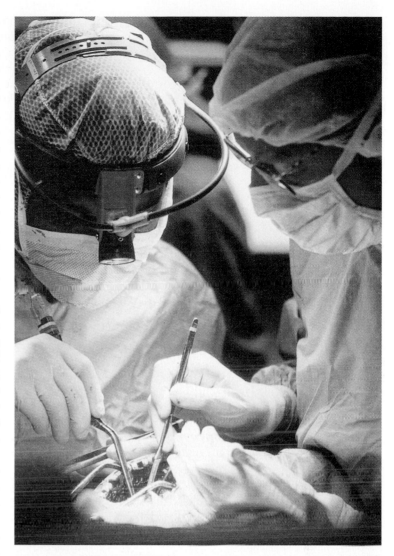

Neurosurgeons need to be sure that any brain tissue that they remove does not control a critical function, like language.

might show a different pattern (Ojemann et al., 1989). If different areas of the brain govern language in different people, presumably the areas associated with aphasias will also vary in different individuals.

Thinking Critically

Now that you have some idea of the units and levels of language (e.g., phonemes, words, semantics, syntax, speaker's intentions), apply these notions to learning a second language. Which components do you think will be the easiest to learn? Which do you think will be the hardest? Why?

How Do We Acquire Language?

Our discussion of language should indicate the enormity of the task confronting children. They must master all levels of language—not only the proper speech sounds but also how these sounds are combined into thousands of words and how these words can be combined into sentences to express thoughts. It is a wonder that virtually all children in all cultures accomplish so much of this in a mere 4 to 5 years. We will first discuss *what* is acquired at each level of language and then consider *how* it is acquired—specifically, what roles learning and innate factors play.

What Is Acquired?

Development occurs at all three levels of language. It starts at the level of phonemes, proceeds to the level of words and other morphemes, and then moves on to the level of sentence units, or syntax. In what follows, we adopt a chronological perspective, tracing the child's development in both understanding and producing language.

Phonemes   Recall that adult listeners are good at discriminating among sounds that correspond to different phonemes in their language, but poor at discriminating between different sounds that correspond to the same phoneme in their language. Remarkably, at birth infants are able to discriminate among sounds that correspond to different phonemes in *any* language. What changes over the first year of life is that infants learn which phonemes are relevant to their language. (In essence, they lose the ability to make distinctions that will be of no use to them in their language.)

These remarkable facts were determined by experiments in which infants were presented with pairs of sounds in succession while they sucked on pacifiers. Since infants suck more in response to a novel stimulus than in response to a familiar one, their rate of sucking can be used to tell whether they perceive two successive sounds as the same or different. Six-month-old infants increase their rate of sucking when the successive sounds correspond to different phonemes in any language, whereas 1-year-olds increase their rate of sucking only when the successive sounds correspond to different phonemes in their own language. Thus, a 6-month-old Japanese child can distinguish between the phonemes /l/ and /r/ but loses this ability by the end of the first year (Eimas, 1985).

While children learn which phonemes are relevant in their first year of life, it takes several years for them to learn how phonemes

During the first year of life, children learn which speech sounds (phonemes) are relevant to their language.

can be combined to form words. When children first begin to talk, they occasionally produce "impossible" words, such as "dlumber" for "lumber." They do not yet know that in English /l/ cannot follow /d/ at the beginning of a word. By age 4, children have learned most of what they need to know about phoneme combinations.

Words and Concepts   At about 1 year of age, children begin to speak. One-year-olds already have concepts for many things (including family members, household pets, food, toys, and body parts), and when they begin to speak, they are associating these concepts with words that adults use. The beginning vocabulary is roughly the same for all children. Children 1 to 2 years old talk mainly about people ("Dada," "Mama," "baby"), animals ("dog," "cat," "duck"), vehicles ("car," "truck," "boat"), toys ("ball," "block," "book"), food ("juice," "milk," "cookie"), body parts ("eye," "nose," "mouth"), and household implements ("hat," "sock," "spoon").

Children between 18 and 30 months of age learn to combine words in phrases and sentences.

Thereafter, vocabulary development virtually explodes. At 1½ years, a child might have a vocabulary of 25 words; at 6 years, the child's vocabulary is around 15,000 words. To achieve this incredible growth, children have to learn new words at the rate of almost 10 per day (Miller & Gildea, 1987; Templin, 1957). Children seem to be tuned to learning new words. When they hear a word they do not know, they may associate it with one of their concepts that is as yet unlabeled, and they use the context in which the word was spoken to find that concept (Clark, 1983; Markman, 1987).

From Primitive To Complex Sentences   At 1½ to 2½ years, the acquisition of phrase and sentence units, or syntax, begins. Children start to combine single words into two-word utterances such as "There cow" (where the underlying thought is "There's the cow"), "Jimmy bike" (the thought is "That's Jimmy's bike"), or "Towel bed" (the thought is "The towel's on the bed"). There is a telegraphic quality about two-word speech. The child leaves out the grammatical words (such as "a," "an," "the," and "is"), as well as other grammatical morphemes (such as the suffixes "ing," "ed," and "s") and puts in only the words that carry the most important content.

Children progress rapidly from two-word utterances to more complex sentences that express thoughts more precisely. Thus, "Daddy hat" may become "Daddy wear hat" and finally "Daddy is wearing a hat." The next step is the use of conjunctions like "and" and "so" to form compound sentences ("You play with the doll *and* I play with the blocks") and the use of grammatical morphemes like the past tense "ed." The sequence of language development is remarkably similar for all children.

Learning Processes

Now that we have discussed what children acquire in the language process, we can ask how they acquire it. Learning *must* play a role; that is why children who are brought up in an English-speaking household learn English while children raised in a French-speaking household learn French. Innate factors *must* also play a role; that is why all the children in a household learn language but none of the pets do (Gleitman, 1986). We discuss learning next, and then turn to an examination of innate factors. In both discussions, we emphasize sentence units and syntax, for it is at this level of language that the important issues about language acquisition are illustrated most clearly.

Imitation and Conditioning   One possibility is that children learn language by imitating adults. While imitation plays some role in learning words (a parent points to a telephone and says "phone," and the child tries to repeat it), it cannot be the principal means by which children learn to produce and understand sentences. Young children constantly utter sentences that they have never heard an adult say, such as "All gone milk." Even when children at the two-word stage try to imitate longer adult sentences (for example, "Mr. Miller will try"), they produce their usual telegraphic utterances ("Miller try"). In addition, the mistakes children make (such as, "Daddy taked me") suggest that they are trying to apply rules, not simply trying to copy what they have heard adults say (Ervin-Tripp, 1964).

A second possibility is that children acquire language through conditioning. Adults may reward children when they produce a grammatical sentence, and reprimand them when they make mistakes. For this to work, parents would have to respond to every detail in a child's speech. However, Roger Brown, Courtney Cazden, and Ursula Bellugi (1969) found that parents do not pay attention to how the child says something as long as the statement is comprehensible. Also, attempts to correct a child (and hence to apply conditioning) are often futile, as the following example shows:

CHILD: Nobody don't like me.

MOTHER: No, say, "nobody likes me."

CHILD: Nobody don't like me.

MOTHER: No, now listen carefully; say "nobody likes me."

CHILD: Oh! Nobody don't LIKES me. (McNeill, 1966, p. 49)

Hypothesis Testing   The problem with imitation and conditioning is that they focus on specific utterances (one can imitate or reinforce only something specific). However, children often learn something general, such as a rule; they seem to form a hypothesis about a rule of language, test it, and retain it if it works.

Consider the grammatical morpheme "ed." As a general rule in English, "ed" is added to the present tense of verbs to form the past tense (as in "cook–cooked"). Many common verbs, however, are irregular and do not follow this rule ("go–went" and "break–broke" are examples). Many of these irregular verbs express concepts that children use from the beginning. So at an early point children use the past tense of some irregular verbs correctly (probably because they learned them by imitation). Then they learn the past tense for some regular verbs and discover the hypothesis "add 'ed' to the present tense to form the past tense." This hypothesis leads them to add the "ed" ending to many verbs, including irregular ones. They say things like "Annie goed home" and "Jackie breaked the cup," which they have never heard before. Eventually they learn that some verbs are irregular, and they stop overgeneralizing their use of "ed."

How do children generate these hypotheses? There are a few operating principles that all children may use as a guide to forming hypotheses. One is to pay attention to the ends of words. Another is to look for prefixes and suffixes that indicate a change in meaning. A child armed with these two principles is likely to hit upon the hypothesis that "ed" at the end of verbs signals the past tense, since "ed" is a word ending associated with a change in meaning. A third operating principle is to avoid exceptions, which explains why children initially generalize their "ed"-equals-past-tense hypothesis to irregular verbs. Some of these principles appear in Table 8-2 and they seem to hold for the 40 languages studied by Slobin (1971; 1985).

Table 8-2

Operating Principles Used by Young Children

Children from many countries seem to follow these principles in learning to talk and to understand speech. (After Slobin, 1971)

1. Look for systematic changes in the form of words.
2. Look for grammatical markers that clearly indicate changes in meaning.
3. Avoid exceptions.
4. Pay attention to the ends of words.
5. Pay attention to the order of words, prefixes, and suffixes.
6. Avoid interruption or rearrangement of constituents (that is, sentence units).

Innate Factors

As noted earlier, some of our knowledge about language is inborn, or innate. There are, however, controversial questions about the extent and nature of this innate knowledge. One question concerns its *richness.* If our innate knowledge is very rich, or detailed, the process of language acquisition should be similar for different languages even if opportunities for learning differ among cultures. A second question about innate factors involves *critical periods.* As noted in Chapter 4, a common feature of innate behavior is that it will be acquired more readily if the organism is exposed to the right cues during a critical time period. Are there such critical periods in language acquisition? A third question about the innate contribution

Research has shown that there is a critical period for learning syntax. Deaf people can use American Sign Language more effectively if they learn it at an early age.

to language concerns its possible *uniqueness:* Is the ability to learn a language system unique to the human species? We will consider these three questions in turn.

The Richness of Innate Knowledge All children, regardless of their culture and language, seem to go through the same sequence of language development. At age 1, the child speaks a few isolated words; at about age 2, the child speaks two- and three-word sentences; at age 3, sentences become more grammatical; and at age 4, the child sounds much like an adult. Because cultures differ markedly in the opportunities they provide for children to learn from an adult, the fact that this sequence is so consistent across cultures suggests that our innate knowledge about language is very rich.

Indeed, our innate knowledge of language seems to be so rich that children can go through the normal course of language acquisition even when there are no language users around them to serve as models or teachers. A group of researchers studied six deaf children of parents who could hear and had decided not to have their children learn sign language. Before the children received any instruction in lipreading and vocalization, they began to use a system of gestures called *home sign,* which included individual signs and combinations of signs. These deaf children essentially created their own language, and they went through the same stages of development as normal hearing children. Thus, the deaf children initially gestured one sign at a time and later put their pantomimes together into two- and three-concept "sentences" (Feldman, Goldin-Meadow, & Gleitman, 1978).

Critical Periods Like other innate behaviors, language acquisition has some critical periods. This is particularly evident when it comes to acquiring the sound system of a new language—that is, learning new phonemes and their rules of combination. We have already noted that infants less than 1 year old can discriminate among the phonemes of any language but lose this ability by the end of their first year. Hence, the first months of life are a critical period for honing in on the phonemes of one's native language. There also seems to be a critical period for acquiring the sound system of a second language. After a few years of learning a second language, young children are more likely than adults to speak it without an accent (Lenneberg, 1967; Snow, 1987).

More recent research indicates that there is also a critical period for learning syntax. The evidence comes from studies of deaf people who know American Sign Language (ASL), which is a fully developed language and not a pantomime system. The studies of interest involved adults who had been using ASL for 30 years or more but varied in the age at which they had learned it. Although all the participants were born to hearing parents, some were native signers who were exposed to ASL from birth, others first learned ASL between ages 4 and 6, and still others did not encounter ASL until after they were 12. If there is a critical period for learning syntax, the early learners should have shown greater mastery of some aspects of syntax than the later learners, even 30 years after acquisition. This is exactly what the researchers found. With respect to understanding and producing words with multiple morphemes, for example, native signers did better than those who learned ASL when entering school, who in turn did better than those who learned ASL after age 12 (Meier, 1991; Newport, 1990).

The fact that there is a critical stage for the acquisition of syntax fits with the finding that some children raised in extreme circumstances never fully acquire language. Perhaps the best-documented case is that of "Genie," who suffered an unimaginably horrible childhood. She was 14 when she was discovered. Apparently, since the age of 20 months she had lived tied to a chair without ever being spoken to. She had had virtually no social contact. Her blind mother would feed her hurriedly, and she was punished if she ever uttered a sound. Not surprisingly, Genie had developed no language. After she was discovered, she was taught language, but she never became proficient at syntax. Although Genie learned to use many words and to combine them into simple phrases, she could not combine phrases to form elaborate sentences (Curtiss, 1977). The crucial factor behind her lack of syntax development seems to be the relatively late age at which she learned language—tragically, she had missed the critical period for learning syntax.

Can Another Species Learn Human Language?   Some experts believe that the innate capacity to learn language is unique to our species (Chomsky, 1972). They acknowledge that other species have communication systems but argue that these are qualitatively different from ours. Consider the communication system of the chimpanzee. Chimpanzees' vocalizations and gestures are limited in number, and the productivity of their communication system is very low compared to that of human language. Another difference is that chimpanzees do not vary the order of their symbols to vary the meaning of their messages, whereas humans do. For instance, for us, "Jonah ate the whale" means something quite different from "The whale ate Jonah"; there is no evidence for a comparable difference in chimpanzee communications.

The fact that chimpanzee communication is impoverished compared to our own does not prove that chimpanzees lack the capacity for a more productive system. Their system may be adequate for their needs. To determine whether chimpanzees have the same innate capacity that we do, we must see if they can learn our language.

In one of the best-known studies of this question, Alan Gardner and Beatrice Gardner (1972) taught a female chimpanzee named Washoe signs adapted from ASL. (Sign language was used because chimps lack the vocal equipment to pronounce human sounds.) Training began when Washoe was about 1 year old and continued until she was 5. During this time Washoe's caretakers communicated with her only by means of sign language. They first used shaping to teach her signs, waiting for her to make a gesture that resembled a sign and then reinforcing her. Later Washoe learned signs simply by observing and imitating. By age 4, Washoe could produce 130 different signs and could understand even more. She could also generalize a sign from one situation to another. For example, she first learned the sign for "more" in connection with more tickling and then generalized it to indicate more milk.

Other chimpanzees acquired comparable vocabularies. Some of these studies used methods of manual communication other than sign language. For example,

David Premack (1971; 1983) taught a chimpanzee named Sarah to use plastic symbols as words and to communicate by manipulating these symbols. In a series of similar studies, Penny Patterson (1978) taught sign language to a gorilla named Koko, starting when Koko was 1 year old. By age 10 Koko had a vocabulary of more than 400 signs (Patterson & Linden, 1981).

Do these studies prove that apes can learn human language? There seems to be little doubt that the apes' signs are equivalent to our words and that the concepts behind some of these signs are equivalent to ours. But many experts doubt that these studies show that apes can learn syntax, that is, learn to combine signs the way humans combine words into a sentence. Thus, not only can we combine the words "snake," "Eve," "killed," and "the" into the sentence "The snake killed Eve," but we can also combine the same words in a different order to produce a sentence with a different meaning: "Eve killed the snake." Although the studies we have reviewed provide some evidence that apes can combine signs into a sequence resembling a sentence, there is little evidence that apes can alter the order of the signs to produce a different sentence (Brown, 1986; Slobin, 1979).

A researcher studying the gorilla Koko, who was trained to communicate using sign language.

Even the evidence that apes can combine signs into a sentence has come under attack. In early studies, researchers reported cases in which an ape produced what seemed to be a meaningful sequence of signs, such as "Gimme flower" and "Washoe sorry" (Gardner & Gardner, 1972). As data accumulated, it became apparent that, unlike human sentences, the utterances of an ape are often highly repetitious. Thus, "You me banana me banana you" is typical of the signing chimps but would be most odd for a human child. In the cases in which an ape utterance is more like a sentence, the ape may have simply been imitating the sequence of signs made by its human teacher. Thus, some of Washoe's most sentencelike utterances occurred when she was answering a question; for example, the teacher signed "Washoe eat?" and then Washoe signed "Washoe eat time." Here, Washoe's combination of signs may have been a partial imitation of her teacher's combination, which is not how human children learn to combine words (Terrace et al., 1979).

The evidence we have considered thus far supports the conclusion that, although apes can develop a humanlike vocabulary, they cannot learn to combine their signs in the systematic way that we do. Some more recent studies, however, seem to challenge this conclusion. Researchers taught a 7-year-old pygmy chimpanzee named Kanzi to communicate by manipulating symbols that stand for words. Kanzi learned to manipulate the symbols in a relatively natural way—for example, by listening to his caretakers as they uttered English words while pointing to the symbols. After a few years of language training, Kanzi demonstrated some ability to vary word order to communicate changes in meaning. For example, if Kanzi were going to bite his half-sister Mulika he would signal "bite Mulika"; but if his sister bit him, he would sign "Mulika bite." Kanzi thus seems to have some syntactic knowledge, roughly that of a 2-year-old human (Greenfield and Savage-Rumbaugh, 1990).

These results are tantalizing, but they need to be interpreted with caution. For one thing, so far Kanzi is among the few chimpanzees who have shown any syntactic ability; hence, one may ask how general the results are. Another matter is that, although Kanzi may have the linguistic ability of a 2-year-old, it took him substantially

The chimpanzee on the left has been trained to communicate using a keyboard. The one on the right has learned a kind of sign language; here he makes the sign for "toothbrush."

longer to get to that point than it does a human; also, we do not yet know whether Kanzi, or any other chimpanzee, can get much beyond that point. But perhaps the main reason to be skeptical about any ape developing comparable linguistic abilities to a human has been voiced by Chomsky:

> If an animal had a capacity as biologically advantageous as language but somehow hadn't used it until now, it would be an evolutionary miracle, like finding an island of humans who could be taught to fly. (1991)

Summary

1. Thought occurs in different modes, including symbolic and imaginal. The basic component of a thought is a *concept,* the set of properties that we associate with a class. Concepts provide cognitive economy by allowing us to code many different objects as instances of the same concept; and they also allow us to predict information that is not readily perceptible.

2. A concept includes both a *prototype* (properties that describe the best examples) and a *core* (properties that are more defining of concept membership). Core properties play a major role in well-defined concepts, such as "bachelor"; prototype properties dominate in fuzzy concepts, such as "bird." Most natural concepts are fuzzy. For many natural concepts, including color and animal concepts, the prototypes are surprisingly universal.

3. People can use different processes to categorize objects. For well-defined concepts, people can categorize an object by applying a rule. For fuzzy concepts, they can categorize an object by determining its similarity to a protoype or its similarity to a known exemplar of the concept. These different processes seem to be controlled by different structures in the brain; structures in the medial temporal lobe are critical for the exemplar process, while structures in the frontal lobes are involved in applying rules.

4. Common cases of reasoning symbolically include the evaluation of arguments and hypotheses. Some

arguments are deductively valid: The conclusion of the argument must be true if its premises are true. When evaluating a deductive argument, we sometimes use logical rules to try to prove that the conclusion follows from the premises. Other times, however, we are more sensitive to the content than to the logical form of the argument. In these cases we use mental models, which are concrete representations of the situations described by the premises.

5. Some arguments are inductively strong: The conclusion is probably true if the premises are true. In generating and evaluating such arguments, we often ignore some of the principles of probability theory and rely instead on *heuristics* that focus on similarity or causality. For example, we may estimate the probability that a person belongs to a category by determining the person's similarity to the category's prototype.

6. Not all thoughts are expressed in symbols; some take the form of visual images. Such images contain the kind of visual detail found in perceptions. The mental operations performed on images (such as scanning and rotation) are like the operations carried out on perceptions. Imagery seems to be like perception because it is controlled by the same parts of the brain. Thus, brain damage that results in certain perceptual problems, known as visual neglect, also results in comparable problems in imagery. Furthermore, experiments using brain scanning techniques indicate that the specific regions of the brain involved in an imagery task are the same as those involved in a perceptual task.

7. Problem solving requires breaking down a goal into subgoals that are easier to obtain. Strategies for doing this include reducing differences between the current state and the goal state; means–ends analysis (eliminating the most important differences between the current

and goal states); and working backward. A useful method for studying problem-solving strategies is computer simulation, in which one tries to write a computer program that solves problems the same way people do. Some problems are easier to solve using a symbolic representation; for other problems, a visual representation works best.

8. Expert problem solvers differ from novices in four basic ways: They have more representations to bring to bear on the problem; they represent novel problems in terms of concepts based on solution principles rather than on surface features, they form a plan before acting; and they tend to reason forward rather than working backward.

9. Language, our primary means for communicating thoughts, is structured at three levels. At the highest level are sentence units, including phrases that can be related to units of symbolic thoughts. The next level is that of *words* and parts of words that carry meaning. The lowest level contains speech sounds. The phrases of a sentence are built from words (and other parts of words), whereas the words themselves are constructed from speech sounds.

10. A *phoneme* is a category of speech sounds. Every language has its own set of phonemes and rules for combining them into words. A morpheme is the smallest unit that carries meaning. Most morphemes are words; others are prefixes and suffixes that are added onto words. A language also has rules of *syntax,* for combining words into phrases and phrases into sentences. Understanding a sentence requires not only analyzing phonemes, morphemes, and phrases but also using context and understanding the speaker's intention.

11. Language development occurs at three different levels. At birth infants are able to learn phonemes, but they need several years to learn the rules for combining them. When children begin to speak, they learn

words that name familiar concepts. In learning to produce sentences, children begin with one-word utterances, progress to two-word "telegraphic" speech, and then progress to more complex sentences.

12. Children learn language at least partly by testing hypotheses. Children's hypotheses appear to be guided by a small set of operating principles, which call the child's attention to critical characteristics of utterances, such as word endings. Innate factors also play a role in language acquisition. Our innate knowledge of language seems to be very rich and detailed, as suggested by the fact that all children seem to go through the same stages in acquiring a language. Like other innate behaviors, some language abilities are learned only during a critical period.

13. Our innate capacity to learn language may be unique to our species. Many studies suggest that chimpanzees and gorillas can learn signs that are equivalent to our words, but have difficulty learning to combine these signs in the systematic way in which human beings combine words.

Suggested Readings

Two relatively recent introductions to the psychology of thinking are Osherson and Smith, *Invitation to Cognitive Science: Vol. 3, Thinking* (2nd ed., 1995); and Garnhman and Oakhill, *Thinking and Reasoning* (1994). The study of concepts is reviewed in Smith and Medin, *Categories and Concepts* (1981).

Research on reasoning is reviewed by Kahneman, Slovic, and Tversky, *Judgment Under Uncertainty: Heuristics and Biases* (1982). For more advanced treatments of reasoning, see Holland, Holyoak, Nisbett, and Thagard, *Induction: Processes of Inference, Learning, and Discovery* (1986); Johnson-Laird and Byrne, *Deduction* (1991); and Rips, *The Psychology of Proof* (1994).

For an introduction to the study of imagery, see Kosslyn, *Ghosts in the Mind's Machine* (1983). For more advanced treatments of imagery, see Kosslyn, *Image and Mind* (1980); Shepard and Cooper, *Mental Images and Their Transformations* (1982); and Kosslyn, *The Resolution of the Imagery Debate* (1994).

For an introduction to problem solving, see Anderson, *Cognitive Psychology and Its Implications* (4th ed., 1995); Hayes, *The Complete Problem Solver* (2nd ed., 1989); and Mayer, *Thinking, Problem Solving, and Cognition* (1983). For an advanced treatment, see the classic by Newell and Simon, *Human Problem Solving* (1972).

Numerous books deal with the psychology of language. Standard introductions include Clark and Clark, *Psychology and Language: An Introduction to Psycholinguistics* (1977); and Foss and Hakes, *Psycholinguistics: An Introduction to the Psychology of Language* (1978). For more recent surveys, see Gleitman and Liberman, *Invitation to Cognitive Science: Vol. 1, Language* (2nd ed., 1995); Tartter, *Language Processes* (1986); and Carroll, *Psychology of Language* (1985). For a more advanced treatment, particularly of issues related to Chomsky's theory of language and thought, see Chomsky, *Rules and Representations* (1980). For an introduction to early language development (and other aspects of language), see Pinker, *The Language Instinct* (1994). For more advanced treatments, consult Pinker, *Language Learnability and Language Development* (1984).

Enhance and Explore

To enhance your understanding of the psychological concepts found in this chapter, please consult the following aids:

Study Guide

Learning Objectives, p. 146
Define the Terms, p. 149
Test Your Knowledge, p. 151
Essay Questions, p. 154
Thinking Independently, p. 156

PowerPsych CD-ROM

HOW DO WE SOLVE COMPLEX PROBLEMS?
Ill-Structured Problems
Mental Set
Forming Subgoals
Gambler's Fallacy

PsychCentral

For more information concerning the topics found in this chapter, access psychology links on the Word Wide Web made through the Harcourt Web page at:
http://www.harcourtcollege.com/psych/Fundamentals

www.harcourtcollege.com

http://www.harcourtcollege.com/psych/index.html

How Language Can Direct Thought: Linquistic Relativity and Linguistic Determinism

Dan I. Slobin, *University of California, Berkeley*

Dan I. Slobin

No one would disagree with the claim that language and thought interact in many significant ways. There is disagreement, however, about the proposition that each language has its own influence on the thought and action of its speakers. On the one hand, anyone who has learned more than one language is struck by the many ways in which languages differ from one another. On the other hand, we expect human beings everywhere to have similar ways of experiencing the world.

There are two issues here: linguistic relativity and linguistic determinism. Relativity is easy to demonstrate. While speaking any language, you have to pay attention to the meanings that are grammatically marked in that language. For example, in English you must mark the verb to indicate the time of occurrence of an event you are speaking about: "It's raining"; "It rained"; and so forth. Turkish, however, like many Native-American languages, has more than one past tense, depending on one's source of knowledge of the event. There are two past tenses—one to report direct experience and the other to report events that you know about only by inference or hearsay. Thus, if you were out in the rain last night, you will say, "It rained last night," using the form that indicates you were a witness to the rain; but if you wake up in the morning and see the wet street and garden, you are obliged to use the other past-tense form—the one that indicates that you were not a witness to the rain itself.

Differences of this sort have long fascinated linguists and anthropologists, who have provided hundreds of facts about "exotic" languages—for example, that the form of a verb of handling can depend on the shape of an object that is being handled (Navajo). But it must be pointed out that "non-exotic" languages also have their surprises. For example, in English it is not appropriate to say, "Richard Nixon has worked in Washington," but it is perfectly okay to say, "George Bush has worked in Washington." Why? English restricts the present-perfect tense ("has worked") to assertions about people who are alive. Exotic!

Proponents of linguistic determinism argue that such differences between languages influence the ways people think—perhaps the ways in which whole cultures are organized. Among the strongest statements of this position are those by Benjamin Lee Whorf and his teacher, Edward Sapir, in the first half of the 20th century—hence the label, "The Sapir-Whorf Hypothesis," for the theory of linguistic relativity and determinism. How can such bold claims be substantiated? If one takes the hypothesis seriously, it should be possible to show that Turks are more sensitive to evidence than are Americans, but that Americans are more aware of death than Turks. Clearly, the hypothesis cannot be supported on so grand a level. Rather, experimental psychologists and cognitive anthropologists have sought to find small differences, on controlled tasks, between speakers of various languages.

The results have been mixed. In most cases, human thought and action are overdetermined by an array of causes, so the structure of language may not play a central causal role. Linguistic determinism can best be demonstrated in situations in which language is the principal means of drawing people's attention to particular aspects of experience. Some of the most convincing empirical research demonstrating some degree of linguistic determinism is being conducted under the direction of Stephen C. Levinson. For example, Levinson and his collaborators distinguish between languages that describe spatial relations in terms of the body (such as English "right/left," "front/back") and those that orient to fixed points in the environment (such as "north/south/east/west" in some aboriginal Australian languages). In a language of the second type one would refer, for example, to "your north shoulder" or "the west end of the table"; in narrating a past event, one would have to remember how the actions related to the compass points. Thus, in order to speak this type of language, you always have to know where you are with respect to the compass points, whether you are speaking or not. And Levinson's group has shown, in extensive cross-linguistic and cross-cultural studies, that this is, in fact, the case.

The Influence of Thought on Language

Eleanor Rosch, *University of California, Berkeley*

Are we trapped by our language into a particular view of the world? According to the most dramatic form of the hypothesis of linguistic determinism (Whorf, 1956), the grammar of each language embodies a complete metaphysic. For example, while English has nouns and verbs, Nootka has only verbs, and Hopi divides the world into the two principles of manifest and unmanifest. Whorf claims that such linguistic differences mold the minds of speakers into mutually incomprehensible ways of thinking.

What evidence do we have for the effect of linguistic differences on thought? At the level of metaphysic, Whorf used bizarre sounding literal translations from Native American languages to make his case. But *literal* translations from any language, even familiar ones such as French or German, sound equally strange. At the level of whole societies, language, culture, and thought cannot be separated experimentally. Even in the case where a difference in world view or "metaphysic" has been documented, such as in the Eastern meditation traditions, peoples' ability to understand those traditions has been found to depend on the practices they do, not on the languages they speak or learn (Rosch, 1997).

A less-sweeping Whorfian claim is that grammatical form classes (such as nouns and verbs in English or shape classifiers in Navajo) affect aspects of thought such as classification or memory. Here one can do experiments, but the findings have been largely negative. For example, grammatical classes do not aid memory the way semantic classes (meaning units such as *plants* or *animals*) do. And speaking a language with shape classifiers does not assure that one will prefer to classify items by shape rather than color. Perhaps grammatical form classes become so automatically processed that they lose much of their semantic meaningfulness for speakers. Or perhaps there is a separate module of thinking, specifically for speaking, which does not necessarily interact with the rest of the meaning system (Slobin, 1997).

Most research on the language and thought issue has been at the still narrower level of vocabulary items. Do the Inuit really have many words for snow, and do the words as such, rather than the snow, affect their thought? But even vocabulary is not easy to isolate from other factors. Languages have names for things in their environments (such as *microchip*); words that map important social and cultural distinction (such as separate terms for *older brother* and *younger brother*); ways of referring to distinctions not encoded by single vocabulary items (skiers find many ways to refer to different kinds of snow); and changes in vocabulary to reflect social change (the disappearance of the polite *you* and familiar *thou* distinction in English). Color categories were once thought to be an ideal domain for vocabulary research since one can measure both color (using the physics of light) and aspects of thought (such as color memory) independently of language. However, the findings have suggested that most facts about both color vocabulary and cognition are determined by the human visual system, with only a secondary role played by language (Hardin & Maffi, 1997; Rosch, 1974). As Slobin (this volume) has indicated, location words are the domain in which there is the most persuasive evidence for effects of a linguistic reference system on thinking. But note that this is a circumscribed domain and that the pragmatics of location (finding objects and finding one's way around) are adequately conveyed by all systems.

Eleanor Rosch

What can we learn from all this? Certainly language differences are intriguing and important, but they do not exist in *isolation*. Posing scientific questions as a dichotomy of isolated extremes on which contributors must take adversarial positions, as in a courtroom or political debate, may be more a matter of our culture (Peng & Nisbett, in press; Tannen, 1998) than of good science that leads to lasting knowledge. We need to learn to think about the relation of language and thought, as well as other polarities in psychology, in terms of interesting, but complex, mutually determining units.

CHAPTER 9

Motivation and Emotion

You're driving along the highway, trying to get to an important job interview on time. You were running late this morning, so you skipped breakfast and you are starving. It seems as if every billboard on the highway is advertising food—egg and ham muffins, juicy hamburgers, cool, sweet juice. Your stomach rumbles and you try to ignore it, but that is impossible. With every mile you are that much hungrier. You nearly rear-end the car in front of you as you stare at a billboard advertising pizza.

You finally arrive at the correct building and find the office of the person you are supposed to meet—potentially your future boss. The minute you meet this person you feel certain twinges. This person is absolutely gorgeous.

Advertisements often appeal to our basic motives, such as sexual motives.

You try to keep your mind on the interview, but your sexual attraction to your potential boss is overwhelming and distracting.

As you are driving home, the only thing that is stronger than your lingering hunger is your anger with yourself for your lack of self-control. How could you let sexual attraction interfere with your performance in that interview? Your anger with yourself is compounded by anger at the traffic jam you find yourself stuck in. In a moment of exasperation, you shake your fist at a driver who cuts you off. He stops his car and gets out. He is huge. Your heart starts racing and you begin to look for an escape route . . .

Sounds like a pretty bad day, doesn't it? If you were to have such a day, you might conclude that you had been a victim of your feelings—of deep desires and motivations and powerful emotions—that are difficult to control through conscious effort.

Those motivations and emotions are the topic of this chapter. *Motivations* run the gamut from basic motivations like hunger and thirst to complex social motivations like achievement or self-fulfillment. In this chapter we focus on the basic motivations—hunger, thirst, and sex; we discuss the higher-order motivations in Chapter 10. Similarly, *emotions* can range from everyday experiences of fear, anger, sadness, or joy to emotional extremes such as those seen in depression and anxiety. In this chapter we focus on the everyday emotions that most people experience. Depression, mania, and other pathological extremes will be taken up in Chapter 12.

What Motivates You?

A **motivation** is *a condition that energizes behavior and gives it direction.* Motivation is experienced subjectively as conscious desire—the desire for food, for drink, for sex. Most of us can choose whether or not to act on our desires. Perhaps we can even deliberately choose not to think about the desires that we refuse to act on. But it is considerably more difficult—perhaps impossible—to control our basic motivations directly. They seem to exist apart from our volition. When we are hungry, it is hard not to want food. When we are hot and thirsty, we cannot help wanting a cool breeze or cold drink. Conscious choice appears to be the consequence, rather than the cause, of our motivational states. What, then, controls our motivation, if not our own rational choice?

This question defines the psychology of motivation. For basic motivations like hunger and thirst, psychologists have traditionally made a distinction between two

motivation a condition that energizes behavior and gives it direction

types of theories. The difference between the theories concerns where the motivation comes from, what causes it, and how the motivation controls behavior. On the one hand are *drive theories,* which stress the role of internal factors in motivation. Some internal drives, such as those related to hunger or thirst, reflect basic physiological needs. For motivations like sex, drive factors seem less tied to absolute physiological needs. After all, you do not need to have sex to the same extent that you need to drink and eat, do you? Still, sex has drive aspects in that internal factors like hormonal state are important in some species and that sex originally evolved to fulfill basic ancestral needs.

On the other hand are *incentive theories,* which stress the motivational role of external events or objects of desire. Incentives are the objects of our motivation—food, drink, sexual partners. Our motivations don't operate in a vacuum—when we want, we seem always to want *something.* The nature of this something pulls us in one or another direction, and so we seek out and work for that particular incentive. Many incentives are rewards: They can produce pleasure and reinforce behavior that leads to them. Some incentives are *primary reinforcers,* able to act as rewards regardless of any prior learning. For example, a sweet taste or a sexual sensation may be pleasant the first time they are experienced. Other incentives are *secondary reinforcers,* which have become rewards partly by association with other reinforcers. For example, money or a good grade can be effective incentives, based on our cultural experience with them and with what they represent. In every case, learning is crucial to the formation of secondary reinforcers—these objects are reinforcing not in their own right but because they are associated with other reinforcers. Learning can also play a part in modulating the effectiveness of some primary reinforcers. For example, you may have been hungry when you were born, but you weren't born specifically desiring the foods that are now your favorites. Incentive theories of motivation focus on the role of learning and experience in the control of motivation.

Incentive and drive theories offer different perspectives on the control of motivation. But the difference between the theoretical perspectives is primarily in their points of view rather than in substance. There is actually no conflict between the two. It is widely acknowledged that both types of pro-

The causes of motivation range from physiological events such as thirst to social aspirations and cultural influences such as those that create the desire to excel.

cesses exist for almost every kind of motivation (Toates, 1986). For example, drive factors can enhance the motivational effect of incentives. The taste of food, for instance, becomes more pleasant to most people when they are hungry (Cabanac, 1979). Have you ever skipped lunch so that you would enjoy an evening feast? Conversely, incentive factors can awaken drive states. Have you ever walked by the delicious aroma coming from a bakery or restaurant and suddenly realized that you were hungry?

Homeostasis and Drives

Our lives depend on keeping certain things the same. If the temperature of your brain were to change by more than several degrees, you would quickly become unconscious. If the proportion of water within you were to rise or fall by more than a few percentage points, your brain and body could not function and you would risk death. Humans and animals walk a tightrope between physiological extremes. Like finely tuned machines, we cannot work unless our internal environment stays in balance. But unlike most machines, we've been designed to maintain this balance ourselves. Even when the outside world changes, our internal states remain relatively stable.

A great deal of basic motivation is directed toward helping to maintain our internal balance. In order to keep our internal world within the narrow limits of physiological survival, we have active control processes to maintain **homeostasis**—that is, *a constant internal state* (*homeo* means "equal" and *stasis* means "static" or "constant"). A homeostatic control process is a system that actively works to maintain a constant state (that is, homeostasis).

homeostasis a constant internal state

Homeostatic control processes can be psychological, physiological, or mechanical. A familiar example is the thermostat that runs your furnace or air conditioner. Thermostats are designed to maintain temperature homeostasis. We have many physiological processes within us that work in homeostatic ways. These processes activate motivations that help maintain homeostasis.

What Causes Thirst?

If you stop eating food, chances are that you could survive quite well (if uncomfortably) for up to several weeks as long as you drank plenty of fluids. But if you tried to go without water you probably could not survive more than a week. And under a hot sun with nothing to drink, a person might not last beyond a single day. Water is crucial to human life. **Thirst** is the *psychological manifestation of the need for water.* What controls our thirst for water?

thirst the psychological manifestation of the need for water

One reservoir of water in the body—*the extracellular reservoir*—is made up of water outside the body cells, contained in blood and other types of body fluid. When water is extracted from the body by the kidneys in the form of urine, excreted by sweat glands in the skin, or breathed out of the lungs as vapor, it comes most directly from the extracellular reservoir. Depletion of the extracellular reservoir reduces blood volume, resulting in a reduction in blood pressure. Pressure receptors within the kidneys, heart, and major blood vessels detect the slight drop in blood pressure and send a signal to the brain that results in the experience of thirst (see Figure 9-1).

When the brain receives this signal, the pituitary gland releases *antidiuretic hormone (ADH)* into the bloodstream. ADH causes the kidneys to retain water from the blood as they filter it. Rather than send this water on to become urine, the kidneys deliver it back to the blood. In addition, the brain sends a neural signal to the kidneys that causes them to release hormones of their own. These hormones activate neurons deep within the brain, producing the desire to drink. You may recall that this entire chain of events is triggered by a drop in blood pressure caused by dehydration. Other events that cause dramatic loss of blood pressure can also produce thirst. For example, soldiers wounded on the battlefield and injured people who have

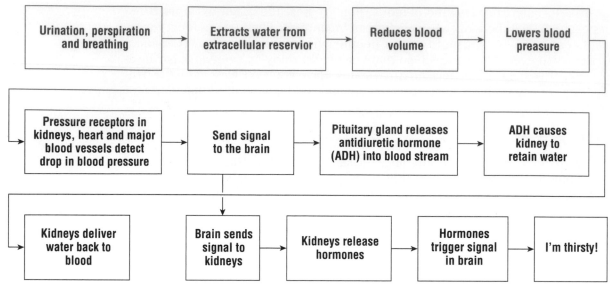

Figure 9-1

The Extracellular Reservoir and Thirst   Depletion of the extracellular reservoir lowers blood pressure, resulting in a series of signals in the kidneys, other organs, and brain that result in the experience of thirst.

bled extensively may feel intense thirst. The cause of their craving is the activation of pressure receptors. This activation triggers the same chain of hormone production, which results in the experience of thirst (Fitzsimons, 1990).

A separate system for producing thirst usually operates in the brain, in parallel with the extracellular thirst system. The intracellular thirst system monitors the level of water inside neurons of the brain, in the *intracellular reservoir.* As the body loses water, the concentrations of "salt" ions of sodium, chloride, and potassium in the bloodstream begin to rise (see Figure 9-2). In essence, the blood becomes saltier. This causes water to migrate from the relatively dilute insides of body cells—including neurons—toward the blood. Neurons within the hypothalamus are activated when higher salt concentration in the blood pulls water from them. This activation produces a desire to drink. Drinking replaces water in the blood, reducing the concentration of salt, which in turn allows water to return to neurons and other cells. That is why people become thirsty after eating salty food—even though they

Figure 9-2

The Intracellular Reservoir and Thirst   When the body loses water, the concentration of salt ions increases, causing water to migrate out of cells into the blood, triggering the hypothalamus to signal thirst.

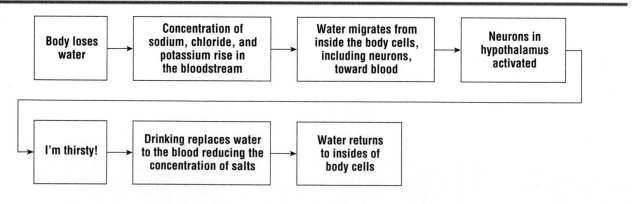

might not have lost water. The salt in the food is absorbed into the blood, where the higher concentrations pull water out of neurons and other cells. When the hypothalamic neurons are forced to give up their water, you experience thirst.

What Makes You Hungry?

Hunger involves many of the same homeostatic concepts as thirst, but eating is much more complex than drinking. When we're thirsty, we generally need only water, and our thirst is directed toward anything that will provide it. But there are lots of different things to eat. We need to eat several kinds of things (proteins, carbohydrates, fats, minerals) in order to be healthy. We need to select the proper balance of foods that contain these things. Evolution has given the brain ways of helping us select the foods we need (and to help us avoid eating things that might poison us). Some of these ways involve the basic taste preferences with which we were born. Others involve mechanisms for learning preferences for particular foods and aversions to others.

Humans are born with preferences for sweet tastes and dislike of bitter tastes.

Flavor is the most important determinant of food preferences. Humans are born "programmed" with likes and dislikes for particular tastes. Even infants respond to sweet tastes with lip-smacking movements and facial expressions that indicate pleasure (Steiner, 1979). The same newborns respond to bitter tastes by turning away and pulling up their faces into expressions of disgust (apes, monkeys, and a number of other species of animals respond the same way). Modern food manufacturers have capitalized on our natural "sweet tooth" to devise sweet foods that spur many people to overconsume.

Why do we find sweet foods and drinks so attractive? Evolutionary psychologists suggest that it is because sweetness is an excellent "label" that told our ancestors, foraging among unknown plants, that a particular food or berry was rich in sugar. Eating sweet foods is an excellent way to gain calories—as any dieter knows—and calories were hard to come by in our evolutionary past. A similar evolutionary explanation has been proposed for our dislike of bitterness. The naturally bitter compounds that occur in certain plants can make the plant toxic to humans. Bitterness, in other words, is a label for a natural type of poison that occurs commonly. Ancestors who avoided bitter plants may have been more successful at avoiding such poisons (Rozin & Schulkin, 1990).

We also develop food preferences through learning. If your first sample of a tasty food or drink is followed by strong symptoms of nausea, you may find that the food seems not at all tasty the next time you try it. The food hasn't changed, but you have—you have formed an association between the food and nausea, and you now experience the food as unpleasant. These learned food aversions are called *conditioned aversions.* Conditioned aversions tend to be strong and permanent only if the food is new to you at the time you become ill. This is why someone who has become ill after drinking too much of a familiar alcoholic beverage may find the thought of that particular drink unpleasant for a few days but then find it palatable again.

Physiological Hunger Cues

How do we know when we're hungry? A common answer is: "My stomach growls." Stomach contractions indeed are most frequent when you are hungry and likely to feel that your stomach is empty. Stomach sensations from contractions are not the real cause of hunger, however. In fact, people who have had their stomachs surgically removed for medical reasons, so that food passes directly to the intestines, can still have strong feelings of hunger even though they lack a stomach and its stretch receptors.

The brain itself senses the need for food. Brain neurons use *glucose* as their principal source of energy. Neurons in particular parts of the brain, especially the brain stem and hypothalamus, are especially sensitive to levels of glucose. When the level falls too low, the activity of these neurons is disrupted. This signals the rest of the brain, producing hunger.

Perhaps surprisingly, the brain's most sensitive signal of nutrient availability comes from neuronal receptors that are separate both from the brain and from food: They are located in the liver (Friedman, 1990). Receptors in the liver are exquisitely sensitive to changes in blood nutrients after digestion, and they send signals about satiety to the brain. A hungry animal will stop eating almost immediately after a tiny infusion of nutrients into the blood supply that goes directly to the liver.

Why should the brain rely on nutrient signals from the liver rather than on its own detectors? The answer may be that the liver can more accurately measure the various types of nutrients used by the body. The brain detects chiefly glucose, but other forms of nutrients, such as complex carbohydrates, proteins, and fats, can be measured, stored, and sometimes converted into other nutrients by the liver. Its role as a general "currency exchange" for nutrients may allow the liver to make the best estimate of the total energy stores available to the body.

Your stomach may not directly signal when you are hungry, but it does signal when you are full. Both the physical expansion of the stomach and the chemicals within the food activate receptors in the stomach's walls, which then relay a signal to the brain that says "fullness" or *satiety*. A second kind of satiety message comes from the duodenum, the part of the intestines that receives food directly from the stomach. When food reaches the duodenum, it causes this structure to release a hormone (cholecystokinin, or CCK) into the many blood vessels that run through it. CCK helps promote physiological digestion, but it also has a psychological consequence. It travels through the blood until it reaches the brain, where it is detected by special receptors. This produces feelings of satiety. Hungry animals can be fooled into a false sense of satiety if microscopic amounts of CCK are infused into their brains shortly after they have begun a meal (Smith & Gibbs, 1994).

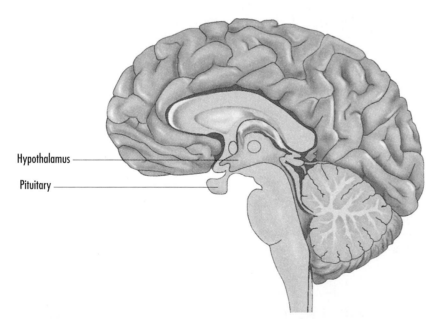

Hypothalamus

Pituitary

Figure 9-3

The Hypothalamus and Pituitary   The hypothalamus is critical in the regulation of hunger.

Integration of Hunger Signals Within the Brain

The brain processes signals for hunger and satiety in two stages to produce the motivation to eat. First, signals from hunger receptors in the brain itself and satiety signals relayed from the stomach and liver are added together in the brain stem to detect the overall level of need (Grill & Kaplan, 1990). In order to become the conscious experience that we know as hunger, and in order to stimulate the seeking of food, the hunger signal must be processed further in the forebrain.

A chief site for hunger processing is the hypothalamus (see Figure 9-3). Hunger is affected in two dramatically different ways by manipulations of two parts of the hypothalamus: the lateral hypothalamus (the parts on each side) and the ventromedial hypothalamus (the lower [ventral] and middle [medial] portion). Destruction of the lateral hypothalamus produces an apparent total lack of hunger, at least until the rest of the brain recovers (Teitelbaum & Epstein, 1962). When small lesions are made in the lateral hypothalamus, an animal may simply ignore food. It may even reject it as though it tasted bad (for example, it will grimace and vigorously spit it out). Unless it is fed artificially, it will voluntarily starve to death. Nearly the exact opposite pattern of behavior is produced by a lesion of the ventromedial hypothalamus. These animals eat voraciously, consuming large quantities of food, especially if it is palatable. Not surprisingly, these animals gain weight until they become quite obese, up to double their normal body weight (see Figure 9-4).

It's clear, however, that many other brain systems interact with the hypothalamus to produce hunger and satiety. Even for animals with lateral hypothalamic lesions, appetite will eventually return. If the rats are fed artificially for several weeks or months after the lesion has been made, they will begin to eat again, but only enough to maintain their lower

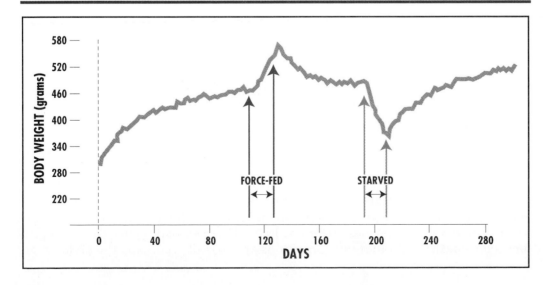

Figure 9-4

Hypothalamic Lesions and Hunger   Damage to the ventromedial hypothalamus produces overeating and obesity.

body weight. They seem to have reached homeostasis at a lower **set point**—*the level at which the body strives to maintain weight.* Similarly, animals with ventromedial hypothalamic lesions do not gain weight infinitely. Eventually they stop at a new, obese body weight. At that point they eat only enough to maintain the new set point. But if they are put on a diet and drop below that set point, they will resume overeating when they are finally given the opportunity (see Figure 9-5). Once they regain that

set point   the level at which the body strives to maintain weight

Figure 9-5

Effects of Forced Feeding and Starvation on Rats with VMH Lesions   Following lesioning of the ventromedial hypothalamus, the rat overeats and gains weight until it stabilizes at a new, obese level. Forced feeding or starvation alters the weight level only temporarily; the rat returns to its stabilized level. (After Hoebel & Teitelbaum, 1966)

level of obesity, they will halt once again. It seems that hypothalamic lesions raise or lower the homeostatic set point for body weight that ordinarily controls hunger. Changing the set point is like resetting a thermostat: The system attempts to achieve the new body weight.

If there are so many ways in which the body regulates how much we eat by signaling hunger and satiety, you may be wondering why we have so much trouble stopping eating when we are munching on potato chips or downing an entire box of candy or scarfing pizza even though we know we are not hungry. So far, we have emphasized homeostatic processes in hunger, but there are many other factors, both biological and environmental, that affect how much we eat. We address some of these factors in the next sections.

What Causes Obesity?

obesity a condition defined as being 30% or more in excess of the recommended weight for one's height and frame

Obesity is common in our culture. Roughly one third of Americans are **obese,** *a condition defined as being 30% or more in excess of the recommended weight for one's height and frame.* The standards for what people should weigh come from insurance industry statistics on the weights at which people of given heights or body frames are thought to live longest. The prevalence of obesity varies from one group to another within society. Physical obesity occurs about equally in both sexes, but the psychological self-perception of being overweight is more common among women. More than 50% of American women, compared to about 35% of men, consider themselves overweight (Brownell & Rodin, 1994; Horm & Anderson, 1993). In the United States, obesity is more prevalent in lower socioeconomic groups than higher ones; however, in developing countries, the reverse is true (Logue, 1991; Sobel & Stunkard, 1989).

Obesity is associated with a higher incidence of diabetes, high blood pressure, and heart disease (Manson et al., 1990; Pi-Sunyer, 1991). As if this were not bad enough, in our culture obesity can also be a social stigma, as obese people are often perceived as being indulgent and lacking willpower. This allegation can be most unfair, since as we will see, in many cases obesity is due to genetic factors rather than overeating. Given all the problems associated with obesity, it is not surprising that each year millions of people spend billions of dollars on diets and drugs to lose weight.

Most researchers agree that obesity is a complex problem that can involve metabolic, nutritional, psychological, and sociological factors. Obesity probably is not a single disorder but a host of disorders that all have excess weight as their major symptom (Rodin, 1981). The question of how one becomes obese is like that of how one gets to Pittsburgh—there are many ways to do it, and the route you take depends on where you are coming from (Offir, 1982). In what follows, we divide the factors that lead to weight gain into two broad classes: (1) genetics and (2) calorie intake (overeating). Roughly speaking, people may become obese because they are genetically predisposed to metabolize nutrients into fat even if they don't eat more than other people (metabolic reasons), or because they eat too much (for psychological or sociological reasons). Both factors may be involved in some cases of obesity, while in others just genetics or just overeating may be the culprit.

Genetic Factors in Obesity

It has long been known that obesity runs in families. In families in which neither parent is obese, only about 10% of the children will be obese; if one parent is obese, about 40% of the children will be too; and if both parents are obese, approximately 70% of the children will also be obese (Gurney, 1936). These statistics suggest a biological basis for obesity, but other interpretations are possible (perhaps the children are simply imitating their parents' eating habits). Research findings, however, strongly support a genetic basis for obesity.

One way to get evidence about the role of genetics in obesity is to study identical twins. Identical twins have the same genes. If genes play a role in weight gain, identical twins should be alike in their patterns of weight gain. In one experiment, 12 pairs of identical twins (all males) agreed to stay in a college dormitory for 100 days. The intent of the experiment was to get the twins to gain weight. Each man ate a diet that contained 1,000 extra calories per day. Also, the men's physical activity was restricted; they were not allowed to exercise, and instead spent much of their time reading, playing sedentary games, and watching television. By the end of the 100 days, all of the men had gained weight, but the amount

Both biological and psychological factors play roles in body weight.

gained varied considerably, from 9 to 30 pounds. However—and this is the critical point—there was hardly any variation in the amount gained *within* a pair of twins (the variation being between pairs of twins). Identical twins gained almost identical amounts. Moreover, identical twins tended to gain weight in the same places. If one member of a pair of twins gained weight in his middle, so would the other; if one member of another pair of twins gained weight on his hips and thighs, so would the other (Bouchard et al., 1990).

These results make it clear why we should not assume that obese people necessarily eat more than nonobese people. Despite eating roughly the same amount (1,000 extra calories), the weight gain of the twins varied. This difference between pairs of twins seems to arise from how their bodies metabolized the extra calories. The bodies of obese people tend to convert a larger proportion of calories into fat stores, whereas the bodies of nonobese people are likely to burn off the same calories through different metabolic processes, regardless of how much is eaten (Ravussin et al., 1988).

Another factor that may be controlled by genes is the number of fat cells in the body. Obese people may have as many as three times as many fat cells as nonobese people (Knittle & Hirsch, 1968). There is a link between genes and the number of fat cells, and another link between the number of fat cells and obesity; by this chain, genes are connected to obesity.

Genes may also influence the set point at which the body regulates weight (Bouchard et al., 1989). There is a strong tendency for obese adults, both humans and animals, to return to their original body weight after a particular diet has ended. The brain may detect changes in the level of body fat and influence the sensation of hunger accordingly (Weigle, 1994).

Overeating and Obesity

While physiological factors such as fat regulation and metabolic rate are important determinants of body weight, there is no question that overeating can also cause obesity. What are the psychological factors that contribute to overeating?

Table 9-1

Weight Loss Following Different Treatments   People who learned new eating and exercise habits through behavioral modification were more successful at weight loss than those who used only diet drugs.

	Weight Loss After Treatment	Weight Loss One Year Later
Treatment groups		
Behavior modification only	24.0	19.8
Drug therapy only	31.9	13.8
Combined treatment	33.7	10.1
Control groups		
Waiting list	2.9 (gain)	—
Physician office visits	13.2	—

Many overweight people are constantly dieting. Dieting is an exercise of conscious restraint on eating, and this restraint may change the ability to read the body's cues about hunger and satiety. A laboratory study shows what happens when restrained eaters (people who chronically restrict what they eat) drop their restraints. Restrained and unrestrained eaters (both of normal weight) were required to drink either two milk shakes, one milk shake, or none; they then sampled several flavors of ice cream and were encouraged to eat as much as they wanted. The more milk shakes the unrestrained eaters were required to drink, the less ice cream they consumed later. In contrast, the restrained eaters who had drunk two milk shakes ate more ice cream than did those who had drunk one milk shake or none before tasting the ice cream. Thus, individuals who are trying to restrain their eating, ignoring their ordinary impulse to eat more, may also come to ignore the feelings of satiety that would ordinarily halt their desire to eat (Herman & Mack, 1975).

Overweight individuals often report that they tend to eat more when they are tense or anxious, and experiments support this. Obese participants eat more in a high-anxiety situation than they do in a low-anxiety situation, while normal-weight participants eat more in low anxiety situations (McKenna, 1972). Other research indicates that any kind of emotional arousal seems to increase food intake in some obese people. In one study, overweight and normal-weight participants saw a different film in each of four sessions. Three of the films aroused various emotions: One was distressing; one, amusing; and one, sexually arousing. The fourth film was a boring travelogue. After viewing each of the films, the participants were asked to taste and evaluate different kinds of crackers. The obese participants ate significantly more crackers after viewing any of the arousing films than they did after seeing the travelogue. Normal-weight individuals ate the same amount of crackers regardless of which film they had seen (White, 1977).

Can obese people ever lose weight? Unfortunately, most dieters are not successful, and those who succeed in shedding pounds often regain them (Jeffery & Wing, 1995). This state of affairs seems to be partly due to the fact that people often overeat after depriving themselves of food. In addition, food deprivation decreases metabolic rate, and the lower one's metabolic rate, the fewer calories expended and the greater one's weight. Consequently, the calorie reduction during dieting is partly offset by the lowered metabolic rate, making it difficult for dieters to meet their goal. The reduction in metabolic rate with dieting may also explain why many people find it harder and harder to lose weight with each successive diet: The body responds to each bout of dieting with a reduction in metabolic rate (Brownell, 1988).

To lose weight and keep it off, it seems that overweight individuals need to establish a new set of permanent eating habits (as opposed to temporary dieting) and engage in a program of exercise. Studies comparing weight control programs find that those that teach people healthy eating and exercise habits result in more successful long-term weight loss than those that simply use appetite suppression drugs to reduce weight (see Table 9-1).

***

Thinking Critically   To what extent do you think your own eating patterns are driven by your body's physiological needs? To what extent are they driven by genetic factors? To what extent by environmental factors?

What Causes Anorexia and Bulimia?

While obesity is the most common eating problem, the opposite problem has also surfaced in the form of anorexia nervosa and bulimia. Both of these disorders involve a pathological desire not to gain weight.

Anorexia nervosa is distinguished by *an extreme, self-imposed weight loss—at least 15% of minimal normal weight.* Some anorexics actually weigh less than 50% of their normal weight. Despite the extreme loss of weight and the problems it leads to, the typical anorexic denies there is a problem and refuses to gain weight. In fact, anorexics frequently think that they look too fat. For females to be diagnosed as anorexic, in addition to the weight loss they must also have stopped menstruating. The weight loss can lead to a number of dangerous side effects, including emaciation, susceptibility to infection, and other symptoms of undernourishment. In extreme cases, the side effects can lead to death.

Anorexia is relatively rare; its incidence in the United States is about 1% (Fairburn, Welch, & Hay, 1993). However, this incidence represents more than a doubling since the 1960s, and the frequency may still be rising (McHugh, 1990). The disorder is 20 times more likely to occur in women than in men, and is particularly prevalent in young women between their teens and their thirties. Typically, anorexics are entirely focused on food, carefully calculating the amount of calories in anything they might consume. Sometimes this concern reaches the point of obsession, as when one anorexic commented to her therapist, "Of course I had breakfast; I ate my Cheerio" or when another anorexic said, "I won't lick a postage stamp—one never knows about calories" (Bruch, 1973). Obsession with food and possible weight gain leads some anorexics to become compulsive exercisers, sometimes exercising vigorously several hours a day (Logue, 1991).

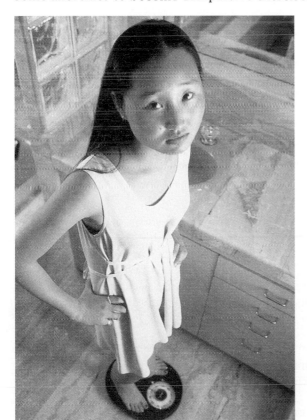

Obsessive concern about weight can develop into an eating disorder.

Bulimia nervosa is characterized by *recurrent episodes of binge eating* (rapid consumption of a large amount of food in a discrete period of time), *often followed by attempts to purge the excess eating by means of vomiting and laxatives.* The binges can be frequent and extreme. A survey of bulimic women found that most of the women binged at least once per day (usually in the evening) and that an average binge involved consuming some 4,800 calories (often sweet or salty carbohydrate foods). However, because of the purges that follow the binges, a bulimic's weight may stay relatively normal; this allows bulimics to hide their eating disorder. This behavior can have high physiological costs: Vomiting and use of laxatives can disrupt the balance of potassium in the body, which can result in problems like dehydration, cardiac arrhythmias, and urinary infections.

Like anorexia, bulimia primarily afflicts young women. Bulimia is somewhat more frequent than anorexia, with an estimated 1% to 3%

anorexia nervosa
a disorder characterized by extreme, self-imposed weight loss—at least 15% of minimal normal weight

bulimia nervosa a disorder characterized by recurrent episodes of binge eating, often followed by attempts to purge the excess eating by means of vomiting and laxatives

Figure 9-6

Icons of Beauty   Jayne Mansfield (left) represented a perfect figure for the 1950s, whereas Julia Roberts (right) was considered the perfect figure for the 1990s.

of American women affected to some degree. Rather than being restricted to the upper classes, bulimia is found in all socioeconomic groups in our society, as well as in all racial and ethnic groups.

An Integrated Model

A number of different causes of anorexia and bulimia have been proposed, including social, biological and personality or family factors. A combination of these factors is probably needed for any individual to develop an eating disorder.

Many psychologists have suggested that social factors, particularly society's emphasis on thinness in women, play a major role in anorexia and bulimia. This emphasis has increased markedly in the past 40 years, which fits with the claim that the incidence of eating disorders has also increased during that period. An indication of this societal influence is the change in what people regard as a "perfect" female figure. Figure 9-6 shows a photograph of Jayne Mansfield, who was popularly thought to have an ideal figure in the 1950s, next to a photograph of actress Julia Roberts, one of today's ideals. Roberts is clearly much thinner than Mansfield. Presumably these "perfect" figures influence women's ideals, which results in the feeling that their own figure is much heavier than the ideal (Garner & Garfinkel, 1980; Logue, 1991).

Clearly not everyone who is exposed to these societal pressures develops an eating disorder. Certain biological vulnerabilities may increase some people's tendencies to develop eating disorders. One hypothesis is that anorexia is caused by malfunctions of the hypothalamus, the part of the brain that helps regulate eating. Anorexic people show lowered functioning of the hypothalamus and abnormalities in several of the neurochemicals that are important to the functioning of the hypothalamus (Fava, Copel, Schweiger, & Herzog, 1989). With regard to bulimia, deficiencies in the neurotransmitter serotonin, which plays a role in both mood regulation and appetite, may be present (Mitchell & deZwaan, 1993).

Personality and family factors may also play a role in anorexia and bulimia. Many young women with eating disorders report that their families demanded "perfection" and extreme self-control but did not allow expressions of warmth or conflict (Bruch, 1973; Minuchin, Rosman, & Baker, 1978). Some young women may seek to gain a sense of control and to elicit expressions of concern from their parents by controlling their eating, and they may eventually develop anorexia. Others may turn to binge eating when they feel emotionally upset or painfully aware of their low self-esteem (Polivy & Herman, 1993).

Therapies designed to help people who have eating disorders regain healthy eating habits and deal with the emotional issues they face have proven useful (Agras, 1993; Fairburn & Hay, 1992). Drugs that regulate the neurotransmitter serotonin can also be helpful, particularly for people with bulimia (FNBC Study Group, 1992). Anorexia and bulimia are serious disorders, however, and those who suffer from them often continue to have significant problems for several years.

What Influences Sexuality?

Like hunger and thirst, sexual desire is a powerful motivation. There are some important differences, however. Sex is a social motive—it typically involves another individual—whereas the survival motives of thirst and hunger concern only the biological self. In addition, hunger and thirst stem from physiological needs, whereas sex does not involve physiological deficits that need to be remedied if the individual is to survive. Consequently, social motives do not lend themselves to a homeostatic analysis.

People vary greatly in their sexual desire and activity and in what they find sexually arousing (see Figures 9-7a and 9-7b). Many scientists have studied whether sexual behaviors and feelings are products of biology—particularly

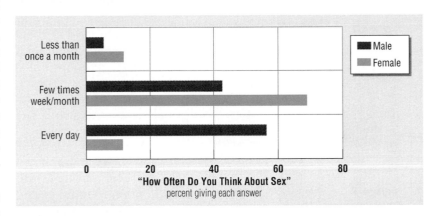

Figure 9-7a

Variations in Sexual Desire   People vary greatly in their levels of sexual desire.

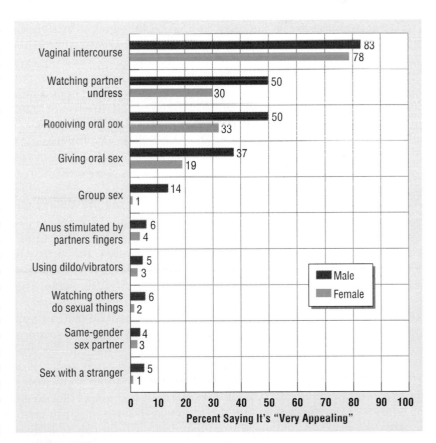

Figure 9-7b

What Kind of Sexual Practices Do People Find Appealing?   A national survey of 18–44-year-olds found that many different sexual practices appeal to people, with men finding more activities appealing than women. (Michael et al., 1994)

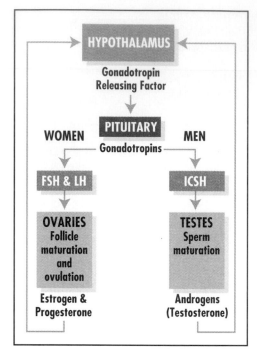

Figure 9-8

The Hormonal System Involved in Sex By way of hormones, the hypothalamus directs the pituitary, which in turn directs the gonads to secrete the sex hormones.

hormones—or environment and learning (early experiences and cultural norms), or of an interaction between the two.

Biological Influences

Changes in body hormone systems begin to occur at puberty, which usually occurs between ages 11 and 14. These changes activate processes of psychological sexuality and trigger the development of physical sexual characteristics such as hair growth and breast development. Control of sexual hormone secretion in adults begins in the hypothalamus (see Figure 9-8). The hypothalamus triggers a series of processes that affect first the pituitary gland, then the rest of the body, and then the brain once again. Thus signals related to sexual function keep a feedback loop operating between body and brain.

At puberty, the hypothalamus begins to secrete chemicals, called *gonadotropin releasing factors.* These stimulate the pituitary gland, which lies immediately below the hypothalamus. The function of the pituitary gland is to secrete hormones into the bloodstream. The pituitary gland's sexual hormones, called *gonadotropins,* circulate through the body to reach the gonads—ovaries in females and testes in males, which generate egg or sperm cells for sexual reproduction. Gonadotropins activate the gonads, causing them to secrete sexual hormones of their own into the bloodstream.

In women, the hypothalamus secretes its gonadotropin releasing factors on a monthly cycle, with hormone levels rising and falling approximately every 28 days. This stimulates the female pituitary to secrete two gonadotropin hormones: *follicle stimulating hormone (FSH)* and *luteinizing hormone (LH),* also on a monthly cycle. These hormones activate the ovaries. Follicle stimulating hormone stimulates the ovaries to generate *follicles,* clusters of cells in the ovaries that allow fertile eggs to develop. Once a follicle has been generated, it begins to secrete the female hormone *estrogen.* Estrogen is released into the bloodstream, where it affects sexual development and, in many species, activates sexual motivation. The second gonadotropin, luteinizing hormone, is released from the pituitary just slightly later than follicle stimulating hormone. It causes ovulation, the release of a mature fertile egg cell from the follicle. When the follicle releases its egg, it also secretes a second female hormone, *progesterone,* which prepares the uterus for implantation of a fertilized egg and, in some species, also activates sexual motivation.

In men, the hypothalamus secretes gonadotropin releasing factor in a constant fashion rather than in a monthly cycle. This causes the male pituitary to constantly release its gonadotropin, called *interstitial cell stimulating hormone (ICSH),* into the bloodstream. ICSH causes male testes to produce mature sperm cells and to dramatically boost secretion of the male hormones called *androgens*—especially *testosterone.* Testosterone and other androgens stimulate the development of male physical characteristics and, in most species, act on the brain to activate sexual desire (and, in some species, facilitate some forms of aggression).

What role do these hormones play in adult sexual desire and arousal? If you experienced the scenario described at the beginning of the chapter, you might conclude that hormones play a strong role in sexual desire and arousal, because you would never *choose* to be sexually aroused during an important job interview. In other species, sexual arousal is closely tied to variations in hormonal levels; in humans, however, social factors may be as important as hormones. Observations of men with serious illnesses (for example, cancer of the testes) who have undergone chemical castration (synthetic hormones administered to suppress or block the use of androgen) typically show that some men lose interest in sex while others continue to lead a normal sex life (Money et al., 1976; Walker, 1978). Apparently, androgen contributes to sexual desire only in some cases. Similarly, some women who have had radical hysterectomies (which remove the ovaries, the main source of estrogen) can experience reductions in sexual desire and arousal, but many do not (Sherwin, 1991).

Studies of the relationship between hormonal fluctuation and sexual interest in healthy people also suggest a mixed picture. For men, testosterone level may have no effect on copulatory function (as indicated by the ability to have an erection) but does increase desire (as indicated by sexual fantasies) (Davidson, 1988). Among women, low levels of estrogen can cause decreased vaginal lubrication, which leads to diminished sexual arousal, pain during sexual activity, and therefore, lowered sexual desire (Sherwin, 1991). Levels of estrogen drop greatly at menopause, and thus postmenopausal women sometimes complain of lowered sexual desire and arousal. Among premenopausal women, however, sexual desire and arousal seem to be barely influenced by the fertility cycle, being affected much more by social and emotional factors (Beck, 1995; Schiavi & Segraves, 1995).

Environmental Influences

Every society places some restrictions on sexual behavior. For example, incest (sexual relations within the immediate family) is prohibited in almost all cultures. Other aspects of sexual behavior—homosexuality, masturbation, sexual activity by children, and premarital sex—are permitted in varying degrees. Among preliterate cultures, acceptable sexual activity varies widely. Some very permissive cultures encourage autoerotic activities and sex play among children of both sexes and allow them to observe adult sexual activity. The Chewa of Africa, for example, believe that if children are not allowed to exercise themselves sexually, they will be unable to produce offspring later. The Sambia of New Guinea have institutionalized bisexuality: From prepuberty until marriage, a boy lives with other males and engages in homosexual practices (Herdt, 1984).

In contrast, very restrictive cultures try to control preadolescent sexual behavior and keep children from learning about sex. The Cuna of South America believe that children should be totally ignorant about sex until they are married; they do not even permit their children to watch animals give birth.

We can also look at changes that occur within countries over time. One such change occurred in the United States and other Western countries between the 1940s and the 1970s. In the 1940s and 1950s, the United States and most other Western countries would have been classified as sexually restrictive. Traditionally, the existence of prepubertal sexuality had been ignored or denied. Marital sex was considered the only legitimate sexual outlet, and other forms of sexual expression (homosexual activities, premarital and extramarital sex) were generally condemned and often prohibited by law. Of course, many members of these societies engaged in such activities, but often with feelings of shame.

Over the years, sexual activities became less restricted. Premarital intercourse, for example, became more acceptable and more frequent. Among American college-educated individuals interviewed in the 1940s, 27% of the women and 49% of the men had engaged in premarital sex by the age of 21 (Kinsey et al., 1953; Kinsey, Pomeroy, & Martin, 1948). In contrast, several surveys of American college students in the 1970s reported percentages ranging from 40 to over 80 for both males and females (Hunt, 1974; Tavris & Sadd, 1977). Furthermore, over the past several decades there has been a gradual trend toward initiating sex at an earlier age. Roughly 50% of both men and women report having had sexual intercourse by age 16 or 17 (Laumann et al., 1994). The change in sexual behavior was greater among women than among men, and the biggest changes occurred in the late 1960s. These changes led many observers of the social scene in the 1970s to conclude that there had been a sexual "revolution."

In the early 1900s, the United States and other Western countries would have been classified as sexually restrictive. Over the years, environmental influences became less restrictive.

Today, it seems that the sexual revolution has been stymied by the fear of sexually transmitted diseases, particularly acquired immunodeficiency syndrome (AIDS). Moreover, the revolution may always have pertained more to behavior than to feelings. In interviews conducted with American college-student couples in the 1970s, only 20% thought that sex between casual acquaintances was completely acceptable (Peplau, Rubin, & Hill, 1977). In a similar vein, while women are becoming more like men with regard to sexual behavior, they continue to differ from men in certain critical attitudes toward sex before marriage. The majority of women who engage in premarital sex do so with only one or two partners with whom they are emotionally involved. Men, in contrast, are more likely to seek sex with multiple partners (Laumann et al., 1994). However, within a given 5-year period, the majority of both men and women are likely to have no more than one sexual partner (Laumann et al., 1994).

Sexual Orientation

sexual orientation
the degree to which an individual is sexually attracted to persons of the opposite sex and/or to persons of the same sex

An individual's **sexual orientation** is *the degree to which he or she is sexually attracted to persons of the opposite sex and/or to persons of the same sex.* Most behavioral scientists conceptualize sexual orientation as a continuum ranging from exclusive heterosexuality to exclusive homosexuality. This oversimplifies the situation, however, because sexual orientation comprises several distinct components, including sexual attraction, sexual behavior, romantic feelings, and self-identification as a heterosexual, homosexual, or bisexual person. Many people who are sexually attracted to persons of the same sex have never participated in any homosexual behaviors; many who have had frequent homosexual encounters do not identify themselves as homosexual or bisexual. To further complicate matters, individuals may shift over time on one or more of the components.

Frequency of Different Sexual Orientations   In a national survey of sexuality in the United States, approximately 10% of adult men and 9% of adult women reported that they experienced predominantly same-sex desire or had engaged in sexual behavior with a person of the same sex since age 18 (Laumann et al., 1994). In terms of self-identification, 2.8% of the men and 1.4% of the woman identified themselves as

homosexual (or gay or lesbian) or bisexual. As the authors of the survey acknowledge, these percentages are undoubtedly underestimates because many people are reluctant to report desires or behaviors that are considered by some to be immoral or pathological. Also, the interviews were conducted in the respondents' homes, and for about 20% of the interviews other family members were present in the home at the time of the interview (though not in the same room). This could have made the respondents even more reluctant to report their sexual desires and practices truthfully.

Links to Biology The determinants of sexual orientation—specifically homosexuality—are currently a subject of debate both in the behavioral sciences and in the public arena. At issue, once again, is the nature-nurture question: Is an adult's sexual orientation determined primarily by innate biological influences, such as genes, or by earlier life experiences?

Evidence for a genetic link comes from recent studies of identical and fraternal twins. As we saw in Chapter 2, identical twins share all their genes, whereas fraternal twins are like ordinary siblings in that they share only about half their genes. To the extent that identical twins are more alike on a trait than fraternal twins, the trait has a genetic component (assuming that other factors, such as differential parental treatment of identical and fraternal twins, can be ruled out).

According to the theory described in the text, both heterosexual and homosexual attraction are based on the same principles.

A study of gay men who had twin brothers found that 52% of the identical twin brothers were also gay, compared with only 22% of the fraternal twin brothers (Bailey & Pillard, 1991). In a comparable study of lesbians, 48% of identical twin sisters were also lesbian, compared with only 16% of fraternal twin sisters (Bailey et al., 1993). These patterns show that there is a correlation between genetic factors and sexual orientation.

But we need to observe two cautions. First, a correlation does not necessarily imply that there is a direct cause-and-effect relationship. As we will see shortly, the

Table 9-2

Gender Nonconformity in Childhood   In a large-scale interview study, gay men and lesbians were more likely than heterosexual men and women to report that they were gender nonconforming during childhood. (After Bell, Weinberg, & Hammersmith, 1981b)

Gender Nonconforming Preferences and Behaviors	Men		Women	
	Gay	Heterosexual	Lesbian	Heterosexual
Had not enjoyed sex-typical activities	63%	10%	63%	15%
Had enjoyed sex-atypical activities	48%	11%	81%	61%
Atypically sex-typed (masculinity/femininity)	56%	8%	80%	24%
Most childhood friends were opposite sex	42%	13%	60%	40%

genes could be influencing some intermediate personality variable that is a more direct precursor of sexual orientation. Second, the percentages themselves reveal that genes cannot be the entire story. If you knew that a man was gay or that a woman was lesbian and you guessed that a genetic clone of this individual—his or her identical twin—would also be gay or lesbian, you would be right only about half the time (i.e., 52% of the time for the gay man and 48% for the lesbian woman). This is no better than a coin flip.

Links to Childhood   The most extensive study of sexual orientation and childhood experiences conducted to date is a large-scale interview study of approximately 1,000 homosexual and 500 heterosexual men and women living in the San Francisco Bay area (Bell, Weinberg, & Hammersmith, 1981). The study uncovered one—and only one—major factor that predicted homosexual orientation in adulthood for both men and women: childhood gender nonconformity—that is, the degree to which a child's activity and playmate preferences are not typical for children of that sex. For example, 63% of both gay men and lesbians said that they had not enjoyed play activities typical of their sex during childhood, compared with only 10% to 15% of heterosexual men and women (see Table 9-2). Gay men and lesbians were also more likely to report that more than half of their childhood friends were members of the opposite sex.

The results of this study also disconfirmed several common theories about the childhood antecedents of a homosexual orientation. For example, contrary to Freud's psychoanalytic theory, an individual's identification with the opposite-sex parent while growing up appears to have no significant effect on whether he or she turns out to be homosexual or heterosexual. In fact, no family-related factors were strongly related to sexual orientation for either men or women.

The study also disconfirmed theories based on learning or conditioning processes (including the common notion that an individual can become gay by being seduced by a person of the same sex or by having contact with an admired teacher, parent, clergyperson, or TV character who is openly gay). Gay men and lesbians were no more likely than their heterosexual counterparts to report having had their first sexual encounter with a person of the same sex. Moreover, they neither lacked heterosexual experiences during their childhood and adolescent years nor found such experiences unpleasant. In fact—contrary to learning or conditioning theories—sexual feelings tended to *precede* rather than *follow* sexual experiences. Gay men and lesbians typically experienced same-sex attractions about 3 years before they engaged in same-sex sexual activity.

Finally, it is clear from all the studies that one's sexual orientation is not simply a matter of choice. Gay men and lesbians do not choose to have erotic feelings toward persons of the same sex any more than heterosexual individuals choose to have erotic feelings toward persons of the opposite sex. Behavioral scientists do disagree over the nature-nurture question—whether the major determinants of sexual orientation are rooted in biology or experience—but the public often misconstrues the question to be whether sexual orientation is determined by variables beyond the individual's control or is freely chosen. That is not the same question.

Exotic Becomes Erotic   A recent theory attempts to integrate all the findings we have reviewed here. It is called the Exotic-Becomes-Erotic (EBE) theory of sexual orientation (Bem, 1996). The central proposition of the theory is that individuals can become erotically attracted to a class of persons from whom they felt different during childhood. Figure 9-9 shows how this is embedded into the overall sequence of events that, according to the theory, lead to an individual's sexual orientation. The sequence begins at the top of the figure with Biological Variables (labeled A) and ends at the bottom with Erotic Attraction (F).

A → B. The theory proposes, first, that biological factors such as genes or prenatal hormones do not influence adult sexual orientation directly but, rather, influence a child's temperaments and personality traits. There is good evidence that most personality traits have a genetic component, including such childhood temperaments as aggression and activity level.

B → C. A child's temperament predisposes him or her to enjoy some activities more than others. One child will enjoy rough-and-tumble play and competitive team sports (male-typical activities); another will prefer to socialize quietly or play jacks or hopscotch (female-typical activities). Thus, depending on the sex of the child, he or she will be genetically predisposed to be gender conforming or gender nonconforming. Children will also prefer to play with peers who share their activity preferences; for example, a child who enjoys baseball or football will selectively seek out boys as playmates.

C → D. Gender-conforming children will feel different from opposite-sex peers, and gender-nonconforming children will feel different from same-sex peers. In the San Francisco study mentioned earlier, 70% to 71% of the gay men and lesbians reported that they had felt different from their same-sex peers during childhood for gender-related reasons, compared with fewer than 8% of heterosexual men and women who did so.

D → E. These feelings of being different produce heightened physiological arousal in the presence of peers from whom the child feels different.

E → F. In later years, this arousal is transformed into erotic arousal or attraction. Evidence for this last step in the process comes, in part, from laboratory studies in which male participants were physiologically aroused in one of several nonsexual ways (for example, by running in place or by watching a videotape of a comedy routine or a grisly killing). When these men subsequently watched a videotape of an attractive woman, they found her more attractive and expressed more interest in dating and kissing her than did men who had not been physiologically aroused. Moreover, it did not matter what caused the initial arousal (White, Fishbein, & Rutstein, 1981). In short, general physiological arousal can be subsequently experienced as, interpreted as, or actually transformed into sexual arousal.

The theory has not been extensively tested; it may well be wrong. But it provides an excellent illustration of how biological and environmental variables might interact to produce a complex human motivation like sexual orientation.

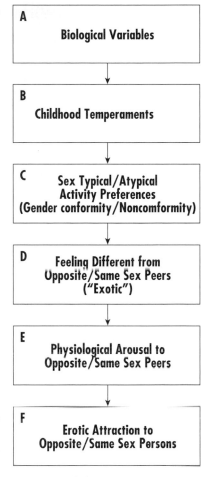

Figure 9-9

The sequence of events leading to sexual orientation for most men and women.

Why do you think many people believe that sexual desire and activity in humans is strongly influenced by hormones when the evidence suggests that it is not?

Thinking Critically

What About the Motivations for Achievement and Power?

You may be suprised that we have not discussed some of the motivations that people often think about when they are describing themselves or other people. For example, you may feel that you don't have enough motivation to do well in your schoolwork. We often describe political leaders as power-hungry, as motivated by a deep desire to control others. Althletes are often highly motivated to perform at their best and to win competitions in their sport.

The motivations for achievement and power have been studied primarily by personality psychologists. Many of the theories that have been used to explain why some people seem to have more achievement motivation or more power motivation are described in Chapter 10. One theory that directly links the more basic motives with higher-order motives is that of Abraham Maslow. Maslow argues that there is a hierarchy of needs ranging from basic physiological needs such as hunger and thirst, to higher-order needs to be loved by others, to achieve and be recognized for one's achievements, to understand and explore, to enjoy art, music and beauty, and finally to realize one's full potential. We decscribe Maslow's theory in detail in Chapter 10. Here it will suffice to say that a fundamental point in Maslow's theory is that we cannot achieve higher-order goals unless our basic physiological needs are being met.

Why Are We So Emotional?

The most basic feelings that we experience include not only motives such as hunger and sex but also emotions such as joy and anger. Emotions and motives are closely related. Emotions can activate and direct behavior in the same way that basic motives do. Emotions may also accompany motivated behavior: Sex, for example, is not only a powerful motive but a potential source of joy as well.

Despite their similarities, emotions need to be distinguished from motives. One common distinction is that emotions are triggered from the outside whereas motives are activated from within. That is, emotions are usually aroused by external events, and emotional reactions are directed toward these events; motives, in contrast, are often aroused by internal events (a homeostatic imbalance, for example) and are naturally directed toward particular objects in the environment (such as food, water, or a mate). Another distinction between motives and emotions is that a motive is usually elicited by a specific need, whereas an emotion can be elicited by a wide variety of stimuli (think of all the different things that can make you angry, for example). These distinctions are not absolute. An external source can sometimes trigger a motive, as when the sight of food triggers hunger. And the discomfort caused by a homeostatic imbalance—severe hunger, for example—can arouse emotions. Nevertheless, emotions and motives are different enough in their sources of activation, subjective experience, and effects on behavior that they merit separate treatment.

What's an Emotion?

emotion   a complex condition that arises in response to certain affectively toned experiences

Emotion is *a complex condition that arises in response to certain affectively toned experiences.* An intense emotion includes several general components (see Figure 9-10) (Frijda, Kuipers, & Schure, 1989; Lazarus, 1991). The component we most frequently recognize in an emotion is the subjective experience of the emotion—the *affective state* or feelings associated with the emotion. A second component is bodily reaction. When angered, for example, you may sometimes tremble or raise your voice, even though you don't want to. A third component is the collection of thoughts and beliefs that accompany the emotion and seem to come to mind automatically. Experiencing joy, for example, often involves thinking about the reasons for the joy ("I did

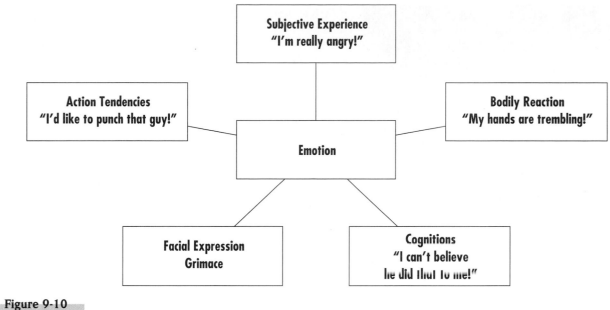

Figure 9-10

Components of Emotion Emotions include at least these five components.

it—I'm accepted into college!"). A fourth component of an emotional experience is facial expression. When you experience disgust, for example, you probably frown, often with your mouth open wide and your eyelids partially closed. A fifth compo-nent is the action tendencies associated with the emotion—the set of behaviors that people tend to engage in when experiencing a certain emotion. Anger may lead you to aggression, for instance.

None of these components by itself is an emotion. All the components come to-gether to create a particular emotion. In addition, each component can influence the others. For example, your **cognitive appraisal** of a situation—*the way you interpret it with respect to your personal goals and well-being*—can lead to a specific emotion: If you believe that a store clerk is trying to cheat you, you are likely to experience anger. But if you enter that situation already angry, you will be even more likely to appraise the clerk's behavior as dishonest.

Emotion theorists are moving toward a *systems perspective* on emotion, in which the components of an emotion are seen as having reciprocal effects on each other. The critical questions in modern theories of emotion concern the detailed nature of each of these components and the specific mechanisms by which they influence each other. For example, one set of questions concerns how bodily responses, be-liefs and cognitions, and facial expressions contribute to the intensity of an experi-enced emotion. Do you feel angrier, for example, when you experience more auto-nomic arousal? Indeed, could you even feel angry if you had no autonomic arousal? Similarly, does the intensity of your anger depend on your having a certain kind of thought, or a certain kind of facial expression? In contrast to these questions about the intensity of an emotion, there are also questions about which components of an emotion are responsible for making the different emotions feel different. Which com-ponents differentiate the emotions?

These questions will guide us as we consider autonomic arousal, cognitive ap-praisal, and facial expression. In the final part of the chapter, we will focus on an ac-tion tendency of an emotion, considering in detail the topic of aggression. Through-out, we will be concerned primarily with the more intense affective states—like those involved in happiness, sadness, anger, fear, and disgust—although the ideas and prin-ciples that will emerge in our discussion are relevant to a variety of feelings.

cognitive appraisal the interpretation of an event or action according to one's own personal goals and well-being

Arousal is common across several emotions, and particular patterns of arousal may be tied to specific emotions.

Arousal and Emotion

When we experience an intense emotion such as fear or anger, we may be aware of a number of bodily changes—including rapid heartbeat and breathing, dryness of the throat and mouth, perspiration, trembling, and a sinking feeling in the stomach. Most of the physiological changes that take place during emotional arousal result from activation of the sympathetic division of the autonomic nervous system as it prepares the body for emergency action (see Chapter 2). The sympathetic system gears the organism for energy output. As the emotion subsides, the parasympathetic system—the energy-conserving system—takes over and returns the organism to its normal state.

Heightened physiological arousal is characteristic of emotional states such as anger and fear, during which the organism must prepare for action—for example, to fight or flee. (The role of this fight-or-flight response in threatening or stressful situations is elaborated in Chapter 11.) Some of the same responses may also occur during joyful excitement or sexual arousal. During emotions such as sorrow or grief, however, some bodily processes may be depressed, or slowed down.

What is the relationship between heightened physiological arousal and the subjective experience of an emotion? In particular, does our perception of our own arousal make up part of the experience of the emotion? To answer this question, researchers have studied the emotional life of individuals with spinal cord injuries. When the spinal cord is severed or lesioned, sensations below the point of injury cannot reach the brain. Since some of these sensations arise from the sympathetic nervous system, the injuries reduce the contributions of autonomic arousal to felt emotion. In one study, army veterans with spinal cord injuries were divided into five groups according to the location on the spinal cord at which the lesion had occurred. In one group, the lesions were near the neck, and no sensations from the sympathetic system could reach the brain. In another group, the lesions were near the base of the spine, allowing at least some sensations from the sympathetic nervous system to reach the brain. The other three groups fell between these two extremes. The five groups represented a continuum of bodily sensation: The higher the location of lesion on the spinal cord, the less the feedback from the autonomic nervous system to the brain.

The participants were interviewed to determine their feelings in situations of fear, anger, grief, and sexual excitement. Each person was asked to recall an emotion-arousing incident prior to the injury and a comparable incident following the injury, and to compare the intensity of their emotional experience in each case. The data for states of fear and anger are shown in Figure 9-11. The higher the person's lesion on the spinal cord (that is, the less the feedback from the autonomic nervous system), the more his emotionality decreased following the injury. The same relationship was true for states of sexual excitement and grief. A reduction in autonomic arousal resulted in a reduction in the intensity of experienced emotion.

Comments by patients with the highest spinal cord lesions suggested that they could react emotionally to arousing situations but that they did not really *feel* emotional. For example: "It's sort of a cold anger. Sometimes I act angry when I see some injustice. I yell and cuss and raise hell, because if you don't do it sometimes, I've learned people will take advantage of you; but it doesn't have the heat to it that it used to. It's a mental kind of anger." Or: "I say I am afraid, like when I'm going into a real stiff exam at school, but I don't really feel afraid, not all tense and shaky with the hollow feeling in my stomach, like I used to."

Clearly, autonomic arousal contributes to the intensity of emotional experience. But does it differentiate among the emotions? Is there one pattern of physiological activity for joy, another for anger, still another for fear, and so on? This question dates back to a seminal paper written by William James more than a century ago (James, 1884). In it, James proposed that the perception of bodily changes is the subjective experience of an emotion: "We are afraid because we run"; "we are angry because we strike." The Danish physiologist Carl Lange arrived at a similar position at about the same time, but for him the bodily changes included autonomic arousal. Their combined position is referred to as the *James-Lange theory,* and it argues as follows: Because the perception of autonomic arousal (and perhaps of other bodily changes) constitutes the experience of an emotion, and because different emotions feel different, there must be a distinct pattern of autonomic activity for each emotion. The James-Lange theory therefore holds that autonomic arousal differentiates among the emotions.

The theory, particularly the part dealing with autonomic arousal, came under severe attack in the 1920s. The attack was led by the physiologist Walter Cannon (1927), who offered three major criticisms. First, since the internal organs are relatively insensitive structures and are not well supplied with nerves,

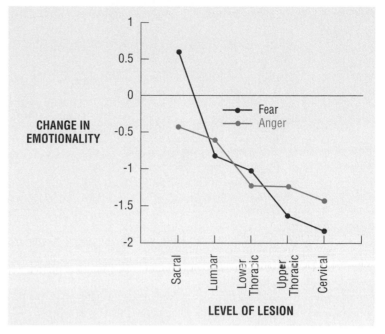

Figure 9-11

The Relationship Between Spinal Cord Lesions and Emotionality
People with spinal cord lesions compared the intensity of their emotional experiences before and after injury. Their reports were coded according to the degree of change: 0 indicates no change; a mild change ("I feel it less, I guess") is scored −1 for a decrease or +1 for an increase; and a strong change ("I feel it a helluva lot less") is scored −2 or +2. Note that the higher the lesion, the greater the decrease in emotionality following injury. (After Schachter, 1971; Hohmann, 1962)

internal changes occur too slowly to be a source of emotional feeling. Second, artificially inducing the bodily changes associated with an emotion—for example, injecting a drug like epinephrine—does not produce the experience of a true emotion. Third, the pattern of autonomic arousal does not seem to differ much from one emotional state to another; for example, while anger makes our heart beat faster, so does the sight of a loved one. The third argument, then, explicitly denies that autonomic arousal can differentiate among the emotions.

Psychologists have tried to rebut Cannon's third point while developing increasingly more accurate measures of the subcomponents of autonomic arousal. Although a few experiments in the 1950s reported distinct physiological patterns for different emotions (Ax, 1953; Funkenstein, 1955), until the 1980s most studies had found little evidence for different patterns of arousal being associated with different emotions. A study by Levenson, Ekman, and Friesen (1990), however, provides strong evidence that there are autonomic patterns distinct to different emotions. Participants produced emotional expressions for each of six emotions—surprise, disgust, sadness, anger, fear, and happiness—by following instructions about which particular facial muscles to contract. While they held an emotional expression for 10 seconds, the researchers measured their heart rate, skin temperature, and other indicators of autonomic arousal. A number of these measures revealed differences between the emotions (see Figure 9-12). Heart rate was faster for the negative emotions of anger, fear, and sadness than it was for happiness, surprise, and disgust; and the former three emotions themselves could be partially distinguished by the fact that skin temperature was higher in anger than in fear or sadness. Thus, even though both anger and the sight of a loved one make our heart beat faster, only anger makes it beat much

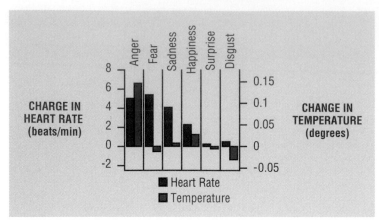

Figure 9-12

Differences in Arousal for Different Emotions   Changes in heart rate (purple) and right finger temperature (green). For heart rate, the changes associated with anger, fear, and sadness were all significantly greater than those for happiness, surprise, and disgust. For finger temperature, the change associated with anger was significantly different from that for all other emotions. (After Ekman, Levenson, & Friesen, 1990)

faster; and although anger and fear have much in common, anger is hot and fear cold (no wonder people describe anger as making their "blood boil," and fear as "bone-chilling" or as "getting cold feet").

Other research suggests that these distinctive arousal patterns may be universal. Levenson, Ekman, and their colleagues studied members of the Minangkabau culture in Western Sumatra, a culture very different from American culture. Again, participants produced facial expressions for various emotions—this time, fear, anger, sadness, and disgust—while measures were taken of their heart rate, skin temperature, and other indicators of arousal. Although the magnitude of the physiological changes was less for the Sumatrans than it was for the Americans reported earlier, the patterns of arousal for the different emotions were the same; again, heart rate was faster for anger, fear, and sadness than for disgust, and skin temperature was highest in anger (Levenson et al., 1992).

These results are important, but they do not provide unequivocal evidence for the James-Lange theory nor for the claim that autonomic arousal is the only component that differentiates among the emotions. The studies demonstrated only that there are some physiological differences between emotions, not that these differences are perceived and experienced as the qualitative differences between the emotions. Even if autonomic arousal does help differentiate some emotions from others, it is unlikely that it differentiates among all emotions; the difference between contentment and pride, for example, is unlikely to be found in visceral reactions. Also, the first two points that Cannon raised against the James-Lange theory still stand: Autonomic arousal is too slow to differentiate among emotional experiences, and artificial induction of arousal does not yield a true emotion. For these reasons, many psychologists still believe that something other than autonomic arousal must be involved in differentiating among the emotions. That something else (or part of it) is usually thought to be the person's cognitive appraisal of the situation.

Cognition and Emotion

When we experience an event or action, we interpret the situation with respect to our personal goals and well-being ("I won the match and I feel happy" or "I failed the test and I feel depressed"). This interpretation, as mentioned earlier, is known as a *cognitive appraisal.*

Clearly, our appraisal of a situation can contribute to the intensity of our emotional experience. If we are in a car that starts to roll down a steep incline, we experience fear, if not terror; but if we know that the car is part of a roller coaster, the fear is usually much less. If we are told by someone that he or she cannot stand the sight of us, we may feel very angry or hurt if that person is a friend, but barely perturbed if the person is someone whom we have never met before. In these cases and countless others, our cognitive appraisal of the situation determines the intensity of our emotional experience (Lazarus, 1991; Lazarus, Kanner, & Folkman, 1980).

Cognitive appraisal may also be heavily responsible for differentiating among the emotions. Unlike autonomic arousal, appraisals are varied enough to distinguish among many different kinds of feelings, and the appraisal process itself may be fast enough to account for the speed with which some emotions arise. Also, we often emphasize cognitive appraisals when we describe the quality of an emotion. We say, "I felt angry because she was unfair" or "I felt frightened because I was abandoned"; unfairness and abandonment are clearly beliefs that result from a cognitive process.

These observations suggest that cognitive appraisals are often enough to determine the quality of emotional experience. This in turn suggests that if people could be induced to be in a neutral state of autonomic arousal, the quality of their emotion would be determined solely by their appraisal of the situation. Schachter and Singer (1962) first tested this claim in an experiment that had a major impact on theories of emotion for the next two decades.

Participants were given an injection of epinephrine, which typically causes autonomic arousal, such as an increase in heart and respiration rates, muscle tremors, and a jittery feeling. The experimenter then manipulated the information the participants were given regarding the effects of epinephrine. Some participants were correctly informed about the arousal consequences of the drug (heart rate acceleration, muscle tremors, and so on); others were given no information about the physiological effects of the drug. The informed participants thus had an explanation for their arousal, while the uninformed participants did not. Schachter and Singer predicted that how the uninformed participants interpreted their symptoms would depend on the situation they were placed in.

Participants were then left in a waiting room with another person, ostensibly another participant but actually a confederate of the experimenter. This confederate created either a happy situation (by making paper airplanes, playing basketball with wads of paper, and so on) or an angry situation (by complaining about the experiment, tearing up a questionnaire, and so on). The results of this study suggested that uninformed participants who were placed in the happy situation rated their feelings as happier than informed participants in that situation did, and uninformed participants in the angry situation rated their feelings as angrier than the informed participants in that situation did. In other words, the subjective state of participants who had a physiological explanation for their arousal was less influenced by the situation than that of participants who did not have the explanation.

The Schachter and Singer experiment was extremely influential, but that influence may not have been justified. The pattern of results in the study did not strongly support the experimenters' hypotheses, in that the differences between certain important groups did not reach statistical significance (a concept explained in the Appendix) and a placebo control group did not react to the experimental manipulations in a manner consistent with the hypotheses. In addition, the type and degree of autonomic arousal may not have been the same in the happy and angry situations, and it certainly was not neutral.

Follow-up experiments found that participants rate their experiences more negatively (less happy or more angry) than the situation warrants, suggesting that the physiological arousal produced by epinephrine is experienced as somewhat unpleasant. Also, these follow-up experiments have sometimes had difficulty reproducing Schachter and Singer's results (Marshall & Zimbardo, 1979; Maslach, 1979). Hence, we need supporting evidence that completely neutral arousal may be misattributed.

Our cognitive appraisal of a situation helps determine the type of emotion we feel as well as its intensity. Cognitive appraisal contributed to the different ways in which people reacted to the verdict in the murder trial of O. J. Simpson.

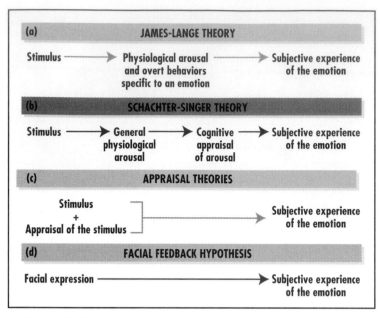

Figure 9-13

Major Theories of Emotion   Different theories of emotion propose different relationships between the components of an emotion.

A different study supplied such evidence. Participants first engaged in strenuous physical exercise and then performed a task in which they were provoked by a confederate of the experimenter. The exercise induced physiological arousal that was neutral and that persisted until the participant was provoked; this arousal should have combined with any that was elicited by the provocation, thereby resulting in a more intense experience of anger. In fact, participants who exercised responded more aggressively to the provocation than participants who did not exercise (Zillman & Bryant, 1974).

The conclusions that emerge from this line of research are that an eliciting event typically results in both autonomic arousal and cognitive appraisal. The perceived arousal and cognitive appraisal are not experienced as independent; rather, the arousal is attributed to the appraisal—"My heart is racing because I'm so angry about what Mary said." These studies indicate that both arousal and appraisal contribute to the intensity of experience—and that sometimes appraisal alone can determine the quality of experience. While research indicates that arousal may aid in differentiating among emotions, it seems to play less of a role than does appraisal. This line of reasoning has been referred to as the *Schacter-Singer theory*.

The top two sections of Figure 9-13 summarize how the components of an emotion interrelate for the two major theories we have discussed so far. Although each of these theories has been supported to some extent, they clearly oversimplify the emotion process. The components, autonomic arousal and cognitive appraisal, are themselves complex events that have subcomponents, and these subcomponents do not all occur at the same time. For example, suppose that an acquaintance says something insulting to you. You may first be aware of the unpleasantness of the remark, then feel a tinge of arousal, next appraise the remark in more detail while experiencing more arousal, and so on. Thus, autonomic arousal and cognitive appraisal are events stretched out in time, and their subcomponents can go on in parallel (Ellsworth, 1991).

Table 9-3

Primary Emotions and Their Causes   Eight primary emotions and their associated appraisals. (After Plutchik, 1980)

Emotion	Appraisal
Grief (sorrow)	Loss of loved one
Fear	Threat
Anger	Obstacle
Joy	Potential mate
Trust	Group member
Disgust	Gruesome object
Anticipation	New territory
Surprise	Sudden novel object

Dimensions of Appraisal   In the third section of Figure 9-13 is a third major theory of emotion, which we have labeled *appraisal theory*. Actually, this is a collection of theories suggesting that it is people's appraisals of situations (not their appraisals of general physiological arousal) that lead to the subjective experience of emotion and the physiological arousal associated with the emotions.

According to one group of appraisal theories, there is a relatively small set of "primary" emotions, each of which is elicited by specific appraisals of an event. Table 9-3 lists several emotions (such as fear) and their respective triggering appraisals (threat). These primary emotions can be found in every human culture and throughout the animal kingdom. Some events may be appraised the same way by everyone; for example, large hissing snakes tend to be appraised as threats by most animals and humans. The types of threats that elicit the appraisals listed in Table 9-3 may differ

Frontiers of Psychology

What Good Is Feeling Good?

Psychologists who are interested in emotions have traditionally focused on the negative emotions—sadness, fear, anger, disgust. As we discuss in this chapter, one of the most popular explanations of the function of negative emotions is an evolutionary one: Negative emotions have evolved to help humans respond quickly to dangerous situations (Levenson, 1994; Tooby & Cosmides, 1990). Negative emotions trigger specific behaviors or action tendencies. When we are frightened, our bodies are mobilized to fight or flee from the threat. When we are disgusted, our face contorts in a way that makes it easier to spit out any disgusting material that might be in our mouth. When we are sad, we "shut down" and reserve our resources.

So what might be the evolutionary value of positive emotions such as joy, contentment, interest, and love? The answer might be obvious—to make us feel good. But this is a somewhat circular argument that doesn't give us much insight. Perhaps surprisingly, few researchers have been interested in positive emotions. A recent exception is Barbara Fredrickson (1998, in press), who has advanced a new and exciting theory of the function of positive emotions, that she calls the *broaden and build theory*.

Fredrickson argues that positive emotions broaden our thinking and actions: Joy creates the urge to play, interest the urge to explore, contentment the urge to savor, and love a recurring cycle of each of these urges. Positive emotions expand our typical ways of thinking and being in the world, pushing us to be more creative, more curious, or more connected to others. By momentarily broadening our thinking and actions, positive emotions promote the discovery of novel and creative ideas, actions, and social bonds. Playing, for instance, can build our physical and social skills; exploring can generate knowledge; and savoring can set our life priorities. It is important to note that these outcomes can endure long after the initial positive emotion has vanished. In this way, positive emotions build up our store of resources to draw upon in times of trouble, including physical resources (such as the ability to outmaneuver a predator), intellectual resources (such as mental maps for finding our way), and social resources (such as someone to turn to for help).

How are positive emotions adaptive? Those of our ancestors who engaged in the behaviors sparked by positive emotions (such as playing, exploring, and savoring) would have acquired more physical, intellectual, and social resources. When those same ancestors later faced threats to life and limb, these resources would have increased their chances of survival. To the extent that the capacities to experience positive and negative emotions are genetically encoded, these capacities, through the process of natural selection, are likely to have become part of our universal human nature.

So, argues Fredrickson, positive emotions may do more for us than we typically acknowledge. Feeling good may broaden our typical ways of thinking and acting, and, in turn, build our personal resources, making us more complex and resilient than we would be otherwise. So the next time you're laughing with friends, pursuing an interest, or enjoying a walk through the park, consider that you may be cultivating more than just fleeting good feelings. You may also be optimizing your long-term health and well-being.

---

across species and human cultures, however (Scherer, 1988). Among humans, for example, many Americans would be shocked to walk onto a beach and discover that everyone is nude, but many Brazilians would be unmoved by such a scene because nude sunbathing is more common in Brazil than in America.

Another group of appraisal theories is concerned with specifying primary dimensions of appraisals (rather than a primary set of emotions) and the emotional consequences of these dimensions. An example is given in Table 9-4. One dimension is the desirability of an anticipated event; another is whether or not the event occurs. When we combine these two dimensions, we get four possible appraisals, each of which seems to produce a distinct emotion. (We are using only four emotions in our example just to keep things simple.) When a desired event occurs (such as falling in love), we experience joy; when a desired event does not occur (the person we are in love with does not love us), we experience

Table 9-4

Primary Appraisal Dimensions and Their Consequences Combinations of two appraisal dimensions and their associated emotions. (After Roseman, 1984; 1979)

	Occur	Not Occur
Desirable	Joy	Sorrow
Undesirable	Distress	Relief

sorrow; when an undesired event occurs (doing poorly on an exam), we experience distress; and when an undesired event does not occur (not doing poorly on an exam), we experience relief.

The preceding example invokes only two dimensions, but most theories of cognitive appraisal assume that multiple dimensions are involved. For example, Smith and Ellsworth (1985, 1987) found that at least six dimensions were needed to describe 15 different emotions (including, for example, anger, guilt, and sadness). These dimensions included (1) the desirability of the situation (pleasant or unpleasant); (2) the effort that one anticipates spending on the situation; (3) the certainty of the situation; (4) the amount of attention that one wants to devote to the situation; (5) the amount of control that one feels over the situation; and (6) the amount of control that one attributes to forces in the situation. To illustrate how the last two dimensions operate, anger is associated with an unpleasant situation caused by another person; guilt is associated with an unpleasant situation brought about by oneself; and sadness is associated with an unpleasant situation controlled by circumstances. Thus, if you and your friend miss a concert that you had your heart set on hearing, you will feel anger if you missed it because your friend carelessly misplaced the tickets, guilt if you misplaced the tickets, and sadness if the performance is canceled due to a performer's illness. The virtue of this kind of approach is that it specifies the appraisal process in detail and accounts for a wide range of emotional experiences.

Expression and Emotion

The facial expression that accompanies an emotion clearly serves to communicate that emotion. Since the publication of Charles Darwin's 1872 work, *The Expression of Emotion in Man and Animals,* psychologists have regarded the communication of emotion as an important function, one with survival value for the species. Thus, looking frightened may warn others that danger is present, and perceiving that someone is angry tells us that he or she may be about to act aggressively. More recent work goes beyond the Darwinian tradition, suggesting that, in addition to their communicative function, emotional expressions contribute to the subjective experience of emotion, just as arousal and appraisal do. This is the emotion theory depicted in the bottom panel of Figure 9-13.

Communication of Emotional Expressions   Certain facial expressions seem to have universal meaning, regardless of the culture in which an individual is raised (see Figure 9-14). The universal expression of anger, for example, involves a flushed face, brows lowered and drawn together, flared nostrils, a clenched jaw, and bared teeth. When people from five countries (the United States, Brazil, Chile, Argentina, and Japan) viewed photographs showing facial expressions of happiness, anger, sadness, disgust, fear, and surprise, they had little difficulty identifying the emotion that each expression conveyed. Even members of remote groups that had had virtually no contact with Western cultures (the Fore and Dani peoples in New Guinea) were able to identify the facial expressions of people from Western cultures correctly. Likewise, American college students who viewed videotapes of emotions expressed by Fore natives identified the emotions accurately, although they sometimes confused fear and surprise (Ekman, 1982).

The universality of certain emotional expressions supports Darwin's claim that they are innate responses with an evolutionary history. According to Darwin, many of the ways in which we express emotion are inherited patterns that originally had some survival value. For example, the expression of disgust or rejection is based on the organism's attempt to rid itself of something unpleasant that it has ingested. To quote Darwin (1872):

> The term "disgust," in its simplest sense, means something offensive to the taste. But as disgust also causes annoyance, it is generally accompanied by a frown, and often by ges-

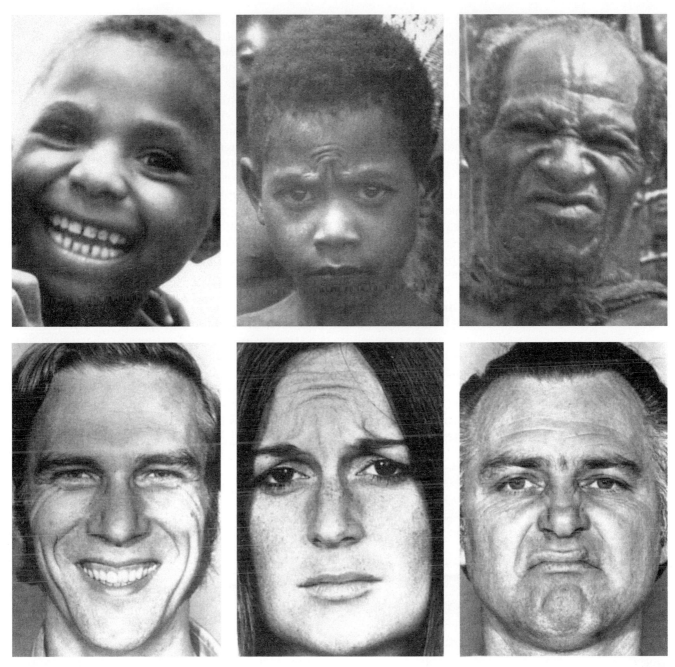

Figure 9-14

The Universality of Facial Expressions of Emotion   Facial expressions are universal in the emotions they convey. Photographs of people from New Guinea and from the United States demonstrate that specific emotions are conveyed by the same facial expressions. Shown here are, from left to right, happiness, sadness, and disgust.

tures as if to push away or to guard oneself against the offensive object. Extreme disgust is expressed by movements around the mouth identical with those preparatory to the act of vomiting. The mouth is opened widely, with the upper lip strongly retracted. The partial closure of the eyelids, or the turning away of the eyes or of the whole body, are likewise highly expressive of disdain. These actions seem to declare that the despised person is not worth looking at, or is disagreeable to behold. Spitting seems an almost universal sign of contempt or disgust; and spitting obviously represents the rejection of anything offensive from the mouth.

While some facial expressions and gestures seem to be closely associated with particular emotions, others are learned from culture. Each culture has its own set of display rules for emotion. These rules specify the types of emotions people should experience in certain situations and the behaviors that are appropriate for each. As an example, in some cultures people who lose a loved one are expected to feel sad and to express the sadness by openly crying and wailing for the loved one to return. In other cultures bereaved people are expected to sing, dance, and be merry. Thus, superimposed on the basic expressions of emotion, which appear to be universal, are conventional forms of expression—a kind of language of emotion that is recognized by others within a culture but often misunderstood by people from other cultures.

Localization in the Brain   The emotional expressions that are universal (for example, those associated with joy, anger, and disgust) are also highly specific: Particular muscles are used to express particular emotions. This combination of universality and specificity suggests that a specialized neurological system may have evolved in humans to interpret the primitive emotional expressions. Evidence indicates that there is indeed such a system and that it is located in the right cerebral hemisphere.

One source of evidence is studies in which pictures of emotional expressions are presented briefly to either the left side or the right side of the participant's visual field. Recall from Chapter 2 that a stimulus presented to the left visual field projects to the right hemisphere whereas a stimulus presented to the right visual field projects to the left hemisphere. When participants have to decide which of two emotions the picture manifests, they are faster and more accurate when the picture is projected to their right hemisphere. In addition, when the two halves of the face convey different emotions (one half may be smiling while the other is frowning), the expression projected to the right hemisphere has the greatest impact on the participant's decision. Another source of evidence about the localization of emotional expressions is studies of patients who have suffered brain damage from strokes or accidents. Patients with damage only in the right hemisphere have more difficulty recognizing facial expressions of emotion than patients with damage only in the left hemisphere (Etcoff, 1985).

In addition to being communicated by facial expressions, emotions are expressed by variations in voice patterns (particularly pitch, timing, and stress). Some of these variations appear to be universal and specific; for example, a sharp increase in pitch indicates fear. The specialized neurological system for perceiving these emotional clues is located in the right cerebral hemisphere, and the evidence for this is similar to that for facial expressions. Individuals are more accurate in identifying the emotional tone of a voice presented to the left ear (which projects information primarily to the right hemisphere) than of one presented to the right ear (which projects primarily to the left hemisphere). And patients who have damage only in the right hemisphere have more trouble identifying emotions from voice clues than do patients who have damage only in the left hemisphere (Ley & Bryden, 1982).

The idea that facial expressions, in addition to their communicative function, also contribute to our experience of emotions is sometimes called the *facial feedback hypothesis* (Tomkins, 1962). According to the hypothesis, just as we receive feedback about (or perceive) our autonomic arousal, so we receive feedback about our facial expression, and this feedback combines with the other components of

The facial feedback hypothesis suggests that the act of smiling actually makes you feel happier.

an emotion to produce a more intense experience. This implies that if you make yourself smile and hold the smile for several seconds, you will begin to feel happier; if you scowl, you will feel tense and angry. (Try it.)

In support of the facial feedback hypothesis, people who exaggerate their facial reactions to emotional stimuli report more emotional response than people who do not. In one study, participants judged the pleasantness of various odors while posing either a smile or a frown. Those who posed the smile perceived the odors as more pleasant; those who posed the frown perceived the odors as less pleasant (Kraut, 1982). In another experiment, participants rated cartoons for funniness while holding a pen either in their teeth or in their lips. Holding a pen in one's teeth forces your face into a smile, while holding it in one's lips forces your face into a frown (try it). As expected, the cartoons were rated as funnier when the pen was held in the teeth than when it was held in the lips (Strack, Martin, & Stepper, 1988).

Some researchers also believe that facial expressions can determine the quality of emotions. Since the expressions for the primary emotions are distinct and occur rapidly, they are at least plausible candidates for contributing to the differentiation of emotions. Tomkins (1980) has proposed that the feedback from a facial expression is inherently positive or negative, thereby suggesting a means by which facial expressions can distinguish positive from negative emotions. Should this suggestion prove true, we are back (in part) to the James-Lange theory mentioned earlier, which holds that emotion is the perception of certain bodily changes. Facial expressions are bodily changes—we are happy because we smile.

Exactly which aspects of a facial expression make it inherently positive or negative? A possible answer may be found in the fact that the contraction of certain facial muscles can affect the blood flow in neighboring blood vessels. This, in turn, may affect cerebral blood flow, which can determine brain temperature, which in turn can facilitate or inhibit the release of various neurotransmitters—and the latter may well be part of the cortical activity that underlies emotion. For example, when we smile, the configuration of facial muscles may lead to a lowering of the temperature in a region of the brain in which the neurotransmitter serotonin is released; this temperature change may block the release of the neurotransmitter, resulting in a positive feeling. The critical path, then, moves from facial expression to blood flow to brain temperature to emotional experience (Zajonc, Murphy, & Inglehart, 1989).

This path from expression to emotion is supported by experiments. One study takes advantage of the fact that pronunciation of the German vowel "ü" (as in *Brücke*, the German word for "bridge") requires extending a facial muscle that is contracted when smiling. This suggests that the facial expression associated with pronouncing ü can lead to a negative feeling. In a study designed to test this hypothesis, German participants read aloud stories that contained either many words with ü or no words with ü; the stories were matched for content and emotional tone. When asked how much they liked the stories, participants rated those with ü-words as less favorable than those with no ü-words. Also, while participants read the stories, the temperature of their foreheads was measured to provide an estimate of brain temperature. Temperatures rose during stories with ü words but not during stories without such words. Thus, the facial expression needed to produce ü led to both increased brain temperature and negative feeling, which supports the proposed path from facial expression to brain temperature to emotional experience (Zajonc, Murphy, & Inglehart, 1989).

Emotion and Action Tendencies

Emotions cause specific action tendencies as well. We may laugh when happy, withdraw when frightened, become aggressive when angry, and so forth. Among these typical action tendencies, psychologists have singled out aggression for extensive study because of the social significance of this action tendency.

According to Freud's early psychoanalytic theory, many of our actions are determined by instincts, particularly the sexual instinct. When expression of these instincts is frustrated, an aggressive drive is induced. Later psychoanalytic theorists broadened this *frustration-aggression hypothesis* to the following claim: Whenever a person's effort to reach any goal is blocked, an aggressive drive is induced that motivates behavior intended to injure the obstacle (person or object) causing the frustration (Dollard et al., 1939). This hypothesis thus has two critical aspects: One is that the usual cause of aggression is frustration; the other is that aggression has the properties of a basic drive, being a form of energy that persists until its goal is satisfied as well as being an inborn reaction (hunger, sex, and other basic drives have these properties). As we will see, it is the drive aspect of the frustration-aggression hypothesis that has been particularly controversial.

Biological Bases of Aggression in Humans   One biological factor that may be related to aggression in human males is testosterone level. Testosterone has been linked to aggression in monkeys. Some studies suggest that in humans as well, higher levels of testosterone are associated with higher levels of aggression. One large-scale study involved more than 4,400 male U.S. veterans. The men were given various psychological tests, some of which measured aggressiveness; blood samples were taken so that their testosterone levels could be determined. Men who had higher levels of testosterone were more likely to have a history of aggression. Since aggressive behavior in males can sometimes lead to antisocial behavior, we might expect that high testosterone levels would be an impediment to success in American life. Indeed, men with extremely high testosterone levels were more likely to have low-status than high-status positions (Dabbs & Morris, 1990).

These findings provide some evidence for a biological basis of aggression in humans, and hence for the view that aggression is like a drive. Still, in these studies the link between testosterone and aggression is often tenuous—large numbers of participants are needed to find the effect—which suggests the need to look elsewhere for determinants of aggression.

Aggression as a Learned Response   Social-learning theory focuses on the behavior patterns that people develop in response to environmental contingencies. Some social behaviors may be rewarded while others may produce unfavorable results; through the process of differential reinforcement, people eventually select the more successful behavior patterns. Social-learning theory differs from strict behaviorism, however, in that it stresses the importance of cognitive processes. Because people can represent situations mentally, they are able to foresee the likely consequences of their actions and to alter their behavior accordingly.

With this emphasis on learning, it is no surprise that social-learning theory rejects the concept of aggression as a frustration-produced drive; the theory proposes instead that aggression is similar to any other learned response. Aggression can be learned through observation or imitation, and the more often it is reinforced, the more likely it is to occur. A person who is frustrated by a blocked goal or disturbed by some stressful event experiences an unpleasant emotion. The response that this emotion elicits will differ, depending on the kinds of responses the individual has learned to use in coping with stressful situa-

Is aggression a drive or a learned response?

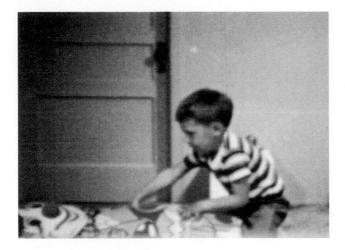

Figure 9-15

Children's Imitation of Adult Aggression   Nursery-school children observed an adult expressing various forms of aggressive behavior toward an inflated doll. After watching the adult, both boys and girls behaved aggressively toward the doll, performing many of the detailed acts of aggression that the adult had displayed, including lifting and throwing the doll, striking it with a hammer, and kicking it.

tions. The frustrated individual may seek help, aggress, withdraw, try even harder to surmount the obstacle, or anesthetize himself or herself with drugs or alcohol. The chosen response will be the one that has relieved frustration most successfully in the past. According to this view, frustration provokes aggression mainly in people who have learned to respond to adverse situations with aggressive behavior (Bandura, 1977).

One source of evidence for social-learning theory is studies showing that aggression, like any other response, can be learned through imitation. Nursery school children who observed an adult expressing various forms of aggression toward a large, inflated doll subsequently imitated many of the adult's actions, including unusual ones (see Figure 9-15). The experiment was expanded to include two filmed versions of aggressive modeling (one showing an adult behaving aggressively toward the doll, the other showing a cartoon character displaying the same aggressive behavior). The results were equally striking. Children who watched either of the two films behaved as aggressively toward the doll as children who had observed a live model displaying aggression.

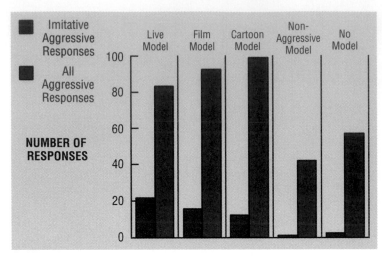

Figure 9-16

Imitation of Aggression Observing aggressive models (either live or on film) greatly increases the amount of aggressive behavior displayed by children, compared to observing a nonaggressive model or no model at all. Note that observation of the live model results in imitation of more specific aggressive acts, whereas observation of filmed (either real-life or cartoon) models instigates more aggressive responses of all kinds. (After Bandura, 1973)

Figure 9-16 shows the measures of aggressive behavior for each of the groups and for two control groups who observed either no model or a nonaggressive model. The conclusion of such studies is that observation of either live or filmed models of aggression increases the likelihood of aggression in the viewer. This may be part of the reason why children whose parents punish them severely are likely to be more aggressive than average: The parents provide the model (Eron, 1987). Similarly, children who watch more violent television shows, including violent cartoons, engage in more violent interactions with their peers (Wood, Wong, & Charchere, 1991).

Aggressive Expression and Catharsis

Studies that try to distinguish between aggression as a drive and aggression as a learned response often focus on *catharsis* (purging an emotion by experiencing it intensely). If aggression is a drive, then the expressions of aggression should be cathartic, resulting in a reduction in the intensity of aggressive feelings and actions (analogous to the way eating leads to a reduction of hunger-based feelings and actions). On the other hand, if aggression is a learned response, the expression of aggression could result in an increase in such actions (if the aggression is reinforced). Psychologists have conducted numerous laboratory studies to determine whether or not aggression decreases once it has been partially expressed. Studies of children indicate that participation in aggressive activities either increases aggressive behavior or maintains it at the same level. Experiments with adults produce similar results. When given repeated opportunities to administer an electric shock to another person (who cannot retaliate), college students become more and more punitive. Participants who are angry become even more punitive on successive attacks than participants who are not angry. If aggression were cathartic, the angry participants should reduce their aggressive drive by acting aggressively and become less punitive the more they aggress (Berkowitz, 1965; Green & Quanty, 1977).

Some evidence about catharsis comes from real-life situations. In one case, California aerospace workers who had been laid off were first interviewed about how they felt about their companies and supervisors, and then asked to describe their feelings in writing. If aggression were cathartic, men who expressed a lot of anger in the interviews should have expressed relatively little in the written reports. The results, however, showed otherwise: The men who let out anger in conversation expressed even more in their reports. Fuming in conversation may have kindled the aggression. In sum, aggression seems to breed aggression rather than dissipate it (Ebbesen, Duncan, & Konecni, 1975).

Thinking Critically

1. If humans develop emotions over the course of evolutionary history because they served useful purposes, what purposes, if any, might be served by extreme manifestations of emotion, such as severe depression or chronic anger?

2. In recent years the notion of emotional intelligence—the ability to understand and regulate your emotions—has become popular. What do you think it means to be emotionally intelligent in our society? How do you think emotional intelligence might vary or remain the same across cultures?

Summary

1. *Motivations* direct and activate our behavior. We can consciously choose whether to act upon a motive, but the processes that directly control motivational states operate in advance of conscious choice. They arise from two sources: internal drive factors and external incentive factors.

2. Incentive factors are goals in the outside world, such as food, water, and partners. Incentives are the targets of motivated behavior and typically are rewarding when achieved. Although some incentives—such as a sweet food when we are hungry—are powerful motivators by themselves, most incentives are established through learning.

3. Drive factors tend to promote *homeostasis:* the preservation of a constant internal state.

4. *Thirst* is a homeostatic motive. There are two regulated variables: intracellular fluid and extracellular fluid. Loss of intracellular fluid is detected by neurons in the hypothalamus that respond to dehydration. Loss of extracellular fluid is detected by blood pressure sensors, neurons in major veins and organs that respond to a drop in pressure. Intracellular and extracellular signals act in parallel to produce thirst.

5. Hunger has evolved to allow us to select an array of nutrients. Humans have innate taste preferences, such as for sweetness, and innate aversions, such as for bitterness, that guide our choice of foods. In addition, we may develop a wide variety of learned preferences and aversions.

6. Hunger is controlled largely by homeostatic deficit and satiety signals. Certain neurons in the brain detect shortages in glucose availability and trigger hunger. Other nutrient detectors, especially in the liver, detect rising levels of energy stores and trigger satiety. A satiety signal, in the form of the hormone cholecystokinin, is released from the intestines to help stop hunger and eating.

7. Two regions of the brain are critical for hunger: the lateral hypothalamus and the ventromedial hypothalamus. Destruction of the lateral hypothalamus leads to undereating; destruction of the ventromedial hypothalamus leads to overeating. Although these regions were originally thought to be centers for hunger and satiety, hunger is not destroyed by any lesion. Another interpretation of these effects is that the lateral and ventromedial regions of the hypothalamus exert reciprocal effects on the homeostatic *set point* for body weight. Damage to the lateral hypothalamus may lower the set point, while damage to the ventromedial hypothalamus may raise the set point.

8. People become *obese* primarily because (1) they are genetically predisposed to be overweight or (2) they overeat (for psychological reasons). The influence of genes is mediated by their effect on fat cells, metabolic rate, and set points. As for overeating and obesity, obese people tend to overeat when they break a diet and eat more when emotionally aroused. Extreme diets appear ineffective in treating obesity, because the deprivation leads to subsequent overeating and to a lowered metabolic rate. What seems to work best is to establish a new permanent set of eating habits and to engage in a program of exercise.

9. *Anorexia nervosa* is characterized by an extreme, self-imposed weight loss. The weight loss may be due to a distorted body image—that is, the anorexic erroneously thinks that she looks too fat. *Bulimia nervosa* is characterized by recurrent episodes of binge eating, followed by attempts to purge the excess eating

by means of vomiting and laxatives. Possible causes include personality factors (for example, need for control), society's emphasis on thinness, and biological factors (for example, a deficit in the neurotransmitter serotonin).

10. The female hormones (estrogen and progesterone) and the male hormones (androgens) are responsible for the body changes that occur at puberty but play only a limited role in human sexual arousal. For humans, environmental determinants of adult sexuality include cultural norms. Although Western society has become increasingly flexible regarding female and male sex roles during the past 30 years, men and women may still differ in their attitudes toward sex and relationships.

11. Although it seems clear that for most people *sexual orientation* is caused, not freely chosen, the nature of the causes is obscure. Recent studies have bolstered the claim that biological, genetic, hormonal, or neural factors may partly determine whether an individual will be heterosexual or homosexual, but the evidence is not conclusive. It is also unknown whether biological factors may influence sexual orientation directly or instead contribute to other traits, such as gender conformity, that indirectly influence the development of sexual orientation.

12. The components of an *emotion* include the subjective experience of emotion, autonomic arousal, cognitive appraisal, emotional expression, and action tendencies. One critical question is: What is the nature of these components? Other critical questions are: How do arousal, appraisal, and expression contribute to the intensity of an emotional experience? and Which components differentiate the emotions?

13. Intense emotions usually involve physiological arousal caused by activation of the sympathetic division of the autonomic nervous system. People with spinal cord injuries, which limit feedback from the autonomic nervous system, report experiencing less intense emotions. Autonomic arousal may also help differentiate among the emotions, since the pattern of arousal (for example, heartbeat, skin temperature) differs for different emotions.

14. A *cognitive appraisal* is an analysis of a situation that results in an emotion. Such appraisals affect both the intensity and the quality of an emotion. When people are induced into a state of undifferentiated arousal, the quality of their emotional experience may be influenced by their appraisal of the situation.

15. The facial expressions that accompany primary emotions have a universal meaning: People from different cultures agree on what emotion a person in a particular photograph is expressing. Cultures may differ in the factors that elicit certain emotions and in their rules for the proper display of emotion. The ability to recognize emotional expression is localized in the right cerebral hemisphere. In addition to their communicative functions, emotional expressions may contribute to the subjective experience of an emotion (the facial feedback hypothesis). In support of this hypothesis, people report a more emotional experience when they exaggerate their facial reactions to emotional stimuli.

16. Aggression is a typical action tendency in response to anger (though it can occur for other reasons as well). According to early psychoanalytic theory, aggression is a drive produced by frustration; according to social-learning theory, it is a learned response. There may be some biological bases of aggression in humans (such as testosterone level in men), but aggressive responses can be learned through imitation and increased in frequency when they are positively reinforced.

Suggested Readings

A general summary of incentive and drive theories of motivation, and their interaction with learning, is provided by Toates, *Motivational Systems* (1986). An overview of biological factors in motivation can be found in Kalat, *Biological Psychology* (6th ed., 1998); and in Carlson, *Physiology of Behavior* (5th ed., 1994). The neural substrates of reward are discussed in detail by Stellar and Stellar, *The Neurobiology of Motivation and Reward* (1985); and by Hoebel in *Stevens' Handbook of Experimental Psychology* (2nd ed., 1988). For analyses of factors controlling eating and drinking, see E. M. Stricker (ed.), "Neurobiology of Food and Fluid Intake," *Handbook of Behavioral Neurobiology* (1990); and Logue, *The Psychology of Eating and Drinking* (1991). A discussion of diverse aspects of human sexuality can be found in McWhirter et al. (eds.), *Homosexuality/Heterosexuality* (1990); and in LeVay, *The Sexual Brain* (1994).

For an introduction to various views on emotion, some chapters in Kavanaugh, Zimmerberg, and Fein (eds.), *Emotion: Interdisciplinary Perspectives* (1996), are very useful. For a more technical treatment of emotion, see Edwards, *Motivation and Emotion: Evolutionary Physiological, Cognitive, and Social Influences* (1999); Lazarus, *Emotion and Adaptation* (1991); Frijda, *The Emotions* (1986); Mandler, *Mind and Emotion* (1982); and Plutchik and Kellerman (eds.), *Emotion: Theory, Research, and Experience* (1980). The role of cognition in emotion is discussed in detail in Dagleish and Power, *Handbook of Cognition and Emotion* (1999).

Interesting books on facial expressions and emotion include Ekman's *Emotion in the Human Face* (2nd ed., 1982), and his *Telling Lies: Clues to Deceit in the Marketplace, Politics, and Marriage* (1985).

The psychoanalytic theory of emotion is presented in two books by Freud: *Beyond the Pleasure Principle* (1920/1975) and *New Introductory Lectures on Psychoanalysis* (1933/1965). For the social-learning approach, see Bandura, *Social Foundations of Thought and Action* (1986).

Books on aggression include Bandura, *Aggression: A Social Learning Analysis* (1973); Tavris, *Anger: The Misunderstood Emotion* (1984); Hamburg and Trudeau (eds.), *Biobehavioral Aspects of Aggression* (1981); and Averill, *Anger and Aggression: An Essay on Emotion* (1982).

Enhance and Explore

To enhance your understanding of the psychological concepts found in this chapter, please consult the following aids:

Study Guide

Learning Objectives, p. 160
Define the Terms, p. 163
Test Your Knowledge, p. 166
Essay Questions, p. 170
Thinking Independently, p. 172

PowerPsych CD-ROM

WHAT MAKES YOU HUNGRY?
Sensitivity to External Cues

WHAT INFLUENCES SEXUALITY?
Psychological Reactions to Orgasm

WHAT'S IN AN EMOTION?
Facial Expressions of Emotion
Genuine or Fake Smile?

PsychCentral

For more information concerning the topics found in this chapter, access psychology links on the Word Wide Web made through the Harcourt Web page at:
http://www.harcourtcollege.com/psych/Fundamentals

www.harcourtcollege.com

http://www.harcourtcollege.com/psych/index.html

Individual Differences, Intelligence, and Personality

CHAPTER **10**

Oskar Stohr and Jack Yufe are identical twins who were born in Trinidad and separated shortly after birth. Oskar was taken to Germany by his mother, where he was raised by his grandmother as a Catholic and a Nazi. Jack remained in Trinidad with his Jewish father, was raised as a Jew, and spent part of his youth on an Israeli kibbutz. The two families never corresponded.

When they were in their late forties, Oskar and Jack were brought together by researchers at the University of Minnesota who were studying sets of twins who had been reared apart. Although Oskar and Jack had met only once before, they showed some remarkable similarities. Both men showed up for the study wearing blue double-breasted shirts, mustaches, and wire-rimmed glasses. Their mannerisms and temperaments were similar, and they shared certain idiosyncrasies: Both liked spicy foods and sweet liqueurs, were absentminded, flushed the toilet before using it, liked to dip buttered toast in their coffee, and enjoyed surprising people by sneezing in elevators.

Many other sets of identical twins studied by the Minnesota researchers also displayed striking similarities. For example, the twins shown in the accompanying photo were separated at birth and were not reunited until they were 31 years old; both had become firefighters. What causes such similarities? Surely there aren't firefighting genes or genes for dipping toast in coffee or genes for surprising people in elevators; such similarities reflect the inherited components of more basic personality characteristics. And indeed, both similarities *and* differences among individuals provide challenges for psychology.

In many ways, every person is like every other person. The biological and psychological processes discussed in this book—development, consciousness, perception, learning, remembering, thinking, motivation, and emotion—are basically the same for all of us. But in other ways every person is different from every other person. Each of us has a distinctive pattern of abilities, beliefs, attitudes, motivations, emotions, and personality traits that makes us unique. It is this individuality that concerns us in this chapter.

These twins, separated at birth, showed remarkable similarities in interests and habits when they first met at age 31.

We begin by returning to a theme we discussed in Chapter 3: the interaction between nature and nurture. In that chapter, we discussed how innate biological factors interact with events in an individual's environment to determine the course of development, focusing particularly on factors that make us all alike. We considered, for example, how innately determined sequences of maturation cause all children to go through the same stages of development in the same sequence, relatively independently of differences in their rearing environments. In this chapter, we focus on the biological and environmental factors that make us different from one another—in other words, the factors that create individuality. We also survey some of the methods used to measure individual differences, including differences in intellectual abilities and personality traits, and we review several general approaches to personality.

How Do Nature and Nurture Interact to Make Each Person an Individual?

If you were asked why one person is taller than another, you would probably give a "nature" (biological) explanation: The taller person has inherited taller "height genes" from his or her parents than the shorter person. Even though health and nutrition can affect a person's growth, you would be correct in assuming that, in general, environmental factors play a minor role in determining a person's height. If, however, you were asked why one person prefers classical music over rock music but another person has the reverse preference, you would be much more inclined to give a "nurture" (environmental) explanation: The different preferences probably developed because the two individuals were exposed to different kinds of music at home or in school; the possibility that there might be genes for musical preference seems unlikely.

But might there be genes for musical talent? Or intelligence, sociability, or sexual orientation? Here the answers are not obvious. Moreover, advocates of particular political positions and social policies frequently invoke one answer or another in support of their viewpoint (for example, Herrnstein & Murray, 1994; also see the discussion of sexual orientation in Chapter 9). Because these debates reveal widespread public misunderstanding about the empirical issues involved, we will describe in some detail the reasoning and methods behavioral scientists use to assess how genetic and environmental factors contribute to individual differences.

Sources of Individual Differences

We begin with Table 10-1, which lists (in descending order) a hypothetical set of scores achieved on an examination by two groups of students. As shown in the last row, the average (mean) score of the students within each group is 82.0. But we can also see that the scores for Group A are much more spread out—that is, more variable—than the scores for Group B. In other words, the scores of students in Group A are more different from one another than scores of students in Group B. As explained in the Appendix, *the degree to which a set of scores differ from one another* can be expressed mathematically by a quantity called their **variance.**

Now consider the scores for Group A. Why are they different from one another? Why do some students do better than others? What accounts for the variance we observe? One obvious possibility is that some students studied for the exam longer than other students. To find out whether and to what extent this is true, we could conduct a hypothetical experiment in which we "controlled for" (that is, held constant) the variable of study time by requiring all

variance　the degree to which a set of scores differ from one another

Table 10-1

Hypothetical Examination Scores of Two Groups of Students

Group A		Group B	
Alice	100	Greta	89
Bob	95	Harold	88
Carol	89	Ilene	83
Dan	83	John	80
Emily	67	Karen	77
Fred	58	Leon	75
Average	82.0	Average	82.0

If all students in a class were required to study for an examination the same length of time, the students' scores would be more alike. The variance of the class's scores would decrease.

students to study exactly 3 hours for the exam, no more and no less. If study time really does affect students' scores, what would happen to the variance of those scores?

First, some of the students who did particularly well because they had studied for more than 3 hours will now do less well. For example, if Alice—who might have studied for 6 hours to achieve her perfect score of 100—had been permitted to study for only 3 hours, her score might have been more like Greta's score of 89. Second, some of the students who did poorly on the exam because they studied less than 3 hours will now do better. Fred—who only had time to skim the reading for the exam—might have obtained a score higher than 58 if he had studied for 3 hours. Like Leon, he might at least have obtained a score of 75. In other words, if we held constant the study time of Group A, the students' scores would bunch closer together, looking more like those for Group B; the variance of their scores would decrease. If we actually did this experiment and observed that the variance of Group A's scores decreased by 60%, we could claim that study time accounted for 60% of the variance of the original scores for this class. In this hypothetical example, then, a major reason that the exam scores differed so much from one another in Group A is that students differed in how much time they spent studying.

Theoretically, we could test for any other potential sources of variance in the same way. If we think that having a good breakfast might affect students' scores, we could feed all the students the same breakfast (or deny breakfast to all the students) and observe whether the variance of their scores is reduced as a result. In general, holding constant any variable that "makes a difference" will reduce the variance of the scores. In the extreme case, if we held all the relevant variables constant, the variance would diminish to zero: Every student would obtain the same score.

It is important to note, however, that we cannot say what will happen to the mean of the scores when we hold a variable constant. For example, if the students in Group A had originally studied for the exam for only 2 hours on the average, then by requiring them all to study 3 hours we will raise the class average. If, however, the students had originally studied 4 hours on the average, then we will lower the class average by limiting everybody to only 3 hours of study time.

Heritability

We are now prepared to ask the "nature" question: To what extent do some students do better than others on the exam because they are genetically more capable? To put it another way, what percentage of the variance in exam scores is accounted for by genetic differences among the students? In general, *the percentage of the variance of any trait that is accounted for by genetic differences among the individuals in a population* is called the trait's **heritability.** The more individual differences on a trait are due to genetic differences, the closer the heritability is to 100%. For example, height is heavily influenced by genetics: Its heritability ranges from about 85% to 95% across different studies.

Now, however, we face a practical difficulty. We cannot conduct an experiment to determine how much of the variance of exam scores is accounted for by students'

heritability   the percentage of the variance of any trait that is accounted for by genetic differences among the individuals in a population

genetic differences the way we did for study time. Such an experiment would require holding the genetic variable constant—that is, turning all the students into genetic clones. But we can take advantage of the fact that nature sometimes does produce genetic clones: identical twins.

As we mentioned in Chapter 2, identical twins (who are called *monozygotic twins* because they come from a single zygote, or fertilized egg) share all their genes. Fraternal twins (called *dizygotic twins* because they develop from two separate eggs) are like ordinary siblings in that they share about half their genes. To the extent that identical twins are more alike on a trait than fraternal twins, we can infer that the trait has a genetic or heritable component (assuming that other factors, such as differences in how parents treat identical and fraternal twins, can be ruled out).

For example, across many studies the mean correlation between intelligence test scores for identical twins was .86; the comparable correlation for fraternal twins was .60. Mathematically, a difference of this magnitude implies that about 52% of the variance in intelligence test scores in the tested population is due to genetic differences (Bouchard & McGue, 1981). Similar studies have examined the heritability of personality traits. One large Swedish study assessed the traits of extraversion (sociability) and emotional stability in a sample of more than 12,000 pairs of adult twins. On both traits, the estimate of heritability was about 60% (Floderus-Myred, Petersen, & Rasmuson, 1980).

One difficulty in interpreting the results of twin studies is that identical twin pairs may be treated more alike than fraternal twin pairs, which may account for the greater similarity of their personalities. That is one reason the researchers at the University of Minnesota decided to study sets of twins who had been reared apart (Bouchard, 1984). They report that twins reared apart are just as similar to one another across a wide range of personality characteristics as twins reared together, permitting us to conclude with greater confidence that identical twins are more similar to each other on personality characteristics than are fraternal twins because they are more similar genetically (Bouchard et al., 1990; Lykken, 1982; Tellegen et al., 1988).

For the most part, the correlations found in the Minnesota studies are in accord with results from many other twin studies. In general, the highest heritabilities are found in measures of abilities and intelligence (60% to 70%); the next highest heritabilities are typically found in measures of personality (about 50%); and the smallest heritabilities are found for religious and political beliefs and vocational interests (30% to 40%).

The recurring public debate over nature-nurture questions reveals widespread misunderstanding about the concept of heritability. Therefore, it is important to be clear about the following points:

- *Heritability refers to a population, not to individuals.* The heritability of a trait refers to differences among individuals within a population, not to percentages of a trait within an individual. To say that height has a heritability of 90% does not mean that 90% of your height came from your genes and 10% came from the environment. It means that 90% of the differences in height among individuals observed in a particular population are due to genetic differences among those individuals.
- *The heritability of a trait is not a single, fixed number.* Heritability refers to an attribute of a trait in a particular population at a particular point in time. If something happens to change the variance of a trait in a population, the heritability of the trait will also change. For example, if everyone in our society were suddenly given equal educational opportunities, the variance of intellectual performance in the society would decrease; scores on standardized measures of intellectual ability would be more similar. (This is what happened in our hypothetical experiment in which everyone had to study the same length of time for the exam.) And because heritability is the *percentage* of variance

due to inherited differences among individuals, the heritability would actually *increase* because the percentage of the variance due to an important environmental factor, education, would have decreased.

- *Heritability does not tell us about the source of mean differences between groups.* One of the most contentious and recurring debates in American society is over the question of whether average differences in the intelligence test scores of different ethnic groups are due to genetic differences between the groups. In the early 20th century, the debate concerned the relatively low intelligence scores obtained by Hungarian, Italian, and Jewish immigrants when they were tested upon arrival in the United States. The test scores of these immigrants led some researchers to conclude that the majority of them were "feeble-minded" (Kamin, 1974). Today the debate concerns the lower scores on tests of intellectual performance obtained by African Americans and Hispanic Americans compared with white Americans (Ceci, 1996; Herrnstein & Murray, 1994). In these debates, the heritability of intelligence is often used to support the genetic argument. But this claim is based on a logical fallacy, as illustrated by the following "thought experiment":

> We fill a white sack and a black sack with a mixture of different genetic varieties of corn seed. We make certain that the proportions of each variety of seed are identical in each sack. We then plant the seed from the white sack in fertile Field A, while that from the black sack is planted in barren Field B. We will observe that within Field A, as within Field B, there is considerable variation in the height of individual corn plants. This variation will be due largely to genetic factors (seed differences). We will also observe, however, that the average height of plants in Field A is greater than that in Field B. That difference will be entirely due to environmental factors (the soil). The same is true of IQs: differences in the average IQ of various human populations could be entirely due to environmental differences, even if within each population all variation were due to genetic differences! (Eysenck & Kamin, 1981, p. 97)

- *Heritability does not tell us about the effects of environmental changes on the average level of a trait.* Another incorrect claim about heritability is that a trait with high heritability cannot be changed by a change in the environment. For example, it has been argued that it is futile to use preschool programs to help disadvantaged children enhance their intellectual abilities because those abilities have high heritabilities. But between 1946 and 1982 the height of young adult males in Japan increased by 3.3 inches, mainly owing to improved nutrition (Angoff, 1988). Yet height is one of the most heritable traits we possess. Then, as now, taller Japanese parents have taller children than do shorter Japanese parents. Similarly, a survey covering 14 countries has shown that the average IQ test score has increased significantly in recent years (Flynn, 1987). In sum, heritability is about variances, not average levels.

Personality–Environment Interactions

In shaping an individual's personality, genetic and environmental influences are intertwined from the moment of birth. Parents give their biological offspring both their genes and a home environment, and both are functions of the parents' own genes. As a result, there is a built-in correlation between the child's *inherited characteristics,* or **genotype,** and the environment in which he or she is raised. For example, because general intelligence is partially heritable, parents with high intelligence are likely to have children with high intelligence. But parents with high intelligence are likely to provide an intellectually stimulating environment for their children—both through their own interactions with them and through books, music lessons, trips to museums, and other intellectual experiences. Because the child's genotype and environment are positively correlated in this way, he or she will get a double dose of intellectual advantage. Similarly, children born to parents with low intelligence are likely

genotype inherited characteristics

to encounter a home environment that exacerbates whatever intellectual disadvantage they may have inherited directly.

The child's genotype also shapes the environment itself (Bouchard, et al., 1990; Plomin, DeFries, & Loehlin, 1977; Scarr, 1988; Scarr & McCartney, 1983). In particular, the environment becomes a function of the child's personality through three forms of interaction: *reactive, evocative,* and *proactive.*

Reactive Interaction   Different individuals exposed to the same environment interpret it, experience it, and react to it differently. An anxious, sensitive child will experience and react to harsh parents differently from the way a calm, resilient child does; the sharp tone of voice that provokes the sensitive child to tears might pass unnoticed by his sister. An extraverted child will attend to people and events around her; her introverted brother will ignore them. A brighter child will get more out of being read to than a less bright child. In other words, each child's personality extracts a subjective psychological environment from the objective surroundings, and it is that subjective environment that shapes subsequent personality development. Even if parents provided exactly the same environment for all their children—which they usually do not—it will not be psychologically equivalent for all of them. Reactive interaction occurs throughout life. One person will interpret a hurtful act as the product of deliberate hostility and react to it quite differently from a person who interprets the same act as the product of unintended insensitivity.

Evocative Interaction   Every individual's personality evokes distinctive responses from others. An infant who squirms and fusses when picked up will evoke less nurturance from a parent than will one who likes to be cuddled. Docile children will evoke a less controlling style of child rearing from parents than will aggressive children. For this reason, we cannot simply assume that an observed correlation between the child-rearing practices of a child's parents and his or her personality reflects a simple cause-and-effect sequence. Instead, the child's personality can shape the parents' child-rearing style, which, in turn, further shapes his or her personality. Like reactive interaction, evocative interaction also occurs throughout life: Gentle people evoke gentle environments; hostile people evoke hostile environments.

Proactive Interaction   Individuals select and construct their own environments. As children grow older, they can move beyond the environments imposed by their parents and begin to select and construct environments of their own. These environments, in turn, further shape their personalities. A sociable child will choose to go to the movies with friends rather than stay home alone and watch television; her sociable personality prompts her to select an environment that reinforces her sociability. And what she cannot select she will construct: If nobody invites her to the movies, she will organize the event herself. As the term implies, proactive interaction is a process through which individuals become active agents in their own personality development.

The relative importance of these different forms of personality–environment interaction shifts over the course of development (Scarr, 1988; Scarr & McCartney, 1983). The built-in correlation between a child's genotype

Parents not only pass their genes down to their children, but they also provide them with an environment that is partly a function of the parents' genes. Thus, the child's genotype and his or her environment are correlated from the moment of birth.

Once genetic similarities are subtracted out, the children from the same family seem to be no more alike in personality than two children chosen randomly from the population.

and his or her environment is strongest when the child is young and confined almost exclusively to the home environment. As the child grows older and begins to select and construct his or her own environment, this initial correlation decreases and the influence of proactive interaction increases. As we have noted, reactive and evocative interactions remain important throughout life.

Why Are Siblings So Different?   Twin studies enable researchers to estimate not only how much of the variation among individuals is due to genetic variation but also how much of the environmentally related variation is due to aspects of the environment that family members share with one another (for example, socioeconomic status) as compared with aspects of the environment that family members do not share (for example, friends outside the family). Surprisingly, differences due to shared aspects of the environment seem to account for almost none of the environmental variation: After their genetic similarities are subtracted out, two children from the same family seem to be no more alike in personality than two children chosen randomly from the population (Plomin & Daniels, 1987). This implies that the kinds of variables that psychologists typically study (such as child-rearing practices, socioeconomic status, and parents' education) are contributing virtually nothing to individual differences in personality. How can this be so?

One possible explanation might be that twin studies do not include a wide enough variety of families; for example, most twin studies are conducted within a single society, almost always a Western industrial society. Twin studies that included families from many cultures might demonstrate that differences between families do indeed produce different personalities in their children. Other kinds of studies of different cultures certainly suggest that this is a likely possibility.

Another possible explanation might be that the reactive, evocative, and proactive processes act to enhance differences among children from the same families and diminish differences between different family environments. A bright child from a neglecting or impoverished home is more likely than a less bright sibling to absorb more information from a television program (reactive interaction), to attract the attention of a sympathetic teacher (evocative interaction), and to go to the library on his or her own (proactive interaction). This child's genotype acts to counteract the potentially debilitating effects of the home environment, and therefore he or she develops differently from a less bright sibling. Only if the environment is severely restrictive will these personality-driven processes be thwarted (Scarr, 1988; Scarr & McCartney, 1983). This explanation is supported by the finding that the most dissimilar pairs of identical twins reared apart are those in which one was reared in a severely restricted environment.

Although this explanation seems plausible, there is no direct evidence that it is correct. In any case it appears that research will have to shift from the usual comparisons of children from different families to comparisons of children within the same families—with particular attention to the personality–environment interactions within those families. Similarly, more attention must be given to influences outside the family; one writer has suggested that the peer group is a far more important source of personality differences among children than is the family (Harris, 1995).

Thinking Critically   If you have any siblings, how different are you from them? Can you discern how some of the personality–environment interactions described in this chapter may have contributed to those differences? Can you see ways in which your parents' child-rearing strategies varied in reaction to the different personalities of each child?

How Are Individual Differences Assessed?

Tests for assessing intellectual ability or attainment, such as the Scholastic Assessment Test (SAT) are familiar to most of us; tests for measuring interests, attitudes, and personality traits are also familiar to many of us. Beyond practical concerns of helping college admissions committees, vocational counselors, and psychotherapists make more informed decisions, methods for measuring such variables are essential to theory and research on individual differences. But before they can be useful for any purpose, they must satisfy the requirements of *reliability* and *validity*.

A test or method of assessment is said to have **reliability** if it gives *reproducible and consistent results*. If a test yielded different results when it was administered on different occasions or when scored by different people, it would be unreliable. A simple analogy is a rubber yardstick. If we did not know how much the yardstick stretched each time we took a measurement, the results would be unreliable no matter how carefully we made each measurement. Reliability of a test is typically assessed by correlating two sets of scores. For example, if a test is given twice to the same group of people and their scores on the two occasions correlate highly, the test is said to have *test-retest reliability*. If scores on alternate versions of the same test—such as different administrations of the Scholastic Assessment Test (SAT)—correlate highly, the test is said to have *alternate-form reliability*. If scores on individual questions or items on a test correlate highly, the test is said to have *internal consistency*.

Although most tests and assessment instruments are scored objectively, it is sometimes necessary to use subjective judgments to evaluate intellectual performance or social behavior. A familiar example is an essay examination. To assess the reliability of such subjective judgments, two or more sets of ratings made by independent raters or judges are correlated. For example, two observers might independently rate several nursery school children for aggression or two or more judges might be asked to read past presidential inaugural addresses and rate them for optimism or count the number of negative references to Iraq. If the correlation between raters or judges is high, the method is said to possess *interrater agreement* or *interjudge reliability*.

In general, a well constructed, objectively scored test of ability should have a reliability of .90 or greater. For personality tests and subjective judgments, reliability coefficients of .70 or even lower can sometimes be satisfactory for research purposes, but inferences about particular individuals must be made with great caution.

A test with demonstrated reliability is measuring *something*, but this does not guarantee that the test is measuring what the test developer claims it is measuring. In other words, a good test must also have **validity:** There must be evidence that *the test measures what it is supposed to measure*. For example, if the final examination in your psychology course contained especially difficult vocabulary words or trick questions, it might be a test of your verbal ability or test sophistication rather than a test of the material learned in the course. Such an examination might be reliable—students would achieve about the same scores on a retest and the separate items might all be measuring the same thing—but it would not be a valid assessment of what students had learned from the course. (Note, however, that a test *must* have reliability if it is to have validity.)

In some instances the validity of a test can be assessed by correlating the test score with some external criterion. This correlation is called a *validity coefficient*. For example, the relatively strong positive correlation between scores on the SAT and freshman grades in college indicates that the test has reasonable validity. This kind of validity is called *criterion* or *empirical validity*. Because of sensitivity to race and sex discrimination, the courts are increasingly requiring companies or government agencies that use tests for personnel selection to provide empirical evidence that those tests correlate with the criterion of on-the-job performance—in other words, to prove that the tests have criterion or empirical validity. For example, a police department that used a test to select new officers would have to present evidence to a

reliability   the extent to which a test or method of assessment gives reproducible and consistent results

validity   the extent to which a test measures what it is supposed to measure

court demonstrating that scores on the test correlated significantly with actual performance as a police officer.

In personality research, however, there may not be an external criterion that the researcher would be willing to consider a "true" measure of the trait being assessed. This is known as the *criterion problem* in personality psychology. How, for example, should a researcher assess the validity of a test for achievement motivation? One can think of a number of possibilities. The test could be given to business executives to see whether it correlates with their salaries. Perhaps the test will correlate with teachers' ratings of the ambitiousness of their students. It would be reassuring if the test correlated with executive salaries, but if it did not, the researcher would not be willing to judge the test to be invalid. In such cases, a researcher attempts to establish its *construct validity*—to validate the concept or "construct" that lies behind the measuring instrument.

This is done through the research process itself. The researcher uses his or her theory of the concept both to construct the test and to generate predictions from the theory. Studies using the test are then conducted to test those predictions. To the extent that the results of several converging studies confirm the theory's predictions, both the theory and the test are validated simultaneously, and the test itself is said to have achieved some degree of construct validity. Most often, mixed results suggest ways in which both the theory and the test need to be modified.

Assessment of Intellectual Abilities

The first person to attempt to develop tests of intellectual ability was Sir Francis Galton. A naturalist and mathematician, Galton developed an interest in individual differences from the evolutionary theory of his famous cousin, Charles Darwin. Galton believed that certain families are biologically superior—stronger and smarter—than others. Intelligence, he reasoned, is a question of exceptional sensory and perceptual skills, which are passed from one generation to the next. Because all information is acquired through the senses, the more sensitive and accurate an individual's perceptual apparatus, the more intelligent the person. In 1884 Galton administered a set of tests (measuring such variables as head size, reaction time, visual acuity, auditory thresholds, and memory for visual forms) to more than 9,000 visitors at the London Exhibition. To his disappointment, he discovered that eminent scientists could not be distinguished from ordinary citizens on the basis of their head size and that measurements such as speed of reaction were not particularly related to other measures of intelligence. Although his test did not prove very useful, Galton did invent the *correlation coefficient,* which plays an important role in psychology.

The first tests that approximated contemporary intelligence tests were devised by the French psychologist Alfred Binet. In 1881 the French government passed a law making school attendance compulsory for all children. Previously, slow learners had usually been kept at home; now teachers had to cope with a wide range of individual differences. The government asked Binet to create a test that would detect children who were too slow intellectually to benefit from a regular school curriculum.

Binet assumed that intelligence should be measured by means of tasks that required reasoning and problem-solving abilities rather than perceptual–motor skills. In collaboration with another French psychologist, Théophile Simon, Binet published such a test in 1905, revising it in 1908 and again in 1911.

Binet reasoned that a slow or dull child was like a normal child whose mental growth was retarded. On tests, the slow child would perform like a normal child of a younger age, a bright child would perform like a normal older child. Binet devised a scale of test items of increasing difficulty that measured the kinds of changes in intelligence ordinarily associated with growing older. The higher a child could go on the scale in correctly answering items, the higher his or her *mental age (MA)*. The concept of mental age was critical to Binet's method; using this method, one could compare the MA of a child with his or her *chronological age (CA)* as determined by date of birth.

The Stanford-Binet Intelligence Scale   The test items originally developed by Binet were adapted for American schoolchildren by Lewis Terman at Stanford University. Terman standardized the administration of the test and developed age-level norms by giving the test to thousands of children. In 1916 he published the Stanford revision of the Binet tests, now referred to as the *Stanford-Binet Intelligence Scale.* It has been revised several times and, despite its age, is still one of the most frequently used psychological tests.

Terman retained Binet's concept of mental age. Each test item was age-graded at the level at which a substantial majority of the children pass it. A child's mental age could be obtained by summing the number of items passed at each level. In addition, Terman adopted a convenient index of intelligence suggested by the German psychologist William Stern. This index is the **intelligence quotient (IQ),** which expresses intelligence as a *ratio of mental age to chronological age:*

$$IQ = MA/CA \times 100$$

The number 100 is used as a multiplier so that the IQ will have a value of 100 when MA is equal to CA. If MA is lower than CA, then the IQ will be less than 100; if MA is higher than CA, then the IQ will be more than 100.

Test materials from the 1986 Stanford-Binet Intelligence Scale.

intelligence quotient (IQ) the ratio of mental age to chronological age (times 100); now defined in terms of standard scores rather than an actual mathematical ratio

Revisions of the Stanford-Binet use *standard age scores* instead of IQ scores. These can be interpreted in terms of *percentiles,* which show the percentage of examinees in the standardization group falling above or below a given score (Thorndike, Hage, & Sattler, 1986). And although the concept of IQ is still used in intelligence testing, it is no longer calculated using the equation shown above. Instead, tables are used to convert raw scores to standard scores, which are adjusted so that the mean at each age equals 100. Because intelligence is thought to be a composite of different abilities, the more recent versions of the test group the different tests into four broad areas of intellectual abilities: verbal reasoning, abstract/visual reasoning, quantitative reasoning, and short-term memory (Sattler, 1988).

The Wechsler Intelligence Scales   In 1939 David Wechsler developed a new test because he thought the Stanford-Binet depended too heavily on language ability and was also not appropriate for adults. The *Wechsler Adult Intelligence Scale,* or *WAIS* (1939, 1955, 1981, 1997), is divided into two parts—a verbal scale and a performance scale—that yield separate scores as well as a full-scale IQ. Test items similar to those on the actual test are described in Table 10-2. Wechsler later developed a similar test for children, the *Wechsler Intelligence Scale for Children (WISC)* (1958, 1974, 1991).

Items on the performance scale require the manipulation or arrangement of blocks, pictures, or other materials. The Wechsler scales also provide scores for each of the subtests, so that the examiner can gain a clearer picture of the individual's intellectual strengths and weaknesses. For example, a discrepancy between

Table 10-2

Tests Composing the Wechsler Adult Intelligence Scale   The tests of the Wechsler Intelligence Scale for Children are similar, with some modifications.

Test	Description
Verbal Scale	
Information	Questions tap a general range of information; for example, "What is the capital of Italy?"
Comprehension	Tests practical information and ability to evaluate past experience; for example, "Why do we put stamps on a letter to be mailed?"
Arithmetic	Verbal problems testing arithmetic reasoning.
Similarities	Asks in what way two objects or concepts (for example, *recipe* and *map*) are similar; assesses abstract thinking.
Digit Span	A series of digits presented auditorily (for example, 7-5-6-3-8) is repeated in a forward or backward direction; tests attention and memory.
Vocabulary	Assesses word knowledge
Letter Number Sequencing	Orally presented letters and numbers presented in a mixed-up order must be reordered and repeated, first with the numbers in ascending order and then with the letters in alphabetical order; assesses working memory.
Performance Scale	
Digit Symbol	A timed coding task in which numbers must be associated with marks of various shapes; assesses speed of learning and writing.
Picture Completion	The missing part of an incompletely drawn picture must be discovered and named; assesses visual alertness, visual memory, and perceptual organization.
Block Design	Pictured designs must be copied with blocks; assesses ability to perceive and analyze patterns.
Picture Arrangement	A series of comic-strip pictures must be arranged in the right sequence to tell a story; assesses understanding of social situations.
Matrix Reasoning	A geometric shape that is similar in some way to a sample shape must be selected from a set of possible alternatives; assesses perceptual organization.
Object Assembly	Puzzle pieces must be assembled to form a complete object; assesses ability to deal with part-whole relationships.
Symbol Search	A series of paired groups of symbols are presented, a target group of two symbols and a search group. Examinee must determine if either target symbol appears in the search group; assesses processing speed.

verbal and performance scores prompts the examiner to look for specific learning problems, such as reading disabilities or language handicaps.

Both the Stanford-Binet and the Wechsler scales show good reliability and validity. They have test-retest reliabilities of about .90, and both correlate about .50 with school performance (Sattler, 1988).

Group Ability Tests   The Stanford-Binet and the Wechsler scales are individual ability tests; that is, they are administered to a single individual by a specially trained tester. Group ability tests, in contrast, can be administered to a large number of people by a single examiner and are usually in pencil-and-paper form.

The Scholastic Assessment Test (SAT) and the American College Test (ACT) are both examples of group-administered, general-ability tests that are likely to be familiar to most college students in the United States. Virtually all four-year colleges require applicants to take one of these as a way of setting a common standard for students from high schools with different curricula and grading standards. The SAT underwent a major revision in 1994 and now includes an essay section and open-ended (rather than multiple-choice) mathematics questions, among other changes. These changes, like some of those in recent revisions of the ACT, are in response to high school curriculum trends that place a premium on more sophisticated reading, writing, and mathematics skills.

Correlations between SAT scores and freshman grade-point averages vary across studies, with a median correlation of about .38 for the verbal section of the SAT and

Scores on the Scholastic Aptitude Test are used to predict academic achievement in college. The correlation between SAT scores and freshman grade point averages is about .50.

.34 for the mathematics section (Linn, 1982). When these correlations are corrected for the fact that many students with very low scores do not end up attending college (and hence cannot be included in the calculation of the validity correlation), the resulting correlations are about .50. Thus, SAT scores improve prediction considerably, but it is also clear that the freshman grades of students with identical SAT scores will vary widely.

The Factorial Approach   Some psychologists view intelligence as a general capacity for comprehension and reasoning that manifests itself in various ways. This was Binet's assumption. Although his test contained many kinds of items, Binet observed that a bright child tended to score higher than dull children on all of them. He assumed, therefore, that the different tasks sampled a basic underlying ability. Similarly, despite the diverse subscales that compose the WAIS, Wechsler also believed that "intelligence is the aggregate or global capacity of the individual to act purposefully, to think rationally, and to deal effectively with his environment" (Wechsler, 1958).

Other psychologists, however, question whether there is such a thing as "general intelligence." They believe that intelligence tests sample a number of mental abilities that are relatively independent of one another. One method of obtaining more precise information about the kinds of abilities that determine performance on intelligence tests is **factor analysis,** *a statistical technique that examines the intercorrelations among a number of tests and, by grouping those that are most highly correlated, reduces them to a smaller number of independent dimensions, called factors.* The basic idea is that two tests that correlate very highly with each other are probably measuring the same underlying ability, and the goal is to discover the minimum number of factors, or abilities, that are required to explain the observed pattern of correlations among an array of different tests.

It was the originator of factor analysis, Charles Spearman (1904), who first proposed that all individuals possess *a general intelligence factor* (called *g*) in varying

factor analysis a statistical technique that examines the intercorrelations among a number of tests and, by grouping those that are most highly correlated, reduces them to a smaller number of independent dimensions, called factors

amounts. A person could be described as generally bright or generally dull, depending on the amount of *g* he or she possessed. According to Spearman, the *g* factor is the major determinant of performance on intelligence test items. In addition, *special factors,* each called *s,* are specific to particular abilities or tests. For example, tests of arithmetic or spatial relationships would each tap a separate *s.* An individual's tested intelligence would reflect the amount of *g* plus the magnitude of the various *s* factors. Performance in mathematics would be a function of a person's general intelligence and mathematical aptitude.

A later investigator, Louis Thurstone (1938), objected to Spearman's emphasis on general intelligence, feeling that it could be broken down into a number of primary abilities using factor analysis. After many rounds of administering tests, factor-analyzing the results, purifying the scales, and retesting, Thurstone identified seven factors, which he used to construct his *Test of Primary Mental Abilities.*

Revised versions of this test are still widely used, but its predictive power is no greater than that of general intelligence tests such as the Wechsler scales. Thurstone's hope of discovering the basic elements of intelligence through factor analysis was not fully realized for several reasons. For one, his primary abilities are not completely independent; indeed, the significant intercorrelations among them provide support for the concept of a general intelligence factor that underlies the specific abilities. For another, the number of basic abilities identified by factor analysis depends on the nature of the test items. Other investigators, using different test items and alternative methods of factor analysis, have identified from 20 to 150 factors to represent the range of intellectual abilities (Ekstrom, French, & Harman, 1979; Ekstrom, French, Harman, & Derman, 1976; Guilford, 1982).

This lack of consistency in the number and kinds of factors raises doubts about the value of the factorial approach. Nevertheless, factor analysis continues to be a principal technique for studying intellectual performance (Carrol, 1988; Comrey & Lee, 1992), and we will encounter it again when we discuss personality traits.

Information-Processing Approach and Multiple Intelligences   Until the 1960s, research on intelligence was dominated by the factorial approach. However, with the development of cognitive psychology and its emphasis on information-processing models, a new approach emerged. This approach is defined somewhat differently by different investigators, but the basic idea is to try to understand intelligence in terms of the cognitive processes that operate when we engage in intellectual activities (Carpenter, Just, & Shell, 1990; Hunt, 1990): What mental processes are involved in the various tests of intelligence? How rapidly and accurately are these processes carried out? What types of mental representations of information do these processes act upon? Thus, rather than trying to explain intelligence in terms of factors, this approach attempts to identify the mental processes that underlie intelligent behavior.

The information-processing approach is illustrated by Robert Sternberg's *componential theory* of intelligence (which is a subtheory of his more comprehensive *triarchic theory* of intelligence) (1988). Sternberg assumes that the test-taker possesses a set of mental processes, which he calls *components,* that operate in an organized way to produce the responses observed on an intelligence test. Sternberg selects a specific task from an intelligence test and uses it in a series of experiments to try to identify the components involved in the task.

For example, consider analogy problems of the following kind:

lawyer is to *client* as *doctor* is to _____

(a) *medicine*   (b) *patient*

A series of experiments with such problems led Sternberg to conclude that the critical components were an *encoding process* and a *comparison process.* The test-taker encodes or interprets each of the words in the analogy by forming a mental repre-

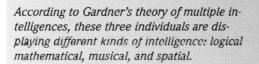

According to Gardner's theory of multiple intelligences, these three individuals are displaying different kinds of intelligence: logical mathematical, musical, and spatial.

sentation of the word—in this case, a list of attributes of the word that are retrieved from long-term memory. For example, a mental representation of the word *lawyer* might include the following attributes: college-educated, versed in legal procedures, represents clients in court, and so on. Once the test-taker has formed a mental representation for each word in the analogy, the comparison process scans the representations looking for matching attributes that solve the analogy. Although other processes are involved in analogy problems, research has shown that individuals who do well on analogy problems spend more time encoding but less time matching attributes than do individuals who do poorly (Galotti, 1989; Pellegrino, 1985).

The factorial and information-processing approaches provide complementary interpretations of performance on intelligence tests. Factor-based tests are useful in identifying broad areas of strengths and weaknesses. They may indicate that a person is strong in word fluency and verbal comprehension but weak in reasoning. If additional testing is conducted, an information-processing analysis could provide a diagnostic profile of the processes responsible for the observed deficiency. A process analysis may indicate a deficiency at the level of *metacomponents* (such as the choice of strategies used to attack the problem) or *retention components* (such as slow or inaccurate recall of relevant information) or *transfer components* (such as poor ability to transfer what has been learned in one situation to another).

Sternberg also argues that current intelligence tests tap only "academic" or analytic intelligence and ignore both practical and creative intelligence (1988). A similar argument for multiple intelligences is made by Howard Gardner (1993), who believes

Table 10-3

Gardner's Seven Intelligences   (Adapted from Gardner, Kornhaber, & Wake, 1996)

1. **Linguistic Intelligence**   The capacity for speech, along with mechanisms dedicated to phonology (speech sounds), syntax (grammar), semantics (meaning), and pragmatics (implications and uses of language in various settings).
2. **Musical Intelligence**   The ability to create, communicate, and understand meanings made of sound, along with mechanisms dedicated to pitch, rhythm, and timbre (sound quality).
3. **Logical-Mathematical Intelligence**   The ability to use and appreciate relationships in the absence of action or objects—that is, to engage in abstract thought.
4. **Spatial Intelligence**   The ability to perceive visual or spatial information, modify it, and re-create visual images without reference to the original stimulus. Includes the capacity to construct images in three dimensions and to move and rotate those images.
5. **Bodily-Kinesthetic Intelligence**   The ability to use all or part of the body to solve problems or fashion products; includes control over fine and gross motor actions and the ability to manipulate external objects.
6. **Intrapersonal Intelligence**   The ability to distinguish among one's own feelings, intentions, and motivations.
7. **Interpersonal Intelligence**   The ability to recognize and make distinctions among other people's feelings, beliefs, and intentions.

that there are at least seven distinct kinds of intelligence, each operating as a separate system (or module) in the brain according to its own rules. These are (1) linguistic, (2) musical, (3) logical-mathematical, (4) spatial, (5) bodily-kinesthetic, (6) intrapersonal, and (7) interpersonal. These are described more fully in Table 10-3. Standard intelligence tests assess only linguistic, logical-mathematical, and spatial kinds of intelligence, and Gardner argues that Western society has emphasized these three to the virtual exclusion of the others, which deserve comparable status.

Assessment of Personality Traits

personality   the distinctive and characteristic patterns of thought, emotion, and behavior that define an individual's personal style of interacting with the physical and social environment

Personality can be defined as *the distinctive and characteristic patterns of thought, emotion, and behavior that define an individual's personal style of interacting with the physical and social environment.* When we are asked to describe an individual's personality, we are likely to use personality trait terms—adjectives such as intelligent, extraverted, conscientious, and so forth. Personality psychologists have attempted to devise formal methods for describing and measuring personality. These go beyond our everyday use of trait terms in three ways. First, they seek to reduce the potential set of trait terms to a manageable set that will still encompass the diversity of human personality. Second, they attempt to ensure that their instruments for measuring personality traits are reliable and valid. Finally, they do empirical research to discover the relationships among traits and between traits and specific behaviors.

One way to begin the task of deriving a comprehensive but manageable number of traits is to consult a dictionary. It is assumed that through linguistic evolution a language will encode most, if not all, of the distinctions among individuals that make a difference in everyday life. Language embodies the accumulated experience of the culture, and the unabridged dictionary is the written record of that experience. In the 1930s, two personality psychologists actually undertook this task. They found approximately 18,000 words that refer to characteristics of behavior—nearly 5% of all English words. Next, they reduced the list to about 4,500 terms by eliminating obscure words and synonyms. Finally, they organized the list into psychologically meaningful subsets (Allport & Odbert, 1936).

Subsequent researchers have used such trait terms to obtain personality ratings of an individual. Peers who know the individual well are asked to rate him or her on a scale of each trait. For example, a rater might be asked to rate the person on the trait of friendliness using a 7-point scale ranging from "not at all friendly" to "very friendly." Often such scales are labeled at the two ends with opposite traits—for example, "domineering–submissive" or "conscientious–unreliable." Individuals can also be asked to rate themselves on the scales. The researchers then used factor analysis to reduce these ratings to a smaller number of "basic" traits. As noted in the discussion of intelligence tests, factor analysis is a statistical technique that examines the intercorrelations among a number of test items and, by grouping together those that are most highly correlated, reduces them to a smaller number of independent dimensions called *factors*.

How many basic personality factors are there? Even with a rigorous analytic procedure like factor analysis, there is no definitive answer. Thus, one researcher arrived at 16 factors (Cattell, 1957, 1966), another at 3 (Eysenck & Eysenck, 1976). Other investigators arrive at still different numbers. We encountered a similar situation earlier when we noted that the number of factors defining the concept of intelligence could be 1 (Spearman's general intelligence factor, *g*), 7 (Thurstone's primary mental abilities), or as many as 150 (Guilford, 1982).

Some of the discrepancy occurs because different traits are initially put into the analysis, some occurs because different types of data are being analyzed (for example, peer ratings versus self-ratings); and some occurs because different factor-analytic methods are employed. But much of the disagreement is a matter of taste. A researcher who prefers a more differentiated or fine-grained description of personality will set a lower criterion for a factor and hence accept more factors, arguing that important distinctions would be lost if the factors were further merged. Another researcher will prefer to merge several lower-level factors into more general ones, arguing that the resulting factors will be more reliable (more likely to reemerge in other analyses).

Despite these disagreements, a consensus is emerging among many trait researchers that five trait dimensions may provide the best compromise (John, 1990). Although the five factors—now called the "Big Five"—were originally identified through a factor analysis of the Allport-Odbert trait list (Norman, 1963), the same five have emerged from a wide variety of personality tests (Digman & Inouye, 1986; McCrae & Costa, 1987). There is still disagreement about how best to name and interpret the factors, but one reasonable way to summarize them is with the acronym OCEAN: Openness to experience, Conscientiousness, Extraversion, Agreeableness, and Neuroticism. Table 10-4 displays some representative examples of the trait scales that characterize each of the five factors. Many personality psychologists consider the discovery and validation of the Big Five to be one of the major breakthroughs of contemporary personality psychology.

Most personality tests do not actually ask individuals to directly rate themselves on personality traits. Instead, they ask them to respond to a set of questions about how they react in certain situations. For example, individuals might be asked to indicate how much they agree or disagree with the statement "I often try new and foreign foods" or "I really like most people I meet." Such questionnaires—called *personality inventories*—resemble structured interviews in that they ask the same questions of each person, and the answers are usually given in a form that can be easily scored, often by computer. Each item on a personality inventory is selected to exemplify a particular personality trait, and subsets of similar items are summed to give the individual a score on each trait scale. For example, the item "I often try new and foreign foods" is on the Openness to experience scale of one inventory designed to measure the

Table 10-4

Five Trait Factors　This table presents five trait factors that reliably emerge when a wide variety of assessment instruments are factor analyzed. The adjective pairs are examples of trait scales that characterize each of the factors. (After McCrae & Costa, 1987)

Trait Factor	Representative Trait Scales
Openness	Conventional-Original
	Unadventurous-Daring
	Conservative-Liberal
Conscientiousness	Careless-Careful
	Undependable-Reliable
	Negligent-Conscientious
Extraversion	Retiring Sociable
	Quiet-Talkative
	Inhibited-Spontaneous
Agreeableness	Irritable-Good natured
	Ruthless-Soft hearted
	Selfish-Selfless
Neuroticism	Calm-Worrying
	Hardy-Vulnerable
	Secure-Insecure

Frontiers of Psychology

Neurotransmitters and Personality

There is considerable evidence that certain neurotransmitters play a role in the development and expression of various personality traits. The functioning of the nervous system is affected by the amounts of various neurotransmitters available at any given time, which can vary quite widely. People also seem to differ in their average levels of those transmitters, and these differences seem to be related to particular personality traits.

The most important neurotransmitters from the standpoint of personality are norepinephrine and dopamine. Norepinephrine affects heart rate, blood pressure, and energy level. People with chronically high levels of norepinephrine seem to be more anxious, dependent, and sociable (Gray, 1987), while those with lower levels of this neurotransmitter are less inhibited and more impulsive. Those with chronically low levels are more likely to be socially detached nonconformers (Zuckerman, 1991).

Dopamine plays a role in the control of body movements and is involved in brain systems that cause the person to approach attractive objects and people. It therefore is thought to affect sociability and general activity level. Some researchers suggest that dopamine is related to extraversion and impulsivity (Sacks, 1983; Zuckerman, 1991).

Another important neurotransmitter is serotonin, which seems to be involved in the inhibition of behavioral impulses, including emotional impulses. One author believes that people with abnormally low levels of serotonin suffer from "serotonin depletion" (Metzner, 1984). The symptoms of this condition include irrational anger, hypersensitivity to rejection, pessimism, obsessive worry, and fear of risk-taking.

The popular antidepressant drug Prozac is a selective serotonin reuptake inhibitor; its effect is to raise serotonin levels. According to Peter Kramer, author of *Listening to Prozac,* the drug can ac-

tually give people new personalities. It can prevent a person from worrying needlessly and overreacting to minor stresses, thereby giving him or her a more cheerful outlook on life. People who have taken Prozac often report that they feel like "better people" who get more work done and are more attractive to members of the opposite sex.

Prozac's success has given rise to speculation that personality is actually determined by the presence or absence of certain chemicals in the brain. However, it should be noted that Prozac does not work on people with adequate levels of serotonin (Metzner, 1994). Moreover, Prozac and other drugs that affect serotonin levels have widely varying effects on different individuals; they do not create a predictable new personality in everyone who takes them. Thus, while it seems clear that neurotransmitters affect personality, there is insufficient evidence to conclude that they create it.

Big Five; the item "I really like most people I meet" is on the Extraversion scale of that inventory.

Thinking Critically

1. By providing a national yardstick, standardized tests like the SAT and the ACT enable high school seniors of all ethnicities and from unknown high schools to compete equally for openings in the nation's top colleges. Before standardized testing, such students rarely had a chance to show that they were qualified, and colleges tended to favor students from well-known high schools or with "family connections." But critics argue that the very success of standardized tests in selecting qualified students has led admissions committees to give them too much weight and has led high schools to gear their curricula toward the tests themselves. In addition, critics argue that standardized tests are biased against certain ethnic groups. On balance, do you think the widespread use of standardized tests has helped or hindered our society in realizing its goal of equal opportunity?

2. How would you rate yourself on the "Big Five" personality traits? Do you think your personality can be accurately described in this way? What important aspect of your personality seems to be left out of such a description? If you and a close friend (or a family member) were to describe your personality, on which characteristics would you be likely to disagree? Why? Are there traits on which

you think the other person might actually be more accurate than you are in describing your personality? If so, why?

What Are the Major Theoretical Approaches to Personality?

Earlier we defined personality as the distinctive and characteristic patterns of thought, emotion, and behavior that define an individual's personal style of interacting with the physical and social environments. One of the major tasks of personality psychology is to describe individual differences—the diverse ways in which individuals differ from one another. The trait approach to personality that we have just described is the most common way of addressing this task.

By itself, however, the trait approach is not a theory of personality but a general orientation and set of methods for assessing stable characteristics of individuals. By themselves personality traits do not tell us anything about the dynamic processes of personality functioning, and trait psychologists who have sought to develop complete theories of personality have had to look to other approaches to address the second major task of personality psychology: synthesizing all the processes that influence an individual's interactions with the physical and social environments—biology, development, learning, thinking, emotion, motivation, and social interaction—into an integrated account of the total person. This task requires going far beyond the general nature-nurture interactions discussed at the beginning of this chapter and makes the study of personality one of the most challenging and ambitious subfields of psychology.

In this section we look at the three theoretical approaches that have dominated the history of personality psychology in the 20th century: the psychoanalytic, behavioral, and phenomenological. Today most personality psychologists would not identify themselves as "pure" adherents to any one of these three approaches, and the differences among the approaches are no longer as sharp as they once were. This is because most contemporary personality theorists, whatever their historical allegiances, have joined the rest of psychology in becoming more "cognitive." As we proceed, we will point out how each approach has become more cognitive in recent years.

The Psychoanalytic Approach

Sigmund Freud, the creator of psychoanalytic theory, is one of the towering intellectual figures of the 20th century. Whatever its shortcomings as a scientific theory, the psychoanalytic account of personality remains the most comprehensive and influential theory of personality ever created. Its impact extends well beyond psychology, influencing the social sciences, the humanities, the arts, and society generally. Even though psychoanalytic theory plays a less central role today than it did 50 or 60 years ago, many of its ideas have been absorbed into the mainstream of psychological thinking. Even parents who have done nothing more than raise their children with the occasional guidance of psychiatrist Benjamin Spock's best-selling *Baby and Child Care* are more like Freudian psychologists than they realize.

Freud began his scientific career as a neurologist, using conventional medical procedures to treat patients suffering from various "nervous" disorders. Because these procedures often failed, Freud took up, but later abandoned, the technique of hypnosis. Eventually he discovered the method of *free association,* in which a patient is instructed to say everything that comes to mind, regardless of how trivial or embarrassing it may seem. By listening carefully to these verbal associations, Freud detected consistent themes that he believed were manifestations of unconscious wishes and fears. He found similar themes in the recall of dreams and early childhood memories.

Freud compared the human mind to an iceberg. The small part that shows above the surface of the water consists of the *conscious*—our current awareness—and the

"Very well, I'll introduce you. Ego, meet Id. Now get back to work."

preconscious, all the information that is not currently "on our mind" but that we could bring into consciousness if called upon to do so (for example, the name of the president of the United States). The much larger mass of the iceberg lying below the water represents the *unconscious,* a storehouse of impulses, wishes, and inaccessible memories that affect our thoughts and behavior. This "iceberg" model was Freud's earliest attempt to map out the nature of the human mind. He was not the first to discover unconscious mental influences—even Shakespeare includes them in his plays—but Freud gave them primary importance in the everyday functioning of the normal personality.

Closely allied with Freud's focus on unconscious processes was his belief in the determinism of human behavior. *Psychological determinism* is the doctrine that all thoughts, emotions, and actions have causes. Freud maintained not only that all psychological events are caused but that most of them are caused by unsatisfied drives and unconscious wishes. In one of his earliest publications, *The Psychopathology of Everyday Life* (1901), Freud argued that dreams, humor, forgetting, and slips of the tongue ("Freudian slips") all serve to relieve psychological tension by gratifying forbidden impulses or unfulfilled wishes.

Freud's writings fill 24 volumes. His first major contribution, *The Interpretation of Dreams,* was published in 1900, and his final treatise, *An Outline of Psychoanalysis,* was published in 1940, a year after his death. We can present only the barest outline of Freud's theory of personality here.

Personality Structure   Freud discovered that his "iceberg" model was too simple to describe the human personality, and so he went on to develop his structural model, which divided personality into three major systems that interact to govern human behavior: the id, the ego, and the superego.

id in Freud's theory, the most primitive part of the personality, which contains the basic biological impulses (or drives) such as sex and aggression

The **id** is *the most primitive part of the personality, which contains the basic biological impulses (or drives) such as sex and aggression.* It is present in the newborn infant and consists of the basic biological impulses (or drives): the need to eat, to drink, to eliminate wastes, to avoid pain, and to gain sexual (sensual) pleasure. Freud believed that aggression is also a basic biological drive. In fact, he believed that the sexual and aggressive drives were the most important instinctual determinants of personality throughout life. The id seeks immediate gratification of these impulses. Like a young child, it operates on the *pleasure principle:* It endeavors to obtain pleasure and to avoid pain, regardless of the external circumstances.

Children soon learn that their impulses cannot always be gratified immediately. Relieving hunger must wait until someone provides food. Relieving bladder or bowel pressure must be delayed until the bathroom is reached. Certain impulses—playing with one's genitals or hitting someone—may be punished. A new part of the personality develops as the young child learns to consider the demands of reality. This is the **ego,** *the executive of the personality,* which decides what actions are appropriate and which id impulses will be satisfied and in what manner. The ego obeys the *reality principle:* Gratification of impulses must be delayed until the situation is appropriate. The ego mediates among the demands of the id, the realities of the world, and the demands of the superego.

ego in Freud's theory, the executive of the personality

The third part of the personality is the superego, which judges whether actions are right or wrong. More generally, the **superego** is *the internalized representation of the values and morals of society.* It comprises the individual's conscience as well as his or her image of the morally ideal person (called the *ego ideal*). The superego develops in response to parental rewards and punishments.

superego in Freud's theory, the internalized representation of the values and morals of society (the conscience)

Initially, parents control children's behavior directly by means of reward and punishment. Through the incorporation of parental standards into the superego, a child brings behavior under his or her own control. Children no longer need anyone to tell them it is wrong to steal; their superego tells them. Violating the superego's standards, or even the impulse to do so, produces anxiety—which was originally the anxiety over the loss of parental love. According to Freud, this anxiety is largely unconscious but may be experienced as guilt. If parental standards are overly rigid, the individual may be guilt ridden and may inhibit all aggressive or sexual impulses. In contrast, an individual who fails to incorporate any standards for acceptable social behavior will have few behavioral constraints and may engage in excessively self-indulgent or criminal behavior. Such a person is said to have a weak superego.

The three components of personality are often in opposition: The ego postpones the gratification that the id wants immediately, and the superego battles with both the id and the ego because behavior often falls short of the moral code it represents. In the well-integrated personality, the ego remains in firm but flexible control; the reality principle governs. In terms of his earlier "iceberg" model, Freud proposed that all of the id and most of the ego and superego are submerged in the unconscious; small parts of the ego and superego are in either the conscious or the preconscious (see Figure 10-1).

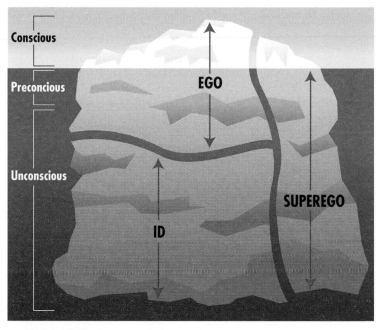

Figure 10-1

Freud's Structural Model of the Mind In Freud's "iceberg" model of the mind, all of the id and most of the ego and superego are submerged in the unconscious. Small parts of the ego and superego are either in the conscious or in the preconscious.

Personality Dynamics The science of physics was remarkably successful in the 19th century, and Freud was greatly influenced by the German physicist Hermann von Helmholtz, who argued that physiological events could be explained by the same principles that had been so successful in physics. Freud was particularly impressed by the principle of the *conservation of energy*—which states that energy may be changed into different forms but is neither created nor destroyed—and he postulated that humans are also closed energy systems. There is a constant amount of psychic energy for any given individual, which Freud called *libido* (Latin for "lust"), reflecting his view that the sexual drive was primary.

One corollary of the conservation of energy principle is that if a forbidden act or impulse is suppressed, its energy will seek an outlet somewhere else in the system, possibly appearing in disguised form. The desires of the id contain psychic energy that must be expressed in some way, and prohibiting their expression does not abolish them. Aggressive impulses, for example, may be displaced to racing sports cars, playing chess, or indulging in a sarcastic sense of humor. Dreams and neurotic symptoms are also manifestations of psychic energy that has been prevented from being expressed directly.

Individuals who feel an urge to do something forbidden experience anxiety. Freud described several strategies—called the *defense mechanisms of the ego*—that the individual can use to prevent or reduce this anxiety. The most basic defense mechanism is *repression,* in which the ego pushes a threatening thought or forbidden impulse out of awareness into the unconscious; from the outside it appears that the individual has simply forgotten the thought or impulse. Another way of reducing anxiety is to express the impulse in a disguised form that will avoid punishment either by society or by its internal representative, the superego. Individuals differ both in their thresholds for anxiety and in the defenses they use to deal with such anxiety. Anxiety and mechanisms of defense are central to Freud's theory of psychopathology.

Personality Development   Freud believed that during the first 5 years of life the individual progresses through several developmental stages that affect personality. Applying a broad definition of sexuality, he called these periods *psychosexual stages.* During each stage, the pleasure-seeking impulses of the id focus on a particular area of the body and on activities connected with that area.

Freud called the first year of life the *oral stage* of psychosexual development. During this period, infants derive pleasure from nursing and sucking and begin to put anything they can reach into their mouths. Freud called the second year of life the beginning of the *anal stage* and believed that during this time children find pleasure both in withholding and in expelling feces. These pleasures come into conflict with parents who are attempting toilet training, the child's first experience with imposed control. In the *phallic stage,* from about age 3 to age 6, children begin to derive pleasure from fondling their genitals. They observe the differences between males and females and begin to direct their awakening sexual impulses toward the parent of the opposite sex.

It is during the phallic stage that children must resolve the *Oedipal conflict.* Freud described this conflict most clearly in the case of a boy. Around the age of 5 or 6, the boy's sexual impulses are directed toward the mother. This leads him to perceive his father as a rival for his mother's affection. Freud called this situation the Oedipal conflict, after Sophocles' play in which Oedipus unwittingly kills his father and marries his mother. According to Freud, the boy also fears that his father will retaliate against these sexual impulses by castrating him. Freud labeled this fear *castration anxiety* and considered it the prototype of all later anxieties provoked by forbidden internal desires. Normally, the boy simultaneously reduces this anxiety and settles for vicarious gratification of his feelings toward his mother by *identifying* with his father—internalizing an idealized perception of his father's attitudes and values. The same process in a girl—resulting in her identification with her mother—is analogous, but more complicated and even more controversial.

Resolution of the Oedipal conflict terminates the phallic stage and is succeeded by the *latency period,* which lasts from about age 7 to age 12. During this sexually quiescent time, children become less concerned with their bodies and turn their attention to the skills needed for coping with the environment. Finally, adolescence and puberty usher in the *genital stage,* the mature phase of adult sexuality and functioning.

Freud felt that special problems at any stage could arrest (or *fixate*) development and have a lasting effect on the personality. Libido would remain attached to the activities appropriate for that stage. Thus, a person who was weaned very early and did not have enough sucking pleasure might become fixated at the oral stage. As an adult, he or she may be excessively dependent on others and overly fond of oral pleasures such as eating, drinking, and smoking. Such a person is said to have an *oral personality.* A person fixated at the anal stage of psychosexual development might be abnormally concerned with cleanliness, orderliness, and saving and tend to resist external pressure; this is called the *anal personality.* Inadequate resolution of the Oedipal conflict can lead to a weak sense of morality, difficulties with authority figures, and many other problems.

According to psychoanalytic theory, a child resolves the Oedipal conflict by identifying with the same-sex parent.

Modifications of Freud's Theories   Freud modified his theories throughout his life. Like a good scientist, he remained open to new data, revising earlier positions as new observations accumulated that could not be accommodated by the original theory. For example, he completely revised his theory of anxiety quite late in his career. Freud's theory was further extended by his daughter Anna, who played a particularly important role in clarifying the mechanisms of defense (1946/1967) and applying psychoanalytic theory to the practice of child psychiatry (1958).

But if Freud was open to new data, he was not open to dissenting opinions. He was particularly adamant that his colleagues and followers not question the libido theory and the centrality of sexual motivation in the functioning of the personality. This dogmatism forced a break between Freud and many of his most brilliant associates—some of whom went on to develop rival theories that placed more emphasis on motivational processes other than sexuality. These former associates included Carl Jung and Alfred Adler as well as later theorists such as Karen Horney, Harry Stack Sullivan, and Erich Fromm.

Freud's daughter, Anna, extended his theory, clarifying the mechanisms of defense and applying the theory to the practice of child psychiatry.

These dissidents and other, more recent psychoanalytic theorists all place more stress on the role of the ego. They believe that the ego is present at birth, develops independently of the id, and performs functions other than finding realistic ways of satisfying id impulses. These ego functions are learning how to cope with the environment and making sense of experience. Ego satisfactions include exploration, manipulation, and competence in performance. This approach ties the concept of the ego more closely to cognitive processes.

An important part of this new direction is *object relations theory,* which deals with a person's attachments and relationships to other people over the life course. Object relations theorists have not rejected the concept of the id or the importance of biological drives in motivating behavior, but they have an equal interest in such questions as degree of psychological separateness from parents, degree of attachment to and involvement with other people versus self-preoccupation, and the strength of the individual's feelings of self-esteem and competence.

The psychoanalyst Erik Erikson, who was discussed in Chapter 3, revised Freud's theory of development. Instead of viewing developmental stages in terms of their psychosexual functions, Erikson saw them as psychosocial stages involving primarily ego processes. For Erikson, the important feature of the first year of life is not that it focuses on oral gratification but that the child is learning to trust (or mistrust) the environment as a satisfier of needs. The important feature of the second year of life is not that it focuses on anal concerns such as toilet training but that the child is learning autonomy. Toilet training just happens to be a frequent arena of conflict in which the child's striving for autonomy clashes with new demands for obedience. Erikson's theory also adds more stages in order to encompass the entire life span.

Projective Tests   The fixed structure of personality inventories—specific questions to which the individual must respond by selecting one of the answers presented—is not well suited to assessing the kinds of unconscious aspects of personality of central interest to psychoanalytic theorists. Accordingly, they prefer tests that resemble Freud's technique of free association, in which the individual is free to say whatever comes to mind. For this reason, they developed projective tests. A **projective test** *presents an ambiguous stimulus to which the person may respond as he or she wishes.* Because the stimulus is ambiguous and does not demand a specific response, it is assumed that the individuals project their personality onto the stimulus and thus

projective test a test that presents an ambiguous stimulus to which the person may respond as he or she wishes

reveal something about themselves. The most widely used projective technique, the Rorschach test developed by the Swiss psychiatrist Hermann Rorschach in the 1920s, consists of a series of 10 cards, each displaying a rather complex inkblot like the one shown in Figure 10-2. Some of the blots are in color; some are black-and-white. The participant is instructed to look at one card at a time and report everything the inkblot resembles. After the participant has looked at all 10 cards, the examiner usually goes over each response, asking the participant to clarify some responses and to tell what features of the blot gave a particular impression.

The participant's responses may be scored in various ways. Three main categories are *location* (whether the response involves the entire inkblot or a part of it), *determinants* (whether the participant responds to the shape of the blot, its color, or differences in texture and shading), and *content* (what the response represents). Most testers also score responses according to frequency of occurrence; for example, a response is "popular" if many people assign it to the same inkblot.

Unfortunately, the Rorschach test is not highly reliable because the interpretation of responses is too dependent on the clinician's judgment; the same test protocol may be evaluated quite differently by two trained examiners. And attempts to demonstrate the Rorschach's validity—its ability to predict behavior or discriminate between groups—have had limited success. In 1974 a system was introduced that attempted to extract and combine the validated portions of all the scoring systems into one complete system. It has undergone extensive revision and is now supplemented by a computer scoring service and software for microcomputers (Exner, 1986). Although this system looks more promising than previous efforts, not enough studies have been done to evaluate its validity with any confidence.

In addition to the Rorschach, many other projective tests have been devised. Some ask the participant to tell a story in response to an ambiguous picture, to draw pictures, or to complete sentences (for example, "I often wish . . ." or "My mother . . ." or "I feel like quitting when they . . ."). Defenders of projective tests point out that it is not fair to expect accurate predictions based on test responses alone; responses to inkblots and projective responses are meaningful only when they are considered in light of additional information, such as the person's life history, other test data, and observations of behavior. A skilled clinician uses the results of projective tests to make tentative interpretations about the individual's personality and then verifies or discards them, depending on further information. The tests are helpful primarily because they suggest possible areas of conflict to be explored.

Figure 10-2

A Rorshach Inkblot   The person is asked to tell what he or she sees in the blot; it may be viewed from any angle.

An Evaluation of the Psychoanalytic Approach   Psychoanalytic theory is so broad in scope that it cannot simply be pronounced true or false. But whether it is correct or incorrect in its details has little bearing on its overall impact on our culture and the value of some of its scientific contributions. For example, Freud's method of free association opened up an entirely new database of observations that had never before been explored systematically. Second, the recognition that our actions often reflect a compromise between our wishes and our fears accounts for many of the apparent contradictions in human behavior better than any other theory of personality; as a theory of *ambivalence*, psychoanalytic theory has no peer. Third, Freud's recognition that unconscious processes play an important role in much of our behavior is almost universally accepted—although these processes are now often reinterpreted in learning-theory or information-processing terms.

Nevertheless, as a scientific theory the psychoanalytic account has been persistently criticized for its inadequacy (Grünbaum, 1984). One of the main criticisms is that many of its concepts are ambiguous and difficult to define or measure objectively. A more serious criticism concerns the validity of the observations that Freud obtained through his psychoanalytic procedure. Critics have pointed out that it often is not clear what Freud's patients told him spontaneously about past events in their lives, what he may have planted in their minds, and what he simply inferred. For example, Freud reported that many of his patients recalled being seduced or sexually molested as children. At first he believed them, but then he decided that these reports were not literally true, but reflected patients' own early sexual fantasies. He regarded this realization as one of his major theoretical insights. But one writer has argued that Freud's original assumption about the reality of the seductions was probably more accurate, an argument that seems more reasonable in light of our increased awareness of child sexual abuse (Masson, 1984). Other critics have gone further and suggested that Freud may have questioned his patients so persistently with leading questions and suggestions that they were led to reconstruct memories of seductions that never occurred—a hypothesis that Freud considered but rejected (Powell & Boer, 1994). Others charge that in many cases Freud simply inferred that seduction had occurred even though the patient never reported such an incident; he actually substituted his theoretical expectations for actual data (Esterson, 1993; Scharnberg, 1993).

When Freud's theories have actually been tested empirically, the results have been mixed. Efforts to link adult personality characteristics to psychosexually relevant events in childhood have generally had negative outcomes (Sears, Maccoby, & Levin, 1957; Sewell & Mussen, 1952). When relevant character traits are identified, they appear to be related to similar character traits in the parents (Beloff, 1957; Hetherington & Brackbill; 1963). Thus, even if a relationship were to be found between toilet-training practices and adult personality traits, it could have arisen because both are linked with parental emphasis on cleanliness and order. In such a case, a simple learning-theory explanation—parental reinforcement and the child's imitation of the parents—would be a more economical explanation of the adult traits than the psychoanalytic hypothesis.

This outcome should also remind us that Freud based his theory on observations of a very narrow range of people—primarily upper-middle-class men and women in Victorian Vienna who suffered from neurotic symptoms. In hindsight, many of Freud's cultural biases are obvious, particularly in his theories about women. For example, his theory that female psychosexual development is shaped largely by "penis envy"— a girl's feelings of inadequacy because she doesn't have a penis—is almost universally rejected as reflecting the sex bias of Freud and the historical period in which he lived. A little girl's personality development during the Victorian era surely was shaped more decisively by awareness that she lacked the greater independence, power, and social status of her brother than by envy of his penis.

Despite these criticisms, however, the remarkable feature of Freud's theory is how well it managed to transcend its narrow observational base. For example, many experimental studies of defense mechanisms and reactions to conflict have supported the theory in contexts quite different from those in which Freud originally developed it (Blum, 1953; Erdelyi, 1985; Holmes, 1974; Sears, 1943, 1944).

In general, however, the structural theory (ego, id, and superego), the psychosexual theory, and the energy concept have not fared well over the years. Even some psychoanalytic writers are prepared to abandon them or to modify them substantially (Kline, 1972; Schafer, 1976). On the other hand, Freud's dynamic theory—his theory of anxiety and the mechanisms of defense—has withstood the test of time, research, and observation. A recent survey of psychoanalytically oriented psychologists and psychiatrists found widespread agreement with a number of ideas that were controversial when Freud first introduced them, including the importance of early childhood in shaping adult personality and the centrality of both conflict and the unconscious in human mental life (Westen, 1999).

The Behavioral Approach

In contrast to the psychodynamic approach to personality, the behavioral approach emphasizes the importance of *environmental* or *situational* determinants of behavior. Behavior is the result of a continuous interaction between personal and environmental variables. Environmental conditions shape behavior through learning; a person's behavior, in turn, shapes the environment.

Individuals and situations influence each other reciprocally. To predict behavior, we need to know how the characteristics of the individual interact with the characteristics of the situation (Bandura, 1986). In its contemporary formulation, the behavioral approach is now called the social-learning approach or the social cognitive approach. It is the descendant of behaviorism and its outgrowth, stimulus-response psychology, which were dominant in the first half of the 20th century (see Chapter 1).

Social Learning and Conditioning   The effect of other people—the rewards and punishments they provide—is an important influence on an individual's behavior. Accordingly, one of the most basic principles of social-learning theory is *operant conditioning* and the processes related to it, discussed in Chapter 6. The basic tenet of social-learning theory is that people behave in ways that are likely to produce reinforcement (reward). Individual differences in behavior result primarily from differences in the kinds of learning experiences a person encounters in the course of growing up.

Although individuals learn many behavior patterns through direct experience by being rewarded or punished for behaving in a certain manner, they also acquire many responses through observational learning. People can learn by observing the actions of others and noting the consequences of those actions. It would be a slow and inefficient process indeed if all of our behavior had to be learned through direct reinforcement of our responses. Similarly, the reinforcement that controls the expression of learned behaviors may be direct (tangible rewards, social approval or disapproval, alleviation of aversive conditions), vicarious (observation of someone receiving reward or punishment for behavior similar to one's own), or self-administered (evaluation of one's own performance with self-praise or self-reproach).

Because most social behaviors are not uniformly rewarded in all settings, the individual learns to discriminate between contexts in which certain behavior is appropriate and contexts in which it is not. To the extent that a person is rewarded for the same response in many different situations, generalization takes place, ensuring that the same behavior will occur in a variety of settings. Thus, a boy who is reinforced for physical aggression at home, as well as at school and at play, is likely to develop a personality that is pervasively aggressive. More often, aggressive responses are rewarded in some situations and not in others, and learned discriminations determine the situations in which the individual will display aggression (for example, aggression is acceptable on the football field but not in the classroom).

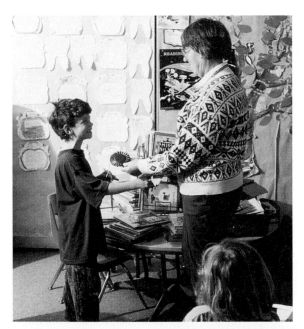

According to the behavioral approach, social learning through positive reinforcement, such as praise, plays an important role in shaping both behavior and personality.

For this reason, social-learning theorists challenge the usefulness of characterizing individuals with trait terms like "aggressive," arguing that such terms obscure the variability of behavior across situations.

Operant conditioning and its related processes apply to behavior, the major focus of social-learning approaches. To account for emotion or affect, social-learning theorists add *classical conditioning* to their account of personality (see Chapter 6). For example, when a child is punished for engaging in a forbidden activity, the punishment elicits the physiological responses that we associate with guilt or anxiety. Subsequently, the child's behavior may itself elicit those same responses; he or she will feel guilty when engaging in the forbidden behavior. In the terminology of classical conditioning, we would say that the behavior becomes a conditioned stimulus by being paired with the unconditioned stimulus of punishment; the anxiety becomes the conditioned response. For the social-learning theorist, it is classical conditioning that produces the internalized source of anxiety that Freud labeled the superego. Like operant conditioning, classical conditioning can also operate vicariously and can generalize to stimuli that have not been directly conditioned.

Social-learning theory has come a long way from its roots in early radical behaviorism, which explicitly avoided any reference to internal cognitive processes. As early as 1954, Julian Rotter (1954, 1982) was introducing cognitive variables into the behavioral approach. Albert Bandura (1986), one of the leading contemporary theorists in this area, calls his version of the approach *social cognitive theory.* His theory emphasizes *reciprocal determinism,* in which external determinants of behavior (such as rewards and punishments) and internal determinants (such as beliefs, thoughts, and expectations) are part of a system of interacting influences that affect both behavior and other parts of the system.

We noted earlier that personality psychology seeks to specify both the variables on which individuals differ from one another and the general processes of personality functioning. Trait approaches have focused on the first task, describing personality differences in detail, while saying virtually nothing about the processes of personality functioning. Psychoanalytic theory has attempted to do both. In contrast, the social-learning approach has focused primarily on process, with little attention devoted to describing individual differences. Because the approach sees every individual's personality as the unique product of that person's reinforcement history and emphasizes the degree to which behavior varies across situations, it has not attempted to classify individuals into types or rate them on traits. But social-learning theorist Walter Mischel (1973, 1993) has attempted to incorporate individual differences into social learning theory by introducing such cognitive variables as the differences among individuals in what they expect to happen in a particular situation, the ways in which they regulate their own behaviors, and their abilities to make realistic plans for reaching their goals.

An Evaluation of the Behavioral Approach   Through its emphasis on specifying the environmental variables that evoke specific behaviors, social-learning theory has made a major contribution to both clinical psychology and personality theory. It has led us to see human actions as reactions to specific environments, and it has helped us focus on the ways in which environments control our behavior and how they can be changed to modify behavior. As we will see in Chapter 13, the systematic application of learning principles has proved successful in changing many maladaptive behaviors.

Social-learning theorists have been criticized for overemphasizing the importance of situational influences on behavior and thus losing the "person" in personality psychology (Carlson, 1971), There is still some merit in this criticism despite the recent cognitive processes and variables that have been incorporated into the theories in recent decades. But the social-learning theorists have forced other personality psychologists to reexamine their assumptions about the flexibility of behavior across situations. As a result, personality psychologists have emerged with a clearer understanding of the interactions between persons and situations and an enhanced appreciation of each person's individuality.

The Phenomenological Approach

phenomenology the individual's subjective experience of the world

The phenomenological approach to the study of personality focuses on the individual's **phenomenology,** *his or her subjective experience of the world.* Phenomenological theories differ from the theories we have discussed so far in that they generally are not concerned with the person's motivational or reinforcement history or with predicting behavior. They focus instead on how the individual perceives and interprets events in his or her current environment. Among the subvarieties of the phenomenological approach, the most central is *humanistic psychology.*

During the first half of the 20th century, the psychoanalytic and behavioral approaches were dominant in psychology. In 1962 a group of psychologists founded the Association of Humanistic Psychology. They labeled humanistic psychology a "third force," an alternative set of assumptions and concerns to those that characterized the other two approaches. To define its mission, the association adopted a set of principles that emphasized the experiencing person and his or her quest for personal meaning ("Who am I?") as the primary focus of study.

In their statement of principles, humanistic psychologists rejected the psychoanalytic approach, believing that a psychology based on crippled personalities could only produce a crippled psychology. They also rejected behaviorism, a psychology that was devoid of consciousness. People, they argued, are not simply motivated by basic drives like sex or aggression or physiological needs like hunger and thirst. They have a need to develop their potentials and capabilities. Growth and self-actualization should be the criteria of psychological health, not merely ego control or adjustment to the environment. Moreover, we should study important human and social problems, even if that sometimes means adopting less rigorous methods. And although psychologists should strive to be objective in collecting and interpreting observations, their choice of research topics can and should be guided by values. In this sense, research is not value-free; values are not something psychologists should pretend not to have or feel they must apologize for. Finally, the humanistic psychologists placed a high value on the dignity of the person. Persons are basically good; the objective of psychology is to understand, not to predict or control them. Even referring to those who participate in research as "subjects" is considered by many humanistic psychologists to degrade their dignity as full partners in the quest for understanding human personality. (In 1994, journals published by the American Psychological Association began using the term "participants" rather than "subjects" when humans were being studied.)

Psychologists who share the values of the association come from diverse theoretical backgrounds. For example, several psychoanalysts such as Carl Jung, Alfred Adler, and Erik Erikson held humanistic views of motivation that diverged from Freud's views. But it is Carl Rogers and Abraham Maslow whose theoretical views lie at the center of the humanistic movement.

Carl Rogers believed that individuals have an innate tendency to move toward growth, maturity, and positive change. He referred to this as the actualizing tendency.

Carl Rogers   Like Freud, Carl Rogers (1902–1987) developed his theory from work with patients or clients in the clinic (Rogers, 1951, 1959, 1963, 1970). Rogers was impressed with what he saw as individuals' innate tendency to move in the direction of growth, maturity, and positive change. He came to believe that the basic force motivating the human organism is the *actualizing tendency*—a tendency toward fulfillment or actualization of all the capacities of the organism. A growing organism seeks to fulfill its potential within the limits of its heredity. A person may not always clearly perceive which actions lead to growth and which actions are regressive. But once the course is clear, the individual chooses to grow rather than to regress. Rogers did not deny that there are other needs, some of them biological, but he saw them as subservient to the organism's motivation to enhance itself.

Rogers's belief in the primacy of actualization forms the basis of his *nondirective* or *client-centered therapy*. This method of psychotherapy assumes that every individual has the motivation and ability to change and that the individual (or client) is best qualified to decide on the direction that such change should take. The therapist's role is to act as a sounding board while the client explores and analyzes his or her problems. This approach differs from psychoanalytic therapy, during which the therapist analyzes the patient's history to determine the problem and devise a course of remedial action. (See Chapter 13 for a discussion of various approaches to psychotherapy.)

The central concept in Rogers's theory of personality is the *self*. The self consists of all the ideas, perceptions, and values that characterize "I" or "me," including awareness of "what I am" and "what I can do." This self-concept does not necessarily reflect reality: A person may be highly successful and respected but still view himself or herself as a failure. A well-adjusted person has a self-concept that is consistent with thought, experience, and behavior; the self is not rigid but flexible, and can change as it assimilates new experiences and ideas. Rogers also emphasized the person's *ideal self*, a conception of the kind of person we would like to be. The closer the ideal self is to the real self, the more fulfilled and happy the individual becomes. A large discrepancy between the ideal self and the real self results in an unhappy, dissatisfied person.

Abraham Maslow The psychology of Abraham Maslow (1908–1970) overlaps that of Carl Rogers in many ways. Maslow was first attracted to behaviorism and carried out studies in primate sexuality and dominance. He was already moving away from behaviorism when his first child was born, at which time he remarked that anyone who observes a baby cannot be a behaviorist. He was influenced by psychoanalysis, but eventually became critical of its theory of motivation and developed his own. Specifically, he proposed that there is a *hierarchy of needs*, ascending from the basic biological needs to the more complex psychological motivations, which become important only after the basic needs have been satisfied (see Figure 10-3). The needs at one level must be at least partially satisfied before those at the next level become important determiners of action. When food and safety are difficult to obtain, efforts to satisfy those needs dominate a person's actions and higher motives are of little significance. Only when basic needs can be satisfied easily will the individual have the time and energy to devote to

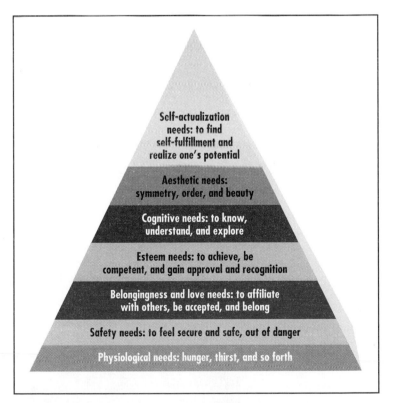

Figure 10-3

Maslow's Hierarchy of Needs Needs that are low in the hierarchy must be at least partially satisfied before needs that are higher in the hierarchy become important sources of motivation. (After Maslow, 1970)

self-actualization in Maslow's theory, the highest motive, which can be fulfilled only after all other needs are fulfilled

aesthetic and intellectual interests. Artistic and scientific endeavors do not flourish in societies in which people must struggle for food, shelter, and safety. *The highest motive—***self-actualization***—can be fulfilled only after all other needs are fulfilled.*

Maslow decided to study *self-actualizers*—men and women who had made extraordinary use of their potential. He began by studying the lives of eminent historical figures such as Spinoza, Thomas Jefferson, Abraham Lincoln, Jane Addams, Albert Einstein, and Eleanor Roosevelt. In this way he was able to create a composite picture of a self-actualizer. The distinguishing characteristics of such individuals are listed in Table 10-5, along with some of the behaviors that Maslow believed could lead to self-actualization.

An Evaluation of the Phenomenological Approach   By focusing on the individual's unique perception and interpretation of events, the phenomenological approach brings the role of private experience back to the study of personality. More than other theories we have discussed, the theories of Rogers and Maslow also concentrate on the whole, healthy person and emphasize a positive, optimistic view of human personality. Moreover, phenomenological psychologists emphasize that they study important problems even if they do not always have rigorous methods for investigating them. They have a point: Investigating trivial problems just because one has a convenient method for doing so does little to advance the science of psychology. Moreover, phenomenological psychologists have been increasingly ingenious over the years at devising new methods for assessing self-concepts and conducting studies that treat the individual as an equal partner in the research enterprise.

Nevertheless, critics can and do question the quality of the evidence given to support the humanistic psychologists' claims. For example, to what extent are the characteristics of self-actualizers a consequence of a psychological process called self-actualization and to what extent are they merely reflections of the particular value systems held by Rogers and Maslow? Where, they ask, is the evidence for Maslow's hierarchy of needs? Phenomenological psychologists are also vulnerable to a criticism that is the mirror image of a criticism they have leveled at Freud. They

Albert Einstein and Eleanor Roosevelt were among the individuals Maslow identified as self-actualizers.

have criticized Freud for attempting to build a complete theory of personality on observations of neurotic individuals. But critics point out that Rogers and Maslow built their theories on observations of relatively healthy people (mainly college students, in the case of Rogers). Accordingly, their theories are best suited to well-functioning people who have the luxury of worrying about needs at the top of Maslow's hierarchy. The application of these theories to seriously malfunctioning individuals or to socially, culturally, or economically disadvantaged individuals is less apparent.

And finally, some have even criticized the values espoused by the humanistic theorists. Many observers believe that American society already has too great a concern for the individual and too little concern for the welfare of the larger society. A psychology that raises individual self-fulfillment and actualization to the top of the value hierarchy is *too* compatible with American ideology; some critics believe that it even provides a psychological "sanction for selfishness" (Wallach & Wallach, 1983). Although Maslow lists concern for the welfare of humanity among his characteristics of self-actualizers (again see Table 10-5) and some of the self actualizers identified by Maslow—such as Eleanor Roosevelt—clearly possessed this characteristic, It is conspicuously absent from the hierarchy of needs that is so central to Maslow's formal theory.

Table 10-5

Self-Actualization   Listed here are the personal qualities that Maslow found to be characteristic of self-actualizers and the behaviors he considered important to the development of self-actualization. (After Maslow, 1967)

Characteristics of Self-Actualizers

Perceive reality efficiently and are able to tolerate uncertainty
Accept themselves and others for what they are
Spontaneous in thought and behavior
Problem-centered rather than self-centered
Have a good sense of humor
Highly creative
Resistant to enculturation, although not purposely unconventional
Concerned for the welfare of humanity
Capable of deep appreciation of the basic experiences of life
Establish deep, satisfying interpersonal relationships with a few, rather than many, people
Able to look at life from an objective viewpoint

Behaviors Leading to Self-Actualization

Experience life as a child does, with full absorption and concentration
Try something new rather than sticking to secure and safe ways
Listen to your own feelings in evaluating experiences rather than to the voice of tradition or authority or the majority
Be honest; avoid pretenses or "game playing"
Be prepared to be unpopular if your views do not coincide with those of most people
Assume responsibility
Work hard at whatever you decide to do
Try to identify your defenses and have the courage to give them up

---

Personality psychologists differ in how appealing they find the three major approaches to personality discussed in this chapter. Some prefer to avoid such formal theories and to use the relatively nontheoretical trait approach. What about you? What do you find appealing or unappealing about each of these approaches?

Thinking Critically

Summary

1. A major task in psychology is to discover how genetic or biological factors ("nature") and environmental factors ("nurture") interact to create differences among individuals. Behavioral scientists typically quantify the extent to which a group of people differ on some measure of a trait or ability by computing the *variance* of the scores obtained. The more the individuals in the group differ from one another, the higher the variance. Researchers can then seek to determine how much of that variance is due to different causes. The percentage of variance in a trait that is accounted for by genetic differences among the individuals is called the *heritability* of the trait. For example, the heritability of height is approximately 90%: Differences among people in their heights are due almost entirely to differences in their genetic makeup.

2. Heritabilities can be estimated by comparing correlations obtained for pairs of identical twins (who share all their genes) and correlations

obtained on pairs of fraternal twins (who, on the average, share about half of their genes). If identical twin pairs are more alike on the trait than fraternal twin pairs, the trait probably has a genetic component.

3. There are many misunderstandings about heritability: Following are some important facts to remember: (1) Heritability is about differences among individuals. It does not indicate how much of a trait in an individual is due to genetic factors. (2) Heritability is not a fixed attribute of a trait. If something happens to change the variability of a trait in a group, the heritability will also change. (3) Heritability is about the variance within a group. It does not indicate the source of mean differences between groups. (4) Heritability does not indicate how much possible environmental changes might change the mean level of a trait in a population.

4. In shaping personality, genetic and environmental influences do not act independently but are intertwined. Because both a child's personality and his or her home environment are functions of the parents' genes, there is a built-in correlation between the child's *genotype* (inherited personality characteristics) and that environment.

5. Three dynamic processes of personality–environment interaction are (1) reactive interaction, in which different individuals exposed to the same environment experience, interpret, and react to it differently; (2) evocative interaction, in which an individual's personality evokes distinctive responses from others; and (3) proactive interaction, in which individuals select or create environments of their own. As a child grows older, the influence of proactive interaction becomes increasingly important.

6. When their genetic similarities are subtracted out, children from the same family seem to be no more alike than children chosen randomly from the population. This surprising finding implies that the kinds of variables that psychologists typically study (such as child-rearing practices and the family's socioeconomic status) contribute virtually nothing to individual differences in personality. It could be that twin studies have not included a wide enough variety of families. Another possibility is that the reactive, evocative, and proactive processes act to enhance the differences among children from the same families and to diminish the differences between different family environments. In any case, future research will have to look more closely at differences between children within the same family and at sources of influence outside the family, such as the peer group.

7. Tests for assessing intelligence or personality must demonstrate that they yield reproducible and consistent results *(reliability)* and that they measure what they are intended to measure *(validity)*.

8. The first successful intelligence tests were developed by the French psychologist Alfred Binet, who proposed the concept of mental age. A bright child's mental age is above his or her chronological age; a slow child's mental age is below his or her chronological age. The concept of the *intelligence quotient (IQ)*, the ratio of mental age to chronological age (multiplied by 100), was introduced into the revision of the Binet scales (the Stanford-Binet). Many intelligence test scores are still expressed as IQ scores, but they are no longer actually calculated according to this formula.

9. Both Binet and David Wechsler, developer of the Wechsler Adult Intelligence Scale (WAIS), assumed that intelligence is a general capacity for reasoning. Similarly, Charles Spearman proposed that a general factor *(g)* underlies performance on different kinds of test items. A method for determining the kinds of abilities that underlie performance on intelligence tests is *factor analysis*.

10. An alternative approach to intelligence is the information-processing approach, which seeks to understand intellectual behavior in terms of the underlying cognitive processes brought into play when an individual attempts to solve an intelligence test problem.

11. Some psychologists believe that there are multiple intelligences and that current tests tap only "academic intelligence" rather than practical intelligence, creative intelligence, or other aspects of intelligent behavior (for example, musical or interpersonal intelligence).

12. *Personality* refers to the distinctive and characteristic patterns of thought, emotion, and behavior that define an individual's personal style of interacting with the physical and social environments. Personality psychology seeks (1) to describe and explain individual differences and (2) to synthesize the processes that can influence an individual's interactions with the environment into an integrated account of the total person.

13. To arrive at a comprehensive but manageable number of personality traits on which individuals can be assessed, investigators first collected all the trait terms found in the unabridged dictionary (about 18,000); these were then reduced to a smaller number. Ratings of individuals on these terms were factor-analyzed to determine how many underlying dimensions were needed to account for the correlations among the scales. Although different investigators arrive at different numbers of factors, the recent consensus is that five factors provide the best compromise. These have been labeled the "Big Five" and form the acronym OCEAN: <u>O</u>penness to experience, <u>C</u>onscientiousness, <u>E</u>xtraversion, <u>A</u>greeableness, and <u>N</u>euroticism.

14. Freud's psychoanalytic theory holds that many behaviors, including dreams and slips of the tongue, are caused by unconscious motiva-

tions. Personality is determined primarily by the biological drives of sex and aggression and by experiences that occur during the first 5 years of life. Freud's theory of personality structure views personality as composed of the *id*, the *ego,* and the *superego,* which are often in conflict. The id operates on the pleasure principle, seeking immediate gratification of biological impulses. The ego obeys the reality principle, postponing gratification until it can be achieved in socially acceptable ways. The superego (conscience) imposes moral standards on the individual. In a well-integrated personality, the ego remains in firm but flexible control over the id and superego; the reality principle governs.

15. Freud's theory of personality dynamics proposes that there is a constant amount of psychic energy (libido) in each individual. If a forbidden act or impulse is suppressed, its energy will seek an outlet in some other form, such as dreams or neurotic symptoms. The theory assumes that unacceptable id impulses cause anxiety, which can be reduced by defense mechanisms.

16. Freud's theory of personality development proposes that individuals pass through psychosexual stages (such as oral, anal, phallic) and must resolve the Oedipal conflict, in which the young child sees the same-sex parent as a rival for the affection of the opposite-sex parent. Freud's theory of anxiety and defense mechanisms has fared better over the years than his structural and developmental theories have. Psychoanalytic theory has been modified by others, such as Jung, Adler, Horney, Sullivan, Fromm, and Erikson—all of whom place more emphasis on functions of the ego and on motives other than sex and aggression.

17. Psychologists who take the psychoanalytic approach prefer less structured assessment instruments called *projective tests,* such as the

Rorschach test. Because the test stimuli are ambiguous, it is assumed that the individual projects his or her personality onto the stimulus, thereby revealing unconscious wishes and motives.

18. Social-learning theory is the contemporary version of the behavioral approach to personality. It assumes that personality differences result from variations in learning experiences—which includes learning by observation in addition to direct operant or classical conditioning. Social-learning theory, which has become increasingly cognitive over the past few decades, now emphasizes the recip-

rocal interaction between external determinants of behavior (such as rewards and punishments) and internal determinants (such as beliefs, thoughts, and expectations).

19. The *phenomenological* approach is concerned with the individual's subjective experience. Humanistic psychology, a branch of this approach, was proposed as a "third force," an explicit alternative to psychoanalytic and behavioral approaches. Humanistic psychologists like Carl Rogers and Abraham Maslow emphasize a person's self-concept and striving for growth, or *self-actualization.*

Suggested Readings

Plomin, *Nature and Nurture: An Introduction to Behavioral Genetics* (1996), provides an accessible discussion of behavioral genetics, including the twin method of assessing heritability. For a complete discussion of the differences among children from the same family, see Dunn and Plomin, *Separate Lives: Why Siblings Are So Different* (1992). A more advanced treatment of the genetics of intelligence is Plomin, DeFries, and McClearn, *Behavioral Genetics: A Primer* (2nd ed., 1989). Plomin and McClearn (eds.), *Nature, Nurture & Psychology* (1993), provide a collection of essays on the nature-nurture problem in several areas. Harris, *The Nurture Assumption* (1998), argues that peers are more important than the family in shaping children's personalities.

For an introduction to individual differences and psychological testing, see Anastasi, *Psychological Testing* (7th ed., 1996); and Sattler, *Assessment of Children* (1988).

For a more general overview of intellectual abilities, see Gardner, Kornhaber, and Wake, *Intelligence: Multiple Perspectives* (1996); and Brody, *Intelligence* (2nd ed., 1992). A theory of multiple intelligences is presented in Gardner, *Frames of Mind: The The-*

ory of Multiple Intelligences (2nd anniversary reprint ed., 1993). Other recent theories may be found in Anderson, *Intelligence and Development: A Cognitive Theory* (1992); Ceci, *On Intelligence . . . More or Less: A Bio-Ecological Treatise on Intellectual Development* (1996); and Sternberg, *Metaphors of Mind: Conceptions of the Nature of Intelligence* (1990).

A very controversial book on intelligence in American society is Herrnstein and Murray, *The Bell Curve* (1994). Ceci (ed.) *The Nature-Nurture Debate: The Essential Readings* (1999) includes several essays that address issues raised in *The Bell Curve.* For personality assessment, see Aiken, *Assessment of Personality* (1989).

There are several general textbooks on personality psychology that blend theory and contemporary research. They include Funder, *The Personality Puzzle* (1997); Mischel, *Introduction to Personality* (6th ed., 1998); and Burger, *Personality* (4th ed., 1996). A classic text that compares and contrasts the formal theories of personality is Hall, Lindzey, Loehlin, and Manosevitz, *Introduction to Theories of Personality* (1985).

Among Freud's most readable writings are his *New Introductory Lectures on*

Psychoanalysis (1933; reprint ed., 1965) and *Psychopathology of Everyday Life* (1901/1960), in which he discusses "Freudian slips" as well as dreams and humor. An excellent summary of psychoanalytic theory and its development since Freud is Mitchell and Black, *Freud and Beyond: A History of Modern Psychoanalytic Thought* (1995). An unsparingly harsh critique of Freud as both scientist and therapist can be found in Crews (ed.), *Unauthorized Freud: Doubters Confront a Legend* (1998).

The social-learning approach to personality is represented by one of its leading theorists in Bandura, *Social Foundations of Thought & Action: A Social Cognitive Theory* (1985).

Two classic statements of the humanistic viewpoint are Maslow, *Toward a Psychology of Being* (1998); and Rogers, *On Becoming a Person: A Therapist's View of Psychotherapy* (1995). Fadiman and Frager, *Personality and Personal Growth* (4th ed., 1997), focuses on the personality theories that are most concerned with understanding human nature and includes sections on Eastern theories of personality such as yoga, Zen Buddhism, and Sufism—topics that are not usually found in more traditional academic treatments of personality.

Enhance and Explore

To enhance your understanding of the psychological concepts found in this chapter, please consult the following aids:

Study Guide

Learning Objectives, p. 177
Define the Terms, p. 179
Test Your Knowledge, p. 183
Essay Questions, p. 189
Thinking Independently, p. 191

PowerPsych CD-ROM

HOW ARE INDIVIDUAL DIFFERENCES ASSESSED?

CONTEXT AND INTELLIGENCE

The "Chitling" Test
Culture-Fair Intelligence Test

GENDER AND INTELLIGENCE

Mental Rotation Test
Embedded-Figures Test

ASSESSMENT OF PERSONALITY TRAITS

Five-Factor Personality Test

PsychCentral

For more information concerning the topics found in this chapter, access psychology links on the Word Wide Web made through the Harcourt Web page at:
http://www.harcourtcollege.com/psych/Fundamentals

www.harcourtcollege.com

http://www.harcourtcollege.com/psych/index.html

Freud's Ideas Are Alive and Vibrant

Joel Weinberger, *Adelphi University*

Of course Freud is dead. He died on September 23, 1939. No one asks whether Isaac Newton or William James is dead. For some odd reason this is reserved for Freud. If the question is whether psychoanalysis, the branch of psychology he founded, is dead, the answer is clearly no. Psychoanalysis survived Freud and thrives today. The American Psychological Association's division of psychoanalysis is the second largest division in the association. There now exists several schools of psychoanalysis, some of which Freud would probably not recognize. That is just what you would expect from a discipline whose founder is now 60 years dead.

Are Freud's ideas dead? They certainly are not. They have entered our common vernacular. They have entered and forever changed our culture. Think of the terms of *id, ego, superego, Freudian slip,* and so on. There are psychoanalytic writers, historians, psychiatrists, and of course, psychologists. The real question, I suppose, is whether Freud's ideas are still *valid.* The answer is that some are and some are not. A surprising number remain relevant, even central, to modern psychology. So I suppose the charge is to state which of his ideas remain valid. And that is what I will address.

Let's look at some of Freud's central ideas and see how they stack up with today's psychology. Freud said that all human motives could be traced back to biological sources, specifically to sex and aggression. There is a branch of psychology now termed evolutionary psychology (Buss, 1994); there is also sociobiology (Wilson, 1975) and ethology (Hinde, 1982). All champion the importance of biological factors in our behavior.

And all have data to back up their claims. This aspect of Freud's thinking is certainly not dead. As for the importance of sex and aggression? Just look at the best selling books, hit movies, and TV shows around you. What characterizes virtually all of them? Sex and violence. Hollywood and book publishers seem all to be Freudians, and so are the people who sample their wares.

Another idea of Freud's that was very controversial in his time was his notion that children have sexual feelings. Now that is simply commonplace knowledge.

Psychoanalysts have long held that one of the major factors accounting for the effectiveness of psychotherapy is the therapeutic relationship. For many years this was not accepted, particularly by the behaviorist school (Emmelkamp, 1994). We now know that this is a critical factor in therapeutic success (Weinberger, 1996). The related idea that we carry representations of early relationships around in our heads, an idea expanded upon by object relations theory (a school of psychoanalysis) and attachment theory (the creation of a psychoanalyst, John Bowlby), is also now commonly accepted in psychology.

The most central idea usually attributed to Freud is the importance of unconscious processes. According to Freud, we are most often unaware of why we do what we do. For a long while, mainstream academic psychology rejected this notion. Now it seems to have finally caught up to Freud. Modern thinkers now believe that unconscious processes are central and account for most of our behavior. Discussion of unconscious processes permeate research in memory (Graf & Masson, 1993), social psychology (Bargh, 1997),

cognitive psychology (Baars, 1988), and so on. In fact, it is now a mainstream belief in psychology. More specific notions of Freud's such as his ideas about defense have also received empirical support (Shedler, Mayman, & Manis, 1993; D. Weinberger, 1990). So have some of his ideas about unconscious fantasies (Siegel & Weinberger, 1997). There is even some work afoot to examine Freud's conceptions of transference (Andersen & Glassman, 1996; Crits-Christoph, Cooper, & Luborsky, 1990).

Of course, many of the particulars of Freud's thinking have been overtaken by events and have turned out to be incorrect. What thinker who died over 60 years ago has had all of his or her ideas survive intact, without change? In broad outline, however, Freud's ideas are not only alive, they are vibrant. We should probably be testing more of them. Any notion that Freud should be ignored because some of his assertions have been shown to be false is just plain silly. It is throwing out the baby with the bath water. And, he is so much fun to read!

Freud's Influence on Psychology Has Been That of a Dead Weight

John F. Kihlstrom, *University of California, Berkeley*

If the 20th century has been "The American Century," it has also been the century of Sigmund Freud (Roth, 1998), because Freud changed our image of ourselves. Copernicus showed that the Earth did not lie at the center of the universe, and Darwin showed that humans were descended from "lower" animals, but Freud claimed to show that human experience, thought, and action was determined not by our conscious rationality, but by irrational forces outside our awareness and control—forces which could only be understood and controlled by an extensive therapeutic process called psychoanalysis.

Freud also changed the vocabulary with which we understand ourselves and others. Before you ever opened this textbook, you already knew something about the id and the superego, penis envy and phallic symbols, castration anxiety and the Oedipus complex. In popular culture, psychotherapy is virtually identified with psychoanalysis. Freudian theory, with its focus on the interpretation of ambiguous events, lies at the foundation of "postmodern" approaches to literary criticism such as deconstruction. More than anyone else, Freud's influence on modern culture has been profound and long-lasting.

Freud's cultural influence is based, at least implicitly, on the premise that his theory is scientifically valid. But from a scientific point of view, classical Freudian psychoanalysis is dead as both a theory of the mind and a mode of therapy (Crews, 1998; Macmillan, 1996). No empirical evidence supports any specific proposition of psychoanalytic theory, such as the idea that development proceeds through oral, anal, phallic, and genital stages, or that little boys lust after their mothers and hate and fear their fathers. No empirical evidence indicates that psychoanalysis is more effective, or more efficient, than other forms of psychotherapy, such as systematic desensitization or assertiveness training. No empirical evidence indicates that the mechanisms by which psychoanalysis achieves its effects, such as they are, are those specifically predicated on the theory, such as transference and catharsis.

Freud lived at a particular period of time, and it might be argued that his theories were valid when applied to European culture at that time, even if they are no longer apropos today. However, recent historical analyses show that Freud's construal of his case material was systematically distorted by his theories of unconscious conflict and infantile sexuality, and that he misinterpreted and misrepresented the scientific evidence available to him. Freud's theories were not just a product of his time: They were misleading and incorrect even as he published them.

Drew Westen (1988), a psychologist at Harvard Medical School, agrees that Freud's theories are archaic and obsolete, but argues that Freud's legacy lives on in a number of theoretical propositions that are widely accepted by scientists: the existence of unconscious mental processes; the importance of conflict and ambivalence in behavior; the childhood origins of adult personality; mental representations as a mediator of social behavior; and stages of psychological development. However, some of these propositions are debatable. For example, there is no evidence that childrearing practices have any lasting impact on personality. More important, Westen's argument skirts the question of whether *Freud's* view of these matters was correct. It is one thing to say that unconscious motives play a role in behavior. It is something quite different to say that our every thought and deed is driven by repressed sexual and aggressive urges; that children harbor erotic feelings toward the parent of the opposite sex; and that young boys are hostile toward their fathers, who they regard as rivals for their mothers' affections. This is what *Freud* believed, and so far as we can tell *Freud* was wrong in every respect. For example, the unconscious mind revealed in laboratory studies of automaticity and implicit memory bears no resemblance to the unconscious mind of psychoanalytic theory (Kihlstrom, 1998).

Westen also argues that psychoanalytic theory itself has evolved since Freud's time, and that it is therefore unfair to bind psychoanalysis so tightly to the Freudian vision of repressed, infantile, sexual and aggressive urges. But again, this avoids the issue of whether *Freud's* theories are correct. Furthermore, it remains an open question whether these "neo-Freudian" theories are any more valid than are the classically Freudian views which preceded them. For example, it is not at all clear that Erik Erikson's stage theory of psychological development is any more valid than Freud's is.

While Freud had an enormous impact on 20th century culture, his influence on psychology has been that of a dead weight. The broad themes that Westen writes about were present in psychology before Freud, or arose more recently independent of his influence. At best, Freud is a figure of only historical interest for psychologists. He is perhaps better studied as a writer than as a scientist.

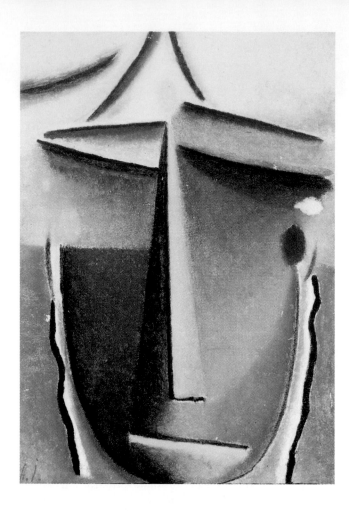

CHAPTER **11** *Stress, Health, and Coping*

Can Interventions Reduce Stress and Improve Health?
Behavioral Techniques
Cognitive Techniques
Modifying Type A Behavior
Slowing the Progress of Cancer

People who are overwhelmed by demands on their attention and time often say they are "stressed."

Janet was feeling near the end of her rope. All day long she had endured one hassle after another. At breakfast, she spilled orange juice on the only clean blouse she had. When she got to work, there were 32 e-mail messages and 15 phone messages waiting for her. In the afternoon, her boss told her to prepare a financial report for the board meeting that was to occur at 9 A.M. the next morning, but her computer crashed and she could not access the financial records for her division. Tired and overwhelmed, when she got home, she called her mother for support, only to discover that her father had been hospitalized with chest pains. After hanging up, Janet felt disoriented, her heart was racing, and she began to get a migraine.

The kind of stress Janet was experiencing is familiar to many of us—silly mistakes that cause stress, the stress of a demanding boss, and stress in our personal relationships. Exposure to stress can lead to painful emotions such as anxiety or depression. It can also lead to physical illnesses, both minor and severe. But people's reactions to stressful events differ widely: Some people who are faced with a stressful event develop serious psychological or physical problems, whereas other people who are faced with the same type of stressful event develop no problems and may even find the event challenging and interesting. In this chapter we discuss the concept of stress and its effects on the mind and the body. We also look at the differences between people's ways of thinking about and coping with stressful events, and how these differences contribute to adjustment.

Stress has become a popular topic. The media often attribute unusual behavior or illness to burnout due to stress or a nervous breakdown resulting from stress. For example, when a celebrity attempts suicide, it is often said that he or she was burned out from the pressures of public life. In their daily lives at school, students often talk about each other's levels of stress. "I'm so stressed out!" is a common claim. But what is stress? In general terms, **stress** occurs *when people are faced with events that they perceive as endangering their physical or psychological well-being.* These events are usually referred to as *stressors,* and people's reactions to them as *stress responses.*

The study of how stress and other social, psychological, and biological factors come together to contribute to illness is known as *behavioral medicine* or *health psychology.* In this chapter we will review research on how psychosocial factors interact with biological vulnerabilities to affect cardiovascular health and the functioning of the immune system. Finally, we will describe ways in which people manage stress so as to improve their health.

stress a condition that occurs when people are faced with events that they perceive as endangering their physical or psychological well-being

What Makes Events Stressful?

Countless events create stress. Some are major events that affect large numbers of people—events such as war, nuclear accidents, and earthquakes. Others are major events in the lives of individuals—for instance, having an ill family member, moving to a new area, changing jobs, getting married, or losing a friend. Everyday hassles

Table 11-1

Characteristics of Stressful Events　Most events that people find stressful have one or more of these characteristics.

Characteristic	Examples
Traumatic—situations of extreme danger outside the range of normal experience	Being in a severe automobile accident; being sexually assaulted.
Uncontrollable	Death of a loved one; having one's home damaged in a hurricane.
Unpredictable	Being mugged on a busy street; sudden onset of an unexpected disease.
Require substantial adjustment or change	Getting married; birth of a child.
Create internal conflict	Having two attractive, but very different, job offers; wanting to spend more time both with one's children and at one's work.

can also be experienced as stressors—spilling juice on your clothes, losing your wallet, getting stuck in traffic, and so on. Events that are perceived as stressful usually fall into one or more of the following categories: traumatic events outside the usual range of human experience, uncontrollable events, unpredictable events, events that require significant change, and internal conflicts (see Table 11-1).

Traumatic Events

traumatic events situations of extreme danger that are outside the range of usual human experience

The most obvious sources of stress are **traumatic events**—*situations of extreme danger that are outside the range of usual human experience.* These include natural disasters, such as earthquakes and floods; human-made disasters, such as wars and nuclear accidents; catastrophic accidents, such as car or plane crashes; and physical assaults, such as rape or attempted murder.

There is a series of psychological reactions that many people experience following a traumatic event (Horowitz, 1986) (see Figure 11-1). At first, survivors are stunned and dazed, and appear to be unaware of their injuries or of the danger. They may wander around in a disoriented state, perhaps putting themselves at risk for further injury. For example, an earthquake survivor may wander through buildings that are on the verge of collapse, unaware of the obvious danger. In the next stage, survivors are still passive and unable to initiate even simple tasks, but they may follow orders readily. For example, days after her assault a rape survivor may not even think to make herself something to eat, but if a close friend calls and insists they go out to eat, she will comply. In the third stage, survivors become anxious and apprehensive, have difficulty concentrating, and may repeat the story of the catastrophe over and over again. The survivor of a car crash may become extremely nervous when near a car, be unable to go back to work because he or she cannot concentrate, and repeatedly tell friends about the details of the crash.

Fortunately, most of us never experience traumatic events. More common events can lead to stress responses, however.

Uncontrollable Events

The more uncontrollable an event seems, the more likely it is to be perceived as stressful. Major uncontrollable events include the

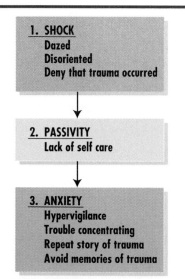

Figure 11-1

Stages of the Stress Response　People often experience shock, then passivity, then anxiety in response to a traumatic event.

1. **SHOCK**
   Dazed
   Disoriented
   Deny that trauma occurred

2. **PASSIVITY**
   Lack of self care

3. **ANXIETY**
   Hypervigilance
   Trouble concentrating
   Repeat story of trauma
   Avoid memories of trauma

Major traumas, such as losing your home in an earthquake, are experienced as stressful by most people.

death of a loved one, being laid off from work, or serious illness. Minor uncontrollable events are such things as having a friend refuse to accept your apology for some misdeed or being bumped off a flight because the airline oversold tickets. One obvious reason uncontrollable events are stressful is that if we cannot control them, we cannot stop them from happening.

It appears that our *perceptions* of the controllability of events are as important to our assessment of their stressfulness as the actual controllability of those events. Consider this study. Participants were shown color photographs of victims of violent deaths. The experimental group could terminate the viewing by pressing a button. The control participants saw the same photographs for the length of time determined by the experimental group, but they could not terminate the exposure. The level of arousal or anxiety in both groups was measured by the *galvanic skin response (GSR),* a drop in the electrical resistance of the skin that is widely used as an index of arousal and anxiety. The experimental group showed much less anxiety in response to the photographs than did the control group, even though the two groups were exposed to the photographs for the same amount of time (Geer & Maisel, 1972).

Even if we never exercise control over events, simply believing that they are controllable appears to reduce the impact of the events. This was demonstrated in a study in which two groups of participants were exposed to a loud, extremely unpleasant noise. Participants in one group were told that they could terminate the noise by pressing a button, but they were urged not to do so unless it was absolutely necessary. Participants in the other group had no control over the noise. None of the participants who had a control button actually pressed it, so the noise exposure was the same for both groups. Nevertheless, performance on subsequent problem-solving tasks was significantly worse for the group that had no control, indicating that they were more disturbed by the noise than the group that had the potential for control (Glass & Singer, 1972).

Unpredictable Events

Being able to predict the occurrence of a stressful event—even if we cannot control it—usually reduces the severity of the stress. Laboratory experiments show that both humans and animals prefer predictable aversive events over unpredictable ones. In one study, rats were given a choice between a signaled shock and an unsignaled shock. If the rat pressed a bar at the start of a series of shock trials, each shock was preceded by a warning tone. If the rat failed to press the bar, no warning tones sounded during that series of trials. All of the rats quickly learned to press the bar, showing a marked preference for predictable shock (Abbott, Schoen, & Badia, 1984). Humans generally choose predictable shocks over unpredictable ones, too. They also show less emotional arousal and report less distress while waiting for predictable shocks to occur, and they perceive predictable shocks as less aversive than unpredictable ones of the same intensity (Katz & Wykes, 1985).

How do we explain these results? One possibility is that a warning signal before an aversive event allows the person or animal to initiate some sort of preparatory process that acts to lessen the effects of a noxious stimulus. An animal receiving the signal that a shock is about to happen may shift its feet in such a way as to reduce the experience of the shock. A man who knows that he is about to receive a shot in the doctor's office can try to distract himself to lessen the pain. A woman who hears warnings of an impending hurricane can board up her windows in an attempt to prevent damage to her house. Another possibility is that with unpredictable shock, there is no safe period; with predictable shock, the person or animal can relax to some extent until the signal warns that shock is about to occur. This has been called the *safety signal hypothesis* (Seligman & Binik, 1977). A real-life example of the presence of a safety signal occurs when an employee's boss, who tends to criticize the employee in front of others, is out of town on a business trip. The boss's absence is a signal to the employee that it is safe to relax. In contrast, an employee whose boss never goes out of town, and who criticizes him unpredictably throughout the day, has no safety signals and may chronically feel stressed.

Even happy events, such as getting married, can be stressful because they require substantial changes in our everyday lives.

Events Requiring Substantial Change

Although we enter some high-pressure situations enthusiastically and joyfully, they still may be stressful. Marriage is a good example; it entails many, many new adjustments. Individuals are often challenged to the limits of their patience and tolerance as they become accustomed to the idiosyncrasies of the new spouse (for example, a habit of leaving clothes lying around everywhere). When minor irritations or major disagreements over important matters (for instance, financial decisions) lead to arguments between newlyweds, the belief that they married the right person may be challenged.

Researchers Holmes and Rahe (1967) argued that any change in life that requires numerous readjustments can be perceived as stressful. In an attempt to measure the impact of life changes, they developed the Life Events Scale, shown in Table 11-2. The life events are ranked in order of most stressful (death of a spouse) to least stressful (minor violations of the law). To arrive at this scale, the investigators examined thousands of interviews and medical histories to identify the kinds of events that people found stressful. Because marriage appeared to be a critical event for most people, it was placed in the middle of the scale and assigned an arbitrary value of 50. The investigators then asked approximately 400 men and women of varying ages, backgrounds, and marital status to compare marriage with a number of other life events. They were asked such questions as, "Does the event call for more or less readjustment than marriage?" Those interviewed were then asked to assign a point value to each event on the basis of their evaluation of its severity and the time required for adjustment. These ratings were used to construct the Life Events Scale.

Although positive events often require adjustment and are therefore sometimes stressful, most research indicates that negative events have a much greater impact on our psychological and physical health than positive events. In addition, there are large differences in how people are affected by events. Some of these differences are linked to age and cultural background (Masuda & Holmes, 1978; Ruch & Holmes, 1971). Also, some people do not find major changes or high-pressure situations such as exam week stressful. They experience such situations as challenging and are invigorated by them. Later we will discuss characteristics of individuals that affect whether they view situations as stressors or challenges.

Internal Conflicts

So far, we have discussed only external events in which something or someone in the environment challenges our well-being. Stress can also be brought about by internal processes—unresolved conflicts that may be conscious or unconscious. Conflict occurs when a person must choose between incompatible, or mutually exclusive, goals or courses of action. Many of the things that people desire prove to be incompatible. You want to play on your college volleyball team but cannot give it the time required and still earn the grades necessary to apply to graduate school. You want to join your friends for a pizza party but are afraid that you will fail tomorrow's exam if you don't stay home and study. You don't want to go to your uncle's for dinner, but you don't want to listen to your parents' complaints if you reject the invitation. The goals in these instances are incompatible because the action needed to achieve one goal automatically prevents you from reaching the other.

Even if two goals are equally attractive—for example, you receive two good job offers—you may agonize over the decision and experience regrets after making a choice. This stress would not have occurred if you had been offered only one job.

Conflict may also arise when two inner needs or motives are in opposition. In our society, the conflicts that are most pervasive and difficult to resolve generally occur between the following motives (Erikson, 1963):

- *Independence versus dependence:* Particularly when faced with a difficult situation, we may want someone to take care of us and solve our problems. But we are taught that we must stand on our own and assume responsibilities. At other times we may wish for independence, but circumstances or other people force us to remain dependent.
- *Intimacy versus isolation:* The desire to be close to another person and to share our innermost thoughts and emotions may conflict with the fear of being hurt or rejected if we expose too much of ourselves.

Table 11-2

The Life Events Scale   This scale, also known as the Holmes and Rahe Social Readjustment Rating Scale, measures stress in terms of life changes. (After Holmes & Rahe, 1967)

Life Event	Value
Death of spouse	100
Divorce	73
Marital separation	65
Jail term	63
Death of close family member	63
Personal injury or illness	53
Marriage	50
Fired from job	47
Marital reconciliation	45
Retirement	45
Change in health of family member	44
Pregnancy	40
Sex difficulties	39
Gain of a new family member	39
Business readjustment	39
Change in financial state	38
Death of a close friend	37
Change to a different line of work	36
Foreclosure of mortgage	30
Change in responsibilities at work	29
Son or daughter leaving home	29
Trouble with in-laws	29
Outstanding personal achievement	28
Wife begins or stops work	26
Begin or end school	26
Change in living conditions	25
Revision of personal habits	24
Trouble with boss	23
Change in residence	20
Change in school	20
Change in recreation	19
Change in church activities	19
Change in social activities	18
Change in sleeping habits	16
Change in eating habits	15
Vacation	13
Christmas	12
Minor legal violations	11

- *Cooperation versus competition:* Our society places much emphasis on competition and success. Competition begins in early childhood among siblings, continues through school, and culminates in business and professional rivalry. At the same time, we are urged to cooperate and to help others.
- *Expression of impulses versus moral standards:* Impulses must be regulated to some degree in all societies. Much of childhood learning involves internalizing cultural restrictions placed on impulses. Sex and aggression are two areas in which our impulses are frequently in conflict with moral standards, and violation of these standards can generate feelings of guilt.

These four areas present the greatest potential for serious conflict. Trying to find a workable compromise between opposing motives can create considerable stress.

Thinking Critically

1. Would having complete control over most situations in your life mean you experienced no stress?

2. If change of any sort can be experienced as stressful, why do most people seek out change at least occasionally?

How Do We React Psychologically to Stress?

Stressful situations produce emotional reactions ranging from exhilaration (when the event is demanding but manageable) to the common emotions of anxiety, anger, discouragement, and depression. If the stressful situation continues, our emotions may switch back and forth among any of these, depending on the success of our coping efforts. The accumulation of all these emotional reactions in one person at one time is often referred to as "burnout."

Anxiety

anxiety the unpleasant emotion characterized by such terms as "worry," "apprehension," "tension," and "fear"

posttraumatic stress disorder (PTSD) a condition in which people (1) feel numb to the world, with a lack of interest in former activities and a sense of estrangement from others; (2) repeatedly relive the trauma in memories and dreams; and (3) have sleep disturbances, difficulty concentrating, and over-alertness

The most common response to a stressor is anxiety. By **anxiety,** we mean *the unpleasant emotion characterized by such terms as "worry," "apprehension," "tension," and "fear"* that we all experience at times in varying degrees.

People who live through events that are beyond the normal range of human suffering (for example, natural disasters, rape, kidnapping) sometimes develop a severe set of anxiety-related symptoms known as **posttraumatic stress disorder (PTSD).** The major symptoms include (1) feeling numb to the world, with a lack of interest in former activities and a sense of estrangement from others; (2) repeatedly reliving the trauma in memories and dreams; and (3) sleep disturbances, difficulty concentrating, and over-alertness. Some individuals also feel guilty about surviving when others did not.

Posttraumatic stress disorder may develop immediately after the disaster, or it may be brought on by some minor stress that occurs weeks, months, or even years later. And it may last a long time. A study of victims of the 1972 flood that wiped out the community of Buffalo Creek, West Virginia, found that shortly after the flood, 63% of the survivors were showing symptoms of PTSD. Fourteen years later, 25% still suffered from PTSD symptoms (Green et al., 1992). Similarly, a study of Florida children who survived Hurricane Andrew in 1992 found that nearly 20% were still suffering from PTSD a year after the disaster (La Greca et al., 1996).

Traumas for which humans are responsible, such as sexual or physical assault, terrorist attacks, and war, may be even more likely to cause PTSD than natural disasters, for at least two reasons. First, human-made disaster can challenge our basic beliefs about the goodness of life and other people, and when these beliefs are shattered, PTSD appears more likely (Janoff-Bulman, 1992). Second, human-made disasters often strike individuals rather than whole communities, and suffering through a trauma alone seems to increase a person's risk for PTSD.

A study of survivors of the Holocaust found that almost half were still suffering from posttraumatic stress disorder 40 years later (Kuch & Cox, 1992). Those who had been in concentration camps were three times more likely to have PTSD as survivors who had not been in the camps. Many still relived the traumas of persecution in their dreams and were afraid that something terrible would happen to their spouses or their children whenever they were out of sight. More recent atrocities also have resulted in widespread PTSD. A study of Bosnian refugees just after they resettled in the United States found that 65% suffered from posttraumatic stress disorder (Weine et al., 1995).

Studies of rape survivors have found that about 95% experience posttraumatic stress symptoms severe enough to qualify for a diagnosis of the disorder in the first 2 weeks following the rape (see Figure 11-2). About 50% still qualify for the diagnosis 3 months after the rape. As many as 25% still suffer from PTSD 4 to 5 years after the rape (Foa & Riggs, 1995; Resnick et al., 1993).

Posttraumatic stress disorder became widely accepted as a diagnostic category because of difficulties experienced by Vietnam veterans. Although stress reactions to the horrors of battle had been noted in earlier wars (in World War I it was called "shell shock" and in World War II "combat fatigue"), veterans of Vietnam seemed especially prone to develop the long-term symptoms we have described. A survey estimated that 15% of Vietnam veterans have suffered from posttraumatic stress disorder since their discharge (Centers for Disease Control, 1988). Substance abuse, violence, and interpersonal problems are common correlates of posttraumatic stress disorder. In a study of 713 men who served in Vietnam, 16% reported having problems resulting from drinking heavily, such as trouble at school or work, problems with friends, and passing out; 16% had been arrested at least once; and 44% said they had war memories that they were still trying to forget (Yager, Laufer, & Gallops, 1984).

The soldiers who fought in Vietnam were young (average age 19), and the conditions of warfare were

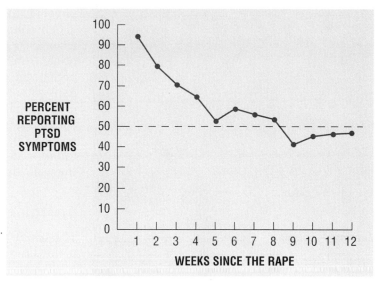

Figure 11-2

Posttraumatic Symptoms in Rape Almost all women who have been raped show symptoms of posttraumatic stress disorder severe enough to be diagnosed with PTSD in the first or second week following the rape. Over the three months following the rape, the percentage of women continuing to show PTSD declines. However, almost 50% of women continue to be diagnosed with PTSD three months after a rape. (After Foa & Riggs, 1995)

Posttraumatic stress disorder affects about one-sixth of the Vietnam War veterans, and almost half of the vets still have memories about the war that they are trying to forget.

The theory of learned helplessness may explain why some women remain in abusive relationships even when they have opportunities to leave.

unusual: absence of clear front lines, unpredictable attacks in dense jungle, difficulty distinguishing between Vietnamese allies and enemies, and the lack of support for the war on the home front. To this day, some Vietnam veterans still reexperience in memories or in dreams the traumatic events that happened to them. As one veteran wrote: "The war is over in history. But it never ended for me" (Marbly, 1987, p. 193).

Soldiers and noncombatants in more recent wars also suffer PTSD. A study of veterans of the 1991 Persian Gulf War found that 13% were suffering from PTSD in the year after the war (Sutker et al., 1995).

Apathy and Depression

The theory of learned helplessness (Seligman, 1975) explains how experience with aversive, uncontrollable events can lead to apathy and depression. A series of experiments showed that dogs placed in a shuttle box (an apparatus with two compartments separated by a barrier) quickly learn to jump to the opposite compartment in order to escape from a mild electric shock delivered to their feet through a grid on the floor. If a light is turned on a few seconds before the grid is electrified, the dogs can learn to avoid the shock entirely by jumping to the safe compartment when signaled by the light. However, if the dog has had a previous history of being in another enclosure in which shocks were unavoidable and inescapable—in which nothing the animal did terminated the shock—it is very difficult for the dog to learn the avoidance response in a new situation in which that response is appropriate. The animal simply sits and endures the shock in the shuttle box, even though an easy jump to the opposite compartment would eliminate dis-

learned helplessness
a condition characterized by apathy, withdrawal, and inability to see opportunities to regain control

comfort. Some dogs never learn, even if the experimenter demonstrates the proper procedure by carrying them over the barrier. The experimenters concluded that the animals had learned through prior experience that they were helpless to avoid the shock, so they gave up trying to do so, even in a new situation. The researchers gave the label **learned helplessness** to the cluster of symptoms the animals showed—*apathy, withdrawal, and the inability to see opportunities to regain control* (Overmeier & Seligman, 1967).

Some humans also appear to develop learned helplessness in response to uncontrollable events. Not all do, however. The original theory of learned helplessness has had to be modified to take into account the fact that some people become helpless following uncontrollable events, while others are invigorated by the challenge that such events pose (Wortman & Brehm, 1975). This modified theory will be discussed later in the chapter.

The original learned helplessness theory is useful, however, in helping us understand why some people seem to give up when exposed to difficult events. For example, the theory has been used to explain why prisoners in Nazi concentration camps did not revolt against their captors more often: They had come to believe that they were helpless to do anything about their captivity and therefore did not try to escape. Women whose husbands or partners beat them frequently do not try to escape. These women often say that they feel helpless to do anything about their situation because they fear what their husband or partner would do if they tried to leave, or because they do not have the economic resources to support themselves and their children.

Cognitive Impairment

In addition to the emotional reactions to stress we have just discussed, people often show substantial cognitive impairment when faced with serious stressors. They find it hard to concentrate and to organize their thoughts logically. They may be easily distracted. As a result, their performance on tasks, particularly complex tasks, tends to deteriorate.

This cognitive impairment may come from two sources. High levels of emotional arousal can interfere with the processing of information. The curve in Figure 11-3 represents the relationship between a person's level of emotional arousal and his or her effectiveness on a task. At very low levels of emotional arousal (for example, at the point of waking up), we may not attend well to sensory information, and our performance will be relatively poor. Performance is optimal at moderate levels of arousal. At high levels of emotional arousal, our performance begins to decline, probably because we cannot devote enough cognitive resources to the task. The optimal level of arousal and the shape of the curve differ for different tasks. A simple, well-learned routine would be much less susceptible to disruption by emotional arousal than a more complex activity that depends on the integration of several thought processes. Thus, during a moment of intense fear you would probably still be able to spell your name but not be able to play chess well.

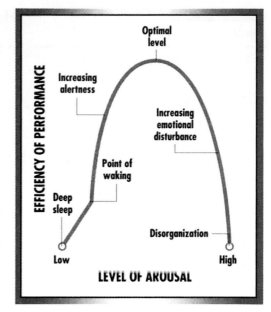

Figure 11-3

Emotional Arousal and Performance   The curve shows the hypothetical relationship between level of emotional arousal and efficiency of performance. The precise shape of the curve differs for various tasks. (After Hebb, 1972)

People vary in how emotionally aroused they become during crises, and hence in how much their behavior is disrupted. Studies of people faced with fires or sudden floods find that about 15% show organized, effective behavior, suggesting that their optimal level of emotional arousal has not been exceeded. The majority, about 70%, show various degrees of disorganization but are still able to function with some effectiveness. The remaining 15% are so disorganized that they are unable to function at all; they may panic or exhibit aimless and completely inappropriate behavior, suggesting that they are far above their optimal level of emotional arousal (Tyhurst, 1951).

Cognitive impairment may also result from the distracting thoughts that go through our heads when we are faced with a stressor. We contemplate possible sources of action, worry about the consequences of our actions, and may berate ourselves for not being able to handle the situation better. For instance, students who have a condition called *test anxiety* tend to worry about possible failures and about their inadequacies while trying to work on a test. They can become so distracted by these negative thoughts that they fail to follow instructions and neglect or misinterpret obvious information provided by questions. As their anxiety mounts, they have difficulty retrieving facts they had learned well.

Cognitive impairment during stressful periods often leads people to adhere rigidly to behavior patterns because they cannot consider alternative patterns. People have been trapped in flaming buildings because they persisted in pushing against exit doors that opened inward; in their panic, they failed to consider the possibility of an alternate action. Some people resort to old, childlike behavior patterns that are not appropriate to the situation. The cautious person may become even more cautious and withdraw entirely, whereas the aggressive person may lose control and strike out heedlessly in all directions.

Some people say they have been able to learn and grow from their experiences with trauma. What might account for this?

Thinking Critically

Table 11-3
Reactions to Stress

Psychological Reactions

Anxiety
Anger and aggression
Apathy and depression
Cognitive impairment

Physiological Reactions

Increased metabolic rate
Increased heart rate
Dilation of pupils
Higher blood pressure
Increased breathing rate
Tensing of muscles
Secretion of endorphins and ACTH
Release of extra sugar from the liver

fight-or-flight response the body's characteristic response to stress, designed to help the body flee from or fight a threat

general adaptation syndrome a physiological response to stress that consists of three phases: alarm, resistance, and exhaustion

How Do We React Physiologically to Stress?

Whether you fall into an icy river, encounter a knife-wielding assailant, or are terrified by your first parachute jump, your body responds in similar ways (see Table 11-3). Regardless of the stressor, your body automatically prepares to handle the emergency. This *characteristic response to stress, designed to help the body fight or flee from a perceived threat,* has been called the **fight-or-flight response.** Quick energy is needed, so the liver releases extra sugar (glucose) to fuel the muscles, and hormones are released that stimulate the conversion of fats and proteins into sugar. The body's metabolism increases in preparation for the need to expend energy on physical action. Heart rate, blood pressure, and breathing rate increase, and the muscles tense. At the same time, certain unessential activities, such as digestion, are curtailed. Saliva and mucus dry up, thereby increasing the size of air passages to the lungs. Thus, an early sign of stress is a dry mouth. The body's natural painkillers, endorphins, are secreted, and the surface blood vessels constrict in order to reduce bleeding in case of injury. The spleen releases more red blood cells to help carry oxygen.

Most of these physiological changes result from activation of two neuroendocrine systems controlled by the hypothalamus: the sympathetic system and the adrenal-cortical system. The hypothalamus has been called the brain's stress center because of its dual function in emergencies. Its first function is to activate the sympathetic division of the autonomic nervous system (see Chapter 2). The hypothalamus transmits nerve impulses to nuclei in the brain stem that control the functioning of the autonomic nervous system. The sympathetic division of the autonomic system acts directly on the smooth muscles and internal organs to produce some of the bodily changes described earlier—for example, increased heart rate, elevated blood pressure, dilated pupils. The sympathetic system also stimulates the inner core of the adrenal glands (the adrenal medulla) to release the hormones epinephrine (adrenaline) and norepinephrine into the bloodstream. Epinephrine has the same effect on the muscles and organs as the sympathetic nervous system does (for example, it increases heart rate and blood pressure) and thus serves to perpetuate a state of arousal. Norepinephrine, through its action on the pituitary gland, is indirectly responsible for the release of extra sugar from the liver (see Figure 11-4).

The events just described concern only the first function of the hypothalamus: activation of the sympathetic system. The hypothalamus carries out its second function, activation of the adrenal-cortical system, by signaling the pituitary gland, which lies just below it, to secrete adrenocorticotropic hormone (ACTH), the body's "major stress hormone." ACTH stimulates the outer layer of the adrenal glands (the adrenal cortex), resulting in the release of a group of hormones (the major one is cortisol) that regulate the blood levels of glucose and of certain minerals. The amount of cortisol in blood or urine samples is often used as a measure of stress. ACTH also signals other endocrine glands to release about 30 hormones, each of which plays a role in the body's adjustment to emergency situations.

In groundbreaking work that continues to be influential today, researcher Hans Selye (1979) described the physiological changes we just discussed as part of a general syndrome that all organisms show in response to stress. The **general adaptation syndrome** is *a physiological and behavioral response that consists of three phases: alarm, resistance, and exhaustion* (see Figure 11-5). In the alarm phase, the body mobilizes to confront a threat by triggering sympathetic nervous system activity. In the resistance phase, the organism makes efforts to cope with the threat by fleeing from it or fighting it. The exhaustion phase occurs if the organism is unable to flee from or fight the threat and depletes physiological resources while trying to do so.

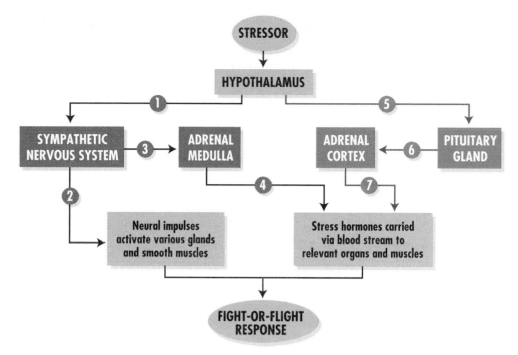

Figure 11-4

The Fight-or-Flight Response A stressful situation activates the hypothalamus, which, in turn, controls two neuroendocrine systems: the sympathetic system (shown in red) and the adrenal-cortical system (shown in green). The sympathetic nervous system, responding to neural impulses from the hypothalamus (1), activates various organs and smooth muscles under its control (2). For example, it increases heart rate and dilates the pupils. The sympathetic nervous system also signals the adrenal medulla (3) to release epinephrine and norepinephrine into the bloodstream (4). The adrenal-cortical system is activated when the hypothalamus secretes CRF, a chemical that acts on the pituitary gland, which lies just below the hypothalamus (5). The pituitary gland, in turn, secretes the hormone ACTH, which is carried via the bloodstream to the adrenal cortex (6), where it stimulates the release of a group of hormones, including cortisol, that regulate blood glucose levels (7). ACTH also signals the other endocrine glands to release some 30 hormones. The combined effects of the various stress hormones carried via the bloodstream plus the neural activity of the sympathetic division of the autonomic nervous system constitute the fight-or-flight response.

Selye argued that a variety of physical and psychological stressors triggers this response pattern. He also argued that repeated or prolonged exhaustion of physiological resources, due to exposure to prolonged stressors that one cannot flee from or fight, is responsible for an array of physiological diseases. He conducted laboratory studies in which he exposed animals to several types of prolonged stressors—such as extreme cold and fatigue—and found that, regardless of the stress, certain bodily changes inevitably occurred: enlarged adrenal glands, shrunken lymph nodes, and stomach ulcers (Selye, 1979). These changes decrease the organism's ability to resist other stressors, including infectious and disease-producing agents. As we will see later, chronic arousal can make both animals and people susceptible to illness.

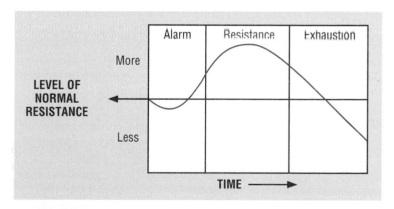

Figure 11-5

The General Adaptation Syndrome According to Hans Selye, the body reacts to a stressor in three phases. In the first phase, alarm, the body mobilizes to confront the threat, which temporarily expends resources and lowers resistance. In the resistance phase, the body actively confronts the threat and resistance is high. If the threat continues, the body moves into the exhaustion phase.

So far we have focused on the negative aspects of the physiological arousal elicited by stressors. Studies have shown, however, that exposure to intermittent stressors can have benefits in the form of physiological toughness. In essence, intermittent stress (occasional exposure but with recovery periods) leads to greater tolerance for stress later on (Dienstbier, 1989). For example, young rats that are removed from their cages and handled daily (a stressor for them) are less fearful when exposed to other stressors as adults and show a quicker return to normal levels of the stress hormones (Levine, 1960; Meaney et al., 1987). Similarly, rats that were toughened by having to swim in cold water for 14 consecutive days performed better on a later swim test and showed less depletion of epinephrine and norepinephrine than rats with no prior exposure to cold water (Weiss et al., 1975).

The physiological responses that appear to be beneficial involve arousal of the sympathetic system and occur when a person makes active efforts to cope with the stressful situation (Frankenhauser, 1983). Increases in epinephrine and norepinephrine correlate positively with performance on a variety of tasks (from students taking tests to paratroopers engaged in training jumps): High levels of these hormones in blood and urine were related to better performance (Johansson & Frankenhauser, 1973; Ursin, 1978). The physiological responses that appear to be harmful involve arousal of the adrenal-cortical system and occur when a person experiences distress but does not actively attempt to cope with the stressful situation.

Thinking Critically

What does the research on the toughening effects of early stress experiences suggest would be important in how parents help their children cope with stressors they may encounter early in their lives?

How Does Stress Affect Health?

Attempts to adapt to the continued presence of a stressor may deplete the body's resources and make it vulnerable to illness. Chronic stress can lead to physical disorders such as ulcers, high blood pressure, and heart disease. It may also impair the immune system, decreasing the body's ability to fight invading bacteria and viruses. Indeed, researchers estimate that emotional stress plays an important role in more than half of all medical problems. Stress probably interacts with an underlying biological vulnerability to certain disorders. In other words, most people who develop a serious medical disorder in the face of chronic stress probably have some vulnerability to that disorder anyway, such as a high genetic risk for the disorder. Chronic stress makes it more likely that they will go on to develop a serious case of the disorder.

psychophysiological disorders physical disorders in which psychological factors are believed to play a critical role

Psychophysiological disorders are *physical disorders in which emotions are believed to play a critical role*. A common misconception is that people with psychophysiological disorders are not really sick and do not need medical attention. On the contrary, the symptoms of psychophysiological illness reflect physiological disturbances associated with tissue damage and pain; a peptic ulcer caused by stress is indistinguishable from an ulcer caused by a factor unrelated to stress, such as long-term heavy usage of aspirin.

In this section we consider how stress may directly affect the body's ability to fight disease, and how it can indirectly affect disease by leading us to engage in unhealthy behaviors (see Figure 11-6).

Direct Effects

The body's physiological response to a stressor may have a direct, negative effect on physical health if this response is maintained over a long period. Long-term overarousal of the sympathetic system or the adrenal-cortical system can cause damage to arteries and organ systems. Stress may also have a direct effect on the immune system's ability to fight off disease.

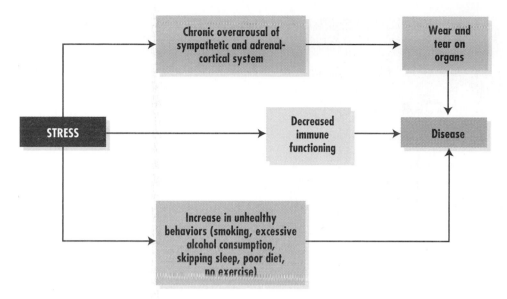

Figure 11-6

Pathways by Which Stress May Affect Health   Stress may affect health directly by causing chronic overarousal of the sympathetic or adrenal-cortical system, or indirectly by contributing to unhealthy behaviors.

Coronary Heart Disease   The chronic overarousal caused by prolonged stressors may contribute to coronary heart disease, particularly in people with a genetic predisposition to this disease. **Coronary heart disease (CHD)** *occurs when the blood vessels that supply the heart muscles are narrowed or closed by the gradual buildup of a hard, fatty substance called* plaque, *blocking the flow of oxygen and nutrients to the heart.* This can lead to pain, called *angina pectoris,* that radiates across the chest and arm. When oxygen to the heart is completely blocked, it can cause a *myocardial infarction*—a heart attack.

Coronary heart disease is a leading cause of death and chronic illness. About 40% of deaths in the United States every year are caused by coronary heart disease, many before the age of 75 (American Heart Association, 1993). There seems to be a genetic contribution to coronary heart disease: People with family histories of CHD are at increased risk for the disease. CHD is also linked to high blood pressure, high serum cholesterol, diabetes, smoking, and obesity.

People in high-stress jobs are at increased risk for CHD. This is particularly true in the case of jobs that are highly demanding (in terms of workload, responsibilities, and role conflicts) but provide little control (the worker has little control over the speed, nature, and conditions of work). An example of such a high-stress job is an assembly line in which rapid, high-quality production is expected and the work is machine-paced rather than self-paced. In one study, 416 middle-aged men in blue-collar jobs were followed over 6 years and examined for the development of heart disease. Men in jobs with a high workload and low control were three to four times more likely than other men to develop coronary heart disease (Siegrist et al., 1990).

coronary heart disease (CHD)   a condition occurring when blood vessels that supply heart muscles are narrowed or closed by the buildup of plaque, blocking the flow of oxygen and nutrients to the heart

A heart attack is one result of coronary heart disease.

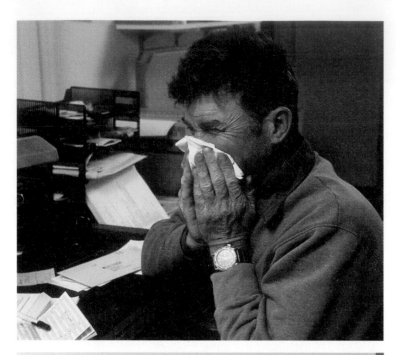

Research has confirmed that we are more prone to immune system disorders, such as colds, when we are under stress.

High family demands in addition to a stressful job can adversely affect a woman's cardiovascular health. Employed women in general are not at higher risk for coronary heart disease than full-time homemakers. However, employed mothers are more likely to develop heart disease. The likelihood of disease increases with the number of children for working mothers but not for homemakers (Haynes & Feinleib, 1980). Women who have control and flexibility over their work and a good income, so that they can afford to hire help with housecleaning and child care, seem not to suffer as much physically and psychologically from their role overload, however (Lennon & Rosenfield, 1992).

One group that lives in chronically stressful settings and has particularly high rates of high blood pressure is low-income African Americans. They often do not have adequate financial resources for daily living, may be poorly educated and therefore have trouble finding good employment, live in violent neighborhoods, and are frequently exposed to racism. All these conditions have been linked to higher blood pressure (Williams & Collins, 1995).

Experimental studies with animals have shown that disruption of the social environment can induce pathology that resembles coronary artery disease (Manuck, Kaplan, & Matthews, 1986; Sapolsky, 1990). Some of the key experiments have been conducted with a type of macaque monkey whose social organization involves the establishment of stable hierarchies of social dominance: Dominant and submissive animals can be identified within a given group based on the animals' social behavior. The introduction of unfamiliar monkeys into an established social group is a stressor that leads to increased aggressive behavior as group members attempt to reestablish a social dominance hierarchy (Manuck, Kaplan, & Matthews, 1986).

In these studies, some monkey groups remained stable, with fixed memberships; other groups were stressed by the repeated introduction of new members. After about 2 years under these conditions, the high-ranking or dominant males in the unstable social condition showed more extensive atherosclerosis (buildup of plaque on the artery walls) than the subordinate males (Sapolsky, 1990).

The Immune System   One relatively new area of research in behavioral medicine is *psychoneuroimmunology,* the study of how the body's immune system is affected by stress and other psychological variables. The immune system, by means of specialized cells called *lymphocytes,* protects the body from disease-causing microorganisms. It affects our susceptibility to infectious diseases, allergies, cancers, and autoimmune disorders (that is, diseases such as rheumatoid arthritis, in which the immune cells attack the normal tissue of the body).

immunocompetence
the quality of an individual's immune system functioning

There is no single index of *the quality of an individual's immune system functioning,* or **immunocompetence.** It is a complex system with many interacting components, and different investigators have chosen to focus on different components of the system. Evidence from a number of areas suggests that stress affects the ability of the immune system to defend the body. The results of one study, for example, support the common belief that we are more likely to catch a cold when we are under stress (Cohen, Tyrel, & Smith, 1991). Researchers exposed 400 healthy volunteers to a nasal wash containing one of five cold viruses or an innocuous salt solution. Participants answered questions about the number of stressful events they had experienced in the past year, the degree to which they felt able to cope with daily demands, and the frequency of negative emotions such as anger and depression. Based on these data, each participant was assigned a stress index ranging from 3 (lowest stress) to 12 (highest stress). The volunteers were examined daily for cold symptoms and for the presence of cold viruses or virus-specific antibodies in their upper respiratory secretions.

The majority of the virus-exposed volunteers showed signs of infection, but only about a third actually developed colds. The rates of viral infection and of actual cold symptoms increased in accordance with the reported stress levels. Compared with the lowest-stress group, volunteers who reported the highest stress were significantly more likely to become infected with the cold virus and almost twice as likely to develop a cold (see Figure 11-7). These results held even after the researchers controlled statistically for a number of variables that might influence immune functioning, such as age, allergies, cigarette and alcohol use, exercise, and diet.

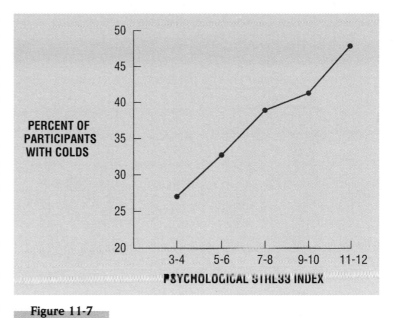

Figure 11-7

Stress and Colds   This graph shows the percentage of virus-exposed people who developed colds as a function of the degree of stress reported. (Psychological Stress and Susceptibility to the Common Cold" by S. Cohen et al., *New England Journal of Medicine,* 3325: 606–612. Copyright © 1991 Massachusetts Medical Society. All rights reserved.)

This study is unusual in that the participants were exposed to a virus, lived in special quarters near the laboratory for a number of days both before and after exposure, and were carefully monitored. Such controlled conditions for studying the effects of stress on health are seldom feasible. Most studies look at individuals undergoing a particularly stressful event—such as academic pressures, bereavement, or marital disruption—and evaluate their immunocompetence, using various indices (Cohen, 1996). For example, one study found that during examination periods college students have lower blood levels of an antibody that defends against respiratory infections (Jemmott et al., 1985), and another found that medical students show lowered immune functioning on a number of blood-sample measures before exams (Glaser et al., 1985, 1986). A study of men whose wives had died from breast cancer demonstrated that the responsiveness of the men's immune system functioning declined significantly within the month following their wives' deaths, and in some cases remained low for a year thereafter (Schleifer et al., 1979). Similarly, a series of studies revealed that individuals of both sexes who had recently been separated or divorced show poorer immune functioning than matched control participants who were still married, even though no significant differences were found between the two groups in health-related behaviors such as smoking and diet (Kiecolt-Glaser et al., 1994).

Recall that controllability is one of the variables that determines the severity of stress. A series of animal studies demonstrates that uncontrollable shock has a much greater effect on the immune system than controllable shock (Laudenslager et al., 1983; Visintainer, Volpicelli, & Seligman, 1982). In these experiments (similar to the learned helplessness described earlier in this chapter), rats were subjected to electric shock. One group could press a lever to turn off the shock. The other animals, the yoked controls, received an identical sequence of shocks, but their levers were ineffective (see Figure 11-8).

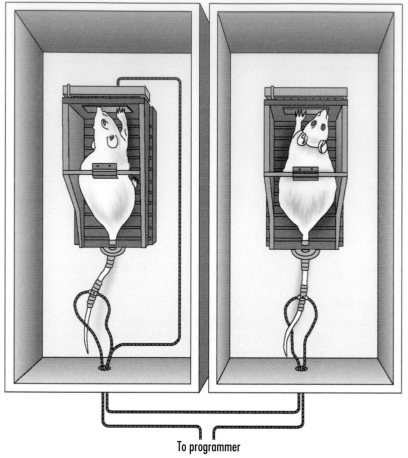

To programmer

Figure 11-8

Yoked Controls in a Stress Experiment   A series of electrical shocks are preprogrammed to be delivered simultaneously to the tails of the two male rats. The rat on the left can terminate a shock when it occurs by pressing the lever in front of him. The rat on the right has no control in the situation (his lever is inoperative), but he is yoked to the first rat. That is, when the first rat receives a shock, the yoked rat simultaneously receives the same shock, and the shock remains on until the first rat presses his lever. The lever presses of the yoked rat have no effect on the shock sequence for either animal.

In one study using this procedure, the investigators looked at how readily a rat's T-cells multiplied when it was challenged by harmful cells. T-cells are lymphocytes that secrete chemicals that kill harmful cells, such as cancer cells. They found that T-cells from rats that could control the shock multiplied as readily as did those from rats that were not stressed at all. T-cells from rats exposed to uncontrollable shock, on the other hand, multiplied only weakly. Thus, shock (stress) interfered with the immune response only in rats that could not control it (Laudenslager et al., 1983).

In another study, the investigators implanted tumor cells into rats, gave them shocks, and recorded whether the rats' natural defenses rejected the cells or whether they developed into tumors. Only 27% of the rats given uncontrollable shocks rejected the tumors, but 63% of the rats that could turn the shocks off rejected the tumors—even though the rats received identical amounts of shock (Visintainer, Volpicelli, & Seligman, 1982).

Perceptions of control also appear to affect the influence of stress on the immune system in humans (Benschop et al., 1998). In a study of the effects of marital separation or divorce on immune functioning, the partner who had initiated the separation (the one more in control of the situation) was less distressed, reported better health, and showed better immune system functioning than the other partner (Kiecolt-Glaser et al., 1988). Most other studies of humans simply have compared the immunocompetence of persons undergoing particular stressors with that of persons not undergoing these stressors (see Cohen, 1996). For example, a study of people who survived Hurricane Andrew in 1992 found that those who experienced more damage to their home or whose lives were more threatened by the storm showed poorer immune system functioning than people whose homes and lives had been safer (Ironson et al., 1997). Similarly, following the 1994 Northridge earthquake in the Los Angeles area, people whose lives had been more severely disrupted showed more decline in immune system functioning than those who had not experienced as much stress as a result of the earthquake (Solomon et al., 1997). People who worried more about the impact of the earthquake on their lives were especially likely to show detriments in natural killer cell activity, one indicator of poor immune functioning (Segerstrom et al., 1998).

The immune system is incredibly complicated, employing a number of different weapons that interact to defend the body. Much remains to be discovered about the immune system and even more about its relationship to the nervous system. Scientists once believed that the immune system operated quite independently, isolated from other physiological systems. But current studies are making it increasingly evident that the immune system and the nervous system have numerous anatomical and physiological connections. For example, researchers are discovering that lymphocytes have receptors for a number of different neurotransmitters. Thus, these immune system cells are equipped to receive messages from the nervous system that may alter the way they behave. One of the reasons a link between neurotransmitters and the immune system is important is that negative emotional states (for example, anxiety or depression) can affect neurotransmitter levels. Thus, stressful situations may affect immune system functioning only if these situations arouse negative emotional states.

Health-Related Behaviors

Our behaviors can greatly affect our susceptibility to illness. Smoking is one of the leading causes of cardiovascular disease and emphysema. A high-fat diet contributes to many forms of cancer as well as to cardiovascular disease. People who do not regularly engage in a moderate amount of exercise are at increased risk for heart disease and earlier death (Blumenthal et al., 1990; Paffenberger et al., 1986). Chronic sleep deprivation is associated with a higher mortality rate due both to illness and to increased accidents (Kryger, Roth, & Dement, 1994). Excessive alcohol consumption can lead to liver disease, cardiovascular disease, and perhaps contribute to some cancers. And failure to use condoms during sex significantly increases the risk of contracting HIV. In sum, scientists estimate that most of the diseases that people in industrialized countries die from these days are heavily influenced by health care behaviors such as these (Taylor, 1999).

When we are stressed, we may be less likely to engage in healthy behaviors. Students taking exams stay up all night, often for several nights in a row. They may skip meals, snacking only on junk food. Many men whose wives have died do not know how to cook for themselves, and therefore may eat poorly or hardly at all. In their grief, some bereaved men increase their alcohol consumption and smoking. People under stress cease normal exercise routines and become sedentary. Thus, stress may indirectly affect health by reducing positive health behaviors and increasing negative ones.

Engaging in negative behaviors may also increase people's subjective sense of stress. Drinking too much alcohol on a regular basis can interfere with cognitive functioning—you can't think as clearly or quickly as you need to when put on the spot. It can also induce lethargy, fatigue, and a mild or moderate sense of depression that makes it difficult to overcome stressful situations or to just keep up with daily life.

People who chronically do not get the sleep they need show impairments in memory, learning, logical reasoning, arithmetic skills, complex verbal processing, and decision making. Reducing your amount of sleep to 5 hours per night for just two nights significantly reduces your performance on math problems and creative thinking tasks. Thus, staying up late to prepare for exams can significantly decrease your performance on those exams (Dinges & Broughton, 1989). In contrast, people who engage in a healthy lifestyle—eating a low-fat diet, drinking alcohol only in moderation, getting enough sleep, and exercising regularly—often report that stressful events seem more manageable and that they feel more in control of their lives. Thus, engaging in healthy behaviors can help to reduce the stressfulness of life as well as reducing the risk of a number of serious diseases.

---

1. What are some of your most unhealthy behaviors, and what prevents you from changing them?

2. What might make some cultures more prone to stress-related health problems than others?

**Thinking
Critically**

Table 11-4

Psychological Factors that Influence Stress Responses   These psychological factors may influence people's physiological response to stress and thus their likelihood of developing stress-related diseases.

Factor	Definition
Attributional Style	Habitual way of explaining events.
Hardiness	Tendency to be actively involved in life, oriented toward challenge, and to feel in control.
Type A Behavior Pattern	Chronic time urgency, hostility, and competitiveness. Hostility may be the most important component.

How Do Psychological Factors Influence Stress Responses?

As we have noted, events that are uncontrollable or unpredictable, that require extensive changes, or that cause internal conflicts tend to be experienced as stressful. Some people appear more likely than others to appraise events in these ways, and thus to experience stress responses to the events (see Table 11-4).

Attributional Style

causal attribution   a type of appraisal that helps determine our sense of control

attributional style a consistent style of making attributions for the events in one's life

The ways we appraise or interpret events can significantly impact how much control we feel we have over them. According to the reformulated learned helplessness theory, **causal attributions** are *a type of appraisal that helps determine our sense of control* (Abramson, Metalsky, & Alloy, 1989; Abramson, Seligman, & Teasdale, 1978). When people attribute negative events to causes that are internal to them ("it's my fault"), are stable in time ("it's going to last forever"), and affect many areas of their lives ("it will affect everything I do"), they are most likely to feel that the events are uncontrollable and to show a helpless, depressed response to negative events. For example, if a person whose spouse left him attributed the breakup of his marriage to his "bad" personality (an internal, stable, and global attribution), he would tend to lose self-esteem and expect future relationships to fail as well. In turn, he would show lowered motivation, passivity, and sadness. In contrast, if he made a less pessimistic attribution, such as attributing the failure of his marriage to simple incompatibility between himself and his wife, he would tend to maintain his self-esteem and motivation for the future (for similar arguments, see Weiner, 1972).

People seem to have *consistent styles of making attributions for the events in their lives,* called **attributional styles,** and these styles influence the degree to which people view events as stressful and have helpless, depressive reactions to difficult situations (Peterson & Seligman, 1984). In one study, researchers assessed the attributional styles of students a few weeks before they were to take a midterm exam. Just before the exam, they also asked the students what grade they would consider a failure and what grade they would be happy with. Then, after the students received their grades from the exam, the researchers measured the students' levels of sadness and depression. Among students who received a grade below their standards, those who had a pessimistic attributional style were significantly more depressed than those who had a more optimistic attributional style (Metalsky, Halberstadt, & Abramson, 1987).

Our responses to stressors, such as conflict with a spouse, will depend on the attributions we make for these events.

A pessimistic attributional style is also linked to physical illness. Students with more pessimistic attributional styles report more illness and make more visits to the health center than students with a more optimistic attributional style. In a 35-year-long study of men in the Harvard classes of 1939 to 1940, researchers found that men who had a pessimistic attributional style at age 25 were more likely to develop physical illness over the subsequent years than men with a more optimistic attributional style (Peterson, Seligman, & Vaillant, 1988).

How does attributional style affect health? A pessimistic attributional style has been linked to lowered immune system functioning. For example, a study of older adults found that those who were pessimistic had poorer immune system functioning than did those who were optimistic (Kamen-Siegel et al., 1991). A study of gay men who were HIV-positive found that those who blamed themselves for negative events showed more decline in immune functioning over 18 months than those who engaged in less self-blaming attributions (Segerstrom et al., 1996). Another study of gay men found that among both HIV-positive and HIV-negative men, those who were more pessimistic and fatalistic were less likely to engage in healthy behaviors such as maintaining a proper diet, getting enough sleep, and exercising (Taylor et al., 1992). This was particularly important for the HIV-positive men, because engaging in healthy behaviors can reduce the risk of developing AIDS. Thus, a pessimistic outlook may affect health directly, by reducing immune system functioning, or indirectly, by reducing a person's tendency to engage in health-promoting behavior.

Hardiness

Another line of research has focused on people who are most resistant to stress—who do not become physically or emotionally impaired even in the face of major stressful events (Kobasa, 1979; Kobasa, Maddi, & Kahn, 1982). In one study, more than 600 men who were executives or managers in the same company were given checklists and asked to describe all the stressful events and illnesses they had experienced over the previous 3 years. Two groups were selected for comparison. The first group scored above average on both stressful events and illness; the second group scored equally high on stress but below average on illness. Members of both groups filled out detailed personality questionnaires. Analysis of the results indicated that the high-stress/low-illness men differed from the men who became ill under stress on three major dimensions: *They were more actively involved in their work and social lives, they were more oriented toward challenge and change, and they felt more in control of events in their lives*—a cluster of characteristics that was labeled **hardiness** (Kobasa, 1979).

These personality differences could be the result rather than the cause of illness. For example, it is hard for people to be involved in work or in social activity when they are ill. The investigators therefore conducted a longitudinal study that considered the personality characteristics of business executives before they became ill, and then monitored their life stress and the extent of their illnesses for a period of 2 years. The results showed that the executives whose attitudes toward life could be rated high on involvement, sense of control, and positive responses to change remained healthier over time than men who scored low on these dimensions (Kobasa, Maddi, & Kahn, 1982). The most important factors appear to be a sense of control and commitment to personal goals (Cohen & Edwards, 1989). Although this study was conducted with men only, similar results have been found in a study of women (Wiebe & McCallum, 1986).

The personality characteristics of stress-resistant or hardy individuals are summarized by the terms "commitment," "control," and "challenge." These characteristics are interrelated with the factors we have discussed as influencing the perceived severity of stressors. For example, the sense of being in control of life events reflects feelings of competence and also influences the appraisal of stressful events. Challenge

hardiness a cluster of characteristics consisting of active involvement in work and social life, orientation toward challenge and change, and a feeling of being in control of events in one's life

also involves cognitive evaluation—that it was based on the belief that change is normal in life and should be viewed as an opportunity for growth rather than as a threat to security.

The Type A Pattern

One behavior pattern or personality style that has received a great deal of attention is the Type A pattern. Over the years, physicians noted that heart attack victims tend to be hostile, aggressive, impatient individuals who were overinvolved in their work. In the 1950s two cardiologists defined a set of behaviors (the Type A pattern) that seemed to characterize patients with coronary heart disease (Friedman & Rosenman, 1974). People who exhibit this **Type A** behavior pattern are *extremely competitive and achievement oriented, have a sense of time urgency, find it difficult to relax, and become impatient and angry when confronted with delays or with people they view as incompetent.* Although outwardly self-confident, they are prey to constant feelings of self-doubt; they push themselves to accomplish more and more in less and less time. Some common Type A behaviors are listed in Table 11-5. Those classified as Type B people do not exhibit the characteristics listed for Type A. Type B people are able to relax without feeling guilty and to work without becoming agitated; they lack a sense of urgency, with its accompanying impatience, and are not easily roused to anger.

Type A a behavior pattern in which the person is extremely competitive and achievement oriented, has a sense of time urgency, finds it difficult to relax, and becomes impatient and angry when confronted with delays or incompetence

To examine the relationship between Type A behavior and coronary heart disease, more than 3,000 healthy middle-aged men were evaluated by means of a structured interview. The interview was designed to be irritating. The interviewer kept the participant waiting without explanation and then asked a series of questions about being competitive, hostile, and pressed for time. For instance: "Do you ever feel rushed or under pressure?" "Do you eat quickly?" "Would you describe yourself as ambitious and hard driving or relaxed and easy-going?" "Do you resent it if someone is late?" The interviewer interrupted, asked questions in a challenging manner, and threw in non sequiturs. The interview was scored more on the way the person behaved in answering the questions than on the answers themselves. For example, extreme Type A men spoke loudly in an explosive manner, talked over the interviewer so as not to be interrupted, appeared tense and tight-lipped, and described hostile incidents with great emotional intensity. Type B men sat in a relaxed manner, spoke slowly and softly, were easily interrupted, and smiled often.

After the participants were classified as Type A or Type B, they were studied for 8½ years. During that period Type A men had twice as many heart attacks or other forms of coronary heart disease as Type B men. These results held up even after diet, age, smoking, and other variables were taken into account (Rosenman et al., 1975). Other studies confirmed this twofold risk and linked Type A behavior to heart disease in both men and women (Haynes, Feinlieb, & Kannel, 1980; Kornitzer et al., 1982). In addition, Type A behavior is associated with severity of coronary artery blockage as determined at autopsy or in X-ray studies of the inside of coronary blood vessels (Friedman et al., 1968; Williams et al., 1988).

Table 11-5

Type A Behaviors   Some behaviors that characterize people prone to coronary heart disease. (After Friedman & Rosenman, 1974)

Thinking of or doing two things at once
Scheduling more and more activities into less and less time
Failing to notice or be interested in the environment or things of beauty
Hurrying the speech of others
Becoming unduly irritated when forced to wait in line or when driving behind a car you think is moving too slowly
Believing that if you want something done well, you have to do it yourself
Gesticulating when you talk
Frequent knee jiggling or rapid tapping of your fingers
Explosive speech patterns or frequent use of obscenities
Making a fetish of always being on time
Having difficulty sitting and doing nothing
Playing nearly every game to win, even when playing with children
Measuring your own and others' success in terms of numbers (number of patients seen, articles written, and so on)
Lip clicking, head nodding, fist clenching, table pounding, or sucking in of air when speaking
Becoming impatient while watching others do things you think you can do better or faster
Rapid blinking or tic-like eyebrow lifting

After reviewing the evidence, in 1981 the American Heart Association decided that Type A behavior should be classified as a risk factor for coronary heart disease. However, it should be noted that two other studies failed to find a link between Type A behavior and heart disease (Case et al., 1985; Shekelle et al., 1983). While some researchers attribute this failure to the way Type A individuals were assessed in these studies, others believe that the definition of Type A behavior, as originally formulated, is too diffuse. They argue that time urgency and competitiveness are not the most important components; the crucial variable may be hostility.

In fact, several studies have found that a person's level of hostility is a better predictor of heart disease than his or her overall level of Type A behavior (Booth-Kewley & Friedman, 1987; Dembroski et al., 1985; Thoresen, Telch, & Eagleston, 1981). To examine further the anger component of Type A behavior, several studies used personality tests rather than interviews to measure hostility. For example, a 25-year study of 118 male lawyers found that those who scored high on hostility traits on a personality inventory taken in law school were five times as likely to die before age 50 as classmates who were not hostile (Barefoot et al., 1989). In a similar follow-up study of physicians, hostility scores obtained in medical school predicted the incidence of coronary heart disease as well as mortality from all causes (Barefoot, Williams, & Dahlstrom, 1983). In both studies, this relationship is independent of the effects of smoking, age, and high blood pressure.

One characteristic of Type A people is doing two or more things at the same time.

How does Type A behavior or its component trait of hostility lead to coronary heart disease? One plausible biological mechanism is the way the individual's sympathetic nervous system responds to stress. When exposed to stressful experimental situations (for example, when faced with threat of failure, harassment, or competitive task demands), most people report feeling angry, irritated, and tense. However, people who score high on hostility as a trait show much larger increases in blood pressure, heart rate, and the secretion of stress-related hormones than people with low hostility scores (Benotsch, Christensen, & McKelvey, 1997; Lepore, 1995). The same results are found when Type A people are compared with Type B people (Manuck & Kranz, 1986). The sympathetic nervous systems of hostile and/or Type A individuals appear to be hyper-responsive to stressful situations. All these physiological changes can damage the heart and blood vessels.

Hostile and nonhostile people may have fundamentally different nervous systems. When nonhostile individuals are aroused and upset, their parasympathetic nervous systems act like a stop switch to calm them down. In contrast, hostile individuals may have a weak parasympathetic nervous system. When they are angered, their adrenaline fires off and they stay unpleasantly aroused. As a consequence, they interact differently with the world (Williams, 1989).

The good news about the Type A behavior pattern is that it can be modified through well-established therapy programs, and people who are able to reduce their Type A behavior show lowered risk of coronary heart disease. We will discuss this therapy later in the chapter.

**Thinking
Critically**
What might be some of the benefits of Type A behavior that help to reinforce and maintain it?

How Does Coping Influence Health?

The emotions and physiological arousal created by stressful situations are highly uncomfortable, and this discomfort motivates the individual to do something to alleviate it. *The process by which a person attempts to manage stressful demands* is called **coping,** and it takes two major forms. A person can focus on the specific problem or situation that has arisen, trying to find some way of changing it or avoiding it in the future. This is called *problem-focused coping*. A person can also focus on alleviating the emotions associated with the stressful situation, even if the situation itself cannot be changed. This process is called *emotion-focused coping* (Lazarus & Folkman, 1984). When dealing with a stressful situation, most people use both problem-focused and emotion-focused coping.

coping   the process by which a person attempts to manage stressful demands

Problem-Focused Coping

Strategies for solving problems include defining the problem, generating alternative solutions, weighing the alternatives in terms of costs and benefits, choosing among them, and implementing the selected alternative. Problem-focused strategies can also be directed inward: The person can change something about himself or herself instead of changing his or her environment. Changing levels of aspiration, finding alternative sources of gratification, and learning new skills are examples. How well the individual employs these strategies depends on his or her range of experiences and capacity for self-control.

Suppose you receive a warning that you are about to fail a course required for graduation. You might confer with the professor, devise a work schedule to fulfill the requirements, and then follow it; or you might decide that you cannot fulfill the requirements in the time remaining and sign up to retake the course in summer school. Both of these actions are problem-focused methods of coping.

People who tend to use problem-focused coping in stressful situations show lower levels of depression both during and after the stressful situation (Billings & Moos, 1984). Of course, people who are less depressed may find it easier to use problem-focused coping. But longitudinal studies show that problem-focused coping leads to shorter periods of depression, even taking into account people's initial levels of depression. In addition, therapies that teach depressed people to use problem-focused coping can be effective in helping them overcome their depressions and react more adaptively to stressors (Nezu, Nezu, & Perri, 1989).

Talking with a professor to understand deficits in your coursework is one form of problem-focused coping.

Emotion-Focused Coping

Often you cannot do anything about the causes of your negative emotions—for example, when they are caused by the death of a loved one. We are left to manage the emotional fallout of such events. One maladaptive way is *to simply deny that we have any negative emotions and to push these emotions out of our conscious awareness,* a strategy that is referred to as **repressive coping.** People who engage in repressive coping tend to show more autonomic nervous system activity (such as higher heart rate) in response to stressors than those people who tend not to employ this strategy (Brown et al., 1996; Weinberger, Schwartz, & Davidson, 1979). Pushing emotions out of awareness may require real physical work, which results in chronic overarousal and, in turn, in physical illness.

Repressing important aspects of your identity may also be bad for your health. One intriguing study showed that gay men who conceal their homosexual identity may suffer health consequences (Cole et al., 1996). Men who concealed their homosexuality were about three times more likely to develop cancer and several infectious diseases (pneumonia, bronchitis, sinusitis, and tuberculosis) over a 5-year period than men who were open about their homosexuality (see Figure 11-9). All of these men were HIV-negative. Another study by this same research group focused on HIV-positive gay men and found that in those who concealed their homosexuality the HIV infection progressed faster than in those who did not conceal their identity (Cole et al., 1995). The differences in health between the men who were "out" and those who were "closeted" did not reflect differences in health care behaviors (smoking or exercise). It may be that chronic inhibition of one's identity, like chronic inhibition of emotions, can lead directly to changes in health.

In contrast, talking about important issues in one's life and about negative emotions appears to have positive effects on health. In a large series of studies, James Pennebaker (1990) found that having people reveal personal traumas in diaries or essays improves their health. For example, in one study, 50 healthy undergraduates were randomly assigned to write either about the most traumatic and upsetting events in their lives or about trivial topics for 20 minutes on each of 4 consecutive days. Blood samples were taken from the students the day before they began writing, on the last day of writing, and 6 weeks after writing; these samples were tested for several markers of immune system functioning. The number of times the students visited the college health center over the 6 weeks after the writing task was also recorded and compared to the number of health center visits the students had made before the study. As Figures 11-10a and 11-10b show, students who revealed their personal traumas in essays had more positive immune system functioning and a greater decline in health center visits than the control group who wrote about trivial events (Pennebaker, Kiecolt-Glaser, & Glaser, 1988).

Some people may get too involved in thoughts about their personal traumas and negative emotions, however. They become caught up in **rumination,** *the tendency to passively and repetitively focus on one's distress without taking any action to relieve that distress* (Nolen-Hoeksema, 1995). People who engage in rumination after experiencing a stressor tend to show longer periods of depression and anxiety and poorer physical health than those who do not. For example, researchers in the San Francisco Bay area happened to have taken measures of emotion-focused coping tendencies and levels of depression and anxiety in a large group of students 2 weeks before the major earthquake that hit the area in 1989. They remeasured the students' levels of depression and anxiety again both 10 days and 7 weeks after the earthquake. They also estimated how much environmental stress the students experienced

repressive coping a maladaptive coping strategy by which a person denies that he or she has any negative emotions and pushes those emotions out of conscious awareness

rumination the tendency to passively and repetitively focus on one's distress without taking any action to relieve that distress

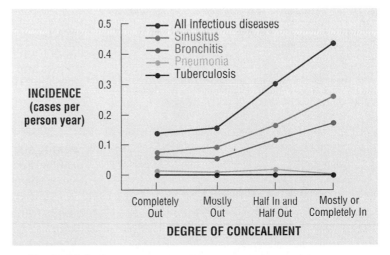

Figure 11-9

Infectious Diseases as a Function of Concealing One's Sexual Orientation Homosexual men who concealed their homosexuality from others were more prone to several infectious diseases. (After Cole et al., 1996)

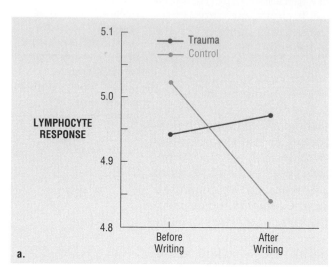

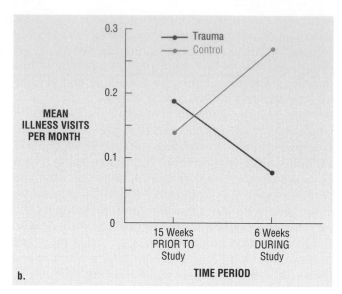

Figure 11-10

Students' Health after Writing about Traumas or Trivialities   Students who revealed personal traumas in a series of essays had stronger immune system functioning and fewer health-care visits than students who wrote about trivial events in their essays. (After Pennebaker, Krecolt-Glaser, & Glaser, 1988)

as a result of the earthquake (that is, injury to themselves, to their friends or family, and to their homes). The results showed that students who evidenced a ruminative style of coping with emotions before the earthquake were more likely to be depressed and anxious 10 days and even 7 weeks after the quake. This was true even after the students' levels of depression and anxiety before the earthquake were taken into account (Nolen-Hoeksema & Morrow, 1991a). Students who used dangerous activities, such as drinking alcohol, to avoid their moods also tended to remain depressed and anxious.

There seems to be some happy medium between repression and rumination, in which people confront and deal with their traumas and negative emotions, but do not get caught up in rumination. As we shall see next, having friends and family members who will support them as they confront stressors can help people find that middle ground.

Seeking Social Support

Seeking social support from others may help people avoid both repression and rumination and engage in more adaptive problem-solving, which in turn improves health (Uchino, Uno, & Holt-Lunstad, 1999). One study of recently bereaved people found that those with good social support were less likely to engage either in rumination or in denial and avoidance of their emotions, and, in turn, showed better adjustment to their loss (Nolen-Hoeksema & Larson, 1999). In a study of women who had just received surgery for breast cancer, Levy and colleagues (1990) found that those who actively sought social support from others had higher natural killer cell activity, indicating that their immune systems were more aggressively attacking their cancer.

Positive emotional support is an important buffer against the effects of stress.

Frontiers of Psychology

Is religion good for your health?

Psychologists have had an ambivalent relationship with religion. William James, a founder of modern psychology, noted that religion can be sick or healthy, debilitating or vitalizing. Freud considered religion an unhealthy coping strategy, and psychological theories have generally viewed religiosity in a less than positive light over the years.

But in recent years secular researchers have had to face the fact that study after study shows religious people to be happier and healthier, on average, than nonreligious people (for reviews, see Ellison & Levin, 1998; Koenig, 1998; Myers, 1992). The links between religiosity and psychological well-being are especially clear. People who have a strong religious faith and are active in a religious community report that they have higher life satisfaction and seem to recover better psychologically after traumas than nonreligious people (Koenig, 1998). For ex-

ample, a study of parents who had lost an infant to sudden infant death syndrome found that those who were active in their churches were better able to cope with the loss of their child (McIntosh, Silver, & Wortman, 1993). Religion probably helps people to cope in several ways: by providing them with a social support system, by helping them to give some meaning to traumatic events, and by giving them a "prescription" for how to deal with stress. Religious people would also say that God helps them directly.

The links between religiosity and physical health have been studied less, but there is some evidence for such links (Ellison & Levin, 1998; Oman & Reed, 1998). Actively religious people have lower mortality rates from a variety of diseases than nonreligious people (Oman & Reed, 1998). They are generally in better physical health (Koenig et al., 1997). Religious beliefs may affect health be-

cause they influence health-related behaviors. Many religions have prohibitions against unhealthy behaviors, such as excessive drinking, drug use, and smoking, and in fact religious people do smoke and drink less than nonreligious people (Koenig et al., 1998). In addition, positive social support is linked to better health, and religious groups provide social support for their members.

For now, just how religiosity affects mental and physical health is largely unknown (Ellison & Levin, 1998). In addition, most of the research to date has been on people who ascribe to Christian or Jewish beliefs, and little work has been done with people of other faiths. But old assumptions that religion is a danger to health and that religiosity is an unhelpful defense mechanism are being replaced by more open-minded views on the benefits religion offers.

The quality of the social support a person receives from others after a trauma strongly influences the impact on health, however (Rook, 1984). Some friends or relatives can be burdens instead of blessings in times of stress. People who have a high degree of conflict in their social networks tend to show poorer physical and emotional health following a major stressor, such as bereavement (Nolen-Hoeksema & Larson, 1999). Conflicted social relationships may affect physical health through the immune system. In one study, newlywed couples who became hostile and negative toward each other while discussing a marital problem showed more decrements in four indicators of immune system functioning than couples who remained calm and nonhostile in discussing marital problems (see Figure 11-11). Couples who became hostile during these discussions also showed elevated blood pressure for a longer period of time than those who did not become hostile (Kiecolt-Glaser et al., 1993; Malarkey et al., 1994).

Figure 11-11

Changes in Immune System Functioning in Newlyweds in High versus Low Conflict Marriages Newlyweds in high conflict relationships showed greater decline in immune system functioning following a discussion with their spouse than those in low conflict relationships. (Adapted from Krecolt-Glaser et al., 1993, Figure 3, page 403.)

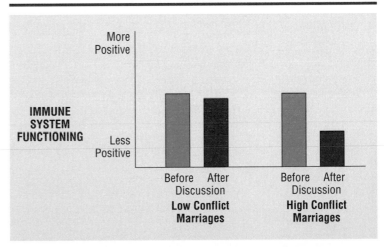

Thus, coping effectively with stress can be a tricky business. Directly confronting and attempting to solve problems seems to be adaptive most of the time. When there is no problem to solve, or while you are solving the problem, negative emotions must be managed. Finding supportive others who will help you avoid rumination or repression is helpful, but not always easy.

Thinking Critically

1. In what ways might the environment in which a child grows up affect the development of his or her coping strategies?

2. Is there anything a person can do to increase the quality of social support he or she obtains from family and friends?

Can Interventions Reduce Stress and Improve Health?

A major focus of much research in behavioral medicine is on helping people reduce stress and thereby improve their psychological and physical health. We will review some behavioral and cognitive techniques that can be helpful for people with a variety of problems. Then we will discuss how they are applied to reduce Type A behavior and to assist cancer patients.

Behavioral Techniques

Among the behavioral techniques that have been used to help people control their physiological responses to stressful situations are biofeedback and relaxation training. In *biofeedback training,* individuals receive information (feedback) about an aspect of their physiological state and then attempt to alter that state. For example, in a procedure for learning to control tension headaches, electrodes are attached to the forehead so that any movement in the forehead muscle can be electronically detected, amplified, and fed back to the person as an auditory signal. The signal, or tone, increases in pitch when the muscle contracts and decreases when it relaxes. By learning to control the pitch of the tone, the individual learns to keep the muscle relaxed. (Relaxation of the forehead muscle usually ensures relaxation of scalp and neck muscles also.) After 4 to 8 weeks of biofeedback training, the person learns to recognize the onset of tension and to reduce it without feedback from the machine (Taylor, 1999).

Physiological processes that are controlled by the autonomic nervous system, such as heart rate and blood pressure, have traditionally been assumed to be automatic and not under voluntary control. However, laboratory studies have demonstrated that people can learn to modify heart rate and blood pressure (see Figure 11-12). The results of these studies have led to new procedures for treating patients with high blood pressure (hypertension). One procedure is to show

Figure 11-12

Operant Conditioning of Blood Pressure and Heart Rate   One group of participants received biofeedback (a light and a tone) whenever their blood pressure and heart rate decreased simultaneously (Group 1); the other group received the same feedback whenever their blood pressure and heart rate increased simultaneously (Group 2). The participants achieved significant simultaneous control of blood pressure and heart rate during a single conditioning session. The group who were reinforced for lowering both functions achieved greater control over trials; the group who were reinforced for raising both functions was less consistent. (After Schwartz, 1975)

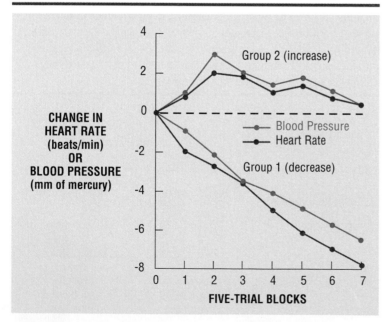

patients a graph of their blood pressure while it is being monitored and to teach them techniques for relaxing different muscle groups. The patients are instructed to tense their muscles (for example, to clench a fist or to tighten the abdomen), release the tension, and notice the difference in sensation. By starting with the foot and ankle muscles and progressing through the body to the muscles that control the neck and face, the patients learn to modify muscular tension. This combination of biofeedback with relaxation training has proved effective in lowering blood pressure for some individuals (Nakao et al., 1997).

Reviews of numerous studies using biofeedback and relaxation training to control headaches and hypertension conclude that the most important variable is learning how to relax (Runck, 1980). Some people may learn to relax faster when they receive biofeedback training. Others may learn to relax equally well when they receive training in muscle relaxation without any specific biofeedback training. The usefulness of relaxation training seems to depend on the individual. Some people who are not conscientious about taking drugs to relieve high blood pressure are more responsive to relaxation training, whereas others who have learned to control their blood pressure through relaxation may eventually drop the procedure because they find it too time-consuming.

Cognitive Techniques

An additional approach to stress management focuses on changing the individual's cognitive responses to stressful situations. *Cognitive behavior therapy* attempts to help people identify the kinds of stressful situations that produce their physiological or emotional symptoms and to change the way they think about and cope with these situations. For example, a man who suffers from tension headaches would be asked to begin by keeping a record of their occurrence and rating the severity of each headache and the circumstances in which it occurred. Next he is taught how to monitor his responses to these stressful events and is asked to record his feelings, thoughts, and behavior prior to, during, and following each event. After a period of self-monitoring, certain relationships among situational variables often become evident. For example, the situation of receiving criticism by a supervisor or coworker may often be accompanied by thoughts such as "I can't do anything right," and emotional, behavioral, and physiological responses such as depression, withdrawal, and headache.

The next step is to identify the expectations or beliefs that might explain the headache reactions (for example, "I expect to do everything perfectly, so the slightest criticism upsets me" or "I judge myself harshly, become depressed, and end up with a headache"). The final and most difficult step is to change something about the stressful situation, the individual's way of thinking about it, or the individual's behavior. The options might include finding a less stressful job, recognizing that the need to perform perfectly leads to unnecessary anguish over errors, or learning to behave more assertively in interactions instead of withdrawing.

Modifying Type A Behavior

Several studies suggest that a combination of cognitive and behavioral techniques effectively reduces Type A behavior. In one study, the participants were more than 1,000 individuals who had experienced at least one heart attack (Friedman et al., 1986). Participants in the treatment group were helped to reduce their sense of time urgency by practicing standing in line (a situation that Type A individuals find extremely irritating) and using the opportunity to reflect on things that they do not normally have time to think about, or to watch people, or to strike up a conversation with a stranger. Treatment also included learning to express themselves without exploding at people and to alter certain specific behaviors (such as interrupting others or talking or eating hurriedly). Therapists helped the participants reevaluate basic beliefs (such as the notion that success depends on the quantity of work produced) that might drive much of a Type A person's urgent and hostile behavior. Finally, participants found ways to make the home and work environment less stressful (such as reducing the number of unnecessary social engagements).

The critical dependent variable in this study was the occurrence of another heart attack. By the end of the study 4½ years later, the experimental group had experienced about half as many new heart attacks as control participants who were not taught how to alter their lifestyles. Clearly, learning to modify Type A behavior was beneficial to these participants' health.

Slowing the Progress of Cancer

Many scientists are skeptical that psychological interventions can significantly affect the course of major disease processes, such as cancer. They argue that suggestions that cancer patients can control their disease through willpower have done more harm than good because cancer patients are made to feel that they are to blame if they cannot cure themselves. However, evidence increasingly suggests that at least some types of supportive psychological interventions can slow the progress of cancer.

One study focused on people with malignant melanoma who had had the cancer surgically removed. Half the participants received a 6-week group intervention that included health education, training in problem-solving skills, stress management techniques such as relaxation, and psychosocial support. Compared to a control group that received no intervention, the intervention group showed more positive changes in several indicators of immune system functioning over the next 6 months, in addition to better psychological well-being. In addition, over the next 6 years the intervention group was less likely than the control group to have a recurrence of their cancer or to die from their cancer (Fawzy et al., 1990; Fawzy et al., 1993).

Another study focused on women with metastatic breast cancer (Spiegel et al., 1989). The researchers began their study by randomly assigning women with metastatic breast cancer either to a series of weekly support groups or to no support groups (all women were receiving standard medical care for their cancers). The focus of the groups was on facing death and learning to live one's remaining days to the fullest. The researchers had no intention of affecting the course of the cancers—they did not believe that this was possible. They only wanted to improve the quality of these women's lives.

The researchers were quite surprised when, 48 months after the study began, all the women who had not been in the support groups had died of their cancers whereas a third of the women in the support groups were still alive. The average survival time (from the time the study began) for the women in the support groups was about 40 months, compared to about 19 months for the women who were not in the support groups.

There were no differences between the groups, other than their participation in the weekly support meetings, that could explain the differences in average survival time. That is, the two groups did not differ in the initial seriousness of their cancers, the type of therapy received, or other variables that might have affected their survival time. The researchers were forced to believe that their intervention actually increased the number of months that the women in the support group lived (for similar results, see Richardson et al., 1990).

Further studies are under way to determine exactly how psychological interventions can affect the course of illness. It may be that reducing distress leads to improved

Interventions that increase people's problem-solving skills and sense of social support may slow the progression of some diseases.

immune system functioning, which slows the progression of disease. Studies such as this one are intriguing, however, and hold promise for new ways of helping people facing serious illness.

_____

How can we help people with serious diseases like cancer change in ways that might slow the progress of their disease without making them feel that they are being blamed for their disease?

Summary

1. Events are often considered *stressful* when they are *traumas* outside the range of normal human experience, are perceived as uncontrollable or unpredictable, require many changes, or cause internal conflicts between competing goals.

2. Common psychological reactions to stress include *anxiety,* apathy and depression, and cognitive impairment (for example, problems in concentration and performance).

3. The body reacts to stress with the *fight-or-flight response.* The sympathetic nervous system causes increased heart rate, elevated blood pressure, dilated pupils, and the release of extra sugar from the liver. The adrenal-cortical system causes the release of adrenocorticotropic hormone (ACTH), which stimulates the release of cortisol in the blood. These reactions prepare the body to fight the stressor or to flee from it. When a person is chronically aroused, however, these physiological responses can cause wear and tear on the body.

4. Researcher Hans Selye described the body's response to stress as the *general adaptation syndrome,* and delineated three phases: alarm, resistance, and exhaustion. Prolonged exposure to stress can result in *psychophysiological disorders*—physical disorders that are affected by psychological factors.

5. Stress may affect health directly by creating chronic overarousal of the sympathetic system or the adrenal-cortical system or by impairing the immune system. In addition, people under stress also may not engage in positive health behaviors, and this may lead to illness.

6. The ways in which people appraise events may influence their vulnerability to illness after events. For example, people who tend to explain bad events by internal, stable, and global causes—a tendency known as a negative *attributional style*—are more likely to develop *learned helplessness* after bad events and to become ill. *Hardy* individuals, however, seem to appraise difficult events as challenging.

7. People with the *Type A* behavior pattern tend to be hostile, aggressive, impatient individuals who are overinvolved in their work. Studies of men and women show that people with this style are at increased risk for *coronary heart disease (CHD).*

8. *Coping* strategies are divided into problem-focused strategies and emotion-focused strategies. People who take active steps to solve problems are less likely to show depression and illness after negative life events. Two maladaptive strategies for emotion-focused coping include *repression* and *rumination.* Seeking social support from others often helps people cope with stress, but only if others provide positive support.

9. Behavioral techniques, such as relaxation training, and cognitive techniques, such as challenging negative thoughts, can help people react more adaptively to stress. Type A behavior can be changed through behavioral and cognitive techniques, resulting in lower risk for coronary heart disease. Psychosocial interventions may also help to slow the progress of some cancers.

Suggested Readings

Peterson, *Stress at Work* (1999), describes psychological and sociological approaches to occupational stress. Steptoe (ed.), *Psychosocial Processes and Health* (1994), is a reader with chapters by some of the leading researchers in health psychology. Schafer, *Stress Management for Wellness* (1996), provides practical tips for reducing stress and teaches relaxation techniques.

The developing field of health psychology is described in Sapolsky, *Why Zebras Don't Get Ulcers* (1994). Pennebaker (1990) summarizes his research on the effect of confiding in others on physical health in *Opening Up: The Healing Powers of Confiding in Others*. For a comprehensive review of the literature on psychology and health, see Taylor, *Health Psychology* (1999).

Enhance and Explore

To enhance your understanding of the psychological concepts found in this chapter, please consult the following aids:

Study Guide

Learning Objectives, p. 198
Define the Terms, p. 201
Test Your Knowledge, p. 204
Essay Questions, p. 207
Thinking Independently, p. 208

PowerPsych CD-ROM

WHAT MAKES LIFE STRESSFUL?
Social Readjustment Rating Scale

HOW DO PSYCHOLOGICAL FACTORS INFLUENCE STRESS RESPONSES?
Type A/Type B Scale

PsychCentral

For more information concerning the topics found in this chapter, access psychology links on the Word Wide Web made through the Harcourt Web page at:
http://www.harcourtcollege.com/psych/Fundamentals

www.harcourtcollege.com
http://www.harcourtcollege.com/psych/index.html

CHAPTER 12 *Abnormal Psychology*

Why Can't That Child Calm Down? (Attention Deficit Hyperactivity Disorder)
Understanding Attention Deficit Hyperactivity Disorder

> Mike was a 32-year-old father who had many concerns. When driving, he felt compelled to stop the car often to check whether he had run over people, although there was no reason to think he had. Before flushing the toilet, Mike inspected the toilet to be sure that a live insect had not fallen into it—he did not want to be responsible for killing any live creature. In addition, he repeatedly checked the doors, stoves, lights, and windows of his house, making sure that all were shut or turned off so that no harm, such as fire or burglary, would befall his family as a result of his "irresponsible" behavior. In particular, he worried about the safety of his 15-month-old daughter, repeatedly checking the gate to the basement to be sure that it was locked. He did not carry his daughter while walking on concrete floors, in order to avoid killing her by accidentally dropping her. Mike performed these and many other checks for an average of 4 hours a day. (Adapted from Foa & Steketee, 1989, p. 189)

Most of us have some concerns, but Mike's concerns seem extreme. Some people might say that his concerns are so extreme that they are abnormal, disordered, or crazy. In this chapter we explore our understanding of what it means to be abnormal, disordered, or crazy. We will see that sometimes the line between normal and abnormal is clear, but most of the time it is fuzzy. We will investigate in detail several specific types of abnormality and theories of why some people develop psychological disorders while others do not. Then, in the next chapter, we will discuss the treatments available for people suffering from psychological disorders.

A word of warning: It is common for students who are studying abnormal psychology for the first time to see signs of psychological disorders in themselves, just as medical students diagnose themselves as suffering from every new disease they read about. Most of us have at one time or another had some of the symptoms we will be describing, and that is no cause for alarm. However, if you have been bothered by distressing thoughts or feelings for quite a while, it is a good idea to talk to someone about them, perhaps someone in your school's counseling service or student health service.

How Are Psychological Disorders Defined and Diagnosed?

What do we mean by "abnormal" behavior? Definitions of abnormality have varied over time, and in our own time they vary across cultures. Most of these definitions have significant weaknesses and leave many questions unanswered (see Figure 12-1).

In its most literal sense, *abnormality* means "away from the norm." Sometimes when we say that a behavior is abnormal, we mean that it is *unusual;* it is a behavior we seldom see. For example, Mike's compulsions to stop his car and check whether he had run over anyone or to check the doors and windows of his house dozens of times each

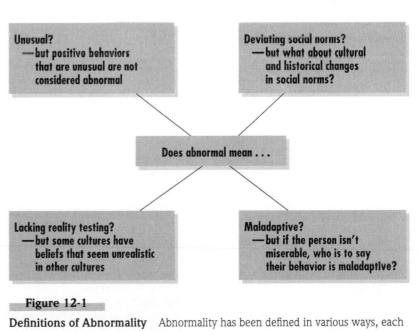

Figure 12-1

Definitions of Abnormality   Abnormality has been defined in various ways, each of which has its disadvantages.

Deviant behavior changes with the times: 50 years ago women would never have worn the common fashions of today.

night are highly unusual, and this is one reason that they seem abnormal. Yet there are many behaviors that are unusual but do not match our sense of what it means to be abnormal. Gifted musicians are unusual—they are infrequent in the population. Yet we don't tend to think of gifted musicians as abnormal—only as unusual.

Behaviors are often labeled as abnormal when they *deviate from social norms.* For example, many societies have norms against nudity in public, and people who violate those norms (such as women going topless on the street, or men displaying their genitals to others) may be labeled as abnormal. Societies differ greatly in their norms, however, and what is abnormal in one society may be completely normal in others. There are societies in which women never wear garments above the waist and men's genitals are always exposed. Social norms also change greatly with time. Fifty years ago a woman wearing a halter top and shorts in public might have been branded as "crazy" in many societies, but today she would be considered perfectly normal in most of those societies.

Lack of reality testing is one criterion that many societies use to label certain thoughts or behaviors as abnormal. People lack reality testing when they cannot tell the difference between what is real and what is unreal. They may hear voices or see objects that are not there. They may believe that they are someone they are not—such as Jesus or Buddha. They may believe that others are plotting against them when this is not true. Such a *lack of reality testing* is often referred to as **psychosis.** The presence of psychosis is currently one of the primary criteria that many societies use to designate abnormality.

psychosis   lack of reality testing

Lack of reality testing may seem like a clear and uncontroversial criterion for defining abnormality, but it is not. Religious people often report having visions or hearing the voices of the deities they worship. Many cultures believe that spirits and deceased family members converse with the living. Labeling these religious and cultural beliefs as abnormal and due to lack of reality testing is not acceptable to many social scientists. Still, within these religious and cultural communities some members may cross the line into psychosis, and leaders in these communities often differentiate between perceptual experiences and beliefs that are manifestations of the community's beliefs, and those that represent a loss of reality testing. For example, among the Yoruba of Africa traditional healers often jump around on their hands and feet and bark like a dog as part of a healing ritual. Healers who do this with the full realization that they are enacting an ancient ritual are thought to be completely normal. A healer who actually believed he was a dog during one of these ceremonies would be considered to have lost touch with reality.

One criterion for defining abnormality that many psychologists find acceptable is *maladaptiveness.* A behavior is abnormal if it causes the individual or important others significant distress or interferes greatly with the ability to function in everyday life. For example, in the story at the beginning of this chapter, Mike was spending 4 hours a day in his checking rituals, and these rituals were causing him severe distress. Many of the conditions we will consider in this chapter—depression, anxiety,

Many religious practices, such as praying to an unseen deity, might be considered signs of lack of reality testing by some people, but most psychologists would not label them as abnormal.

schizophrenia—make people acutely miserable and make it very difficult for them to hold jobs or enjoy relationships with others. Other conditions, such as some of the personality disorders, do not cause personal distress for the people with the disorders, but they cause a great deal of trouble for other people. For example, people with antisocial personality disorder, who are abusive and have little regard for the basic rights of other people, may not be distressed about their own behavior but can make the other people in their lives miserable.

As reasonable as this criterion of maladaptiveness may seem, we can still raise many questions about it. First, just how maladaptive does a behavior, thought, or feeling have to be before it is labeled as abnormal? For example, most of us feel at least somewhat sad or depressed occasionally. How sad or depressed do we have to be before labeling these feelings as maladaptive? Second, do we really have a right to call some people abnormal because they make their friends and family members unhappy, if these people do not wish to change their behaviors and are not distressed by their behaviors? For example, people who join a religious cult are often very happy about their new life, although their families and friends are very unhappy about the changes they see in them. What right does society have to label some people's life choices as abnormal and others as normal, just because their families and friends don't like their choices? Finally, the criterion of maladaptiveness is still highly susceptible to social norms. What is considered adaptive in

Joining a cult may appear maladaptive to some, but not to others.

one society may be considered maladaptive in another. For example, in societies with a collectivist orientation—in which devotion to one's family and social group is the highest goal—being modest and self-sacrificing is highly adaptive, while promoting oneself and being independent from others is considered highly maladaptive. In contrast, in individualist cultures—in which individualism and achievement are prized—promoting oneself and being independent from others is adaptive, but being extremely modest and self-sacrificing is considered maladaptive.

The bottom line is that there is no clear-cut definition of abnormality. Lack of reality testing and maladaptiveness are currently the most widely used criteria and, as we will see, form the basis for diagnosing most psychological disorders. Even these criteria have their weaknesses, however.

Historical Perspectives

Many of the ancient theories of abnormality viewed people with unusual behavior as possessed by evil spirits. These demons could supposedly be exorcised by prayer, incantation, magic, and the use of purgatives concocted from herbs. If these interventions were unsuccessful, more extreme measures were taken to ensure that the body would be an unpleasant dwelling place for the evil spirit. Flogging, starving, burning, and causing the person to bleed profusely were frequent forms of intervention.

Biological explanations of mental disorders can be found as far back as ancient Chinese texts written around 2600 B.C. Chinese medicine was based on the concept of Yin and Yang; the human body was said to contain a positive force and a negative force that both confront and complement each other. If the two forces are in balance, the individual is healthy. If not, illness, including insanity, can result. For example, insane excitement was considered to be the result of an excessive positive force:

> The person suffering from excited insanity initially feels sad, eating and sleeping less; he then becomes grandiose, feeling that he is very smart and noble, talking and scolding day and night, singing, behaving strangely, seeing strange things, hearing strange voices, believing that he can see the devil or gods, etc. As treatment for such an excited condition withholding food was suggested, since food was considered to be the source of positive force and the patient was thought to be in need of a decrease in such force. (Tseng, 1973, p. 570)

In Western medicine, progress toward a biological model of mental disorders was made by the Greek physician Hippocrates (circa 460–377 B.C.), who rejected demonology and maintained that unusual behaviors were the result of a disturbance in the balance of bodily fluids. Hippocrates, and the Greek and Roman physicians who followed him, argued for more humane treatment of the mentally ill. They stressed the importance of pleasant surroundings, exercise, proper diet, massage, and soothing treatments, as well as some less desirable treatments, such as purging, and mechanical restraints. Although there were no institutions

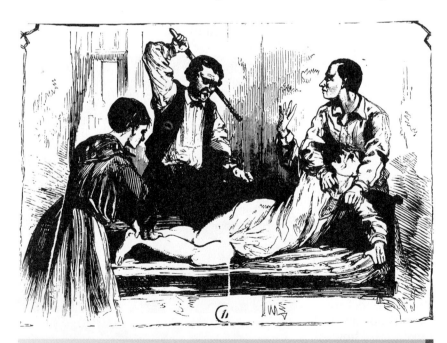

Early forms of "treatment" for mental illness often included floggings.

for the mentally ill during this period, many individuals were cared for with great kindness in temples dedicated to the Greek and Roman gods.

Supernatural theories of mental illness reemerged with great force in the late Middle Ages. The mentally ill were considered to be in league with Satan and to possess supernatural powers that they could employ to cause floods, pestilence, and injuries to others. Seriously disturbed people were treated cruelly. People believed that by beating, starving, and torturing the mentally ill, they were punishing the devil. Some mentally ill individuals were accused of being witches and sentenced to death by burning at the stake.

As early as the 12th century, some cities began to create asylums to cope with the mentally ill. Many of these asylums were simply prisons; the inmates were chained in dark, filthy cells and treated more as animals than as human beings. It was not until the 18th century, when the humanitarian movement swept across Europe and America, that improvements were made. Proponents of this movement argued that people became mad because they had become separated from nature and had succumbed to the stresses imposed by rapid social changes.

In 1792, French physician Philippe Pinel was placed in charge of an asylum in Paris. As an experiment, he removed the chains that restrained the inmates. Much to the amazement of skeptics who thought Pinel was mad to unchain such "animals," the experiment was a success. When released from their restraints, placed in clean, sunny rooms, and treated kindly, many people who for years had been considered hopelessly insane improved enough to leave the asylum.

By the beginning of the 20th century, the fields of medicine and psychology were making great advances. In 1905 a mental disorder known as *general paresis* was shown to have a physical cause: a syphilis infection acquired many years before the symptoms of the disorder appeared. General paresis is characterized by a gradual decline in mental and physical functions, marked personality changes, and delusions and hallucinations. If the disease is not treated, death occurs within a few years. The syphilis spirochete remains in the body after the initial genital infection disappears, and it gradually destroys the nervous system. At one time, general paresis accounted for more than 10% of all admissions to mental hospitals, but today few cases are reported due to the effectiveness in penicillin in treating syphilis (Dale, 1975).

The discovery that general paresis was the result of a disease encouraged those who believed that mental illness was biological in origin. At about the same time, Sigmund Freud and his followers laid the groundwork for understanding mental illness in terms of psychological factors; likewise, Pavlov's laboratory experiments demonstrated that animals could become emotionally disturbed if they were forced to make decisions beyond their capabilities.

Modern Theories

These days, attempts to understand the causes of mental disorders generally fall under several general approaches to psychology (see Figure 12-2). The *biological perspective,* also called the medical or disease model,

Philippe Pinel in the courtyard of the hospital of Saltpêtrière.

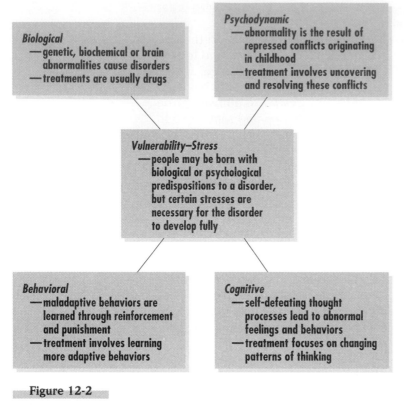

Figure 12-2

Different Perspectives on Abnormality   There are at least four different theoretical perspectives on abnormality. Vulnerability-stress models try to integrate these perspectives.

suggests that bodily disturbances cause disordered thought, behavior, and emotion. Researchers using this approach look for genetic irregularities that may predispose a person to develop a particular mental disorder. They also look for abnormalities in specific parts of the brain, defects in neurotransmitter systems, or problems in the functioning of the autonomic nervous system. The primary method used by proponents of this perspective to treat disorders is drug therapy.

The *psychodynamic perspective* on mental disorders emphasizes the importance of unconscious conflicts, usually originating in early childhood, and the use of defense mechanisms to handle the anxiety generated by repressed impulses and emotions. Bringing the unconscious conflicts and emotions into awareness presumably eliminates the need for the defense mechanisms and alleviates the disorder.

The *behavioral perspective* investigates how fears become conditioned to specific situations and the role that reinforcement plays in the origin and maintenance of inappropriate behaviors. This approach looks at mental disorders from the standpoint of learning theory and assumes that maladaptive behaviors are learned.

The *cognitive perspective* suggests that some mental disorders stem from disordered cognitive processes and can be alleviated by changing these faulty cognitions. Rather than stressing hidden motivations, emotions, and conflicts, however, it emphasizes conscious mental processes. The way we think about ourselves and the way we appraise stressful situations, and our strategies for coping with them, are all interrelated.

The ideas embodied in these summaries will become clearer as we discuss them in relation to specific mental disorders. Each of these approaches has something important to say about mental disorders, but none has the complete answer. One way of integrating these factors is in *vulnerability-stress models,* which consider the interaction between a predisposition that makes a person vulnerable for developing an illness and the stressful environmental conditions encountered by that person. On a biological level, the vulnerability might be genetic. On a psychological level, a chronic feeling of hopelessness and inadequacy might make an individual vulnerable to depression. Being vulnerable to a disorder does not, by any means, guarantee that the person will develop the disorder. Whether or not the predisposition leads to an actual disorder often depends on the kinds of stressors the individual encounters.

The key point of vulnerability-stress models is that both vulnerability and stress are necessary. They help explain why some people develop psychological disorders when confronted with a minimum of stress, while others remain healthy regardless of how difficult their lives may be.

Diagnosis of Psychological Disorders

The system used in the United States for diagnosing psychological disorders is the *Diagnostic and Statistical Manual of the American Psychiatric Association,* currently in its fourth edition and widely known as the DSM or the DSM-IV. In the first two editions, the criteria for diagnosing each disorder were vague and heavily influenced by theory. In the more recent editions, the authors of the manual have attempted to make the criteria for each disorder as clear and nontheoretical as possible. Generally, the criteria include specific numbers and types of symptoms that must be observed in an individual before a given diagnosis can be made. In addition, the criteria usually require that the symptoms be long-lasting and severe enough to significantly interfere with the individual's ability to function in everyday life. You can see how the notion that abnormality equals maladaptiveness is built into the manual. Dozens of specific disorders are listed in the DSM-IV. The major groups of disorders are listed in Table 12-1. The disorders recognized in the DSM correspond generally to those in the manual used in Europe and much of the rest of the world, known as the *International Classification of Diseases.*

Just how does a disorder come to be listed in the DSM? For the fourth edition, committees of experts on psychological disorders were convened to decide what groups of symptoms constitute discrete disorders and how many symptoms of each disorder must be present and to what degree in order for a diagnosis to be made. It would be nice if there were some objective standard against which we could test the committees' decisions—some blood test or brain scan that could definitively say that an individual has a given disorder. Then we could determine whether or not the committees had identified the correct criteria for diagnosing each disorder. But unfortunately there are no definitive standards for identifying any of the psychological disorders. Although, as we will see, people with certain disorders often show abnormalities in brain scans or blood tests, they do not always do so, and to date there is no reliable test for determining the presence or absence of a psychological disorder.

Many cultures recognize mental disorders that do not correspond to any listed in DSM-IV (see Table 12-2). Although some of these disorders may have the same underlying causes as certain disorders recognized by the DSM-IV, they are manifested by different symptoms. Other culture-bound disorders may be truly unique to the societies in which they are found.

The fact that there is no objective standard by which to define psychological disorders raises questions about the validity of the diagnoses in the DSM-IV. One influential critic of psychiatry, Thomas Szasz, has argued that there are so many biases inherent in who is labeled as having a mental disorder that the entire system of diagnosis is corrupt and should be abandoned. Szasz (1961) believes that people in power use psychiatric diagnoses to label and dispose of people who do not "fit in." He suggests that mental disorders do not really exist, and that people who seem to be suffering from mental disorders are only suffering from oppression by a society that does not accept their alternative ways of behaving and looking at the world. Even psychiatrists and psychologists who do not fully agree with Szasz's perspective recognize the great danger of labeling behaviors or people as abnormal. The person labeled as abnormal is treated differently by society, and this treatment can continue long after the person stops exhibiting behaviors labeled as abnormal.

Yet diagnostic systems serve a vital role. If the various types of abnormal behavior have different causes, we can hope to uncover them by grouping individuals according to similarities in their behavior, and then looking for other ways in which they may be similar. A diagnostic label also helps those who work with disturbed individuals to communicate information more quickly and concisely. The diagnosis of schizophrenia, for instance, indicates quite a bit about a person's behavior. Knowing that an individual's symptoms are similar to those of other people whose disorder followed a particular course or who benefited from a certain kind of treatment is helpful in deciding how to treat this person.

---

1. If you were experiencing distressing feelings, thoughts, or behaviors, would you feel better or worse if these experiences could be diagnosed as a psychological disorder? Explain your answer. What would having a diagnosis mean to you?

Thinking Critically

Table 12-1

Categories of Mental Disorders   Listed here are the main diagnostic categories of DSM-IV. Each category includes numerous subclassifications. (After American Psychiatric Association, 1994)

1. Disorders usually first evident in infancy, childhood, or adolescence	Includes mental retardation, autism, attention deficit disorder with hyperactivity, separation anxiety, speech disorders, and other deviations from normal development.
2. Delirium, dementia, amnestic, and other cognitive disorders	Disorders in which the functioning of the brain is known to be impaired, either permanently or transiently; may be the result of aging, degenerative diseases of the nervous system (for example, syphilis or Alzheimer's disease), or the ingestion of toxic substances (for example, lead poisoning or drugs).
3. Psychoactive substance use disorders	Includes excessive use of alcohol, barbiturates, amphetamines, cocaine, and other drugs that alter behavior. Marijuana and tobacco are also included in this category, which is controversial.
4. Schizophrenia	A group of disorders characterized by loss of contact with reality, marked disturbances of thought and perception, and bizarre behavior. At some phase, delusions or hallucinations almost always occur.
5. Mood disorders	Disturbances of normal mood; the person may be extremely depressed, abnormally elated, or may alternate between periods of elation and depression.
6. Anxiety disorders	Includes disorders in which anxiety is the main symptom (generalized anxiety or panic disorders) or anxiety is experienced unless the individual avoids feared situations (phobic disorders) or tries to resist performing certain rituals or thinking persistent thoughts (obsessive-compulsive disorders). Also includes post-traumatic stress disorder.
7. Somatoform disorders	The symptoms are physical, but no organic basis can be found and psychological factors appear to play the major role. Included are conversion disorders (for example, a woman who resents having to care for her invalid mother suddenly develops a paralyzed arm) and hypochondriasis (excessive preoccupation with health and fear of disease when there is no basis for concern). Does *not* include psychosomatic disorders that have an organic basis.
8. Dissociative disorders	Temporary alterations in the functions of consciousness, memory, or identity due to emotional problems. Included are amnesia (the individual cannot recall anything about his or her history following a traumatic experience) and dissociative identity disorder (better known as multiple personality disorder, involving two or more independent personality systems existing within the same individual).
9. Sexual disorders	Includes problems of sexual identity (for example, transsexualism), sexual performance (for example, impotence, premature ejaculation, and frigidity), and sexual aim (for example, sexual interest in children, sadism, and masochism).
10. Eating disorders	Self-induced starvation (anorexia) or patterns of binge eating followed by self-induced purging (bulimia).
11. Sleep disorders	Includes chronic insomnia, excessive sleepiness, sleep apnea, sleepwalking, and narcolepsy.
12. Factitious disorders	Physical or psychological symptoms that are intentionally produced or feigned. Differs from malingering in that there is no obvious goal, such as disability payments or the avoidance of military service. The best-studied form of this disorder is called Münchausen syndrome: The individual's plausible presentation of factitious physical symptoms results in frequent hospitalizations.
13. Impulse control disorder	Includes kleptomania (compulsive stealing of objects not needed for personal use or their monetary value), pathological gambling, and pyromania (setting fires for the pleasure or relief of tension derived thereby).
14. Personality disorders	Long-standing patterns of maladaptive behavior that constitute immature and inappropriate ways of coping with stress or solving problems. Antisocial personality disorder and narcissistic personality disorder are two examples.
15. Other conditions that may be the focus of clinical attention	This category includes many of the problems for which people seek help, such as marital problems, parent-child difficulties, and academic or occupational problems.

2. What are the attitudes of some of your friends and family members toward people with a psychological disorder? What theories about the causes of psychological disorders do these attitudes seem to represent?

Table 12-2

Culture-Bound Syndromes Some cultures have syndromes or mental disorders that are found only in that culture and that do not correspond to any DSM-IV categories. (Based on Carson & Butcher, 1992, p. 89)

Syndrome	Cultures Where Found	Symptoms
amok	Malaysia, Laos, Philippines, Papua New Guinea, Puerto Rico, Navajos	Brooding, followed by violent behavior, persecutory ideas, amnesia, exhaustion. More often seen in men than in women.
ataque de nervios	Latin America	Uncontrollable shouting, crying, trembling, heat in the chest rising to the head, verbal or physical aggression, seizures, fainting.
ghost sickness	American Indians	Nightmares, weakness, feelings of danger, loss of appetite, fainting, dizziness, hallucinations, loss of consciousness, sense of suffocation.
koro	Malaysia, China, Thailand	Sudden and intense anxiety that the penis (in males) or the vulva and nipples (in females) will recede into body and cause death.
latah	East Asia	Hypersensitivity to sudden fright, trance-like behavior. Most often seen in middle-aged women.
susto	Mexico, Central America	Appetite disturbances, sleep disturbances, sadness, loss of motivation, feelings of low self-worth following a frightening event. Sufferers believe that their soul has left their body.
taijin kyofusho	Japan	Intense fear that one's body displeases, embarrasses, or is offensive to others.

Why Are You So Afraid? (Anxiety Disorders)

Hazel was walking down a street near her home one day when she suddenly felt flooded with intense and frightening physical symptoms. Her whole body tightened up, she began sweating and her heart was racing, she felt dizzy and disoriented. She thought, "I must be having a heart attack! I can't stand this! Something terrible is happening! I'm going to die." Hazel stood frozen in the middle of the street until an onlooker stopped to help her.

The symptoms that Hazel was experiencing—tension, sweating, racing heart, fear, worry, dread—are ones that we all experience at least occasionally. Hazel's symptoms, however, were more severe than those most of us experience, and they occurred in a situation that is usually not stressful for most people—just walking down the street. Hazel may suffer from an **anxiety disorder.** This term refers to *a group of disorders in which anxiety either is the main symptom or is experienced when a person attempts to control certain maladaptive behaviors.*

There are four types of symptoms of anxiety (see Table 12-3); Hazel was experiencing some of each of these types. First, she had *physiological* or *somatic symptoms:* Her heart was racing, she was perspiring, and her muscles tensed. You may recognize these symptoms as part of the fight-or-flight response we discussed in Chapter 11. This is the body's natural reaction to a challenging situation—the physiological changes of the fight-or-flight response prepares our body to

anxiety disorders a group of disorders in which anxiety either is the main symptom or is experienced when a person attempts to control certain maladaptive behaviors

Anxiety can involve overwhelming physical, emotional, cognitive, and behavioral symptoms.

Table 12-3

Symptoms of Anxiety   The symptoms of anxiety fall into four clusters.

Somatic	Behavioral	Emotional	Cognitive
Goosebumps	Escape	Dread	Hypervigilance
Tense muscles	Avoidance	Terror	Worry
Heart rate increases	Aggression	Restlessness	Fear of losing control
Respiration increases	Freezing	Irritability	Fear of dying
Peripheral blood vessels dilate			Sense of unreality
Bronchioles widen			Problems concentrating
Pupils dilate			
Perspiration			
Adrenaline secreted			
Salivation decreases			
Bladder relaxes			

fight against a threat or flee from it. Second, Hazel had *cognitive symptoms* of anxiety: She was sure she was having a heart attack and dying. Third, she had a *behavioral symptom* of anxiety: She froze, unable to move until help arrived. Fourth, she had the sense of dread and terror, which is an *emotional symptom* of anxiety.

All of these symptoms can be highly adaptive when an individual is facing a real threat, such as a saber-toothed tiger in ancient times or a burglar today. They become maladaptive when there is no real threat to fight against or flee from. For example, Hazel's symptoms came "out of the blue"; they were not triggered by a tiger, a burglar, or any other truly dangerous situation. Even when these symptoms do arise in response to some perceived threat, they can be maladaptive if they are extreme given the nature of the threat, or if they persist after the threat passes. Many people with an anxiety disorder seem to view as highly threatening situations that most of us would think are benign, and they worry about those situations even when they are very unlikely to occur. For example, people with social phobias are terrified of the possibility that they might embarrass themselves in public; they therefore go to great lengths to avoid social situations.

generalized anxiety disorder   a disorder in which a person has a chronic sense of tension and dread

In one form of anxiety disorder, **generalized anxiety disorder,** the person walks around with *a chronic sense of tension and dread,* all day every day. People with this disorder are unable to relax; they suffer from disturbed sleep, headaches, dizziness, and a rapid heart rate, and are fatigued much of the time. They continually worry about potential problems and have difficulty concentrating or making decisions. When they finally make a decision, it becomes the source of further worry ("Did I think about all the possible consequences?" "What if it doesn't work out the way I want it to?"). Other anxiety disorders, such as panic disorder, phobias, and obsessive-compulsive disorder, are characterized by more focused anxiety and are discussed in more detail in the remainder of this section (see also Figure 12-3). (Posttraumatic stress disorder, in which people experience prolonged and severe anxiety symptoms following a traumatic event, was discussed in Chapter 11.)

Panic Disorder

panic attack   an episode of acute and overwhelming apprehension or terror

Hazel's symptoms suggest that she is experiencing a **panic attack**—*an episode of acute and overwhelming apprehension or terror.* During panic attacks, people feel certain that they are having a heart attack or stroke, that they will suffocate, that they are going crazy and losing control. They may have all the physiological symptoms of anxiety, including heart palpitations, shortness of breath, perspiration, muscle tremors, faintness, and nausea. Often these panic attacks are triggered by

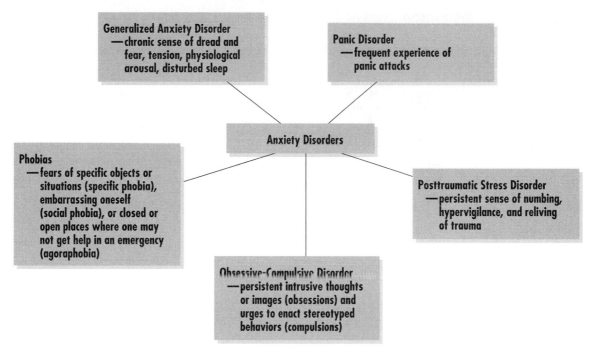

Figure 12-3

The Anxiety Disorders   In anxiety disorders, anxiety is either the main symptom or experienced when the person attempts to control certain behaviors.

certain situations, but sometimes they seem to come completely out of the blue, as in Hazel's case.

As many as 40% of young adults have occasional panic attacks, especially during times of intense stress, such as exam week (King et al., 1993). For most people, panic attacks are annoying but isolated events and do not change how they live their lives. But when *panic attacks become a common occurrence and people begin to worry about having attacks,* they may receive a diagnosis of **panic disorder.** Whereas the experience of isolated panic attacks is fairly common, panic disorder is relatively rare: Only about 1.5% to 3.5% of people will ever develop a panic disorder (American Psychiatric Association, 1994). Usually, people who develop panic disorder do so sometime between late adolescence and their mid-thirties. Without intervention, panic disorder tends to be chronic (Ehlers, 1995).

People with panic disorder may believe that they have a life-threatening illness, such as heart disease, or a susceptibility to stroke, even after such illnesses have been ruled out by medical examinations. They may seek out frequent medical care, going from one physician to another searching for the one who can diagnose their ailments. People with panic disorder also may believe that they are "going crazy" or "losing control." If their symptoms go untreated, they may become depressed and demoralized.

Agoraphobia   Panic disorder can be debilitating in its own right. Unfortunately, about one third to one half of people with panic disorder also develop another disorder known as agoraphobia (American Psychiatric Association, 1994). People with **agoraphobia** *fear any place where they might be trapped or unable to receive help in an emergency.* The emergency they most often fear is having a panic attack. The term *agoraphobia* is Greek for "fear of the marketplace"—and indeed, people with agoraphobia fear being in a busy, crowded marketplace (or, in our day, a mall). They may also fear being in tightly enclosed spaces from which escape can be difficult, such as

panic disorder a disorder in which panic attacks are a common occurrence and the person begins to worry about having attacks

agoraphobia a disorder characterized by fear of any place where the person might be trapped or unable to receive help in an emergency

People with agoraphobia may become confined to their homes, terrified of panicking should they venture out.

a bus, an elevator, or a subway. They may fear being alone in wide-open spaces, such as a meadow or a deserted beach. All of these places are frightening for people with agoraphobia because if a panic attack or some other emergency were to happen, it would be very difficult for them to escape or get help. They may also fear that they will embarrass themselves when others see that they are having a panic attack, although other people usually cannot tell when a person is having a panic attack.

People with agoraphobia avoid all of the places they fear. They may significantly curtail their activities, staying in a few "safe" places, such as their home and within a few blocks of their home. Sometimes they can venture to "unsafe" places if a trusted family member or friend accompanies them. If they attempt to enter "unsafe" places on their own, however, they may experience a great deal of general anxiety in anticipation, which will trigger a full panic attack.

Hazel, the woman in our example, developed agoraphobia. She continued to have panic attacks every few days, sometimes on the same street where she had the first panic attack, but increasingly in places where she'd never had a panic attack before. It seemed she was especially likely to have a panic attack if there were lots of people standing around her, and she became confused about how she would get out of the crowd if she began to panic. The only place Hazel had not had any panic attacks was in her apartment. Thus, she began to spend more and more time in her apartment, and refused to go anyplace where she had previously had a panic attack. After a few months, she had called in sick to work so often that she was fired. Yet Hazel could not bring herself to leave her apartment. She had her groceries delivered so she wouldn't have to go out to get them. She would only see friends if they would come to her apartment. Hazel's savings were becoming depleted, however, because she had lost her job. Hazel began looking for a job that she could do from her apartment.

Hazel's situation is not unique. Although people can develop agoraphobia without panic attacks, the vast majority of them do have panic attacks or panic-like symptoms in social situations (McNally, 1994). Usually, agoraphobia develops within a year of the onset of recurrent panic attacks. Obviously, the symptoms of agoraphobia can severely interfere with people's ability to function in daily life. People with agoraphobia often turn to alcohol and other drugs to cope with their symptoms. Fortunately, we have learned a great deal about the causes of panic and agoraphobia in the last few years.

Understanding Panic Disorder

Many people who develop panic disorder probably have a genetic or other biological vulnerability to the disorder. Panic disorder runs in families (Fyer et al., 1990, 1993). This does not mean, of course, that panic disorders are entirely hereditary, because family members also live together in the same environment. However, the results of twin studies provide firmer evidence for an inherited predisposition for panic disorder. Identical twins, as you recall, develop from the same egg and share the same heredity; fraternal twins develop from different eggs and are no more alike genetically than ordinary siblings. If a disorder is transmitted entirely genetically, then if one identical twin suffers from the disorder the other twin should be highly likely to suffer from it as well. In contrast, when one fraternal twin suffers from the disorder the other twin should not be at greatly increased risk for it because the fraternal twins are quite different genetically. Twin studies have shown that an identical twin is twice as likely to suffer panic disorder if the other twin does than are fraternal twins (Kendler et al., 1992, 1993).

One characteristic that may be inherited in people who are prone to panic attacks is an overreactive fight-or-flight response (McNally, 1994). A full panic attack can be induced easily by having these people engage in certain activities that stimulate the initial physiological changes of the fight-or-flight response. For example, when people with panic disorder purposely hyperventilate, breathe into a paper bag, or inhale a small amount of carbon dioxide, they experience an increase in subjective anxiety, and many will experience a full panic attack (Bourin et al., 1998; Rapee et al., 1992). In contrast, people without a history of panic attacks may experience some physical discomfort while doing these activities, but rarely experience a full panic attack.

This overreactive fight-or-flight response may be the result of deficiencies in areas of the brain that regulate this response, especially the limbic system (Bell & Nutt, 1998). Some studies show low levels of the neurotransmitter serotonin in the limbic system and other brain circuits involved in the fight-or-flight response in people with panic disorder. Serotonin deficiencies cause chronic hyperactivation of these areas of the brain, putting the individual on the verge of a panic attack most of the time.

An overreactive fight-or-flight response may not be enough to create a full panic disorder, however. Cognitive-behavioral theories of panic and agoraphobia suggest that people who are prone to panic attacks tend to pay very close attention to their bodily sensations, misinterpret those sensations in a negative way, and engage in catastrophic thinking (Barlow, 1988; Clark, 1988). So when Hazel first began feeling a bit of tightness in her muscles, she began thinking, "I'm having a heart attack! I'm going to die!" Not surprisingly, these thoughts increased her emotional symptoms of anxiety, which exacerbated her physiological symptoms—her heart rate increased even more and her muscles felt even tighter. She then interpreted these physiological changes catastrophically, and she was on her way to a full panic attack. Between full panic attacks, Hazel was hypervigilant for any bodily sensations. Her constant vigilance made her autonomic nervous system chronically aroused, making it more likely that she would experience another panic attack (Ehlers & Breuer, 1992).

So far we have talked only about the causes of panic disorder. But how does agoraphobia develop? According to the cognitive-behavioral theory, people who experience panic attacks remember vividly the places where these attacks have occurred. They greatly fear those places and generalize that fear to similar places. By avoiding those places, they reduce their symptoms of anticipatory anxiety, and so their avoidance behavior is highly reinforced. They may also find that they experience few symptoms of anxiety in particular places, such as their own home, and this reduction of their anxiety is also highly reinforcing, leading them to confine themselves to these "safe" places. Thus, through straightforward classical and operant conditioning, people's behaviors are shaped into what we call agoraphobia. For example, Hazel found that she could reduce her panic attacks by avoiding places where she had experienced attacks before, including work, and by staying in her apartment.

What is the evidence for this cognitive-behavioral theory of panic and agoraphobia? Several laboratory studies support the contentions that cognitive factors play a strong role in panic attacks and that agoraphobic behaviors may be conditioned through learning experiences (see McNally, 1994, for a review). In one study, researchers asked two groups of patients with panic disorder to wear breathing masks through which they would inhale air infused with slight amounts of carbon dioxide. Both groups were told that, although inhaling a slight amount of carbon dioxide was not dangerous to their health, it could induce a panic attack. One group was told that they

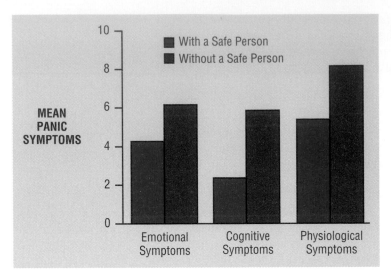

Figure 12-4

Panic Symptoms in Panic Patients with and without a Safe Person Available   Panic patients were much more likely to show symptoms of panic when a safe person was not with them. (After Carter et al., 1995)

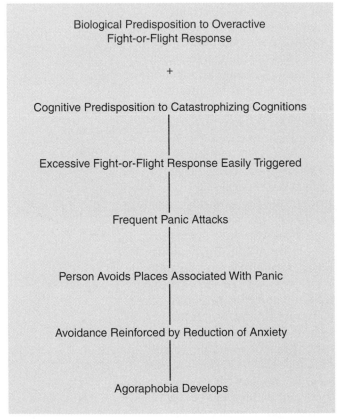

Figure 12-5

A Vulnerability-Stress Model of Panic and Agoraphobia   A combination of biological vulnerability to an overreactive fight-or-flight response plus cognitive vulnerability to catastrophizing cognitions may begin a chain of processes leading to panic and agoraphobia.

could not control the amount of carbon dioxide that came through their masks. The other group was told that they could control how much carbon dioxide they inhaled by turning a knob. Actually, neither group had control over the amount of carbon dioxide they inhaled, and both groups inhaled the same small amount. Eighty percent of the patients who believed that they had no control experienced a panic attack, but only 20% of those who believed that they could control the carbon dioxide had a panic attack. These results clearly suggest that beliefs about control over one's panic symptoms play a strong role in panic attacks (Sanderson, Rapee, & Barlow, 1989).

In a study focusing on agoraphobic behaviors, researchers examined whether people with panic disorder could avoid having a panic attack, even after inhaling carbon dioxide, by having a "safe person" nearby. Panic patients who were exposed to carbon dioxide with their safe person present were much less likely to experience the emotional, cognitive, and physiological symptoms of panic than panic patients who were exposed to carbon dioxide without their safe person present (Carter et al., 1995) (see Figure 12-4). These results show that the symptoms of panic become associated with certain situations, and that operant behaviors such as sticking close to a "safe person" can be reinforced by the reduction of panic symptoms.

Thus, the biological and cognitive-behavioral theories of panic and agoraphobia can be integrated into a vulnerability-stress model (Barlow, 1988) (see Figure 12-5). People who develop panic disorder may carry a genetic or biochemical vulnerability to an overreactive fight-or-flight response, so that at the slightest trigger, their bodies experience all of the physiological symptoms of this response. In order for a full panic disorder to develop, however, it may be necessary for them also to be prone to catastrophizing these physiological symptoms and to worrying excessively about having panic attacks. These cognitions further heighten their physiological reactivity, making it even more likely that they will experience a full fight-or-flight response at the slightest provocation. Agoraphobia develops when these people begin to avoid places that they associate with their panic symptoms and confine themselves to places in which they experience fewer anxiety symptoms. This integrated vulnerability-stress model has led to exciting breakthroughs in the treatment of panic disorder and agoraphobia, which we will discuss in Chapter 13.

Phobias

Although phobias are extremely common, they can significantly interfere with people's lives. People with **phobias** experience *such intense fear upon confronting a certain object or situation—to the point of having a panic attack—that they will take extreme steps to avoid it.* They usually realize that their fear is irrational, but the fear is nonetheless overwhelming. Many people have some fear of particular objects or situations, but the lives of people with a phobic disorder are quite disrupted by their fears. Examples might include a man whose phobia of bridges keeps him from traveling about town or a woman whose phobia of dogs causes her to lock herself in her home for fear of confronting a dog. There are three types of phobias: agoraphobia, specific phobias, and social phobia. We have already discussed agoraphobia, so will focus here on specific phobias and social phobia.

phobia a disorder characterized by such intense fear upon confronting a certain object or situation that the person will take extreme steps to avoid it

Specific Phobias   People with **specific phobias** *fear specific objects or situations.* These objects or situations usually fall into four categories. *Animal type phobias* are focused on specific animals or insects, such as dogs, cats, snakes, or spiders. *Natural environment type phobias* are focused on events or situations in the natural environment, such as storms, heights, or water. *Situational type phobias* usually involve fear of public transportation, tunnels, bridges, elevators, or flying. Claustrophobia, or fear of enclosed spaces, is a common situational phobia. Finally, people with *blood-injection-injury type phobias* fear seeing blood or an injury, or receiving an injection or some other invasive medical procedure.

specific phobia a disorder characterized by fear of a specific object or situation

There is great consistency across cultures in the objects of phobias. These tend to be objects or situations that were actually dangerous to our early ancestors. Natural selection may have favored those who learned quickly that spiders, snakes, heights, and deep water were dangerous. As a result, modern humans may be biologically predisposed, or prepared, to develop fears of these objects (Seligman, 1971). In contrast, it may be more difficult for humans to develop phobias of objects and situations that are not dangerous, or that have only been dangerous in recent history (such as guns and electric outlets).

social phobia a disorder characterized by a deep and abiding fear of embarrassing oneself or being judged by other people

Social Phobia   People with a **social phobia** have a *deep and abiding fear of embarrassing themselves or being judged by other people.* They will go to great lengths to avoid being in a situation in which others might evaluate them. For example, they may refuse to eat in public for fear that they might dribble food or someone might see their hand shake. They may take jobs that are solitary and isolating in order to avoid other people. If they find themselves in a feared social situation, they may begin trembling and perspiring, feel confused and dizzy, have heart palpitations and eventually have a full panic attack. They are sure that others see their nervousness and are judging them as inarticulate, weak, stupid, or "crazy." Social phobia is quite common, with about 8% of the U.S. adult population qualifying for the diagnosis in a 12-month period (Schneier

We may be biologically disposed to develop phobias to objects that have been dangerous to humans for most of evolutionary history, such as spiders.

et al., 1992). It typically begins in the adolescent years (Blazer et al., 1991) and tends to be a chronic and often debilitating problem if not treated (Kessler et al., 1998).

Understanding Phobias

Historically, phobias have been the focus of a major clash between psychodynamic and behavioral theories. Freud's theory of the development of phobias was one of his most famous and controversial. He argued that phobias result when people displace their anxiety over unconscious motives or desires onto objects that symbolize those motives or desires. His classic example was the case of Little Hans, a 5-year-old who developed an intense fear of horses. Freud interpreted the boy's phobia in terms of Oedipal fears. As Freud saw it, Hans was in love with his mother, jealously hated his father, and wanted to replace him (the Oedipal conflict). He feared that his father would retaliate by castrating him; the anxiety produced by this conflict was enormous because these wishes were unacceptable to the child's conscious mind. Hans's unconscious anxiety was displaced onto an innocent object that symbolized Hans's father (a large horse that Hans had seen fall down and thrash about violently on the street).

Freud's evidence for the foregoing explanation of Hans's horse phobia consisted of Hans's answers to a series of rather leading questions about what he was "really" afraid of, and the fact that Hans appeared to lose his horse phobia after his conversations with Freud. Freud suggested that Hans had gained insight into the true source of his phobia and that this insight had cured the phobia. Critics of Freud's theory, however, pointed out that Hans never provided any spontaneous or direct evidence that his real concerns were with his father rather than with the horse, and that Hans's phobia diminished gradually over time, rather than abruptly in response to some sudden insight.

Some of the severest critics of Freud's analysis of phobias were behaviorists (Watson & Raynor, 1920). They argued that phobias do not develop from unconscious anxieties, but rather are the results of classical and operant conditioning. Many phobias emerge after a traumatic experience—a child nearly drowns and develops a phobia of water; another child is bitten by a dog and develops a phobia of dogs; an adolescent stumbles through a speech at school and is laughed at by peers then develops a phobia of public speaking. In these cases, a previously neutral stimulus (the water or dog or public speaking) is paired with a traumatic event (drowning or biting or embarrassment) that elicits a natural anxiety reaction. Through classical conditioning, the previously neutral stimulus now is able to elicit the anxiety reaction. In addition, many people with such fears come to avoid the feared objects because this avoidance helps reduce anxiety. Thus, through operant conditioning the phobic behavior is maintained.

While some phobias appear to result from actual frightening experiences, others may be learned vicariously, through observation (Bandura, 1969; Mineka et al., 1984). Fearful parents tend to produce children who share their fears. A child who observes his or her parents reacting with fear to specific situations may develop the same reactions to those situations. Indeed, studies find that phobias

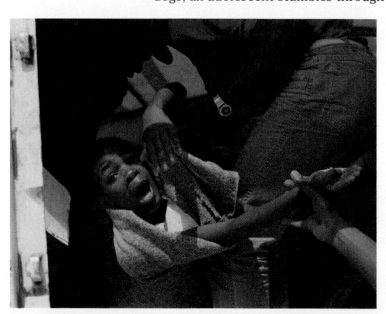
Traumatic events, such as nearly drowning, can induce phobias.

clearly run in families (Fyer et al., 1993). Whether this is largely due to children learning phobias from their parents, or also partially due to genetic transmission of phobias, is unclear.

Behavioral theories have led to highly successful treatments for phobias, lending further support to these theories. In contrast, treatments based on psychodynamic theories of phobias do not tend to be successful.

Obsessive-Compulsive Disorder

Obsessive-compulsive disorder, in which a person *experiences obsessions and compulsions,* is classified as an anxiety disorder, but it has many features that distinguish it from the other anxiety disorders. **Obsessions** are *persistent intrusions of unwelcome thoughts, images, or impulses that cause great anxiety.* Obsessive thoughts cover a variety of topics, but most often they are concerned with causing harm to oneself or others (as in Mike's obsession, described at the beginning of the chapter, that he might drop his child and kill her), fears of contamination, and doubt that a completed task, such as turning off the stove, has been accomplished satisfactorily (Rachman & Hodgson, 1980). The focus of obsessive thoughts seems to be similar across cultures, with the most common type of obsession focusing on contamination (Akhtar et al., 1975; Insel, 1984; Kim, 1993; Rachman & Hodgson, 1980).

Compulsions are *irresistible urges to carry out certain acts or rituals.* Obsessive thoughts are often linked with compulsive acts (for example, people with obsessions about germs may be compelled to wash their eating utensils many times before using them). "Checking" compulsions are extremely common and are tied to obsessional doubts, as is illustrated in the following story:

> I'm driving down the highway doing 55 mph. I'm on my way to take a final exam. My seat belt is buckled and I'm vigilantly following all the rules of the road. No one is on the highway—not a living soul.
>
> Out of nowhere an Obsessive-Compulsive Disorder (OCD) attack strikes. It's almost magical the way it distorts my perception of reality. While in reality no one is on the road, I'm intruded with the heinous thought that I *might* have hit someone . . . a human being! God knows where such a fantasy comes from.
>
> I think about this for a second and then say to myself, "That's ridiculous. I didn't hit anybody." Nonetheless, a gnawing anxiety is born. An anxiety I will ultimately not be able to put away until an enormous emotional price has been paid.
>
> I try to make reality chase away this fantasy. I reason, "Well, if I hit someone while driving, I would have *felt* it." This brief trip into reality helps the pain dissipate . . . but only for a second. Why? Because the gnawing anxiety that I really did commit the illusionary accident is growing larger—so is the pain.
>
> The pain is a terrible guilt that I have committed an unthinkable, negligent act. At one level, I know this is ridiculous, but there's a terrible pain in my stomach telling me something quite different.
>
> Again, I try putting to rest this insane thought and that ugly feeling of guilt. "Come on," I think to myself, "this is *really* insane!"
>
> But the awful feeling persists. The anxious pain says to me, *"You Really Did Hit Someone."* The attack is now in full control. Reality no longer has meaning. My sensory system is distorted. I have to get rid of the pain. Checking out this fantasy is the only way I know how.
>
> I start ruminating, "Maybe I did hit someone and didn't realize it. . . . Oh my God! I might have killed somebody! I have to go back and check." Checking is the only way to calm the anxiety. It brings me closer to truth somehow. I can't live with the thought that I actually may have killed someone—I have to check it out.
>
> Now I'm sweating . . . literally. I pray this outrageous act of negligence never happened. My fantasies run wild. I desperately hope the jury will be merciful. I'm particularly concerned about whether my parents will be understanding. After all, I'm now a criminal. I

obsessive-compulsive disorder a disorder in which the person experiences obsessions and compulsions

obsession a persistent intrusion of an unwelcome thought, image, or impulse that causes great anxiety

compulsion an irresistible urge to carry out a certain act or ritual

must control the anxiety by checking it out. Did it really happen? There's always an infinitesimally small kernel of truth (or potential truth) in all my OC fantasies.

I think to myself, "Rush to check it out. Get rid of the hurt by checking it out. Hurry back to check it out. God, I'll be late for my final exam if I check it out. But I have no choice. Someone could be lying on the road, bloody, close to death." Fantasy is now my only reality. So is my pain.

I've driven five miles farther down the road since the attack's onset. I turn the car around and head back to the scene of the mythical mishap. I return to the spot on the road where I "think" it "might" have occurred. Naturally, nothing is there. No police car and no bloodied body. Relieved, I turn around again to get to my exam on time.

Feeling better, I drive for about twenty seconds and then the lingering thoughts and pain start gnawing away again. Only this time they're even more intense. I think, "Maybe I should have pulled *off* the road and checked the side brush where the injured body was thrown and now lies? Maybe I didn't go *far enough* back on the road and the accident occurred a mile farther back."

The pain of my possibly having hurt someone is now so intense that I have no choice—I really see it this way.

I turn the car around a second time and head an extra mile farther down the road to find the corpse. I drive by quickly. Assured that this time I've gone far enough, I head back to school to take my exam. But I'm not through yet.

"My God," my attack relentlessly continues, "I didn't get *out* of the car to actually *look* on the side of the road!"

So I turn back a third time. I drive to the part of the highway where I think the accident happened. I park the car on the highway's shoulder. I get out and begin rummaging around the brush. (Rapaport, 1990, pp. 21–23)

This man's compulsive checking makes some sense, given what he is thinking. But what he is thinking—that he hit someone on the road without knowing it—is highly implausible. Moreover, the compulsive checking quells obsessional thoughts briefly, but the obsessional thoughts soon return with even more force.

Often the link between the obsession and compulsion is the result of "magical thinking." For example, one young boy who had an obsession about losing his saliva felt compelled to touch his shoulders to his chin whenever he had the obsession (Rapaport, 1990). Similarly, many people with the disorder feel compelled to repeat a behavior, ritual, or thought a certain number of times, as if there was something magical about the specific number of repetitions. Their rituals often become stereotyped and rigid, and they develop obsessions and compulsions about not performing the ritual correctly.

Obsessive-compulsive disorder often begins when the person is young (American Psychiatric Association, 1994; Rasmussen & Eisen, 1990). It tends to be chronic if left untreated. Obsessional thoughts are very distressing to people with this disorder, and engaging in compulsive behaviors can take a great deal of time and even be harmful (for example, washing your hands so often that they bleed). Among people with anxiety disorders, those with obsessive-compulsive disorder are among the most psychologically impaired. Between 1.0% and 2.5% of people develop obsessive-compulsive disorders at some time in their lives (Karno & Golding, 1991; Robins et al., 1984).

Understanding Obsessive-Compulsive Disorder

There is strong evidence that obsessive-compulsive disorder may have biological causes. People with this disorder may have deficiencies in the neurotransmitter serotonin in the areas of the brain that regulate primitive impulses about sex, violence, and cleanliness—impulses that are often the focus of obsessions (Baxter et al., 1992; Rapaport, 1990; Swedo et al., 1992). As a result of poor functioning in this brain system, these primitive impulses may break through to consciousness and motivate the performance of stereotyped behaviors much more often for people with obsessive-compulsive disorder than for those without the disorder.

PET scans of people with obsessive-compulsive disorder show more activity in the areas of the brain involved in this primitive circuit than do people without the disorder (Baxter et al., 1990; Saxena et al., 1998) (see Figure 12-6). In addition, people with the disorder often get some relief from their symptoms when they take drugs that better regulate serotonin; in turn, serotonin plays an important role in the proper functioning of this primitive circuit in the brain (Rapaport, 1991). Finally, patients who do respond to serotonin-enhancing drugs tend to show more reductions in the rate of activity in these areas of the brain than patients who do not respond well to these drugs (Baxter et al., 1992; Swedo et al., 1992).

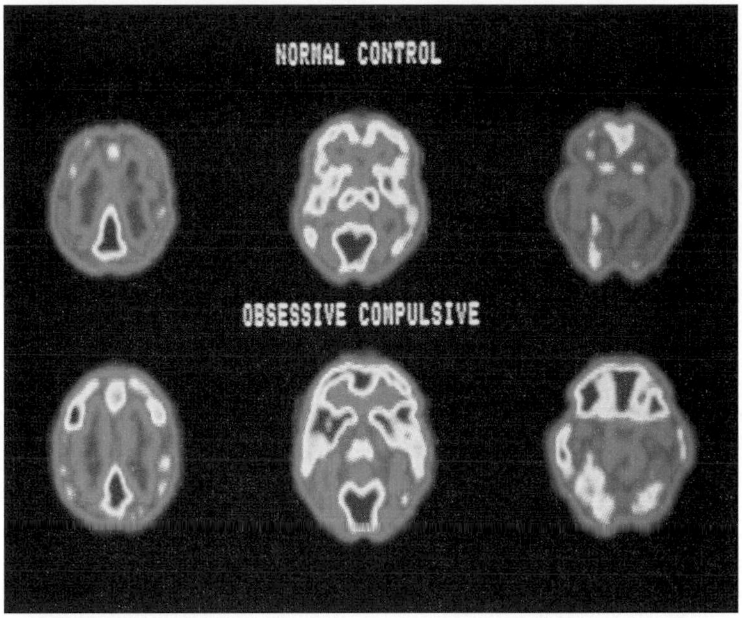

As with panic disorder, however, people may develop a full obsessive-compulsive disorder only if they also have certain cognitive and behavioral vulnerabilities, in addition to a biological vulnerability. Cognitive and behavioral theorists suggest that people with

Figure 12-6

A Normal Brain versus an Obsessive-Compulsive Brain   This PET scan shows the metabolic differences between areas of the brain of a person with obsessive-compulsive disorder and the same areas in the brain of a normal person.

obsessive-compulsive disorder have more trouble "turning off" the intrusive thoughts that all of us have occasionally, because they have a tendency toward rigid, moralistic thinking (Rachman, 1993; Salkovskis et al., 1997). They judge the negative, intrusive thoughts they have as more unacceptable than most people would, and they become more anxious and guilty over having these thoughts. This anxiety then makes it even harder for them to dismiss the thought (Clark & de Silva, 1985). People with obsessive-compulsive disorder may also believe that they *should* be able to control all thoughts, and may have trouble accepting that everyone has horrific thoughts from time to time (Clark & Purdon, 1993; Freeston et al., 1992). They tend to believe that having these thoughts means they are going crazy, or to equate having the thought with actually engaging in the behavior (e.g., "If I'm thinking about hurting my child, I'm as guilty as if I actually did hurt my child"). Of course, this makes them even much more anxious when they have the thoughts, which makes it harder for them to dismiss the thoughts.

Compulsions may develop fortuitously when an obsessional person discovers that some behavior helps to quell the obsession, and anxiety about it, temporarily. This reduction in anxiety reinforces the behavior, and a compulsion is born: Every time the person has the obsession, she or he will feel compelled to engage in the behavior in order to reduce the anxiety.

Again, some of the best evidence in favor of cognitive and behavioral perspectives on obsessive-compulsive disorder is that therapies based on these perspectives are helpful to people with the disorder, as we will discuss in Chapter 13.

In contrast, psychodynamic theories of obsessive-compulsive disorder have not led to successful treatments, although these theories have been very influential in clinical writings and in lay notions of anxiety. Briefly, according to psychodynamic theories, obsessions are unacceptable impulses (hostility, destructiveness, inappropriate sexual urges) that have been repressed and have reappeared in a disguised form. The individual feels that the obsessions are not a part of herself or himself and may commit compulsive acts in order to undo or atone for forbidden impulses. A mother who is obsessed with thoughts of murdering her child may feel compelled to check many times during the night to assure herself that the child is well. Compulsive rituals also serve to keep threatening impulses out of the individual's conscious awareness: A person who is continually busy has little opportunity to think improper thoughts or commit improper actions. According to psychodynamic theory, bringing the unconscious conflict to light and gaining insight into this conflict should cure an obsessive-compulsive disorder. What little research has been done to test this theory, however, suggests that insight-oriented therapy does not cure obsessive-compulsive disorder in most cases.

In sum, biological and psychological factors probably combine in creating many of the anxiety disorders. Many people who develop these disorders probably have a genetic, neurological, or biochemical vulnerability to anxiety. But it may be necessary for them also to have a tendency toward catastrophizing cognitions and to develop maladaptive avoidant behaviors to reduce their anxiety in order for the full syndrome of an anxiety disorder to develop.

Thinking Critically

1. How might a therapist help a person suffering from panic disorder confront his or her tendency to catastrophize distressing bodily symptoms without seeming to dismiss the person's concerns?

2. We noted evidence that evolution has prepared humans to develop phobias of objects that were dangerous to our ancient ancestors, such as spiders and snakes. In a few thousand years, what types of phobias might evolution predispose humans to have?

Is Life Worth Living? (Mood Disorders)

I was a senior in high school when I had my first attack. . . . At first, everything seemed so easy. I raced about like a crazed weasel, bubbling with plans and enthusiasms, immersed in sports, and staying up all night, night after night, out with friends, reading everything that wasn't nailed down, filling manuscript books with poems and fragments of plays, and making expansive, completely unrealistic plans for my future. The world was filled with pleasure and promise; I felt great. Not just great, I felt *really* great. I felt I could do anything, that no task was too difficult. My mind seemed clear, fabulously focused, and able to make intuitive mathematical leaps that had up to that point entirely eluded me. Indeed, they elude me still. At the time, however, not only did everything make perfect sense, but it all began to fit into a marvelous kind of cosmic relatedness. My sense of enchantment with the laws of the natural world caused me to fizz over, and I found myself buttonholing my friends to tell them how beautiful it all was. They were less than transfixed by my insights into the webbings and beauties of the universe, although considerably impressed at how exhausting it was to be around my enthusiastic ramblings: You're talking too fast, Kay. Slow down, Kay. You're wearing me out, Kay. Slow down, Kay. And those times when they didn't actually come out and say it, I still could see it in their eyes: For God's sake, Kay, slow down.

I did, finally slow down. In fact, I came to a grinding halt. . . . The bottom began to fall out of my life and my mind. My thinking, far from being clearer than a crystal, was tortuous. I would read the same passage over and over again only to realize that I had no memory at all for what I had just read. . . . My mind had turned on me: It mocked me for my vapid enthusiasms; it laughed at all my foolish plans; it no longer found anything interesting or enjoyable or worthwhile. It was incapable of concentrated thought and turned time and again to the subject of death: I was going to die, what difference did anything make? Life's run was only a short and meaningless one, why live? I was totally exhausted and could scarcely pull myself out of bed in the mornings. It took me twice as long to walk anywhere as it ordinarily did, and I wore the same clothes over and over again, as it was otherwise too much of an effort to make a decision about what to put on. I dreaded having to talk with people, avoided my friends whenever possible, and sat in the school library in the early mornings and late afternoons, virtually inert, with a dead heart and a brain as cold as clay (Jamison, 1995, pp. 35–38).

The author of this passage is Kay Redfield Jamison, one of the foremost researchers of mood disorders, and a person who suffers from bipolar disorder (also known as manic depression). Jamison describes tremendous emotional highs, known as **mania,** which are characterized by *unlimited energy, agitation, and expansive self-esteem.* She also describes tortuous lows, known as **depression,** which are characterized by *sadness, hopelessness, fatigue, and low self-esteem.*

There are many different types of mood disorders, but they can be divided into two groups. In **depressive disorders,** people have *one or more periods of depression without a history of mania.* In **bipolar disorders,** people *alternate between periods of depression and periods of mania,* usually with a return to normal mood in between the two extremes. Manic episodes without some history of depression are quite uncommon.

Depression

Most of us have periods when we feel sad, lethargic, and uninterested in doing anything. Depression is a normal response to many of life's stresses, especially losses. It is considered abnormal only when it is out of proportion to the event and continues past the point at which most people begin to recover (see Figure 12-7). Depression is a relatively common disorder; about 17% of people experience an episode of severe depression at some time in their lives (Kessler et al., 1994).

Sadness and dejection are the best known emotional symptoms in depression. Equally pervasive, however, is loss of pleasure in life. Activities that used to bring satisfaction seem dull and joyless. Depressed people lose interest in hobbies, recreation, and family activities. Many report that they do not feel pleasure in anything they do.

The cognitive symptoms of depression consist primarily of negative thoughts. Depressed people tend to have low self-esteem, feel inadequate, and blame themselves for their failures. They feel hopeless about the future and doubt that they can do anything to improve their lives. They may contemplate suicide because of this hopelessness. Depressed people also report that they have trouble concentrating and remembering, and that their thinking feels slow and confused.

Motivation is at a low ebb in depression. Depressed people tend to be passive and do not initiate activities. They may sit for hours just staring out the window. They have trouble getting their work done. They don't call friends and often will refuse to go out with friends, saying that they don't have the energy or want to be alone. They often lose all interest in sexual activity.

The physical symptoms of depression include changes in appetite, sleep disturbances, and unrelenting fatigue. Depressed people may not feel like eating

mania a condition characterized by unlimited energy, agitation, and expansive self-esteem

depression a condition characterized by sadness, hopelessness, fatigue, and low self-esteem

depressive disorders disorders in which the person has one or more periods of depression without a history of mania

bipolar disorders disorders in which the person alternates between periods of depression and periods of mania

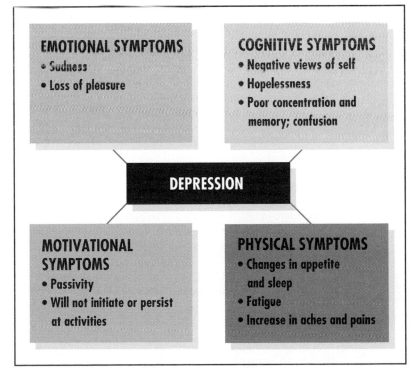

Figure 12-7

The Symptoms of Depression Depression includes emotional, cognitive, motivational, and physical symptoms.

Suicide

Suicide is the ninth leading cause of death in the United States. More than 30,000 people kill themselves each year, which averages to nearly 85 people per day or one person every 17 minutes. In addition, there are approximately 600,000 nonfatal suicide attempts per year (McIntosh, 1991). Internationally, at least 160,000 people die by suicide every year and 2 million others make suicide attempts each year (McIntosh, 1991; World Health Organization, 1992). In truth, these numbers probably underestimate the actual numbers of attempted and completed suicides by two to three times, since many suicide attempts and completions are not reported or are misreported as accidents. As many as 3% of the population contemplates suicide at some time in their lives, and between 5% and 16% report having had suicidal thoughts at some time (Statham et al., 1998).

The overall rate of suicide in the general population has increased slightly over the last 60 years, but the rate among 15- to 24-year-olds has skyrocketed by nearly 300% (Hendin, 1995). Much of this increase has taken place among African American youth. In the last decade, the suicide rate has risen by 50% for African American males and by 40% for African American females between 15 and 24 years of age. In contrast, the rate among Caucasian males between the ages of 15 and 24 has risen 10% in the last decade, and there has been no increase in suicide rates among young Caucasian females. The increase in suicide among African American youth is probably tied, in part, to their perceptions that there are few opportunities open to them and that they face a constant battle to succeed and be accepted for their talents. The increase in *completed* suicide among young adults is also associated with the increased availability of guns. As it becomes easier for young people to acquire guns, the chances that they will use them impulsively to end their lives become greater.

College students are twice as likely to kill themselves as are non-students of the same age. The increased suicide rate among college students is found not only in the United States but in European countries, India, and Japan as well. There are a number of possible reasons for the greater despair among college students: living away from home for the first time and having to cope with new problems; trying to stay at the top academically when the competition is much fiercer than it had been in high school; and loneliness caused by the absence of long-time friends and anxiety about new ones.

One group of researchers was able to conduct a study of people who attempted suicide during a year-long study of 13,673 adults randomly chosen from a community sample. All these adults were interviewed twice, one year apart. An interview was used to determine whether each adult qualified for the diagnosis of some type of psychological disorder. During the year between the two interviews, 40 people in the sample attempted suicide. The researchers randomly chose 40 other people from the rest of the sample who had not attempted suicide to make comparisons with the 40 suicide attempters. The attempters tended to have lower educational levels and were more likely than the nonattempters to be unemployed, separated, or divorced. When the researchers examined the data from the first interview, they found that 53% of the suicide attempters had been diagnosed with major depressive disorders, compared to 6% of the nonattempters (Petronis et al., 1990).

You may be surprised that not everyone who attempts or commits suicide is depressed. As many as half the people with bipolar disorder attempt suicide, and perhaps one in five will complete suicide (Goodwin & Jamison, 1990). It might seem strange that a manic person would attempt suicide, because the symptoms of mania include elation and heightened self-esteem. However, often the predominant feelings of mania are agitation and irritation mixed with despair over having the illness or contemplating falling into depression. Kay Jamison (1995b, pp. 113–114) describes one of her suicide attempts, which occurred when she was in a mixed manic and depressive state and highly agitated:

> In a rage I pulled the bathroom lamp off the wall and felt the violence go through me but not yet out of me. "For Christ's sake," he said, rushing in—and then stopping very quietly. Jesus, I must be crazy, I can see it in his eyes a dreadful mix of concern,

and may lose weight, or they may binge and gain weight. They may sleep very little, or a great deal. They may experience aches and pains more acutely and may worry about their health. In some cultures, including certain Asian cultures, people may experience and report depression primarily in the form of physical aches and pains (Kleinman & Kleinman, 1985).

terror, irritation, resignation, and why me, Lord? "Are you hurt?" he asks. Turning my head with its fast-scanning eyes I see in the mirror blood running down my arms. . . . I bang my head over and over against the door. God, make it stop, I can't stand it, I know I'm insane again. He really cares, I think, but within ten minutes he too is screaming, and his eyes have a wild look from contagious madness, from the lightning adrenaline between the two of us. "I can't leave you like this," but I say a few truly awful things and then go for his throat in a more literal way, and he does leave me, provoked beyond endurance and unable to see the devastation and despair inside. I can't convey it and he can't see it; there's nothing to be done. I can't think, I can't calm this murderous cauldron, my grand ideas of an hour ago seem absurd and pathetic, my life is in ruins, and worse still—ruinous; my body is uninhabitable. It is raging and weeping and full of destruction and wild energy gone amok. In the mirror I see a creature I don't know but must live and share my mind with.

I understand why Jekyll killed himself before Hyde had taken over completely. I took a massive overdose of lithium with no regrets.

A major factor contributing to suicide is drug abuse (Statham et al., 1998). In the study we have been discussing, 33.0% of the attempters were identified as heavy drinkers, compared to 2.5% of the nonattempters. Alcohol makes people more likely to engage in impulsive acts, even self-destructive ones like suicide attempts. Also, people with chronic alcohol problems may have a general tendency toward self-destructive acts and may wreck many of their relationships and their careers, making them feel that they do not have much reason to live.

About 10% of people with schizophrenia commit suicide (Clark, 1995). They may kill themselves to end the torment of hallucinations telling them they are evil or to end the excruciating social isolation they may feel. Most suicide attempts among people with schizophrenia happen not when the people are psychotic but when they are lucid but depressed. The schizophrenics who are most likely to commit suicide are young males who have frequent relapses into psychosis but who had a good educational history and high expectations for themselves before they developed schizophrenia. It seems that these young men cannot face a future that is likely to be so much less than what they envisioned for themselves (Hendin, 1995).

Recent studies suggest that there is a biological predisposition to commit suicide. Twin studies suggest that genetics play a role in suicide (Statham et al., 1998). Many studies have found a link between suicide and low serotonin levels (Goodwin & Jamison, 1990; Malone & Mann, 1997). Low serotonin levels are linked with suicidality even among people who are not depressed, suggesting that the connection between serotonin and suicidality is not due entirely to a common connection to depression. Serotonin may generally be linked to impulsive and aggressive behavior (Linnoila & Virkkunen, 1992). Low serotonin levels are most strongly associated with impulsive and violent suicides. Although these pieces of evidence do not prove that low serotonin levels cause suicidal behavior, they suggest that people with low serotonin levels may be at high risk for impulsive and violent behavior that sometimes results in suicide.

What should you do if you suspect that a friend or family member is suicidal? First, take the situation seriously. Although most people who express suicidal thoughts do not go on to attempt suicide, most people who do commit suicide have communicated their suicidal intentions to friends or family members before attempting suicide (Shneidman, 1976). The most important thing to do if you suspect that someone is suicidal is get help from mental health professionals as soon as you can, by calling a suicide hotline to ask for help in dealing with the person, calling the local county mental health association, or asking a psychologist or psychiatrist at your local health clinic for advice. Even seasoned mental health professionals can find helping a person who is suicidal challenging and unnerving, so you should not expect to be able to deal with a person's suicidality on your own.

Women are twice as likely as men to develop depression (Nolen-Hoeksema, 1990). This seems to be true across many cultures, suggesting that women's vulnerability to depression may have a biological basis. But women also have lower status compared to men in most cultures, and their lack of power may contribute to a sense of helplessness and a vulnerability to depression.

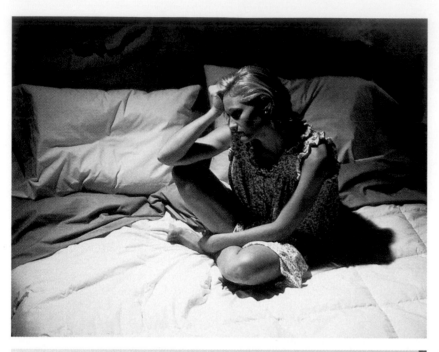

Depressed people may have insomnia and be chronically tired and unmotivated.

Clearly, depression can be a debilitating disorder. Unfortunately, severe depressions can also be long-lasting. On average, a severe episode of depression lasts between 6 months and a year, and half of all people who become depressed go on to experience multiple episodes of depression during their lives if they are not properly treated (Judd et al., 1998; Keller et al., 1982).

Bipolar Disorder

The majority of depressions occur without episodes of mania. But about 1 or 2 people in 100 will experience both depression and mania. They can be diagnosed with bipolar disorder, commonly known as manic depression (Kessler et al., 1994).

People experiencing manic episodes behave in a way that appears, on the surface, to be the opposite of depression. During mild manic episodes they are energetic, enthusiastic, and full of self-confidence. They talk continually, rush from one activity to another with little need for sleep, and make grandiose plans, paying little attention to their practicality. Kay Redfield Jamison writes of spending thousands of dollars on impulse purchases of things she "just had to have," such as 12 snakebite kits. Unlike the kind of joyful exuberance that characterizes normal elation, manic behavior has a driven quality and is often expressed as hostility more than as elation.

People experiencing severe manic episodes behave somewhat like the popular concept of a "raving maniac." They are extremely excited and constantly active. They may pace about, sing, shout, or pound the walls for hours. They are angered by attempts to interfere with their activities, and may become abusive. Impulses (including sexual ones) are immediately expressed in actions or words. These individuals are confused and disoriented, and may experience delusions of great wealth, accomplishment, or power.

For instance, Tony was a middle-aged man, quite ragged in appearance, who was brought to the hospital by his family because he was "out of control" and "going crazy." Tony had been a sensible, rather subdued man until about a month ago, when his behavior changed dramatically. A bus driver in Philadelphia, Tony had taken to stopping his bus in busy traffic, turning to his passengers, and breaking into song. When asked about these incidents, Tony said that he had decided he wanted to be a nightclub singer and he was glad he had been fired from his bus-driving job because it gave him more time to devote to his singing career. By all accounts, Tony actually had a terrible singing voice. Two weeks before coming to the hospital, he had traveled to Las Vegas, where he tried to meet with managers of several casinos to convince them he should have a headline show at their casino. He was arrested for making threatening remarks when he was thrown out of the casinos. Tony then decided he should open his own nightclub in Philadelphia so that he could sing every night. He cashed out the family savings account and put the house up for sale to finance his plan.

Usually, people who experience manic episodes like Tony's will eventually fall into a depressive episode. The depressions are similar to what we have already described. Manic-depressive cycles almost always recur if the individual is untreated.

Cultures do not seem to differ greatly in the prevalence of bipolar disorder, but they may differ in the manifestation of the disorder. This is illustrated in a fascinating study of the prevalence of mood disorders among the Old Order Amish (Egeland, Hostetter, & Eshleman, 1983). The Amish have strict rules against acting in prideful ways that call attention to oneself. Thus, the behaviors that indicate grandiosity and inflated self-esteem in Amish society can seem like normal behaviors to people from the rest of North American society. For example, an Amish person who tells others at length about a recent accomplishment or who dresses in fine modern clothes is violating the norms of his or her society to such a degree that these behaviors might be signs of grandiosity. Of course, we would not diagnose mania in an Amish person simply on the basis of isolated behaviors such as these. The diagnosis would only be made if the person also seemed to fit all the other criteria for a manic episode. But this study of the Amish provides striking examples of how social factors can influence the manifestation of a disorder.

A manic episode involves feelings of elation and energy far beyond what most people ever experience.

Understanding Mood Disorders

As with the anxiety disorders, a combined biological and psychological model may best explain the mood disorders. Most people who develop depression, and particularly a bipolar disorder, may have a biological vulnerability to these disorders. But the experience of certain types of life events and the tendency to think in negative ways also clearly increase people's vulnerability to develop the disorders.

The Biological Perspective   A tendency to develop the mood disorders, particularly bipolar disorder, appears to be inherited. Family history studies of people with bipolar disorder find that their first-degree relatives (that is, parents, children, and siblings) have at least two to three times higher rates of both bipolar disorder and depressive disorders than relatives of people without bipolar disorder (MacKinnon, Jamison, & DePaulo, 1997). Twin studies have also consistently suggested that bipolar disorder has a genetic component (Faraone, Kremen, & Tsuang, 1990).

The evidence regarding the heritability of unipolar depression is less consistent. Family history studies do find higher rates of unipolar depression in the first-degree relatives of people with unipolar depression than among control groups (Gershon, 1990; Keller & Baker, 1991). Interestingly, relatives of depressed people do not tend to have any greater risk for bipolar disorder than relatives of people with no mood disorder. This suggests that bipolar disorder has a different genetic basis from that of unipolar depression. Twin studies have provided mixed evidence concerning the heritability of unipolar depression. Some studies find evidence of heritability (Kendler et al., 1992), but other studies do not (McGuffin et al., 1991; Torgersen, 1986).

The specific role of genetic factors in the mood disorders is unclear. However, it seems likely that a biochemical abnormality is involved. Two neurotransmitters that

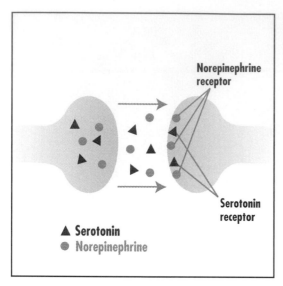

Figure 12-8

Neurotransmission in Depression   The neuronal receptors for norepinephrine and serotonin may not work efficiently in depressed people, so that norepinephrine and serotonin released from one neuron cannot bind to receptor sites on other neurons.

are believed to play an important role in mood disorders are norepinephrine and serotonin. (We noted that serotonin is implicated in anxiety disorders as well. Anxiety and depression often occur together, and one reason may be that both disorders involve serotonin abnormalities.)

Recall from Chapter 2 that neurotransmitters and their receptors interact like locks and keys (see Figure 12-8). Each neurotransmitter will fit into a particular type of receptor on the neuronal membrane. If there is the wrong number of receptors for a given type of neurotransmitter, or if the receptors for that neurotransmitter are too sensitive or not sensitive enough, the neurons do not efficiently use the neurotransmitter that is available in the synapse. Several studies suggest that people with depression or bipolar disorder may have abnormalities in the number and sensitivity of receptor sites for serotonin and norepinephrine particularly in areas of the brain that are involved in the regulation of emotion, such as the hypothalamus (e.g., Malone & Mann, 1993; McBride et al., 1994). In major depressive disorder, receptors for serotonin and norepinephrine appear to be too few or insensitive. In bipolar disorder, the picture is less clear, but it is likely that receptors for these neurotransmitters undergo poorly timed changes in sensitivity that are correlated with mood changes (Goodwin & Jamison, 1990).

The Cognitive Perspective   Cognitive theories have focused primarily on depression. According to these theories, people become depressed because they tend to interpret the events in their lives in pessimistic, hopeless ways (Abramson, Metalsky, & Alloy, 1989; Beck et al., 1979; Peterson & Seligman, 1984). One of the most influential cognitive theorists, Aaron Beck, grouped the negative thoughts of depressed people into three categories, which he called the *cognitive triad:* negative thoughts about the self, about present experiences, and about the future. Negative thoughts about the self include beliefs that one is worthless and inadequate. Any present misfortune is blamed on these personal inadequacies or defects. A negative view of the future is one of hopelessness. Depressed people believe that their inadequacies and defects will prevent them from ever improving their situation.

Beck proposes that the depressed person's negative self-beliefs ("I am worthless," "I can't do anything right," "I am unlovable") are formed during childhood or adolescence through such experiences as loss of a parent, social rejection by peers, criticism by parents or teachers, or a series of tragedies. These negative beliefs are activated whenever a new situation resembles in some way, perhaps only remotely, the conditions in which the beliefs were learned, and depression may result. Moreover, according to Beck, depressed people make systematic errors in thinking that lead them to misperceive reality in a way that contributes to their negative self-beliefs. Some of these errors are listed in Table 12-4.

Another cognitive approach to depression, which focuses on the kinds of attributions or causal explanations that people make when bad things happen, was discussed in Chapter 11. This theory proposes that people who characteristically attribute negative events to causes that are internal ("it's my fault"), are stable over time ("it's going to last forever"), and affect many areas of their lives ("it will affect everything I do") are more prone to depression than individuals who have a less pessimistic attributional style (Abramson, Metalsky, & Alloy, 1989; Peterson & Seligman, 1984).

Critics of cognitive theories of depression have argued that these negative cognitions are symptoms or consequences of depression, rather than causes. While it is clear that depressed people do have negative cognitions, there has been less evidence that negative cognitive styles precede and cause depressive episodes (see Haaga,

Table 12-4

Cognitive Distortions in Depression   According to Beck's theory, these are the principal errors in thinking that characterize depressed individuals.

Overgeneralization	Drawing a sweeping conclusion on the basis of a single event. For example, a student concludes from his poor performance in one class on a particular day that he is inept and stupid.
Selective Abstraction	Focusing on an insignificant detail while ignoring the more important features of a situation. For example, from a conversation in which her boss praises her overall job performance, a secretary remembers the only comment that could be construed as mildly critical.
Magnification and Minimization	Magnifying small bad events and minimizing major good events in evaluating performance. For example, a woman gets a small dent in her car fender and views it as a catastrophe (magnification), while the fact that she gave an excellent presentation in class does nothing to raise her self-esteem (minimization).
Personalization	Incorrectly assuming responsibility for bad events in the world. For example, when rain dampens spirits at an outdoor buffet, the host blames himself rather than the weather.
Arbitrary Inference	Drawing a conclusion when there is little evidence to support it. For example, a man concludes from his wife's sad expression that she is disappointed in him; if he had checked out the situation, he would have discovered that she was distressed by a friend's illness.

Dyck, & Ernst, 1991). Also, there is some evidence that depressed people are not the ones whose thinking is distorted: When asked to make judgments about how much control they have over situations that are actually uncontrollable, depressed people are quite accurate. In contrast, nondepressed people greatly overestimate the amount of control they have, especially over positive events (Alloy & Abramson, 1979).

On the other hand, a recent study that followed students through their college careers has provided strong evidence that negative cognitive styles in fact do precede and predict depression. Researchers measured the students' tendencies toward negative thinking patterns early in their first year of college then followed them for the next few years. Students who evidenced a negative cognitive triad or a pessimistic attributional style were much more likely to develop episodes of depression during their college years than those who did not, even if they had never been depressed before college (Alloy & Abramson, 1999).

The Psychodynamic Perspective Psychodynamic theories interpret depression as a reaction to loss (see Figure 12-9). Whatever the nature of the loss (rejection by a loved one, being fired from a job), the depressed person reacts to it intensely because

A recent study of college students found that those who tended to have negative views of the world were more likely to develop depression during their college years.

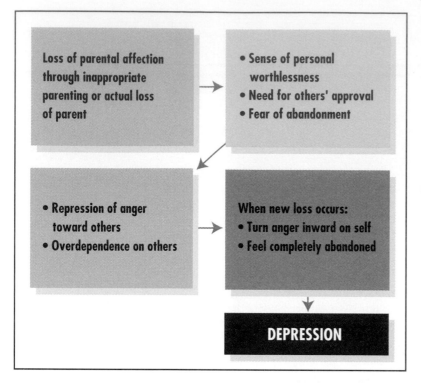

Figure 12-9

Psychodynamic Theories of Depression   Psychodynamic theories suggest that depressed people did not receive enough parental affection in childhood and that subsequent losses in adulthood trigger feelings of dejection and worthlessness.

the current situation brings back all the fears of an earlier loss that occurred in childhood—the loss of parental affection. The individual's needs for affection and care were not satisfied in childhood. A loss in later life causes the individual to regress to his or her helpless, dependent state at the time that the original loss occurred. Part of the depressed person's behavior, therefore, represents a cry for love—a display of helplessness and an appeal for affection and security (Bibring, 1951; Blatt, 1974).

Reaction to loss is complicated by angry feelings toward the deserting person. An underlying assumption of psychodynamic theories is that people who are prone to depression have learned to repress their hostile feelings because they are afraid of alienating those on whom they depend for support. When things go wrong, they turn their anger inward and blame themselves. For example, a woman may feel extremely hostile toward the employer who fired her. But because her anger arouses anxiety, she internalizes her feelings: She is not angry; rather, others are angry at her. She assumes that the employer had a reason for rejecting her: She is incompetent and worthless.

Psychodynamic theories suggest that the depressed person's low self-esteem and feelings of worthlessness stem from a childlike need for parental approval. A small child's self-esteem depends on the approval and affection of parents. But as a person matures, feelings of worth also should be derived from the individual's sense of his or her own accomplishments and effectiveness. The self-esteem of a person who is prone to depression depends primarily on external sources: the approval and support of others. When these supports fail, the individual may be thrown into depression.

In sum, psychodynamic theories of depression focus on loss, overdependence on external approval, and internalization of anger. They seem to provide a reasonable explanation for some of the behaviors of depressed individuals, but they are difficult to prove or to refute.

Thinking Critically

1. Why might some people, when faced with a stressful event, become highly anxious while other people, faced with the same event, become highly depressed?

2. Is it possible that some people might be able to put the symptoms of mania to good use for themselves? What would determine whether these symptoms were useful or destructive?

What Is Real? (Schizophrenia)

schizophrenia a disorder in which the person loses touch with reality and often cannot function in daily life

Schizophrenia is one of the most severe forms of psychological disorder. People with **schizophrenia** *lose touch with reality and often cannot function in daily life.* As mentioned at the beginning of this chapter, the loss of reality testing is often referred to as *psychosis.* The symptoms of schizophrenia are complex and vary from one person

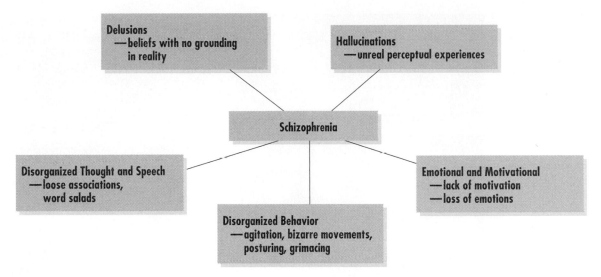

Figure 12-10

The Symptoms of Schizophrenia   The symptoms of schizophrenia vary from one person to another but generally fall into these five groups.

to another. They generally fall into five groups, however: *delusions, hallucinations, disorganized thought and speech, disorganized behavior,* and the *emotional and motivational symptoms of schizophrenia* (see Figure 12-10).

Delusions are *beliefs with little or no grounding in reality.* The most common delusions are beliefs that external forces are trying to control one's thoughts and actions—that one's thoughts are being broadcast on the evening news, that strange thoughts are being inserted into one's head, that feelings are actions are being imposed by some external force. Also frequent are beliefs that certain people or certain groups are threatening or plotting against you, known as delusions of persecution. Grandiose delusions involve beliefs that one is powerful and important, such as the belief that one is the Messiah.

delusion a belief with little or no grounding in reality

Hallucinations are *perceptual experiences that are unreal*—seeing, hearing, feeling, or smelling things that are not there. Auditory hallucinations (usually voices telling the person what to do or commenting on his or her actions) are the most common. These hallucinations are often frightening, even terrifying:

hallucination a perceptual experience that is unreal

> At one point, I would look at my coworkers and their faces would become distorted. Their teeth looked like fangs ready to devour me. Most of the time I couldn't trust myself to look at anyone for fear of being swallowed. I had no respite from the illness. Even when I tried to sleep, the demons would keep me awake, and at times I would roam the house searching for them. I was being consumed on all sides whether I was awake or asleep. I felt I was being consumed by demons. (Long, 1995–1996)

The strange perceptual experiences of people with schizophrenia may also include feeling that their bodies have changed (that their hands have grown smaller or larger, their legs are overly extended, their eyes are dislocated in their faces). Some people fail to recognize themselves in a mirror, or see their reflection as a triple image. The whole world may seem different—voices are louder, colors more intense. They may feel barraged by sensations and unable to determine what is real and what is unreal.

Both the process and the content of thinking and speech may be disturbed. People with schizophrenia may see associations between events that no one else sees, as in the following passage:

> If things turn by rotation of agriculture or levels in regards and timed to everything; I am referring to a previous document when I made some remarks that were facts also tested

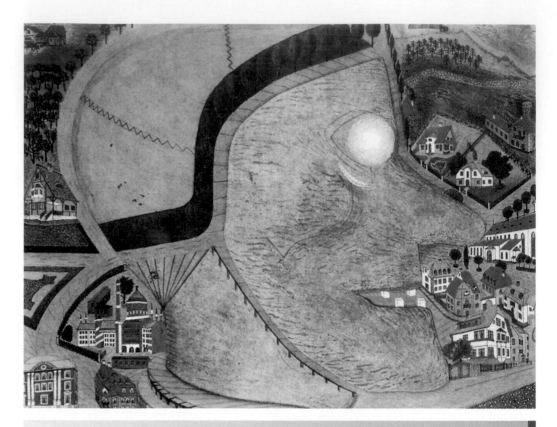

German psychiatrist Hans Privizhorn is responsible for the most extensive collection of artwork by mental patients available. The painting from the collection, by August Neter, illustrates the hallucinations and paranoid fantasies from which many schizophrenic patients suffer.

and there is another that concerns my daughter she has a lobed bottom right ear, her name being Mary Lou. Much of abstraction has been left unsaid and undone in these productmilk syrup, and others, due to economics, differentials, subsidies, bankruptcy, tools, buildings, bonds, national stocks, foundation craps, weather, trades, government in levels of breakages and fuses in electronics too all formerly states not necessarily factuated. (Maher, 1966, p. 395)

By themselves, the words and phrases make sense, but they are meaningless in relation to each other. The juxtaposition of unrelated words and phrases and the idiosyncratic word associations (sometimes called a *word salad*) are characteristic of the writing and speaking of people with schizophrenia. They may make associations between words that are based on the sounds of the words rather than their content; these are known as *clang associations*. For example, in response to the question, "Is that your dog?" a person with schizophrenia might say, "Dog. Dog is Spog. Frog. Leap. Heap, steep, creep, deep, gotta go beep."

The disorganized behavior of people with schizophrenia sometimes frightens others. People with schizophrenia may engage in bizarre activities, continuously flapping their hand, suddenly shouting and running down the street, grimacing or adopting strange facial expressions. They may become very agitated and move about in continual activity. Or they may become totally unresponsive and immobile, adopting unusual poses and maintaining them for long periods. For example, a person may stand like a statue with one foot extended and maintain this state for hours.

Finally, people with schizophrenia experience a set of emotional and motivational symptoms that are often called the *negative symptoms* of schizophrenia because they represent losses or deficits rather than the presence of strange symptoms.

Emotionally, people with schizophrenia may appear completely flat—they show no emotional reactions to events, they may have no emotional tone in their voices, and they may not make eye contact with anyone. People with schizophrenia may also lose the motivation to do almost anything, even feed and care for themselves. They may sit around doing nothing all day. They may withdraw from others completely.

What must it be like to have this disorder? The following account by a woman with schizophrenia who later recovered and became a psychiatrist gives some sense of the experience of schizophrenia. Along with these descriptions of her thoughts and emotions, drawn from memory and a diary, is an excerpt from her medical records:

> The helicopters. Oh no, not the helicopters. Have come to tear the feathers out of my frontal lobes. Help me, nurse, help me, can't you hear them? Gotta get back into my body to save it. Am so far away. Out of reach of the neural connections. The doctor is thinking I would make good glue. He is a witch doctor. He is sending radio messages to the helicopters to help them find me. Big pieces are cracking off the edge of my consciousness I will never be back. The universe disappears with one slight wave of my hand.
>
> A nurse observed in my chart:
>
> *Date. patient acting out in response to voices, i.e., posturing, crying out. States she's frightened, refused to undress for sleep for fear of needing to get out of room quickly . . . was found standing in one place for long periods of time, eyes wide open, staring . . . patient standing in room facing wall, arms outstretched to wall. . . .*
>
> "Would you like to be made into hotdog meat?" Ah, the voices. Where have they been? I must be on track again.
>
> "Hotdogs for lunch!"
>
> My head splits down the middle, brains falling out all over the floor, and I put out an awkward hand to catch them. They slip right through my metal fingers. Do they put brain meat in hotdogs?
>
> "You can put down your hand Carol. You don't have to hold it there." Had the nurse said that or had I said it? Or had the voices said it? Or was it a slice from another Dimension? Hand back to my side. Try to think straight. There is a logical way out of this maze. Just don't forget your thoughts. Don't forget. (North, 1987, pp. 282–284)

Understanding Schizophrenia

Schizophrenia occurs in all cultures, even those that are remote from the stresses of industrialized civilization, and appears to have plagued humanity for at least 200 years. The disorder affects about 1% of the population, occurs equally in men and women, and usually appears in late adolescence or early adulthood. Sometimes schizophrenia develops slowly, as a gradual process of increasing seclusiveness and inappropriate behavior. Sometimes the onset of schizophrenia is sudden, marked by intense confusion and emotional turmoil. Such acute cases are usually precipitated by a period of stress in individuals whose lives have tended toward isolation, self-preoccupation, and feelings of insecurity.

Schizophrenia probably has strong biological roots, but environmental stress may push people with a vulnerability to schizophrenia into more severe forms of the disorder or new episodes of acute schizophrenia.

The Biological Perspective   Family studies show that there is a hereditary predisposition toward developing schizophrenia; relatives of people with schizophrenia are more likely to develop the disorder than people from families free of schizophrenia (Gottesman, 1991). Figure 12-11 shows how likely an individual is to develop schizophrenia as a function of how closely he or she is genetically related to a person diagnosed with schizophrenia. Note that an identical twin of a person with schizophrenia is 3 times as likely as a fraternal twin and 46 times as likely as an unrelated person to develop the disorder. However, fewer than half of the identical twins of people with schizophrenia develop the disorder themselves, even though they share the same genes. This fact demonstrates the importance of nongenetic variables.

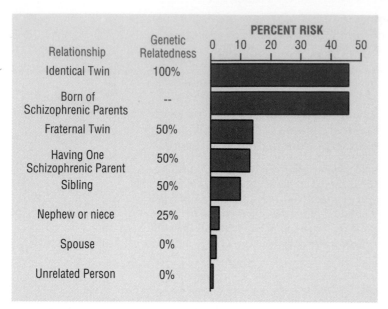

Figure 12-11

Risks of Developing Schizophrenia   People's risk of developing schizophrenia depends on their genetic closeness to a relative with schizophrenia. (After Gottesman, 1991)

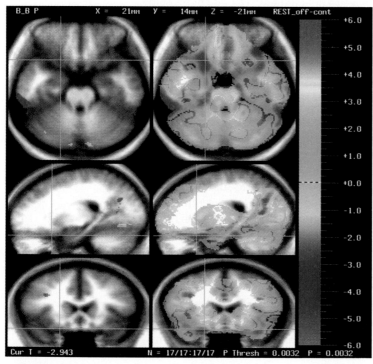

Figure 12-12

Lower Activity in the Prefrontal Cortex in Schizophrenia   This neuroimaging scan shows lower levels of activity in the frontal areas of the brain (as indicated in blue) in schizophrenic patients compared to healthy people.

How do the genetic abnormalities that predispose an individual to schizophrenia affect the brain? Current research focuses on two areas: *brain structure* and *biochemistry*. Two types of structural deficits have been found in the brains of people with schizophrenia. First, the prefrontal cortex is smaller and shows less activity in some people with schizophrenia compared to people without schizophrenia (Andreason et al., 1997; Berman et al., 1992; Buchsbaum et al., 1992; Gur et al., 1998) (see Figure 12-12). The prefrontal cortex is the single largest brain region in human beings, constituting nearly 30% of the total cortex. It has connections to all other cortical regions, as well as to the limbic system, which is involved in emotion and cognition, and the basal ganglia, which is involved in motor movement. The prefrontal cortex is important in language, emotional expression, planning and producing new ideas, and social interactions. Thus, it seems logical that people with a prefrontal cortex that is unusually small or inactive would show a wide range of deficits in cognition, emotion, and social interaction, as people with schizophrenia do.

Second, people with schizophrenia have enlarged ventricles (Andreason et al., 1990; Zorilla et al., 1998). The ventricles are fluid-filled spaces in the brain. Enlarged ventricles suggest atrophy or deterioration in other brain tissue. The specific areas of the brain that have deteriorated to create ventricular enlargement could lead to different manifestations of schizophrenia (Breier et al., 1992).

While biochemical theories of the mood and anxiety disorders center on norepinephrine and serotonin, the culprit in schizophrenia is believed to be dopamine. Early dopamine theories of schizophrenia held that the disorder was the result of too much dopamine present in key areas of the brain. This theory is now considered too simple. The most recent theories suggest that there is a complicated imbalance in levels of dopamine in different areas of the brain (Davis et al., 1991). First, there may be excess dopamine activity in the mesolimbic system, a subcortical part of the brain that is involved in cognition and emotion. This might produce to the positive symptoms of schizophrenia—the hallucinations, delusions, and thought disorder. On the other hand, there may be unusually low dopamine activity in the prefrontal area of the brain, which is involved in attention, motivation, and in organization of behavior. Low dopamine activity in the prefrontal area may lead to the negative symptoms of schizophrenia—lack of motivation, inability to care for oneself in daily activities, and blunting of affect.

The Social and Psychological Perspectives
Although it is clear that stressful events cannot cause someone to develop the full syndrome of schizophrenia, psychosocial factors may play an important role in determining the eventual severity of the disorder in people with a biological vulnerability and in triggering new episodes of schizophrenia.

The particular kind of stress that has received most attention in recent studies is family-related stress. Members of families that are high in *expressed emotion* are overinvolved with each other, are overprotective of their disturbed family member, and voice self-sacrificing attitudes toward their disturbed family member, while at the same time

The odds of all four of a set of identical quadruplets being diagnosed as schizophrenic are 1 in 2 billion—yet these quadruplets, the Genain sisters, all suffer from schizophrenia and have been hospitalized at various times since high school.

being critical, hostile, and resentful of their disturbed family member (Brown, Birley, & Wing, 1972; Vaughn & Leff, 1976). People with schizophrenia whose families are high in expressed emotion are three to four times more likely to suffer a relapse than those whose families are low in expressed emotion (Butzlaff & Hooley, 1998). Being in a high-expressed-emotion family may create stresses for the person with schizophrenia that overwhelm his or her ability to cope and thus trigger new episodes of psychosis.

Critics of the literature on expressed emotion argue that the hostility and intrusiveness observed in some families of people with schizophrenia might be the result of the symptoms exhibited by the person with schizophrenia, rather than a contributor to relapse (Parker, Johnston, & Hayward, 1988). Although families are often forgiving of the positive symptoms of schizophrenia (hallucinations, delusions, thought disturbances) because they view them as uncontrollable, they can be unforgiving of the negative symptoms (lack of motivation, blunted affect), viewing them as controllable (Brewin et al., 1991; Hooley et al., 1987). People with schizophrenia who have more of these symptoms may elicit more negative expressed emotion from their families, and they may be especially prone to relapse.

Another alternative explanation for the link between family expressed emotion and relapse comes from evidence that family members who are particularly high on expressed emotion are themselves more likely to have some form of mental disorder (Goldstein et al., 1992). Thus, it may be that people with schizophrenia have high rates of relapse because they have a greater risk of mental disorder, as evidenced by the presence of mental disorder in their family members, rather than because their family members are high in expressed emotion. Perhaps the best evidence that expressed emotion actually influences relapse in schizophrenic patients is that interventions that reduce expressed emotion tend to reduce the relapse rate in schizophrenic family members.

---

1. People are often very fearful when they encounter a person with schizophrenia. Why do you think this happens?

2. How could a family high on expressed emotion be helped to change their interactions without feeling blamed for creating their schizophrenic member's problems?

Thinking Critically

Who Are You? (Personality Disorders)

personality disorders disorders in which personality traits become so inflexible and maladaptive that they significantly impair the individual's ability to function

Personality disorders are long-standing patterns of maladaptive behavior. *Personality traits* are enduring ways of perceiving or relating to the environment and thinking about oneself. *When personality traits become so inflexible and maladaptive that they significantly impair the individual's ability to function,* they are called **personality disorders.** Personality disorders constitute immature and inappropriate ways of coping with stress or solving problems. They are usually evident by early adolescence and may continue throughout adult life.

Unlike people with mood or anxiety disorders, which also involve maladaptive behavior, people who have personality disorders often do not feel upset or anxious and may not be motivated to change their behavior. They do not lose contact with reality or display marked disorganization of behavior, unlike individuals suffering from schizophrenia.

DSM-IV lists a number of personality disorders (see Table 12-5). For example, someone who has a *narcissistic personality disorder* is described as having an inflated sense of self-importance, being preoccupied with fantasies of success, constantly seeking admiration and attention, and being insensitive to the needs of others and often exploiting them. *Dependent personality disorders* are characterized by a passive orientation to life, an inability to make decisions or accept responsibility, a tendency to be self-deprecating, and a need for continual support from others.

Most of the personality disorders listed in DSM-IV have not been the subject of much empirical research. The characteristics of the various personality disorders overlap, so that agreement in classifying individuals is poor. Moreover, it is even more difficult to say when a person's behavior is simply different from other people's behaviors and when the behavior is so severe that it warrants a diagnosis. The personality disorder that has been studied the most and is the most reliably diagnosed is the antisocial personality (formerly called *psychopathic personality* or *sociopathy*).

Antisocial Personality Disorder

antisocial personality disorder a disorder diagnosed in people who have little sense of responsibility, morality, or concern for others

People who have **antisocial personality disorder** seem to have *little sense of responsibility, morality, or concern for others.* Their behavior is determined almost entirely

Table 12-5

Types of Personality Disorders   The DSM-IV recognizes several different personality disorders.

Diagnosis	Description
Antisocial Personality Disorder	Impulsive, callous behavior based on disregard for others and lack of respect for social norms.
Borderline Personality Disorder	Chronic instability of mood, relationships, and self-concept; self-destructive impulsiveness.
Histrionic Personality Disorder	Chronic intense need for attention and approval sought by dramatic behavior, seductiveness, and dependence.
Narcissistic Personality Disorder	Frequent grandiosity and obliviousness to others' needs; exploitative behavior; arrogance.
Paranoid Personality Disorder	Chronic and pervasive mistrust of others that is unwarranted.
Schizoid Personality Disorder	Chronic lack of interest in interpersonal relationships; emotional coldness.
Schizotypal Personality Disorder	Chronically inhibited or inappropriate emotional and social behavior; aberrant cognitions; disorganized speech.
Avoidant Personality Disorder	Avoidance of social interactions and restrictiveness in interactions due to chronic worry over being criticized.
Dependent Personality Disorder	Pervasive selflessness, need to be cared for, and fear of rejection.
Obsessive-Compulsive Personality Disorder	Pervasive rigidity in activities and relationships; extreme perfectionism.

by their own needs. In other words, they lack a conscience. Whereas the average person realizes at an early age that some restrictions are placed on behavior and that pleasures must sometimes be postponed in consideration of the needs of others, individuals who have antisocial personalities seldom consider any desires except their own. They behave impulsively, seek immediate gratification of their needs, and cannot tolerate frustration.

The term *antisocial personality* is somewhat misleading, because these characteristics do not describe most people who commit antisocial acts. Antisocial behavior results from a number of causes, including membership in a delinquent gang or a criminal subculture, the need for attention and status, loss of contact with reality, and inability to control impulses. Most juvenile delinquents and adult criminals do have some concern for others (for family or gang members) and some code of moral conduct ("you don't betray a friend"). In contrast, antisocial personalities have little feeling for anyone except themselves and seem to experience little guilt or remorse, regardless of how much suffering their behavior may cause others. Other characteristics of the antisocial personality (*sociopath*, for short) include a great facility for lying, a need for thrills and excitement with little concern for possible injury, and inability to alter behavior as a consequence of punishment. Such individuals are often attractive, intelligent, charming people who are quite facile in manipulating others—in other words, good

Gary Gilmore, who was convicted of a brutal murder, probably suffered from antisocial personality disorder.

con artists. Their façade of competence and sincerity wins them promising jobs, but they have little staying power. Their restlessness and impulsiveness soon lead them into an escapade that reveals their true nature; they accumulate debts, desert their families, squander company money, or commit crimes. When they are caught, their declarations of repentance are so convincing that they often escape punishment and are given another chance. But people with antisocial personality disorder seldom live up to these declarations; what they say has little relationship to what they feel or do.

Understanding Antisocial Personality Disorder

What factors contribute to the development of the antisocial personality? Current research focuses on biological determinants, the quality of the parent–child relationship, and thinking styles that promote antisocial behaviors.

Biological Factors   Genes seem to play a role in the development of antisocial personality. Twin studies show that if one identical twin has antisocial personality characteristics, the other twin also shows these characteristics about 50% of the time; in contrast, among fraternal twins the concordance rate for antisocial personality is only about 20% (Carey & Goldman, 1997; Rutter et al., 1990). Adoption studies find that the criminal records of adopted sons are more similar to the records of their biological fathers than to those of their adoptive fathers (Cloninger & Gottesman, 1987; Crow, 1983; Mednick et al., 1987).

Many investigators have argued that individuals with antisocial personality disorder have low levels of arousability, which lead them to seek stimulation and sensation through impulsive and dangerous acts (Raine, 1997). For example, one study compared two groups of adolescent male delinquents selected from the detention unit of a juvenile court. One group had been diagnosed as having antisocial personality disorders; the other had been diagnosed as having adjustment reactions to negative life events. The experimenters measured galvanic skin response (GSR) under stress. Dummy electrodes were attached to each participant's leg, and he was told that in 10 minutes he would be given a very strong but not harmful shock. A large clock was visible so that the participant knew precisely when the shock was supposed to occur. No shock was actually administered. The two groups showed no difference in GSR measures during periods of rest or in response to auditory or visual stimulation. However, during the 10 minutes of shock anticipation, the group with adjustment reactions showed significantly more tension than the antisocial group. At the moment when the clock indicated that the shock was due, most of the group with adjustment reactions showed GSR responses indicating a sharp increase in anxiety. None of the antisocial participants showed this reaction (Lippert & Senter, 1966). Low arousability in response to anxiety-provoking stimuli may also make it more difficult for people with antisocial personality disorder to learn from the punishments they do receive because they will not experience punishment to be as aversive as most people do, and they will not be anxious in anticipation of the punishment.

Social Factors   Although children who develop antisocial personalities may have some biological predisposition to this disorder, studies suggest that they are unlikely to develop it unless they are also exposed to environments that promote antisocial behavior (Dishion & Patterson, 1997). The parents of children with the disorder often appear to be simultaneously neglectful and hostile toward their children. The children are frequently unsupervised for long periods. The parents often are not involved in the children's everyday life, not knowing where they are or who their friends are. But when these parents do interact with their children, these interactions are often characterized by hostility, physical violence, and ridicule (Patterson, DeBaryshe, & Ramsey, 1989). This description does not fit all parents of children who develop antisocial personality, but parental noninvolvement and hostility are two good predictors of children's vulnerability to the disorder.

The biological factors and family factors that contribute to antisocial personality may often coincide. Children who develop the disorder often suffer neuropsychological problems that are the result of maternal drug use, poor prenatal nutrition, prenatal and postnatal exposure to toxic agents, child abuse, birth complications, and low birth weight (Moffitt, 1993). Children with these neuropsychological problems are more irritable, impulsive, awkward, overreactive, and inattentive, and learn more slowly than their peers. This makes them difficult for parents to care for, and they are at increased risk for maltreatment and neglect. In turn, the parents of these children are more likely to be teenagers or to have psychological problems of their own that contribute to ineffective or harsh or inconsistent parenting. Thus, these children may carry a biological predisposition to disruptive, antisocial behaviors and experience parenting that contributes to these behaviors. In a study of 536 boys, Moffitt (1990) found that those who had both neuropsychological deficits and adverse home environments scored four times higher on an aggression scale than those with neither neuropsychological deficits nor adverse home environments.

Harsh and inconsistent parenting may contribute to antisocial personality disorder.

Personality Factors   Children who develop antisocial tendencies tend to process information about social interactions in ways that promote aggressive reactions to these interactions (Crick & Dodge, 1994). They assume that other children will be aggressive toward them, and they interpret the actions of their peers in line with these assumptions. In addition, they tend to believe that any negative actions a peer might take against them—for example, taking their favorite pencil—are intentional rather than accidental. When deciding what action to take in response to a perceived provocation by a peer, these children tend to think of a narrow range of responses, usually including aggression. When pressed to consider responses other than aggression, these children generate ineffective or vague responses, and often consider responses other than aggression to be useless or unattractive.

Children who think about their social interactions in this way are likely to engage in aggressive behaviors toward others. They then may be retaliated against: Other children will hit them, parents and teachers will punish them, and they will be more often perceived negatively by others. In turn, these actions may feed their assumptions that the world is against them, causing them to misinterpret future actions by others. A cycle of interactions can be created that maintains and encourages aggressive, antisocial behaviors in a child.

Children who are prone to antisocial behavior tend to overinterpret the acts of others as provocation.

Borderline Personality Disorder

Borderline personality disorder has been the focus of considerable attention in the popular press and in clinical and research writings in psychology in the last couple of decades. The diagnosis of borderline personality disorder was added to the DSM only in its third edition in 1980. Clinicians have long used the label "borderline," however, to refer to people who seem to teeter between severe neurotic traits (such as emotional instability) and bouts of psychosis (Millon, 1981).

Borderline personality disorder is characterized by *unstable moods, self-concept, and interpersonal relationships*. People with this disorder have frequent bouts of severe depression, anxiety, or anger that may be triggered by almost nothing. They have periods of extreme self-doubt and periods of grandiose self-importance. They may have transient episodes in which they feel unreal, lose track of time, and may even forget who they are. They can switch from idealizing other people to despising them without provocation. They often feel desperately empty and will initially cling to a new acquaintance or therapist in hopes that he or she will fill the tremendous void they feel in themselves. They are nearly paranoid about abandonment, however, and misinterpret other people's innocent actions as abandonment or rejection. People with borderline personality disorder are prone to impulsive self-damaging behaviors, including self-mutilation and suicidal behavior. The following case describes a person with borderline personality disorder:

borderline personality disorder a disorder in which the person's moods, self-concept, and interpersonal relationships are highly unstable

> Ms. Q was a 28-year-old, white single woman when admitted voluntarily [to a psychiatric hospital]. . . . In late adolescence, Ms. Q became romantically and sexually involved with a young artist. When he informed her that she was "just another woman" in his life, she became morose and moody. She began hallucinating his face on movie screens and newspapers. Shortly after the accidental drowning of a young boy from her neighborhood, Ms. Q started feeling guilty for his death and feared imminent apprehension by the

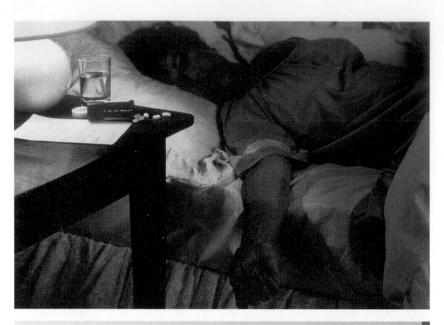

People with borderline personality disorder are at high risk for suicide attempts.

police. In an act later described as a "manipulative gesture," she took an overdose of sleeping medication and was hospitalized briefly.

Over the next five years, Ms. Q attended college sporadically. She moved often between a variety of living situations: alone in hotels or dormitories or with one or the other of her divorced parents. Changes of domicile were often precipitated by quarrels. Although seldom alone, she developed relatively superficial social relationships. The few women whom she befriended tended to be older. She would frequently become attached to their parents and call them "mama and papa." Sexually she had three or four intense affairs, each lasting less than six months and each terminating painfully with one or the other partner refusing to marry. In all of her relationships, Ms. Q was described as manipulative, dependent, masochistic, hostile, and derogatory.

Mood swings between anger and despondency occurred weekly and sometimes daily. She frequently abused alcohol and barbiturates and made numerous manipulative suicidal threats. For the latter she was hospitalized briefly on two more occasions (one month or less in duration). . . .

Her hospitalization at [the psychiatric hospital] arose out of a visit home to her mother. She felt slighted in several ways. First, her mother's welcome was less than "gushing." Second, she felt insulted when her mother's boyfriend showed her a brochure describing a psychiatric residential treatment facility. Third, she discovered that a certain choice piece of family real estate was being willed to her least favorite sibling. Feeling rejected, she took an overdose of aspirin and was hospitalized at (the psychiatric hospital) shortly thereafter. (McGlashan, 1984, pp. 87–88)

Studies suggest that only about 1% to 2% of adults will ever develop a borderline personality disorder (Weissman, 1993). This disorder is diagnosed in women much more often than in men (Fabrega et al., 1991; Swartz et al., 1990).

Understanding Borderline Personality Disorder

Psychodynamic theorists have taken the greatest interest in borderline personality disorder and have provided the most comprehensive explanation of the disorder. They suggest that people with this disorder have just enough reality testing to retain a foothold in the real world, but rely on primitive defenses such as denial rather than more advanced defenses against their conflicts (Kernberg, 1979). In addition, the borderline person has very poorly developed views of self and others, stemming from poor early relationships with caregivers. Their early caregivers were comforting and rewarding when the children remained dependent and compliant toward the caregivers, but hostile and rejecting when they tried to pursue their own interests. As a result, they did not develop a strong sense of self separate from their caregivers. This makes them extremely reactive to others' opinions of them and to the possibility of being abandoned by others. When others are perceived as rejecting them, they reject themselves and may engage in self-punishment or self-mutilation.

Other research suggests that many people with borderline personality disorder have experienced physical and sexual abuse during childhood (Perry & Herman,

1993). This abuse could lead to the problems in self-concept that most theorists suggest are at the core of this disorder. In addition, a child whose parent alternates between being abusive and being loving could develop a fundamental mistrust of others and a tendency to see others as either all good or all bad.

Thinking Critically

1. The personality disorders are extremely hard to diagnose reliably. Why might this be true?

2. Often people with a personality disorder do not want treatment. Should they ever be forced to receive treatment?

Why Can't That Child Calm Down? (Attention Deficit Hyperactivity Disorder)

The final disorder we will discuss in this chapter is *attention deficit hyperactivity disorder,* abbreviated as ADHD. This is considered a disorder of childhood, although increasing attention has been paid to adults who have ADHD but were not diagnosed with the disorder as children. ADHD is only one of several disorders that can be diagnosed in children. We highlight ADHD in this chapter because it has been the focus of much public attention in the last decade and is frequently diagnosed in children.

Children with **attention deficit hyperactivity disorder (ADHD)** have *fundamental problems in the ability to maintain attention and control impulsive behaviors* that go far beyond the usual inattentiveness and impulsivity of young children (see Figure 12-13). Consider the following example of a young boy with ADHD (adapted from Spitzer et al., 1994, pp. 351–352):

attention deficit hyperactivity disorder (ADHD) a disorder in which a person has fundamental problems in the ability to maintain attention and control impulsive behaviors

Eddie, age 9, was referred to a child psychiatrist at the request of his school because of the difficulties he creates in class. His teacher complains that he is so restless that his classmates are unable to concentrate. He is hardly ever in his seat and mostly roams around the class, talking to other children while they are working. When the teacher is able to get him to stay in his seat, he fidgets with his hands and feet and drops things on the floor. He never seems to know what he is going to do next and may suddenly do something quite outrageous. His most recent suspension from school was for swinging from the fluorescent light fixture over the blackboard. Because he was unable to climb down again, the class was in an uproar.

His mother says that Eddie's behavior has been difficult since he was a toddler and that, as a 3-year-old, he was unbearably restless and demanding. He has always required little sleep and been awake before anyone else. When he was small, "he got into everything," particularly in the early morning, when he would awaken at 4:30 A.M. or 5:00 A.M. and go downstairs by himself. His parents would awaken to find the living room or kitchen "demolished."

Eddie has no interest in TV and dislikes games or toys that require any concentration or patience. He is not popular with other children and at home prefers to be outdoors playing with his

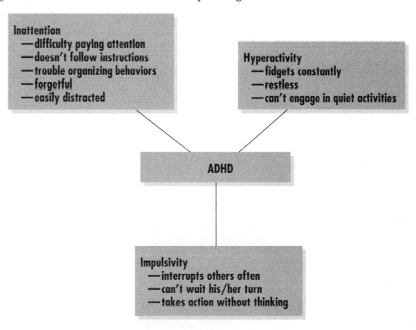

Figure 12-13

The Symptoms of Attention Deficit Hyperactivity Disorder (ADHD) The symptoms of ADHD include inattention, hyperactivity, and impulsivity.

dog or riding his bike. If he does play with toys, his games are messy and destructive and his mother cannot get him to keep his things in any order.

Not surprisingly, children like Eddie often do poorly in school because they cannot pay attention or quell their hyperactivity (Henker & Whalen, 1998). Perhaps 25% of children with ADHD may have serious learning disabilities that make it even harder for them to learn (Barkley, 1990). Children like Eddie also tend to be disliked by other children because they are disorganized, intrusive, irritable, and demanding (Hinshaw & Melnick, 1995). When things don't go their way, they are prone to angry outbursts and may become physically violent. Between 45% and 60% of children with ADHD develop antisocial problems or abuse drugs (Barkley et al., 1990).

Although there would seem to be an epidemic of ADHD according to some media accounts and the number of children informally given this diagnosis in school settings, careful studies suggest that only 1% to 7% of children have ADHD (Hinshaw, 1994). Boys are about three times more likely to develop ADHD than girls (Cohen et al., 1993).

Understanding Attention Deficit Hyperactivity Disorder

Attention deficit hyperactivity disorder appears to have neurological underpinnings. Studies show that children with ADHD differ from children with no psychological disorders on a variety of measures of neurological functioning, such as cerebral blood flow and EEG readings (Barkley, 1996). One hypothesis is that the brains of children with ADHD are maturing at a slower rate than those of children without the disorder, and thus they are not able to maintain a level of attention appropriate for their age. This would explain why many children "grow out" of ADHD as they age.

Children with ADHD often have histories of prenatal and birth complications, including low birth weight, premature delivery, and oxygen deprivation during delivery (Barkley, 1996; Sprich-Buckminster et al., 1993). Moderate to severe alcohol ingestion or use of nicotine or barbiturates during pregnancy may contribute to ADHD in children. Exposure to high concentrations of lead may also contribute to ADHD (Fergusson, Horwood, & Lynskey, 1993). The notion that consumption of large amounts of sugar or other dietary factors can lead to hyperactivity in children has not been supported in controlled studies (Milich, Wolrach, & Lindgren, 1986).

Children with ADHD are more likely than children without the disorder to come from families that are prone to hostility, conflict, and antisocial behavior (Barkley et al., 1990). It is not clear, however, whether these family factors are causes, correlates, or perhaps consequences of the child's disorder. Children with ADHD can be highly disruptive of family life. In addition, there may be some third factors—such as a genetic predisposition to impulsive and hostile behaviors—that accounts both for the conflict in the family and for the presence of ADHD in the child (Barkley, 1991).

The foregoing descriptions of psychological disorders may seem daunting and depressing. Fortunately, in recent decades great strides have been made in treating many of them. The next chapter describes the most common treatments.

Thinking Critically

Diagnosing psychological disorders in children is more difficult than diagnosing disorders in adults. Why might this be true?

Summary

1. Some criteria that are used to judge behaviors as abnormal include unusualness, deviation from social norms, lack of reality testing, and maladaptiveness. Each of these criteria is open to judgment and biases. The last two criteria are most accepted in the social sciences.

2. DSM-IV is the system used in the United States to diagnose psycho-

logical disorders. It lists specific symptoms and the degree and length of time that these symptoms must be present in order for a psychological disorder to be diagnosed. There are a number of other disorders not included in the DSM-IV that are found in other cultures.

3. Theories about the causes of psychological disorders and treatments for these disorders can generally be grouped into biological, psychodynamic, behavioral, and cognitive perspectives. The vulnerability-stress model emphasizes the interaction between a predisposition (biological and/or psychological) that makes a person vulnerable for a disorder and the environmental conditions that individual encounters.

4. *Anxiety disorders* include *generalized anxiety disorder* (constant worry and dread), *panic disorder* (sudden attacks of overwhelming apprehension), *phobias* (irrational fears of specific objects or situations), and *obsessive-compulsive disorders* (persistent unwanted thoughts, or *obsessions,* combined with urges, or *compulsions,* to perform certain acts).

5. Biological theories attribute anxiety disorders to genetic predispositions or to biochemical or neurological abnormalities. Most anxiety disorders run in families, and twin studies strongly suggest an inherited component to panic disorder and obsessive-compulsive disorder. People with *panic attacks* have an overreactive fight-or-flight response, perhaps because of serotonin deficiencies in the limbic system. People with obsessive-compulsive disorder may have serotonin deficiencies in areas of the brain that regulate primitive impulses.

6. Cognitive and behavioral perspectives suggest that people with anxiety disorders are prone to catastrophizing cognitions and to rigid, moralistic thinking. Maladaptive behaviors, such as avoidant behaviors and compulsions, arise through operant conditioning when the individual discovers that the behaviors reduce anxiety. Phobias may emerge through classical conditioning. Psychodynamic theories of anxiety attribute them to unconscious conflicts that are disguised as phobias, obsessions, or compulsions.

7. Mood disorders are divided into *depressive disorders* (the person has one or more periods of depression) and *bipolar disorders* (the person alternates between periods of depression and periods of mania). *Depression* is characterized by sadness, negative thinking, low motivation, and physical disturbances. *Mania* is characterized by elation, excessive energy and self-confidence, grandiosity, and agitation.

8. Biological theories attribute mood disorders to genetic factors and to poor regulation of the neurotransmitters serotonin and norepinephrine. Cognitive theories attribute depression to pessimistic views of the self, the world, and the future, and to maladaptive attributional styles. Psychodynamic theories view depression as a reactivation of the loss of parental affection in a person who is dependent on external approval and tends to turn anger inward.

9. *Schizophrenia* is characterized by *delusions* (beliefs with no grounding in reality), *hallucinations* (unreal perceptual experiences), disturbed thought and speech, disorganized behavior, and loss of motivation and emotional tone.

10. Schizophrenia clearly is transmitted genetically. People with schizophrenia also show poor regulation in the neurotransmitter dopamine, and two types of brain abnormalities: the prefrontal cortex is smaller and less active, and the ventricles are enlarged. Difficult environments probably cannot create schizophrenia, but they may worsen the disorder and contribute to relapses.

11. *Personality disorders* are lifelong patterns of behavior that constitute immature and inappropriate ways

of coping with stress or solving problems. People are diagnosed with *antisocial personality disorder* if they are impulsive, show little guilt, and have no regard for the rights of others. Antisocial personality disorder probably has genetic and biological roots, but neglectful and hostile parenting also may contribute to the disorder. People with *borderline personality disorder* show instability in mood, self-concept, and interpersonal relationships.

Psychodynamic theories suggest that the caregivers of people with this disorder required dependence from their children and alternated between extreme expressions of love and hostility.

12. *Attention deficit hyperactivity disorder (ADHD)* is diagnosed in children who show fundamental deficits in the ability to pay attention and control impulsive behaviors. ADHD probably has strong neurological roots.

Suggested Readings

Mending Minds (1992), a paperback by Heston, provides a brief description of the major mental disorders, with case histories and descriptions of treatment options. Also see Torrey, *Out of the Shadows: Confronting America's Mental Illness* (1997).

The hereditary aspects of mental illness are reviewed in Plomin, De-Fries, and McClearn, *Behavioral Genetics: A Primer* (2nd ed., 1989). *Schizophrenia Genesis: The Origins of Madness* (1991), a paperback by Gottesman, presents research findings on the genetics of this disorder, a discussion of social and psychological factors, and personal accounts by schizophrenic patients and their families. Another important work is Torrey, *Schizophrenia and Manic-Depressive Disorder: The Biological Roots of Mental Illness as Revealed by the Landmark Study of Identical Twins* (1994).

Agras, *Panic: Facing Fears, Phobias, and Anxiety* (1985), provides an interesting discussion of the way fears develop into phobias. Rapaport, *The Boy Who Couldn't Stop Washing: The Experience and Treatment of Obsessive-Compulsive Disorder* (1989), provides a fascinating account of this disorder, including descriptions of clinical cases and research findings on treatment.

For a fascinating look at the link between mental illness and creativity, see Jamison, *Touched With Fire: Manic Depressive Illness and the Artistic Temperament* (1996), and *An Unquiet Mind* (1995).

The world of psychosis from the patient's viewpoint is graphically described in Green, *I Never Promised You a Rose Garden* (1971); and in North, *Welcome Silence* (1987). Nassar writes of Nobel prize winner John Nash, who suffered schizophrenia, in *A Beautiful Mind* (1998). In Endler, *Holiday of Darkness* (1982), a well-known psychologist provides an account of his personal battle with depression and discusses the effects of various treatments. Donna Williams writes of her childhood experiences with autism in two gripping books, *Nobody Nowhere* (1992) and *Somebody Somewhere* (1994). Another fascinating account of autism is given by Temple Grandin in *Thinking in Pictures: My Life with Autism* (1995).

People with family members suffering from mental illness will find useful advice in Marsh, Dickens, & Torrey, *How to Cope With Mental Illness in Your Family: A Self-Care Guide for Siblings, Offspring, and Parents* (1998). A comprehensive and sensitive overview of suicide can be found in Jamison, *Darkness Falls Fast* (1999).

Enhance and Explore

To enhance your understanding of the psychological concepts found in this chapter, please consult the following aids:

Study Guide

Learning Objectives, p. 214
Define the Terms, p. 217
Test Your Knowledge, p. 222
Essay Questions, p. 225
Thinking Independently, p. 226

PowerPsych CD-ROM

HOW ARE PSYCHOLOGICAL DISORDERS DEFINED AND DIAGNOSED?

Mystery Client: Anxiety (Phobia), Depression, Schizophrenia

PsychCentral

For more information concerning the topics found in this chapter, access psychology links on the Word Wide Web made through the Harcourt Web page at:

http://www.harcourtcollege.com/psych/Fundamentals

www.harcourtcollege.com

http://www.harcourtcollege.com/psych/index.html

ADHD Is Overdiagnosed

Caryn L. Carlson, *The University of Texas at Austin*

The growing public attention to ADHD over the past decade has increased the detection of legitimate cases and led to much-needed research. We must be cautious, however, that we do not allow the diagnostic pendulum to swing too far, since finding answers about ADHD depends on the rigor and integrity of our classification system.

There is reason to believe that ADHD is currently being overdiagnosed in some areas of the United States. Prescriptions of stimulant medications, which are almost exclusively for ADHD, provide a "proxy" for diagnostic rates

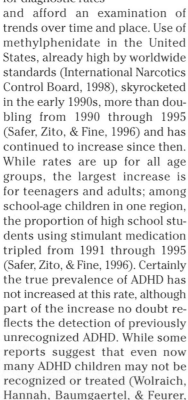

Caryn Carlson

and afford an examination of trends over time and place. Use of methylphenidate in the United States, already high by worldwide standards (International Narcotics Control Board, 1998), skyrocketed in the early 1990s, more than doubling from 1990 through 1995 (Safer, Zito, & Fine, 1996) and has continued to increase since then. While rates are up for all age groups, the largest increase is for teenagers and adults; among school-age children in one region, the proportion of high school students using stimulant medication tripled from 1991 through 1995 (Safer, Zito, & Fine, 1996). Certainly the true prevalence of ADHD has not increased at this rate, although part of the increase no doubt reflects the detection of previously unrecognized ADHD. While some reports suggest that even now many ADHD children may not be recognized or treated (Wolraich, Hannah, Baumgaertel, & Feurer,

1998), the average rates are now quite high (Safer, Zito, & Fine, 1996).

Part of the dramatic increase probably reflects overdiagnosis, particularly when considered in light of the vast disparities across geographical locales in the United States. The rate of methylphenidate consumption per capita in 1995 was 2.4 times higher in Virginia than in neighboring West Virginia, and nearly 4 times higher than in California (Spanos, 1996). Even more troubling are the high discrepancies across counties within states. For example, although the per capita rate for males of ages 6–12 in 1991 in New York was 4.1% statewide, rates varied by a factor of 10 among counties, ranging up to 14% (Kaufman, 1995).

What factors might lead to overdiagnosis of ADHD? We know from epidemiological research that unreasonable prevalence rates (e.g., up to nearly 23% of school-age boys [Wolraich, Hannah, Baumgaertel, & Feurer, 1998]) are obtained when ADHD is identified based merely on simple ratings from one source, but become much lower when full diagnostic criteria—including age of onset by 7, presence across settings, and confirmation of impairment—are imposed. The wide variability in diagnostic rates across locations suggests that clinicians are applying diagnostic criteria inconsistently. Some clinicians diagnose without assessing all criteria, and often they rely only on parent reports. While underdiagnosis may be occurring in some places, over-

diagnosis is occurring in others.

When is overdiagnosis most likely? It seems that the diagnosis of ADHD has become fashionable for those who experience some negative life event—such as school failure or job loss—and desire to attribute such problems to a disorder rather than accept personal responsibility. This tendency is apparent even in more mundane arenas, such as feeling bored or unmotivated—"What a relief: the fact that I find it difficult to pay attention in my 'history of Swedish cartographers' class isn't my fault. I have ADHD."

One safeguard against misdiagnosis is the current criteria that symptoms must onset by age 7. But how early and by what means can we detect ADHD if we agree that it is present from an early age? Since objective measures that can reliably identify ADHD are currently unavailable, we must rely on symptom reports from others. Setting the age of onset at 7 years recognizes that normal behavior patterns may be similar to symptoms of ADHD up to about age 5, when normal activity decreases and attention increases (but not in children with ADHD). Also, impairment may not occur outside the demands of a classroom environment. But if individuals do not have symptoms early but develop them later for a variety of reasons, including life situations or stress, then diagnosis does not seem warranted. Should such problems be recognized? By all means. Should they be treated? Of course, by teaching people organizational and behavior management strategies, and possibly even with medication. But significant problems in living are not the equivalent of disorders, and to call them that will deter us in the search for etiologies of ADHD.

ADHD Is Neither Overdiagnosed nor Overtreated

William Pelham, *SUNY Buffalo*

Because ADHD is the most widely diagnosed mental health disorder of childhood and because its frequency of treatment with medication has been increasing exponentially through the 1990s, it has become fashionable in many quarters—particularly among educators—to argue that it is overdiagnosed and consequently overtreated. Histrionic diatribes aside, there is no solid empirical evidence that ADHD is overdiagnosed or overtreated.

First, consider the accusation that ADHD is only a relatively recent phenomenon. To the contrary, the diagnosis was often widely used in the past but played second fiddle to other diagnoses. For example, one of the more important early studies in treatment of conduct disordered children (Patterson, 1974) noted, almost as an aside that more than two-thirds of the boys had hyperkinesis, an early label for ADHD. Thus while ADHD may well be *diagnosed* more often than in the past 30 years, it is simply being diagnosed more appropriately and given the prominence it deserves.

It is important to note that the major reason for the increasing rate of ADHD identification in the 1990s is a result of the 1991 change in the status of ADHD in the Individuals with Disabilities Education Act (IDEA), the federal law that governs special education throughout the United States. This change included ADHD as a handicapping condition. Further, the U. S. Office of Education sent a memorandum to all state officers of education directing them to consider ADHD as a condition eligible for special education. As a result of this directive, school districts throughout the country for the first time were required to establish screening and diagnostic procedures for ADHD. The increase in diagnosis for ADHD is thus not a conspiracy or a fatal flaw in education or an indictment of current parenting practices, but is instead a natural by-product of a change in federal regulations governing education in the United States.

What about the criticism that ADHD is a disorder with diagnostic rates that vary widely both within North America and across the world? The explanation is that local school districts and states vary dramatically in the degree to which they have implemented the mandated changes in the IDEA. Furthermore, ADHD when similar diagnostic criteria are applied, comparable rates to those in North America exist in a diverse collection of countries that include Italy, Spain, South Africa, Israel, Argentina, and Vietnam.

The most important factor in deciding whether a mental health disorder is overdiagnosed is whether the diagnosed individuals have impairments in daily life functioning sufficient to justify the label. ADHD is a particularly compelling example of this issue because the children suffer from dramatic impairment in relationships with peers, parents, teachers, and siblings, as well as in classroom behavior and academic performance. To take a single example, in one classic study of consecutive referrals to a clinic, 96% of ADHD children were rejected by their peers on sociometric nominations at a rate higher than their class averages (Pelham & Bender, 1982). In the field of child psychopathology, the number of negative nominations received on a classroom peer nomination inventory in elementary school is widely thought to be the best indicator of severe impairment in childhood and poor outcome in adulthood, so this elevated rate of negative nominations highlights the impairment that ADHD children suffer in the peer domain.

A corollary of the argument that many children are inappropriately diagnosed with ADHD is the complaint that these children are being inappropriately treated—usually with medication. In fact, the literature shows that only a small minority of diagnosed ADHD children (or all children with mental health disorders for that matter) receive treatment—medication or otherwise. We should be happy that treatment rates for the disorder are increasing. The dramatic rise in the treatment of ADHD—pharmacological or otherwise—clearly results from the increase in the rates of diagnosis, which are secondary to the change in the IDEA noted above. Notably, one of the studies that supports these arguments regarding impairment and treatment was conducted with children identified using only teacher ratings, which have been the main target for complaints of overdiagnosis (Wolraich et al., 1998).

In summary, ADHD is the most common mental health disorder of childhood, and it is one of the most impairing and refractory, and one with poor long-term prognosis. Current diagnostic rates are in line with scientific views of the nature of the disorder. If anything, we need to accurately identify *more* children with ADHD and provide the evidence-based treatments—both behavioral and pharmacological—that they need.

CHAPTER **13** *Treatment of Psychological Disorders*

Phil knew he needed help. He hadn't been functioning well for months. In recent weeks all he could do was lie in bed, eat a little when his roommate brought him food, and listen to the thoughts wildly swirling in his head. But whom could he turn to? What could be done for him? Was there really any hope for him?

Many people suffering from psychological disorders or more minor psychological problems ask the same questions that Phil asked. In this chapter we explore the various treatments available for people suffering from psychological problems. We begin by reviewing the different types of mental health professionals who provide treatment to people with psychological disorders. We then review the major biological treatments, focusing on drugs used to treat disorders, and then the most commonly used psychological techniques. Then we address the complex social and legal issues concerning the rights of people with mental disorders and society's obligations to them. And finally, we present guidelines for staying psychologically healthy as we cope with everyday problems and stresses.

Many people suffering from psychological disorders never seek help, although their symptoms can be effectively treated.

Who Treats People With Psychological Disorders?

Most people who receive treatment for a psychological disorder are treated as outpatients in private offices or clinics. Some people must be hospitalized because their symptoms are more severe. When they are discharged from the hospital, they may go back home to their families or they may go to a residential treatment facility, where they live with other people who have psychological disorders and receive ongoing treatment from live-in mental health professionals. There are also day treatment facilities where people receive treatment during the day but go home to sleep at night. Regardless of where a person receives mental health treatment, several different types of professionals may be involved.

A *psychiatrist* has an M.D. degree and has completed a three-year residency (after medical school) in a mental health facility, during which he or she received supervision in the diagnosis of abnormal behavior, drug therapy, and psychotherapy. As a physician, the psychiatrist can prescribe medication and, in most states, hospitalization.

Psychologists who work as therapists have obtained graduate training in clinical, counseling, or school psychology. They usually hold a Ph.D. (doctor of philosophy) or a Psy.D. (doctor of psychology) degree. The Ph.D. emphasizes training in research as well as diagnosis and therapy. The Psy.D. is a more applied degree, focusing mainly on diagnosis and therapy. Both degrees require 4 or 5 years of postgraduate study plus a year or more of internship. In addition, most states require psychologists to pass a licensing or certification examination. Psychologists cannot prescribe drugs, but they often work in conjunction with physicians who will prescribe drugs to patients while the psychologists provide psychotherapy.

The term *psychoanalyst* is reserved for individuals who have received specialized training at a psychoanalytic institute learning the methods and theories derived from Freud. Once, most psychoanalytic institutes required their graduates to have an M.D. degree, but now psychologists can become psychoanalysts as well.

Several different kinds of mental health professionals practice psychotherapy.

Psychiatric social workers have completed a two-year master's degree program (M.S.W.), which includes training in interviewing, therapy, and extending treatment to the home and community. The psychiatric social worker is often called upon to collect information about a patient's home situation and to assist the patient in getting help from community resources (such as hospitals, clinics, and social agencies).

Sometimes these professionals work as a team. The psychiatrist prescribes psychotherapeutic medications and monitors their effectiveness; the psychologist sees the same person in psychotherapy; the social worker monitors the home environment and acts as a liaison with community agencies for the client. In mental hospitals, a fourth professional is available: the *psychiatric nurse*. Psychiatric nursing is a field within the nursing profession that requires special training in the understanding and treatment of mental disorders. In our discussion of therapeutic techniques, we will not specify the profession of the therapists, but instead we will assume that they are trained and competent members of any one of these professions.

Thinking Critically

If you were suffering a psychological disorder, what type of mental health professional would you seek out, and why?

Can We Change How the Body Works? (Biological Treatments)

Biological therapies most often involve the use of drugs (see Table 13-1). Most of the drugs that are effective in treating mental disorders have been discovered in the last 50 years, leading to a revolution in the care of people with these disorders.

Antipsychotic Drugs

antipsychotic drugs drugs used to treat symptoms of psychosis

Antipsychotic drugs are *drugs used to treat the symptoms of psychosis*—delusions (beliefs that are out of touch with reality), hallucinations (sensory experiences that are not real), and severe disorganization of thought. These drugs appear to work by blocking certain receptors for the neurotransmitter dopamine, thereby reducing the action of dopamine in the brain. People with schizophrenia typically must take these drugs prophylactically (that is, even when they are not experiencing acute symptoms) in order to prevent new onsets of symptoms. The antipsychotic drugs have revolutionized the treatment of schizophrenia, making it possible for many people with this disorder to lead productive lives.

The antipsychotic drugs are not without problems, however. First, although these drugs are effective in treating psychotic symptoms, they tend not to reduce the negative symptoms in schizophrenia—lack of motivation and deficits in interpersonal relations. Thus, some people with schizophrenia who take these drugs may no longer be actively psychotic, but they still are not able to lead normal lives, holding a job and building positive social relationships. Second, a substantial minority (around 25%) of people with schizophrenia do not respond at all to these drugs, and hence do not get relief even from the psychotic symptoms of schizophrenia (Liberman et al., 1994). Third, these drugs have significant side effects, including grogginess, dry mouth, blurred vision, visual disturbances and a variety of motor disturbances. One of the most serious side effects is **tardive dyskinesia,** *a neurological disorder that involves involuntary movements of the tongue, face, mouth, or jaw.* People

tardive dyskinesia a neurological disorder that involves involuntary movements of the tongue, face, mouth, or jaw

Table 13-1

Drugs Used to Treat Psychological Disorders These drugs are some of the most commonly used to treat psychological disorders.

Antipsychotic Drugs
  Examples: Thorazine, Clozapine
  Effective in treating: delusions, hallucinations, thought disorganization
  Side effects: grogginess, dry mouth, blurred vision, motor disturbances, tardive dyskinesia

Antidepressant Drugs
  Examples: Prozac, Wellbutrin, Tofranil
  Effective in treating: depression, anxiety, obsessive-compulsive behavior, impulsive behavior
  Side effects: dry mouth, perspiration, constipation, urinary retention, weight gain, sexual dysfunction,
    nervousness, nausea

Lithium
  Effective in treating: mania
  Side effects: abdominal pain, nausea, vomiting, diarrhea, tremors, twitches

Antianxiety Drugs
  Examples: Valium, Xanax, Librium
  Effective in treating: anxiety symptoms, sleeplessness
  Side effects: addictive, cause heart rate acceleration, irritability, profuse sweating in withdrawal

Stimulant Drugs
  Example: Ritalin
  Effective in treating: attention deficit hyperactivity disorder
  Side effects: insomnia, headaches, tics, nausea

with this disorder may involuntarily smack their lips, make sucking sounds, stick out their tongue, puff their cheeks, or make other bizarre movements, over and over again. Tardive dyskinesia is often irreversible and may occur in more than 20% of people who use antipsychotic drugs over long periods (Morganstern & Glazer, 1993).

Some of the side effects of antipsychotic drugs are described in this personal account:

> My muscles became rigid, my vision blurred and I slept about 20 hours a day; however, within two weeks my symptoms had remitted and I was able to be discharged from the hospital. When I say my symptoms had remitted, I should point out that I am referring to the positive symptoms of schizophrenia, that is the delusions, the hallucinations, and the thought disorder. The so-called negative symptoms such as lack of motivation and depression actually got worse and were made more severe by the medication. . . . Another of the side effects of the medication for me was gaining weight. Within six months from first starting the treatment I had gained 40 or 50 pounds. This only added to my depression and my poor self-esteem. (Long, 1995–1996)

Fortunately, a relatively new drug called *clozapine* seems to be effective in treating schizophrenia without inducing the same serious side effects as the older drugs (Wilson & Clausen, 1995). It seems to work by binding to a different type of dopamine receptor than the other drugs, although it also influences several other neurotransmitters, including serotonin.

Antidepressant Drugs

Antidepressant drugs *help relieve the symptoms of depression by regulating the neurotransmitters serotonin and norepinephrine.* There are three major classes of antidepressants: the *tricyclic antidepressants,* the *monoamine oxidase inhibitors (MAOIs),* and the *selective serotonin reuptake inhibitors (SSRIs).* You are probably most familiar with the selective serotonin reuptake inhibitors, whose trade names include Prozac,

antidepressant drugs drugs that help relieve the symptoms of depression by regulating the neurotransmitters serotonin and norepinephrine

Figure 13-1

Advertisement for PAXIL   PAXIL and other selective serotonin reuptake inhibitors have become the widest-selling antidepressants.

Zoloft, and Paxil (see Figure 13-1). All of these drugs can reduce depression in the majority of people taking them (Guze & Gitlin, 1994). In addition, the SSRIs appear to be helpful in treating a number of other problems, including panic disorders, obsessive-compulsive disorders, and impulsive behaviors.

Unfortunately, however, like antipsychotic drugs, antidepressants have a number of side effects. The tricyclic antidepressants can cause dry mouth, excessive perspiration, blurring of vision, constipation, urinary retention, weight gain, and sexual dysfunction. The MAOIs can interact with certain foods, including hard cheeses, chocolate, and red wine, to cause a rise in blood pressure that can be fatal. In addition, these drugs can cause liver damage, weight gain, severe lowering of blood pressure, and several of the side effects caused by the tricyclic antidepressants. The SSRIs seem to cause fewer side effects than the other antidepressants, but many people taking them experience nervousness, nausea and diarrhea, and decreased sexual functioning.

Still, the antidepressants have been lifesavers for thousands of people, as can be seen in this account by a person who began taking an SSRI:

And then something just kind of changed in me. Over the next few days, I became all right, safe in my own skin. It happened just like that. One morning I woke up, and I really did want to live, really looked forward to greeting the day, imagined errands to run, phone calls to return, and it was not with a feeling of great dread, not with the sense that the first person who stepped on my toe as I walked through the square may well have driven me to suicide. It was as if the miasma of depression had lifted off me, gone smoothly about its business, in the same way that the fog in San Francisco rises as the day wears on. (Wurtzel, 1995, p. 329)

Antidepressants are also used to help people with bipolar disorder cope with their depressed moods. *Lithium* is the drug most often used to treat mania. Between 80% and 90% of patients experience significant reductions in symptoms of bipolar disorder under lithium (Goodwin & Jamison, 1990). Unfortunately, many people cannot take lithium because of its side effects, which include abdominal pain, nausea, vomiting, diarrhea, tremors, and twitches. Says Kay Redfield Jamison:

I found myself beholden to a medication that also caused severe nausea and vomiting many times a month—I often slept on my bathroom floor with a pillow under my head and my warm, woolen St. Andrews gown tucked over me. . . . I have been violently ill more places than I choose to remember, and quite embarrassingly so in public places. (1995, p. 93)

People who take lithium complain of blurred vision and problems in concentration and attention that interfere with their ability to work. Lithium can cause a form of diabetes, kidney dysfunction, and birth defects if taken by pregnant women during the first trimester of pregnancy.

Frontiers of Psychology

Herbal Remedies for Psychological Problems

One of the hottest debates in psychology and psychiatry these days involves "medicines" that have been used for centuries to treat psychological symptoms. These products, which are usually derived from common plants, are referred to by scientists as *phytomedicines,* and by laypeople as *herbal remedies.* Phytomedicines are a regular part of modern mainstream medicine in Asia and parts of western Europe, particularly Germany (Grunwald, 1995). Only recently have Americans begun to turn to herbal remedies for psychological problems.

Probably the best-known herbal remedy these days is St. John's wort (technically known as hypericum perforatum). Although it has been used for decades in Europe as an effective treatment for mild depression, Americans did not know much about St. John's wort until psychiatrist Harold Bloomfield popularized it in his book *Hypericum and Depression.* Since then, sales of this over-the-counter product have increased phenomenally, hitting $48 million in the United States in 1997.

Altogether, herbal products account for more than $1 billion in sales in the United States annually, with as many as 40% of Americans reporting they use herbal products at least occasionally (Astin, 1998; Cott, 1995). These products are typically sold as foods. They can range from simple and mild products such as chamomile and peppermint to products with potent pharmacological activity, such as foxglove, from which digitalis is derived. Only a few of these products have been tested in rigorous research. Studies in the United States have supported the European studies in showing that St. John's wort is effective in the treatment of mild to moderate depression, although it may not be potent enough to relieve more serious depressions (Cott, 1995; Cott & Fugh-Berman, 1998; Linde, Ramirez, Mulrow, Pauls, Weidenhammer, & Melchart, 1996). In addition, people tend to experience fewer side effects to St. John's wort than to prescription antidepressant medications, although some people experience gastrointestinal symptoms, fatigue, and increased sensitivity to ultraviolet light (Linde et al., 1996).

Two products used to treat anxiety—valerian and kava—have also undergone scientific study. Valerian is made from the root of the Valeriana officinalis, a common herb native to both Europe and Asia (Cott, 1995). Valerian appears to be a safe, mild sedative that produces no morning hangover (Balderer & Borbely, 1985; Fugh-Berman & Cott, 1999). Kava is the psychoactive member of the pepper family, widely used in Polynesia, Micronesia, and Melanesia as a ceremonial, tranquilizing beverage, and in Europe and the United States for anxiety and insomnia. Several placebo-controlled studies have shown that kava is a safe herb for short-term relief from stress and anxiety (Volz & Keiser, 1997). Although most people who take kava report no side effects, some report mild gastrointestinal complaints or allergic skin reactions. Kava may also interact with prescription antianxiety drugs.

Ginkgo biloba is an antioxidant, and some reports suggest it may enhance cognitive functioning in people with Alzheimer's disease and other memory impairments (e.g., Kanowksi, Herrmann, Stephan, Wierich, & Hoerr, 1996; LeBars, Katz, Berman, Itil, Freedman, & Schatzberg, 1997). Germany has approved the use of ginkgo biloba for the treatment of dementia. Although it is rare for humans to experience significant side effects from gingko, it does have anticoagulant effects and in rare cases has been associated with serious bleeding problems, usually in people who are already taking anticoagulant drugs.

Many scientists are concerned that people are using these potent substances without any consultation with their physicians, putting themselves at risk for side effects or interactions with drugs or other substances. Much more research is needed before guidelines on the safe use of these drugs will be formulated. Unfortunately, doing research on drugs, including herbal remedies, is extremely expensive. Pharmaceutical companies generally are not interested in funding this research because botanicals are not patentable and are chemically very complex. Thus, research sufficient to allay the fears of skeptics of herbal remedies may never be done.

In the meantime, millions of people around the world are using these products to treat their psychological symptoms. If you ever consider using an over-the-counter herbal treatment, it is wise to consult your physician about possible side effects and interaction effects with other medications, alcohol, or other drugs you may be exposed to. Even though these remedies are "natural," they are still potent and some carry significant risks.

Anticonvulsant medications are now also commonly used to treat bipolar disorder. These drugs can be highly effective in reducing the symptoms of severe and acute mania, but they do not seem as effective as lithium in the long-term treatment of bipolar disorder. The side effects of the anticonvulsants include dizziness, rash, nausea, and drowsiness (Goodwin & Jamison, 1990).

Antianxiety Drugs

antianxiety drugs
drugs that reduce tension and cause drowsiness by depressing the action of the central nervous system

Antianxiety drugs *reduce tension and cause drowsiness by depressing the action of the central nervous system.* Most drugs that reduce anxiety belong to the family called benzodiazepines. They are commonly known as tranquilizers and are marketed under such trade names as Valium, Librium, and Xanax. The most frequent use of these drugs is as sleeping pills. Each year, as many as 70 million prescriptions are written for benzodiazepines in the United States. The drugs are also used to treat anxiety disorders, withdrawal from alcohol, and physical disorders related to stress. Unfortunately, the benzodiazepines are highly addictive, and up to 80% of people who take them for 6 weeks or more show withdrawal symptoms, including heart rate acceleration, irritability, and profuse sweating.

Antianxiety drugs can help people feel more calm and relaxed.

Stimulant Drugs

stimulant drugs drugs used to treat the attentional problems of people with attention deficit hyperactivity disorder

Finally, **stimulant drugs** are *used to treat the attentional problems of attention deficit hyperactivity disorder.* One of the most commonly used stimulants has the trade name Ritalin. Although it may seem odd to give a stimulant to a hyperactive person, between 60% and 90% of children with ADHD respond to these drugs with decreases in disruptive behavior and increases in attention (Gadow, 1992). For that matter, children *without* ADHD also show increases in attention span when they take Ritalin. These drugs have been controversial because some schools and physicians have been too quick to diagnose ADHD and to prescribe Ritalin for schoolchildren (Hinshaw, 1994). Stimulant drugs have significant side effects, including insomnia, headaches, tics, and nausea (Gadow, 1991, 1992). Thus, it is important that children be accurately diagnosed with ADHD before stimulant drugs are prescribed. Recently, many more adults have been diagnosed with ADHD and also have begun to take stimulant drugs.

Drug therapy has reduced the severity of many types of mental disorders. However, many clinicians believe that they should be used in conjunction with psychotherapy to help people overcome their psychological problems more fully. We turn now to an overview of some of the main types of psychotherapy.

Thinking Critically

If a drug became available that allowed people who were not suffering a psychological disorder to feel a little more self-confident, energetic, and creative, while not inducing any significant side effects, do you think this drug should be made widely available? Why or why not?

Can We Help People Change Thoughts and Behaviors? (Psychotherapy)

Psychotherapy refers to *the treatment of mental disorders by psychological means.* The term embraces a variety of techniques, all of which are intended to help people modify their behavior, thoughts, and emotions so that they can develop more useful ways of dealing with stress and with other people. We will discuss some of the major types of psychotherapy in terms of their application in one-on-one therapist–client interactions. All of these therapies, however, can and have been delivered to families, couples, and groups of people with similar problems, as well as to individuals.

Over the last 30 years, many claims have been made about the general effectiveness of psychotherapy (Eysenck, 1952; Roth & Fogary, 1996; Smith, Glass, & Singer, 1980). Today, most researchers argue that it is not enough to ask simply, "Does psychotherapy work?" Rather, the appropriate question is this: "What types of psychotherapy work for what types of disorders?" (Chambless & Hollon, 1998). Several controlled studies have been done in which different types of psychotherapy were compared to drug therapy or to controls in which people received no therapy for a specific disorder. These studies clearly suggest that certain forms of psychotherapy can be highly effective in the treatment of depression, anxiety disorders, eating disorders, substance abuse disorders, sexual disorders, and several childhood disorders, including conduct disorders and attention deficit hyperactivity disorder (DeRubeis & Crits-Cristoph, 1998; Kazdin & Weisz, 1998; Roth & Fogary, 1996) (see Table 13-2). Psychotherapy can also help reduce symptoms of autism and schizophrenia and lower the risk of relapse in schizophrenia (Hogarty et al., 1986; Kazdin & Weisz, 1998).

Not all forms of psychotherapy have been put to rigorous empirical tests for effectiveness, however. In general, proponents of behavioral and cognitive approaches to therapy have been interested in empirically testing the efficacy of their therapies, so many studies have focused on these types of therapies. In contrast, proponents of psychodynamic and humanistic therapies have been less concerned with empirical

psychotherapy the treatment of mental disorders by psychological means

---

Table 13-2

Psychotherapies Shown to Be Effective for Specific Adult Disorders   Controlled studies have shown that some psychotherapies are effective in the treatment of many of the adult disorders. (Sources: DeRubeis & Crits Cristoph, 1998; Markowitz & Weissman, 1995; Roth & Fogary, 1996).

Depression	**Generalized Anxiety Disorder**
Cognitive Therapy	Cognitive Therapy
Behavior Therapy	Relaxation Techniques
Interpersonal Therapy	**Social Phobia**
Schizophrenia (reduction of symptoms only)	Cognitive + Behavior Therapy
Social Skills Training (through Behavior Therapy)	**Obsessive-Compulsive Disorder**
Family Education on Symptoms and Management	Behavior Therapy
of Schizophrenia	Behavior + Cognitive Therapy
Substance Abuse & Dependence	**Agoraphobia**
Behavior Therapy	Behavior Therapy
Cognitive + Behavior Therapy	**Panic Disorder**
Interpersonal Therapy	Cognitive + Behavior Therapy
Eating Disorders	**Posttraumatic Stress Disorder**
Cognitive + Behavior Therapy	Behavior Therapy
Interpersonal Therapy	Stress Reduction (through
Sexual Disorders	Cognitive + Behavior Therapy)
Behavior Therapy	
Marital Therapy	

tests of their therapies (DeRubeis & Crits-Cristoph, 1998). As we describe each type of psychotherapy, we will note the findings in empirical research on its effectiveness for specific disorders.

Psychodynamic Therapies

psychodynamic therapies therapies based on the assumption that a person's problems cannot be successfully resolved without a thorough understanding of their unconscious basis in early relationships with parents and siblings

free association a technique in which the client is encouraged to give free rein to thoughts and feelings and to say whatever comes to mind without editing or censoring

resistance a condition that results from the individual's unconscious control over sensitive areas

dream analysis talking about the content of one's dreams and then free-associating to that content

A key assumption of **psychodynamic therapies** is that *a person's current problems cannot be successfully resolved without a thorough understanding of their unconscious basis in early relationships with parents and siblings.* The goal of these therapies is to bring conflicts (repressed emotions and motives) into awareness so that they can be dealt with in a more rational and realistic way. The psychodynamic therapies include traditional Freudian psychoanalysis and more recent therapies derived from psychoanalysis.

One of the main techniques traditional psychoanalysts use to facilitate the recovery of unconscious conflicts is **free association,** whereby *the client is encouraged to give free rein to thoughts and feelings and to say whatever comes to mind without editing or censoring.* This is not easy to do, however. In conversation, we usually try to keep a connecting thread running through our remarks and to exclude irrelevant ideas. We also learn to withhold thoughts that seem inappropriate, stupid, or shameful. With practice, free association becomes easier. But even people who are trying to "say it all" will find themselves blocked occasionally, unable to recall the details of an event, or to finish a thought. Freud believed that blocking, or **resistance,** results from *the individual's unconscious control over sensitive areas,* and that these are precisely the areas that should be explored. Another technique often used in traditional psychoanalytic therapy is **dream analysis,** or *talking about the content of one's dreams and then free-associating to that content.* Freud believed that dreams are the "royal road to the unconscious," representing an unconscious wish or fear in disguised form.

Freud's office in Vienna offered the comfort of his famous couch, as well as a collection of Egyptian, Greek, and Roman antiquities.

As the therapist and client interact during therapy, the client will often react to the therapist in ways that seem exaggerated or inappropriate. The client may become enraged when the therapist must reschedule an appointment, or may be excessively deferential to the therapist. The tendency for the client to make the therapist the object of emotional responses is known as **transference:** *The client expresses attitudes toward the therapist that the client actually feels toward other people who are, or were, important in his or her life.* By pointing out how their clients are reacting to them, therapists help their clients achieve a better understanding of how they react to others. The following excerpt shows an analyst's use of transference, followed by the use of free association (adapted from Woody & Robertson, 1988, p. 129):

CLIENT: I don't understand why you're holding back on telling me if this step is the right one for me at this time in my life.

THERAPIST: This has come up before. You want my approval before taking some action. What seems to be happening here is that one of the conflicts you have with your wife is trying to get her approval of what you have decided you want to do, and that conflict is occurring now between us.

CLIENT: I suppose so. Other people's approval has always been very important to me.

THERAPIST: Let's stay with that for a few minutes. Would you free-associate to that idea of getting approval from others? Just let the associations come spontaneously—don't force them.

Traditional psychoanalysis is a lengthy, intensive, and expensive process. The client and analyst usually meet for 50-minute sessions several times a week for at least a year, and often for several years. Many people find self-exploration under traditional psychoanalysis to be extremely valuable. For some people, however, it is unaffordable. In addition, people suffering from acute depression, anxiety, or psychosis typically cannot tolerate the lack of structure in traditional psychoanalysis, and need more immediate relief from their symptoms.

In response to these pressures and to changes in psychodynamic theories since Freud's time, newer psychodynamic therapies tend to be more structured and short-term than traditional psychoanalysis. **Interpersonal therapy** is *a relatively recent form of psychodynamic therapy* (Klerman et al., 1986). Sessions are scheduled less frequently, usually once a week. There is less emphasis on complete reconstruction of childhood experiences and more attention to problems arising from the way the individual is currently interacting with others. Free association is often replaced with direct discussion of critical issues, and the interpersonal therapist may be more direct, raising pertinent topics when it seems appropriate rather than waiting for the client to bring them up. While transference is still considered an important part of the therapeutic process, the therapist may try to limit the intensity of the transference process. Some research has shown that interpersonal therapy is helpful in the treatment of depression, anxiety, drug addiction, and eating disorders (Markowitz & Weissman, 1995).

Still central, however, is the psychodynamic therapist's conviction that unconscious motives and fears are at the core of most emotional problems and that insight is essential to cure. As we will see next, behavior therapists do not agree with these ideas.

Behavior Therapies

Behavior therapists point out that, although achieving insight is a worthwhile goal, it does not ensure behavior change. Often we understand why we behave the way we do in a certain situation but are not able to change our behavior. If you are timid about speaking in class, you may be able to trace this fear to past events (your father criticized your opinions when you expressed them, your mother corrected your grammar constantly), but this may not make it much easier for you to speak up in class.

---

transference a condition in which the client expresses attitudes toward the therapist that the client actually feels toward other people who are, or were, important in his or her life

interpersonal therapy a recent form of psychodynamic therapy, focused more on current relationships

behavior therapies
therapies that focus on changing people's maladaptive behaviors in specific situations

Behavior therapies focus on *changing people's maladaptive behaviors in specific situations,* rather than on changing broad aspects of their personality. The first step in behavior therapy is to define the problem behaviors clearly and to break them down into a set of specific therapeutic goals. If, for example, the client complains of general feelings of inadequacy, the therapist will try to help the client pinpoint the kinds of situations in which these feelings occur and the kinds of behaviors associated with them. Once the behaviors that need to be changed have been specified, the therapist and client work out a treatment program that employs a number of different strategies to create change.

Relaxation exercises are often part of behavioral therapy.

systematic desensitization   a strategy for changing anxious responses to stimuli and the maladaptive behaviors that accompany this anxiety by substituting a response that is incompatible with anxiety—namely, relaxation

Systematic desensitization is *a strategy for changing anxious responses to stimuli and the maladaptive behaviors that accompany this anxiety by substituting a response that is incompatible with anxiety—namely, relaxation.* This strategy is highly effective in treating anxiety disorders.

The client is first trained in relaxation exercises. He or she is taught to use deep breathing and progressive tensing and relaxing of muscle groups to relax the whole body. The next step is to make up a hierarchy of the situations that produce anxiety. The situations are ranked in order from one that produces little anxiety to one that produces most anxiety. The client is then asked to relax and imagine each situation in the hierarchy, starting with the one that is least anxiety-producing and eventually proceeding to more anxiety-producing situations.

Table 13-3

Anxiety Hierarchy for a Person With a Snake Phobia
A person with a snake phobia might be asked to list his or her feared situations, from the least anxiety-provoking ones, to the most anxiety-provoking ones, to create an anxiety hierarchy such as the one below.

(Least Anxiety-Provoking)

1. Seeing a picture of a snake
2. Seeing a picture of someone else near a snake
3. Touching a toy snake
4. Seeing a live snake in a cage
5. Seeing another person touching a live snake
6. Being near a live snake by myself
7. Touching a live snake
8. Handling a live snake

(Most Anxiety-Provoking)

An example will make these procedures clearer. Suppose that the client is a woman who suffers from a phobia of snakes. This phobia is so strong that the woman is afraid to walk in her own backyard for fear of encountering a snake, let alone go for a walk in the countryside or on a vacation to a resort in the woods. Her anxiety hierarchy might begin with a picture of a snake in a book (see Table 13-3). Somewhere around the middle of her hierarchy might be viewing a snake in a glass cage at the zoo. At the top of her list would be actually handling a large snake. After the woman has learned to relax and has constructed the hierarchy, the therapist would begin to take her through her list. She would sit with her eyes closed in a comfortable chair while the therapist describes the least anxiety-provoking situation to her. If she can imagine herself in the situation without any increase in anxiety, the therapist proceeds to the next item on the list. If the woman reports any anxiety while visualizing a scene, she concentrates on relaxing. The same scene is visualized until all anxiety is neutralized. This process continues through a series of sessions until the situation that originally provoked the most anxiety now elicits only relaxation. At this point, the woman has been systematically desensitized to anxiety-provoking situations through the strengthening of an incompatible response—relaxation.

Sometimes it is not enough to imagine the anxiety-provoking situations—the client must actually experience these situations and learn to relax in them in order to overcome the anxiety. This is known as *in vivo exposure therapy*. During this type of therapy, the woman with a snake phobia would actually experience each of the situations on her list, beginning with the one she fears least. Before the woman actually handled a snake herself, the therapist might model handling the snake without being fearful. The therapist would hold the snake in the client's presence, displaying confidence and no anxiety. Eventually the woman would handle the snake herself, allowing it to crawl on her, while using relaxation to control her anxiety. In vivo exposure therapy has proven extremely effective in the treatment of specific phobias, agoraphobia, and obsessive-compulsive disorder (Bandura, Blanchard, & Rifter, 1969; Emmelkamp & Kuipus, 1979; Steketee & White, 1990) (see Figure 13-2).

Often, clients seeking therapy want to learn how to interact with other people more effectively. They may become extremely anxious when they meet a new person, or are depressed because they feel socially isolated or rejected. **Behavioral rehearsal,** more commonly referred to as **role-playing,** is *a behavioral technique for helping clients learn more effective behaviors, especially social behaviors.* In the following excerpt, a therapist helps a young man overcome his anxieties about asking women for dates. The young man has been pretending to talk to a woman over the phone and finishes by asking for a date:

Behavior therapy has proven very effective in treating the anxiety disorders, such as a snake phobia.

behavioral rehearsal (role-playing) a behavioral technique for helping clients learn more effective behaviors, especially social behaviors

CLIENT:	Um, I was wondering, you wouldn't want to go out on a date Saturday night or anything, would you?
THERAPIST:	Okay, that's a start. Can you think of another way that sounds a bit more positive and confident? For example, "There's a concert I'd like to see on Saturday night and I'd like very much to take you, if you are free."
CLIENT:	That's great!
THERAPIST:	Okay, you try it.
CLIENT:	Um, I've got two tickets to the concert Saturday night. If you don't have anything to do, you might want to come along.
THERAPIST:	That's better. Try it again, but this time try to convey to her that you'd really like her to go.
CLIENT:	I've got two tickets for Saturday's concert. It would be great if you'd go with me, if you're not busy.
THERAPIST:	That's terrific, you're making great progress!

This example illustrates the use of behavioral rehearsal in one type of assertiveness training.

Figure 13-2

Treatment of Snake Phobia   The mean number of snake-approach responses by individuals before and after they received different behavior therapy treatments. (After Bandura, Blanchard, & Ritter, 1969)

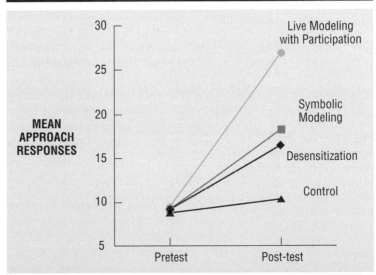

selective reinforcement a behavioral technique that can help clients change maladaptive behaviors by setting up reinforcements for positive behaviors and removing reinforcements for negative behaviors

Like the young man in the example, many people have trouble asking for what they want or refusing to allow others to take advantage of them. By practicing assertive responses (first in role-playing with the therapist and then in real-life situations), the individual not only reduces anxiety but also develops more effective coping techniques (see Table 13-4).

Selective reinforcement is another *behavioral technique that can help clients change maladaptive behaviors by setting up reinforcements for positive behaviors and removing reinforcements for negative behaviors*. Take the example of a third-grade student who was inattentive in school, refused to complete assignments or participate in class, and spent most of her time daydreaming. The behavior that her teachers and family wanted to reinforce was "on task" behavior, including paying attention to schoolwork, completing reading assignments, and taking part in class discussions. Every time the girl completed one of these

Table 13-4

Some Elements of an Assertive Response

- Decide what you want to say and stick with it rather than giving into others the minute they disagree with you. For example, when a clerk says you cannot return a defective product, say "This is defective and I want to return it" repeatedly until the clerk allows you to return it or at least calls the manager, whom you tell "This is defective and I want to return it" until you get your money back.

- Ask for small, specific changes in a situation or another person's behavior rather than requesting global changes. For example, rather than saying, "I want you to be more loving," say, "I want you to listen to me when I talk."

- Use "I" phrases instead of accusatory phrases when discussing a difficult situation with another person. Four pieces to an "I" statement are:
  I feel . . .
  when you . . .
  because . . .
  what I want . . .
  For example, *"I feel* angry *when you* don't show up for an appointment *because* it wastes my time. *What I want* is for you to call me and cancel our appointment when you think you won't be able to make it."

behaviors, she was given a bean or a token that could be exchanged for special privileges that the girl valued, such as standing first in line (three beans) or being allowed to stay after school to help the teacher with special projects (nine beans). If she did not complete one of her on task behaviors during the school day, she received no beans.

During the first 3 months of treatment, the girl completed 12 units of schoolwork, compared to zero units during the 3 months before the selective reinforcement regime started. In the final 3 months, she completed 36 units of schoolwork and was performing at the same level as the rest of the class. A follow-up in the next year showed that the girl was maintaining her academic performance. She also showed a marked improvement in social skills and was accepted more by the other children (Walker et al., 1981). This is a common finding: Improving behavior in one area of life often produces added benefits (Kazdin, 1982).

A number of mental hospitals have instituted "token economies" on wards with very impaired people with schizophrenia. Tokens (which can later be exchanged for privileges such as watching television) are given for dressing properly, interacting with other patients, eliminating "psychotic talk," helping on the wards, and so on. Such programs have proven useful in improving both clients' behavior and the general functioning of inpatient psychiatric wards (Paul & Lentz, 1977).

Cognitive Therapies

cognitive therapy a form of therapy that attempts to help people control disturbing emotional reactions, such as anxiety and depression, by teaching them more effective ways of interpreting and thinking about their experiences

A therapist using **cognitive therapy** attempts to *help people control disturbing emotional reactions, such as anxiety and depression, by teaching them more effective ways of interpreting and thinking about their experiences*. For example, in treating depression, cognitive therapists try to help their clients recognize the distortions in their thinking and make changes toward more adaptive ways of thinking. The following dialogue illustrates how a therapist, by means of carefully directed questioning, makes a client aware of the unrealistic nature of her beliefs.

CLIENT: Without my boyfriend, I can't go on, I just don't want to live.

THERAPIST: What has your relationship with your boyfriend been like?

CLIENT: It's been miserable lately. He clearly has been pulling away. I think he's got another girlfriend.

THERAPIST: You say you can't be happy without your boyfriend. Have you been happy with your boyfriend?

CLIENT: Not for the last several months. We fight all the time and I feel terrible.

THERAPIST: You say you are nothing without your boyfriend. Before you met your boyfriend, did you feel you were nothing?

CLIENT: No, I felt I was somebody. In fact, he's always put me down. I felt a lot better about myself before I met him.

THERAPIST: If you felt better before you met him, and he puts you down a lot, why do you think you would feel good if he stayed?

CLIENT: Well, maybe I wouldn't.

Although supportive friends can help us get through stressful times, we may need psychotherapy to get through more severe problems.

Many cognitive therapists also employ behavioral techniques to help clients challenge their negative beliefs and learn new skills. For example, the woman in this dialogue may be encouraged to spend an evening with friends other than her boyfriend, then to record her feelings at the end of the evening. This information could serve to challenge her belief that she can't be happy without her boyfriend. It could also reinstill skills at interacting with others.

In working with a person with panic attacks and agoraphobia, a cognitive therapist might help the client replace self-defeating internal dialogues ("I'm so nervous, I know I'll faint as soon as I leave the house") with positive self-instructions ("Be calm; I'm not alone; even if I have a panic attack, I can cope"). The therapist might go with the client on excursions into the situations the client finds most frightening. This in vivo exposure to frightening situations will help extinguish the client's anxiety and allow the therapist to help the client practice cognitive skills to quell the anxiety-producing thoughts that arise in those situations.

Combined cognitive-behavioral therapies have proven highly effective in treating an array of nonpsychotic conditions, including depression, anxiety disorders, eating disorders, drug and alcohol addiction, and sexual dysfunctions (Fairburn et al., 1995; Jacobson & Hollon, 1996; Margraf et al., 1993; Marlatt et al., 1993; Rosen & Lieblum, 1995) (see Figure 13-3). These therapies tend not only to

Figure 13-3

Percentage of Panic Patients Remaining Symptom-Free After 15 Months People receiving cognitive-behavioral therapy for panic disorder were more likely to remain symptom-free over 15 months than people receiving only drug therapy or relaxation training. (After Clark et al., 1994)

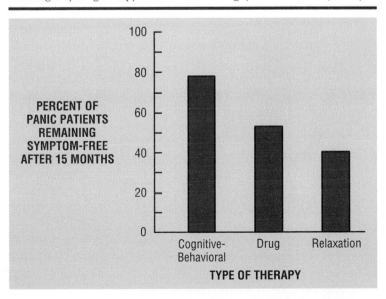

help people overcome troubling thoughts, feelings, and behaviors, but also to prevent relapses into their problems after therapy has ended.

Humanistic Therapies

While there are different varieties of humanistic therapies, all emphasize the individual's natural tendency toward growth and self-actualization. Psychological disorders are assumed to arise when the process of reaching one's potential is blocked by circumstances or by other people (parents, teachers, spouses) who try to channel the person's development along lines that they find acceptable. When this occurs, the person begins to deny his or her true desires. The person's awareness of his or her uniqueness becomes narrowed and the potential for growth is reduced. **Humanistic therapies** seek to *help people get in touch with their real selves and to make deliberate choices regarding their lives and behavior, rather than letting external events determine their behavior.* The goal of humanistic therapy is to help the client become more like the person he or she is capable of becoming.

humanistic therapies therapies that seek to help people get in touch with their real selves and to make deliberate choices regarding their lives and behavior, rather than letting external events determine their behavior

Like the psychoanalyst, the humanistic therapist attempts to increase the person's awareness of underlying emotions and motives. But the emphasis is on what the individual is experiencing in the here and now, rather than in the past. The humanistic therapist does not interpret the person's behavior (as a psychoanalyst might) or try to modify it (as a behavior therapist would) because such actions would impose the therapist's own views on the patient. The goal of the humanistic therapist is to facilitate exploration of the individual's own thoughts and feelings and to assist the individual in arriving at his or her own solutions. This approach will become clearer as we look at client-centered therapy (also called nondirective therapy), one of the first humanistic therapies.

client-centered therapy a form of therapy based on the assumption that the individual is the best expert on himself or herself and that people are capable of working out solutions to their own problems

Client-centered therapy, developed in the 1940s by the late Carl Rogers, is based on the assumption that *the individual is the best expert on himself or herself and that people are capable of working out solutions to their own problems.* The task of the therapist is to facilitate this progress, not to ask probing questions, make interpretations, or suggest courses of action. In fact, Rogers preferred the term "facilitator" to "therapist," and he called the people he worked with "clients" rather than "patients" because he did not view emotional difficulties as an indication of an illness to be cured. The therapist facilitates the client's progress toward self-insight by restating to the client what the therapist hears the client saying about his or her needs and emotions. The goal is to help the client clarify his feelings.

Rogers believed that the most important qualities for a therapist are empathy, warmth, and genuineness. *Empathy* refers to the ability to understand the feelings the client is trying to express and the ability to communicate this understanding to the client. The therapist must adopt the client's frame of reference and strive to see the problems the way the client sees them. By *warmth,* Rogers meant a deep acceptance of the individual as he or she is, including the conviction that this person has the capacity to deal constructively with his or her problems. A therapist who is *genuine* is open and honest and does not play a role or operate behind a professional façade. People are reluctant to reveal themselves to those whom they perceive as phony. Rogers believed that a therapist who possesses these three attributes will facilitate the client's growth and self-exploration (Rogers, 1970; Truax & Mitchell, 1971).

Client-centered therapists listen to their clients, conveying a genuine empathy and warmth.

Client-centered therapy has some limitations, however. Like psychoanalysis, it appears to be successful only with individuals who are fairly verbal and are motivated to discuss their problems. For people who do not voluntarily seek help or are seriously disturbed and are unable to discuss their feelings, more directive methods are usually necessary.

An Eclectic Approach

There are many variations of psychotherapy in addition to the ones we have discussed here. Most psychotherapists do not adhere strictly to any single method. Instead, they take an eclectic approach, selecting from the different techniques the ones they feel are most appropriate given the client's personality and specific symptoms. In addition, many psychotherapists use both psychotherapeutic techniques and drug therapies in treating clients. Psychotherapists who are not physicians will work with a physician who will prescribe drugs for their clients.

Despite differences in the specific techniques employed, most methods of psychotherapy have certain basic features in common. They involve a helping relationship between two people: a client (patient) and the therapist. The client is encouraged to discuss intimate concerns, emotions, and experiences freely without fear of being judged by the therapist or having confidences betrayed. The therapist, in turn, offers sympathy and understanding, engenders trust, and tries to help the client develop more effective ways of handling his or her problems. Several theorists have argued that these common components of psychotherapy account for their effectiveness more than any method specific to a type of psychotherapy (Garfield, 1980; Luborsky et al., 1985; Orlinsky & Howard, 1987).

Group and Family Therapy

Many emotional problems involve an individual's difficulties in relating to others, including feelings of isolation, rejection, and loneliness and inability to form meaningful relationships. Although the therapist can help the individual work out some of these problems, the final test lies in how well the person can apply the attitudes and responses learned in therapy to relationships in everyday life. **Group therapy** *permits clients to work out their problems in the presence of others, to observe how other people react to their behavior, and to try out new methods of responding when old ones prove unsatisfactory.* It is often used as a supplement to individual psychotherapy.

Therapists of various orientations (psychoanalytic, humanistic, and cognitive-behaviorist) have modified their techniques so that they can be applied to therapy groups. Group therapy has been used in a variety of settings—in hospital wards and outpatient psychiatric clinics, with parents of disturbed children, and with teenagers in correctional institutions, to name a few. Typically, the groups consist of a small number of individuals (6 to 8 is considered optimal) who have similar problems. The therapist usually remains in the background, allowing the members to exchange experiences, comment on one another's behavior, and discuss their own problems as well as those of the other members. However, in some groups the therapist is quite active. For example, in a group desensitization session, people who share the same phobias (such as fear of flying or test anxiety) may be led together through a systematic desensitization hierarchy. Or in a session for training social skills, a group of shy and unassertive individuals may be coached by the therapist in a series of role-playing

group therapy a form of therapy that permits clients to work out their problems in the presence of others, observe how other people react to their behavior, and try out new methods of responding when old ones prove unsatisfactory

Group therapy often involves people with similar problems working together.

scenes. Group therapy has several advantages over individual therapy. It uses the therapist's resources more efficiently because one therapist can help several people at once. An individual can derive comfort and support from observing that others have similar, perhaps more severe problems. A person can learn vicariously by watching how others behave and can explore attitudes and reactions by interacting with a variety of people, not just with the therapist. Groups are particularly effective when they give the participants opportunities to acquire new social skills through modeling and to practice these skills in the group.

Most groups are led by a trained therapist. However, the number and variety of self-help groups—groups that are conducted without a professional therapist—are increasing. *Self-help groups* are voluntary organizations of people who meet regularly to exchange information and support one another's efforts to overcome a common problem. Alcoholics Anonymous is the best known of the self-help groups. Another is Recovery, Inc., an organization open to former mental patients. Other groups help people cope with specific stressful situations such as bereavement, divorce, and single parenthood.

In group homes or therapeutic communities, people who share certain psychological problems live together in a supportive atmosphere, usually with the aid of other residents who are mental health professionals. A classic example of this is The Lodge, a residential treatment center established by George Fairweather and colleagues (1969) for people with schizophrenia. At The Lodge, residents were responsible for running the household and working with other residents to encourage appropriate behaviors. The residents also established their own employment agency to help each other find jobs. Studies showed that Lodge residents were less likely to be rehospitalized and much more likely to hold jobs than people with schizophrenia who were simply discharged from a hospital into the care of their families or less intensive treatment programs (Fairweather et al., 1969).

marital therapy a form of therapy that focuses on helping the partners communicate their feelings, develop greater understanding and sensitivity to each other's needs, and work on more effective ways of handling their conflicts

Marital and Family Therapy   Problems in communicating feelings, satisfying one's needs, and responding appropriately to the needs and demands of others become intensified in the intimate context of marriage and family life. To the extent that they involve more than one client and focus on interpersonal relationships, marital therapy and family therapy can be considered specialized forms of group therapy. The high divorce rate and the number of couples seeking help for difficulties centering on their relationship have made marital, or couple, therapy a growing field. Studies show that joint therapy for both partners is more effective in solving marital problems than is individual therapy for only one partner (Baucom et al., 1998). Marital therapy can also be very helpful when one member of a couple has a psychological disorder, and the marriage is being disrupted by the symptoms or consequences of the disorder.

There are many approaches to **marital therapy,** but most focus on *helping the partners communicate their feelings, develop greater understanding and sensitivity to each other's needs, and work on more effective ways of handling their conflicts.* Some couples enter marriage with very different, and often unrealistic, expectations about each other's roles, which can wreak havoc with their relationship. The therapist can help them clarify their expectations and work out a mutually agreeable compromise. Sometimes the couple negotiates behavioral contracts, agreeing on the behavior changes each person is willing to make in order to create a more satisfying relationship, and specifying the rewards

Many family therapists view an individual's problems as part of a maladaptive pattern of family interactions.

and penalties they can use with each other to ensure that the changes are made.

Family therapy overlaps with marital therapy but has a somewhat different origin. It developed in response to the discovery that many people who improved in individual therapy while away from their family—often in institutional settings—relapsed when they returned home. It became apparent that many of these people came from a disturbed family setting that must itself be modified if the individual's gains were to be maintained. When the person with a psychological problem is a child, it is particularly important that the family be treated, because children are entirely dependent on their families. The basic premise of family therapy is that the problem shown by the identified patient is a sign that something is wrong with the entire family—in other words, the family system is not operating properly. The difficulty may lie in poor communication among family members or in an alliance between some family members that excludes others. For example, a mother whose relationship with her husband is unsatisfactory may focus all her attention on her son. As a result, the husband and daughter feel neglected and the son, upset by his mother's smothering and the resentment directed toward him by his father and sister, develops problems in school. While the boy's school difficulties may be the reason for seeking treatment, it is clear that they are only a symptom of a more basic family problem.

In **family therapy**, the family meets regularly with one or two therapists (usually a male and a female). *The therapist, while observing the interactions among family members, tries to help each member become aware of the way he or she relates to the others and how his or her actions may be contributing to the family's problems.* Sometimes videotape recordings are played back to make the family members aware of how they interact. Other times, the therapist may visit the family in the home to observe conflicts and verbal exchanges as they occur in their natural setting. It often becomes apparent that problem behaviors are being reinforced by the responses of family members. For example, a young child's temper tantrums or a teenager's eating problems may be inadvertently reinforced by the attention they elicit from the parents. The therapist can teach the parents to monitor their own and their children's behavior, determine how their reactions may be reinforcing the problem behavior, and then alter the reinforcement situations. Family therapy has been shown to be effective in the treatment of a number of childhood disorders (Kaslow & Rascussen, 1994).

One important application of family therapy involves teaching the families of people with schizophrenia to communicate more positively and clearly with one another (Goldstein, 1987). Schizophrenics in families in which conflict and hostility are expressed in hurtful ways and family members are overinvolved in one another's lives tend to have more frequent relapses than schizophrenics in families in which conflict and hostility are expressed more calmly and family members respect each other's independence. Training programs that enhance families' skills in expressing negative emotion and interacting in positive ways can reduce relapse rates for people with schizophrenia (Hogarty et al., 1986) (see Figure 13-4).

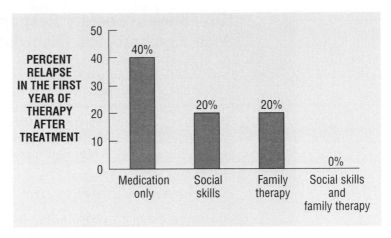

Figure 13-4

Effects of Psychosocial Intervention With Medication on Relapse Rates   Schizophrenic patients who received either social skills training, family therapy, or both in addition to medication had much lower relapse rates in the first year after treatment than did patients who received only medication.

family therapy a form of therapy in which the therapist observes the interactions among family members and tries to help each member become aware of the way he or she relates to the others and how his or her actions may be contributing to the family's problems

How might a psychotherapist adapt the other therapeutic methods described in this chapter to help a person with schizophrenia? Which of these methods do you think would be helpful for a person with schizophrenia? Which methods would not be helpful?

Thinking Critically

How Should Society Respond to People With Psychological Disorders?

People with psychological disorders raise a number of difficult issues for societies. What obligation do societies have toward these people? Should people with serious psychological disorders be forced to obtain treatment even if they do not want it? Should they be held responsible for their behavior in the same way as people without psychological disorders? The answers to these questions are complex and vary across cultures and in different historical periods.

The Deinstitutionalization Movement

Until the 1960s many people with serious psychological disorders (particularly people who became psychotic) were kept in mental hospitals, often against their will. Clifford Beers, who lived around the turn of the 20th century, was one of these people. As a young man, Beers developed a bipolar disorder and was confined for 3 years in several private and state hospitals. Although chains and other methods of torture had been abandoned long before, the straitjacket was still widely used to restrain excited patients. Lack of funds made the average state mental hospital—with its overcrowded wards, poor food, and unsympathetic attendants—a far from pleasant place to live. After his recovery, Beers wrote about his experiences in the now-famous book *A Mind That Found Itself* (1908), which aroused considerable public interest. Beers worked ceaselessly to educate the public about mental illness, and helped organize the National Committee for Mental Hygiene. In 1950 this organization joined with two related groups to form the National Association for Mental Health. The mental hygiene movement played an invaluable role in stimulating the organization of child guidance clinics and community mental health centers to aid in the prevention and treatment of mental disorders.

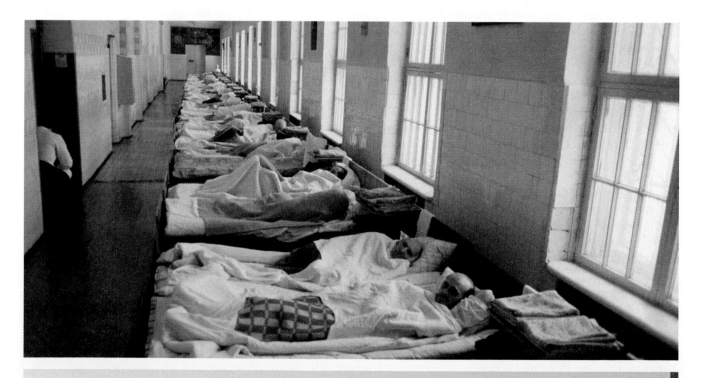

Patients with mental disorders were formerly warehoused in mental institutions.

Mental hospitals have been upgraded considerably since Beers's time, but there is still much room for improvement. The best of these hospitals are comfortable and well-kept places that provide drug therapies and a number of therapeutic activities: individual and group psychotherapy, recreation, training in occupational skills, and educational courses. The worst are primarily custodial institutions where patients lead a boring existence in run-down, overcrowded wards and receive little treatment except for medication. Most mental hospitals fall somewhere between these two extremes.

Beginning in the early 1960s, emphasis shifted from treating mentally disturbed people in hospitals to treating them in their own communities. This movement toward deinstitutionalization was motivated partly by the recognition that hospitalization has some inherent disadvantages, regardless of how good the facilities may be. Hospitals remove people from the social support of family and friends and from their patterns of daily life. They tend to make people feel "sick" and unable to cope with the world. They encourage dependence. They are also very expensive.

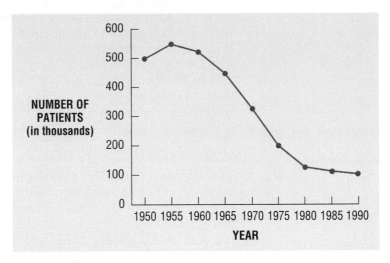

During the 1950s drugs that could relieve depression and anxiety and reduce psychosis were discovered. When these drugs became widely available in the 1960s, it was possible for many hospitalized patients to be discharged and returned home, where they could be treated as outpatients (see Figure 13-5). Community mental health centers were built to provide outpatient treatment and other services, including short-term hospitalization and partial hospitalization. (Partial hospitalization allows people to receive treatment at the center during the day and return home in the evening, or work during the day and spend nights at the center.)

Figure 13-5

Patients in Mental Hospitals　The number of patients cared for in the United States' state and county mental hospitals has decreased dramatically over the past 35 years.

The number of patients treated in mental hospitals has decreased dramatically over the past 40 years. For some patients, deinstitutionalization has worked. For others, however, deinstitutionalization has had unfortunate consequences, largely because the facilities in most communities are far from adequate. Follow-up care for people who have been released from inpatient facilities is often lacking, and as a consequence they lead a revolving-door existence, going in and out of institutions between unsuccessful attempts to cope on their own. About half of all patients discharged from state mental hospitals are readmitted within a year.

Some people do not make it back into care. They may live in dirty, overcrowded housing or roam the streets. The disheveled man standing on the

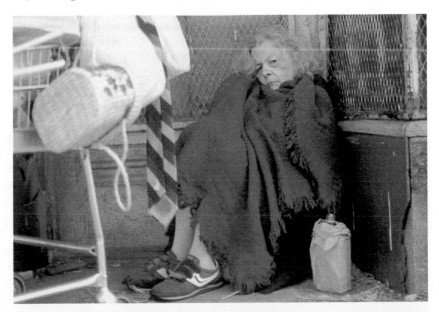

Some people with mental disorders end up on the streets.

corner talking to himself may be one victim of deinstitutionalization. The woman with all her worldly possessions in a shopping bag, who spends one night in the doorway of an office building and the next in a subway station, may be another. Estimates of the rates of serious mental illness among the homeless are typically around 20% to 30% (Koegel, Burnam, & Farr, 1988; Morse & Calsyn, 1992). In emergencies, these people end up in general or private hospitals that often are not equipped to treat them appropriately (Kiesler & Sibulkin, 1983).

Civil Commitment

The increasing visibility of homeless mentally ill people has aroused public concern and prompted a move toward reinstitutionalization. However, an important ethical issue is involved. If such people are not readjusting to society, should they be involuntarily committed to a mental hospital? One of the most cherished civil rights in a democratic society is the right to liberty.

civil commitment
committing people to mental health facilities against their will

Three different criteria are used in the process known as **civil commitment,** in which *people are committed to mental health facilities against their will.* In most states in the United States, people who show *grave disability*—who are so incapacitated by a mental disorder that they cannot care for their basic needs of food, clothing, and shelter—can be committed to a mental institution against their will. Yet it has proven difficult for public officials to use the grave disability criterion to institutionalize the homeless mentally ill. For example, in the bitter winter of 1988, former New York Mayor Ed Koch invoked the legal principle of *parens patriae* ("sovereign as parent") to have mentally ill homeless people picked up from the streets of New York City and taken to mental health facilities. He argued that it was the city's duty to protect these people when they were unable, because of grave disability due to their mental disorder, to protect themselves from the ravages of the winter weather. One of the homeless people who were involuntarily hospitalized in this campaign was Joyce Brown, a 40-year-old woman with schizophrenia who had been living on the streets for years, despite her family's attempts to house her and obtain treatment for her. Brown contested her commitment, with the help of the American Civil Liberties Union, and won her release on the grounds that the city had no right to incarcerate her if she had no intention of being treated.

Most people who are involuntarily committed based on the grave disability criterion, however, do not have the wherewithal that Joyce Brown did to contest her commitment. They often have long histories of serious mental disorders and few financial resources. Often they are committed to psychiatric facilities because there are no less restrictive facilities available in their communities and no family members to care for them (Turkheimer & Parry, 1992).

Another criterion used to commit people to a mental health facility against their will is that they are an *imminent danger to themselves*—that is, they appear highly likely to harm themselves if left alone. In such cases, people can be held in an inpatient psychiatric facility for a few days while undergoing further evaluation and possibly treatment.

Finally, people can be involuntarily committed if they pose an *imminent danger to others.* The rare, but highly publicized, occasions when a mentally ill person experiencing a psychotic episode attacks an innocent bystander have generated fears for public safety. But dangerousness is difficult to predict (Gardner et al., 1996; Lidz, Mulvey, & Gardner, 1993). Although people with serious mental disorders do appear in general to commit violent crimes more often than people with no psychological disorders (Monahan, 1992), expert opinions of whether any specific individual with a mental disorder will commit violent crimes are as often wrong as they are correct (Monahan & Walker, 1990) (see Figure 13-6).

Moreover, our legal system is designed to protect people from preventive detention. A person is assumed to be innocent until he or she has been proven guilty by thc courts, and prisoners are released from penitentiaries even though statistics show that most will commit additional crimes. Many people argue that people with psychological disorders should have the same rights.

The Insanity Defense and Competence to Stand Trial

How should the law treat a mentally disturbed person who commits a criminal offense? Should individuals whose mental faculties are impaired be held responsible for their actions? Over the centuries, an important part of Western law has been the concept that a civilized *society should not punish a person who is mentally incapable of controlling his or her conduct*—a principle leading to what we call the **insanity defense.** In 1724, an English court maintained that a man was not responsible for an act if "he doth not know what he

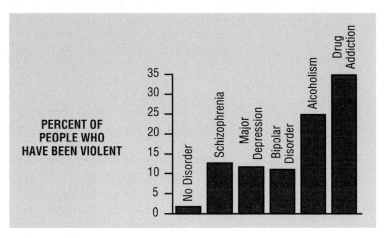

Figure 13-6

Percentage of People Who Have Been Violent as a Function of Diagnosed Psychiatric Disorders   People with severe psychiatric disorders do appear to be at increased risk for being violent compared to people with no psychiatric diagnosis. (After Monahan, 1992)

insanity defense
legal defense based on the principle that society should not punish a person who is mentally incapable of controlling his or her conduct

is doing, no more than . . . a wild beast". Modern standards of legal responsibility, however, have been based on the M'Naghten decision of 1843.

M'Naghten, a Scotsman, suffered the paranoid delusion that he was being persecuted by the English prime minister, Sir Robert Peel. In an attempt to kill Peel, he mistakenly shot Peel's secretary. Everyone involved in the trial was convinced by M'Naghten's senseless ramblings that he was insane. He was judged not responsible by reason of insanity and sent to a mental hospital, where he remained until his death. But Queen Victoria was not pleased with the verdict—apparently she felt that political assassinations should not be taken lightly—and called upon the House of Lords to review the decision. The decision was upheld, and rules for the legal definition of insanity were put into writing. The *M'Naghten Rule* states that a defendant may be found not guilty by reason of insanity only if he was so severely disturbed at the time of his act that he did not know what he was doing or, if he did know what he was doing, that he did not know it was wrong.

The M'Naghten Rule was adopted in the United States, and the distinction of knowing right from wrong remained the basis of most decisions of legal insanity for more than a century. Some states added to their statutes the doctrine of "irresistible impulse," which recognizes that some mentally ill individuals may respond correctly when asked if a particular act is morally right or wrong but may be unable to control their behavior.

During the 1970s, a number of state and federal courts adopted a broader legal definition of insanity proposed by the American Law Institute. This rule states that "A person is not responsible for criminal conduct if at the time of such conduct, as a result of mental disease or defect, he lacks substantial capacity either to appreciate the wrongfulness of his conduct or to conform his conduct to the requirements of the law." The word *substantial* suggests that any incapacity is not enough to avoid criminal responsibility but that total incapacity is not required either. The use of the word *appreciate* rather than *know* implies that intellectual awareness of right or wrong is not enough; individuals must have some understanding of the moral or legal consequences of their behavior before they can be held criminally responsible.

The problem of legal responsibility in the case of mentally disordered individuals became a topic of increased debate in the wake of John Hinckley, Jr.'s, acquittal, by reason of insanity, for the attempted assassination of President Ronald Reagan in 1981. Many Americans were outraged by the verdict and felt that the insanity defense was a legal loophole that allowed too many guilty people to go free. In response, Congress enacted the Insanity Defense Reform Act (1984), which contains a number of provisions designed to make it more difficult to absolve a defendant of legal responsibility. For example, the act changes the American Law Institute's "lacks substantial capacity . . . to appreciate" to "is unable to appreciate"; it stipulates that the mental disease or defect must be "severe" (the intent being to exclude nonpsychotic disorders such as antisocial personality); and it shifts the burden of proof from the prosecution to the defense (instead of the prosecution having to prove that the person was sane beyond a reasonable doubt at the time of the crime, the defense must prove that he or she was not sane, and must do so with "clear and convincing evidence"). This law applies to all federal courts and about half the state courts.

John Hinckley was acquitted by reason of insanity for shooting President Ronald Reagan, setting off a firestorm of public protest.

Another attempt to clarify the legal defense of insanity is the verdict of guilty but mentally ill. Initially proposed by Michigan, it has been adopted by several states. (In some of these states, this verdict replaces the verdict of not guilty by reason of insanity, in others it is an additional option.) Generally, the laws permit a verdict of guilty but mentally ill when a defendant is found to have suffered from a substantial disorder of thought or mood at the time of the crime, which significantly impaired his or her judgment, behavior, capacity to recognize reality, or ability to cope with the ordinary demands of life. The effect of this mental illness defense, however, falls short of legal insanity. The verdict of guilty but mentally ill allows jurors to convict a person they perceive as dangerous while also attempting to ensure that he or she receives psychotherapeutic treatment. The individual could be given treatment in prison or be treated in a mental hospital and returned to prison when deemed fit to complete the sentence. In reality, however, many prisoners receive little treatment or highly inadequate treatment (Tanay, 1992).

Public concern that the insanity defense may be a major loophole in the criminal law is largely groundless (see Figure 13-7). The defense is rarely used, and actual cases of acquittal by reason of insanity are even rarer. Jurors seem reluctant to believe that people are not morally responsible for their acts, and lawyers, knowing that an insanity plea is apt to fail, tend to use it only as a last resort. Fewer than 1 in 400 defendants charged with serious crimes are found not guilty by reason of insanity (McGreevy, Steadman, & Callahan, 1991).

Figure 13-7

Comparison of Public Perceptions of the Insanity Defense With Actual Use and Results   The public perceives that the insanity defense is used and is successful much more often than is the case. (Silver et al., 1994)

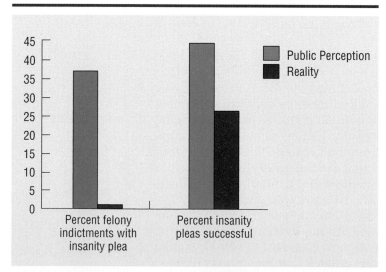

The question of mental disorder exerts its greatest impact earlier in the legal process. Many accused people who are mentally ill never come to trial. In the United States, the law requires that the defendant be competent to stand trial. An individual is judged competent to stand trial if he or she is able (1) to understand the charges and (2) to cooperate with a lawyer in preparing a defense. The competence issue is basic to the American ideal of a fair trial and is separate from the question of whether the person was "insane" at the time the crime was committed. In a preliminary hearing, the judge receives evidence about the accused's mental competence.

The judge may drop the charges and commit the individual to a psychiatric facility (if the crime is not serious) or commit the accused and file the charges until he or she is deemed competent to stand trial. Because court calendars are congested and trials are expensive, judges often prefer to deal with mentally disturbed defendants in this way, particularly if they believe that the mental hospital will provide adequate treatment and secure confinement.

Many more individuals are confined to mental institutions because they are found incompetent to stand trial than because they are found not guilty by reason of insanity. Before the widespread use of antipsychotic drugs, individuals deemed incompetent to stand trial were often committed to mental institutions for life. However, in 1972 the Supreme Court ruled that defendants found incompetent to stand trial due to mental illness could not be held indefinitely. Judges now attempt to bring such individuals to trial or to release them within 18 months. In deciding on release, the seriousness of the crime and the potential for future dangerous behavior are important considerations. But as we have already discussed, judgments of the dangerousness of individuals are generally unreliable.

Unabomber Ted Kaczynski had a long history of schizophrenia. During his trial he wanted to represent himself, but most legal scholars believed he was not competent to do so.

Thinking Critically

1. What do you think are society's obligations to people with serious mental disorders? What laws should be enacted to protect the rights of these people?

2. Does society have a right or obligation to see to it that children with serious mental disorders receive treatment even if their parents do not want their children to be treated?

How Can You Stay Mentally Healthy?

In this chapter we have focused on treatments for people with serious psychological problems. But many people who do not have serious psychological problems could still use some help in just coping with life. The problems that people face vary greatly, and there are no universal guidelines for staying psychologically healthy. However, a few general suggestions have emerged from the experiences of therapists.

Accept Your Feelings   Anger, sorrow, fear, and a feeling of having fallen short of ideals or goals are all unpleasant emotions, and we may try to avoid anxiety by denying them. Sometimes we try to avoid anxiety by facing situations unemotionally, which leads to a false kind of detachment or cool that may be destructive. We may try to suppress all emotions, thereby losing the ability to accept as normal the joys and sorrows that are a part of our involvement with other people.

Unpleasant emotions are a normal reaction to many situations. There is no reason to be ashamed of feeling homesick, of being afraid when learning to ski, or of becoming angry at someone who has disappointed us. These emotions are natural, and

Developing your talents and interests can help you stay mentally healthy.

it is better to recognize them than to deny them. When emotions cannot be expressed directly (for example, it may not be wise to tell off your boss), it helps to find another outlet for releasing tension. Taking a long walk, pounding a tennis ball, or discussing the situation with a friend can help dissipate anger. As long as you accept your right to feel emotion, you can express it in indirect or substitute ways when direct channels of expression are blocked.

Know Your Vulnerabilities   Discovering the kinds of situations that upset you or cause you to overreact may help guard against stress. Perhaps certain people annoy you. You could avoid them, or you could try to understand just what it is about them that disturbs you. Maybe they seem so poised and confident that they make you feel insecure. Trying to pinpoint the cause of your discomfort may help you see the situation in a new light. Perhaps you become very anxious when you have to speak in class or present a paper. Again, you could try to avoid such situations, or you could gain confidence by taking a course in public speaking. (Many colleges offer courses specifically aimed at learning to control speech anxiety.) You could also reinterpret the situation. Instead of thinking, "Everyone is waiting to criticize me as soon as I open my mouth," you could tell yourself, "The class will be interested in what I have to say, and I'm not going to let it worry me if I make a few mistakes."

Many people feel especially anxious when they are under pressure. Careful planning and spacing of work can help you avoid feeling overwhelmed at the last minute. The strategy of purposely allowing more time than you think you need to get to classes or to appointments can eliminate one source of stress.

Develop Your Talents and Interests   People who are bored and unhappy seldom have many interests. Today's college and community programs offer almost unlimited opportunities for people of all ages to explore their talents in many areas, including sports, academic interests, music, art, drama, and crafts. Often, the more you know about a subject, the more interesting it (and life) becomes. In addition, the feeling of competence gained from developing skills can do a great deal to bolster self-esteem.

Become Involved With Other People   Feelings of isolation and loneliness are at the core of most emotional disorders. We are social beings, and we need the support, comfort, and reassurance provided by other people. Focusing all your attention on your own problems can lead to an unhealthy preoccupation with yourself. Sharing your concerns with others often helps you view your troubles from a clearer perspective. Also, being concerned for the welfare of other people can reinforce your feelings of self-worth.

Know When to Seek Help   Although these suggestions can promote emotional well-being, there are limits to self-understanding and self-help. Some problems are difficult to solve alone. Our tendency toward self-deception makes it hard to view problems objectively, and we may not know all the possible solutions. When you feel that you are making little headway in gaining control over a problem, it is time to seek professional help from a counseling or clinical psychologist, a psychiatrist, or some other trained therapist. Willingness to seek help is a sign of emotional maturity, not of weakness; do not wait until you feel overwhelmed. Obtaining psychological help when it is needed should be as accepted as going to a physician for help with medical problems.

Do you think self-help books are good or bad for people's mental health?

Summary

1. Biological therapies often involve the use of *antipsychotic drugs* to treat psychotic symptoms, *antidepressants* and lithium to treat mood disorders, *antianxiety drugs* (called the benzodiazepines) to treat anxiety, and *stimulants* to treat attention deficit hyperactivity disorder. Each of these drugs has proven effective, but each has significant side effects.

2. *Psychodynamic therapies,* including traditional psychoanalysis developed by Freud, focus on uncovering and resolving unconscious conflicts through *free association, dream analysis,* and analysis of *transference* and *resistance.*

3. *Behavior therapies* focus on changing maladaptive behaviors by extinguishing anxiety responses to situations (as in *systematic desensitization* and in vivo *exposure*), reinforcing more positive behaviors (as in *selective reinforcement* techniques), and teaching new behaviors through *rehearsal* and *role playing.*

4. *Cognitive therapy* focuses on changing maladaptive thinking styles by challenging clients' interpretations of stressful events in their lives.

5. *Humanistic therapies* seek to free individuals from concerns over the wishes and demands of others so that they can realize their own goals and potential. Carl Rogers, who developed *client-centered psychotherapy,* believed that certain characteristics in the therapist are necessary for the client's growth and self-exploration. Those characteristics are empathy, warmth, and genuineness.

6. *Group therapy* provides an opportunity for the individual to explore his or her attitudes and behavior in interaction with others who have similar problems. *Marital therapy* and *family therapy* are specialized forms of group therapy that help couples, or parents and children, learn more effective ways of relating to one another and dealing with their problems.

7. The policy of *deinstitutionalization,* despite its good intentions, has left many people with psychological disorders in situations in which they cannot obtain appropriate care.

8. Through the process of *civil commitment,* people can be involuntarily committed to a psychiatric facility if they show grave disability due to a mental disorder, are imminently dangerous to themselves, or are judged to be dangerous to others.

9. The *insanity defense* is based on the principle that people who cannot understand the criminality of their actions or cannot control their behaviors as a result of a mental disorder should not be held accountable for criminal acts. This defense is rarely used and is even more rarely successful.

10. People are judged incompetent to stand trial for a crime if they are unable to understand the charges against them or to cooperate with a lawyer in preparing a defense. They may be held for treatment until such time as they become competent to stand trial, with certain restrictions.

11. We can promote our own emotional health by accepting our feelings as natural, discovering our vulnerabilities, developing our talents and interests, becoming involved with others, and recognizing when to seek professional help.

Suggested Readings

Interesting material on the historical treatment of the mentally ill can be found in Veith, *Hysteria: The History of a Disease* (1970); and Grob (1994), *The Mad Among Us.*

A review of the various methods of psychotherapy is provided by Gurman and Messer (eds.), *Essential Psychotherapies* (1995). Garfield, *Psychotherapy: An Eclectic Approach* (1980), describes the process of psychotherapy, the features common to most psychotherapies, and psychotherapy research. Seligman reviews the effectiveness of therapies for a wide range of psychological disorders in *What You Can Change and What You Can't* (1993).

For an introduction to psychoanalytic methods, see Luborsky, *Principles of Psychoanalytic Psychotherapy* (1984), and Auld and Hyman, *Resolution of Inner Conflict: An Introduction to Psychoanalytic Therapy* (1991). For client-centered therapy, see Carl Rogers, *On Becoming a Person: A Therapist's View of Psychotherapy* (1970), and *Carl Rogers on Personal Power* (1977). The principles of behavior therapy are presented in Thorpe and Olson, *Behavior Therapy: Concepts, Procedures and Application* (1997). The application of cognitive-behavior therapy to a variety of mental disorders is described in J. S. Beck, *Cognitive Therapy: Basics and Beyond* (1995).

An overview of group therapy is presented in Yalom, *The Theory and Practice of Group Psychotherapy* (3rd ed., 1985).

Medicine and Mental Illness (1991), a paperback by Lickey and Gordon, presents a very readable summary of biological research on the major mental disorders. It describes symptoms and DSM-III-R diagnostic criteria, evidence of drug effectiveness, and how psychotherapeutic drugs affect the brain. Valenstein, *Blaming the Brain* (1998), presents a stinging critique of biological theories and treatments of mental disorders.

For ways to modify your own behavior, see Watson and Tharp, *Self-Directed Behavior: Self-Modification for Personal Adjustment* (5th ed., 1989). Burns, *Feeling Good* (1981), is a paperback that provides a step-by-step program for using cognitive therapy techniques to understand and to change feelings of depression, anxiety, and anger. *Necessary Losses* (1986) by Viorst, written from a psychoanalytic viewpoint, is a sensitive and wise analysis of how we grow and change through the losses that are an inevitable part of life.

Enhance and Explore

To enhance your understanding of the psychological concepts found in this chapter, please consult the following aids:

Study Guide

Learning Objectives, p. 232
Define the Terms, p. 234
Test Your Knowledge, p. 238
Essay Questions, p. 241
Thinking Independently, p. 243

PowerPsych CD-ROM

CAN WE CHANGE HOW THE BODY WORKS?

Synaptic Changes: Anxiety, ADHD, Depression, Schizophrenia

Effects of Drugs at the Synapses: Anxiety, ADHD, Depression, Schizophrenia

CAN WE HELP PEOPLE CHANGE THOUGHTS AND BEHAVIORS?

Treatment of Phobias

PsychCentral

For more information concerning the topics found in this chapter, access psychology links on the Word Wide Web made through the Harcourt Web page at:

http://www.harcourtcollege.com/psych/Fundamentals

www.harcourtcollege.com

http://www.harcourtcollege.com/psych/index.html

CHAPTER **14** *Social Behavior*

How do we form our impressions of other people and interpret their actions? How are our beliefs and attitudes—including our stereotypes and prejudices—formed and changed? How do we influence one another? What determines whom we like or love?

These are examples of the kinds of questions that are addressed by **social psychology,** *the study of how people think and feel about their social world and how they interact and influence one another.* In seeking answers to such questions, social psychologists begin with the basic observation that human reactions are a function of both the person and the situation. Each individual brings a unique set of personal attributes to a situation, leading different people to think, feel, and act in different ways in the same situation. But each situation also brings a unique set of forces to bear on an individual, leading him or her to think, feel, and act in different ways in different situations. Research in social psychology has repeatedly shown that situations—especially social influences—are more powerful determinants of our beliefs, attitudes, and behaviors than our intuitions lead us to believe.

Individuals, however, do not react simply to the objective features of a situation but to their subjective interpretations of it. The person who interprets a hurtful remark as a deliberate insult reacts differently from the person who interprets it as an unintended faux pas. Accordingly, we begin our examination of social behavior by examining the ways in which we perceive and interpret the motives and behaviors of others.

social psychology
the study of how people think and feel about their social world and how they interact and influence one another

How Do We Think About Our Social World?

We are all psychologists. In attempting to understand people, we are like informal scientists who construct our own intuitive theories of human behavior. In doing so, we face the same basic tasks as the formal scientist (Nisbett & Ross, 1980). First, we collect data ("My friend Chris asserts that women should have the right to obtain abortions"; "Kyoko achieved the highest score on the math test"). Second, we attempt to detect *covariation* or *correlation*—that is, to discern what goes with what ("Do most people who support the right to abortion also oppose the death penalty?" "On average, do Asians seem to do better in math and science than non-Asians?"). And third, we try to infer cause and effect, to evaluate what causes what ("Does Chris support the right to abortion out of genuine conviction or because of peer pressure to express liberal attitudes?" "Do Asian students excel in math and science because they are inherently smarter or because their families stress the value of education?").

Our intuitive attempts to apply scientific reasoning to everyday life work remarkably well. Social interaction would be chaos if our informal theories of human behavior did not have considerable validity. But we also make a number of systematic errors in arriving at social judgments, and, ironically, our intuitive theories themselves often interfere with making accurate judgments. As we will see, our theories can actually shape our perceptions of the data, distort our estimates of covariation, and bias our evaluations of cause and effect.

Storing and Retrieving Data

The first difficulty we face as informal scientists is that of collecting data in a systematic and unbiased way. When a survey researcher wants to estimate how many Americans support a woman's right to abortion, he or she takes great care to ensure that a random or representative sample of people are contacted so that the numbers of Catholics, Protestants, men, women, and so forth who are interviewed are proportional to the percentage of these groups in the total population. But when we, as informal survey researchers, try to make this estimate intuitively, our major source of data is likely to be the people we know personally. Obviously, this is not a representative sample of the population.

Another major source is the mass media, which also provide a nonrandom and nonrepresentative sample of data. For example, the media necessarily give more

Vivid events are more likely to influence our judgments than less vivid events.

attention to a small number of antiabortion protesters publicly demonstrating at a medical clinic than they do to a larger number of people who silently support the clinic's abortion service. The media are not being biased here in the usual sense; they are simply reporting the news. But the data they give us do not comprise a reliable sample from which to estimate public opinion.

A survey researcher also keeps accurate records of the data. But in everyday life we constantly accumulate information in our heads and then attempt to recall it from memory when we are later called upon to make some judgment. Thus, not only are the data we collect a biased sample in the first place, but the data we actually bring to bear on our social judgments are further biased by problems of selective recall.

Vividness   One of the factors that influence the information we notice and remember is its *vividness.* Research has shown that when both vivid and nonvivid information compete for our attention, our estimates and judgments are influenced more by the vivid information—even when the nonvivid information is more reliable and potentially more informative (Nisbett & Ross, 1980; Taylor & Thompson, 1982).

In one study, introductory psychology students who planned to major in psychology were given information about upper-level psychology courses and then asked to indicate which courses they planned to take. The participants either heard two or three students make some informal remarks about each course in a face-to-face session or saw a statistical summary of course evaluations made by past students in the courses. The participants were influenced more by the face-to-face remarks than by the statistical summary—even when the summary was accompanied by written quotations of those same remarks. The vivid face-to-face information was more influential than the nonvivid written information even though it was based on less complete and less representative data (Borgida & Nisbett, 1977).

The vividness effect is a particular problem with information from the mass media. Even if reporters scrupulously gave equal coverage to both the vivid and the nonvivid sides of an issue, our own information-processing tendencies would supply the bias. Thus, even if a television newscast reports the results of a survey showing that a national majority supports abortion rights, we are more likely to store and later recall the vivid pictures of the antiabortion protest when we intuitively try to estimate public opinion.

Schemas

Even if we could collect data in a systematic and unbiased way, our perceptions of the data can still be biased by our existing expectations and preconceptions—our theories—of what the data *should* look like. Whenever we perceive any object or event, we compare the incoming information with our memories of previous encounters with similar objects and events. Our memories of objects and events are not photograph-like reproductions of the original stimuli; rather, they are simplified reconstructions of our original perceptions. Such representations or memory structures are called **schemas,** *organized beliefs and knowledge we hold about people, objects, events, and situations. The process of searching in memory for the schema that is most consistent with the incoming data* is called **schematic processing.** Schemas and schematic processing permit us to organize and process an enormous amount of information with great efficiency. Instead of having to perceive and remember all the details of each new object or event, we can simply note that it is like one of our preexisting schemas and encode or remember only its most prominent features. Schematic processing typically occurs rapidly and automatically; usually we are not even aware that any processing of information is taking place at all (Fiske, 1993; Fiske & Taylor, 1991).

schemas organized beliefs and knowledge we hold about people, objects, events, and situations

schematic processing the process of searching in memory for the schema that is most consistent with the incoming data

For example, we have schemas for different kinds of people. When someone tells you that you are about to meet an extravert, you retrieve your extravert schema in anticipation of the coming encounter. The extravert schema consists of a set of interrelated traits such as sociability, warmth, and possibly loudness and impulsiveness. *General person-schemas* such as these are sometimes called **stereotypes.** We also have schemas of particular people, such as the president of the United States or our parents. We even have a **self-schema**—*a set of organized self-concepts stored in memory* (Markus, 1977). When you see an advertisement for the job of peer counselor, you can evaluate the match between your counselor schema and your self-schema to decide whether you should apply for the job.

stereotypes general person-schemas

self-schema a set of organized self-concepts stored in memory

Research confirms that schemas help us process information. For example, if people are explicitly instructed to remember as much information as they can about a person, they actually remember less than if they are simply told to try to form an impression of the person (Hamilton, 1979). The instruction to form an impression induces the participants to search for various person-relevant schemas that help them organize and recall material better. The self-schema also permits us to organize and process information efficiently. For example, people can recall a list of words better if they are told to decide whether each word describes themselves as they go through the list (Ganellen & Carver, 1985; Rogers, Kuiper, & Kirker, 1977). This has become known as the *self-reference effect* and occurs for two reasons: (1) because relating each word to the self leads the person to think more deeply and elaborately about it as he or she decides whether it is self-relevant, and (2) because the self-schema serves to link in memory what would otherwise be unrelated information (Klein & Loftus, 1989; Klein, Loftus, & Burton, 1989).

Stereotypes

Detecting covariation or correlation—discovering what goes with what—is a fundamental task in every science. Discovering that symptoms of an illness covary with the amount of environmental pollution or correlate with the presence of a virus is the first step toward a cure. And as intuitive scientists of human behavior, we perceive—or think we perceive—such correlations all the time ("People who are against capital punishment seem likely to hold a pro-choice position on abortion"; "Asians seem to do better in math and science than non-Asians"). Our schemas of classes of persons—that is, our stereotypes—are actually minitheories of covariation: The stereotype of an extravert, a gay person, or a college professor is a theory of what particular traits or behaviors go with certain other traits or behaviors.

Research shows that we are not very accurate at detecting covariations. This is because our theories distort our perceptions. When our schemas or theories lead us to expect two things to covary, we overestimate the correlation between them, even seeing illusory correlation that do not exist. But when we do not have a theory that

Stereotypes can lead people who observe a man with effeminate gestures to assume he is gay even though they have no knowledge of his sexual orientation.

leads us to expect them to covary, we underestimate the correlation, even failing to detect a correlation that is strongly present in the data.

This was demonstrated by two researchers who were intrigued by the fact that clinical psychologists routinely report correlations between their clients' responses to projective tests (see Chapter 10) and their personality characteristics, even though controlled research studies fail to find such correlations. For example, experienced clinicians have often reported that gay men are more likely than heterosexual men to see anal images, feminine clothing, and similar kinds of images in Rorschach inkblots. Controlled studies, however, have not found any of these images to be correlated with a homosexual orientation (Chapman & Chapman, 1969). The researchers hypothesized that psychologists see these correlations because the reported images fit a popular stereotype, or schema, of male homosexuality. Several experiments have confirmed this hypothesis.

In one, college students were asked to study a set of Rorschach cards. Each card contained the inkblot, a description of the image a client had reported seeing in it, and a statement of two personal characteristics that the client possessed. The images described included the five stereotyped images reported by clinical psychologists to be correlated with male homosexuality plus a number of unrelated images (for example, images of food). The characteristics reported were either homosexuality ("has sexual feelings toward other men") or unrelated characteristics (for example, "feels sad and depressed much of the time"). The cards were carefully constructed so that no image was systematically associated with homosexuality.

After studying all the cards, participants were asked to report whether they had noticed "any general kind of thing that was seen most often by men" with the different characteristics. The results revealed that the students in this study—like experienced clinical psychologists—erroneously reported a correlation between the stereotyped images and homosexuality. They did not report any correlations between the nonstereotyped images and homosexuality.

The researchers then repeated the study, modifying the cards so that two of the nonstereotyped images (a monster image in one inkblot and an animal-human image in another) always appeared with the characteristic of homosexuality—a perfect correlation. Despite this, participants still reported seeing the nonexistent correlation with the stereotyped images more than twice as often as the perfect correlation with the nonstereotyped images.

As intuitive psychologists, we are schema- or theory-driven. We see covariations that our theories have prepared us to see and fail to see covariations that our theories have not prepared us to see.

Persistence of Stereotypes   Perhaps it is not surprising that the inexperienced students in the study just described are misled by their stereotypes to see nonexistent correlations in the data. But why should this be true of experienced clinical psychologists? Why doesn't their daily contact with real data correct their mistaken perceptions of covariation? More generally, why do our stereotypes persist in the face of nonconfirming data?

We can illustrate some of the factors involved by representing the covariation task in a 2 × 2 table, as shown in Figure 14-1. It displays some hypothetical data relevant to a popular stereotype similar to that explored in the Rorschach inkblot study described earlier—in this case, the stereotype that gay men display effeminate gestures. The table classifies a hypothetical sample of 1,100 men into the four cells of the table according to whether they have a homosexual or a heterosexual orientation and whether they do or do not display effeminate gestures.

The correct way to assess whether the two factors are correlated is to examine whether the *proportion* of gay men who display effeminate gestures (the left-hand column) is different from the *proportion* of heterosexual men who display effeminate gestures (the right-hand column). To do this, we must first add up the two cells in each column to find how many men with each kind of orientation there are in the sample. When we do this, we see that 10 out of 100, or 10%, of the gay men display effeminate gestures and 100 out of 1,000, or 10%, of the heterosexual men do so. In other words, these data reveal no correlation between sexual orientation and effeminate gestures. It is important to note that to assess the correlation we had to take into account all four cells of the table.

Now consider what our intuitions would tell us if we encountered these data in daily life—where we do not have the data neatly laid out in front of us. In our society men with a homosexual orientation are in a minority, as are men who display effeminate gestures. When the two occur together (as in cell A, gay men with effeminate gestures), it is a particularly distinctive occurrence. This has two consequences. First, research has shown that people *overestimate* the frequency with which they have actually encountered such distinctive combinations (Hamilton & Gifford, 1976; Hamilton & Sherman, 1989). Second, even if we did not overestimate their frequency, we are still most likely to notice and remember instances that fall into cell A and remain oblivious to instances that fall into the other cells of the table.

Part of the reason for this is that the relevant information is almost never available to us. In particular, we rarely have the opportunity to assess the frequency of cell C, the number of gay men who do *not* display effeminate gestures. Cell B also sets a trap for some people. When they observe a man with effeminate gestures, they may simply *assume* that he is gay even though they have no knowledge of his sexual orientation. He could in fact belong to either cell A or cell B. But through circular reasoning, they illegitimately convert cell B disconfirmations of their stereotype into cell A confirmations. Note that it is the stereotype itself that leads them to make this error—another instance of how our information processing is schema- or theory-driven.

But even if the data from cells other than cell A were available to us, it would not typically occur to us that we need to know this other information. We find it particularly difficult to take into account—or to understand why we *need* to take into account—cell D, the frequency of *non*gay men who do *not* display effeminate gestures. Why is this so difficult?

We noted earlier that we are more likely to notice and remember vivid rather than nonvivid information. This is why cell A is noticed, remembered, and overestimated: Gay men with effeminate gestures are distinctive and, hence, vivid. In contrast, there are not many events that are less vivid—and hence, less noticeable and less memorable—than events that do *not* occur. But this is precisely what cell D events are: nonevents. The nongay man who does not display effeminate gestures does not constitute a psychological event for us. It is difficult to notice or appreciate the relevance of nonevents in daily life.

This difficulty was cleverly employed by Arthur Conan Doyle in his Sherlock Holmes story "The Adventure of Silver Blaze," in which the famous detective is asked

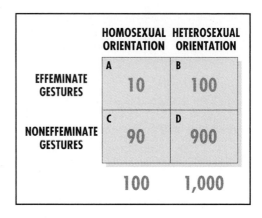

	HOMOSEXUAL ORIENTATION	HETEROSEXUAL ORIENTATION
EFFEMINATE GESTURES	A 10	B 100
NONEFFEMINATE GESTURES	C 90	D 900
	100	1,000

Figure 14-1

Stereotypes as Covariations To determine whether there is a correlation between sexual orientation and effeminate gestures, we need to know whether the proportion of men with effeminate gestures differs as a function of sexual orientation. This requires taking all four cells into account so that the column totals can be computed. Invalid stereotypes often persist because we attend only to cell A and neglect the other cells. There is, in fact, no correlation between the two factors in these hypothetical data.

Self-Fulfilling Stereotypes   *Our stereotypes can lead us to interact with those whom we stereotype in ways that cause them to respond, in turn, in ways that fulfill our expectations.*

to discover who had stolen a prize racehorse from its private stable during the night. Holmes draws the police inspector's attention to "the curious incident of the dog in the night-time." Puzzled, the inspector says, "The dog did nothing in the night-time." To which Holmes replies: "That was the curious incident." Holmes then deduces correctly that the horse was stolen by its own trainer—because the dog had *not* barked and, hence, must have known the intruder (Doyle, 1892/ 1981, p. 197).

The nonvividness of nonevents also leads the news media to promote and sustain stereotypes. When a gay man commits a murder—especially one with sexual overtones—both his sexual orientation and the murder are featured in the news story; when a heterosexual man commits a murder—even one with sexual overtones—sexual orientation is not mentioned. Thus, cell A events are widely publicized—thereby fueling the stereotype—whereas cell B events are not seen as relevant to sexual orientation. And of course, cell C and cell D events—men of any sexual orientation who do *not* commit murder—are not news. They are nonevents.

Self-Fulfilling Stereotypes   Our schemas influence not only our perceptions and inferential processes, but also our behavior and social interactions. And this, too, can sustain our stereotypes. In particular, our stereotypes can lead us to interact with those whom we stereotype in ways that cause them to fulfill our expectations. Thus, our stereotypes can become both self-perpetuating and self-fulfilling.

In a study of this process, the investigators first observed that white interviewers displayed a less friendly manner when interviewing African American job applicants than when interviewing white applicants. They hypothesized that this could cause African American applicants to perform less well in the interviews. To test this hypothesis, they trained interviewers to reproduce both the less friendly and the more friendly interviewing styles. Applicants (all white) were then videotaped while being interviewed by an interviewer using one of these two styles. Judges who later viewed the tapes rated applicants who had been interviewed in a less friendly manner significantly lower on their interview performance than those who had been interviewed in the more friendly manner (Word, Zanna, & Cooper, 1974). The study thus confirmed the hypothesis that prejudiced individuals can interact in ways that actually evoke the stereotyped behaviors that sustain their prejudice.

Attributions

At the heart of most sciences is the discovery of causes and effects. Similarly, as intuitive psychologists, we feel that we truly understand some instance of human behavior when we know why it occurred or what caused it. Suppose, for example, that a famous athlete endorses a breakfast cereal on television. Why does she do it? Does she really like the cereal or is she doing it for the money? Suppose that you give a $20 donation to Planned Parenthood. Why? Do you believe in the work of the organization? Were you being pressured? Did you need a tax write-off?

Each of these cases creates an attribution problem. We see a behavior—perhaps our own—and must decide which of many possible causes the action should be attributed to. Our intuitive attempt to infer the causes of behavior has been a central topic in social psychology for a long time (Heider, 1958; Kelley, 1967).

Is this woman giving money to the Salvation Army because she supports its work, because she feels pressured, or because she is generally altruistic?

The Fundamental Attribution Error

As the two examples just given illustrate, one of the major attribution tasks we face daily is deciding whether an observed behavior reflects something unique about the person (his or her attitudes, personality characteristics, and so forth) or something about the situation in which we observe the person. If we infer that something about the person is primarily responsible for the behavior (for instance, the athlete really loves the cereal), our inference is called an internal or *dispositional attribution* ("disposition" here refers to a person's beliefs, attitudes, and personality characteristics). If, however, we conclude that some external cause is primarily responsible for the behavior (for instance, money, social norms, threats), it is called an external or *situational attribution.*

Research has demonstrated that an individual's behavior is so compelling to us that we take it at face value and give insufficient weight to the circumstances surrounding it. That is, we underestimate the situational causes of behavior, jumping too easily to conclusions about the person's disposition. If we observe someone behaving aggressively, we too readily assume that the person has an aggressive personality rather than considering the possibility that the situation might have provoked aggression in almost anyone. Another way of stating this is that we have a schema of cause and effect for human behavior that gives too much weight to the person and too little to the situation. One psychologist has termed this *bias toward dispositional attributions rather than situational attributions* the **fundamental attribution error** (Ross, 1977).

An experiment designed as a quiz game illustrates how we can make the fundamental attribution error when judging not only the behavior of others but our own as well. Pairs of male or female participants were recruited to participate in a question-and-answer game of general knowledge. One member of the pair was randomly assigned to be the questioner and to make up 10 difficult questions to which he or she knew the answers (for example, "What is the world's largest glacier?"). The other participant served as the contestant and attempted to answer the questions. When the contestant failed a question, the questioner would give the answer. In a reenactment of the study, observers also watched the contest. After the game was completed, both participants and observers were asked to rate the level of general knowledge possessed by the questioner and the contestant relative to the "average student." It is important to note that participants and observers all knew that the roles of questioner and contestant had been assigned randomly.

As Figure 14-2 shows, questioners judged both themselves and the contestant to be about average in level of general knowledge. But contestants rated the questioner as superior and themselves as inferior to the average student. They attributed the outcome of the game to their (and the questioner's) level of knowledge rather than to the overwhelming situational advantage enjoyed by the questioner—who gets to decide which questions to ask and can therefore omit any questions to which he or

fundamental attribution error the bias toward dispositional attributions rather than situational attributions

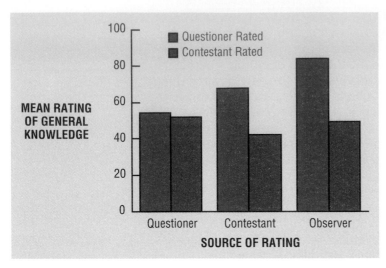

MEAN RATING OF GENERAL KNOWLEDGE

Questioner Rated
Contestant Rated

SOURCE OF RATING

Questioner   Contestant   Observer

Figure 14-2

The Fundamental Attribution Error   Ratings of questioners and contestants after they had participated in a quiz game. The questioner is rated as superior by both the contestant and observer even though the questioner had an overwhelming situational advantage. Both contestants and observers gave too much weight to dispositional causes and too little to situational causes. (After Ross, Amabile, & Steinmetz, 1977)

she does not know the answer. Observers, seeing the questioner ask questions to which neither they nor the contestant knew the answer, rated the questioner's level of knowledge even higher. In other words, both contestants and observers gave too much weight to dispositional causes and too little to situational causes—the fundamental attribution error (Ross, Amabile, & Steinmetz, 1977).

One implication of this study is that people who select the topics discussed in a conversation will be seen as more knowledgeable than those who passively let others set the agenda, even if everyone is aware of the differential roles being played. This, in turn, has implications for contemporary sex roles. Research has shown that men talk more than women in mixed-sex interactions (Henley, Hamilton, & Thorne, 1985); they interrupt more (West & Zimmerman, 1983); and they are more likely to raise the topics discussed (Fishman, 1983). The quiz game study implies that one consequence of these conversational patterns is that women leave most mixed-sex interactions thinking themselves less knowledgeable than the men, with bystanders of both sexes sharing this illusion. The moral is clear: The fundamental attribution error can work for or against you. If you want to appear knowledgeable both to yourself and to others, learn how to structure the situation so that you control the choice of topics discussed. Be the questioner, not the contestant.

Self-Attributions   In the experiment just described, the contestants made the fundamental attribution error about their own behavior. One social psychologist has proposed that, in general, we make judgments about ourselves using the same inferential processes—and making the same kinds of errors—that we use for making judgments about others. Specifically, this *self-perception theory* proposes that individuals come to know their own attitudes, emotions, and other internal states partially by inferring them from observations of their own behavior and the circumstances in which the behavior occurs. Thus to the extent that internal cues are weak, ambiguous, or uninterpretable, the individual is like any outside observer who must rely on external cues to infer the individual's inner state (Bem, 1972).

These propositions are illustrated by the common remark, "This is my second sandwich; I guess I was hungrier than I thought." Here the speaker has inferred an internal state by observing his or her own behavior. Similarly, the self-observation that "I've been biting my nails all day; something must be bugging me" is based on the same external evidence that might lead a friend to remark, "You've been biting your nails all day; something must be bugging you."

Attitudes

attitudes favorable or unfavorable evaluations of and reactions to objects, people, situations, or any other aspects of the world

So far our discussion has focused on processes of perceiving and thinking—our cognitive reactions to the social world. The concept of attitude, one of social psychology's most central concepts, refers to some of our emotional reactions to that world. Specifically, **attitudes** are likes and dislikes—*favorable or unfavorable evaluations of and reactions to objects, people, situations, or any other aspects of the world,* including abstract ideas and social policies.

We often express our attitudes in opinion statements: "I love oranges" or "I can't abide Republicans." But even though attitudes express feelings, they are often linked to cognitions, specifically to beliefs about the attitude objects ("Oranges contain lots of vitamins"; "Republicans have no compassion for the poor"). Moreover, attitudes are sometimes linked to actions we take with respect to the attitude objects ("I eat an orange every morning"; "I never vote for Republican candidates").

Accordingly, social psychologists usually conceive of attitudes as comprising a *cognitive* component, an *affective* component, and a *behavioral* component. For example, in studying negative attitudes toward groups, social psychologists distinguish between negative stereotypes (negative beliefs and perceptions about a group—the cognitive component), prejudice (negative feelings toward the group—the affective component), and discrimination (negative actions against members of the group—the behavioral component).

Consistency of Attitudes   Certain attitudes seem to go together. For example, people who support affirmative action seem likely to advocate stronger gun control, to oppose capital punishment, and to hold a pro-choice position on abortion. On the surface these diverse attitudes do not seem to follow one another logically. Yet knowing that a person holds one of these attitudes often permits us to predict with pretty fair accuracy that he or she holds the others as well. There seems to be a kind of logic involved: The attitudes all appear to follow more or less from a common set of underlying values that we might label as "liberal."

The same kind of logic can be discerned among "conservative" attitudes. Many people who oppose affirmative action and gun control laws cite the value of individual freedom as the basis for their opinions. Even those who disagree with such opinions can appreciate the logic involved. But many such freedom-loving individuals also feel that a woman's place is in the home, that marijuana use should be more heavily penalized, and that homosexual behavior should be illegal. Here the logic is less than clear, yet these attitudes, too, seem strangely predictable.

In short, people's attitudes often appear to have a kind of internal logic, but it is a kind of psycho-logic, not strict formal logic. It is this kind of psycho-logic that social psychologists have studied under the label of *cognitive consistency*. The basic premise of cognitive consistency theories is that we all strive to be consistent in our beliefs, attitudes, and behaviors, and that inconsistency acts as an irritant or a stimulus that motivates us to modify or change them until they form a coherent, if not logical, package. Throughout the years, the consistency theorists have amassed a great deal of evidence for this basic premise (Abelson et al., 1968).

Cognitive Dissonance   One of the most influential consistency theories has been Leon Festinger's *theory of cognitive dissonance* (1957). Like cognitive consistency theories in general, cognitive dissonance theory assumes that there is a drive toward cognitive consistency: Two cognitions that are inconsistent with one another will produce discomfort that motivates the person to remove the inconsistency and bring the cognitions into harmony. This *inconsistency-produced discomfort* is called **cognitive dissonance.**

cognitive dissonance discomfort produced by inconsistency

Although cognitive dissonance theory addresses several kinds of inconsistency, it has been the most provocative in predicting that engaging in behavior that is counter to one's attitudes creates pressure to change the attitudes so that they are consistent with the behavior. The theory further states that engaging in counter-attitudinal behavior produces the most dissonance, and hence the most attitude change, when there are no consonant (that is, consistent) reasons for engaging in the behavior.

This was illustrated in an experiment in which male college students participated one at a time in an experiment in which they worked on dull, repetitive tasks. After completing the tasks, some participants were offered $1 to tell the next participant that the tasks had been fun and interesting. Others were offered $20 to do this.

All participants complied with the request. Later they were asked how much they had enjoyed the tasks. As shown in Figure 14-3, participants who had been paid only $1 stated that they had, in fact, enjoyed the tasks. But participants who had been paid $20 did not find them significantly more enjoyable than participants who were not required to tell another person that the tasks were fun and interesting. The small incentive for complying with the experimenter's request—but not the large incentive—led individuals to believe what they had heard themselves say (Festinger & Carlsmith, 1959). Why should this be so?

Cognitive dissonance theory suggests that this man might come to believe that his job is less boring if he could be induced to tell other people that he finds it very interesting.

According to cognitive dissonance theory, saying that the tasks were fun and interesting was inconsistent—and hence dissonant—with the actual experience of performing them. This created pressure on the participants to become more favorable toward the tasks. But being paid $20 to say that the tasks were fun provided a very consonant reason for complying with the experimenter's request, and hence the $20 participants experienced little or no dissonance. The inconsistency between the person's behavior and his or her attitude toward the tasks was outweighed by the far greater consistency between the compliance and the incentive for complying. Accordingly, the participants who were paid $20 did not change their attitudes. The participants who were paid $1, however, had no consonant reason for complying. Accordingly, they experienced dissonance, which they reduced by coming to believe that they really did enjoy the tasks. The general conclusion is that dissonance-causing behavior will lead to attitude change in induced-compliance situations when the behavior can be induced with a minimum amount of incentive.

Nonconsistency of Public Opinion   Most of the research on consistency of attitudes has been conducted with college students in laboratory studies, and many psychologists and political scientists who have analyzed the public mind outside the laboratory are not convinced that members of the general public feel any strong need to be consistent in their opinions on social and political issues (Kinder & Sears, 1985). For example, in national surveys, a majority of Americans say that they disapprove of "most government-sponsored welfare programs." Yet more than 80% say that they support each of the following: the government's "program providing fi-

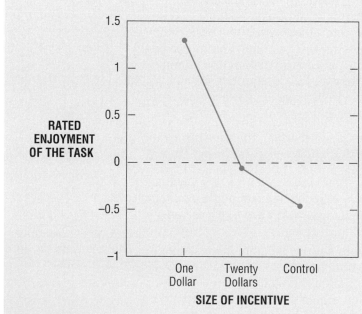

Figure 14-3

An Induced-Compliance Experiment   The smaller incentive for agreeing to say that the tasks were interesting led participants to infer that they had actually enjoyed the tasks. The larger incentive did not. (After Festinger & Carlsmith, 1959)

nancial assistance for children raised in low-income homes where one parent is missing" (the former Aid to Families with Dependent Children, a major welfare program); the government's program for "helping poor people buy food for their families at cheaper prices" (the federal food stamp program); and the government's program for paying for health care for poor people (the Medicaid program). The strong support for these major welfare programs is similar among all types of people—rich and poor, liberal and conservative, Democratic and Republican. One survey found that about 25% of Americans are ideologically conservative on questions concerning the general concept of welfare but pragmatically liberal on questions concerning specific welfare programs (Free & Cantril, 1967). It should also be noted that the public does not usually define government subsidies that primarily benefit the middle class—such as federally subsidized college loans and tax deductions for mortgage interest payments—as welfare.

Despite these findings, however, we should be cautious about accusing someone of being inconsistent, because his or her attitudes may simply be inconsistent with our own ideological framework; in other words, inconsistency may be in the eye of the beholder. For example, opposition to capital punishment (the death penalty) is usually characterized as a liberal position, whereas opposition to legalized abortion is usually thought of as a conservative position. Yet there is a quite logical consistency to the views of a person who, being against all taking of life, opposes both capital punishment and legalized abortion. (Most Catholic clergy hold this set of views.) Another example is provided by libertarians, who are opposed to any government interference in our lives. They are conservative on economic issues—the free market, not the government, should control the economic system—and in their opposition to civil rights laws. But they are liberal on personal social issues, believing, for example, that the government should not criminalize the use of marijuana or concern itself with private sexual behavior. To libertarians, it is conservatives and liberals who are being inconsistent.

Nevertheless, the evidence suggests that most citizens do not organize their beliefs and attitudes according to any kind of overall ideology; nonconsistency, if not inconsistency, seems to be more prevalent than consistency. This has led one psychologist to propose that many of our attitudes come packaged as *opinion molecules*. Each molecule is made up of a belief, an attitude, and a perception of social support; or, as he cleverly put it, a fact, a feeling, and a following (Abelson, 1968): "It's a fact that when my aunt Sylvia had back pain, she was cured by acupuncture [*fact*]"; "I feel that acupuncture has been sneered at for too long by the medical establishment [*feeling*], and I know a lot of people who feel exactly the same way [*following*]." Or, "Americans don't really want universal health insurance [*following*], and neither do I [*feeling*]. It would lead to socialized medicine [*fact*]."

Opinion molecules serve important social functions. First, they act as conversational units, giving us something coherent to say when a particular topic comes up in conversation. They also give a rational appearance to our unexamined agreement with friends and neighbors on social issues. But most important, they serve as badges of identification with important social groups, reinforcing our sense of belonging to a social community. Thus, the fact and the feeling are less important ingredients of an opinion molecule than the following. In fact, one reason that citizens may appear to have sets of coherent political opinions is that their social groups—families, friends, churches, and political parties—have provided them with prepackaged ideologies. Such groups are called *reference groups,* and we will examine how they influence our beliefs and attitudes in the next section.

---

1. Suppose that in preparation for buying a new car, you carefully read *Consumer Reports'* survey of several thousand car owners and become convinced that a particular model has the highest reliability and owner satisfaction. But then your neighbor tells you that she owned that model and it was a terrible car. Which

Thinking Critically

source of information should be more valid, the survey of several thousand owners or your neighbor? Which source is more influential in your buying decision? If these are not the same, why not?

2. How might the fundamental attribution error contribute to the tendency of many people to blame the poor for their condition?

3. Can you identify any inconsistencies among your beliefs and attitudes?

How Do Other People Influence Us?

To most people, the term *social influence* connotes direct and deliberate attempts to change our beliefs, attitudes, or behaviors. Parents attempt to get their children to eat spinach; television commercials attempt to induce us to buy a product or vote for a candidate; a religious cult attempts to persuade a person to abandon school, job, or family and serve a "higher" mission.

We react to such influences in many ways. In some cases, we publicly comply with the wishes of the influencer but do not necessarily change our private beliefs or attitudes—the child eats the spinach but may continue to dislike it. Social psychologists have called this *compliance*. In other cases, we are convinced that the influencer is correct and change our private beliefs and attitudes as well. This has been called *internalization*.

Many forms of social influence are indirect or unintentional; for example, just being in the presence of other people can affect us in many ways. And even when we are alone, we continue to be influenced by **social norms**—*implicit rules and expectations that dictate what we ought to think and feel and how we ought to behave.* These range from the trivial to the profound. Social norms tell us to face forward when riding in an elevator, and they govern how long we can gaze at a stranger before being considered rude. More profoundly, social norms can create and maintain racism, sexism, or homophobia in a society. And as we will see, compliance itself often depends on unwitting allegiance to internalized social norms.

social norms implicit rules and expectations that dictate what we ought to think and feel and how we ought to behave

Social interaction and influence are central to communal life. Cooperation, altruism, and love all involve social interaction and influence. But practical social problems have historically prompted social psychologists to focus much of their attention on the negative effects of social influence. Accordingly, just as the chapter on psychopathology dwells on the dark side of individual behavior, this section focuses disproportionately on the dark side of social behavior. Some of the findings are disturbing, even depressing. But just as the study of psychopathology has led to effective therapies, so too the study of problematic social interactions has led to more effective ways of dealing with them. By understanding the principles underlying many of our social problems, we simultaneously understand the principles underlying their solutions.

Social norms—such as the informal rule to face forward in an elevator— are a subtle but powerful source of influence over our beliefs, attitudes, and behaviors.

Bystander Intervention

In the introduction to this chapter we noted that people react not just to the objective features of a situation but to their subjective interpretations of it as well. As we will now see, defining or interpreting the situation is often the mechanism through which individuals influence one another.

In 1964 Kitty Genovese was murdered outside her apartment building in New York City late at night. She fought back, and the murder took more than half an hour. At least 38 neighbors heard her screams for help, but nobody came to her aid. No one even called the police. The American public was horrified by this incident, and social psychologists began to investigate the causes of what at first was termed "bystander apathy." The research, however, showed that "apathy" was not an accurate term; it is not simple indifference that prevents bystanders from intervening in emergencies. First, there are realistic deterrents such as physical danger. Second, getting involved may mean lengthy court appearances or other entanglements. Third,

There are many features of emergencies that realistically prevent bystanders from intervening, including genuine physical danger, subsequent legal entanglements, and our unpreparedness for the quick, unplanned action required.

emergencies are unpredictable and require quick, unplanned action; few people are prepared for such situations. Finally, bystanders risk making fools of themselves by misinterpreting a situation as an emergency when it is not. Two of the major researchers in this area concluded that "the bystander to an emergency situation is in an unenviable position. It is perhaps surprising that anyone should intervene at all" (Latané & Darley, 1970, p. 247).

Although we might suppose that the presence of other bystanders would embolden an individual to act despite the risks, research demonstrates the reverse: Often it is the very presence of other people that deters us from intervening. In fact, by 1980, there were more than 50 studies of bystander intervention, most of them showing that people are *less* likely to help when others are present (Latané, Nida, & Wilson, 1981). Bibb Latané and John Darley (1970) suggest that the presence of other people deters an individual from intervening by (1) defining the situation as a nonemergency and (1) diffusing the responsibility for acting.

Defining the Situation   Many emergencies begin ambiguously. Is the man who is staggering about ill or simply drunk? Is the woman being threatened by a stranger or is she arguing with her husband? Is that smoke from a fire or just steam pouring out the window? One common way to deal with such dilemmas is to postpone action, act as if nothing is wrong, and look around to see how others are reacting. What you are likely to see, of course, are other people who, for the same reasons, are also acting as if nothing is wrong. Everybody in the group misleads everybody else by defining the situation as a nonemergency. We have all heard about crowds panicking because each person leads everybody else to overreact. The reverse situation—in which a crowd lulls its members into inaction—may be even more common. Several experiments demonstrate this effect.

In one experiment, male college students were invited to an interview. As they sat in a small waiting room filling out a questionnaire, a stream of smoke began to pour through a wall vent. Some participants were alone in the waiting room when this occurred; others were in groups of three. The experimenters observed them through a one-way window and waited 6 minutes to see if anyone would take action or report the situation. Of the participants who were tested alone, 75% reported the smoke within about 2 minutes. In contrast, fewer than 13% of the people who were tested in

Although many passers-by have noticed the man lying on the side-walk, no one has stopped to help—to see if he is asleep, sick, drunk, or dead. Research shows that people are more likely to help if no other bystanders are present.

groups reported the smoke within the entire 6-minute period, even though the room was filled with smoke. Those who did not report the smoke subsequently reported that they had decided that it must have been steam, air-conditioning vapors, or smog—practically anything but a real fire or an emergency. This experiment thus showed that bystanders can define situations as nonemergencies for one another (Latané & Darley, 1968).

But perhaps these men were simply afraid to appear cowardly. To check this out, a similar study was designed in which the "emergency" did not involve personal danger. Male participants in the testing room heard a female experimenter in the next office climb up on a chair to reach a bookcase, fall to the floor, and yell, "Oh my God—my foot. . . . I can't move it. Oh . . . my ankle. . . . I can't get this thing off me." She continued to moan for about a minute longer. The entire incident lasted about 2 minutes. Only a curtain separated the woman's office from the testing room in which participants waited, either alone or in pairs. The results confirmed the findings of the smoke study. Of the participants who were alone, 70% came to the woman's aid, but only 40% of those in two-person groups offered help. Again, those who had not intervened claimed later that they had been unsure of what had happened but had decided that it was not serious (Latané & Rodin, 1969). The presence of other people led each individual, observing the calmness of the others, to resolve the ambiguity of the situation by deciding that no emergency existed.

Diffusion of Responsibility   The observation that the presence of others can lead individuals to define a situation as a nonemergency does not explain incidents such as the Genovese murder in which the emergency is not at all ambiguous. Moreover, Kitty Genovese's neighbors could not observe one another behind their curtained windows and hence could not tell whether others were calm or panicked. The crucial process here was *diffusion of responsibility:* When each individual knows that many others are present, the burden of responsibility does not fall solely on him or her. Each can think, "Someone else must have done something by now; someone else will intervene."

To test this hypothesis, experimenters placed participants in individual booths and told them that they would participate in a group discussion about personal problems faced by college students. They were told that, to avoid embarrassment, the discussion would be held through an intercom. Each person would speak for 2 minutes. The microphone would be turned on only in the booth of the person speaking, and the experimenter would not be listening. Actually, all the voices other than the participant's were tape recordings. On the first round, one of the taped participants mentioned that he had problems with seizures. On the second round, this individual sounded as if he were actually starting to have a seizure and begged for help. The experimenters waited to see if the participant would leave the booth to report the emergency, and how long it would take. Note that (1) the emergency is not at all ambiguous, (2) the participant could not tell how the bystanders in the other booths were reacting, and (3) the participant knew that the experimenter could not hear the emergency. Some participants were led to believe that the discussion group consisted only of themselves and the seizure victim. Others were told that they were part of a three-person group; and still others that they were part of a six-person group.

Of the participants who thought that they alone knew of the victim's seizure, 85% reported it; of those who thought that they were in a three-person group, 62% reported the seizure; and of those who thought that they were part of a six-person group only 31% reported it (see Figure 14-4). Interviews showed that all the participants perceived the situation to be a real emergency. Most were very upset by the conflict between letting the victim suffer and rushing for help. In fact, the participants who did not report the seizure appeared more upset than those who did. Clearly, we cannot interpret their nonintervention as apathy or indifference. Instead, the presence of others diffused the responsibility for acting (Darley & Latané, 1968; Latané & Darley, 1968).

If the ambiguity of the situation and diffusion of responsibility are minimized, will people help one another? To find out, three psychologists used the New York City subway system as their laboratory (Piliavin, Rodin, & Piliavin, 1969). Two male and two female experimenters boarded a subway train separately. The female experimenters took seats and recorded the results, while the two men remained standing. As the train moved along, one of the men staggered forward and collapsed, remaining prone and staring at the ceiling until he received help. If no help came, the other man finally helped him to his feet. Several variations of the study were tried: The victim either carried a cane (so he would appear ill) or smelled of alcohol (so he would appear drunk). Sometimes the victim was white; at other times, black. There was no ambiguity; the victim clearly needed help. Diffusion of responsibility was minimized because each bystander could not continue to assume that someone else was intervening. Therefore, people should help.

The results supported this optimistic expectation. The victim with the cane received spontaneous help within an average of 5 seconds on more than 95% of the trials. The drunk victim received help in half of the trials, on average within 2 minutes. Both black and white cane victims were aided by black and white bystanders. There was no relationship between the number of bystanders and the speed of help, suggesting that diffusion of responsibility had indeed been minimized.

The Role of Information   Now that you have read about the factors that deter bystanders from intervening in an emergency, would you be more likely to act in such a situation? An experiment conducted at the University of Montana suggests that you would. Undergraduates were either given a lecture or shown a film based on the material we have discussed here. Two weeks later, each undergraduate was confronted with a simulated emergency while walking with one other person (a confederate of the experimenters). A male college student was sprawled on the floor of a hallway. The confederate did not react as if the situation were an emergency. Those who had heard the lecture or seen the film were significantly more likely than others to offer help (Beaman et al., 1978). For society's sake, perhaps you should reread this section!

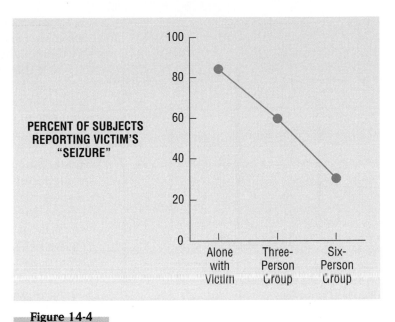

PERCENT OF SUBJECTS REPORTING VICTIM'S "SEIZURE"

Figure 14-4

Diffusion of Responsibility   The percentage of individuals who reported a victim's apparent seizure declined as the number of other people the individual believed were in his or her discussion group increased. (After Darley & Latané, 1968)

Conformity to a Majority

When we are in a group, we may find ourselves in the minority on some issue. This is a fact of life to which most of us have become accustomed. If we decide that the majority

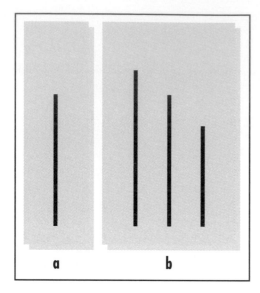

Figure 14-5

A Representative Stimulus in Asch's Study   After viewing display (a), participants were told to pick the matching line from display (b). The displays shown here are typical in that the correct decision is obvious.

is a more valid source of information than our own experience, we may change our minds and conform to the majority opinion. But imagine yourself in a situation in which you are sure that your own opinion is correct and that the group is wrong. Would you yield to social pressure and conform under those circumstances? This is the kind of conformity that social psychologist Solomon Asch decided to investigate in a series of classic studies (1952, 1955, 1958).

In Asch's standard procedure, a single participant was seated at a table with a group of seven to nine others (all confederates of the experimenter). The group was shown a display of three vertical lines of different lengths, and members of the group were asked to judge which line was the same length as a standard drawn in another display (see Figure 14-5). Each individual announced his or her decision in turn, and the participant sat in the next-to-last seat. The correct judgments were obvious, and on most trials everyone gave the same response. But on several predetermined trials the confederates had been instructed to give the wrong answer. Asch then observed the amount of conformity this procedure would elicit from the participants.

The results were striking. Even though the correct answer was always obvious, the average participant conformed to the incorrect group consensus about one third of the time; about 75% of the participants conformed at least once. Moreover, the group did not have to be large to obtain such conformity. When Asch varied the size of the group from 2 to 16, he found that a group of 3 or 4 confederates was just as effective at producing conformity as larger groups (Asch, 1958).

Why didn't the obviousness of the correct answer provide support for the individual's independence from the majority? Why isn't a person's confidence in his or her ability to make simple sensory judgments a strong force against conformity?

According to one line of argument, it is precisely the obviousness of the correct answer in the Asch experiment that produces the strong forces toward conformity (Ross, Bierbrauer, & Hoffman, 1976). Disagreements in real life typically involve difficult or subjective judgments such as which economic policy will be more effective in reducing inflation or which of two paintings is more aesthetically pleasing. In such cases, we expect to disagree with others occasionally; we even know that being a minority of one in an otherwise unanimous group is a plausible, if uncomfortable, possibility.

The Asch situation is much more extreme. Here the individual is confronted with unanimous disagreement about a simple physical fact, a bizarre and unprecedented occurrence that appears to have no rational explanation. Participants are clearly puzzled and tense. They rub their eyes in disbelief and jump up to look more closely at the lines. They squirm, mumble, giggle in embarrassment, and look searchingly at other members of the group for some clue to the mystery. After the experiment, they offer halfhearted hypotheses about optical illusions or suggest—quite aptly—that perhaps the first person occasionally made a mistake and each successive person followed suit because of conformity pressures (Asch, 1952).

Consider what it means to dissent from the majority under these circumstances. Just as the judgments of the group seem incomprehensible to the participant, so the participant believes that his or her dissent will be incomprehensible to the group. Group members will surely judge him or her to be incompetent, even out of touch with reality. Similarly, if the participant dissents repeatedly, this will seem to constitute a direct challenge to the group's competence, a challenge that requires enormous courage when one's own perceptual abilities are suddenly and inexplicably called into question. Such a challenge violates a strong social norm against insulting others. This fear of "What will they think of me?" and "What will they think I think of them?" inhibits dissent and generates the strong pressure to conform in the Asch situation.

Pressure to conform is far less strong when the group is not unanimous. If even one confederate breaks with the majority, the amount of conformity drops from 32% of the trials to about 6%. In fact, a group of eight containing only one dissenter produces less conformity than a unanimous majority of three (Allen & Levine, 1969; Asch, 1958). Surprisingly, the dissenter does not even have to give the correct answer. Even when the dissenter's answers are more inaccurate than the majority's, their influence is broken and participants are more inclined to give their own, correct judgments (Asch, 1955). Nor does it matter who the dissenter is. An African American dissenter reduces the conformity rate among racially prejudiced white participants just as effectively as a white dissenter (Malof & Lott, 1962). In a variation that approaches the absurd, conformity was significantly reduced even though the participants thought the dissenter was so visually handicapped that he could not see the stimuli (Allen

In a study of conformity to majority opinion, (top) all of the group members except the man sixth from the left are confederates who have been instructed to give uniformly wrong answers on 12 of the 18 trials. Number 6, who has been told that he is participating in an experiment on visual judgment, therefore finds that he is a lone dissenter when he gives the correct answers. (bottom left) The participant, showing the strain of repeated disagreement with the majority, leans forward anxiously to look at the exhibit in question. (bottom right) This particular participant persists in his opinion, saying that "he has to call them as he sees them." (After Asch, 1958)

& Levine, 1971). It seems clear that the presence of only one other deviant to share the potential disapproval or ridicule of the group permits the participant to dissent without feeling totally isolated.

If Asch's conformity situation is unlike most situations in real life, why did Asch use a task in which the correct answer was obvious? The reason is that he wanted to study pure public conformity, uncontaminated by the possibility that participants were actually changing their minds about the correct answers; he was interested in compliance, not internalization. Several variations of Asch's study have used more difficult or subjective judgments, and although they may reflect life more faithfully, they do not permit us to assess the effects of pure pressure to conform to a majority when we are certain that our own minority judgment is correct (Ross, Bierbrauer, & Hoffman, 1976).

Minority Influence

A number of European scholars have been critical of social psychological research in North America because of its preoccupation with conformity and the influence of the majority on the minority. As they correctly point out, intellectual innovation, social

Social change—such as the end of apartheid in South Africa—is sometimes brought about because a few people manage to persuade the majority to change its attitudes.

change, and political revolution often occur because an informed and articulate minority—sometimes a minority of one—begins to convert others to its point of view (Moscovici, 1976). Why not study innovation and the influence that minorities can have on the majority?

To make their point, these investigators began their experimental work by setting up a laboratory situation virtually identical to Asch's conformity situation. Participants were asked to make a series of simple perceptual judgments in the face of confederates who consistently gave the incorrect answer. But instead of placing a single participant in the midst of several confederates, the investigators planted two confederates, who consistently gave incorrect responses, in the midst of four real participants. The experimenters found that the minority was able to influence about 32% of the participants to make at least one incorrect judgment. For this to occur, however, the minority had to remain consistent throughout the experiment. If they wavered or showed any inconsistency in their judgments, they were unable to influence the majority (Moscovici, Lage, & Naffrechoux, 1969).

Since this initial demonstration of minority influence, more than 90 related studies have been conducted in both Europe and North America, including several that required groups to debate social and political issues rather than to make simple perceptual judgments (Wood et al., 1994). The general finding is that minorities can move majorities toward their point of view if they present a consistent position without appearing rigid, dogmatic, or arrogant. Such minorities are perceived to be more confident and, occasionally, more competent than the majority (Maass & Clark, 1984).

But the most interesting finding from this research is that the majority members in these studies show a change of private attitude—that is, internalization—not just the public conformity that was found in the Asch experiments. In fact, minorities sometimes obtain private attitude change from majority members even when they fail to obtain public conformity. One investigator has suggested that minorities are able to produce attitude change because they lead majority individuals to rethink the issues. Even when they fail to convince the majority, they broaden the range of acceptable opinions. In contrast, unanimous majorities are rarely prompted to think carefully about their position (Nemeth, 1986).

These findings remind us that the majorities of the world typically have the social power to approve and disapprove, to accept or reject, and it is this power that can obtain public compliance or conformity. In contrast, minorities rarely have such social power. But if they have credibility, they have the power to produce genuine attitude change and, hence, innovation, social change, and revolution.

Obedience to Authority

From 1933 to 1945, millions of innocent people were systematically put to death in concentration camps in Nazi Germany. The mastermind of this horror, Adolf Hitler, may well have been a psychopathic monster. But he could not have done it alone. What about the people who ran the day-to-day operations, who built the ovens and gas chambers, filled them with human beings, counted bodies, and did the necessary paperwork? Were they all monsters, too?

Not according to social philosopher Hannah Arendt (1963), who covered the trial of Adolf Eichmann, a Nazi war criminal who was found guilty and executed for causing the murder of millions of Jews. She described him as a dull, ordinary bureaucrat who saw himself as a little cog in a big machine. The publication of a partial transcript of Eichmann's pretrial interrogation supports Arendt's view. Several psychiatrists found Eichmann to be quite sane, and his personal relationships were quite normal. In fact, he believed that the Jews should have been allowed to emigrate to a separate territory, and had argued for such a policy within Hitler's security service. Moreover, he had a Jewish mistress in secret—a crime for an SS officer—and a Jewish half-cousin whom he arranged to have protected during the war (Von Lang & Sibyll, 1983).

In *Eichmann in Jerusalem: A Report on the Banality of Evil,* Arendt concluded that most of the "evil men" of Nazi Germany were ordinary people who were just following orders from superiors. This suggests that all of us might be capable of such evil and that Nazi Germany was less alien from the normal human condition than we might like to think. As Arendt put it, "In certain circumstances the most ordinary decent person can become a criminal." This is not an easy conclusion to accept because it is more comforting to believe that monstrous evil is done only by monstrous people. In fact, our emotional attachment to this explanation of evil was vividly shown by the intensity of the attacks on Arendt and her conclusions.

In 1969 the problem of obedience to authority arose again in Vietnam, when a group of American soldiers, claiming that they were simply following orders, deliberately killed a large number of civilians in the community of My Lai. Again the public was forced to ponder the possibility that ordinary citizens are willing to obey authority in violation of their own moral conscience.

This issue was explored empirically in a series of important and controversial studies conducted by Stanley Milgram (1963, 1974) at Yale University. Ordinary men and women were recruited through a newspaper ad that offered $4 for an hour's participation in a "study of memory." On arriving at the laboratory, the participant was told that he or she would be playing the role of teacher in the study. The participant was to read a series of word pairs to another participant and then test that learner's memory by reading the first word of each pair and asking him to select the correct second word from four alternatives. Each time the learner made an error, the participant was to press a lever that delivered an electric shock to him.

The participant watched while the learner was strapped into a chair and an electrode was attached to his wrist. The participant was then seated in an adjoining room in front of a shock generator whose front panel contained 30 lever switches set in a horizontal line. Each switch was labeled with a voltage rating, ranging in sequence from 15 to 450 volts, and groups of adjacent switches were labeled descriptively, ranging from "Slight Shock" up to "Danger: Severe Shock." When a switch was depressed, an electric buzzer sounded, lights flashed, and the needle on a voltage meter deflected to the right. To illustrate how it worked, the participant was given a sample shock of 45 volts from the generator. As the procedure began, the experimenter instructed the participant to move one level higher on the shock generator after each successive error (see Figure 14-6).

The learner did not actually receive any shocks. He was a mild-mannered, 47-year-old man who had been specially trained for his role. As he began to make errors and the shock levels escalated, he could be heard protesting through the adjoining wall. As the shocks became stronger, he began to shout and curse. At 300 volts he began to kick the wall, and at the next shock level (marked "Extreme Intensity Shock"), he no longer answered the questions or made any noise. As you might expect, many participants began to object to this excruciating procedure, pleading

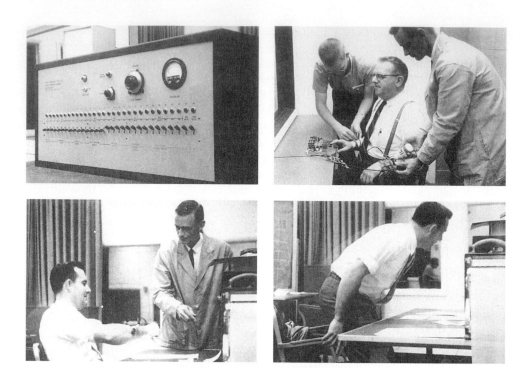

(top left) The "shock generator" used in Milgram's experiment on obedience. *(top right)* The "learner" is strapped into the "electric chair." *(bottom left)* A participant receives a sample shock before starting the "teaching session." *(bottom right)* A participant refuses to go on with the experiment. Most participants became deeply disturbed by the role they were asked to play, whether they remained in the experiment to the end or refused at some point to go on. (From the film Obedience, *distributed by New York University Film Library, copyright 1965 by Stanley Milgram)*

Figure 14-6

Milgram's Experiment on Obedience   The "teacher" was told to give the "learner" a more intense shock after each error. If the "teacher" objected, the experimenter insisted that it was necessary to go on.

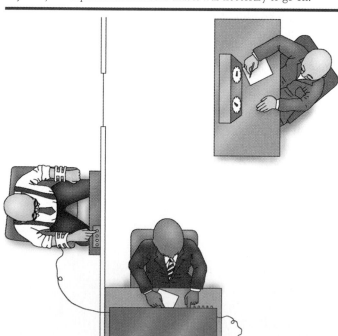

with the experimenter to call a halt. But the experimenter responded with a sequence of prods, using as many as necessary to get the participant to go on: "Please continue"; "The experiment requires that you continue"; "It is absolutely essential that you continue"; and "You have no other choice—you must go on." Obedience to authority was measured by the maximum amount of shock the participant would administer before refusing to continue.

Milgram found that 65% of the participants continued to obey throughout the experiment, going all the way to the end of the shock series (450 volts). Not one participant stopped prior to administering 300 volts, the point at which the learner began to kick the wall (see Figure 14-7). What produces such obedience?

Milgram suggests that the potential for obedience to authority is such a necessary requirement for communal life that it has probably been built into our species by evolution. The division of labor in a society requires that individuals be willing at times to subordinate and coordinate their own independent actions to serve the goals and purposes of the larger social organization. Parents, school systems, and businesses all nurture this willingness further by reminding the individual about the importance of following the directives of others who "know the big picture." To understand obedience in a particular situation, then, we need to understand the factors that persuade individuals to relinquish their autonomy and become voluntary agents of the system. Milgram's experiments illustrate four such factors: social norms, surveillance, buffers, and ideological justification.

Social Norms   By replying to the advertisement and agreeing to be in the study, participants in Milgram's experiments had voluntarily assented to an implicit contract to cooperate with the experimenter, to follow the directions of the person in charge, and to see the job through to completion. This is a very strong social norm, and we tend to underestimate how difficult it is to break such an agreement and go back on our implied word to cooperate.

The experiment was also designed to reinforce this norm by making it particularly difficult to stop once it had begun. The procedure starts rather innocently as an experiment in memory and then gradually escalates. Once participants begin to give shocks and to raise the shock levels, there is no longer a natural stopping point. By the time they want to quit, they are trapped. The experimenter makes no new demands, only that they continue to do what they are already doing. In order to break off, they must suffer the guilt and embarrassment of acknowledging that they were wrong to begin at all. And the longer they put off quitting, the harder it is to admit their misjudgment in going as far as they have. It is easier to continue. (Imagine how much less obedience there would be if participants had to begin by giving the strongest shock first.)

Finally, the potential quitter faces a dilemma over violating a norm of etiquette (not being rude). Dissenting is equivalent to accusing the experimenter of being immoral—a compelling force that pushes the participant toward going along with the experiment.

If social norms like these can produce so much obedience in Milgram's studies, then it is easy to imagine how much more powerful the penalties for quitting would be in Nazi Germany or in military service once one has already "signed on."[1]

Surveillance   An obvious factor in Milgram's experiments is the constant presence or surveillance of the experimenter. When the experimenter left the room and issued his orders by telephone, obedience dropped from 65% to 21% (Milgram, 1974). Moreover, several of the participants who continued under these conditions cheated by administering shocks of lower intensity than they were supposed to. This clearly shows that participants were merely complying with the orders; they were not privately assenting to the correctness or the necessity of the procedure. In other words, they were showing compliance, not internalization.

Buffers   Milgram's participants believed that they were committing acts of violence, but there were several buffers that obscured this fact or diluted the immediacy

Figure 14-7

Obedience to Authority   The percentage of participants who are willing to administer a punishing shock did not begin to decline until the intensity level of the shock reached 300 volts (the danger level). (After Milgram, 1963)

---

[1]Daniel Goldhagen, the author of *Hitler's Willing Executioners: Ordinary Germans and the Holocaust* (1996), argues that Milgram's studies of obedience do not in fact provide an explanation for Nazi atrocities.

Modern warfare allows individuals to distance themselves from the actual killing, giving them the feeling that they are not responsible for enemy deaths.

of the experience. For example, the learner was in the next room, out of sight and unable to communicate. Milgram reports that obedience drops from 65% to 40% if the learner is in the same room as the participant. If the participant must personally ensure that the learner holds his hand on a shock plate, obedience declines to 30%. The more direct the person's experience with the victim—the fewer buffers between the person and the consequences of his or her act—the less the person will obey.

The most common buffer found in warlike situations is the remoteness of the person from the final act of violence. Thus, Adolf Eichmann argued that he was not directly responsible for killing Jews; he merely arranged for their deaths indirectly. Milgram conducted an analog to this "link-in-the-chain" role by requiring a participant only to pull a switch that enabled another teacher (a confederate) to deliver the shocks to the learner. Under these conditions, obedience soared: A full 93% of the participants continued to the end of the shock series. In this situation, the participant can shift responsibility to the person who actually delivers the shock.

The shock generator itself served as a buffer—an impersonal mechanical agent that actually delivered the shock. Imagine how obedience would have declined if participants were required to hit the learner with their fists. In real life, we have analogous technologies that permit us to destroy distant fellow humans by remote control, thereby removing us from the sight of their suffering. Although we probably all agree that it is worse to kill thousands of people by pushing a button that releases a guided missile than it is to beat one individual to death with a rock, it is still psychologically easier to push the button. Such are the effects of buffers.

Ideological Justification   The fourth and most important factor producing voluntary obedience is the individual's acceptance of an *ideology*—a set of beliefs and attitudes—that legitimates the authority of the person in charge and justifies following his or her directives. Nazi officers such as Eichmann believed in the primacy of the German state and hence in the legitimacy of orders issued in its name. Similarly, the

American soldiers who followed orders to shoot enemy civilians in Vietnam had already committed themselves to the premise that national security requires strict obedience to military commands.

In Milgram's experiments, the "importance of science" is the ideology that legitimates even quite extraordinary demands. Some critics have argued that the Milgram experiments were artificial, that the prestige of a scientific experiment led people to obey without questioning the dubious procedures in which they participated, and that in real life people would never do such a thing (Baumrind, 1964). Indeed, when Milgram repeated his experiment in a rundown set of offices and removed any association with Yale University from the setting, obedience dropped from 65% to 48% (Milgram, 1974).

But this criticism misses the major point. The prestige of science is not an irrelevant artificiality but an integral part of Milgram's demonstration. "Science" serves the same legitimating role in the experiment that the German state served in Nazi Germany and that national security serves in wartime killing. It is precisely their belief in the importance of scientific research that prompts individuals to subordinate their personal moral autonomy and independence to those who claim to act in behalf of science.

Resistance to Obedience   Milgram's procedure involves a lone individual. If the participant were not alone, would he or she be less obedient? Milgram tested this possibility by modifying the standard procedure so that two additional confederates were present. They were introduced as participants who would also play teacher roles. Teacher 1 would read the list of word pairs; Teacher 2 would tell the learner whether he was right or wrong; and Teacher 3 (the participant) would deliver the shocks. The confederates complied with the instructions through the 150-volt shock, at which point Teacher 1 informed the experimenter that he was quitting. Despite the experimenter's insistence that he continue, Teacher 1 got up from his chair and sat in another part of the room. After the 210-volt shock, Teacher 2 also quit. The experimenter then turned to the participant and ordered him to continue alone. In this situation only 10% of the participants were willing to complete the series. In a second variation, there were two experimenters rather than two additional teachers. After a few shocks, they began to argue—one of them saying that they should stop the experiment, the other saying that they should continue. Under these circumstances, not a single participant would continue despite orders to do so by the second experimenter (Milgram, 1974). Just as a participant in the Asch conformity situation is less likely to go along with the group's incorrect judgments if there is at least one other dissenter, so, too, having a role-model for disobedience in the Milgram experiment made it much easier for the participant to disobey.

Ethical Issues in Milgram's Obedience Experiments   Over the years, Milgram's obedience experiments have become as well known for the ethical questions they raise about the conduct of psychological research as they have for their results. The first published criticism appeared soon after Milgram published his early findings (Baumrind, 1964), and an entire book has been written about the controversy itself (Miller, 1986).

First, critics argued that Milgram's procedure created an unacceptable level of stress in the participants during the experiments. Second, they expressed concern about the long-term psychological effects on participant's self-esteem of having learned that they would be willing to give potentially lethal shocks to a fellow human being. And finally, critics argued that participants were likely to feel foolish and "used" when told the true nature of the experiment, thereby making them less trusting of psychologists in particular and of authority in general.

Milgram replied to these and other criticisms. His major defense was that, in general, the participants themselves did not agree with the critics. After each session, Milgram conducted a careful "debriefing," explaining the reasons for the procedures and reestablishing positive rapport with the participant. This included a reassuring chat with the "victim" who the participant had thought was receiving the shocks. After the completion of an experimental series, participants were sent a detailed report of the results and purposes of the experimental project. Milgram then conducted a survey of the participants, asking them how they felt about their participation "now that [you] have read the report, and all things considered."

Milgram found that 84% of the participants indicated that they were glad to have taken part in the study; 15% reported neutral feelings; and 1% stated that they were sorry to have participated. These percentages were about the same for those who had obeyed and for those who had defied the experimenter during the experiment itself. In addition, 80% felt that more experiments of this sort should be carried out, and 74% indicated that they had learned something of personal importance as a result of being in the study. Milgram also hired a psychiatrist to interview 40 of the participants in person to determine whether the study had had any injurious effects. This follow-up revealed no indications of long-term distress or traumatic reactions among participants; typically they felt that their participation had been instructive and enriching (Milgram, 1964).

With respect to the concern that participants might be less trusting of authority in the future, Milgram noted that "the experimenter is not just any authority: he is an authority who tells the participant to act harshly and inhumanely against another man. I would consider it of the highest value if participation in the experiment could inculcate a skepticism of this kind of authority" (1964, p. 852).

In Chapter 1 we noted that research guidelines set forth by the United States government and the American Psychological Association emphasize two major principles. The principle of *minimal risk* specifies that the risks anticipated in a research study should be no greater than those ordinarily encountered in daily life. The principle of *informed consent* specifies that participants must enter a study voluntarily and be permitted to withdraw from it at any time without penalty if they so desire. They must also be told ahead of time about any aspects of the study that could be expected to influence their willingness to cooperate. When this requirement cannot be strictly met, a thorough "debriefing" must eliminate any negative feelings the participant might have experienced.

Milgram's studies were conducted in the early 1960s, before these guidelines were in effect. Despite the importance of the research and the precautions that Milgram took, it seems likely that most of the review boards that must now approve federally funded research projects would not permit these experiments to be conducted today. Although many replications of Milgram's experiments were conducted in earlier years, the last one conducted in the United States was published in 1976 (Blass, 1991).

The Power of Situations

Earlier in the chapter we noted that people typically overestimate the role of dispositional

Figure 14-8

Predicted and Actual Compliance The upper curve presents Milgram's data and shows the percentage of participants who remained obedient in the situation, continuing to administer shocks as the voltage increased. The lower curve is from a study in which role-playing participants reenacted the Milgram experiment. They were asked to estimate the percentage of the participants who would continue to be obedient as shock increased. The role-playing participants vastly underestimated the magnitude of the situational forces and the likelihood of obedience in Milgram's experimental situation. (After Bierbrauer, 1973)

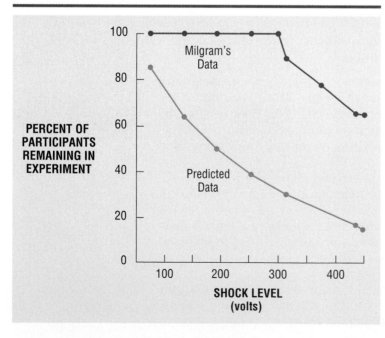

factors and underestimate that of situational factors in controlling behavior—the fundamental attribution error. The Milgram studies illustrate this point—not through their results, but through our surprise at their results. We simply do not expect the situational forces to be as effective as they are. When college students are told about Milgram's procedures (but not given the results) and are asked whether they would continue to administer the shocks in the Milgram situation after the learner begins to pound on the wall, about 99% say they would not (Aronson, 1995). Milgram himself surveyed psychiatrists at a leading medical school. They predicted that most participants would refuse to go on after reaching 150 volts, that only about 4% would go beyond 300 volts, and that fewer than 1% would go all the way to 450 volts. In one study, participants were asked to estimate obedience rates after they had reenacted the entire Milgram procedure, complete with shock apparatus and a tape recording of the protesting learner. Whether they played the role of the actual participant or the role of an observer, all participants continued to vastly underestimate the compliance rates actually obtained by Milgram, as shown in Figure 14-8 (Bierbrauer, 1973).

In sum, our reactions to the obedience experiments dramatically illustrate a major lesson of social psychology: We seriously underestimate the extent and power of social and situational forces on human behavior.

Reference Group Influence

Nearly every group to which we belong, from our family to the society as a whole, has an implicit or explicit set of beliefs, attitudes, and behaviors that it considers correct. Any member of the group who strays from these social norms risks isolation and social disapproval. Thus, through social rewards and punishments, the groups to which we belong obtain compliance from us. In addition, if we respect or admire other individuals or groups, we may *obey their norms and adopt their beliefs, attitudes, and behaviors in order to be like them, to identify with them.* This process is called **identification.**

Groups with whom we identify are called our **reference groups,** because we refer to them in order to evaluate our own opinions and actions. Reference groups can also serve as a *frame of reference* by providing us not only with specific beliefs and attitudes but also with a general perspective from which we view the world—an *ideology* or set of ready-made interpretations of social issues and events. If we eventually adopt these views and integrate the group's ideology into our own value system, then the reference group will have produced internalization. The process of identification, then, can provide a bridge between compliance and internalization.

An individual does not necessarily have to be a member of a reference group in order to be influenced by its values. For example, lower-middle-class individuals often use the middle class as a reference group. A young, aspiring athlete may use professional athletes as a reference group, adopting their views and otherwise trying to model himself or herself after them.

Life would be simple if each of us identified with only one reference group. But most of us identify with several reference groups, and this often leads to conflicting pressures on us. For example, a Jewish businessperson might experience cross-pressures because his or her ethnic reference group usually holds more liberal political positions than his or her business reference group. But perhaps the most enduring example of competing reference groups is

identification the process in which we obey the norms and adopt the beliefs, attitudes, and behaviors of others in order to be like them

reference groups groups with whom we identify

Identification With Reference Groups *A young aspiring athlete might use professional athletes as a reference group, adopting their views—as well as their athletic shoes—in order to be more like them.*

When they first arrive at college, young people often experience a conflict between their family reference group and their college or peer reference group on many social attitudes and issues.

the conflict that many young people experience between their family reference group and their college or peer reference group. The most extensive study of this conflict is Theodore Newcomb's classic Bennington Study—an examination of the political attitudes of the entire population of Bennington College, a small, politically liberal college in Vermont. The dates of the study (1935–1939) are a useful reminder that this is not a new phenomenon.

Today Bennington College tends to attract politically liberal students, but in 1935 most students came from wealthy, conservative families. (It is also coeducational today, but in 1935 it was a women's college.) More than two thirds of the parents of Bennington students were affiliated with the Republican party. The Bennington College community was liberal during the 1930s, but this was not why most of the women selected the college.

Newcomb's main finding was that with each year at Bennington, students moved further away from their parents' attitudes and closer to the attitudes of the college community. For example, in the 1936 presidential campaign about 66% of parents favored the Republican candidate, Alf Landon, over the Democratic candidate, Franklin Roosevelt. Landon was supported by 62% of the Bennington freshmen and 43% of the sophomores, but by only 15% of the juniors and seniors.

For most of the women, increasing liberalism reflected a deliberate choice between the two competing reference groups. Two of them describe how they made this choice:

1. All my life I've resented the protection of governesses and parents. At college I got away from that, or rather, I guess I should say, I changed it to wanting the intellectual approval of teachers and more advanced students. Then I found that you can't be reactionary and be intellectually respectable.
2. Becoming radical meant thinking for myself and, figuratively, thumbing my nose at my family. It also meant intellectual identification with the faculty and students that I most wanted to be like. (Newcomb, 1943, pp. 131, 134)

Note that this woman actually uses the term *identification* in the sense that we have defined it. Note, too, how the women describe a mixture of change produced by social rewards and punishments (compliance) and change produced by attraction to an admired group whom they strive to emulate (identification).

From Identification to Internalization   As mentioned earlier, reference groups also serve as frames of reference by providing their members with new perspectives on the world. The Bennington community, particularly the faculty, gave students a perspective on the depression of the 1930s and the threat of world war that their wealthy and conservative home environments had not, and this began to move them from identification to internalization:

1. It didn't take me long to see that liberal attitudes had prestige value. . . . I became liberal at first because of its prestige value; I remain so because the problems around which my liberalism centers are important. What I want now is to be effective in solving problems.
2. Prestige and recognition have always meant everything to me. . . . But I've sweat blood in trying to be honest with myself, and the result is that I really know what I want my atti-

tudes to be, and I see what their consequences will be in my own life. (Newcomb, 1943, pp. 136–37)

Many of our most important beliefs and attitudes are probably based initially on identification. Whenever we start to identify with a new reference group, we engage in a process of "trying on" the new set of beliefs and attitudes they prescribe. What we "really believe" is in flux, capable of changing from day to day. The first year of college often has this effect on students; many of the views they bring from the family reference group are challenged by alternative perspectives held by students and faculty from very different backgrounds. Students often "try on" the new beliefs with great intensity and strong conviction, only to discard them for still newer beliefs when the first set does not quite fit. As we noted in our discussion of adolescent identity development in Chapter 3, this is a natural process of growth. Although the process never really ends for people who remain open to new experiences, it is greatly accelerated during the college years, before the person has formed a nucleus of permanent beliefs on which to build more slowly and less radically. Some of the real work of college is to evolve an ideological identity from the several beliefs and attitudes that are tested in order to move from identification to internalization.

As noted earlier, one advantage of internalization over compliance is that the changes are self-sustaining. The original source of influence does not have to monitor the individual to maintain the induced changes. The test of internalization, then, is the long-term stability of the induced beliefs, attitudes, and behaviors. Was the identification-induced liberalism of Bennington women maintained when the students returned to the "real world"? The answer is yes. Two follow-up studies of the Bennington women done 25 and 50 years later found that they had remained liberal. For example, in the 1984 presidential election 73% of Bennington alumnae preferred the Democratic candidate, Walter Mondale, over the Republican candidate, Ronald Reagan, compared with fewer than 26% of women of the same age and educational level. Moreover, about 60% of Bennington alumnae were politically active, most (66%) within the Democratic party (Alwin, Cohen, & Newcomb, 1991; Newcomb et al., 1967).

But we never outgrow our need to identify with supporting reference groups. The political attitudes of Bennington women remained stable, in part, because after college they selected new reference groups—friends and husbands—who supported the attitudes they had developed in college. Those who married more conservative men were more likely to be politically conservative in later life. As Newcomb noted, we often select our reference groups because they share our attitudes, and our reference groups, in turn, help to develop and sustain our attitudes. The relationship is circular. The distinction between identification and internalization is a useful one for understanding social influence, but in practice it is not always possible to disentangle them.

---

1. If you were a member of a university review board that was asked to consider the risks and benefits of proposed research programs, would you vote to approve Milgram's obedience experiments? Why or why not?

2. Can you identify any changes in your beliefs and attitudes that have come about by being exposed to new reference groups?

Thinking Critically

How Do We Select Our Friends and Lovers?

Interpersonal Attraction

We cannot all be beautiful film stars, but when two such people become a couple, they illustrate several of the determinants of interpersonal attraction that apply even to us ordinary mortals: *physical attractiveness, proximity, familiarity,* and *similarity.*

As the high divorce rate also illustrates, however, these factors are not always sufficient to sustain a long-term relationship.

Physical Attractiveness   To most of us there is something mildly undemocratic about the possibility that a person's physical appearance is a determinant of how well he or she is liked by others. Unlike character and personality, physical appearance is a factor over which we have little control, and hence it seems unfair to use it as a criterion for liking someone. In fact, surveys taken over a span of several decades have shown that people do not rank physical attractiveness as very important in their liking of other people (Buss & Barnes, 1986; Hudson & Hoyt, 1981; Perrin, 1921; Tesser & Brodie, 1971).

But research on actual behavior shows otherwise (Brehm, 1992). One group of psychologists set up a "computer dance" in which college men and women were randomly paired. At intermission everyone filled out an anonymous questionnaire evaluating his or her date. In addition, the experimenters obtained several personality test scores for each person, as well as an independent estimate of his or her physical attractiveness. The results showed that only physical attractiveness played a role in how much the person was liked by his or her partner. None of the measures of intelligence, social skills, or personality was related to the partners' liking for one another (Walster et al., 1966). There have been many replications of this experiment, including one that focused on gay men (Sergios & Cody, 1985), and all have shown similar results. Moreover, the importance of physical attractiveness operates not only on first dates but on subsequent ones as well (Mathes, 1975).

Why is physical attractiveness so important? Part of the reason is that our own social standing and self-esteem are enhanced when we are seen with physically attractive companions. Both men and women are rated more favorably when they are with an attractive romantic partner or friend than when they are with an unattractive companion (Sheposh, Deming, & Young, 1977; Sigall & Landy, 1973). But there is an interesting twist to this: Both men and women are rated less favorably when they are seen with a stranger who is physically more attractive than they (Kernis & Wheeler, 1981). Apparently they suffer by comparison. This effect has been found in other studies. For example, male college students who had just watched a television show starring beautiful young women gave lower attractiveness ratings to a photograph of a more typical-looking woman—as did both men and women who were first shown a photograph of a highly attractive woman (Kenrick & Gutierres, 1980).

Fortunately, there is hope for the unbeautiful among us. First of all, physical attractiveness appears to be less important in the choice of a permanent partner (Stroebe et al., 1971). And as we will see, several other factors can work in our favor.

Proximity   An examination of 5,000 applications for marriage licenses in Philadelphia in the 1930s found that one third of the couples lived within five blocks of each other (Rubin, 1973). Research shows that the best single predictor of whether two people are friends is how far apart they live. In a study of friendship patterns in apartment houses, residents were asked to name the three people they saw socially most often. Residents mentioned 41% of neighbors who lived in the apartment next door, 22% of those who lived two doors away (about 30 feet), and only 10% of those who lived at the other end of the hall (Festinger, Schachter, & Back, 1950). Studies of college dormitories show the same effect. After a full academic year, roommates were twice as likely as floormates to be friends, and floormates were more than twice as likely as dormitory residents in general to be friends (Priest & Sawyer, 1967).

Those who believe in miracles when it comes to matters of the heart may think that there is a perfect mate chosen for each of us waiting to be discovered somewhere in the world. But if this is true, the far greater miracle is the frequency with which fate conspires to place that person within walking distance.

Familiarity   One of the major reasons proximity creates liking is that it increases familiarity, and there is abundant evidence that familiarity all by itself—sheer exposure—increases liking (Zajonc, 1968). This "familiarity-breeds-liking" effect is a very general phenomenon. For example, rats that are repeatedly exposed either to the music of Mozart or to that of Schönberg enhance their liking for the composer they have heard, and humans who are repeatedly exposed either to selected nonsense syllables or to Chinese characters come to prefer those they have seen most often. The effect even occurs when individuals are unaware that they have been previously exposed to the stimuli (Bornstein, 1992; Bornstein & D'Agostino, 1992; Moreland & Zajonc, 1979; Wilson, 1979). In one clever demonstration of this familiarity-breeds-liking effect, the investigators took photographs of college women and prepared prints of both the original face and its mirror image. These prints were then shown to the women themselves, their female friends, and their lovers. The women themselves preferred the mirror-image prints by a margin of 68% to 32%, but the friends and lovers preferred the nonreversed prints by a margin of 61% to 39% (Mita, Dermer, & Knight, 1977). Can you guess why?

More germane to the present discussion is a study in which participants were exposed to pictures of faces and then asked how much they thought they would like the person shown. The more frequently they had seen a particular face, the more they said that they liked it and thought they would like the person (Zajonc, 1968). Similar results are obtained when individuals are exposed to one another in real life (Moreland & Beach, 1992). The moral is clear. If you are not beautiful or you find your admiration of someone unreciprocated, be persistent and hang around. Proximity and familiarity are your most powerful weapons.

Similarity   An old saying declares that opposites attract, and lovers are fond of recounting how different they are from each other: "I love boating, but she prefers mountain climbing." "I'm in engineering, but he's a history major." What such lovers overlook is that they both like outdoor activities; they are both preprofessionals; they are both Democrats; they are both the same nationality, the same religion, the same social class, the same educational level; and they probably are within 3 years of each other in age and within 5 IQ points of each other in intelligence. In short, the old saying is mostly false.

Research all the way back to 1870 supports this conclusion. More than 99% of the married couples in the United States are of the same race, and most are of the same religion. Moreover, statistical surveys show that husbands and wives are significantly similar to each other not only in sociological characteristics such as age, race, religion, education, and socioeconomic class but also with respect to psychological

Partners in successful long-term relationships tend to be similar to each other in characteristics such as age, race, and education, as well as in their interests, personality traits, and even physical attractiveness.

characteristics like intelligence and physical characteristics such as height and eye color (Rubin, 1973). A study of dating couples found the same patterns, in addition to finding that couples were also similar in their attitudes about sexual behavior and sex roles. Moreover, couples who were most similar in background at the beginning of the study were most likely to be together a year later (Hill, Rubin, & Peplau, 1976). Especially pertinent to our earlier discussion is the finding that couples are closely matched in physical attractiveness as well (Feingold, 1988).

For example, in one study, judges rated photographs of each partner of 99 couples for physical attractiveness without knowing who was paired with whom. The physical attractiveness ratings of the couples matched each other significantly more closely than did the ratings of photographs that were randomly paired into couples (Murstein, 1972). Similar results were obtained in a field study in which separate observers rated the physical attractiveness of members of couples in bars and theater lobbies and at social events (Silverman, 1971).

This matching of couples on physical attractiveness appears to come about because we weigh a potential partner's attractiveness against the probability that the person would be willing to pair up with us. To put it bluntly, less attractive people seek less attractive partners because they expect to be rejected by someone who is more attractive than themselves. A study of a video dating service found that both men and women were most likely to pursue a relationship with someone who matched them in physical attractiveness. Only the most attractive people sought dates with the most attractive partners (Folkes, 1982). The overall result of this marketplace process is similarity in attractiveness: Most of us end up with partners who are about as attractive as we are.

But similarities on dimensions other than physical attractiveness are probably even more important over the long-term course of a relationship. A longitudinal study of 135 married couples found that spouses who were more similar to each other in personality also resembled each other more in terms of how much they enjoyed similar daily activities like visiting friends, going out for dinner, and participating in community activities and professional meetings. These couples also reported less marital conflict and greater closeness, friendliness, and marital satisfaction than less similar spouses (Caspi & Herbener, 1990).

In an ambitious study of similarity and friendship, male students received free room for the year in a large house at the University of Michigan in exchange for their participation. On the basis of information from tests and questionnaires, some men were assigned roommates who were quite similar to them and others were assigned roommates who were quite dissimilar. The investigator observed the friendship patterns that developed over the course of the year, obtaining more questionnaire and attitude data from the participants at regular intervals. In all other respects, the men lived as they would in any dormitory.

Roommates who were initially similar generally liked each other and ended up as better friends than those who were dissimilar. When the study was repeated with a new group of men the next year, however, the familiarity-breeds-liking effect turned out to be even more powerful than similarity. Regardless of whether low or high similarity had been the basis for room assignments, roommates came to like each other (Newcomb, 1961).

One reason similarity produces liking is probably that people value their own opinions and preferences and enjoy being with others who validate their choices, possibly boosting their self-esteem in the process. But perhaps the major reason is just a repeat of factors we have seen before—proximity and familiarity. Both social norms and situational circumstances throw us together with people who are like us. Most religious groups prefer (or insist) that their members date and mate within the religion, and cultural norms regulate what is considered acceptable in terms of race and age matches—a couple comprising an older woman and a younger man is still viewed as inappropriate. Situational circumstances also play an important role. Many couples meet in college or graduate school, thus ensuring that they will be similar in educational level, general intelligence, professional aspirations, and probably age and socioeconomic status. Moreover, tennis players will have met on the tennis courts, political liberals at a pro-choice rally, and gay people at a meeting of the Lesbian, Gay, and Bisexual Task Force.

Despite all this, it is often suggested that the notion that opposites attract may still apply to certain complementary traits (Winch, Ktsanes, & Ktsanes, 1954). To take the most obvious example, one partner may be quite dominant and hence may need someone who is relatively more submissive. A person with strong preferences may do best with someone who is very flexible or even wishy-washy. Despite the plausibility of this complementarity hypothesis, there is not much evidence for it (Levinger, Senn, & Jorgensen, 1970). In one study, marital adjustment among couples who had been married for up to 5 years was found to depend more on similarity than on complementarity (Meyer & Pepper, 1977). Attempts to identify the pairs of personality traits that bring about complementarity have not been very successful (Strong et al., 1988).

In later life the passionate component of romantic love tends to become less important than the companionate component.

Love

Love is more than just strong liking. Most of us know people whom we like very much but do not love, and some of us have even felt passionate attraction for someone we did not particularly like. Research confirms these everyday observations. One of the first researchers to study romantic love compiled a number of statements that people thought reflected liking and loving, and constructed separate scales to measure each (Rubin, 1973). Items on the liking scale tap the degree to which the other person is regarded as likable, respected, admired, and having maturity and good judgment. Items on the love scale tap three main themes: a sense of attachment ("It would be hard for me to get along without _____"), a sense of caring for the other person ("I would do almost anything for _____"), and a sense of trust ("I feel that I can confide in _____ about virtually everything"). The two scales are only moderately correlated: .56 for men and .36 for women.

Love and Marriage   The concept of romantic love is an old one, but the belief that it has much to do with marriage is more recent and far from universal. In some non-Western cultures, marriage is still considered to be a contractual or financial arrangement that has nothing whatever to do with love. In our own society, the link between love and marriage has actually become stronger over the past 30 years. In 1967, college students were asked "If a man (woman) had all the other qualities you desired, would you marry this person if you were not in love with him (her)?" About 65% of the men said no, but only 24% of the women said no (only 4% actually said yes; the majority of women were undecided) (Kephart, 1967). The women's rights movement had just begun at that time, and it may be that women were more likely then than they are now to consider marriage a necessary condition for their own financial security. When the survey was repeated in 1984, 85% of both men and women said that they would refuse to marry without being in love (Simpson, Campbell, & Berscheid, 1986).

Producing Passion With Extrinsic Arousal

In his 1st-century Roman handbook *The Art of Love,* Ovid offered advice about romantic conquest to both men and women. Among his more intriguing suggestions was for a man to take a woman in whom he is interested to the gladiatorial contests, where she could be easily aroused to passion. He did not say why this should be so, however. It was not until 1887 that a psychological explanation for this bit of wisdom was offered:

> Love can only be excited by strong and vivid emotion, and it is almost immaterial whether these emotions are agreeable or disagreeable. The Cid wooed the proud heart of Donna Ximene, whose father he had slain, by shooting one after another of her pet pigeons. (Adolf Horwicz, quoted in Finck, 1887, p. 240)

These romantic tactics should strike a familiar chord. As discussed in Chapter 9, we sometimes judge what emotion we are experiencing through a process of cognitive appraisal. Although the physiological arousal of our autonomic nervous system provides the cues that we are experiencing an emotion, the more subtle judgment of precisely which emotion we are experiencing often depends on our cognitive appraisals of the surrounding circumstances.

Ovid and Horwicz thus were suggesting that a person who is physiologically aroused (by whatever means) might attribute that arousal to love or sexual passion—to the advantage of any would-be lover who happens to be at hand. There is now solid experimental evidence for this phenomenon, but psychologists disagree about the process underlying it. In one set of studies, male participants were physiologically aroused by running in place, hearing an audiotape of a comedy routine, or hearing an audiotape of a grisly killing. They then viewed a taped interview with a woman who was either attractive or unattractive. Finally, they rated the woman on several dimensions, including her attractiveness, her sexiness, and the degree to which they would be interested in dating her and kissing her. The results showed that no matter how the arousal had been elicited, participants were more sexually responsive to the attractive woman and less sexually responsive to the unattractive woman than were control participants who had not been aroused. In other words, the arousal intensified both positive or negative reactions to the woman, depending on which was cognitively appropriate (White, Fishbein, & Rutstein, 1981).

This effect can also be observed physiologically. In two studies, men or women watched a sequence of two videotapes. The first portrayed either an anxiety-inducing or non-anxiety-inducing scene; the second videotape portrayed a nude heterosexual couple engaging in sexual foreplay. Measurements made by instruments connected to the participants' genitals showed that, for both men and women, preexposure to the anxiety-inducing scene produced greater sexual arousal in response to the erotic scene than did preexposure to non-anxiety-inducing scenes (Hoon, Wincze, & Hoon, 1977; Wolchik et al., 1980).

Several explanations for this effect have been offered. The *attribution* (or misattribution) explanation is that the individual mistakenly attributes his or her arousal to the target person, thereby interpreting it as romantic or sexual feelings (or possibly as revulsion in the presence of a particularly unattractive person). A second explanation is that the effect reflects *excitation transfer* in which arousal experienced from one source can carry over to intensify the arousal experienced from a different source. For example, a man will show more aggression when provoked if he has first been exposed to sexually stimulating materials, including nonviolent materials (Zillmann, 1978, 1984; Zillmann & Bryant, 1974). By extension, arousal produced by exercise might carry over to intensify sexual arousal.

A third explanation is *response facilitation,* a well-known phenomenon in psychology. When an organism is aroused, whatever response it is most likely to make in the situation—called the *dominant response*—will be facilitated or intensified. If the dominant response is attraction to the woman, this response will be intensified by the additional arousal. If the subject's dominant response in the situation is *not* to be attracted to the woman, the arousal would intensify this negative response. This is exactly what was found in the study just described (Allen, Kenrick, Linder, & McCall, 1989).

Experimental attempts to determine which explanation is the most valid have produced mixed results and the dispute is not yet settled (Allen et al., McCall, 1989; McClanahan et al., 1990; White & Kight, 1984). But whatever the specific mechanism, the phenomenon itself appears to be genuine and solidly established. Would-be lovers of both sexes should feel encouraged to buy a pair of tickets to the hockey game.

Passionate and Companionate Love   Several social scientists have attempted to distinguish among different kinds of love. One of the most widely accepted distinctions is between passionate love and companionate love (Hatfield, 1988; Peele, 1988). **Passionate love** is defined as *an intensely emotional state in which tender and sexual feelings, elation and pain, anxiety and relief, altruism and jealousy coexist in a confusion of feelings* (Berscheid & Walster, 1978, p. 177). In contrast, **companionate love** is defined as *the affection we feel for those with whom our lives are deeply intertwined* (Berscheid & Walster, 1978, p. 177; Hatfield, 1988, p. 205).

The characteristics of companionate love are trust, caring, tolerance of the partner's flaws and idiosyncrasies, and an emotional tone of warmth and affection rather than high-pitched emotional passion. As a relationship continues over time, interdependence grows and the potential for strong emotion actually increases. This can be seen when long-time partners experience intense feelings of loneliness and desire when temporarily separated from each other or in the emotional devastation typically experienced by someone who loses a long-time partner. But, paradoxically, because companionate couples become so compatible and coordinated in their daily routines, the actual frequency of strong emotions is usually fairly low (Berscheid, 1983).

Many of the young men and women in the 1967 study, cited earlier, stated that if love disappears from a marriage, that is sufficient reason to end it. Young people who equate love with its passionate variant, however, are likely to be disappointed. Most successful long-term couples emphasize the companionate elements of their relationship, and both theory and research suggest that the intense feelings that characterize passionate love are unlikely to persist over time (Berscheid, 1983; Solomon & Corbit, 1974). As the 16th-century writer Giraldi put it, "The history of a love affair is in some sense the drama of its fight against time."

This point is illustrated in a study that compared long-term marriages in the United States—where couples claim to marry for love—with marriages in Japan that had been arranged by the couples' parents. As expected, the American marriages started out with a higher level of expressed love and sexual interest than the Japanese arranged marriages. But in both groups the amount of love expressed decreased until there were no differences between the two groups after 10 years. Nevertheless, many couples in this study reported quite gratifying marriages, marriages that had evolved into a deep companionate love characterized by communication between the partners, an equitable division of labor, and equality of decision-making power (Blood, 1967).

The moral is that passionate love might be terrific for starters, but the sustaining forces of a good long-term relationship are less exciting, undoubtedly require more work, and have more to do with equality than with passion.

We have focused primarily on the factors that cause people to be attracted to each other. What do you think are the most important factors in people remaining together for a long time?

Thinking Critically

passionate love an intensely emotional state in which tender and sexual feelings, elation and pain, anxiety and relief, altruism and jealousy coexist in a confusion of feelings

companionate love the affection we feel for those with whom our lives are deeply intertwined

Summary

1. *Social psychology* is the study of how people perceive, think, and feel about their social world and how they interact and influence one another. Beginning with the premise that human behavior is a function of both the person and the situation, social psychologists emphasize the power of a situation and the importance of the person's interpretation of a situation in determining social behavior.

2. In attempting to understand others and ourselves, we construct intuitive theories of human behavior by performing the same tasks as a formal scientist: collecting data, detecting covariation, and inferring

causality. Our theories themselves, however, can shape our perceptions of the data, distort our estimates of covariation, and bias our evaluations of cause and effect. For example, we tend to notice and recall vivid information more than nonvivid information, and this biases our social judgments.

3. *Schematic processing* is the perceiving and interpreting of incoming information in terms of simplified memory structures called *schemas.* Schemas constitute minitheories of everyday objects and events. They enable us to process social information efficiently by permitting us to encode and to remember only the unique or most prominent features of a new object or event. But because schemas are simplifications of reality, schematic processing produces biases and errors in our processing of social information.

4. We are not very accurate at detecting covariations or correlations between events in everyday life. When our schemas or theories lead us to expect two things to covary, we overestimate their actual correlation; but when we do not have a theory, we underestimate their correlation.

5. *Stereotypes* can be thought of as theories or schemas of covariation. Like other schemas, they are resistant to change. In particular, they lead us overlook data that would disconfirm them. Moreover, they can be self-perpetuating and self-fulfilling because they influence those who hold them to behave in ways that actually evoke the stereotyped behavior.

6. Attribution is the process by which we attempt to interpret and explain the behavior of other people—that is, to discern the causes of their actions. One major attribution task is to decide whether someone's action should be attributed to dispositional causes (the person's personality or attitudes) or to situational causes (social forces or other external circumstances). We tend to give too much weight to dispositional factors and too little to situational factors. This bias has been called the *fundamental attribution error.*

7. *Attitudes* are likes and dislikes—favorable or unfavorable evaluations of and reactions to objects, people, events, or ideas. Attitudes have a cognitive component, an affective component, and a behavioral component.

8. A major issue in attitude research is the degree of consistency among a person's attitudes. *Cognitive dissonance* theory proposes that when a person's behaviors are inconsistent with his or her attitudes, the discomfort produced by this dissonance leads the person to change the attitudes so that they will be consistent with the behavior.

9. Despite evidence for attitude consistency in laboratory studies, those who have analyzed the public mind outside the social psychology laboratory are far less convinced that members of the general public display ideological consistency on social and political issues.

10. To most people, the concept of social influence connotes direct and deliberate attempts to change our beliefs, attitudes, or behaviors. If we respond to such influence by complying with the wishes of an influencer—without necessarily changing our private beliefs or attitudes—our reaction is called compliance. If we change our private beliefs and attitudes as well, our reaction is called internalization. Many forms of social influence are indirect or unintentional. We are also influenced by *social norms,* implicit rules and expectations about how we ought to think and behave. The success of direct and deliberate social influence often depends on our allegiance to social norms.

11. A bystander to an emergency is less likely to intervene or help if in a group than if alone. Two major factors that deter intervention are

defining the situation and diffusion of responsibility. By attempting to appear calm, bystanders may define the situation for each other as a nonemergency, thereby deterring one another from intervening. The presence of other people also diffuses responsibility so that no one person feels the necessity to act. Bystanders are more likely to intervene when these factors are minimized.

12. In a series of classic studies on conformity, Solomon Asch found that a unanimous group exerts strong pressure on an individual to conform to the group's judgments—even when those judgments are clearly wrong. Much less conformity is observed if even one person dissents from the group.

13. A minority within a larger group can move the majority toward its point of view if it maintains a consistent dissenting position without appearing to be rigid, dogmatic, or arrogant. Minorities sometimes obtain private attitude change (internalization) from majority members even when they fail to obtain public conformity (compliance).

14. In a series of classic studies of obedience, Stanley Milgram demonstrated that ordinary people would obey an experimenter's order to deliver strong electric shocks to an innocent victim. Factors conspiring to produce the high obedience rates include social norms (for example, the implied contract to continue the experiment until completed); the surveillance of the experimenter; buffers that distance the person from the consequences of his or her acts; and the legitimating role of science, which leads people to abandon their autonomy to the experimenter. There has also been controversy about the ethics of the experiments themselves. Most people's surprised reactions to the results of the obedience studies reveal that situational factors exert more influence over behavior than most of us realize. We tend to underestimate situational forces on behavior.

15. In the process of *identification,* we obey the norms and adopt the beliefs, attitudes, and behaviors of groups that we respect and admire. We use such *reference groups* to evaluate and regulate our opinions and actions. A reference group can regulate our attitudes and behavior by administering social rewards and punishments or by providing us with a frame of reference, a ready-made interpretation of events and social issues.

16. Most of us identify with more than one reference group, and this can lead to conflicting pressures on our beliefs, attitudes, and behaviors. College students frequently move away from the views of their family reference group toward those of the college reference group. These new views are usually sustained in later life because (1) they become internalized and (2) after college we tend to select new reference groups—spouses and friends—who share our views.

17. Many factors influence whether we will be attracted to a particular person. The most important of these are physical attractiveness, proximity, familiarity, and similarity. The old saying that "opposites attract" has not been upheld by research.

18. The link between love and marriage is historically recent and far from universal. In our own society the link has become closer over the past 30 years, with more women and men refusing to marry someone they do not love. Among attempts to classify types of love, the most widely accepted is the distinction between *passionate love,* which is characterized by intense and often conflicting emotions, and *companionate love,* which is characterized by trust, caring, tolerance of the partner's flaws, and an emotional tone of warmth and affection. Because passionate love decreases over time, the success of most long-term relationships is based

primarily on the sustaining forces of companionate love. Because companionate couples become so compatible in their daily routines, the actual frequency of strong emotions is fairly low, but the potential for strong emotion actually increases.

Suggested Readings

Three comprehensive textbooks in social psychology are Aronson, Wilson, and Akert, *Social Psychology* (3rd ed., 1998); Baron and Byrne, *Social Psychology* (8th ed., 1997); and Lord, *Social Psychology* (1996). More advanced treatments are available in Gilbert, Fiske, and Lindzey (eds.), *The Handbook of Social Psychology* (4th ed., 1998).

A major theme of this chapter—that people act as informal scientists in arriving at social judgments—is treated in detail in Nisbett and Ross, *Human Inference: Strategies and Shortcomings of Social Judgment* (1980). A delightful extension of this basic theme is presented by Gilovich in *How We Know What Isn't So: The Fallibility of Human Reason in Everyday Life* (1991).

A number of books deal in more depth with other topics discussed in this chapter. Recommended are Aronson, *The Social Animal* (7th ed., 1995); Brehm, *Intimate Relationships* (2nd ed., 1992); and Ross and Nisbett, *The Person and the Situation: Perspectives of Social Psychology* (1991).

Many of the topics in this chapter are covered in paperback books written for general audiences, often by the original investigators. Milgram, *Obedience to Authority* (1974), is well worth reading, especially before forming an opinion about this controversial series of studies. Latané and Darley, *The Unresponsive Bystander: Why Doesn't He Help?* (1970), is a report by two of the original researchers in that area.

Enhance and Explore

To enhance your understanding of the psychological concepts found in this chapter, please consult the following aids:

Study Guide

Learning Objectives, p. 250
Define the Terms, p. 252
Test Your Knowledge, p. 254
Essay Questions, p. 257
Thinking Independently, p. 258

PowerPsych CD-ROM

HOW DO WE SELECT OUR FRIENDS AND LOVERS?

Triangular Love Scale

PsychCentral

For more information concerning the topics found in this chapter, access psychology links on the Word Wide Web made through the Harcourt Web page at:
http://www.harcourtcollege.com/psych/Fundamentals

www.harcourtcollege.com
http://www.harcourtcollege.com/psych/index.html

Evolutionary Origins of Sex Differences in Mate Preferences

David M. Buss, *University of Texas at Austin*

Evolutionary psychology provides a powerful theoretical guide to identifying both commonalities and differences between men and women. The logic stems from understanding the *adaptive problems* the sexes have faced over the long course of human evolutionary history—problems of survival and reproduction. Both sexes have faced many similar survival problems—the need to select food, combat diseases, and fend off predators. Where men and woman have confronted similar adaptive problems, evolutionary psychologists predict the sexes will be similar. Both sexes, for example, have similar taste preferences (e.g., sugar, protein, and fat) and similar fears (e.g. snakes).

In reproduction, however, the sexes have faced fundamentally different adaptive problems, and here we expect sex differences in adaptive solutions. Women, for example, bear the burdens and joys of a nine-month minimum obligatory investment (pregnancy) to produce a single child; men's minimum investment is as low as a few hours, a few minutes, or a few seconds.

Much evidence, emerging from varied data sources—self-reports, behavioral studies, and laboratory studies—confirms several sex differences predicted in advance by evolutionary psychologists. One pertains to choosiness. When approached by an opposite-sex stranger, 50% of women agreed to a date, 6% agreed to go back to his apartment, and 0% agreed to sex. In contrast, of the men approached by women, 50% agreed to a date, 69% agreed to go back to her apartment, and 75% agreed to sex (Clarke & Hatfield, 1989). This is one among hundreds of studies that document that women are more selective and discriminating in short-term mating contexts (Buss, 1994). This psychological sex difference stems from a long evolutionary history of an asymmetry between the sexes in parental investment.

Humans, unlike most other primates, also pursue long-term mating. Because of women's heavy parental investment, they are predicted to value mates who are able and willing to invest resources in them and their children. In my study of 10,047 individuals in 37 cultures located on six continents and five islands, from coastal Australia to the Zulu tribe in South Africa, this prediction was soundly supported. Women placed a greater premium on a mate's financial resources, ambition, and industriousness. Women also desired spouses who were roughly three years older.

Sometimes an alternative explanation is proposed—women do not have an evolved desire for resourceful men, but rather are forced to prefer such men because they have been excluded from other means to economic resources (Buss & Barnes, 1986). Although reasonable, the available evidence fails to support it. Women living in more economically equal cultures, such as Sweden and Norway, show just as strong a desire for mates with resources as women in more economically unequal cultures such as Japan or Iran (Buss, 1989). Furthermore, women in the United States who are economically successful place even more emphasis on a man's resources. Although more tests are needed, the available evidence supports the hypothesis that women have an evolved desire for resourceful mates.

Another key sex difference stems from ovulation. Unlike most other primate females, who experience estrus cycles with large red genital swellings, women's ovulation evolved to be cryptic or concealed. This posed a unique adaptive problem for ancestral men—how to identify fertile women in the absence of obvious estrus cues. According to one evolutionary hypothesis, men evolved to value certain features of physical appearance because appearance provides a wealth of cues to a woman's age and health, and hence to her fertility. The 37-culture study supports this explanation. Men worldwide, from Zambia to Austria, value women who are young and physically attractive, precisely as predicted.

Although these findings and their evolutionary explanations are upsetting to some people, there are three important qualifications. First, discoveries that men and women have evolved psychological differences does not justify discrimination based on sex, nor does it excuse behavior some consider immoral, such as sexual infidelity. Second, neither men nor women can be considered superior or inferior; each sex has evolved adaptations to solve its own unique problems. Third, in most psychological domains, the sexes are similar since both sexes have faced similar adaptive problems, such as identifying who will be a good long-term cooperator. Both sexes equally value a potential mate's intelligence, kindness, dependability, creativity, and adaptability. And both sexes in all 37 cultures place a premium on love and mutual attraction, which may be evolution's way of bringing the sexes together over the long term to transcend whatever differences they display.

Problems With the Evolutionary Model of Sex Differences in Mate Preferences, Cindy Hazan, *Cornell University*

The theory proposed by David Buss is one among several perspectives on how humans go about the business of mating, and it is a highly controversial one. According to his theory, sex differences in mate preferences are the ultimate result of differences in what it costs each sex to reproduce. Because the cost to males can be as little as a few minutes and a few sperm, males are "naturally" inclined to have sex with as many fertile (i.e., young and attractive) females as possible. In stark contrast, the cost to a female—including pregnancy, lactation, and childcare—is usually years of investment, which in theory predisposes her to hold out for one male with resources that he is willing to commit to her and the offspring she will have to nurture. Thus, Buss's theory makes two predictions: (1) sex differences in the best mating strategy for achieving reproductive success and (2) sex differences in what qualities are sought in a mate.

Consider first the plausibility of the prediction that men have an evolved, innate predisposition to move quickly from one sex partner to the next as a means of maximizing their reproductive success. Back when natural selection was sculpting human mating behavior, tens of thousands of years before birth control was available, women were pregnant or lactating during an estimated 24 of the 26 or so years between puberty and menopause, and thus fertile during only a small fraction of that time. The probability that any random copulation would result in conception was only about 1%. Although a one-night stand can result in pregnancy, on average it actually takes several months of

unprotected sex. Further, women ovulate more often, more regularly, and reach menopause later if they have a stable sexual partner. Perhaps most important is the fact that more human infants survive when their fathers stick around to help with their upbringing. Therefore, the prediction that men would maximize their reproductive success by being promiscuous is less plausible than the competing prediction that they would be more successful in passing their genes down to successive generations if they stayed with one female for an extended period of time and invested in their joint offspring.

Consider next the prediction about sex differences in mate preferences. Are women "naturally" attracted to men with resources? Buss's own cross-cultural survey data show clearly that the more socioeconomic inequity that exists between the sexes in a particular culture, the more females in that culture care about the socioeconomic status of potential mates (Eagly & Wood, 1999). It stands to reason that a woman who has little chance of being able to provide adequately for herself or her children would pay attention to the financial status of her suitors. Caring more about a man's looks or personality than his income is a luxury that many women simply cannot afford. Even at the dawning of the 21st century, and even in the most modern of human societies, females still cannot expect equal pay for equal work.

In describing his study of 37 cultures, Buss emphasizes the few minor sex differences he found but, as he himself acknowledges in the final sentence of his essay, the *mate qualities ranked highest by both sexes are exactly the same:*

More than anything, men and women alike report that they want a mate who is kind, understanding, and intelligent. Moreover, one of the most well documented facts of human mating is that people typically choose mates who are similar to them in a wide variety of ways, *including* socioeconomic status and physical attractiveness.

There is also a methodological problem with the studies that appear to support Buss's claims about sex differences in mate preferences. Most of these studies have used a hypothetical scenario. Study participants, often undergraduates, are asked to make a list of the traits they *think* will be important when they eventually get around to mating. A far better approach would be to study individuals who already have mates and then use an objective means of identifying the criteria used to select them. That's exactly what one team of investigators did (Lykken & Tellegen, 1993). By comparing the spouses of identical twins with those of unrelated individuals, the researchers discovered that *chance* plays a big role in human mating. That is, rather than making a list of preferences and then searching far and wide for the best possible match, most people instead end up with a partner who happened to be available, acceptable, and interested at the time they were looking to mate. More importantly, *no support was found for Buss's theory.*

Although Buss's theory may fit well with familiar sex-role stereotypes, the logical and empirical evidence for it is seriously flawed. For an alternative evolutionary model of human mating, see Hazan and Diamond (in press).

Statistical Methods and Measurement

Psychologists study a great variety of phenomena: the activity of certain brain regions under different conditions; the progression of human development; the causes and treatments of psychopathology; how people behave in social groups. Regardless of the specific focus of these studies, the outcome of the studies is usually in the form of numbers. The researchers' problem, then, is to interpret these numbers and arrive at some general conclusions. Basic to this task is *statistics*—the discipline that deals with collecting numerical data and making inferences from these data.

In this appendix we review some basic statistics. An introductory acquaintance with statistics is not beyond the scope of anyone who understands enough algebra to use plus and minus signs and to substitute numbers for letters in equations. Understanding some basic statistics will help you understand much of what is presented in this book. You are also confronted with statistics in your daily life in newspapers, advertisements, and other media. Understanding more about these statistics will help you develop more informed decisions and opinions.

Descriptive Statistics

Statistics, first of all, provide a shorthand description of large amounts of data. Suppose that we want to study the college entrance examination scores of 5,000 students, which are recorded on cards in the registrar's office. These scores are the *raw data*. Thumbing through the cards will give us some impressions of the students' scores, but it will be impossible for us to keep all of them in mind. So we need to make some kind of summary of the data, possibly averaging all the scores or finding the highest and lowest scores. These statistical summaries make it easier to remember and to think about the data. Such summarizing statements are called *descriptive statistics*.

Frequency Distributions

Items of raw data become comprehensible when they are grouped in a *frequency distribution*. To group data, we must first divide the scale along which they are measured into intervals and then count the number of items that fall into each interval. An interval in which scores are grouped is called a *class interval*. The decision as to how many class intervals the data are to be grouped into is not fixed by any rule but is based on the judgment of the investigator.

Table 1 provides a sample of raw data representing college entrance examination scores for 15 students. The scores are listed in the order in which the students were tested (the first student tested had a score of 84; the second, 61; and so on). Table 2 shows these data arranged in a frequency distribution for which the class interval has been set at 10. One score falls in the 50–59 interval, three scores fall in the 60–69 interval, and so on. Note that most scores fall in the 70–79 interval and that no scores fall below the 50–59 interval or above the 90–99 interval.

A frequency distribution is often easier to understand if it is presented graphically. The most widely used form of graph is the *frequency histogram;* an example is shown in the top panel of Figure 1. Histograms are constructed by drawing bars whose bases are given by the class intervals and whose heights are determined by the corresponding class frequencies. An alternative way of presenting frequency distributions in graphical form is to use a *frequency polygon,* an example of which is shown in the bottom panel of Figure 1. Frequency polygons are constructed by plotting the class frequencies at the center of the class interval and connecting the points obtained with straight lines. To complete the picture, one extra class is added at each end of the distribution; since these classes have zero frequencies, both ends of the figure will touch the horizontal axis. The frequency polygon gives the same information as the frequency histogram but by means of a set of connected lines rather than bars.

In practice, we would obtain a much greater number of items than those plotted in Figure 1, but a minimum amount of data is shown in all of the illustrations in this appendix so that you can easily check the steps in tabulating and plotting.

Measures of Central Tendency

A *measure of central tendency* is simply a representative point on our scale—a central point that summarizes important information about the data. Three such measures are commonly used: the mean, the median, and the mode.

The *mean* is the familiar arithmetic average, which is obtained by adding the scores and dividing by the number of scores. The sum of the raw scores in Table 1 is 1,125. If we divide this by 15 (the number of scores), the mean turns out to be 75.

The *median* is the score of the middle item, which is obtained by arranging the scores in order and then counting into the middle from either end. When the 15 scores in Table 1 are placed in order from highest to lowest, the eighth score from either end turns out to be 75. If the number of cases is even, we simply average the two cases on each side of the middle.

Table 1

Raw Scores   College entrance examination scores for 15 students, listed in the order in which they were tested.

84	75	91
61	75	67
72	87	79
75	79	83
77	51	69

Table 2

A Frequency Distribution   Scores from Table 1, accumulated by class intervals.

Class Interval	Number of Persons in Class
50–59	1
60–69	3
70–79	7
80–89	3
90–99	1

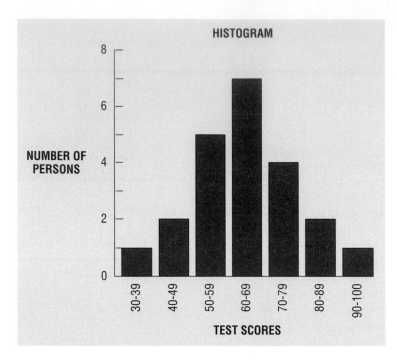

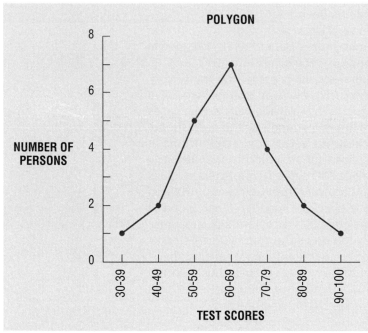

Frequency Diagrams   The data from Table 2 are plotted here. A frequency histogram is on the top, a frequency polygon on the bottom.

The *mode* is the most frequent score in a given distribution. In Table 1, the most frequent score is 75; hence, the mode of the distribution is 75.

In a *normal distribution,* in which the scores are distributed evenly on either side of the middle (as in Figure 1), the mean, median, and mode all fall together. This is not true for distributions that are *skewed,* or unbalanced. Suppose that we want to analyze the departure times of a morning train. The train usually leaves on time; occasionally it leaves late, but it never leaves early. For a train with a scheduled departure time of 8:00 A.M., one week's record might be as follows:

M	8:00	Mean = 8:07
Tu	8:04	Median = 8:02
W	8:02	Mode = 8:00
Th	8:19	
F	8:22	
Sat	8:00	
Sun	8:00	

The distribution of departure times in this example is skewed because of the two late departures; they raise the mean departure time but do not have much effect on the median or the mode.

Skewness is important because, unless it is understood, the differences between the median and the mean may sometimes be misleading (see Figure 2). If, for example, company executives and the company's union are arguing about the prosperity of the company's workforce, it is possible for the mean and median incomes to move in opposite directions. Suppose that a company raises the wages of most of its employees but cuts the wages of its top executives, who were at the extremely high end of the pay scale. The median income of the company might have gone up while the mean went down. The party wanting to show that incomes were getting higher would choose the median, while the party wanting to show that incomes were getting lower would choose the mean.

The mean is the most widely used measure of central tendency, but there are times when the mode or the median is a more meaningful measure.

Measures of Variation

Usually more information is needed about a distribution than can be obtained from a measure of central tendency. For example, we need a measure to tell us whether scores cluster closely around their average or whether they scatter widely. A measure of the spread of scores around the average is called a *measure of variation.*

Measures of variation are useful in at least two ways. First, they tell us how representative the average is. If the variation is small, we know that individual scores are close to the average. If the variation is large, we cannot use the mean as a representative value with as much assurance. Suppose that clothing is being designed for a group of people without the benefit of precise measurements. Knowing their average size would be helpful, but it also would be important to know the spread of sizes. The second measure provides a yardstick that we can use to measure the amount of variability among the sizes.

To illustrate, consider the data in Figure 3, which show frequency distributions of entrance examination scores for two classes of 30 students. Both classes have the same mean of 75, but they exhibit clearly different degrees of variation. The scores of all the students in Class I are clustered close to the mean, whereas those of the students in Class II are spread over a wide range. Some measure is required to specify more exactly how these two distributions differ. Three measures of variation often used by psychologists are the range, the variance, and the standard deviation.

To simplify arithmetic computation, we will suppose that five students from each class seek entrance to college and that their entrance examination scores are as follows:

Student scores from Class I:
73, 74, 75, 76, 77 (mean = 75)

Student scores from Class II:
60, 65, 75, 85, 90 (mean = 75)

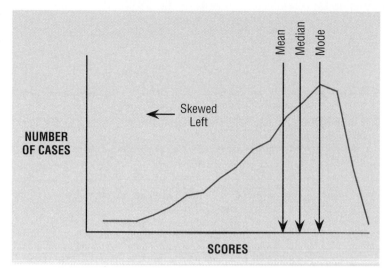

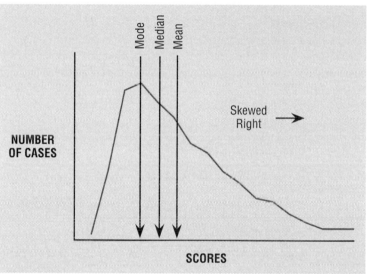

Figure 2

Skewed Distribution Curves   Note that skewed distributions are designated by the direction in which the tail falls. Also note that the mean, median, and mode aren't identical for a skewed distribution; the median commonly falls between the mode and the mean.

We will now compute the measures of variation for these two samples.

The *range* is the spread between the highest score and the lowest score. The range of scores for the students from Class I is 4 (from 73 to 77); the range of scores for the students from Class II is 30 (from 60 to 90).

The range is easy to compute, but the variance and standard deviation are more frequently used. They are more sensitive measures of variation because they account for every score, not just extreme values as the range does. The *variance* measures how far the scores making up a distribution depart from that distribution's mean. To compute the variance, first compute the deviation (*d*) of each score from the mean of the distribution by subtracting each score from the mean (see Table 3). Then, each of the deviations is squared to get rid of negative numbers. Finally, the deviations are added together and divided by the total number of deviations to obtain

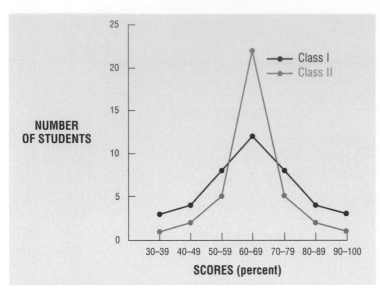

NUMBER OF STUDENTS

SCORES (percent)

Figure 3

Distributions Differing in Variation   It is easy to see that the scores for Class I cluster closer to the mean than the scores for Class II, even though the means of the two classes are identical (75). For Class I, all the scores fall between 60 and 89, with most of the scores falling in the interval from 70 through 79. For Class II, the scores are distributed fairly uniformly over a wide range from 40 through 109. This difference in variability between the two distributions can be measured using the standard deviation, which is smaller for Class I than for Class II.

Table 3

Computation of the Variance and Standard Deviation

Class I Scores (Mean = 75)		
	d	d^2
77 − 75 =	2	4
76 − 75 =	1	1
75 − 75 =	0	0
74 − 75 =	−1	1
73 − 75 =	−2	4
		10

Sum of d^2 = 10
Variance = mean of d^2 = 10/5 = 2.0
Standard Deviation (σ) = $\sqrt{2.0}$ = 1.4

Class II Scores (Mean = 75)		
	d	d^2
90 − 75 =	15	225
85 − 75 =	10	100
75 − 75 =	0	0
65 − 75 =	−10	100
60 − 75 =	−15	225
		650

Sum of d^2 = 650
Variance = mean of d^2 = 650/5 = 130
Standard Deviation (σ) = $\sqrt{130}$ = 11.4

the average deviation. This average deviation is the variance. When this is done for the data in Figure 3, we find that the variance for Class I is 2.0 and the variance for Class II is 130. Obviously, Class II exhibits much more variability in its scores than Class I.

One disadvantage of the variance is that it is expressed in squared units of measurement. Thus, to say that Class I has a variance of 2 does not indicate that, on average, scores varied by an average of 2 points from the mean. Instead, it indicates that 2 is the average of the squared number of points by which scores varied from the mean. In order to obtain a measure of variability that is expressed in the original units of measurement (in this case, points on an exam), simply take the square root of the variance. This is known as the *standard deviation*. The standard deviation is denoted by the lowercase Greek letter *sigma* (σ), which also is used in several other statistical calculations, as we will discuss shortly. The formula for the standard deviation is given as follows:

$$\sigma = \sqrt{\frac{\text{Sum of } d^2}{N}}$$

Statistical Inference

Now that we have become familiar with statistics as a way of describing data, we are ready to turn to the processes of interpretation—that is, to making inferences from data.

Populations and Samples

First, it is necessary to distinguish between a population and a sample drawn from that population. The U.S. Census Bureau attempts to describe the whole population by obtaining descriptive material on age, marital status, and so on from everyone in the country. The word *population* is appropriate to the census because it represents all the people living in the United States.

In statistics, the word *population* is not limited to people or animals or things. The population may be all the temperatures registered on a thermometer during the last decade, all the words in the English language, or all of any other specified supply of data. Often we do not have access to the total population, so we try to represent it by a *sample* selected in a random (unbiased) fashion. We may ask some questions of a random fraction of the people, as the Census Bureau has done as part of recent censuses; we may derive average temperatures by reading the thermometer at specified times, without taking a continuous record; we may estimate the number of words in the encyclopedia by counting the words on random pages. These illustrations all involve the selection of a sample from the population. If these processes are repeated, we will obtain slightly different results due to the fact that a sample does not fully represent the whole population and therefore contains errors of sampling. This is where *statistical inference* enters.

A sample of data is collected from a population in order to make inferences about that population. A sample of census data may be examined to see whether the population is getting older, for example, or whether there is a trend of migration to the suburbs. Similarly, experimental results are studied to determine what effects experimental manipulations have had on behavior—whether the threshold for pitch is affected by loudness, whether child-rearing practices have detectable effects later in life. To make statistical inferences, we have to evaluate the relationships revealed by the sample data. These inferences are always made under some degree of uncertainty due to sampling errors (discussed later in this appendix). If the statistical tests indicate that the magnitude of the effect found in the sample is fairly large (relative to the estimate of the sampling error), we can be confident that the effect observed in the sample holds for the population as a whole.

Thus, statistical inference deals with the problem of making an inference or judgment about a feature of a population based solely on information obtained from a sample of that population. As an introduction to statistical inference, we will consider the normal distribution and its use in interpreting standard deviations.

Normal Distribution

When large amounts of data are collected, tabulated, and plotted as a histogram or polygon, they often fall into a roughly bell-shaped symmetrical distribution known as the *normal distribution.* Most items fall near the mean (the high point of the bell), and the bell tapers off sharply at very high and very low scores. This form of curve is of special interest because it also arises when the outcome of a process is based on a large number of chance events all occurring independently. The demonstration device displayed in Figure 4 illustrates how a sequence of chance events gives rise to a normal distribution. The chance factor of whether a steel ball will fall to the left or right each time it encounters a point where the channel branches results in a symmetrical distribution: More balls fall straight down the middle, but occasionally one reaches one of the end compartments. This is a useful way of visualizing what is meant by a chance distribution closely approximating the normal distribution.

The normal distribution (Figure 5) is the mathematical representation of the idealized distribution approximated by the device shown in Figure 4. The normal distribution represents the likelihood that items within a normally distributed population will depart from the mean by any stated amount. The percentages shown in Figure 5 represent the percentage of the area lying under the curve between the indicated scale values; the total area under the curve represents the whole population. Roughly two thirds of the cases (68%) will fall between ±1 standard deviation from the mean; 95% of the cases will fall within ±2 standard deviations; and virtually all cases (99.7%) within ±3 standard deviations. A more detailed listing of areas under portions of the normal curve is given in Table 4.

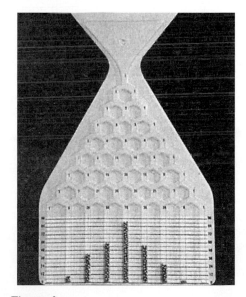

Figure 4

A Device to Demonstrate a Chance Distribution　The board is held upside down until all the steel balls fall into the reservoir. Then the board is turned over and held vertically until the balls fall into the nine columns. The precise number of balls falling into each column will vary from one demonstration to the next. On average, however, the heights of the columns of balls will approximate a normal distribution, with the greatest height in the center column and gradually decreasing heights in the outer columns.

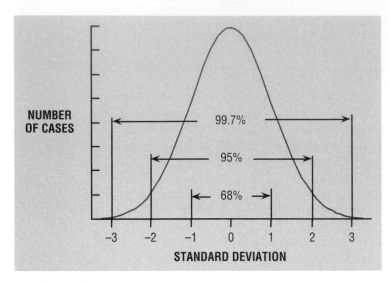

NUMBER OF CASES

99.7%

95%

68%

-3 -2 -1 0 1 2 3

STANDARD DEVIATION

Figure 5

The Normal Distribution   The normal distribution curve can be constructed using the mean and the standard deviation. The area under the curve below -3σ and above $+3\sigma$ is negligible.

Using Table 4, let us trace how the 68% and 95% values in Figure 5 are derived. We find from Column 3 of Table 4 that between -1 standard deviation and the mean lies .341 of the total area and between $+1$ standard deviation and the mean also lies .341 of the area. Adding these values gives us .682, which is expressed in Figure 5 as 68%. Similarly, the area between -2 standard deviations and $+2$ standard deviations is $2 \times .477 = .954$, which is expressed as 95%.

The standard deviation is convenient because we can interpret how far away 1σ or 2σ is from the mean (see Table 4). A score based on a multiple of the standard deviation is known as a *standard score*. Expressing a number in terms of a standard score gives some indication where that number is relative to the mean for the group from which that number came and relative to the distribution of numbers in that group. Let's explore an example.

Table 1 presented college entrance scores for 15 students. What is the standard score for a student who had a grade of 90 on the examination? On this examination, we will assume that the mean is 75 and the standard deviation is 10. Thus, a standard score for grade of 90 is 1.5, meaning it is 1½ standard deviations from the mean score:

$$\frac{90 - 75}{10} - \frac{15}{10} = 1.5$$

As a second example, consider a student with a score of 53. The standard score for a grade of 53 is computed as follows:

$$\frac{53 - 75}{10} = \frac{-22}{10} = -2.2$$

Table 4

The Area of the Normal Distribution as a Proportion of Total Area

Standard Deviation	(1) Area to the Left of This Value	(2) Area to the Right of This Value	(3) Area Between This Value and Mean
-3.0σ	.001	.999	.499
-2.5σ	.006	.994	.494
-2.0σ	.023	.977	.477
-1.5σ	.067	.933	.433
-1.0σ	.159	.841	.341
-0.5σ	.309	.691	.191
0.0σ	.500	.500	.000
$+0.5\sigma$	.691	.309	.191
$+1.0\sigma$	.841	.159	.341
$+1.5\sigma$	.933	.067	.433
$+2.0\sigma$	.977	.023	.477
$+2.5\sigma$	.994	.006	.494
$+3.0\sigma$	.999	.001	.499

In this answer, the negative sign tells us that the student's score is below the mean by 2.2 standard deviations. Thus, the sign of the standard score (+ or −) indicates whether the score is above or below the mean, and its value indicates how far from the mean the score lies in standard deviations.

How Representative Is a Mean?

How useful is the mean of a sample in estimating the mean of the population? If we measure the height of a random sample of 100 college students, how well does the sample mean predict the true population mean (that is, the mean height of all college students)? These questions raise the issue of making an inference about a population based on information from a sample.

The accuracy of such inferences depends on errors of sampling. Suppose that we were to select two random samples from the same population and compute the mean for each sample. What differences between the first and the second mean could be expected to occur by chance?

Successive random samples drawn from the same population will have different means, forming a distribution of sample means around the true mean of the population. These sample means are themselves numbers for which the standard deviation can be computed. We call this standard deviation the *standard error of the mean,* or σ_M, and we can estimate it on the basis of the following formula:

$$\sigma_M = \frac{\sigma}{\sqrt{N}}$$

where σ is the standard deviation of the sample and N is the number of cases from which each sample mean is computed.

According to the formula, the size of the standard error of the mean decreases as the size of the sample increases; thus, a mean based on a large sample is more trustworthy (more likely to be close to the actual population mean) than a mean based on a smaller sample. Common sense would lead us to expect this. Computations of the standard error of the mean permit us to make clear assertions about the degree of uncertainty in our computed mean. The more cases there are in the sample, the more uncertainty has been reduced.

Significance of a Difference

In many psychological experiments, data are collected on two groups of subjects; one group is exposed to certain specified experimental conditions, and the other serves as a control group. The question is whether there is a difference in the mean performance of the two groups, and if such a difference is observed, whether it holds for the population from which these groups of subjects have been drawn. Basically, we are asking whether a difference between two sample means reflects a true difference or whether this difference is simply the result of sampling error.

As an example, assume we are comparing the scores on a reading test for a sample of first-grade boys with the scores for a sample of first-grade girls. The boys in our hypothetical sample score lower than the girls as far as mean performances are concerned, but there is a great deal of overlap; some boys do extremely well, and some girls do very poorly. Thus, we cannot accept the obtained difference in means without making a test of its statistical significance. Only then can we decide whether the observed differences in sample means reflect true differences in the population or are due to sampling error. If some of the brighter girls and some of the duller boys are selected by sheer chance, the difference could be due to sampling error.

As another example, suppose that we have set up an experiment to compare the grip strength of right-handed and left-handed men. The top panel of Table 5 presents hypothetical data from such an experiment. A sample of five right-handed men

The Significance of a Difference   Two examples that compare the difference between means are shown. The difference between means is the same (8 kilograms) in both the top and bottom panel. However, the data in the bottom panel indicate a more reliable difference between means than do the data in the top panel.

Strength of Grip In Kilograms, Right-Handed Men	Strength of Grip in Kilograms, Left-Handed Men
40	40
45	45
50	50
55	55
100	60
Sum 290	Sum 250
Mean 58	Mean 50

Strength of Grip In Kilograms, Right-Handed Men	Strength of Grip in Kilograms, Left-Handed Men
56	48
57	49
58	50
59	51
60	52
Sum 290	Sum 250
Mean 58	Mean 50

averaged 8 kilograms stronger than a sample of five left-handed men. In general, what can we infer from these data about left-handed and right-handed men? Can we argue that right-handed men are stronger than left-handed men? Obviously not, because the averages derived from most of the right-handed men would not differ from those derived from the left-handed men; the one markedly deviant score of 100 tells us that we are dealing with an uncertain situation.

Now suppose that the results of the experiment were those shown in the bottom panel of Table 5. Again, we find the same mean difference of 8 kilograms, but we are now inclined to have greater confidence in the results, because the left-handed men scored consistently lower than the right-handed men. Statistics provides a precise way of taking into account the reliability of the mean differences so that we do not have to depend solely on intuition to determine that one difference is more reliable than another.

These examples suggest that the significance of a difference will depend on both the size of the obtained difference and the variability of the means being compared. From the standard error of the means, we can compute the *standard error of the difference between two means,* or σD_M. We can then evaluate the obtained difference by using a *critical ratio*—the ratio of the obtained difference between the means D_M to the standard error of the difference between the means:

$$\text{Critical ratio} = \frac{D_M}{\sigma D_M}$$

This ratio helps us to evaluate the significance of the difference between the two means. As a rule of thumb, a critical ratio should be 2.0 or larger for the difference between means to be accepted as significant. Throughout this book, statements that the difference between means is "statistically significant" indicate that the critical ratio is at least that large.

Why is a critical ratio of 2.0 selected as statistically significant? Simply because a value this large or larger can occur by chance only 5 out of 100 times. Where do we get the 5 out of 100? We can treat the critical ratio as a standard score because it is merely the difference between two means, expressed as a multiple of its standard error. Referring to Column 2 in Table 4, we note that the likelihood is .023 that a standard deviation as high as or higher than +2.0 will occur by chance. Because the chance of deviating in the opposite direction is also .023, the total probability is .046. This means that 46 times out of 1,000, or about 5 times out of 100, a critical ratio as large as 2.0 would be found by chance if the population means were identical.

The rule of thumb that says a critical ratio should be at least 2.0 is just that—an arbitrary but convenient rule that defines the "5% level of significance." Following this rule, we will make fewer than 5 errors in 100 decisions by concluding on the basis of sample data that a difference in means exists when in fact there is none. The 5% level need not always be used; a higher level of significance may be appropriate in certain experiments, depending on how willing we are to make an occasional error in inference.

The Coefficient of Correlation

We often want to know how two things are related: Do people who exercise have better emotional or physical health? Do people with certain forms of brain damage show specific cognitive problems? Do people who are prejudiced tend to have parents who are prejudiced? One way to address such questions is through *correlational studies,* which examine how two or more things vary with one another. A *correlation* is a statistic that indicates the degree of covariation between two things.

Let us say that we want to know the correlation between scores on a certain standardized test and college grades. We could obtain test scores and college grades for a group of students. The most frequently used method of determining the coefficient of correlation is the *product-moment method,* which yields the index conventionally designated by the lowercase letter r. The product-moment coefficient r varies between perfect positive correlation ($r = +1.00$) and perfect negative correlation ($r = -1.00$). Lack of any relationship yields $r = .00$.

The formula for computing the product-moment correlation is:

$$r = \frac{\text{Sum } (dx)(dy)}{N\sigma_x\sigma_y}$$

Here, one of the paired measures has been labeled the x-score; the other, the y-score. The dx and dy refer to the deviations of each score from its mean; N is the number of paired measures; and σ_x and σ_y are the standard deviations of the x-scores and the y-scores.

Computation of the coefficient of correlation requires that we determine the sum of the $(dx)(dy)$ products. This sum, in addition to the computed standard deviations for the x-scores and y-scores, can then be entered into the formula.

Suppose that we have collected the data shown in Table 6. For each participant, we have obtained two scores—the first being a score on a college entrance test (to be labeled arbitrarily the x-score) and the second being freshman grades (the y-score). Figure 6 is a *scatter diagram* of these data. Each point represents the x-score and y-score for a given participant; for example, the uppermost right-hand point is for Adam's score. Looking at these data, we can easily detect that there is some positive correlation between the x-scores and the y-scores. Adam attained the highest score on the entrance test and also earned the highest freshman grades; Edward received the lowest scores on both. The other students' test scores and grades are a little irregular, so we know that the correlation is not perfect; hence, r is less than 1.00.

We will compute the correlation to illustrate the method, although in practice no researcher would consent to determining a correlation for so few cases. The details are given in Table 6. Following the procedure outlined in Table 3, we compute the standard deviation of the x-scores and then the standard deviation of the y-scores.

Table 6

Computation of a Product-Moment Correlation

Student	Entrance Test (x-score)	Freshman Grades (y-score)	(dx)	(dy)	(dx)(dy)
Adam	71	39	6	9	+54
Bill	67	27	2	−3	−6
Charles	65	33	0	3	0
David	63	30	−2	0	0
Edward	59	2	−6	−9	+54
Sum	325	150	0	0	+102
Mean	65	30			

$$\sigma_x = 4$$
$$\sigma_y = 6$$

$$r = \frac{\text{Sum } (dx)(dy)}{N\sigma_x\sigma_y} = \frac{+102}{5 \times 4 \times 6} = +.85$$

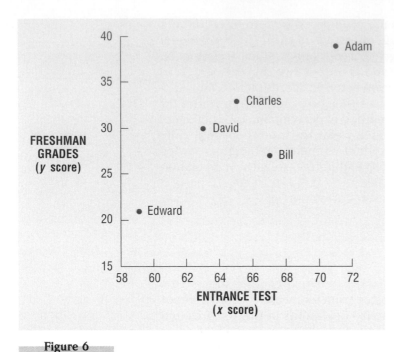

Figure 6

A Scatter Diagram Each point represents the *x*- and *y*-scores for a particular student.

Next, we compute the (*dx*)(*dy*) products for each subject and total the five cases. Entering these results in our equation yields an *r* of 1.85.

Interpreting a Correlation Coefficient

We can use correlations in making predictions. For example, if we know from experience that a certain entrance test correlates with freshman grades, we can predict the freshman grades for beginning college students who have taken the test. If the correlation were perfect, we could predict their grades without error. But *r* is usually less than 1.00, and some errors in prediction will be made; the closer *r* is to 0, the greater the sizes of the errors in prediction.

Although we cannot go into the technical problems of predicting freshman grades from test scores or making other similar predictions, we can consider the meanings of correlation coefficients of different sizes. It is evident that with a correlation of 0 between *x* and *y*, knowledge of *x* will not help to predict *y*. If weight is unrelated to intelligence, it does us no good to know a person's weight when we are trying to predict his or her intelligence. At the other extreme, a perfect correlation would mean 100% predictive efficiency—knowing *x*, we can predict *y* perfectly. What about intermediate values of *r?* Some appreciation of the meaning of correlations of intermediate sizes can be gained by examining the scatter diagrams in Figure 7.

In the preceding discussion, we did not emphasize the sign of the correlation coefficient, since this has no bearing on the strength of a relationship. The only distinction between a correlation of *r* = +.70 and *r* = −.70 is that increases in *x* are accompanied by increases in *y* for the former, while increases in *x* are accompanied by decreases in *y* for the latter.

Although the correlation coefficient is one of the most widely used statistics in psychology, it is also one of the most widely misused procedures. Those who use it sometimes overlook the fact that *r* does not imply a cause-and-effect relationship between *x* and *y*. When two sets of scores are correlated, we may suspect that they have some causal factors in common, but we cannot conclude that one of them causes the other.

Correlations sometimes appear paradoxical. For example, the correlation between study time and college grades has been found to be slightly negative (about −.10). If a causal interpretation were assumed, we might conclude that the best way to raise grades would be to stop studying. The negative correlation arises because some students have advantages over others in grade-making (possibly due to better college preparation), so that often those who study the hardest are those who have difficulty earning the best grades.

This example provides sufficient warning against assigning a causal interpretation to a coefficient of correlation. It is possible, however, that when two variables are correlated, one may in fact be the cause of the other. The search for causes is a logical one, and correlations can help us by providing leads to experiments that can verify cause-and-effect relationships.

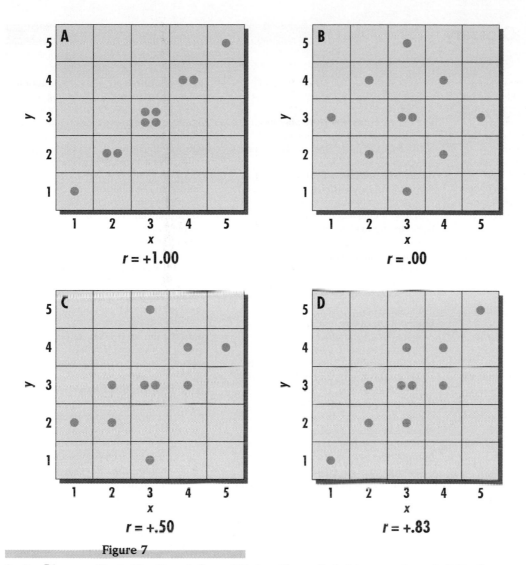

Figure 7

Scatter Diagrams Illustrating Correlations of Various Sizes   Each dot represents one individual's score on two tests, *x* and *y*. In A, all cases fall on the diagonal and the correlation is perfect (*r* = +1.00); if we know a subject's score on *x*, we know that it will be the same on *y*. In B, the correlation is 0; knowing a subject's score on *x*, we cannot predict whether it will be at, above, or below the mean on *y*. In both C and D, there is a diagonal trend to the scores, so that a high score on *x* is associated with a high score on *y* and a low score on *x* with a low score on *y*, but the relationship is imperfect.

absolute threshold the minimum magnitude of a stimulus that can be reliably discriminated from no stimulus at all

action potential an electrochemical impulse that travels from the dendritic area down to the end of the axon

adolescence the period of transition from childhood to adulthood

agoraphobia a disorder characterized by fear of any place where the person might be trapped or unable to receive help in an emergency

amnesia partial loss of memory

anorexia nervosa a disorder characterized by extreme, self-imposed weight loss—at least 15% of minimal normal weight

antianxiety drugs drugs that reduce tension and cause drowsiness by depressing the action of the central nervous system

antidepressant drugs drugs that help relieve the symptoms of depression by regulating the neurotransmitters serotonin and norepinephrine

antipsychotic drugs drugs used to treat symptoms of psychosis

antisocial personality disorder a disorder diagnosed in people who have little sense of responsibility, morality, or concern for others

anxiety the unpleasant emotion characterized by such terms as "worry," "apprehension," "tension," and "fear"

anxiety disorders a group of disorders in which anxiety either is the main symptom or is experienced when a person attempts to control certain maladaptive behaviors

aphasia the language deficits of patients with brain damage

attachment an infant's tendency to seek closeness to particular people and to feel more secure in their presence

attention deficit hyperactivity disorder (ADHD) a disorder in which a person has fundamental problems in the ability to maintain attention and control impulsive behaviors

attitudes favorable or unfavorable evaluations of and reactions to objects, people, situations, or any other aspects of the world

attributional style a consistent style of making attributions for the events in one's life

automaticity habituation of responses that initially required conscious attention

autonomic system the portion of the peripheral nervous system that connects with the internal organs and glands

behavioral rehearsal (role-playing) a behavioral technique for helping clients learn more effective behaviors, especially social behaviors

behavior genetics a field of study that combines the methods of genetics and psychology to study the inheritance of behavior characteristics

behavior therapies therapies that focus on changing people's maladaptive behaviors in specific situations

binocular disparity the difference between the retinal images on the two eyes when we look at an object from a distance

binocular parallax the fact that any visible point will differ slightly in its direction to the two eyes

bipolar disorders disorders in which the person alternates between periods of depression and periods of mania

borderline personality disorder a disorder in which the person's moods, self-concept, and interpersonal relationships are highly unstable

bulimia nervosa a disorder characterized by recurrent episodes of binge eating, often followed by attempts to purge the excess eating by means of vomiting and laxatives

case history a biography obtained for scientific use

categorization assigning an object to a concept

causal attribution a type of appraisal that helps determine our sense of control

central nervous system all the neurons in the brain and spinal cord

cerebrum the brain's two cerebral hemispheres

chromosomes structures found in the nucleus of each cell in the body

civil commitment committing people to mental health facilities against their will

classical conditioning a learning process in which a previously neutral stimulus becomes associated with another stimulus through repeated pairings

client-centered therapy a form of therapy based on the assumption that the individual is the best expert on himself or herself and that people are capable of working out solutions to their own problems

cognitive appraisal the interpretation of an event or action according to one's own personal goals and well-being

cognitive dissonance discomfort produced by inconsistency

cognitive therapy a form of therapy that attempts to help people control disturbing emotional reactions, such as anxiety and depression, by teaching them more effective ways of interpreting and thinking about their experiences

color constancy the tendency for the perceived color of an object to remain roughly the same with different light sources

companionate love the affection we feel for those with whom our lives are deeply intertwined

compulsion an irresistible urge to carry out a certain act or ritual

concept the set of properties that we associate with a class

concrete operational stage a period when, although the child is using abstract terms, he or she is doing so only in relation to concrete objects

conditioned response (CR) the learned or acquired response to a stimulus that did not evoke the response originally (i.e., a conditioned stimulus)

conditioned stimulus (CS) a previously neutral stimulus that comes to elicit a conditioned response through association with an unconditioned stimulus

consciousness monitoring ourselves and our environment so that perceptions, memories, and thoughts are represented in awareness, and controlling ourselves and our environment so that we are able to initiate and terminate behavioral and cognitive activities

conservation the understanding that the amount of a substance remains the same even when its form is changed

constructive memory a condition in which top-down processes add information to the input in creating a memory

control group a group in which the condition under study is absent

coping the process by which a person attempts to manage stressful demands

core the properties that are most important for defining a concept

coronary heart disease (CHD) a condition occurring when blood vessels that supply heart muscles are narrowed or closed by the buildup of plaque, blocking the flow of oxygen and nutrients to the heart

correlation coefficient an estimate of the degree to which two variables are related

critical or sensitive periods stages in development during which the organism is optimally ready to acquire certain abilities

delusion a belief with little or no grounding in reality

dependent variable the variable hypothesized to depend on the value of the independent variable

depressants drugs that depress the central nervous system

depression a condition characterized by sadness, hopelessness, fatigue, and low self-esteem

depressive disorders disorders in which the person has one or more periods of depression without a history of mania

difference threshold (just noticeable difference) the minimum difference in stimulus magnitude or quality necessary to tell two stimuli apart

discrimination a reaction to differences between stimuli

dissociation a condition in which some thoughts and actions become split off, or dissociated, from the rest of consciousness and function outside of awareness

distance cues two-dimensional aspects that a perceiver uses to infer distance in a three-dimensional world

dream analysis talking about the content of one's dreams and then free-associating to that content

dreaming an altered state of consciousness in which remembered images and fantasies are temporarily confused with external reality

drug abuse continued use of a drug by a person who is not dependent on it, yet continues to use it despite serious consequences

drug dependence a condition in which an individual develops tolerance for a drug, suffers withdrawal upon discontinuing use of the drug, and engages in compulsive use of the drug

ego in Freud's theory, the executive of the personality

emotion a complex condition that arises in response to certain affectively toned experiences

encoding transforming a physical input into the kind of code or representation that memory accepts, and placing that representation in memory

escape (avoidance) use of an aversive event to cause the organism to learn a new response

ethologists biologists and psychologists who study animal behavior in the natural environment

experimental group a group in which the condition under study is present

explicit memory memory that is manifested in conscious recollection of the past

factor analysis a statistical technique that examines the intercorrelations among a number of tests and, by grouping those that are most highly correlated, reduces them to a smaller number of independent dimensions, called factors

family therapy a form of therapy in which the therapist observes the interactions among family members and tries to help each member become aware of the way he or she relates to the others and how his or her actions may be contributing to the family's problems

fetal alcohol syndrome a condition characterized by mental retardation and multiple deformities of the face and mouth

fight-or-flight response the body's characteristic response to stress, designed to help the body flee from or fight a threat

flashbulb memory a vivid and relatively permanent record of the circumstances in which one learned of an emotionally charged, significant event

forebrain the structures located in the front, or anterior, part of the brain

formal operational stage a period in which a person has the ability to reason in purely symbolic terms

free association a technique in which the client is encouraged to give free rein to thoughts and feelings and to say whatever comes to mind without editing or censoring

frequency in sound, the number of cycles per second in a pure tone

functionalism the study of how the mind works so that an organism can adapt to and function in its environment

fundamental attribution error the bias toward dispositional attributions rather than situational attributions

gene a segment of a deoxyribonucleic acid (DNA) molecule

general adaptation syndrome a physiological response to stress that consists of three phases: alarm, resistance, and exhaustion

generalization the principle that the more similar new stimuli are to the original CS, the more likely they are to evoke the conditioned response

generalized anxiety disorder a disorder in which a person has a chronic sense of tension and dread

genotype inherited characteristics

group therapy a form of therapy that permits clients to work out their problems in the presence of others, observe how other people react to their behavior, and try out new methods of responding when old ones prove unsatisfactory

habituation the process through which an organism learns to weaken its reaction to a weak stimulus that has no serious consequences

hallucination a perceptual experience that is unreal

hallucinogens drugs whose main effect is to change perceptual experience

hardiness a cluster of characteristics consisting of active involvement in work and social life, orientation toward challenge and change, and a feeling of being in control of events in one's life

heritability the percentage of the variance of any trait that is accounted for by genetic differences among the individuals in a population

heuristic a short-cut procedure that is relatively easy to apply and can often yield the correct answer but does not inevitably do so

hierarchical an organizational system that progresses from lower-level to higher-level attributes

hindbrain all the structures located in the hind, or posterior, part of the brain, closest to the spinal cord

homeostasis a constant internal state

hue the quality of light described by a color name

humanistic therapies therapies that seek to help people get in touch with their real selves and to make deliberate choices regarding their lives and behavior, rather than letting external events determine their behavior

hypnosis a condition in which a willing and cooperative participant relinquishes some control over his or her behavior to the hypnotist and accepts some reality distortion

hypothesis a statement that can be tested

iconic memory visual, sensory memory

id in Freud's theory, the most primitive part of the personality

identification the process in which we obey the norms and adopt the beliefs, attitudes, and behaviors of others in order to be like them

identity crisis active process of self-definition

illusion   a perception that is false or distorted

immunocompetence   the quality of an individual's immune system functioning

implicit memory   memory that is manifested in the performance of a skill

independent variable   a variable independent of what the participant does

informed consent   the principle that participants must enter a study voluntarily and be permitted to withdraw from it at any time without penalty if they so desire

insanity defense   legal defense based on the principle that society should not punish a person who is mentally incapable of controlling his or her conduct

intelligence quotient (IQ)   the ratio of mental age to chronological age; now defined in terms of standard scores rather than an actual mathematical ratio

intensity   in sound, the pressure difference between the peak and the trough in a pressure-versus-time graph

interference   a condition in which the ability to retrieve an item is reduced because other items are associated with the same cue

interpersonal therapy   a recent form of psychodynamic therapy

interval schedules   schedules of reinforcement in which reinforcement is available only after a certain time interval has elapsed

introspection   an individual's observation and recording of the nature of his or her own perceptions, thoughts, and feelings

language comprehension   the process of hearing sounds, attaching meanings to them in the form of words, combining the words to create a sentence, and extracting a thought from the sentence

language production   the process of translating a symbolic thought into a sentence and expressing the sentence with sounds

learned helplessness   a condition characterized by apathy, withdrawal, and inability to see opportunities to regain control

learning   a relatively permanent change in behavior that results from practice

lightness   how white a light appears

lightness constancy   the tendency for the perceived lightness of an object to remain roughly the same even when the amount of reflected light changes dramatically

limbic system   a set of structures that are closely interconnected with the hypothalamus and appear to impose

additional controls over some of the instinctive behaviors regulated by the hypothalamus and brain stem

location constancy   the tendency for the perceived positions of fixed objects to remain roughly the same when the retinal image changes

long-term memory   a system that retains information for intervals ranging from a few minutes to a lifetime

mania   a condition characterized by unlimited energy, agitation, and expansive self-esteem

marital therapy   a form of therapy that focuses on helping the partners communicate their feelings, develop greater understanding and sensitivity to each other's needs, and work on more effective ways of handling their conflicts

maturation   innately determined sequences of growth and change that are relatively independent of environmental events

mean   technical term for an arithmetic average

measurement   a system for assigning numbers to variables

meditation   achieving an altered state of consciousness by performing certain rituals and exercises

memory span   the number of items a person can retain in working memory

mental practice   the imagined rehearsal of a perceptual–motor skill in the absence of any gross body movements

meta-analysis   a statistical technique that treats the accumulated studies of a particular phenomenon as a single grand experiment and each study as a single observation

midbrain   the middle of the brain

minimal risk   the principle that the risks anticipated in the research should be no greater than those ordinarily encountered in daily life

mnemonic systems   a system for aiding memory

moral realism   a confusion between moral and physical laws

motivation   a condition that energizes behavior and gives it direction

multivariate experiment   a study involving the simultaneous manipulation of several variables

nerve   a bundle of elongated axons belonging to hundreds or thousands of neurons

neuron   a specialized cell that transmits neural impulses or messages to other neurons, glands, and muscles

neurotransmitter   a chemical that diffuses across the synaptic gap and stimulates the next neuron

non-REM sleep   stages of sleep other than REM sleep

obesity   a condition defined as being 30% or more in excess of the recommended weight for one's height and frame

object permanence   the awareness that an object continues to exist even when it is not present to the senses

object recognition   determining what objects are

obsession   a persistent intrusion of an unwelcome thought, image, or impulse that causes great anxiety

obsessive-compulsive disorder   a disorder in which the person experiences obsessions and compulsions

operant conditioning   a learning process in which responses are learned because they operate on, or affect, the environment

operation   a mental routine for separating, combining, and otherwise transforming information mentally in a logical manner

opiates   drugs that diminish physical sensation and the capacity to respond to stimuli by depressing the central nervous system

panic attack   an episode of acute and overwhelming apprehension or terror

panic disorder   a disorder in which panic attacks are a common occurrence and the person begins to worry about having attacks

passionate love   an intensely emotional state in which tender and sexual feelings, elation and pain, anxiety and relief, altruism and jealousy coexist in a confusion of feelings

perception   the integration and meaningful interpretation of sensations

perceptual constancy   the tendency toward constancy in perceiving the appearance of objects

peripheral nervous system   the nerves connecting the brain and spinal cord to the other parts of the body

personality   the distinctive and characteristic patterns of thought, emotion, and behavior that define an individual's personal style of interacting with the physical and social environment

personality disorders   disorders in which personality traits become so inflexible and maladaptive that they significantly impair the individual's ability to function

phenomenology   the individual's subjective experience of the world

pheromones   chemicals that float through the air to be sniffed by other members of the species

phobia   a disorder characterized by such intense fear upon confronting a certain object or situation—to the point of having a panic attack—that the person will take extreme steps to avoid it

phoneme   a discrete speech sound

physiology   the study of the functions of the living organism and its parts

pitch   the prime quality of sound, ordered on a scale from low to high

posttraumatic stress disorder (PTSD)   a condition in which people (1) feel numb to the world, with a lack of interest in former activities and a sense of estrangement from others; (2) repeatedly relive the trauma in memories and dreams; and (3) have sleep disturbances, difficulty concentrating, and over-alertness

preconscious memories   memories that are accessible to consciousness

preoperational stage   a period when the child does not yet comprehend certain rules or operations

priming   a condition in which prior exposure to a stimulus facilitates or primes later processing of that stimulus

projective test   a test that presents an ambiguous stimulus to which the person may respond as he or she wishes

prototype   the best example of a concept

psi   anomalous processes of information and/or energy transfer that cannot currently be explained in terms of known biological or physical mechanisms

psychoactive drugs   drugs that affect behavior, consciousness, and/or mood

psychodynamic therapies   therapies based on the assumption that a person's problems cannot be successfully resolved without a thorough understanding of their unconscious basis in early relationships with parents and siblings

psychology   the scientific study of behavior and mental processes

psychophysiological disorders   physical disorders in which psychological factors are believed to play a critical role

psychosis   lack of reality testing

psychotherapy   the treatment of mental disorders by psychological means

punishment   use of an aversive event to weaken an existing response

ratio schedules   schedules of reinforcement in which reinforcement is available only after a certain number of responses have been made

reductionism   reducing psychological notions to biological ones

reference groups   groups with whom we identify

rehearsal   saying an item over and over to oneself

reliability   the extent to which a test or method of assessment gives reproducible and consistent results

REM sleep   a stage of sleep in which the sleeper's eyes move rapidly beneath the closed eyelids

repressive coping   a maladaptive coping strategy by which a person denies that he or she has any negative emotions and pushes those emotions out of conscious awareness

resistance   a condition that results from the individual's unconscious control over sensitive areas

retrieval   recovering an item from memory

retrieval cue   anything that can help retrieve a memory

right to privacy   the principle that information about a participant that might be acquired during a study must be treated as confidential and not made available to others without his or her consent

rumination   the tendency to passively and repetitively focus on one's distress without taking any action to relieve that distress

saturation   the colorfulness or purity of light

schema   a mental representation of a class of people, objects, events, or situations

schematic processing   the process of searching in memory for the schema that is most consistent with the incoming data

schizophrenia   a disorder in which the person loses touch with reality and often cannot function in daily life

selective attention   the process by which we select stimuli for further processing

selective reinforcement   a behaviorist technique that can help clients change maladaptive behaviors by setting up reinforcements for positive behaviors and removing reinforcements for negative behaviors

self-actualization   in Maslow's theory, the highest motive, which can be fulfilled only after all other needs are fulfilled

self-schema   a set of organized self-concepts stored in memory

sensations   experiences associated with simple stimuli

sensitization   the process whereby an organism learns to strengthen its reaction to a weak stimulus if a threatening or painful stimulus follows

sensorimotor stage   a period in which the infant is busy discovering the relationships between his or her actions and the consequences of those actions

set point   the level at which the body strives to maintain weight

sexual orientation   the degree to which an individual is sexually attracted to persons of the opposite sex and/or to persons of the same sex

shape constancy   the tendency for the perceived shape of an object to remain roughly the same when the retinal image changes

shaping   conditioning that is accomplished by reinforcing only variations in response that deviate in the direction desired by the experimenter

size constancy   the tendency for an object's perceived size to remain relatively constant no matter what its distance

social norms   implicit rules and expectations that dictate what we ought to think and feel and how we ought to behave

social phobia   a disorder characterized by a deep and abiding fear of embarrassing oneself or being judged by other people

social psychology   the study of how people think and feel about their social world and how they interact and influence one another

somatic system   the portion of the peripheral nervous system that carries messages to and from the sense receptors, muscles, and the surface of the body

spatial localization   determining where objects are

specific phobia   a disorder characterized by fear of a specific object or situation

state-dependent learning   a condition in which memory is partly dependent on the internal state prevailing during learning

statistics   mathematical methods for sampling data from a population of individuals and then drawing inferences about the population from those data

stereotypes   general person-schemas

stimulant drugs   drugs used to treat the attentional problems of people with attention deficit hyperactivity disorder

stimulants   drugs that increase alertness and general arousal

storage   retaining an item in memory

stress   a condition that occurs when people are faced with events that they perceive as endangering their physical or psychological well-being

structuralism   the analysis of mental structure

superego   in Freud's theory, the internalized representation of the values and morals of society (the conscience)

syntax   an analysis of the relations between words in phrases and sentences

systematic desensitization   a strategy for changing anxious responses to stimuli and the maladaptive behaviors that accompany this anxiety by substituting a response that is incompatible with anxiety—namely, relaxation

tardive dyskinesia   a neurological disorder that involves involuntary movements of the tongue, face, mouth, or jaw

temperament   mood-related personality characteristics

theory   an interrelated set of propositions about a particular phenomenon

thirst   the psychological manifestation of the need for water

transduction   the translation of physical energy into electrical signals in the brain

transference   a condition in which the client expresses attitudes toward the therapist that the client actually feels toward other people who are, or were, important in his or her life

traumatic events   situations of extreme danger that are outside the range of usual human experience

Type A   a behavior pattern in which the person is extremely competitive and achievement oriented, has a sense of time urgency, finds it difficult to relax, and becomes impatient and angry when confronted with delays or incompetence

unconditioned response (UCR)   the response originally given to the unconditioned stimulus, used as the basis for establishing a conditioned response to a previously neutral stimulus

unconditioned stimulus (UCS)   a stimulus that automatically elicits a response, typically via a reflex, without prior conditioning

unconscious   the thoughts, attitudes, impulses, wishes, motivations, and emotions of which we are unaware

validity   the extent to which a test measures what it is supposed to measure

variable   something that can occur with different values

variance   the degree to which a set of scores differ from one another

word   the name of a concept

working memory   a system that keeps a limited amount of information in an active state for a brief period and performs mental operations on it

References

ABBOTT, B. B., SCHOEN, L. S., & BADIA, P. (1984). Predictable and unpredictable shock: Behavioral measures of aversion and physiological measures of stress. *Psychological Bulletin, 96,* 45–71.

ABELSON, R. P. (1968). Computers, polls, and public opinion—Some puzzles and paradoxes. *Transaction, 5,* 20–27.

ABRAMSON, L. Y., METALSKY, G. I, & ALLOY, L. B. (1989). Hopelessness depression: A theory-based subtype of depression. *Psychological Review, 96,* 358–372.

ABRAMSON, L. Y., SELIGMAN, M. E. P., & TEASDALE, J. (1978). Learned helplessness in humans: Critique and reformulation. *Journal of Abnormal Psychology, 87,* 49–74.

ADAMS, J. L. (1974). *Conceptual blockbusting.* Stanford, CA: Stanford Alumni Association.

ADAMS, M., & COLLINS, A. (1979). A schema-theoretic view of reading. In R. O. Freedle (Ed.), *New Directions Discourse Processing,* Vol. 12. Norwood, NJ: Ablex.

ADKINS-REGAN, E. (1988). Sex hormones and sexual orientation in animals. *Psychobiology, 16,* 335–347.

ADORNO, T. W., FRENKEL-BRUNSWIK, E., LEVINSON, D. J., & SANFORD, R. N. (1950). *The authoritarian personality.* New York: Harper.

AGRAS, W. S. (1993). Short term psychological treatments for binge eating. In C. G. Fairburn & G. T. Wilson (Eds.), *Binge eating: Nature, assessment, and treatment.* New York: Guilford.

AINSWORTH, M. D. S., BLEHAR, M. C., WALTERS, E., & WALL, S. (1978). *Patterns of attachment: A psychological study of the strange situation.* Hillsdale, NJ: Erlbaum.

AKERS, C. (1984). Methodological criticisms of parapsychology. In S. Krippner (Ed.), *Advances in parapsychological research* (Vol. 4). Jefferson, NC: McFarland.

AKHTAR, S., WIG, N. N., VARMA, V. K., PERSHARD, D., & VERMA, S. K. (1975). A phenomenological analysis of symptoms in the obsessive-compulsive neurosis. *British Journal of Psychiatry, 127,* 342–348.

ALBERTS, B., BRAY, D., LEWIS, J., RAFF, M., ROBERTS, K., & WATSON, J. D. (1994). *Molecular biology of the cell* (3rd ed.). New York: Garland.

ALDAG, R. J., & FULLER, S. R. (1993). Beyond fiasco: A reappraisal of the groupthink phenomenon and a new model of group decision processes. *Psychological Bulletin, 113,* 533–552.

ALLEN, J. B., KENRICK, D. T., LINDER, D. E., & MCCALL, A. M. (1989). Arousal and attraction: A response-facilitation alternative to misattribution and negative-reinforcement models. *Journal of Personality and Social Psychology, 57,* 261–270.

ALLEN, V. L., & LEVINE, J. M. (1969). Consensus and conformity. *Journal of Experimental Social Psychology, 5,* 389–399.

ALLEN, V. L., & LEVINE, J. M. (1971). Social support and conformity: The role of independent assessment of reality. *Journal of Experimental Social Psychology, 7,* 48–58.

ALLOY, L., & ABRAMSON, L. Y. (1997, May). *The cognitive vulnerability to depression project.* Paper presented to the Midwestern Psychological Association, Chicago, IL.

ALLOY, L. B., & ABRAMSON, L. Y. (1979). Judgment of contingency in depressed and nondepressed students: Sadder but wiser? *Journal of Experimental Psychology: General, 108,* 441–485.

ALLOY, L. B., & TABACHNIK, N. (1984). Assessment of covariation by animals and humans: Influence of prior expectations and current situational information. *Psychological Review, 91,* 112–149.

ALLPORT, F. H. (1920). The influence of the group upon association and thought. *Journal of Experimental Psychology, 3,* 159–182.

ALLPORT, F. H. (1924). *Social psychology.* Boston: Houghton Mifflin.

ALLPORT, G. W., & ODBERT, H. S. (1936). Trait-names: A psycholexical study. *Psychological Monographs, 47* (1, Whole No. 211).

ALTEMEYER, B. (1988). *Enemies of freedom: Understanding right-wing authoritarianism.* San Francisco: Jossey-Bass.

ALWIN, D. F., COHEN, R. L., & NEWCOMB, T. M. (1991). *Personality and social change: Attitude persistence and changes over the lifespan.* Madison: University of Wisconsin Press.

AMACHAI, Y. (1999). The precision of pain and the blurriness of joy. *New York Review of Books, 46,* 10.

AMERICAN ACADEMY OF PAIN MEDICINE AND AMERICAN PAIN SOCIETY CONSENSUS STATEMENT. (1997). The use of opioids for the treatment of chronic pain. *Pain Forum, 6,* 77–79.

AMERICAN PSYCHIATRIC ASSOCIATION (1994). *Diagnostic and statistical manual of mental disorders* (4th ed.). Washington, DC: American Psychiatric Association.

AMERICAN PSYCHOLOGICAL ASSOCIATION (1990). Ethical principles of psychologists. *American Psychologist, 45,* 390–395.

AMERICAN PSYCHOLOGICAL ASSOCIATION (1996). *Affirmative action: Who benefits?* Washington, DC: American Psychological Association.

ANCH, M. A., BROWMAN, C. P., MITLER, M. M., & WALSH, J. K. (1988). *Sleep: A scientific perspective.* Englewood Cliffs, NJ: Prentice-Hall.

ANCOLI-ISRAEL, S., KRIPKE, D. F., & MASON, W. (1987). Characteristics of obstructive and central sleep apnea in the elderly: An interim report. *Biological Psychiatry, 22,* 741–750.

ANDERSEN, S. M., & GLASSMAN, N. S. (1996). Responding to significant others when they are not there: Effects on interpersonal inference, motivation, and affect. In R. M. Sorrentino & E. T. Higgins (Eds.), *Handbook of motivation and cognition, Volume 3* (pp. 262–321). New York: Guilford.

ANDERSON, J. R. (1983). *The architecture of cognition.* Cambridge, MA: Harvard University Press.

ANDERSON, J. R. (1987). Skill acquisition: Compilation of weak-method problem solutions. *Psychological Review, 94,* 192–210.

ANDERSON, J. R. (1990). *Cognitive psychology and its implications* (3rd ed.). New York: Freeman.

ANDERSON, M. (1992). *Intelligence and development: A cognitive theory.* Oxford: Blackwell.

ANDERSSON, B-E. (1992). Effects of daycare on cognitive and socioemotional competence of thirteen-year-old Swedish schoolchildren. *Child Development, 63,* 20–36.

ANDREASEN, N. C. (1988). Brain imaging: Applications in psychiatry. *Science, 239,* 1381–1388.

ANDREASEN, N. C., FLAUM, M., SCHULTZ, S., DUZYUREK, S., & MILLER, D. (1997). Diagnosis, methodology, and subtypes of schizophrenia. *Neuropsychobiology, 35,* 61–63.

ANDREASEN, N. C., FLAUM, M., SWAYZE, V. W., TYRRELL, G., & ARNDT, S. (1990). Positive and negative symptoms in schizophrenia: A critical reappraisal. *Archives of General Psychiatry, 47,* 615–621.

ANDREWS, K. H., & KANDEL, D. B. (1979). Attitude and behavior. *American Sociological Review, 44,* 298–310.

ANGOFF, W. H. (1988). The nature-nurture debate, aptitudes, and group differences. *American Psychologist, 43,* 713–720.

ANGHOFF, W. H., & JOHNSON, E. G. (1988). A study of differential impact of curriculum on aptitude test scores. *Research Report 88–46.* Princeton, NJ: Educational Testing Service.

ANTROBUS, J. (1983). REM and NREM sleep reports: Comparisons of word frequencies by cognitive classes. *Psychophysiology, 20,* 562–568.

ANTROBUS, J. (1991). Dreaming: Cognitive processes during cortical activation and high afferent thresholds. *Psychological Review, 98,* 96–121.

ANTROBUS, J. (1993). Dreaming: Could we do without it? In A. Moffitt, M. Kramer, & R. Hoffman (Eds.), *The functions of dreaming.* Albany: State University of New York Press.

ARCHER, D., & MCDANIEL, P. (1995). Violence and gender: Differences and similarities across societies. In R. B. Ruback & N. A. Weiner (Eds.), *Interpersonal violent behaviors: Social and cultural aspects* (pp. 63–87). New York: Springer.

ARDREY, R. (1966). *The territorial imperative.* New York: Dell.

ARENDT, H. (1963). *Eichmann in Jerusalem: A report on the banality of evil.* New York: Viking Press.

ARMOR, D. A., & TAYOR, S. E. (1998). Situated optimism: Specific outcome expectancies and self-regulation. In M. P. Zanna (Ed.), *Advances in experimental social psychology* (Vol. 30, pp. 309–379). New York: Academic Press.

ARMSTRONG, S. L., GLEITMAN, L. R., & GLEITMAN, H. (1983). What some concepts might not be. *Cognition, 13,* 263–308.

ARNOLD, M. (1949). A demonstrational analysis of the TAT in a clinical setting. *Journal of Abnormal and Social Psychology, 44,* 97–111.

ARONSON, E. (1995). *The social animal* (7th ed.). San Francisco: Freeman.

ARONSON, E., & CARLSMITH, J. M. (1963). The effect of the severity of threat on the devaluation of forbidden behavior. *Journal of Abnormal and Social Psychology, 66,* 584–588.

ARRIGO, J. M., & PEZDEK, K. (1997). Lessons from the study of psychogenic amnesia. *Current Directions in Psychological Science, 6,* 148–152.

ARTMAN, L., & CAHAN, S. (1993). Schooling and the development of transitive inference. *Developmental Psychology, 29,* 753–759.

ASCH, S. E. (1952). *Social psychology.* Englewood Cliffs, NJ: Prentice-Hall.

ASCH, S. E. (1955). Opinions and social pressures. *Scientific American, 193,* 31–35.

ASCH, S. E. (1958). Effects of group pressure upon modification and distortion of judgments. In E. E. Maccoby, T. M. Newcomb, & E. L. Hartley (Eds.), *Readings in social psychology* (3rd ed.). New York: Holt, Rinehart & Winston.

ASHMEAD, D. H., DAVIS, D. L., WHALEN, T., & ODOM, R. D. (1991). Sound localization and sensitivity to interaural time differences in human infants. *Child Development, 62,* 1211–1226.

ASLIN, R. N. (1987). Visual and auditory development in infancy. In J. D. Osofsky (Ed.), *Handbook of infant development* (2nd ed.). New York: Wiley.

ASLIN, R. N., & BANKS, M. S. (1978). Early visual experience in humans: Evidence for a critical period in the development of binocular vision. In S. Schneider, H. Liebowitz, H. Pick, & H. Stevenson (Eds.), *Psychology: From basic research to practice.* New York: Plenum.

ASLIN, R. N., PISONI, D. V., & JUSCZYK, P. W. (1983). Auditory development and speech perception in infancy. In P. H. Mussen (Ed.), *Handbook of child psychology* (Vol. 2). New York: Wiley.

ASPINWALL, L. G., & BRUNHART, S. M. (1996). Distinguishing optimism from denial: Optimistic beliefs predict attention to health threats. *Personality and Social Psychology Bulletin, 22,* 993–1003.

ASSAD, G., & SHAPIRO, B. (1986). Hallucinations: Theoretical and clinical overview. *American Journal of Psychiatry, 143,* 1088–1097.

ASTIN, J. A. (1998). Why patients use alternative medicine: Results of a national study. *Journal of the American Medical Association, 279,* 1548–1553.

ATKINSON, D. (1983). Ethnic similarity in counseling psychology: A review of the research. *Counseling Psychologist, 11,* 79–92.

ATKINSON, D., MARUYAMA, M., & MATSUI, S. (1978). The effects of counselor race and counseling approach on Asian Americans' perceptions of counselor credibility and utility. *Journal of Counseling Psychology, 25,* 76–83.

ATKINSON, D. R. (1983). Ethnic similarity in counseling psychology: A review of the research. *Counseling Psychologist, 11,* 79–92.

ATKINSON, R. C. (1975). Mnemotechnics in second-language learning. *American Psychologist, 30,* 821–828.

ATKINSON, R. C., HERRNSTEIN, R. J., LINDZEY, G., & LUCE, R. D. (Eds.) (1988) *Stevens' handbook of experimental psychology* (Vols. 1 and 2). New York: Wiley.

ATKINSON, R. C., & SHIFFRIN, R. M. (1971a). The control of short-term memory. *Scientific American, 225,* 82–90.

ATKINSON, R. C., & SHIFFRIN, R. M. (1971b). Human memory: A proposed system and its control processes. In K. W. Spence (Ed.), *The psychology of learning and motivation: Advances in research and theory* (pp. 89–195). New York: Academic Press.

AULD, F., & HYMAN, M. (1991). *Resolution of inner conflict: An introduction to psychoanalytic therapy.* Washington, DC: American Psychological Association.

AVERILL, J. R. (1983). Studies on anger and agression: Implications for theories of emotion. *American Psychologist, 38,* 1145–1160.

AWAYA, S., MIYAKE, Y., IMAYUMI, Y., SHIOSE, Y., KNADA, T., & KOMURO, K. (1973). Amblyopia. *Japanese Journal of Ophthalmology, 17,* 69–82.

AX, A. (1953). The physiological differentiation between fear and anger in humans. *Psychosomatic Medicine, 15,* 433–442.

BAARS, B. J. (1988). *A cognitive theory of consciousness.* New York: Cambridge Universities Press.

BAARS, BERNARD J. (1988), Momentary forgetting as a "resetting" of a conscious global workspace due to competition between incompatible contexts. In Mardi J. Horowitz (Ed.) et al., *Psychodynamics and cognition.* (pp. 269–293). Chicago: University of Chicago Press.

BABKOFF, H., CASPY, T., MIKULINCER, M., & SING, H. C. (1991). Monotonic and rhythmic influences: A challenge for sleep deprivation research. *Psychological Bulletin, 19,* 411–428.

BACHMAN, J. G., JOHNSTON, L. D., & O'MALLEY, M. (1998). Explaining recent increase in students' marijuana use: Impacts of perceived risks and disapproval, 1976 through 1996. *American Journal of Public Health, 88,* 887–892.

BADDELEY, A. (1986). *Working memory.* Oxford: Clarendon.

BADDELEY, A. D. (1990). *Human memory: Theory and practice.* Boston: Allyn and Bacon.

BADDELEY, A. D., & HITCH, G. J. (1974). Working memory. In G. H. Bower (Ed.), *The psychology of learning and motivation* (Vol. 8). New York: Academic Press.

BADDELEY, A. D., THOMPSON, N., & BUCHANAN, M. (1975). Word length and the structure of short-term memory. *Journal of Verbal Learning and Verbal Behavior, 14,* 575–589.

BAER, P. E., & FUHRER, M. J. (1968). Cognitive processes during differential tracc and dclaycd conditioning of the G. S. R. *Journal of Experimental Psychology, 78,* 81–88.

BAHRICK, H. P., & PHELPHS, E. (1987). Retention of Spanish vocabulary over eight years. *Journal of Experimental Psychology: Learning, Memory and Cognition, 13,* 344–349.

BAILEY, J. M., & MARTIN, N. G. (1995, September). A twin registry study of sexual orientation. Paper presented at the twenty-first annual meeting of the International Academy of Sex Research, Provincetown, MA.

BAILEY, J. M., & PILLARD, R. C. (1991). A genetic study of male sexual orientation. *Archives of General Psychiatry, 48,* 1089–1096.

BAILEY, J. M., & PILLARD, R. C. (1995). Genetics of human sexual orientation. *Annual Review of Sex Research, 6,* 126–150.

BAILEY, J. M., PILLARD, R. C., NEALE, M. C., & AGYEI, Y. (1993). Heritable factors influence sexual orientation in women. *Archives of General Psychiatry, 50,* 217–223.

BAILEY, J. M., & ZUCKER, K. J. (1995). Childhood sex-typed behavior and sexual orientation: A conceptual analysis and quantitative review. *Developmental Psychology, 31,* 43–55.

BAILLARGEON, R. (1987). Object permanence in 3½- and 4½-month-old infants. *Developmental Psychology, 23,* 655–664.

BAILLARGEON, R., & DEVOS, J. (1991). Object permanence in young infants: Further evidence. *Child Development, 62,* 1227–1246.

BAILLARGEON, R., SPELKE, E. S., & WASSERMAN, S. (1985). Object permanence in five-month-old infants. *Cognition, 20,* 191–208.

BALDERER, G., & BORBELY, A. A. (1985). Effect of valerian on human sleep. *Psychopharmacology, 87,* 406–409.

BANDURA, A. (1969). *Principles of behavior modification.* New York: Holt, Rinehart and Winston.

BANDURA, A. (1973). *Aggression: A social learning analysis.* Englewood Cliffs, NJ: Prentice-Hall.

BANDURA, A. (1977). *Social learning theory.* Englewood Cliffs, NJ: Prentice-Hall.

BANDURA, A. (1986). *Social foundations of thought and action: A social cognitive theory.* Englewood Cliffs, NJ: Prentice-Hall.

BANDURA, A. (1995). *Self-efficacy in changing societies.* New York: Cambridge University Press.

BANDURA, A., BLANCHARD, E. B., & RITTER, B. (1969). The relative efficacy of desensitization and modeling approaches for inducing behavioral, affective, and attitudinal changes.

Journal of Personality and Social Psychology, 13, 173–199.

BANKS, W. P., & PRINTZMETAL, W. (1976). Configurational effects in visual information processing. *Perception and Psychophysics, 19,* 361–367.

BANKS, W. P., & SALAPATEK, P. (1983). Infant visual perception. In P. H. Mussen (Ed.), *Handbook of child psychology* (Vol. 2). New York: Wiley.

BANYAI, E. I., & HILGARD, E. R. (1976). A comparison of active-alert hypnotic induction with traditional relaxation induction. *Journal of Abnormal Psychology, 85,* 218–224.

BAREFOOT, J. C., WILLIAMS, R. B., & DAHLSTROM, W. G. (1983). Hostility, CHD incidence and total mortality: A 25-year follow-up study of 255 physicians. *Psychosomatic Medicine, 45,* 59–63.

BARGH, J. A. (1997). The automaticity of everyday life. In R. S. Wyer, Jr. (Ed.), *Advances in social cognition, volume X.* Mahway, NJ: Lawrence Erlbaum.

BARGH, J. A., CHEN, M., & BURROWS, L. (1996). Automaticity of social behavior: Direct effects of trait construct and stereotype activation on action. *Journal of Personality and Social Psychology, 71,* 230–244.

BARKOW, J., COSMIDES, L., & TOOKY, J. (1990). *The adapted mind: Evolutionary psychology and the generation of culture.* Oxford University Press.

BARLOW, D. H. (1988). *Anxiety and its disorders: The nature and treatment of anxiety and panic.* New York: Guilford.

BARLOW, H. B., & MOLLON, J. D. (1982). *The senses.* Cambridge, England: Cambridge University Press.

BARON, R. S. (1986). Distraction-conflict theory: Progress and problems. In L. Berkowitz (Ed.), *Advances in experimental social psychology* (Vol. 19). New York: Academic Press.

BARRERA, M. E., & MAURER, D. (1981). Recognition of mother's photographed face by the three-month-old infant. *Child Development, 52,* 714–716.

BARSALOU, L. W. (1985). Ideals, central tendency, and frequency of instantiation as determinants of graded structure in categories. *Journal of Experimental Psychology: Learning, Memory, and Cognition, 11,* 629–654.

BARSALOU, L. W. (1992). *Cognitive psychology: An overview for cognitive scientists.* Hillsdale, NJ: Erlbaum.

BARTLETT, F. C. (1932). *Remembering: A study in experimental and social psychology.* Cambridge, England: Cambridge University Press.

BARTOSHUK, L. M. (1979). Bitter taste of saccharin: Related to the genetic ability to taste the bitter substance

propylthiourial (PROP). *Science, 205,* 934–935.

BARTOSHUK, L. M. (1993). Genetic and pathological taste variation: What can we learn from animal models and human disease? *Ciba Foundation Symposium (D7X), 179,* 251–262.

BASOGLU, M. (Ed.). (1992). *Torture and its consequences: Current treatment approaches.* Cambridge, England: Cambridge University Press.

BATESON, P. (1978). Sexual imprinting and optimal outbreeding. *Nature, 273,* 659–660.

BATSON, C. D. (1991). *The altruism question: Toward a social-psychological answer.* Hillsdale, NJ: Erlbaum.

BAUCOM, D. H., SHOHAM, V., MUESSER, K. T., DAIUTO, A. D., & STICKLE, T. R. (1998). Empirically supported couple and family interventions for marital distress and adult mental health problems. *Journal of Consulting and Clinical Psychology, 66,* 53–88.

BAUMEISTER, R. F., & TICE, D. M. (1984). Role of self-presentation and choice in cognitive dissonance under forced compliance: Necessary or sufficient causes? *Journal of Personality and Social Psychology, 43,* 838–852.

BAUMRIND, D. (1964). Some thoughts on ethics of research: After reading Milgram's "Behavioral study of obedience." *American Psychologist, 19,* 421–423.

BAUMRIND, D. (1967). Child care practices anteceding three patterns of preschool behavior. *Genetic Psychology Monographs, 75,* 43–88.

BAUMRIND, D. (1971). Current patterns of parental authority. *Developmental Psychology Monographs, 1,* 1–103.

BAXTER, L., SCHWARTZ, J., BERGMAN, K., & SZUBA, M. (1992). Caudate glucose metabolic rate changes with both drug and behavior therapy for obsessive-compulsive disorder. *Archives of General Psychiatry, 49,* 681–689.

BAXTER, L. R., SCHWARTZ, J. M., GUZE, B. H., & BERGMAN, K. (1990). PET imaging in obsessive compulsive disorder with and without depression. *Journal of Clinical Psychiatry, 51*(suppl.), 61–69.

BEAMAN, A. L., BARNES, P. J., KLENTZ, B., & MCQUIRK, B. (1978). Increasing helping rates through information dissemination: Teaching pays. *Personality and Social Psychology Bulletin, 4,* 406–411.

BECHARA, A., TRANEL, D., DAMASIO, H., ADOLPHS, R., ROCKLAND, C., & DAMASIO, A. R. (1995). *Science, 269,* 1115–1118.

BECK, A. T. (1976). *Cognitive therapy and the emotional disorder.* New York: International Universities Press.

BECK, A. T., RUSH, A. J., SHAW, B. F., & EMERY, G. (1979). *Cognitive therapy of depression*. New York: Guilford.

BEECHER, H. K. (1961). Surgery as placebo. *Journal of the American Medical Association, 176,* 1102–1107.

BÉKÉSY, G. VON (1960). *Experiments in hearing* (E. G. Weaver, Trans). New York: McGraw-Hill.

BELL, A. P. (1982, November). Sexual preference: A postscript. *Siecus Report, 11,* 1–3.

BELL, A. P., & WEINBERG, M. S. (1978). *Homosexualities: A study of diversity among men and women*. New York: Simon & Schuster.

BELL, A. P., WEINBERG, M. S., & HAMMERSMITH, S. K. (1981). *Sexual preference: Its development in men and women*. Bloomington: Alfred C. Kinsey Institute of Sex Research.

BELL, A. P., WEINBERG, M. S., & HAMMERSMITH, S. K. (1981a). *Sexual preference: Its development in men and women*. Bloomington: Indiana University Press.

BELL, A. P., WEINBERG, M. S., & HAMMERSMITH, S. K. (1981b). *Sexual preference: Its development in men and women. Statistical appendix*. Bloomington: Indiana University Press.

BELL, C. J., & NUTT, D. J. (1998). Serotonin and panic. *British Journal of Psychiatry, 172,* 465–471.

BELL, S. M., & AINSWORTH, M. D. (1972). Infant crying and maternal responsiveness. *Child Development, 43,* 1171–1190.

BELOFF, H. (1957). The structure and origin of the anal character. *Genetic Psychology Monographs, 55,* 141–172.

BELSKY, J., FISH, M., & ISABELLA, R. A. (1991). Continuity and discontinuity in infant negative and positive emotionality: Family antecedents and attachment consequences. *Developmental Psychology, 27,* 421–431.

BELSKY, J., & ROVINE, M. J. (1987). Temperament and attachment security in the strange situation: An empirical rapprochement. *Child Development, 58,* 787–795.

BELSKY, J., & ROVINE, M. J. (1988). Nonmaternal care in the first year of life and the security of infant-parent attachment. *Child Development, 59,* 157–167.

BEM, D. J. (1972). Self-perception theory. In L. Berkowitz (Ed.), *Advances in experimental social psychology* (Vol. 6). New York: Academic Press.

BEM, D. J. (1995). *Exotic becomes erotic: A developmental theory of sexual orientation*. Unpublished manuscript, Cornell University at Ithaca, New York.

BEM, D. J. (1996). Exotic becomes erotic: A developmental theory of sexual orientation. *Psychological Review, 103,* 320–335.

BEM, D. J., & HONORTON, C. (1994). Does psi exist? Replicable evidence for an anomalous process if information transfer. *Psychological Bulletin, 115,* 4–18.

BEM, D. J., WALLACH, M. A., & KOGAN, N. (1965). Group decision-making under risk of aversive consequences. *Journal of Personality and Social Psychology, 1,* 453–460.

BEM, S. L. (1975). Sex role adaptability: One consequence of psychological androgyny. *Journal of Personality and Social Psychology, 31,* 634–643.

BEM, S. L. (1981). Gender schema theory: A cognitive account of sex typing. *Psychological Review, 88,* 354–364.

BEM, S. L. (1985). Androgyny and gender schema theory: A conceptual and empirical integration. In T. B. Sonderegger (Ed.), *Nebraska symposium on motivation 1984: Psychology and gender* (pp. 179–226). Lincoln, NE: University of Nebraska Press.

BEM, S. L. (1987). Gender schema theory and the romantic tradition. In P. Shaver & C. Hendrick (Eds.), *Review of personality and social psychology* (Vol. 7, pp. 251–271). Newbury Park, CA: Sage.

BEM, S. L. (1989). Genital knowledge and gender constancy in preschool children. *Child Development, 60,* 649–662.

BEM, S. L. (1993). *The lenses of gender: Transforming the debate on sexual inequality*. New Haven, CT: Yale University Press.

BENJAMIN, J., LI, L., PATTERSON, C., GREENBERG, B. D., MURPHY, D. L., & HAMER, D. H. Population and familial association between the D4 dopamine receptor gene and measures of novelty seeking. *Nature Genetics, 12,* 81–84.

BENSON, D. F. (1985). Aphasia in K. M. Heilman & E. Valenstein (Eds.), *Clinical neuropsychology* (2nd ed., pp. 17–47). New York: Oxford University Press.

BERGER, T. W. (1984). Long-term potentiation of hippocampal synaptic transmission affects rate of behavioral learning. *Science, 224,* 627–630.

BERGIN, A. E., & LAMBERT, M. J. (1978). The evaluation of therapeutic outcomes. In S. L. Garfield & A. E. Bergin (Eds.), *Handbook of psychotherapy and behavior change* (2nd ed.). New York: Wiley.

BERGIN, A. E., & LAMBERT, M. J. (1979). Counseling the researcher. *Counseling Psychologist, 8,* 53–56.

BERK, L. E. (1997). *Child development* (4th ed.). Needham Heights, MA: Allyn and Bacon.

BERKOWITZ, L. (1965). The concept of aggressive drive. In L. Berkowitz (Ed.), *Advances in experimental social psychology* (Vol. 2). New York: Academic Press.

BERLIN, B., & KAY, P. (1969). *Basic color terms: Their universality and evolution*. Los Angeles: University of California Press.

BERMAN, A. L., & JOBES, D. A. (1991). *Adolescent suicide assessment and intervention*. Washington, DC: American Psychological Association.

BERMAN, K. F., TORREY, E. F., DANIEL, D. G., & WEINBERGER, D. R. (1992). Regional cerebral blood flow in monozygotic twins discordant and concordant for schizophrenia. *Archives of General Psychiatry, 49,* 927–934.

BERNSTEIN, I. L. (1978). Learned taste aversions in children receiving chemotherapy. *Science, 200,* 1302–1303.

BERRIDGE, K. C., & VALENSTEIN, E. S. (1991). What psychological process mediates feeding evoked by electrical stimulation of the lateral hypothalamus? *Behavioral Neuroscience, 105,* 3–14.

BERSCHEID, E. (1983). Emotion. In H. H. Kelley, E. Berscheid, A. Christensen, J. H. Harvey, T. L. Hutson, G. Levinger, E. McClintock, L. A. Peplau, & D. R. Peterson (Eds.), *Close relationships* (pp. 110–168). New York: Freeman.

BERSCHEID, E., & WALSTER, E. H. (1974). A little bit about love. In T. Huston (Ed.), *Foundation of interpersonal attraction*. New York: Academic Press.

BEST, J. B. (1992). *Cognitive psychology*. New York: West.

BIBRING, E. (1953). The mechanism of depression. In P. Greenacre (Ed.), *Affective disorders* (pp. 13–48). New York: International Universities Press.

BIEDERMAN, I. (1987). Recognition by components: A theory of human image understanding. *Psychological Review, 94,* 115–1947.

BIEDERMAN, I. (1990). Higher-level vision. In D. N. Osherson, S. M. Kosslyn, & J. M. Hollerbach (Eds.). *An invitation to cognitive science: Visual cognition and action* (Vol. 2). Cambridge, MA: MIT Press.

BIEDERMAN, I., & JU, G. (1988). Surface versus edge-based determinants of visual recognition. *Cognitive Psychology, 20,* 38–64.

BIERBRAUER, G. (1973). *Attribution and perspective: effects of time, set, and role on interpersonal inference*. Unpublished Ph.D. dissertation, Stanford University.

BILLINGS, A. G., & MOOS, R. H. (1984). Coping, stress, and social resources among adults with unipolar depression. *Journal of Personality and Social Psychology, 46,* 887–891.

BINET, A., & SIMON, T. (1905). New methods for the diagnosis of the intellectual level of subnormals. *Annals of Psychology, 11,* 191.

BINNS, K. E., & SALT, T. E. (1997). Post eye-opening maturation of visual receptive field diameters in the superior colliculus of normal- and dark-reared rats. *Brain Research: Developmental Brain Research, 99,* 263–266.

BISIACH, E., & LUZZATI, C. (1978). Unilateral neglect of representational space. *Cortex, 14,* 129–133.

BLAGROVE, M. (1992). Dreams as a reflection of our waking concerns and abilities: A critique of the problem-solving paradigm in dream research. *Dreaming, 2,* 205–220.

BLAGROVE, M. (1996). Problems with the cognitive psychological modeling of dreaming. *Journal of Mind and Behavior, 17,* 99–134.

BLAKE, R. (1981). Strategies for assessing visual deficits in animals with selective neural deficits. In R. N. Aslin, J. R. Alberts, & M. R. Petersen (Eds.), *Development of perception: Vol. 2. The visual system* (pp. 95–110). New York: Academic Press.

BLAKESLEE, S. (1998, October 13). Placebos prove so powerful even experts are surprised. *New York Times,* pp. F1, F4.

BLAMEY, P. J., DOWELL, R. C., BROWN, A. M., CLARK, G. M., & SELIGMAN, P. M. (1987). Vowel and consonant recognition of cochlear implant patients using formant-estimating speech processors. *Journal of the Acoustical Society of America, 82,* 48–57.

BLANCK, G. (1990). Vygotsky: The man and his cause. In L. C. Moll (Ed.), *Vygotsky and education.* New York: Cambridge University Press.

BLATT, S. J. (1974). Levels of object representation in anaclitic and introjective depression. *Psychoanalytic Study of the Child, 29,* 107–159.

BLAZER, D. G., GEORGE, L., & HUGHES, D. (1991). The epidemiology of anxiety disorders. In C. Salzman & B. Liebowitz (Eds.), *Anxiety disorders in the elderly* (pp. 17–30). New York: Springer-Verlag.

BLISS, E. L. (1980). Multiple personalities: Report of fourteen cases with implications for schizophrenia and hysteria. *Archives of General Psychiatry, 37,* 1388–1397.

BLISS, T. V. P., & LMO, T. (1973). Long-lasting potentiation of synaptic transmission in the dentate area of the anesthetized rabbit following stimulation of the preforant path. *Journal of Physiology, 232,* 331–356.

BLOCK, J. (1961/1978). *The Q-sort method in personality assessment and psychiatric research.* Palo Alto: Consulting Psychologists Press.

BLOOD, R. O. (1967). *Love match and arranged marriage.* New York: Free Press.

BLUM, G. S. (1953). *Psychoanalytic theories of personality.* New York: McGraw-Hill.

BLUM, K., CULL, J. G., BRAVERMAN, E. R., & COMINGS, D. E. (1996). Reward deficiency syndrome. *American Scientist, 84,* 132–145.

BLUMENTHAL, J. A., EMERY, C. F., MADDEN, D. J., SCHNIEBOLK, S., WALSH-RIDDLE, M., GEORGE, L. K., MCKEE, D. C., HIGGINBOTHAM, M. B., COBB, F. R., & COLEMAN, R. E. (1991). Long term effects of exercise on psychological functioning in older men and women. *Journal of Gerontology, 46,* 352–361.

BOFF, K. R., KAUFMAN, L., & THOMAS, J. P. (Eds.). (1986). *Handbook of perception and human performance* (Vol. 1). New York: Wiley.

BOLLES, R. C. (1970). Species-specific defense reactions and avoidance learning. *Psychological Review, 77,* 32–48.

BONANNO, G. A., & SINGER, J. L. (1990). Repressive personality style: Theoretical and methodological implications for health and pathology. In J. L. Singer (Ed.), *Repression and dissociation* (pp. 435–465). Chicago: University of Chicago Press.

BOND, C. F. (1982). Social facilitation: A self-presentational view. *Journal of Personality and Social Psychology, 42,* 1042–1050.

BOON, S., & DRAIJER, N. (1993). Multiple personality disorder in The Netherlands: A clinical investigation of 71 patients. *American Journal of Psychiatry, 150,* 489–494.

BOOTH, A., SHELLEY, G., MAZUR, A., THARP, G., & KITTOK, R. (1989). Testosterone and winning and losing in human competition. *Hormones and Behavior, 23,* 556–571.

BOOTH, D. (1990). Learned role of tastes in eating motivation. In E. D. Capaldi & P. T. L. (Eds.), *Taste, experience, and feeding* (pp. 179–194). Washington, DC: American Psychological Association.

BOOTH, D. A. (1991). Learned ingestive motivation and the pleasures of the palate. In R. C. Bolles (Eds.), *The hedonics of taste* (pp. 29–58). Hillsdale, NJ: Erlbaum.

BOOTH-KEWLEY, S., & FRIEDMAN, H. S. (1987). Psychological predictors of heart disease: A quantitative review. *Psychological Bulletin, 101,* 343–362.

BOOTZIN, R. R., KIHLSTROM, J. F., & SCHACTER, D. L. (Eds.) (1990). *Sleep and cognition.* Washington, DC: American Psychological Association.

BORGIDA, E., & NISBETT, R. E. (1977). The differential impact of abstract vs. concrete information on decisions. *Journal of Applied Social Psychology, 7,* 258–271.

BORING, E. G. (1930). A new ambiguous figure. *American Journal of Psychology, 42,* 444–445.

BORNSTEIN, R. F. (1992). Subliminal mere exposure effects. In R. F. Bornstein & T. S. Pittman (Eds.), *Perception without awareness: Cognitive, clinical and social perspectives* (pp. 191–210). New York: Guilford.

BORNSTEIN, R. F., & D'AGOSTINO, P. R. (1992). Stimulus recognition and the mere exposure effect. *Journal of Personality and Social Psychology, 63,* 545–552.

BOTMAN, H., & CROVITZ, H. (1992). Dream reports and autobiographical memory. *Imagination, Cognition and Personality, 9,* 213–214.

BOUCHARD, C., et al. (1990). The response to long-term overeating in identical twins. *New England Journal of Medicine, 322,* 1477–1482.

BOUCHARD, T. J., JR. (1984). Twins reared apart and together: What they tell us about human diversity. In S. Fox (Ed.), *The chemical and biological bases of individuality.* New York: Plenum.

BOUCHARD, T. J., JR. (1995). *Nature's twice-told tale: Identical twins reared apart—What they tell us about human individuality.* Paper presented at the annual meeting of the Western Psychological Association, Los Angeles.

BOUCHARD, T. J., JR., LYKKEN, D. T., MCGUE, M., SEGAL, N. L., & TELLEGEN, A. (1990). Sources of human psychological differences: The Minnesota study of twins reared apart. *Science, 250,* 223–228.

BOUCHARD, T. J., & MCGUE, M. (1981). Familial studies of intelligence: A review. *Science, 212,* 1055–1059.

BOURNE, L. E. (1966). *Human conceptual behavior.* Boston: Allyn and Bacon.

BOWEN, W. G., & BOK, D. (1998). *The shape of the river: Long-term consequences of considering race in college and university admissions.* Princeton, NJ: Princeton University Press.

BOWER, G. H. (1981). Mood and memory. *American Psychologist, 6,* 129–148.

BOWER, G. H., BLACK, J. B., & TURNER, T. R. (1979). Scripts in memory for text. *Cognitive Psychology, 11,* 177–220.

BOWER, G. H., & CLARK, M. C. (1969). Narrative stories as mediators for serial learning. *Psychonomic Science, 14,* 181–182.

BOWER, G. H., CLARK, M. C., WINZENZ, D., & LESGOLD, A. (1969). Hierarchical retrieval schemes in recall of categorized word lists. *Journal of Verbal Learning and Verbal Behavior, 8,* 323–343.

BOWER, G. H., & SPRINGSTON, F. (1970). Pauses as recoding points in letter series. *Journal of Experimental Psychology, 83,* 421–430.

BOWER, J. E., KEMENY, M. E., TAYLOR, S. E., & FAHEY, J. L. (1998). Cognitive processing, discovery of meaning, CD4 decline, and AIDS-related mortality among bereaved HIV-seropositive men. *Journal of Consulting and Clinical Psychology, 66,* 979–986.

BOWLBY, J. (1969). *Attachment and loss. Volume 1. Attachment.* New York: Basic Books.

BOWLBY, J. (1973). *Attachment and loss: Separation, anxiety and anger* (Vol. 2). London: Hogarth Press.

BOYNTON, R. M. (1979). *Human color vision.* New York: Holt, Rinehart & Winston.

BRADLEY, S. J., OLIVER, G. D., CHERNICK, A. B., & ZUCKER, K. J. (1998). Experiment of nurture: Ablatio penis at 2 months, sex reassignment at 7 months, and a psychosexual follow-up in young adulthood. *Pediatrics, 102,* e9.

BRADSHAW, G. L., & ANDERSON, J. R. (1982). Elaborative encoding as an explanation of levels of processing. *Journal of Verbal Learning and Verbal Behavior, 21,* 165–174.

BRANSFORD, J. D., & JOHNSON, M. K. (1973). Considerations of some problems of comprehension. In W. G. Chase (Ed.), *Visual information processing.* New York: Academic Press.

BRAUN, B. G. (1986). *Treatment of multiple personality disorder.* Washington, DC: American Psychiatric Press.

BRAZELTON, T. B. (1978). The remarkable talents of the newborn. *Birth & Family Journal, 5,* 4–10.

BREEDLOVE, S. M. (1994). Sexual differentiation of the human nervous system. *Annual Review of Psychology, 45,* 389–418.

BREGMAN, A. S. (1990). *Auditory scene analysis.* Cambridge, MA: MIT Press.

BREHM, S. S. (1992). *Intimate relationships* (2nd ed.). New York: McGraw-Hill.

BREIER, A., SCHREIBER, J. L., DYER, J., & PICKAR, D. (1992). Course of illness and predictors of outcome in chronic schizoprenia: Implications for pathophysiology. *British Journal of Psychiatry, 161,* 38–43.

BRELAND, K., & BRELAND, M. (1966). *Animal behavior.* New York: Macmillan.

BRENNER, C. (1980). A psychoanalytic theory of affects. In R. Plutchik & H. Kellerman (Eds.), *Emotion: Theory, research, and experience* (Vol. 1). New York: Academic Press.

BREWIN, C. R., MACCARTHY, B., DUDA, K., & VAUGHN, C. E. (1991). Attribution and expressed emotion in the relatives of patients with schizophrenia. *Journal of Abnormal Psychology, 100*(4), 546–554.

BRIDGER, W. H. (1961). Sensory habituation and discrimination in the human neonate. *American Journal of Psychiatry, 117,* 991–996.

BRIONES, B., ADAMS, N., STRAUSS, M., ROSENBERG, C., WHALEN, C., CARSKADON, M., ROEBUCK, T., WINTERS, M., & REDLINE, S. (1996). Relationship between sleepiness and general health status. *Sleep, 19,* 583–588.

BROADBENT, D. E. (1958). *Perception and communication.* London: Pergamon.

BROMAN, C. L. (1987). Race differences in professional help seeking. *American Journal of Community Psychology, 15,* 473–489.

BROOKS-GUNN, J., & RUBLE, D. N. (1983). The experience of menarche from a developmental perspective. In J. Brooks-Gunn & A. C. Petersen (Eds.), *Girls at puberty: Biological and psychological perspectives.* New York: Plenum.

BROWN, A. E. (1936). Dreams in which the dreamer knows he is asleep. *Journal of Abnormal Psychology, 31,* 59–66.

BROWN, D. P. (1977). A model for the levels of concentrative mediation. *International Journal of Clinical and Experimental Hypnosis, 25,* 236–273.

BROWN, E. L., & DEFFENBACHER, K. (1979). *Perception and the senses.* Oxford: Oxford University Press.

BROWN, G. W., BIRLEY, J. L., & WING, J. K. (1972). Influence of family life on the course of schizophrenic disorders: A replication. *British Journal of Psychiatry, 121,* 241–258.

BROWN, J. (1991). Staying fit and staying well: Physical fitness as a moderator of life stress. *Journal of Personality and Social Psychology, 60,* 555–561.

BROWN, J. D. (1986). Evaluations of self and others: Self-enhancement biases in social judgments. *Social Cognition, 4,* 353–376.

BROWN, L. L., TOMKARKEN, A. J., ORTH, D. N., LOOSEN, P. T., KALIN, N. H., & DAVIDSON, R. J. (1996). Individual differences in repressive-defensiveness predict basal salivary cortisol levels. *Journal of Personality and Social Psychology, 70,* 362–371.

BROWN, R. (1973). *A first language: The early stages.* Cambridge, MA: Harvard University Press.

BROWN, R. (1974). Further comment on the risky shift. *American Psychologist, 29,* 468–470.

BROWN, R. (1986). *Social psychology: The second edition.* New York: Free Press.

BROWN, R., CAZDEN, C. B., & BELLUGI, U. (1969). The child's grammar from 1 to 3. In J. P. Hill (Ed.), *Minnesota symposium on child psychology* (Vol. 2). Minneapolis: University of Minnesota Press.

BROWN, R., & KULIK, J. (1977). Flashbulb memories. *Cognition, 5,* 73–99.

BROWN, R. W., & MCNEILL, D. (1966). The "tip-of-the-tongue" phenomenon. *Journal of Verbal Learning and Verbal Behavior, 5,* 325–337.

BROWNELL, K. (1988, January). Yo-yo dieting. *Psychology Today, 22,* 20–23.

BROWNELL, K. D., & RODIN, J. (1994). The dieting maelstrom: Is it possible and advisable to lose weight? *American Psychologist, 49,* 781–791.

BRUCH, H. (1973). *Eating disorders: Obesity, anorexia nervosa, and the person within.* New York: Basic Books.

BRUNER, J. S. (1957). Going beyond the information given. In *Contemporary approaches to cognition: A symposium held at the University of Colorado.* Cambridge, MA: Harvard University Press.

BRUNER, J. S., GOODNOW, J. J., & AUSTIN, G. A. (1956). *A study of thinking.* New York: Wiley.

BRUNER, J. S., OLVER, R. R., GREENFIELD, P. M., & collaborators (1966). *Studies in cognitive growth.* New York: Wiley.

BRUYER, R., LATERRE, C., SERON, X., & collaborators (1983). A case of prosopagnosia with some preserved covert remembrance of familiar faces. *Brain and Cognition, 2,* 257–284.

BRYAN, J. H., & TEST, M. A. (1967). Models and helping: Naturalistic studies in aiding behavior. *Journal of Personality and Social Psychology, 6,* 400–407.

BUB, D., BLACKS, S., & HOWELL, J. (1989). Word recognition and orthographic context effects in a letter-by-letter reader. *Brain and Language, 36,* 357–376.

BUCHANAN, C. M., ECCLES, J. S., & BECKER J. B. (1992). Are adolescents the victims of raging hormones? Evidence for activational effects of hormones on moods and behavior at adolescence. *Psychological Bulletin, 111,* 62–107.

BUCHSBAUM, M. S., HAIER, R. J., POTKIN, S. G., & NUECHTERLEIN, K. (1992). Fronostriatal disorder of cerebral metabolism in never-medicated schizophrenics. *Archives of General Psychiatry, 49,* 935–942.

BUCK, L., & AXEL, R. (1991). A novel multigene family may encode odorant receptors: A molecular basis for odor recognition. *Cell, 65,* 175–187.

BURNAM, M. A., STEIN, J. A., GOLDING, J. M., SIEGEL, J. M., SORENSON, S. B., FORSYTHE, A. B., & TELLES, C. A. (1988). Sexual assault and mental disorders in a community population. *Journal of Consulting and Clinical Psychology, 56,* 843–850.

BURNSTEIN, E., & VINOKUR, A. (1973). Testing two classes of theories about group-induced shifts in individual choice. *Journal of Experimental Social Psychology, 9,* 123–137.

BURNSTEIN, E., & VINOKUR, A. (1977). Persuasive arguments and social comparison as determinants of attitude polarization. *Journal of Experimental Social Psychology, 13,* 315–332.

BUSBY, P. A., TONG, Y. C., & CLARK, G. M. (1993). Electrode position, repetition rate, and speech perception by early- and late-deafened cochlear implant patients. *Journal of the Acoustical Society of America, 93,* 1058–1067.

BUSS, A. H., & PLOMIN, R. (1975). *A temperament theory of personality development.* New York: Wiley.

BUSS, D. M. (1989). Sex differences in human mate preference: Evolutionary hypotheses tested in 37 cultures. *Brain and Behavior Sciences, 12,* 1–49.

BUSS, D. M. (1991). Evolutionary personality psychology. *Annual Review of Psychology, 42,* 459–491.

BUSS, D. M. (1994a). *The evolution of desire: Strategies of human mating.* New York: Basic Books.

BUSS, D. M. (1994b). Personality evoked: The evolutionary psychology of stability and change. In T. F. Heatherton & J. Weinberger (Eds.), *Can personality change?* Washington, DC: American Psychological Association Press.

BUSS, D. M., & BARNES, M. (1986). Preferences in human mate selection. *Journal of Personality and Social Psychology, 50,* 559–570.

BUSS, D. M., LARSEN, R. J., WESTEN, D., & SEMMELROTH, J. (1992). Sex differences in jealousy: Evolution, physiology, and psychology. *Psychological Science, 3,* 251–255.

BUSSEY, K., & BANDURA, A. (in press). Social cognitive theory of gender development and differentiation. *Psychological Review.*

BUTLER, J. M., & HAIGH, G. V. (1954). Changes in the relation between self-concepts and ideal concepts consequent upon client centered counseling. In C. R. Rogers & R. F. Dymond (Eds.), *Psychotherapy and personality change: Coordinated studies in the client-centered approach* (pp. 55–76). Chicago: University of Chicago Press.

BUTTERFIELD, E. L., & SIPERSTEIN, G. N. (1972). Influence of contingent auditory stimulation on nonnutritional sucking. In J. Bosma (Ed.), *Oral sensation and perception: The mouth of the infant.* Springfield, IL: Charles B. Thomas.

CABANAC, M. (1979). Sensory pleasure. *Quarterly Review of Biology, 54,* 1–29.

CABANAC, M. (1992). Pleasure: The common currency. *Journal of Theoretical Biology, 155,* 173–200.

CACIOPPO, J. T., KLEIN, D. J., BEMSTON, G. G., & HATFIELD, E. (1993). The psychophysiology of emotion. In M. Lewis & J. M. Haviland (Eds.), *The handbook of emotions.* New York: Guilford.

CADORET, R. J., & CAIN, C. A. (1980). Sex differences in predictors of antisocial behavior in adoptees. *Archives of General Psychiatry, 37,* 1171–1175.

CAHILL, L., BABINSKY, R., MARKOWITSCH, H. J., & MCGAUGH, J. L. (1996). The amygdala and emotional memory. *Nature, 377,* 295–296.

CAHILL, L., PRINS, B., WEBER, M., & MCGAUGH, J. L. (1994). Adrenergic activation and memory for emotional events. *Nature, 371.*

CAIN, W. S. (1988). Olfaction. In R. C. Atkinson, R. J. Hernstein, G. Lindzey, & R. D. Luce (Eds.), *Stevens' handbook of experimental psychology* (Vol. 1). New York: Wiley, 409–459.

CALLAWAY, M. R., MARRIOTT, R. G., & ESSER, J. K. (1985). Effects of dominance on group decision making: Toward a stress-reduction explanation of group-think. *Journal of Personality and Social Psychology, 49,* 949–952.

CAMPOS, J. J., BARRETT, K. C., LAMB, M. E., GOLDSMITH, H. H., & STENBERG, C. (1983). Socioemotional development. In P. Mussen (Ed.), *Handbook of child psychology* (Vol. 1, pp. 1–101). New York: Wiley.

CANNON, W. D. (1927). The James-Lange theory of emotions: A critical examination and an alternative theory. *American Journal of Psychology, 39,* 106–124.

CARAMAZZA, A., & ZURIF, E. B. (1976). Dissociation of algorithmic and heuristic processes in language comprehension: Evidence from aphasia. *Brain and Language, 3,* 572–582.

CARDON, L. R., FULKER, D. W., DEFRIES, J. C., & PLOMIN, R. (1992). Continuity and change in general cognitive ability from 1 to 7 years of age. *Developmental Psychology, 28,* 64–73.

CARLSON, N. R. (1998). *Foundations of physiological psychology* (4th ed.). Boston: Allyn and Bacon.

CARLSON, N. R. (1994). *Physiology of behavior* (5th ed.). Boston: Allyn and Bacon.

CARLSON, N. R. (1998). *Foundations of physiological psychology* (4th ed.). Boston: Allyn and Bacon.

CARLSON, R. (1971). Where is the person in personality research? *Psychological Bulletin, 75,* 203–219.

CARLSON, W. R. (1986). *Physiology of behavior* (3rd ed.). Boston: Allyn and Bacon.

CARPENTER, P. A., JUST, M. A., & SHELL, P. (1990). What one intelligence test measures: A theoretical account of the processing in the Raven Progressive Matrices Test. *Psychological Review, 97,* 404–431.

CARROLL, D. W. (1985). *Psychology of language.* Monterey, CA: Brooks/Cole.

CARROLL, J. B. (1988). Individual differences in cognitive functioning. In R. C. Atkinson, R. J. Herrnstein, G. Lindzey, & R. D. Luce (Eds.), *Stevens' handbook of experimental psychology* (Vol. 2). New York: Wiley.

CARROLL, J. B. (1993). *Human cognitive abilities: A survey of factor-analytic studies.* New York: Cambridge University Press.

CARSKADON, M. A. (1989). Ontogeny of human sleepiness as measured by sleep latency. In D. F. Dinges & R. J. Broughton (Eds.), *Sleep and alertness: Chronobiological, behavioral, and medical aspects of napping* (pp. 53–69). New York: Raven Press.

CARSKADON, M. A., MITLER, M. M., & DEMENT, W. C. (1974). A comparison of insomniacs and normals: Total sleep time and sleep latency. *Sleep Research, 3,* 130.

CARTER, M. M., HOLLON, S. D., CARON, R. S., & SHELTON, R. C. (1995). Effects of a safe person on induced distress following a biological challenge in panic disorder with agoraphobia. *Journal of Abnormal Psychology, 104,* 156–163.

CARTERETTE, E. C., & FRIEDMAN, M. P. (Eds.) (1974–1978). *Handbook of perception* (Vols. 1–11). New York: Academic Press.

CARTWRIGHT, R. (1978, December). Happy endings for our dreams. *Psychology Today,* pp. 66–67.

CARTWRIGHT, R. (1992). Masochism in dreaming and its relation to depression. *Dreaming, 2,* 79–84.

CARTWRIGHT, R. (1996). Dreams and adaptation to divorce. In D. Barrett, (Ed.), *Trauma and dreams.* Cambridge, MA: Harvard University Press.

CARTWRIGHT, R. D. (1974). The influence of a conscious wish on dreams. A methodological study of dream meaning and function. *Journal of Abnormal Psychology, 83,* 387–393.

CARVER, C. S., & SCHEIER, M. F. (1981). *Attention and self-regulation: A control-theory approach to human behavior.* New York: Springer-Verlag.

CASE, R. (1985). *Intellectual development: A systematic reinterpretation.* New York: Academic Press.

CASE, R. B., HELLER, S. S., CASE, N. B., & MOSS, A. J. (1985). Type A behavior and survival after acute myocardial infarction. *The New England Journal of Medicine, 312,* 737.

CASPI, A., & HERBENER, E. S. (1990). Continuity and change: Assortative marriage and the consistency of personality in adulthood. *Journal of Personality and Social Psychology, 58,* 250–258.

CASPI, A., & MOFFIT, T. E. (1991). Individual differences are accentuated during periods of social change: The sample case of girls at puberty. *Journal of Personality and Social Psychology, 61,* 157–168.

CATTELL, R. B. (1957). *Personality and motivation structure and measurement.* Yonkers-on-Hudson, NY: World.

CATTELL, R. B. (1966). *The scientific analysis of personality.* Chicago: Aldine.

CAVALLERO, C., CICOGNA, P., NATALE, V., & OCCIONERO, M. (1992). Slow wave sleep dreaming. *Sleep, 15,* 562–566.

CECI, S. J. (1990). *On intelligence . . . more or less: A bio-ecological treatise on intellectual development.* Englewood Cliffs, NJ: Prentice-Hall.

CECI, S. J., & ROAZZI, A. (1994). The effect of context on cognition: Postcards from Brazil. In R. J. Sternberg & R. K. Wagner (Eds.), *Mind in context: Interactionist perspectives on human intelligence.* Cambridge, England: Cambridge University Press.

CENTERS FOR DISEASE CONTROL (1988). Health status of Vietnam veterans: Psychosocial characteristics. *Journal of the American Medical Association, 259,* 2701–2707.

CERNOCH, J. M., & PORTER, R. H. (1985). Recognition of maternal axillary odors by infants. *Child Development, 56,* 1593–1598.

CHAIKEN, S. (1987). The heuristic model of persuasion. In M. P. Zanna, J. N. Olson, & C. P. Herman (Eds.), *Social influence: The ontario symposium* (Vol. 5, pp. 3–39). Hillsdale, NJ: Erlbaum.

CHAMBLESS, D. L., & HOLLON, S. D. (1998). Defining empirically supported therapies. *Journal of Consulting and Clinical Psychology, 66,* 7–18.

CHAPMAN, L. J., & CHAPMAN, J. P. (1969). Illusory correlation as an obstacle to the use of valid psychodiagnostic signs. *Journal of Abnormal Psychology, 74,* 271–280.

CHASE, W. G., & SIMON, H. A. (1973a). The mind's eye in chess. In W. G. Chase (Ed.), *Visual information processing.* New York: Academic Press.

CHASE, W. G., SIMON, H. A. (1973b.) Perception in chess. *Cognitive Psychology, 4,* 55–81.

CHAUDURI, H. (1965). *Philosophy of meditation.* New York: Philosophical Library.

CHEN, S. C. (1937). Social modification of the activity of ants in nest-building. *Physiological Zoology, 10,* 420–436.

CHEN, X. H., GELLER, E. B., & ADLER, M. W. (1996). Electrical stimulation at traditional acupuncture sites in periphery produces brain opoid-receptor-mediated antinociception in rats. *Journal of Pharmacology and Experimental Therapy, 277,* 654–660.

CHENG, P. W., HOLYOAK, K. J., NISBETT, R. E., & OLIVER, L. (1986). Pragmatic versus syntactic approaches to training deductive reasoning. *Cognitive Psychology, 18,* 293–328.

CHESS, S., & THOMAS, A. (1984). *Origins and evolution of behavior disorders: Infancy to early adult life.* New York: Brunner/Mazel.

CHI, M. (1978). Knowledge structures and memory development. In R. S. Siegler (Ed.), *Children's thinking: What develops?* Hillsdale, NJ: Erlbaum.

CHI, M., GLASER, R., & REES, E. (1982). Expertise in problem solving. In R. Sternberg (Ed.), *Advances in the psychology of human intelligence* (Vol. 1). Hillsdale, NJ: Erlbaum.

CHOCOLLE, R. (1940). Variations des temps de réaction auditifs en fonction de l'intensité à diverses fréquences. *Année Psychologique, 41,* 65–124.

CHOMSKY, N. (1965). *Aspects of the theory of syntax.* Cambridge, MA: MIT Press.

CHOMSKY, N. (1972). *Language and mind* (2nd ed.). New York: Harcourt Brace Jovanovich.

CHOMSKY, N. (1980). *Rules and representations.* New York: Columbia University Press.

CHOMSKY, N. (1991, March). Quoted in *Discover.*

CHORNEY, M. J., CHORNEY, K., SEESE, N., OWEN, M. J., DANIELS, J., MCGUFFIN, P., THOMPSON, L. A., DETTERMAN, D. K., BENBOW, C., LUBINSKI, D., ELEY, T., & PLOMIN, R. (1998). A quantitative trait locus associated with cognitive ability in children. *Psychological Science, 13,* 159–166.

CHRISTIE, R., & JOHODA, M. (Eds.) (1954). *Studies in the scope and method of "the authoritarian personality."* New York: Free Press.

CHURCHLAND, P. M. (1995) *The engine of reason, the seat of the soul.* Cambridge, MA: MIT Press.

CHURCHLAND, P. S., & SEJNOWSKI, T. J. (1988). Perspectives on cognitive neuroscience. *Science, 242,* 741–745.

CLARK, D. A., & DESILVA, P. (1985). The nature of depressive and anxious, intrusive thoughts: Distinct or uniform phenomena? *Behaviour Research & Therapy, 23,* 383–393.

CLARK, D. A., & PURDON, C. (1993). New perspectives for a cognitive theory of obsessions. *Australian Psychologist, 28,* 161–167.

CLARK, D. M. (1988). A cognitive model of panic attacks. In S. Rachman & J. D. Maser (Eds.), *Panic: Psychological perspectives.* Hillsdale, NJ: Erlbaum

CLARK, D. M., SALKOVSKIS, P. M., HACKMANN, A., MIDDLETON, H., and collaborators (1994). A comparison of cognitive therapy, applied, relaxation, and imipramine in the treatment of panic disorder. *British Journal of Psychiatry, 164,* 759–769.

CLARK, E. V. (1983). Meanings and concepts. In P. H. Mussen (Ed.), *Handbook of child psychology* (Vol. 3). New York: Wiley.

CLARK, H. H. (1984). Language use and language users. In G. Lindzey & E. Aronson (Eds.), *The handbook of social psychology* (Vol. 2, 3rd. ed.). New York: Harper & Row.

CLARK, H. H., & CLARK, E. V. (1977). *Psychology and language: An introduction to psycholinguistics.* New York: Harcourt Brace Jovanovich.

CLARKE, R. D., & HATFIELD, E. (1989). Gender differences in receptivity to sexual offers. *Journal of Psychology and Human Sexuality, 2,* 39–55.

CLARKE-STEWART, K. A. (1973). Interactions between mothers and their young children: Characteristics and consequences. *Monographs of the Society for Research in Child Development, 38* (6 & 7, Serial No. 153).

CLARKE-STEWART, K. A. (1989). Infant day care: Maligned or malignant? *American Psychologist, 44,* 266–273.

CLONINGER, C. R., & GOTTESMAN, I. I. (1987). Genetic and environmental factors in antisocial behavior disorders. In S. A. Mednick, T. E. Moffitt, & S. A. Stack (Eds.), *The causes of crime: New biological approaches* (pp. 92–109). New York: Cambridge University Press.

CLORE, G. L. (1992). Cognitive phenomenology: Feelings and the construction of judgment. In L. L. Martin & A. Tesser (Eds.), *The construction of social judgments* (pp. 133–163). Hillsdale, NJ: Erlbaum.

COHEN, C. E. (1981). Person categories and social perception: Testing some boundaries of the processing effects of prior knowledge. *Journal of Personality and Social Psychology, 40,* 441–452.

COHEN, D., & NISBETT, R. E. (1994). Self-protection and culture of honor: Explaining Southern violence. *Personality and Social Psychology Bulletin, 20,* 551–567.

COHEN, N. J., & SQUIRE, L. R. (1980). Preserved learning and retention of pattern analyzing skill in amnesia: Dissociation of knowing how and knowing that. *Science, 210,* 207–209.

COHEN, S. (1980, September). *Training to understand TV advertising: Effects and some policy implications.* Paper presented at the American Psychological Association convention, Montreal.

COHEN, S. (1996). Psychological stress, immunity, and upper respiratory infections. *Current Directions in Psychological Science, 5,* 86–90.

COHEN, S., & EDWARDS, J. R. (1989). Personality characteristics as moderators of the relationship between stress and disorder. In R. J. Neufeld (Ed.), *Advances in the investigation of psychological stress* (pp. 235–283). New York: Wiley.

COHEN, S., TYRRELL, D. A. J., & SMITH, A. P. (1991). Psychological stress and susceptibility to the common cold. *The New England Journal of Medicine, 325,* 606–612.

COLBY, A., KOHLBERG, L., GIBBS, J., & LIEBERMAN, M. A. (1983). A longitudinal study of moral judgment. *Monographs of the Society for Research in Child Development, 48,* 1–2.

COLE, M., & COLE, S. R. (1993). *The development of children.* (2nd ed.) New York: Scientific American Books.

COLE, S. W., KEMENY, M. E., TAYLOR, S. E., & VISSCHER, B. R. (1996). Elevated physical health risk among gay men who conceal their homosexual identity. *Health Psychology, 15,* 243–251.

COLE, S. W., KEMENY, M. E., TAYLOR, S. E., VISSCHER, B. R., & FAHEY, J. L. (1996). Accelerated course of human immunodeficiency virus infection in gay men who conceal their homosexual identity. *Psychosomatic Medicine, 58,* 219–238.

COLEGROVE, F. W. (1899). Individual memories. *American Journal of Psychology, 10,* 228–255.

COLLINS, A. M., & LOFTUS, E. G. (1975). A spreading-activation theory of semantic processing. *Psychological Review, 82,* 407–428.

COMREY, A. L., & LEE, H. B. (1992). *A first course in factor analysis* (2nd ed.). Hillsdale, NJ: Erlbaum.

CONRAD, R. (1964). Acoustic confusions in immediate memory. *British Journal of Psychology, 55,* 75–84.

COOK, M., & MINEKA, S. (1990). Selective associations in the observational conditioning of fear in rhesus monkeys. *Journal of Experimental Psychology: Animal Behavior Processes, 16,* 372–389.

COOPER, L. A., & SHEPARD, R. N. (1973). Chronometric studies of the rotation of mental images. In W. G. Chase (Ed.), *Visual information processing.* New York: Academic Press.

COOPER, L. M. (1979). Hypnotic amnesia. In E. Fromm & R. E. Shor (Eds.), *Hypnosis: Developments in research and new perspectives* (rev. ed.). New York: Aldine.

CORBETTA, M., MIEZIN, F.M., SHULMAN, G. L., & PETERSEN, S. E. (1991). Selective attention modulates extrastriate visual regions in humans during visual feature discrimination and recognition. In D. J. Chadwick & J. Whelan (Eds.), *Ciba Foundation symposium 163, exploring brain functional anatomy with positron tomography* (pp. 165–180). Chichester: Wiley.

CORBETTA, M., MIEZIN, F. M., SHULMAN, G. L., & PETERSEN, S. E. (1993). A PET study of visuospatial attention. *The Journal of Neuroscience, 13,* 1202–1226.

COREN, S. (1992). The moon illusion: A different view through the legs. *Perceptual & Motor Skills, 75,* 827–831.

COREN, S., & GIRGUS, J. S. (1980). Principles of perceptual organization and spatial distortion: The gestalt illusions. *Journal of Experimental Psychology: Human Perception & Performance, 6,* 404–412.

COREN, S., WARD, L. M., & ENNS, J. T. *Sensation and perception* (5th ed.). Fort Worth: Harcourt Brace.

COSCINA, D. V., & DIXON, L. M. (1983). Body weight regulation in anorexia nervosa: Insights from an animal model. In F. L. Darby, P. E. Garfinkel, D. M. Garner, & D. V. Coscina (Eds.), *Anorexia nervosa: Recent developments.* New York: Allan R. Liss.

COTT, J. (1995). Natural product formulations available in Europe for psychotropic indications. *Psychopharmacology, 31,* 131–137.

COTT, J. M., & FUGH-BERMAN, A. (1998). Is St. John's Wort (hypericum perforatum) an effective antidepressant? *Journal of Nervous and Mental Disease, 186,* 500–501.

COTTRELL, N. B. (1972). Social facilitation. In C. G. McClintock (Ed.), *Experimental social psychology.* New York: Holt, Rinehart & Winston.

COTTRELL, N. B., RITTLE, R. H., & WACK, D. L. (1967). Presence of an audience and list type (competitional or noncompetitional) as joint determinants of performance in paired-associates learning. *Journal of Personality, 25,* 425–434.

COTTRELL, N. B., WACK, D. L., SEKERAK, G. J., & RITTLE, R. H. (1968). Social facilitation of dominant responses by the presence of an audience and the mere presence of others. *Journal of Personality and Social Psychology, 9,* 245–250.

COURAGE, M. L., & ADAMS, R. J. (1990a). Visual acuity assessment from birth to three years using the acuity card procedures: Cross-sectional and longitudinal samples. *Optometry and Vision Science, 67,* 713–718.

COURAGE, M. L., & ADAMS, R. J. (1990b). The early development of visual acuity in the binocular and monocular peripheral fields. *Infant Behavioral Development, 13,* 123–128.

COURTRIGHT, J. A. (1978). A laboratory investigation of groupthink. *Communications Monographs, 43,* 229–246.

COUSINS, S. D. (1989). Culture and self-perception in Japan and the U.S. *Journal of Personality and Social Psychology, 56,* 124–131.

CRAIGHEAD, L. W., STUNKARD, A. J., & O'BRIEN, R. M. (1981). Behavior therapy and pharmacotherapy for obesity. *Archives of General Psychiatry, 38,* 763–768.

CRAIK, F. I. M., & TULVING, E. (1975). Depth of processing and the retention of words in episodic memory. *Journal of Experimental Psychology: General, 104,* 268–294.

CRARY, W. G. (1966). Reactions to incongruent self-experiences. *Journal of Consulting Psychology, 30,* 246–252.

CRASILNECK, H. B., & HALL, J. A. (1985). *Clinical hypnosis: Principles and applications* (2nd ed.). Orlando: Grune & Stratton.

CREWS, F. C. (Ed.) (1998). *Unauthorized Freud: Doubters confront a legend.* New York: Viking.

CRICK, F. (1994). *The astonishing hypothesis: The scientific search for the soul.* New York: Macmillan.

CRICK, N. R., & DODGE, K. A. (1994). A review and reformulation of social information-processing mechanisms in children's social adjustment. *Psychological Bulletin, 115,* 74–101.

CRITS-CHRISTOPH, P., COOPER, A., & LUBORSKY, L. (1990). The measurement of accuracy of interpretations. In L. Luborsky & P. Crits-Christoph (Eds.), *Understanding transference: The CCRT method* (pp. 173–188). New York: Basic Books.

CROMWELL, P. F., MARKS, A., OLSON, J. N., & AVARY, D. W. (1991). Group effects on decision-making by burglars. *Psychological Reports, 69,* 579–588.

CROSBY, F., & CORDOVA, D. I. (1996). Words worth of wisdom. *Journal of Social Issues, 52,* 33–49.

CROSS, G. M., MORGAN, C. W., MARTIN, C. A., & RAFTER, J. A. (1990). Alcoholism treatment: A ten-year follow-up study. *Alcoholism: Clinical and Experimental Research, 14,* 169–173.

CROYLE, R. T., SUN, Y., & HART, M. (1997). Processing risk factor information: Defensive biases in health-related cognitions. In J. A. Petrie & J. A. Weinman (Eds.), *Perceptions of health and illness: Current research and applications* (pp. 267–290). Singapore: Harwood Academic Publishers.

CURTISS, S. (1977). *Genie: A psycholinguistic study of a modern-day "wild child."* New York: Academic Press.

CURTISS, S. (1989). The independence and task-specificity of language. In M. H. Bornstein & J. S. Bruner (Eds.), *Interaction in human development.* Hillsdale, NJ: Erlbaum.

CUTLER, W. B., PRETI, G., KRIEGER, A., HUGGINS, G. R., GARCIA, C. R. & LAWLEY, H. J. (1986). Human axillary secretions influence women's menstrual cycles: The role of donor extract from men. *Hormones and Behavior, 20,* 463–473.

CUTTING, J. E. (1986). *Perception with an eye for motion.* Cambridge, MA: MIT Press.

CYANDER, M., TIMNEY, B. N., & MITCHELL, D. E. (1980). Period of susceptibility of kitten visual cortex to the effects of monocular deprivation extends beyond 6 months of age. *Brain Research, 191,* 545–550.

CZEISLER, C. A., DIJK, D. J., DUFFY, J. F. (1995). Entrained phase of the circadian pacemaker serves to stabilize alertnesss and performance throughout the habitual waking day. In R. D. Ogilvie & J. R. Harsh (Eds.), *Sleep onset normal and abnormal processes* (pp. 89–110). Washington, DC: American Psychological Association.

DABBS, J. M., & MORRIS, R., JR. (1990). Testosterone, social class, and antisocial behavior in a sample of 4,462 men. *Psychological Science, 1,* 209–211.

DALE, A. J. D. (1975). Organic brain syndromes associated with infections. In A. M., Freeman, H. I. Kaplan, & B. J. Sadock (Eds.), *Comprehensive textbook of psychiatry* (Vol. 2, pp. 1121–1130). Baltimore, MD: Williams & Wilkins.

DAMASIO, A.R. (1985). Disorders of complex visual processing: Agnosia, achromatopsia, Balint's syndrome, and related difficulties of orientation and construction. In M. M. Mesulam (Ed.), *Principles of behavioral neurology* (pp. 259–288). Philadelphia: F. A. Davis.

DAMASIO, A. R. (1990). Category-related recognition defects as a clue to the neural substrates of knowledge. *Trends in Neurosciences, 13,* 95–98.

DAMASIO, A. R. (1994). *Descartes' error.* New York: Putnam.

DAMON, W. (1977). *The social world of the child.* San Francisco: Jossey-Bass.

DAMON, W. (1983). *Social and personality development.* New York: Norton.

DANEMAN, M., & CARPENTER, P. A. (1980). Individual differences in working memory and reading. *Journal of Verbal Learning and Verbal Behavior, 19,* 450–466.

DARIAN-SMITH, I. (Ed.) (1984). *Handbook of physiology: The nervous system:*

Section 1, vol. 3. Sensory processes. Bethesda, MD: American Physiological Society.

DARLEY, C. F., TINKLENBERG, J. R., ROTH, W. T., HOLLISTER, L. E., & ATKINSON, R. C. (1973a). Influence of marijuana on storage and retrieval processes in memory. *Memory and Cognition, 1,* 196–200.

DARLEY, C. F., TINKLENBERG, J. R., ROTH, W. T., HOLLISTER, L. E., & ATKINSON, R. C. (1973b). Marijuana and retrieval from short-term memory. *Psychopharmacologia, 29,* 231–238.

DARLEY, C. F., TINKLENBERG, J. R., ROTH, W. T., VERNON, S., & KOPELL, B. S. (1977). Marijuana effects on long-term memory assessment and retrieval. *Psychopharmacology, 52,* 239–241.

DARLEY, J. M., & LATANÉ, B. (1968). Bystander intervention in emergencies: Diffusion of responsibility. *Journal of Personality and Social Psychology, 8,* 377–383.

DARWIN, C. (1859). *On the origin of the species.* London: Murray.

DARWIN, C. (1872). *The expression of emotion in man and animals.* New York: Philosophical Library.

DASHIELL, J. F. (1930). An experimental analysis of some group effects. *Journal of Abnormal and Social Psychology, 25,* 190–199.

DASHIELL, J. F. (1935). Experimental studies of the influence of social situations on the behavior of individual human adults. In C. Murchison (Ed.), *Handbook of social psychology.* Worcester, MA: Clark University.

DAVIDSON, K., & PRKACHIN, K. (1997). Optimism and unrealistic optimism have an interacting effect on health-promoting behavior and knowledge changes. *Personality and Social Psychology Bulletin, 23,* 617–625.

DAVIS, K. L., KAHN, R. S., KO, G., & DAVIDSON, M. (1991). Dopamine in schizophrenia: A review and conceptualization. *American Journal of Psychiatry, 148,* 1474–1486.

DEAKIN, J. W., & GRAEFF, F. G. (1991). 5-HT and mechanisms of defense. *Journal of Psychopharmacology, 5,* 305–315.

DEARY, I. (1992). Multiple minds. *Science, 259,* 28.

DEARY, I. J., WHALLEY, L. J., LEMMON, H., CRAWFORD, J. R., & STARR, J. M. (in press). The stability of individual differences in mental ability from childhood to old age: Follow-up of the 1932 Scottish mental survey. *Intelligence.*

DECASPER, A. J., & FIFER, W. P. (1980). Of human bonding: Newborns prefer their mothers' voices. *Science, 208,* 1174–1176.

DECASPER, A. J., & PRESCOTT, P. A. (1984). Human newborns' perception

of male voices: Preference, discrimination and reinforcing value. *Developmental Psychobiology, 17,* 481–491.

DECASPER, A. J., & SPENCE, M. J. (1986). Prenatal maternal speech influences newborns' perception of speech sounds. *Infant Behavior and Development, 9,* 133–150.

DEIKMAN, A. J. (1963). Experimental meditation. *Journal of Nervous and Mental Disease, 136,* 329–373.

DEMBROSKI, T. M., MACDOUGALL, J. M., WILLIAMS, B., & HANEY, T. L. (1985). Components of Type A hostility and anger: Relationship to angiographic findings. *Psychosomatic Medicine, 47,* 219–233.

DEMENT, W. C., & KLEITMAN, N. (1957). The relation of eye movements during sleep to dream activity: An objective method for the study of dreaming. *Journal of Experimental Psychology, 53,* 339–346.

DEMENT, W. C., & WOLPERT, E. (1958). The relation of eye movements, bodily mobility, and external stimuli to dream content. *Journal of Experimental Psychology, 55,* 543–553.

DENNIS, W., & DENNIS, M. (1940). The effects of cradling practices upon the onset of walking in Hopi children. *Journal of Genetic Psychology, 56,* 77–86.

DERUBEIS, R. J., & CRITS-CHRISTOPH, P. (1998). Empirically supported individual and group psychological treatments for adult mental disorders. *Journal of Abnormal Psychology, 101,* 371–382.

DEVALOIS, R. L., & DEVALOIS, K. K. (1980). Spatial vision. *Annual Review of Psychology, 31,* 309–341.

DEVALOIS, R. L., & JACOBS, G. H. (1984). Neural mechanisms of color vision. In I. Darian-Smith (Ed.), *Handbook of physiology* (Vol. 3). Bethesda, MD: American Physiological Society.

DE WAAL, F. B. M. (1996). *Good natured: The origins of right and wrong in humans and other animals.* Cambridge, MA: Harvard University Press.

DEWEY, J. (1916). *Democracy and education.* New York: Macmillan.

DIAMOND, M. (1982). Sexual identity, monozygotic twins reared in discordant sex roles and a BBC follow-up. *Archives of Sexual Behavior, 11,* 181–6.

DIAMOND, M., & SIGMUNDSON, K. (1996). Sex reassignment at birth: A long term review and clinical implications. *Journal of the American Medical Association* (in press).

DIAMOND, M., & SIGMUNDSON, K. (1997). Sex reassignment at birth: Long-term review and clinical implications. *Archives of Pediatric Medicine, 151,* 298.

DIENER, E. (1979). Deindividuation, self-awareness, and disinhibition. *Journal of Personality and Social Psychology, 37,* 1160–1171.

DIENER, E. (1980). Deindividuation: The absence of self-awareness and self-regulation in group members. In P. B. Paulus (Ed.), *The psychology of group influence.* Hillsdale, NJ: Erlbaum.

DIENER, E., FRASER, S. C., BEAMAN, A. L., & KELEM, R. T. (1976). Effects of de-individuation variables on stealing among Halloween trick-or-treaters. *Journal of Personality and Social Psychology, 33,* 178–183.

DIENSTBIER, R. A. (1989). Arousal and physiological toughness: Implications for mental and physical health. *Psychological Review, 96,* 84–100.

DIGMAN, J. M., & INOUYE, J. (1986). Further specification of the five robust factors of personality. *Journal of Personality and Social Psychology, 50,* 116–123.

DIJK, D. J., DUFFY, J. F., & CZEISLER, C. A. (1992). Circadian and sleep-wake dependent aspects of subjective alertness and cognitive performance. *Journal of Sleep Research, 1,* 112–117.

DILLBECK, M. C., & ORME-JOHNSON, D. W. (1987). Physiological differences between transcendental meditation and rest. *American Psychologist, 42,* 879–881.

DINGES, D. F., & BROUGHTON, R. J. (Eds.) (1989). *Sleep and alertness: Chronobiological, behavioral, and medical aspects of napping.* New York: Raven.

DOBB, E. (1989, November–December). The scents around us. *The Sciences, 29,* 46–53.

DOBELLE, W. H., MEADEJOVSKY, M. G., & GIRVIN, J. P. (1974). Artificial vision for the blind: Electrical stimulation of visual cortex offers hope for a functional prosthesis. *Science, 183,* 440–444.

DOLLARD, J., DOOB, L. W., MILLER, N. E., MOWRER, O. H., & SEARS, R. R. (1939). *Frustration and aggression.* New Haven, CT: Yale University Press.

DOMHOFF, G. W. (1985). *The mystique of dreams.* Berkeley: University of California Press.

DOMHOFF, G. W. (1996). *Finding meaning in dreams: A quantitative approach.* New York: Plenum.

DOMHOFF, G. W., & SCHNEIDER, A. (1998). The quantitative study of dreams. http://www.ucsc.edu.

DOMJAN, M., & BURKHARD, B. (1986). *The principles of learning and behavior.* Monterey, CA: Brooks/Cole.

DONCHIN, E. (1981). Surprise! . . . Surprise? *Psychophysiology, 18,* 493–513.

DOWLING, J. E., & BOYCOTT, B. B. (1966). Organization of the primate retina. *Proceedings of the Royal Society of London, Series b, 166,* 80–111.

DOYLE, A. C. (1892/1981). *The original illustrated Sherlock Holmes.* Secaucus,

NJ: Castle Books. (Originally published in America by Harper & Bros. in *McClure's Magazine,* 1893)

DUCLAUX, R., & KENSHALO, D. R. (1980). Response characteristics of cutaneous warm fibers in the monkey. *Journal of Neurophysiology, 43,* 1–15.

DUJARDIN, K., GUERRIEN, A., & LECONTE, P. (1990). Sleep, brain activation and cognition. *Physiology & Behavior, 47,* 1271–1278.

DUNCAN, J., & HUMPHREYS, G. W. (1989). Visual search and simulus similarity. *Psychological Review, 96,* 433–458.

DUNCAN, P. D., and collaborators (1985). The effects of pubertal timing on body image, school behavior, and deviance. *Journal of Youth and Adolescence, 14,* 227–235.

DUNCAN, R. D., SAUNDERS, D. E., KILPATRICK, D. G., HANSON, R. F., & RESNICK, H. S. (1996). Childhood physical assault as a risk factor for PTSD, depression, and substance abuse: Findings from a national survey. *American Journal of Orthopsychiatry, 66,* 437–448.

DUTTON, D. G., & ARON, A. P. (1974). Some evidence for heightened sexual attraction under conditions of high anxiety. *Journal of Personality and Social Pychology, 30,* 510–517.

EAGLY, A. H., & CHAIKEN, S. (1984). Cognitive theories of persuasion. In L. Berkowitz (Ed.), *Advances in experimental social psychology* (Vol. 17, pp. 267–359). New York: Academic Press.

EAGLY, A. H., & WOOD, W. (1999). The origins of sex differences in human behavior: Evolved dispositions versus social roles. *American Psychologist, 54,* 408–423.

EBBESEN, E., DUNCAN, B., & KONECNI, V. (1975). Effects of content of verbal aggression on future verbal aggression: A field experiment. *Journal of Experimental Psychology, 11,* 192–204.

EBBINGHAUS, H. (1885). *Uber das gedachthis.* Leipzig: Dunckes and Humbolt.

EDGAR, D. M., & DEMENT, W. C. (1992). Evidence for opponent processes in sleep/wake regulation. *Sleep Research, 20A,* 2.

EHLERS, A. (1995). A 1-year prospective study of panic attacks: Clinical course and factors associated with maintenance. *Journal of Abnormal Psychology, 104,* 164–172.

EHLERS, A., & BREUER, P. (1992). Increased cardiac awareness in panic disorder. *Journal of Abnormal Psychology, 101,* 371–382.

EHRHARDT, A. A., MEYER-BAHLBURG, H. F., ROSEN, L. R., FELDMAN, J. F., VERIDIANO, N. P., ELKIN, E. J., & MCEWEN, B. S. (1989). The development of gender-related behavior in females follow-

ing prenatal exposure to diethylstilbestrol (DES). *Hormones & Behavior, 23,* 526–541.

EIBL-EIBESFELDT, I. (1970). *Ethology: The biology of behavior* (E. Klinghammer, Trans.). New York: Holt, Rinehart & Winston.

EICH, J. E. (1980). The cue-dependent nature of state-dependent retrieval. *Memory and Cognition, 8,* 157–173.

EIMAS, P. D. (1975). Speech perception in early infancy. In L. B. Cohen & P. Salapatek (Eds.), *Infant perception: From sensation to cognition* (Vol. 2). New York: Academic Press.

EIMAS, P. D. (1985). The perception of speech in early infancy. *Scientific American, 252,* 46–52.

EKMAN, P. (1982). *Emotion in the human face* (2nd ed.). New York: Cambridge University Press.

EKSTROM, R. B., FRENCH, J. W., HARMAN, H. H., & DERMAN, D. (1976). *Manual for kit of factor-referenced cognitive tests, 1976.* Princeton, NJ: Educational Testing Service.

EKSTROM, R. B., FRENCH, J. W., & HARMAN, H. H. (1979). Cognitive factors: Their identification and replication. *Multivariate behavioral research monographs.* Fort Worth: Society for Multivariate Experimental Psychology.

ELKIN, I., SHEA, T., WATKINS, J. T., IMBER, S. D., SOTSKY, S. M., COLLINS, J. F., GLASS, D. R., PILKONIS, P. A., LEBER, W. R., DOCHERTY, J. P., FIESTER, S. J., & PARLOFF, M. B. (1989). National Institute of Mental Health treatment of depression collaborative research program: General effectiveness of treatments. *Archives of General Psychiatry, 46,* 971–982.

ELKIN, R. A., & LEIPPE, M. R. (1986). Physiological arousal, dissonance, and attitude change: Evidence of a dissonance-arousal link and a "don't remind me" effect. *Journal of Personality and Social Psychology, 51,* 55–65.

ELLIOT, A. J., & DEVINE, P. G. (1994). On the motivational nature of cognitive dissonance: Dissonance as psychological discomfort. *Journal of Personality and Social Psychology, 67,* 382–394.

ELLIS, L., & AMES, M. A. (1987). Neurohormonal functioning and sexual orientation: A theory of homosexuality-heterosexuality. *Psychological Bulletin, 2,* 233–258.

ELLISON, C. G., & LEVIN, J. S. (1998). The religion-health connection: Evidence, theory, and future directions. *Health Education & Behavior, 25,* 700–720.

ELLSWORTH, P. (1991). Some implications of cognitive appraisals on theories of emotion. In K. T. Strongman (Ed.), *International review of studies on emotion* (Vol. 1). New York: Wiley.

ELLSWORTH, P. C., & SMITH, C. A. (1988). Shades of joy: Patterns of appraisal differentiating pleasant emotions. *Cognition and Emotion, 2,* 301–331.

ELMES, D. G., KANTOWITZ, B. H., & ROEDIGER, H. L. (1989). *Research methods in psychology* (3rd ed.). St. Paul, MN: West.

EMMELKAMP, P. M. G. (1994). Behavior therapy with adults. In A. E. Bergin & S. L. Garfield (Eds.), *Handbook of psychotherapy and behavior change* (4th ed.) (pp. 379–427). New York: Wiley.

EMMELKAMP, P., & KUIPERS, A. (1979). Agoraphobia: A follow-up study four years after treatment. *British Journal of Psychiatry, 134,* 352–355.

ENGEN, T. (1982). *The perception of odors.* New York: Academic Press.

ENNS, J. T., & GIRGUS, J. S. (1985). Perceptual grouping and spatial distortion: A developmental study. *Developmental Psychology, 21,* 241–246.

ENNS, J. T., & PRINZMETAL, W. (1984). The role of redundancy in the object-line effect. *Perception & Psychophysics, 35,* 22–32.

ENNS, J. T., & RENSINK, R. A. (1990). Sensitivity to three-dimensional orientation in visual search. *Psychological Science, 1,* 323–326.

EPSTEIN, S., & MEIER, P. (1989). Constructive thinking: A broad coping variable with specific components. *Journal of Personality and Social Psychology, 57,* 332–350.

ERDELYI, M. H. (1985). *Psychoanalysis: Freud's cognitive psychology.* New York: Freeman.

ERICSSON, K. A., CHASE, W. G., & FALOON, S. (1980). Acquisition of a memory skill. *Science, 208,* 1181–1182.

ERICSSON, K. A., & SIMON, H. A. (1993). *Protocol analysis: Verbal reports as data* (rev. ed.). Cambridge, MA: MIT Press.

ERIKSON, E. H. (1963). *Childhood and society* (2nd ed.). New York: Norton.

ERIKSON, E. H. (1968). *Identity: Youth and crisis.* New York: Norton.

ERON, L. D. (1987). The development of aggressive behavior from the perspective of a developing behaviorism. *American Psychologist, 42,* 435–442.

ERON, L. D., HUESMANN, L. R., LEFKOWITZ, M. M., & WALDER, L. O. (1972). Does television violence cause aggression? *American Psychologist, 27,* 253–263.

ERVIN-TRIPP, S. (1964). Imitation and structural change in children's language. In E. H. Lenneberg (Ed.), *New directions in the study of language.* Cambridge, MA: MIT Press.

ESTERSON, A. (1993). *Seductive mirage: An exploration of the work of Sigmund Freud.* Chicago: Open Court.

ESTES, W. K. (1972). An associative basis for coding and organization in memory. In A. W. Melton & E. Martin (Eds.), *Coding processes in human memory.* Washington, DC: Winston.

ESTES, W. K. (1994). *Classification and cognition.* New York: Oxford University Press.

ESTES, W. K. (Ed.) (1975–1979). *Handbook of learning and cognitive processes* (Vols. 1–6). Hillsdale, NJ: Erlbaum.

ETCOFF, N. L. (1985). The neuropsychology of emotional expression. In G. Goldstein & R. E. Tarter (Eds.), *Advances in clinical neuropsychology* (Vol. 3). New York: Plenum.

EVANS, C. (1984). *Landscapes of the night: How and why we dream.* New York: Viking.

EXNER, J. (1986). *The Rorschach: A comprehensive system* (2nd ed., Vol. 1). New York: Wiley.

EYSENCK, H. J. (1953). *The structure of human personality.* New York: Wiley.

EYSENCK, H. J., & KAMIN, L. (1981). *The intelligence controversy.* New York: Wiley.

FABREGA, H. ULRICH, R. PILKONIS, P., & MEZZICH, J. (1991). On the homogeneity of personality disorder clusters. *Comprehensive Psychiatry, 32,* 373–386.

FAGOT, B. I. (1978). The influence of sex of child on parenteral reactions to toddler children. *Child Development, 49,* 459–465.

FAIRBURN, C. G., & HAY, P. J. (1992). Treatment of bulimia nervosa. *Annals of Medicine, 24,* 297–302.

FAIRBURN, C. G., NORMAN, P. A., WELCH, S. L., O'CONNOR, M. E., DOLL, H. A., & PEVELER, R. C. (1995). A prospective study of outcome in bulimia nervosa and the long-term effects of three psychological treatments. *Archives of General Psychiatry, 52,* 304–312.

FAIRBURN, C. G., WELCH, S. L., & HAY, P. J. (1993). The classification of recurrent overeating: The "binge eating disorder" proposal. Fifth International Conference on Eating Disorders (1992, New York). *International Journal of Eating Disorders, 13,* 155–159.

FALBO, T., & POLIT, D. F. (1986). Quantitative research of the only child literature: Research evidence and theory development. *Psychological Bulletin, 100,* 176–189.

FANTZ, R. L. (1961). The origin of form perception. *Science, 204,* 66–72.

FANTZ, R. L. (1970). Visual perception and experience in infancy: Issues and approaches. In *National Academy of Science, early experience and visual information processing in perceptual and reading disorders* (pp. 351–381). New York: National Academy of Science.

FARAH, M, HAMMOND, K. M., & LEVINE, D. N. (1988). Visual and spatial mental imagery: Dissociable systems of representation. *Cognitive Psychology, 20,* 439–462.

FARAH, M. J., & MCCLELLAND, J. L. (1991). A computational model of semantic memory impairment. *Journal of Experimental Psychology: General, 120,* 339–357.

FARAH, M. J. (1990). *Visual agnosia: Disorders of object recognition and what they tell us about normal vision.* Cambridge, MA: MIT Press.

FARAONE, S. V., KREMEN, W. J., & TSUANG, M. T. (1990). Genetic transmission of major affective disorders: Quantitative models and linkage analyses. *Psychological Bulletin, 108,* 109–127.

FARTHING, G. W. (1992). *The psychology of consciousness.* Englewood Cliffs, NJ: Prentice Hall.

FAUST, I. M. (1984). Role of the fat cell in energy balance physiology. In A. T. Stunkard & E. Stellar (Eds.), *Eating and its disorders.* New York: Raven Press.

FAVA, M., COPELAND, P. M., SCHWEIGER, U., & HERZOG, D. B. (1989). Neurochemical abnormalities of anorexia nervosa and bulimia nervosa. *American Journal of Psychiatry, 146,* 963–971.

FAZIO, R. H. (1990). Multiple processes by which attitudes guide behavior: The MODE model as an integrative framework. In M. P. Zanna (Ed.), *Advances in experimental social psychology* (Vol. 23). San Diego: Academic Press.

FAZIO, R., ZANNA, M. P., & COOPER, J. (1977). Dissonance and self-perception: An integrative view of each theory's proper domain of application. *Journal of Experimental Social Psychology, 13,* 464–479.

FECHNER, G. T. (1860/1966). *Elements of psychophysics* (H. E. Adler, Trans.). New York: Holt, Rinehart & Winston.

FEINGOLD, A. (1988). Cognitive gender differences are disappearing. *American Psychologist, 43,* 95–103.

FEINGOLD, A. (1990). Gender differences in effects of physical attractiveness on romantic attraction. *Journal of Personality and Social Psychology, 59,* 981–993.

FELDMAN, H., GOLDIN-MEADOW, S., & GLEITMAN, L. R. (1978). Beyond Herodotus: The creation of language by linguistically deprived children. In A. Lock (Ed.), *Action, gesture, and symbol: The emergence of language.* London: Academic Press.

FELDMAN, H., MEYER, & QUENZER. (1997). *Neuropharmacology.* New York: Sinauer.

FENWICK, P. (1987). Meditation and the EEG. In M. A. West (Ed.), *The psychol-*

ogy of meditation. Oxford, England: Oxford University Press.

FESHBACH, N. D. (1980, September). *The child as psychologist and economist: Two curricula.* Paper presented at the American Psychological Association convention, Montreal.

FESTINGER, L. (1957). *A theory of cognitive dissonance.* Stanford: Stanford University Press.

FESTINGER, L., & CARLSMITH, J. M. (1959). Cognitive consequences of forced compliance. *Journal of Abnormal and Social Psychology, 58,* 203–210.

FESTINGER, L., PEPITONE, A., & NEWCOMB, T. M. (1952). Some consequences of deindividuation in a group. *Journal of Abnormal and Social Psychology, 47,* 383–389.

FESTINGER, L., SCHACHTER, S., & BACK, K. (1950). *Social pressures in informal groups: A study of human factors in housing.* New York: Harper & Row.

FIELD, J. (1987). The development of auditory-visual localization in infancy. In B. E. McKenzie & R. H. Day (Eds.), *Perceptual development in early infancy.* Hillsdale, NJ: Erlbaum.

FIELD, T. (1991). Quality infant day care and grade school behavior and performance. *Child Development, 62,* 863–870.

FINCK, H. T. (1887). *Romantic love and personal beauty: Their development, causal relations, historic and national pecularities.* London: Macmillan.

FINKE, R. A. (1985). Theories relating mental imagery to perception. *Psychological Bulletin, 98,* 236–259.

FISHER, G. H. (1967). Preparation of ambiguous stimulus materials. *Perception and Psychophysics, 2,* 421–422.

FISHER, S., & GREENBERG, R. (1977). *The scientific credibility of Freud's theories and therapy.* New York: Basic Books.

FISHER, S., & GREENBERG, R. (1996). *Freud scientifically appraised.* New York: Wiley.

FISHMAN, P. (1983). Interaction: The work women do. In B. Thorne, C. Kramarae, & N. Henley (Eds.), *Language, gender, and society.* Rowley, MA: Newbury House.

FISKE, S. T. (1993). Social cognition and social perception. In L. Porter & M. R. Rosenzweig (Eds.), *Annual review of psychology* (Vol. 44, pp. 155–194).

FISKE, S. T., & TAYLOR, S. E. (1991). *Social cognition* (2nd ed.). New York: McGraw-Hill.

FITZSIMONS, J. T. (1969). The role of a renal thirst factor in drinking induced by extra cellular stimuli. *Journal of Physiology, London, 201,* 349–368.

FITZSIMONS, J. T. (1990). Thirst and sodium appetite. In E. M. Stricker

(Ed.), *Neurobiology of food and fluid intake* (pp. 23–44). New York: Plenum.

FIVUSH, R., & HAMOND, N. R. (1991). Autobiographical memory across the preschool years: Toward reconceptualizing childhood memory. In R. Fivush & N. R. Hamond (Eds.), *Knowing and remembering in young children.* New York: Cambridge University Press.

FIXSEN, D. L., PHILLIPS, E. L., PHILLIPS, E. A., & WOLF, M. M. (1976). The teaching-family model of group home treatment. In W. E. Craighead, A. E. Kazdin, & M. J. Mahoney (Eds.), *Behavior modification: Principles, issues, and applications.* Boston: Houghton Mifflin.

FLAVELL, J. H. (1992). *Cognitive development* (3rd ed.). Englewood Cliffs, NJ: Prentice Hall.

FLEMING, J., & DARLEY, J. M. (1986). *Perceiving intention in constrained behavior: The role of purposeful and constrained action cues in correspondence bias effects.* Unpublished manuscript, Princeton University, Princeton, NJ.

FLODERUS-MYRED, B., PETERSEN, N., & RASMUSON, I. (1980). Assessment of heritability for personality based on a short form of the Eysenck Personality Inventory. *Behavior Genetics, 10,* 153–161.

FLOR, H., FYDRICH, T., & TURK, D. C. (1992). Efficacy of multidisciplinary pain treatment: A meta-analytic review. *Pain, 49,* 221–230.

FLOWERS, M. L. (1977). A laboratory test of some implications of Janis's groupthink hypothesis. *Journal of Personality and Social Psychology, 35,* 888–896.

FLUOXETINE BULIMIA NERVOSA STUDY GROUP (1992). Fluoxetine in the treatment of bulimia nervosa: A multicenter, placebo-controlled, double-blind trial. *Archives of General Psychiatry, 49,* 156–162.

FLYNN, J. R. (1987). Massive IQ gains in 14 nations: What IQ tests really measure. *Psychological Bulletin, 101,* 171–191.

FOA, E., & STEKETEE, G. (1989). Obsessive-compulsive disorder. In C. Lindemann (Ed.), *Handbook of phobia therapy.* Northvale, NJ: Jason Aronson.

FOA, E. D., & RIGGS, D. S. (1995). Posttraumatic stress disorder following assault: Theoretical considerations and empirical findings. *Current Directions in Psychological Science, 4,* 61–65.

FODOR, J. A., BEVER, T. G., & GARRETT, M. F. (1974). *The psychology of language: An introduction to psycholinguistics and generative grammar.* New York: McGraw-Hill.

FOLKES, V. S. (1982). Forming relationships and the matching hypothesis.

Personality and Social Psychology Bulletin, 8, 631–636.

FORDYCE, W. E. (1976). *Behavioral methods for chronic pain and illness.* St. Louis, MO: C. V. Mosby.

FORGE, K. L., & PHEMISTER, S. (1987). The effect of prosocial cartoons on preschool children. *Child Development Journal, 17,* 83–88.

FOSS, D. J., & HAKES, D. T. (1978). *Psycholinguistics: An introduction to the psychology of language.* Englewood Cliffs, NJ: Prentice-Hall.

FOULKES, D. (1985). *Dreaming: A cognitive-psychological analysis.* Hillsdale, NJ: Erlbaum.

FOULKES, D. (1993). Data constraints on theorizing about dream function. In A. Moffitt, M. Kramer, & R. Hoffman (Eds.), *The functions of dreaming.* Albany: State University of New York Press.

FOULKES, D., & SCHMIDT, M. (1983). Temporal sequence and unit comparison composition in dream reports from different stages of sleep. *Sleep, 6,* 265–280.

FRABLE, D. E. (1989). Sex typing and gender ideology: Two facets of the individual's gender psychology that go together. *Journal of Personality and Social Psychology, 56,* 95–108.

FRANK, R. H. (1988). *Passions within reason: The strategic role of the emotions* (Ch. 1, pp. 1–19). New York: W. W. Norton.

FRANKENHAEUSER, M. (1983). The sympathetic-adrenal and pituitary-adrenal response to challenge: Comparison between the sexes. In T. M. Dembroski, T. H. Schmidt, & G. Blumchen (Eds.), *Biobehavioral bases of coronary heart disease.* Basel: Karger.

FRANKLIN, J. (1987). *Molecules of the mind.* New York: Atheneum.

FRANTZ, R. L. (1966). Pattern discrimination and selective attention as determinants of perceptual development from birth. In A. H. Kikk & J. F. Rivoire (Eds.), *Development of perception: Vol. 2. The visual system* (pp. 143–173). New York: International University Press.

FRAZIER, K. (1987). Psychic's imagined year fizzles (again). *Skeptical Inquirer, 11,* 335–336.

FREDRICKSON, B. L. (1998). What good are positive emotions? *Review of General Psychology, 2,* 300–319.

FREDRICKSON, B. L. (in press). Cultivating positive emotions to optimize health and well-being. *Prevention and Treatment.*

FREE, L. A., & CANTRIL, H. (1967). *The political beliefs of Americans.* New Brunswick, NJ: Rutgers University Press.

FREEDMAN, J. L. (1965). Long-term behavioral effects of cognitive dissonance. *Journal of Experimental Social Psychology, 1,* 145–155.

FREESTON, M. H., LADOUCEUR, R., THIBODEAU, N., & GAGNON, F. (1992). Cognitive intrusions in a non-clinical population: II. Associations with depressive, anxious, and compulsive symptoms. *Behaviour Research and Therapy, 30,* 263–271.

FREUD, A. (1958). Adolescence. *The Psychoanalytic Study of the Child, 13,* 255–278.

FREUD, A. (1946/1967). *The ego and the mechanisms of defense* (rev. ed.). New York: International Universities Press.

FREUD, S. (1885). *Ueber coca.* Vienna: Mortiz Perles. (Translated in Freud, 1974).

FREUD, S. (1885/1974). *Cocaine papers* (edited and introduction by R. Byck; notes by A. Freud). New York: Stonehill.

FREUD, S. (1900/1953). *The interpretation of dreams* (Reprint ed., Vols. 4, 5). London: Hogarth Press.

FREUD, S. (1901/1960). *Psychopathology of everyday life* (Standard ed., Vol. 6). London: Hogarth Press.

FREUD, S. (1905/1948). *Three contributions to theory of sex* (4th ed.; A. A. Brill, Trans.). New York: Nervous and Mental Disease Monograph.

FREUD, S. (1915/1976). Repression. In J. Strachey (Ed. and Trans.), *The complete psychological works: Standard edition* (Vol. 14). London: Hogarth Press.

FREUD, S. (1920/1975). *Beyond the pleasure principle.* New York: Norton.

FREUD, S. (1925/1961). Some psychical consequences of the anatomical distinctions between the sexes. In J. Strachey (Ed. and Trans.), *The complete psychological works: Standard edition* (Vol. 18). London: Hogarth Press.

FREUD, S. (1933/1964). *New introductory lectures on psychoanalysis* (J. Strachey, Ed. and Trans.). New York: Norton.

FREUD, S. (1933/1965). Revision of the theory of dreams. In J. Strachey (Ed. and Trans.), *New introductory lectures on psychoanalysis* (Vol. 22, Lect. 29). New York: Norton.

FREUD, S. (1940). An outline of psychoanalysis. *International Journal of Psychoanalysis, 21,* 27–84.

FRIEDMAN, M., & ROSENMAN, R. H. (1974). *Type A behavior.* New York: Knopf.

FRIEDMAN, M., THORESEN, C. E., GILL, J. J., ULMER, D., POWELL, L. H., PRICE, V., BROWN, B., THOMPSON, L., RABIN, D. D., and collaborators (1994). Alteration of Type A behavior and its effect on cardiac recurrences in post myocardial infarction patients: Summary results of the recurrent coronary prevention project. In A. Steptoe (Ed.), *Psychosocial processes and health: A reader.* Cambridge, England: Cambridge University Press.

FRIEDMAN, M. I. (1990). Making sense out of calories. In E. M. Stricker (Eds.), *Neurobiology of food and fluid intake* (pp. 513–528). New York: Plenum.

FRIJDA, N. H. (1986). *The emotions.* Cambridge, England: Cambridge University Press.

FRIJDA, N. H., KUIPERS, P., & SCHURE, E. (1989). Relations among emotion, appraisal, and emotional action readiness. *Journal of Personality and Social Psychology, 57,* 212–228.

FRISCHHOLZ, E. J. (1985). The relationship among dissociation, hyponosis, and child abuse in the development of multiple personality disorder. In R. P. Kluft (Ed.), *Childhood antecedents of multiple personality.* Washington, DC: American Psychiatric Press.

FRODI, A., & THOMPSON, R. (1985). Infants' affective responses in the strange situation: Effects of prematurity and of quality of attachment. *Child Development, 56,* 1280–1290.

FUGH-BERMAN, A., & COTT, J. M. (1999). Dietary supplements and natural products as psychotherapeutic agents. *Psychosomatic Medicine, 61,* 712–728.

FUNKENSTEIN, D. (1955). The physiology of fear and anger. *Scientific American, 192,* 74–80.

FYER, A. J., MANNUZZA, S., CHAPMAN, T. F., & LIEBOWITZ, M. R. (1993). A direct interview family study of social phobia. *Archives of General Psychiatry, 50,* 286–293.

FYER, A. J., MANNUZZA, S., GALLOPS, M. S., & MARTIN, L. Y. (1990). Familial transmission of simple phobias and fears: A preliminary report. *Archives of General Psychiatry, 47,* 252–256.

GADOW, K. D. (1991). Clinical issues in child and adolescent psychopharmacology. *Journal of Consulting and Clinical Psychology, 59,* 842–852.

GADOW, K. D. (1992). Pediatric psychopharmacotherapy: A review of recent research. *Journal of Child Psychology and Psychiatry,* 153–195.

GALANTER, E. (1962). Contemporary psychophysics. In R. Brown & collaborators (Eds.), *New directions in psychology* (Vol. 1). New York: Holt, Rinehart & Winston.

GALINSKY, E., HOWES, C., KONTOS, S., & SHINN, M. (1994). The study of children in family child care and relative care: Highlights of findings.

GALLUP ORGANIZATION (1995). *Sleep in America: A national survey of U.S. adults.* Poll conducted for the National Sleep Foundation. Princeton, NJ: National Sleep Foundation.

GALOTTI, K. M. (1989). Approaches to studying formal and everyday reasoning. *Psychological Bulletin, 105,* 331–351.

GAMSON, W. B., FIREMAN, B., & RYTINA, S. (1982). *Encounters with unjust authority.* Homewood, IL: Dorsey Press.

GANELLEN, R. J., & CARVER, C. S. (1985). Why does self-reference promote incidental encoding? *Journal of Personality and Social Psychology, 21,* 284–300.

GARCIA, L. T., ERSKINE, N., HAWN, K., & CASMAY, S. R. (1981). The effect of affirmative action on attributions about minority group members. *Journal of Personality, 49,* 427–437.

GARCIA, J., & KOELLING, R. A. (1966). The relation of cue to consequence in avoiding learning. *Psychonomic Science, 4,* 123–124.

GARDNER, B. T., & GARDNER, R. A. (1972). Two-way communication with an infant chimpanzee. In A. M. Schrier & F. Stollnitz (Eds.), *Behavior of nonhuman primates* (Vol. 4). New York: Academic Press.

GARDNER, E. L. (1992). Brain reward mechanisms. In J. H. Lowinson, P. Ruiz, & R. B. Millman (Eds.), *Substance abuse: A comprehensive textbook* (2nd ed.). Baltimore, MD: Williams & Wilkins.

GARDNER, H. (1975). *The shattered mind.* New York: Knopf.

GARDNER, H. (1985). *The mind's new science: A history of the cognitive revolution.* New York: Basic Books.

GARDNER, H. (1993a). *Frames of mind: The theory of multiple intelligences.* New York: Basic Books.

GARDNER, H. (1993b). *Multiple intelligences: The theory in practice.* New York: Basic Books.

GARDNER, H. KORNHABER, M. L., & WAKE, W. K. (1996). *Intelligence: Multiple perspectives.* Fort Worth: Harcourt Brace.

GARDNER, M. (1981). *Science: Good, bad, and bogus.* New York: Prometheus.

GARDNER, W., LIDZ, C. W., MULVEY, E. P., & SHAW, E. C. (1996). Clinical versus actuarial predictions of violence in patients with mental illnesses. *Journal of Consulting and Clinical Psychology, 64,* 602–609.

GARFIELD, S. L. (1994). Research on client variables in psychotherapy. In S. L. Garfield & A. E. Bergen (Eds.), *Handbook of psychotherapy and behavior change* (pp. 190–228). New York: Wiley.

GARNER, D. M., & GARFINKEL, P. E. (1980). Socio-cultural factors in the development of anorexia nervosa. *Psychological Medicine, 10,* 647–656.

GARRETT, M. (1997). The effects of infant child care on infant-mother attachment security: Results of the NICHD Study of Early Child Care. *Child Development, 68,* 860–879.

GARRETT, M. F. (1990). Sentence processing. In D. N. Osherson & H. Lasnik, *An invitation to cognitive science: Language* (Vol. 1). Cambridge, MA: MIT Press.

GARRY, M., MANNING, C., LOFTUS, E. F., & SHERMAN, S. J. (1996). Imagination inflation. *Psychonomic Bulletin and Review, 3,* 208–214.

GATES, A. I. (1917). Recitation as a factor in memorizing. *Archives of Psychology,* No. 40.

GAW, A. (1993). *Culture, ethnicity, and mental illness.* Washington, DC: American Psychiatric Press.

GAZZANIGA, M. S. (1985). *The social brain: Discovering the networks of mind.* New York: Basic Books.

GEEN, R. G. (1990). *Human aggression.* Pacific Grove, CA: Brooks/Cole.

GELLATLY, A. R. H. (1987). Acquisition of a concept of logical necessity. *Human Development, 30,* 32–47.

GENTER, D., & STEVENS, A. L. (1983). *Mental models.* Hillsdale, NJ: Erlbaum.

GERSHON, E. S. (1990). Genetics. In F. K. Goodwin & K. R. Jamison (Eds.), *Manic-depressive illness* (pp. 373–401). New York: Oxford University Press.

GESCHWIND, N. (1972). Language and the brain. *Scientific American, 226,* 76–83.

GESCHWIND, N. (1979). Specializations of the human brain. *Scientific American, 241,* 180–199.

GESELL, A., & THOMPSON, H. (1929). Learning and growth in identical twins: An experimental study by the method of co-twin control. *Genetic Psychology Monographs, 6,* 1–123.

GHEORGHIU, V. A., NETTER, P. EYSENCK, H. J., & ROSENTHAL, R. (Eds.) (1989). *Suggestion and suggestibility: Theory and research.* New York: Springer-Verlag.

GIANOULAKIS, C., KRISHNAN, B., & THAVUNDAYIL, J. (1996). Enhanced sensitivity of pituitary ß-endoorphin to ethanol in subjects at high risk of alcoholism. *Archives of General Psychiatry, 53,* 250–257.

GIBSON, E. J., & WALK, R. D. (1960). The "visual cliff." *Scientific American, 202,* 64–71.

GILBERT, D. T., & JONES, E. E. (1986). Perceiver-induced constraint: Interpretations of self-generated reality. *Journal of Personality and Social Psychology, 50,* 269–280.

GILCHRIST, A. L. (1988). Lightness contrast and failures of constancy: A common explanation. *Perception & Psychophysics, 43,* 415–424.

GILLGAN, C. (1982). *In a different voice.* Cambridge, MA: Harvard University Press.

GILLIN, J. C. (1985). Sleep and dreams. In G. L. Klerman, M. M. Weissman, P. S. Applebaum, & L. H. Roth (Eds.), *Psychiatry* (Vol. 3). Philadelphia: Lippincott.

GINSBERG, A. (1983). *Contrast perception in the human infant.* Unpublished manuscript.

GLANZER, M. (1972). Storage mechanisms in recall. In G. H. Bower & J. T. Spence (Eds.), *The psychology of learning and motivation* (Vol. 5). New York: Academic Press.

GLASER, R., RICE, J., SPEICHER, C. E., STOUT, J. C., & KIECOLT-GLASER, J. K. (1986). Stress depresses interferon production by leukocytes concomitant with a decrease in natural killer cell activity. *Behavioral Neuroscience, 100,* 675–678.

GLASS, D. C., & SINGER, J. E. (1972). *Urban stress: Experiments on noise and social stressors.* New York: Academic Press.

GLASS, G. V., MCGAW, B., & SMITH, M. L. (1981). *Meta-analysis in social research.* Beverly Hills, CA: Sage

GLEITMAN, H. (1986). *Psychology* (2nd ed.). New York: Norton.

GLEITMAN, L. R. (1986). Biological predispositions to learn language. In P. Marler & H. S. Terrace (Eds.), *The biology of learning.* New York: Springer-Verlag.

GODDEN, D., & BADDELEY, A. D. (1975). Context-dependent memory In two natural environments: On land and under water. *British Journal of Psychology, 66,* 325–331.

GOETHALS, G. P., & ZANNA, M. P. (1979). The role of social comparison in choice shifts. *Journal of Personality and Social Psychology, 37,* 1469–1476.

GOLDEN, H., HINKLE, S., & CROSBY, F. J. (1998). Affirmative action: Semantics and Substance. *Institute for Research on Women and Gender Working Papers.* Ann Arbor, MI: University of Michigan.

GOLDIN-MEADOW, S. (1982). The resilience of recursion: A structure within a conventional model. In E. Wanner & L. R. Gleitman (Eds.), *Language acquisition: The state of the art.* Cambridge, England: Cambridge University Press.

GOLDMAN-RAKIC, P. S. (1987). Circuitry of primate prefrontal corex and regulation of behavior by representational memory. In F. Plum (Ed.), *Handbook of physiology: The nervous system.* Bethesda, MD: American Physiology Society.

GOLDMAN-RAKIC, P. S. (1996). Regional and cellular fractionation of working memory. *Proceedings of the National Academy of Science of the United States of America, 93,* 13473–13480.

GOLDSTEIN, A. (1994). *Addiction: From biology to drug policy.* New York: Freeman.

GOLDSTEIN, E. B. (1989). *Sensation and perception* (3rd ed.). Belmont, CA: Wadsworth.

GOLDSTEIN, M. (1987). Family interaction patterns that antedate the onset of schizophrenia and related disorders: A further analysis of data from a longitudinal prospective study. In K. Hahlweg & M. Goldstein (Eds.), *Understanding major mental disorders: The contribution of family interaction research* (pp. 11–32). New York: Family Process Press.

GOLDSTEIN, M. J., TALOVIC, S. A., NUECHTERLEIN, K. H., & FOGELSON, D. L. (1992). Family interaction versus individual psychopathology: Do they indicate the same processes in the families of schizophrenia? *British Journal of Psychiatry, 161,* 97–102.

GOLEMAN, D. (1995, May 2). Biologists find the site of working memory. *New York Times.*

GOLEMAN, D. J. (1988, October 18). Chemistry of sexual desire yields its elusive secret. *New York Times.*

GOODALL, J. (1978). Chimp killings: Is it the man in them? *Science News, 113,* 276.

GOODGLASS, H., & BUTTERS, N. (1988). Psychobiology of cognitive processes. In R. C. Atkinson, R. J. Hernstein, G. Lindzey, & R. D. Luce (Eds.), *Stevens' handbook of experimental psychology* (Vol. 2). New York: Wiley.

GOODWIN, F. K., & JAMISON, K. R. (1990). *Manic-depressive illness.* New York: Oxford University Press.

GORDON, W. (1989). *Learning & memory.* Pacific Grove, CA: Brooks/Cole.

GOTTESMAN, I. I. (1991). *Schizophrenia genesis: The origins of madness.* New York: W. H. Freeman.

GOTTFRIED, A. E., FLEMING, J. S., & GOTTFRIED, A. W. (1998). The role of cognitively stimulating home environment on children's academic intrinsic motivation. *Child Development, 69,* 1448–1460.

GOY, R. W. (1968). Organizing effect of androgen on the behavior of rhesus monkeys. In R. F. Michael (Ed.), *Endocrinology of human behaviour.* London: Oxford University Press.

GRADY, C. L., HAXBY, J. V., HORWITZ, B., SCHAPIRO, M. B., RAPOPORT, S. I., UNGERLEIDER, L. G., MISHKIN, M., CARSON, R. E., & HERSCOVITCH, P. (1992). Dissociation of object and spatial vision in human extrastriate cortex: Age-related changes in activation of regional cerebral blood flow measured with [15O] water and positron emission tomography. *Journal of Cognitive Neuroscience, 4,* 23–34.

GRAF, P., & MANDLER, G. (1984). Activation makes words more accessible, but not necessarily more retrievable. *Journal of Verbal Learning and Verbal Behavior, 23,* 553–568.

GRAF, P., & MASSON, M. E. J. (Eds.) (1993). *Implicit memory: New directions in cognition, development, and neuropsychology.* Hillsdale, NJ: Lawrence Erlbaum.

GRAHAM, J. R. (1990). *The MIMPI-2: Assessing personality and psychopathology.* New York: Oxford University Press.

GRANRUD, C. E. (1986). Binocular vision and spatial perception in 4- and 5-month old infants. *Journal of Experimental Psychology: Human Perception and Performance, 12,* 36–49.

GRAY, E., & COSGROVE, J. (1985). Ethnocentric perception of childbearing practices in protective services. *Child Abuse and Neglect 9,* 389–396.

GRAY, J. (1982). Precis of the neuropsychology of anxiety: An enquiry into the functions of the septo-hippocampal system. *Behavioural & Brain Sciences, 5,* 469–534.

GRAY, J. A. (1987). *The psychology of fear and stress* (2nd ed.). Cambridge, England: Cambridge University Press.

GRAY, J. A. (1971). *The psychology of fear and stress.* London: Weidenfeld & Nicholson.

GREEN, B. L., LINDY, J. D., GRACE, M. C., & LEONARD, A. C. (1992). Chronic post-traumatic stress disorder and diagnostic comorbidity in a disaster sample. *Journal of Nervous and Mental Disease, 180,* 760–766.

GREEN, D. M., & WIER, C. C. (1984). Auditory perception. In I. Darian-Smith (Ed.), *Handbook of physiology* (Vol. 3). Bethesda, MD: American Physiological Society.

GREEN, J. G., FOX, N. A., & LEWIS, M. (1983). The relationship between neonatal characteristics and three-month mother-infant interaction in high-risk infants. *Child Development, 54,* 1286–1296.

GREEN, R. (1987). *The "sissy boy syndrome" and the development of homosexuality.* New Haven, CT: Yale University Press.

GREENFIELD, P. M., & SAVAGE-RUMBAUGH, S. (1990). Grammatical combination in *Pan Paniscus:* Processes of learning and invention in the evolution and development of language. In S. Parker & K. Gibson (Eds.), *"Language" and intelligence in monkeys and apes: Comparative developmental perspectives.* New York: Cambridge University Press.

GREENWALD, A. G. (1968). Cognitive learning, cognitive response to persuasion, and attitude change. In A. G. Greenwald, T. C. Brock, & T. M. Ostrom (Eds.), *Psychological foundations of attitudes.* New York: Academic Press.

GREENWALD, A. G. (1992). Unconscious cognition reclaimed. *American Psychologist, 47,* 766–779.

GRICE, H. P. (1975). Logic and conversation. In G. Harman & D. Davidson (Eds.), *The logic of grammar.* Encino, CA: Dickinson.

GRIGGS, R. A., & COX, J. R. (1982). The elusive thermatic-materials effect in Watson's selection task. *British Journal of Psychology, 73,* 407–420.

GRILL, H. J., & KAPLAN, J. M. (1990). Caudal brainstem participates in the distributed neural control of feeding. In E. M. Stricker (Ed.), *Neurobiology of food and fluid intake* (pp. 125–149). New York: Plenum Press.

GRODZINSKY, Y. (1984). The syntactic characterization of agrammatism. *Cognition, 16,* 99–120.

GROVES, P. M., & REBEC, G. V. (1992). *Introduction to biological psychology* (4th ed.). Dubuque, IA: Brown.

GRÜNBAUM, A. (1984). *The foundations of psychoanalysis.* Berkeley, CA: University of California Press.

GRUNWALD, J. (1995). The European phytomedicines: Market figures, trends, analyses. *Herbalgram, 34,* 60–65.

GUILFORD, J. P. (1982). Cognitive psychology's ambiguities: Some suggested remedies. *Psychological Review, 89,* 48–49.

GUMPERZ, J. J., & LEVINSON, S. C. (Eds.) (1996). *Rethinking linguistic relativity.* Cambridge: Cambridge University Press.

GURNEY, R. (1936). The hereditary factor in obesity. *Archives of Internal Medicine, 57,* 557–561.

HAAGA, D. A. F., DYCK, M. J., & ERNST, D. (1991). Empirical status of cognitive theory of depression. *Psychological Bulletin, 110,* 215–236.

HABER, R. N. (1969). Eidetic images. *Scientific American, 220,* 36–55.

HABER, R. N. (1979). Twenty years of haunting edetic imagery: Where's the ghost? *Behavioral and Brain Sciences, 24,* 583–629.

HABERLANDT, K. (1993). *Cognitive psychology.* Boston, MA: Allyn and Bacon.

HAITH, M. M. (1998), Who put the cog in infant cognition? Is rich interpretation too costly? *Infant Behavior & Development, 21,* 167–180.

HAITH, M. M., BERGMAN, T., & MOORE, M. J. (1977). Eye contact and face scanning in early infancy. *Science, 198,* 853–855.

HALL, C., & VAN DE CASTLE, R. (1966). *The content analysis of dreams.* New York: Appleton-Century-Crofts.

HALL, C. S. (1947). Diagnosing personality by the analysis of dreams. *Journal of Abnormal and Social Psychology, 42,* 68–79.

HALL, C. S. (1953). A cognitive theory of dreams. *Journal of General Psychology, 48,* 169–186.

HAMER, D. H., HU, S., MAGNUSON, V. L., HU, N., et al. (1993). A linkage between DNA markers on the X chromosome and male sexual orientation. *Science, 261,* 321–327.

HAMER, D., & COPELAND, P. (1994). *The science of desire: The search for the gay gene and the biology of behavior.* New York: Simon & Schuster.

HAMILTON, D. L. (1979). A cognitive-attributional analysis of stereotyping. In L. Berkowitz (Ed.), *Advances in experimental social psychology* (Vol. 12). New York: Academic Press.

HAMILTON, D. L., & GIFFORD, R. K. (1976). Illusory correlation in interpersonal perception: A cognitive basis of stereotypic judgments. *Journal of Experimental Social Psychology, 12,* 392–407.

HAMILTON, D. L., & SHERMAN, S. J. (1989). Illusory correlations: Implications for stereotype theory and research. In D. Bar-Tal, C. F. Gravmann, A. W. Kruglanski, & W. Stroebe (Eds.), *Stereotypes and predjudice: Changing conceptions.* New York: Springer-Verlag.

HARDIN, C. L., & MAFFI, L. (Eds.) (1997). *Color categories in thought and language.* Cambridge: Cambridge University Press.

HARE, R. D. (1980). A research scale for the assessment of psychopathy in criminal populations. *Personality and Individual Differences, 1,* 111–119.

HARLOW, H. F. (1971). *Learning to love.* San Francisco: Albion.

HARLOW, H. F., & HARLOW, M. K. (1969). Effects of various mother-infant relationships on rhesus monkey behaviors. In B. M. Foss (Ed.), *Determinants of infant behavior* (Vol. 4). London: Methuen.

HARRIS, B. (1979). Whatever happened to little Albert? *American Psychologist, 34,* 151–160.

HARRIS, J. R. (1995). Where is the child's environment? A group socialization theory of development. *Psychological Review, 102,* 458–489.

HARRIS, J. R. (1998). *The nurture assumption.* New York: Free Press.

HARRIS, M. J., & ROSENTHAL, R. (1988). *Interpersonal expectancy effects and human performance research.* Washington, DC: National Academy Press.

HARRIS, P. R. (1996). Sufficient grounds for optimism?: The relationship between perceived controllability and optimistic bias. *Journal of Social and Clinical Psychology, 15,* 9–52.

HARTMANN, E. (1968). The day residue: Time distribution of waking events. *Psychophysiology, 5,* 222.

HATFIELD, E. (1988). Passionate and companionate love. In R. J. Sternberg & M. L. Barnes (Eds.), *The psychology of love* (pp. 191–217). New Haven, CT: Yale University Press.

HATHAWAY, S. R., & MCKINLEY, J. C. (1943). *Manual for the Minnesota Multiphasic Personality Inventory.* New York: Psychological Corporation.

HAWKINS, R. D., & KANDEL, E. R. (1984). Is there a cell-biological alphabet for simple forms of learning? *Psychological Review, 91,* 375–391.

HAXBY, J. V., GRADY, C. L., HORWIZ, B., UNGERLEIDER, L. G., MISHKIN, M., CARSON, R. E., HERSCOVITCH, P., SCHAPIRO, M. B., & RAPOPORT, S. I. (1990). Dissociation of object and spatial visual processing pathways in human extrastriate cortex. *Neurobiology, 88,* 1621–1625.

HAYES, J. R. (1989). *The complete problem solver* (2nd ed.). Hillsdale, NJ: Erlbaum.

HAYES, L. A., & WATSON, J. S. (1981). Neonatal imitation: Fact or artifact. *Developmental Psychology, 17,* 655–660.

HAYNE, H., ROVEE-COLLIER, C., & BORZA, M. A. (1991). Infant memory for place information. *Memory and Cognition, 19,* 378–386.

HAYNES, S. G., & FEINLEIB, M. (1980). Women, work, and coronary heart disease: Prospective findings from the Framingham heart study. *American Journal of Public Health, 70,* 133–141.

HAYNES, S. G., FEINLEIB, M., & KANNEL, W. B. (1980). The relationship of psychosocial factors to coronary heart disease in the Framingham study: Pt. 3. Eight-year incidence of coronary heart disease. *American Journal of Epidemiology, 111,* 37–58.

HAZAN, C., & DIAMOND, L. (in press). Place of attachment in human mating. *Review of General Psychology,* 186–204.

HE, Z. J., & NAKAYAMA, K. (1992). Surfaces versus features in visual search. *Nature, 359,* 231–233.

HEATH, R. G. (1972). Pleasure and brain activity in man. Deep and surface electroencephalograms during orgasm. *Journal of Nervous and Mental Disease, 154,* 3–18.

HEBB, D. O. (1982). Understanding psychological man: A state-of-the-science report. *Psychology Today, 16,* 52–53.

HECHT, S., SHALER, S., & PIREENE, M. H. (1942). Energy, quanta, and vision. *Journal of General Physiology, 25,* 819–840.

HEIDER, F. (1958). *The psychology of interpersonal relations.* New York: Wiley.

HEILBRUN, K. S. (1982). Silverman's subliminal psychodynamic activation: A failure to replicate. *Journal of Abnormal Psychology, 89,* 560–566.

HEILMAN, M. E. (1994). Affirmative action: Some unintended consequences for working women. In B. M. Staw & L. L. Cummings (Eds.), *Research in organizational behavior* (Vol. 16, pp. 125–169). Greenwich, CT: JAI Press.

HEILMAN, M. E., BLOCK, C. J., & LUCAS, J. A. (1992). Presumed incompetent? Stigmatization and affirmative action efforts. *Journal of Applied Psychology, 77,* 536–544.

HEILMAN, M. E., BLOCK, C. J., & STATHATOS, P. (1997). The affirmative action stigma of incompetence: Effects of performance information. *Academy of Management Journal, 40,* 603–625.

HEILMAN, M. E., MCCULLOUGH, W. F., & GILBERT, D. (1996). The other side of affirmative action: Reactions of non-beneficiaries to sex-based preferential selection. *Journal of Applied Psychology, 81*(4), 346–357.

HELBURN, S. W. (Ed.) (1995). *Cost, quality and child outcomes in child care centers.* Denver: University of Colorado.

HELD, R. (1965). Plasticity in sensory motor systems. *Scientific American, 21,* 84–94.

HELD, R., & HEIN, A. (1963). Movement produced stimulation in the development of visually guided behavior. *Journal of Comparative and Physiological Psychology, 56,* 872–876.

HELLIGE, J. B. (1990). Hemispheric asymmetry. *Annual Review of Psychology, 41,* 55–80.

HELLIGE, J. B. (1993). Unity of thought and action: Varieties of interaction between left and right hemispheres. *Current Directions in Psychological Science, 2,* 21–25.

HEMMI, T. (1969). How we have handled the problem of drug abuse in Japan. In F. Sjoqvist & M. Tottie (Eds.), *Abuse of central stimulants.* New York: Raven Press.

HENCHY, T., & GLASS, D. C. (1968). Evaluation apprehension and social facilitation of dominant and subordinate responses. *Journal of Personality and Social Psychology, 10,* 445–454.

HENDIN, H. (1995). *Suicide in America.* New York: W.W. Norton.

HENLEY, N., HAMILTON, M., & THORNE, B. (1985). Womanspeak and manspeak: Sex differences and sexism in communication, verbal and nonverbal. In A. G. Sargent (Ed.), *Beyond sex roles.* St. Paul, MN: West.

HENSEL, H. (1973). Cutaneous thermoreceptors. In A. Iggo (Ed.), *Handbook of sensory physiology* (Vol. 2). Berlin: Springer-Verlag.

HERDT, G. H. (Ed.) (1984). *Ritualized homosexuality in melanesia.* Berkeley: University of California Press.

HEREK, G. M. (1986). The instrumentality of attitudes: Toward a neofunctional theory. *Journal of Social Issues, 42,* 99–114.

HEREK, G. M. (1987). Can functions be measured? A new perspective on the functional approach to attitudes. *Social Psychology Quarterly, 50,* 285–303.

HERING, E. (1878). *Outlines of a theory of the light sense* (L. M. Hurvich & D. Jameson, Trans.). Cambridge, MA: Harvard University Press.

HERING, E. (1920). Memory as a universal function of organized matter. In S. Butler (Ed.), *Unconscious memory.* London: Jonathon Cape.

HERMAN, C. P., & MACK, D. (1975). Restrained and unrestrained eating. *Journal of Personality, 43,* 647–660.

HERMAN, C. P., & POLIVY, J. (1980). Restrained eating. In A. J. Stunkard (Ed.), *Obesity.* Philadelphia: Saunders.

HERRNSTEIN, R. J., & MURRAY, C. (1994). *The bell curve: Intelligence and class structure in American life.* New York: Free Press.

HESS, E. H. (1972). "Imprinting" in a natural laboratory. *Scientific American, 227,* 24–31.

HETHERINGON, E. M., & BRACKBILL, Y. (1963). Etiology and covariation of obstinacy, orderliness, and parsimony in young children. *Child Development, 34,* 919–943.

HILGARD, E. R. (1965). *Hypnotic susceptibility.* New York: Harcourt Brace Jovanovich.

HILGARD, E. R. (1968). *The experience of hypnosis.* New York: Harcourt Brace Jovanovich.

HILGARD, E. R. (1986). *Divided consciousness: Multiple controls in human thought and action.* New York: Wiley-Interscience.

HILGARD, E. R. (1987). *Psychology in America: A historical survey.* San Diego: Harcourt Brace Javanovich.

HILGARD, E. R., & HILGARD, J. R. (1975). *Hypnosis in the relief of pain.* Los Altos, CA: Kaufmann.

HILGARD, E. R., HILGARD, J. R., MACDONALD, H., MORGAN, A. H., & JOHNSON, L. S. (1978). Covert pain in hypnotic analgesia: Its reality as tested by the real-simulator design. *Journal of Abnormal Psychology, 87,* 655–663.

HILL, C., RUBIN, Z., & PEPLAU, L. A. (1976). Breakups before marriage: The end of 103 affairs. *Journal of Social Issues, 32,* 147–168.

HILLIER, L., HEWITT, K. L., & MORRONGIELTO, B. A. (1992). Infants' perception of illusions in sound localization: Reaching to sounds in the dark. *Journal of Experimental Child Psychology, 53,* 159–179.

HILLYARD, S. A. (1985). Electrophysiology of human selective attention. *Trends in Neuroscience, 8,* 400–406.

HINDE, R. (1982). *Ethology: Its nature and relations with other sciences.* New York: Oxford Universities Press.

HINSHAW, S. P. (1994). *Attention deficits and hyperactivity in children.* Thousand Oaks, CA: Sage.

HIRSCH, J., & BATCHELOR, B. R. (1976). Adipose tissue cellularity and human obesity. *Clinical Endocrinology and Metabolism, 5,* 299–311.

HOBSON, J. A. (1988). *The dreaming brain.* New York: Basic Books.

HOBSON, J. A. (1989). *Sleep.* New York: Freeman.

HOBSON, J. A. (1994). *The chemistry of conscious states, how the brain changes its mind.* New York: Little, Brown.

HOBSON, J. A. (1997). Dreaming as delirium: A mental status analysis of our nightly madness. *Seminars in Neurology, 1,* 121–128.

HOEBEL, B. G., & TEITELBAUM, P. (1966). Effects of force-feeding and starvation on food intake and body weight on a rat with ventromedial hypothalamic lesions. *Journal of Comparative and Physiological Psychology, 61,* 189–193.

HOFLING, C. K., BROTZMAN, E., DALRYMPLE, S., GRAVES, N., & PIERCE, C. M. (1966). An experimental study in nurse-physician relationships. *Journal of Nervous and Mental Disease, 143,* 171–180.

HOGARTY, G. E. (1986). Family psychoeducation, social skills training, and maintenance chemotherapy in the aftercare treatment of schizophrenia: I. One-year effects of a controlled study on relapse and expressed emotion. *Archives of General Psychiatry, 43,* 633–642.

HOGARTY, G. E., SCHOOLER, N. R., ULRICH, R., MUSSARE, F., FERRO, P., & HERRON, E. (1979). Fluphenazine and social therapy in the after care of schizophrenic patients. *Archives of General Psychiatry, 36,* 1283–1294.

HOHMANN, G. W. (1962). Some effects of spinal cord lesions on experienced emotional feelings. *Psychophysiology, 3,* 143–156.

HOLLAND, J. H., HOLYOAK, K. J., NISBETT, R. E., & THAGARD, P. R. (1986). *Induction: Processes of inference, learning, and discovery.* Cambridge, MA: MIT Press.

HOLLOWAY, F. A. (1989). What is affirmative action? In F. A. Blanchard & F. J. Crosby (Eds.), *Affirmative action in perspective* (pp. 9–19). New York: Springer Verlag.

HOLMES, D. S. (1974). Investigations of repression: Differential recall of material experimentally or naturally associated with ego threat. *Psychological Bulletin, 81,* 632–653.

HOLMES, D. S. (1984). Meditation and somatic arousal reduction: A review of the experimental evidence. *American Psychologist, 39,* 1–10.

HOLMES, D. S. (1985a). To meditate or rest? The answer is rest. *American Psychologist, 40,* 728–731.

HOLMES, D. S. (1985b). Self-control of somatic arousal: An examination of the effects of meditation and feedback. *American Behavioral Scientist, 28,* 486–496.

HOLMES, T. H., & RAHE, R. H. (1967). The social readjustment rating scale. *Journal of Psychosomatic Research, 11,* 213–218.

HOLROYD, K. A., APPEL, M. A., & ANDRASIK, F. (1983). A cognitive behavioral approach to psychophysiological disorders. In D. Meichenbaum & M. E. Jaremko (Eds.), *Stress reduction and prevention.* New York: Plenum.

HONIG, W. K., & STADDON, J. E. R. (Eds.) (1977). *Handbook of operant behavior.* Englewood Cliffs, NJ: Prentice-Hall.

HONORTON, C. (1985). Meta-analysis of psi ganzfeld research: A response to Hyman. *Journal of Parapsychology, 49,* 51–91.

HOOLEY, J. M., RICHTERS, J. E., WEINTRAUB, S., & NEALE, J. M. (1987). Psychopathology and marital distress: The positive side of positive symptoms. *Journal of Abnormal Psychology, 96,* 27–33.

HOON, P. W., WINCZE, J. P., & HOON, E. F. (1977). A test of reciprocal inhibition: Are anxiety and sexual arousal in women mutually inhibitory? *Journal of Abnormal Psychology, 86,* 65–74.

HOPKINS, J. R. (1977). Sexual behavior in adolescence. *Journal of Social Issues, 33,* 67–85.

HORM, J., & ANDERSON, K. (1993). Who in America is trying to lose weight? *Annals of Internal Medicine, 119,* 672–676.

HORNE, J. A., & MCGRATH, M. J. (1984). The consolidation hypothesis for REM sleep function: Stress and other confounding factors—A review. *Biological Psychology, 18,* 165–84.

HOROWITZ, F. D. (1974). Visual attention, auditory stimulation, and language stimulation in young infants. *Monographs of the Society for Research in Child Development, 31,* Serial No. 158.

HOROWITZ, M. (1986). Stress-response syndromes: A review of posttraumatic and adjustment disorders. *Hospital & Community Psychiatry, 37,* 241–249.

HOVLAND, C., JANIS, I., & KELLEY, H. H. (1953). *Communication and persuasion.* New Haven, CT: Yale University Press.

HOWES, C. (1990). Can the age of entry into child care and the quality of child care predict adjustment in kindergarten? *Developmental Psychology, 26,* 292–803.

HOWES, C., PHILLIPS, D. A., & WHITEBOOK, M. (1992). Thresholds of quality: Implications for the social development of children in center-based child care. *Child Development, 63,* 449–460.

HSER, Y. I., ANGLIN, D., & POWERS, K. (1993). A 24-year follow-up of California narcotics addicts. *Archives of General Psychiatry, 50,* 577–584.

HU, S., PATTATUCCI, A. M. L., PATTERSON, C., LI, L., FULKER, D. W., CHERNY, S. S., KRUGLYAK, L., & HAMER, D. H. (1995). Linkage between sexual orientation and chromosome Xq28 in males but not in females. *Nature Genetics, 11,* 248–256.

HUBEL, D. H., & WIESEL, T. N. (1963). Receptive fields of cells in striate cortex of very young visually inexperienced kittens. *Journal of Neurophysiology, 26,* 994–1002.

HUBEL, D. H., & WIESEL, T. N. (1968). Receptive fields and functional architecture of monkey striate cortex. *Journal of Physiology, 195,* 215–243.

HUDSON, J. W., & HOYT, L. L. (1981). Personal characteristics important in mate preference among college students. *Social Behavior and Personality, 9,* 93–96.

HUESMANN, L. R., ERON, L. D., LEFKOWITZ, M. M., & WALDER, L. O. (1984). The stability of aggression over time and generations. *Developmental Psychology, 20,* 1120–1134.

HUMMEL, J. E., & BIEDERMAN, I. (1992). Dynamic binding in a neutral network for shape recognition. *Psychological Review, 99,* 480–517.

HUMPHREYS, K., & MOOS, R. (1996). Reduced substance abuse-related health care costs among voluntary participants in Alcoholics Anonymous. *Psychiatric Services, 47,* 709–713.

HUMPHREYS, K., MOOS, R. H., & COHEN, C. (1997). Social and community resources and long-term recovery from treated and untreated alcoholism. *Journal of Studies on Alcohol, 58,* 231–238.

HUNT, E. (1990). A modern arsenal for mental assessment. *Educational Psychologist, 25,* 223–241.

HUNT, E. (1995). *Will we be smart enough?* New York: Russell Sage Foundation.

HUNT, M. (1974). *Sexual behavior in the 1970's.* Chicago: Playboy Press.

HUNT, P. J., & HILLERY, J. M. (1973). *Social facilitation at different stages in learning.* Paper presented at the Midwestern Psychological Association Meetings, Cleveland.

HUNTER, I. M. L. (1974). *Memory.* Baltimore: Penguin.

HURVICH, L. M., & JAMESON, D. (1974). Opponent processes as a model of neural organizations. *American Psychologist, 29,* 88–102.

HUTTON, D. C., & BAUMEISTER, R. F. (1992). Self-awareness and attitude change: Seeing oneself on the central route to persuasion. *Personality and Social Psychology Bulletin, 18,* 68–75.

HYMAN, R. (1985). The ganzfield psi experiment: A critical appraisal. *Journal of Parapsychology, 49,* 3–49.

HYMAN, R. (1994). Anomaly or Artifact? Comments on Bem and Honorton. *Psychological Bulletin, 115,* 19–24.

HYMAN, R., & HONORTON, C. (1986). A joint communiqué: The psi ganzfeld controversy. *Journal of Parapsychology, 50,* 351–364.

HYMAN I. E., HUSBAND. T. H., & BILL INGS, F. J. (1995). False memories of childhood experiences. *Applied Cognitive Psychology, 9,* 181–197.

IMPERATO-MCGINLEY, J., PETERSON, R. E., GAUTIER, T., & STURLA, E. (1979). Androgens and the evolution of male gender identity among male pseudohermaphrodites with 5 alpha reductase deficiency. *New England Journal of Medicine, 300,* 1233–1237.

INSTITUTE OF MEDICINE (1982). *Marijuana and health.* Washington, DC: National Academy Press.

INTERNATIONAL NARCOTICS CONTROL BOARD (1998). *Psychotropic substances: Statistics for 1996.* New York: United Nations.

ISABELLA, R. A., & BELSKY, J. (1991). Interactional synchrony and the origins of infant-mother attachment: A replication study. *Child Development, 62,* 373–384.

ISBELL, L., CLORE, G. L., & WYER, R. S. (1999). Affect as feedback about accessible knowledge. *Journal of Personality and Social Psychology.*

ISEN, A. M. (1987). Positive affect, cognitive processes, and social behavior. *Advances in Experimental Social Psychology, 20,* 203–253.

ISEN, P. M. (1985). The assymmetry of happiness and sadness in effects on memory in normal college students. *Journal of Experimental Psychology: General, 114,* 388–391.

ISEN, P. M., SHALKER, T. E., CLARK, M., & KARP, L. (1978). Affect, accessibility of material in memory, and behavior: A cognitive loop? *Journal of Personality and Social Psychology, 36,* 1–12.

ISENBERG, D. J. (1986). Group polarization: A critical review and meta-analysis. *Journal of Personality and Social Psychology, 50,* 1141–1151.

ISOZAKI, M. (1984). The effect of discussion on polarization of judgments. *Japanese Psychological Research, 26,* 187–193.

JACKENDOFF, R. (1990). *Consciousness and the computational mind.* Cambridge, MA: MIT Press.

JACOBS, W. J., & NADEL, W. (1985). Stress-induced recovery of fears and phobias. *Psychological Review, 92,* 512–531.

JACOBSON, A. L., FRIED, C., & HOROWITZ, S. D. (1967). Classical conditioning, pseudoconditioning, or sensitization in the planarian. *Journal of Comparative and Physiological Psychology, 64,* 73–79.

JACOBSON, N. S., & HOLLON, S. D. (1996). Cognitive-behavior therapy versus pharmacotherapy: Now that the jury's returned its verdict, it's time to present the rest of the evidence. *Journal of Consulting and Clinical Psychology, 64,* 74–80.

JAMES, W. (1884). What is an emotion? *Mind, 9,* 188–205.

JAMISON, K. R. (1995, February). Manic-depressive illness and creativity. *Scientific American.*

JAMISON, K. R. (1995). An unquiet mind: A memoir of moods and madness. New York: Alfred A. Knopf.

JAMISON, R. N. (1996). *Mastering chronic pain. A professional's guide to behavioral treatment.* Sarasota, FL: Professional Resource Press.

JAMISON, R. N., RAYMOND, S. A., SLAWSBY, E. A., NEDELJKOVIC, S. S., & KATZ, N. P. (1998). Opioid therapy for noncancer back pain: A randomized prospective study. *Spine, 23,* 2591–2600.

JANET, P. (1889). *L'automisme psychologique.* Paris: Félix Alcan.

JANIS, I. L. (1982). *Groupthink: Psychological studies of policy decisions and fiascoes* (2nd ed.). Boston: Houghton Mifflin.

JANIS, I. L. (1985). Sources of error in strategic decision making. In J. M. Pennings (Ed.), *Organizational strategy and change.* San Francisco: Jossey-Bass.

JANOFF-BULMAN, R. (1992). *Shattered assumptions: Toward a new psychology of trauma.* New York: Maxwell Macmillan International.

JASMOS, T. M., & HAKMILLER, K. L. (1975). Some effects of lesion level and emotional cues on affective expression in spinal cord patients. *Psychological Reports, 37,* 859–870.

JEMMOTT, J. B., III, BORYSENKO, M., MCCELLAND, D. C., CHAPMAN, R., MEYER, D., & BENSON, H. (1985). Academic stress, power motivation, and decrease in salivary secretory immunoglubulin: A secretion rate. *Lancet, 1,* 1400–1402.

JENNINGS, D., AMABILE, T. M., & ROSS, L. (1982). Informal covariation assessment: Data-based vs. theory-based judgments. In A. Tversky, D. Kahneman, & P. Slovic (Eds.), *Judgment under uncertainty: Heuristics and biases.* New York: Cambridge University Press.

JOHANSSON, G., & FRANKENHAEUSER, J. (1973). Temporal factors in sympatho-adrenomedullary activity following acute behavioral activation. *Biological Psychology, 1,* 63–73.

JOHANSSON, G., VON HOFSTEN, C., & JANSON, G. (1980). Event perception. *Annual Review of Psychology, 31,* 27–63.

JOHN, O. P. (1990). The "Big Five" factor taxonomy: Dimension of personality in the natural language and in questionnaires. In L. A. Pervin (Ed.), *Handbook of personality: Theory and research* (pp. 66–100). New York: Guilford.

JOHNSON, M. H. (1997). *Developmental cognitive neuroscience: An introduction.* Boston: Blackwell.

JOHNSON, R. D., & DOWNING, L. L. (1979). Deindividuation and valence of cues: Effect on prosocial and antisocial behavior. *Journal of Personality and Social Psychology, 37,* 1532–1538.

JOHNSON-LAIRD, P. N. (1985). The deductive reasoning ability. In R. J. Sternberg (Ed.), *Human abilities: An information processing approach.* New York: Freeman.

JOHNSON-LAIRD, P. N. (1988). *The computer and the mind: An introduction to cognitive science.* Cambridge, MA: Harvard University Press.

JOHNSON-LAIRD, P. (1988). A computational analysis of consciousness. In A. J. Marcel & E. Bisiach (Eds.), *Consciousness in contemporary science.* New York: Oxford University Press.

JOHNSON-LAIRD, P. N. (1989). Mental models. In M. I. Posner (Ed.), *Foundations of cognitive science.* Cambridge, MA: MIT Press.

JOHNSON-LAIRD, P. N., & BYRNE, R. M. J. (1991). *Deduction.* Hillsdale, NJ: Erlbaum.

JOHNSTON, L. D., O'MALLEY, P. M., & BACHMAN, J. G. (1995). *National survey results on drug use.* Rockville, MD: National Institute on Drug Abuse.

JONES, E. E. (1978). Effects of race on psychotherapy process and outcome: An exploratory investigation. *Psychotherapy: Theory, Research, and Practice, 15,* 226–236.

JONES, E. E. (1990). *Interpersonal perception.* New York: Freeman.

JONES, E. E., & HARRIS, V. A. (1967). The attribution of attitudes. *Journal of Experimental Social Psychology, 3,* 1–24.

JONES, E. E., ROCK, L., SHAVER, K. G., GOETHALS, G. R., & WARD, L. M. (1968). Pattern of performance and ability attribution: An unexpected primacy effect. *Journal of Personality and Social Psychology, 9,* 317–340.

JONES, H. C., & LOVINGER, P. W. (1985). *The marijuana question and science's search for an answer.* New York: Dodd, Mead.

JUDD, L., AKISKAL, H., MASER, J., ZELLER, P. J., ENDICOTT, J., CORYELL, W., PAULUS, M., KUNOVAC, J., LEON, A., MUELLER, T., RICE, J., & KELLER, M. (1998). A prospective 12-year study of subsyndromal and syndromal depressive symptoms in unipolar major depressive disorders. *Archives of General Psychiatry, 55,* 694–700.

JULIEN, R. M. (1988). *Drugs and the body.* New York: Freeman.

JULIEN, R. M. (1992). *A primer of drug action: A concise, nontechnical guide to the actions, uses, and side effects of psychoactive drugs* (6th ed.). New York: Freeman.

JUST, M. A., & CARPENTER, P. A. (1980). A theory of reading: From eye fixations to comprehension. *Psychological Review, 87,* 329–354.

JUST, M. A., & CARPENTER, P. A. (1992). A capacity theory of comprehension: Individual differences in working memory. *Psychological Review, 99,* 122.

KAGAN, J. (1979). Overview: Perspectives on human infancy. In J. D. Osofsky (Ed.), *Handbook of infant development.* New York: Wiley-Interscience.

KAGAN, J. (1998). *Three seductive ideas.* Cambridge, MA: Harvard University Press.

KAGAN, J., KEARSLEY, R. B., & ZELAZO, P. (1978). *Infancy: Its place in human development.* Cambridge, MA: Harvard University Press.

KAGAN, J., & SNIDMAN, N. (1991). Temperamental factors in human development. *American Psychologist, 46,* 856–862.

KAGAN, N. (1984). *The nature of the child.* New York: Basic Books.

KAGAN, N., & MOSS, H. A. (1962). *Birth to maturity.* New York: Wiley.

KAHNEMAN, D., SLOVIC, P., & TVERSKY, A. (Eds.) (1982). *Judgment under uncertainty: Heuristics and biases.* New York: Cambridge University Press.

KAIL, R. (1989). *The development of memory in children* (3rd ed.). New York: Freeman.

KAMEN-SIEGEL, L., RODIN, J., SELIGMAN, M. E., & J. D. (1991). Explanatory style and cell-mediated immunity in elderly men and women. *Health Psychology, 10,* 229–235.

KAMIN, L. J. (1974). *The science and politics of IQ.* Hillsdale, NJ: Erlbaum.

KANDEL, E. R., SCHWARTZ, J. H., & JESSELL, T. M. (Eds.) (1991). *Principles of neural science* (3rd ed.). New York: Elsevier.

KANOWSKI, S., HERRMANN, W. M., STEPHAN, K., WIERICH, W., & HOERR, R. (1996). Proof of efficacy of the gingko Biloba special extract EGb761 in outpatients suffering from mild to moderate primary degenerative dementia of the Alzheimer type or multi-infarct dementia. *Pharmacopsychiatry, 29,* 47–56.

KAPLAN, M. R., & MILLER, C. E. (1987). Group decision making and normative versus informational influence: Effects of type of issue and assigned decision rule. *Journal of Personality and Social Psychology, 53,* 306–313.

KARASEK, R., BAKER, D., MARXER, F., AHLBOM, A., & THEORELL, T. (1981). Job decision latitude, job demands, and cardiovascular disease: A prospective study of Swedish men. *American Journal of Public Health, 71,* 694–705.

KARASEK, R. A., THEORELL, T. G., SCHWARTZ, J., PIEPER, C., & ALFREDSSON, L. (1982). Job, psychological factors and coronary heart disease: Swedish prospective findings and U.S. prevalence findings using a new occupation inference method. *Advances in Cardiology, 29,* 62–67.

KARNI, A., TANNE, D., RUBENSTEIN, B. S., ASKENASY, J. J. M., & SAGI, D. (1994). Dependence on REM sleep of overnight improvement of a perceptual skill. *Science, 265,* 679–682.

KARNO, M., & GOLDING, J. M. (1991). Obsessive compulsive disorder. In L. R. Robins & D. A. Regier (Eds.), *Psychiatric disorders in America: The epidiologic Catchment area study.* New York: Maxwell Macmillan International.

KARYLOWSKI, J. J. (1990). Social reference points and accessibility of trait-related information in self-other similarity judgments. *Journal of Personality and Social Psychology, 58,* 975–983.

KATZ, D. (1960). The functional approach to the study of attitudes. *Public Opinion Quarterly, 24,* 163–204.

KATZ, L. C., & SHATZ, C. J (1996). Synaptic activity and the construction of cortical circuits. *Science, 274,* 1133.

KATZ, R., & WYKES, T. (1985). The psychological difference between temporally predictable and unpredictable stressful events: Evidence for information control theories. *Journal of Personality and Social Psychology, 48,* 781–790.

KAUFMAN, G. (1995, November). *Methylphenidate findings from New York's triplicate prescription data.* Presented at the annual conference of the National Association of State Controlled Substances Authorities.

KAUFMAN, L., & ROCK, I. (1989). The moon illusion thirty years later. In M. Hershenson (Ed.), *The moon illusion* (pp. 193–234). Hillsdale, NJ: Erlbaum.

KAZDIN, A. E. (1982). Symptom substitution, generalization, and response covariation: Implications for psychotherapy outcome. *Psychological Bulletin, 91,* 349–365.

KAZDIN, A. E., & WEISZ, J. R. (1998). Identifying and developing empirically supported child and adolescent treatments. *Journal of Consulting and Clinical Psychology, 66,* 19–36.

KEIL, F. C. (1989). *Concepts, kinds, and cognitive development.* Cambridge, MA: MIT Press.

KEIL, F. C., & BATTERMAN, N. A. (1984). Characteristic-to-defining shift in the development of word meaning. *Journal of Verbal Learning and Verbal Behavior, 23,* 221–236.

KELLER, M. B., & BAKER, L. A. (1991). Bipolar disorder: Epidemiology, course, diagnosis, and treatment. *Bulletin of the Menninger Clinic, 55,* 172–181.

KELLEY, H. H. (1967). Attribution theory in social psychology. In D. Levine (Ed.), *Nebraska symposium on motivation* (Vol. 15). Lincoln: University of Nebraska Press.

KELLMAN, P. J. (1984). Perception of three-dimensional form by human infants. *Perception and Psychophysics, 36,* 353–358.

KELLY, G. A. (1955). *The psychology of personal constructs.* New York: Norton.

KENDLER, K. S., NEALE, M. C., KESSLER, R. C., & HEATH, A. C. (1992). Major depression and generalized anxiety disorder: Same genes, (partly) different environments? *Archives of General Psychiatry, 49,* 716–722.

KENDLER, K. S., NEALE, M. C., KESSLER, R. C., & HEATH, A. C. (1993). Panic disorder in women: A population-based twin study. *Psychological Medicine, 23,* 397–406.

KENDRICK, D. T., & GUTIERRES, S. E. (1980). Contrast effects and judgments of physical attractiveness: When beauty becomes a social problem. *Journal of Personality and Social Psychology, 38,* 131–140.

KENSHALO, D. R., NAFE, J. P., & BROOKS, B. (1961). Variations in thermal sensitivity. *Science, 134,* 104–105.

KEPHART, W. M. (1967). Some correlates of romantic love. *Journal of Marriage and the Family, 29,* 470–474.

KERNBERG, P. F. (1979). Psychoanalytic profile of the borderline adolescent. *Adolescent Psychiatry, 7,* 234–256.

KERNIS, M. H., & WHEELER, L. (1981). Beautiful friends and ugly strangers: Radiation and contrast effects in perception of same-sex pairs. *Journal of Personality and Social Psychology, 7,* 617–620.

KESSLER, R. C., BROWN, R. L., & BROMAN, C. L. (1981). Sex differences in psychiatric help-seeking: Evidence from four large-scale surveys. *Journal of Health and Social Behavior, 22,* 49–64.

KESSLER, R. C., DAVIS, C. G., & KENDLER, K. S. (1997). Childhood adversity and adult psychiatric disorder in the US National Comorbidity Survey. *Psychological Medicine, 27,* 1101–1119.

KESSLER, R. C., MCGONAGLE, K. A., ZHAO, S., NELSON, C., HUGHES, M., ESHLEMAN, S., WITTCHEN, H., & KENDLER, K. (1994). Lifetime and 12-month prevalence of DSM-III-R psychiatric disorders in the United States. *Archives of General Psychiatry, 51,* 8–19.

KETELAAR, T., & AU, W. T. (1999). The role of guilty feelings in cooperative behavior in the prisoner's dilemma: An emotion-as-information interpretation of Frank's Commitment model. Unpublished manuscript, UCLA.

KIECOLT-GLASER, J. K., and collaborators (1985). Psychosocial enhancement of immunocompetence in a geriatric population. *Health Psychology, 4,* 25–41.

KIECOLT-GLASER, J. K., GLASER, R., CACIOPPO, J. T., & MALARKEY, W. B. (1998). Marital stress: Immunologic, neuroendocrine, and autonomic correlates. In S. M. McCann (Ed.), *Annals of the New York Academy of Sciences, Vol. 840: Neuroimmunomodulation: Molecular aspects, integrative systems, and clinical advances* (pp. 656–663). New York: New York Academy of Sciences.

KIECOLT-GLASER, J. K., KENNEDY, S., MALKOFF, S., FISHER, L., SPEICHER, C. E., & GLASER, R. (1988). Marital discord and immunity in males. *Psychosomatic Medicine, 50,* 213–229.

KIESLER, C. A., & SIBULKIN, A. E. (1987). *Mental hospitalization: Myths and facts about a national crisis.* Newbery Park, CA: Sage.

KIHLSTROM, J. F. (1984). Conscious, subconscious, unconscious: A cognitive view. In K. S. Bowers & D. Meichenbaum (Eds.), *The unconscious: Reconsidered.* New York: Wiley.

KIHLSTROM, J. F. (1985). Hypnosis. *Annual Review of Psychology, 36,* 385–235.

KIHLSTROM, J. F. (1987). The cognitive unconscious. *Science, 237,* 1445–1452.

KIHLSTROM, J. F. (1998). Conscious and unconscious cognition. In R. J. Sternberg (Ed.), *The concept of cognition.* Cambridge, MA: MIT Press.

KIMMEL, D. C., & WEINER, I. B. (1985). *Adolescence: A developmental transition.* Hillsdale, NJ: Erlbaum.

KINDER, D. R., & SEARS, D. O. (1985). Public opinion and political action. In G. Lindzey & E. Aronson, (Eds.), *The handbook of social psychology* (3rd ed., Vol. 2). New York: Random House.

KING, N. J., GULLONE, E, TONGE, B. J., & OLLENDICK, T. H. (1993). Self-reports of panic attacks and manifest anxiety in adolescents. *Behavior Research & Therapy 31,* 111–116.

KINSEY, A. C., POMEROY, W. B., & MARTIN, C. E. (1948). *Sexual behavior in the human male.* Philadelpia: Saunders

KINSEY, A. C., POMEROY, W. B., & MARTIN, C. E. & GEBHARD, P. H. (1953). *Sexual behavior in the human female.* Philadelphia: Saunders.

KISHLINE, A. (1994). *Moderate drinking.* New York: Three Rivers Press.

KLAHR, D. (1982). Nonmonotone assessment of monotone development: An information processing analysis. In S. Strauss (Ed.), *U-shaped behavioral growth.* New York: Academic Press.

KLATZKY, R. L., LEDERMAN, S. J., & METZGER, V. A. (1985). Identifying objects by touch: An expert system. *Perception and Psychophysics, 37,* 299–302.

KLEIN, S. B., & LOFTUS, J. (1988). The nature of self-referent encoding: The contributions of elaborative and organizational processes. *Journal of Personality and Social Psychology, 55,* 5–11.

KLEIN, S. B., & LOFTUS, J., & BURTON, H. A. (1989). Two self-reference effects: The importance of distinguishing between self-descriptiveness judgments and autobiographical retrieval in self-referent encoding. *Journal of Personality and Social Psychology, 56,* 853–865.

KLERMAN, G. L., WEISSMAN, M. M., ROUNSAVILLE, B., & CHEVRON, E. (1984). *Interpersonal psychotherapy of depression.* New York: Basic Books.

KLINE, P. (1972). *Fact and fancy in Freudian theory.* London: Methuen.

KLINEBERG, O. (1938). Emotional expression in Chinese literature. *Journal of Abnormal and Social Psychology, 33,* 517–520.

KLÜVER, H., & BUCY, P. C. (1937). "Psychic blindness" and other symptoms following temporal lobectomy in rhesus monkeys. *American Journal of Physiology, 119,* 352–353.

KNITTLE, J. L., & HIRSCH, J. (1968). Effect of early nutrition on the development of rat epididymal fat pads: Cellularity and metabolism. *Journal of Clinical Investigation, 47,* 2091.

KNOBLICH, G., & KING, R. (1992). Biological correlates of criminal behavior. In J. McCord (Ed.), *Advances in criminological theory: Facts, frameworks, and forecasts* (pp. 1–21). New Brunswick, NJ: Transaction Publishers.

KOBASA, S. C. (1979). Stressful life events, personality, and health: An inquiry into hardiness. *Journal of Personality and Social Psychology, 37,* 1–11.

KOBASA, S. C., MADDI, S. R., & KAHN, S. (1982). Hardiness and health: A prospective study. *Journal of Personality and Social Psychology, 42,* 168–177.

KOENIG, H. G. (Ed.). (1998). *Handbook of religion and mental health.* San Diego: Academic Press.

KOENIG, H. G., GEORGE, L. K., COHEN, H. J., HAYS, J. C., LARSON, D. B., & BLAZER, D. G. (1998). The relationship between religious activities and cigarette smoking in older adults. *Journals of Gerontology, Series A, Biological Sciences and Medical Sciences, 53A,* M426–M434.

KOENIG, H. G., HAYS, J. C., GEORGE, L. K., BLAZER, D. G., LARSON, D. B., & LANDERMAN, L. R. (1997). Modeling the cross-sectional relationships between religion, physical health, social support, and depressive symptoms. *American Journal of Geriatric Psychology, 5,* 131–144.

KOHLBERG, L. (1966). A cognitive developmental analysis of children's sex role concepts and attitudes. In E. E. Maccoby (Ed.), *The development of sex differences* (pp. 82–173). Stanford, CA: Stanford University Press.

KOHLBERG, L. (1969). Stage and sequence: The cognitive-developmental approach to socialization. In D. A. Goslin (Ed.), *Handbook of socialization theory and research.* Chicago: Rand McNally.

KOHLBERG, L. (1976). Moral stages and moralization: The cognitive-developmental approach. In T. Lickong (Ed.), *Moral development and behavior.* New York: Holt, Rinehart & Winston.

KOHLER, W. (1925). *The mentality of apes.* New York: Harcourt Brace. (Reprint ed., 1976. New York: Liveright.)

KOHNSTAMM, G. A., BATES, J. E., & ROTHBART, M. K. (Eds.) (1989). *Temperament in childhood.* Chichester: Wiley.

KOLB, B., & WHISHAW, I. Q. (1985). *Fundamentals of human neuropsychology* (2nd ed.). San Francisco: Freeman.

KOLODNY, J. A., (1994). Memory processes in classification learning. *Psychological Science, 5,* 164–169.

KOOB, G. F., & BLOOM, F. E. (1988). Cellular and molecular mechanisms of drug dependence. *Science, 242,* 715–723.

KORNER, A. F. (1973). Individual differences at birth: Implications for early experience and later development. In J. C. Westman (Ed.), *Individual differences in children.* New York: Wiley.

KORNHABER, M., & GARDNER, H. (1991). Critical thinking across multiple intelligences. In S. Maclure & P. Davies (Eds.), *Learning to think: Thinking to learn.* Oxford, England: Pergamon.

KORNHABER, M., KRECHEVSKY, M., & GARDNER, H. (1990). Engaging intelligence. *Educational Psychologist, 25,* 177–199.

KOSAMBI, D. D. (1967). Living prehistory in India. *Scientific American, 215,* 105.

KOSS, M., & BOESCHEN, L. (1998). Rape. In *Encyclopedia of Mental Health,* (Vol. 3). New York: Academic Press.

KOSSLYN, S. M. (1980). *Image and mind.* Cambridge, MA: Harvard University Press.

KOSSLYN, S. M. (1983). *Ghosts in the mind's machine.* New York: Norton.

KOSSLYN, S. M. (1988). Aspects of a cognitive neuroscience of mental imagery: *Science, 240,* 1621–1626.

KOSSLYN, S. M. (1994). *The resolution of the imagery debate.* Cambridge, MA: MIT Press.

KOSSLYN, S. M., ALPERT, N. M., THOMPSON, W. L., MALJKOVIC, V., WEISE, S. B., CHABRIS, C. F., HAMILTON, S. E., RAUCH, S. L., & BUONANNO, F. S. (1993). Visual mental imagery activates topographically organized visual cortex. *Journal of Cognitive Neuroscience, 5,* 263–287.

KOSSLYN, S. M., BALL, T. M., & REISER, B. J. (1978). Visual images preserve metric spatial information: Evidence from studies of image scanning. *Journal of Experimental Psychology: Human Perception and Performance, 4,* 47–60.

KOSSLYN, S. M., & KOENIG, O. (1992). *Wet mind: The new cognitive neuroscience.* New York: Free Press.

KOULACK, D., & GOODENOUGH, D. R. (1976). Dream recall and dream recall failure: An arousal-retrieval model. *Psychological Bulletin, 83,* 975–984.

KRAUT, (1982). Social presence, facial feedback, and emotion. *Journal of Personality and Social Psychology, 42,* 853–863.

KRAVITZ, D., & PLATANIA, J. (1993). Attitudes and beliefs about affirmative action: Effects of target and of respondent sex and ethnicity. *Journal of Applied Psychology, 78,* 928–938.

KRAVITZ, D. A., HARRISON, D. A., TURNER, M. E., LEVINE, E. L., CHAVES, W., BRANNICK, M. T., DENNING, D. L., RUSSELL, C. J., & CONARD, M. A. (1997). *Affirmative action: A review of psychological and behavioral research.*

Bowling Green, OH: Society for Industrial and Organizational Psychology.

KRIPKE, D. F. (1985). Biological rhythms. In G. L. Klerman, M. M. Weissman, P. S. Applebaum, & L. H. Roth (Eds.), *Psychiatry* (Vol. 3). Philadelphia: Lippincott.

KRIPKE, D. F., & GILLIN, J. C. (1985). Sleep disorders. In G. L. Klerman, M. M. Weissman, P. S. Applebaum, & L. N. Roth (Eds.), *Psychiatry* (Vol. 3). Philadelphia: Lippincott.

KRYGER, M. H., ROTH, T., & DEMENT, W. C. (Eds.) (1994). *Principles and practice of sleep medicine.* Philadelphia: Saunders.

KUCH, K., & COX, B. J. (1992). Symptoms of PTSD in 124 survivors of the Holocaust. *American Journal of Psychiatry, 149,* 337–340.

KUHL, P. K., WILLIAMS, K. A., LACERDA, F., STEVENS, K. N., & LINDBLOM, B. (1992). Linguistic experience alters phonetic perception in infants by 6 months of age. *Science, 255,* 606–608.

KUHN, C., SWARTZWELDER, S., & WILSON, W. (1998). *Buzzed: The straight facts about the most used and abused drugs.* New York: Norton.

KUIPER, N. A., MACDONALD, M. R., & DERRY, P. A. (1983). Parameters of a depressive self-schema. In J. Suls & A. G. Greenwald (Eds.), *Psychological perspectives on the self* (Vol. 2). Hillsdale, NJ: Erlbaum.

KUIPER, N. A., OLINGER, L. J., MACDONALD, M. R., & SHAW, B. F. (1985). Self-schema processing of depressed and nondepressed content: The effects of vulnerability on depression. *Social Cognition, 3,* 77–93.

KUIPER, N. A., & ROGERS, T. B. (1979). Encoding of personal information: Self-other differences. *Journal of Personality and Social Psychology, 37,* 499–514.

KUMAN, I. G., FEDROV, C. N., & NOVIKOVA, L. A. (1983). Investigation of the sensitive period in the development of the human visual system. *Journal of Higher Nervous Activity, 33,* 434–441.

KURTINES, W., & GREIF, E. B. (1974). The development of moral thought: Review and evaluation of Kohlberg's approach. *Psychological Bulletin, 81,* 453–470.

LA BERGE, D. (1995). *Attentional processing: The brain's art of mindfulness.* Cambridge, MA: Harvard University Press.

LAGERSPETZ, K., VIEMERO, V., & AKADEMI, A. (1986). Television and aggressive behavior among Finnish children. In L. R. Huesmann & L. D. Eron (Eds.), *Television and the aggressive child.* New York: Erlbaum.

LAGRECA, A. M., SLIVERMAN, W. K., VERNBERG, E. M., & PRINSTEIN, M. J. (1996). Symptoms of posttraumatic stress in children after Hurricane

Andrew: A prospective study. *Journal of the American Academy of the Child and Adolescent Psychiatry, 27,* 330–335.

LAMB, M. E., & BORNSTEIN, M. H. (1987). *Development in infancy: An introduction* (2nd ed.). New York: Random House.

LAMBERT, M. J., & BERGIN, A. E. (1994). The effectiveness of psychotherapy. In A. Bergin (Ed.), *Handbook of psychotherapy and behavior change* (4th ed., pp. 143–189). New York: Wiley.

LAND, E. H. (1977). The retinex theory of color vision. *Scientific American, 237,* 108–128.

LAND, E. H. (1986). Recent advances in retinex theory. *Vision Research, 26,* 7–21.

LANGLOIS, J. H., & DOWNS, A. C. (1980). Mothers, fathers, and peers as socialization agents of sex-typed play behaviors in young children. *Child Development, 51,* 1237–1247.

LAPIERE, R. (1934). Attitudes versus actions. *Social Forces, 13,* 230–237.

LARKIN, J. H., MCDERMOTT, J., SIMON, D. P., & SIMON, H. A. (1980). Expert and novice performance in solving physics problems. *Science, 208,* 1335–1342.

LARSEN, R. J., & SEIDMAN, E. (1986). Gender schema theory and sex role inventories: Some conceptual and psychometric considerations. *Journal of Personality and Social Psychology, 50,* 205–211.

LATANÉ, B., & DARLEY, J. M. (1968). Group inhibition of bystander intervention in emergencies. *Journal of Personality and Social Psychology, 10,* 215–221.

LATANÉ, B., & DARLEY, J. M. (1970). *The unresponsive bystander: Why doesn't he help?* New York: Appleton-Century-Crofts.

LATANÉ, B., NIDA, S. A., & WILSON, D. W. (1981). The effects of group size on helping behavior. In J. P. Rushton & R. M. Sorrentino (Eds.), *Altruism and helping behavior: Social personality, and developmental perspectives.* Hillsdale, NJ: Erlbaum.

LATANÉ, B., & RODIN, J. (1969). A lady in distress: Inhibiting effects of friends and strangers on bystander intervention. *Journal of Experimental and Social Psychology, 5,* 189–202.

LAUDENSLAGER, M. L., RYAN, S. M., DRUGAN, R. C., HYSON, R. L., & MAIER, S. F. (1983). Coping and immunosuppression: Inescapable but not escapable shock suppresses lymphocyte proliferation. *Science, 221,* 568–570.

LAUMANN, E. O., GAGNON, J. H. MICHAEL, R. T., & MICHAELS, S. (1994). *The social organization of sexuality: Sexual practices in the United States.* Chicago: University of Chicago Press.

LAZARUS, R. S. (1991a). Cognition and motivation in emotion. *American Psychologist, 46,* 352–367.

LAZARUS, R. S. (1991b). *Emotion and adaptation.* New York: Oxford University Press.

LAZARUS, R. S., & FOLKMAN, S. (1984). *Stress, appraisal, and coping.* New York: Springer.

LAZARUS, R. S., KANNER, A. D., & FOLKMAN, S. (1980). Emotions: A cognitive-phenomenological analysis. In R. Plutchik & H. Kellerman (Eds.), *Emotion: Theory, research, and experience* (Vol. 1). New York: Academic Press.

LE BARS, P. L., KATZ, M. M., BERMAN, N., ITIL, T. M., FREEDMAN, A. M., & SCHATZBERG, A. F. (1997). *A placebo-controlled, double-blind, randomized trial of an extract of ginkgo biloba for dementia. Journal of the American Medical Association, 278,* 1327–1332.

LE BON, G. (1895). *The crowd.* London: Ernest Benn.

LE DEOX, J. E. (1989). Cognitive-emotional interactions in the brain. *Cognition and Emotion, 3,* 267–289.

LEEDHAM, B., MEYEROWITZ, B. E., MUIRHEAD, J., & FRIST, M. H. (1995). Positive expectations predict health after heart transplantation. *Health Psychology, 14,* 74–79.

LEFF, J. P., & VAUGHN, C. E. (1981). The role of maintenance therapy and relatives' expressed emotion in relapse of schizophrenia: A two-year follow-up. *British Journal of Psychiatry, 139,* 102–104.

LENNEBERG, E. H. (1967). *Biological foundations of language.* New York: Wiley.

LENNON, M. C., & ROSENFIELD, S. (1992). Women and mental health: The interaction of job and family conditions. *Journal of Health and Social Behavior, 33,* 316–327.

LEONARD, J. S. (1986). The effectiveness of equal employment law and affirmative action regulation. In R. G. Ehrenberg (Ed.), *Research in labor economics* (vol. 8, 319–350). Greenwich, CT: JAI Press.

LERNER, B. (1972). *Therapy in the ghetto: Political impotence and personal disintegration.* Baltimore: Johns Hopkins University Press.

LESHNER, A. I. (1997). Addiction is a brain disease, and it matters. *Science, 278,* 45–47.

LEVAV, I., FRIEDLANDER, Y., KARK, J. D., & PERITZ, E. (1988). An epidemiologic study of mortality among bereaved parents. *New England Journal of Medicine, 319,* 457–461.

LEVAY, S. (1991). A difference in hypothalmic structure between heterosexual and homosexual men. *Science, 253,* 1034–1037.

LEVAY, S. (1996). *Queer science: The use and abuse of research into homosexuality.* Cambridge, MA: MIT Press.

LEVENSON, R. W. (1994). Human emotions: A functional view. In P. Ekman & R. Davidson (Eds.), *The nature of emotion: Fundamental questions* (pp. 123–126). New York: Oxford University Press.

LEVENSON, R. W., EKMAN, P., & FRIESEN, W. V. (1990). Voluntary facial action generates emotion-specific nervous system activity. *Psychophysiology, 27,* 363–384.

LEVENSON, R. W., EKMAN, P., HEIDER, K., & FRIESIN, W. V. (1992). Emotion and automic nervous system activity in an Indonesian culture. *Journal of Personality and Social Psychology, 62,* 927–988.

LEVINE, S. (1960). Stimulation in infancy. *Scientific American, 202,* 80–86.

LEVINGER, G., SENN, D. J., & JORGENSEN, B. W. (1970). Progress toward permanence in courtship: A test of the Kerckhoff-Davis hypotheses. *Sociometry, 33,* 427–443.

LEVY, J. (1985). Right brain, left brain: Facts and fiction. *Psychology Today, 19,* 38–44.

LEVY, S. M., & HEIDEN, I., (1991). Depression, distress and immunity: Risk factors for infectious disease. *Stress Medicine, 7,* 45–51.

LEVY, S., HERBERMAN, R., WHITESIDE, T., SANZO, K., LEE, J., & KIRKWOOD, J. (1990). Perceived social support and tumor estrogen/progesterone receptor status as predictors of natural killer cell activity in breast cancer patients. *Psychosomatic Medicine, 52,* 73–85.

LEWINSOHN, P. M., MISCHEL, W., CHAPLIN, W., & BARTON, R. (1980). Social competence and depression: The role of illusory self-perceptions. *Journal of Abnormal Psychology, 89,* 203–212.

LEY, R. G., & BRYDEN, M. P. (1982). A dissociation of right and left hemispheric effects for recognizing emotional tone and verbal content. *Brain and Cognition, 1,* 3–9.

LIBERMAN, A. M., COOPER, F., SHANKWEILER, D., & STUDERT-KENNEDY, M. (1967). Perception of the speech code. *Psychological Review, 74,* 431–459.

LICKEY, M. E. & GORDON, B. (1991). *Medicine and mental illness.* New York: Freeman.

LIDZ, C. W., MULVEY, E. P., & GARDNER, W. (1993). The accuracy of predictions of violence to others. *Journal of the American Medical Association, 269,* 1007–1011.

LIEBERMAN, L. R., & DUNLAP, J. T. (1979). O'Leary and Borkovec's conceptualization of placebo: The placebo paradox. *American Psychologist, 34,* 553–554.

LIGHT, P., & PERRETT-CLERMONT, A. (1989). Social context effects in learning and testing. In A. R. H. Gellatly, D. Rogers, & J. Sloboda (Eds.), *Cognition and social worlds.* Oxford: Clarendon Press.

LINDE, K. RAMIREZ, G., MULROW, C. D., PAULS, A., WEIDENHAMMER, W., & MELCHART, D. (1996). St. John's wort for depression: An overview and meta-analysis of randomized clinical trials. *British Medical Journal, 313,* 253–258.

LINE, L. (1998, August–September). Leader of the flock. *National Wildlife,* pp. 20–27.

LINN, R. L. (1982). Ability testing: Individual differences, prediction, and differential prediction. In A. Wigdor & W. Gardner (Eds.), *Ability testing. Uses, consequences, and controversies.* Washington, DC: National Academy Press.

LINNOILA, N., VIRKUNNEN, M., SCHEININ, M., NUTTILA, A., RIMON, R., & GOODWIN, F. (1983). Low cerebrospinal fluid 5-Hydroxyindoleacetic acid concentration differentiates impulsive from nonimpulsive violent behavior. *Life Sciences, 33,* 2609–2624.

LINNOILA, V. M. & VIRKKUNEN, M. (1992). Aggression, suicidality, and serotonin. *Journal of Clinical Psychiatry, 53,* 46–51.

LIPPERT, W. W., & SENTER, R. J. (1966). Electrodermal responses in the sociopath. *Psychonomic Science, 4,* 25–26.

LIVINGSTONE, M., & HUBEL, D. (1988). Segregation of form, color, movement, and depth: Anatomy, physiology, and perception. *Science, 240,* 740–750.

LOFTUS, E. F. (1997, September). Creating false memories. *Scientific American, 277*(3), 70–75.

LOFTUS, E. F., & LOFTUS, G. R. (1980). On the permanence of stored information in the human brain. *American Psychologist, 35,* 409–420.

LOFTUS, E. F., & PICKRELL, J. E. (1995). The formation of false memories. *Psychiatric Annals, 25,* 720–725.

LOFTUS, E. F., SCHOOLER, J. W., & WAGENAAR, W. A. (1985). The fate of memory: Comment on McCloskey and Zaragoza. *Journal of Experimental Psychology: General, 114,* 375–380.

LOGUE, A. W. (1991). *The psychology of eating and drinking: An introduction* (2nd ed.). New York: Freeman.

LONG, P. W. (1996). Internet mental health. http://www.mentalhealth.com/

LONGLEY, J., & PRUITT, D. G. (1980). Groupthink: A critique of Janis's theory. In L. Wheeler (Ed.), *Review of personality and social psychology* (Vol. 1). Beverly Hills, CA: Sage.

LOOMIS, A. L., HARVEY, E. N., & HOBART, G. A. (1937). Cerebral states during sleep as studied by human potentials. *Journal of Experimental Psychology, 21,* 127–144.

LOPEZ, A., ATRAN, S., MEDIN, D. L., COOLEY, J., & SMITH, E. E. (1997). The tree of life: Universals of folkbiological taxonomies and inductions. *Cognitive Psychology, 32,* 251–295.

LORD, C. G. (1980). Schemas and images as memory aids: Two modes of processing social information. *Journal of Personality and Social Psychology, 38,* 257–269.

LORD, C. G., ROSS, L., & LEPPER, M. R. (1979). Biased assimilation and attitude polarization: The effects of prior theories on subsequently considered evidence. *Journal of Personality and Social Psychology, 37,* 2098–2109.

LORENZ, K. (1966). *On aggression.* New York: Harcourt Brace Jovanovich.

LOVE, R. E., & GREENWALD, A. C. (1978). Cognitive responses to persuasion as mediators of opinion change. *Journal of Social Psychology, 104,* 231–241.

LOVIBOND, P. F., SIDDLE, D. A. T., & BOND, N. W. (1993). Resistance to extinction of fear-relevant stimuli: Preparedness or selective sensitization? *Journal of Experimental Psychology: General, 122,* 449–461.

LUBORSKY, L. L., MCLELLAN, A. T., WOODY, G. E., O'BRIEN, E. P., & AUERBACH, A. (1985). Therapist success and its determinants. *Archives of General Psychiatry, 42,* 602–611.

LUBORSKY, L. L., SINGER, B., & LUBORSKY, L. (1975). Comparative studies of psychotherapies: Is it true that "everyone has won and all must have prizes"? *Archives of General Psychiatry, 32,* 995–1008.

LUCHINS, A. (1957). Primacy-recency in impression formation. In C. L. Hovland (Ed.), *The order of presentation in persuasion.* New Haven: Yale University Press.

LUNDIN, R. W. (1985). *Theories and systems of psychology* (3rd ed.). Lexington, MA: Heath.

LURIA, Z., & RUBIN, J. Z. (1974). The eye of the beholder: Parents' views on sex of newborns. *American Journal of Orthopsychiatry, 44,* 512–519.

LYKKEN, D. T. (1980). *Tremor in the blood: Uses and abuses of the lie detector.* New York: McGraw-Hill.

LYKKEN, D. T. (1982). Research with twins: The concept of emergenesis. *The Society for Psychophysiological Research, 19,* 361–373.

LYKKEN, D. T. (1984). Polygraphic interrogation. *Nature, 307,* 681–684.

LYKKEN, D. T., MCGUE, M., TELLEGEN, A., & BOUCHARD, T. J., JR. (1992). Emergenesis: Genetic traits that may not run in families. *American Psychologist, 47,* 1565–1577.

LYKKEN, D. T., & TELLEGEN, A. (1993). Is human mating adventitious or the result of lawful choice? A twin study of mate selection. *Journal of Personality and Social Psychology, 65,* 56–68.

LYUBOMIRSKY, S., & NOLEN HOEKSEMA, S. (1995). Effects of self-focused rumination on negative thinking and interpersonal problem solving. *Journal of Personality and Social Psychology, 69,* 176–190.

MAAS, J. B. (1998). *Power sleep: The revolutionary program that prepares your mind for peak performance.* New York: HarperCollins.

MAASS, A., & CLARK, R. D., III (1984). Hidden impact of minorities: Fifteen years of minority influence research. *Psychological Bulletin, 95,* 428–450.

MACAULAY, J. (1970). A shill for charity. In J. Macaulay & L. Berkowitz (Eds.), *Altruism and helping behavior* (pp. 43–59). New York: Academic Press.

MACCOBY, E. E. (1980). *Social development: Psychological growth and the parent-child relationship.* New York: Harcourt Brace Jovanovich.

MACCOBY, E. E., & JACKLIN, C. N. (1974). *The psychology of sex differences.* Stanford, CA: Stanford University Press.

MACKINNON, D., JAMISON, R., & DEPAULO, J. R. (1997). Genetics of manic depressive illness. *Annual Review of Neuroscience, 20,* 355–373.

MACMILLAN, M. B. (1996). *Freud evaluated: The completed arc.* Cambridge, MA: MIT Press.

MAHER, B. A. (1966). *Principles of psychotherapy: An experimental approach.* New York: McGraw-Hill.

MAIER, S. F., & SELIGMAN, M. E. P. (1976). Learned helplessness: Theory and evidence. *Journal of Experimental Psychology: General, 105,* 3–46.

MAIN, M., & CASSIDY, J. (1988). Categories of response to reunion with parents at age 6: Predictable from infant attachment classifications and stable over a 1-month period. *Developmental Psychology, 24,* 415–426.

MAIN, M., & SOLOMON, J. (1986). Discovery of an insecure-disorganized/disoriented attachment pattern: Procedures, findings and implications for the classification of behavior. In T. B. Brazelton, & M. Yogman (Eds.), *Affective development in infancy* (pp. 95–124). Norwood, NJ: Ablex.

MALINOW, R., OTMAKHOV, N., BLUM, K. I., & LISMAN, J. (1994). Visualizing hippocampal synaptic function by optical detection of Ca2 entry through the N-methyl-D-aspartate channel. *Proceedings of the National Academy of Sciences of the United States of America, 91,* 8170–8174.

MALOF, M., & LOTT, A. J. (1962). Ethnocentrism and the acceptance of Negro support in a group pressure situation. *Journal of Abnormal and Social Psychology, 65,* 254–258.

MALONE, K., & MANN, J. J. (1993). Serotonin and major depression. In J. J. Mann & D. J. Kupfer (Eds.), *Biology of depressive disorders: Part A. A systems perspective* (pp. 29–49). New York: Plenum Press.

MALONEY, L. T., & WANDELL, B. A. (1986). Color constancy: A method for recovering surface spectral reflectance. *Journal of the Optical Society of America, 3,* 29–33.

MANDLER, J. (1983). Representation. In P. H. Mussen (Ed.), *Handbook of child psychology* (Vol. 3). New York: Wiley.

MANUCK, S. B., KAPLAN, J. R., & MATTHEWS, K. A. (1986). Behavioral antecedents of coronary heart disease and atherosclerosis. *Arteriosclerosis, 6,* 1–14.

MARBLY, N. (1987). But you weren't there. In T. Williams (Ed.), *Posttraumatic stress disorders: A handbook for clinicians.* Cincinnati, OH: Disabled American Veterans.

MARCIA, J. E. (1966). Development and validation of ego identify status. *Journal of Personality and Social Psychology, 3,* 551–558.

MARCIA, J. E. (1980). Identity in adolescence. In J. Adelson (Ed.), *Handbook of adolescent psychology.* New York: Wiley.

MARCUS, G. F. (1996). Why do children say "breaked"? *Current Directions in Psychological Science, 5,* 81–85.

MAREN, S., & FANSELOW, M. S. (1996). The amygdala and fear conditioning: Has the nut been cracked? *Neuron, 16,* 237–240.

MARGRAF, J., BARLOW, D. H., CLARK, D. M., & TELCH, M. J. (1993). Psychological treatment of panic: Work in progress on outcome, active ingredients, and follow-up. *Behaviour Research & Therapy, 31,* 1–8.

MARKMAN, E. M. (1979). Classes and collections: Conceptual organization and numerical abilities. *Cognitive Psychology, 11,* 395–411.

MARKMAN, E. M. (1987). How children constrain the possible meanings of words. In U. Neisser (Ed.), *Concepts and conceptual development: Ecological and intellectual factors in categorizations.* New York: Cambridge University Press.

MARKOWITZ, J. C., & WEISSMAN, M. M. (1995). Interpersonal psychotherapy. In E. E. Beckham & W. R. Leber (Eds.),

Handbook of depression (2nd ed.). New York: Guilford.

MARKUS, H. (1977). Self-schemata and processing information about the self. *Journal of Personality and Social Psychology, 35,* 63–78.

MARKUS, H., & NURIUS, P. (1986). Possible selves. *American Psychologist, 41,* 954–969.

MARKUS, H., & SENTIS, K. (1982). The self in social information processing. In J. Suls (Ed.), *Psychological perspectives on the self* (Vol. 1). Hillsdale, NJ: Erlbaum.

MARKUS, H., & SMITH, J. (1981). The influence of self-schema on the perception of others. In N. Cantor & J. F. Kihlstrom (Eds.), *Personality, cognition, and social interaction.* Hillsdale, NJ: Erlbaum.

MARLATT, G. A., LARIMER, M. E., BAER, J. S., & QUIGLEY, L. A. (1993). Harm reduction for alcohol problems: Moving beyond the controlled drinking economy. *Behavior Therapy, 24,* 461–503.

MARR, D. (1982). *Vision.* San Francisco: Freeman.

MARSHALL, D. A., BLUMER, L., & MOULTON, D. G. (1981). Odor detection curves for n-pentanoic acid in dogs and humans. *Chemical Senses, 6,* 445–453.

MARSHALL, G., & ZIMBARDO, P. G. (1979). Affective consequences of inadequately explained physiological arousal. *Journal of Personality and Social Psychology, 37,* 970–988.

MARTIN, N., BOOMSMA, D., & MACHIN, G. (1997). A twin-pronged attack on complex traits. *Nature Genetics, 17,* 387–392.

MASLACH, C. (1979). The emotional consequences of arousal without reason. In Izard, C. E. (Ed.), *Emotion in personality and psychopathology.* New York: Plenum.

MASLOW, A. H. (1970). *Motivation and personality* (2nd ed.). New York: Harper and Row.

MASSON, J. M. (1984). *The assault on truth.* New York: Farrar, Straus & Giroux, Inc.

MASTERS, W. H., & JOHNSON, V. E. (1966). *Human sexual response.* Boston: Little, Brown.

MASUDA, M. & HOLMES, T. H. (1978). Life events: Perceptions and frequencies. *Psychosomatic Medicine, 40,* 236–261.

MATAS, L., AREND, R. A., & SROUFE, L. A. (1978). Continuity of adaption in the second year: The relationship between quality of attachment and later competence. *Child Development, 49,* 547–556.

MATHES, E. W. (1975). The effects of physical attractiveness and anxiety on heterosexual attraction over a series of five encounters. *Journal of Marriage and the Family, 37,* 769–773.

MATTHEWS, D. F. (1972). Response patterns of single neurons in the tortoise olfactory epithelium and olfactory bulb. *Journal of General Physiology, 60,* 166–180.

MAYER, R. E. (1983). *Thinking, problem solving and cognition.* New York: Freeman.

MAZZONI, G. A. L., & LOFTUS, E. F. (1998). Dreaming, believing and remembering. In J. DeRivera & T. R. Sarbin (Eds.), *Believed-in imaginings* (pp. 145–156). Washington, DC: American Psychological Association Press.

MCALISTER, A., PERRY, C., KILLEN, J., SLINKARD, L. A., & MACCOBY, N. (1980). Pilot study of smoking, alcohol and drug abuse prevention. *American Journal of Public Health, 70,* 719–721.

MCBRIDE, P., BROWN, R. P., DEMEO, M., & KEILP, J. (1994). The relationship of platelet 5-HT-sub-2 receptor indices to major depressive disorder, personality traits, and suicidal behavior. *Biological Psychiatry, 35,* 295–308.

MCBURNEY, D. H. (1978). Psychological dimensions and the perceptual analysis of taste. In E. C. Carterette & M. P. Friedman (Eds.), *Handbook of perception* (Vol. 6). New York: Academic Press.

MCCLANAHAN, K. K., GOLD, J. A., LENNEY, E., RYCKMAN, R. M., & KULBERG, G. E. (1990). Infatuation and attraction to a dissimilar other: Why is love blind? *Journal of Social Psychology, 130,* 433–445.

MCCLELLAND, D. C. (1987). *Human motivation.* New York: Cambridge University Press.

MCCLELLAND, J. L., & RUMELHART, D. E. (1981). An interactive model of context effects in letter perception: Pt. 1. An account of basic findings. *Psychological Review, 88,* 375–407.

MCCLINTOCK, M. K. (1971). Menstrual synchrony and suppression. *Nature, 229,* 244–245.

MCCOLSKEY, M., WIBLE, C. G., & COHEN, N. J. (1988). Is there a flashbulb-memory system? *Journal of Experimental Psychology, 117,* 171–181.

MCCONAGHY, M. J. (1979). Gender permanence and the genital basis of gender. Stages in the development of constancy of gender identity. *Child Development, 50,* 1223–1226.

MCCRAE, R. R., & COSTA, P. T., JR. (1987). Validation of the five-factor model of personality across instruments and observers. *Journal of Personality and Social Psychology, 52,* 81–90.

MCDOUGALL, W. (1908). *Social psychology.* New York: Putnam.

MCDOUGALL, W. B. (1923). *Outline of psychology.* New York: Scribner's Sons.

MCELREE, B. DOSHER, B. A. (1989). Serial position and set size in short-term memory. The time course of recognition. *Journal of Experimental Psychology: General, 118,* 346–373.

MCFARLAND, S. G., AGEYEV, V. S., & ABALAKINA-PAAP, M. A. (1992). Authoritarianism in the former Soviet Union. *Journal of Personality and Social Psychology, 63,* 1004–1010.

MCGHIE, A., & CHAPMAN, J. (1961). Disorders of attention and perception in early schizophrenia. *British Journal of Medical Psychology, 34,* 103–116.

MCGLASHAN, T. H. Omnipotence, helplessness, and control with the borderline patient. *American Journal of Psychotherapy, 37,* 49–61.

MCGRATH, E., KEITA, G. P., STRICKLAND, B. R., & RUSSO, N. F. (1990). *Women and depression: Risk factors and treatment issues.* Washington, DC: American Psychological Association.

MCGRAW, M. B. (1975). *Growth: A study of Johnny and Jimmy.* New York: Acno Press. (Originally published 1935)

MCGUFFIN, P., KATZ, R., & RUTHERFORD, J. (1991). Nature, nurture and depression: A twin study. *Psychological Medicine, 21,* 329–335.

MCHUGH, P. R. (1990). Clinical issues in food ingestion and body weight maintenance. In E. M. Stricker (Ed.), *Neurobiology of food and fluid intake* (pp. 531–547). New York: Plenum.

MCINTOSH, J. L. (1991). *Epidemiology of suicide in the United States.* In A. A. Leenaars (Ed.), *Life span perspectives on suicide: Time-lines in the suicide process.* New York: Plenum.

MCINTOSH, D. N., SILVER, R. C., & WORTMAN, C. B. (1993). Religion's role in adjustment to a negative life event: Coping with the loss of a child. *Journal of Personality and Social Psychology, 65,* 812–821.

MCKENNA, R. J. (1972). Some effects of anxiety level and food cues on the eating behavior of obese and normal subjects. *Journal of Personality and Social Psychology, 22,* 311–319.

MCNALLY, R. J. (1994). Choking phobia: A review of the literature. *Comprehensive Psychiatry, 35,* 83–89.

MCNALLY, R. J., & REISS, S. (1984). The preparedness theory of phobias: The effects of initial fear level on safety-signal conditioning to fear-relevant stimuli. *Psychophysiology, 21,* 647–652.

MCNEILL, D. (1966). Developmental psycholinguistics. In F. Smith & G. A. Miller (Eds.), *The genesis of language: A psycholinguistic approach.* Cambridge, MA: MIT Press.

MEANEY, M. J., AITKENS, D. H., BERKEL, C., BHATNAGAR, S., SARRIEAU, A., &

SAPOLSKY, R. M. (1987). *Post-natal handling attenuates age-related changes in the adrenocortical stress response and spatial memory deficits in the rat.* Paper presented at the 17th Annual Meeting of the Society of Neuroscience, New Orleans.

MECHANIC, D. (1962). *Students under stress.* New York: Free Press.

MEDCOF, J., & ROTH, J. (Eds.) (1988). *Approaches to psychology.* Philadelphia: Open University Press, Milton Keynes.

MEDIN, D. L., & ROSS, B. H. (1992). *Cognitive psychology.* Fort Worth: Harcourt Brace.

MEDNICK, B., REZNICK, C., HOCEVAR, D., & BAKER, R. (1987). Long-term effects of parental divorce on young adult male crime. *Journal of Youth & Adolescence, 16,* 31–45.

MEDNICK, S. A., GABRIELLI, W. F., & HUTCHINGS, B. (1984). Genetic influences in criminal convictions: Evidence from an adoption cohort. *Science, 224,* 891–894.

MEEHL, P. E., & DAHLSTROM, W. G. (1960). Objective configural rules for discriminating psychotic from neurotic MMPI profiles. *Journal of Consulting Psychology, 24,* 375–387.

MEGARGEE, E. I. (1972). *The California psychological inventory handbook.* San Francisco: Jossey-Bass.

MEIER, R. P. (1991). Language acquisition by deaf children. *American Scientist, 79,* 60–76.

MELAMED, B. G., & SIEGEL, L. J. (1975). Reduction of anxiety in children facing hospitalization and surgery by use of filmed modeling. *Journal of Consulting and Clinical Psychiatry, 43,* 511–521.

MELTON, A. W. (1963). Implications of short-term memory for a general theory of memory. *Journal of Verbal Learning and Verbal Behavior, 1,* 1–21.

MELZAK, R. (1973). *The puzzle of pain.* New York: Basic Books.

MELZAK, R. (1990). The tragedy of needless pain. *Science, 362,* 27–33.

MELZAK, R., & WALL, P. D. (1982, 1988). *The challenge of pain.* New York: Basic Books.

MERVIS, C. B., & PANI, J. R. (1981). Acquisition of basic object categories. *Cognitive Psychology, 12,* 496–522.

MERVIS, C. B., & ROSCH, E. (1981). Categorization of natural objects. In M. R. Rosenz & L. W. Porter (Eds.), *Annual review of psychology* (Vol. 21). Palo Alto, CA: Annual Reviews.

MESQUITA, B., & FRIJDA, N. H. (1992). Cultural variations in emotions: A review. *Psychological Bulletin, 112,* 179–204.

MESSICK, S. (1992). Multiple intelligences or multilevel intelligence? Selective emphasis on distinctive properties of hierarchy: On Gardner's *Frames of mind* and Sternberg's *Beyond IQ* in the context of theory and research on the structure of human abilities. *Journal of Psychological Inquiry, 1,* 305–384.

METALSKY, G. I., HALBERSTADT, L. J., & ABRAMSON, L. Y. (1987). Vulnerability to depressive mood reactions: Toward a more powerful test of the diathesis-stress and causal meditation components of the reformulated theory of depression. *Journal of Personality and Social Psychology, 52,* 386–393.

METZNER, R. J. (1994, March 14). Prozac is medicine, not a miracle. *Los Angeles Times,* p. B7.

MEYER, J. P., & PEPPER, S. (1977). Need compatability and marital adjustment in young married couples. *Journal of Personality and Social Psychology, 8,* 331–342.

MIDDLETON, F. A., & STRICK, P. L. (1994). Anatomic evidence for cerebellar and basal ganglia involvement in higher cognitive function. *Science, 266,* 458–463.

MILGRAM, S. (1963). Behavioral study of obedience. *Journal of Abnormal and Social Psychology, 67,* 371–378.

MILGRAM, S. (1974). *Obedience to authority: An experimental view.* New York: Harper & Row.

MILLAR, M. G., & TESSER, A. (1989). The effects of affective-cognitive consistency and thought on the attitude-behavior relation. *Journal of Experimental Social Psychology, 25,* 189–202.

MILLER, D. T., & ROSS, M. (1975). Self-serving biases in attribution of causality: Fact or fiction? *Psychological Bulletin, 82,* 213–225.

MILLER, G. A. (1956). The magical number seven plus or minus two: Some limits on our capacity for processing information. *Psychological Review, 63,* 81–97.

MILLER, G. A., & GILDEA, P. M. (1987). How children learn words. *Scientific American, 257,* 94–99.

MILLER, J. G. (1984). Culture and the development of everyday social explanation. *Journal of Personality and Social Psychology, 46,* 961–978.

MILLER, J. M., & SPELMAN, F. A. (1990). *Cochlear implants: Models of the electrically stimulated ear.* New York: Springer-Verlag.

MILLER, N. E., & KESSEN, M. L. (1952). Reward effects of food via stomach fistula compared with those of food via mouth. *Journal of Comparative and Physiological Psychology, 45,* 555–564.

MILLER, P. A., & EISENBERG, N. (1988). The relation of empathy to aggressive and externalizing/antisocial behavior. *Psychological Bulletin, 103,* 324–344.

MILLER, P. H. (1993). *Theories of developmental psychology* (3rd ed.). New York: Freeman.

MILLON, T. (1981). *Disorders of personality: DSM-III.* New York: Wiley.

MILNER, B. (1970). Memory and the medial temporal regions of the brain. In K. H. Pribram & D. E. Broadbent (Eds.), *Biology of memory.* New York: Academic Press.

MILNER, B., CORKIN, S., & TUEBER, H. L. (1968). Further analysis of the hippocampal amnesic syndrome: 14-year follow-up study of H. M. *Neuropsychologia, 6,* 215–234.

MINARD, R. D. (1952). Race relations in the Pocahontas coal field. *Journal of Social Issues, 8,* 29–44.

MINEKA, S. (1987). A primate model of phobic fears. In H. Eysenck & I. Martin (Eds.), *Theoretical foundations of behavior therapy* (pp. 81–111). New York: Plenum Press.

MINEKA, S., DAVIDSON, M., COOK, M., & KEIR, R. (1984). Observational conditioning of snake fear in rhesus monkeys. *Journal of Abnormal Psychology, 93,* 355–372.

MINTZ, L. I., LIEBERMAN, R. P., MIKLOWITZ, D. J., & MINTZ, J. (1987). Expressed emotion: A call for partnership among relatives, patients, and professionals. *Schizophrenia Bulletin, 13,* 227–235.

MINUCHIN, S., ROSMAN, B. L., & BAKER, L. (1978). *Psychosomatic families: Anorexia nervosa in context.* Cambridge, MA: Harvard University Press.

MISCHEL, W. (1966). A social learning view of sex differences in behavior. In E. E. Maccoby (Ed.), *The development of sex differences.* Stanford, CA: Stanford University Press.

MISCHEL, W. (1973). Toward a cognitive social learning reconceptualization of personality. *Psychological Review, 80,* 272–283.

MISCHEL, W. (1993). *Introduction to personality* (5th ed.). Fort Worth: Harcourt Brace Jovanovich.

MISHKIN, M., UNGERLEIDER, L. G., & MACKO, K. A. (1983). Object vision and spatial vision: Two cortical pathways. *Trends in Neuroscience, 6,* 414–417.

MITA, T. H., DERMER, M., & KNIGHT, J. (1977). Reversed facial images and the mere-exposure hypthoses. *Journal of Personality and Social Psychology, 35,* 597–601.

MITCHELL, J. E., & DEZWAAN, M. (1993). Pharmacological treatments of binge eating. In C. E. Fairburn & G. T. Wilson (Eds.), *Binge eating: Nature, assessment, and treatment.* New York: Guilford.

MOFFITT, T. E. (1993). The neuropsychology of conduct disorder. *Development and Psychopathology, 5,* 135–151.

MONAHAN, J. (1992). Mental disorder and violent behavior: Perceptions and evidence. *American Psychologist, 47,* 511–521.

MONAHAN, J., & WALKER, L. (1990). *Social science in law: Cases and materials.* Westbury, NY: Foundation Press.

MONEY, J. (1980). Endocrine influences and psychosexual status spanning the life cycle. In H. M. Van Praag (Ed.), *Handbook of biological psychiatry* (Part 3). New York: Marcel Dekker.

MONEY, J. (1987). Sin, sickness, or status? Homosexual gender identity and psychoneuroendocrinology. *American Psychologist, 42,* 384–400.

MONEY, J., & EHRHARDT, A. A. (1972). *Man and woman, boy and girl: The differentiation and dimorphism of gender identity from conception to maturity.* Baltimore: Johns Hopkins University Press.

MONEY, J., SCHWARTZ, M., & LEWIS, V. G. (1984). Adult heterosexual status and fetal hormonal masculinization and demasculinization: 46, XX congenital virilizing adrenal hyperplasia and 46, XY androgen-insensitivity syndrome compared. *Psychoneuroendocrinology, 9,* 405–414.

MONEY, J., WEIDEKING, C., WALKER, P. A., & GAIN, D. (1976). Combined antiandrogenic and counseling programs for treatment for 46 XY and 47 XXY sex offenders. In E. Sacher (Ed.), *Hormones, behavior and psychopathology.* New York: Raven Press.

MONSELL, S. (1979). Recency, immediate recognition memory, and reaction time. *Cognitive Psychology, 10,* 465–501.

MOORE, B. C. J. (1982). *An introduction to the psychology of hearing* (2nd ed.). New York: Academic Press.

MOOS, R. H. (1988). *Coping responses inventory manual.* Palo Alto, CA: Social Ecology Laboratory, Department of Psychiatry, Stanford University and Veterans Administration Medical Centers.

MORAN, J., & DESIMONE, R. (1985). Selective attention gates visual processing in the extrastriate cortex. *Science, 229,* 782–784.

MORAY, N. (1969). *Attention: Selective processes in vision and hearing.* London: Hutchinson.

MORELAND, R. L., & BEACH, S. R. (1992). Exposure effects in the classroom: The development of affinity among students. *Journal of Experimental Social Psychology, 28,* 255–276.

MORELAND, R. L., & ZAJONC, R. B. (1979). Exposure effects may not depend on stimulus recognition. *Journal of Personality and Social Psychology, 37,* 1085–1089.

MOREY, L. C. (1993). Psychological correlates of personality disorder. *Journal of Personality Disorders* (suppl.), 149–166.

MORGENSTERN, H., & GLAZER, W. M. (1993, September). Identifying risk factors for tardive dyskinesia among long-term outpatients maintained with neuroleptic medications: Results of the Yale tardive dyskinesia study. *Archives of General Psychiatry, 50.*

MOSCOVICI, S. (1976). *Social influence and social change.* London: Academic Press.

MOSCOVICI, S., LAGE, E., & NAFFRECHOUX, M. (1969). Influence of a consistent minority on the responses of a majority in a color perception task. *Sociometry, 32,* 365–379.

MOSCOVICI, S., & ZAVALLONI, M. (1969). The group as a polarizer of attitudes. *Journal of Personality and Social Psychology, 12,* 125–135.

MOSKOWITZ, H. R., KUMRAICH, V., SHARMA, H., JACOBS, L., & SHARMA, S. D. (1975). Cross-cultural difference in simple taste preference. *Science, 190,* 1217–1218.

MOVSHON, J. A., & VAN SLUYTERS, R. C. (1981). Visual neural development. *Annual Review of Psychology, 32,* 477–522.

MOWRER, O. H. (1947). On the dual nature of learning—A reinterpretation of "conditioning" and "problem-solving". *Harvard Educational Review, 17,* 102–148.

MOYER, K. E. (1976). *The psychobiology of aggression.* New York: Harper & Row.

MUKHERJEE, S., SHUKLA, S., WOODLE, J., ROSEN, A. M., & OLARTE, S. (1983). Misdiagnosis of schizophrenia in bipolar patients: A multiethnic comparison. *American Journal of Psychiatry, 140,* 1571–1574.

MUKHOPADHYAY, P., & TURNER, R. M. (1997). Biofeedback treatment of essential hypertension. *Social Science International, 13,* 1–9.

MURDOCK, B. B., JR. (1962). The serial position effect in free recall. *Journal of Experimental Psychology, 64,* 482–488.

MURPHY, G. L., & BROWNELL, H. H. (1985). Category differentiation in object recognition: Typicality constraints on the basic category advantage. *Journal of Experimental Psychology, 11,* 70.

MURSTEIN, B. I. (1972). Physical attractiveness and marital choice. *Journal of Personality and Social Psychology, 22,* 8–12.

MUSSEN, P. H. (Ed.) (1983). *Handbook of child psychology* (4th ed.). New York: Wiley.

MYERS, D. G. (1992). *The pursuit of happiness.* New York: Morrow.

MYERS, D. G. (1993). *Social psychology* (4th ed.). New York: McGraw-Hill.

MYERS, D. G., & DIENER, E. (1995). Who is happy? *Psychological Science, 6,* 10–19.

MYERS, D. G., & LAMM, H. (1976). The group polarization phenomenon. *Psychological Bulletin, 83,* 602–627.

NACOSTE, R. W. (1987). But do they care about fairness? The dynamics of preferential treatment and minority interest. *Basic and Applied Social Psychology, 8,* 177–185.

NARROW, W. E., REGIER, D. A., RAE, D., MANDERSCHEID, R. W., & LOCKE, B. Z. (1993). Use of services by persons with mental and addictive disorders. *Archives of General Psychiatry, 50,* 95–107.

NATHANS, J. (1987). Molecular biology of visual pigments. *Annual Review of Neuroscience, 10,* 163–194.

NEISSER, U. (Ed.) (1982). *Memory observed: Remembering in natural contexts.* New York: Freeman.

NEMETH, C. (1986). Differential contributions of majority and minority influence. *Psychological Review, 93,* 23–32.

NEWCOMB, M. D., RABOW, J., & HERNANDEZ, A. C. R. (1992). A cross-national study of nuclear attitudes, normative support, and activist behavior: Additive and interactive effects. *Journal of Applied Social Psychology, 22,* 780–200.

NEWCOMB, T. M. (1943). *Personality and social change.* New York: Dryden Press.

NEWCOMB, T. M. (1961). *The acquaintance process.* New York: Holt, Rinehart & Winston.

NEWCOMB, T. M., KOENING, K. E., FLACKS, R., & WARWICK, D. P. (1967). *Persistence and change: Bennington College and its students after twenty-five years.* New York: Wiley.

NEWELL, A., & SIMON, H. A. (1972). *Human problem solving.* Englewood Cliffs, NJ: Prentice-Hall.

NEWPORT, E. L. (1990). Maturational constraints on language learning. *Cognitive Science, 14,* 11–28.

NEZU, A. M., NEZU, C. M., & PERRI, M. G. (1989). *Problem-solving therapy for depression: Theory, research, and clinical guidelines.* New York: Wiley.

NICHD EARLY CHILD CARE RESEARCH NETWORK. (1998). Early child care and self-control, compliance, and problem behavior at 24 and 36 months. *Child Development, 69,* 1145–1170.

NIELSON, T., & POWELL, R. (1992). The day-residue and dream-lag effect. *Dreaming, 2,* 67–77.

NILSON, D. C., NILSON, L. B., OLSON, R. S., & MCALLISTER, B. H. (1981). *The planning environment report for the Southern California Earthquake Safety Advisory Board.* Redlands, CA: Social

Research Advisory & Policy Research Center.

NINIO, A. (1980). Picture book reading in mother-infant dyads belong to two subgroups in Israel. *Child Development, 51,* 587–590.

NISAN, M., & KOHLBERG, L. (1982). Universality and variation in moral judgment: A longitudinal and cross-sectional study in Turkey. *Child Development, 53,* 865–876.

NISBETT, R. E., KRANZ, D. H., JEPSON, D., & KUNDA, Z. (1983). The use of statistical heuristics in everyday inductive reasoning. *Psychological Review, 90,* 339–363.

NISBETT, R. E., & ROSS, L. (1980). *Human inference: Strategies and shortcomings of social judgment.* Englewood Cliffs, NJ: Prentice-Hall.

NISBETT, R. E., & WILSON, T. D. (1977). Telling more than we can know: Verbal reports on mental processes. *Psychological Review, 84,* 231–259.

NOLEN-HOEKSEMA, S. (1991). Responses to depression and their effects on the duration of depressive episodes. *Journal of Abnormal Psychology, 100,* 569–582.

NOLEN-HOEKSEMA, S., & LARSON, J. (1999). *Coping with loss.* Mahwah, NJ: Erlbaum.

NOLEN-HOEKSEMA, S., & MORROW, J. (1991). A prospective study of depression and distress following a natural disaster: The 1989 Loma Prieta earthquake. *Journal of Personality and Social Psychology, 61,* 105–121.

NORTH, C. (1987). *Welcome silence.* New York: Simon and Schuster.

NUCCLI, L. (1981). The development of personal concepts: A domain distinct from moral or societal concepts. *Child Development, 52,* 114–121.

OFFIR, C. (1982). *Human sexuality.* San Diego: Harcourt Brace Jovanovich.

OGBORNE, A. C. (1993). Assessing the effectiveness of Alcoholics Anonymous in the community: Meeting the challenges. In B. S. McCrady & W. R. Miller (Eds.), *Research on Alcoholics Anonymous: Opportunities and alternatives.* New Brunswick, NJ: Rutgers Center of Alcohol Studies.

OHMAN, A. (1986). Face the beast and fear the face: Animal and social fears as prototypes for evolutionary analyses of emotion. *Psychophysiology, 23,* 123–145.

OJEMANN, G. (1983). Brain organization for language from the perspective of electrical stimulation mapping. *Behavioral and Brain Sciences, 6,* 189–230.

OLTON, D. S. (1978). Characteristics of spatial memory. In S. H. Hulse, H. F. Fowler, & W. K. Honig (Eds.), *Cognitive processes in animal behavior.* Hillsdale, NJ: Erlbaum.

OLTON, D. S. (1979). Mazes, maps, and memory. *American Psychologist, 34,* 583–596.

OLWEUS, D. (1969). *Prediction of aggression.* Scandanavian Test Corporation.

OLWEUS, D., MATTSSON, A., SCHALLING, D., & LOW, H. (1988). Circulating testosterone levels and aggression in adolescent males: A causal analysis. *Psychosomatic Medicine, 50,* 261–272.

OMAN, D., & REED, D. (1998). Religion and mortality among the community dwelling elderly. *American Journal of Public Health, 88,* 1469–1475.

ORLINSKY, D. E., & HOWARD, K. I. (1987). A generic model of psychotherapy. *Journal of Integrative and Eclectic Psychotherapy, 6,* 6–27.

ORNE, M. T., & HOLLAND, C. C. (1968). On the ecological validity of laboratory deceptions. *International Journal of Psychiatry, 6,* 282–293.

ORNE, M. T., SOSKIS, D. A., DINGES, D. F., & ORNE, E. C. (1984). Hypnotically induced testimony. In G. L. Wells & E. F. Loftus (Eds.), *Eyewitness testimony: Psychological perspectives* (pp. 171–213). Cambridge: Cambridge University Press.

ORTONY, A., CLORE, G. L., & COLLINS, A. (1988). *The cognitive structure of emotions.* New York: Cambridge University Press.

OSHERSON, D. N., KOSLYN, S. M. & HOLLERBACH, J. M. (1990). *An invitation to cognitive science* (Vol. 2). Cambridge, MA: MIT Press.

OSHERSON, D. N., & LASNIK, H. (1990). *An invitation to cognitive science* (Vol. 1). Cambridge, MA: MIT Press.

OSHERSON, D. N., & SMITH, E. E. (1990). *An invitation to cognitive science* (Vol. 3). Cambridge, MA: MIT Press.

OSHERSON, D. N., SMITH, E. E., WILKIE, O., LOPEZ, A., & SHAFIR, E. B. (1990). Category based induction. *Psychological Review, 97,* 185–200.

OSOFSKY, J. D. (Ed.) (1987). *Handbook of infant development* (2nd ed.). New York: Wiley.

OVERMEIER, J. B., & SELIGMAN, M. E. P. (1967). Effects of inescapable shock upon subsequent escape and avoidance responding. *Journal of Comparative and Physiological Psychology, 63,* 28.

PAFFENBERGER, R. S., HYDE, R. T., WING, A. L., & HSIEH, C. (1986). Physical activity, all-cause mortality, and longevity of college alumni. *New England Journal of Medicine, 314,* 605–613.

PAICHELER, G. (1977). Norms and attitude change: Pt. 1. Polarization and styles of behavior. *European Journal of Social Psychology, 7,* 5–14.

PALLIS, C. A. (1955). Impaired identification of faces and places with agnosia for colors. *Journal of Neurology, Neurosurgery, and Psychiatry, 18,* 218–224.

PALMER, S. E. (1975). The effect of contextual scenes on the identification of objects. *Memory and Cognition, 3,* 519–526.

PARKER, G., JOHNSTON, P., & HAYWARD, L. (1988). Parental "expressed emotion" as a predictor of schizophrenic relapse. *Archives of General Psychiatry, 45,* 806–813.

PARKER, G., & HADZZI-PAVLOVIC, D. (1990). Expressed emotion as a predictor of schizophrenic relapse: An analysis of aggregated data. *Psychological Medicine, 20,* 961–965.

PASZTOR, A. (1996, July 1). An air-safety battle brews over the issue of pilots' rest time. *The Wall Street Journal.*

PATEL, V. L., & GROEN, G. J. (1986). Knowledge based solution strategies in medical reasoning. *Cognitive Science, 10,* 91.

PATTERSON, F. G. (1978). The gestures of a gorilla: Language acquisition in another pongid. *Brain and Language, 5,* 72–97.

PATTERSON, F. G., & LINDEN, E. (1981). *The education of Koko.* New York: Holt, Rinehart & Winston.

PATTERSON, G. R., DEBARSHYE, B. D., & RAMSEY, E. (1989). A developmental perspective on antisocial behavior. *American Psychologist, 44,* 329–335.

PATTERSON, G. R., LITTMAN, R. A., & BRICKER, W. A. (1967). Assertive behavior in children: A step toward a theory of aggression. *Monographs of the Society for Research in Child Development* (Serial No. 113), 5.

PATTERSON, G. R., REID, J. B., & DISHION, T. J. (1992). *Antisocial boys.* Eugene, OR: Castalia Press.

PAUL, G. L. (1967). Insight versus desensitization in psychotherapy two years after termination. *Journal of Consulting Psychology, 31,* 333–348.

PAUL, G. L., & LENTZ, R. J. (1977). *Psychosocial treatment of chronic mental patients: milieu versus social learning programs.* Cambridge, MA: Harvard University Press.

PAULHUS, D. (1982). Individual differences, self-presentation, and cognitive dissonance: Their concurrent operation in forced compliance. *Journal of Personality and Social Psychology, 43,* 838–852.

PAULUS, P. B., & MURDOCK, P. (1971). Anticipated evaluation and audience presence in the enhancement of dominant responses. *Journal of Experimental Social Psychology, 7,* 280–291.

PAVLOV, I. P. (1927). *Conditioned reflexes.* New York: Oxford University Press.

PECHURA, C. M., & MARTIN, J. B. (Eds.) (1991). *Mapping the brain and its functions.* Washington, D.C.: National Academy Press.

PEDERSEN, N. L., PLOMIN, R., MCCLEARN, G. E., & FRIBERG, L. (1988). Neuroticism, extraversion and related traits in adult twins reared apart and reared together. *Journal of Personality and Social Psychology, 55,* 905–957.

PEELE, S. (1988). Fools for love: The romantic ideal, psychological theory, and addictive love. In R. J. Sternberg & M. L. Barnes (Eds.), *The psychology of love* (pp. 159–188). New Haven, CT: Yale University Press.

PELLEGRINO, J. W. (1985). Inductive reasoning ability. In R. J. Sternberg (Ed.), *Human abilities: An information-processing approach.* New York: Freeman.

PENG, K., & NISBETT, R. E. (in press). Naïve dialecticism and its effects on reasoning and judgment about contradiction. *American Psychologist.*

PENNEBAKER, J. W. (1990). *Opening up: The healing power of confiding in others.* New York: William Morrow.

PENNEBAKER, J. W. (1997). *Opening up: The healing power of expressing emotions* (rev. ed.). New York: Guilford.

PENNEBAKER, J. W., KIECOLT-GLASER, J. K., & GLASER, R. (1988). Disclosure of traumas and immune function: Health implications for psychotherapy. *Journal of Consulting and Clinical Psychology, 56,* 239–245.

PENNEBAKER, J. W., & O'HEERON, R. C. (1984). Confiding in others and illness rates among spouses of suicide and accidental-death victims. *Journal of Abnormal Psychology, 93,* 473–476.

PEPLAU, L. A., RUBIN, Z., & HILL, C. T. (1977). Sexual intimacy in dating relationships. *Journal of Social Issues, 33,* 86–109.

PERRIN, F. A. C. (1921). Physical attractiveness and repulsiveness. *Journal of Experimental Psychology, 4,* 203–217.

PERRY, D. G., & BUSSEY, K. (1984). *Social development.* Englewood Cliffs, NJ: Prentice-Hall.

PERRY, D. G., PERRY, L.C., & BOLDIZAR, J. P. (1990). Learning of aggression. In M. Lewis & S. Miller (Eds.), *Handbook of developmental psychopathology* (pp. 135–146). New York: Plenum.

PERRY, J. C. (1993). Longitudinal studies of personality disorders. *Journal of Personality Disorders,* Suppl. 1, 63–85.

PETERSEN, A. C. (1989). Adolescent development. In M. R. Rosenzweig & L. W. Porter (Eds.), *Annual review of psychology* (Vol. 39). Palo Alto, CA: Annual Reviews.

PETERSON, C., & SELIGMAN, M. E. P. (1984). Causal explanations as a risk factor for depression: Theory and evidence. *Psychological Review, 91,* 347–374.

PETRIE, K. J., BOOTH, R. J., & PENNEBAKER, J. W. (1998). The immunological effects of thought suppression. *Journal of Personality and Social Psychology, 75,* 1264–1272.

PETRONIS, K. R., SAMUELS, J. F., MOSCICKI, E. K., & ANTHONY, J. C. (1990). An epidemiologic investigation of potential risk factors for suicide attempts. *Social Psychiatry and Psychiatric Epidemiology, 25,* 193–199

PETTIGREW, T. F. (1959). Regional differences in anti-Negro prejudice. *Journal of Abnormal and Social Psychology, 59,* 28–36.

PETTY, R. E., & CACIOPPO, J. T. (1981). *Attitudes and persuasion: Classic and contemporary approaches.* Dubuque, IA: Wm. C. Brown.

PETTY, R. E., & CACIOPPO, J. T. (1984). The effects of involvement on responses to argument quantity and quality: Central and peripheral routes to persuasion. *Journal of Personality and Social Psychology, 46,* 69–81.

PETTY, R. E., & CACIOPPO, J. T. (1986). Elaboration likelihood model of persuasion. In L. Berkowitz (Ed.), *Advances in experimental social psychology* (Vol. 19, pp. 123–205). New York: Academic Press.

PETTY, R. E., & CACIOPPO, J. T. & GOLDMAN, R. (1981). Personal involvement as a determinant of argument-based persuasion. *Journal of Personality and Social Psychology, 41,* 847–855.

PETTY, R. E., OSTROM, T. M., & BROCK, T. C. (1981). Historical foundations of the cognitive response approach to attitudes and persuasion. In R. E. Petty, T. M. Ostrom, & T. C. Brock (Eds.), *Cognitive responses in persuasion.* Hillsdale, NJ: Erlbaum.

PEZDEK, K., FINGER, K., & HODGE, D. (1997). Planting false childhood memories: The role of event plausibility. *Psychological Science, 8,* 437–441.

PHILLIPS, D. A., MCCARTNEY, K., & SCARR, S. (1987). Child-care quality and children's social development. *Developmental Psychology, 23,* 537–543.

PHILLIPS, D. A., VORAN, M., KISKER, E., HOWES, C., & WHITEBROOK, M. (1994). Child care for children in poverty: Opportunity or inequity? *Child Development, 65,* 472–492.

PHILLIPS, J. L., JR. (1981). *Piaget's theory: A primer.* San Francisco: Freeman.

PHILLIPS, J. L., JR. (1992). *How to think about statistics* (rev. ed.). New York: Freeman.

PHOENIX, C. H., GOY, R. H., & RESKO, J. A. (1968). Psychosexual differentiation as a function of androgenic stimulation. In M. Diamond (Ed.), *Reproduction and sexual behavior.* Bloomington: Indiana University Press.

PIAGET, J. (1932/1965). *The moral judgment of the child.* New York: Free Press.

PIAGET, J. (1950a). *The origins of intelligence in children.* New York: International Universities Press.

PIAGET, J. (1950b). *The psychology of intelligence.* New York: International Universities Press.

PIAGET, J., & INHELDER, B. (1956). *The child's conception of space.* London: Routledge & Kegan Paul. (originally published 1948)

PIAGET, J., & INHELDER, B. (1969). *The psychology of the child.* New York: Basic Books.

PICCIONE, C., HILGARD, E. R., & ZIMBARDO, P. G. (1989). On the degree of stability of measured hypnotizability over a 25-year period. *Journal of Personality and Social Psychology, 56,* 289–295.

PICKERING, T. G., DEVEREUX, R. B., JAMES, G. D., GERIN, W., LANDSBERGIS, P., SCHNALL, P. L., & SCHWARTZ, J. E. (1996). Environmental influences on blood pressure and the role of job strain. *Journal of Hypertension, 14* (Suppl.), S179–S185.

PILIAVIN, I. M., RODIN, J., & PILIAVIN, J. A. (1969). Good Samaritanism: An underground phenomenon: *Journal of Personality and Social Psychology, 13,* 289–299.

PINKER, S. (1984). *Language learnability and language development.* Cambridge, MA: Harvard University Press.

PINKER, S. (1991). Rules of language. *Science, 253,* 530–555.

PINKER, S., & PRINCE, A. (1988). On language and connectionism: Analysis of a parallel distributed processing model of language acquisition. *Cognition, 28,* 71–193.

PION, G. M. (1991). Psychologists wanted: Employment trends over the past decade. In R. R. Kilburg (Ed.), *How to manage your career in psychology.* Washington, D.C.: American Psychological Association.

PLATT, J. J., YAKSH, T., & DARBY, C. L. (1967). Social facilitation of eating behavior in armadillos. *Psychological Reports, 20,* 1136.

PLOMIN, R. (1989). Environment and genes: Determinants of behavior. *American Psychologist, 44,* 105–111.

PLOMIN, R., & DANLIES, D. (1987). Why are children in the same family so different from one another? *Behavioral and Brain Sciences, 10,* 1–60.

PLOMIN, R., DEFRIES, J. C., & LOEHLIN, J. C. (1977). Genotype-environment interaction and correlation in the analysis of human behavior. *Psychological Bulletin, 84,* 309–322.

PLOMIN, R., FULKER, D. W., CORLEY, R., & DEFRIES, J. C. (1997). Nature, nurture, and cognitive development from 1 to 16 years: A parent-offspring adoption study. *Psychological Science, 8,* 442–447.

PLOMIN, R., OWEN, M. J., & MCGUFFIN, P. (1994). The genetic basis of complex human behaviors. *Science, 264,* 1733–1739.

POLIVY, J., & HERMAN, C. P. (1985). Dieting and bingeing: A causal analysis. *American Psychologist, 40,* 193–201.

POLIVY, J., & HERMAN, C. P.. (1993). Etiology of binge eating: Psychological mechanisms. In C. E. Fairburn & G. T. Wilson (Eds.), *Binge eating: Nature, assessment, and treatment.* New York: Guilford.

PORTENOY, R. K. (1990). Chronic opioid therapy in nonmalignant pain. *Journal of Pain and Symptom Management, 5,* S46–S62.

PORTENOY, R. K., & FOLEY, K. M. (1986). Chronic use of opioid analgesics in non-malignant pain: Report of 38 cases. *Pain, 25,* 171–186,

PORTER, R. H., MAKIN, J. W., DAVIS, L. B., & CHRISTENSEN, K. M. (1992). An assessment of the salient olfactory environment of formula-fed infants. *Physiology and Behavior, 50,* 907–911.

PORTER, S. (1998). The nature of real, created, and fabricated memories for emotional childhood events. Unpublished doctoral dissertation, University of British Columbia.

POSNER, M. I. (1988). Structures and functions of selective attention. In T. Boll & B. K. Bryant (Eds.), *Clinical neuropsychology and brain function: Research, measurement, and practice.* Washington, DC: American Psychological Association.

POSNER, M. I. (1993). Seeing the mind. *Science, 262,* 673–674.

POSNER, M. I., & DEHAENE, S. (1994). Attentional networks. *Trends in Neuroscience, 17,* 75–79.

POSNER, M. I., & RAICHLE, M. E. (1994). *Images of mind.* New York: Scientific American Library.

POWELL, R. A., & BOER, D. P. (1994). Did Freud mislead patients to confabulate memories of abuse? *Psychological Reports, 74,* 1283–1298.

PREMACK, D. (1971). Language in chimpanzees? *Science, 172,* 808–822.

PREMACK, D. (1985). "Gavagi!" Or the future history of the animal language controversy. *Cognition, 19,* 207–296.

PREMACK, D., & PREMACK, A. J. (1983). *The mind of an ape.* New York: Norton.

PRESSLEY, M., LEVIN, J. R., & DELANEY, H. D. (1982). The mnemonic keyword method. *Review of Educational Research, 52,* 61–91.

PRETI, G., CUTLER, W. B., GARCIA, C. R., HUGGINS, G. R., and collaborators (1986). Human axillary secretions influence women's menstrual cycles: The role of donor extract of females. *Hormones & Behavior, 20,* 474–482.

PRIEST, R. F., & SAWYER, J. (1967). Proximity and peership: Bases of balance in interpersonal attraction. *American Journal of Sociology, 72,* 633–649.

PRINZMETAL, W. (1981). Principles of feature integration in visual perception. *Perception & Psychophysics, 30,* 330–340.

PROJECT MATCH RESEARCH GROUP (1997). Matching alcoholism treatments to client heterogeneity: Project MATCH posttreatment drinking outcomes. *Journal of Studies on Alcohol, 58,* 7–29.

PROTHRO, E. T., (1952). Ethnocentrism and anti-Negro attitudes in the deep South. *Journal of Abnormal and Social Pathology, 47,* 105–108.

PUTNAM, F. W. (1991). Recent research on multiple personality disorder. *Psychiatric Clinics of North America, 14,* 489–502.

QUIRK, G. J., REPA, C., & LEDOUX, J. E. (1995). *Neuron, 15,* 1029–1039.

RAAIJMAKERS, J. G., & SHIFFRIN, R. M. (1981). Search of associative memory. *Psychological Review, 88,* 93–134.

RAAIJMAKERS, J. G., & SHIFFRIN, R. M. (1992). Models for recall and recognition. *Annual Review of Psychology, 43,* 205–234.

RACHMAN, S. (1993). Obsessions, responsibility and guilt. *Behaviour Research & Therapy, 31,* 149–154.

RACHMAN, S. J., & HODGSON, R. J. (1980). *Obsessions and compulsions.* Englewood Cliffs, NJ: Prentice-Hall.

RACHMAN, S. J., & WILSON, G. T. (1980). *The effects of psychological therapy* (2nd ed.). Elmsford, NY: Pergamon Press.

RAEIKKOENEN, K., MATTHEWS, K. A., FLORY, J. D., & OWENS, J. F. (1999). Effects of hostility on ambulatory blood pressure and mood during daily living in healthy adults. *Health Psychology 18,* 44–53.

RAGSDALE, D. S., MCPHEE, J. C., SCHEUER, T., & CATTERALL, W. A. (1994). Molecular determinants of state-dependent block of Na channels by local anesthetics. *Science, 265,* 1724–1728.

RAICHLE, M. E. (1994). Images of the mind: Studies with modern imaging techniques. *Annual Review of Psychology, 45,* 333–356.

RAMACHANDRAN, V. S., & BLAKESLEE, S. (1998). *Phantoms in the brain.* New York: William Morrow.

RAMACHANDRAN, V. S., & GREGORY, R. L. (1991). Perceptual filling in of artificially induced scotomas in human vision. *Nature, 350,* 699–702.

RAMACHANDRAN, V. S., LEVI, L., STONE, L., ROGERS-RAMACHANDRAN, D., and collaborators (1996). Illusions of body image: What they reveal about human nature. In R. R. Llinas & P. S. Churchland (Eds.) et al., *The mind-brain continuum: Sensory processes* (pp. 29–60). Cambridge, MA: MIT Press.

RANDI, J. (1982). *Flim-flam! Psychics, ESP, unicorns and other delusions.* Buffalo: Prometheus Books.

RAPAPORT, D. (1942). *Emotions and memory.* Baltimore: Williams & Wilkins.

RAPAPORT, J. L. (1990). *The boy who couldn't stop washing.* New York: Plume.

RAPAPORT, J. L. (1991). Recent advances in obsessive-compulsive disorder. *Neuropsychopharmacology, 5,* 1–10.

RAPEE, R. M., BROWN, T. A., ANTONY, M. M., & BARLOW, D. H. (1992). Response to hyperventilation and inhalation of 5.5% carbon dioxide-enriched air across the DSM III-R anxiety disorders. *Journal of Abnormal Psychology, 101,* 538–552.

RASMUSSEN, S. A., & EISEN, J. L. (1990). Epidemiology of obsessive compulsive disorder. *Journal of Clinical Psychiatry, 51* (suppl.), 10–13.

RATHBUN, C., DIVIRGLIO, L., & WALDFOGEL, S. (1958). A restitutive process in children following radical separation from family and culture. *American Journal of Orthopsychiatry, 28,* 408–415.

RAVENS, J. C. (1965). *Advanced progressive matrices, sets II and II.* London: H. K. Lewis. (Distributed in the U.S. by The Psychological Corporation, San Antonio, TX)

RAVUSSIN, E., and collaborators (1988). Reduced rate of energy expenditure as a risk factor for body-weight gain. *New England Journal of Medicine, 318,* 467–472.

RAY, W. J., & RAVIZZA, R. (1988). *Methods toward a science of behavior and experience* (3rd ed.). Belmont, CA: Wadsworth.

RAYNER, K. (1978). Eye movements, reading and information processing. *Psychological Bulletin, 6,* 618–660.

REED, G. M., KEMENY, M. E., TAYLOR, S. E., WANG, H.-Y. J., & VISSCHER, B. R. (1994). "Realistic acceptance" as a predictor of decreased survival time in gay men with AIDS. *Health Psychology, 13,* 299–307.

REGAN, D., BEVERLEY, K. I., & CYNADER, M. (1979). The visual perception of motion depth. *Scientific American, 241,* 136–151.

REGAN, D. T., & FAZIO, R. (1977). On the consistency between attitudes and behavior: Look to the method of attitude information. *Journal of Experimental Social Psychology, 13,* 28–45.

REICHER, G. M. (1969). Perceptual recognition as a function of the meaningfulness of the material. *Journal of Experimental Psychology, 81,* 275–280.

REINISCH, J. M. (1981). Prenatal exposure to synthetic progestins increases potential for aggression in humans. *Science, 211,* 1171–1173.

REISS, D. (1997). Mechanisms linking genetic and social influences in adolescent development: Beginning a collaborative search. *Current Directions in Psychological Science, 6,* 100–105.

RESCORLA, R. A. (1967). Pavlovian conditioning and its proper control procedures. *Psychological Review, 74,* 71–80.

RESCORLA, R. A. (1972). Informational variables in Pavlovian conditioning. In G. H. Bower (Ed.), *Psychology of learning and motivation* (Vol. 6). New York: Academic Press.

RESCORLA, R. A. (1980). Overextension in early language development. *Journal of Child Language, 7,* 321–335.

RESCORLA, R. A. (1987). A Pavlovian analysis of goal-directed behavior. *American Psychologist, 42,* 119–129.

RESCORLA, R. A. & SOLOMON, R. L. (1967). Two-process learning theory: Relations between Pavlovian conditioning and instrumental learning. *Psychological Review, 74,* 151–182.

RESKIN, B. (1998). *The realities of affirmative action in employment.* Washington, DC: American Sociological Association.

RESNICK, H. S., KILPATRICK, D. G., DANSKY, B. S., & SAUNDERS, B. E. (1993). Prevalence of civilian trauma and posttraumatic stress disorder in a representative national sample of women. *Journal of Consulting and Clinical Psychology, 61,* 984–991.

REUBENS, A. B., & BENSON, D. F. (1971). Associative visual agnosia. *Archives of Neurology, 24,* 305–316.

REYNOLDS, D. V. (1969). Surgery in the rat during electrical analgesia induced by focal brain stimulation. *Science, 164,* 444–445.

RHEINGOLD, H. F., & COOK, K. V. (1975). The content of boys' and girls' rooms as an index of parent behavior. *Child Development, 46,* 459–463.

RICE, B. (1978). The new truth machine. *Psychology Today, 12,* 61–78.

RICHARDSON, J. L., SHELTON, D. R., KRAILO, M., & LEVINE, A. M. (1990). The effect of compliance with treatment in survival among patients with hematologic malignancies. *Journal of Clinicial Oncology, 8,* 356.

RICHARDSON, K. (1986). Theory? Or tools for social selection? *Behavioral and Brain Sciences, 9,* 579–581.

RIESEN, A. H. (1947). The development of visual perception in man and chimpanzee. *Science, 106,* 107–108.

RIMM-KAUFMAN, S., & KAGAN, J. (1996). The psychological significance of changes in skin temperature. *Motivation and Emotion, 20,* 63–78.

RIPS, L. J. (1983). Cognitive processes in propositional reasoning. *Psychological Review, 90,* 38–71.

RIPS, L. J. (1994). *The psychology of proof.* Cambridge, MA: MIT Press.

ROBERT, M. (1989). Reduction of demand characteristics in the measurement of certainty during modeled conservation. *Journal of Experimental Child Psychology, 47,* 451–466.

ROBINS, L. N., HELZER, J. E., WEISSMAN, M. M., ORVASCHEL, H., GRUENBERG, E., BURKE, J. D., & REIGIER, D. A. (1984). Lifetime prevalence of specific psychiatric disorders in three sites. *Archives of General Psychiatry, 41,* 949–958.

ROBINSON, T. E., & BERRIDGE, K. C. (1993). The neural basis of drug craving: an incentive-sensitization theory of addiction. *Brain Research Review, 18,* 247–291.

RODIN, J. (1981). Current status of the internal-external hypothesis of obesity: What went wrong? *American Psychologist, 36,* 361–372.

ROFFWARG, H. P., HERMAN, J. H., BOWER-ANDERS, C., & TAUBER, E. S. (1978). The effects of sustained alterations of waking visual input on dream content. In A. M. Arkin, J. S. Antrobus, & S. J. Ellman (Eds.), *The mind in sleep.* Hillsdale, NJ: Erlbaum.

ROGERS, C. R. (1959). A theory of therapy, personality, and interpersonal relationships as developed in the client-centered framework. In S. Koch (Ed.), *Psychology: A study of a science: Vol. 3. Formulations of the person and the social context.* New York: McGraw-Hill.

ROGERS, C. R. (1951). *Client-centered therapy.* Boston: Houghton Mifflin.

ROGERS, C. R. (1963). The actualizing tendency in relation to motives and to consciousness. In M. Jones (Ed.), *Nebraska symposium on motivation* (pp. 1–24). Lincoln: University of Nebraska Press.

ROGERS, C. R. (1970). *On becoming a person: A therapist's view of psychotherapy.* Boston: Houghton Mifflin.

ROGERS, T. B., KUIPER, N. A., & KIRKER, W. S. (1977). Self-reference and the encoding of personal information. *Journal of Personality and Social Psychology, 35,* 677–688.

ROGOFF, B. (1990). *Apprenticeship in thinking.* New York: Oxford University Press.

ROITBLAT, H. L. (1986). *Introduction to comparative cognition.* New York: Freeman.

ROLAND, P. E., & FRIBERG, L. (1985). Localization of cortical areas activated by thinking. *Journal of Neurophysiology, 53,* 1219–1243.

ROOK, K. (1984). The negative side of social interaction: Impact on psychological well-being. *Journal of Personality and Social Psychology, 46,* 1097–1108.

ROSCH, E. (1974). Linguistic relativity. In A. L. Silverstein (Ed.), *Human communication: Theoretical explorations.* New York: Halsted Press.

ROSCH, E. (1978). Principles of categorization. In E. Rosch & B. L. Lloyd (Eds.), *Cognition and categorization.* Hillsdale, NJ: Erlbaum.

ROSCH, E. (1997). Transformation of the wolf man. In J. Pickering (Ed.), *The authority of experience: Essays on Buddhism and psychology.* Surrey, Eng.: Curzon Press.

ROSE, J. E., BRUGGE, J. F., ANDERSON, D. J., & HIND, J. E. (1967). Phase-locked response to lower frequency tones in single auditory nerve fibers of the squirrel monkey. *Journal of Neurophysiology, 390,* 769–793.

ROSEN, R. C., & LEIBLUM, S. R. (1995). Treatment of sexual disorders in the 1990s: An integrated approach. *Journal of Consulting and Clinical Psychology, 63,* 877–890.

ROSENBLITH, J. F. (1992). *In the beginning: Development from conception to age two years* (2nd ed.). Newbury Park, CA: Sage.

ROSENBLOOM, P. S., LAIRD, J. E., NEWELL, A., & MCCARL, R. (1991). A preliminary analysis of the foundations of Soar. *Artificial Intelligence, 47,* 289–325.

ROSENMAN, R. H., BRAND, R. J., JENKINS, C. D., FRIEDMAN, M., STRAUS, R., & WRUM, M. (1976). Coronary heart disease in the Western Collaborative Group Study: Final follow-up experience of 8½ years. *Journal of the American Medical Association, 233,* 878–877.

ROSENTHAL, R. (1984). *Meta-analytic procedures for social research.* Beverly Hills, CA: Sage.

ROSENZWEIG, M. R., & LEIMAN, A. L. (1989). *Physiological psychology* (2nd ed.). Lexington, MA: Heath.

ROSS, L. (1977). The intuitive psychologist and his shortcomings: Distortions in the attribution process. In L. Berkowitz, (Ed.), *Advances in experimental social psychology* (Vol. 10). New York: Academic Press.

ROSS, L., AMABILE, T. M., & STEINMETZ, J. L. (1977). Social roles, social control, and biases in social-perception processes. *Journal of Personality and Social Psychology, 35,* 485–494.

ROSS, L., BIERBRAUER, G., & HOFFMAN, S. (1976). The role of attribution processes in conformity and dissent. Revisiting the Asch situation. *American Psychologist, 31,* 148–157.

ROSS, L., LEPPER, M. R., & HUBBARD, M. (1975). Perseverance in self perception and social perception: Biased attributional processes in the debriefing paradigm. *Journal of Personality and Social Psychology, 32,* 880–892.

ROSS, L., LEPPER, M. R., STRACK, F., & STEINMETZ, J. L. (1977). Social explanation and social expectation: The effects of real and hypothetical explanations upon subjective likelihood. *Journal of Personality and Social Psychology, 35,* 817–829.

ROSS, L., & NISBETT, R. E. (1991). *The person and the situation: Perspectives of social psychology.* New York: McGraw-Hill.

ROSSI, P. (1990). The old homelessness and the new homelessness in historical perspective. *American Psychologist, 45,* 954–959.

ROTH, A., FONAGY, P., PARRY, G., TARGET, M., and collaborators (1996). *What works for whom? A critical review of psychotherapy research.* New York: Guilford.

ROTH, M. (1998). *Freud: Conflict and culture.* New York: Knopf.

ROTTER, J. B. (1954). *Social learning and clinical psychology.* Englewood Cliffs, NJ: Prentice-Hall.

ROTTER, J. B. (1982). *The development and applications of social learning theory: Selected papers.* New York: Praeger.

ROVEE-COLLIER, C., & HAYNE, H. (1987). Reactivation of infant memory: Implications for cognitive development. In H. W. Reese (Ed.), *Advances in child development and behavior* (Vol. 20). New York: Academic Press.

ROWLAND, N. E., & ANTELMAN, S. M. (1976). Stress-induced hyperphagia and obesity in rats: A possible model for understanding human obesity. *Science, 191,* 310–12.

ROYCE, J. R., & MOS, L. P. (Eds.) (1981). *Humanistic psychology: Concepts and criticisms.* New York: Plenum.

ROZIN, P. N., & SCHULKIN, J. (1990). Food selection. In E. M. Stricker (Ed.), *Neurobiology of food and fluid intake* (pp. 297–328). New York: Plenum.

RUBIN, Z. (1973). *Liking and loving.* New York: Holt, Rinehart & Winston.

RUCH, J. C. (1975). Self-hypnosis: The result of heterohypnosis or vice versa? *International Journal of Clinical and Experimental Hypnosis, 23,* 282–304.

RUCH, J. C., MORGAN, A. H., & HILGARD, E. R. (1973). Behavioral predictions from hypnotic responsiveness scores when obtained with and without prior induction procedures. *Journal of Abnormal Psychology, 82,* 543–546.

RUDERMAN, A. J. (1986). Dietary restraint: A theoretical and empirical review. *Psychological Bulletin, 99,* 247–262.

RUMELHART, D. E., & MCCLELLAND, J. L. (1987). Learning the past tenses of English verbs: Implicit rules or parallel distributed processing? In B. MacWhinney (Ed.), *Mechanisms of language acquisition.* Hillsdale, NJ: Erlbaum.

RUMELHART, D. E., MCCLELLAND, J. L., & THE PDP RESEARCH GROUP (1986). *Parallel distributed processing: Explorations in the microstructure of cognition. Volume 1: Foundations.* Cambridge, MA: Bradford Books/ MIT Press.

RUSSELL, M. J. (1976). Human olfactory communication. *Nature, 260,* 520–522.

RUSSELL, M. J., SWITZ, G. M., & THOMPSON, K. (1980). Olfactory influence on the human menstrual cycle. *Pharmacology, Biochemistry and Behavior, 13,* 737–738.

RUSSO, N. F., & SOBEL, S. B. (1981). Sex differences in the utilization of mental health facilities. *Professional Psychology, 12,* 7–19.

RUTTER, M., MACDONALD, H., CONTEUR, A. L., HARRINGTON, R., BOLTON, P., & BAILEY, A. (1990). Genetic factors in child psychiatric disorders: II. Empirical findings. *Journal of Child Psychology and Psychiatry, 31,* 39–83.

RUTTER, M., QUINTON, D., & HILL, J. (1990). Adult outcome of institution-reared children: Males and females compared. In L. Robins (Ed.), *Straight and devious pathways from childhood to adulthood* (pp. 135–157). Cambridge, England: Cambridge University Press.

RYMER, R. (1992a, April 13). A silent childhood. *New Yorker,* pp. 41–53.

RYMER, R. (1992b, April 20). A silent childhood, pt. II. *New Yorker,* pp. 43–47.

SACHS, J. D. S. (1967). Recognition memory for syntactic and semantic aspects of connected discourse. *Perception and Psychophysics, 2,* 437–442.

SACKS, O. (1985). *The man who mistook his wife for a hat and other clinical tales.* New York: Harper Perennial.

SACKS, O. W. (1983). *Awakenings.* New York: Dutton.

SAFER, D. J., ZITO, J. M., & FINE, E. M. (1996). Increased methylphenidate usage for Attention Deficit Disorder in the 1990s. *Pediatrics, 98,* 1084–1088.

SALAMY, J. (1970). Instrumental responding to internal cues associated with REM sleep. *Psychonomic Science, 18,* 342–343.

SALAPATEK, P. (1975). Pattern perception in early infancy. In L. B. Cohen & P. Salapatek (Eds.), *Infant perception: From sensation to cognition* (Vol. 1). New York: Academic Press.

SALKOVSKIS, P. M. (1989). Cognitive-behavioral factors and the persistence of intrusive thoughts in obsessional problems. *Behaviour Research & Therapy, 27,* 677–682.

SANDERS, G. S. (1984). Self-presentation and drive in social facilitation. *Journal of Experimental Social Psychology, 20,* 312–322.

SANDERS, G. S., & BARON, R. S. (1975). The motivating effects of distraction on task performance. *Journal of Personality and Social Psychology, 32,* 956–963.

SANDERS, G. S., & BARON, R. S. (1977). Is social comparison irrelevant for producing choice shifts? *Journal of Experimental Social Psychology, 13,* 303–314.

SANDERSON, W. C., RAPEE, R. M., & BARLOW, D. H. (1989). The influence of illusion of control on panic attacks induced via inhalation of 5.5% carbon dioxide-enriched air. *Archives of General Psychology, 46,* 157–162.

SAPOLSKY, R. M. (1990). Stress in the wild. *Scientific American, 262,* 116–123.

SATINOFF, E. (1964). Behavioral thermoregulation in reponse to local cooling of the rat brain. *American Journal of Physiology, 206,* 1389–1394.

SATINOFF, E. (1983). A reevaluation of the concept of the homeostatic organization of temperature regulation. In E. Satinoff & P. Teitelbaum (Eds.), *Motivation* (pp. 443–474). New York: Plenum Press.

SAUNDERS, D. R. (1985). On Hyman's factor analyses. *Journal of Parapsychology, 49,* 86–88.

SAXE, L., DOUGHERTY, D., & CROSS, T. (1985). The validity of polygraph testing. *American Psychologist, 40,* 355–366.

SAYLER, R. D. (1992). Ecology and evolution of brood parasitism in waterfowl. In B. D. J. Batt et al. (Eds.), *Ecology and Management of Breeding Waterfowl* (pp. 290-322). Minneapolis: University of Minnesota Press.

SCARR, S. (1985). An author's frame of mind: Review of *Frames of mind,* by Howard Gardner. *New Ideas in Psychology, 3,* 95–100.

SCARR, S. (1988). How genotypes and environments combine: Development and invidual differences. In N. Bolger, A. Caspi, G. Downey, & M. Moorehouse (Eds.), *Persons in context: Developmen-*

tal processes (pp. 217–244). New York: Cambridge University Press.

SCARR, S., & EISENBERG, M. (1993). Child care research: Issues, perspectives, and results. *Annual Review of Psychology, 44,* 613–644.

SCARR, S., & MCCARTNEY, K. (1983). How people make their own environments: A theory of genotype-environment effects. *Child Development, 54,* 424–435.

SCARR, S., PHILLIPS, D., MCCARTNEY, K., & ABBOTT-SHIM, M. (1993). Quality of child care as an aspect of family and child care policy in the United States. *Pediatrics, 91,* 182–188.

SCARR, S., WEINBERG, R. A., & LEVINE, A. (1986). *Understanding development.* San Diego: Harcourt Brace Javanovich.

SCHACHTEL, E. G. (1982). On memory and childhood amnesia. In U. Neisser (Ed.), *Memory observed: Remembering in natural contexts.* San Francisco: Freeman.

SCHACHTER, S., & SINGER, J. E. (1962). Cognitive, social and physiological determinants of emotional state. *Psychological Review, 69,* 379–399.

SCHACTER, D. L. (1989). Memory. In M. Posner (Ed.), *Foundations of cognitive science.* Cambridge, MA: MIT Press.

SCHAFER, R. (1976). *A new language for psychoanalysis.* New Haven, CT: Yale University Press.

SCHARNBERG, M. (1993). *The nonauthentic nature of Freud's observations: Vol. 1. The seduction theory.* Philadelphia: Coronet.

SCHEIER, M. F., BUSS, A. H., & BUSS, D. M. (1978). Self-consciousness, self-reports of aggressiveness, and aggressions. *Journal of Research in Personality, 12,* 133–140.

SCHEIER, M. F., & CARVER, C. S. (1992). Effects of optimism on psychological and physical well-being: Theoretical overview and empirical update. *Cognitive Therapy and Research, 16,* 201–228.

SCHEIER, M. F., MATTHEWS, K. A., OWENS, J., MAGOVERN, G. J., SR., LEFEBVRE, R. C., ABBOTT, R. A., & CARVER, C. S. (1989). Dispositional optimism and recovery from coronary bypass surgery: The beneficial effects on physical and psychological well-being. *Journal of Personality and Social Psychology, 57,* 1024–1040.

SCHIFF, W., & FOULKE, E. (Eds.) (1982). *Tactual perception: A sourcebook.* Cambridge, England: Cambridge University Press.

SCHIFFENBAUER, A., & SCHIAVO, R. S. (1976). Physical distance and attraction: An intensification effect. *Journal of Experimental Social Psychology, 12,* 274–282.

SCHINDLER, R. A., & MERZENICH, M. M. (Eds.) (1985). *Cochlear implants.* New York: Raven Press.

SCHLEIDT, M., HOLD, B., & ATTILI, G. (1981). A cross-cultural study on the attitude toward personal odors. *Journal of Chemical Ecology, 7,* 19–31.

SCHLEIFER, S. J., KELLER, S. E., MCKEGNEY, F. P., & STEIN, M. (1979, March). The influence of stress and other psychosocial factors on human immunity. Paper presented at the 36th Annual Meeting of the Psychosomatic Society, Dallas.

SCHLESINGER, A. M., JR. (1965). *A thousand days.* Boston: Houghton Mifflin.

SCHMERMUND, A., SELLERS, R., MUELLER, B., & CROSBY, F. (1998). *Attitudes toward affirmative action as a function of racial identity among Black college students.* Manuscript under review.

SCHMITT, B. H., GILOVICH, T., GOORE, N., & JOSEPH, L. (1986). Mere presence and social facilitation: One more time. *Journal of Experimental Social Psychology, 22,* 242–248.

SCHNEIDER, A. M., & TARSHIS, B. (1986). *An introduction to physiological psychology* (3rd ed.). New York: Random House.

SCHNEIDER, D. J., & MILLER, R. S. (1975). The effects of enthusiasm and quality of arguments on attitude attribution. *Journal of Personality, 43,* 693–708.

SCHNEIER, F. R., JOHNSON, J., HORNIG, C. D., & LIEBOWITZ, M. R. (1992). Social phobia: Comorbidity and morbidity in an epidemiologic sample. *Archives of General Psychiatry, 49,* 282–288.

SCHULTZ, D. (2000). *A history of modern psychology* (7th ed.). Fort Worth: Harcourt.

SCHULZ, R., BOOKWALA, J., KNAPP, J., et al. (1994, April 15). *Pessimism and mortality in young and old recurrent cancer patients.* Paper presented at the American Psychosomatic Society annual meetings, Boston, MA.

SCHWARTZ, B. (1989). *Psychology of learning and behavior* (3rd ed.). New York: Norton.

SCHWARTZ, B., & REISBERG, D. (1991). *Learning and memory.* New York: Norton.

SCHWARTZ, B., SNIDMAN, N., & KAGAN, J. (1996). Early childhood temperament as a determinant of externalizing behavior in adolescence. *Development and Psychopathology, 8,* 527–537.

SCHWARZ, N., & CLORE, G. L. (1996). Feelings and phenomenal experiences. In E. T. Higgins & A. Kruglanski (Eds.), *Social psychology: A handbook of basic principles* (pp. 433–465). New York: Guilford Press.

SCOTT, T. R., & MARK, G. P. (1986). Feeding and taste. *Progress in Neurobiology, 27,* 293–317.

SEARS, R. R. (1943). Survey of objective studies of psychoanalytic concepts. *Social Science Research Council Bulletin,* No. 51.

SEARS, R. R. (1944). Experimental analyses of psychoanalytic phenomena. In J. Hunt (Ed.), *Personality and the behavior disorders* (Vol. 1, pp. 306–332). New York: Ronald.

SEARS, R. R., MACCOBY, E. E., & LEVIN, H. (1957) *Patterns of child rearing.* New York: Harper &Row.

SEGERSTROM, S. C., TAYLOR, S. E., KEMENY, M. E., REED, G. M., & VISSCHER, B. R. (1996). Causal attributions predict rate of immune decline in HIV-seropositive gay men. *Health Psychology, 15,* 485–493.

SEIFERT, C. M., ROBERTSON, S. P., & BLACK, J. B. (1985). Types of inferences generated during reading. *Journal of Memory and Language, 24,* 405–422.

SEGERSTROM, S. C., TAYLOR, S. E., KEMENY, M. E., & FAHEY, J. L. (1998). Optimism is assicoated with mood, coping, and immune change in response to stress. *Journal of Personality and Social Psychology, 74,* 1646–1655.

SEKULER, R. (1975). Visual motion perception. In E. C. Carterette & M. Friedman (Eds.), *Handbook of perception: Vol. 5* (pp. 387–433). New York: Academic Press.

SEKULER, R., & BLAKE, R. (1985). *Perception.* New York: Knopf.

SELIGMAN, M. E. P. (1975). *Helplessness.* San Francisco: Freeman.

SELIGMAN, M. E. P. & BINIK, Y. M. (1977). The safety signal hypothesis. In H. Davis & H. Hurwitz (Eds.), *Pavlovian operant interactions.* Hillsdale, NJ: Erlbaum.

SELYE, H. (1978). *The stress of life.* New York: McGraw-Hill.

SERBIN, L. A., POWLISHTA, K. K., & GULKO, J. (1993). The development of sex typing in middle childhood. *Monographs of the Society for Research in Child Development, 58* (2, Serial No. 232).

SEWELL, W. H., & MUSSEN, P. H. (1952). The effects of feeding, weaning, and scheduling procedures on childhood adjustment and the formation of oral symptoms. *Child Development, 23,* 185–191.

SHALLICE, T. (1988). *From neuropsychology to mental structure.* Cambridge, England: Cambridge University Press.

SHALLICE, T., FLETCHER, P., FRITH, C. D., GRASBY, P., FRACKOWIAK, R. S. J., & DOLAN, R. J. (1994). Brain regions associated with acquisition and retrieval of verbal episodic memory. *Nature, 368,* 633–635.

SHANKS, D. R., & DICKINSON, A., (1987). Associative accounts of causality judgment. *The Psychology of Learning and Motivation, 21,* 229–261.

SHANNON, R. V., & OTTO, S. R. (1990). Psychophysical measures from electrical stimulation of the human cochlear nucleus. *Hearing Research, 47,* 159–168.

SHAPIRO, A. K., & MORRIS, L. A. (1978). The placebo effect in medical and psychological therapies. In S. L. Garfield & A. E. Bergin (Eds.), *Handbook of psychotherapy and behavior change* (2nd ed.). New York: Wiley.

SHAPIRO, D. A., & SHAPIRO, D. (1982). Meta-analysis of comparative therapy outcome studies: A replication and refinement. *Psychological Bulletin, 92,* 581–604.

SHAPLEY, R., & LENNIE, P. (1985). Spatial frequency analysis in the visual system. *Annual Review of Neurosciences, 8,* 547–583.

SHAW, D. W., & THORESEN, C. E. (1974). Effects of modeling and desensitization in reducing dentist phobia. *Journal of Counseling Psychology, 21,* 415–420.

SHEDLER, J., MAYMAN, M., & MANIS, M. (1993). The illusion of mental health. *American Psychologist, 48,* 1117–1131.

SHEINGOLD, K., & TENNEY, Y. J. (1982). Memory for a salient childhood event. In U. Neisser (Ed.), *Memory observed: Remembering in natural contexts.* San Francisco: Freeman.

SHEKELLE, R., NEATON, J. D., JACOBS, D., HULLEY, S., & BLACKBURN, H. (1983). Type A behavior pattern in MRFIT. A paper presented to the American Heart Association Council on Epidemiology Meetings, San Diego.

SHEPARD, R. N., & COOPER, L. A. (1982). *Mental images and their transformations.* Cambridge, MA: MIT Press, Bradford Books.

SHEPHER, J. (1971). Mate selection among second generation kibbutz adolescents and adults: Incest avoidance and negative imprinting. *Archives of Sexual Behavior, 1,* 293–307.

SHEPOSH, J. P., DEMING, M., & YOUNG, L. E. (1977, April). The radiating effects of status and attractiveness of a male upon evaluating his female partner. Paper presented at the annual meeting of the Western Psychological Association, Seattle.

SHERWIN, B. (1988a). A comparative analysis of the role of androgen in human male and female sexual behavior: Behavioral specificity, critical thresholds, and sensitivity. *Psychobiology, 16,* 416–425.

SHERWIN, B. (1988b). Critical analysis of the role of androgens in human male and female sexual behavior: Behavioral specificity, critical thresholds, and sensitivity. *Psychobiology, 16,* 416–423.

SHNEIDMAN, E. S. (1976). *Suicidology: Contemporary developments.* New York: Grune & Stratton.

SHWEDER, R. A. (1984). Anthropology's romantic rebellion against the enlightenment, or there's more to thinking than reason and evidence. In R. A. Shweder & R. A. LeVine (Eds.), *Culture theory: Essays on mind, self, and emotion* (pp. 27–66). Cambridge, England: Cambridge University Press.

SIEGEL, P., & WEINBERGER, J. (1998). Capturing the "MOMMY AND I ARE ONE" merger fantasy: The oneness motive. In R. F. Bornstein & J. M. Masling (Eds.), *Empirical perspectives on the psychoanalytic unconscious* (pp. 71–98). Washington, DC: American Psychological Association Press.

SIEGLER, R. S. (1991). *Children's thinking* (2nd ed.). Englewood Cliffs: NJ: Prentice-Hall.

SIGALL, H., & LANDY, D. (1973). Radiating beauty: The effects of having a physically attractive partner on person perception. *Journal of Personality and Social Psychology, 31,* 410–414.

SILVERMAN, I. (1964). Self-esteem and differential responsiveness to success and failure. *Journal of Abnormal and Social Psychology, 69,* 115–119.

SILVERMAN, I. (1971). Physical attractiveness and courtship. *Sexual Behavior, 1,* 22–25.

SIMMONS, J. V. (1981). *Project sea hunt: A report on prototype development and tests.* Technical Report 746, Naval Ocean Systems Center, San Diego.

SIMMONS, R. G., & BLYTH, D. A. (1988). *Moving into adolescence: The impact of pubertal change and school context.* Hawthorne, NY: Aldine.

SIMON, H. A. (1985, June). Using Cognitive Science to Solve Human Problems. Paper presented at Science and Public Policy Seminar, Federation of Behavioral, Psychological, and Cognitive Sciences.

SIMON, H. A., & GILMARTIN, K. (1973). A simulation of memory for chess positions. *Cognitive Psychology, 5,* 29–46.

SIMPSON, J. A., CAMPBELL, B., & BERSCHEID, E. (1986). The association between romantic love and marriage: Kephart (1967) twice revisited. *Personality and Social Psychology Bulletin, 12,* 363–372.

SINGER, J. L., & SINGER, D. G. (1981). *Television, imagination and aggression.* Hillsdale, NJ: Erlbaum.

SIQUELAND, E. R., & LIPSITT, J. P. (1966). Conditioned head-turning in human newborns. *Journal of Experimental Child Psychology, 3,* 356–376.

SIZEMORE, C. C., & PITTILLO, E. S. (1977). *I'm Eve.* Garden City, NY: Doubleday.

SKINNER, B. F. (1938). *The behavior of organisms.* New York: Appleton-Century-Crofts.

SKINNER, B. F. (1948). "Superstition" in the pigeon. *Journal of Experimental Psychology, 38,* 168–172.

SKINNER, B. F. (1971). *Beyond freedom and dignity.* New York: Knopf.

SKINNER, B. F. (1981). Selection by consequences. *Science, 213,* 501–504.

SKYRMS, B. (1986). *Choice and chance: An introduction to inductive logic.* Belmont, CA: Dickenson.

SLOBIN, D. (1997). From "thought and language" to "thinking for speaking."

SLOBIN, D. I. (1971). Cognitive prerequisites for the acquisition of grammar. In C. A. Ferguson & D. I. Slobin (Eds.), *Studies of child language developments.* New York: Holt, Rinehart & Winston.

SLOBIN, D. I. (1979). *Psycholinguistics* (2nd. ed.). Glenville, IL: Scott, Foresman.

SLOBIN, D. I. (Ed.) (1985). *The cross-linguistic study of language acquisition.* Hillsdale, NJ: Erlbaum.

SMITH, A. (1759/1937). *A Theory of Moral Sentiments.*

SMITH, C. A., & ELLSWORTH, P. C. (1985). Patterns of cognitive appraisal in emotion. *Journal of Personality and Social Psychology, 48,* 813–848.

SMITH, C. A., & ELLSWORTH, P. C. (1987). Patterns of appraisal and emotion related to taking an exam. *Journal of Personality and Social Psychology, 52,* 475–488.

SMITH, D., KING, M., & HOEBEL, B. G. (1970). Lateral hypothalamic control of killing: Evidence for a cholinoceptive mechanism. *Science, 167,* 900–901.

SMITH, E. E. (1989). Concepts and induction. In M. I. Posner (Ed.), *Foundations of cognitive science.* Cambridge, MA: MIT Press.

SMITH, E. E. (1995). Concepts and categorization. In E. E. Smith & D. Osherson (Eds.), *Invitation to cognitive science, Vol. 3, Thinking* (2nd ed.). Cambridge, MA: MIT Press.

SMITH, E. E., & JONIDES, J. (1994). Neuropsychological studies of working memory. In M. Gazzaniga (Ed.), *The cognitive neurosciences.* Cambridge, MA: MIT Press.

SMITH, E. E., JONIDES, J., & KOEPPE, R. A. (1996). Dissociating verbal and spatial working memory using PET.

SMITH, E. E., & MEDIN, D. L. (1981). *Categories and concepts.* Cambridge, MA: Harvard University Press.

SMITH, E. E., PATALANO, A. L., & JONIDES, J. (1998). Alternative strategies of categorization. *Cognition, 65,* 167–196.

SMITH, G. P., & GIBBS, J. (1994). Satiating effect of cholecystokinin. *Annals of the New York Academy of Sciences, 713,* 236–41.

SMITH, M. B., BRUNER, J. S., & WHITE, R. W. (1956). *Opinions and personality.* New York: Wiley.

SMITH, M. L., GLASS, G. V., & MILLER, T. I. (1980). *The benefits of psychotherapy.* Baltimore: Johns Hopkins University Press.

SMITH, V. C., & POKORNY, J. (1975). Spectral sensitivity of the foveal cones between 400 and 500 nm. *Vision Res.* 15, 161.

SMUTS, B. B. (1986). Gender, aggression, and influence. In B. Smuts, D. Cheney, R. Seyfarth, R. Wrangham, & T. Struhsaker (Eds.), *Primate societies.* Chicago: University of Chicago Press.

SNAITH, P. (1998). Meditation and psychotherapy. *British Journal of Psychiatry, 173,* 193–195.

SNODGRASS, J. G., LEVY-BERGER, G., & HAYDON, M. (1985). *Human experimental psychology.* New York: Oxford University Press.

SNOW, C. (1987). Relevance of the notion of a critical period to language acquisition. In M. H. Bornstein (Ed.), *Sensitive periods in development: Interdisciplinary perspectives.* Hillsdale, NJ: Erlbaum.

SNOWDEN, L. R. (1988). Ethnicity and utilization of mental health services: An overview of current findings. In *Oklahoma Mental Health Research Institute, 1988 professional symposium* (pp. 227–238). Oklahoma City: Oklahoma Mental Health Research Institute.

SNOWDEN, L., & CHEUNG, F. (1990, March). Use of inpatient mental health services by members of ethnic minority groups. *American Psychologist, 45,* 347–355.

SOLOMON, R. L., & CORBIT, J. D. (1974). An opponent-process theory of motivation: I. Temporal dynamics of affect. *Psychological Review, 81,* 119–145.

SONTHEIMER, H. (1995). Glial neuronal interactions: A physiological perspective. *The Neuroscientist, 1,* 328–337.

SPANOS, B. (1996, December). Quotas, ARCOs, UN report, and statistics. In G. Feussner (Moderator), *Prevalence of ADHD and psychostimulant utilization for treatment.* Symposium conducted at Drug Enforcement Administration meeting on stimulant use in the treatment of ADHD.

SPANOS, N. P. (1986). Hypnotic behavior: A social-psychological interpretation of amnesia, analgesia, and "trance logic." *The Behavioral and Brain Sciences, 9,* 449–502.

SPANOS, N. P., & HEWITT, E. C. (1980). The hidden observer in hypnotic analgesia: Discovery or experimental creation? *Journal of Personality and Social Psychology, 39,* 1201–1214.

SPEARMAN, C. (1904). "General intelligence" objectively determined and measured. *American Journal of Psychology, 15,* 201–293.

SPELKE, E. S. (1998). Nativism, empiricism, and the origins of knowledge. *Infant Behavior & Development, 21,* 181–200.

SPENCER, S., STEELE, C. M., & QUINN, D. (1997). *Under suspicion of inability: Stereotype threat and women's math performance.* Unpublished manuscript, Stanford University.

SPERLING, G. (1960). The information available in brief visual presentations. *Psychological Monographs, 74,* 329.

SPERRY, R. W. (1968). Perception in the absence of neocortical commissures. In Association for Research in Nervous and Mental Disease, *Perception and its disorders.* New York: Williams & Wilkins.

SPIEGEL, D. (1991). Mind matters: Effects of group support on cancer patients. *Journal of NIH Research, 3,* 61–63.

SPIEGEL, D., BLOOM, J. R., KRAEMER, H. C., & GOTTHEIL, E. (1989). Psychological support for cancer patients. *Lancet, II,* 1447.

SPIELBERGER, C. D., JOHNSON, E. H., RUSSELL, S. F., CRANE, R. S., JACOBS, G. A., & WORDEN, T. J. (1985). The experience and expression of anger: Construction and validation of an anger expression scale. In M. A. Chesney & R. H. Rosenman (Eds.), *Anger and hostility in cardiovascular and behavioral disorders.* New York: Hemisphere/McGraw-Hill.

SPIVEY, C. B., & PRENTICE-DUNN, S. (1990). Assessing the directionality of deindividuated behavior: Effects of deindividuation, modeling, and private self-consciousness on aggressive and prosocial responses. *Basic and Applied Social Psychology, 11,* 387–403.

SPRAFKIN, J. N., LIEBERT, R. M., & POULOUS, R. W. (1975). Effects of a prosocial televised example on children's helping. *Journal of Personality and Social Psychology, 48,* 35–46.

SPRINGER, S. P., & DEUTSCH, G. (1989). *Left brain, right brain* (3rd ed.). San Francisco: Freeman.

SQUIER, L. H., & DOMHOFF, G. W. (1998). The presentation of dreaming and dreams in introductory psychology textbooks: A critical examination. Unpublished paper.

SQUIRE, L. R. (1987). *Memory and brain.* New York: Oxford University Press.

SQUIRE, L. R. (1992). Memory and the hippocampus: A synthesis from findings with rats, monkeys, and humans. *Psychological Review, 99,* 195–231.

SQUIRE, L. R., & BUTTERS, N. (Eds.) (1984). *The neuropsychology of memory.* New York: Guilford.

SQUIRE, L. R., & FOX, M. M. (1980). Assessment of remote memory: Validation of the television test by repeated testing during a seven-day period. *Behavioral Research Methods and Instrumentation, 12,* 583–586.

SQUIRE, L. R., KNOWLTON, B., & MUSEN, G. (1993). The structure and organization of memory. *Annual Review of Psychology, 44,* 453–495.

SQUIRE, L. R., OJEMANN, J. G., MIEZIN, F. M., PETERSEN, S. E., VIDEEN, T. O., & RAICHLE, M. E. (1992). Activation of the hippocampus in normal humans: A functional anatomical study of memory. *Proceedings of the National Academy of Sciences, 89,* 1837–1841.

SQUIRE, L. R., & ZOLA, S. M. (1996). Ischemic brain damage and memory impairment: A commentary. *Hippocampus, 6,* 546–552.

SQUIRE, L. R., ZOLA-MORGAN, S., CAVE, C. B., HAIST, F., MUSEN, G., & SUZUKI, W. A. (1990). Memory: Organization of brain systems and cognition. In *Symposium on quantiative biology, the brain* (Vol. 55). Cold Spring Harbor, NY: Cold Spring Harbor Laboratory.

STAATS, A. W. (1968). *Language, learning, and cognition.* New York: Holt, Rinehart & Winston.

STANGOR, C., & MCMILLAN, D. (1992). Memory for expectancy-congruent and expectancy-incongruent information: A review of the social and social developmental literature. *Psychological Bulletin, 111,* 42–61.

STATHAM, D. J., HEATH, A. C., MADDEN, P., BUCHOLZ, K., BIERUT, L., DINWIDDIE, S. H., SLUTSKE, W. S., DUNNE, M. P., & MARTIN, N. G. (1998). Suicidal behavior: An epidemiological study. *Psychological Medicine, 28,* 839–855.

STASSER, G., TAYLOR, L. A., & HANNA, C. (1989). Information sampling in structured and unstructured discussion of three- and six-person groups. *Journal of Personality and Social Psychology, 57,* 67–78.

STASSER, G., & TITUS, W. (1985). Pooling of unshared information in group decision making: Biased information sampling during discussion. *Journal of Personality and Social Psychology, 48,* 1467–1478.

STATTIN, H., & MAGNUSSON, D. (1990). *Pubertal maturation in female development.* Hillsdale, NJ: Erlbaum.

STAYTON, D. J. (1973, March). *Infant responses to brief everyday separations: Distress, following, and greeting.* Paper presented at the meeting of the Society for Research in Child Development.

STEELE, C. M. (1997). A threat in the air: How stereotypes shape intellectual identify and performance. *American Psychologist, 52,* 613–629.

STEELE, C. M., & ARONSON, J. (1995). Stereotype threat and the intellectual test performance of African Americans. *Journal of Personality and Social Psychology, 69,* 797–811.

STEIN, D. J. (Ed.). (1997). *Cognitive science and the unconscious.* Washington, DC: American Psychiatric Press.

STEINBERG, L. (1996). *Adolescence* (4th ed.). New York: Knopf.

STEINER, J. E. (1979). Human facial expressions in response to taste and smell stimulation. *Advances in Child Development and Behavior, 13,* 257–295.

STEKETEE, G., & WHITE, K. (1990). *When once is not enough.* Oakland, CA: New Harbinger.

STELLAR, J. R., & STELLAR, E. (1985). *The neurobiology of motivation and reward.* New York: Springer-Verlag.

STERN, R. S., & COBB, J. P. (1978). Phenomology of obsessive-compulsive neurosis. *Britis Journal of Psychiatry, 132,* 233–239.

STERNBERG, R. J. (1985). *Beyond IQ: A triarchic theory of human intelligence.* Cambridge, England: Cambridge University Press.

STERNBERG, R. J. (1986). *Intelligence applied: Understanding and increasing your intellectual skills.* San Diego: Harcourt Brace Jovanovich.

STERNBERG, R. J. (1988). *The triarchic mind: A new theory of human intelligence.* New York: Viking.

STERNBERG, R. J., & WILLIAMS, W. M. (1997). Does the Graduate Record Examination (GRE) predict meaningful success in the graduate training of psychologists? A case study. *American Psychologist, 52,* 630–651.

STERNBERG, S. (1966). Highspeed scanning in human memory. *Science, 153,* 652–654.

STERNBERG, S. (1975). Memory scanning: New findings and current controversies. *Quarterly Journal of Experimental Psychology, 27,* 1–32.

STEUER, F. B., APPLEFIELD, J. M., & SMITH, R. (1971). Televised aggression and the interpersonal aggression of preschool children. *Journal of Experimental Child Psychology, 11,* 422–447.

STEVENSON, H. W., LEE, S., & GRAHAM, T. (1993). Chinese and Japanese kindergartens: Case study in comparative research. In B. Spodek (Ed.), *Handbook of research on the education of young children.* New York: Macmillan.

STILES, W. B., SHAPIRO, D. A., & ELLIOTT, R. (1986). Are all psychotherapies equivalent? *American Psychologist, 41,* 165–180.

STONER, J. A. F. (1961). *A comparison of individual and group decisions involving risk.* Unpublished master's thesis, Massachusetts Institute of Technology.

STRACK, F., MARTIN, L. L., & STEPPER, S. (1988). Inhibiting and facilitating conditions of the human smile: A nonobtrusive test of the facial feedback hypothesis. *Journal of Personality and Social Psychology, 54,* 768–777.

STREISSGUTH, A. P., CLARREN, S. K., & JONES, K. L. (1985). Natural history of the fetal alcohol syndrome: A 10-year follow-up of eleven patients. *Lancet, 2,* 85–91.

STROEBE, W., INSKO, C. A., THOMPSON, V. D., & LAYTON, B. D. (1971). Effects of physical attractiveness, attitude similarity and sex on various aspects of interpersonal attraction. *Journal of Personality and Social Psychology, 18,* 79–91.

STRONG, S. R., HILLS, H. J., KILMARTIN, C. T., DEVRIES, H., LANIER, A, K., NELSON, B. N., STRICKLAND, D., & MEYER, C. W., III (1988). The dynamic relations among interpersonal behaviors: A test of complementarity and anti-complementarity. *Journal of Personality and Social Psychology, 54,* 798–810.

STUNKARD, A. J. (1982). Obesity. In M. Hersen, A. Bellack, & A. Kazdin (Eds.), *International handbook of behavior modification and therapy.* New York: Plenum.

STUNKARD, A. J. (1996). *The origins and consequences of obesity.* Chichester: Wiley.

STUNKARD, A. J., HARRIS, J. R., PEDERSEN, N. L., & MCCLEARN, G. E. (1990). A separated twin study of the body mass index. *The New England Journal of Medicine, 322,* 1483–1487.

SUAREZ, E. C., KUHN, C. M., SCHANBERG, S. M., WILLIAMS, R. B., JR., & ZIMMERMAN, E. A. (1998). Neuroendocrine, cardiovascular, and emotional responses of hostile men: The role of interpersonal challenge. *Psychosomatic Medicine, 60,* 78–88.

SUE, S., ALLEN, D., & CONAWAY, L. (1978). The responsiveness and equality of mental health care to Chicanos and Native Americans. *American Journal of Community Psychology, 6,* 137–146.

SUE, S., & ZANE, N. (1987). The role of culture and cultural techniques in psychotherapy: A critique and reformulation. *American Psychologist, 42,* 37–51.

SULLIVAN, H. S. (1953). *The interpersonal theory of psychiatry.* New York: Norton.

SUTKER, P. B., DAVIS, J. M., UDDO, M., & DITTA, S. R. (1995). Assessment of psychological distress in Persian Gulf troops: Ethnicity and gender comparisons. *Journal of Personality Assessment, 64,* 415–427.

SVENSON, O. (1981). Are we all less risky and more skillful than our fellow drivers? *Acta Psychologica, 47,* 143–148.

SWARTZ, M., BLAZER, D., GEORGE, L., & WINFIELD, I. (1990). Estimating the prevalence of borderline personality disorder in the community. *Journal of Personality Disorders, 4,* 257–272.

SWEDO, S. PIETRINI, P., & LEONARD, H. (1992). Cerebral glucose metabolism in childhood-onset obsessive-compulsive disorder. *Archives of General Psychiatry, 49,* 690–694.

SWETS, J. A., & BJORK, R. A. (1990). Enhancing human performance: An evaluation of "new age" techniques considered by the U.S. Army. *Psychological Science, 1,* 85–96.

SWINNEY, D. A. (1979). Lexical access during sentence comprehension: Consideration of context effects. *Journal of Verbal Learning and Verbal Behavior, 18,* 645–659.

SYMONS, D. (1992). On the use and misuse of Darwinism in the study of human behavior. In J. H. Barkow & L. Cosmides (Eds.) et al., *The adapted mind: Evolutionary psychology and the generation of culture* (pp. 137–159). New York: Oxford University Press.

TANENHAUS, M. G., LEIMAN, J., & SEIDENBERG, M. (1979). Evidence for multiple stages in the processing of ambiguous words in syntactic contexts. *Journal of Verbal Learning and Verbal Behavior, 18,* 427–441.

TANNEN, D. (1998). *The argument culture.* New York: Ballantine Books.

TARTTER, V. C. (1986). *Language processes.* New York: Holt, Rinehart & Winston.

TAVRIS, C., & SADD, S. (1977). *The Redbook report on female sexuality.* New York: Dell.

TAYLOR, S. (1999). *Health psychology* (4th ed.). Boston: McGraw-Hill.

TAYLOR, S. E., & BROWN, J. D. (1988). Illusion and well-being: A social psychological perspective on mental health. *Psychological Bulletin, 103,* 193–210.

TAYLOR, S. E., KEMENY, M. E., ASPINWALL, L. G., SCHNEIDER, S. C., RODRIGUEZ, R., & HERBERT, M. (1992). Optimism, coping, psychological distress, and high-risk sexual behavior among men at risk for AIDS. *Journal of Personality and Social Psychology, 63,* 460–473.

TAYLOR, S. E., & THOMPSON, S. C. (1982). Stalking the elusive "vividness" effect. *Psychological Review, 89,* 155–181.

TEITELBAUM, P., & EPSTEIN, A. N. (1962). The lateral hypothalamic syndrome: Recovery of feeding and drinking after lateral hypothalamic lesions. *Psychological Review, 69,* 74–90.

TELLEGEN, A., BOUCHARD, T. J., WILCOX, K. J., SEGAL, N. L., LYKKEN, D. T., & RICH, S. (1988). *Journal of Personality and Social Psychology, 54,* 1031–1039.

TELLER, D. Y., & MOVSHON, J. A. (1986). Visual development. *Vision Research, 26,* 1483–1506.

TEMPLIN, M. C. (1957). *Certain language skills in children: Their development and interrelationships.* Minneapolis: University of Minnesota Press.

TERMAN, L. M., & ODEN, M. H. (1959). *Genetic studies of genius, Vol. IV: The gifted group at midlife.* Stanford, CA: Stanford University Press.

TERRACE, H. S., PETITTO, L. A., SANDERS, D. J., & BEVER, T. G. (1979). Can an ape create a sentence? *Science, 206,* 891–902.

TESSER, A., & BRODIE, M. (1971). A note on the evaluation of a "computer date." *Psychonomic Science, 23,* 300.

THIGPEN, C. H., & CLECKLEY, H. (1957). *The three faces of eve.* New York: McGraw-Hill.

THOMAS, A., & CHESS, S. (1977). *Temperament and development.* New York: Brunner/Mazel.

THOMAS, A., & CHESS, S. (1986). The New York longitudinal study: From infancy to early adult life. In R. Plomin & J. Dunn (Eds.), *The study of temperament: Changes, continuities and challenges* (pp. 39–52). Hillsdale, NJ: Erlbaum.

THOMAS, A., & CHESS, S., BIRCH, H., HERTZIG, M., & KORN, S. (1963). *Behavioral individuality in early childhood.* New York: New York University Press.

THOMAS, E. L., & ROBINSON, H. A. (1982). *Improving reading in every class.* Boston: Allyn and Bacon.

THOMPSON, R. A., LAMB, M., & ESTES, D. (1982). Stability of infant-mother attachment and its relationship to changing life circumstances in an unselected middle-class sample. *Child Development, 53,* 144–148.

THOMPSON, S. K. (1975). Gender labels and early sex role development. *Child Development, 46,* 339–347.

THOMPSON, W. R. (1954). The inheritance and development of intelligence. *Proceedings of the Association for Research on Nervous and Mental Disease, 33,* 209–231.

THORESEN, C. E., TELCH, M. J., & EAGLESTON, J. R. (1981). Altering Type A behavior. *Psychosomatics, 8,* 472–482.

THORNDYKE, E. L. (1898). Animal intelligence: An experimental study of the associative processes in animals. *Psychological Monographs, 2.*

THORPE, G. L., & OLSON, S. L. (1997). *Behavior therapy: Concepts, procedures, and applications* (2nd ed.). Boston: Allyn and Bacon.

THURSTONE, L. L. (1938). Primary mental abilities. *Psychometric Monographs,* No. 1. Chicago: University of Chicago Press.

TIZARD, B., & REES, J. (1975). The effect of early institutional rearing on the behavioural problems and affectional relationships of four-year-old children. *Journal of Child Psychology and Psychiatry, 16,* 61–73.

TOATES, F. (1986). *Motivational systems.* Cambridge, England: Cambridge University Press.

TOLMAN, E. C. (1932). *Purpose behavior in animals and men.* New York: Appleton-Century-Crofts. (Reprinted 1967. New York: Irvington.)

TOMASSON, R. F., CROSBY, F. J., & HERZBERGER, S. D. (1996). *Affirmative action: The pros and cons of policy and practice.* Washington, DC: American University Press.

TOMPKINS, S. S. (1962). *Affect, imagery, consciousness: Vol. 1. The positive affects.* New York: Springer.

TOMPKINS, S. S. (1980). Affect as amplification: Some modifications in theory. In R. Plutchik & H. Kellerman (Eds.), *Emotion: Theory, research and experience* (Vol. 1). New York: Academic Press.

TOOBY, J., & COSMIDES, L. (1990). The past explains the present: Emotional adaptations and the structure of ancestral environments. *Ethology and Sociobiology, 11,* 375–424.

TORGERSEN, S. (1986). Genetic factors in moderately severe and mild affective disorders. *Archives of General Psychiatry, 49,* 690–694.

TOWNSHEND, B., COTTER, N., VAN COMPERNOLLE, D., & WHITE, R. L. (1987). Pitch perception by cochlear implant subjects. *Journal of the Acoustical Society of America, 82,* 106–115.

TRAFIMOW, D., TRIANDIS, H. C., & GOTO, S. G. (1991). Some tests of the distinction between the private self and the collective self. *Journal of Personality and Social Psychology, 60,* 649–655.

TREISMAN, A. (1969). Strategies and models of selective attention. *Psychological Review, 76,* 282–299.

TREISMAN, A. M. (1986). Features and objects in visual processing. *Scientific American, 255,* 114B–125.

TRIANDIS, H. C. (1989). The self and social behavior in different cultures. *Psychological Review, 96,* 506–520.

TRINDER, J. (1988). Subjective insomnia without objective findings: A pseudo-diagnostic classification. *Psychological Bulletin, 103,* 87–94.

TRIPP, C. A. (1987). *The homosexual matrix* (2nd ed.). New York: New American Library.

TRUAX, K., WOOD, A., WRIGHT, E., CORDOVA, D. I., & CROSBY, F. J. (1998). Undermined? Affirmative action from the targets' point of view. In J. K. Swim & C. Stagnor (Eds.), *Prejudice: The target's perspective* (pp. 171–188). New York: Academic Press.

TULVING, E. (1974). Cue-dependent forgetting. *American Scientist, 62,* 74–82.

TULVING, E. (1983). *The elements of episodic memory.* New York: Oxford University Press.

TULVING, E. (1985). How many memory systems are there? *American Psychologist, 40,* 385–398.

TULVING, E., KAPUR, S., CRAIK, F. I. M., MOSCOVITCH, M., & HOULE, S. (1994). Hemispheric encoding/retrieval asymmetry in episodic memory: Positron emission tomography findings. *Proceedings of the National Academy of Science of the United States of America, 91,* 2016–2020.

TULVING, E., KAPUR, S., MARKOWITSCH, H. J., CRAIK, F. I. M., HABIB, R., & HOULE, S. (1994). Neuroanatomical correlates of retrieval in episodic memory: Auditory sentence recognition. *Proceedings of the National Academy of Science of the United States of America, 91,* 2012–2015.

TULVING, E., & PEARLSTONE, Z. (1966). Availability versus accessibility of information in memory for words. *Journal of Verbal Learning and Verbal Behavior, 5,* 381–391.

TUMA, J. M. (1989). Mental health services for children: The state of the art. *American Psychologist, 44,* 188–199.

TUNNELL, G. (1981). Sex role and cognitive schemata: Person perception in feminine and androgynous women. *Journal of Personality and Social Psychology, 40,* 1126–1136.

TURIEL, E. (1983). *The development of social knowledge: Morality and convention.* Cambridge, England: Cambridge University Press.

TURK, D. C. (1996). Clinician attitudes about prolonged use of opioids and the issue of patient heterogeneity. *Journal of Pain and Symptom Management, 11,* 218–230.

TURK, D. C., & OKIFUJI, A. (1997). What factors affect physicians' decisions to prescribe opioids for chronic non-cancer pain patients? *The Clinical Journal of Pain, 13,* 330–336.

TURNER, M. E., & PRATKANIS, A. R. (1994). Affirmative action as help: A review of recipient reactions to preferential selection and affirmative action. *Basic and Applied Social Psychology, 15,* 43–69.

TURNER, M. E., PRATKANIS, A. R., PROBASCO, P., & LEVER, C. (1992). Threat, cohesion, and group effectiveness:

Testing a social identity maintenance perspective in groupthink. *Journal of Personality and Social Psychology, 63,* 781–796.

TVERSKY, A., & KAHNEMAN, D. (1973). On the psychology of prediction. *Psychological Review, 80,* 237–251.

TVERSKY, A., & KAHNEMAN, D. (1983). Extensional versus intuitive reasoning: The conjunction fallacy in probability judgment. *Psychological Review, 90,* 293–315.

TYE-MURRAY, N., SPENCER, L., & WOOD-WORTH, G. G. (1995). Acquisition of speech by children who have prolonged cochlear implant experience. *Journal of Speech and Hearing Research, 38,* 327–337.

TYLER, H. (1977). The unsinkable Jeane Dixon. *The Humanist, 37,* 6–9.

URSIN, H. (1978). Activation, coping, and psychosomatics. In H. Ursin, E. Baade, & S. Levine (Eds.), *Psychobiology of stress: A study of coping men.* New York: Academic Press.

UTTS, J. (1986). The gansfeld debate: A statistician's perspective. *Journal of Parapsychology, 50,* 393–402.

VAN VORT, W., & SMITH, G. P. (1987). Sham feeding experience produces a conditioned increase of meal size. *Appetite, 9,* 21–29.

VAUGHN, B. E., LEFEVER, G. B., SEIFER, R., & BARGLOW, P. (1989). Attachment behavior, attachment security, and temperament during infancy. *Child Development, 60,* 728–737.

VAUGHN, C. E., & LEFF, J. P. (1976, August). The influence of family and social factors on the course of psychiatric illness: A comparison of schizophrenic and depressed neurotic patients. *British Journal of Psychiatry, 129,* 125–137.

VELMANS, M. (1991). Is human information processing conscious? *Behavioral and Brain Sciences, 14,* 651–726.

VISINTAINER, M. A., VOLPICELLI, J. R., & SELIGMAN, M. E. P. (1982). Tumor rejection in rats after inescapable or escapable shock. *Science, 216,* 437–439.

VOGT, T., & BELLUSCIO, D. (1987). Controversies in plastic surgery: Suction-assisted lipectomy (SAL) and the HCG (human chorionic gonadotropin) protocol for obesity treatment. *Aesthetic Plastic Surgery, 11,* 131–56.

VOLZ, H. P., & KIESER, M. (1997). Kava-kava extract WS 1490 versus placebo in anxiety disorders: A randomized placebo-controlled 25-week outpatient trial. *Pharmacopsychiatry, 30,* 1–5.

VON LANG, J., & SIBYLL, C. (Eds.) (1983). *Eichmann interrogated* (R. Manheim, Trans.). New York: Farrar, Straus & Giroux.

VYGOTSKY, L. S. (1986). *Thought and language* (A. Kozulin, Trans.). Cambridge, MA: MIT Press. (originally published 1934)

WADDEN, T. A., BERKOWITZ, R. I., VOGT, R. A., STEEN, S. N., STUNKARD, A. J., & FOSTER, G. D. (1997). Lifestyle modification in the pharmacological treatment of obesity: A pilot investigation of a potential primary care approach. *Obesity Research, 5,* 218–226.

WAGNER, W. M., & MONNET, M. (1979). Attitudes of college professors toward extrasensory perception. *Zetetic Scholar, 5,* 7–17.

WALKER, C. E., HEDBERG, A., CLEMENT, P. W., & WRIGHT, L. (1981). *Clinical procedures for behavior therapy.* Englewood Cliffs, NJ: Prentice-Hall.

WALKER, E. (1978). *Explorations in the biology of language.* Montgomery, VT: Bradford.

WALLACH, M. A., KOGAN, N., & BEM, D. J. (1962). Group influence on individual risk taking. *Journal of Abnormal and Social Psychology, 65,* 75–86.

WALLACH, M. A., KOGAN, N., & BEM, D. J. (1964). Diffusion of responsibility and level of risk taking in groups. *Journal of Abnormal and Social Psychology, 68,* 263–274.

WALLACH, M. A., & WALLACH, L. (1983). *Psychology's sanction for selfishness.* San Francisco: Freeman.

WALSTER, E., ARONSON, E., ABRAHAMS, D., & ROTTMAN, L. (1966). Importance of physical attractiveness in dating behavior. *Journal of Personality and Social Psychology, 4,* 508–516.

WALTERS, J., & GARDNER, H. (1985). The development and education of intelligences. In F. Link (Ed.), *Essays on the intellect.* Washington, DC: Curriculum Development Associates/ Association for Supervision and Curriculum Development.

WALZER, M. (1970). *Obligations.* Cambridge, MA: Harvard University Press.

WAMPOLD, B. E., MONDIN, G. W., MOODY, M., STICH, F., BENSON, K., & AHN, H. (1997). A meta-analysis of outcome studies comparing bona fide psychotherapies: Empirically, "all must have prizes." *Psychological Bulletin, 122,* 203–215.

WARD, I. L. (1992). Sexual behavior: The products of perinatal hormonal and prepubertal social factors. In A. A. Gerall, H. Motz, & I. L. Ward (Eds.), *Sexual differentiation* (pp. 157–179). New York: Plenum.

WARRINGTON, E. K., & SHALLICE, T. (1984). Category specific semantic impairments. *Brain, 107,* 829–853.

WARRINGTON, E. K., & WEISKRANTZ, L. (1978). Further analysis of the prior

learning effect in amnesic patients. *Neuropsychologica, 16,* 169–177.

WASON, P. C., & JOHNSON-LAIRD, P. N. (1972). *Psychology of reasoning: Structure and content.* London: Batsford.

WASSERMAN, E. A. (1990). Detecting response-outcome relations: Toward an understanding of the causal texture of the environment. *Psychology of Learning and Motivation, 26,* 27–82.

WATERMAN, A. S. (1985). Identity in the context of adolescent psychology. In A. S. Waterman (Ed.), *Identity in adolescence: Progress and contents (New directions for child development, no. 30).* San Francisco: Jossey-Bass.

WATSON, J. B. (1930). *Behaviorism* (rev. ed.). New York: Norton.

WATSON, J. B., & RAYNER, R. (1920). Conditioned emotional reactions. *Journal of Experimental Psychology, 3,* 1–14.

WEAVER, E. G. (1949). *Theory of hearing.* New York: Wiley.

WECHSLER, D. (1958). *The measurement and appraisal of adult intelligence.* Baltimore: Williams.

WECHSLER, H., DAVENPORT, A., DOWDALL, G., MOEYKENS, B., & CASTILLO, S. (1994). Health and behavioral consequences of binge drinking in college, a national survey of students at 140 campuses. *Journal of the American Medical Association, 272,* 1672–1677.

WECHSLER, H., DOWDALL, G. W., MAENNER, G., GLEDHILL-HOYT, J., & LEE, H. (1998). Changes in binge drinking and related problems among American college students between 1993 and 1997. *Journal of American College Health, 47,* 57–68.

WEGNER, D. M., SCHNEIDER, D. J., CARTER, S., III, & WHITE, L. (1987). Paradoxical consequences of thought suppression. *Journal of Personality and Social Psychology, 53,* 1–9.

WEIGLE, D. S. (1994). Appetite and the regulation of body composition. *Faseb Journal, 8,* 302–10.

WEINBERG, M. S., SCHWARTZ, G. E., & DAVIDSON, R. E. (1979). Low-anxious, high-anxious, and repressive coping styles: Psychometric patterns and behavioral and physiological responses to stress. *Journal of Abnormal Psychology, 88,* 369–380.

WEINBERGER, D. (1990). The construct validity of the repressive coping style. In J. L. Singer (Ed.), *Repression and dissociation: Implications for personality theory, psychopathology, and health* (pp. 337–385). Chicago: University of Chicago Press.

WEINBERGER, J. (1996). Common factors aren't so common: The common factors dilemma. *Clinical Psychology: Science and Practice, 2,* 45–69.

WEINBERGER, J., & MCCLELLAND, D. C. (1990). Cognitive vs. traditional motivational models: Irreconcilable or complementary? In R. Sorrentino & E. T. Higgins (Eds.), *Handbook of motivation and cognition* (pp. 562–597). New York: Guilford.

WEINE, S. M., BECKER, D. F., MCGLASHAN, T. H., LAUB, D., LAZROVE, S., VOJVODA, D., & HYMAN, L. (1995). Psychiatric consequences of "ethnic cleansing": Clinical assessments and trauma testimonies of newly resettled Bosnian refugees. *American Journal of Psychiatry, 152,* 536–542.

WEINE, S. M., VOJVODA, D., BECKER, D. F., MCGLASHAN, T. H., HODZIC, E., LAUB, D., HYMAN, L., SAWYER, M., & LAZROVE, S. (1998). PTSD symptoms in Bosnian refugees 1 year after resettlement in the United States. *American Journal of Psychiatry, 155,* 562–564.

WEINSTEIN, N. D. (1980). Unrealistic optimism about future events. *Journal of Personality and Social Psychology, 39,* 806–820.

WEINSTEIN, N. D. (1987). Unrealistic optimism about susceptibility to health problems: Conclusions from a community-wide sample. *Journal of Behavioral Medicine, 10,* 481–500.

WEINSTEIN, N. D. (1989). Optimistic biases about personal risks. *Science, 246,* 1232–1233.

WEINSTEIN, N. D. (1998). Accuracy of smokers' risk perceptions. *Annals of Behavioral Medicine, 20,* 135–140.

WEISNER, C., GREENFIELD, T., & ROOM, R. (1995). Trends in the treatment of alcohol problems in the U.S. general population. *American Journal of Public Health, 85,* 55–60.

WEISS, J. M., GLAZER, H. I., POHORECKY, L. A., BRICK, J., & MILLER, N. E. (1975). Effects of chronic exposure to stressors on avoidance-escape behavior and on brain norepinephrine. *Psychosomatic Medicine, 37,* 522–534.

WEISS, R. D., MIRIN, S. M., & BARTEL, R. L. (1994). *Cocaine* (2nd ed.). Washington, DC: American Psychiatric Press, Inc.

WEISSMAN, M. M. (1993). Family genetic studies of panic disorder. Conference on panic and anxiety: A decade of progress. *Journal of Psychiatric Research, 27* (Suppl.), 69–78.

WEISSTEIN, N. A., & WONG, E. (1986). Figure-ground organization and the spatial and temporal responses of the visual system. In E. C. Schwab & H. C. Nusbaum (Eds.), *Pattern recognition by humans and machines. Volume 2. Visual perception* (pp. 31–64). Orlando: Academic Press.

WEISZ, J. R., DONENBERG, G., HAN, S., & KAUNECKIS, D. (1995). Child and adolescent psychotherapy outcomes in experiments versus clinics: Why the disparity? *Journal of Abnormal Child Psychology, 23,* 83–106.

WELLER, L., & WELLER, A. (1993). Human menstrual synchrony: A critical assessment. *Neuroscience & Behavioral Reviews, 17,* 427–439.

WERTHEIMER, M. (1912/1932). Experimentelle studien uber das sehen von beuegung. *Zeitschrift Fuer Psychologie, 61,* 161–265.

WERTHEIMER, M. (2000). *A brief history of psychology* (6th ed.). Fort Worth: Harcourt.

WEST, C., & ZIMMERMAN, D. H. (1983). Small insults: A study of interruptions in cross-sex conversations between unacquainted persons. In B. Thorne, C. Kramarae, & N. Henley (Eds.), *Language, gender, and society*. Rowley, MA: Newbury House.

WESTBROOK, G. L. (1994). Glutamate receptor update. *Current Opinion in Neurobiology, 4,* 337–346.

WESTEN, D. (1988). The scientific legacy of Sigmund Freud: Toward a psychodynamically informed psychological science. *Psychological Bulletin, 124,* 333–371.

WHITE, C. (1977). Unpublished Ph.D. dissertation, Catholic University, Washington, DC.

WHITE, G. L., FISHBEIN, S., & RUTSTEIN, J. (1981). Passionate love and the misattribution of arousal. *Journal of Personality and Social Psychology, 41,* 56–62.

WHITE, G. L., & KIGHT, T. D. (1984). Misattribution of arousal and attraction: Effects of salience of explanations for arousal. *Journal of Experimental Social Psychology, 20,* 55–64.

WHITAM, F. L., & MATHY, R. M. (1986). *Male homosexuality in four societies: Brazil, Guatemala, the Philippines, and the United States* (Vol. Special Studies). New York: Praeger.

WHITAM, F. L., & MATHY, R. M. (1991). Childhood cross-gender behavior of homosexual females in Brazil, Peru, the Philippines, and the United States. *Archives of Sexual Behavior, 20,* 151–170.

WHORF, B. L. (1956). *Language, thought and reality: Selected writings of Benjamin Lee Whorf* (J. B. Carroll, Ed.). Cambridge, MA: MIT Press.

WHYTE, W. H. (1956). *The organization man.* New York: Simon & Schuster.

WIEBE, D. J., & MCCALLUM, D. M. (1986). Health practices and hardiness as mediators in the stress-illness relationship. *Health Psychology, 5,* 425–438.

WILCOXIN, H. C., DRAGOIN, W. B., & KRAL, P. A. (1971). Illness-induced aversions in rat and quail: Relative salience of visual and gustatory cues. *Science, 171,* 823–828.

WILKES, A. L., & KENNEDY, R. A. (1969). Relationship between pausing and retrieval latency in sentences of varying grammatical form. *Journal of Experimental Psychology, 79,* 241–245.

WILKINS, W. (1984). Psychotherapy: The powerful placebo. *Journal of Consulting and Clinical Psychology, 52,* 570–573.

WILLIAMS, D. C. (1959). The elimination of tantrum behavior by extinction procedures. *Journal of Abnormal and Social Psychology, 59,* 269.

WILLIAMS, GEORGE C. (1996). *Plan and purpose in nature.* London: Weidenfeld & Nicholson.

WILLIAMS, M. D., & HOLLAN, J. D. (1981). The process of retrieval from very long-term memory. *Cognitive Science, 5,* 87–119.

WILLIAMS, R. B. (1995). Somatic consequences of stress. In M. J. Friedman (Ed.), *Neurobiological and clinical consequences of stress: From normal adaptation to post-traumatic stress disorder.* Philadelphia: Lippincott-Raven.

WILLIAMS, R. B., JR., BAREFOOT, J. C., HANEY, T. L., HARRELL, F. E., BLUMENTHAL, J. A., PRYOR, D. B., & PETERSON, B. (1988). Type A behavior and angiographically documented coronary atherosclerosis in a sample of 2,289 patients. *Psychosomatic Medicine, 50,* 139–152.

WILSON, E. O. (1975). *Sociobiology: The new synthesis.* Cambridge, MA: Harvard University Press.

WILSON, E. O. (1978). *On human nature.* Cambridge, MA: Harvard University Press.

WILSON, E. O. (1963). Pheromones. *Scientific American, 208,* 100–114.

WILSON, M. A., & MCNAUGHTON, B. L. (1994). Reactivation of hippocampal ensemble memories during sleep. *Science, 265,* 676–679.

WILSON, T. D., DUNN, D. S., KRAFT, D., & LISLE, D. J. (1989). Introspection, attitude change, and attitude-behavior consistency: The disruptive effects of explaining why we feel the way we do. In L. Berkowitz (Ed.), *Advances in experimental social psychology* (Vol. 22). San Diego: Academic Press.

WILSON, T. D., LASER, P. S., & STONE, J. I. (1982). Judging the predictors of one's mood: Accuracy and the use of shared theories. *Journal of Experimental Social Psychology, 18,* 537–556.

WILSON, W. H., & CLAUSEN, A. M. (1995). 18-month outcome of clozapine treatment for 100 patients in a state psychiatric hospital. *Psychiatric Services, 46,* 386–389.

WILSON, W. R. (1979). Feeling more than we can know: Exposure effects without learning. *Journal of Personality and Social Psychology, 37,* 811–821.

WINCH, R. F., KTSANES, T., & KTSANES, V. (1954). The theory of complementary needs in mate selection: An analytic and descriptive study. *American Sociological Review, 29,* 241–249.

WINDHOLZ, M. J., MARMAR, C. R., & HOROWITZ, M. J. (1985). A review of the research on conjugal bereavement: Impact on health and efficacy of intervention. *Comprehensive Psychiatry, 26,* 433–447.

WINGER, G., HOFFMAN, F. G., & WOODS, J. H. (1992). *A handbook on drug and alcohol abuse* (3rd ed.). New York: Oxford University Press.

WINSON, J. (1990). The meaning of dreams. *Scientific American, 262,* 86–96.

WISE, R. A. (1982). Neuroleptics and operant behavior: The anhedonia hypothesis. *Behavioral and Brain Sciences,* 539–587.

WISNIEWSKI, E. J., & MEDIN, D. L. (1991). Harpoons and longsticks: The interaction of theory and similarity in rule induction. In D. Fisher, M. Pazzani, & P. Langley (Eds.), *Concept formation: Knowledge and experience in unsupervised learning.* San Mateo, CA: Morgan-Kaufman.

WOLCHIK, S. A., BEGGS, V. E., WINCZE, P. P., SAKHEIM, D. K., BARLOW, D. H., & MAVISSAKALIAN, M. (1980). The effect of emotional arousal on subsequent sexual arousal in men. *Journal of Abnormal Psychology, 89,* 595–598.

WOLMAN, B. B., DALE, L. A., SCHMEIDLER, G. R., & ULLMAN, M. (Eds.) (1986). *Handbook of parapsychology.* New York: Van Nostrand & Reinhold.

WOLPE, J. (1958). *Psychotherapy by reciprocal inhibition.* Stanford, CA: Stanford University Press.

WOLRAICH, M. L., HANNAH, J. N., BAUMGAERTEL, A., & FEURER, I. D. (1998). Examination of DSM-IV criteria for ADHD in a country-wide sample. *Developmental and Behavioral Pediatrics, 19,* 162–168.

WOOD, G. (1986). *Fundamentals of psychological research* (3rd ed.). Boston: Little, Brown.

WOOD, W., LUNDGREN, S., OUELLETTE, J. A., BUSCEME, S., & BLACKSTONE, T. (1994). Minority influence: A meta-analytic review of social influence processes. *Psychological Bulletin, 115,* 323–345.

WOOD, W., WANG, F. Y. & CHACHERIE, J. G. (1991). Effects of media violence on viewers' aggression in unconstrained social situations. *Psychological Bulletin, 109,* 371–383.

WOODY, R. H., & ROBERTSON, M. (1988). *Becoming a clinical psychologist.* Madison, CT: International Universities Press.

WORD, C. O., ZANNA, M. P., & COOPER, J. (1974). The nonverbal mediation of self-fulfilling prophecies in interracial interaction. *Journal of Experimental Social Psychology, 10,* 109–120.

WORTMAN, C. B., & BREHM, J. W. (1975). Responses to uncontrollable outcomes: An integration of reactance theory and the learned helplessness model. *Advances in Experimental and Social Psychology, 8,* 277–236.

WRIGHT, L. (1988). The Type A behavior pattern and coronary artery disease, quest for the active ingredients and the elusive mechanism. *American Psychologist, 43,* 2–14.

WURTZ, R. H., GOLDBERG, M. E., & ROBINSON, D. L. (1980). Behavioral modulation of visual responses in monkeys. *Progress in Psychobiology and Physiological Psychology, 9,* 42–83.

YAGER, T., LAUFER, R., & GALLOPS, M. (1984). Some problems associated with war experience in men of the Vietnam generation. *Archives of General Psychiatry, 41,* 327–333.

YARBUS, D. L. (1967). *Eye movements and vision.* New York: Plenum.

YESAVAGE, J. A., LEIER, V. O., DENARI, M., & HOLLISTER, L. E. (1985). Carry-over effect of marijuana intoxication on aircraft pilot performance: A preliminary report. *American Journal of Psychiatry, 142,* 1325–1330.

YOST, W. A., & NIELSON, D. W. (1985). *Fundamentals of hearing* (2nd ed.). New York: Holt, Rinehart & Winston.

YU, B., ZHANG, W., JING, Q., PENG, R., ZHANG, G., & SIMON, H. A. (1985). STM capacity for Chinese and English language materials. *Memory and Cognition, 13,* 202–207.

ZAJONC, R. B. (1965). Social facilitation. *Science, 149,* 269–274.

ZAJONC, R. B. (1968). Attitudinal effects of mere exposure. *Journal of Personality and Social Psychology,* Monograph Supplement 9 (No. 2), 1–29.

ZAJONC, R. B. (1980). Compresence. In P. B. Paulus (Ed.), *Psychology of group influence.* Hillsdale, NJ: Erlbaum.

ZAJONC, R. B. (1984). On the primacy of affect. *American Psychologist, 39,* 117–123.

ZAJONC, R. B., HEINGARTNER, A., & HERMAN, E. M. (1969). Social enhancement and impairment of performance in the cockroach. *Journal of Personality and Social Psychology, 13,* 83–92.

ZAJONC, R. B., MURPHY, S. T., & INGLEHART, M. (1989). Feeling and facial efference: Implications of the vascular theory of emotion. *Psychological Review.*

ZALUTSKY, R. A., & NICOLL, R. A. (1990). Comparison of two forms of longterm potentiation in single hippocampal neurons. *Science, 248,* 1619–1624.

ZAMANSKY, H. S., & BARTIS, S. P. (1985). The dissociation of an experience: The hidden observer observed. *Journal of Abnormal Psychology, 94,* 243–248.

ZEKI, S. (1993). *A vision of the brain.* Boston: Blackwell Scientific Publications.

ZELAZO, P. R., ZELAZO, N. A., & KOLB, S. (1972). Walking in the newborn. *Science, 176,* 314–315.

ZHANG, Y., PROENCA, R., MAFFEI, M., BARONE, M., LEOPOLD, L., & FRIEDMAN, J. M. (1994). Positional cloning of the mouse *obese* gene and its human homologue. *Nature, 372,* 425–431.

ZILLMANN, D. (1984). *Connections between sex and aggression.* Hillsdale, NJ: Erlbaum.

ZILLMANN, D., & BRYANT, J. (1974). Effect of residual excitation on the emotional response to provocation and delayed aggressive behavior. *Journal of Personality and Social Psychology, 30,* 782–791.

ZIMBARDO, P. G. (1970). The human choice: Individuation, reason and order versus deindividuation, impulse and chaos. In W. J. Arnold & D. Levine (Eds.), *Nebraska symposium on motivation* (Vol. 16). Lincoln: University of Nebraska Press.

ZIMBARDO, P. G. (1972). Pathology of imprisonment. *Society, 9,* 4–8.

ZOLA-MORGAN, S., & SQUIRE, L. R. (1985). Medial-temporal lesions in monkeys impair memory on a variety of tasks sensitive to human amnesia. *Behavioral Neuroscience, 99,* 22–34.

ZOLA-MORGAN, S. M., SQUIRE, L. R., & AMARAL, D. G. (1989). Lesions of the hippocampal formation but not lesions of the fornix or the mamalary nuclei produce long-lasting memory impairments in monkeys. *Journal of Neuroscience, 9,* 898–913.

ZOLA-MORGAN, S. M., & SQUIRE, L. R. (1990). The primate hippocampal formation: Evidence for a time-limited role in memory storage. *Science, 250,* 228–290.

ZUBER, J. A., CROTT, H. W., & WERNER, J. (1992). Choice shift and group polarization: An analysis of the status of arguments and social decision schemes. *Journal of Personality and Social Psychology, 62,* 50–61.

ZUCKER, K. J., & BRADLEY, S. J. (1995). *Gender identity disorder and psychosexual problems in children and adolescents.* New York: Guilford.

ZUCKER, K. J., BRADLEY, S. J., OLIVER, G., & BLAKE, J. (1996). Psychosexual development of women with congenital adrenal hyperplasia. *Hormones & Behavior, 30,* 300–318.

ZUCKERMAN, M. (1979). *Sensation seeking: Beyond the optimal level of arousal.* Hillsdale, NJ: Erlbaum.

ZUCKERMAN, M. (1991). *Psychobiology of personality.* Cambridge, England: Cambridge University Press.

ZUCKERMAN, M. (1995). Good and bad humors: Biochemical bases of personality and its disorders. *Psychological Science, 6,* 325–332.

ZURIF, E. B., (1990). Language and the brain. In D. N. Osherson & H. Lasnik (Eds.), *An invitation to cognitive science: Language* (Vol. 1). Cambridge, MA: MIT Press.

ZURIF, E. B., CARAMAZZA, A., MYERSON, R., & GALVIN, J. (1974). Semantic feature representations for normal and aphasic language. *Brain and Language, 1,* 167–187.

Copyrights, Acknowledgments and Illustration Credits

American Psychological Association. Reprinted with permission.

Figure 2-1 Schematic Diagram of a Neuron from Gaudin and Jones, *Human Anatomy and Physiology,* fig. 11.3a, p. 263. Reprinted by permission of the author. **Figure 2-2** Synapses at the Cell Body, fig. 11.16 Gaudin and Jones, *Human Anatomy and Physiology.* Reprinted by permission of the author. **Figure 2-3** Shapes and Sizes of Neurons, fig. 11.17 Gaudin and Jones, *Human Anatomy and Physiology.* Reprinted by permission of the author. **Figure 2-5** "Synapse" from *In Search for the Human Mind* by Robert Sternberg, p. 105. Copyright © 1995 by Harcourt, Inc. reproduced by permission of the publisher. **Figure 2-8** Human Brain from Gaudin and Jones, *Human Anatomy and Physiology.* Reprinted by permission of the author., fig. 12.1, p. 291. **Figure 2-9** Cerebral Hemispheres fig. 12.2, p. 294 Gaudin and Jones, *Human Anatomy and Physiology.* Reprinted by permission of the author. **Figure 2-11** Visual Pathways, fig. 16.14, p. 393 from Gaudin and Jones, *Human Anatomy and Physiology.* Reprinted by permission of the author. **Figure 2-12** Reprinted from *Neuropsychologia,* Vol. 9, R.D. Nebes and R.W. Sperry, "Cerebral Dominance in Perception", p. 247. Copyright © 1970 with permission from Elsevier Science. **Figure 2-13** Reprinted from *Neuropsychologia,* Vol. 9, R.D. Nebes and R.W. Sperry, "Cerebral Dominance in Perception," p. 247. Copyright © 1970 with permission from Elsevier Science. **Figure 2-15** Motor Fibers" fig. 14.2, p. 345 from Gaudin and Jones, *Human Anatomy and Physiology.* Reprinted by permission of the author. **Figure 2-18** Reprinted from "The Inheritance and Development of Intelligence" by R.W. Thomson in *Proceedings of the Association for Research in Nervous and Mental Diseases,* Vol. 33, 1954, pp. 209–231. Reprinted by permission.

Table 3-1 "Piaget's States of Cognitive Development" from *Review of Child Development Research.* Vol. 1, 1964, by M.L. Hoffman and L.W. Hoffman, eds. Copyright © 1964 Russell Sage Foundation. Used with permission. **Figure 3-6** "Testing Object Permanence" adapted from "Object Permanence in 3½ and 4½ Month Old Infants" by R. Baillargeon from *Developmental Psychology,* Vol. 23, 1987, pp. 655–664. Copyright © 1987 Academic Press, Inc. Reprinted by permission. **Table 3-2** "Stage and Sequence: The Cognitive Developmental Approach to Socialization" from *Handbook of Socialization Theory and Research,* D.A. Goslin, ed. **Figure 3-7** Reprinted by permission of the publishers from Infancy: It's Place in Human Development by Jerome Kagan, Richard B. Kearsley and Phillip R. Zelazo, Cambridge, Mass.: Harvard University Press. Copyright © 1978 by the President and Fellows of Harvard College.

Table 4-1 From "Contemporary Psychophysics" by E. Galanter in *New Directions in Psychology,* Vol. 1, ed. Roger Brown, 1962. Reprinted by permission. **Figure 4-5** Figure from *Sensation and Perception,* Third Edition, by Stanley Coren and Laurence Ward. Copyright © 1989 by Harcourt, Inc., reproduced by permission of the publisher. **Figure 4-4** "Cross-section of the Ear" Gaudin and Jones, *Human Anatomy and Physiology,* fig. 16.16, p. 399. Reprinted by permission of the author. **Figure 4-8** "Taste Areas" from "Sensory Neural Patterns in Gustation" by E. Erickson, from *Olfaction and Taste,* ed. by Zotterman, Vol. 1, 1963, pp. 205–213. **Figure 4-9** "Culture and Pain" from "Living Prehistory in India" by D.D. Kosambi, *Scientific American,* Vol. 215, 1967, p. 105. **Figure 4-10** "Top View of R. Eye" from *Human Color Vision* by Robert M. Boynton, 1979. **Figure 4-11** "Image Formation in the Eye" from *Human Color Vision* by Robert M. Boynton, 1979. **Figure 4-12** "Organization of the Primate Retina" by Dowling and Boycott from *Proceedings of the Royal Society of London,* Series B, Vol. 166, pp. 80–111. Copyright © 1966 Royal Society of London. Reprinted by permission. **Figure 4-18** "Trichromatic Theory" from "Spectral Sensitivity of the Foveal Cone Photopigments between 400 and 500 nm," *Vision Research,* Vol. 15, pp. 161–171. Copyright © 1975 with permission from Elsevier Science. **Figure 4-19** Reprinted with permission from *in Trends in Neurosciences,* Vol. 6, No. 10, Mishkin et al., pp. 414–417. Copyright by Elsevier Science. **Figure 4-27** "Recognition of Components: A Theory of Human Image Understanding" by I. Biederman from *Computer Vision, Graphics, and Image Processing,* Vol. 32, 1985, pp. 92–73. Copyright © 1985 Academic Press, Inc. Reprinted by permission. **Figure 4-28** "Recognition of Components: A Theory of Human Image Understanding" by I. Biederman from *Computer Vision, Graphics, and Image Processing,* Vol. 32, 1985, pp. 92–73. Copyright © 1985 Academic Press, Inc. Reprinted by permission. **Figure 4-29** W.E. Hill, "My Wife and My Mother-in-Law," *Puck* (November 6, 1915). **Figure 4-30** From "Perception of Ambiguous Stimulus Materials" by G.H. Fisher in *Perception and Psychophysics,* Vol. 2, pp. 421–422, 1967. Reprinted by permission of Psychonomic Society, Inc. **Figure 4-33** From *Sensation and Perception, 3rd edition* by E. Goldstein, © 1989. Reprinted with permission of Wadsworth, a division of Thomson Learning. Fax 800-730-2215. **Figure 4-38** "Movement Produced in the Development of Visually Guided Behavior" by R. Held and A. Hein in *Journal of Comparative and Physiological Psychology,* Vol. 56, pp. 872–876. Copyright © 1963 American Psychological Association. Reprinted by permission.

Figure 5-5 From *Illicit Drug Use, Smoking and Drinking by America's High School Students, College Students and Young Adults, 1975–1995* by Jerome Johnston, P.M. O'Malley and Jerald G. Bachman. Rockville, MD: National Institute on Drug Abuse. **Figure 5-6** From "Historical and Clinical Considerations of the Relaxation Response" by H. Benson et al., *American Scientist,* Vol. 65, pp. 441–443, 1977. Reprinted by permission of The Scientific Research Society.

Table 6-1 "Predictability, Surprise, Attention Conditioning" by Leon J. Kamin in *Punishment and Aversive Behavior* edited by B.A. Campbell and R.M. Church, 1969. **Figure 6-2** Adapted from *Conditioned Reflexes* by E.P. Pavlov. Copyright © 1927 by Oxford University Press. Ltd. **Figure 6-3** "The Sensory Generalization of Conditioned Responses with Varying Frequencies of Tone" by C.I. Hovland from *Journal of General Psychology,* Vol. 17, pp. 125–148, 1937. Reprinted with the permission of the Helen Dwight Reid Educational Foundation. Published by Heldref Publications, 1319 Eighteenth St., NW, Washington, DC 20036-1802. Copyright © 1937. **Figure 6-4** Adapted with permission from "Differential Classical Conditioning Verbalization of Stimulus Contingencies" by M.J. Fuhrer and P.E. Baer, *Science,* Vol. 150, December 10, 1965, pp. 1479–1481. Copyright © 1965 American Association for the Advancement of Science. **Figure 6-5** "Pavlovian Conditioning & Its Proper Control Procedures" by R.A. Rescorla, *Psychological Review,* Vol. 74:71–80. Copyright © 1967 American Psychological Association. Reprinted by permission. **Table 6-2** "Predictability, Surprise, Attention and Conditioning" by L.J. Kamin from *Punishment and Aversive Behavior,* edited by B.A. Campbell and R.M. Church, 1969. **Table 6-3** "The Relation of Cue to Consequence in Avoidance Learning" by J. Garcia and R.A. Loekling, *Psychonomic Science* Vol. 4, pp. 123–124, 1966. Reprinted by permission of Psychonomic Society, Inc. **Figure 6-8** From *Brain, Mind and Behavior* by Bloom and Lazerton. Copyright © 1985, 1988 by Educational Broadcasting Corporation. Used with permission by W.H. Freeman and Company.

Figure 7-1 "Implication of Short-Term Memory for a General Theory of Memory" by A.W. Melton from *Journal of Verbal Learning and Verbal Behavior* 2:1–21. Copyright © 1963 Academic Press, Inc. Reprinted by permission. **Figure 7-3** "Spatial Working Memory in Humans as Revealed by PET" by John Jonides et al, *Nature,* 363:623–625. Copyright © 1994 Macmillan Magazines Ltd. Reprinted by permission. **Figure 7-4** Reprinted with permission from "High-Speed Scanning in Human Memory" by S. Sternberg, *Science* Vol. 153, August 5, 1966, pp. 652–654. Copyright © 1966 American Association for the Advancement of Science. **Figure 7-5** "What One Intelligence Test Measures: A Theoretical Account of the Processing in the Raven Progressive Matrices Test" by P.A. Carpenter et al, *Psychological Review,* 97(3):404–431. Copyright © 1990 American Psychological Association. Reprinted by permission. **Table 7-1** "Availability and Accessibility" by E. Tulving and Z. Pearlstone, *Journal of Memory and Language* 5:381–391, 1976. Copyright © 1976 Academic Press, Inc. Reprinted by permission. **Figure 7-7** "Context-Dependent Memory in Two Natural Environments; On Land & Under Water" by D. Godden and A.D. Baddeley, *British Journal of Psychology,* 66:321–331, 1975. **Table 7-2** Reprinted from *Neuropsychologia,* Vol. 16, "Further Analysis of the Proper Learning Effect in Amnesiac Patients," pp.169–177, W.K. Warrinton and L. Weiskrantz, Copyright ©1978 with permission from Elsevier Science, Ltd. **Figure 7-8** "Memory, Hippocampus, and Brain Systems" by L.R. Squire and B.J. Knowlton in M.S. Gazzaniga (Ed.), *The Cognitive Neurosciences,* p. 826, Fig. 53.1. Copyright © 1995 MIT Press. Reprinted by permission. **Figure 7-10** Adapted from "Acquisition of a Memory Skill" reprinted by permission from *Science,* Vol. 208, 1980, pp. 1181–1182 by I.A. Ericsson et al. Copyright © 1980 by American Association for the Advancement of Science. **Figure 7-12** From "Narrative Stories as Mediators for Serial Learning" by G.H. Bower and M.C. Clark, *Psychonomic Science,* Vol.14, pp.181–182, 1969. Reprinted by permission of Psychonomic Society, Inc.

Excerpt chapter 8 from *Memory* by I.M.L. Hunter, pp. 265–266. (Penguin Books 1957, revised edition 1964). Copyright © Ian M.L. Hunter, 1957, 1964.

Figure 9-5 "Effects of Force Feeding and Starvation, Food Intake and Body Weight of a Rat with Ventromedial Hypthalamic Lesions" by B.G. Hoebel and P. Teitelbaum, *Journal of Comparative & Physio logical Psychology,* 61:189–193. Copyright © 1966 American Psychological Association. Reprinted by permission. **Table 9-1** "Behavior Therapy and Pharmacotherapy for Obesity" by L.W. Craighead et al., *Archives of General Psychiatry,* 38: 763–768, 1981. Copyright © 1981 American Medical Association. Reprinted by permission. From A.P. Bell et al., *Sexual Preference: Its Development in Men & Women.* Copyright © 1981 by Indiana University Press. Reprinted by permission of the publisher. **Figure 9-7b** "What Kind of Sexual Practices do People Find Appealing?" from *Sex in America,* R.T. Michael et al.,1994. **Figure 9-11** "The Interaction of Cognitive and Physiological Determination of Emotional State" by S. Schachter, in P.H.Lederman and D. Shapiro (eds.) *Psychobiological Approaches to Human Behavior,* Stanford: Stanford University Press. Adapted from Hohmann, "The Effect of Dysfunctions of the Autonomic Nervous System on Experienced Feelings and Emotions," paper read at Conference on Emotions and Feelings at The New School for Social Research, New York, October, 1962. **Figure 9-12** Adapted from article by P. Ekman et al., "Autonomic Nervous System Activity Distinguishes Among Emotions" *Science* Vol. 221, pp. 1208–1210, September 16, 1983. Copyright © 1983 American Association for the Advancement of Science. Reprinted by permission of AAAS and Paul Ekman. **Table 9-3** From *Emotion: Theory, Research and Experience* edited by R. Plutchick and H. Kellerman, Vol. 1. 1980. Copyright © 1980 Academic Press, Inc. Reprinted by permission. **Figure 9-16** Adapted from Bandura, A., et al., "Imitation of Film-Mediated Aggressive Models" in *Journal of Abnormal and Social Psychology,* 66:8. Copyright © 1963 American Psychological Association. Adapted by permission.

Table 10-2 "Stanford-Binet Items (for 6 to 8 year Olds)." Copyright © 1986 by The Riverside Publishing Company. Reproduced from *Stanford Binet Intelligence Scale,* Fourth Edition, by Robert L. Thorndike, et al. **Table 10-3** Adapted from *Intelligence: Mutliple Perspectives* by Howard Gardner and Mindy Kornhaber. Copyright © 1996 by Holt, Rinehart and Winston, reproduced by permission of the publisher. **Table 10-4** R.R. McCrae and P.T. Costa, Jr., "Validation of the Five-Factor Model of Personality Across Instruments and Observers" *Journal of Personality and Social Psychology,* 52:81–90, 1987. **Excerpt chapter 10** from *The Intelligence* by Eysenck & Kamin, p. 97. Copyright © 1981 John Wiley & Sons Limited. Reproduced with permission. **Figure 10-3** Maslow's Hierarchy of Needs" from *Motivation and Personality* by Maslow. Copyright © 1998. Reprinted by permission of Prentice-Hall, Upper Saddle River, NJ. **Table 10-5** Maslow, A.H. "Self-Actualization and Beyond" in *Challenges of Humanistic Psychology,* J.F.T. Bugental (ed.). Copyright © 1967 by Abraham H. Maslow. Used with permission of James Bugental.

Figure 11-2 From "Posttraumatic Stress Disorder Following Assault: Theoretical Considerations and Empirical Findings" by E.D. Foa and D.S. Riggs, *Current Direction in Psychological Science,* Vol. 4, pp. 61–65, 1995. Reprinted by permission of Blackwell Science, Ltd. **Table 11-2** Reprinted *from Journal of Psychosomatic Research,* Vol. 11, No. 2, "The Social Readjustment Rating Scale" pp. 213–218, T.H. Holmes & R.H. Rahe, copyright 1967 with permission from Elsevier Science. **Figure 11-3** Figure from *Textbook of Psychology,* Third Edition by Donald O. Hebb. Copyright © 1972 by Holt, Rinehart and Winston, reproduced by permission of the publisher. **Figure 11-7** "Psychological Stress and Susceptibility to the Common Cold" by S. Cohen et al., *New England Journal of Medicine,* 3325: 606–612. Copyright © 1991 Massachusetts Medical Society. All rights reserved. **Table 11-5** From *Type A Behavior and Your Heart* by Meyer Friedman M.D. and Ray Rosenman, M.D. Copyright © 1974 by Meyer Friedman. Reprinted by permission of Alfred A. Knopf, a Division of Random House, Inc. **Figure 11-9** From Cole, Kemeny, Taylor & Visscher. "Elevated Physical Health Risks among Gay

Name Index

Subject Index